W0007734

SELENA BY MARY TIGHE

Mary Tighe's unpublished novel *Selena* is one of the great unknown treasures of British Romanticism. Completed in 1803, this brilliant, compulsively readable, beautifully written, and psychologically astute courtship novel is finally available in a scholarly edition that reveals Mary Tighe to have been as talented a fiction writer as she was a poet. The history of this amazing work's long journey from manuscript to print is only one of the stories Harriet Kramer Linkin recounts in this scrupulously annotated edition based on the only known copy of the manuscript, currently part of the National Library of Ireland's holdings. Linkin's introduction situates the novel in its historical context, draws attention to significant aspects of the plots and characters, and makes a strong case for *Selena*'s importance for understanding the history of the novel, fiction by women, Anglo-Irish fiction, silver-fork novels, and the Romantic period. Explanatory notes explain obscure references and contexts, identify allusions to other writers, and provide translations of any non-English or archaic words. *Selena* itself is a revelation in its frank treatment of the darker aspects of Tighe's world, including parents who mistreat, cheat, or fail their children and spouses who commit adultery or betray one another emotionally. At the same time, it is magnificent in its stunning and moving portrayals of romantic love, of the possibility and importance of female friendship, of the difficult necessity of choosing sense over sensibility, and of the need for women and men to choose self-enhancing vocations. This extraordinary novel is destined to open up new ways of thinking by scholars of the Romantic era and the history of the novel.

Selena by Mary Tighe
A Scholarly Edition

Edited by

HARRIET KRAMER LINKIN
New Mexico State University, USA

ASHGATE

Published by
Ashgate Publishing Limited
Wey Court East
Union Road
Farnham
Surrey, GU9 7PT
England

Ashgate Publishing Company
Suite 420
101 Cherry Street
Burlington
VT 05401-4405
USA

www.ashgate.com

British Library Cataloguing in Publication Data
Linkin, Harriet Kramer, 1956–
Selena by Mary Tighe. – Scholarly ed.
   1. Tighe, Mary, 1772–1810. Selena.
   I. Title
   823.7–dc23

Library of Congress Cataloging-in-Publication Data
Tighe, Mary, 1772–1810.
  Selena / by Mary Tighe; a scholarly edition edited by Harriet Kramer Linkin.
    p. cm.
  An annotated edition of the unpublished courtship novel, based on the only known copy of the manuscript, housed in the National Library of Ireland, it traces the work's long journey from manuscript to print.
  Includes bibliographical references.
    1. Courtship—Ireland—Fiction. 2. Psychological fiction. I. Linkin, Harriet Kramer, 1956– II. Title.

PR5671.T2S45 2012
823'.7—dc23

2011046391

ISBN 9781409405498 (hbk)
ISBN 9781409405504 (ebk)

Printed and bound in Great Britain by the
MPG Books Group, UK

Contents

List of Figures

Acknowledgments

I owe deep thanks to the many friends, colleagues, scholars, librarians, and institutions that made it possible to produce this edition of Mary Tighe's *Selena*, but first and foremost I am grateful to Mary Tighe for writing this wonderful novel, and to the Tighe family for preserving it. I am also very grateful to New Mexico State University for providing multiple resources to support this project; to the trustees of the National Library of Ireland for granting permission to reproduce the original manuscripts 4742–4746 for this edition, and for granting permission to include eight illustrations from manuscript accession 5495/C/8/1; to the National Gallery of Ireland for granting permission to reproduce NPG 1164 for the cover of the print edition; and to Ashgate Press and Ann Donahue for a superb publication experience from start to finish. This project could never have been completed without the generous assistance of librarians at the National Library of Ireland (notably Tom Desmond and Barry Houlihan), Trinity College Dublin, the Dublin City Library (especially Clodagh Kingston), and the New Mexico State University Interlibrary Loan Office, and without the encouragement, enthusiasm, and expertise of many generous souls, including Stephen Behrendt, Averill Buchanan, Lucia Greene, Jacqueline Labbe, Laura Mandell, Tracey Miller-Tomlinson, Miranda O'Connell, Brian Rourke, Elizabeth Schirmer, Antony Tighe, Gary Tomlinson, Mónica Torres, Sylvia Webber, Tom Whyte, and Julia Wright. Special thanks go to my very dear friend, Kathleene West, for poring through transcriptions and paragraphing conventions, and to my truly better half, Larry Linkin, for more than I know how to put in words (and I think he knows that says everything, since I'm rarely at a loss for words).

Mary Tighe:
A Brief Chronology

1770   William Blachford and Theodosia Tighe marry.

1771   John Blachford is born.

1772   Mary Blachford is born on 9 October in Dublin.

1773   William Blachford dies.

1786   Mary Blachford attends day school at Este's Academy in London for a year while John Blachford attends Eton.

1787   Theodosia Blachford publishes her translation of *The Life of the Baroness de Chantal*.

1793   Mary Blachford marries her cousin Henry Tighe on 5 October and the Tighes spend the next eight years in England (with frequent visits to Ireland).

1795   George Romney completes a portrait of Mary Tighe.

1801   The Tighes return to Ireland. Mary Tighe completes *Psyche; or, The Legend of Love* by 1802 and *Selena* by 1803.

1802   Theodosia Blachford co-founds the Dublin House of Refuge on Baggot Street.

1804   Mary and Henry Tighe go to England with Theodosia Blachford to seek a cure for Mary Tighe's tuberculosis. Friends urge Mary Tighe to publish a collection of poetry.

1805   Mary Tighe privately publishes *Psyche; or, The Legend of Love* in June and distributes 50 copies to family and friends. She also prepares a two-volume collection of her poems in manuscript (with illustrations) for Henry Tighe while they are in Brompton seeking a cure for her health: *Verses Transcribed for H.T.* (Brompton, 1805). The Tighes return to Ireland in September.

1806   Mary Tighe begins a "Reading Journal" that she continues through 1809.

1810   Mary Tighe dies on 24 March at Woodstock, the estate of her cousin William Tighe.

1811   *Psyche, with Other Poems by the late Mrs. Henry Tighe* is published by Longman. *Mary, a Series of Reflections During Twenty Years* is privately published and distributed to family and friends.

1817   John Blachford dies in August; Theodosia Blachford dies in November.

1818   Henry Tighe contacts Longman to see whether they might publish *Selena*.

1836   Henry Tighe dies.

Notes on the Text

The text is a direct transcription of the manuscript copy of *Selena* archived at the National Library of Ireland in Dublin (MSS 4742–4746), which acquired all five volumes in 1953 (as noted in the Introduction). These five volumes may or may not be a single copy of the novel: the hand changes, the spelling changes ("apartment" is sometimes spelled "appartment," "chestnut" is usually spelled "chesnut" but sometimes "chestnut," "symmetry" is sometimes spelled "symmetry," and words with a silent "p" such as "symptom" or "presumptive" are sometimes spelled without that "p"), and the punctuation style changes. Although Tighe's mother states that Tighe wrote out her copy of *Selena* "fair" in 1801–1803, Volume III is dated "Feb. 6, 1811" and watermarks for Volumes IV and V indicate a later inscription date (1809 for Volume IV, and 1807, 1808, and 1810 for Volume V).

Tighe used an amanuensis and dictated her manuscript. There are at least two hands that make editorial changes: one matches the mostly neat hand of the original manuscript, and is either Tighe herself (whose handwriting was closely emulated by the amanuensis) or the copyist. The other hand resembles Henry Tighe's, who may have made corrections when he considered submitting the manuscript for publication. Many of Henry Tighe's corrections in Volume I make the occasionally unladylike language more ladylike (especially for Lord Dallamore's speech). Sometimes his corrections are fussy grammatical changes, comparable to the changes made in Tighe's "Psyche" for the 1811 edition of *Psyche, with Other Poems* (see the notes to "Psyche" in the *Collected Poems and Journals of Mary Tighe*, 294–303). This edition of *Selena* incorporates Mary Tighe's corrections and notes the corrections Henry Tighe wanted to make.

I have provided a great deal of punctuation to facilitate reading: the manuscript uses different lengths of dashes for commas, semicolons, and periods as well as quotation marks (although there are occasional periods and semicolons and quotation marks). New paragraphs in the manuscript are indicated with additional space between the dashes, which I have transformed into indented paragraphs. Specifically, I have punctuated accurately for all dialogue (inserting quotation marks and commas to match the conventions of our time: "Hello," she said, "it is good to see you" versus Tighe's "Hello she said it is good to see you—"). I have used periods to end sentences when it is clear that a sentence is completed (either through the size of the dash or capitalization). I have preserved Tighe's use of dashes within sentences because she does use commas and semicolons in some instances (but not with regularity); there would be too much editorial interpretation to insert commas, semicolons, and colons to regularize the manuscript with a uniform style. The manuscript contains many errors which I have left as is, such as the capitalizing of the first letter after a semicolon, to preserve the work as it is.

I have not indicated obvious corrections: words struck out because they were written twice by the amanuensis, for instance. I have silently corrected missing apostrophes that indicate possession (Mrs. Vallard's) or elided letters ('tis, thro', tho'). I have silently corrected some missing commas that might have faded from the manuscript pages. I have not corrected spelling ("comparatively," "feind"), but I have made the spelling of names consistent: Belle (sometimes Bell), Le Roi (sometimes LeRoi), Bently (sometimes Bentley), Anne (sometimes Ann), and Sidney (sometimes Sydney).

I have indicated any editorial insertions to facilitate understanding of the sense of a sentence with brackets: [insertion]. Words that were difficult to decipher due to faded ink are enclosed with special brackets: {uncertain}.

Introduction

This edition offers readers a real rarity: the first printing of Mary Tighe's unpublished manuscript novel *Selena* (c. 1803), a brilliant, compulsively readable, beautifully written, and psychologically astute courtship novel that explores and critiques society, manners, morality, class, fashion, gender roles, sexual identity, familial relationships, inheritance laws, economics, education, the marriage market, religious bias, animal cruelty, female dependence, and more in late eighteenth-century England, Ireland, and Scotland. It is one of the great unknown treasures of the British Romantic era, a work that not only invokes (and stands on par with) Burney's *Cecilia* (1782), Smith's *Emmeline* (1788), Radcliffe's *The Mysteries of Udolpho* (1794), and Edgeworth's *Belinda* (1801), but one that uncannily anticipates Austen's *Sense and Sensibility* (1811) and *Persuasion* (1818), and displays the scope, poignance, and sly wit of so much of Dickens and Eliot. A highly crafted, wonderfully capacious work, *Selena* makes a powerful addition to our understanding of the history of the novel, fiction by women, Anglo-Irish fiction, silver-fork novels, and Romantic-era novels that incorporate poetry. It may well stand as Tighe's greatest contribution to literary history.

The Secret History of Tighe's Novel

Tighe is now recognized as a premier poet of the Romantic era for her epic romance *Psyche; or, the Legend of Love* (1805), completed during the same prolific two-year period as *Selena* (1801–1803), but her work as a novelist remained something of a secret because *Selena* was never made available to the public.[1] Unlike some women writers, Tighe did not need to publish to support her family: born on 9 October 1772 in Dublin to an Anglo-Irish family of wealth, privilege, connection, and learning, she was the second child of Marsh librarian Rev. William Blachford (1730–73) and Methodist leader Theodosia Tighe Blachford (1744–1817), who married in 1770 and had their son John in 1771. Tighe's mother gave her a solid education and encouraged her to write; she herself had published a translation of *The Life of the Baroness de Chantal* (1787) and several religious tracts, and came from a family of writers: her oldest brother William Tighe won prizes for

---

[1]   Tighe's mother Theodosia Blachford establishes the composition and completion dates of both *Psyche* and *Selena* as 1801–1803 (see her "Observations" in *The Collected Poems and Journals of Mary Tighe*, ed. Harriet Kramer Linkin [Lexington: University Press of Kentucky, 2005], 234), but several of the poems Tighe wrote in the voice of characters in *Selena* are dated earlier, including "Verses Written for Emily 1799" and "Stanzas. Written for Angela, 1800" (so titled in Tighe's *Verses Transcribed for H.T.* [Brompton, 1805], Acc. 5495, National Library of Ireland, Dublin).

his poetry at Cambridge, brother Edward Tighe (the theater critic "Melantius") published plays, poetry, and pamphlets; and brother Richard Tighe published a life of William Law, hymns, and religious tracts. Tighe's surviving literary works date from the late 1780s through her marriage to first cousin Henry Tighe on 5 October 1793 to her death on 24 March 1810. Although she evinced steadfast reluctance to publish any of it, she circulated her poetry amongst a set of prominent friends and relatives who ultimately established her literary reputation.[2] In 1804 they urged her to publish a volume of poetry for Longman while she was in England seeking treatment for the tuberculosis that would end her life six years later. She seems to have taken that recommendation quite seriously before deciding against publication, as she reveals in a 24 December 1804 letter to Joseph Cooper Walker:

> I have myself been on the very verge of a most frightful auspice & had almost been persuaded to expose to the mercy of the reviewers, Edinburg butchers & all, my poor little Psyche & a volume of smaller poems which I was advis'd to add, as I might, to serve like the straw appendages of a kite, that she might not fall to the ground by her own weight — however after a few nights agitation I found that I have not nerves for it.[3]

Instead she printed 50 copies of *Psyche* in a private 1805 edition dedicated and distributed to the members of her circle; those copies were borrowed, loaned, and recopied with such enthusiasm that *Psyche* made Tighe famous for the remainder of her life, despite her refusal to publish. In tandem with the 1805 print edition of *Psyche* Tighe prepared a uniquely illustrated two-volume hardbound handwritten copy of 121 of her lyrics and lyric translations for her husband, *Verses Transcribed for H.T.* (Brompton, 1805).[4] A year after Tighe's death, her family published the very work Tighe decided not to publish, an edition of *Psyche, with Other Poems* (Longman, 1811), the first of multiple editions that brought Tighe tremendous posthumous success and acclaim as a poet throughout the nineteenth century and then again in the late twentieth century, when *Psyche* was reappraised as "one of the neglected masterpieces of English poetry."[5]

---

[2]   These friends included Thomas Moore, Sydney Owenson (later Lady Morgan), Alicia LeFanu, the Llangollen Ladies (Eleanor Butler and Sarah Ponsonby), Anna Seward, Barbarina Dacre, Joseph Cooper Walker, William Hayley, and William Roscoe; for a comprehensive listing see Harriet Kramer Linkin, "Mary Tighe and the Coterie of Women Poets in *Psyche*," *The History of British Women's Writing, 1750–1830*, ed. Jacqueline Labbe (England: Palgrave Macmillan, 2010), 303.

[3]   Letter to Joseph Cooper Walker, December 1804, MS 1461/7/194, Trinity College Library, Dublin.

[4]   Acc. 5495, National Library of Ireland, Dublin.

[5]   Adam Roberts, *Romantic and Victorian Long Poems* (England: Ashgate, 1999), 201. For a comprehensive reception history, see Harriet Kramer Linkin, "Mary Tighe and Literary History: the Making of a Critical Reputation," *Literature Compass* 7:7 (July 2010), 564–76.

Selena remained buried in obscurity, despite the delight Tighe herself expressed over her novel undertaking. When Walker first urged her to consider publishing *Psyche* after his initial reading of the poem in 1802, she replied "As to my Psyche — my maternal vanity & fondness for her has been moved alone by your flattery — & I have almost forgotten her in the new fancy of my imagination — but I am a great coward as to publication."[6] She seems to have shared *Selena* with family and friends as she did her poetry, though not quite as extensively. Her cousin and sister-in-law Caroline Hamilton reports that Tighe read portions aloud at family gatherings, "leaving us to guess how she meant to conclude it. Unlike Miss Edgeworth, who, I remember, told me that she generally finished the entire rough sketch of her story before she filled it up."[7] It's clear that her cousin and brother-in-law William Tighe read the manuscript in its entirety, because she records a series of critical comments he made in a late 1809 journal entry: "WT's objections to Selena — She adheres too pedantically to her principles — Ld T. should not make a doubt as to Selena's society tho' LT had not express'd his consent — Ldy Trevallyn swears — no {hopes} for ever — Sidney should not call suicide cowardly — nor should he be capriciously jealous."[8] She also gave friends like Walker "a peep," as Walker puts it in a letter to William Hayley, with the usual caveat that "it is not intended for the press."[9] But at 2,481 manuscript pages the prospect of printing a private edition of *Selena* like the 1805 *Psyche* may have been too costly to consider; nor is there a clear (or carefully preserved) record of advocacy for printing *Selena* as there was for *Psyche*.

Nevertheless, in January 1818 Henry Tighe contacted Longman about the possibility of publishing a posthumous edition of *Selena* (rather precipitously after the death of Tighe's mother in November 1817 and her brother in August 1817; the Tighes had no children). Longman not only expressed interest but wanted to commence immediate production, having recently printed the fifth lucrative edition of *Psyche* in 1816 (totaling 5,500 copies since 1811). The Longman archives copy of a letter drafted to Henry Tighe on 17 January 1818 states "As in the regular course of printing, the doing of the 5 vols would occupy about 8 weeks, it would be very desirable if the Novel could be proceeded upon immediately. We consider the Months of January & February as the best for the publication of books, and we never, if possible, wish to exceed March: for, in general, few books are sold when the season is more advanced. Indeed the sooner we had the MS the more valuable it would be to us." A month later, on 21 February 1818, a second letter

---

[6]   Undated letter to Joseph Cooper Walker, MS 1461/7/221, Trinity College Library, Dublin.

[7]   Caroline Hamilton, "Mary Tighe," in *The Collected Poems and Journals of Mary Tighe*, ed. Harriet Kramer Linkin (Lexington: University Press of Kentucky, 2005), 260.

[8]   Mary Tighe, "Reading Journal," MS 4804, National Library of Ireland, Dublin (the last page contains this undated upside-down note).

[9]   Joseph Cooper Walker letter to William Hayley, 27 January 1808, MS 146/79, Gilbert Collection, Dublin City Library, Dublin.

from the Longman group is even more encouraging (and solicitous): "We beg to acknowledge receipt of your letter of the 16th, & to state that we shall be most happy to treat with you for the Novel whenever it may be determined to print it & to commence printing it at any time of the year most convenient to you."[10]

Although Henry Tighe experienced periodic financial difficulties, he withdrew the novel from consideration, perhaps after hearing from Thomas Moore in November 1818, who advised him against the project's profitability: "Wrote to Tighe advising him not to publish Mrs. Tighe's novel, as I could not in conscience encourage the Longmans to give such a price as would be worth *his* while to accept."[11] That he was intent on pursuing the project is clear from his abundant editorial marks (especially in his correction of unladylike language, replacing words like "cursed" with "great" or deleting phrases like "devil of a" and "damn it"). Perhaps a close rereading prompted him to evaluate the impact publication would have on Tighe's delicately constructed reputation as a beautiful dead poetess, "an angel, if ever there was one on earth, beautiful, airy, and evanescent as her own immortal Psyche."[12] *Selena* is far more risqué in its presentation of erotic desire than the more seemly allegorical sensuality of *Psyche*, and daringly overt in addressing some of the darker aspects of Tighe's world: parents mistreat, cheat, or fail their children; innocents are seduced and abandoned; rejected lovers attempt suicide; spouses commit adultery or betray one another; husbands incarcerate wives; wives humiliate husbands; mothers-to-be miscarry; false friends treat one another with psychological, emotional, and physical cruelty; and animals frequently bear the brunt of human vengeance. Perhaps, even closer to home, the story's main plot line of a young woman maneuvered into an ill-fated marriage with her first cousin—in part because she had not yet learned the art of "gracefully pronouncing the ungraceful monosyllable *No*" (1.85)—too painfully echoed the origins of the Tighes's troubled marriage. According to Theodosia Blachford, Tighe did not know how to refuse her cousin Henry's proposal, "a heart that she was unwilling, indeed seemingly unable to wound by a positive refusal" (233), though she loved someone else.

Whatever prompted Henry Tighe's decision not to pursue publication with Longman, after that brief flurry of letters, *Selena* dropped out of view for more than a century. The novel is not mentioned in any of the letters, journals, or poems Felicia Hemans wrote about her 1831 visit to Tighe's tomb at Woodstock, where she had the opportunity to view Tighe's papers; it is not mentioned by Mrs. Richard Smith in her 1844 biography of Rev. Henry Moore, which not only reproduces letters to and from Theodosia Blachford on Mary Tighe's literary achievements

---

[10]   Archives of the Longman Group, MS 1393, Longman I, 100: 209, 227, Reading University Library, Reading, UK.

[11]   Thomas Moore, Diary for 14 November 1818, *Memoirs, Journal, and Correspondence*, volume 2, ed. Lord John Russell (London: Longman, 1853), 216.

[12]   Timothy Tickler, "Noctes Ambrosianae XXI," *Blackwood's Magazine* vol. 18, no. 104 (September 1825): 381.

but contains a lengthy description of those achievements by Smith herself, who viewed the family papers; it is not mentioned by Elizabeth Blackburne in her 1877 biographical essay on Tighe, who also had the opportunity to view the family papers then in the possession of Charles Hamilton of Hamwood; it is not mentioned by the otherwise indefatigable Earle Vonard Weller in his 1928 overview of Tighe's work for his oddly conceived edition of *Keats and Mary Tighe: The Poems of Mary Tighe with Parallel Passages from the Work of John Keats* (which footnotes Tighe's poetry with references to Keats's poetry); nor is it mentioned by Eva Mary Bell in her 1930 *The Hamwood Papers of the Ladies of Llangollen and Caroline Hamilton*, which prints and describes a multitude of Tighe and Hamilton family papers. The 1898 *Dictionary of National Biography* entry on Tighe does note that she "seems to have written a novel" (389) based on the footnote to "The Picture: Written for Angela" in the 1811 *Psyche, with Other Poems*, which reads "This, with some other poems, belong to a novel written by Mrs. H. Tighe, and which is now in the possession of the editor" (313). So too does Arthur Harcourt Mountain in his 1921 MA thesis on Tighe, "The Romantic Elements in Mrs. Tighe's 'Psyche,' with an Account of Her Life and a Review of Her Reliques," who assumes the novel is lost but freely speculates on its contents as follows:

> The unprinted novel of Mrs. Tighe's, which William Tighe in one of his editorial notes refers to as being in his possession and from which he tells us he extracted certain of the poems, is probably lost. No other reference to it has been found, though it may have been preserved as a curious family heirloom .... The novel may be safely assumed to have been a blend of genteel romance and morality, with the actors moving back and forth between the elegance of Georgian town-houses and the sentimental simplicity of country prospects. And even as her poems are still faintly redolent of her personality, like old rose-petals grown brown and rusty from long being pressed in some favorite volume, so this lost novel, too, must have been gently instinct with the unassuming and gracious spirit of Mary Tighe. (54)

Although *Selena* was preserved by the family, exactly which member or branch of the family remains unclear (as does the identity of the editor of the 1811 *Psyche, with Other Poems*, once assumed to be William Tighe); it is not mentioned by Wilfrid Tighe in the Tighe family history he produced in the 1950s, which includes a chapter on "Henry Tighe and Mary ('Psyche')."[13]

---

[13]   See Henry Chorley, *Memorials of Mrs. Hemans with Illustrations of Her Literary Character from Her Private Correspondence*, 2 vols (London: Saunders and Otley, 1836), who includes a copy of Hemans's 1834 sonnet "On Records of Immature Genius: Written after Reading Memorials of the late Mrs. Tighe"; Mrs. Richard Smith, *The Life of the Rev. Henry Moore; The Biographer and Executor of the Rev. John Wesley; including the Autobiography; and the Continuation, Written from His Own Papers* (London: Simpkin, Marshall, 1844); Elizabeth Blackburne, "Mrs. Mary Tighe," *Illustrious Irishwomen*, 2 vols (London: Tinsley Brothers, 1877), 2:52–63; Earle Vonard Weller, *Keats and Mary Tighe: The Poems of Mary Tighe with Parallel Passages from the Work of John Keats* (New York:

The novel apparently remained in the family's possession until 10 November 1953, when third-party Seamus Fenning of Ranelagh sold the five volumes of Tighe's *Selena* to the National Library of Ireland (MSS 4742–4746), along with the first two cantos of William Tighe's long poem "The Plants" (MSS 4752–4753) and additional family papers.[14] Just four days earlier, the National Library had acquired a copy of the rare *Mary, a Series of Reflections During Twenty Years* (a second posthumous collection of Tighe's poetry privately printed and distributed to 20 intimates in 1811). When the National Library shortly thereafter acquired Hamilton's *Anecdotes of Our Family Written for My Children* (MS 4810), which contained her biography of Tighe, transcriptions from Tighe's journals, and a transcription of Theodosia Blachford's account of her daughter's life, the great National Library keeper and Samuel Beckett scholar Patrick Henchy published an essay on "The Works of Mary Tighe: Published and Unpublished" (1957) for the *Bibliographic Society of Ireland* that may well have plunged *Selena* into archival oblivion for the rest of the twentieth century.[15] Henchy used the valuable information Hamilton's journals provided to expand bibliographical knowledge of Tighe's works as well as biographical knowledge of her life. While most of the essay offers an unexpectedly sympathetic discussion of Tighe's life (unexpected in light of the article's bibliographic focus), Henchy took a decidedly negative view of the novel, which he read through the prism of Tighe's life:

> This unpublished novel was recently identified among some manuscripts offered for sale to the National Library where it now is. It consists of five large quarto volumes on paper bearing a watermark dated 1809 and is in the neat hand of William Tighe. The heroine, Selena, is tricked by parental maneuvering into marrying her first cousin with whom she is not in love. Indeed, in the pages of this novel there are many shadows cast from the life of the authoress. It is a long and tedious work and is not a good novel. Perhaps its chief interest lies in the picture it gives us of the life and times in which it was written.
>
> *The Picture* is the only poem of the seven woven into this novel which has been published. All show literary merit and are worthy of note in this paper ....
>
> If I have dwelt on the circumstances of Mary Tighe's marriage and married life it is because they are essential to an understanding of her writings, and in

Modern Language Association, 1928); Eva Mary Bell, *The Hamwood Papers of the Ladies of Llangollen and Caroline Hamilton* (London: Macmillan, 1930); Elizabeth Lee, "Mary Tighe," *Dictionary of National Biography*, ed. Sidney Lee, vol. 56 (New York: Macmillan, 1898); Arthur Harcourt Mountain, "The Romantic Elements in Mrs. Tighe's 'Psyche,' with an Account of Her Life and a Review of Her Reliques" (MA Thesis, University of Chicago, 1921); Wilfrid Tighe, "The Tighe Story" (privately printed, 1951–59), MS D/2685/14/1, Public Record Office of Northern Ireland, Belfast.

[14]   William Tighe (1766–1816), Henry's older brother, was the learned author of *Statistical Observations Relative to the County of Kilkenny* (1802). Both he and Henry served as members of the Irish Parliament; both voted against the 1800 Act of Union.

[15]   Patrick Henchy, "The Works of Mary Tighe: Published and Unpublished," *The Bibliographic Society of Ireland* 6.6 (1957): 1–14.

following the course of her life in all its phases we are able to solve a number of bibliographical problems. One cannot read her novel *Selena* without seeing Mary Tighe's dark clouded life in every line of the heroine; and though Selena does not die of T.B., nor indeed at all in the pages of the novel, her devoted mother does. And in her long drawn-out illness we get a vivid picture of Mary Tighe's last years. (8–9, 10)

These comments, invoked in one form or another in nearly every reference to *Selena*, set the terms for the novel's extremely sparse reception history in the latter half of the twentieth century, and surely discouraged prospective readers from poring through those 2,481 manuscript pages if they had the opportunity to work in the National Library's manuscripts reading room.

Most references to *Selena* simply identify it as an unpublished autobiographical novel,[16] but some add very specific details from Henchy: that it was "copied out by hand by her brother-in-law William after her death" (Angeline Kelly, 33), that "it is the mother, not daughter, who dies of TB: see booklet by Patrick Henchy, 1957" (Virginia Blain et al., 1081), or that the heroine is "tricked by parental manoeuvring [sic] into marrying her first cousin with whom she is not in love" (Duncan Wu, 371). Two notable exceptions occur: Paula Feldman's paragraph on *Selena* in *British Women Poets of the Romantic Period* observes that the "epigraphs are an index to Tighe's wide reading in classical as well as seventeenth- and eighteenth-century literature; they include quotations from Charlotte Smith, Mary Wortley Montagu, Jane Porter, Anna Seward, Joanna Baillie, and Hannah More, as well as Shakespeare, Milton, Dryden, Petrarch, Beaumont, and Fletcher" (757); and Debnita Chakravarti's essay on *Psyche* suggests that "Tighe's awareness of the potency of the gaze is also evident in her unpublished novel *Selena*, where she describes her protagonist's promptness to employ it in her first meeting with her cousin" (106). Even so, in 2005, when the manuscripts became slightly more accessible to readers not working at the National Library via the Adam Matthew microfilm series *Irish Women Writers of the Romantic Era* (reels 3–4), the publisher's description drew on Henchy to note that Tighe "wrote a long autobiographical novel entitled *Selena*, which was never published. It is interesting that this described the death of a mother from consumption and the impact that this had on the family. In the real world, it was Mary Tighe who died of tuberculosis in 1810." Similarly, the magisterial *Guide to Irish Fiction, 1650–1900*

---

[16]   See entries on "Mary Tighe" by John Anderson, *The Encyclopedia of Romanticism: Culture in Britain, 1780s–1830s*, ed. Laura Dabundo (New York: Garland, 1992), 576; Joanne Shattock, *The Oxford Guide to British Women Writers* (Oxford: Oxford University Press, 1994), 427; Isobel Armstrong, et al., *Nineteenth Century Women Poets* (Oxford: Clarendon Press, 1996), 115; Mary K. DeShazer, *The Longman Anthology of Women's Literature* (New York: Longman, 2000), 682; Pam Perkins, *The Oxford Dictionary of National Biography* (Oxford: Oxford University Press, 2004), 25 September 2005; or Maureen Mulvihill, *Irish Women Writers: An A-to-Z Guide*, ed. Alexander G. Gonzalez (Westport, CT: Green Press, 2006), 310.

that appeared in 2006 cited Henchy directly in its commentary on *Selena*: "A partly-autobiographical novel whose heroine, Selena, is tricked by parental manoeuvring into marrying her first cousin with whom she is not in love. The novel contains seven poems interwoven with the text" (1294). Happily, as this edition was going to press, Averill Buchanan published the first serious essay-length article on *Selena*, pointing excellent attention to Tighe's dark wit and taking Henchy to task in arguing that "*Selena* is not as autobiographical as he suggests" (176).[17]

It is not surprising that Henchy would dismiss Tighe's novel, given the dominant tastes of the times and his own admiration for Beckett; it is surprising, however, that Henchy made a few factual errors in reporting the contents of MSS 4742–4746, including the total number of pages, which he tallies at "more than 1,700" (13) rather than 2,481, and in omitting five of the eleven rather than seven poems woven into the novel (he lists "The Picture" twice).[18] Also surprising is his conclusion that William Tighe himself copied out the manuscript, given the unlikelihood that a man of William Tighe's education and authorial expertise would have made the numerous, often revealing spelling mistakes the manuscripts contain (which are not in his hand but the less practiced hand and ear of Tighe's amanuensis, who spells "temps" as "tems," "chestnut" as "chesnut," or "fiend" as "feind"), and, more obviously, easy access to a direct handwriting comparison.

---

[17]   Angeline Kelly, *Pillars of the House: An Anthology of Verse by Irishwomen from 1690 to the Present* (1987; Dublin: Wolfhound Press, 1997); Virginia Blain, Patricia Clements, and Isobel Grundy, *The Feminist Companion to Literature in English* (New Haven and London: Yale University Press, 1990); Duncan Wu, *Romantic Women Poets* (Oxford: Blackwell, 1997); Paula Feldman, *British Women Poets of the Romantic Period* (Baltimore: Johns Hopkins University Press, 1997); Debnita Chakravarti, "The Female Epic and the Journey Toward Self-Definition in Mary Tighe's *Psyche*" in *Approaches to the Anglo and American Female Epic, 1621–1982*, ed. Bernard Schweizer (England: Ashgate, 2006), 99–116; *Irish Women Writers of the Romantic Era*, 9 reels (Adam Matthew, 2005); Rolf Loeber and Magda Loeber with Anne Mullin Burnham, *A Guide to Irish Fiction, 1650–1900* (Dublin: Four Courts, 2006), 1293–4; and Averill Buchanan, "'Selena,' the 'New Favorite of My Imagination': Mary Tighe's Unpublished Novel," *Irish University Review* 41:1 (2011): 169–82. Also see Linkin's "Mary Tighe: A Portrait of the Artist for the Twenty-First Century" in *A Companion to Irish Literature*, ed. Julia M. Wright (Oxford: Wiley-Blackwell, 2010), 1:306–7.

[18]   Although the manuscripts were incorrectly numbered (Volume I is 484 versus 504 pages; Volume II is 444 versus 394 pages; Volume III is 585 pages; Volume IV is 421 pages; and Volume V is 577 versus 547 pages), it is hard to see how Henchy came to 1,700 versus 2,481 pages. Of the five poems he omits—"Lord of Hearts benignly callous" (1.65–6), "'Tis thy command, and Edwin shall obey" (I.136–7), "When the bitter source of sorrow" (II.168–9), "Here let us rest, while with meridian blaze" (V.733), "How soft the pause! the notes melodious cease" (V.734)—the last two were the already famous Killarney sonnets, "Written at the Eagle's Nest, Killarney. July 26, 1800" and "Written at Killarney. July 29, 1800," published in *Psyche, with Other Poems* (and frequently reprinted elsewhere).

Even more curious is Henchy's comment on the death of Selena's mother, who actually dies of a "rapid consumption" (I.148) in the last four pages of the first volume rather than of a long drawn-out illness. After brief mention of a "sudden sickness" she experiences in Chapter V during a tense scene with her husband (I.46), the novel makes no reference to her health until Chapter XVIII, when Selena receives a shocking letter urging her return home before her mother expires (I.141). It seems possible that Henchy did not read the novel as thoroughly as he might have, and more's the pity, because *Selena* eminently rewards reading.

While *Selena* offers an unflinching portrait of some of the darker aspects of Tighe's life and world, the novel is magnificent in presenting stunning and moving portrayals of romantic love, of the possibility and importance of female friendship, of the difficulty but necessity of choosing sense over sensibility, and of the need for men and women to pursue self-enhancing vocations (as poets, artists, musicians, educators, farmers, ministers, and more) in conjunction with companionable sociality. It contains some of Tighe's most important and direct statements about the function and power of art in narrative commentaries, as well as conversations that feature Lady Emily Trevallyn (a poet and botanist), Edwin Stanmore (a poet and singer), Selena Miltern, and her younger sister Clara (musicians who may have served as models for Austen's Elinor and Marianne Dashwood), and Angela Harley (a poet and portrait artist). Above all, *Selena* is an aesthetically rich and elegantly constructed novel filled with interesting characters, complex plots, witty external dialogues, moving internal monologues, biting social satire, fascinating sketches of country and city life, lyrically and metaphorically resonant descriptive passages, intriguing remarks on a wide range of invoked literary texts, and sophisticated multi-layered narrative perspectives that eloquently complicate the story being told, including a remarkable 43-page inset narrative (150 manuscript pages) titled "Angela's Narrative Written for her Mother," a confessional self-justification Angela Harley prepares for her Methodist mother as she lays dying (of physical and mental exhaustion exacerbated by the excessive consumption of opium).

The Story of *Selena*

Focused foremost on the romantic and moral entanglements of title character Selena Miltern, the novel begins as if it is a classic fairy tale, with Selena leaving her family home in the Wye valley to visit her godmother Mrs. Vallard in Derbyshire, and therein fulfill a promise her mother made long ago that Selena would visit Hillbarton the summer she turned 17. Within the first three pages she meets her wealthy cousin Lord Dallamore, an indolent, fey, self-indulgent but impulsively generous 20-year-old who, of course, falls madly in love with her for all the wrong reasons except her talent as a musician. Identified as a true connoisseur of music, Dallamore escapes his characteristic restiveness whenever Selena plays the pianoforte or harp, but since he is usually surrounded by sycophants seeking his favor, he mistakes Selena's polite attention for interest, her amused response to his odd behavior as attraction, and her readiness to play as a demonstration of her desire to please him rather than herself:

> The look of fixed attention which surprise at his strange conversation often gave her expressive face, the innocent familiarity with which she often laughed at his extravagant sallies, or his unaccountable fits of distraction, and the obliging cheerfulness with which she was always ready to comply with his desire to hear her sing and play, all conspired to convince him that her young heart had become sensible to his attractions which from the intercourse he had had hitherto with the fair sex he was well inclined to consider as irresistible. The hours which she past at the pianoforte or harp tho' really almost unconscious of his presence were all placed to the account of her wish to fascinate him .... with pleasure to herself she devoted hour after hour to those musical reveries while the indolent Dallamore stretched upon the sopha either held a volume in his hand which he did not even appear to read or played with his favourite Rolla a large spaniel whose fawning caresses alone interrupted the stillness with which he listened to Selena's melody. (I.46)

Although her mother experiences justified anxiety that these cousins from estranged branches of her husband's family have met (and in Selena's case, first learned of the other's existence), her father is secretly pleased at the opportunity he realizes the meeting might provide for him to revenge himself upon his oldest brother, who humiliated him when both were young men by marrying the woman Frederick Miltern (then Dallamore) imagined he loved (Mr. Miltern pointedly fulfills the unfulfilled terms of *Cecilia* by taking his wife's last name for her fortune).

Through a series of gothic machinations worthy of Radcliffe's Montoni, Frederick Miltern engineers a clandestine marriage between the cousins in Scotland, despite Selena's conviction that her mother would never approve her marrying a man of Lord Dallamore's quixotic character (a conviction her father fails to undermine by forging a letter in her mother's handwriting). Miltern is ultimately aided in his plot by his wife's deathbed summons, which prompts Selena's hasty consent so that she can return home as the first volume ends. Many complications ensue: Selena discovers that her mother did not sanction (or even know of) the marriage; her father disinherits her in light of her presumed new status as Lady Dallamore (to leave a more generous legacy for her siblings) but dies of a violent stroke upon learning that his brother plans to contest the Scottish wedding of his underage son; and because Lord Dallamore himself continually neglects to acknowledge the marriage (much less consummate it through a series of mostly homosocial misadventures that keep distracting his ever-wandering attention and body from Selena for much of the novel), Selena cannot or will not openly identify herself as Selena Dallamore. Most complicated of all, it is only after the clandestine marriage that Selena meets the man she belatedly recognizes as her perfect mate, her far more suitable cousin Sidney Dallamore (the son of yet a third estranged Dallamore brother, and not only fellow cousin to Lord Dallamore but childhood friend), who falls in love with her for all the right reasons:

> Sidney had not been many days at Hillbarton before he began to think it impossible to behold and converse with Selena with indifference—and every hour this persuasion grew stronger, whether he gazed upon the perfect loveliness of her light and graceful form, the beauty of her ever varying countenance and complexion, or listened to the simple and unaffected conversation which shewed the justice and delicacy of her sentiments, or admired her uncommon talents displayed with unobtrusive modesty which never seemed to consider herself in the applause which they excited, whatever she said, or however she was employed, whether he observed her mind or mind-illumined face he still saw in her excellence which he had hitherto considered but as the creature only of his own warm imagination, "so lovely fair / That what seemed fair in all the world, seemed / Mean, or in her summed up, in her contained." (II.195, citing *Paradise Lost* 8:471–3)

At this point Sidney does not know that the woman he envisions as his Eve is actually married to another Adam. Nor do the several other prospective suitors who fall desperately and obsessively in love with Selena, including the poet Edwin Stanmore, the son of her father's boyhood friend, who is rather wickedly described as simply waiting for his "Laura" to arrive on the scene:

> The altar had been already raised in the unoccupied temple, and the divinity to whom it was to be consecrated now appeared. Selena was indeed all that his poetical fancy had hitherto painted, every impassioned line which had hitherto kindled his vague and undirected sensibility in his favourite amatory poets now hung upon his lips as he gazed with earnest admiration upon his fair guest, and drank with eagerness love's delicious poison from her eyes. His soul was in a tumult of pleasure. A new existence seemed open to him. Here was a centre towards which all the enthusiastic ardour of his feelings should henceforth for ever be directed. She was at once his Laura, his Cinthia, his Delia, his Saccharissa and his Amoret. The representative of all that hitherto had been celebrated and the theme of every future song; here was the beautiful, the perfect object where his fancy might hereafter repose with passionate tenderness. No solicitous fears disturbed the delightful sensation with which he hailed the power he had so long been prepared to adore. His ambition was only to love, and he had not yet asked himself whether he should be beloved again. (I.134)

While the narrator pokes a little fun at the idealizing, objectifying desire Edwin experiences when he first meets Selena (the chapter just before Selena's secret marriage to Lord Dallamore), the novel treats the dilemma of unfulfilled desire with Tighe's characteristically acute sensitivity: Edwin may imagine that he can safely transform the outpouring of desire for what will prove to be an unattainable object into Petrarchan poetry, but that option will not prove viable for himself or most of the other characters in the novel, including Selena and Sidney, who struggle with the difficulty of channeling their desires for one another into appropriate venues and relationships.

For Selena the greatest internal challenge is recognizing and negotiating a path that leads through the maze of feeling and sensibility to right reason and good moral judgment. Although everyone in the novel identifies her as a model of rectitude for her seemingly infallible morality and ethical judgment (including a few mean-spirited detractors who resent her for it), she herself questions the inner voice that keeps steering her towards sometimes excessively high standards, wondering whether she overcorrects or adheres to those impossibly high standards to avoid censure, or, more troubling, allowing herself to experience the intensity of her emotions. Before she meets Sidney, she puts sincere effort into reconciling herself to the marriage she expects will begin in earnest the minute Lord Dallamore returns, whose disappearance after the wedding for the first of his many larks is the first of her many reasons for repudiating the marriage (which includes his failure to acknowledge the marriage, his aborted engagement to another woman after the marriage, and, ultimately, his notorious affair with one of her relatives). After she meets Sidney, she becomes uncertain how her feelings for him figure into her insistence that she, at least, adhere to the sanctity of the holy promise she and Lord Dallamore made: despite abundant legal justification for annulling the secret marriage, and despite abundant ethical justification for annulling a marriage her father tricked her into by counterfeiting her mother's approval (whose near-last words were "I am contented, you have resolution, you will remember your mother and never be Lord Dallamore's" [I:150]), Selena keeps puzzling through whether she betrays the promise she freely gave by falling in love with Sidney, or betrays herself and her beloved by adhering to the promise. Does true love trump a sacred promise? Is she being perversely moral in denying herself, or has she already lost the moral high ground by allowing herself to feel what she feels for Sidney?

Tighe compounds the psychological difficulties Selena experiences with her material circumstances. She must fend for herself in terms of her precarious economic status: although Lord Dallamore makes funds available to her, she feels unjustified in using them (particularly since Lord Dallamore makes Sidney his agent), but after her father's ill-conceived revision of his will, she has no access to the Miltern family money (and her older brother and younger sister are unable to help her, given various circumstances that afflict them). With no money or room of her own, Selena becomes dependent on the kindness of whoever will house her, and in turn, as a classic dependent (or toad eater, as her unkind sister-in-law puts it), is expected to socialize for her supper. But since the marriage is clandestine and remains unacknowledged, her social status is questioned by all beyond the very small circle acquainted with her dilemma, including the several men who pursue her: not just the lovelorn poet Edwin Stanmore, whose social position, economic standing, and relation to Selena's family makes him an appropriate suitor, but the even more eligible Lord Louverney, charming, socially skilled, wealthy, and of rank, who recognizes in her the ideal mate, but is too late on the scene, given her marriage to one cousin and desire for the other (and whose rejection becomes doubly complicated for Selena to manage because of her unacknowledged marriage to Dallamore and her inappropriate desire for Sidney). It will take all five volumes for Selena Miltern to sort through her material and psychological circumstances, and to combine sense with sensibility so that she can emerge at story's end as Selena Dallamore.

Counterpointing and informing Selena's story is the story of the woman who becomes Selena's best friend, the exquisitely beautiful Lady Emily Trevallyn, compelled by her mother's dying wish to marry a man old enough to be her grandfather when her beloved first cousin Lord Henry Ortney deserts her after their public four-year romance, only to have him pursue her with greater vigor as a newly married countess, whose vain husband Lord Trevallyn lives to display her at various assemblies and parties as his latest acquisition (and in doing so perhaps too closely parallels what Henry Tighe did with Mary Tighe according to Hamilton, who notes how his idle acquaintances would "admire his pretty wife" and that he "made no acquaintances in the world, where he let his wife go by herself" ["Mary Tighe," 254]). Just 25, immured in an uncongenial marriage that her older friend and neighbor Mrs. Vallard sympathetically refers to as "Beauty and the Beast" (I.44–5), striving to let go of the love she still feels for Lord Henry, Lady Emily understands all too well the problem Wollstonecraft wisely analyzed in *A Vindication of the Rights of Woman*, as she tells Selena how her lack of education prepared her to do nothing but make a splendid marriage:

> Upon the first sensations of disgust which I felt for a life of dissipation and what is called the world I became sensible of the great defect in my education. Too much engrossed by the unfortunate idea entertained by my family, that my shewy person was to provide my future settlement, company, dress and amusements were the business of those years which should have been devoted to the cultivation of my mind. The only accomplishment I had ever practised was drawing, and this I rather prosecuted malgré ma minerve, for in spite of all my wishes to excel I have no genius. (I.121)

Although Lady Emily reads widely, writes poetry, and continues to draw, those activities plunge her ever more deeply into reexperiencing the emotional morass of her fatal attachment to Lord Henry; what provides a powerful alternative to her tendency towards excessive sensibility is her charity work: keeping a school for 12 orphan girls managed by Methodist school-mistress Mrs. Harley, who also oversees a manufactory and a shop "where she sold to the labourers every article which was necessary for their comfort at a considerably reduced price" (I.60), including More's *Cheap Repository Tracts*.[19] That Selena understands the prospective parallel between her own story and Lady Emily's is clear when she repeats Lady Emily's

---

[19]   Tighe would have been very familiar with such schools through her mother (Theodosia Blachford was one of the founding members of the House of Refuge in Baggot Street), her mother-in-law (Sarah Tighe had such a school at Rossana, one of the Tighe family estates), and her aunt (Mrs. Edward Tighe was a founding member of the Female Orphan House in Dublin); all of them knew Hannah More as fellow Methodists. For more information, see Angela Bourke, et al., *Irish Women's Writing and Traditions*, vols 4 and 5 of *The Field Day Anthology of Irish Writing* (Cork: Cork University Press; New York: New York University Press, 2002).

telling sentence "Self-sacrificed happiness and I have taken leave of each other for ever" (I.61) just before her marriage to Lord Dallamore (I.129). The parallel becomes even more instructive when she falls in love with Sidney, and tries to control the feelings Lady Emily fails to control for Lord Henry, who sympathetically observes "Alas Selena! our cousins are too amiable!" (III.316).

Juxtaposed to Lady Emily's story is the tragic story of Mrs. Harley's daughter Angela, a successful portrait painter raised as a dependent in the household of Lady Anne Ortney (aunt to both Lady Emily and Lord Henry), whose deeply unsettling, intensely romantic relationship with her seducer (and sometime art instructor) Lord Henry gives the multi-layered narrative of *Selena* a brilliant polyphony, as she and Lady Emily present alternate versions and pieces of the same events from their class-inflected vantage points (rendered with exceptional skill in extended discourses that relate stories surrounding a geranium plant and a portrait of Lord Henry, gift objects that come to reveal the depth of Lord Henry's duplicitous relations with both). Although Tighe carefully underscores the class distinctions that differentiate Lady Emily and Angela, she just as carefully highlights their similarities in her initial descriptions of both. Selena's first glimpse of Lady Emily depicts her as a rare botanical specimen, a hothouse flower ensconced in her luxurious octagon room:

> She was seated at a table covered with plants, botanical instruments, and materials for drawing. On the ground lay open some volumes of Sowerby's plates and other books, and on the little stool at her feet she had thrown her gloves and a white silk handkerchief—the heat of the day thus having inclined her to discover arms and a neck of the most perfect shape and colour. A muslin veil thrown back in graceful drapery confined the luxuriance of her bright chestnut hair and appeared to form a part of the loose folds of her gown which but half declared the symmetry of that beautiful form which the Grecian artists might have selected as the model of their most perfect specimens. (I.42)

When Selena first sees Angela she comes upon her in a "wildly romantick spot" on Lady Emily's plantation, embowered in an abandoned arbor where she has been reading Milton:

> A book lay open on the rude table before her, but she was not reading. Both her arms were also upon it and her head rested upon them with her face turned from that side on which Selena entered. For a moment Selena paused unwilling to disturb her and when she heard with compassion her deep and repeated sighs, she felt still less inclined to intrude and would have retreated gently when Angela suddenly started and turned towards her a face covered with the tears which she had not thought of wiping away.
>
> In spite of those tears Selena beheld her with admiration, her complexion was indeed pale, and her skin tho' of the finest texture was even sallow. Her features were small and delicate, and her long silky eyelashes softened her large black eyes. A close cap covered her dark hair except where a few locks had escaped which shaded her neck and forehead. The beauty of her arms,

the exquisite fineness of her hands and the delicacy of her whole form plainly shewed her education had been superior to her present dress, which was of the coarsest materials tho' put on with an air of good taste which once obtained is perhaps never lost. (I.67)

Those initial descriptions all too accurately anticipate the fates in store for both as a consequence of their self-destructive relationships with Lord Henry. Lady Emily's story takes an even more sinister turn than Selena's, when the jealous Lord Trevallyn temporarily incarcerates his wife in an old mansion in Wales under the watchful gaze of his illegitimate son Edward Guise (whose sanguinary interest in Lord Trevallyn's fortune makes him an unfortunate choice). While Lady Emily is eventually rescued and restored from exile, for Angela there is no return after her expulsion from the garden: her fall results in death.

The fate Tighe scripts for Angela is a very harsh one (and is preceded by pregnancy, miscarriage, illness, opium addiction, and shame). Selena and Sidney evince compassion for her (and thereby show their higher natures), but the narrative is unequivocal in showing that Angela falls further than Lady Emily in terms of actual "criminal" acts and expresses no remorse for the acts themselves, only the pain the consequences of those acts bring to her mother. Nevertheless it is telling that despite the difference in social position (and degree of criminality), both characters feel the same romantic/sexual feelings, both fall into the same seductive traps, and both undergo comparable moments of psychological torment. Both succumb to Lord Henry's false sympathy, and both, lacking Selena's moral self-sufficiency, wither when it is withdrawn, like plants that have been "fostered in factitious warmth":

How sheltered how supported do we feel in every sorrow, in every difficulty when we are confident that the heart whose affection we are most solicitous to preserve is near us to take as it were our part "Against ill fortune and the world."

Yet exquisitely powerful as may be this consolation, the philosopher will perhaps never abandon himself to that weak sensibility which opens the heart to receive it since it is certain that when deprived of that external support by any of the thousand chances to which mortal attachments are liable it is then infinitely less able to struggle with the afflictions or the mortifications of life. It is like the plant which fostered in factitious warmth and covered by the protecting glass is encouraged to expand its delicate leaves and unfold its feeble and premature blossoms to the heat of the reflected sun. But suddenly expelled from the green house, exposed at once to the nipping frost or the overwhelming tempest its pride its beauties instantly languish, its withering branches by degrees drop off and the perishing stem alone remains, stripped sapless and faded the encumbrance of the garden; while its more hardy companions, natives of the same soil but accustomed unshielded to "bear the pitiless storm" are still able to defy its keen[n]ess and resist its force. (V.577, citing *The Fair Penitent* 4.1.335 and *King Lear* 3.4.29)

Expelled from the greenhouse, exposed in the arbor, stripped sapless by the knowledge of Lord Henry's faithlessness, Angela perishes and Lady Emily nearly does, but is saved from the brink of death by Selena's active friendship, the hardy companion whose internal resources enable her to penetrate Lord Henry's ruses early on (because he, of course, contemplates adding Selena to his harem of conquests when he first meets her, in a scene that intriguingly prefigures the first meeting of Anne Elliott and Mr. Elliot in *Persuasion*). In the passage above, the narrator goes on to offer a stern warning:

> Bosoms endowed with sensibility! who now repose upon affection and enjoy the balmy sweets of mutual confidence, can the foreboding mind envy your felicity? Too well assured that the time must come when one at least will bitterly feel how insupportable is such a deprivation—will it not rather be inclined to utter the selfish but prudent precept of the inconsistent Rousseau "O Homme resserre ton existence en [sic] dedans de toi & tu ne seras pas plus misérable." (V.577, citing *Émile* 2)

However that cold advice to follow Rousseau—"O man, constrain your existence within yourself, and you will no longer be miserable"—utterly fails Selena, who becomes more miserable the more she seeks to contain her existence within herself. Neither can she find complete satisfaction in dedicating herself to others: much like Tighe's Psyche, Selena must find the midway between dependence and independence. As her mother predicted, "Selena's loving heart can only find its happiness in well placed affection" (I.150). By story's end Selena locates that perfect balance as she rightly assumes her identity as Lady Dallamore in a fairy tale marriage to Sidney that the narrator believes will only strengthen over time, happily ever after: "Happy lovers! Revolving periods find you more endearing, more endeared unto each other, for you there is no honey moon! Your love knows how to perpetuate itself, and built upon the solid basis of just esteem has nothing to fear from time which can but strengthen the beautiful and perfect edifice, as the weight which oppresses the arch adds to its firmness and ensures its durability" (V.738).

Characters of Interest

While *Selena* focuses primarily on the stories of Selena, Lady Emily, and Angela, and how they succeed or fail to integrate the forces of desire and self control in navigating the constructs of female identity, it is also the story of several young men who need to learn how to make more appropriate choices, such as Edwin Stanmore, who must overcome his obsession with Selena to understand the truer value (for him) of her younger sister Clara Miltern, which he explains as a kind of Petrarchan transference of the ideal to the real:

"Do not dear Selena," cried he earnestly, "Judge me of a fickle disposition, and that my love is of a transient nature because I have proved it possible to be transferred. The sentiments, the graces that I have loved and yet love with a passion which never can be changed are the same. You are all that is lovely, all that is excellent upon earth, I know, I feel it, but give credit to my sincerity when I declare that had I seen Clara at Inverathie, my unfortunate folly should never have tormented you and injured myself as it has done. I blush for what has past, but not for that love which has never changed, for in you I did but love the virtues and the charms of Clara." (V.737)

So too Selena's older brother Robert Miltern, who falls head over heels in love with Lady Harriet Modely because of her "shewy figure," as Mrs. Vallard somewhat tactfully puts it (II.210), deploying greater delicacy than the happily snide narrator:

Lady Harriet's brilliant complexion indeed owed the advantages of its striking colours not to rouge alone, and the large and completely exposed neck and shoulders which dazzled the eye by their uncommon whiteness, as well as the snowy lustre of her arms, more covered by their bracelets than the small and delicate web which could scarcely boast the name of sleeve shewed as little of their natural hue as the less artificial and more acknowledged painting of her cheek. And yet it was to the shewy contrast formed by this complexion with a profusion of dark hair for which also she was not entirely indebted to Nature, that she owed her having been a much celebrated tho' questioned beauty. For except for her eyes which were large and of the very darkest hazle she possessed not one feature which could be called fine and certainly did not by the expression or animation of her countenance compensate for the want of perfect regularity. (II.203)

Like Edwin, Robert experiences a passion for what in his case proves to be a false erotic idol that he subsequently transfers to the innocent, childlike Ophelia Lawder, whom he sees as embodying a familial domestic ideal as the favorite adopted daughter in the Bently clan:

"I am not sure that you would allow her to be beautiful and she is certainly not so perfect a model as Lady Trevallyn, but a sweeter dimpled smile nor a finer natural complexion it is impossible to shew. Add to these a profusion of flaxen ringlets with the softest clear blue eyes—and you may form some idea of Ophelia Lawder's person. But the innocent interesting expression, the playful childish grace which accompanies all her words, looks, and actions, and to which her foreign accent perhaps contributes—you certainly cannot imagine for I never saw any thing like it except with herself. I have more than once seen infantine naiveté affected and turned from it with disgust, but this peculiarity in the simplicity of Ophelia's manners are as perfectly unattainable as the features of her face." (IV.503)

Just as Clara naturalizes the almost terrible perfection that Selena represents to Edwin, Ophelia (French accent and all) naturalizes the false affectations Lady

Harriet assumes and reverses her simmering sexual sophistication with a perhaps too sweetly simpering simplicity.

Lady Harriet is one of several memorable secondary female characters whose exploits or histories cast light on the alternate paths Selena, Lady Emily, and Angela might take: a woman who only lives to be admired, who is vain, shallow, bored and boring, who is unwilling to walk, talk, read, or play music (much less pursue charitable occupations), who is marginally interested in netting and always interested in mean-spirited gossip, she manages to have affairs with most of the men in the novel (except the ever-virtuous Sidney and the otherwise-engaged Edwin), and therein contrasts with the woman she sees as her chief competitor for admiration, Lady Emily, fully demonstrating the logic of Wollstonecraft's argument that women who are raised to attract men only know how to attract men and do so, resulting, ultimately, in betrayal. Although Lady Harriet's narcissistic actions bring real harm to others—and illuminate how thoroughly and deliberately women can hurt one another—she is also the source of an immense font of humor, and frequently enables other women to make feeling connections with one another, as Selena and Clara do in witnessing the "ceremony" of the sneeze during their first evening with her:

> Lady Harriet listened in silence with a vacant eye and a smile which Selena could not help thinking was a smile not of satisfaction but contempt.
> In the midst of her eulogium she was however interrupted by Lady Harriet's asking with a yawn, "Pray may I ring the bell?"
> "Certainly, but can I do any thing for you Lady Harriet," answered Selena.
> "No I thank you," answered her Ladyship who had touched the bell which was at her elbow while she spoke.
> Upon the servant's entrance she said in even a lower voice than usual, "Be so good as to tell my maid to bring me my handkerchief."
> "My Lady!" said the servant approaching to hear if possible the yet inaudible commands; Selena repeated her orders, Lady Harriet appearing in silent despair of making herself understood by ears so vulgar.
> The maid entered with the perfumed handkerchief which she presented on a salvar, and again receiving it in a few moments retired as she had approached with an unnoticed and silent curtsey.
> Selena thought this ceremony must be rather troublesome in case her Ladyship was ever unfortunate enough to be troubled with so vulgar a thing as a cold and turned her eye fearfully from the arch smile of Clara. (II.208–9)

Similarly, when Lady Emily finally makes a requisite visit to Lady Harriet which she has been avoiding because she "could not bear the idea of submitting to the inquisitive stare of Lady Harriet in a morning visit where there was nothing else to divert her great black eyes from counting the moles on my face, or the hairs in my eyelashes; for as she does not draw, I cannot conceive for what other purpose she always takes such an accurate survey of features which I am sure it gives her no pleasure to look at" (II.229), that visit demonstrates the immense affection she feels for Selena; she not only makes the visit at Selena's express request, but says so:

> Lady Trevallyn then turning round to Selena softly whispered as she pressed her hand, "You see your power."
>
> Selena blushed and fearful of Lady Harriet's scrutinizing eye occupied herself in drawing a chair for Lady Trevallyn while Clara ran to look for Mrs. Vallard. A silence of some instants ensued, while Lady Trevallyn's expressive "Hem!" told Selena how much she was suffering under the expected stare. (II.233)

Here the gaze that so often initiates obsession and possession in male-female relations becomes an object of humor and connection for female-female relations.

Like Lady Harriet, the quirky Lady Greysville provides some keen comic relief, but from a generally more benevolent position (at least to the women she considers sincere, versus those she identifies as hypocrites, to whom she is merciless). One of the most interesting characters in the novel, Lady Greysville is a Freudian dream come true: physically diminutive but beautiful, almost always depicted in a riding "habit and large man's hat" (I.85), thoroughly obsessed with horses, most attractive, according to Lord Louverney, when she places herself in danger on large animals, constantly torturing her extremely jealous husband by flirting with other men (indeed treating him like a child, which is what Selena imagines he must be when she first hears Lady Greysville referring to him as "Tom"), she is ultimately "corrected" of her displaced desire through a pregnancy that removes her from the pages of the novel and purportedly brings peace or at least "the prospect of an heir to the house of Greysville which had been for some time despaired of" (V.593). So reports her Aunt Rolleham, who is not only "excessively shortsighted" (V.592) but excessively concerned with keeping her house in order (and tellingly restores gender power relations by identifying her niece as "Charlotte"). A well-intentioned and supportive friend to Lady Emily and Selena, Lady Greysville recognizes the dangers of seduction and warns Selena against falling into the emotional sinkhole Lady Trevallyn inhabits:

> "How much happier would she have been, how much more estimable if she had acted wisely and given up her foolish love and her wicked cousin when she saw he had no intention of acting fairly by her .... there is no man worth being unhappy about believe me. A lover is a very charming thing but when he begins once to give you a pain, good bye all that is charming, let him go without a struggle. Treat him as you would a pen knife—nothing looks more brilliant at a distance but where it dazzles most if clasped too closely nothing can give a sorer wound. Handle it rightly nothing is more useful, but attempt not to detain it if withdrawn for if you do depend upon it, it will cut you most severely." (III.393)

Although she frequently flirts with Lord Henry, it is usually a comic flirtation in which she seeks to maintain the upper hand: "He was indeed then submitting to the whim of Lady Greysville who had covered his cheeks with rouge, and tied on his head her own white hat and feathers" (I.105). She knows how to handle circulating material and keep herself clean, whether it be the effluvia of books or men, as when she is "seated at the open window occupied in reading a novel which

she had sent for to the circulating library as she said to drive away the ill temper
of Sir Thomas. She had placed the book on the outside that she might at the same
time watch the arrival of her horses and avoid its effluvia, and to protect herself
from the filth of the leaves turned them over with a knife and fork" (I.95). The
diametrical opposite of Lady Harriet, who spreads malicious gossip to put down
other women and elevate herself, Lady Greysville tells a spurious tale to distract
attention from Selena at an embarrassing moment, and then pointedly admits the
tale is spurious:

> "half the scandalous stories you hear are told like mine for the sole purpose
> of your entertainment, only those who relate them have seldom the sincerity
> to own as I do their true origin …. Who ever tells any story simply as it is and
> when the luxuriant branches of exxageration, malice or interest, or the mere
> desire of exciting astonishment are lopped off who will pay any attention to the
> dull unornamented trunk that is left, if even any thing whatever should remain."
> (III.382–3)

However, when Lady Greysville herself is the subject of a scandalous story that
she tricked Lord Dallamore and her husband in a monetary exchange over a gift
horse (that Lord Dallamore is said to have shot because she ruined it through hard
riding), the unornamented trunk of the tale is anything but dull and revelatory of
violence between men:

> "he offered me a beautiful thorough bred chesnut mare that I took a fancy to,
> and I would have given one of my eyes to Tom with pleasure if he would but
> have allowed me to keep her, but nothing could prevail upon him, so after two
> days riding I sent her back with a heavy heart. But any thing for a quiet life you
> know. I took care however to make my complaint to Dallamore and what do you
> think he did?"
>
> "Gave her to his groom I dare say."
>
> "Oh I wish to Heaven he had. No but the savage took a pistol and shot her
> thro' the head before Tom's face, I really cried with vexation when I heard it."
> (III.388)

Exacerbating the patriarchal violence of the unornamented version is Lord
Louverney's chilling response, who simply smiles "at the strange misrepresentation
with which this annecdote had so lately been repeated" (III.388) and considers
using it to humble the female teller of the false one.

Art and Aesthetics

Lady Greysville's shrewd comments on the function of exaggeration in
storytelling instance one of the several places in *Selena* where Tighe offers some
intriguingly self-reflexive remarks on artistic production and aesthetic pleasure
through the voices of her characters. The very words Tighe used to describe her
own anxieties about the "vanity of authorship" in letters to Walker reappear in a

major conversation Selena and Edwin have on the dangers of public performance, which provides a tantalizing glimpse into Tighe's rationale for not publishing.[20] When Selena expresses the hope that Edwin's "talents if rightly exercised must ensure him reputation," Edwin assumes she is "ambitious of hearing that your friend is applauded on the stage where perhaps my voice may please while it is a novelty," an assumption Selena quickly dispels to assert the value of private study over social success:

> "Ridiculous!" said Selena, "you could not imagine that I meant that, nay I should be sorry to hear that you yielded to the solicitations of those who will call themselves your friends and the natural impulse of vanity by devoting your time to the exhibition of your musical talents even in a less public manner. Grieved indeed should I be to know that you were ensnared in that dangerous and *bruyante* society, to which you will undoubtedly be courted, and which it will I am sensible cost you some courage to resist. It is not in scenes of dissipation and at the tables of riot that I wish my friend to seek for applause—it is in the fruits of your study that I hope you will taste the sweeter and more valuable praise of genius and of virtue." (III.314)

Unfortunately, Edwin will find himself ensnared by an especially bruyante society and succumb to even more than the vanity of its applause, but at this point he tells Selena that he writes not for fame but to relieve himself. After a characteristic citation from Petrarch—"certo ogni mio studio in quel tempo era / Pur di sfogare il doloroso core / In qualche modo, non d'acquistar fama / Pianger cercai, non già del pianto honore" (sonnet 293, lines 9–12: "in truth my efforts at that time / were to ease the saddened heart / in that manner, not to acquire fame. / I sought to weep, not gain honour from tears")—Edwin explains

> "I have never felt much alive to the pleasures of an unlimited confidence, and this has the rather inclined me to write my sensations—for oh how soothing is it to fix upon paper and to behold with my eyes the feelings deeply engraven on my heart but known only to myself. This embosoming of my soul affords indeed a charm sweet and consolatory, far superior to that which could arise from a detail of sentiments to ears which never can fully understand and still less sympathise with our emotions for vain is the effort to communicate by any expressions the ideas which memory and sensibility can sometimes reproduce to the mind by a single line." (III.315)

---

[20]   When Walker asks permission to show his copy of *Psyche* to William Hayley in 1803, with an eye towards prospective publication, Tighe replies "You are very good to receive with such indulgence my compositions but I fear others (to whom your flattering partiality might incline you to show them) cannot be expected to look upon them with the same favoring eye — I hope my vanity of authorship may never conquer the repugnance I now feel to stand forth to the public & say Hear me, but I will not deny that I feel any thing more delightful to self love than to be listen'd to with a smile, nor is that pleasure in any degree lessen'd by a consciousness that I should place the smile to the account of partiality" (Postmark 16 August 1803, MS 1461/5/43, Trinity College, Dublin).

Selena's reply not only echoes Tighe's words to Walker, but will subsequently resonate in both Blachford's and Hamilton's biographical descriptions of Tighe: "tho' you may despise the vanity of authorship, or not feel inclined to undertake any work which might benefit others, yet I hope you will never lose in dissipation or indolence your taste for literature, nor forget the instructions of your father, nor the prayers of your mother—and that for the sake of those friends whom you still possess, you will pay some attention to your health, which has been so near suffering irreparably by your neglect" (III.315).

While Edwin's Petrarchan and semi-Wordsworthian sensibility views poetry as a means of expressing and thereby relieving the spontaneous overflow of powerful feelings, in the next chapter Lady Emily broadens Edwin's masculinist perspective by telling Selena that the act of poetic composition can actually induce or intensify strong emotion. After Lady Emily recites Angela's poem "The Picture" (a beautifully refractive moment in the novel where Lady Emily speaks the words Angela has written about the portrait Lord Henry uses to seduce them both), Selena is stunned by the overt sexual passion it conveys and hopes it is only a copy: "if poor Angela did indeed write those verses, I fear she is lost not only to happiness and her poor Mother, but even to innocence. What virtuous girl could bear thus openly to boast a passion for which it is evident she even then doubted of meeting a faithful return? But I can hardly think they are her own; perhaps she has only copied them" (III.324). Lady Emily certifies that Angela did indeed compose the verses—"there were one or two lines scratched out and others to the same purpose written over them evidently done for the sake of the rhyme"—but suggests that Angela's imagination could have fleshed out her experience: "I do not quite agree with you as to the necessary conclusion you have drawn from them, for I know when the fit of writing seizes a person who is in the habit of this dangerous indulgence, one is inclined to express in even stronger language than the heart at other times feels the sentiments we scarce allow ourselves in plain prose to speak" (III.325). One of the grand meta-moments in the novel, Lady Emily's words go far toward explaining or justifying the risks Tighe herself takes as the actual author of "The Picture" and in scripting so much more that suggests she might be "lost not only to happiness and her poor Mother, but even to innocence," comparable to her strategic defense of *Psyche* (which she dedicates to her mother): "my subject might be condemned by the frown of severer moralists; however I hope, that if such have the condescension to read through a poem which they may perhaps think too long, they will yet do me the justice to allow, that I have only pictured innocent love, such love as the purest bosom might confess" (*Collected Poems* 53).

Another such wonderful meta-moment occurs when Lord Trevallyn berates his niece Jane Aston for associating with scholars, with his toady brother-in-law Mr. Montrose following suit. Modeled in large part on Theodosia Blachford, the former Jane Trevallyn educated herself by reading the works in her father's library and was only able to marry a propertied but miserly reverend when she was past her prime because, as Lady Emily explains to Selena, despite her youthful beauty "she had the odious character of being a very learned Lady" (III.327):

> "She is entirely self taught, educated in great retirement with a very confined circle of illiterate, self conceited ignorant card players her mind really superior to all around took its ideas wholly from books. No one took any pains either to amuse or improve her time, and as she had naturally an inquisitive turn and that there happened to be a large old library at Trevallyn hall where the first five and twenty years of her life were exclusively past reading became almost her sole occupation …. When at length she escaped from her confinement and mixed with the world, she saw that even among the most distinguished literary characters there were perhaps none who sacrificed to study so large a portion of their time as she had been accustomed to devote." (III.328)[21]

The moment Lord Trevallyn happens upon Mrs. Aston discoursing enthusiastically about an old book she found in the Montrose library, which she believes will assist her researches for a Dr. Proclus and his treatise on polytheism and Plato, he chastises her severely:

> "I have frequently told you Jane that people of a certain rank and women in particular should have nothing to do with Pedants and scholars who are for the most part people of low birth and in no respect such as we should like to associate with."
> "Faith my Lord it's very true," cried Mr. Montrose, "I wonder for my part how people can have any pleasure in poring over books and besides one must get so d—d sick of all these old stories about the Gods and one stuff or another of that kind over and over again for the same stupid nonsense these thousand years I dare say." (III.377)

Situated at the near-center of the novel, it is no accident that Lady Emily's husband and brother seek to demonstrate their power but instead reveal their meanness by insulting self-educated women who pored over old books about the gods to write their own, just like Tighe herself.

The Real and Literary Worlds of Mary Tighe's *Selena*

The self-reflexive attention Tighe calls to herself as the author of *Psyche* and to her mother via the figure of Jane Aston in this central moment in the novel provides a portion of what Henchy rightly recognizes as the autobiographical elements of *Selena*, with one major critical distinction: like all great writers, Tighe transforms the elements of her life into art. Comparable to the *roman à clef* aspects of Smith's *Emmeline*, or Wollstonecraft's *Mary*, or Lamb's *Glenarvon*, or Shellley's *Frankenstein*, *Selena* contains multiple characters and episodes clearly

---

[21] See Hamilton's strikingly similar description of Theodosia Blachford's early education in the library at Rossana ("Mary Tighe," 247–8).

drawn from Tighe's experience: if Jane Aston evokes Tighe's mother, Edwin Stanmore evokes Thomas Moore, Robert Miltern evokes Tighe's brother John Blachford (who eventually divorced his flashy first wife Camilla for the more decorous Mary Anne Grattan, daughter of Henry Grattan), Lady Anne Ortney evokes Lady Selina Hutchinson, Angela Harley's parents follow a John Wesley-like Methodist preacher to America for a stint (the Wesleys were very close to the Tighes), and the details for a particularly nasty affair may have been drawn from Tighe's cousin Robert Tighe's court case (who successfully sued his wife's lover for "criminal conversation" in 1800).[22] The more we learn about Tighe's life, the more opportunities there will be to appreciate how she refashions her world into Selena's, a literary world Henchy also rightly recognizes as interesting for its depiction of late eighteenth-century life and culture. Tighe offers a compelling portrait of her times as characters from various social strata interact at country houses, gardens, parks, parties, private clubs, alehouses, theaters, and inns within England (Derbyshire, Harrogate, Harewood House, The Green Dragon, The Star, Strawberry Hill, Herefordshire, Bath, London), Ireland (Dublin, Clonagh, Killarney), Scotland (Inverathie, Carlisle), Wales, and Germany (Frankfurt), not only voicing their feelings about one another but about the social concerns of the day, which range from humorous commentaries on the amount of rouge it takes to cover Belle Richmond's ample cheeks to more serious reflections on the impact of absentee landlords on the people of Ireland.

Above all, the literary world Tighe creates in *Selena* is a world immersed in literature, with significant invocations of work in Latin, Italian, English, French, Spanish, and German by Homer, Horace, Ovid, Petrarch, Tasso, Guarini, Drayton, Shakespeare, Rinuccini, Milton, Beaumont, Fletcher, Dryden, Otway, Lee, Cervantes, Rowe, Pope, Young, Thomson, Gray, Akenside, Brooke, Rousseau, Macpherson, Metastasio, Lillo, Goldsmith, Beattie, Barbauld, More, Monti, Burns, Goethe, Walpole, Cowper, Fenton, Seward, Baillie, Hayley, Smith, Moore, Porter, Southey, and others. In addition to the 94 authorial epigraphs that provide emotionally meaningful keys to the events of the chapters that follow, the narrator offers dozens upon dozens of internal references that brilliantly contextualize the lives and feelings of the characters, often through the sophisticated use of free indirect discourse, which enables the narrator to seamlessly pass into a character's mind. Even more important than the authorial epigraphs and narrator references are the literary texts that the characters themselves invoke directly, particularly Lady Emily, Selena, Sidney, Clara, Edwin, and Angela, who encode or express their feelings through citation. Almost all the characters have frequent recourse to

---

[22] See *An act to dissolve the marriage of John Blachford ... with Maria Camilla Blachford, his now wife, and to enable him to marry again; and for other purposes therein mentioned* (London: Clayton & Scott, 1812) for the details on John Blachford's divorce; see *Report of the trial ... between Robert Tighe ... plaintiff, and Dive Jones ... for crim. con. with Esther Francis Tighe, otherwise Wade ...* (Dublin: William Folds, 1800) for the details on Robert Tighe's suit.

Shakespeare, self-consciously addressing their own situations (or those observed) in a literary shorthand that draws on *Romeo and Juliet* (Mrs. Miltern, Angela), *Two Gentlemen of Verona* (Selena), *A Midsummer Night's Dream* (Lord Henry, Clara), *Henry IV, Part 1* (Lady Greysville), *Much Ado About Nothing* (Lord Henry), *As You Like It* (Lady Emily, Selena), *Hamlet* (Mrs. Miltern, Clara), *Troilus and Cressida* (Sidney), *All's Well that Ends Well* (Edwin), *Othello* (Sidney), *Macbeth* (Lady Emily, Selena), *Antony and Cleopatra* (Selena), and *Coriolanus* (Sidney).[23] They also communicate their feelings about one another by sharing physical texts, such as Akenside's *The Pleasures of the Imagination* (Sidney and Selena), Baillie's *Count Basil* (Edwin and Clara), Bernardin de Saint-Pierre's *Paul et Virginie* (which Selena gives to Angela), Florian's *Estelle et Némorin* (which Edwin gives to Selena), or Rousseau's *Julie, ou La Nouvelle Héloïse* (which Selena cites to Edwin, and, more importantly, Lady Emily and Selena read aloud to one another). Lady Emily instructs Selena in the pleasures of botanizing through books as well as flowers (Chaptal's *Elements of Chemistry*, Sowerby's *English Botany*, Withering's *The Botanical Arrangement*), Thomson's *The Seasons* seems to run through everyone's mind, and there are more references to Milton (20) than the Bible (8), a surprise given Hamilton's representation of Tighe's opinion of Milton: "I have great reason to be dissatisfied with my want of taste if Milton does indeed deserve all the admiration that has been lavished upon him" ("Mary Tighe," 259).

Even more surprising, although Tighe populates the world of *Selena* with several active poets, there are as many references to plays as there are to poems, and her characters are as quick to see themselves enacting roles in Restoration and eighteenth-century dramas as they are to romance one another with Petrarch and Monti, adverting, via the narrator or themselves, to Lee's *Mithridates* (1678) and *Theodosius* (1680); Dryden's *All For Love* (1678) and *Don Sebastian* (1690); Otway's *Venice Preserved* (1682); Rowe's *Tamerlane* (1701), *The Fair Penitent* (1703), and *Jane Shore* (1714); Young's *The Revenge* (1721); Thomson's *The Tragedy of Sophonisba* (1730), *Agamemnon* (1738), and *Tancred and Sigismunda* (1745); Brooke's *The Earl of Essex* (1761); More's *Percy* (1778) and *The Fatal Falsehood* (1779); Jephson's *The Count of Narbonne* (1781); Walpole's *The Mysterious Mother* (1781); Fenton's *Mariamne* (1723); Schiller's *Cabal and Love* (1785); and Baillie's *Count Basil* (1798), with a rueful self-awareness.[24]

---

[23] The narrator and epigraphs also cite *Henry VI, Part II, Twelfth Night, Measure for Measure, King Lear,* and *The Tempest*. Interestingly, Edwin only cites Shakespeare once, although Selena comments that it is Edwin who made Clara so fond of him (II.200).

[24] These are all the plays cited more than once; Tighe also includes references to Baillie's *De Montfort* (1798), Beaumont and Fletcher's *The Nice Valour* (1615), *The Custom of the Country* (1647), *The Maid in the Mill* (1647), Brooke's *Earl of Westmoreland* (1789), Congreve's *The Mourning Bride* (1697), Corneille's *Othon* (1664), Dryden's *The Rival Ladies* (1664), *The Royal Martyr* (1670), *The Conquest of Granada* (1672), *The Spanish Fryar* (1681), and his translation of Flaucus's *The Second Satyr* (1693), Fletcher's *The Lovers' Progress* (1647), Kotzebue's *Count Benyowsky* (1798), Lee's *The Massacre of Paris* (1690), Lillo's *Arden of Feversham* (1762), Mallet's *Mustapha* (1739), Plautus's

Almost all these dramas evidence Tighe's taste for "she-tragedies" (the term Rowe himself coined to describe pathetic tragedies like his own that focused on the domestic sufferings of innocent, virtuous women), and allusively overwhelm the handful of references to continental and British novels (Cervantes's *Don Quixote*, Smollett's *The Adventures of Peregrine Pickle*, Richardson's *Sir Charles Grandison*, Rousseau's *Julie*, Goethe's *Werther*, Montolieu's *Caroline de Lichtfield*, Florian's *Estelle et Némorin* and *Gonsalve de Cordoue*, and Bernardin's *Paul et Virginie*).[25] While Tighe did not situate her five-volume novel in the emerging tradition of women's fiction through direct citation, she recognized its consonance with other women writers' texts. In a late reading journal entry dated 27 January 1807, she records the following notes on Parsons's four-volume novel *Murray House* (1801): "Deficient in style & in force of character as this novel is, it yet instructs far more than the normal run of the same class — there were two or three striking resemblances in points of story & character to Selena which I confess annoy'd me & had I read it some years ago mine must have been a plagiary."[26]

Whether or not Parsons would have found *Selena* to be a plagiary, it is tantalizing to wonder how other women writers might have responded to Tighe's novel, and whether there were additional readers of the manuscripts whose comments may yet emerge, such as Austen, whose path most likely crossed Tighe's when both were in residence at Bath, or Edgeworth, who sustained an ongoing friendship with Hamilton, or Owenson, whose novels came in for a sharp but appreciative drubbing in Tighe's journal, despite their purported friendship (a friendship Hamilton saw Owenson pushing forward rather than Tighe), or Lamb, connected to Tighe through their common Ponsonby relations (as well as her friendship with Owenson as Lady Morgan), or Shelley, who sustained a close friendship with Tighe's cousin George Tighe and Lady Mountcashell (and wrote "Maurice, or the Fisher's Cot" for their daughter Laurette Tighe), or the Brontës, whose father went to St. Johns College at Cambridge under the sponsorship of Tighe's uncle Thomas Tighe (half-brother of Theodosia Blachford). It is equally tantalizing to wonder what further impact Tighe might have had on the development of women's literature had *Selena* been published, and the greater reputation she might have sustained in nineteenth- and twentieth-century literary history. Readers will have time in the twenty-first century to figure it out anew.

Stichus (200 BC), Rowe's *The Ambitious Stepmother* (1702) and *The Royal Convert* (1708), Thomson's *Edward and Eleanora* (1739) and *Alfred: A Masque* (1740), Trapp's *Abra-Mule* (1708), and Young's *Busiris* (1719) and *The Brothers* (1753).

[25]   Somewhat tellingly, the only work that succeeds in absorbing Lord Dallamore's attention is a French novel.

[26]   MS 4804, National Library of Ireland, Dublin.

Volume I

Chapter I

As the buds of wild roses, the cheeks of the maid
    Were just tinted with youth's lovely hue;
Her form like the aspen mild graces displayed
And her eyes over which her luxuriant locks strayed
    As the skies of the summer were blue.
    Charlotte Smith[1]

The Summer was already advanced before Mrs. Vallard could prevail upon her friend Mrs. Miltern to part with her beloved Selena tho' a promise had been long given that she should receive a visit from her godchild when the spring should have completed her seventeenth year. At last conquered by her importunity, at the advice of her husband, Mrs. Miltern consented with some pain that Selena should spend a month with the friend for whom tho' long divided by distance, she still retained the warmest affection, and in whose care she placed the utmost confidence. Selena herself accustomed from her birth to the exclusive retirement of Miltern Abbey considered this separation from her family, and in particular a mother so tenderly loved, as well as the interruption to her pursuits and studies as a sacrifice which she must reluctantly make to the amiable character of the person whom from her infancy she had been taught to consider as a second mother. She was received by Mrs. Vallard as the most precious deposit with a tenderness which could not have been exceeded had she welcomed the return of her only daughter, yet in the pleasure which she felt in her society there mingled a kind of anxiety and regret that she should be removed from the protection of her excellent instructress, an anxiety which was hourly encreased while she gazed upon the improved talents of her very lovely charge, and continually beheld some new demonstration of the most cultivated understanding, the most polished mind, and a judgment almost supernatural when compared with her years and inexperience. Mrs. Vallard had been for many years a widow, and since the death of her husband had resided at Hillbarton, which was a small but beautiful estate situated in the most delightful part of Derbyshire left to her by her fond husband as almost the only unsettled part of the immense property which as he had no children devolved upon his sister married to the Earl of Mount Villars.

---

[1]   Charlotte Smith, "The Forest Boy," *Elegiac Sonnets and Other Poems*, 8th ed., 2 vols (London: Cadell and Davies, 1797–1800), 2:64, lines 25–30.

Lady Mount Villars had not long survived her brother and the estate now became the property of her only son Lord Dallamore who tho' not yet of age was suffered to consider it already as his own by an indulgent father.

As Mrs. Vallard and her young companion were one evening returning from their accustomed walk they crossed that side of the park next the high road where the paling was low; when the sound of an approaching carriage directed thither their attention; a cloud of dust and the swiftness with which the equipage flew past prevented their being able to distinguish more than that it was a curricle[2] attended by two grooms on horseback.

Selena with the curiosity natural to a young mind ran from her companion and standing on a little bank near the paling pursued with her eyes the new and lively object which had gone by, and when she perceived it take the direction which by a turn in the road led down to Hillbarton she returned as speedily to inform Mrs. Vallard of her visitor and to be herself informed whom they might expect to meet on their return home. In this point she however received no satisfaction; and they were amusing themselves with conjectures when they came within view of the house and perceived on the lawn a young man walking slowly towards them.

"My dear Selena," exclaimed Mrs. Vallard, "I cannot be deceived that is your cousin Lord Dallamore."

"My cousin! I never before heard his name."

"That surprises me," returned Mrs. Vallard, "I knew indeed that your father had not been on friendly terms with his family, but that you should never have heard them spoken of is astonishing."

"If that is the case," said Selena with some hesitation, "I am afraid my father will consider this meeting as unfortunate."

"There is no help for it now my dear, you must be introduced to him, and your father who knows my connexion with Dallamore must have reflected that this was at least probable. He is a very charming young man and will not I am sure intrude himself upon Mr. Miltern."

While she was speaking the subject of their conversation approached; his hat was off and with his handkerchief he wiped the dust from a face which had he worn his hair in its natural state might have gained him the appelation of a beautiful child, unless the tall and manly figure to which it was associated had rendered such a comparison ridiculous.

With a smile and a careless air replacing his hat upon his head he gave his hand to Mrs. Vallard addressing her with a familiarity which proved him no stranger.

"You see," said he, "I have fulfilled my promise even sooner than you expected, I dare say you did not believe I meant to come."

"You are a good boy, indeed I did not think you could so soon have torn yourself from your gay town friends to visit an old aunt in the country, to reward you I will introduce you to a new cousin, a pleasure which I should not have been

---

2   Curricle: light, two-wheeled carriage only large enough for a driver and passenger.

able to procure you, had you long delayed your visit. Selena Miltern I must present you to your cousin Lord Dallamore."

The young man now first looked at Selena, who on her part had not been so unobservant of him, tho' when they joined him she had timidly left Mrs. Vallard's arm and retired a few steps from whence unnoticed she had gazed with some degree of wonder and interest upon this unknown relation.

Dallamore felt himself surprised at the introduction; not that Selena's name was also a stranger to his ears, but to find one of that family with his aunt, with whom he knew not that they had any acquaintance and thus suddenly to be presented to a relation whom he had been taught never to consider as such startled and gave him an air of hesitation and even of restraint which he was very little accustomed to wear.

Recovering himself however he complained of the dust and heat, and upon Mrs. Vallard's enquiring how far he had driven he exclaimed "Why I left Derby today with Peters and Richmond on our way to Harrogate and I have promised to follow them there; but upon my soul the roads are so insufferable that I think I must stay with you till there is some rain; There ought positively be an act of parliament against those odious waggons and stage coaches; Don't you think so? For there is no travelling in dry weather they poison one to such a degree. And rain is a cursed bore too. How pretty and cool Hillbarton looks after those d--d dusty roads, you will let me stay here while this hot weather lasts I hope—Won't you?"[3]

"Dear Dallamore you will make me quite happy, and I have now an additional reason to join with my haymakers in praying for a continuance of this dry season."

They were by this time at the hall door but as they were entering Dallamore who perceived the grooms leading round the horses insisted upon Mrs. Vallard's accompanying him to the stable yard to look at them and his new curricle.

Selena mean while stole up stairs to write to her mother an account of the arrival of her cousin and to ask for an explanation of the mystery with which her relationship to the house of Mount Villars had been hitherto concealed.

Mrs. Vallard took the opportunity of her absence to express her surprise that not only persons so nearly related should never had met but that Selena had actually never heard of Dallamore's connexion with her family.

"D--n it," said the young man with a vacant air, "there has been always so much mystery about those Milterns that I never gave myself the trouble to know what they would be at—and my father always flies into such a cursed passion when their names even are mentioned, that it is quite a treat to see it."[4]

"A treat do you call it Dallamore!"

"Oh I only mean that I wonder anyone should give himself so much uneasiness about nothing for I am sure they never come across him. I could amuse you for an hour telling you all the plots Richmond and I laid to get him to talk of them, that

---

[3]   The MS editor crosses out "upon my soul," and replaces "cursed" with "great."

[4]   The MS editor deletes "D--n it" and "cursed."

we might find out what crimes they had committed against his serene highness; I suppose he forced his poor devil of a brother to change his name from Dallamore."[5]

"No that he certainly did not for your uncle took the name of Miltern for a very large estate when he married my dear friend Selena who about twenty years ago was almost as pretty as your little cousin that I have just introduced to you. So if that was all the information you got Mr. Richmond might have saved himself the trouble of laying plots to vex your poor father."

"Oh we never got any information at all that was the devil of it, for he saw what we were at, and at last put an end to that fun, for he turned Richmond out of the house, and told me I might follow him and that he never desired to see my face again."[6]

"My dear Dallamore you are not serious?"

"Absolute fact, and what do you think all that storm was for?"

"I really cannot guess but I dare say you were very provoking."

"Well you shall hear: We were sitting after dinner, and Richmond began to talk of his Herefordshire tour last year to amuse us, for we were devilish stupid as usual, and he wanted to divert us by seeing my father who looked the moment before as if he was asleep begin to work and shake his ears the way he always does you know when he is vexed. At last Richmond asked him with a very grave face had he ever been to see his brother's house near the Wye; Miltern Hall, or Miltern something I forgot the name.[7] No Sir says my father as gruff as a bear. Lord how odd says Richmond; why sir it is the prettiest place you ever beheld and he lives like a prince. Dallamore I'll introduce you to your cousins next Summer and we can have nice boating parties on the Wye with the young Milterns. Oh if you had but seen my father! I would give the world I could make a face like him now just to shew you; I never can think of it without laughing, and there he stood raging while Richmond and I stuffed our napkins into our mouths till he flew out of the room."

"Oh fie Dallamore," said Mrs. Vallard gravely, "don't talk that way of your father when I know you are the best son in the world."

"I love him well enough, but why is he so amazingly absurd as to quarrel about nothing."

"But surely you do not mean that you have really quarrel'd about it?"

"Oh not I; I never minded it, but Richmond went off in a huff and would not come to Cavendish square any more. But apropos Aunt I am going to be married."

"Very apropos indeed and very likely too," said Mrs. Vallard smiling.

"Upon my soul I am in earnest."[8]

"And pray may I ask you to whom?"

"Oh a cursed big devil a sister of Richmond's."[9]

---

5   The MS editor deletes "devil of a."

6   The MS editor replaces "devil" with "misfortune."

7   The MS editor replaces "ears" with "head."

8   The MS editor replaces "soul" with "word."

9   The MS editor replaces "cursed" with "great" and deletes "devil a."

"Upon my word you describe your bride in very flattering terms."

"Oh I can assure you she is a remarkably fine woman, and has been reckon'd so every where I cannot tell how long."

"That is certainly in her favour at present; but do you really mean that you have any thoughts of being married?"

"I mean that I have actually proposed for Belle Richmond; she plays so divinely on the harp that I could not help it."

"Oh, I am sure she does not play so well as Selena."

"Who is Selena?"

"Why your little cousin that you saw just now, is not she a pretty creature?"

"Pretty no … I don't think she seemed to be any thing extraordinary. I did not much look at her tho'."

"I suppose you were thinking of Miss Richmond."

"Not I faith, but do you like the match?"[10]

"Oh nonsense you are always romancing about marrying, and I do not believe you will ever be married."

"Why? because I am so old?"

"Oh no, you are certainly rather *too* young yet, but I know men like you who are always proposing for every girl they see grow old bachelors at last."

"Well I'll bet you a thousand guineas I'll be married before six months are over."[11]

"I'll take your bet with all my heart provided you let me add with my consent."

"Oh I like that as if you would ever give your consent in that case."

"You don't think so Dallamore. You know there is nothing upon earth I wish more than to see you well married, as I think of all the young men I ever saw you most want a good wife."

"Oh well stay till you see Belle Richmond!"

"And where shall I see her."

"Why I dare say they will all come here soon to look after me."

"What you don't think your bride elect can amuse herself at Harrogate without you?"

"No to be sure," said he yawning, adding, "I wish she was here now to play for me with all my heart."

"Why Selena shall play for you and sing too and I am sure you will allow her to be superior to Miss Richmond or perhaps anyone you have ever heard."

"Are you in earnest?"

"I am indeed but you know I am not a very great judge myself; and perhaps you who are only accustomed to hear those who have had the advantage of instructions from the best modern professors, may not think her so wonderful a performer as I do, who can only know that her voice and manner of playing are the sweetest harmony I ever heard."

---

[10] The MS editor deletes "faith."

[11] The MS editor replaces "I'll" with "I shall."

"And will she play? Where is she?"

"Tea is just coming in, and I daresay she will be down directly; she always plays for me after tea 'till the candles come."[12]

"Tea! why you have dined then now!"

"And have not you?"

"Not I—but never mind."

"Never mind ... indeed I shall mind dear Dallamore I beg a thousand pardons but why did not you remember your unfashionable aunt's early hours and speak sooner?"

"Faith I did not think of dinner and I am not hungry."[13]

While the kind and hospitable lady is bustling to expedite the second dinner we shall leave Dallamore to strum with his right hand upon the keys of the pianoforte and in as few words as possible explain the causes which had made such a breach between Lord Mount Villars and his youngest brother Frederick the father of our heroine.

Chapter II

What so sweet
So beautiful on earth, and ah so rare
As kindred love and family repose?
Young[14]

Frederick Dallamore third son of the late Earl of Mount Villars had been the favoured lover of Miss Vallard some years before the marriage of that lady's brother to the present possessor of Hillbarton and while she was considered as the heiress of all his wealth and the large estate which was settled upon her in case of her brother's dying without heirs which was at that time highly probable, as he was already advanced in life, and had declared his intention of never marrying, so fondly was he attached to his sister who had from her birth been to him as a darling daughter. But fortune had not been Mr. Dallamore's principal object; her beauty had captivated him and her wit had given her a power over his fancy fatal to the future peace of his mind naturally violent in its pursuits and strong in its prepossessions. While she flattered him that his attentions were pleasing to her, and encouraged his constant assiduities her heart was in fact disengaged, tho' she heard him with regret declare the necessity he was under to return for a short time to Ireland upon the death of his father.

The tenderness she shewed at parting and the smile with which she received his promise of expediting his affairs as much as possible to shorten his banishment, enchanted him with hope and he prevailed upon his brother now Lord Mount

---

[12]   The MS editor replaces "down" with "here" and "come" with "are brought."

[13]   The MS editor deletes "Faith."

[14]   Antigonus in Edward Young's *The Brothers: A Tragedy* (1753), 1.1.400–402.

Villars to accompany him in a few weeks back to London where they were both welcomed with equal smiles by the bewitching Charlotte.

It was not without uneasiness that Dallamore beheld his brother share the conversation and the apparent favour which he had so long considered as his richest possession, but every day encreased the torments of a jealousy which it became impossible for him to disguise. Every circumstance declared the encreasing preference. When the brothers appeared together, the first glance, the first smile were for the young Earl, and often the gloom which overspread his brother's countenance was the subject of their mirth.

Unable to endure this unfeeling and as he thought unjust conduct he at length took an opportunity of reproaching her coquetry in terms which provoked her to declare that she had never given him any right over her actions and that she was determin'd not to subject herself in future to his reproaches by holding with him any conversation. Stung with resentment and rendered desperate by this reply the unfortunate Frederick flew to his brother and overwhelmed him with the most furious upbraidings which were received by the Earl with a cool contempt which for ever destroyed all sentiments of fraternal affection in the bosom of Frederick.

Lord Mount Villars declared his hope of soon presenting him with a sister of whose perfections he had so often heard him speak in such high terms. To all his threats and reproaches he returned no other answer than with a smile advising him to have recourse to a celebrated mad doctor and protested that in the mean time he should have his doors watched and guard himself against assassination. "As to fighting you my dear Frederick," added he, "because Charlotte Vallard so foolishly prefers my title and fortune and perhaps without vanity I might even say myself also to my younger brother it is quite out of the question. You cannot be such a fool as not to see that at present the stakes are too unequal and I have not the least disposition just now to part with my life, either by the hand of the hangman or that of my kind brother. But for God's sake Frederick don't go with that ridiculous face of yours and frighten Charlotte or she will really be obliged to call the servants to turn you out of doors which would be a great disgrace to her future brother-in-law."

The powerless rage and the gloomy despair of disappointed love were thus alike unheeded by the gay coquet and the unfeeling brother, and the advice which he had given the wretched Frederick became but too seriously necessary, so that at the time Lord Mount Villars gave his name to the fair Charlotte his brother was actually suffering under confinement requisite to restore his disorder'd reason. For some time his cure was considered nearly hopeless, but youth and a vigorous constitution overcame the shock which his bodily as well [as] mental frame had sustained from passion and disappointment; and in a few years he consoled his sorrows and repaired his fortunes by a most splendid marriage with the accomplished heiress of Miltern Abbey, for whose hand and estates he changed a name become hateful to him by having shared it with a brother so detested.

Mr. Vallard who had highly disapproved of his sister's conduct in the whole of this affair, upon her going over to Ireland soon after her marriage found himself so much weaned from his blind attachment to her that he yielded to the inclination he felt to bestow his hand upon an amiable young woman whose conduct and affectionate attention towards him during the remainder of his life justified the step and to whom at his death he bequeathed all that it was in his power to withold from Lady Mount Villars, who as was already observed did not long survive her brother leaving but one son who has been now introduced to the reader in company with his very partial aunt, whose presumptive heir he was generally also considered.

Lord Mount Villars tho' selfish and passionate was not illnatured, and contrary to the approved opinion which has said

> Forgiveness to the injured doth belong
> But they ne'er pardon who have done the wrong[15]

he was the first to seek reconciliation with his brother.

Upon his marriage with Miss Miltern he wrote a congratulatory letter which was returned torn across and enclosed in a blank cover. In about a year after this another attempt was made with even worse success. The beautiful domain of Mount Villars, the favourite residence of the family in the most romantic part of Ireland contained an uncommonly beautiful island formed by the windings of a noble river. The late Earl passionately fond of his youngest son, while a boy delighted to call it Frederick's island, and built in the center of it an highly ornamented pavilion. The estate unfortunately as it afterwards proved, being unsettled, in a whimsical will he bequeathed this island to his third son, and expressed a hope that his brother would rather rejoice in a circumstance which would tend to encourage Frederick to reside a part of every year at Mount Villars.

Their new connexions in England had rendered both brothers absentees for sometime after their father's death, but when the young Earl wished to settle at his princely abode in Ireland, knowing that his brother could never have any pleasure in his insulated possession, he wrote in the kindest and most conciliatory terms to offer him any compensation he could desire for the little estate, for which he proposed to give him in exchange one of more than equal value in England and concluded with an affectionate hope that all animosities might be forgotten and that he and his unknown sister Mrs. Miltern might visit them and settle the purchase on the ensuing summer at Mount Villars. To this was returned the following answer.

> "The meaness which prompts you to crouch for a favour to the man you treated with treachery and insult when you thought it in your power to injure him, can alone be equaled by the absurdity which inclines you to hope you shall again be able to cheat him into confidence by your perfidy and cunning. Of my inheritance you never shall deprive me and I wish not again to be provoked to declare that contempt and detestation alike concur in rendering me desirous to hear from you no more.
>
> Frederick Miltern"

---

[15]   Zulema in John Dryden's *The Conquest of Granada* (1672), Part 2, 1.2.5–6.

Mr. Miltern's future conduct was consistent with this letter, scarcely was it received before the enraged Earl had the mortification to behold the picturesque but little valuable trees of Frederick's island felled to the ground. Divided into small farms, and covered with the most miserable mud hovels without windows or chimneys and let at will to tenants of the most wretched poverty this island soon became so gross a deformity to Mount Villars of which it had once formed the most striking beauty that no longer able to bear the insulting prospect which it was impossible by any means entirely to exclude the Earl at length resolved forever to abandon the long loved and lovely abode of his forefathers, and in future never visited Mount Villars except as a temporary guest.

Indeed the country had become odious to him upon another account. He had warmly espoused the interest of his favourite second brother of whom we have hitherto not spoken in a sharply contested election. Their mutual affection had rendered his brother Sidney scarcely less obnoxious to Mr. Miltern than the Earl himself. He on this occasion therefore exerted all his influence against his brothers and exulted to find that he had chosen the strongest and by his assistance the successful party. Mortified and provoked at their defeat the Earl instantly quitted Ireland leaving Sidney to superintend his affairs at Mount Villars whose studious and domestic disposition inclined him to remain there almost entirely from the period of his marriage till his death. After this open and avowed implacability on the part of Mr. Miltern no farther attempt had been made towards a reconciliation, and indeed on every opportunity which had since that time occurred he had studied to prove that the enmity had rather been strengthened than diminished by time.

Lord Mount Villars on his side considered him with a species of horror as his evil daemon who pursued him with malice and appeared to exist only to torment him.

Chapter III

> Thus on the sands of Africk's burning plains
> However deeply made no long impress remains,
> The lightest leaf can leave its image there
> The strongest form is scattered by the air
> So yielding the soft temper of his mind
> So touched by every eye, so tossed by every wind.
>   Lady Mary Wortley Montagu[16]

From such black traits of the human heart there can be no doubt that the reader will with pleasure return to behold the innocent Selena with unreluctant obedience seat herself at her harp, and in compliance with Mrs. Vallard's desire pour forth notes

---

[16] Lady Mary Wortley Montagu, "An Epistle to Lord B----," *Poetical Works of the Right Honourable Lady M—y W—y M——e* (1781), lines 59–64. Line 61 should read as "The slightest leaf can leave its figure there;", the pronoun in line 63 should be "your" ("So yielding the warm temper of your mind"), and line 64 should not include a second "every" ("So touch'd by every eye, so toss'd by wind").

of the softest melody accompanied by the most brilliant & graceful execution; Dallamore who was really what young men of fashion generally affect, a nice connoisseur in musick from a naturally quick ear and fine taste was as much pleased as his indolent and uninjoying disposition ever allowed him to feel; he stretched himself upon the opposite sopha and while attempting to accompany her forgot he had no voice.

Nay when upon the entrance of candles Selena according to her usual custom rose from her harp to seek her work basket, her cousin so far exerted himself as to pay her some half expressed and very inarticulate compliments and entreated her to continue, endeavouring but in vain to recollect the names of some of his favourite opera airs, or explain which were the songs he particularly wished to hear. Selena smiled at his unsuccessful efforts, but unable to comprehend him handed over a number of musick books, in turning over which he amused himself 'till supper was announced.

Selena saw no more of her cousin till dinner time the following day. She had long quitted the breakfast room and retired to her usual daily studies before Dallamore's valet had softly opened his master's windows, and the first dinner bell had just rung when Mrs. Vallard met her nephew at the hall door preparing for his morning's ride.

He expressed however neither surprise or regret at being thus prevented[17] what he had projected only as the best means he could himself devise of passing the time and returned whistling a tune with both his hands in his waistcoat pockets in his usual lounging gait to take off the boots which had been drawn on scarcely one hour.

The dinner party was too small to suffer his uncommon mode of eating to pass unobserved by his aunt or Selena, tho' to the former, before acquainted with his peculiarities it gave less surprise. Filling his glass the moment he sat down with the wine which stood nearest his hand, he accepted Mrs. Vallard's offer of helping him from the dish before her. Scarcely tasting it he dismissed his plate, and in the same manner, refusing nothing which was offered, but seemingly unconscious of what he did he received and sent away a part of every dish, at the hospitably and elegantly served table.

Of Selena he took no notice, and indeed said little while the servants remained in the room, but as soon as they had retired and that Mrs. Vallard began to *row* him as he called it[18] on the subject of Belle Richmond his spirits seemed to return, and talking in the wildest and most unconnected manner, by turns of his intended bride, and his intended tour thro' Germany, in which she seemed not in the least to be included, Selena gazed at him with surprise, and for a moment imagined that his deficiency in intellect had occasioned the strange silence of her family concerning so near a relation.

---

[17]   The MS editor inserts "doing" after "prevented."

[18]   The MS editor replaces "row" with "banter" and deletes "as he called it."

This opinion however she relinquished when Mrs. Vallard assured her on their retiring from the dinner parlour that he was "remarkably clever, only a little odd and spoiled by his connexion with a few fashionable young men who found it extremely convenient to keep him in their society and make use of his horses, dogs, and carriages."

We must however in some degree differ from his partial aunt; Lord Dallamore was not clever; he was however possessed of a natural quickness of perception and delicacy of taste which his unfortunate indolence had prevented him from ever cultivating. When a boy he had passed all his holy days with his aunt, the generous easiness of his temper had captivated her fondness and the pliability with which at her instigation he pursued the lighter studies of the belles lettres deceived her judgment. His indolence was rather habitual than natural. Had Dallamore been obliged for his subsistance to adhere with steadiness to some pursuit, in that pursuit he might probably have excelled. But left to himself and devoted to pleasure, with every blessing of fortune except the art of enjoyment he became a prey to ennui, a jest to the fools he called his friends while he shared with them his fortune, and yawned through his tedious existence, a proof to the discerning observer that the secret of enjoying life is to employ it.

The taste with which nature had endowed him served but to destroy the sweetness of his temper in some degree, by disgusting him with almost every thing he saw and giving him really that unfortunate fastidiousness of character so generally affected by young men of fashion. He was in fact all they with so mistaken a judgment affect.[19] He was very absent, very careless of every thing which he possessed, might possess, very inattentive to all but his immediate gratification, and in any mode of gratification extremely difficult to be satisfied. Celebrated among his companions for generosity and good nature a severe critic of his character would perhaps attribute the appearance of both to the indifference which made him ever comply with the most unreasonable solicitations or even hints to the momentary trouble of giving a refusal.

From that incessantly quick attention to self interest which however studiously concealed forms so striking a feature in the characters of most young men of fashion Dallamore was entirely free—and was ever led about[20] without enjoyment to himself as the convenience or inclination of his companions directed. If he had now given them the slip it was because both his selfish friends Peters and Richmond had refused to accompany him in the curricle during the intense heat of the day, chusing to shield themselves from the dust in Dallamore's travelling chaise, and for this purpose relinquishing one of their horses to his valet who in their journey from town had before this alone occupied the covered carriage.

Dallamore was not offended, to offend him was indeed impossible—but once out of their influence he put a sudden thought into execution which had they been present, they would never have suffered him to have effected. Arriving at Norton

---

[19]   The MS editor corrects this sentence as follows: "He was in fact all that they with mistaken judgment affect."

[20]   The MS editor deletes "about."

about four o'clock while the sun was yet in its full power, choaked with dust, and oppressed with heat, he resolved to go no further till night; when fortunately for the first time recollecting that he was now within ten miles of his aunt whom he had promised to visit on his way to Yorkshire, he left orders for his carriage to follow him and turned down the shady lane which led to Hillbarton desiring the waiter to inform his friends that he would meet them at Harrogate in a few days; never once imagining their rage and disappointment at thus losing the various accommodations his company afforded them, and the prodigious difference it would produce in their future orders for wine and dinners on their[21] road, recollecting that there was no longer a valet ready to discharge the bills without the teizing delay of being themselves obliged to settle them before setting out.

Nor was this all that Mr. Richmond feared from this most inauspicious separation. He had eagerly entered into his sister's designs upon Dallamore, and had taken uncommon pains to free him from any other interested claim upon his society, and by his assistance to the great disappointment of two or three less cunning competitors Dallamore was prevailed upon to quit London some weeks earlier in the summer than he could otherwise have been able to do, in order that Richmond himself might be *pranked*[22] to Harrogate without any expense and that Dallamore might be brought under the immediate and continual influence of Arabella Richmond's charms.

Dallamore's character was too well known by his artful and speculating companion not to make him justly dread this unforeseen interruption to his scheme, and besides Richmond felt ashamed to join his sister at Harrogate unattended by Dallamore after his many boastful promises of conveying to her her captive Knight in triumph.

Chapter IV

Wise beauteous, good, with every grace combined
That charms the eye, or captivates the mind:
Fair as the flowret opening on the morn
Whose leaves bright drops of liquid pearl adorn;
Sweet as the downy pinioned gale that roves,
To gather fragrance in arabian groves;
Mild as the strains that at the close of day
Warbling remote along the vales decay!
Yet why with these compared? What tints so fine
What sweetness mildness can be matched with thine.
Beattie[23]

---

21   The MS editor replaces "their" with "the."

22   Pranked: to make an ostentatious display with; to show off (OED).

23   James Beattie, "An Elegy Occasioned by the Death of a Lady," *Original Poems and Translations* (1760), lines 21–30. Line 21 should read "Wise, beauteous, good! O every grace combined."

As Mrs. Vallard accompanied by Selena passed the windows of the parlour, intending to enjoy the coolness of the evening breeze under the fragrant shade of a lime which spread half of its branches over a rapid river, they were seen by Dallamore and immediately joined, any thing to him appearing preferable to solitude.[24]

Ever restless however he would not allow them to take their usual seat, but after repeatedly saying "Come let us walk" without attempting to stir from a little wooden bridge on which he leaned with his eyes fixed upon the running stream, he at length followed Mrs. Vallard in silence, who stopped to ask him for his arm and endeavoured to discover from him whether there was really any danger of his being drawn in to marry a lady no longer young, and who for many years had been considered in the no very respectable light of a female fortune hunter.

Tho' Mrs. Vallard knew him sufficiently to make her hardly believe it possible he should like thus to shackle himself without even the pretence of being in love yet she dreaded his being so far entangled as to render a retreat with honor extremely doubtful, and therefore resolved to detain him for the present at Hillbarton, and if possible devise some other pursuit or at least amusement to occupy her fickle kinsman. For this purpose she enquired from him whether he knew Lord Trevallyn.

"What that horrid old brute married to I forget whom some remarkable girl."[25]

"Yes the beautiful Emily Montrose."

"Oh I remember now, and she hates him already I suppose confoundly."[26]

"No," answered Mrs. Vallard warmly, "I am sure on the contrary she feels for him every sentiment of affection and duty."

"Pooh, nonsense, why she was forced to marry him you know."

"No not absolutely forced," answered Mrs. Vallard with a sigh which she could not suppress, "her dying Mother anxious at the thoughts of her being left only to an unkind brother, upon whom her large jointure[27] had hitherto prevented her being dependant, recommended her acceptance of Lord Trevallyn's offers with her dying breath, and Emily the most inconsolable of daughters gave a promise which she afterwards considered as not less sacred than that which in consequence of it soon after united her at the alter to a man old enough I will allow you to be her grandfather."

"Very pathetic indeed!" said Dallamore yawning, "but why do you ask me about the wretch?"

"Because he is at present my next neighbour, he has at last returned to Esselberrie park and intends to pass here the greatest part of every year at least my dear Emily tells me she hopes so."

"And is Emily Montrose at Esselberrie now?" cried Dallamore eagerly.

---

[24]   The MS editor deletes "of" before "its branches" and inserts "by him" after "joined."

[25]   The MS editor replaces "brute" with "man."

[26]   The MS editor deletes "confoundly."

[27]   Jointure: the holding of property to the joint use of a husband and wife for life or in tail, as a provision for the latter, in the event of her widowhood (OED).

"She is indeed to my great satisfaction tho' I have seen but little of her as yet."

"I must go[28] visit her then," answered he with unusual alacrity, "for she was always my greatest favourite."

"What greater than Miss Richmond?"

"Oh ridiculous, you would not compare Belle to the prettiest woman in England."

"Not I indeed," said Mrs. Vallard laughing, "but I thought it odd *you* should compare them or have any greater favourite than your intended bride, much less Emily Montrose whose very name you had forgotten."

"I did not forget her name did I?"

"Have you not just asked me who it was Lord Trevallyn married?"

"Oh I forgot she was married that was quite *autre chose*[29] but do let us come to Esselberrie."

"You do not mean now?"

"Yes why not?"

"Because in the first place they would think our illtimed visit rather strange, and a better reason is that whatever you and Selena may be, your old aunt could by no means be able to take such a walk."

"Oh never mind that, I can send for the curricle and drive you home."

"And Selena," cried Mrs. Vallard smiling.

"Yes to be sure we can easily go three; you are both together not half so much weight as Miss Richmond that my horses are so well used to. So pray come now ..."

It was with some difficulty that Mrs. Vallard persuaded him to put this scheme out of his head and recommended him to ride over the next morning to breakfast at Esselberrie, and invite the Earl and his fair bride to dinner which he readily promised to do.

During the rest of the evening he could however speak of nothing but Lady Trevallyn or rather Emily Montrose as he persisted in still calling her—repeatedly asking in almost the same words "Do you think she will come to dinner? ... Is she certainly at Esselberrie?" 'till his aunt tired of the subject she had herself started requested Selena to play her favourite air of Roy's wife.[30] While she sung the simple and truly musical scotch melody giving to it by her peculiar expression "a tuneful grace it never knew before"[31] Emily Montrose and Belle Richmond were alike forgotten and as Dallamore passed his aunt's dressing room after they had retired for the night she heard him still whistling the notes which had last enchanted his ears.

When Selena entered the drawing room as usual the next day at one o'clock to read for an hour to Mrs. Vallard, she expressed her fears lest Dallamore might

---

[28]   The MS editor inserts an "&" after "go."

[29]   Autre chose: different thing (French). The MS editor replaces "quite" with "une."

[30]   Roy's Wife: "Roy's Wife of Aldivalloch," a traditional Scots air ("The Ruffians Rant") with lyrics composed by Elizabeth Grant of Carron in the late 18th century.

[31]   An allusion to James Beattie's *The Minstrel* (1771), especially 2:31.

be ill, as notwithstanding his eagerness to visit Lady Trevallyn she perceived his window shutters were yet unclosed.

Mrs. Vallard herself apprehended no such thing but rung the bell to enquire whether he had been called.

"My Lord gave no orders," said his valet, "and does not in general like to be disturbed so early."

Selena stared and involuntarily repeated "so early!"

"Go to him," cried Mrs. Vallard, "however now from me and tell him I beg to know what day Lord and Lady Trevallyn have appointed to dine with me."

The servant did not return, but in a little more than an hour they heard Dallamore open the door of the breakfast parlour, when seeing none of the usual morning tea equipage he rang the bell and enquired if the ladies had breakfasted. Having been answered in the affirmative, and the servant desiring to know if he chose breakfast, he replied as he walked towards the drawing room "Oh no, 'tis no matter ... never mind!!"

"Well Dallamore you have seen Lady Trevallyn I suppose," said Mrs. Vallard as he opened the door.

"Not I. I never thought of it but I will go and breakfast there now."

"Dine you mean rather at this hour."

"Why is it too late do you think?"

"Indeed I am sure of it, so you may as well call for breakfast here and take your ride afterwards."

Dallamore said nothing for at that moment, with his face turned to the back of the chair which he bestrode he was deeply engaged in platting thro' the rails of it his slender whip. Seated at breakfast he forgot to order his horses so that at four o'clock Mrs. Vallard perceiving him upon the lawn advised him once more to defer his visit. To this however he would not assent and said he was just going to mount[32] and that he would be back in less than an hour and at all events not to wait dinner. Mrs. Vallard nevertheless gave orders to postpone dinner till six but Dallamore not appearing at that hour they sat down without him, and Selena expressed her hopes that Lady Trevallyn might accept Mrs. Vallard's invitation as she was longing to see a person of whose beauty she had already heard so much.

"I assure you Selena," said Mrs. Vallard, "that her uncommon beauty is almost the least captivating of her natural advantages, I never saw manners so insinuating or gentleness so bewitching. She only wants spirits, but for one so young she seems strangely grave and even dejected."

"But my dear Madam if married to so old a man can you wonder she should look dejected?"

"Her want of spirits can certainly not be attributed justly to that cause, however obvious it might appear as I knew her long before her marriage and have always lamented that kind of languor in her constitution. On the contrary in the little I

---

[32]   The MS editor inserts "his horse" after "mount."

have seen of her since she was Lady Trevallyn I have thought her spirits improved. But look, here is Dallamore! and certainly he has had no dinner."

The cloth was however changed and the dinner once more prepared before Dallamore who went up to dress immediately upon his return, was ready to sit down, and when he again joined the ladies he professed himself more than ever in love with Emily tho' he had not been invited to stay and had himself forgotten to ask them to Hillbarton as he had been commissioned.

"It was certainly my fault for trusting your memory without a written message," said Mrs. Vallard, "but we shall see to-morrow Selena if you and I can be more successful."

The next day Selena impatient to be introduced to the fair Emily watched with anxiety Dallamore's windows, who tho' repeatedly called at Mrs. Vallard's desire seemed little inclined to rise in pursuance of the promise he had given the evening before of accompanying the ladies to Esselberrie at twelve o'clock. At length to Selena's great joy, Mrs. Vallard despairing of his appearance ordered the carriage to the door and leaving a request for Dallamore to follow them drove with her young companion to Esselberrie park.

The french servant who appeared on their driving up to the door said his lady was not at home, but upon hearing Mrs. Vallard's name respectfully approached and requested she might enter and he would enquire if his Lady had walked out, as she had given particular orders never to be denied to Mrs. Vallard. He then preceded them thro' a covered corridore open to the south and filled with a profusion of the most fragrant and beautiful plants. The door of the octagon room at the end of this was open, and as the passage was covered with green cloth Lady Trevallyn almost started when the servant tho' in a low voice announced her visitors.

She was seated at a table covered with plants, botanical instruments, and materials for drawing. On the ground lay open some volumes of Sowerby's plates[33] and other books, and on the little stool at her feet she had thrown her gloves and a white silk handkerchief—the heat of the day thus having inclined her to discover arms and a neck of the most perfect shape and colour. A muslin veil thrown back in graceful drapery confined the luxuriance of her bright chestnut hair and appeared to form a part of the loose folds of her gown which but half declared the symmetry of that beautiful form which the Grecian artists might have selected as the model of their most perfect specimens.

In her reception of her visitors were at once displayed the easy manners of a woman accustomed to what is called fashionable life, the softness of natural timidity and the engaging simplicity of an affectionate disposition. After having embraced Mrs. Vallard and half reproached her for her long absence, she turned with a smile to Selena, whose eyes were intently fixed upon her with an admiration which almost conquered civility, and accused her of having alienated from her, "her now best and dearest friend" laying a melancholy emphasis upon the word *now*.

---

[33]   The naturalist and illustrator James Sowerby contributed plates for numerous botanical works, including his own 36-volume series on *English Botany* (1790–1814).

"No indeed," cried Mrs. Vallard, "on the contrary my dear Lady Trevallyn it is solely in compliance with Selena's wishes that I came now in defiance of all etiquette, ill humour and proper pride to pay you my third unreturned visit."

"Oh say nothing of that for you know I cannot go to you."

"I know it!" returned Mrs. Vallard, "no indeed I know no such thing, pray what do you mean?"

"Oh because I have visited no one since I came to the country, and if I was once to begin, farewell to all the dear quiet of my sweet Esselberrie, you know I must go the complete rounds of a neighbourhood of about twenty miles. And then the dinners! Oh do not let us think of it any more the very idea kills me."

"Well and how do you avoid mortally offending your good neighbours who will not come like me in spite of form to interrupt your dear quiet at sweet Esselberrie?"

"God forbid they should!" cried Lady Trevallyn smiling, "but I have really not been well and Lord Trevallyn is so good as to go every where and lament as I do the weakness of my health which keeps me so entirely a prisoner at Esselberrie."

"My dear Emily this is really ridiculous—you called me just now your friend—I must use the privilege of friendship and tell you honestly what I think of a conduct you will believe me hereafter repent, when you have provoked the illnature of a hundred tongues, which a little condescension would have made unanimous in your praises."

"Oh you are quite mistaken; I am sure they are all as happy as I am to be saved the trouble of making dinners for a person who cannot possibly afford them any entertainment—especially as I detest cards, and am quite determined never to play. At all events I cannot make the sacrifice so my dear, dear Mrs. Vallard let us talk of something else, and you will see I will not oppose your judgment in any other point on which you will give me your advice."

Mrs. Vallard shook her head but changing the subject told her of the invitation which she had sent by Dallamore the preceeding day tho' she now almost despaired of prevailing upon her to accept it.

"Impossible my dear Madam," answered she, "but Lord Trevallyn will I am sure be happy to wait upon you any day you and Miss Miltern shall shew that you are not formal and illnatured as you kindly represent the rest of our neighbours, but come and spend at least one day in every week with the invalid at Esselberrie."

Mrs. Vallard at first protested against accepting any invitation on such terms but Lady Trevallyn pressed her suit in so graceful a manner that to resist her was impossible, and Selena heard with pleasure Mrs. Vallard's promise of dining at Esselberrie the ensuing Friday.

"But you have not invited Dallamore," said Mrs. Vallard with a smile, "and he is not the least of your admirers."

At the mention of Dallamore a short cloud passed over the fine features of Emily but recovering herself in a moment she said "Oh certainly Lord Trevallyn will be extremely happy to see your nephew."

The voice in which this was said as well as the look which had preceeded it convinced Selena that the admiration felt by Dallamore for the lovely Countess was at least not mutual—but if Mrs. Vallard also perceived it it was unnoticed by her, who when they were returning home openly declared that she was delighted at the engagement she had made to dine at Esselberrie, on Dallamore's account who she was now sure would not be tempted to leave Derbyshire.

Selena for her part was in raptures, and as much fascinated by the soft manners of the enchanting Emily as the beauty of her figure. She had indeed never before seen any thing half so lovely, except in the glass, and there she had been accustomed hitherto to behold without admiration the promise of a beauty almost as perfect as that of the celebrated Emily Montrose.

But it was a beauty of a very different character and as yet wanted all that easy polish which women so particularly admire in each other, and which is perhaps never acquired without considerable sacrifices at the shrine of fashion. While Lady Trevallyn's loveliness was acknowledged by every eye, Selena might have been overlooked by some even less absent than Dallamore, and some might even have refused to allow her any pretentions to eminent beauty. Selena's countenance ever changing scarcely concealed a thought of her heart, while the fair Emily's face presented one almost uninterrupted picture of a sweetness unrivaled rendered more interesting by a cast of quiet melancholy which peculiarly agreed with the fine contour of her regular Madonna features.

"But my dear Madam," said Selena as they drove home, "why did she marry such an old man?"

"I told you already my love," said Mrs. Vallard with some restraint, "that it was the wish of her dying Mother."

"Yes but how could *she* wish her to marry so, and she so very beautiful and so very young."

"She is indeed beautiful and young but she had been out five winters and is full seven years older than my Selena."

"Well I never should have taken her for more than eighteen! But still I cannot think she loves Lord Trevallyn did you hear how she called you her *dearest* friend, and I never shall forget the sad smile she had when she was telling you how happy she was at Esselberrie—she sighed too afterwards, and I thought she blushed as she caught your eye looking earnestly upon her, and then she looked down and gave another sad smile."

"You are a very nice observer my love," said Mrs. Vallard with more assumed cheerfulness than she at that moment really felt, "but indeed I hope you are mistaken. I have not for years seen Lady Trevallyn look more contented than since she came to Esselberrie, and her *sad smiles* as you call them are I really think her natural smiles and not the consequence of unhappiness."

"I am sure," said Selena, "she ought to be happy, she looks so mild and so innocent."

"She is indeed a sweet creature," answered Mrs. Vallard, "but you must not look when you see Lord Trevallyn next Friday as if you thought of Beauty and the Beast,[34] nor give him many of your inquisitive glances, for fear he should suspect that you thought him unworthy of his young countess, of whom he is not a little proud, tho' perfectly sensible of the advantages of that rank to which he has raised her."

On their return they met Dallamore in his curricle, who instead of proceeding to Esselberrie stopped and so earnestly invited Selena to take a drive in the park that encouraged by Mrs. Vallard she alighted from the chaise, and assisted by the hand which Dallamore exerted himself so far as to extend sprung into the vacant seat at his side.

The tete-a-tete[35] was not very lively or interesting, but Selena had never before thought her cousin so little disagreeable, and Dallamore began to agree with his aunt in thinking that Selena might one day be as pretty as Emily Montrose.

Scarcely had the chaise driven from the door that morning which conveyed Mrs. Vallard and Selena to Esselberrie, when Dallamore's valet who had some time before opened his master's windows exclaimed "I am sure my Lord Miss Miltern did not expect you would have let them set out without your Lordship."

Dallamore not appearing to hear this observation Le Roi who did not chuse his discernment should be overlooked and knew besides how he could best flatter his master in a few minutes continued thus, "It is no wonder so fine a young lady should look a little disappointed at being so neglected."

"What are you muttering Le Roi," cried Dallamore throwing back the curtain.

"I say my Lord it was a pity Miss Miltern should be disappointed at last after her watching for two hours on the lawn in hopes of seeing these windows opened."

"Has she faith? And why did you not tell me so?"[36]

"Oh my Lord I would not take the liberty only now your Lordship asked me."

While Dallamore was dressing he began to think with Le Roi that it was a pity so fine a young lady should be disappointed, and this idea produced the exertion to entertain his cousin which may perhaps have surprised our readers, and which did indeed flatter and please Selena.

There was no sensation which had so much influence over Dallamore as the belief that he was of consequence to the fair sex—and when art or casual circumstances had flattered him with such an idea, he lost for a moment all the supiness of his character, and was ready to comply with every thing required of him let it cost not only expense but trouble.

With such a disposition it is not surprising that he was the dupe of every designing female cast in his way by chance or art—and if he had hitherto escaped from forming any lasting connexion it was because the number of rival schemers by seizing in turns upon his fickle mind defeated each other's plans.

Having once had the idea suggested to his imagination that he was not indifferent to Selena every trifling occurrence assisted in confirming the deception.

---

[34] Beauty and the Beast: reference to the traditional fairy tale.

[35] Tête-à-tête: private conversation (French).

[36] The MS editor deletes "faith."

The look of fixed attention which surprise at his strange conversation often gave her expressive face, the innocent familiarity with which she often laughed at his extravagant sallies, or his unaccountable fits of distraction, and the obliging cheerfulness with which she was always ready to comply with his desire to hear her sing and play, all conspired to convince him that her young heart had become sensible to his attractions which from the intercourse he had had hitherto with the fair sex he was well inclined to consider as irresistible. The hours which she past at the pianoforte or harp tho' really almost unconscious of his presence were all placed to the account of her wish to fascinate him. Her uncommon talents for musick had rendered it even in childhood her chief amusement and often when her thoughts were engaged by the studies she had just quitted or the entertainments she was promised, her well practised fingers still called from the instrument at which she sat almost involuntary harmony in accompaniment to her sentiments or the images of her fancy.

When Mrs. Vallard anxious to dissipate the mortal ennui which appeared to oppress Dallamore entreated Selena to endeavour to charm away that foul fiend by her magic notes, with pleasure to herself she devoted hour after hour to those musical reveries while the indolent Dallamore stretched upon the sopha either held a volume in his hand which he did not even appear to read or played with his favourite Rolla a large spaniel whose fawning caresses alone interrupted the stillness with which he listened to Selena's melody.

Chapter V

> How stands the great account twixt me and vengeance
> Tho' much is paid yet still it owes me much
>   Young[37]

Let us for a while leave the little party at Hillbarton, while Mrs. Vallard and the cheerful Selena are exerting themselves to amuse the listless Dallamore and follow the letter written at his arrival to Mrs. Miltern by her daughter curious to know the meaning of this secret relationship with the Mount Villars family.

"What is the matter?" "Is Selena ill?" exclaimed almost in a breath Mr. Miltern and his son while they behold the evident perturbation with which Selena's letter trembled in the hands of her agitated mother.

"Nothing my dear," said Mrs. Miltern to her husband and then observing the affectionate solicitude painted in the countenance of her son she continued, "Robert my love do not be frightened, Selena is thank God quite well which is more than I can say of myself I think," added she smiling as she rose from the breakfast table vainly endeavouring to disguise the trouble which the letter had occasioned her. "The sudden sickness I have been subject to of late has come over me—ring the bell my dear Robert for Wilson and I will go to my room."

---

[37] Zanga in Edward Young's *The Revenge: A Tragedy* (1721), 5.2.241–2.

In less than half an hour Mrs. Miltern softly knocked at the library door, and being desired by her husband to come in, she said to him in a voice trembling with emotion and apprehension "I am come to tell you the purport of Selena's letter."

"She has met Mount Villars I suppose," abruptly interrupted Mr. Miltern.

"No but Lord Dallamore is at Hillbarton and what am I to say in answer to her enquiries?"

"I suppose there is no necessity to satisfy the curiosity of girls at all times, but I should like to know what violent consequence there can be in Lord Dallamore's being at Hillbarton."

"None I hope but do you not think we had better send Robert for Selena?"

"No certainly. Robert has other business to attend to at present, and I have no idea of having any part of my family run away from …."

Here he rose in evident tho' suppressed rage, and standing with his back to the fireplace while he pushed from him with one foot the chair on which he had been sitting after a momentary pause endeavouring to assume a careless air he asked "Well and pray what does Selena say of her cousin?"

"She had scarcely seen him when she wrote to question me concerning their relationship, which seemed so extraordinary …"

"Tell her what you please," again impatiently interrupted Mr. Miltern, "only do not teize me at present for I am busy." While he spoke he resumed his seat and took the pen into his hand as his wife silently withdrew.

Mrs. Miltern tho' gentle and submissive in her deportment and disposition, was keen in her penetration into the designs of others, and firm in acting herself as she thought right. Her husband tyrant as he ruled in his domestic circle yet felt ashamed to confess to her the latent hope he entertained from his knowledge of Dallamore's character and frequent visits at Hillbarton that thro' Selena he might yet torment again the still abhorred Mount Villars. It was with this view he had urged her journey to Derbyshire, and this made him receive with apparent indifference but in reality secret joy the news Mrs. Miltern so much dreaded to communicate. She had herself thought more than once on the possibility of a meeting with some of the family but feared introducing a subject always painful and sometimes attended with the most intemperate fits of passion. This apprehension was therefore never alleged among the many objections she had made to sending from her, her darling Selena. When the evil so dreaded actually arrived an unaccountable sensation of sorrow and terror struck upon her heart with a cold presentiment of future ill arising from this rencounter to Selena. A thousand sources of disquiet pressed upon her imagination and the sickness of which she complained upon retiring from the breakfast table was not merely assigned as an excuse but real almost to fainting. Her answer to Selena was short, and for the first time in her life constrained; she merely told her in vague terms that "Lord Mount Villars had behaved in so unbrotherly a manner to Mr. Miltern that all connexion had with mutual consent ceased between them for many years—and that the subject was so disagreeable that the less it was touched upon the better, so that on her return which she hoped would not now be long delayed she entreated she might never introduce Dallamore into her conversation."

But to Mrs. Vallard she thought it prudent to write with more freedom, that she might be on her guard timely to prevent what she at present thought the greatest misfortune which could befal her Selena. She had heard that Dallamore was amiable in his disposition and prepossessing in his appearance and trembled lest a young person educated in such seclusion from the world as that in which Selena's years had hitherto been past, might receive an impression which should be injurious at least to her present tranquility if not her future happiness.

Resolving therefore to caution her friend against encouraging what is termed the innocent flirtation of young people whom chance has brought together she wrote by the next post the following letter to Mrs. Vallard.

"My dearest Mrs. Vallard,

"The length of time which has separated us in person has made no diminution in the confidence I place in your affection and judgment, tho' it has made us in a great measure strangers to the circumstances of each other's situation. I have not loved to trouble you with the little vexations which you could not remove or weary you with particulars which could not interest from their relating in so great a degree to persons unknown to you. But my reliance on the friend of my youth is unshaken and I have therefore no scruple of opening to you my whole heart at present when your assistance is perhaps necessary to save my child from danger. You have heard I am persuaded some of the circumstances which caused the unfortunate breach between Mr. Miltern and his brothers, and it is now unnecessary to recal particulars so painful. But you do not know the resentment with which those offences are yet remembered. Nor can you conceive how grievous a crime it would be considered should my Selena dare to look with a partial eye upon 'one of the house of Montague.'[38] She is so gentle that I have no fears of her ever resisting the will of her father, but I wish to spare that gentleness the suffering it may possibly feel from too familiar an intimacy with so charming a young man as I have heard your nephew represented.

"Do not therefore be offended my dear friend if I own that I am impatient to recal my child from a situation I consider as dangerous, nor press a continuation of her visit at this time if I can prevail upon Mr. Miltern to suffer me to send directly for Selena. In the mean time look I beseech you with a mother's eye upon the conduct of the young people and give my inexperienced girl, who knows not the habitual gallantry of all young men, the necessary cautions which Laertes bestowed upon his sister at parting when he feared that she might look with too serious an eye upon 'Hamlet and the trifling of his favours.'[39]

"Besides you can let fall a casual hint which it is impossible for me to introduce in a letter that were Dallamore a Prince and my portionless Selena of a rank even far below that in which she is placed, her father would still scorn all thoughts of such an alliance which events that had passed long before her birth

---

[38]   Imprecise reference to Shakespeare's *Romeo and Juliet* (1594), 1.2.81–2 where a servant invites Romeo to a feast at the Capulet's "if you be not of the house of Montague."

[39]   Laertes's warning to Ophelia in Shakespeare's *Hamlet* (1600), 1.3.5.

have rendered forever impossible. Forgive my dear friend perhaps the idle fears
of a too anxious mother and be such for the present to my poor Selena.
                    Yours with the truest affection & esteem,
                            Selena Miltern"

While Mrs. Miltern with maternal solicitude was considering with terror her
daughter's present situation Selena engrossed far differently her father's thoughts.
Various and unconnected plans floated in his mind. Determined that Dallamore
should be captivated and troubled with little doubt as to that material point, he
at one time resolved to reject with scorn and insult the proposed alliance, and at
another projected means to precipitate a union which must be so displeasing to
the proud Earl. All the hatred and revenge which want of opportunity had alone
prevented him for some years from continuing to exercise was now tumultuously
tormenting in various schemes his unquiet imagination, at length however he
determined to engage in this design the open and unsuspicious nature of his son
and thro' him endeavour to allure Dallamore to Miltern Abbey.

With this view when Mrs. Miltern had retired after dinner with the french
governess and her little Clara he invited Robert to walk with him to a distant part
of the farm where he intended to make a new plantation.

Robert was beginning an eloquent description of the beauty of a course which
he had seen that morning in the park when Mr. Miltern abruptly interrupted him
by saying "Have you found out yet what vexed your Mother so much when she
got Selena's letter."

"No indeed Sir and I do not think she has been well all day."

"I will tell you then, her former jealousy towards Lady Mount Villars to whom
you must know I was once to have been married has descended to her Ladyship's
son and heir and she is now fretting herself to death because Selena has met this
dreaded cousin."

"Oh Sir," cried Robert, "I am sure nothing would delight my Mother so much
as to have all that business quite forgotten."

"She has told you so then … has she?" asked Mr. Miltern with a rage which he
could not entirely disguise.

"Not exactly that," hesitatingly answered Robert, "but when I have asked why
I was never to speak of my uncle's family she has lamented that your dislike of
such near relations made it necessary."

"Well no matter for that," said Mr. Miltern impatiently, "it shall not be my fault
if you do not speak of them as often as you please in future and to shew you how
ready *I* am for a reconciliation you are welcome when you go for Selena to invite
her cousin to return with you here, only you must promise me, not to tell your
mother who I know will only make herself miserable about it till the time comes
and you know it is a thousand to one if Dallamore will accept the invitation."

Robert who had little doubt that Mrs. Miltern would rejoice in any step towards
a reconciliation which he knew she so ardently desired readily promised to comply
with a precaution he thought quite unnecessary in his father's scheme—and

Mrs. Miltern heard with evident satisfaction her husband declare on his return from his evening's walk that to gratify her he had resolved to send immediately for Selena.

As Mr. Miltern past thro' the hall on quitting the parlour after supper he perceived on the table the post bag. He took it up and returned with it into the library recollecting he had left there an unsealed letter which he wished should go by the next day's post.

Upon opening the bag the letter to Mrs. Vallard struck his eye, and fearing lest it might contain some advice which should defeat his plans he with little hesitation opened, read, and committed it to the flames. That to Selena he next read, but meeting in it nothing which opposed his wishes after sealing he returned it into the post bag.

Mrs. Miltern satisfied in some degree with having committed Selena to the prudence of her friend saw with less impatience than she would otherwise have felt the many delays which still retarded the purposed journey of her son, who was himself eager to execute the commission with which he had been entrusted and which he considered so important and so pleasing.

Chapter VI

Qui sait remplir ses heures à trouvé la route des virtues
Mercier[40]

The Friday expected by Selena with so much impatience as the day which they were to pass with the interesting Lady Trevallyn at length arrived—and perhaps Selena had never before taken so much pains at her toilet or felt so little satisfied at the success.

When the carriage was at the door Dallamore as usual was not ready. While Mrs. Vallard and Selena waited for him the former was more than commonly struck by the beautiful carnation that glowed upon her young companion's cheek and the animation which sparkled with more than usual lustre in her fine blue eyes.

"You look very nice my love today," said she with a smile as she parted over her dark and regular eye brows the thick curls of bright hair that concealed them from view, "But I am too old fashioned not to wish to see a little of your fair forehead."

"Yet you admired as I did," cried Selena "the beautiful manner in which Lady Trevallyn's fine hair fell over her face when we saw her the other morning. How much that veil became her! and do you remember how gracefully her muslin gown hung about her like soft drapery. I wish my cloaths would set the same way. I am

---

[40]   The MS misquotes this line from Louis-Sébastien Mercier's *Tableau de Paris*, vol. 5 (Neuchâtel, 1783) which should read as "Qui fait remplir ses heures à trouvé la route des vertus" (116): who fills his hours has found the road of virtue (French).

sadly afraid Lady Trevallyn must think you are bringing her a very vulgar country girl who has never seen any one dressed like those she has been used to live with."

"Well," cried Mrs. Vallard smiling, "I did not suspect you would have made so foolish a speech Selena. I see it is quite in vain to expect sense or education will conquer female vanity, or prevent your looking up with admiration and envy to that Goddess of female hearts fashion; you need not however be ashamed of your looks, and if you want compliments I can tell you that your figure put me in mind just now of Lady Trevallyn only you are not so tall, and I believe you have been dressing after her."

While Selena blushing owned with smiles this accusation their conversation was interrupted by a message from Dallamore who hearing that the ladies were in the hall sent down to beg they might not wait for him as he would follow them in his curricle, and to this Mrs. Vallard reluctantly assented, unwilling to risk offending by any appearance of deficiency in proper respect the known haughty temper of the Earl.

Dinner was indeed called for immediately upon their arrival at Esselberrie—and the gloom which lowered on Lord Trevallyn's brow while Mrs. Vallard made some apologies heightened the wonder and pity Selena still felt in spite of all Mrs. Vallard had told her "that one so very young and beautiful should have married such an old man."

The dinner was long and tedious, Lady Trevallyn said but little and the Earl seemed to think he did enough by supplying her place in doing the honours of the sumptuous repast. Long and tedious however as it was Dallamore appeared not and almost immediately upon the servants withdrawing after having placed the dessert Lady Trevallyn rose and led the way to the drawing room.

"Well I wish that I had known your nephew would not have come," said she taking Mrs. Vallard's hand, "and you should not have been punished with such a dinner. But thank God it is over and we may have a little ease and comfort now."

As she spoke she led Mrs. Vallard to a sopha and placed herself at her side pointing with a graceful smile to a footstool on which she invited Selena to seat herself.

"It was your own fault," continued she, "if you had said nothing of Lord Dallamore we should have had a delightful day and Lord Trevallyn would have gone to dine at Mrs. Johnson's or Mr. Thompson's or some of your good neighbours who are so wonderfully fond of asking him."

"Dear Emily how you talk, as if the absence of Lord Trevallyn was necessary to give us a delightful day!"

"Oh no! I do not mean that, you know I could not mean that; far from it, except my dear Mrs. Vallard I never desire to see any other company but Lord Trevallyn. But then all that parade and form which he thought necessary for strangers almost killed me and I was sure you were both in misery as well as myself but what shall we do now? Do you like to walk after dinner? Or will Miss Miltern play for us; I hear she is an uncommon fine performer—at least Lord Dallamore says so."

The blush with which this compliment was received was attributed both by the speaker and Mrs. Vallard to the arch look by which it was accompanied which however in fact had been totally lost upon the unconscious Selena.

"Let us walk before the dew falls," said Mrs. Vallard, "and on our return Selena will shew you that her cousin has not exaggerated her praises."

While they walked Lady Trevallyn who had taken an arm of each of her guests under hers evidently exerted herself to talk with cheerfulness and even gaiety, avoiding all particular conversation with Mrs. Vallard and pointing to their observation the most beautiful scenes thro' which they past.

In the midst of a thick tuft of evergreens close to the flower-garden the smoke of a chimney attracted Mrs. Vallard's attention.

"That is my little school," said Lady Trevallyn in answer to her enquiries; "But I will not shew it to you now, because I will keep it as an inducement for you and Miss Miltern to come to me some morning. I have besides a shop and a manufactory, all managed by my school-mistress who is the best of women and without whom I could do nothing; for you know I never could make much exertion, tho' you see I am less indolent than I used to be and this is all owing to that excellent creature."

Mrs. Vallard and Selena were impatient to enter the school, but with a half playful obstinacy she refused to comply with their wishes, and made them promise to spend a few days entirely at Esselberrie Lord Trevalynn being obliged to go to town on business of consequence.

Upon their return Lady Trevallyn brought them thro' the green house into her dressing room which opened into the study where Selena had first seen her.

In the window stood her harp and on the desk beside it a folded paper which Lady Trevallyn hastily put into a portfolio that lay on her writing table.

"You have been playing," said Selena timidly; "will you not let me hear you?"

"Oh I play so seldom, and know so little of music that I must not expose myself. I never play except when I cannot do any thing else." She added this in a tone of voice which as it struck upon the hearts of both her auditors she seemed eager to recal, or at least to divert their attention, hastily inviting Selena to play and repeating the composers' names as she turned over a variety of music, while she kept her face averted from the fixed eye of Mrs. Vallard.

Selena mean while seated herself and was beginning Roy's wife in compliance with Mrs. Vallard's taste when her quick eye caught a glance from hers which arrested her fingers.

"Play something of your own my love," said Mrs. Vallard in some compassion at the unexpected stop while Lady Trevallyn gave what Selena might indeed justly call a "sad smile."

"I will play you a lullaby which I composed for my sister Clara," said Selena. "She is rather too old to be sure to be sung to sleep but it is a whim of hers, and she loves me to sing it after we are in bed."

"Are the words your own?" asked Lady Trevallyn.

"Oh no, the words are Italian and have been set before but Clara did not like the music."

Lady Trevallyn appeared so much delighted with the simple and pathetic air that Selena blushing offered to write it out directly which Lady Trevallyn gratefully accepted providing her with pen and ink and music-paper and while Selena was thus employed called for tea.

"Shall I write the words which I sing?" asked Selena, "the music I think is rather adapted to something more plaintive."

"Write those which you sing," answered Lady Trevallyn, "as a guide, and I may perhaps find some verses of Metastasio[41] more suited to your charming notes than that lullaby which does not much hit my fancy as I have no Clara to sing to sleep."

Mrs. Vallard sighed for there was no blush on Lady Trevallyn's cheek to sanction the smile with which her friend was at first ready to wish that she might soon have occasion for the lullaby she now declared useless to her.

Selena and the lovely Countess parted almost equally delighted with each other and with an admiration nearly equal—for Selena's was still the most ardent, her imagination being occupied with fewer objects, and her young mind more susceptible of receiving new and lively impressions.

As they drove home Mrs. Vallard expressed much surprise at Dallamore's conduct, and uneasiness to know where he had dined. During a pause in her conjectures Selena ventured with a hesitating voice to ask Mrs. Vallard why she had prevented her from playing her favourite air.

"I did not mean to prevent you my dear," answered she with evident embarrassment, "but Lady Trevallyn's match appears so unequal that I believe I felt awkward lest any allusion might strike her. But it was very ridiculous and I hope she did not mind it."

"I hope at least," said Selena with a smile, "that Lady Trevallyn has left no Johnny."

Mrs. Vallard made not reply, but a reply was unnecessary for they now drove up to the door and immediately upon enquiring for Dallamore Mrs. Vallard to her infinite surprise was informed he was still sitting in the dinner parlour with two gentlemen who had arrived just after she had left Hillbarton.

"Do you know the gentlemen Philip?"

"No Madam but they enquired for Lord Dallamore and Le Roi says they came with my Lord from town."

It was indeed the selfish and designing Richmond who had prevailed upon his yet more empty companion Peters to accompany him from Harrogate in order to engage Dallamore to return to their society, which they had in vain endeavoured to accomplish by daily letters which during his stay at Hillbarton he had not only received in silence but scarce given himself the trouble to read. It is true those epistles were not penned with much of the eloquence of a Cicero or the grace of

---

[41]   Pietro Metastasio, the pen name of Pietro Antonio Domenico Trapassi (1698–1782), the Italian poet and librettist.

a Sevigne.[42] They cost their author however unusual labour and were not perhaps wanting in artfulness of design. They were calculated to represent Harrogate as the scene of all gaiety and to mock the stupidity of Dallamore who could thus immure himself with a quiz[43] of an old aunt. In a postscript it had even been added that Belle's singing was more admired than ever but that she was too much offended with Dallamore to send him any message.

When this chef d'oeuvre[44] of the epistolary art was found to have failed also in the desired effect the provoked and impatient Richmond with many a curse bestowed on the fool he called his dear Dallamore resolved to go in person and take his prisoner, never doubting of his usual success. To take however so long a ride in such weather was insupportable, and to post alone in a hired chaise was almost an equal bore, and besides more expensive, which was a circumstance this fine gentleman secretly never forgot, however he affected the air of extravagance. To lessen in some degree both these evils he determined that Peters should accompany him but as he was less interested in Dallamore's arrival than Richmond it required some generalship to achieve this.

"It is d--d vulgar Peters," said he one day as they were entering the billiard room together, "to be so long stationary at this hell of a place. You see Dallamore is too fashionable to come near it, and for my part I am tired to death of those informal city faces one sees every day at dinner. D--m me if I don't go to morrow and rusticate with Dallamore rather than stay in such a hole as this any longer."

"You are acquainted with his aunt then," said Peters in a mortified voice.

"Not I but a young man of fashion is always welcome any where, and I will introduce you there if you like to join Dallamore rather than stay here where there is not a soul one knows."

Peters who had but one ambition upon earth trembled at the idea of being abandoned to a society thus pronounced destitute of all fashion and eagerly bit at the proposal of sharing Richmond's chaise to Hillbarton both relying on Dallamore for their conveyance from thence.

In spite however of all his natural assurance and acquired airs of self consequence Richmond felt some degree of awkwardness when the chaise drove down the beautifully shaded avenue to Hillbarton, tho' he was far from acknowledging such a humiliating sensation to Peters who asked him with a half frightened face "would not Mrs. Vallard think their intrusion very odd?"

"Odd! Not at all man! Nothing can be more natural than that I should call on my friend, and Mrs. Vallard has lived too much with people of fashion to think this any thing extraordinary."

---

42   The Roman philosopher and orator Marcus Tullius Cicero was particularly admired for his prose style; Marie de Rabutin-Chantal, Marquise de Sévigné (1626–96) was famous for her letter writing, especially to her daughter, Madame de Grignan.

43   Quiz: odd or eccentric person (OED).

44   Chef d'oeuvre: masterpiece (French).

The reflection which the latter part of this speech was calculated to cast upon his fears determined Peters to assume all that easy freedom he thought so fashionable, notwithstanding which the two friends felt equally relieved when on Dallamore's appearance they discovered that the lady of the mansion was from home.

Now then was Richmond's opportunity and he now exerted all his influence to induce Dallamore to return with them directly to Harrogate.

"Why how can I go with you? Don't I tell you that I am engaged and that Emily Montrose is actually waiting dinner this moment for me?" repeated the annoyed Dallamore while Richmond took upon himself to order Le Roi to make preparations for his Master's immediate departure, and desired the post boy to hasten for the four post horses he had already bespoke at an inn about half a mile from Hillbarton.

"And are we to get no dinner in the mean time?" said Peters in a dissatisfied voice not a little amazed at Richmond's violent impatience to return to the place he had quitted with such disgust.

"Oh you shall have dinner here directly," said Dallamore ringing the bell to give the unexpected orders.

"What the devil matter when you dine or whether you dine at all?" exclaimed Richmond turning furiously to Peters provoked beyond concealment at a delay which he thought might prove so critical to the undetermined mind of his devoted future brother-in-law.

"No," said Dallamore coolly, "Peters is in the right, we had certainly better dine here at all events and then you shall hear Selena play this evening."

"Selena! What Selena?"

"Why Selena Miltern that plays like an angel."

"Selena Miltern My God what brought her to Derbyshire?"

"I do not know what brought her, but she is the prettiest little girl you ever saw, and you shall hear her play I tell you this evening."

"Oh I have heard her play and seen her too tho' I cannot say I agree with your taste."

"What you do not think her pretty?"

"No faith she did not strike me as being at all pretty."

"Perhaps it was her sister you saw. What sort of a girl was it?"

"Oh d--m it I never look at raw girls but I saw them both. I dined at Miltern Abbey last Summer and I remember a little insipid awkward Miss was called down from the nursery to entertain me by playing some long stupid concertos and old fashioned ballads."

Now this speech like most other narrative exercises of Mr. Richmond's tongue possessed neither the merit of total invention nor still less of strict truth. He had indeed dined almost self-invited at Miltern Abbey in the preceding summer and admired during dinner the promising charms of the young Selena. But she had appeared no more in the evening, and her musical abilities he took upon trust. His speech was not however uttered without design. He began to fear that Dallamore's delay at Hillbarton had been occasioned by this new object—and that in Selena might be found a formidable rival to oppose the united schemes of himself and his sister.

The best way he thought of preventing any such competition was to make Dallamore ashamed of the admiration he had bestowed upon an unfashioned girl, "a gawky Miss" the appellation with which he honoured Selena when he enquired with a loud laugh whether Dallamore had fallen in love with his cousin, and "damn it," added he, "that will make fine sport with the old bashaw[45] in Cavendish square. Then I suppose Peters we may as well go off with ourselves for this sighing Philander[46] will never make good company for our noisy merry friends at Harrogate."

"What nonsense you do run on with Richmond, I have not thought of the girl, nor any other girl faith since I came here—for there is Emily Montrose within two miles of us and here you have kept me dawdling till it is too late to go dine there."

"Well since it is too late let us be off," said Richmond. "See there are the horses coming and I dare say Le Roi has got every thing ready. I am sure he has had time enough."

The irresolute Dallamore stood whistling and looking thro' the window at the preparations thus making for his departure when the butler entered to enquire if they were ready for dinner.

"Yes to be sure," answered Dallamore not attending to Richmond's persuasions to the contrary who was more than ever anxious to quit the field before the return home of Mrs. Vallard and Selena.

"What kind of stockings do you call those?" said Dallamore fixing his eyes with unusual attention upon Peters' legs where below his pantaloons was exhibited a most fancifully embroidered clock.[47]

"Aye did you ever see such things in your life," exclaimed Richmond glad of the opportunity to vent his spite against Peters, and knowing well that had he slandered his mother and cursed his father he would have been heard with more indifference by the wretched Peters than while he thus derided his attempts at appearing the best dressed and most fashionable young man in the circle in which it cost him so much pains to move.

"Don't you like them?" said Peters, drawing in the leg he had before extended with such a well satisfied air, his face in a flame. "Well I can't help that, I got them from town yesterday and you said yourself Richmond when you saw them first that they were quite the thing."

"Who I? I am sure I must have been drunk or asleep then. But why the devil can you never dress like any body else? One would think you were born to be a merry andrew."[48]

---

45 Bashaw: important or pompous person (OED).
46 Philander: lover (OED).
47 Dallamore refers to the elaborate embroidery on Peters's stockings, known as a clock.
48 Merry andrew: clown or buffoon (OED).

It was fortunate that the entrance of dinner diverted in some degree the excess of rage and chagrin this attack had occasioned its unfortunate object, whose first thoughts upon Mrs. Vallard's return home reverted to the ridicule which he now feared had been justly cast upon his conspicuous stockings. He would gladly indeed have joined with Richmond in urging the precipitation of their retreat but by the time the first bottle had circulated Richmond had found his courage and assurance so much strengthened that he felt well satisfied to defer their journey till next morning and enjoy for the present the comfortable hospitality Hillbarton afforded in preference to the fatigue of travelling all night or the chance of a bad bed in a country inn.

Immediately on the return of the ladies Richmond took Dallamore's arm and desired him to present him to his aunt and as Peters followed them into the drawing room with an awkward confusion which he in vain tried to disguise by an air of familiar gaiety and much grimace, he congratulated himself that as it was already dark his stockings might have the better chance to escape observation.

Whatever Mrs. Vallard might have thought of their forwardness she did not forget that she was in her own house and as the friends of Dallamore she received them with much civility.

Richmond treated her with particular attention and conversed with her the remainder of the evening on the subjects which he guessed would prove the most agreeable so that Mrs. Vallard who was blessed with that happy disposition which is inclined to like every one till there appears some just reason for dislike expressed herself to Selena when they retired much pleased with his manners.

To Selena he had merely bowed, and indeed at the moment that she returned that bow she scarcely remembered that he had a right to claim her as an acquaintance tho' his name afterwards confirmed her recollection of having once before seen him at Miltern Abbey.

As Dallamore never once thought of his intended departure and as his friends purposely avoided mentioning it before Mrs. Vallard, she saw with surprise his chaise drive to the door the next morning while they were sitting at breakfast according to Richmond's directions; Dallamore himself however not having yet made his appearance.

"What upon earth has Dallamore got into his head now I wonder!" she exclaimed; when observing the curricle and other preparations for his departure, the purpose for which she had been honoured by their visit instantly occurred to her, and turning to Richmond with rather a serious air she enquired if he was going to run away with her nephew.

Before he could reply Dallamore opened the door, having been roused completely at this unusual early hour by the impatient Richmond.

"What a cursed fuss you are in!" said he as he entered, "without exception you are the greatest pest upon earth when one is to go any where."

"Where are you to go and pray whom do you mean?" said Mrs. Vallard half displeased and much mortified.

"Why Richmond to be sure, he has been boring me for two hours to get up this way in the middle of the night because we have about forty miles to go today."

"Why where are you going?"

"To Harrogate to be sure. Did not you know?"

"No indeed and I am very sorry to know now that you are so soon tired of Hillbarton."

"I am not in the least tired of it, on the contrary nothing could give me greater pleasure than to stay—but I don't know ... Richmond says I cannot be off—indeed I *am* engaged to a party there but I will see you again very soon."

"Oh yes, I have great reliance on your promises. Unless I go for you," returned she looking slightly at Richmond, "I have much chance of your returning to Hillbarton."

"I wish you would come for me," cried Dallamore eagerly, "or rather come with me, I will take you in the curricle or you and Selena shall go in the chaise, and we shall have the best fun in the world at Harrogate. Do pray come."

"Ridiculous! What should I do at Harrogate?" said Mrs. Vallard laughing and half inclined to accept his proposal in order to disappoint the schemes she could not help seeing were laid to entangle her nephew, but the thought was but for a moment and the deep blushes on Selena's cheek reminded her of the delicate situation in which she stood towards her cousin, and how little probability there was that Mr. Miltern would approve any farther intimacy.

She was not however so positive in her refusal as to deprive Dallamore of all expectation of her accompanying him back to Harrogate in case he really came for her in a week, which he positively promised, a promise which Richmond in secret determined should not be performed.

Chapter VII

> Art thou dejected? is thy mind o'ercast?
> Thy gloom to chace go fix some weighty truth
> Chain down some passion, do some generous good
> Teach ignorance to see, or grief to smile;
> Thy gloom is scattered, sprightly spirits flow
> Tho' withered is the vine, and harp unstrung.
>   Young[49]

Mrs. Vallard strove to forget the vexation which she could not help feeling on Lord Dallamore's account, in the gentle but lively society of Selena, who exerted

---

[49]   Edward Young, "Night VIII," *Night Thoughts* (1742–45), lines 735–44. The epigraph omits lines 736 ("Amid her fair ones, thou the fairest choose") and 740–42 ('Correct thy friend; befriend thy greatest foe; / Or, with warm heart, and confidence Divine, / Spring up, and lay strong hold on Him who made thee").

her talents to divert her mind from the apprehensions she confessed to her she entertained lest her nephew should be drawn in to make so imprudent a connexion.

In a day or two after this they received the expected summons from Lady Trevallyn who having heard of Dallamore's departure from Hillbarton expressed her impatience to see her friends in pursuance of their promise Lord Trevallyn's journey to town having been hastened even sooner than was expected.

"I am now," she added, "quite alone and long to renew the pleasures and advantage I have so often found in my dear Mrs. Vallard's society, besides that I expect great delight in cultivating the acquaintance of her charming Selena."

Mrs. Vallard gladly accepted the invitation, as she was really interested for Lady Trevallyn's happiness and wished to discover if her present prospects were likely to produce it and besides she feared that Selena might naturally feel Hillbarton unusually dull after the departure of so fine a young man, not reflecting how very little that fine young man had contributed to their entertainment.

She therefore without delay complied with Lady Trevallyn's request who received them with the most affectionate cordiality.

Mrs. Vallard tho' accustomed herself to the regular quiet of a well ordered Dowager's family was yet struck with the extreme stillness which Selena bid her observe reigned at Esselberrie. The numerous servants that waited upon Lord Trevallyn accustomed to the haughty superiority which required their obedience not as fellow creatures, but as machines created for his service, performed their duties with a quiet submission which the softness of Lady Trevallyn's manners rather assisted to encrease than encouraged to diminish. She could not enjoy the attendance of the mutes who watched her plate and were ready to offer her bread before she herself perceived that she was unprovided, but was glad in Lord Trevallyn's absence to find herself at dinner with her friends attended only by a waiter dumb as the domesticks she had dismissed but happily also deaf.

When they rose from table Mrs. Vallard reminded Lady Trevallyn of her promise and with pleasure she conducted them to her little school, where innocent mirth danced in the eyes of twelve little girls over whose cheeks plenty and cleanliness had but lately spread the ruddy bloom attendant upon health and youth. They had not however been so powerful in their effects over the pale countenance of a woman apparently past the middle age of life who met Lady Trevallyn at the door with an air of respectful affection that speaks a welcome more eloquently than any words.

"I was afraid my Lady," said she, "that you were not well as we have not seen you since yesterday morning."

"Oh I have been very busy Mrs. Harley but I have brought to visit you now my dear Mrs. Vallard of whom you have so often heard me speak, and here is Miss Miltern who says she will help you to teach our girls to sing hymns."

She then seated herself in the midst of the whispering and chuckling group who crowded around her and by their loving familiarity and their sly side long glances at the strangers demonstrated that it was not Lady Trevallyn's presence which had stilled the noisy merriment which had saluted their ears as they approached the jessamine covered windows of the school room.

"But where is Angela?" said Lady Trevallyn looking round. "I missed her reading as usual in her little bower tho' I came by there now on purpose to get a peep at her."

"She has not been well today and has lain down I believe My Lady," said Mrs. Harley with a sigh.

"Angela!" cried Mrs. Vallard, "that is a still finer name than yours Selena."

"Yes Madam," said Mrs. Harley modestly, "it is a fine name for one so humble as my daughter; but it was given to her by a kind benefactress who was disposed indulgently to give her many things unsuitable to her rank."

"It is a very pretty name, and she is a very pretty girl too," said Lady Trevallyn rising, "tho' I am sorry to say she does not seem well. But shall we take these ladies to your dairy?"

"Certainly My Lady" answered Mrs. Harley shewing them the way thro' the kitchen and laundry all of which for their wonderful cleanliness and regularity well deserved to be admired.

"And this is all done by my girls," said Lady Trevallyn, "or rather indeed I should say by Mrs. Harley, for notwithstanding all my persuasions she will not allow herself a maid—and it is for my own sake I am so anxious that she should not wear herself out for where should I find her equal. As for you Mrs. Harley the more you exhaust yourself, certainly the sooner you will go to Heaven but you ought to remember that you have not done me all the good you are intended to do on earth, and there is Angela who cannot spare you yet."

"I should indeed be sorry to leave my poor Angela at present if it is the will of God to allow me to be of any use to her," said Mrs. Harley her eyes filled with tears which she in vain tried to conceal while Lady Trevallyn affectionately took her hand and turned the discourse by asking her whether Angela wanted wine or any thing which the house could supply.

When they were quitting the school Mrs. Harley asked with a smile would they not look at her shop where she sold to the labourers every article which was necessary for their comfort at a considerably reduced price.

A young and worthy couple settled in a little lodge near one of the gates into the park had the care of the stock and Mrs. Harley herself superintended the sale which was only during stated hours while Angela at those hours taught the girls in the absence of Mrs. Harley to read and write.

"All the good that has resulted from this," said Lady Trevallyn, "and all that I expect to result from the little manufactory I boasted of but which is yet only in its infancy I owe to Mrs. Harley, it was originally all her own plan and she has herself conducted it."

"Pardon me My Lady *my* plan was far less expensive and perhaps the advantages might be equal—for except in times of particular scarcity the labourers can well afford to buy all their necessaries at first cost, and in that way the shop would be attended with but little expence tho' of the utmost benefit to the poor creatures who are often so much imposed upon and besides get a habit of running in debt with those little country shop-keepers which often proves their ruin."

"Well I must raise your prices I believe," said Lady Trevallyn, "in order to advance our manufactory and I expect in return you will assist me by giving me your stuff cheaper than I can get it."

Mrs. Vallard saw with delight her lovely friend turn her mind to occupations so useful and at the same time capable of affording so much enjoyment to a benevolent heart, and while she conversed with Mrs. Harley on the subject of the manufactory Selena who had followed Lady Trevallyn into the little flower garden before the lodge putting her arm round her waist softly exclaimed in an endearing voice "How happy you are dear Lady Trevallyn to be able to do so much good."

"Happy my love, Oh no!" and turned toward her her beautiful mild eyes swimming in tears. The affectionate address of Selena had for a moment banished the natural reserve of Lady Trevallyn's disposition while she returned her pressure and added in a low plaintive voice, "Self-sacrificed happiness and I have taken leave of each other for ever."

Selena was surprised and inexpressibly affected but Lady Trevallyn disengaging herself from her arm, and turning from her appeared to recollect herself and repent the words which had escaped her.

Hearing Mrs. Vallard's voice she hastily dashed the tears from her eyes and drawing Selena towards the gate as if to observe something whispered to her smiling, "Don't take any notice of me now and I will tell you some other time what I meant by saying I was self-sacrificed."

Selena in silence obeyed her and turned to Mrs. Vallard who now brought out for her inspection some of Miss Hannah More's cheap publications[50] with which Lady Trevallyn had provided her shop for the benefit of her uncultivated neighbours who shared with her tho' in an humbler way the pleasures which reading can afford.

On their return home as Selena leaned upon Lady Trevallyn's arm, and reflected upon the few words which she had just heard, her uncommon absence and the silent thoughtfulness of her manner were noticed by Mrs. Vallard who asked her if she was not well, a question which was felt by her as a reproach, especially as Lady Trevallyn seemed to exert herself particularly to amuse both her guests.

Selena wishing in her turn to say something asked Lady Trevallyn "What was the matter with Angela of whom she had heard her enquire from Mrs. Harley."

"I am afraid," answered she "that the poor girl is in a consumption. I believe she met very unkind treatment lately at an aunt's, where she was sent upon the death of Lady Anne Ortney."[51]

---

[50] Hannah More's series of *Cheap Repository Tracts* (1795–97) were short sketches designed to provide moral instruction and literacy for the working class.

[51] Lady Anne is probably based on Selina Hastings, Countess of Huntingdon (1707–91), an important figure in the rise of Methodism in England.

"Was she an eleve[52] of Lady Anne's?" asked Mrs. Vallard.

"She was her favourite and one of those who suffered the most from her dying without a will, tho' the late Marquis settled something upon her, I do not exactly know what."

"Was it Lady Anne who recommended to you Mrs. Harley?" asked Mrs. Vallard after a moment's silence.

"It was and I owe her an eternal obligation."

"I take it for granted then," resumed Mrs. Vallard, "that she is a methodist, indeed I thought so from her dress and manner."

"She is a methodist," said Lady Trevallyn with a smile; "but you must not think the worse of her. She does not intrude upon me any others of her society, nor even her own peculiar principles, neither does she insist upon going to their meetings."

"Her appearance," said Selena, "seems above her situation."

"She was brought up with Lady Anne in the Marquis's family," answered Lady Trevallyn, "and did not quit her patroness 'till after Angela's birth. It was to Mrs. Harley that poor Lady Anne first owed her inclination to those methodists as Mr. Harley was one of their teachers. His enthusiasm induced him to follow one of their chief leaders to America whither Mrs. Harley accompanied him leaving behind at Lady Anne's particular request her little godchild Angela who was thought too delicate to bear the voyage. Mr. Harley never returned to England and when upon his death his poor widow came over thinking to gain an asylum with Lady Anne, she had the additional affliction of finding her benefactress had died suddenly and her poor Angela languishing in oppression with an austere maiden aunt whose appearance when I went to enquire from her for Mrs. Harley made me dread to have any thing to do with methodists, tho' from what I had heard from Lady Anne I was anxious to find out Mrs. Harley when I first thought of my little school. But indeed the sisters are very different. So now I have told you Mrs. Harley's history, but part of Angela's I cannot tell you for she is the most extraordinary girl I ever knew."

"Is she pretty?" asked Selena.

"Yes very pretty *I* think, yet that is a disputed point, but she is so melancholy and so reserved, and the oddest part of her character is pining to return to her aunt in spite of the harshness with which she was treated, and that her poor Mother whose heart is almost breaking is the most indulgent and tenderest of nurses."

"Oh she has left a lover then to be sure," cried Mrs. Vallard.

"Why I should really think so," answered Lady Trevallyn, "but Mrs. Harley when I stated this suspicion told me that she had enquired from her sister who protested no young man ever entered her doors and that Angela never went out while with her except to chapel, nor there except in obedience to her and with great reluctance."

"So she at least is not a methodist!" said Mrs. Vallard.

---

[52]   Élève: student (French).

"Oh no! poor Lady Anne used often to lament that she was always reading profane plays and novels and never loved what was good, that is in the way of sermons and prayers."

"Poor Angela!" said Selena smiling.

"Yes you will say poor Angela indeed when you have seen her—for never was there such a picture of sadness, and there is no soothing her into revealing the cause of her melancholy. She is the most impenetrable girl! It was only the other day that I made the last attempt. A young farmer a tenant of Lord Trevallyn's remarkably well brought up had seen Angela and proposed for her. It would have been an excellent match and I promised to Mrs. Harley to use my influence with Lord Trevallyn to get them a lease for ever of a considerable farm. But Angela would not hear it, and fell into such a gloomy fit of despair upon its being mentioned that her mother with tears advised me not to say any more of it to the poor girl. However when the thing had cooled a little and that I saw Angela still continued as gloomy as ever and that I knew the young man was really in love, I thought I would make one effort, so I asked her the other morning to walk with me to the Woodhouse, which by the bye you have not seen yet and it is too long a walk I am afraid for you.

"Well poor Angela with evident reluctance prepared to follow me, and when I would have taken her arm she looked so miserable and so afraid of me that I felt half affronted and quite uncomfortable. However I began in as delicate a manner as I could devise to say something of her lover's constancy, but I saw her silence was not that of bashful timidity and then she trembled and turned so pale I really had not courage to go on. And when I would have soothed her by assurances of her never being controled, she answered my kindness in so cold a way that it absolutely silenced me and I am sure I felt more afraid of her than she was of me. I was glad to shorten my walk, and indeed poor thing she looked scarce able to keep up with me tho' you know I am not a very stout walker myself. To all my offers of affording her any amusement she could wish I could get no reply except 'You are very good Madam but my health was better at Islington and I should be very glad to return to my Aunt. I am sure I could make myself of more use to her than I can be here.' This was so disheartening and so strange that I have given her up and am determined to torment her no more."

"And would it not be better to indulge her," said Mrs. Vallard, "sick people have sometimes such odd fancies?"

"Why Mrs. Harley," answered Lady Trevallyn, "cannot bear the thoughts of parting with her in such a delicate state, and sure the air and diet she has here must be infinitely better for her than that wretched hole at Islington where she was like a servant to a cross old maid. Poor thing I should really think the change would be her death. She is a great distress to us both, but she will kill her dear Mother if she goes on this way."

Mrs. Vallard retired at night her head full of the interesting account she had heard of Angela; but Selena was far more engrossed by the reflections which

Lady Trevallyn's exclamation had given birth to, aided by the expression of deep melancholy with which it had been accompanied.

The compassionate interest she felt for her, and the expectation which her promised confidence had excited kept her eyes long unclosed after she had lain down and it was late when she heard with surprise the sound of a harp touched indeed very softly but which the stillness of night enabled her perfectly to distinguish. She recalled to mind that her room was not a great distance from the octagon study but was surprised at Lady Trevallyn's chusing such an hour for music. As she listened attentively to her voice with which she softly accompanied the lullaby Selena had given her, tho' it was impossible accurately to distinguish the words yet she heard enough to make her certain they were not italian, and she felt impatient till morning that she might see what Lady Trevallyn had adapted to her musick. The air was repeated several times and the harp then ceased but Selena continued to dream of the interesting performer and awoke early her warm fancy entirely occupied by her new friend.

Chapter VIII

> Slight was her form, and graceful o'er her neck
> Sicklied with primrose tint, her jetty locks
> Fell rich but rudely—whilst her mournful eyes
> Beamed thro' a watry lustre, she was formed
> In Nature's kindness—and tho' the rose
> No longer melted in her cheek, nor blushed
> With deeper brilliance on her lip yet still
> Unnumbered graces decked her, and looked forth
> At every feature—the wreck of better days.
>   Miss Porter[53]

The sun that shone so brightly on the lawn before her windows, strongly marking the shade of the fine trees with which it was scattered, and the early bell that called the labourers to work deceived Selena, so that coming into the breakfast room she was surprised to find no person stirring nor any preparedness for breakfast. The hall door was yet locked and Selena who tempted by the beauty of the morning

---

[53]   Anna Maria Porter, "After Having Seen a Lovely But Miserable Girl," *The Poetical Register and Repository of Fugitive Poetry for 1801* (London: Rivington, 1802), lines 1–14, with liberal modifications from the original: "Slight was her form, and graceful; as she pass'd; / Mine eye fell on her, and with quick surprize / Recoil'd; for the few garments that she wore, / Blew torn on the cold wind, and scarcely clothed / The beauties they so sullied: O'er her neck / (Sicklied with primrose tint) her jetty locks / Fell rich but rudely, whilst her mournful eyes / Beam'd thro' a watery lustre. She was form'd / In Nature's kindliness; and tho' the rose / No longer melted in her cheek, nor blushed / With deepen'd brilliance on her lip, yet still / Unnumber'd graces deck'd her, and look'd forth / At every feature—thro' her rags there shone / The wreck of better days."

wished to walk out went to the octagon room which opened to the green house thro' which she knew she might pass to the garden.

As she entered the study the harp reminded her of the music she had heard the preceding night, and she approached the desk in order to discover what were the words which Lady Trevallyn had chosen. The musick book was closed, but on the leaf in which Selena had written her lullaby was a scrap of paper containing some verses which Selena took up without suspecting that Lady Trevallyn might not have intended them for another's perusal. The verses were as follows.

> Lord of Hearts benignly callous
>   Come Insensibility,
> Stop the streams which feeling hallows
>   Smother each impassioned sigh.

> Let this bosom idly beating
>   Taste at length a moment's peace!
> Passion's tide at length retreating
>   Bid the furious tempest cease.

> O'er my path once sweetly smiling
>   Crowned with flowers, unseen his dart,
> Love with blushes soft beguiling
>   Seized my fascinated heart.

> Soon the traitor rudely rending
>   From my brow the rosy crown,
> Pityless of storms impending
>   Drove me forth to Fate's dark frown.

> Harassed, struggling, faint and weary
>   Long kind Hope reluctant clung,
> Shudd'ring at my prospects dreary
>   All her brilliant chords unstrung.

> Thus the quivering lamp expiring
>   Sudden shines with trembling beams
> Extinguished now, now life desiring
>   Shoots forth momentary gleams.

> Mute her voice, and dropt her lyre
>   Now at last she sinks opprest,
> Day's bright beams with her retire
>   O'er me clouds and darkness rest.

> Joy and Hope and Love and Pleasure!
>   Here I bid you all adieu!
> Thee sweet Peace my last best treasure
>   All my wishes now pursue.

O'er my senses softly stealing
   Blest Indifference kindly come!
From this agony of feeling
   Hide me in thy tranquil gloom.

Banish each bright form delusive,
   From my aching eyes remove,
Fancy's torch with glare obtrusive
   Visions of seductive Love![54]

Fig. I.1   Illustration for "Verses Written for Emily 1799" in *Verses Transcribed for H.T.* (Brompton, 1805), MS Acc 5495/C/8/1, National Library of Ireland, Dublin.

It was not till Selena had finished or nearly finished these verses, that she was shocked by an idea that she was guilty of a breach of honour and confidence in thus opening Lady Trevallyn's papers in her absence, and perhaps had read the effusions of her heart meant to be concealed from every other eye; The moment the thought struck her she replaced the paper hastily without indulging herself in a second glance but the melancholy turn of mind of which the lines were expressive filled her with pity for Lady Trevallyn's fate. And her surprise and sorrow were encreased that her Mother could have wished her so earnestly thus "young and beautiful to marry such an old man."

---

[54]   This poem is titled "Verses Written for Emily 1799" in Tighe's *Verses Transcribed for H.T.* (Brompton, 1805), which contains an additional four stanzas with numerous variations, including the opening stanza: "Poor fond heart with pleasure swelling / What hast thou to do with joy? / Sorrows still usurp the dwelling / Scatters wide each glitt'ring joy."

Unwilling to remain longer in a place where she felt she had already too familiarly intruded she unbolted the doors of the green house and past into the garden where the men were already at work and the gate being open she proceeded from thence into the cooler shade of the closely planted shrubbery in the midst of which the white rails of the school-house were scarcely to be discovered.

It was in a wildly romantick spot of this plantation that the late Lady Trevallyn had a favourite arbour which had been totally neglected for some time, Esselberrie park having been but little inhabited for many years. The little stream which used to enliven with its silver current "the smooth well shaven green"[55] in front was now half choaked with flags[56] and rushes and its extended damp had enriched to rankness the level banks now neglected and over spread with weeds. The great branches of the evergreen shrubs were stretched into uncouth shapes and their leafless stems covered with green lichen. Round the arbour itself "many a garden flower grew wild"[57] and the scene undressed as it was had still many attractions.

Selena recollected that it was into this little spot that Lady Trevallyn had peeped the evening before when she observed that she "had missed Angela at her usual seat."

This idea prompted her now to enter it, and there she indeed discovered the subject of her thoughts. A book lay open on the rude table before her, but she was not reading. Both her arms were also upon it and her head rested upon them with her face turned from that side on which Selena entered. For a moment Selena paused unwilling to disturb her and when she heard with compassion her deep and repeated sighs, she felt still less inclined to intrude and would have retreated gently when Angela suddenly started and turned towards her a face covered with the tears which she had not thought of wiping away.

In spite of those tears Selena beheld her with admiration, her complexion was indeed pale, and her skin tho' of the finest texture was even sallow. Her features were small and delicate, and her long silky eyelashes softened her large black eyes. A close cap covered her dark hair except where a few locks had escaped which shaded her neck and forehead. The beauty of her arms, the exquisite fineness of her hands and the delicacy of her whole form plainly shewed her education had been superior to her present dress, which was of the coarsest materials tho' put on with an air of good taste which once obtained is perhaps never lost.

They were both silent for a moment but Angela rising in confusion to retire Selena stopped and gently asked her pardon for the intrusion.

"Oh Madam it is I that should demand forgiveness for intruding into a place too beautiful for me to occupy. But Lady Trevallyn so seldom comes into it that I some times take the liberty to read here."

---

[55] John Milton's "Il Penseroso" (1645), line 66: "On the dry smooth-shaven Green."

[56] Flags: a kind of grass (OED).

[57] Oliver Goldsmith, *The Deserted Village* (1770), line 138.

"I am sure," cried Selena with the sweetest smile, "Lady Trevallyn will like the place the better if it gives pleasure to Angela, for it is to Angela certainly that I am speaking."

"Her Ladyship is very good indeed," said Angela in a broken voice, with a low curtsey and downcast eye.

Selena wishing to detain her took up the book and seeing it was a volume of Milton asked her if she read a great deal, observing that "she had at least now made a good choice."

"Yes Madam," answered Angela, "but my Mother's library is so small that I have not the merit of chusing much at present."

"I am sure," said Selena, "Lady Trevallyn will be delighted to supply you with any books you would like. Do allow me to be the messenger."

"Oh not for worlds!" cried she eagerly when observing Selena's surprise she added, "would I take such a liberty or encroach so far on Lady Trevallyn's goodness."

Selena pressed the subject no more but endeavoured to draw Angela into some general conversation, and succeeded beyond her hopes. She was indeed modest and diffident but Selena wondered that Lady Trevallyn should think her so very reserved, and still more how she could call her cold. Selena on the contrary thought she perceived in her a susceptibility of accepting kindness which enchanted her, and Angela on her part after the first few moments appeared far from desirous of shortening their interview. They did not part till the breakfast bell summoned Selena home and even Angela smiled when as she left her Selena exacted a promise that she should not run away from her when next they might meet.

"I thought you had eloped," said Mrs. Vallard as Selena entered the breakfast parlour. "Your room was empty and no one had seen or could give any account of you."

"I have been sitting with poor Angela for this hour I believe."

"With Angela!" exclaimed Lady Trevallyn; "and would Angela sit with you?"

"She did indeed and talked a good deal. I do not despair of being her confidant. What a sweet creature she is!"

"Do you think her very pretty?" asked Mrs. Vallard.

"Beautiful I think."

"Oh no! not beautiful," said Lady Trevallyn smiling, "but she has very fine eyes and the nicest teeth that can be."

"Why no," replied Selena, "she certainly is not beautiful, even if she looked healthy she is too little to be called beautiful, but she is more interesting than mere beauty could make her. She looks so amiable and mild, and so *sensible* in the full meaning that the french language gives that word."[58]

Lady Trevallyn was silent and thoughtful.

"You do not seem to join me," said Selena rather disappointed.

---

[58]   Sensible: receptive to impressions or acutely perceptive (OED).

"Why then to say the truth I do not like poor Angela very much … I was at first greatly inclined to like her, but she is so cold and so dark, that either she dislikes *me* particularly as I sometimes think, or there is something not right about her— which I confess has made me afraid of her tho' I would do any thing upon earth for her advantage—for dear Mrs. Harley's sake, and indeed for her own too, poor little soul; for she is certainly very unhappy, and I pity her from my heart tho' some how we do not warm to each other."

Selena said nothing for Mrs. Vallard looked grave, and she began to fear lest some objections might be raised to her future intimacy with poor Angela for whom she felt now deeply interested.

When breakfast was over Lady Trevallyn said she knew Mrs. Vallard too well to think it necessary to make any excuses for leaving her at liberty till dinner; "but I must shew you the library Selena," added she, "the piano forte is there, and I will send the harp which I so seldom use into your room."

As Selena declined this offer she blushed at the recollection of the kind of theft she had committed and following her into the library said hesitating, "I have a confession to make my dear Lady Trevallyn; Will you forgive me and bid me forgive myself for having read the verses which I heard you sing last night?"

It was now Lady Trevallyn's turn to blush, "You heard me sing," answered she in the utmost confusion. "Why! where … how did you hear me?"

"While I lay awake last night thinking of your promise."

"Oh my love you must not think of that promise any more. It was a very foolish one … and I have indeed nothing to tell you. I am or at least ought to be very happy. You must not get every one's secrets," added she smiling, "and you may be satisfied if you can obtain Angela's confidence."

"I have no wish to get your secrets dear Lady Trevallyn—but I should be grieved indeed to think you were not happy."

Lady Trevallyn observed her eyes filled with tears as she fixed them fondly upon her and found them infectious.

"Nobody is quite happy my love. There is poor Angela, when I think of her, tho' I know not the cause of her distress, yet I blame myself for indulging a melancholy which thus preys upon life itself."

"But you are not angry with me," asked Selena smiling, "for having read your verses."

"Oh no I could not be angry with *you* for any thing, and that was my own fault for leaving my nonsense throwing about, I must go however and put them by, for tho' you are welcome to read my compositions yet I should not chuse to give every one that liberty."

Before she quitted the library Selena obtained her free permission to take to Angela whatever books she chose; and she begged Selena would encourage her to change them as frequently as she could wish.

But Selena took care to conceal from her the reluctance which Angela had shewn to demand from Lady Trevallyn this favour, which indeed appeared unaccountable.

Impatient to convey to her what she thought might prove some consolation to her sadness Selena selected a few of her own favourite authors and putting them into her work basket tripped lightly to the school-house.

Mrs. Harley was at the shop and Angela with pallid cheeks and dejected eyes seated amidst the lively group appeared oppressed by the duty she endeavoured to fulfil on teaching the older girls to write, while the others repeated their lessons to her in turns. Selena offered to assist her and said she was sure the confusion around her made her head ache. Humbly and gracefully she declined the offered assistance and praised the children's affectionate gentleness and quiet obedience to her when they saw she was not able to bear much noise.

"My Mother is too indulgent to me," she added, "and will allow me to do nothing else to assist her. How worthless and ungrateful should I be not to perform this easy task. Besides the hours I thus pass are by far the happiest I can now spend; I have read somewhere what I find is very true that they who give to the unfortunate employment give them consolation."

"What you say," answered Selena, "is I am sure very just, but I am sorry to see you number yourself among the unfortunate. With a mother so indulgent you have only to open your heart and I am confident if in her power to gratify you, you will have no reason to think yourself any longer unfortunate."

It was the voice of tenderness in which these words were uttered and not what was said that touched so powerfully Angela's heart and while she wiped with her hand the tears which fell fast upon the spelling book which she held on her lap, half suffocated by the violence of her emotion she said "I am indeed unfortunate but I do not deserve your pity, and I have already met with but too much indulgence."

There was something in her manner which struck even the unsuspicious and inexperienced Selena that her sorrow was too deep and too secret for innocence, and without even allowing herself the idea, she felt a sensation of fear lest Angela should indeed chuse her as her confidant.

There was a short pause and the afflicted Angela still continuing to weep Selena whispered her in a low voice to compose herself before the children and to divert her for the present produced the books from her work basket. She was surprised to find Angela was already acquainted with all she had selected and hearing that she understood french said she would change them for the works of St Pierre[59] which Selena had just finished. Angela again expressed her reluctance to trouble Lady Trevallyn with any of her concerns but she was now in too languid a frame of mind to make much resistance to any thing which Selena might suggest.

Selena then proposed to hear the children sing, and having selected those whose voices appeared most promising asked Angela to come with them before breakfast while she remained at Esselberrie that she might have the assistance of the pianoforte in giving them the instructions which Lady Trevallyn had seemed inclined they should receive from her.

---

[59]   Jacques Henri Bernardin de Saint-Pierre (1737–1814), author of *Paul et Virginie* (1788).

Angela made no reply and looked so distressed that Selena repented having made the proposal, but as if recollecting herself after a minute's silence Angela answered, "Yes certainly Madam, we shall wait on you whatever hour you are pleased to name."

Selena said she should expect her at eight o'clock next morning as that was a time when they might be sure of being undisturbed and then affectionately taking her leave retired to her usual occupations till dinner time.

When her little pupils came next day at the appointed hour they found Selena already at the pianoforte trying some hymns in the collection which Lady Trevallyn had given her at her desire the evening before. Angela looked round with an earnest tho' timid eye as she entered and finding that the lesson was to be given by Selena entirely alone appeared relieved from her fears and remained without reluctance. She was not however to be prevailed upon to join in their little morning concerts, and when pressed by Selena (as she could not positively say she had never sung Lady Trevallyn having told Selena how Lady Anne used to boast of her talents in that and other accomplishments) she said in a voice that silenced the gentle instructress, "No Madam I am not worthy to join with such voices or ever to sing hymns."

She seemed however to listen with pleasure tho' as she sat in the window Selena without appearing to notice her fits of absence often perceived the work fall from her hands and her countenance assume a look of misery very different from that expression of quiet melancholy that even added to the beauty of Lady Trevallyn's features.

One morning Selena had left Angela with the children while she went to the octagon study to look for some musick to which she intended to adapt the words of a psalm. As she passed she plucked a small branch of a very beautiful geranium then in full bloom. On her return with a gentle and graceful playfulness she held it to Angela's face saying, "Is not that delightful!"

Angela shuddered, and with a movement that seemed involuntary repulsed Selena with her hand repeating at the same time "No, no, no" with a kind of energetick wildness that terrified Selena.

In a moment she grew calm and seeing Selena gaze upon her with astonishment and terror arose in confusion, trembling and bursting into tears as she asked her pardon saying she was at the moment seized with a sickness which her sudden paleness and tremor well justified.

Selena threw open the window and when Angela declared herself recovered affected to think no more of a circumstance which she perceived dwelt painfully upon Angela's own mind. She would not either mention it to Mrs. Vallard or Lady Trevallyn for fear they might entertain an idea which for an instant had occurred to herself that Angela's senses were disordered; tho' she was afterwards convinced that the emotion she had discovered arose from some painful remembrances which the peculiar odour of this plant had probably excited—and this idea was confirmed when she watched her sometime afterwards take up the branch which the affrighted Selena had let fall, and thinking herself unnoticed press it to her lips bathe it with her tears and place it in her bosom.

"Perhaps," said Selena, that evening to Lady Trevallyn as they were walking tete-a-tete, "poor Angela is regretting the gayer scenes in which her first youth was spent at Lady Anne Ortney's."

"It is very likely," answered she, "that the loss of her good friend may help to depress her spirits but there must I am persuaded be some secret cause otherwise at her time of life she would be pleased at the novelty of the scene, especially as on her arrival here Lord Trevallyn was so good as to allow me to offer her an appartment at Esselberrie, where she might have been not very gay indeed, as we live so retired but I should think just as lively as ever she was at Lady Anne's, who except her own family saw no company but methodist teachers."

"And how come you My dear Lady Trevallyn to be admitted into such a select society."

"I owed that honour to relationship my Mother was niece to the late Marquis of Ortney Lady Anne's brother; perhaps you did not know I was so nobly connected, but little as you may think of that point," observing Selena smile, "I can tell you but for this circumstance I should never have been raised by Lord Trevallyn to the rank of a countess."

If Selena made any reply it was unheard by Lady Trevallyn and forgotten by herself, for she was immediately struck by the deep thoughtfulness and silence which followed this speech and not a word was uttered on either side, till their walk was interrupted by a little gate which Selena on endeavouring to open found to be locked.

"Have you the key?" asked she in a soft voice.

Lady Trevallyn started and looking round with a heavy sigh as if awakening from an unpleasant dream answered, "Oh no! we have come quite wrong. I beg your pardon a thousand times," and then returning with a quicker pace she seemed anxious to find subjects of conversation most amusing to Selena.

She would have rallied her about Dallamore but the ease with which Selena received the raillery convinced her of her indifference, she confessed that she was surprised at Mrs. Vallard's partiality for so weak a character and declared that for her part she thought him the most tiresome companion she had ever met with, "but then," said she, "I believe he is particularly teizing to me, when a girl I used to dread seeing him in a publick place, for I was sure not to be able to get rid of him from my side, and yet he never attempted any conversation or seemed to pay me the [sic] attention."

"Oh that is exactly his way," said Selena laughing, "he often does not seem to be thinking of any thing but himself or to hear what we are saying for hours together, but he is very entertaining sometimes too, he makes such odd remarks, and then he is so good-natured that I am not surprised that Mrs. Vallard should love him. I happened to say I should like to see the musick of a new ballet he was praising, and he sent for it directly to town, and not only it but I believe all the musick which has been published this year past.

"But what I think a great deal more of was a circumstance which occurred the day before he left Hillbarton. Mrs. Vallard was telling me without thinking of his attending to us in the least, that she was afraid Mrs. Pine a milliner in Derby to whom she had written would not take her own little orphan niece whose poor Mother had died in our neighbourhood, without a premium. He asked directly what premium she wanted and said he would give the little orphan fifty pounds. Mrs. Vallard looked quite proud of him, but I am sure would never have reminded him of it, and for my part I never expected he would have thought of it again. But to our great surprise just before he left Hillbarton his servant brought Mrs. Vallard the fifty pounds, and when she asked him laughing for what he had sent her so much money he answered as if surprised at her asking 'Why for your orphan to be sure, does not she want it.'"

"Yes," said Lady Trevallyn, "I have a thousand good stories of him in that way but I really hope he may not come near me any more in spite of that, for he tires me to death. I beg your pardon for speaking so of your cousin and I suspect your lover too."

Selena laughing assured her that in both characters she was at liberty to attack him as severely as she pleased; and that she could not in the least consider herself as bound to him in either.

Chapter IX

> When she was frighted didst thou not mark
> How far beyond the purity of snow
> The soft wind drives, whiteness of innocence
> Or anything that bears celestial paleness
> She appeared of the sudden? ....
> Didst thou not see those orient tears flowed from her
> The little worlds of love?
>
> Beaumont and Fletcher[60]

A week had thus past peacefully at Esselberrie, in which Selena had gained every day upon the hearts both of Lady Trevallyn and the drooping Angela, when Mrs. Vallard one morning received a few lines which Selena immediately knew to be in her Mother's hand. They were merely intended as a letter of recommendation for her son Robert who now awaited their return at Hillbarton.

"You see therefore my dear Emily I must now positively leave you," said Mrs. Vallard as she handed to her the letter, "unless you will for once break thro' your resolution and accompany me home till Lord Trevallyn returns."

---

[60] Francis Beaumont and John Fletcher, *The Maid in the Mill* (1647), 1.2.27–35, with some important elisions in lines 27–8 ("when she was frighted / At our uncivil Swords, didst thou not mark") and 32–3 ("Didst thou not see her Tears / When she entreated? O thou Reprobate!").

"I have it not in my power," answered she, "to pay you so great a compliment for I expect Lord Trevallyn this very day tho' I would not tell you so before for fear the news might frighten you from Esselberrie."

"We are not so easily frightened," said Mrs. Vallard gravely, "but since you say you cannot come with us I hope you will at least not let our dear Selena go without coming to take leave of her at Hillbarton. I fear we must soon lose her."

Lady Trevallyn would not however part from them till she had received Selena's promise that she would not quit the neighbourhood without once more visiting Esselberrie, a promise which she repeated to the weeping but silent Angela.

Mrs. Vallard was delighted to see in Robert the manly but beautiful portrait of her beloved friend.

"Has Clara too," she asked, "her Mother's sweet blue eyes, which I see you have inherited as well as Selena."

"Yes," said Robert, "we are all like my Mother and that was I suppose to please my father, who certainly would not have liked us the better for any resemblance to his family. But pray where is Lord Dallamore? I was in hopes I should have seen him here."

"And was your father also in hopes you should?" asked Mrs. Vallard with a smile.

"My father I assure you wished nothing more and gave me liberty to invite him to Miltern Abbey if he would acknowledge me as a relation."

Mrs. Vallard was astonished but infinitely pleased at the idea that thro' her mediation it was now possible a family so long divided might at length be reunited.

The thought even struck her that perhaps Mr. Miltern might not be averse to the idea of Selena possessing with Dallamore those very estates the acquisition of which to his brother had been the cause of so much animosity. She herself would have delighted in the thoughts of a union of two persons so dear to her, but she had hitherto checked so improbable an idea.

She now more than ever regretted Dallamore's departure, and was actually meditating schemes for his recovery, when as they were sitting the next day after dinner Selena interrupted her contemplations by an exclamation of surprise and Mrs. Vallard looking up beheld with equal wonder and pleasure Dallamore himself who accompanied by Richmond had stopped his curricle before the parlour windows and was peeping in to discover whether dinner was over, an event which for these two hours past Richmond had been foreboding with no small degree of dissatisfaction.

"Dear Dallamore how glad I am to see you," said Mrs. Vallard running to the door to meet him, "so you really have come back to us."

"Yes to be sure I am come. Did you not promise you would go to Harrogate and I hope you are ready now. Where is Selena? Oh I was afraid you were gone!" said he advancing to shake hands with as he perceived her on entering the parlour, "and I long to shew you Harrogate it will amuse you, there is such a set of quizzes there now."

"I am glad you have been so well amused yourself," answered Selena.

"Oh I never was so *bored* in my whole life. I was coming back here the very next day but Richmond said he would come with me and he has kept me waiting upon him for this month."

"A month Dallamore!" exclaimed Richmond. "Why how much less have we been at Harrogate. We have been there I suppose about four days."

"Well never mind, Richmond that was only like one of your own histories. But I really could bear it no longer—and I was half way here without him today, when he overtook me."

Richmond who from his knowledge of Dallamore did not expect this transaction would have even been remembered far less repeated, shewed as much embarrassment as he was ever capable of displaying upon any occasion, but dreading lest Mrs. Vallard should penetrate into the designs which thus fastened him on her nephew, he with never daunted assurance and his usual presence of mind interrupted him laughing and exclaimed, "Come Dallamore, do not romance, Mrs. Vallard knows you too well to believe that you would have left Harrogate till dooms day by yourself. You have been talking about it indeed ever since you went there, but if I had not taken you at your word this morning when you offered to drive me here, we should both have been stewing this moment in that cursed dinner room at the Green Dragon."[61]

Dallamore did not give himself the trouble to contradict or even to listen to this harangue, and Mrs. Vallard scarcely waited for its conclusion impatient as she was to introduce Dallamore to his cousin Robert who gracefully returned his bow and expressed with some confusion his hope of their being in future well acquainted. Richmond's hint of dinner was however quickly attended to ... and Mrs. Vallard left Robert to do the honours of her table to the new guests and retired with Selena to consult whether she would really comply with Dallamore's proposal that they should spend a day or two at Harrogate.

In spite however of the commission with which Robert said he had been entrusted Selena was still so apprehensive of her father's displeasure, that she entreated Mrs. Vallard to suffer her to return directly to Miltern Abbey as she could not bear to think that she prevented her from going where she might be of use to her nephew, and yet without the knowledge of Mrs. Miltern she could not consent to accompany her.

Mrs. Vallard assured her that she should not think of going unless it was with her and Robert, and begged of her therefore not to hasten her departure from Hillbarton on that account, adding that could she get rid of Mr. Richmond she would infinitely rather detain Dallamore with her, which she had little doubt of being able to accomplish.

She did not however give any positive refusal but allowed her nephew to divert himself part of the evening in forming wild plans for the amusement at Harrogate while she found a pleasure in baffling Mr. Richmond's artful endeavours to discover whether she had in fact any intention to return there with Dallamore

---

[61] The Green Dragon is an inn in Yorkshire (the location of Harrogate).

plainly discerning that while he politely appeared to recommend their compliance with this plan, he was studiously introducing every circumstance which he thought might prevent or discourage them from taking a journey so inimical to his wishes: To humour the design she plainly saw he had in view she enquired with an air of interest what company there was at present at Harrogate and whether there had been many people of fashion there that season.

"Oh not a single soul," cried he, "but the red-faced wives of Bristol merchants and some scorbutick[62] Irish Dowagers, with a swarm of Scotch Misses and fortune hunters, who dance till their high cheek bones blaze like their own fiery hair."

"Is not Lady Greysville there now, she called on me some time ago on her way as she told me to Harrogate with Miss Ludlow?"

Tho' Mrs. Vallard asked this question thro' mere chance yet Richmond ever full of himself, and supposing others equally occupied by his concerns thought it intended to put him out of countenance and that she must already have heard of the attentions he had paid during his stay at Harrogate to this reputed heiress.

He simply therefore answered in the affirmative and turning to Robert asked him did he purpose joining their party at the Green Dragon.

"Nothing would give me greater pleasure if Mrs. Vallard would allow me to attend her, but I am afraid she is not serious in her intentions."

"Do you think so?" asked Richmond eagerly. "Why faith there is not much temptation in the society at present."

"Are you fixed to return there yourself."

"That shall be just as Dallamore pleases; I have given him a month and promised to let him steer me as he chuses for that time."

Mrs. Vallard smiled—but Richmond was not to be disconcerted by a smile. He preserved his temper unmoved and again endeavoured to divert Mrs. Vallard and Robert by a satirical account of the party he had just left, tho' in secret he heartily hated the one as the opposer of his designs, and despised the other as a young man who knew nothing and whom nobody knew.

While he vainly tried to sift Mrs. Vallard concerning her plans Dallamore seated behind Selena with his feet stretched upon an opposite chair, was by times listening to her musick and asking her questions, the answers to which were indeed but little regarded.

She had just concluded a very lively bravura song when Dallamore enchanted with the rapidity of her execution and the spirit with which it was performed exclaimed, "Well Selena I have seen or heard nothing like you since I'll be d--d if I have."

Perhaps this was as fine a speech as ever Dallamore had made, and was indeed received by Selena with a blush as well as a laugh—a blush perhaps caused by the recollection of Lady Trevallyn's raillery tho' at the time it had entirely failed of its effect. Absent as Dallamore in general was, this blush was not unobserved, and if he had ever any degree felt the influence of the tender passion it was not until that moment.

---

[62]   Scorbutick: symptomatic of or proceeding from scurvy (OED).

It was in vain that Richmond endeavoured the next morning to disturb Dallamore in order that he might press his aunt to decide whether she would return with them or not to Harrogate. "To be sure she will go …" "Ask her yourself …" "Pray do not torment me any more" were all the answers he could obtain to his repeated and impatient doubts while he protested "that they should be kept loitering there for nothing, that the day would be lost, and that Mrs. Vallard had not the least idea of leaving Hillbarton."

When breakfast was over Robert followed Selena out of the room to shew her a letter which he had just received from his father and which he advised her to communicate to Mrs. Vallard as in his opinion it entirely removed every objection to their expedition to Harrogate a plan which he felt extremely inclined to put into execution. The letter was as follows.

> "Dear Robert,
> "I have been thinking that many unpleasant consequences might result from inviting Lord Dallamore to Miltern Abbey but I have no objection that you and Selena should cultivate an acquaintance which you may think desirable, nor any wish to perpetuate family quarrels. On the contrary if Mrs. Vallard is not tired of you I should be very glad that you might profit by this opportunity which chance has cast in your way of knowing so near a relation whom in your future intercourse with the world you cannot avoid meeting.
> > Yours affectionately,
> > Frederick Miltern"

Selena who wondered at her Mother's silence felt an extreme reluctance to going any where without her knowledge, yet knew not how to object to what Robert seemed to think so fortunate and so delightful. She still held the letter in her hand at the window when Mrs. Vallard past saying, "In deep contemplation Selena! I hope you are not meditating flight."

"No Madam," said Robert, "on the contrary we are only laying schemes for trespassing farther on your kindness."

"In what way my love?" said Mrs. Vallard, going up to Selena with pleasure and affection painted in her eyes.

"Give her the letter Selena," said Robert taking it from her hastily while she stood silent and debating thoughtfully in her own mind how she might persuade Robert to agree with her in thinking it better to remain where they were, or rather indeed return to her Mother than go on an expedition she thought so wild without her consent.

Mrs. Vallard however was of Robert's opinion for she was ever inclined to forward any scheme for the innocent amusement of young people, and Selena who was yet little skilled in the art so necessary to acquire thro' life of gracefully pronouncing the ungraceful monosyllable *No* gave a passive and silent consent; contrary to her judgment and even wishes.

When Dallamore appeared he had therefore the satisfaction of hearing that they were preparing for their Harrogate expedition but that Mrs. Vallard would not leave home immediately tho' she would not delay Dallamore longer than the next day.

The enraged Richmond in this arrangement was not invited to stay, but he chose to think the invitation was not necessary, as he had come to Hillbarton with Dallamore and had declared his engagement, which indeed was voluntarily made, of remaining with him for a month.

"Do you think it is possible my dear Madam," said Selena as soon as she had decided upon their going, "that Lady Trevallyn would come with us to Harrogate, I should be so delighted to have her and that Robert might know her."

Mrs. Vallard shook her head. "Lady Trevallyn hates the thoughts of all gaiety," said she, "since she was married, and she could not be there without meeting some of those whom she knew formerly in the circle where she so conspicuously moved. Besides poor Lord Trevallyn is hardly rested yet I suppose after his journey to town, and back again, which was a pretty long one for so old a man to perform in a week. However write and try what your eloquence will do."

Selena obeyed her but received not the acquiescence which she indeed hardly hoped to obtain. Lady Trevallyn's note was very kind and she reminded Selena of her promise of visiting her again before she finally quitted her neighbourhood and in a postscript she added, "Poor Angela has been very ill every since you went, and has at last extorted from her unhappy mother a promise that when she is a little better she shall go to her aunt if she is willing again to receive her. I hope we shall be able to make her situation there a little more comfortable than it was before, notwithstanding her strange obstinacy in persisting in her desire to return."

Mrs. Vallard wishing to afford some amusing variety to her guests prepared the next day to dine in a summer house which had been built even long before the house at Hillbarton in a most picturesque part of the wood which overhung the river. The day had been unusually hot, and the evening, lovely as imagination could conceive gave to their view an ever changing sky of the most rich and glorious colouring. They descended the steep bank by steps to a little boat, built for the shallowest water. Dallamore's servant who played remarkably well on the clarionet was seated at one end, his master occupied the stern, while Robert and Richmond, both well accustomed to the exercise rowed them up and down between the beautiful banks of the river as far as the rocky interruptions to its course would suffer their little navigation.

Selena enraptured with the scenery allowed no beauty to pass unnoticed but pointed out with delighted observation now the bright reflection of the sky flaming with gold and purple, and now the deep dark brown that seemed to sleep upon the water beneath the wooded bank. As they passed under the little building where they had dined she bid Dallamore observe the beautiful rose tree which was in luxuriant flower beneath the windows in a spot which now appeared totally inaccessible the river having eaten away the bank below so that that part on which stood the summer house, fringed with wild shrubs and underwood quite overhung the river.

"I wonder," said she, "who planted it there and how many summers it has now flowered secure from any spoiler's hand. I suppose it is because I cannot possibly get it that I long for one of those roses more than for all that are now in blow in the garden."[63]

"Nothing more easy," said Dallamore, "than to get one."

"Easy as it may be," cried Richmond with a sneer, "I'll bet you fifty guineas you do not stick one of those roses in Miss Miltern's hat."

"Done," said Dallamore hastily who never in his whole life had been known to refuse a bet however absurd; and however experience had given him cause to doubt his success.

Selena could not believe him serious but Mrs. Vallard who knew him better was extremely uneasy. Nor was Selena less alarmed when they perceived him turn the little boat towards land. In vain they entreated him to give up such a boyish enterprise. In vain Mrs. Vallard herself took the rudder from his hand. He leaped on shore and in a moment appeared to his aunt and the no less terrified Selena issuing from the window of the summer house and clambring from thence to the spot where the unfortunate roses had attracted their attention.

They remained breathless with suspence, and even Richmond who had at first only laughed at their apprehensions now considered his situation with a degree of alarm which he might perhaps not have shared had he not been conscious how much blame would be imputed to him should any ill consequences ensue.

Dallamore however succeeded in his purpose, but the instant he had seized the branch containing two or three roses in full bloom 'ere he could hold it up in triumph the bank which for years had sustained no weight but that of the shrubs it nurtured suddenly gave way, and the stunned Dallamore fell into the water a height of above thirty feet. Mrs. Vallard screamed but Selena who had all along considered herself as the unfortunate occasion of this hazardous exploit now shocked at what she thought the inevitable destruction of the wretched Dallamore sunk lifeless to the bottom of the boat and Le Roi who had instantly jumped into the river to his Master's assistance had dragged him in perfect safety to shore; long before Selena opened her languid eyes, or by the least breath or motion had given any sign of existence.

When the tumult this had occasioned was subsided and Selena in some degree recovered as she appeared ill able to walk Mrs. Vallard entreated the rowers to make all possible expedition in conveying her home in the boat, and Dallamore dripping as he was insisted upon accompanying them tho' entreated by Mrs. Vallard to save himself a severe cold by running to the house.

As they were thus returning Richmond exclaimed, "Well Dallamore you lost your bet at last for tho' you got the rose you never placed it in Miss Miltern's hat."

"D--n it that's true," cried Dallamore, "where is the branch? I must go back and look for it."

"No my Lord for I have got it safe," said Le Roi producing from the bottom of the boat the roses all wet and dripping as Dallamore himself and far more severely injured as they had indeed received even worse treatment.

---

[63] See Tighe's sonnet "Written at Rossana. November 18, 1799" for a similar image.

The truth was that in the moment of confusion when Le Roi had just saved his master and Selena was yet apparently dead, Richmond ever attentive to self interest perceiving at his foot the branch Dallamore had dropped by a sly kick pushed it again into the river determining at all events to win his bet. Le Roi on their return to the boat perceived the object of the wager gained with such imminent danger floating on the brink and snatched it from threatened destruction. Occupied as he was himself at the moment he had seen Richmond's action and resolved thus to frustrate his design.

When Dallamore therefore proposed returning to search for the branch he presented it to his master saying with a smile he could not suppress, "It would not have been fair my Lord for Mr. Richmond to throw back into the river the roses your Lordship had run such a risk to get for Miss Miltern."

Richmond coloured with rage and even shame but endeavouring to laugh it off answered with assumed carelessness, "D--n me if I saw the roses before 'till this moment."

No one contradicted the assertion; but the trait could never be forgotten by Mrs. Vallard or Selena, tho' Dallamore thought not of it a second time, and Robert could not give any credit to the insinuation of Le Roi. It was indeed scarcely possible for any event to have taken place more provoking to Richmond or better calculated to defeat his designs on Dallamore. He had lost his wager (the payment of which however he intended should be forgotten) and his liberal disregard of money had been placed in a light terribly suspicious.

But besides these unlucky circumstances Selena's particular alarm for Dallamore's danger evinced in so unquestionable a manner had impressed him with a conviction that she really felt for her cousin that interest and regard of which even the affectation had been attended with such promise of success hitherto to his sister. He was not blind to Selena's advantages, tho' he treated her with slight and pretended to think little of her person and despise her for her talents. But he saw with inexpressible mortification that Dallamore was enchanted by her innocent demonstration of affection and captivated by the blooming graces of her form and her uncommon skill in the accomplishment of which Nature had enabled him to feel the power.

Chapter X

> Wild as the wind
> That sweeps the desert of our moving plains,
> Love might as well be sowed upon our sands
> As in a breast so barren.
>
> Dryden[64]

---

[64]   The Emperor in John Dryden's *Don Sebastian: A Tragedy* (1689), 2.1.19–22. The first line should read "wild as winds."

Selena not chusing that Mr. Richmond should forget to pay Dallamore a wager so dearly earned appeared the next morning (which was that fixed for their journey) with the withered trophy still unremoved from her hat, a circumstance which was even more flattering to Dallamore than it was annoying to the person for whose observation it was intended—for Dallamore to their surprise joined them at breakfast notwithstanding that Richmond who knew they were to carry with them the persons whose company he so much detested did not again persecute him with any impatient summons.

Delighted with the compliment of seeing his roses still so much valued Dallamore pressed Selena to accompany him in the curricle unmindful of Richmond who listened on thorns to a proposal every way displeasing to him but particularly so as Selena's accepting the offer would deprive him of the conveyance which he esteemed his right. From this distress he was however freed by Selena's declaration that the sun would certainly give her a head-ache, as she was not accustomed to expose herself to the mid-day heat, tho' Dallamore in vain attempted to persuade her that to go third in a chaise with Mrs. Vallard and her maid was infinitely more likely to make her ill.

With this arrangement he was however obliged to be content, and Richmond recovered his usual good temper as he took his seat in the curricle, while Robert accompanied them on horseback delighted with the party, and the prospect of so motley a scene as he conceived Harrogate would present. When they stopped at Wakefield Dallamore proposed their staying there to dine declaring he could no longer endure the heat and dust of the roads and Mrs. Vallard who felt herself fatigued readily assented.

After dinner he again entreated Selena to take the vacant place in the curricle, and she hesitated, not well knowing what excuse she should make when suddenly recollecting herself, "Oh certainly no," said she, "what would Mr. Richmond do?"

"Oh d--n Richmond, never mind him, he can get a chaise here you know."

"Thank you Dallamore," replied Richmond much piqued, "but there is no necessity for my being damned about it in any way even to a cursed *rattle trap*[65] which really is complete damnation, for if Miss Miltern chuses my place in the curricle we may leave one of your grooms to follow us and I can take his horse."

"Very well do so then," said Dallamore, "it is an excellent plan, so now Selena you see we have settled all things to your satisfaction;" Mrs. Vallard encouraged Selena to make no more objections giving her a handkerchief to defend her from the evening dew, which Dallamore with unexpected gallantry insisted upon tying round her neck himself.

When they drove up to the door of the Green Dragon Dallamore prevented Mrs. Vallard from alighting, assuring her that she could never bear the confounded bustle of the house nor the pest of meeting such quizzes for ever upon the stairs,

---

[65] Rattle trap: old or rickety vehicle (OED).

but offered to undertake procuring for her a small house "where at least they might sleep in peace if they were obliged to dine in the bear-garden."[66]

Mrs. Vallard felt rather discouraged at the picture he thus drew of the residence at the publick lodging house and allowed him to go and ask from the Mistress a more quiet abode; the Lady of the house was eager to go herself and explain to Mrs. Vallard "how the quality always preferred lodging in the house which she was sure they would find much more convenienter."

But if Dallamore was not eloquent he however possessed one art of conquering all difficulties made by whose with whom he had any dealings in the way of business—for he was ever ready to offer them all the compensation which money can afford, upon which he seldom found any so stiff as to continue dissatisfied. Having now settled the point to their mutual contentment the good lady called a waiter and desired him to shew my Lord and his company the way to Tom Crosley's and followed herself to see that her new guests were provided with every accommodation my Lord's rank demanded.

Richmond who had rode on before impatient to seek his fair heiress and acquaint his sister with the unwelcome arrival of Mrs. Vallard now came to see how Dallamore and his party were settled; having found that his friends were still at the play he easily prevailed upon Dallamore to assent to his proposal of accompanying him to see what was going on there and taking his arm they walked out together, leaving Robert to entertain the ladies in their empty lodgings, Selena having no instrument with which she might assuredly have detained Dallamore till supper when they promised to return to conduct them to the Green Dragon.

The play was just over when the gentlemen reached the door of the theatre—and amidst the noisy group by which they were instantly surrounded, and who welcomed the return of their two beaux Richmond was not without hopes of the newly arrived Ladies being totally forgotten by Dallamore, a triumph over the artless Selena to which he looked forward as a consolation for some of the mortifications she had innocently caused him. He was however disappointed for notwithstanding that Belle Richmond had seized hold of his arm, declaring it much too fine a night to go back in the carriage which waited at the door of the theatre yet when they reached the hall Dallamore silently disengaged himself and catching Richmond's eye asked him "would he not come for Selena?"

Richmond had indeed watched his motions tho' apparently listning with admiration to Miss Ludlow's account of the monstrous heat at the play and the monstrous bore it had been to her to accompany Lady Greysville there.

Mortified at this remembrance of Dallamore which defeated his hopes he answered him carelessly, "My dear fellow impossible, can not you send the waiter?"

"No damn it I'll go myself," replied he leaving Richmond amazed at an exertion so unusual and his sister bursting with vexation at finding herself thus left to walk unhanded and unattended by her beau to the supper table.

---

[66]   Bear-garden: a place originally set apart for the baiting of bears, and used for the exhibition of other rough sports, figuratively a scene of strife and tumult (OED).

The company had taken their places when they entered and Dallamore's seat beside Miss Richmond remained vacant. He did not however resume it as had been expected but placed himself at the bottom of the table next the door between his aunt and Selena. They were followed into the room by two young men whom Selena had noticed as they first drove up to the door of the hotel for arriving almost at the same moment as her own party they had stood and stared at her during Dallamore's transaction with the Landlady with an attention which Selena did not feel quite civil and rather unpleasant.[67] One of them in particular struck her as he must have done every observer by the uncommon beauty of his person, the elegance of his appearance, and the easy gracefulness which mingled with a degree of majesty accompanied his most trifling movements. He now seated himself on the outside next Selena and addressed Dallamore by name.

Dallamore who had not before observed the strangers now looked round and nodding his head familiarly returned the salutation with "Oh are you there Ortney, when did you come to Harrogate?" At the name of Ortney Selena again looked at the young man with a degree of interest supposing him to be related to her friend Lady Trevallyn whom she knew to be connected with the noble house of Ortney. She even thought that he bore some resemblance to the beautiful features of Lady Trevallyn and she looked till her modest eye perceived that her attention was more than returned by the stranger.

Ashamed of being thus observed she turned [to] Dallamore and joined with Mrs. Vallard's entreaties that in the mixt company there assembled he should gratify their curiosity and point out to them Miss Richmond, and upon his refusal they diverted themselves by looking round the room and forming guesses. This employment seemed to interest and entertain their unknown neighbour even more than Dallamore. He indeed kept his eyes fixed upon them and tho' he himself eat nothing was far more attentive in offering to help Selena and Mrs. Vallard to every thing within his reach than Dallamore under whose more immediate care the ladies seemed to be placed. He ventured to make some observations to Selena and even ask her some questions. But she who was unaccustomed to the easy and familiar manners of this kind of temporary society felt embarrassed at thus finding herself engaged in conversation with a total stranger.

At length Mrs. Vallard tired of her journey tho' pleased and amused full as much as Selena by the novelty of the scene and the gay observations of their new and courteous acquaintance now rose and requested Dallamore to conduct them home, not chusing she said to depend upon Robert's knowledge of a way he had only come once and that in the dark. Dallamore was but little inclined to stir and got up slowly yawning and stretching himself. The young stranger who on their first movement had stood up with ready civility to allow Selena to pass rallied Dallamore on his listless acceptance of so enviable a charge, and bowing to both the ladies as they retired seemed to bespeak their future acquaintance without the formality of an introduction.

---

[67] The MS editor replaces "and rather unpleasant" with "or pleasant."

Selena was impatient to enquire concerning him from Dallamore on their quitting the room and Mrs. Vallard not having like her heard her nephew return his first salutation by name, now discovered with evident surprise that she had been speaking to Lord Henry Ortney.

"Do you know any thing of him?" said Selena observing the emotion with which she heard his name.

"I have seen him before My dear," answered she with some hesitation, "but tho' I did not directly remember him I am well acquainted with some of his family."

"Is not he related to Lady Trevallyn" asked Selena.

"He is, but did she tell you so?"

"No I did not hear her mention him in particular but she said she was nearly connected with the family of the Marquis, I think he is a little like her, and has a good deal of her sweet expression of countenance and that very remarkable shape of Lady Trevallyn's beautiful eyes."

Mrs. Vallard said nothing and Selena asked her if she did not think him very handsome.

Dallamore saved her the trouble of answering by interrupting her with "d--d handsome and a favourite of the ladies."

Selena felt somewhat disappointed that Mrs. Vallard ever ready to praise did not say any thing in favour of an appearance she thought so remarkably pleasing. Indeed Mrs. Vallard was but little inclined to speak at all of perhaps the only person in the world with whom her benevolent heart did not feel in perfect charity, and she half regretted that her coming hither at that particular time had thrown in her way one for whom tho' unknown she entertained a dislike as nearly amounting to hatred as a mind so amiable was capable of feeling and which she thought some circumstances fully justified.

Before they parted for the night Dallamore requested that they might breakfast at their lodging, and Mrs. Vallard gladly consented; unwilling yet to encounter so many strangers especially as she could not expect Dallamore would be ready to accompany them.

He was up however sooner than they imagined for Le Roi had reminded him that this was the only day in the week in which he could shew Miss Miltern the beautiful domain of Harewood[68]—and Richmond had been sent by Lady Greysville to invite them to join her party who were going to profit by the permission. Mrs. Vallard gave her consent and he then went up to Dallamore's room to enquire whether he intended to keep the engagement he had made some time before by driving Miss Richmond that morning to Harewood.

If such a promise had really been made it had totally escaped Dallamore's memory and at present he would have much preferred offering the place in his curricle to Selena, however this he was ashamed to express, and promising to call for Miss Richmond finished his toilet at leisure, while Le Roi who never

---

[68]   Harewood is a historic house in Yorkshire (owned by the Lascelles).

could conceal his dislike of Miss Richmond in a kind of soliloquy intended for his Master's ear "wondered how Miss Miltern was to go to Harewood."

In the mean time Richmond hastened down to warn his sister to be on the watch, taking care *en passant*[69] to inform Selena that Dallamore had sent him to invite his sister to drive with him to Harewood, tho' he thereby totally failed in his design of mortifying the unsuspecting Selena who had never once considered Miss Richmond as her rival.

Mrs. Vallard however felt herself affronted and when Dallamore appeared reproached him for deserting them so soon.

"Oh never mind," said he, "I'll overturn her very soon and then I can take you or Selena in."

Selena laughing declared for her part she would take care not to make room for any else in the same way.

"Oh you need not be afraid Selena," said Dallamore with unaffected kindness in his look and manner, "I could never wish to get rid of you and I am d--d sorry I cannot take you now."

Selena deeply blushing assured him that at present she preferred a covered carriage and was excessively pleased that she should see Miss Richmond at last.

"Oh you will not like her I am sure."

"Why do you think so?" cried Selena with her eyes fixed upon the window adding immediately, "But who are all those!"

"Confound them!" said Dallamore annoyed and pushing his chair from the breakfast table, "Here is the whole set coming down upon us."

As he spoke the door opened and a pretty but very little woman in a habit and large man's hat entered the room with a laugh which was however not to be heard so completely was it drowned by the more boisterous mirth of the Lady who burst in at the same moment forming a most striking contrast with the delicacy of Lady Greysville's figure which has been just described.

They were both indeed equally highly rouged but the quantity which covered Miss Richmond's ample cheeks might if properly divided have supplied Lady Greysville's miniature face for some days.

They were followed by Richmond upon whose arm leaned Miss Ludlow apparently oppressed by languor and fatigue.

After the first bustle of salutation and introduction was subsided Lady Greysville enquired how they intended to go the purposed party, and hearing that Mrs. Vallard had ordered her chaise exclaimed, "Lord how stupid for Miss Miltern, do let her ride with us, I have a famous horse I will lend her, for I am going to try one for Tom."

While Selena with modest thanks declined the obliging offer she secretly wondered whether by Tom was meant Sir Thomas Greysville or her coachman— till she settled it in her mind that Lady Greysville wished to ascertain the quietness

---

[69] En passant: in passing (French).

of a horse for some little boy tho' she could not think her old enough to have a son yet fit to ride.

"Come Dallamore where is your curricle," said Miss Richmond starting from her seat after having taken a rude and scornful survey of Selena's face and person for a length of time which had called up all the pure and eloquent blood into the glowing cheeks of Selena who had timidly withdrawn her eyes from the singular figure to which curiosity had attracted them as often as they met fixed upon her the undaunted gaze of insolent assurance.

"My God how close this room is!" exclaimed Miss Richmond observing that Dallamore took no notice of her question and throwing up the sash, while Mrs. Vallard who had been seated with her back to the window quietly moved her chair not without some surprise at so much freedom in a total stranger.

"You are always so devilish hot Belle," cried Lady Greysville, "but I wish to God you would take yourself off out of this close room and send me my horses. I cannot conceive," she continued while she looked out of the window, "what my fellows are about they were all ready and I had saddled my own mare myself before I left the stables."

Dallamore however still did not move. He was indeed just then extremely busy feeding his favourite Rolla with the remains of the breakfast table, of which he had himself not tasted after the interruption which the visitors had given him. Perceiving his employment Miss Richmond came over to assist him and patting Rolla's head asked his master in rather a lower voice how he could bear to be stuffed up there the whole morning when the room was like an oven.

"It is confoundedly hot," cried Dallamore rising to ring the bell and order his curricle, the arrival of which Miss Richmond watched impatiently from the window and the moment it appeared ascended calling upon Dallamore to follow her.

"Is that to be the match?" said Lady Greysville as she looked after them.

Mrs. Vallard (to whom this was addressed in a half whisper) pointed towards Mr. Richmond and smiled significantly.

"Oh he does not mind us," continued her ladyship in the same tone, "He is too busy making love to Fanny Ludlow. But I have bet two to one against it in spite of the desperate attack Bella is making on your nephew."

"I am sure," said Mrs. Vallard softly, "I hope your ladyship may not lose."

"Oh she is the devil!" cried she smiling, "But there is my Tom looking every where for me," added she in a louder voice and the next moment exerted its utmost force as she called "Tom, Tom" in order to attract the attention of a mean looking young man who with his neck stretched alternately on one side and the other was sauntering on the green at some distance.

Selena involuntarily rose to look at Tom whose name had already occasioned her some curiosity.

"Lord how like a goose he looks," cried Lady Greysville at the same moment taking a spring from the open window towards him and seized hold of his arm so suddenly that he gave a violent start which almost overset him.

He did not however seem in the least to join in the mirth which this occasioned to Lady Greysville and as they walked slowly towards them Selena heard Richmond observe to Miss Ludlow as they stood at the other window "Greysville's in a d--d sulk today."

Selena did not hear the answer, Miss Ludlow's voice being at all times excessively low and at present not raised above her breath, but just then Lady Greysville approached the window and playfully pushed in Sir Thomas's head while she exclaimed laughing, "Aye look in, you see Lord Henry is not there so now do put on a better face and be a little less gloomy or you will frighten the whole Harewood party. Don't you think so Miss Miltern?"

Sir Thomas in evident struggles between shame and vexation awkwardly paid his compliments to Mrs. Vallard and then bowed to Selena who blushing at Lady Greysville's address endeavoured to laugh off her confusion.

"And now go for my horses like a good boy," said she patting him upon the back, "for we are losing the day terribly and I cannot conceive why these devils do not bring them."

Sir Thomas peevishly drawing back from her playful hand answered dryly, "How can you possibly expect the servants are to guess where you run to if you do not condescend to leave orders. The horses have been standing in the sun at the Green Dragon for this half hour at least, and it was not in my power to give Frank any information as you chuse to fly off the moment I left you."

"Well my dear Tom you must take my advice at last," said Lady Greysville screwing up her little mouth and assuming as grave a face as she could, "you must get a string and tye me to your button-hole for I positively never can think of waiting for your leave when I am tired of any one place."

"Pooh, nonsense!" cried Sir Thomas turning from her, "I should be glad to know Lady Greysville whether you intend to ride to day or not."

"My God how unreasonable you are Tom! Here have I been waiting for you for an hour, and now you are cross with me for my complaisance. But come Fanny for the love of Heaven let us set out at last."

Miss Ludlow protested she was not able to walk back in the sun and upon this Richmond at length offered to go for the horses.

Chapter XI

But truer stars did govern Proteus' birth
His words are bonds, his oaths are oracles,
His love sincere, his thoughts immaculate,
His tears pure messengers sent from his heart,
His heart as far from fraud as Heaven from earth ....
.... Pray heaven he prove so! ...

Shakespear[70]

---

[70]   Julia in Shakespeare's *The Two Gentlemen of Verona* (1594), 2.7.74–8, followed by Lucetta's response (2.7.79).

The business of departure being at last arranged, and Selena at liberty freely to discourse tete-a-tete with Mrs. Vallard as they followed the gay party in her chaise to Harewood, they naturally expressed their mutual surprise how Dallamore could think of a woman so very disagreeable in her person and manners as Miss Richmond appeared to them both.

"Sure you do not think her handsome!" cried Selena in a voice which plainly spoke her opinion.

"Why she certainly has something striking about her from that shewy contrast of colours in her hair, eyes, and complexion," answered Mrs. Vallard, "and her figure tho' so large I believe is uncommonly fine."

"Well for my part I think her quite ugly," said Selena.

Mrs. Vallard smiled and perhaps imagined Selena would not have thought her ugly had she not occupied her place in the curricle. In this she was however mistaken, Selena unused to mix with the fashionable world was really shocked at the bold countenance, glaring rouge and riotous manners of Belle Richmond, and had she been far handsomer would still have seen her with disgust. She owned indeed that her features were all good and her person what is called fine but concluded with declaring that of all the women she had ever seen she most disliked her looks.

"Now there," she cried, "is Miss Ludlow; she is certainly not a bit handsome, yet would not you infinitely rather look like her than Miss Richmond?"

Mrs. Vallard confessed in reply that she should not at all covet the appearance of either were she young and had the liberty to chuse.

"Why sure Madam you do not call Miss Richmond young?"

"Somewhat younger than I am you will allow my dear tho' rather too old indeed for Dallamore."

"Is it possible you can think my cousin has any serious idea of her."

"Indeed I hope not my love."

Selena heard not this reply as she exclaimed at the same moment, "Oh there is Lord Henry Ortney I am sure," looking out while a young man attended by a groom, both mounted on remarkably beautiful horses hastily passed the carriage and overtook the party before them.

"Did he bow?" demanded Mrs. Vallard.

"No he did not look in, but I am pretty certain I know his figure. Oh yes it is for he is turning about now," and as she said this with a blush of the most lovely vermillion she returned his bow.

Lord Henry had indeed expected to find her among the group on horseback, having seen Dallamore drive past accompanied by Belle Richmond and enquiring directly from Richmond where was that pretty little girl whom he had seen the evening before with Dallamore was desired by Lady Greysville to look behind and immediately turning round saw Selena and having caught her eye made her a graceful and smiling bow.

Mrs. Vallard not much pleased with the acquaintance and perhaps fearing his approach complained of the dust and requested Selena to draw up the window till the party had rode on. She was then silent 'till Selena called her attention to another subject by expressing her surprise that so delicate a little woman as Lady Greysville should appear so masculine in her character.

"It is all affectation my love," answered Mrs. Vallard, "I remember her a remarkable timid little girl and believe she has a thousand times more real gentleness than Miss Ludlow who looks so *die away*."[71]

"I suppose," said Selena, "they chuse each other's society by way of foil."

"They both aim at the same end," observed Mrs. Vallard, "Lady Greysville found that her delicate person accompanied by rough manners attracted the admiration of the men more than the softest appearance had obtained for her pretty face and figure, and Miss Ludlow plain and homely as she is must probably have passed totally unnoticed but for the extreme absurdity of her affectation of weakness and softness."

"And does that absurdity gain her admiration," asked Selena with a smile.

"No but it ensures attention and vanity is always contented with that and will never suspect the difference there is between attracting universal admiration and universal attention. But I own I am surprised what can so much attach Mr. Richmond to her conversation. I should think he would aim at something more dashing or at least with more pretention."

"Perhaps," said Selena who had already seen a good deal into the character of Richmond, "perhaps she has a large fortune."

"No she has nothing I believe," answered Mrs. Vallard, "had he indeed paid his attentions to her cousin I should not have been surprised. She has one of the best estates in Yorkshire in her own power or at least will have it when she comes of age in a few months."

When they entered the hall they found the party still assembled there, and they all proceeded together thro' the superb and highly ornamented apartments. They had not however gone thro' many of the rooms when they missed Dallamore and the boistrous spirits of Miss Richmond were a little subdued by the mortifying apprehensions that after some time she could not help entertaining that he actually intended to return to them no more. What was she to do! and how could she endure to be thus exposed to the ridicule of the whole party and above all Lady Greysville from whose unrestrained and humourous raillery she had on more occasions than one smarted. He was not however with Selena, that was one comfort, and when she could reach a front window she had the additional consolation of still seeing the curricle driven about by the groom.

Dallamore was indeed stretched upon a tempting sopha whose downy cushions he had found irresistibly detain him in one of the first apartments they had visited— and on the return of the party to the hall, Richmond who followed Miss Ludlow to look once more into that room, with a loud laugh now exclaimed, "My God, look at Dallamore where he has gone to sleep!"

---

[71] Die away: that dies away or has the air of dying away; languishing (OED).

"No," said Dallamore coolly and slowly rising, "I am not asleep but I should like to know why I should tire myself to death because you all like a parcel of fools chuse to poke into every hole and corner of another person's house. I am sure I should be very sorry to give myself half that trouble if it were my own."

"You are quite right I think Lord Dallamore," said Miss Ludlow throwing herself in an attitude upon the sopha which he had just quitted and vexed that the idea had not been originally her own.

"But you are fond of pictures," said Selena, "and the furniture is really beautiful!"

"Oh I can imagine it perfectly," said he sauntering towards the hall door, "Are you satisfied yet Miss Richmond? Shall we go now?" added he getting into his curricle without once turning round to see if he was followed.

"Well you are capital!" said Lady Greysville looking after him and laughing immoderately. "Is he not a treat Lord Henry? Miss Richmond you do not keep your beau in order, he will go without you, if you do not look sharp, take care," added she archly "or he will slip through your fingers I promise you."

Miss Richmond was not prepared to answer and at the moment would have relinquished all her doubtful hopes of Dallamore for the satisfaction of making some bitter retort which might have paid back Lady Greysville the vexation which she felt. None however occurred and Lord Henry who was in every respect a man of fashion except that the softness of his manners made him always prefer civility to rudeness gave her some relief by offering his hand to assist her in entering the curricle.

The good nature which appeared in this was not lost upon Selena and when again tete-a-tete in the chaise with her friend who always listened with delight to her observations she asked her had she remarked it.

"Lord Henry my dear is a general flirt," answered Mrs. Vallard.

Selena thought she had never made an answer less apropos for this action had surely nothing whatever to say to flirting, tho' perhaps the attention which he had paid both to Selena herself and Lady Greysville during their survey of Harewood might with somewhat more justice have been placed to that account.

Mrs. Vallard and her party who waited some time for Dallamore did not enter the dinner room 'till the company were again seated and again they took the places nearest to the door. Lord Henry was not however their neighbour and Mrs. Vallard with pleasure saw him seated beside Lady Greysville at the upper end of the room and apparently completely happy in his situation. Selena indeed would have probably eat more dinner had Lord Henry been again at her side, for unlike any other repast at which she had been ever before seated she found some kind of exertion was necessary to obtain or rather detain the food which was snatched away with a rapidity which laughably reminded her of Sancho's feasts during his administration at Barataria.[72]

---

[72] A reference to Miguel de Cervantes's *Don Quixote* (1605), when Sancho Panza is inaugurated as governor of the island-city Barataria: during the feast each dish presented to him is whisked away immediately by orders of his doctor.

Dallamore full as little qualified for such a scramble as Selena herself and infinitely more annoyed by the heat, confusion, and noise of the room scarcely eat or uttered a syllable and had it not been for Le Roi Mrs. Vallard and Selena must have arisen from table still hungry after their morning's expedition. As for Robert he had been seized upon by Belle Richmond as a *pis aller*,[73] as she was determined to fill up the vacant seat at her side which at Lady Greysville's particular request her next neighbour persisted in leaving for Lord Dallamore tho' now pretty sure of his not claiming it. When the waiters and servants had withdrawn Dallamore began to recover, but he still appeared to think the scene so uncomfortable that Selena wondered how he who was so completely his own master should like voluntarily so much to mortify himself. She was yet to learn that to the unsatisfied disposition variety is necessary and that "to a craving heart the world is a desert to the contented Kamtschatka is a paradise."[74]

On the ladies retiring Mrs. Vallard was joined by Lady Greysville who had not yet taken off her habit and said she had not returned from her ride till the bell had rung for dinner, "but I cannot help that," she added, "and must go as I am to the play. I hope you and Miss Miltern will come to my box but I vow I will not let Belle put her great foot in it."

Mrs. Vallard complained of a head-ach, and Selena felt really grieved when she insisted upon her not remaining at home with her. Lady Greysville pressed her so strongly to allow Miss Miltern to go with her, that Miss Miltern's assurances of her preference to stay were overpowered and Selena once more yielded with reluctance to the solicitations which she wished, and felt that she ought to resist.

She was however soon sufficiently amused to forget the uneasiness with which she had first reflected that Mrs. Miltern would feel regret that the first play she should see, was by such performers and in such company. Of the play she indeed saw but little after the second act. Towards the end of it Lord Henry entered the box accompanied by Dallamore and Richmond, and from that time the mirth and conversation within it made all attempt to listen to the less noisy performers upon the stage impossible.

Richmond and Miss Ludlow who were as Lady Greysville said "Busy making love" added indeed but little to this loud confusion of tongues—and her ladyship seemed to forget that Miss Richmond's brother was one of the party while she rallied Dallamore unmercifully upon his coyness to Belle's acknowledged passion. She was assisted by Lord Henry whose lively but delicate humour attracted Selena's attention and considerably amused her. Indeed his eyes told her in language sufficiently intelligible that this *persiflage*[75] was intended for her entertainment and while Lady Greysville was engaged with Dallamore, he said in

---

[73] Pis aller: last resort (French).

[74] Theodora in August von Kotzebue's *Count Benyowsky; or, The Conspiracy of Kamtschatka* (1798), 1.1.no lines.

[75] Persiflage: bantering (French).

a lower voice as he bent his head nearer to her glowing face, "Strange indeed if his lovely cousin could not steel his heart against any attack from Miss Richmond."

Selena turned abashed from the earnest gaze of Lord Henry's animated and sparkling eyes, for there was in them an expression of ardent admiration such as Dallamore's had never displayed. Yet Dallamore had really admired his fair cousin, and attractive and beautiful as she had appeared to him, Lord Henry thought not at that moment of Selena—thought not of Selena! of the interesting lovely being whose modest eye he had thus forcibly averted by the eager glance which spoke delighted captivated attention! On what then could his thoughts have been engaged.

The creature of affectation, the habitual deceiver, his very glances were mechanical. Lord Henry thought on Lady Trevallyn—not on the lovely, the beautiful Emily whose opening graces before she had yet reached Selena's years had captivated his boyish affections, not the Emily whose soft smile had awakened in his bosom the first pulsation of love, "and called the first sweet silver tones from the yet unsounded harp."[76] Not on the Emily whose choicest years he had wasted in fruitless, soul consuming expectations and whose bright youth he had blasted with disappointment. These were images he loved not to recall; It was on Lady Trevallyn that he dared to think with delight and hope. On Lady Trevallyn whom, even yet more lovely than Emily Montrose, he had seen presented at court, admired above all that was hitherto esteemed beautiful & graceful in the splendid circle, and whose languid eye seemed to turn with tasteless indifference from the homage which that admiration had extorted from all that was considered gallant and gay in the most brilliant assembles.

Lord Henry had accidently heard from Dallamore of Selena's intimacy at Esselberrie and now felt strongly revived all these soft ideas which dissipation prevented from dwelling with painful constancy upon his mind. The image of Lady Trevallyn was still painted in his memory as he had beheld her on the morning of her bridal presentation when every eye was fixed upon her form and every tongue spoke but of the young Countess whose superior beauty eclipsed all others— where majesty itself struck with the unrivalled loveliness of her figure looked with an applauding smile, and even Envy subdued by the modest and retiring grace of her undemanding charms was content to give to her the praise it had refused more gay and insolent beauties.

Oppressed by the weight of cumbrous ornaments, conscious of the universal attention she excited without sharing the delightful intoxication which this consciousness generally creates in the mind of a lovely woman, the fair bride was impatient to quit the crowded apartment, where the heat and agitation had suffused her cheek with a more than usual glow. A distinguished personage led her towards the door, when her eye which had scarcely raised its soft beams from the

---

[76]   A variant of Lady Milford's lines in Frederich Schiller's *Cabal and Love* (1784; English translation 1795), 1.7.no lines: "Ha! There it is! Sixteen! The first pulsation of love! The first sweet vibration upon the yet unsounded harp! Nothing is more fascinating."

silky fringe of her long eyelashes during her appearance in the circle, now turned a casual glance towards the spot where Lord Henry stood intently gazing upon his beautiful cousin, seen now for the first time since an instance of marked neglect to the poor Emily Montrose had withered the last fading blossoms of hope in her gentle bosom. Her spirits had been already exhausted and she had felt even before this almost overpowered by the fatigue and heat. The sudden unexpected sight was more than she could bear—the beautiful vermillion vanished from her lips, the carnation died upon her cheeks, and her royal conductor catching her in his arms alone prevented her from sinking upon the floor.

Lord Henry whose heart throbbed with mingled sensations of tenderness, regret and triumph could not then approach her and when he seized upon the first opportunity of again presenting himself to her view, he was received with a formal civility and affected indifference which might have deceived the eyes of one possessed of less penetration and vanity. He was not discouraged; he was not the dupe of a coldness too late assumed. Yet great were his advantages. Lord Trevallyn whose age alone might have rendered him unsuitable to the lovely Emily was detested by all the world for his absurd pride and despised for his folly. He had married the celebrated Emily Montrose portionless indeed but highly connected that the world might say, The Countess of Trevallyn was the most beautiful of all that shone in the circle of fashion—and with this he was content.

Lord Henry had been the acknowledged possessor of her young and susceptible heart and might now claim all those opportunities of intimacy which relationship justified. She had been educated by a Mother whose heart was amiable and excellent but whose understanding was remarkably deficient—and the extreme softness of Emily's character gave him hopes that she had inherited much of her Mother's weakness united with the finest sensibility, purest taste, and a liveliness of imagination singularly captivating. What then had he to fear? Lady Trevallyn indeed evidently avoided him and was seldom to be met in the gay circle where Lord Henry hoped to flatter her by the constancy of his assiduities. Her doors were shut to morning visitors, the summer was fast approaching; and she was eager to press Lord Trevallyn's return to Esselberrie. But Lord Henry was consoled by receiving in Lord Trevallyn's farewell visit an invitation to spend some time with them should business or pleasure ever lead him to Derbyshire.

Lord Henry who entertained no doubt that the restraint and coldness of his Emily's manners proceeded from offended pride and love had taken no small pains to remove from her mind the persuasion that he had ever voluntarily relinquished all hopes of being united to her for life. She had listened to him in silence but in her pale cheek and averted eye, her throbbing bosom and the involuntary tear he read the willingness with which lingering love longed to believe the fabricated tale. It was thus they had parted and the sanguine mind of Lord Henry overlooked the months of separation while he already anticipated a meeting of kinder promise to his hopes.

Dallamore had mentioned Esselberrie and Lord Henry's quick ear had caught the well remembered name. He seized on the first opportunity of obtaining from

Dallamore all the information in his power to bestow, and resolved to satisfy himself still more fully from Selena. Nor was he disappointed. Selena warm in her admiration of her friend talked on no other subject with equal animation or delight—and to continue a conversation interesting to both tho' in a very different degree Lord Henry contrived to place himself at supper on one side of Selena while the silent Dallamore as usual occupied the other.

Chapter XII

> For this alliance may so happy prove
> To turn your household rancour to pure love.
>
> Shakespear[77]

Mrs. Vallard saw with some uneasiness the pleasure with which Selena appeared to listen to her gay and insinuating neighbour, tho' she knew not the subject of their discourse, but her mind was diverted from such disagreeable suggestions as Lord Henry's attentions had excited by the delighted surprise expressed by Selena on their return to their lodgings at finding there a piano-forte. Dallamore was also himself much gratified at the unexpected expedition with which Le Roi had executed the commission he had so gladly undertaken of procuring one from Leeds.

Le Roi was indeed very ready to forward any proposal which he thought tended towards the defeat of Mr. Richmond's schemes and he foresaw that while Selena could entertain him at home his master would be less inclined to pass his mornings listening to Miss Richmond's harp, which had also at Dallamore's desire been procured (tho' with considerably less alacrity) from Leeds. Selena impatiently sat down to try the instrument, and touching it with the gentlest skill, the harmony of her voice with which she accompanied her light fingers made Dallamore forget how much out of tune he had discovered it to be during the prelude. It was late before he allowed her to retire and while she undressed in Mrs. Vallard's room, Lord Henry was forgotten amidst the grateful encomiums which she bestowed upon Dallamore's good nature and obliging disposition.

At breakfast the next morning they were again surprised by a visit from Belle Richmond. As she entered the parlour she looked with wonder at the piano forte, saying she had come on purpose to request Miss Miltern to make use of her harp.

"The instrument in the public room being almost continually occupied by squalling Misses. I have heard a vast deal," she added, "of your performance and hope you will not refuse to gratify me."

Selena thought this was said in a voice more expressive of scornful curiosity than of civility tho' she gracefully thanked her for her intended kindness.

"I will send for the harp directly and we may play a duet," said Miss Richmond ringing the bell while Mrs. Vallard and Selena heard her in silence dispatch the

---

[77]   Friar Laurence in Shakespeare's *Romeo and Juliet* (1594), 2.3.91–2.

servant for the instrument which they could not help thinking was only sent for in order to serenade Dallamore who had not yet come down.

While they were preparing their concert they perceived Mr. Richmond and Miss Ludlow walk by, but in such deep conversation that neither of them looked up towards the windows.

"Are you acquainted with Miss Ludlow?" said Miss Richmond to Mrs. Vallard who replied that she had not seen her for many years, till some weeks before that time when she had called at Hillbarton on her way to Harrogate with Lady Greysville, "but I knew her," continued she, "very well when she was a child and lived in this neighbourhood with her uncle the late owner of that fine place in the possession of her cousin."

"Her cousin! What cousin do you mean?" cried Miss Richmond.

"Why Miss Ludlow the great Yorkshire heiress."

"You are mistaken I should imagine for this is the heiress herself."

"Oh no," replied Mrs. Vallard smiling at an idea which now suggested itself from the mistake, "I am certain of the contrary for I have all my life known the family and I have a cousin a young man who is law agent to the present heiress who called on me not many months ago and told me that Miss Ludlow was still in Italy with her guardian and his wife."

The key with which Miss Richmond was tuning the harp fell from her hand as she listened with evident consternation to the intelligence which perhaps considerably shortened the intended concert. She indeed found it impossible to collect her faculties so as to surpass as she designed Selena and astonish her by the power and skill of her performance.

Therefore after the first duet recollecting as she said some engagement with Lady Greysville she returned to the Green Dragon with hasty strides full of the important communication which she had to impart to her deluded brother. He was however not to be found, and was indeed at that very moment busily employed in persuading away the last weak scruples with which Miss Ludlow opposed his entreaty that she should avoid the formalities of tedious preparations and objections of fogram[78] relations by a trip to Scotland which they could most easily accomplish being already so far on the road. Bursting with rage and indignation which she could not dissemble the gentle Belle now flew into Lady Greysville's room determined to vent herself in reproaches for her deception without considering how much more disgrace falls upon the dupe than upon the duper on such occasions.

She found Lady Greysville seated at the open window occupied in reading a novel which she had sent for to the circulating library as she said to drive away the ill temper of Sir Thomas. She had placed the book on the outside that she might at the same time watch the arrival of her horses and avoid its effluvia, and to protect herself from the filth of the leaves turned them over with a knife and fork. She did

---

[78]   Fogram: antiquated or old-fashioned (OED).

not stop on Miss Richmond's entrance, but continued in even a louder and more emphatic voice the interesting scene she had begun.

Miss Richmond sat with impatient vexation meditating how she should commence the enquiries she determined to make concerning Lady Greysville's protégée. At length unable any longer to contain herself she interrupted her rather bluntly with, "I had always understood from you Lady Greysville that Miss Ludlow was the heiress of Harston."

"And I have always had the utmost respect for Miss Richmond's understanding," answered Lady Greysville smiling.

"Your Ladyship is very good but people of better understanding than I pretend to have before this been duped by needy imposters and artful designers."

"It is very possible, but if you please I will ask Lord Dallamore what is his opinion of this judicious remark."

"Lord Dallamore," cried Miss Richmond rising with a fury which she could no longer disguise under the mask of politeness, "Lord Dallamore would I daresay despise as I do those who should endeavour to impose upon others as an heiress a beggarly dependant."

"What is the meaning of all this?" asked Sir Thomas, "and who said Miss Ludlow was an heiress?"

"I have," cried Lady Greysville coolly, "I have said a thousand times that Miss Ludlow was an heiress and no one in Yorkshire will deny that, and a great heiress too."

"What is that to the purpose," said Sir Thomas peevishly, "you know we are speaking of Fanny and I do not believe she has sixpence in the world."

Lady Greysville interrupted the enraged exclamation which Belle was about to address to Sir Thomas by saying hastily, "Well and is it my fault if Mr. Richmond chose to think there could be no other Miss Ludlow but Fanny, or am I answerable for her presumption in daring to listen to his great proposals when she was conscious she had not a suitable fortune to bestow?"

Lord Henry just then coming in, she appealed to him on the justice of her defense which Sir Thomas did not seem much inclined to allow, and they both made themselves so extremely merry on the ridiculous misapprehension that Belle unable to endure so mortifying a jest quitted the room in a fury which considerably added to the amusement of Lady Greysville.

That the delusion into which Richmond had so eagerly assisted to insnare himself should be thus discovered before Miss Ludlow had been able to complete the tacit deception gave Lady Greysville no concern. She had merely humoured the error into which she perceived Richmond had fallen for the sake of the sport which it afforded to her and the rest of the company to whom she had communicated the jest but she had never entertained an idea that the mistake must not have been discovered before any serious engagement had been formed.

Fanny Ludlow however had far more serious expectations, and had artfully hastened matters to such a crisis that had the discovery thus accidentally made by Mrs. Vallard been delayed many hours, Fanny Ludlow would have found herself in possession of a very fashionable tho' rather needy husband and Mr. Richmond would have too late discovered that while he attempted to delude the artless credulity of an ignorant heiress he had himself been the dupe of a more successful and fortuneless schemer.

No sooner had he confirmed beyond the power of doubt the intelligence communicated to him by his sister than he determined to quit the field, unable to endure the raillery to which he knew he should be exposed, and leaving his sister to the care of her companion Mrs. Aston, he wrote a cool billet[79] to Miss Ludlow in which he pretended to have received a sudden summons from a near relation who had been taken ill and lamented that he was prevented having the honour of seeing her as he had hoped that evening. To Dallamore he also wrote accounting for his abrupt departure in the same manner and requested him to take care of Belle in his absence. He then ordered the chaise and four which he had already bespoke for a different purpose and set off for the first stage towards London leaving Belle almost hopeless of doing any good with Dallamore thus deprived of the assistance of her brother.

When the company were assembled before dinner Lady Greysville to whom Miss Ludlow in the utmost vexation had communicated the note she had just received announced Richmond's departure with the most immoderate fits of laughter and the appearance of the deserted Fanny could alone in some degree silence the noisy mirth with which the news was received, and which had not at all yielded to the enraged glances of his sister who upon entering the room found herself alone excluded from the secret of this universal jest.

Dallamore had scarcely stirred from the piano forte during the whole morning and had detained there Selena as long as she would stay. She wished however to write to her Mother at whose silence she felt much uneasiness an account of all she had seen, and to ask her instructions as to their return. As soon as she had left the parlour Dallamore arose and was whistling as he walked towards the window when his servant presented him with Richmond's note.

"What the devil care am I to take of his sister? Is not she of age to take charge of herself?" said he as he tossed the note on the piano-forte.

"Whom do you speak of?" said Mrs. Vallard in some surprise at the soliloquy.

"Why Richmond is gone off and left his sister in my care. Of all the people in the world think of his chusing me for her guardian?"

"Nothing more natural," answered Mrs. Vallard laughing, "since you know she is your intended bride."

"My bride [—] Oh God forbid!"

"Why did not you tell me yourself that you had proposed for her?"

"Oh but that was only in jest. She cannot be such a fool as to think I was in earnest."

"So you really do not intend to marry Miss Richmond!"

"No nor any one else except Selena."

---

[79]   Billet: short, informal letter (OED).

"Selena is much obliged by your kind intentions but have you told her of them?"

"No not yet I will as soon as ever I can get a proper opportunity."

"You are not serious."

"Why not, I suppose you think now that she would not have me."

"I really cannot say, but you have my consent at least to try which is more than I can promise for your father or hers."

"Why what the devil is it to either of them?"

"I have no doubt that they will both be so absurd as to think it is something to them, but you may make the experiment and if you will gain over Lord Mount Villars to your side I will undertake to manage Mr. Miltern."

"Oh d--n it no. I would rather never marry at all than run the gauntlet among the whole set and be obliged to talk to musty lawyers about settlements and devilments. No, no Selena must marry me first, and then we can talk the matter over with the rest at our leisure."

"I can hardly think Selena will agree to those terms."

"Oh yes she will … what will you lay he does not get it in five leaps more."

Mrs. Vallard looked amazed for tho' she observed that while he had been speaking his eyes were fixed upon Rolla who with ineffectual efforts was endeavouring to seize the glove which Dallamore held suspended on his stick at some distance from the floor, yet she could not believe his mind had been occupied by so trifling a circumstance while conversing on a subject so important.

After a moment's silence she said half mortified, "So I see you have only been jesting about Selena after all!"

"No upon my soul I never was in love before and am determined to propose for her this very day. I have said something about it to Robert already."

"You have! And pray what did you say?"

"I really forget exactly, but I believe I bid him ask Selena would she like to come to Scotland. Richmond I suppose is gone there now with Miss Ludlow if he has not changed his mind, for I do not believe one word he says about his sick uncle. He never cared a d--n about any of his relations."

"To Scotland with Miss Ludlow you surely are dreaming Dallamore."

"No I am not dreaming, he told me so himself last night and asked me to come with them for that was what put Selena into my head."

"Selena would be much flattered I confess at the circumstance."

"Oh I only mean our going together to Scotland for I have been thinking of Selena this long time, and indeed Scotland too, for I must go there this summer, I have been intending it every year this great while."

Nothing was farther from Richmond's intentions than such a connexion as Scotland and Selena but he had really entrusted Dallamore with his secret and wished him to accompany them in their expedition for various excellent reasons (besides being thus spared all travelling expences) not the least of which reasons was the immediate separation he thus hoped to effect between Dallamore and his too fascinating cousin. Once out of the sphere of her attractions, closely watched by himself and his sister who in this case should assuredly be of the party, he hoped he could not fail of drawing Dallamore into his snares in a country where the fetters of Hymen are forged with so little difficulty or delay. The unexpected discovery which had prevented and totally defeated all these fine plans was therefore an almost equal disappointment to Miss Richmond as to her brother.

Dallamore expressed not the least surprise when he found that Richmond had suddenly altered his intentions, an event which from his own experience he might very justly have regarded as not in the least extraordinary. He joined however in the publick jest at his expence tho' perhaps he himself would never have suspected that a change of mind so likely to happen must necessarily have arisen from the accidental discovery of the error Richmond perceived he had fallen into respecting the Yorkshire heiress.

When Mrs. Vallard quitted Dallamore she went immediately to Selena's apartment whom she found in deep conversation with her brother. The moment Mrs. Vallard cast her eyes upon her countenance animated as it was with the most lively emotion, and her cheeks suffused with the deepest glow she had not a doubt of the truth of Dallamore's message by Robert.

On her entrance they were a moment silent, 'till taking Selena's hand she said with a smile, "So you have had a proposal my Love."

"Yes," interrupted Robert, "and she is quite provoking, for I cannot persuade her to think it any thing but a jest and yet I promised Dallamore to write this very evening to my father—and now Selena declares she will not suffer it."

Mrs. Vallard was rather surprised at this speech considering Dallamore's late protestations against asking consent, and perhaps felt some degree of doubt with regard to the sincerity of Selena's resistance to having her father consulted. Indeed since the adventure of the roses she scarcely entertained a doubt that Dallamore to whose powers of pleasing she was extremely partial had gained some progress in his cousin's affections tho' she had no apprehensions of its being serious enough to injure her peace in case the alliance should be disapproved.

Selena's astonishment was alone abated by her conviction that Robert unacquainted with Dallamore's character, had mistaken the jest or perhaps the sudden idea of the moment already forgotten for a serious proposal. In vain she declared her certainty of this being the case, and told her brother of her knowledge of his attachment to Miss Richmond.

He laughed at her doubts and protested he was charged with a commission to his father, which nothing should prevent him from executing.

"My dear Mrs. Vallard," said Selena, "do persuade Robert how ridiculous it will make us all appear to take my cousin's oddities thus *au pied de la lettre*.[80] You know very well that he has no more idea of me than I have of him in that way."

"Indeed my love," answered Mrs. Vallard, "I do not know what ideas you may have of him but I know he has very serious designs upon you and am sure he is very anxiously bent to prevail on you to listen to his proposals with some of which

---

[80]   Au pied de la lettre: quite literally (French).

I do not indeed think you will comply since your impatient lover would have you set off this instant for Scotland."

"Can anything my dear Madam be a more convincing proof of the whole business being a jest? Besides tho' I do not like the idea of thus hastily refusing what I am sure was never really proposed yet if Robert persists in writing to my father what I am sure will throw the whole house into very unnecessary confusion, I must beg him to add that for my part I intirely disbelieve the truth of an offer which at all events I could never accept."

"Oh no Selena, sure you will not add the latter part in earnest," said Mrs. Vallard very gravely and with a mortified air that struck the sensible heart of Selena with concern that she should have given her loved and respected friend unnecessary pain.

"There is no occasion," cried she, "my dear Madam to discuss that point at present and I am well persuaded there never will."

"I assure you solemnly," answered Mrs. Vallard, "you are mistaken Selena for Dallamore has this instant been entertaining me with his hopes and plans."

"There now, will you be convinced my positive little sister and am I not right Madam," cried Robert turning to Mrs. Vallard, "to tell my father directly what Dallamore has desired?"

"Certainly I do," said Mrs. Vallard, "and I should like to know what passed between you and Dallamore on the subject."

"Why it was before breakfast this morning, he sent for me while he was dressing to know if I would have the curricle today to drive Mrs. Aston out, and kept me talking for he declared he would not go down till Belle Richmond was gone as we heard her roaring in the parlour and I hardly know how he began for I thought it but a jest at first myself but he swore so solemnly that he never was in love before, and that he would never marry if Selena would not have him, that I must be mad or think him mad to doubt him as she seems to do—but I shall not mind her, for I am determined to write."

"As you please," said Selena, "but I warn you that I have nothing to say to it."

Robert did not wait to make any reply but retired impatient to write the letter which from what had passed between him and his father he thought would not prove unacceptable.

Mr. Miltern had no sooner received this letter which beyond his expectations thus speedily crowned with success his meditated hopes, than he resolved to be himself the bearer of an answer to Lord Dallamore. When on the spot he determined to be guided by the behavior of Lord Mount Villars. If he should receive with approbation the proposed alliance which was to heal a breach so long esteemed incurable Mr. Miltern exulted in the idea of the scorn and contempt with which he should reject it. But if on the contrary, as was natural after so many outrages and insults from the father, the daughter unprovided as she was with a fortune suited to Dallamore's large possessions and expectations, should be refused by the haughty Earl, it was then Mr. Miltern's design to hurry the marriage so displeasing to a brother he detested, which should restore to his offspring the estate he once considered as his right.

In the midst of his agitating contemplations of future malice he felt however some concern as to what he should avow and what conceal from Mrs. Miltern. At length he thought it most prudent to acquaint her that not approving of the apparent intimacy of his children with Lord Dallamore he had determined to go himself directly for Selena, as the best way to put an immediate conclusion to the business and prevent any future unpleasant consequences such as he feared there was some reason to expect. At the same time he secretly resolved to take every precaution to prevent Selena from receiving any letters of advice from her mother.

Chapter XIII

Has he a form that love persuades
Seducing smiles, an angel tongue?
That form, those artful smiles enclose
A heart corrupt and foul beneath,
So towers the Cypress blooms the rose
To veil the hideous caves of Death.

Selim & Zaida[81]

In the mean time Selena heard indeed from Dallamore himself professions of the most ardent love and thro' Mrs. Vallard and her brother even stronger and more continual declarations. But being resolved never to connect herself with a person of so undecided a character, and being besides convinced that the alliance would be displeasing to both sides of so disunited a family she rather hoped that the air of jest which she endeavoured to give to her refusals of listening to Dallamore would render her rejection less offensive and that thus discouraged he would in the end persuade himself he really never had been serious.

Mrs. Vallard whose good sense was apt at all times to yield to her good nature, felt much grieved that a connexion from which she expected so many good consequences was likely to meet with opposition from Selena herself, and began now to question the attachment she had fancied she discovered her to feel for her cousin. She approved however of Selena's conduct in case she sincerely wished to discourage his proposals and thought with her that he might thus be saved the mortification of thinking himself really refused.

Selena took care to avoid as much as possible all particular conversation with Dallamore, she danced with him indeed, and played for him as often as he requested her, when there appeared no sufficient cause to justify her refusal, but she passed the greatest part of her mornings in her own room and was well pleased

---

[81] John Boyd Greenshields, *Selim and Zaida* (Edinburgh, 1800), part 2, lines 213–20. The epigraph uses "smile" for "form" in line 213, and omits lines 215–16 ("That form, these smiles, shall hapless Maids / Oft curse, by shame and anguish stung").

that Lord Henry's attentions often saved her from listening to Dallamore's less agreeable conversation.

Mrs. Vallard on more occasions than that which has been recorded, had repeated that "Lord Henry was a general flirt"—and Selena's penetration left her no doubt that there were some reasons unknown to her which not only prevented her always indulgent friend from looking upon him with that favourable eye which his soft and captivating manners seemed to claim but had not so entirely prejudiced her against him that she was unwilling to allow him any excellence and avoided as much as possible all intercourse and conversation with him.

Selena at the conclusion of a dance had seated herself beside Mrs. Vallard in a window when Dallamore indolently approaching them asked her with a yawn when they were to dance together reminding her of her engagement.

"Not for this set however Dallamore," said Lord Henry who had followed Selena with his eyes, "for I have a prior claim on Miss Miltern."

"I think not," said Mrs. Vallard gravely, "for I am witness Selena promised to dance with her cousin to-night before we came into the room, and I am sure this will be the last set."

Lord Henry was silent but holding his hand to Selena with a smile awaited her decision.

Selena perceiving Mrs. Vallard really wished her to refuse Lord Henry took the hint and said to Dallamore, "I did not think you meant to claim me but since you remember your engagement at last I must make my excuse to Lord Henry and lay the blame of my seeming caprice upon you."

Lord Henry bowed and saying he hoped to be more fortunate another time walked to the upper end of the room where he stood and watched Selena till she had gone down the dance, and then immediately joined her.

"Was Dallamore asleep?" said he, "or was he, as he appears at this moment in some delightful reverie that he could so long forget the happiness you gave him leave to claim?"

Selena laughing looked at her partner and perceived that totally regardless that she was yet standing in the dance he had sunk upon a seat which was fortunately vacant behind him; his head leaned upon his hand, while the bench supported his elbow and one of his legs, the other being also stretched at its full length upon the floor. Selena did not indeed agree with Lord Henry that he looked in "some delightful reverie" for tho' his eye was bent on vacancy the form which his lips had assumed made her rather suppose he was whistling and imagining some tune which the musick so close to his ears could not possibly allow him to hear.[82] She was however prevented from reply by Mrs. Vallard who attentive to Lord Henry's motions did not approve of his pointing out her nephew to the ridicule of Selena, and determined to interrupt a conversation the subject of which their eyes had plainly declared.

---

[82]   In Shakespeare's *Hamlet* (1600) 3.4.120–21 Gertrude asks Hamlet "how is't with you, / That you do bend your eye on vacancy."

"Are you not fatigued by the heat my love?" said she, "you had better sit down Dallamore will make room for us," and taking her arm led her across the room.

Dallamore did indeed make room for them, but seemed just then as little inclined to enter into any conversation with them as with Miss Richmond who had seated herself on the other side and vainly endeavoured to seize upon his attention.

Peters who had all the evening watched for an opportunity of addressing one whom the fashionable Lord Henry had shewed he considered worthy of notice perceiving that he did not follow Selena to the seat (where Mrs. Vallard had evidently brought her to avoid him) now ventured to approach.

Taught to look upon inattention and even a degree of rudeness to youth and beauty especially if not accompanied by high ton[83] as the easiest and surest method of being esteemed a fine man which was the very summit of his ambition, Peters knew not immediately upon Selena's arrival at Harrogate whether or not he should confer upon her the honour of his particular acquaintance. Upon her first entrance into the room happening to be seated close to her he slightly returned her bow and almost in the same moment quickly turned his back and engaged in conversation with his neighbour at the other side.

As it never occurred to Selena that he could intend as it is called to *cut*[84] her she thought from this, if indeed she thought of it at all, that he had for the moment forgotten her face, and she received with her usual sweetness and cheerful affability the awkward attempts he afterwards made while appearing to claim an intimacy which she by no means desired, but which he now ambitiously sought upon discovering that she was certainly the most admired girl at Harrogate and even it was not improbable that from Lord Henry's manifest attention she might in future be raised to that envied rank in London.

He was now beginning to amuse Selena with Richmond's flight, the favourite topick of the day and particularly grateful to him who feared and hated Richmond for the many mortifications he had made him endure on sundry occasions during his connexion which he was yet willing to bear in consideration of the good company to which Richmond introduced him and of the air it gave him to be seen continually with so fashionable a man as Richmond was himself considered.

Selena listened with uneasiness, for she perceived Miss Richmond's large fierce eyes were directed towards them, and she feared increasing the hatred which had not even been attempted to be disguised by civility. Anxious to turn the conversation Selena asked him had he been dancing?

"Me dancing? God forbid!"

Selena looked at him with surprise and asked did he never dance.

"Oh never! We young fellows in town have cut dancing completely."

"Do you mean that you have no balls now in London?" demanded Selena with unaffected naiveté.

---

[83]   High ton: people of fashion (OED).

[84]   Cut: to affect not to see or know; cut dead (OED).

"Oh yes," answered he with a sneering smile, "there are plenty of balls, and I can promise you as much dancing as you please, there are always enough of boys and men one don't know to make up the crowd and do for partners; *they* are obliged to dance to make acquaintances, but for my part I have totally given it up from the impossibility I found of fixing my choice among so many beautiful ladies of quality my particular friends who all love dancing ... very odd that ... is not it?"

Selena was rather in doubt to what part of his speech his question alluded. If it related to his own declaration by which he endeavoured to account for his relinquishing dancing she perfectly agreed with him in thinking it "very odd," but Selena herself fond of an exercise to which her beautiful graceful nymph-like figure was peculiarly adapted thought nothing could be more natural than that the ladies of quality of whom he spoke should love dancing. She waited therefore in silence his farther explanation and satisfied with being listened to he proceeded thus.

"I often used to ask Lady Harriet Modely and Emily Montrose what could induce them to be for ever on their feet going thro' the same wearisome figure and everlasting tunes."

"You know Lady Trevallyn then," said Selena ever happy to speak of her favourite and much admired friend.

"Yes to be sure I do," said Peters who would not have chosen however to have thus familiarly named her had he recollected the intimacy he now remembered there seemed to subsist between Esselberrie and Hillbarton—and indeed any other fashionable name would have answered him full as well.

"Is she not charming?" cried Selena with that animated smile which ever overspread her features when speaking of Lady Trevallyn.

"Oh yes very charming! Quite the ton indeed. But do you know Lady Harriet Modely?" asked he willing to change the subject.

"No," said Selena, "is she reckoned as handsome as Lady Trevallyn?"

"Oh no certainly not so regular a beauty but then she has more life and spirit, more the thing to please me in short. We are great friends and if we meet in London I will[85] have the honour to introduce you to her if you please."

Selena smiled but said she had no idea of going to London.

"Not in the Spring! Why where shall you be then?"

"In Herefordshire I hope."

"Oh horrible! You will never keep such a resolution and bury yourself there when all the world are in town."

"As I have not yet tasted of its pleasures," replied Selena, "I should find no difficulty in keeping this resolution if even it were to depend upon myself."

"You have never been in town then?"

"Never."

"Oh I might have guessed so indeed by your not knowing Lady Harriet, indeed her acquaintance is a test of fashion, for she is amazingly clever and knows how to cut vulgar people incomparably."

---

[85]   The MS editor replaces "will" with "shall."

Selena smiled and perhaps doubted the inference Mr. Peters intended she should draw from this assertion. She did not find his conversation very entertaining and began to wish that Dallamore would recollect that the second dance was now almost half over. Of this however she despaired, and thought it best upon the whole not to appear eager to remind him of his partner.

Rather weary of hearing Peters continually introduce subjects so uninteresting to her as the fine parties to which he had been last year invited, and the various merits of the beauties of rank with whose high-sounding titles she was even for the most part unacquainted, she turned to Mrs. Vallard and bid her observe how extremely merry Lady Greysville and Lord Henry appeared.

"I would rather you would bid me look at any other person in the room than Lord Henry," said Mrs. Vallard hastily.

"By why my dear Madam? Do you know any thing bad of him?"

"I believe he is a very profligate young man and I know his great object is to seduce the affections of women. I have heard many stories of him, some of which I am but too sure are true, and sorry indeed should I be that he was now to fix his designs upon my Selena."

"You think then that I could not resist him," said Selena laughing.

"No my love, on the contrary I am sure when you know him better you would despise him, but I cannot help thinking that there is something baneful in his acquaintance, and I never knew him pay any attention to a young woman married or single that her reputation or happiness did not suffer by it materially. But my dear let us talk of something else for I own I do not love nor like Lord Henry."

"Well then," said Selena to whom this had not appeared so serious a conversation as Mrs. Vallard really felt it, "if you do not love nor like Lord Henry, pray look at him for this once, for he is making himself so excessively ridiculous."

He was indeed then submitting to the whim of Lady Greysville who had covered his cheeks with rouge, and tied on his head her own white hat and feathers.

As she then just caught Selena's eye she led him towards her asking if his face did not look a thousand times more like a woman than Miss Richmond's.

"A pretty woman at least," added she nodding her head at Dallamore in an affected whisper, tho' still loud enough to be heard for tho' it was not absolutely intended for Miss Richmond's ears Lady Greysville gave herself but little concern at perceiving that it had reached them.

Miss Richmond fired and almost inarticulate with passion requested Lady Greysville "would not do her the honour of continually making her the subject of her conversation."

"Oh my dear, I was only saying that you were more like a man than a woman, and all the world can see that you know, as well as whether or not you are handsome: for my part I own I think Lord Henry far handsomer as man or woman, but do not let that discourage you Belle for I can tell you I have the misfortune very often to think differently from the rest of the world, perhaps it may be so in this instance, suppose we put it to the vote, Miss Miltern what do you say Lord Henry or Miss Richmond? …"

"Oh my dear Ladies," interrupted Lord Henry, "spare my blushes and confusion, I am sure I am at present an uncommonly handsome woman, but great indeed must be the pretensions of her that will not yield to Miss Richmond."

While he said this he removed from his own head the hat and began to settle it once more upon that of Lady Greysville, he was then proceeding to arrange some other articles of her dress which it was probable he executed in rather an awkward manner since Lady Greysville rejected his services and gently pushed him from her laughing.

In the mean time Miss Richmond to whom Lord Henry's compliment had restored the use of her speech of which passion seemed to have deprived her, looking scornfully at Lady Greysville's little figure as she stood before her exclaimed, "It is of very little consequence what your Ladyship may think of my person but when I am inclined to envy beauty I shall certainly not look so low as what I can now see."

"This is Hermia and Helena I think," said Lord Henry smiling archly, "is it not Miss Miltern? '*They have no gift at all in shrewishness*' you see."[86]

"Thank you my dear Miss Richmond," said Lady Greysville quickly making her at the same time a bow, "thank you for not attacking me in a more vulnerable point, I am so well content with my person puppet as I am, that it is absolutely impossible for you to say any thing on that subject which can hurt me. I appeal to all the assembly if I am not in the right. What do you say yourself of my face? Will you not at least allow that to be pretty? Then my teeth pray look at them," said she opening her mouth and turning round with a smile which shewed at once two rows of perfect ivory and an inchanting dimple, "are they bad? As for my hair, I have cropped it indeed for convenience but see in what nice curls it falls naturally," and as she said this she once more removed the hat from her small and well shaped head. "Now for my hands and arms there, I will throw my glove and challenge with it the whole room, nor am I a bit more afraid of displaying my foot and ancle."

She accompanied the last part of her speech with a sudden motion which certainly in some little degree exceeded the nice bounds of decorum.

"Bravo," cried Dallamore, raised at last from his reverie by the scene acting before him, "pray proceed Lady Greysville."

"No," said she putting on a demure look, "I can say no more now for here is Tom. I suppose he has lost his rubber[87] on purpose to come and scold me. Lord how cross he looks. Oh such a February face so full of frost and storm and cloudiness! Well Tom what is the matter now?"

"Matter Lady Greysville! I really do not know what you mean."

---

[86]   Lord Henry invokes the quarrel between short Hermia and tall Helena in Shakespeare's *A Midsummer Night's Dream* (1595) when Helena declares "I have no gift at all in shrewishness" (3.2.301).

[87]   Rubber: set of three or five games (such as whist or bridge) in which the winner wins two out of three (or three out of five).

"Oh nothing only I was afraid you were discomposed my love at seeing me play the fool."

"There was at least nothing to surprise me in that," answered he without returning her smiles.

"Why no it does happen pretty often I must confess and tant mieux[88] to teach you patience."

As she said this she walked from him declaring to Lord Henry that there was nothing upon earth she so much disliked to look at as a cross face while Sir Thomas followed her with a countenance not very expressive of the patience which she professed to teach him.

Mrs. Vallard having completely accomplished the design which had at first inclined her to undertake the journey to Harrogate, and seeing Dallamore for the present delivered from the snares which Richmond had laid not indeed with much delicate art but with sufficient perseverance and assurance now began to be impatient to return to Hillbarton and the rather because as she confessed to Selena she did not love to look at Lord Henry and still less that Lord Henry should look as she thought he did upon her innocent and very lovely charge.

Dallamore always glad to change the scene and wearied to death of all around him except Selena and her piano forte willingly assented to the proposal of removing and Selena for her part rejoiced that she might now hope in a few days to set out upon her way home. Robert only of all the party seemed to quit Harrogate with regret, and having prevailed upon them to wait till he shewed to them various beauties and curiosities in the neighbourhood would have discovered as many more to detain them from day to day, had not Selena seriously entreated him to make no more plans for a delay which she was convinced would grieve her Mother.

Indeed Robert had been considerably occupied at Harrogate. Lady Greysville had amused him and attracted his admiration. Belle Richmond even while he laughed at her had contrived to seize upon his attention, but her companion Mrs. Aston, tho' neither young nor beautiful, and avoided as she was by the rest of the assembly had afforded him the highest and most incessant entertainment. He had ever been accustomed to the conversation of women of sense and education but a female pedant was to him a new object, and one in which he took the utmost delight, from the ridiculous view in which her attempts to astonish him had made her character appear to his mind ever open to amusement and pleased instead of disgusted by absurdity.

For her part she was inchanted with the flattery which her young beau had indeed not spared, and she saw the departure of her *hearer* with even more regret than Miss Richmond bestowed upon the final crush to all her schemes upon Dallamore. Mrs. Aston had however to comfort her the promise that a constant literary correspondence should in future subsist between her and one so well gratified by his genius and taste to judge of her extraordinary talents

---

[88]   Tant mieux: so much the better (French).

and learning, and whose studies she should have the pleasure of directing by her superior knowledge—and she was not without hopes of again meeting a youth so promising in a few months in London as he had engaged to visit her in his first excursion thither.

The night before the party left Harrogate Selena could not refuse to dance with Lord Henry who had engaged her in the morning, tho' to prevent giving Mrs. Vallard uneasiness she would have preferred another partner. Seated beside her after the first dance he led the conversation apparently in the most natural manner to Lady Trevallyn.

"You expect to see her on your return to Derbyshire."

"Oh certainly I would not for the world leave the neighbourhood without bidding her farewell."

"You will then perhaps honour me with a moment of remembrance while at Esselberrie."

"I shall be happy to be the bearer of any message you may wish to send."

"You are very good and if you should chance indeed to recollect me pray tell Lady Trevallyn that I had come to this country with an intention of fulfilling my engagement to wait upon Lord Trevallyn but was prevented from having that honour on my way here by meeting his Lordship on the road to town.

"But you must not mention me I think before Mrs. Vallard," continued he as he gently laid her fan upon her lips with an arch smile, "for I am much afraid that I have the *malheur*[89] not to be in that Lady's good graces for some unfortunate reason which alas I can neither discover nor remove."

Selena blushed at his penetration, but without answering this hint to which she could not reply at once with politeness and sincerity she assured him she would not forget to make his apology at Esselberrie.

Lord Henry from his knowledge of the female heart thought it not improbable that Lady Trevallyn might feel piqued at hearing from Selena that he had been amusing himself at Harrogate and wished to prove that he had been still occupied only with her and to make a merit to her of that discretion which had indeed prompted him to defer his visit, as thinking it most likely it would not have been received in the absence of Lord Trevallyn. He besides embraced every opportunity of paying the compliments required by form which he knew were always able to flatter Lord Trevallyn, and without directly announcing his arrival to the soft Emily he wished and perhaps hoped to excite in her susceptible bosom that doubtful and anxious agitation which the uncertain probability of seeing a beloved object always can create.

---

[89]   *Malheur*: misfortune (French).

Chapter XIV

Still shall those sighs heave after one another?
Those trickling drops chace one another still?
As if the posting messengers of grief
Could overtake the hours fled far away
And make old Time come back.

Rowe[90]

When they arrived at Hillbarton Robert who had been in daily expectation of receiving his father's answer not finding it there as he had thought possible agreed with Mrs. Vallard in opinion that they were bound to await its arrival, since at Dallamore's desire he had requested permission to bring him with them on their return to Miltern Abbey.

Selena obliged to submit at once in opposition to her inclination and judgment, wishing for the present to avoid the persecutions of Dallamore who really began now to show himself a more ardent lover than they could have imagined, reminded Mrs. Vallard of her promise to pay a farewell visit to Lady Trevallyn.

Mrs. Vallard declared herself tired with her unusual exertions but consented to Selena's desire of passing the next day at Esselberrie saying she would send the carriage with her if she would not allow Dallamore to drive her there in the curricle. Selena entreated her not to suggest such an idea, or say any thing of her intention, as Dallamore's presence would totally deprive them both of the satisfaction which she hoped Lady Trevallyn as well as herself would experience in the tete-a-tete. Mrs. Vallard complied with her request but sighed at the proof she thought that this displayed of Selena's indifference for her nephew whom she herself could not help considering as worthy of the tenderest regard of any woman whom he should distinguish by a preference.

Selena being told that Lady Trevallyn was in her dressing room impatient to embrace her friend waited not to be announced, but with a light step flew before the servant and gently opening the door was met by Lady Trevallyn with eyes where affection spoke the sweetest language in a tear of pleasure.

The joy of Selena was however in some degree damped by the appearance of Lord Trevallyn who arose stiffly at her entrance and now returned her salutation with a cold but profound bow.

"I am sorry," said he in a voice of solemn displeasure, "to observe Miss Miltern that my servants have been so deficient in the attention due to you and to Lady Trevallyn as to suffer you thus to enter without being properly waited upon and your presence announced and I must discover which of my people have been guilty of this strange remissness."

Selena shocked at the reproach which this speech conveyed to herself and the haughty manner in which it was delivered blushing and hesitating asked pardon

---

[90] Lady Alicia in Nicholas Rowe's *The Tragedy of Jane Shore* (1714), 1.2.64–8.

for the precipitancy which had prevented the servant from the performance of a duty she now heartily repented that her coming at that time had made necessary.

Lady Trevallyn said nothing but affectionately pressing Selena's hand placed her at her side on the little sopha where she had been seated at her dressing table and in a half whisper asked her how she liked Harrogate.

Lord Trevallyn fancying himself thus excluded from the conversation darted a look of sullen displeasure not unmingled with contempt at the lovely friends and stalked out of the room.

A moment's silence ensued, till Lady Trevallyn conquering her confusion once more began her enquiries, but appeared absent and thoughtful, and at length left the room telling Selena she would return in a few moments.

Having employed these in expelling the evil spirit of peevishness from the bosom of her Lord by the invincible sweetness of her accents, when she again entered her brow was unclouded, her soft features were illuminated by their own peculiar placid smile and if Selena thought that she had wept, it was her eyes alone that told the tale for her countenance wore not the semblance of sorrow and her cheek betrayed no traces of a tear.

"I am desired by Lord Trevallyn," said she as she again took Selena's hand, "to ask you in proper form to dinner, but I hope that is not necessary and that you have no idea of leaving me till night."

Selena whose intentions had been indeed frightened away by Lord Trevallyn's ungracious reception now but half reassured consented, and then enquired for Angela.

"You shall go see her after dinner but you must not leave me now, so let me hear your adventures."

Selena who tho' she had a quick sense of the ridiculous had yet but little talent and still less inclination for satire, past over but slightly the characters which had indeed for the time afforded her amusement while present, and impatient to communicate Lord Henry's message began immediately to mention him. Scarcely had the name passed her lips when she was struck by the deep blush it called forth on Lady Trevallyn's face, succeeded almost instantaneously by a paleness even more expressive of extreme agitation. Her eyes remained fixed upon the paper where she had been drawing, but her hands trembled and Selena could plainly perceive the pulse which throbbed with violence beneath her transparent skin. Hardly able to proceed and ashamed to stop Selena delivered the message in so incoherent a manner that Lady Trevallyn feared she had betrayed herself and timidly raised her eyes to Selena's face. But there she met an expression of such enquiring pity and affectionate sadness as completely convinced her that her secret was discovered, or that at least her penetrating friend suspected the interest which the name of Lord Henry had excited.

For an instant the thought that the former fruitless attentions which she had received from her cousin had been communicated perhaps by Mrs. Vallard to Selena flashed upon her mind with a mortifying suspicion and alarmed lest apprised of past circumstances she might now attribute her confusion and sadness to the indulgence of a hopeless passion, pride for a moment conquered the natural extreme softness of her character, and the tenderness which had been all roused by Lord Henry's name now yielded to the indignant recollection of the humiliations to which he had exposed her.

Exerting therefore all her energy she said with quickness, "Oh my dear Selena do not talk to me of my relations, let us have something new."

This was said in a voice and manner so unlike herself that Selena could not at that moment have so much wondered as she had done when she at first perceived that Angela felt afraid of Lady Trevallyn.

In some confusion but glad of the pretence to change the subject she now began to praise the beauty of Lady Greysville.

"Was she much admired at Harrogate," asked Lady Trevallyn.

"Yes very much indeed."

"She is a general flirt," observed she.

Selena half smiled at the remembrance of Mrs. Vallard's very frequent application of that expression.

"Why do you smile," said Lady Trevallyn with some interest, "was she flirting there much with any particular person? Lord Henry perhaps," added she with a forced smile and in a faultering voice.

"No indeed," answered Selena, "I saw no particular flirtation going on I think except between Mr. Richmond and Miss Ludlow, and that had a very comical conclusion."

She then endeavoured to amuse her rather inattentive auditor with the mistake which still afforded so much mirth and table talk at Harrogate. The conversation was however languid and Lady Trevallyn had sunk into a gloomy silence which she in vain sought to conquer by asking now and then an insipid question to the answer of which she forgot to attend. There is no tete-a-tete so tedious as that between two persons who really love each other, when the mind is fixed upon some interesting object without liberty to communicate or ask a communication. The want of confidence is then at once a grief and a reproach and the very wish to disguise the restraint renders it even more insupportable.

Selena now for the first time felt herself not at ease in the society of Lady Trevallyn and while she fancied herself a weight upon her dejected friend sincerely wished herself again at Hillbarton.

Lady Trevallyn was herself distressed at the consciousness that the farewell visit of her amiable friend should leave so disagreeable an impression.

"Shall we walk my love," said she aware that inactive idleness is always the most oppressive when threatened by ennui.

The motion of the feet, the variety presented to the eye, support the spirits in some degree during a change of scene but who is a stranger to the punishment of vainly exploring the barren invention for topicks to fill up the vacancy of conversation where there is nothing to be done by the hand or the foot where all is unimployed except the heart which suffers.

Selena saw thro' her design and rising laid her hand gently on her friend's saying with the sweetest smile, "No *you* shall not walk, I know you never love to go out till evening, but I will go see poor Angela. Mrs. Harley is now at the shop and I would rather find her alone as I think she speaks more."

"Do so my love," answered Lady Trevallyn, gratefully pressing before she released the hand which she held and opening immediately for Selena the door of the green house.

As Selena walked slowly towards the school she pondered over the extraordinary preference of great wealth which she imagined must alone have determined Mrs. Montrose to require such a sacrifice from her child. For Lord Henry had every advantage over Lord Trevallyn except that as a younger brother of a noble family whose possessions equalled not their rank his property was comparatively small. She considered with an almost equal compassion these two young and lovely persons condemned to perpetual regret on the sacrifice of their first affections.

The recollection however of Mrs. Vallard's evident dislike of Lord Henry quickly suggested the idea that perhaps his profligate character might have occasioned Mrs. Montrose's anxious desire of having her daughter united to another—and as this appeared the most probable conjecture her warm heart shared Mrs. Vallard's indignant dislike of the specious being who had thus destroyed the happiness of one so amiable and so lovely. Yet one so amiable and so lovely might surely she thought have reclaimed him young and gentle and sensible as he appeared.

In the midst of such reflections she entered the school; she found Mrs. Harley just returned and perceived Angela who wearied by her exertions in her absence, and now feeling a sad gratification in being at liberty again to return to her own melancholy meditations, was seated in the window, while with her eyes closed and her arms folded she leaned her head languidly against the shutter. At Selena's voice she started and a sudden flash of pleasure for an instant illumined the shade which usually hung over her countenance. But as if joy dare not shew itself in a face so sad without some modest "badge of bitterness"[91] tears rushed to her eyes as Selena held out her hand and affectionately met her salutation.

Mrs. Harley also received her with unaffected pleasure. She indeed felt a lively affection for Selena. Independent of the gratitude she experienced towards her for the kindness which Selena had shewn to Angela she loved the society of innocent young people. She was herself of a disposition naturally active, cheerful and even gay. The afflictions of life thro' which she had been supported by the mild influence of the purest religion, tho' they had injured her constitution had never been able to subdue intirely the spirits which she owed to a sanguine complexion and a temperament the most happy. She was ever ready indeed to weep with those who wept, but she enjoyed that far more rare and enviable disposition which can

---

[91]   The messenger in Shakespeare's *Much Ado About Nothing* (1598), 1.1.22–3, describing Claudio's uncle.

incline the benevolent heart to rejoice at all times (except when under the influence of some peculiar sorrow) with those who rejoice.

Ever ready to contribute to their innocent pleasures, and to interest herself in their concerns, their hopes and their fears, her society was courted by the young and the gay, not only when they sought her counsel or assistance when in difficulty, but even in the intervals of these amusements which still occupied their imagination. She listened with an attentive interest to the scenes they loved to remember and repeat for it was thus she gained the favourable opportunity of understanding the situation in which they stood, and of warning them of the dangers which awaited them. She possessed the art of shewing them their follies without humbling their pride, while flattered by her regard they submitted to her reproof, or gained from her conversation the instruction which she seemed accidentally to bestow.

Angela alone, Angela whom of all upon earth she most desired to serve, Angela the dearest, now almost the sole of her worldly cares and affections, Angela alone seemed to shun her society and shrink from her confidence. With grief and surprise but unmingled with resentment, she saw her anxious desire of once more quitting her protection, and exchanging her soothing tenderness for the cold and purchased hospitality of an aunt whom she did not even profess to love. Of all the sorrows with which Heaven had afflicted her this indeed appeared to be the most severe, for it was attended with some degree of self-reproach. She had abandoned her child, and that beloved child was now desirous to abandon her. Her dear, her only child, loved her not, esteemed her not as a parent and the moment approached when yielding to her discontent she had promised to dismiss from her eyes the beloved object of her solicitude whose ill health even rendered the probability of again beholding her fearfully doubtful.

Under such circumstances it is not surprising that Selena observed an unusual dejection in the placid countenance of Mrs. Harley—and sure of obtaining Lady Trevallyn's concurrence in her friendly design she wished to discover from Angela whether any change in her present habits of life might not reconcile her to remain under the eye of her anxious Mother.

With this view and the better to engage Angela to throw aside that silent reserve which now prevented her from bearing even the smallest share in their conversation Selena asked her should she dislike to walk for a while in some of the shaded paths cut thro' the woods which encircled the house.

Angela said it would do her good, and struggling with her habitual languor rose to accompany her with a readiness which almost surprised them both.

As they slowly proceeded thro' the walks best screened from the sun Selena began to lead the conversation to the days of Angela's childhood and was pleased to observe her animated by the sweet remembrance. She spoke of her lamented benefactress with tears indeed but they were tears of tenderness. She seemed willing to prolong the subject and voluntarily recounted to Selena some anecdotes which represented her lost friend in the most amiable light.

"Did you know Lady Trevallyn at that time?" asked Selena.

"I often saw Mrs. Montrose and her daughter at Lady Anne's, but as it was generally when there was other company, I never had any intimacy with either," answered she coldly with her face averted from Selena.

"Did Lady Anne see much of her relations?"

"Yes a good deal," replied Angela still in the same manner and the same tone.

"Have you ever seen Lord Henry Ortney there?"

"Yes."

"Was he a favourite of Lady Anne's?"

"I cannot tell."

Selena struck with the shortness of her replies and the haste with which they were delivered intending to change the subject, stopped and pointing out to Angela a fungus of an extraordinary size said smiling, "I suppose now if Lady Trevallyn was here she would stoop directly for that ugly plant, for I do not think botanists much mind the beauty of the objects of their curiosity. I have a mind to bring it home to her. Is it common in these woods do you think?"

Angela slowly turned round her face which she had so long held averted and Selena was shocked to behold the deadly hue with which it was overspread.

"Are you ill Angela?" cried she earnestly. "You have walked too much. Do let us sit down."

Her lips which were almost of a purple tint quivered as she forced a smile and assured Selena she was perfectly well gathering at the same time the fungus to which she had directed her attention.

This is strange, thought Selena as they proceeded in silence. They were just then in view of the house.

"Are those Lord Trevallyn's horses?" said Selena pointing to those on the gravel which they saw led by a groom and willing to interrupt the gloomy reverie in which Angela seemed plunged.

Angela looked up, cast around a wild eye which struck Selena with an emotion of terror and catching suddenly hold of her arm exclaimed, "Oh Miss Miltern let us return. I am sick."

Selena in great distress would again have entreated her to sit down, but before she could speak Angela could no longer hear, and was in her arms apparently without sign of life. Excessively terrified, unknowing how to obtain assistance and unable to support her Selena sunk with her unhappy burthen to the ground, and endeavoured for a few moments vainly to recover her by throwing lavender water in her face and unpinning her gown—but perceiving to her extreme horror no symptom of returning life, she flew towards the house and the groom being still on the gravel made signs to him to hasten towards her. He obeyed surprised at the agitation in which she appeared as soon as he could secure his horses, and on her pointing breathless to the apparently lifeless body of Angela he lost no time in flying to her assistance.

"My God Madam Miss Harley is quite dead!" said he with looks of terror.

"Oh no, no," cried Selena, "she has only fainted. Let us carry her to her poor Mother."

"Is it to the house?" replied the groom as he lifted her in his arms.

"No the school is nearer I think," answered Selena running towards it while he followed her steps.

Just as they reached the door a deep sigh from Angela declared her return to life, and Selena then ordered him to place her on the bench at the porch while she sat down beside her to support her till a little come to herself that she might less terrify her Mother.

But Mrs. Harley surprised at the little bustle at the door was now come out and Angela's unclosing eyes beheld her weeping Mother on her knees before her.

"Where am I? What is the matter? Where is he?" said she looking wildly around her as she endeavoured to start from Selena who had thrown her supporting arm about her.

"The young Lady will recover now I hope," said the groom hastening back to his horses before Selena had time to reward or even to thank him for his humane and ready assistance.

"Are you better my Love?" said Mrs. Harley.

"Oh yes I am quite well," cried she again trying to rise and putting her hands to her temples while she seemed recollecting what had passed still looking round as if expecting to behold some other person.

"Will you lye down my child?" said her mother as she brought her a glass of wine.

"Do dear Angela," said Selena, "lye down and repose yourself it was all my fault I have tired you by taking you [for] too long a walk."

Angela made no opposition to their advice tho' she assured them that she was now quite well, and Mrs. Harley told Selena not to reproach herself as Angela had before that terrified her more than once by these sudden illnesses.

Chapter XV

> But when he spoke of Love! thy very soul
> Hung on his lips; say canst thou not repeat
> Each word each syllable—his accent too
> Thou notedst; still it rings upon thine ear;
> And then his eyes, they looked such wondrous truth
> Art thou not sure he cannot have deceived thee?
> Lord Oxford[92]

As soon as Angela was laid upon the bed Selena hastened back, apprehensive that Lady Trevallyn might be surprised at her long absence. As she was about to enter the dressing room thro' the green house, the remembrance of Lord Trevallyn's

---

[92] The Countess in Horace Walpole's (not Lord Oxford's) *The Mysterious Mother* (1781), 3.1.120–25 (addressing her daughter Adeliza, who has fallen in love with her brother/father).

reproof stopped her and she softly knocked at the door—but no one answering she past on to the drawing room. At the window in conversation with Lord Trevallyn to her no small surprise she discovered Lord Henry.

He immediately approached her and professed his pleasure at so soon being able to renew their acquaintance, but after a few expressive words, again turned to Lord Trevallyn and continued the conversation upon the deplorable insult which had lately been done to the peerage of England by raising to that high rank persons of such obscure birth.

In a few minutes the dinner-bell rang and Lady Trevallyn entered the drawing room. She went up immediately to Selena and in a low voice asked her where she had been ever since.

"I have been detained by poor Angela; who gave me a sad fright, she was taken suddenly so ill while we were walking."

"Angela," cried Lord Henry gaily, who on Lady Trevallyn's entrance had approached them, and was now seated on the table at her side, "Angela! who has that fine name?"

"Do not you remember Angela Harley at Lady Anne's?" answered Lady Trevallyn without raising her eyes.

"Oh yes, and is she here."

"She lives here with her Mother but not in the house."

"Under your protection I suppose," resumed Lord Henry carelessly; dinner was now announced and Lord Trevallyn offering his hand to Selena, Lord Henry followed his example and leading Lady Trevallyn to the parlour seated himself at her side.

In Lady Trevallyn's manner there appeared nothing which could either justify or destroy the suspicions which had so recently been excited in the bosom of Selena. She spoke indeed but little and what she did say was chiefly addressed to Selena, but except in a tete-a-tete her silence was so habitual that no inference could be drawn from thence.

While Lord Trevallyn was in a pompous harangue describing to Lord Henry the pains he had of late taken to perform some essential service to government Lady Trevallyn in a lower voice enquired from Selena what had been the matter with Angela.

Selena told her of her sudden fainting adding how much she was obliged to the groom whose accidental presence and prompt assistance had been such a relief to her. Lady Trevallyn seemed desirous to know which of the servants had offered this opportune help saying that Lord Trevallyn had not rode out that day, then suddenly recollecting observed that it must have been Lord Henry's groom who arrived just about that time.

"I should think not," said Selena, "for I remember he knew Angela instantly and called her Miss Harley before I was able myself to speak to him."

Lord Henry at that moment called Lady Trevallyn's attention by enquiring would she not honour him with some commands to town the next day.

"You will surely not go tomorrow my Lord," interrupted the master of the house who felt it in some degree insulted by this sudden departure of a guest he had taken so much pains to entertain.

Lord Henry assured him that nothing but business of the utmost consequence could force him to forego at present the pleasure which he hoped however in a very short time to be able to renew by returning to Esselberrie.

Lady Trevallyn was silent and upon his repeating his offers of service declined them with scarcely any other answer than a bow.

"Pray," said Lord Henry in a half whisper to Lady Trevallyn, "what is the name of that lady at your right hand?"

"Is it Miss Miltern you mean?" answered she looking at him with surprise.

"Oh I was afraid I had been making a mistake in so calling her then she is not yet Lady Dallamore."

"May I answer for you in the negative?" said she turning with a smile to the blushing Selena.

"When Lady Dallamore shall honour us with a bridal visit," said Lord Trevallyn his stately features unrelaxed by any smile, "we will endeavour to receive her in a more festive manner. I am rejoiced to find that I am then soon to congratulate you upon being raised to a rank you will so much adorn." As he added these words he in some degree softened his usual imperious voice in the idea that he was addressing a future countess.

"I assure you my Lord there is not the smallest foundation for the jest with which Lord Henry wishes to entertain you," said Selena half vexed at Lord Trevallyn's compliment and much annoyed at the subject which had occasioned it.

"Nay," said Lord Henry, "Dallamore told me himself that in a few days he was to be the happiest of Benedicts[93] and I did not expect you would have been more reserved to Lady Trevallyn."

"Come Selena you must atone for this want of confidence and tell me all about this," said Lady Trevallyn rising from table, and Lord Henry as he opened the door for them to leave the room said some words softly to Lady Trevallyn while she passed which not only called forth in her cheeks such varying roses as Aurora[94] scatters in the path of the sun, but banished from her recollection for a few minutes the questions with which she had intended to assail Selena.

Her reverie was interrupted by the surprise which Selena expressed at having seen Lord Henry at her return.

"Yes," said Lady Trevallyn, "he came soon after you had left me but you did not expect to have the secret you kept so slyly, betrayed all at once."

"Dear Lady Trevallyn I have no secret for I assure you it is quite a jest."

"But jest or earnest Lord Dallamore *has* proposed for you."

"Yes as he has for you I have no doubt fifty times."

---

[93] Benedict from Shakespeare's *Much Ado About Nothing* (constantly bickering with but ultimately in love with Beatrice).

[94] Aurora: goddess of the dawn.

"Oh no," said Lady Trevallyn, "he never went quite so far with me."

"Well then it was because you did not give him the opportunity which our intimacy necessarily allowed, for I am sure he has thought of you a great deal more than ever he will do of me."

"But supposing him serious my dear Selena what do you think of it?"

"Well then supposing what I never did yet for a moment that he really meant to do me so much honour I should be extremely sorry to have the business at all spoken of, as I could never accept him and know that the very discussion of it must be attended with the most disagreeable consequences in the family, as my father is not on good terms with Lord Mount Villars."

"But perhaps your connexion with Lord Dallamore might be the bond of future amity."

Selena shook her head and assured her that could never be.

"But I must call and see how poor Angela is before it grows dark," cried she after they had dwelt for some time on the uncertain character of Dallamore with which Lady Trevallyn did not disguise her pleasure that Selena was resolved never to unite herself.

"I will walk there with you," answered Lady Trevallyn, and her heart being opened by the freedom with which Selena had spoken to her of her own affairs as she walked before her thro' the green house she asked her in a hurried voice and without turning round her face, "Has Mrs. Vallard told you that it was once thought *I* also should have been married to my cousin?"

"No never indeed, Lord Henry do you mean?"

"Yes," said Lady Trevallyn half repenting to have said so much since it was indeed hitherto unknown to Selena. "Well then you must not tell her that I have mentioned it."

"I will not indeed, I do not think Lord Henry is a favourite with her."

"Oh no, Mrs. Vallard was always so partial to his eldest brother. But indeed she never knew him, if she had I am sure she would have liked him. My poor Mother loved him like her own son, better indeed for he behaved far kinder to her."

"Dear Lady Trevallyn I own you surprise me."

"Why so?" answered she turning for the first time since the commencement of this conversation her glowing face to Selena and stopping to take her arm as they now proceeded thro' the shrubbery.

"Because," said Selena with some hesitation, "I heard that it was at Mrs. Montrose's desire that you married Lord Trevallyn."

"My poor Mother desired nothing but my happiness," answered she as the large drops fell silently from her eyes, "she could not bear to leave me dependant, and thought she prevented this when she engaged me for life to a master."

"But why not Lord Henry?" asked Selena timidly.

"Because," answered she forcing a smile while a still deeper blush burned upon her cheek, "Because Lord Henry was not so fond of proposing as Dallamore."

Selena at once understood, abhorred, and wondered at the conduct of Lord Henry, while she beheld with the deepest compassion the too evident sensibility with which he had so cruelly sported. She was silent—indeed it was impossible for her to express the sensations or sentiments by which she was agitated; but the look of interest and sympathy which spoke so eloquently in her eyes irresistibly seduced the confidence of Lady Trevallyn whose soft and susceptible disposition was ever prone to receive the language of affection.

"I will tell you all," said she, "and you shall see if I am not indeed self-sacrificed." As she spoke they seated themselves on a bank and Lady Trevallyn continued, "I will not disguise from you that my Mother thought I loved Lord Henry too well ever to marry any one else and as she had also reason to believe from his declining to accompany us abroad when I was ordered thither for the recovery of my health that he had not the same sentiments, nor ever seriously thought of her poor Emily, her anguish and despair on my account when she perceived she was going for ever to leave me are not to be imagined. Indeed Selena I cannot even now remember it without shuddering. Hopeless myself of ever again tasting a moment's happiness deprived of her tenderness, life appeared at that time of so little value that I thought the consolation which I was able thus to afford her last hours cheaply purchased by the sacred promise I then made her to accept Lord Trevallyn's offers in case they should be renewed.

"The promise reached his ears, I believe thro' the solicitude of my dying Mother, and scarcely were the last remains of this best and most beloved of parents torn from my arms, before I saw myself for ever bound by the most solemn of all engagements to pass my life with one to whom I was as yet almost a total stranger. I will not make you a half confidence Selena; I will own that having considered my situation my soul revolted against it cruelly and in the latent hope of freeing myself from a fate I esteemed so wretched I persuaded myself it was [right] to confess my unconquerable preference, my attachment to another tho' I named not the object. He was content to accept my hand and trust our mutual honour to the principles which I hope will ever be my defence. I returned to England his wife—and it was then I learned that while I was thus separating myself from him by insurmountable and eternal barriers—while the vain study, the continual desire of my soul was to tear him from my memory, Lord Henry mindful only of our early loves was sacrificing every thing which he thought opposed our union."

Here she for a moment paused unable to proceed and Selena anxiously enquired how she had been assured of this. Lady Trevallyn wiped the tears which had half choked her utterance while she struggled to restrain them, and which on her silence had instantly burst forth.

"I heard it from himself, but in a singular manner," answered she after some hesitation. "At the time when we were almost constantly together he had one day taken from my finger a little ring which I used generally as a seal. It was the antique which representing Love mounted upon a lion seems intended to express his power to subdue all.[95] I never could recover my ring, and he wore it constantly upon his little finger. At Lord Trevallyn's desire on my return to London I sat to a celebrated painter who drew figures in miniature at full length. One day while I waited for my carriage after Lord Trevallyn who always accompanied me there had left me, the painter took from his desk a picture and handed it over for my inspection saying that he had been desired to ask me if the likeness was striking. It was indeed not to be mistaken—it was Lord Henry himself—but scarcely could I conceal my emotion while I examined a portrait intended to convey so much, and manifestly addressed to me. Nothing could be more beautiful than the execution of this design calculated to explain to my eye those motives which had actuated him suddenly to give up his high rank in the army as I had already heard he had so imprudently done, upon being refused to quit Ireland. The utmost sorrow was painted on his countenance as he pointed to a broken sword which he had placed upon an altar where I read those words *For thee alone*[96] immediately beneath the exact impression I so well remembered of my own seal."

"I hope," interrupted Selena, "that there was nothing in your countenance which might betray you to the painter."

"He was fortunately called away almost immediately after he had presented me with the portrait. The moment that I perceived the carriage come to the door I hastened away and this being my last sitting I saw him no more."

"Did Lord Henry ever speak to you of this picture?"

Lady Trevallyn was silent for a while but at length said, "I will not deny that he at first sought every opportunity of speaking to me, and even once shed tears while he said that the severest disappointment of his life, had not been the loss of all his hopes of promotion but the intelligence which reached his ears immediately after he had thus voluntarily resigned them, intelligence which shewed him how vain had been the sacrifice, and delivered him to perpetual regret. These Selena were his words, I cannot it is true forget them but indeed I have nothing with which to reproach myself I trust hitherto in my conduct to Lord Henry since my marriage."

"But why my dear Lady Trevallyn," interrupted Selena, "since this sacrifice was necessary why was it not made before? How unfortunate that it should thus have been delayed till circumstances had rendered it vain!"

"I know not," answered she after a short pause, "for I never would listen to his attempted explanation of the particulars of his conduct, with the utmost care I have avoided all interviews which are indeed painful to me beyond the power of expression, and when ever he has addressed me with that voice and look which I so well remember to accompany any words intended to convey peculiar tenderness I have turned from him with a coldness the most discouraging. The scenes of gaiety

---

[95]   Lady Trevallyn may be referring to Mattheus van Beveren's ivory statue of Cupid mounted on a lion (ca. 1675–90) or other renditions of this image, drawn from Ovid and Virgil.

[96]   For thee alone: a phrase often used in hymns.

once so delightful to me now became irksome. I found it impossible to forget[97] the pleasures which I had been accustomed to derive from them resulted solely from his continual assiduity. It was in vain I turned from him my eyes. While present he occupied my whole attention, and whether he appeared as was too generally the case only there to observe me, or whether he addressed his casual civility to some other woman he was the sole object on which I could fix with the smallest degree of interest. As far as it was in my power I declined all parties in publick, and avoided all mixed assemblies, but tho' this spared me the torment of a restraint so cruel while continually beholding what I had for ever lost, yet our unfortunate family connexion rendered it impossible for me to escape frequently meeting him whose sight I now dreaded. At the houses of my relations, in the dinners which we were obliged to accept and even at those which Lord Trevallyn gave Lord Henry was a never failing guest and generally at my side.

"With unfeigned pleasure I hailed the arrival of that season which was to interrupt this society to me the source of constant disquietudes and ever new tortures. Upon the first sensations of disgust which I felt for a life of dissipation and what is called the world I became sensible of the great defect in my education. Too much engrossed by the unfortunate idea entertained by my family, that my shewy person was to provide my future settlement, company, dress and amusements were the business of those years which should have been devoted to the cultivation of my mind. The only accomplishment I had ever practised was drawing, and this I rather prosecuted malgré ma minerve,[98] for in spite of all my wishes to excel I have no genius. I had no talents like you Selena to occupy those hours which I now chose to pass alone, finding society worse than insipid. I always indeed loved poetry, but it is really true that

> Fancy enervates while it soothes the heart,
> To joy each hightning charm it can impart
> But wraps the hour of woe in tenfold night
>
> Beattie[99]

I confess I began to feel her dangerous influence in cherishing a melancholy which I knew to be at once fatal and criminal. In vain I struggled, no employment interested me, and in town it was impossible to study—the images I sought to avoid pursued me to my solitude, I listened with regret to the account of pleasures I felt I could never more enjoy and watched with a kind of impatient dread for the name which perpetually haunted me. But upon my coming here I no longer experienced that oppressive gloom which used to render my inactive hours so tedious.

"Providence threw in my way my dear Mrs. Harley the comfort and the guide of my life. My efforts to turn my mind from what is wrong have not been

---

[97] The MS editor inserts "that" after "forget."

[98] Malgré my minerve: despite my collar (French).

[99] James Beattie, *The Minstrel; or, the Progress of Genius* (1771), 2:361–4 (Tighe omits line 362: "And while it dazzles, wounds the mental sight").

unsuccessful; moments of embittering sadness do indeed still pursue me, but I have power to banish the torturing reflections that all my prospects are thus early in life for ever shut in. The endearing and natural expressions of affection which I daily receive from those innocent little girls, and the partial approbation of dear Mrs. Harley have been my support in many a sad hour, and my Selena's friendship will now add another charm to impoverished existence."

Selena's affectionate heart afflicted and softened by Lady Trevallyn's confidence, returned with ardour her embrace as she concluded, and mingling her tears with her friend's for a few minutes they were neither of them able to speak any other language.

But Lady Trevallyn quickly making an effort to recover her composure said in a low voice, "It grows late Selena, and I have too much indulged those ideas it is highly wrong in me to cherish; let us go now and enquire for poor Angela, who doubtless has her sorrows, perhaps even more real than mine."

They then rose and proceeded towards the school house. They found the doors already closed for the night. Mrs. Harley on hearing Lady Trevallyn's voice came down, and said she had been reading to Angela who had not since risen from her bed.

"I will tell her," she added, "that you have been so kind to call, for I am sure it will please her."

"Do," said Selena, "ask her if I may go up for a minute to bid her farewell."

Mrs. Harley obliged but in a few minutes returned and said that she was afraid Angela tho' sensible of her kindness was then too weak to see her.

"She talks incessantly my Lady of Islington," continued she, "and I fear I must at length keep my word with the dear strange girl, let it cost me what it may to part with her thus."

Lady Trevallyn said she really thought she would do well to indulge her, and that perhaps she might in a short time be content to return to them.

Mrs. Harley shook her head in silence.

The gentlemen were already in the drawing room when they returned and Lord Trevallyn expressing his surprise at their late walk they accounted for it by saying that had been to enquire for Angela.

"Have you seen her?" said Lord Henry.

"No," answered Lady Trevallyn, "poor thing she was not able to let us up."

"Is she ill?"

"More unhappy than ill I think."

"Why what is the matter," demanded he with a smile as he offered his assistance to Lady Trevallyn taking from her hand the tea-pot.

"That we cannot discover," answered she after a moment's silence.

The conversation then took another turn, and Lady Trevallyn requested Selena to play—after which she returned to Hillbarton but Lady Trevallyn would not take a formal leave, being determined to see her once again before she parted from a friend so lately acquired but so highly valued.

Chapter XVI

Without fear I stood ....
Like one who on the beech descries from far
A labouring bark with which the billows war,
Pities its state, wishing the tempest gone
But views not the near sea come rolling on.

Dryden[100]

Selena on her way back thought over every circumstance of Lady Trevallyn's history—and troubled at the dangerous situation in which she stood—which the excellence of her judgement plainly pointed out to her apprehension, inexperienced as she was. She saw that in spite of all Lady Trevallyn had said, she continued to cherish those sentiments so calculated to involve her in the deepest misery. She saw also the subtle deceit which Lord Henry had employed to persuade her of his former intentions—a fallacy which the delusion of partial affection could only have blinded Lady Trevallyn from herself discovering. How improbable indeed was it, that Lord Henry who for years might at any moment have offered to his cousin a hand he knew too well she would accept, should only then intend to make the offer when his situation and duty in the army should have prevented his being able to join her, and at the critical period of her bestowing herself upon another.

All this was plain to Selena; but love is credulous and Lady Trevallyn loved. Who indeed would persist in believing themselves neglected or slighted by the object they adore, when that most adored object would persuade them of unshaken love and fidelity. Love, child as he is[101] indeed is easily offended, but by how gross a deception, how trifling a concession may he not be consoled? Deeply interested by Lady Trevallyn's confidence Selena yet wished that it had been rather reposed in Mrs. Vallard whose experience and long affection for her young friend might better have entitled her to give those warning cautions which Selena judged necessary but felt of too delicate a nature for her to venture to bestow.

When Selena entered the drawing room at Hillbarton where they were already seated at supper she was not a little surprised to behold Mr. Miltern. Eagerly enquiring for her mother as she flew to embrace him, he told her that impatient at her long absence she had sent him for her and saying this he received her caresses with more than usual kindness in his manner. At the same time he declared his intention of remaining but one night at Hillbarton and desired Selena to be prepared to accompany him. She assured him of her readiness while she affectionately turned to Mrs. Vallard asking her to forgive her impatience again to embrace her Mother from whom she had never before found herself separated.

---

[100] Mithridates in Nathaniel Lee's (not Dryden's) *Mithridates, King of Pontus: A Tragedy* (1678) 1.3.320–24.

[101] "Facilmente l'adira, facilmente si placa. Tasso" (Tighe's note). Tighe quotes from the epilogue spoken by Venus about Cupid in Torquato Tasso's *Aminta* (1573), lines 83–4: easy to anger, easy to placate.

After supper they retired together to Mrs. Vallard's chamber—and reluctant to bid each other good night for the last time prolonged their conversation to a late hour. In consequence of her enquiries after Lady Trevallyn and in the course of Selena's little narrative of her day, Mrs. Vallard heard with an uneasiness she did not disguise of Lord Henry's visit, and when Selena told her that he was determined to leave Esselberrie on the following day she exclaimed "I am glad of it from my heart and trust in God he may never return." Selena was silent, but Mrs. Vallard who half reproached her indiscretion for what had thus escaped her read in her speaking countenance that she was no longer entirely a stranger to the reasons of her strong dislike.

"Ah my dear Selena," cried she, while tears started to her eyes, "only for the base conduct of that cruel young man, my poor Emily would in all probability have been the happy wife of one of the most amiable and estimable characters I ever knew, of an age and appearance suitable to her own and of a rank even superior to that she now possesses."

"Whom do you mean?" demanded Selena with some surprise.

"I am sure I may depend upon you my Love," answered Mrs. Vallard, "and you will yourself see how wrong it would be now to publish a rejection which at the time was I believe known only to Emily, her lover, his unworthy rival and myself. Since I have said so much I will confide to you the whole affair. From the time my poor Emily was quite a child, and a most lovely child she was, her cousin the present Marquis of Ortney, then Lord Lorville fixed all his happiness upon her. Determined however to owe nothing to the ambition of her Mother which Emily's own heart should refuse he concealed his attachment and watched her with an anxiety which poisoned the best hours of life. I believe I was his only confidant and with me he used to love to converse while I deceived by my own wishes unintentionally flattered him with the false hopes that his jealousy had alone discovered the mutual attachment of Lord Henry and his cousin.

"At length he spoke to his brother and confessed his own views, which I believe only made Lord Henry the more eager in his endeavours to gain poor Emily's affections. Sensible of the advantages he possessed in the eyes of her family the Marquis with that noble generosity which accompanies all his actions declared himself alone to Emily—who overwhelmed with confusion and bathed in tears acknowledged to him her attachment for another, and entreated him to spare her the importunities of her Mother and the persecution of her family. She forbore to name the object of her love, but this he could too easily guess, and having assured her that he would never voluntarily counteract her happiness he bade her farewell for ever, and soon after quitted England, telling me that he could not bear the idea of beholding as a sister the only woman upon earth he could ever love. Oh Selena! if you knew the mind, the heart of that excellent young man you would share all my detestation of the being who thus wantonly destroyed all his happiness and that of our poor Emily two creatures so perfect they seemed indeed created for each other."

Selena did indeed share in all Mrs. Vallard's sentiments of just abhorrence for Lord Henry and compassion for the victim of his selfish unfeeling conduct. She also secretly deplored the too evident partiality she yet discovered existed in Lady Trevallyn's heart for him who had so injured her—but of this she forbore to speak and Mrs. Vallard gave no hint of her entertaining a suspicion so melancholy.

When they at length separated for the night Mrs. Vallard shed tears at the thoughts of parting probably for so long a time from her young friend whose amiable disposition, engaging manners, and uncommon talents had endeared her to such a degree to her warm heart already partially prepossessed in her favour before her arrival—and it was with the utmost regret that she surrendered all the wild hopes she had at first indulged of seeing her united to her nephew.

Scarcely had the ladies withdrawn when Mr. Miltern artfully encouraged Dallamore to declare his hopes and wishes with respect to Selena—and upon his endeavouring to draw from this unreserved young man the sentiments of Lord Mount Villars Dallamore forgot the prudent promise he had made to Mrs. Vallard and delivered into the hands of Mr. Miltern a letter which he had that morning received from his irritated father.

How he had been informed of Dallamore's designs upon Selena was a matter of the utmost surprise to all at Hillbarton. But tho' Dallamore had not thought it necessary to ask the consent of his father, Mr. Richmond well aware of its being refused had judged differently. Therefore upon his stopping at Leeds on the very day he left Harrogate he wrote an anonymous letter which he trusted would be attributed to Le Roi containing a caution to Lord Mount Villars with respect to the artful schemes of Miss Miltern, assuring him that if some speedy steps were not taken to prevent it Lord Dallamore would be on his way to Scotland with the pennyless daughter of his malicious brother and referring for the truth of this information to Mr. Richmond whom the informer truly represented as having vainly exerted his influence to defeat the designs which he perceived had been formed.

In consequence of the rage excited by this intelligence Lord Mount Villars had in the first intemperate fit of passion written in the following strong and unjustifiable terms to his son.

"Dallamore!
"I swear by the Eternal God that if you marry or have any connexion whatever with a child of that detestable Miltern no power in Heaven or earth shall prevail upon me to acknowledge you as my son or ever again to hold any conversation with you—and however independant you may consider yourself, you shall find I have yet power to injure you.
Mount Villars"

The indignation and redoubled fury of revenge which this letter excited in the breast of Mr. Miltern he had the art to disguise from Dallamore never very anxious or keen in penetrating into the minds of those with whom he conversed. But while the father of Selena was in the most subtle manner persuading Dallamore to give up to the imperious mandates of Lord Mount Villars the inclination which he felt towards his cousin he by the most artful suggestions enflamed him with the most determined ardour to continue his suit. Mr. Miltern said every thing which was necessary to convince Dallamore of Selena's love, but while actuated as he said merely through pity for their mutual attachment he promised tho' with apparent reluctance to afford his consent and assistance towards the completion of their wishes.

He advised Dallamore for the present to refrain from speaking either to Mrs. Vallard or Selena on the subject but told him that if he would accompany them one day upon their journey he would impart to him the plan which he conceived most likely to be attended with success and at once contribute to his own gratification, the happiness of Selena and the peace of the family.

Dallamore with eagerness acceeded to all he proposed, and both Selena and Mrs. Vallard heard the next day with surprise and some dissatisfaction that Dallamore was to be their travelling companion so far as Birmingham—for now that Mrs. Vallard was convinced of Selena's sincere rejection of her nephew she was as averse as she herself could be to the encouragement of his views which must end only in disappointment.

However on the following morning the party set out professedly for Birmingham tho' in reality Mr. Miltern had no intentions of pursuing that route. Accepting the place which Dallamore offered him in his curricle he explained to him in terms best suited to ensure his warm concurrence, the scheme which it was his design to adopt, but which indeed he had now the art to make Dallamore himself propose and firmly believe his own suggestion. Selena was not yet to be consulted who would certainly resist such a measure without the approbation of her Mother, but they were immediately to take the northern road, and with all possible expedition reach Scotland, where a marriage might be celebrated without delay if Selena could be brought to consent, or if she should refuse they might then part, and in either case the whole was to be kept a profound secret from Lord Mount Villars till by their united efforts his resentment should be appeased and his more brotherly regard conciliated.

Dallamore was indeed even more occupied and delighted with this project than with Selena herself—and tho' it is certain no other woman could so powerfully have made him desire its success, yet it is by no means so certain that no other woman could have prevailed upon him to put such a scheme into execution. At the first stage Mr. Miltern communicated the plan to Robert under a strict injunction of secrecy, as it was indeed impossible to proceed in it without his knowledge. But tho' Robert earnestly desired the union, and consented to keep the promise he had given of not revealing their design to Selena, he could not at all approve of thus precipitating an affair of such consequence to his sister, whose extreme youth was in itself he could not but think a principle objection. Besides he confessed his opinion that she would never consent to unite herself for life without the knowledge and concurrence of her mother.

Mr. Miltern sternly desired him on no account to interfere or dare to offer his advice to Selena, and when they stopped for the night being already fifty miles on the great northern road, aware of the impracticability of proceeding much father without Selena's discovering their route he called her into his own apartment, and telling her he wished to have some serious conversation with her produced from his pocket a letter which he said he had that morning received from her Mother—and the better to ensure her implicit belief in the forgery without delivering it into Selena's hands he then read as follows.

"Your intentions with respect to Selena meet my warmest approbation and I trust my dear girl is inclined to embrace a proposal to which she has already given so much encouragement and which is so likely to afford happiness to herself and peace to our divided family. I have no doubt from what I have heard of Lord Dallamore that we shall find him all we can desire, when a few years shall take from him that apparent want of decision, in which his character alone seems deficient, but which in one so young may proceed from the most amiable suavity of disposition. Tell Selena that she has now an opportunity of gratifying the warmest wish of my heart by her ready compliance with my advice and entreaty, all that duty and affection the profession of which I never doubted. When I next embrace her I hope she will present me to another son in her amiable and deserving cousin, the favourite nephew of my dearest friend. Clara alone detains me here, and prevents me from indulging my ardent desire of being myself present at a union circumstances render it so expedient to hasten. But she has frightened us within this day or two by a feverish cold which seems to foretel the measles, and I think in such a situation I ought not to leave her even to witness the marriage of my still dearer Selena."

Consternation and astonishment held Selena dumb tho' her father in silence seemed to expect her reply.

At length "Well Selena," said he, "now that you know your Mother's opinion you will not I hope make any childish objections to our rather hurrying this business, without the nonsense of wedding finery and formalities of ceremony. I wouldn't however indeed press it so suddenly, but for the folly and malice Lord Mount Villars has displayed in trying to prevent his son's happiness as well as yours, but we will manouvre it in spite of him."

"Oh never Sir!" said Selena timidly but warmly interrupting him, "you cannot I am sure wish to force me into a family where I should be despised and rejected—and besides I am certain Lord Dallamore is not at all what my Mother conceives him to be, nor can I think of yet uniting myself to one a stranger to her and without her even possessing the knowledge of his real character."

"Ridiculous!" cried Mr. Miltern scarcely able to restrain as he thought prudently the violence of his rage at seeing himself thus opposed by a child; "Do you then presume to suppose yourself better qualified to judge of his character than your Mother? or what can you object to in one so generous and every way so amiable?"

"Dear Sir," answered Selena bursting into tears, "do not accuse me of presumption, but indeed you do not know him. You have not seen as I have the strange instances of inconsistency and proofs of a caprice, which tho' it may now lead him to desire me for a wife, believe me would probably in a few days incline him even yet more strongly to another—and render me at the best an object of indifference. Oh Sir do not press me to consent to a union that must make me miserable for life and which you say Lord Dallamore's father is so determined to oppose."

"Listen to me Selena," said her father in a stern voice but assumed calmness, "an opportunity now offers you the power of eternally obliging your Mother and me, by healing that unfortunate breach in the family which we have so long vainly wished to effect. When once indissoluble bonds shall thus closely have connected two beings for whom we are equally and most warmly interested Lord Mount Villars will not refuse my proposals for reconciliation. Lord Dallamore is deserving of your affection, and with the understanding which you naturally possess you will have it in your power to make him exactly what you wish and that understanding will also point out to you that the rank and fortune which he can bestow so superior to what you have a right to expect are recommendations not absolutely contemptible. I have arranged every thing for your immediate marriage, and your mother approves of its taking place without delay. Dallamore himself has no doubt of your consent encouraged by the evident pleasure with which you have listened to his offers."

"Oh," exclaimed Selena, "how much has he misrepresented my conduct! Never did I willingly listen to what I could not accept and what I always considered the mere effect of sudden caprice."

"He has not misrepresented you Selena," continued her father, "but he has expressed his hopes, hopes which from all I have heard he has had just reason to entertain. This is however nothing to the purpose, but be assured if you perversely and childishly oppose me in the chief object of my life, as well as your own happiness, I never will again consider you in affection as my child, tho' I shall still perform my duty in providing for your welfare, and your mother whose advice you thus contemptuously reject shall not again give you an opportunity of slighting her commands. Take therefore your choice, either accompany us on the road we mean to go tomorrow, preparatory to your accepting Dallamore who sincerely loves you, tho' perhaps an innocent and artless young man as he is, may not have so many insinuating ways of displaying affection as a profligate such as Lord Henry Ortney whom you so much admire, either I say consent to our wishes or prepare yourself to a separation from your family and to take up your residence in a boarding school near London with a lady upon whose prudence and good conduct I can depend, and where you shall remain until I can more fortunately point out another alliance which tho' less brilliant and in every respect less eligible may meet your approbation."

Selena answered with her tears alone.

At length she entreated permission at least to write and wait for her Mother's answer, promising to abide by that, be it what it would, and declaring at the same time with a firmness which surprised her father, that in case this was refused she must accept the cruel alternative he had offered, as she was resolved never to unite herself to Dallamore while her Mother remained ignorant as she was persuaded she now was of her strong objections to such a step.

Mr. Miltern after some hesitation accepted the terms, provided that during the interval of receiving the answer to Selena's letter they should proceed on their journey to Scotland, and that her behaviour towards Dallamore should not be more reserved or repulsive than it had hitherto been.

Selena then retired, but for a long time was so bewildered with sorrow and amazement at the scene which had just past that she knew not how to express to her Mother the feelings by which she was agitated. Important indeed was the letter which she was about to write; its answer was to decide the fate of her future life, and by that decision she had promised to abide.

Her confidence in Providence and in the judgment and affection of her Mother however supported her, and having represented the character of Dallamore in what she thought its true colours, and confessed that she felt not for him that partial affection which might blind her to his defects, or incline her to run all risks with the man she preferred in spite of those defects, when she had done this, and urged in the simple and pathetic language of feeling her reluctance to quit the beloved protection of her mother, and the society of her own dear affectionate family to place herself under the direction of a judgment she could not respect, among persons disposed to receive her with aversion and contempt; after stating all her fears and all her objections she felt in some degree satisfied to accept her lot, let what would be the will of Heaven, and of her whom next to Heaven she most loved and respected and resolved to consider it and Dallamore in the most favourable light.

But tho' she endeavoured to think of this as what might possibly be the result of her letter yet she could not without extreme terror and reluctance imagine herself the wife of Dallamore and with tears of sympathy she remembered those of compassion which she had shed for the lot of Lady Trevallyn, at that very moment when one scarcely less pitiable was preparing for herself, while she recollected and internally repeated the melancholy expression of her friend *Self sacrificed happiness and I have taken leave of each other for ever.*

Chapter XVII

Perish the love that deadens young desire!
Pursue poor imp th'imaginary charm,
Indulge gay Hope and Fancy's pleasing fire
Fancy and Hope too soon will of themselves expire.
Beatie[102]

---

[102] James Beattie, *The Minstrel, or, The Progress of Genius* (1771), 1:276–9. Tighe invokes Beattie's minstrel in naming her minstrel Edwin.

In the mean time Mr. Miltern seemed desirous to divert the mind of Selena from consideration of the important subject by the rapidity with which they travelled—while Dallamore forgetful of Mr. Miltern's advice openly expressed his expectations and the future schemes he had in view, endeavouring to amuse Selena by purchasing something that happened to strike his fancy at every town in which they stopped to change horses—so that the carriages soon became the strange and ridiculous repositories of articles of the most extraordinary and various.

It had been agreed to wait at Carlisle for the letter which Selena expected with such agitating suspense. But Mr. Miltern was so well acquainted with the disposition of Dallamore who like an infant accustomed to the rocking of a cradle, could find no repose or contentment but in continual motion, that he began to dread lest exposed to the attacks of ennui during the inactivity of a residence of some days at an hotel in a town where he had no acquaintances Dallamore might for once in his life prudently reflect on the consequences of the step he was about to take, and as with Dallamore a change of conduct was ever the immediate result of a change of inclination Mr. Miltern knew that if once the wish to be free from his present engagement occurred to his mind there was nothing to be expected from his consideration of having bound himself by those engagements to proceed.

Determined therefore to provide some occupation for the restless mind or at least limbs of their companion, and recollecting his passion for musick, by which as Mrs. Vallard had informed him Selena first captivated his attention, Mr. Miltern wished to afford her at this critical period the opportunity of exercising her talent and proposed their leaving Carlisle after they had wandered for some hours about the town, and that they should proceed to Inverathie, a village at about twenty miles distance where he knew had resided constantly for many years one of his former most intimate friends.

When boys indeed Edwin Stanmore and he had been inseparable, but had never met since either of them had married. Mr. Stanmore had early united himself to an interesting young woman, whose birth and fortune being considerably inferior to the connexion which his family had wished him to form, she had been received by them with such marked coldness and even slight that her warm and fondly attached husband resolved to abandon for ever their society, and happening to pass thro' the village of Inverathie at the time that the beautiful little residence he since occupied was untenanted he determined to settle there for life, and having made the purchase continued to embelish the beloved scene where with his amiable wife he devoted himself to the cultivation of the only child they had been able to hear call them by the endearing names to which a parent listens with such inexpressible delight.

Here with their promising boy they had enjoyed almost uninterruptedly all the happiness which heaven can bestow, realizing that exquisite picture of domestick bliss described in language so inimitable by Thompson:

> Where nothing strikes the eye but sights of bliss
> All various nature pressing on the heart
> An elegant sufficiency content

Retirement, rural quiet, friendship, books
Ease and alternate labour, useful Life
Progressive virtue and approving Heaven![103]

The young Edwin the source of their most lively joys was however the sole cause of their uneasiness: he had inherited from his Mother with a delicate constitution uncommon talents for musick and poetry; from his father he possessed a temper warm and romantick to excess and a sensibility the most acute. The education he had received, had served to heighten those dangerous qualities so that his anxious father who at the age of twenty beheld him endowed with what he could not help considering as unrivalled excellence, yet too plainly discovered he was totally unqualified to mingle with a world where his superior talents could never atone for his singularity.

Educated entirely at home, or wandering under the eye of his father amid the romantic scenery within the circle of a pedestrious[104] journey of a few days, acquainted only with his amiable parents and the servants attached to him from his childhood, with no ideas but those drawn from Nature and from books, to dismiss him into mixed society was at once to consign him to ruin and misery; and tho' as yet he appeared contented with the tranquil seclusion of Inverathie Mr. Stanmore looked forward with terror to the time when the ardour of a young mind should demand the attractions of novelty.

Mr. Miltern remembered to have heard of the young Edwin's musical abilities, and the rather resolved to introduce Dallamore to this uncommon family as he had also heard that there was no female there who should be likely to attempt to rival Selena.

"From Inverathie," said he addressing Dallamore, "we can ride over to Carlisle on Friday, which is the soonest that we can expect the letter for which Selena is determined to wait, and in the mean time I can promise you a singular treat, if, as I am sure you must do, you like to observe in a very high degree united genius and oddity, which is indeed generally the case."

Dallamore who had already by whistling and yawning given some accustomed symptoms of ennui eagerly embraced the proposal declaring he "never was so delighted to quit any place as that infernal hotel where the noise of the bells and clamour for chambermaids had almost tormented him to death" and then confessed that he was upon the point of setting out to wait for them at the next stage.

Mr. Miltern secretly congratulated himself upon the penetration that had anticipated a design which so probably would have proved fatal to his plans.

Inverathie situated at the foot of one of the wooded mountains that almost completely encircled a small lake consisted of a few scattered houses the residence of people of more taste than fortune and could indeed scarcely be called a village. Among them Mr. Stanmore's dwelling was not visible—a rocky glen shaded with the most picturesque oak and ash, concealed from the view till it was immediately

---

[103] James Thomson, "Spring," *The Seasons* (1728), lines 1156–61.

[104] Pedestrious: going on foot (OED).

entered the little valley of the softest green watered by a mountain stream in the midst of which stood the small but beautiful building, the residence of the Stanmores. The whiteness of the rocks which in fantastic shapes burst tho' the deep and now richly coloured foliage of the surrounding woods, formed a wild and beautiful contrast with the highly dressed scenery and dazzling verdure which immediately encircled the house—and for the eye which is delighted with the confinement and tranquility of a home scene, there was in this spot nothing to be desired.

Unwilling to intrude upon a friend not seen for so many years Mr. Miltern endeavoured to procure a lodging at the little publick house in the village and while with some difficulty he arranged their accommodations Dallamore fortunately discovered a boat, and fond of amusing himself upon the water accompanied by Le Roi hastened to explore the navigation of the Lake. In the mean time Mr. Miltern sent a few lines to announce his arrival and ask permission to renew their friendship which was immediately answered by Mr. Stanmore in person. With the warmest hospitality and most cordial welcome he insisted upon the instant removal not only of themselves but their attendants to his house, and having succeeded in his urgent importunity when he had introduced Selena to Mrs. Stanmore he hastened to accompany Mr. Miltern in his own boat in search of Dallamore.

Selena grateful for the kindness with which Mrs. Stanmore received her exerted herself to revive the spirits which her present situation had so much damped. At her age the elastic mind naturally bounds from its sorrows and it even requires a kind of voluntary effort of reflection to dwell continually upon any misfortune however deeply it may be felt. Selena for a time forgot her anxiety and her fears while she was charmed with her hostess tho' her manners, devoid of all refinements except those which natural sweetness and good nature bestow, were unlike any she had ever before met with, and even her dress simple as it was yet wore an air of singularity which at first evidently struck Selena and still more Dallamore.

Nor was the young Edwin less the object of their surprise and admiration. He was indeed not handsome and as may be supposed he was entirely destitute of all that is called an air of fashion. Yet his figure was fine, and there was an affectionate gentleness in his address, a look of wild animation in his large dark eyes that irresistibly captivated attention, and his manners tho' far from those of fashion were yet still more removed from all vulgarity.

Mr. Stanmore was the only part of the family that in the least resembled other people, and even he had acquired from studious retirement a manner of expressing himself which Dallamore called extreme pedantry but which had a novel grace that charmed Selena and her brother.

Even the old servants partook of the peculiar air, which the valley seemed to inspire; and tho' the guests were waited upon with officious and anxious care, yet they could not refrain from some surprise at the familiar simplicity with which their attendants would sometimes intrude their observations.

"The Lord has eat nothing scarce I think," whispered the butler to Mrs. Stanmore, when with grief he beheld Dallamore send away almost untouched the plate of excellent trout his own happy morning had been employed in providing.

"Perhaps," he again observed, "he might prefer a nice slice of cold beef," pointing at the same time to the side table which he had covered with a profusion of good things with which his mistress had not suffered him to crowd their dinner. Mrs. Stanmore smiling looked at Dallamore to whom this invitation had been made sufficiently audible, and who as usual accepted it with a bow. When Selena called for a glass of water David softly approached her ear and humbly recommended the flavour of his cyder and Mrs. Stanmore in a whisper cautioned her not to hurt him by a refusal. Robert also shared his attentive solicitude, but the habitual haughty gloom which had settled upon the features of Mr. Miltern appeared to discourage his officious watchfulness.

When dinner was over Dallamore accustomed to enjoy himself at perfect ease looked in some measure annoyed when instead of seeing the ladies withdraw, he beheld Mr. Stanmore himself lead the way to the drawing room. A table was there spread with wines, confectionary and a variety of the finest fruit then in season, in the large wyat window[105] which admitted the entrance of a profusion of roses and honeysuckles, and which opened upon the lawn of the greenest velvet, bounded with the little amphitheatre of wood overtopped by the blue pointed hills. Dallamore soon consoled himself here for the unexpected disturbance by solacing himself with the excellent wine which he drank almost stretched with Roman luxury upon the softest sopha which had been wheeled round to the well spread table. Coffy was after a short time brought in, and Mrs. Stanmore was then called upon to amuse her guests by her husband after he had enquired whether they were fond of musick. Her voice was not strong nor her execution astonishing, but it spoke to the heart and Selena and Dallamore both enchanted by the simplicity and peculiarity of the composition with one voice demanded the author.

"It is Edwin's," cried the delighted Mother. "But you shall hear himself. Are you ready my Son?"

Edwin who had felt unusual gratification at Selena's praises flew with alacrity to comply with her desire before she had quite uttered the entreaty which enforced the request of his mother—and at once delight and wonder suspended every thought but those which his voice and manner excited in the bosom of Selena as well as that of the no less fascinated Dallamore. He had indeed heard the rapidity of execution and these supernatural exertions which astonished a crowded and applauding theatre, he had been enchanted by the grace and melody of Selena's more touching musick, but never had he before heard such "wood-notes wild,"[106] such simple pathos, such nature-taught genius, where the sound which captivated the ear seemed but created to convey the sense to the heart. Edwin's musick was indeed a musick of his own—"Il cantar che nell'anima si senti"[107]—and in singing

---

[105] Designer James Wyatt was known for his Wyatt window.

[106] Popular poetic phrase used to describe a wild or natural note.

[107] From Petrarch's *Canzoniere* 213, line 6 ("e 'l cantar che ne l'anima si sente"): "and singing that is heard within the soul" (Mark Musa translation).

his own compositions he gave them a grace which they could never receive from others, let their musical skill be what it would.

He was however anxious to resign his seat to Selena, who grateful for the entertainment she had received modestly and with doubtful diffidence in her turn tried to please. Edwin's unaffected raptures and the energy with which he expressed them, gave her indeed some confusion, but never perhaps was mutual genius admired with so little envy. In compliance with the wishes of their and Edwin's ardent desire of still listening to Selena, and of taking a part with her in singing the evening was totally devoted to musick, and the reading with which it was generally concluded was for this time omitted.

After supper when Mrs. Stanmore arose to lead Selena to her chamber Dallamore stared and Selena herself almost smiled with Robert at the affectionate embrace with which her son bade her good night.

The embrace was however alas no longer given as it had been accustomed with his whole heart. That *heart* warm and romantic, predisposed to receive the first impressions of a sentiment which it longed to feel was already at least in imagination the willing captive of the lovely stranger. The altar had been already raised in the unoccupied temple, and the divinity to whom it was to be consecrated now appeared. Selena was indeed all that his poetical fancy had hitherto painted, every impassioned line which had hitherto kindled his vague and undirected sensibility in his favourite amatory poets now hung upon his lips as he gazed with earnest admiration upon his fair guest, and drank with eagerness love's delicious poison from her eyes. His soul was in a tumult of pleasure. A new existence seemed open to him. Here was a centre towards which all the enthusiastic ardour of his feelings should henceforth for ever be directed. She was at once his Laura, his Cinthia, his Delia, his Saccharissa and his Amoret.[108] The representative of all that hitherto had been celebrated and the theme of every future song; Here was the beautiful, the perfect object where his fancy might hereafter repose with passionate tenderness. No solicitous fears disturbed the delightful sensation with which he hailed the power he had so long been prepared to adore.

His ambition was only to love, and he had not yet asked himself whether there was a possibility that he should be beloved again. In the bright and glowing pictures which imagination gave to him of Love, its pains and its pleasures were both delightful and courted by his heart which longed only to be occupied while

> Flattering Hope
> Formed endless prospects of encreasing bliss
> And still the credulous heart believed them all
> Ev'n more than Love could promise ....[109]

---

[108] The Laura of Petrarch's sonnets; the Cynthia of Propertius's Latin elegies; the Delia of Tibullus's poetry; the Sacharissa of Waller's poetry; and the Amoret of Spenser's *Faerie Queene*.

[109] Masinissa in James Thomson's *The Tragedy of Sophonisba* (1730), 2.2.120–23.

Oh enviable delusion of inexperienced youth! Why must real life at length convince the warmest bosom that the Deity so worshiped, smiling like innocence itself, adorned with beauty and crowned with flowers, is too often pursued by the fiends of remorse, regret, infamy and jealousy—and even at best is but like the graceful and well sculptured column whose aspiring height attracts our eyes amid the gardens of pleasure while within all is empty, dark and hollow?

Early the next morning Edwin rose to gather for the lovely object who had banished his repose the late roses which yet bloomed in their gardens and which he contrived to weave into a garland and hang upon her door accompanied with some verses composed during his sleepless night wherein tho' he did not yet venture to declare his passion he warmly expressed his admiration of her beauty and talents. Anxiously he watched her appearance at the breakfast table which was spread with the profusion usually attendant on a scotch breakfast accompanied with that elegance by which true taste can alone adorn and give a grace to all things.

Selena blushed as she met Edwin, and knew not how to acknowledge the poetical gallantry with which she had been already saluted, but that blush was to the delighted Edwin the most bewitching acknowledgment. He placed himself at her side for Dallamore was not yet risen, to contend with him that seat which perhaps if he had even been there he might have forgotten to occupy.

Mr. Stanmore was anxious to shew to his guests some of the uncommonly beautiful scenery which his neighbourhood afforded, and the gentlemen readily assented to the proposed ride. Mrs. Stanmore's health allowed her not to join in this party, and Selena requested to be permitted to remain with her kind hostess, finding it at some times difficult to support her spirits in the continual presence of strangers who by unceasing civilities called forth her constant attention. Dallamore eagerly pressed her to accompany them and Edwin silently but with far more expressive earnestness joined in his entreaties. However as Mr. Miltern did not oppose her wishes she was not to be prevailed upon and Edwin after a thousand pretended delays was at length forced to quit the drawing room where she and Mrs. Stanmore were seated at work, to obey the summons of his father and attend his guests. In about an hour however the ladies were not a little surprised to behold Edwin return alone.

"What has happened my Son?" cried Mrs. Stanmore half startled at his unexpected entrance.

"Nothing," answered he a little confused as the heightened colour glowed over his ingenious countenance unused to any disguise, "but I stopped to settle my saddle while our party rode on, and not being able to guess which road they have taken I despaired of finding them again and thought I might as well return."

"Lazy boy," said Mrs. Stanmore smiling, "well you shall help me to shew our own Lions at home to Miss Miltern."

Edwin enraptured to be suffered to attend her wandered with them slowly thro' the wild paths in the woods which over hung the lake, or as they were seated in some of their rustic bowers, repeated at Mrs. Stanmore's desire some passages from her favourite poets.

Selena could not be blind to the passionate language which his ardent eyes fixed upon her with continual attention so plainly spoke and she wished by the coldness of her manner to repel the homage which he seemed so earnest to pay; but the modest diffidence with which he addressed her, and the gratitude she felt for the kind hospitality they all received rendered extremely painful and difficult her attempts at ungracious and discouraging reserve. She resolved however as much as possible to avoid all particular conversation with him during their stay at Inverathie, which as he was for ever at her side she indeed found almost impossible.

Mr. Miltern saw with evident displeasure the enthusiastick admiration this young man addressed to Selena and even declared to her his dislike of his folly.

But Dallamore tho' he himself derived pleasure from the singular talents of Edwin could never once imagine him an object possible to excite the slightest emotion of jealousy in his breast not very susceptible of that most cruel torment of delicate minds.

Three days passed in this manner augmented the romantic passion of Edwin to the most extravagant height. Selena had but one method of diverting the conversation which dwelt upon the detail of his feelings, and this was to play herself or request him to entertain her with his own musick. Often would he obey her with reluctance and seat himself at the piano forte when his eyes declared how much he then preferred listening to the melody of her voice which tho' delivering but short and constrained replies was far more enchanting to his ears than his own exquisite harmony.

She had one day interrupted an effusion of tender sentiment to which in spite of her endeavours to divert the discourse he had for sometime obliged her to listen by desiring him thus to play. It was not till he was threatened with her retiring, that he at length complied and then with a deep sigh, after fixing his eyes upon her in silence during a prelude of some length he sung the following stanzas which he had composed but a few hours before, but Selena made no enquiries concerning the author or their object.

> 'Tis thy command, and Edwin shall obey
>   My voice shall sound submissive to thy will,
> Tho' sad my lute and mournful be my lay
>   Yet 'tis enough, thy slave obeys thee still.
>
> Poor as I am, my love how dare I own
>   No boon to offer, but a faithful heart,
> Unblest with fortune's gifts, obscure, unknown
>   With nought my portion but this tuneful art.
>
> Yet pardon sentiments as warm and pure
>   As tho' by royal lips they were profest,
> My thoughts are noble, tho' my state obscure
>   And truth and honour harbour in this breast.

The Muses too have deign'd to touch my tongue
    Early they charmed my simple ravished ear,
Each rising sun a tender hopeless song
    To thee I'll raise if thou will gently hear.

No hope presumptuous shall my bosom fire,
    My sole ambition only thee to please,
A look shall pay the efforts of my lyre,
    A smile the highest boon my soul would seize.

Attendant on thy steps Oh might I guard
    Protect, defend thee with an anxious eye,
No ill should reach thee which this arm could ward
    Thy servant would I live thy champion die.

Art thou for some blest youth reserved by fate
    The nuptial song I'll raise, the garland weave
Nor mix my woes nor envy his high state
    But boast myself thy minstrel and thy slave.[110]

Fig. I.2   Illustration for "The Minstrel" in *Verses Transcribed for H.T.* (Brompton, 1805), MS Acc 5495/C/8/1, National Library of Ireland, Dublin.

---

[110] Tighe titles this lyric "The Minstrel" in *Verses Transcribed for H.T.* (Brompton, 1805).

Chapter XVIII

Strew all your withered flowers, your autumn sweets
By the hot sun ravished of bud and beauty
.... All joy
That leads a virgin to receive her lover
Keep from the place, all fellow maids that bless her.
And blushing would unloose her zone keep from her;
No merry voice, nor jocund sons be heard there; ....
Sing mournfully that sad Epithalamium
I gave thee now, and prithee let thy lute weep.

> Beaumont and Fletcher[111]

Selena beheld the day arrive which was to decide her fate with an agitation which she found it impossible to disguise from the observant eye of Edwin. But anxious as she herself was for the important letter she felt some surprise that her father should think it necessary to go himself with Dallamore so far, and wondered they did not entrust Le Roi with the commission.

But independant of his design of keeping Dallamore in constant employment Mr. Miltern had other reasons for wishing to be himself the express to Carlisle. He had some preparatory steps to take on their way from thence back to Inverathie which he wished not to declare to Selena but which would expedite the business which alone brought him to the frontiers of Scotland. *He* indeed was perfectly free from any of those disquieting uncertainties which tormented Selena with respect to an answer which he had already forged to a letter which he had taken care should never reach her Mother—he possessed the dangerous art of imitating the characters of hands, and with that of his wife he was so familiar as to leave him no doubt of success with the unsuspicious Selena. He was perfectly at ease as to future consequences, and hoped to influence his wife to silence which she might herself think most prudent when once the business was irrevocably decided.

Dallamore who never could conceal the subject which engrossed his present fancy had let fall many expressions in spite of Mr. Miltern's cautions which had pretty plainly declared the object of their journey to Scotland.

But Edwin tho' he could not avoid seeing what were the expectations of Dallamore, was yet willing to flatter himself that they were not justly founded, or at least that there could be no decided plan formed for an immediate union, the probability of which their delay at Inverathie appeared so strongly to contradict.

But when on Friday morning Dallamore expressed his anxious wishes that they might find at Carlisle the letter which he declared they went purposely to seek, and when Edwin saw at the mention of this expected letter the blood forsake

---

[111] Charino in Beaumont and Fletcher's *The Custom of the Country* (1647), 1.2.1–12. Tighe omits lines 3–4 ("Thus round about her Bride-bed, hang those blacks there / The emblemes of her honour lost; all joy"), slightly changes line 8 ("No merry noise nor lusty songs be heard here"), and omits lines 9–10 ("Nor full cups crown'd with wine make the rooms giddy; / This is no masque of mirth, but murdered honour").

Selena's cheeks and her expressive countenance betray such extreme emotion, all the fairy-bowers which fancy had so lately reared for love appeared suddenly blasted, and doubtful solicitude, and jealous suspicion the bitter attendants of the divinity[112] beautiful only in infancy, and therefore in infancy only represented began to torture his bosom.

Mr. Miltern not chusing to leave him the whole morning to entertain Selena wished Robert not to accompany them to Carlisle but rather to engage Edwin in some excursion in their neighbourhood—but the evident depression which seemed to overwhelm those spirits which so lately appeared all life and animation discouraged Robert from making any proposal which politeness to his guest might have prevented Edwin from declining however disagreeable to himself. He therefore mentioned his intentions of taking Le Roi with him on a fishing party and Edwin entrusting them to the charge of David who was a well practised sailor felt relieved when he saw him depart, that he might yield himself up without constraint to the melancholy which now rendered solitude more than ever delightful to him; for solitude was all he even hoped for on this morning. Selena had retired immediately after breakfast, having pleaded an head-ach to Mrs. Stanmore which Edwin saw was intended as an apology for not again returning.

From the wood which fronted the house he watched her windows and the little smoke which he knew proceeded from the chimney of her room, meditated on the graces of her figure and still more bewitching graces of her mind, and recollected with careful fondness her most trifling observations and her most casual movements—looking forward with terror to the moment which must deprive him of the possibility of indeed beholding with his eyes charms for ever pictured on his heart—while he regretted that even of those few precious hours which yet remained of her residence at Inverathie her coldness should thus exclude him from her presence.

Stung by the impatience which this last idea excited, he returned to the drawing room and taking from thence the Estelle of Florian[113] which he had heard her say she had not yet read he ventured to knock gently at her door.

But when upon her opening it he perceived she had been in tears his courage failed him completely, and forgetful of his pretended business he gazed on her in silence with anxious and tender earnestness. This gave place however to his confusion when he observed that she stood in some surprise and perplexity awaiting the explanation of his unexpected visit.

---

[112] "Mansueto Fanciullo, e fiero reglio—Petrarca" (Tighe's note). From Petrarch's *Trionfo d'Amore* (c. 1351), line 79, which describes Eros as gentle in youth and fierce as he grows old.

[113] Jean-Pierre Claris de Florian's *Estelle et Némorin* (1787), a French pastoral novel in which the shepherd Némorin falls in love with Estelle, who returns his love but promises to marry Méril after he rescues her father but is free to marry Némorin when Méril heroically sacrifices himself.

"Can you forgive my intrusion?" said he at length, "I wished to steal upon your solitude not myself, my presumption aspired not so high but a favourite little work, which I had hoped might have amused your fancy—but alas, I fear more interesting subjects engross your mind, and I have no right …. I must not dare I know to ask a participation …. pardon my impertinence …. deeply indeed must I feel all the concerns you."

Selena pitied his embarrassment and forcing a smile extended her hand for the book, saying if her head would allow her she would look over it, before dinner. Seeing that he still waited, his eyes yet fixed upon her without retiring one step from the door she asked was Mrs. Stanmore below, to which he eagerly replied in the affirmative adding half timidly that it would delight his Mother if she would allow him to read to them in the drawing room, a part of the little story he had now brought for perusal.

Reluctant as Selena was to comply she yet hardly knew how to refuse and returning to him the book promised to follow him down in a few minutes. Indeed having nothing now to do but submit, important and critical as was this day to the whole of her future life, she thought it most prudent as far as depended upon herself to banish the reflections which could only agitate her mind and make her less able to receive the dreaded tidings should they be such as might realize her fears, tho' she could scarce persuade herself to believe the possibility that her mother should indeed require from her such a sacrifice at once of her feelings and her judgment.

Taking therefore the little sketch which she had made on the preceeding day of part of Inverathie and its beautiful lake she prepared to finish it, while Edwin enchanted with her compliance, and the liberty of beholding her, forgot his fears and his sorrows and with his own peculiar silver-toned accents soon irresistibly captivated the attention of Selena and his delighted mother, while he read the simple and pathetic tale he had recommended to their admiration.

Mr. Stanmore who had been absent during the morning upon some business, joined them with Robert returned from his fishing expedition, at their accustomed usual early dinner hour, after which they strolled together to the edge of the lake whose gently ripling waves then reflected in silver streaks the pure light of the autumnal moon, till the heavy evening dews warned them to return to Mrs. Stanmore and the cheerful drawing room, thro' the windows of which the candles and a bright wood fire already courted their approach.

Selena unequal to the task of exerting herself declined joining in their concert, and was listning to the soothing harmony of Edwin's compositions executed by himself and his Mother when with a palpitating heart she distinguished the sound of voices in the hall which announced the arrival of Lord Dallamore and Mr. Miltern. During a few moments general conversation Selena waited in breathless suspense her eye intently fixed upon those of her father as if she expected in them to read her fate. Lord Dallamore then approached her in a fit of sportive gallantry such as sometimes used suddenly to seize upon him and taking the letter from his bosom presented it to her heedless of observation upon one knee.

"See Selena," cried he, "where I have carried it all the way and my heart has felt so light while it was there, that I am certain it contains good news. Come do open it and let us know our fate."

Selena covered with blushes, and trembling with emotion arose, but was scarcely able to move towards the door; whither Edwin little less affected than herself pursued her with sad and eager eyes.

Dallamore finding it impossible to detain her entreated Mr. Miltern to follow, he however with some difficulty at last succeeded in changing the discourse, but as Selena after a considerable time did not return her father at length left the drawing room and knocking at her door Selena flew to open it, exclaiming, "Oh Sir! let us hasten, do with me as you please but let us not lose a moment or I never shall again behold my Mother!"

Her sobs prevented her from uttering another word and having put the letter covered with her tears into his hands, she again sunk upon the floor and laid her weeping face upon the bed. The letter which had filled her with such affliction and alarm contained but the following words.

> "I accept your obedience and wish only to live till I may know it is completed. Hasten my beloved children and receive the blessing and last embrace of your expiring Mother."

Mr. Miltern having left orders at the post town of Hillbarton that his letters should be forwarded to Carlisle on his arrival there that day had really found the last sentence of this letter written with apparent extreme difficulty to Selena by her Mother who felt herself at the point of death. He was at first it is true seized with a sudden horror at the intelligence and the conviction of his own treacherous conduct, yet after the shock had subsided and conscience was once more smothered he determined not to lose this critical and decisive moment but profit by the opportunity thus unexpectedly offered of hastening the business he so much desired.

Nay such monsters does guilt make of those who surrender themselves to its tyranny that he even congratulated himself upon the probability of the death of this most amiable and estimable mother of his family since by that he might purchase the security that his base deception should never be detected.

He now endeavoured to comfort Selena, and inspire her with hope that her mother's apprehensions exaggerated her illness, and her despairing heart catching at the faint ray of consolation uttered the most fervent prayers, for the restoration of her beloved parent, or at least that she might once again receive her blessing. With the most eager impatience she urged her father to set out on their return, and made no opposition nor reply except her tears, as he informed her that he had already prepared all things at a neighbouring village so that without delay the nuptials might be solemnized before their return to Carlisle. He would have endeavoured then to sooth her anguish but she so earnestly entreated him to lose no time in ordering the horses that he left her promising instantly to dispatch a messenger to the next town there being none to be obtained in the village of Inverathie.

Before he gave these orders he communicated to Dallamore and the hospitable family the alarming account which had so terrified Selena and sent the afflicted Robert to offer her some consolation or rather to weep with her. They neither of them undressed or took any repose during the night—but Mrs. Stanmore with kind attention had prevailed upon Selena to swallow some cordial refreshment without which nature would have sunk exhausted with weakness and sorrow. Poor Edwin who had also kept a sad vigil, expected as they did with anxiety the arrival of the horses—but the rest of the family at Mr. Miltern's entreaty at midnight took leave of him and Lord Dallamore—their other two guests being then unable to thank them for their hospitable kindness. Mr. Miltern himself also followed Dallamore's example and lay down having desired Robert to call them when every thing was ready for their setting out.

The morning was just dawning when the sorrowful Edwin pressed the cold hand of Selena as he handed her to the chaise who unable to speak could not refuse his sympathising sadness this small mark of gratitude, or withdraw it with any expression of displeasure when she perceived it moistened by his tears as he held it to his lips. For tho' at another time she would have thought it right to repress by every appearance of coldness the testimonies of a sentiment which she did not and circumstanced as she was ought not to return yet when the heart is softened by the pressure of affliction it receives with the weakness of a child every soothing appearance of tenderness and compassionate affection.

One idea however consoled the melancholy Edwin. He knew not the profound sorrow in which he saw the object of his fondness suddenly plunged instead of retarding, actually precipitated that union which he could not endure to think should really take place tho' he at the same time confessed to himself that his passion was hopeless. He knew not that in less than two hours the lovely weeping victim upon whom he now gazed with passionate regret should pass the most solemn vows of fidelity to another, and that but six miles should separate him from the spot where she should offer those reluctant vows to Heaven. Dallamore and Robert accompanied her in the chaise, but they observed her ceaseless tears in silence nor did either of them attempt vainly to afford her consolation.

Dallamore unaffectedly distressed by the deep affliction in which he beheld one whom he really loved felt besides much discomposed at this interruption to all cheerfulness and gaiety in those whose society he was now compelled to share. It had ever been his practice to fly from all scenes of sadness, not from want of a good natured desire to relieve distress but from his fixed dislike of all trouble to himself. Here there was however nothing for him to do, neither was there a possibility for him to escape.

Mr. Miltern had arranged all things and with little more exertion on his part than on that of the suffering Selena the mutual vows were given the force and consequences of which were but half felt even by her so completely and sadly was her heart engrossed by the danger which threatened her most beloved parent.

Robert was himself nearly as much affected by the situation in which they stood. He trembled for his mother so tenderly loved and he saw his dear his interesting sister while yet almost in the years of childhood hurried against her inclination into a union with a character which even seen with a partial eye as he had been ever disposed to regard it was not such as to ensure happiness or to be relied on for constancy. He was therefore but little able to supply comfort, or to amuse and relieve Dallamore, but as they were borne rapidly along he held his arm around her waist and as she sobbed upon his bosom was not ashamed to mingle his tears with hers.

Poor Dallamore who had pictured to his fancy in the trip to Scotland a far different image of a happy bride in the gay and animated Selena, felt his own spirits unusually low, and on their arrival to Carlisle about noon suffered her without opposition to retire to her apartment in order as she said to obtain a little rest while Mr. Miltern transacted some business which he said must detain him there about an hour.

Left to himself for Mr. Miltern having now gained his point no longer thought it necessary continually to watch his movements and provide him with entertainment Lord Dallamore began to reflect what he was now to do. To accompany his weeping bride to the house of mourning and the bed of death was not a very gay prospect and he was obliged to have recourse to his usual amusement of whistling to divert the chagrin which began to creep over his mind. He indeed persuaded himself that he was only grieving for Selena's distress but in fact it was not the distress that affected him but the dull melancholy which it had thrown over their party.

While he stood at the window thus employed he was not a little surprised to see his father walk past accompanied by Richmond with whom he appeared in deep conversation. Without any one idea but that of astonishment at such an unexpected meeting he hastily threw up the sash and bursting into a loud laugh as they turned round starting in almost equal surprise at the sound of his voice he exclaimed—

"Well d--m me if this is not comical! What the devil sir brought you to Carlisle?"

"What did not you get my letter then?" said Lord Mount Villars gravely.

"Letter no, what letter?"

"I wrote to request if you were not better engaged that you would meet me at Lord Glenmere's who has at present with him a large grousing party ready to proceed with him to the highlands. I have particular business in the north of Ireland and am now on my way to Port Patrick but promised to spend a day or two with the party at Glanmure. I was in hopes you were here with the same intention."

Dallamore had suffered him to proceed so far without interruption feeling himself unprepared for an answer and revolving in his mind the pleasures of the party at Glanmure and the difficulties which must now attend his joining it.

At last looking at Richmond he said in a careless voice, "Are you going to Ireland too?"

"No but I overtook Lord Mount Villars as I was on my way to Glanmure and now we can all go there together. Never was there any thing so lucky. We might have been here twenty times and not met if Lord Mount Villars had not persuaded me to walk out while they were fixing a new check brace to look at that cathedral.

I am sure I might have been here all my life passing thro' Carlisle as I have already done every grousing season and never thought of going to see an old church before. But come Dallamore have you breakfasted; for my part I cannot wait any longer …."

"Breakfasted! Good Lord I have been up since before it was light."

"Why how far have you come today?" said Lord Mount Villars eagerly.

"Oh I have come a good way, and done a good deal of business," answered Dallamore smiling and nodding significantly.

Richmond and Lord Mount Villars looked at each other with evident marks of consternation, but Dallamore who was not much given to the science of Physiognomy getting out of the window to join them Richmond took his arm and again proposed to Lord Mount Villars that they should return to their inn to breakfast.

Dallamore asked a thousand questions with respect to the party at Glanmure and Richmond taking it for granted that he was resolved to accompany them exerted all his eloquence to represent it in the most delightful colours, promising and expatiating upon a thousand agrémens[114] his knowledge of which was indeed completely extempory; the truth of his representations being at all times a matter of the most perfect indifference to Richmond.

Lord Mount Villars in the mean time repeatedly enquired from whence Dallamore came and who accompanied him, circumstances which Richmond without directly interrogating him determined to discover.

But Dallamore for once in his life had a secret which he was in some degree on his guard to preserve from a mixture of shame and apprehension, from the expected ridicule of Richmond and reproaches of his father. He therefore for the present baffled their anxious curiosity and the doubt yet remained important as was the question whether Dallamore and his companions were on their road to Scotland or on their return from thence.

Of his purposed journey they had had certain intelligence which had indeed been the real motive of their present expedition.

While they were now contriving means to detain him till they were ready to resume their journey which some trifling repairs necessary to Lord Mount Villars's carriage had delayed Selena was impatiently waiting his return that they also might proceed upon that journey she was to anxious to pursue.

When in compliance with her entreaties her father had ordered the horses and still Dallamore was no where to be found Robert at her request went in search of him and having been directed by the waiter to the other inn which he told him he had seen Lord Dallamore enter with two gentlemen, unwilling to intrude upon strangers he waited at the door while he sent in a message desiring to speak with him.

Dallamore immediately came out and upon seeing Robert exclaimed, "I will bet you a hundred guineas you can not guess who is here."

---

[114] Agrémens: ornaments or grace notes (French).

"I really have not the least idea, but are you ready? The horses are to the carriage and poor Selena is very impatient."

"Oh yes I am ready, but what the plague shall I say to my father?"

"Your father! You do not surely mean that Lord Mount Villars is here?"

"Yes do not I tell you so? and Richmond too."

"And have you told them of your marriage?"

"Oh not a word they would make such a cursed uproar, but what I shall do I cannot imagine for they are tormenting me to go with them to Lord Glenmere's."

"What stay does Lord Mount Villars make there?"

"Oh only a day or two, had I best go do you think?"

Extremely surprised at this question Robert was for a moment silent but upon reflection dreading the furious and enflamed spirits with whom they were connected, and who upon this sudden important discovery would no doubt burst forth with a mutual bitterness of hatred and rage which might be fatal in its effects and must be peculiarly distressing to Selena in her present situation, he thought it best not to oppose his separating from them for a few days and therefore upon Dallamore again repeating his question what he should do he said, "perhaps you had better comply with your father's wishes and you may thus find a favourable opportunity of declaring the step which you have just taken, which had certainly better not be made known while his brother whom he has not met for so many years is on the spot. You can follow us to Miltern Abbey as soon as possible and I hope poor Selena's spirits will then be better suited to her bridal state, poor thing!"

"Yes but I am afraid she will think it very odd," said Dallamore after a thoughtful pause of some length.

"No," replied Robert, "I will explain the circumstances to her and her mind is at present so much engrossed by uneasiness on my Mother's account that I am sure she will feel relieved that she has not the new duties of a wife as yet to agitate still more her mind—but how soon shall I tell her that we may expect you."

"Oh in a week at farthest. But I will go ask her advice and bid her farewell at all events."

Robert anxious to keep secret from his father the intelligence of the arrival of Lord Mount Villars strongly advised him against this farewel—and hearing Richmond come out of the parlour hastily shook hands with Dallamore and told him he would undertake to make his apology to Selena and that he hoped they should meet in a few days under gayer auspices than they now parted.

Dallamore bad him farewel and dismissing from his mind his lovely bride and her dying mother set off in a few minutes with a light heart to join the gay assembly he was now prepared to expect at Glanmure.

Chapter XIX

Oh let me hunt my traveled thoughts again
Range the wild waste of desolate despair!
Start any hope—alas I lose myself
'Tis' pathless dark and barren all to me.
Thou art my only guide, my light of life
And thou art leaving me!—send out thy beams
Upon the wing—let 'em fly all around
Discover every way is there a dawn
A glimmering of comfort?

Southerne[115]

Having thus parted from Dallamore Robert hurried back and telling his father that Dallamore had met some friends who detained him for a day or two, he deferred a farther explanation till he was tete-a-tete with Selena. She was indeed as he had foretold relieved by his absence and expressed her satisfaction at Robert's prudent conduct in such warm terms as while it gratified him with the confirmation of his judgment that he had acted right in rather encouraging Dallamore in the plan which he himself appeared desirous to adopt yet too surely convinced him that poor Selena looked not for support or consolation from the being she was in future to consider as her protector and her dearest friend.

Strange as Dallamore's conduct appeared to Mr. Miltern, his mind was yet far more occupied by the malicious triumph with which he now longed to communicate the intelligence to his brother that he hoped should prove to him so displeasing. Even the thoughts of his dying wife were banished by these exulting meditations. Had he entertained the smallest idea of Lord Mount Villars being at that moment within his reach no power on earth should have refrained him from finding out his retreat, bursting into his presence and proclaiming the event by which he was so impatient to mortify his pride and resentment. Dreadful indeed might have been the effect of such an interview and in all the future occurrences of Selena's life she yet remembered with gratitude towards Heaven and her brother that she had been saved the probable horrors attendant on such a meeting.

With the utmost unwillingness to make any stop for refreshment or repose she now urged their speed and the evening of the third day terminated her sad and fatiguing journey. As they entered the thick woods which surrounded the beloved abode her heart fainted lest the home she had so earnestly desired to reach, instead of the welcome of tenderness and the smile of delighted affection she had so long looked forward to receive on the happy hour of return should now yield her nothing but despair and the confirmation of all her fears.

Unable to speak and even breathing with difficulty extreme agitation restrained her tears and the terror and anguish which could find no utterance oppressed her bosom and almost smothered her by their ineffectual struggles.

---

[115] Oroonoko in Thomas Southerne's *Oroonoko: A Tragedy* (1696), 5.5.158–66.

But when amid the gloom the lights of the dear mansion first appeared to her view fearfully and eagerly she stretched her eyes towards the windows of her mother's apartment and beholding them illuminated with the light from within, as she clasped the arm of her brother with a trembling and convulsive grasp she exclaimed, "She lives my Robert! she lives—and I shall yet embrace her! I shall hear her dear voice Oh God, Oh God accept my gratitude and disappoint not my hopes!"—as she said this she sunk upon her knees and her tears which now streamed in rivers from her eyes relieved the oppression of her heart.

The servants who crowded to the door on the sound of the carriage bore however on their countenances such traces of melancholy that Robert who had anxiously looked around as he lifted into the hall the fainting Selena almost trembled to break the silence; till Wilson Mrs. Miltern's maid rushing in exclaimed as she flew to Selena, "God be praised you are come! My Mistress will I am sure revive when she hears Miss Miltern is at last arrived."

She was then hastily returning but Selena suddenly restored to strength and hope stopped her to prevent the sudden intelligence which might give her mother too much emotion.

Mean while the physician who had heard the disturbance occasioned by their arrival was already on the stairs and positively forbad her to enter till he had himself prepared his patient for seeing the daughter for whom she had incessantly and anxiously enquired.

While Selena stood impatiently at the door asking in whispers from Wilson every fearful question the answers to which struck with renewed terror on her heart Mr. Miltern approached telling her that he wished to say a few words in private.

Wilson observing that she seemed unwilling to quit her station near the door withdrew and her father then said with some hesitation, "Selena I wish just to caution you not to disturb or agitate your mother in her present dangerous situation by alluding to your marriage. The Doctor insists upon her being kept perfectly quiet, and she will not begin of herself a conversation which must be attended with so much emotion to one of her weak nerves."

Selena bathed in tears readily promised obedience, and continued with anxious ear to watch every stir in her mother's apartment 'till Doctor Lambert gave her at length the liberty she so eagerly desired with a caution to restrain as much as possible her feelings.

The inflamation that had seized on her lungs with such alarming symptoms had indeed subsided but had left her so much exhausted that a relapse which the physician had apprehended as too probable would be attended with the utmost danger.

Such indeed was her weakness that notwithstanding every preparatory caution upon Selena's approach to embrace her mother she fainted in her arms.

But when recovered from this first emotion and that free from present suffering she lay peacefully with her hand held in those of her most beloved child who kneeling by the side of her bed offered up silent prayers for her restoration, when she was satisfied that she should be able to give her an expiring blessing, nature seemed in some degree to revive and slowly and gradually she appeared to gain strength.

Observing Selena's paleness and altered looks she insisted upon her retiring at midnight and upon Dr. Lambert's assurances that a material change for the better had taken place in his patient, Selena with a grateful heart poured forth her thanksgivings to Heaven and enjoyed a few hours repose such as she had not tasted since she quitted Inverathie.

In a few days Mrs. Miltern was so far recovered as to be able to enjoy the conversation of her children and leave her bed for some hours, but alas tho' the shattered building had been propped up for a while the foundations were undermined and Dr. Lambert's anxious countenance too plainly shewed his apprehensions of danger were not yet removed. The cruel and wasting symptoms of a rapid consumption indeed were soon but too visible, and Selena in silent despair watched the progress of the hopeless malady with the same sensations as the wretch escaped from shipwreck to some rocks beholds the resistless tide bring every wave nearer and nearer till the last eminence to which he has vainly retreated washed by its gradual progress betrays him to inevitable fate.

Mrs. Miltern herself read in the countenances of her family and that of the valuable physician who had so long been attached to her as a friend the certainty of her danger which it is the treacherous nature of that disorder to conceal from the patient.

For herself resigned to the will of Heaven and humbly confident in its mercy she felt no regret to leave a world from whose pleasures she had been weaned by the harsh unkindness of the husband of her choice. But to quit her daughters at an age which still asked so much from the watchful eye of a mother, and above all her darling Selena whose gentle and affectionate heart seemed to lean upon her for support thro' a hard world where all its happiness must consist in the fondness of attachment, to quit Selena whose anguish she now beheld with a pang which made her almost wish herself less dear to her beloved child, this was indeed the bitterness of death, and to spare those sorrows she would have even prayed for life had not her faith and resignation rose superior to every earthly care.

Warmly and tenderly she recommended her girls to the protection of their brother who as well as Selena in the midst of his affliction would sometimes wonder at the total silence preserved by Mr. Miltern with respect to Dallamore. This circumstance and Mr. Miltern's repeated cautions to them both to refrain from the subject on the pretence of its being too agitating for their mother yet to bear inspired them both with some vague and terrible suspicions which they felt too injurious to their father's honour to dare to confess to each other or even indeed to themselves.

One day while the family were at dinner and that Selena seated on a little stool beside her mother leaning her face upon the bed held with tenacious fondness that hand which she every moment felt would soon be snatched from her affectionate grasp, while the darkness of the chamber allowed her to indulge the tears which she continually sought to conceal from the anxious eye that gazed upon her with pitying sadness and dying tenderness, Mrs. Miltern having desired the nurse not to interrupt them till she should ring the bell began to urge the duty of resignation and to promise its never failing consolations to her afflicted child, and having besought her tho' life to guard against the dangers of listning with weakness to the dictates of what is called a warm sensibility, which but too often leads to the indulgence of those tormenting and violent passions that destroy the peace of life, smothering by the rankest weeds the simple and delicate plant of virtue in that unhappy breast which cherishes at first their seeds. She then after a short pause, added these important words, without being able to conceive the cruel effect which they should produce on the astonished and now too late undeceived victim of deceit and treachery to whom they were addressed.

"There is one thing my Selena which has dwelt so much upon my mind that tho' I trust my caution is superfluous, I will relieve my solicitude by communicating it to you now that I have this opportunity of speaking to you without reserve. You have heard the unfortunate resentment your father still entertains toward his brother. Some suspicions I trust without foundation have of late crossed my mind that he would not be sorry that your cousin Lord Dallamore should look upon you with a partial eye—and I will confess to you I have imagined that he only desired this that he might have an opportunity of proudly and contemptuously refusing the alliance. Let me entreat you my child never to give the slightest encouragement, or what could ever be construed into the most distant degree of approbation of such a proposal, should chance again throw in your way this young man. I know and am persuaded that eternal discord and misery in some shape or other must be the consequence of your forming such a connexion could it ever be completed, but I have rather dreaded lest my Selena should suffer her affections to be engaged where the power of both parents will I am assured be exerted against a union. Satisfy my beloved girl my perhaps foolish anxiety. Say you do not wish for it, and that it will never be sought by you. Speak my child and I shall die in peace."

The emotions of Selena from the commencement of this speech delivered in the slow accents of a voice weakened already by the hand of death may be better imagined than expressed—in silent horror at her own ruined happiness and her father's guilt she remained after its conclusion unable to answer as her mother expected and unknowing what she ought to say. To shock her last expiring moments by the development of so base so cruel a treachery in the father of her children, the object of her youthful love and her apparent continued affection and esteem, to declare to her, that her name, her influence had been employed to consign her child thus early to irretrievable misery, was what the tender prudence, the calm courage of Selena suddenly and firmly rejected—but to be constrained now for the first time in her existence to use duplicity to the adored parent to whose supposed will she had sacrificed her own judgment and even all her bright prospects of earthly felicity was a task the most difficult, a misery the most painful.

Alarmed by her silence Mrs. Miltern bursting into tears after a long pause exclaimed, "Oh Selena! I see I am too late, you have fallen into the snare I dreaded, you have already given your young and inexperienced heart, and much I fear your cousin will not know its value. Oh why was I persuaded to part with thee my dearest child!"

"Oh no my Mother," cried Selena, roused by her grief, "solemnly I assure you that my silence proceeded not from the cause which you suppose, Lord Dallamore never, never could be my choice, and from my soul could I wish him the husband of another. Believe me when I declare that the idea of a union with him would afford me the utmost misery—a misery which nothing but the loss of you can equal to my imagination. Satisfy yourself then my dearest Mother and let us talk of him no more."

"Enough my child, I know your sincerity, I perceive something has past— you have been ordered secrecy—but I see your heart is not engaged, and I am contented, you have resolution, you will remember your mother and never be Lord Dallamore's."

Selena's tears fell plenteously over the hand which she pressed to her lips in silent agony—and her Mother continued, "May Heaven give to you my Selena such a husband as in my happiest hours of any castle building I have so much delighted to create for her—for my Selena's loving heart can only find its happiness in well placed affection—young and lovely as herself with a sensibility directed by reason, and firmness softened by tenderness, possessed of every virtue and a heart as amiable as affectionate as her own—and may the performance of your loving happy duties be rewarded with such children as mine!" Poor Selena agitated by contending sorrows which she dared not reveal, wished that in the embrace by which her exhausted mother now concluded her parting address they might together quit a world which she shuddering looked upon with despair and abhorrence—and the moment she was at liberty for the first time since her return to Miltern Abbey voluntarily quitted her Mother's apartment.

Having gained her own chamber she sunk on the floor in an agony of sorrow at this conviction of the treachery by which she was devoted to misery for life.

"Oh stay my Mother!" she cried clasping her hands in the deepest anguish; "leave me not quite forlorn, take with thee thy wretched child from the sorrows into which my cruel father has plunged me."

After a few moments however the remembrance of her Mother's exhortations to consider with resignation the will of Heaven calmed her mind. Her lot had not been her own chusing and might be less terrible than she now imagined. Tho' that happiness of fond and mutual affection so often supplicated for her by her Mother never could be hers yet in the performance of her duty tranquility might be the reward of her peaceful days. All future evils appeared at present light compared with that she was too sure must unavoidably await her in the loss of her Mother. Her filial piety even now when she most keenly felt the injury that she had suffered from her father's guilty conduct determined her to conceal even from Robert the discovery she had made. She considered it almost as a duty to banish from her own mind reflections on a conduct she could not help seeing with detestation and contempt, and resolving that he himself should never blush in the eye of his daughter at the conviction of his baseness she made a vow to bury in silence the causes which had precipitated her marriage and trusted that Heaven would in time reconcile her mind to the fate which was now irrevocable.

With undivided sadness of attention she therefore (after the first tumults of her mind had subsided) centered all her anxieties and regrets in the situation of her Mother—watching as a precious relick every expression that fell from her lips,

> that sadly dear
> Her soul should keep or utter with a tear[116]

and never even for a moment quitting her presence without the utmost reluctance.

Dallamore in the mean time made not his appearance, without acquainting his father that Lord Mount Villars had been actually at Carlisle at the moment they left it Robert had confessed that Mr. Richmond had prevailed upon Dallamore to accompany him to Glanmure in order to meet his father at his express desire.

Mr. Miltern who only waited the hourly expected death of his wife to bestow upon his daughter the title to which she had a right could not restrain his impatience himself to communicate the triumphant intelligence to his brother. He therefore in a day or two after his arrival at Miltern Abbey wrote a letter in the must insulting terms acquainting him with the step which his son had taken and at the same time declaring that he would never by the smallest portion enrich the son of his most detested enemy.

But as at that time Lord Mount Villars was rapidly changing the scene in order to divert the mind of Dallamore and prevent the possibility of his escape, passing with him and a chosen party thro' Scotland and the greatest part of Ireland this letter reached him not till after a considerable time had elapsed in which Mr. Miltern congratulated himself that the silence with which it was received proceeded from the excess of mortified and powerless rage.

Three weeks had now been past by Selena in that state of cruel suspence wherein hope refusing to yield to conviction still clings reluctant to quit the sufferer deprived of every other support, when as she lay one night upon her mother's bed exhausted by the melancholy fatigue of watching her difficult respiration Nature sunk into a kind of slumber which those acquainted with sorrow well know to suspend the faculties without delivering the heart from a heavy consciousness of undefined misery. From this she was however roused by the hand of her mother gently laid upon her shoulder and at the same time she heard her feebly pronounce her name.

Starting and pressing the cold hand to her lips she enquired if she wanted any thing.

"Support me my child till I give you my last embrace, my blessing."

As she spoke these words faintly, she raised herself on her elbow and while Selena bent over her imprinted a dying kiss upon her forehead. The impression was still felt but the lips which bestowed it were for ever immoveable!

End of Volume I

---

[116] Alexander Pope's translation of Homer's *The Illiad* (1715–20), 24:936–7 (from Andromache's lament over Hector's dead body).

Volume II

Chapter I

Ah now for comfort whither shall I go?
No more thy soothing voice my sorrow cheers!
Thy placid eyes with smiles no longer glow
My hopes to cherish and allay my fears!
'Tis meet that I should mourn—flow forth afresh my tears.

Beattie[1]

The fatigue of mind and body with which Selena had now for nearly a month been harassed seemed at once to overpower her at the moment when torn for the last time from the parent whose voice should never again delight her ears, she was laid senseless upon her own bed from whence she was for some days unable to rise.

When the burning fever which had seized upon her had subsided she still remained in a state of such despondent dejection that Dr. Lambert alarmed lest the melancholy which seemed to pray upon her nerves should become a fatal and miserable habit of mind earnestly recommended a change of scene, as soon as she should be able to travel which in her present weakness was impossible.

The first thing which appeared to rouse her from the profound sadness in which she was plunged was a letter from Mrs. Vallard. She started with a sensation of terror as she looked at the cover and perceived herself for the first time addressed by the name of Dallamore. It contained only these lines but the tears which they excited seemed salutary to the oppressed bosom of Selena.

> "My dearest child,
>
> "For such you henceforth are to me: by every tie come to my arms and let us weep together the irreparable loss we have sustained. I would go myself for you and our little Clara, but I am not yet sufficiently recovered the illness which was occasioned by the sad tidings that so severely shocked and afflicted me. Refuse me not the only consolation which I desire and let me here behold the union of my beloved and amiable children, whom I pray no power on earth may in future be able to separate. The happiness of each is indeed necessary to that of their most affectionate Aunt.
>
> Clara Vallard"

With the tenderest persuasions to accept an offer from which he trusted Selena would derive such consolation Robert urged her departure from Miltern Abbey which had now nothing to present to her but scenes which momentarily recalled

---

[1] James Beattie, *The Minstrel* (1771), 2:563–7.

her loss—a loss perhaps the most irreparable and most sensibly felt by a young female endowed with gratitude and sensibility.

What can indeed in any degree offer the disinterested affection, the never ceasing solicitude, [the] partial tenderness of a Mother? The passion of a lover may … alas! must be diminished, the constancy of a husband may fail, the attachment of a friend may be alienated, and the most beloved sister by absence and personal perplexities may be forgotten, but on the love of a mother we rely with confidence for it is unchangeable in its nature and unalterable by any circumstances. Selena had ever been deeply conscious of the magnitude of the blessing which she had enjoyed in such a parent but when lost to her for ever how bitterly did she reproach herself that she had not still more ardently prized the counsels, the friendship which never now could be renewed. She blamed herself that she had not by her sorrow and entreaties prevailed upon her to refuse the reluctant consent which she had so unfortunately given to part with her.

"Oh that I had never left her!" she continually exclaimed with bitter and unavailing regret. "Had I watched her in the first moment of her illness perhaps I might yet have been happy perhaps she might now give me that smile which I would gladly purchase with the remainder of my life."

In the midst of her lamentations the indifference shewn by Dallamore would often add to the melancholy with which she considered her future prospects. But she never spoke of it and Robert, who with anxious surprise watched every post and eagerly started to the window at the sound of every horse that entered the court, was equally silent from the impossibility he felt to offer any excuse and his reluctance to notice the apparent neglect. He was however on this account doubly impatient to take his sisters to Mrs. Vallard. From her letter he thought it was probable she was acquainted with some particulars respecting Dallamore, or at least might be able to inform them where he was to be found.

Selena who could not feel much consoled by the society of her father, tho' she suffered no reproach or disrespectful allusion ever to pass her lips, refused not to comply with the advice of her brother to which Mr. Miltern readily consented. The evening before that day which was fixed for their departure from Miltern Abbey she entered her father's study and perceiving him engaged with his man of business would have retired. He stopped her saying he wished to have some conversation with her adding, "I have now concluded for the present what I had to say to Mr. Edwards," who upon this hint immediately made his bow and quitted the room.

Mr. Miltern then continued, "Sit down Selena, I think it is fair to let you know that I have been making my will, as was necessary on the alteration of my family, and have disinherited you—not as you may well suppose from any displeasure at your conduct; but as considering you happily and greatly established."

Selena was silent and the tears which rushed to her eyes owed not their source to the deprivation of her birthright which he thus announced.

"You know," he proceeded, "that by the settlement made at our marriage £10,000 only was allowed for the provision of younger children and that your

Mother and I had a right to divide or bestow this at our pleasure. I find no will nor any expression of your Mother's wishes as to the sum entrusted to her disposal, I am therefore justified in giving to Clara the whole of a sum scarce worth dividing with the wife of a man the yearly rent of whose independent property far exceeds the whole of the settled portion—and you will I am sure agree to the justice of the determination which I wish to explain as your obedient conduct to me deserves not to be rewarded by any apparent slight."

He paused and Selena perceiving that he expected some reply answered, "I shall never murmur Sir at any determination in favour of my sister and I make no claim upon your partiality by the merit of an obedience which I own I considered not as paid exclusively to your will."

Mr. Miltern raised his eyes with fearful confusion to read in the countenance of his daughter whether this speech was intended to convey a reproach for his discovered duplicity. But he there saw no glow of resentment, no glance of scorn, and on her pale cheek and in her meek eye the expression of fixed sadness alone remained. Mr. Miltern was reassured; for it was not thus he could himself have borne an injury. He was not however totally at his ease with respect to the concealment of his treachery—for Mrs. Vallard alarmed at the report she had heard of Dallamore's conduct since his marriage, and surprised by a letter she had received from Mrs. Miltern on her first illness expressive of her uneasiness lest Selena might be betrayed into a connexion she of all others most deprecated could not without indignation receive from Robert the account of Selena's marriage with the previous circumstances which had induced his sister to consent.

In the first warmth of her displeasure Mrs. Vallard had written herself to Mr. Miltern a few lines sufficiently expressive of her suspicion that he had deceived his daughter. This letter he did not receive till the very day on which Selena was to set out and the perusal of it rendered him peculiarly anxious to prevent her journey to Hillbarton—and having advised her strongly to remain at Miltern Abbey to wait for Dallamore (an advice openly and warmly opposed by Robert, and which his father had indeed no arguments to support), he now positively refused to allow Clara to accompany her sister to Derbyshire.

This refusal as he had hoped shook the resolution of Selena, as she could not bear to add to Clara's grief the loss of her society when it might afford her benefit and consolation.

When Robert provoked at this defeat of the plan he had formed for amusing Selena's mind, and discovering the cause of Dallamore's delay, found his persuasions were in vain he resolved to write to Mrs. Vallard and entrust her with these uneasy suspicions which tormented his mind and thro' her endeavour to obtain some direction where to meet with Dallamore. He was in the mean time restless and agitated and under this restraint could neither bear to converse with Selena nor his father, whose conduct he highly disapproved tho' he was ignorant of the extent of its criminality.

While the gloomy and little social party were assembled at breakfast, of which they partook in a sad silence nearly unbroken except by the questions of Clara which for the most part received only the half whispered replies of her governess; the arrival of the post bag awakened as usual the impatient curiosity of Robert. Snatching it from the servant, he threw with a disappointed air the only letter which it contained across the table to his father who hastily tore it open. The terrible expression of his agitated countenance and the convulsive trembling with which he still held it before his overstrained and immoveable features were observed for a few moments in terrified silence by the shocked spectators. But the horrible appearance of sudden disorder in mind and body increasing every instant all arose in confusion—Robert and Selena enquiring in one breath the nature of his illness while Clara screamed and the governess being the most calm approached to offer him assistance.

Suddenly with frightful violence a torrent of blood burst forth from every feature of his disfigured and convulsed face, and the agonies of death appeared to overtake him as he struggled in the arms of his affrighted children. Dr. Lambert was immediately sent for, but his utmost exertions and skill proved in vain to stop the effusion occasioned by the bursting of a blood vessel and in a few hours this wretched victim of his own indulged and intemperate passions expired in the presence of his children without being able to utter one dying expression of repentance or affection.

When Robert next entered the parlour he perceived upon the floor the letter, the perusal of which to all appearance had caused this fatal accident. He eagerly seized it and seeing it signed Mount Villars impatiently perused its contents which were as follows.

> "Your art is defeated and your malice despised. My son denies the marriage in which you so vainly triumph, and in a few months will prove that when of age he is at liberty to escape from the snares, which fraud baseness and folly may have laid for a minor."

Anxious to meet Dallamore and ascertain the truth of this assertion of Lord Mount Villars Robert impatiently urged Selena to hasten her journey to Hillbarton, which she herself earnestly desired, wishing nothing so much as to quit the scene which in so short a space had witnessed her despair on the loss of the tenderest of parents and her horror at the sudden and dreadful termination to the life of her unhappy father.

At her desire tho' in some degree contrary to the opinion of Robert she still retained her maternal name—and the strictest silence was observed as to the transaction which had authorised her to change it.

As Selena with a sad heart prepared to quit the scene of her happy hours and infantine pleasures, the image of her mother as she had seen her on the morning of her last departure from Miltern Abbey overpowered her with the most tender recollections. The tear with which her parting embrace had been accompanied still seemed to bathe her cheek, and with an emotion of passionate tenderness which she could not resist, she pressed her lips to the step where she had last beheld her stand, while she watched her from the windows of the chaise which conveyed her to Hillbarton. Every spot on the road, which she now remembered at that time to have past in a situation so different gave a new pang to her heart and Robert with inexpressible distress observed that the depression of her spirits appeared encreased by the fatigue of her body.

Mrs. Vallard was visibly shocked at the terrible alteration which sorrow and anxiety had in so short a time made in the faded charms of the so lately blooming Selena, and the first moment that she was able to speak in private to Robert freely expressed her warm disapprobation of the means which Mr. Miltern had made use of to bring about the marriage which she now trembled to think might not be for Selena's happiness.

Nothing could equal the astonishment nay indeed horror of Robert at the conviction of his father's unjustifiable conduct too plainly and certainly established by the sight of the letter from Mrs. Miltern which Mrs. Vallard put into his hands. He expressed his doubts as to Selena's knowledge of it, as she had never hinted to him any such discovery.

Mrs. Vallard rightly suggested that her silence must have proceeded from that filial delicacy which could not bear to reproach a parent with guilt, and could not believe that in her constant attendance upon her dying mother she had not been fully acquainted with all her sentiments.

But hastily reverting to the strange conduct of Dallamore and the letter of Lord Mount Villars, Robert enquired from Mrs. Vallard whether she had heard any circumstances which might confirm or destroy this alarming suspicion occasioned by the assertion of so base and injurious a determination in her nephew.

Mrs. Vallard was extremely shocked at the perusal of the insulting and revengeful epistle—and declared herself unable to account for Dallamore's conduct who was as she had heard actually gone to Ireland with his father accompanied by two or three other idle young men, who finding the season too far advanced for grousing had accepted the invitation of Lord Mount Villars to look for the long neglected partridge and hares for which Mount Villars used to be so famous.

"I have no doubt," said Mrs. Vallard, "that the party was made on purpose to divert Dallamore from fixing his thoughts on poor Selena, and that it has in some degree succeeded I am obliged to own I lament, but I never can believe that he was accessory to the writing of that letter or that he will ever be prevailed upon to act in so cruel so dishonourable a manner. I have already written to him strongly to represent the necessity of his immediate return to England and expressing my hope to see him in a very few days meet and acknowledge at Hillbarton his lovely bride. In the mean time as I think men always do more harm than good by their interference in matters so delicate I would advise you to leave the business entirely to ourselves and do not think of calling Dallamore to account for his father's conduct which I am sure he does not mean should injure Selena to whom I am persuaded he is sincerely attached."

Robert consented to wait for a few days the result of Mrs. Vallard's letter saying that if Dallamore accepted not her invitation he must certainly seek him to have a decided explanation of his intentions. In less than the time he had limited to await his answer Mrs. Vallard received from Dallamore this singular letter.

"Dear Aunt,

"Do not mind what they say, I love Selena better than ever and know very well she is my wife in spite of them, but as I cannot get away just now, it is as well to keep them in good humour and not make a fuss by saying any thing about it—but I long to be at Hillbarton, and as soon as possible will shew all the world that she is Selena Dallamore the only girl I ever loved or ever can love. D--m me if I don't. Tell her not to be melancholy nor angry with me for not writing for I think of her all day and all night—love to Robert.

    Yours &c,
     Dallamore"

Mrs. Vallard entirely satisfied with the declaration contained in this letter endeavoured to persuade Robert that it was every thing he could wish and succeeded in at least making him appear contented to Selena, who in silence accepted the apology from the husband whom she blamed herself for not being more anxious to behold; tho' she had not observed his neglect with indifference.

Robert being in some measure reassured by this letter, and convinced that his active interference was not likely for the present to administer to the happiness of Selena, now left her and Clara to the kind care of Mrs. Vallard, and at the desire of Mr. Turner, a distant relation who had been appointed by Mr. Miltern the guardian of his children he returned to meet him at Miltern Abbey and there examine the will of which Mr. Turner was the executor.

Selena persisted in refusing to be called by Dallamore's name, and said that such evidently appeared to be his own wish, by his desiring that "the affair should not be spoken of, till he might himself shew to the world Selena Dallamore."

Mrs. Vallard tho' she could not entirely approve of this design yet was not insensible to the awkward situation in which Selena must appear as a deserted bride should her marriage be avowed before the return of Dallamore, and she knew too well the characters with whom she had to do not to fear to provoke Lord Mount Villars while Dallamore yet continued under his immediate influence.

It was with surprise and encreased indignation that Mrs. Vallard heard the particulars of Mr. Miltern's will which thus left Selena entirely unprovided should Dallamore's death or renunciation of her prevent her ever enjoying the large possessions of which she might one day be mistress as Countess of Mount Villars. Either of these events were possible tho' she trusted equally improbable to take place. Robert was indeed the most affectionate of brothers, and Mrs. Vallard was resolved (Hillbarton being entirely in her own disposal) that even after her death Selena should never want an asylum. But that Mr. Miltern should thus chuse to leave his injured child dependant and portionless was to Mrs. Vallard incomprehensible.

Chapter II

Yes thou shalt smile again! time always heals
In youth the wounds of sorrow ….
………..Yet shall the glow
Of beauty, health, and hope, by soft degrees
Spread o'er thy breast; disperse these storms of woe,
Wake with sweet pleasure's sense, the wish to please
Till from these eyes the wonted lustres flow
Bright as the sun on calm and crystal seas.

Seward[2]

Immediately upon Selena's arrival Lady Trevallyn broke thro' her general rule and flew with impatience to see and weep with her friend in whose misfortunes she had deeply sympathised, Mrs. Vallard having disguised from her nothing which concerned the young and truly mourning bride. Having obtained permission from Mrs. Vallard to seek her in her own apartment, Selena having already expressed her wish to see again her interesting friend, Lady Trevallyn softly opened the door and much affected by the pale countenance, and the melancholy which was written upon the features of Selena aided by the deep mourning in which she was dressed, she burst into tears the moment she beheld her. Selena's flowed freely as they embraced in silence tho' she had recovered her tranquility before Lady Trevallyn was able to utter a syllable or restrain her tears.

Indeed all reminded her most powerfully of the similar loss which she had herself sustained in circumstances she considered even more afflicting—and while she wept over Selena's situation she once more recalled and lamented with self pity her own sufferings and her own sacrifice. She could not indeed imagine that Selena had equal cause with herself to repine at her lot. The tenderest affections of her heart were not fatally engaged to another; Lord Dallamore young and amiable might still be its sole possessor, and reward it by mutual fidelity. She had a brother dearly and warmly attached to her interest, and a sister of whom she had frequently heard her speak with complacent fondness. The soul of the fond Emily from the first moment of her existence had been centered in two objects—death in depriving her of a mother so beloved had ravished from her one of those beings and from the other fate and her own act had for ever separated her. She no longer resisted the consolation of unbosoming herself without restraint, which she had so long denied to her disposition naturally soft, tender, and open to friendship tho' reserved from timidity and Selena's heart melted by distress, and not selfishly wrapt up in her

---

[2] Anna Seward, "Sonnet, to a Young Lady in Affliction, Who Thought She Should Never More Be Happy; Written on the Sea-shore," *Llangollen Vale, with Other Poems* (1796), lines 1–14. The epigraph omits lines 2–9 ("O! survey / Yon now subsided Deep, thro' night a prey / To warring winds, and to their furious peals / Surging tumultuous.—Yet, as in dismay, / The settling billows tremble—Morning steals / Grey on the rocks; and soon, to pour the day / From the streak'd east, the radiant Orb unveils, / In all his pride of light"), uses "Yet" for "Thus" in line 9, and uses "sweet" for "soft" in line 12.

own concerns found a soothing relief in listning to Lady Trevallyn as she repeated the scenes of hopeless sorrow still impressed upon her mind in characters so lively.

Upon Selena's enquiring for Angela Lady Trevallyn informed her that she had at length obtained her desire and in spite of the reluctance of Mrs. Harley was returned to Islington.

"Alas," cried Selena, "the day may come when poor Angela will bitterly repay by self reproach every pain she has inflicted upon her Mother, unless Heaven shall spare her this most cruel misfortune by not suffering her to survive this indulgent parent."

"Indeed," replied Lady Trevallyn, "that appears the most probable from the state in which she left us. She has written since her arrival at her aunt's it is true to declare that she was much better and contented—but on this we have but little dependance. Poor Mrs. Harley," added she, "speaks of you with the utmost tenderness and interest. I have not thought myself at liberty to tell her exactly your real situation but she knows the loss you have sustained, and I have hinted your engagements with your cousin. I am sure you will find a satisfaction in conversing with this most excellent woman who has without exception, the best judgment and the best heart I ever knew united. But I will not ask you to come to us immediately," and while a deep blush glowed on her cheek and her eyes were involuntarily averted, she hesitatingly concluded by saying, "I am sure you would not like just now to meet strangers and Lord Henry is at Esselberrie but he will go in a day or two and then Selena you will not refuse to spend a little while with me in as perfect retirement as you can desire."

Selena consented to give her the promise she asked, and obtained Lady Trevallyn's joyful permission to bring with her Clara her sister and her pupil. Indeed the greatest relief which she found to her sadness consisted in acting towards her as far as it was possible that part which her Mother had so tenderly performed to them both.

Many a heavy hour would have been passed brooding over her own dark prospects but for the exertion which she thought it her duty to make in devoting so much of her time to the instruction of the young orphan so peculiarly her care. Her character more soft and pliable than that of Selena began already to display the necessity of constant and delicate care to guard against the dangers of an excessive sensibility—dangers of which Mrs. Miltern in her last moments had so particularly warned Selena. Yet tender and affectionate as was Selena's heart she possessed with the gentleness of her Mother all her firmness and strength of mind, and the storm of passion nor the torrent of feeling never in her bosom had power by their impetuosity to conquer the still small voice[3] of reason and of duty.

Clara on the contrary ever ardent and even irritable by nature elated to rapture by every pleasure, and overwhelmed into despondency by the slightest mortification, hurried away by the dictates of momentary sentiment, cruelly hurt by imaginary unkindness, and offended at involuntary or unintentional neglect,

---

[3]   Elijah hears the voice of God as a still small voice in 1 Kings 19:12 (KJV).

with a temperament thus threatened with every pang that rends in its difficult and thorny path of life the heart which unarmed by indifference, and refusing to yield with quiet gentleness, struggles with agony against every injury of fate and meets with open bosom the anguish of each pointed dagger of affliction. Clara thus unhappily gifted by Nature with that keen sensibility which tho' so often the object of affectation is yet a source of misery to its real possessor, Clara the susceptible Clara called hourly for the watchful eye of prudence to direct her judgment and restrain those follies which she herself would too late bitterly lament.

When Selena met Mrs. Vallard at dinner after Lady Trevallyn's departure she could not but observe that her mind appeared painfully occupied by some reflections which she did not communicate, and when the servants had retired, and that they had drawn their chairs nearer the fire while Clara still amused herself at the table with the nuts which she peeled for their acceptance, Selena in a half whisper asked her friend had she heard any thing that morning of Dallamore.

"No my love," answered she looking at her with particular kindness, "and I own I have thought of him and even of you (dear as you are to me above all the world) less than of poor Lady Trevallyn since her visit."

"Why what of Lady Trevallyn?" asked Selena eagerly.

"Oh nothing very new except that I cannot I own hear with patience of Lord Henry's daring to go to Esselberrie after behaving so basely so cruelly as he has done to that sweet creature."

Observing that Selena was still silent but that she heard her with a deep sigh and no mark of surprise she added, "I have no doubt that poor Emily has told you how we all expected year after year that she would have been Lady Henry and the reason why her poor Mother was so anxious to have her married."

"She has indeed treated me with a confidence the most flattering," answered Selena, "but I confess I wish you would speak to her on the subject, for I am convinced that the idea she has of his having at last intended to propose for her adds to her present unhappiness by encreasing her regrets, and if as I myself suspect that really was not the case ...."

"Oh never, never," warmly interrupted Mrs. Vallard, "the mean artful creature never had one real intention of contributing to the happiness of the amiable lovely being he has been torturing by his pretended love from the very years of childhood when her beauty first gave the promise of all that unrivalled perfection which it has since justified. But how is it possible to convince her of this mortifying truth when one look one sigh from him would overturn every argument built upon the surest foundations. I cannot tell you how much I suffered when I heard of her marriage. I blamed myself that I had not told Mrs. Montrose of the young Marquis's constant attachment which might have made her less urgent in Lord Trevallyn's favour, tho' I am certain that the Marquis himself would never accept the hand of one whose heart was another's, still less when his rival was his brother. When I first saw her upon her marriage she assured me it was her own choice, and that she was perfectly happy, and ever since she has studiously avoided all particular conversation with me, whether this proceeds from a shame commonly attendant upon disappointed affection, or from her knowledge of my dislike to Lord Henry with a kind of dread lest I should examine too closely into these sentiments which I am sure she retains almost unconsciously, I know not, but it is not for me to urge a confidence which she does not seem willing to bestow. With concern however which I cannot disguise I see her indulge what must produce misery to her gentle well disposed heart, and with indignation I hear of any proofs that Lord Henry still looks upon her as the object of pursuit."

"But what can that pursuit mean," said Selena, "he cannot be so malicious as to wish to see her unhappy on his account when he can now never expect to repay her sufferings?"

Mrs. Vallard shook her head. "Oh Selena you do not know what a hard heart is the sure never failing companion of a profligate character, nor how much unfeeling cruelty and ungenerous selfishness is overlooked by those who receive with smiles a man of pleasure! If Lord Henry has audacity enough to form any designs against Lady Trevallyn's virtue I am sure her innocence and natural delicacy will be her guard and her principles must ever be victorious—but I have no doubt he is at this moment disguising beneath the mask of tenderness and regret that malicious triumph which you cannot suppose him capable of enjoying."

"Has he been long at Esselberrie?" demanded Selena after a silence on both sides of some moments.

"About a week I think Lady Trevallyn said. I had not heard he was there, nor should I have known it, had I not said something about your going to Esselberrie, but I immediately guessed from her sudden change of countenance who was her visitor, and upon my enquiring had she any company found I was right in my suspicion."

"I am sure," replied Selena, "he at least receives from her no encouragement to prolong his visit."

"Ah my dear Selena," said Mrs. Vallard smiling, "the heart is very treacherous. Poor Emily I have no doubt herself thinks that his presence is painful to her, but depend upon it Lord Henry sees involuntary symptoms which make him entertain a different opinion. Otherwise he would never have devoted even so much of his time, from other pursuits less hopeless—for Lady Trevallyn, tho' she has always been his first, is not I assure you his only object. There are other unfortunate nay amiable victims who have had their peace and prospects for ever blasted by this *vile seducer*, for in two words that is my opinion of one upon whom I own I could not once see my Selena smile without a vexation which I fear you thought at the time very capricious."

"No dear Madam I never so unjustly accused you, but I guessed you knew more of him than I did, who saw nothing but what you will allow is much in his favour, indeed I cannot wonder that any woman should be captivated by his gentle manners and pleasing, insinuating conversation."

"Yes Selena and you may add his beautiful person for that must go for something tho' not much with a delicate woman well acquainted with the heart which it conceals."

"I suppose," said Selena, "that one motive for the great anxiety of Mrs. Montrose to have her daughter married was her knowledge of Lord Henry's profligate character."

"No," said Mrs. Vallard, "poor Mrs. Montrose was even more deceived than her daughter. I have seen Emily's cheek pale with suspicion while Mrs. Montrose in the fullness of her heart has been exulting to me in the security of beholding her two beautiful children as she used to call them at length happily united when all those little obstacles were removed, which until the decisive moment of his refusing to accompany them abroad she ever persisted in believing delayed that proposal which she was so well convinced he longed to make. It will be four years next Spring since some business obliged me to spend a few weeks in town. I lived almost constantly with them and my heart ached for the cruel suspense that I saw poor Emily suffer. How many scenes have I witnessed of bitter mortification to her and malicious triumph to her sister-in-law. One day in particular I shall never forget, poor Mrs. Montrose had prevailed upon me to join a large party on the water, who having got permission to see Strawberry Hill[4] were to dine at Richmond. We were all to assemble at young Mrs. Montrose's in Grosvener Street. I saw by the many pretended delays on the part of her mother and the confusion which Emily vainly tried to conceal, that the person whom she expected with most anxiety was not yet arrived. At last Mr. Montrose insisted upon our setting out threatning us that we should lose the tide, and his wife impatient and provoked at seeing us still lingering exclaimed with a bitter laugh that I never could forgive, 'Oh I know what Emily is waiting for. Do Edward for God's sake send for Lord Henry or we shall not get off today, for I am sure he has no notion of coming with us.'"

"How ill-natured," cried Selena, "But did he come?"

"Oh you may be certain there was no more delay on our part, poor Emily who had before this made in secret many a vain effort to urge her Mother's departure was the first to step into the carriage which stood nearest to the door of those that waited to convey us to the river. I followed her and we were accompanied by her sister-in-law and a gay young man, who appeared to my old fashioned ideas to pay her such attentions as no married woman ought to receive. However I believe I am censorious, and am sure there was really nothing in this but what the free manners of the times authorize—and I was perhaps the harder upon them from their ill nature to poor Emily. We drove past Lord Henry's lodgings, I did not know it till I saw young Mrs. Montrose give a significant smile to her beau, while Emily her face in a flame hastily withdrew her eyes from the windows on which they had for an instant been fixed. 'Shall we stop?' said Mrs. Montrose sarcastically addressing poor Emily. 'Aye pray do let us call for Ortney,' said her beau, pretending to suppress a laugh. 'Where is the string—For Heaven's sake, do not stop dear sister, oh pray let us go on,' cried my poor girl quite off her guard for an instant 'till recalled to herself by their maliciously insulting looks. The tears then started to her eyes which however she struggled to disperse while Mrs. Montrose contented at

---

[4]   Horace Walpole's Gothic villa.

having gained her point said in a spiteful voice, 'Why I do think we may as well go on for there are his bed chamber windows close shut and I dare say he has forgot your invitation and is at this moment fast asleep.'

"When we all assembled at the river Emily and I took care not to place ourselves in the same boat with our tormentors—but the Mother's undisguised vexation at Lord Henry's disappointment overwhelmed Emily with nearly as much confusion and distress as her persecutors could have made her suffer. She listened with a vacant countenance to the young man who addressed her, shared not in the least in the gaiety which surrounded us and never was there a party of pleasure more completely defeated than this to poor Emily. At last just as we were about to enter Strawberry hill and were all scattered about the road who should drive up to the gate but Lord Henry in a curricle with a painted flashy looking young woman who from her dress and air altogether I protest to you Selena I was quite convinced was a lady of the town till young Mrs. Montrose exclaimed in her shrill voice, 'Lord—Emily only look I beseech you at Lady Harriet Modely— think of her driving from town in the curricle with Lord Henry!' I looked towards Emily who stood absolutely petrified, so that when they passed her smiling and bowing she continued with her eyes fixed without even thinking of returning Lady Harriet's salutations. She recovered herself however when she heard her mother begin to inveigh against Lady Harriet for her imprudence and strange improper conduct. They had now alighted and Lady Harriet having given her arm to Lord Henry walked towards us and amidst much noise and laughing we heard her reproach young Mrs. Montrose for not waiting for her saying that she had arrived at Grosvener Street just as we had left it, adding, 'I should not have been able to have come to you only for the luckiest accident! Lord Henry drove up just as I was turning from your door and proposed to me to come with him, so for a frolick I consented but you must take care and not tell Mama that I did not go with you for she would be furious.' Mrs. Montrose promised to keep her secret but looked incredulous as to the *accident* which had procured a tete-a-tete so enviable."

"But what did Lord Henry say?" asked Selena.

"Oh he took no notice of us except by a general bow, and continued to flirt with Lady Harriet all day till dinner was over. Poor Emily with every exertion betrayed herself almost as much as her less cautious mother. I saw they were the objects of observation to the whole party, and never did I spend a more uneasy day. At length Lord Henry whether tired of Lady Harriet or forcibly attracted by her lovely dejected rival, I know not which, but upon the party rising up from dinner he approached Emily, and giving her his arm to assist her in getting into the boat quitted her not again during the rest of the evening."

"Did she look offended?" demanded Selena.

"Oh she looked nothing but tenderness and delight! He doubtless knew how to apologize for his neglect—methinks I have them before me that night at supper— she had taken off her hat and her beautiful hair hung in rich curls over her eyes that darted peculiar lustre and her cheeks brightly flushed with an unusual glow from the exercise of mind and body she had past thro' during the day. He had thrown his arm over the back of her chair, and his countenance animated in an uncommon degree he hung over her with eyes expressive of the most passionate tenderness. I could not but pity Mrs. Montrose while she gazed on them with a look which seemed to say *My beautiful children*—which struck me with compassion while it afforded the highest amusement to the other spectators. Tho' very amiable and good-hearted Mrs. Montrose was rather weak and she was for many years completely the dupe of Lord Henry's specious character. He flattered her so constantly and paid her such pretty attentions that she felt for him all a mother's partiality and this was the more natural because her own son always treated her from a boy with such brutal rudeness and unkind disrespect and his sister because her favourite with such contempt and ill-nature, that they both dreaded his society and were never at ease in his presence."

"I am almost surprised still," said Selena, "that Mrs. Montrose should so earnestly have insisted upon Lady Trevallyn's giving up at once every hope of one to whom she knew she was so strongly attached."

"Why my dear besides the melancholy reflection of leaving her child quite dependant upon her unkind brother and his envious narrow-minded wife Mrs. Montrose justly feared that Emily would waste all her youth in vain expectations; she had besides a little weakness in hoping that the great wealth and rank to which Lord Trevallyn would elevate her daughter might console her for her early disappointment and mortify those who had treated her with a slight which the fond mother never could endure. I own I think it would have been better had Emily married a more engaging and amiable character, and of an age better suited to her blooming beauty tho' in an humbler sphere. But Providence I trust will overrule all for her good, and when I saw the dear creature in the midst of her school, looking for happiness in bestowing it upon others I blessed Heaven that had given her so large a portion of wealth by which she was thus disposed to purchase herself true pleasures and consolations."

"Oh my dear Mrs. Vallard," cried Selena warmly, "what a pity that she should now be interrupted in such employments!"

"Dangerously interrupted indeed my dear however I trust not fatally! But come, Clara will kill us with those nuts. Let us go into the drawing room and you shall sing me a duet to divert my mind from a subject on which my meditations can be of no use."

It was not the love of gossiping, or the impossibility of retaining what she knew of the affairs of her friends which had led Mrs. Vallard into this conversation, but she saw that Lady Trevallyn had treated her young friend with that confidence which she denied to her, and she wished to impress Selena with the danger of which her inexperience might not be aware, of cherishing in its infancy the first approaches to a renewed intimacy and a criminal attachment. Selena too, in a situation the most delicate might herself one day stand in need of that prudence with which Mrs. Vallard now wished to furnish her for the advantage of her friend and in the cautions which she advised her to bestow she imagined she was providing Selena with future armour for herself.

Chapter III

So many tender joys and woes
    Have o'er my quivering soul had power
Plain life with heightening passions rose
    The boast or burden of their hour—
Oh what is all we feel! why fled
    Those pains and pleasures o'er my head?
               Gambold[5]

It was now late in September and the autumnal damp allowed not Mrs. Vallard to venture abroad after dinner, but the peculiar melancholy of the calm evenings at this season often invited Selena to steal alone thro' the leaf strewn walks and sadly meditate on the endearing remembrance of her whose spirit seemed then to hover over her "and sooth her throbbing sorrows into peace."[6] Nay often as she slowly trod beneath the silent dusky grove, in fancy she could still hold converse with her beloved Mother, and started when the withered leaf shook by the insensible breeze falling upon her head aroused her from her deep reverie.

She had been tempted one evening by the unusual mildness of the air, and the clear beauty of the full moon that lengthened the lingering light of the parting day with its soft splendor, to wander beyond her usual solitary stroll while Clara promised to play for Mrs. Vallard till her return. Having reached the end of the avenue which by the old trees on either side entirely excluded all prospect she was struck with the beautiful stillness that seemed to reign over heaven and earth as she gazed on the soft uninterrupted blue of the sky, and the surrounding country shaded as it were with a white veil caused by the rising mist.

Seated on a low wall opposite the gate, which with a deep fence on the inner side, enclosed but did not exclude from the road the view of the most beautifully shaped grounds in the park, Selena indulged the irresistible charm with which melancholy when unembittered by any remorse or harassed by anxiety, loves to "woo lone quiet in her silent walks"[7] and would have remained thoughtless of the time which elapsed far beyond that on which Mrs. Vallard looked for her return had she not been surprised and startled by the figure of a man at some distance evidently seeking to conceal himself from view behind the stem of a large tree. She was so near the porter's lodge that she felt little fear tho' she wondered at the circumstance and determined to walk home with more expedition than she was accustomed.

As she opened the gate of the avenue a sudden thought occurred to her that perhaps Dallamore was returned and wished to surprise her in this way which she

---

[5]   John Gambold, "The Mystery of Life," *The Works of the Late Rev. John Gambold* (1789), lines 13–18. Line 14 should read "Have on my quivering soul had power."

[6]   James Thomson, "Autumn," *The Seasons* (1730), line 966. Tighe replaces "passions" with "sorrows."

[7]   James Thomson, "Autumn," *The Seasons* (1730), line 967.

knew was not unlike the whims that used suddenly at times to seize him. This idea for a moment arrested her steps, and bending forward with attention towards the form which she still perceived she sought to discover if it resembled his.

The stranger seeing himself thus observed now slowly came forward and Selena immediately perceived that it could not be Dallamore, the person who approached being much slighter in his figure and not so tall. Rather uneasy in her situation she hastily passed the gate, and looked round to see if she was followed. He had stopped but pursued her with his eyes and upon her turning about she heard her name softly pronounced in a voice which she thought was not unknown to her ears. She paused, and with a timid step the stranger then advanced.

"I beg your pardon Miss Miltern, I fear I have frightened you ... I did not intend ... I did not think ...."

"Is it possible!" exclaimed Selena, "is that Mr. Stanmore? Am I mistaken it is really so dark."

"Yes Selena ... I beg pardon Miss Miltern ... yes it is Edwin Stanmore ... I have brought a letter from my Mother but it was not my intention to intrude at this unseasonable hour at Hillbarton tho' I was tempted by this lovely moon to walk thro' a scene so interesting to me where I hardly expected the happiness which awaited me."

Observing that Selena heard him in silence (for indeed a variety of perplexing considerations prevented her from making any reply) he continued, "May I hope you will allow me permission to present to you tomorrow my Mother's letter?"

"Certainly," said Selena, while she hesitated grieved at the cold return she was now obliged to make for the hospitality so strikingly different which she had received from his family.

But the impropriety of thus introducing a stranger to Mrs. Vallard unauthorised by her permission was not the only motive which deterred Selena from inviting Edwin to Hillbarton. She recollected during their residence at Inverathie his passionate professions of a sentiment which she had not even then wished to encourage, but now must never listen to without a breach of that duty which she was resolved whatever might be Dallamore's conduct on her own part strictly to fulfill. She could not help suspecting that she might have some share in this sudden journey to Derbyshire. The awkwardness of her situation which thus exposed her to receive no longer innocently the innocent affection of the uncorrupted young man who she was assured would have banished her from his mind had he known her irrevocable engagements, now struck forcibly upon her heart, and the sad remembrance of all she had passed thro' since last she beheld him contributed to oppress and agitate her spirits, so that it required her utmost exertions to enable her to make the customary enquiries which civility called for.

The coldness the reserve of her manner was severely felt by poor Edwin while with his eyes mournfully fixed upon her face which the light of the moon shewed in all its pale interesting beauty of sadness he walked slowly by her side towards the house. When they reached the gravel sweep[8] before the door Selena involuntarily stopped uncertain what to do, and Edwin shocked at the idea that she meant this as a dismission to his too forward intrusion hastily bad her good night and returned to the spot where Selena had first perceived him to vent the bitter disappointment which he had just experienced in the meeting so ardently expected so madly desired.

"I have seen her," he exclaimed, "I have beheld her graceful, her beautiful form once more! I have heard those soft accents which breathe the love which alas she feels not but I have seen I have heard her only to be convinced that I am the object of her aversion, of her contempt. Yes she met me with more than indifference. She could not disguise her reluctance to cast her eyes upon the wretched Edwin whose eyes and heart never once beheld any other image but hers since the moment of her first appearance in their sight. She drove me from her terrified lest I should dare to demand to enter once more beneath the roof where she reposes—and I must never again share these bewitching smiles, and I must never again utter in her presence the passion which consumes my soul."

Unaccustomed to restrain any of his emotions he sank upon the damp ground beneath the spot where she had been seated when he watched her unseen with such exquisite rapture—and covering it with his tears and his kisses, gave way to all the idle effusions of a romantic and morbid sensibility. The consolation of reducing into numbers the sorrows which overwhelmed him however calmed by diverting his affliction, and gave him a species of pleasure in being unhappy which none but a poet can know. The verses which he thus suddenly composed were indeed not worth preserving but as they occupied his mind while he transcribed them in the vacant leaf of his pocket Tibullus[9] from the melancholy reflections inspired by his solitary and comfortless abode in the sanded parlour of a poor village inn, they have perhaps some claim for a place in this narrative.

When the bitter source of sorrow
    When the last farewell is sighed,
With no hope to cheer tomorrow
    Joy's kind promises denied.

Yet we dwell with ling'ring pleasure
    On that distant doubtful day,
Which may yield us back our treasure
    All our sorrows to repay.

Can the tender heart declare
    Meeting what it fondly loves
Why the bliss cannot compare
    With the pang which parting proves

---

[8]   Gravel sweep: carriage drive (OED).
[9]   The Latin poet Albius Tibullus (ca. 55–19 BC) was known for his elegies.

Happy hour so long expected!
    Joy impatiently desired
Disappointed half dejected
    What have I from thee acquired?

Take again the transient pleasure
    Willingly I yield it up;
But restore my dearest treasure
    Give me back delicious Hope.[10]

In the mean time Selena pained at the necessity which had compelled her so ungraciously to welcome the amiable young man from whom and his whole house she had received nothing but kindness in no common degree, and grieved at having hurt and perhaps afflicted a heart she knew possessed so much sensitivity entered the drawing room with a look of such absence and concern that Mrs. Vallard hourly in expectation of some intelligence, immediately demanded had she heard any thing unpleasant.

"No," answered Selena smiling, "I was only thinking of a little adventure I have just met with and what you will say to me when I confess I have been walking by moonlight with a young man."

"With Dallamore," cried Mrs. Vallard starting up with a flush of pleasure on her benevolent countenance.

"No dear Madam," said Selena, while the emotion Mrs. Vallard had displayed brought tears of grateful affection into her eyes, and a blush on her cheeks which was perhaps the blush of mortification at conscious neglected worth, "No, I have no such great news yet but I was not a little astonished to meet in the avenue young Mr. Stanmore of whom you have heard Robert talk so much."

"Well and where is he?"

"I parted from him at the door just now."

"Dear Selena did you suffer him to go at this hour?"

"I will tell you," said Selena blushing, "why I did not ask him in …"

"Not ask him in!" interrupted Mrs. Vallard, "well I never heard any thing in my life so savage. Do ring the bell Clara my dear that I may send after him."

"Oh no pray do not," said Selena earnestly, "I have a thousand reasons, and besides I am sure he is gone too far now. He will be here tomorrow and you may lay all the blame upon me for indeed you do not deserve the character of inhospitality."

"And pray Selena what are your reasons for chusing Mr. Stanmore should think me so very terrible that you dare not give shelter for one night nor even invite within my door one to whom you yourself are so much indebted for hospitable reception?"

Selena endeavoured with some confusion to explain her reasons for avoiding all encouragement to a young man she thought so wild and romantic but she found

---

[10]   Tighe titles this lyric "Hope" in *Verses Transcribed for H.T.* (Brompton, 1805).

some difficulty in reconciling Mrs. Vallard to a conduct against which her own good-natured and warm heart so much revolted.

Edwin's partial meditations and the secret delightful satisfaction that he was to behold Selena at least the following day, in some degree consoled him for the mortification and sorrow with which he had felt her chilling reception. He past however a sleepless night and in the morning found himself considerably disordered not only from the anxiety of his mind but from a severe cold which he had caught on the preceeding evening.

Had his fond Mother who reluctantly at last yielded to his urgent solicitations to be allowed to quit Inverathie, had she been acquainted with the manner in which he had spent the night her misery on his account would have indeed far exceeded his. His constitution naturally delicate had been watched with such continual care by his anxious parents that his body was as unequal to struggle with the uncertainties of life, as even his mind enervated as it was by the indulgence of a susceptible imagination. It is therefore not surprising that both should have suffered from his unfortunate moon-light expedition, and the hopes of seeing Selena perhaps look more kindly at him than she had done on their last interview, alone gave him strength to prepare himself for the promised visit to Hillbarton. With the contents of the letter which he had brought from his Mother he was unacquainted for the sole object of his journey had no higher ambition than to be allowed again to behold Selena. He could form no pretentions to offer himself in any other light than as a hopeless adorer and he would have shrunk with timid opposition from being the bearer of proposals which he would have considered as so madly presumptuous.

Mrs. Stanmore partial as she was to her son however hoped otherwise and seeing that his peace and even his life appeared at stake while he dwelt with almost frenzied passion upon the image of Selena she had exerted all her influence with her husband to persuade him to consent that Edwin should make a short excursion and visit this regretted and adored object of his warm affections. They had heard of Dallamore's departure to Ireland, which seemed so certainly to contradict the vague report which had also reached them of her marriage, and they had taken pains to learn the situation in which she stood at the death of her parents. Mr. Miltern's strange will in some degree authorised the idea that he had disinherited his daughter for her refusal to marry Dallamore at his desire, and encouraged as they thought the pretentions of their son, whose paternal family was even noble and his fortune tho' not large yet sufficient to allow all the elegancies and even most of the luxuries of a retired life. From what they had seen of Selena's character they formed strong hopes that she would prefer the virtuous and amiable mind and uncommon talents of Edwin to a more shewy establishment, to which her beauty, rank and accomplishments might perhaps entitle her. Impressed with this idea Mrs. Stanmore wrote to Selena and with affectionate sincerity told her of Edwin's ardent partiality and the united wishes of herself and her husband for the success of his desires. She informed her also that she made this offer without the knowledge of her son, who had only desired the letter as some introduction to a visit he feared Selena might consider as presumptuous and whose timidity would never have dared so highly to aspire a strong fear and a weak hope being the agitating and certain attendants upon true love.

Edwin whose impatience was resisted by the dread of an imputation of forwardness, loitered in the park of Hillbarton till he was convinced the family had separated after breakfast and then half fearfully approached the glass door by which he had seen Selena enter the evening before when he ventured to look back after what he considered her unkind dismissal. Selena's voice, as she accompanied Clara at the harp, arrested him—her back was towards him as she sat and irresistibly fascinated he listened to the sweetest sounds which recalled happier hours to his thrilling heart.

After a few moments Clara looking up started, and Selena then turning round saw Edwin and arose to open the door for his admission. The awkwardness of his situation was immediately relieved by Mrs. Vallard, who quitting her work received him with an open and encouraging kindness which in a moment gained his grateful heart and banished that diffident reserve which deprived him at his first entrance of all his natural grace.

His engaging and singular manners charmed her so forcibly that totally forgetful of Selena's prudence she invited him to take up his abode at Hillbarton during his stay in that country, an invitation which not being seconded by Selena's eyes he with a sigh declined, consenting however to return that day to dinner. His visit was after this lengthened to what in Selena's opinion so much passed the necessary bounds that having received from him Mrs. Stanmore's letter she silently left the room. Poor Edwin once more sunk to the deepest dejection by this manifest indifference was unable after her departure to continue a conversation which had afforded Mrs. Vallard much pleasure—and in a few moments having apologised in a mournful voice for his long intrusion he for the present took his leave receiving with a bow Mrs. Vallard's request that he would remember to come at four o'clock.

When Mrs. Vallard met Selena she felt a little ashamed at having shewn so much less prudence than her young friend and while she acknowledged that her cold and forbidding reserve towards him was right, half wondered how she could maintain it to one so modest and so interesting.

To prevent her farther indulgence of his groundless hopes, Selena thought herself justified in shewing to Mrs. Vallard the letter she had received from Mrs. Stanmore, which she immediately answered in the most decisive terms, declaring that whatever might be her gratitude and affection for her kind friends at Inverathie, her present secret engagements were such as of themselves entirely to preclude all return of that partiality which she regretted should have caused any uneasiness.

When she had concluded this letter she immediately dispatched it to the village under cover to Edwin, in some hopes that her quickness of answering it might be a hint to him that she supposed his stay in the neighbourhood would not be very long—a hint which it was indeed impossible for Edwin's lively sensibility not to feel—and this added to the encreasing indisposition so much overpowered his spirits that he found himself unable to accept the invitation which Mrs. Vallard had so cordially given him; with a sad heart he sent his apology and shutting himself up in his own room threw himself on the bed where he lay in feverish misery which encreased towards evening even to delirium.

The servant to whom his anxious parents had entrusted with many a charge the care of watching over his health and safety and who was himself attached to him with the most partial affection, beheld his illness with terror and having vainly entreated him to take some food and suffer him to assist him in undressing as he lay restless on the bed, by the bustle which his officious cares occasioned in the house while he eagerly enquired for a physician, unintentionally inspired the landlady with higher ideas of his consequence than she at first entertained from their appearance.

She therefore took upon herself to say that she would step down to Hillbarton to acquaint "Madam Vallard with his situation and she was sure of getting from her a cure, as she was a deal more learned in them cases than their potecary or any Doctor that could be had for many a mile round Barton bridge."

The good Lewis miserable and perplexed as he was at seeing his master thus taken ill at what he thought the world's end, when he reflected on the immeasurable distance they had rode since they left Inverathie, eagerly accepted her proposal and watched for her return from his Master's window, till it grew too dark to distinguish distant objects and then at the door in hopes of meeting what he expected would afford his poor Master some relief.

At length he perceived his hostess hurrying across the path which led thro' the fields from Hillbarton full of the important intelligence she had to communicate "How Madam Vallard had ordered the carriage and was coming herself to see young Mr. Stanmore if so be that was his Master's name and she made no doubt but her coming would do him a power of good."

Mrs. Vallard was indeed extremely alarmed at the account given by the landlady who having upon all occasions a love to magnify every trifle into the marvelous had taken care to justify the trouble she now gave Mrs. Vallard by the most frightful picture of the sudden illness with which she said the fine young gentleman was seized when on arriving the evening before had directly enquired the way to Hillbarton.

Selena was no less shocked and considering herself, however innocently, the cause of the despair his parents would feel should any ill befall their darling child at a distance from their care she encouraged Mrs. Vallard to go in person to see his real situation and afford him every assistance in her power till a physician could be sent for to Derby.

On her arrival Mrs. Vallard found him indeed in a high fever but tho' his head appeared considerably disordered he knew her and was so grateful for her kindness that Mrs. Vallard deeply interested in his favour shed tears at his danger, and having sent a woman upon whose care she could depend to sit up by him during the night promised to see him early the next morning.

With the tenderness of a mother she watched over him during his illness which confined him for a week to his bed, and when able to be removed strongly represented to Selena that charity demanded her to allow his being brought to Hillbarton, the accomodations at the village being so uncomfortable for an invalid, from the noise and continual smell of tobacco occasioned by the hourly resort of the neighbouring farmers who passed all their evenings over their pipes and ale in the room immediately beneath that in which poor Edwin was confined.

Selena made no opposition but resolved as much as possible to shun his presence and Mrs. Vallard promised that she would take the very first opportunity to inform him of her engagement tho' without explaining any unnecessary particulars.

Chapter IV

> But I have loved with such transcendent passion
> I soared at first, quite out of Reason's view
> And now am lost above it
>
> Dryden[11]

Once more then was the happy Edwin, for such in spite of Selena's reserve, he now esteemed himself, permitted to repose beneath the roof which sheltered all his heart valued upon earth. For alas this devouring passion when once suffered to assume dominion over a warm imagination allows no other sentiment of nature or duty to retain its former influence. The thoughts have then indeed but one object and those who consider it but as a figurative expression of the lover who declares that not for one moment is his mind diverted from the contemplation of what he thus idly worships, has been happily yet a stranger to the power of Love tho' he may have mistaken for it the impulse of passion, or have been blessed beneath the influence of the milder sentiments of affection. It has been well said by a female writer in her beautiful imitation of Sir John Suckling's "Honest Lover"

> If any hopes thy bosom share
> But those which Love has planted there
> Or any cares but this thy breast enthral
> Thou never yet his power hast known,
> Love sits on a despotic throne
> And reigns a tyrant if he reigns at all.[12]

In the mean time Selena wrote herself to Mrs. Stanmore guessing that Edwin's silence would alarm them at Inverathie, and having repeated all she had before said of the impossibility of his present pursuit meeting with success entreated that

---

[11]   Cleopatra in John Dryden's *All for Love* (1678), 2.1.20–22.

[12]   "Mrs. Barbauld" (Tighe's note). Anna Laetitia Barbauld, "Song I" ("Come here fond youth, whoe'er thou be"), *Poems* (1773), lines 37–42. Tighe replaces "his" with "this" in line 39.

she should advise her son's immediate return home as his delay could only be productive of pain to them both.

Mrs. Vallard delighted with the conversation of Edwin, his genius and the pure sentiments which his warm heart breathed with such enthusiastic ardor, and amused while she was charmed at his total ignorance of the world, yet lost no opportunity of endeavouring to convince him that as his love for Selena was from irrevocable circumstances hopeless he should for his own sake and hers restrain its violence. As his nurse she would not yet suffer him to walk out and Edwin gave up the indulgence of being allowed to follow Selena in her rambles satisfied to be considered as an invalid by which he was furnished with an excuse for prolonging his stay where he at least was at liberty to behold her for some hours in every day, and to listen to the enchanting melody of her voice.

Selena on her part was afflicted with many uneasy considerations. She began to be convinced that Dallamore would indeed be persuaded by those around him to renounce those engagements which by the most solemn vows they were both bound to fulfill—and tho' she expressed not her suspicions to Mrs. Vallard she severely felt the mortifying and cruel situation in which she stood. She had besides the most tormenting dread lest Robert whose silence now so much surprised her should resent too warmly Dallamore's conduct, and the restraint under which she found herself from Edwin's presence added to the distress which preyed upon her mind. She was not insensible to the amiable qualifications of this young man, and his talents were such as she was peculiarly fitted to enjoy, but she was perpetually on the watch to prevent herself from giving the slightest approbation to that excellence which she really admired, lest it should be construed by his watchful eye into encouragement.

She expected therefore with hourly impatience an invitation from Lady Trevallyn which at this time she would have been so peculiarly glad to accept and thus escape from the difficult task of repressing by constant coldness the modest and involuntary demonstrations of a passion the most sincere and the most devoted.

"You will not surely venture out this evening," said Edwin timidly as he observed Selena rise from the table immediately after dinner and go towards the window, where the sullen sky and fast closing gloom afforded no very tempting invitation.

"I am afraid not, for it is raining just now," answered Selena coldly and still attentively looking out.

"No indeed my dear," said Mrs. Vallard, "you must give up your evening walks and I will desire Philip to let us have candles tomorrow at dinner, for it is very melancholy to sit this way without being able to see each other's faces. Let us come into the drawing room where I hope he has now shut the windows and given us a more cheerful fire than this."

As she spoke this she took Selena's arm and Edwin as was his custom immediately followed.

"Oh this is another region," said Mrs. Vallard as she seated herself near the bright wood fire whose blaze perfectly illuminated the gay apartment, and cast a brilliant splendour on the gilded picture frames with which it was hung. "I found the vapours fast creeping over me looking out at this dreary evening do not you find your spirits raised ten degrees since you changed the scene?"

Edwin who had been watching with earnest sadness the averted eye of Selena which she held obstinately fixed upon the screen she had taken in her hand, turned hastily to reply, "Alas 'tis still the same dreary prospect to me! With me 'tis ever

> Nought but gloom around—the darkened sun
> Loses his light; the rosy bosomed spring
> To weeping Fancy pines; and the bright arch
> Contracted bends into a dusky vault
> All nature fades extinct, and she alone
> Heard, felt, and seen, possesses every thought
> Fills every sense and pants in every vein."[13]

Selena, who from the manner in which he repeated these lines, could not pretend to doubt the application, colouring rose in silence and gently laying the screen on the table at the other side, left the room without looking at Edwin.

"There," said Mrs. Vallard turning round to gaze after her as she softly closed the door. "There you have sent Selena away. How can you act so foolishly, or persist in expressing sentiments which I have told you it was wrong in you to feel or in her to hear."

"But why wrong? It is I know absurd, since I am unfortunate and can never hope to please, but why not bear with me, when I only desire her to *listen* to the sorrow which I hope not she will relieve. 'I follow her with no presumptuous suit' but may I not 'Religious in my error' adore her while she shines like the sun heedless upon me as upon all and take no other notice of her worshippers—this is all I implore."[14]

"Ridiculous," exclaimed Mrs. Vallard, "Why will you talk such wild nonsense? She will not and ought to listen to it."

"Why *ought* not."

"Because as I have told you repeatedly she is irrevocably engaged."

"I know of no engagement which ought to prevent her from *hearing* me— unless she were indeed married—which situated as she is here I never can believe."

"Why can you not believe it?"

---

[13] "Thompson" (Tighe's note). James Thomson, "Spring," *The Seasons* (1728), lines 1006–12. Tighe uses "the" for "yon" in line 1008.

[14] Edwin invoke Helena's lines in Shakespeare's *All's Well that Ends Well* (1602), 1.3.194–204: "I follow him not / By any token of presumptuous suit; / Nor would I have him till I do deserve him; / Yet never know how that desert should be. / I know I love in vain, strive against hope; / Yet in this captious and intenible sieve / I still pour in the waters of my love / And lack not to lose still: thus, Indian-like, / Religious in mine error, I adore / The sun, that looks upon his worshipper, / But knows of him no more."

"Oh Heavens! Selena married, and abandoned by the man thus allowed to claim the richest jewel the universe can shew. No, no, it cannot be—you wish to drive me to despair by the false insinuations, but it is impossible."

Mrs. Vallard shook her head.

"Oh relieve me I beseech you from this cruel torture, say she is not indeed married and torment me not thus with an idea which in my cooler moments I must again disbelieve. I promise you I will do all in my power to conquer this self-destroying passion, or at least I will condemn you no longer to bear with its vain language, but say you have only wished to banish from me all hope by this false suggestion. Speak I conjure you speak."

"I cannot Edwin deceive you, and tho' it is of consequence not to betray the situation of Selena yet to you I will not disguise the truth … she *is* married."

"Oh Heavens!" cried Edwin as if struck with sudden anguish violently placing his hands before his face.

"Why surely," continued Mrs. Vallard, "this cannot be an unexpected discovery to you. How often at Selena's own desire have I told you as much almost in express language."

"How could I believe it!" exclaimed Edwin as soon as the violence of his emotions allowed him utterance. "Who, where, is her husband? Has Heaven perceiving him unworthy of the rich prize deprived him of his senses and the possibility of enjoying it—or has he committed some frightful crime that has obliged him to fly from the presence of Selena? Oh tell me I beseech you who is this wretch. Let me know there is a being more to be pitied than myself since he might once have hoped to have been his that blessing of which he is now deprived. Explain this mystery and deliver me from this bewildering perplexity!"

"My dear Mr. Stanmore," said Mrs. Vallard half terrified at his violence, "of what consequence can it be to you to be made acquainted with particulars to which a combination of circumstances have I own given a strange appearance? You can no longer entertain any hope of Selena yourself; why then agitate yourself with useless curiosity about an event which having absolutely taken place your utmost fury and regret can never undo. Reconcile yourself to what you must now at least, be convinced is irremediable, and do not make me regret the confidence I have placed in you by proving yourself unworthy of it and molesting poor Selena's peace."

"I molest her peace! Ah that is out of my power! But is there another being upon earth who would like me perish gladly to ensure it? And if there is tell me is he rewarded by her love? Tell me I beseech you is Selena happy?"

"Happy," answered Mrs. Vallard with some hesitation, "at present I am certain she is not, but I have no doubt of her affection for her husband who is in every respect worthy of it, and I am persuaded that your conduct now contributes to the perplexity and melancholy of her situation."

Edwin heard her with tears of anguish and exclaimed, "I will go then, I will quit her for ever, quit her without one hope, one consolatory reflection upon earth and oh that my death at this instant would release me from this intolerable burden of existence and absolve her from all future molestation from me."

"Now do not talk so strangely, so wickedly—poor Selena suffered cruelly at your illness, and you can only wish for death to torment her."

"Oh cruel, cruel!" said Edwin bitterly, while he accused Mrs. Vallard of hardness of heart, which indeed she never knew, and which she was never farther from feeling than at this moment while she saw and pitied his unaffected transports of grief.

She found however that it was in vain to endeavour to sooth or reason with him and therefore opposed not his leaving her when she perceived him impetuously quit the room.

But when she observed that he appeared not at the usual hour of tea, apprehending that he would suffer from the indulgence of his passions, she determined to interrupt his solitary gloom, and some time before supper knocked at his door to enquire as she said after her patient. It was locked but upon hearing her voice he opened it, and appeared with such a countenance as a painter might have chosen who wished to express the sorrows of Werter.[15]

"You are too good," said he in answer to her enquiries, "but I shall not trouble you long I have given Lewis directions, and shall leave this early tomorrow."

"You will return I hope to Inverathie and I trust that you will there soon find the peace which you have for some time lost."

"Oh never, never," said he sadly, "but I have done with complaints let not Selena receive my farewell with unkind displeasure. Ask her to forgive me. I will not trust myself with the petition, but I bid her not hate nor despise me, if possible."

"Will you not come down," said Mrs. Vallard much affected, "will you not sup with us for the last time?"

"Oh Heavens for the last time," cried Edwin striking his forehead against the wall, "must I then see her for the last time, and must I bear to live with that terrible idea for ever oppressing me—but I am calm, 'calm as the miserable land over which the desolating plague has past.'[16] Yes I *will* see Selena for the last time, and see her without uttering one complaint, one expression which she *ought* not then to hear; Go down then and reassure her, that she may not again fly the wretched Edwin who will not long demand her compassionate endurance."

"Compose yourself then dear Edwin and follow me soon, give me your hand, you must not hate me for the painful advice I have been obliged to give you."

Edwin raised his head from the chimney piece where he had for some time leaned it, and meeting her eyes filled with tears, pressed the hand she extended to him affectionately to his lips, and promising to join them at supper endeavoured to prepare himself for taking his last farewell, without betraying his emotions in too effeminate a weakness.

---

[15]   In Johann Wolfgang von Goethe's epistolary novel *The Sorrows of Young Werther* (1774) Werther falls in love with the engaged and subsequently married Charlotte (and ultimately kills himself).

[16]   A reference to Ferdinand's lines at the end of Friedrich von Schiller's *Cabal and Love* (1784), 5.2.no lines.

Mrs. Vallard apprised Selena of part of what had passed, and of his intention of leaving them the next day—and tho' Selena felt for him more grateful pity than she chose to express yet she heartily rejoiced that he had been prevailed upon by any means to quit Hillbarton. At supper no allusion was made on any side to his purposed departure. He attempted not to join in the conversation which was but feebly supported by Mrs. Vallard and Selena. He thought not of appearing to eat, till Selena asked should she help him from the dish before her—an offer which he eagerly accepted, hastily extending the plate which he refused to suffer the servant to present. Mrs. Vallard looked at him with concern as she saw him vehemently and with evident difficulty swallow in large morsels the food she had thus presented to him and poor Selena took care to offer him no more.

To shorten a scene so distressing to all Mrs. Vallard rose to retire earlier than usual, and Edwin who fearfully and watchfully had anticipated this motion changed colour, and gasping for breath exclaimed, "So soon it is then all over!" then catching hold of Selena's hand he pressed it with sudden wildness to his lips and his heart and endeavouring but in vain to pronounce the farewell blessing which that agonised heart implored tho' these lips refused to utter he rushed from them impetuously and without taking off his cloaths flung himself on the bed to wait the dawn of that morning which was for ever to separate him from all he thought life and happiness.

When Mrs. Vallard came into the breakfast room next day she found Clara alone as Selena who feared again to meet Edwin had not ventured down.

"I wonder," said Clara as soon as she saw her, "how Mr. Stanmore is this morning—he looked very ill last night—do you not think so Madam?"

"I hope," answered Mrs. Vallard, "his journey will be of use to him."

"Journey—what journey?"

"Why he set out this morning at break of day, poor fellow. I trust Mrs. Stanmore will not think that his tour in Derbyshire has hurt him materially."

"And is he gone then," asked Clara with a voice of such melancholy disappointment that Mrs. Vallard said smiling—

"Why Clara are you going to cry for him? You have certainly lost your heart."

"No indeed Madam," said she confused and hesitating, "but only thinking we, that is I mean you and Selena will have a great loss."

She was going on but seeing Mrs. Vallard still smiling as she looked at her, half vexed and half ashamed at the concern which she could not help betraying she burst into tears.

"What is the matter?" cried Selena as she entered the room and stopped with anxious surprise at beholding the glowing face of Clara bathed in tears which as fast as she attempted to wipe away still swelled in her eyes and suffused her blushing cheeks.

Mrs. Vallard made a sign to her not to take any notice and asking Clara to fetch her keys which she had left in her writing desk in her own room gave her an excuse to retire for a few moments which she gladly seized.

"All for Edwin I assure you!" said Mrs. Vallard softly turning round to be convinced the door was shut after her, "poor Clara is in love very early."

"Dear Mrs. Vallard what do you mean?"

"Why the moment I told her that he was gone, she changed colour and with difficulty restrained her tears, which upon my foolishly noticing her confusion burst forth."

"Oh she was only ashamed and distressed at your jesting with her," said Selena smiling, "we had better say no more about it."

"No certainly," answered Mrs. Vallard, "her love will soon wear off at all events, I wish poor Edwin's was not of more dangerous consequence."

"Nay I am sure you need not fear much danger even from his, he is very romantic but I hope will shortly transfer his imaginary attachment."

Mrs. Vallard was prevented from expressing her doubts by the return of Clara who presenting her the keys averted her face with a sullen mixture of displeasure and shame.

Mrs. Vallard putting her arm round her neck gently turned it round and kissed her cheek, which completely softened the affectionate heart of Clara and once more brought the big tears into her eyes while she quickly and warmly returned her embrace.

As she took her usual place Mrs. Vallard and Selena stole a look at each other tho' they would not venture to smile when they observed her take up and put into her own bosom the flowers which she had laid beside Edwin's plate as was her usual custom and general gift to each guest every morning that the weather allowed her to search the garden before breakfast for the autumnal flowers which lingered late or faintly put forth their sweets for the second time.

All day she was unusually pensive and Selena could not help observing that she performed her accustomed exercises with languor and inattention. She would not however appear to notice it, nor express any surprise when at the hour of practice, in which since Edwin's visit she had been accustomed to play with him and receive his instructions, she requested Selena not to ask her that morning to play complaining of a headach. But not chusing that Clara should give way to a fancied melancholy she thought so foolish Selena offered to accompany her in a walk. Clara felt for the first time in her life constrained by the society of her sister and would have preferred a solitary ramble, however she would not decline the proposal and tying on her hat in silence prepared to attend her.

"Where shall we go?" said Selena.

"It is indifferent to me," answered Clara mournfully as she closed the glass door, her thoughts at that moment entirely occupied by the remembrance of Edwin as she had seen him at that spot for the first time.

"We will go towards Esselberrie then," said Selena. "I love that walk now that the sun is not strong it is so cheerful."

"No," replied Clara, "I am tired of that way let us come up the avenue."

"For variety!" said Selena smiling, "but with all my heart," and as she spoke she changed their direction.

Very soon however she thought that she guessed the motive of this little caprice when she perceived Clara's eyes fixed upon the traces left by Edwin's horses upon the soft gravel, a suspicion which was confirmed when on their passing the gate she found that she led still the road which they had taken.

Selena exerted herself to amuse Clara, but in vain, and after proceeding a long time in silence she at last asked her with a smile, "Well are we to go on all the way to Inverathie?"

Clara started and with a blush said, "Dear Selena if you are tired why did you not turn about before? I am sure I am ready whenever you please."

"I am not tired of walking Clara but you are tired of me, for you have not spoken three words since we set out."

"I have really a headach, and you are not as kind as you used to be, or you would pity me."

The tears which started to her eyes struck Selena with a reproach the most sensible and eager to repair the pain she had unintentionally inflicted she exclaimed as she pressed her hand, "I do pity you my love, and beg your pardon from my heart if I have seemed unkind. Here is some aromatic vinegar poor Mrs. Stanmore gave me at Inverathie when I had a headach too, if you will forgive me I will make it a present to you tho' I value it for her sake."

Clara took the little box with a grateful glow of pleasure which would have been considerably augmented had she known that the gift had been really from Edwin tho' he had bestowed it thro' the medium of his mother fearing for himself a refusal.

After dinner while Mrs. Vallard and Selena were in conversation over the fire, Selena bid her friend observe that Clara was playing nothing but Edwin's music, which she had either learned from him or retained in her ear by memory and that she had even caught his peculiar manner of singing which was singularly evident as she repeated his own songs.

Mrs. Vallard smiled at the idea of being able perhaps to transfer Edwin's affection for Selena to her captivated sister.

"Dear Madam do you think it possible a child, for surely she is still a child would indeed be captivated? and by one so grave as Edwin who never flirted or played with her the least."

"Oh he is just that sentimental kind of young man likely to gain the heart of Clara who child as she is, is all alive to sensibility and romantic impressions."

"Perhaps," said Selena, "such follies are more excusable at her age than any other but we must direct her now and not allow this imagination to interrupt her studies or injure her sweet temper."

In a day or two Clara as her friends had prognosticated recovered her spirits and was even more eager in the pursuit of knowledge and accomplishments than she had been before. Music indeed was her chief object and she had no pleasure so great as playing Edwin's songs or conversing with Selena about him and Inverathie, about which she had asked so many questions, and had so repeatedly copied the views which Selena had taken there that she was almost as well acquainted with every spot as Selena herself.

Chapter V

He was the bane and ruin of my peace
This anguish and these tears, these are the legacies
His fatal love has left me ……..
Oh that my head were laid my sad eyes closed
And my cold corse wound in my shroud to rest!
My painful heart will never cease to beat
Will never know a moment's peace till then.

Rowe[17]

At length arrived the expected note from Lady Trevallyn, and Mrs. Vallard with a sigh whispered to Selena as it was put into her hands, "Thank God he is gone at last I hope."

Lord Henry was not however mentioned in the note, but it contained only a few words to remind Selena of her promise, and to assure her she was quite alone, requesting her if possible to prevail on Mrs. Vallard to change her mind and accompany them to Esselberrie.

Mrs. Vallard declined the invitation and when at parting with Selena she limited her stay to one week she secretly hoped that some intelligence respecting Dallamore might shorten even that period.

Lady Trevallyn's spirits did not appear to have been much improved from the visit she had lately had. She confessed to Selena that Lord Henry had only just left her when she dispatched the note, and added blushing, "I was really impatient to let you and Mrs. Vallard know that he did not intend to take up his residence here, he would not indeed have stayed so long only Lord Trevallyn insisted upon his remaining till he had made a great dinner for half the country, and it was but the day before he went that this terrible business was over."

"Lord Henry would have excused the feast I dare say," said Selena smiling.

"Oh yes! but Lord Trevallyn would not excuse *him*—he was quite pleased to shew some of the grand relations of his poor wife."

Selena was silent, and Lady Trevallyn felt inwardly hurt that in her anxiety to give some reason for Lord Henry's stay she had suffered herself to be betrayed into this rather slighting allusion to the failing of Lord Trevallyn. She condemned herself for this conduct and willingly allowed Selena to change the conversation. She was indeed impatient to know whether any thing had since been heard of Dallamore, and could not disguise her astonishment and even indignation at his conduct.

"Lord Henry," said she, "told me that he heard in town that you had made a run away match but that you had been pursued and overtaken immediately after the ceremony by your father and had both since been persuaded to give each other

---

[17]   The first three lines in the epigraph are spoken by Jane Shore in Nicholas Rowe's *The Tragedy of Jane Shore* (1714), 1.2.96–8; the next four lines are spoken by Jane Shore in 2.1.293–6.

up—you see how facts are always misrepresented. Indeed I have ever known them most strangely tortured where there is the least foundation on which to build any story which either from its singularity or affording food for spiteful remarks can interest folly or ill-nature."

"Did he say any thing of Lord Dallamore's present occupations?" asked Selena.

"Yes he said there was a very riotous party now at Mount Villars, and that there was a great deal of drinking going on to the considerable annoyance of Mrs. Dallamore's sober family. I hear she has been living there quietly near twenty years without any disturbance from Lord Mount Villars. You never saw your aunt Dallamore of course?"

"Never but I have heard Mrs. Vallard and my poor Mother speak both of her and my late uncle in the highest terms."

"I have seen," said Lady Trevallyn, "a very fine young man in town with Lord Dallamore that I remember he introduced to me as his irish cousin I suppose he is their son."

"Yes, Sidney Dallamore. Mrs. Vallard mentioned him the other day but I have never seen him."

"That was the name, I recollect I thought him much more pleasing as well as handsomer than Lord Dallamore—and he was very much liked, but not quite so much the ton as his cousin, probably because he had not so large a fortune."

"Mrs. Vallard was saying," replied Selena, "that she supposed the party at Mount Villars detained him in Ireland as she had expected a visit from him about this time on his way to London to keep his term as he is to be a lawyer I understand."

"I wish he would come and bring us some news from Mount Villars," said Lady Trevallyn, "perhaps Dallamore is waiting for him."

"Not improbable," answered Selena half smiling at the idea considering the situation in which Dallamore stood.

"Well my love," continued Lady Trevallyn, "if you are not very impatient, I would rather in that case we should see nothing of either of them for a few days, for I am so selfish I should not like to give you up directly."

Selena took the first moments she had at liberty to visit Mrs. Harley.

She answered her enquiries respecting Angela in a voice expressive of the deepest melancholy.

"I seldom hear from my poor girl," said she, "and what she does write can give me little satisfaction, as I know she treats me not with confidence in regard to her mind, nor sincerity as to her health. I have in vain entreated my sister to write me some particulars, I have been able to get from her but three lines since my child went to Islington, I believe I have them here," added she taking from among some papers in a table drawer, this letter which she handed to Selena.

"Dear Sister,

"I marvel much at your want of resignation and faith. Your daughter is, you ought to know, as well as it is the will of God she should be, and I fear your worldly anxiety will meet its reward. I think it my duty to speak thus plain and hope you will receive it kindly as meant by your loving sister.

Gertrude Blightal"

"Oh what a pity!" cried Selena, as she gave her back this harsh epistle, "what a pity that poor Angela should persist in chusing to reside with one so different from you, dear Mrs. Harley. Can you conceive her motives for this apparently strange caprice."

"I will tell you my dear Miss Miltern my thoughts without disguise, because from your great kindness to my poor Angela I am sure you are interested in her happiness, and from the disposition she seemed to show only towards you to lose that gloomy backwardness and reserve with which she received all other offers of affection I think it possible you may be able to furnish me with some hints which can throw light on her extraordinary conduct. Has my girl ever said any thing to you which could make you suspect she did not feel that gratitude and love for My Lady which her kindness to us so well merits?"

"To say the truth," replied Selena, "from the first conversation that I had with Angela it struck me that she had what I could not help thinking a very strange dislike for Lady Trevallyn."

"Dislike. Oh dear Miss Miltern dislike is a strong word! She could not dislike my Lady who is so amiable so gentle that the very children employed to weed in the walks love to see her approach, and are ready to kiss her gown as she passes. There is not a labourer about Esselberrie that would not work himself almost to death when my Lady has any job to be done and they can talk of nothing else if my Lady has but said one word."

"Well perhaps *it* is a strong word, but Angela certainly did not love to see her approach, and would rather we must allow talk of any one else."

"It is too true," said Mrs. Harley sighing, "and when we used to hear my Lady's soft voice entering the school room Angela always turned pale, and when it was possible hid herself or made her escape before she came into us. It has occurred to me sometimes that having known her at Lady Anne Ortney's, as in some degree a companion, perhaps any unhappy child's proud spirit could not now bear to owe to her charity the bread which supported us. I think this the more as Angela has a talent for drawing by which she maintained herself and even made her aunt large presents during her stay at Islington, and that I never could prevail upon her to exercise it while here—tho' I thought she might have pleased my Lady by exerting herself to make this little offering which nature had qualified her to bestow. There was a circumstance also which occurred a little while before she left me, which I will tell you, if I do not too far trespass on your patience."

Selena assured her that she listened with the deepest interest and entreated her to relate every thing that had past which might tend to a discovery of the source of poor Angela's melancholy.

Mrs. Harley then continued, "You remember Miss Miltern the evening you left her so ill after that walk in which her fainting so much terrified you. Never before had she talked so strangely, and I really began to fear that my poor child's reason was disordered. She that is naturally so quiet and so silent for a few hours spoke almost incessantly, accusing Heaven in language which made me shudder for having created her, and wishing in the most passionate manner with convulsive sobs and clasped hands that I had strangled her at the moment of her birth. So unlike her usual gentleness and dutiful conduct towards me, tho' alas I cannot indeed ever boast of her true affection which would have led her to treat me with more confidence, she now upbraided me with bitterness for having abandoned her in childhood, and carelessly exposed her to misery. She paid no attention to my prayers or my tears, and to all my expressions of tenderness and pity answered only by urging her entreaties that I would suffer her to return to Islington—or that I should put an end to her existence at once, since she could no longer endure the burden."

"But," cried Selena, "you had already promised to indulge her, had you not?"

"Oh yes; but my promises were all in vain, I could not sooth her, she would have risen, and set out upon the spot, had I not almost by force and tears of the sorest anguish I ever shed prevented her. There was no possibility of convincing her that my Lady was not coming to visit her and more than once the most frightful convulsions agitated every limb in the idea of hearing voices upon the stairs. Not one moment of sleep did she get thro' the whole of that cruel night and if I hoped for an instant that she had sunk into forgetfulness her sudden stirring as in agony convinced me of her continued suffering; Towards morning she grew apparently even more composed. Her tears flowed no longer, and her impenetrable silence returned, but it was the silence of despair. Ill able as she was to rise she so strongly insisted upon it that I did not think it well to refuse and the moment it was light she dressed herself, and with secret horror I watched her tie her hat over her face and wrap herself up in her coarse cloak.

"I cannot tell you Miss Miltern," continued the afflicted mother after a pause which her tears had occasioned, "I cannot tell you what were my dreadful suspicions, but when she went to the door, I threw myself upon my knees before it and told her if she passed it must be by stepping over her dying Mother—for indeed I did feel as if that dreadful moment would be my last. I believe my horror struck her with compunction for looking at me wildly for a while she flung herself upon my neck, and exclaimed bursting into tears, 'Oh I am a wretch unworthy indeed to see the light of Heaven forgive me my Mother, forgive me, but do not pray for me—for I am abandoned of God and your prayers would be in vain.'

"You may well imagine all I tried to say which might inspire her with hope and comfort in the mercy of God to the vilest of sinners, that all are his children and that he never abandons any who would seek him, for I now thought her sorrow was not the sorrow of this world, but proceeded from that dreadful malady of the mind which sometimes drives those of a melancholy constitution to despair of ever finding mercy. She heard me with more calmness than I expected and received my endearments with more tenderness than I had been accustomed to receive from her—but her reserve was as strong as ever, and she earnestly persisted in beseeching me to allow her to refresh herself in the air. She solemnly assured me she would return before it was dark, and did not refuse to take the little basket with her dinner and her work as was her practice frequently when she used to ask my permission to pass the day alone in the woods.

"I was not however able to satisfy my mind to let her thus go from me, so resolving to follow I delayed her with one excuse or another till I sent down to the house for one upon whom I could depend to stay with the children, and with a note for my Lady when she got up to excuse my unusual absence. I lost not sight of my poor Angela all day tho' she did not discover my pursuit—and indeed I had not then a doubt of her disordered intellects. As soon as she thought she was out of my sight she threw into a thick bush of laurestina her basket, and hurried towards the house, concealing herself behind a large tree on the lawn she remained on her knees with her eyes fixed upon the windows, and her hands clasped for I am sure above an hour. Two of the labourers who came to roll the gravel before the door and who now advanced whistling and talking drove her thence I believe, for she suddenly started and ran softly towards the stables looking round fearfully at every step.

"Not one of the grooms or stable boys were yet about the court yard and my poor Angela with what intention I could not guess since she surely could not have thus meditated escape, tried the doors of every stable, and finding all were locked slowly walked away as if disappointed. She then proceeded towards the park and I was afraid to approach near enough to listen tho' I had no doubt she often spoke and was now unburdening her poor heart, which she refused to do when any but the eye of God was present. I could only weep when I saw her tears flowing, and pray that God who alone knew her sorrows to pity and relieve them.

"She did not go very far, I suppose she was faint and that her strength failed her in that steep rough path which she had chosen but there is a spot in the park which tho' not far from the house is yet very wild and unfrequented. It is that sharp rock which you know forms so pretty an object from all the domain from which you can plainly look down upon the house and the lawn immediately beneath, with the whole surrounding country like a map. It was there my poor child bent her steps— and with some difficulty I clambered up and seated myself behind her concealed from view as she was herself by the low scraggy oaks which half cover the rock. I felt pleased that she had chosen a situation so cheerful and trusted that the mild air and enlivening prospect would sooth her afflicted spirit but alas her meditations were not calm—and I witnessed her agonies with a torture which I cannot express.

"I think it was about noon when she suddenly started up, and bending forward with her arms extented she seemed fixed breathless in that posture for I am sure many minutes. I was afraid to move, but had I even been able to direct my eyes with hers, I dare say I should have received no information as I have no doubt it was some object in her own mind which then occupied her so eager attention. I could not however resist my curiosity, and when I heard her utter a cry of anguish and fall prostrate with her face upon the hard rock, I softly rose and wiped the tears from my eyes that I might be able to distinguish whether she had really seen any visible object to fix her melancholy regards. A travelling carriage and some horses attending it just turning out of the gate, was all I could see of novelty in the prospect but the groans of my child indeed quickly seized upon all my attention. With difficulty I retained myself from flying to her casting myself by her side and mingling with hers the voice of my sorrows—but after some time she arose, and left the spot where I had indeed wondered at her so long patiently remaining.

"I felt much apprehension when I saw she crossed the fields towards the high road, and could not have been much surprised, had she in her apparent wild disorder purposed to commence thus on foot the journey she was so anxious to undertake. However she stopped upon reaching the end of the path and leaning upon the style only looked with a sad earnestness towards the London road, and remained in that attitude till my limbs were stiff and my spirits weary with watching. At length to my great satisfaction she slowly took the road towards home, and when certain that she meant to return, I hurried in by a shorter path that I might prepare for her reception.

"After a night of such misery, and a day passed without food and in the indulgence of such passionate sorrows you will not be surprised that my poor child was upon her entrance the very true picture of death. She had not however forgotten to look for her basket and I suppose threw away the food it had contained for her dinner. Her own distress did not render her regardless or insensible to mine, and looking at me with a pitying and melancholy eye she said, 'you are very very pale—you had no rest last night—did I stay out too long?' I took her in my arms, comforted by her kindness and with tears entreated her not to refuse me the consolation of seeing her taste some refreshment. She would not grieve me by a denial and having swallowed a large glass of wine lay down as she said to sleep. She was at least quiet and my own spirits were so much exhausted that having recommended my child to Heaven I soon forgot my own distress and even hers, as I laid my head upon the end of her pillow while on my knees at the side of her bed. I only afflict you my dear Miss Miltern by thus dwelling on particulars but I have not told you all."

Selena's whose tears had flowed abundantly with those of the unhappy Mother entreated her to proceed and she went on.

"The gloom which now settled upon her encreased every hour, and tho' I arranged all things preparatory to her departure with the wife of a neighbouring farmer who had business in town and that she was in a very few days to go under her protection in the stage, not even this compliance with her wishes appeared in any degree to rouse her from the extreme despondence in which she was plunged.

"The day before she was to leave me, I resolved to try for her one remedy which I myself have ever experienced to have the most salutary effects in calling back my soul to gratitude and resignation when dejection had seized upon my spirits. I had heard of the distress which had overtaken a family in the neighbouring village, and tho' I knew that from the ever ready benevolence of my Lady I should soon obtain for them the relief which they wanted I delayed informing her of their situation until I had brought my poor Angela to look at their misery. Without communicating my design I invited her for the last time to take with me a melancholy farewell walk—and as she accompanied me in gloomy silence I led her steps to the abode of wretchedness. 'Let us come in here,' said I, 'for a moment to ask how poor Woodford does this afternoon.'

"She followed me but started back at the scene which presented itself to us. On a miserable bed lay extended the speechless and apparently dying support of all the family. His wife the picture of despair, held to his livid lips covered with the deadly symptoms of disease a broken pitcher of water the only refreshment which she had to bestow. Their eldest child, an idiot girl of sixteen half covered with squalid rags and filth pulled our cloaths as we entered and demanded bread with a wild voice of famine, while five other wretched starving objects were contending for a few cabbage stalks which they had stolen from the pigs in a neighbouring yard. 'See my Angela,' I cried, as she turned away shocked and disgusted from this horrid picture, and shrinking sickly from the offensive odour of disease and filth, 'see to what a situation the afflicting hand of our God has reduced this poor family. Think of the blessings you enjoy and receive with gratitude the proofs of love which your heavenly father hourly bestows.'

"'Oh my Mother,' she exclaimed, withdrawing from me the hand I had held, 'it is not to me you should give this lesson. What am I? a wretch despised, existing upon the charity of a stranger. What have I to bestow and my anguish greater than theirs. It is to Lady Trevallyn you should shew this contrast, to Lady Trevallyn rich, innocent, beautiful, to Lady Trevallyn beloved yet daring to repine and call herself unhappy! Take me from this scene of outward misery, that which I incessantly behold within is believe me a sufficient punishment for all my guilt—yes even for my *guilt*—for wretch that I am whom have I injured but myself?'

"I saw that she was not melted, and she even refused to accompany me when I returned to administer to the poor Woodfords the relief I obtained instantly from My Lady's bounty. This however convinced me that pride had some share in my child's distress. But tho' this may account for her wish to quit the asylum with which we might have been here blessed yet still the mystery of her deep anguish is unexplained. I wished indeed to ask you whether you have ever heard her let fall any expression which might lead you to think she had any unfortunate attachment."

"Never," answered Selena, "but I will own a momentary suspicion once crossed my mind upon my asking her some question concerning Lord Henry Ortney."

Mrs. Harley started and turned pale, but besought Selena to tell her exactly what had passed, and tho' there was no positive circumstance on which to found conjecture a deep and unaccountable conviction fell like a heavy weight upon her soul, that she had now discovered the fatal cause of her child's despair and she determined to make one more effort to obtain her confidence and perhaps save her from eternal ruin. For this purpose she resolved to quit Esselberrie and follow her herself to Islington.

She however for the present parted with Selena, with a mutual advice and determination not to reveal their suspicions to Lady Trevallyn, and Mrs. Harley when she requested from her leave to make this journey, as soon as some person could be found to supply her place in her absence, gave not the least hint of the vague surmise which had in truth irresistibly prompted her to take this resolution.

Chapter VI

Digne puer meliore flamma!

Horace[18]

While Selena remained at Esselberrie she received a letter from Robert in which with all the raptures of a lover he announced the favourable reception which his passion had met with from the lovely Lady Harriet Modely whom he had seen at his guardian's and to whom with his consent he had made an offer of his hand. He begged of her to write to him at Mr. Turner's, what she had heard from Dallamore, and excused himself from going to her at present as he could not then endure a separation from his fair treasure—but hoped in less than a fortnight to present her to her new sister—Lady Harriet having promised to accompany him to Hillbarton immediately on their nuptials unless Selena and Clara would meet them at Miltern Abbey.

Selena's surprise was indeed great at this sudden and unexpected intelligence. A confused but disagreeable idea remained upon her mind of Lady Harriet from the praises which Mr. Peters had bestowed upon his fashionable friend—and the anecdote which Mrs. Vallard had related with the impression which she described her appearance to have made when seen in the curricle with Lord Henry was yet more distressing to her recollection.

Impatient to hear Lady Trevallyn's opinion of one in whom she was now so closely interested she flew to her room with the letter still in her hand but stopped at the door, upon hearing the imperious and ever dreaded voice of Lord Trevallyn in a tone even more elevated than usual haranging as it seemed in displeasure to some person whose total silence alone led Selena to fear it could be the gentle Emily. She had never been witness of the least domestic disagreement, and the constraint which her presence always seemed to impose upon him, and the continual sullen silence he almost ever preserved during the tedious, and formal hours of repast made Selena much fear that her society however pleasing it might be to Lady Trevallyn was not much desired by her Lord.

Unwilling now to share in a scene she feared to be so painful she was softly returning to her own room, when the door suddenly bursting open Lord Trevallyn issued forth uttering these words, "Remember Madam in supporting your charities I will never countenance an intimacy with beggars," when perceiving Selena, he cast upon her a look of angry contempt and passed on.

Selena could have no doubt that this speech alluded to Lady Trevallyn's fondness for Mrs. Harley and her little school, but felt now excessively confused at this incident. She however thought it better to advance and found what she had indeed fearfully anticipated her friend in tears.

As soon as she perceived Selena, who timid and irresolute stood yet uncertain at the door whether she should advance or retire, she arose hastily and going to

---

18   Quintus Horace Flaccus, *Odes* (23 BC), 1.27.20: young man worthy of a better flame.

the window to conceal her face while she dried her eyes, said smiling, "Come in Selena, what have you got in your hand?"

"I have brought you a letter to read that I have just got from my brother, only think, he is to be married in a fortnight."

"Married, so soon, and is this the first you have heard of the business?"

"Yes indeed—and it is to Lady Harriet Modely. You know her, do not you?"

"What? You do not say seriously that he is going to marry Lady Harriet Modely?"

"Why dear Lady Trevallyn is she not amiable?"

"Oh I was only amazed, for she is surely older than your brother and not just what I should have expected he would have liked for a wife."

"I am afraid you do not think she will make poor Robert happy?"

"Why I will confess she is no great favourite of mine, but I believe I am rather fastidious and not apt to like people much. Besides as we went out a good deal together I am sure people took it into their heads that I must envy her, for all the men who wished to be civil to me spoke ill of Lady Harriet and tell me a great many little ugly stories, half of which I dare say were lies—but I know she is reckoned very handsome and was greatly the fashion last winter. How upon earth did your brother meet with her?"

"She was on a visit at his guardian Mr. Turner's."

"Oh that is near Worcester—I believe he is her uncle—but I hope they do not insist upon your going to them."

"No, here is the letter, you will see he promises to come to us, but perhaps poor Mrs. Vallard may not quite like the visit of this fine lady, since you say that Lady Harriet is so fine."

As Lady Trevallyn was reading the letter she made no reply to this, but while she was folding it up, she said with a smile, "I wonder Selena how you will like this new sister."

"How old is she? You say she is older than Robert."

"That she is I am sure. We came out together and I was then very young, she cannot possibly be less than four or five and twenty. Your brother is not of age I know."

"He wants only a few months the difference therefore is not great, tho' certainly on the wrong side."

Selena saw indeed that Lady Harriet was not a favourite, but tho' she could not but feel some uneasiness at a connexion which from all she had heard did not seem to promise much domestic happiness to her brother yet she hoped that many of the particulars which had been represented disagreeably wore rather the colour of prejudice to heighten their natural displeasing shade.

She was impatient to communicate this intelligence to Mrs. Vallard and hastened to shew her the letter.

Mrs. Vallard being herself like Selena a total stranger to the disposition of Lady Harriet was willing to hope that the unfavourable circumstance in which she had seen her for the only time, and her very fashionable appearance, had given her a wrong impression of her character, encouraging Selena to hope that Robert had chosen well, and that the rank and beauty which she certainly possessed were not her only recommendations. Her fortune was trifling as they heard from Lady Trevallyn but they knew Robert too well to imagine that this could ever be an object of much consideration in the disposal of his heart.

At Mrs. Vallard's desire Selena wrote to congratulate her brother and to express their hopes of seeing them at the appointed time at Hillbarton. Not having any thing satisfactory to say with respect to Dallamore, she forbore to disturb his present felicity by mentioning him—and indeed calculated her letter for the perusal of his intended bride tho' as she sealed it her heart sighed deep with many a sad presentiment as she inwardly exclaimed, "Alas my Mother why were your fond children deprived of your counsel in the most important moments of their life."

The week allotted to Selena's stay at Esselberrie past rapidly away; The sweetest confidence reigned between Lady Trevallyn and her younger friend— and altho' Lord Henry was seldom mentioned, the subject was rather avoided as one from which they mutually thought it right to divert their minds than because there was on either side any intentional reserve. Lady Trevallyn accustomed to occupy herself during the mornings, except when tempted out by the fineness of the weather left Selena at liberty to direct the studies of Clara, and pursue her own—but the evenings were dedicated to a conversation the most delightful, because each pleased with the other, and assured of mutual sympathy, listened with interest and spoke without restraint. They felt not while in each other's presence the necessity of speaking that bane of society, but their very silence had in it more of intimacy than the usual intercourse of uninterrupted conversation, where to disguise the weariness which we mutually suffer in each other's company, folly and impertinence are on every side abundantly uttered. The two amiable and interesting friends seemed even to forget the melancholy with which both had regarded their unpromising prospects, while they formed plans for passing together much of their future time—and tho' Selena spoke of her establishment as uncertain, Lady Trevallyn could not think it possible that Lord Dallamore should indeed be persuaded to disown a wife of whom he might justly feel so proud.

"But should he," said she to Selena, "indeed behave with such unaccountable baseness, will you not consent to take up your abode entirely with me until you shall make I cannot say a *second* but a better choice?"

"Oh never can I now make a choice," cried Selena. "I have already passed my solemn vows, and never can I think any conduct on the part of Lord Dallamore can absolve me from my duty of promised fidelity. I have taken him ye know," added she smiling, "for better for worse."

Lady Trevallyn looked very thoughtful, but after some pause said, "You have I know a much better judgment than I, but I cannot help thinking you are in this instance quite wrong. I can see no possible reason why you should consider yourself bound to fulfill one part of a conditional promise, when on the other side it is renounced."

"I do not argue the point my dear Lady Trevallyn, but am very sure I can myself never think otherwise than I do at present. But I hope I shall not have a necessity for discussing this except as a matter of meer opinion."

"I sincerely hope so too," answered Lady Trevallyn, "since such are your sentiments."

The friends parted with mutual regret tho' with a promise of often meeting during the uncertain period of Selena's stay at Hillbarton.

Mrs. Harley took leave of Selena with more emotion as she thought it highly probable she might never again be able to share her society, being determined to give up her situation at Esselberrie (desirable as it was for herself) if by so doing she could prevail upon Angela to reside with her constantly. She did not however chuse to acknowledge this intention to Lady Trevallyn who with great reluctance consented, after many vain arguments to detain her, to look out for some substitute finding however so many objections to every person proposed that poor Mrs. Harley's patience was almost worn out by repeated delays to the journey which she felt it so necessary for her to undertake.

Chapter VII

> Such spotless honour, such ingenuous truth,
> Such ripened wisdom in the bloom of youth,
> So mild, so gentle, so composed a mind
> To such heroic warmth and courage joined
> Like polished Sidney nursed in learning's arms
> …………………………..
> Like him possessed of every pleasing art
> The secret wish of every female heart.
> Lord Lyttleton[19]

A few evenings after Selena's return to Hillbarton, she found herself engaged with Mrs. Vallard while seated over the fire in a conversation the most interesting. They had been led insensibly from the approaching marriage of Robert to Selena's own embarrassing situation and the unfortunate tie of relationship which still dangerously connected Lady Trevallyn with the man whom she should above all others avoid. Mean while Clara unobserved was feeding her lively fancy with the yet remembered image of Edwin, as seated upon the sopha she turned over the numerous leaves of the large volume of poetical extracts out of which he had so often captivated her attention by reading to them some of his favourite passages while they worked or drew. While the little party now in the drawing room at Hillbarton were thus occupied, the hours of the usually unemployed

---

[19] George Lyttelton (1709–73), "Epitaph on Captain Grenville; Killed in Lord Anson's Engagement in 1747," *The Poetical Works of George Lord Lyttelton* (1801), lines 5–9, 11–12, with a variation in line 9, which should read "He, too, like Sidney, nursed in Learning's arms."

Sunday evening flew rapidly away—Hours which alas too often in the family circle are dozed away in yawning tediousness, or filled up in a much worse manner by scandalous anecdotes, discordant disputes, or sparring answers to unkind and offensive allusions.

"Can that be ten o clock?" said Mrs. Vallard taking out her watch as she heard the hour strike.

"Impossible!" cried Selena.

"It is really," replied Mrs. Vallard rising, "and I have let slip the time and given the family no sermon. What a shame!"

While she spoke the sound of wheels aroused their attention.

"There is a carriage," cried Clara, "who can that be!"

"It is Dallamore certainly," cried Mrs. Vallard impatiently flying towards the door, while poor Selena without power to move changed colour and would have found the task extremely difficult had she been just then obliged to define her emotions.

The door however opened just as Mrs. Vallard reached it and presented to her eyes a young man of no common appearance but not Dallamore. She started back with an expression of surprise and disappointment which did not escape the penetration of the young stranger dazzled as he was on his first entrance into the glare of the well lighted drawing room.

"Have you forgotten me then dear Mrs. Vallard or have I frightened you at an unseasonable hour?" said he extending with a half mortified air his hand which Mrs. Vallard immediately took with recovered graciousness and warm cordiality.

"No Sidney I am rejoiced to see you. But are you alone?" said she still looking towards the hall.

"Yes I hope so," answered he with a smile hastily turning round with an air of affected terror. "What are you afraid of my admitting any unwelcome guests?"

"On the contrary I hoped you had brought me one most welcome. Did not Dallamore come with you?"

"Oh is that it? No, he is not come and yet I assure you he had half a mind. I think if he was not your nephew I should be very jealous, for he is almost as much in love with you as I have been you know for so many years, and alas, I see his passion has met a kinder return; for at the moment I expected my wife to meet me with a fond embrace she turns from me with disappointment and asks '*Are you alone?*'"

Mrs. Vallard laughed at the ludicrous voice of sorrow with which he repeated her words and said, "Well Husband, I will own that I did not receive you with proper duty, but I will make amends by assuring you now, that I am most sincerely glad to see you, do not however be jealous if I ask you where is Dallamore?"

"Dallamore again! Are you not afraid to dare me thus? Are there no daggers now, nor poisoned bowls for faithless wives?"

"Well but Sidney to be serious tell me is my nephew coming?"

"Well then to be serious it is impossible for me to say what mind your nephew is in at present, as he is seldom of the same for ten minutes together—but I really believe you have kept his heart since his last visit, for he would have been on his road here but for at least an hundred frolicks of Mr. Richmond's to detain him in Ireland. I did think there was a plot to keep him from some one tho' I had little idea it was my own wife. However if I had known your impatience I could easily have eloped with him, and have no doubt he would have embraced such a proposal upon the spot, if I had but started it."

"I wish you had Sidney with all my soul."

"I recollect now that he repeatedly desired me to tell you that he was coming directly, but to say the truth as I did not give the least degree of credit to the message I had no thoughts of delivering it, only I goodnaturedly now would give you the consolation of knowing that he at least wishes to come and that his weakness not his will 'consents to this protracted separation.'"[20]

While he spoke he fixed his beautiful and intelligent blue eyes upon Selena who confused and distressed with heightened colour and full heart could with difficulty restrain her tears—being assured that all his words alluded to her humiliating situation.

Mrs. Vallard struck by the glances which he directed towards Selena once more took his hand and said, "I must now present you to your cousins. Here is Selena ..." she stopped for an instant uncertain what name she should add till he gracefully offering his hand and without waiting for a conclusion said with a smile, "Will Selena Miltern own her cousin Sidney who has long wished for this happy opportunity? And this is I am sure another relation!" added he advancing to Clara while Mrs. Vallard and Selena exchanged a mutual glance expressive of their conviction that Sidney was uninformed of Dallamore's situation.

"Yes," said Mrs. Vallard, seeing him turn round expecting some reply, "that is Clara Miltern and if you stop here for a few days you shall see two more new cousins."

"Two indeed! I expect impatiently to be introduced to Robert, but who is the second?"

"Robert's new wife, now Lady Harriet Modely."

Sidney with some surprise and doubt in his expressive countenance repeated the question which Lady Trevallyn had already asked.

"Do you mean that Robert Miltern is really going to marry Lady Harriet Modely?" But being assured of the truth of the intelligence he said with a smile, "Oh I have no occasion for an introduction there. Lady Harriet and I are old friends, at least old partners. We have danced together at many a ball last Spring."

"I hope you approve of your cousin's choice," said Mrs. Vallard.

"Lady Harriet is very handsome—dances charmingly, and seems lively and good humoured. This is almost all I know of her indeed but she is amazingly admired—and I hope hereafter we shall be better acquainted—for I trust none of my fair cousins will resist my desire of further intimacy."

---

[20] Direct source of quotation unlocated; legal language for divorce.

Tho' the fair cousins, to whom the latter part of this speech had been addressed, made not any immediate answer yet their smiles of complacency sufficiently declared they felt no repulsive inclination to repel the offered intimacy.

There was indeed in his unaffected manners, graceful figure and beautiful countenance an irresistible charm, a bewitching attraction, which even where he appeared with indifference rendered him an object of universal attention—but which when he peculiarly desired to please possessed a fascination that had never failed, tho' opposed against the most stupid prejudice or the most cold insensibility.

His lively conversation and the interest with which his auditors listened to the account he gave of the party which he had left at Mount Villars insensibly held them wakeful to a much later hour than that upon which they usually retired—notwithstanding which Mrs. Vallard accompanied Selena to her room and closed the door to express her displeasure and surprise at what she had heard, and at the secrecy which it was too plain Dallamore preserved even to so near a relation. So little were they inclined to terminate a conversation so interesting to each that with their candles still lighted in their hands they yet stood engaged in deep discourse when the clock striking two, startled and gave them a hint to separate.

Sidney, the only son of the second brother of Lord Mount Villars, had been when a boy the school fellow and chosen friend of Lord Dallamore. Tho' not more than one year older than his cousin he had always possessed the most unbounded influence over his inclinations, and Lord Dallamore ever in the company of Sidney, was like Sidney generous, noble, amiable, active and happy. But their situations were now different, and tho' Dallamore still loved Sidney above all his other companions, yet separated from him he had acquired other friendships, or rather made other acquaintances, for of friendship his uncertain character was indeed incapable, and had unfortunately found other guides less favourable to improve his heart and direct his head. They had passed their holy days together, chiefly at Mrs. Vallard's, and in spite of her fond partiality for her nephew, the talents, understanding and graces of Sidney were admired and loved by her with almost equal affection. On his part, finding himself ever received by her with the most flattering indulgence he loved her above all women except his mother, and had been accustomed in sportive fondness to call her his wife, a name which she still retained among that branch of the family.

Aware of the ascendency which he possessed over the mind of Dallamore, Mrs. Vallard wished to engage him in their interests—but Selena struck with the unusual reserve of Dallamore entreated her not to betray what he so evidently wished to preserve still a secret. Mrs. Vallard yielded to her advice the more readily as she reflected that Sidney could not at present return to Ireland, without great inconvenience, his influence therefore, which she was sensible extented not beyond his presence could not now be exerted for Selena's advantage. Sidney was not however himself without some suspicions that the strong inclination repeatedly evinced by Dallamore to return to Hillbarton, and the artful opposition it had received not only from Richmond but Lord Mount Villars, proceeded from his admiration of Selena tho' he had little idea of the real truth, a truth which

Dallamore himself had carefully concealed from a consciousness that Sidney would disapprove of his conduct.

Indeed Sidney had not been many days at Hillbarton before he began to think it impossible to behold and converse with Selena with indifference—and every hour this persuasion grew stronger, whether he gazed upon the perfect loveliness of her light and graceful form, the beauty of her ever varying countenance and complexion, or listened to the simple and unaffected conversation which shewed the justice and delicacy of her sentiments, or admired her uncommon talents displayed with unobtrusive modesty which never seemed to consider herself in the applause which they excited, whatever she said, or however she was employed,[21] whether he observed her mind or mind-illumined face he still saw in her excellence which he had hitherto considered but as the creature only of his own warm imagination

> so lovely fair
> That what seemed fair in all the world, seemed
> Mean, or in her summed up, in her contained
> And in her looks; while to consumate all
> Greatness of mind and nobleness their seat
> Built in her loveliest.[22]

Determined however to guard his heart, lest he should irrevocably bestow it upon one whose affections were already given to another he avoided paying to Selena that exclusive attention to which the admiration he felt for her continually inclined him; nay he even appeared to prefer the innocent familiarity with which Clara treated him to the more reserved but soul captivating conversation of her sister.

Clara's conduct to him was indeed strikingly different from that which she had observed towards Edwin. To Edwin she had listened in timid silence, and in his presence seemed to lose the gaiety natural to her age and character. With her cousin all animated and even sportive she was ever ready to converse with the utmost ease, and even solicitated his company when preparing for their morning's walk or evening's lecture. She was not satisfied when she sung with Selena if Sidney did not accompany them with his fine mellow voice, and when at her call he joined in their concert she then exerted herself with delighted success. Her cheeks were not then covered with blushes nor did the tremulous notes expire but half expressed while her faltering accents betrayed her agitated confusion as had ever been the case when receiving the instructions of Edwin.

Selena felt half displeased at her levity, and suspecting that she had already transferred these affections which she so early had bestowed, asked Mrs. Vallard one day did she not think that Clara now liked her cousin better than she had once done Edwin.

---

[21] MS: "employment" (my correction).

[22] "Milton" (Tighe's note). John Milton, *Paradise Lost* (1674), 8:471–4, 556–8 (Adam's first meeting with Eve). Tighe omits "now" after "seemed" in line 472.

Mrs. Vallard acknowledged that she had herself imagined she perceived the commencement of a mutual inclination, and expressed much pleasure at the circumstance, saying they would make a lovely couple, and that it could not be expected that Clara at her age would very faithfully cherish an unreturned love which she rejoiced to perceive she had now forgotten.

Selena tho' not romantic enough to esteem a first love of that kind invincible and irrecoverable, yet could not approve the lightness with which affection could in a few weeks be thus changed, and tho' she was silent on the subject secretly lamented the want of delicacy which she thought was thus discovered in the character of Clara.

Sidney in the mean time while he directed to Clara almost all his manifest attention, carefully and anxiously watched every word which fell from Selena and every look that spoke in her eloquent eye as often as Dallamore was the theme of conversation. The sadness which at those times peculiarly overspread her mild countenance, and the enquiring interest which at the mention of his name ever aroused her silent attention almost convinced him of her partiality and while he wondered at the eager curiosity with which he sought to discover her secret he felt provoked at the uneasy sensations which so often prompted him to lament that a heart so excellent and capable of such sensibility should be thrown away upon Dallamore whose apparent indifference seemed not to merit its worth.

Convinced from a thousand little circumstances which can only be known to the persons themselves most interested that Clara did not mistake his playful gallantry for any serious regard, and that on her part she saw and conversed with him in perfect indifference—he was not displeased that Mrs. Vallard and Selena should be diverted from discovering the real situation of his heart by the suspicions which he saw they entertained. He hoped not to be able to supplant Dallamore if Selena had really looked upon him with partial eyes. He owned not to himself that he even wished it, but already deeply and forever interested in her welfare, he resolved if he was convinced that her happiness depended upon Dallamore, to exert all his efforts in fixing his inconstant and volatile mind only upon her who so well deserved his love and admiration.

This idea seized with such strong force upon his generous mind that he even persuaded himself that he now desired nothing upon earth more ardently than to be able by his influence to bring Dallamore to her feet, and see her happy in the complete possession of his heart. In the midst of all these enthusiastic plans a doubt would sometimes occur which he loved to indulge that perhaps he was yet mistaken, and that Selena's bosom was a stranger to those sentiments he had supposed her to feel.

However it might be, his whole soul was occupied by his schemes and his doubts with respect to Selena, and if possible he was resolved to gain her confidence. With this view he now took all opportunities of leading her into conversation on subjects of a less gay and general nature than he had at first been used to discuss, and tho' she sought not his society, yet she did not refuse his advances to an intimacy she could not but see he wished to establish on the basis of friendship.

With Clara still in her eye she thought it natural that Sidney really captivated by her early graces should wish to cultivate the regard and conciliate the esteem of her sister who might in future aid his wishes by her partiality in his favour and she was not sorry that he thus gave her an opportunity of learning his sentiments and becoming more intimately acquainted with his character.

Selena had one morning been so much engaged with his conversation after breakfast that neither noticed the departure of Mrs. Vallard and Clara, while they stood in a window, where Sidney had followed her to mark the fading beauties of the autumnal scene, when upon looking round and seeing the room deserted she was about to retire in some confusion, but Sidney smiling as he took her hand said softly, "Who are you looking for there now?[23] There is no one at present at Hillbarton that can dispute my claims on your attention. Clara is gone to play some of your friend Edwin's songs, and when that is the case you and I are alike intruders. Mrs. Vallard is too busy mixing physic for her poor neighbours to mind us at present. Let us then not mind them but come out and enjoy this lovely mild day. We cannot expect many more such days for a long long dreary season, and soon too soon I must relinquish such society."

Selena was surprised, and surprise held her dumb; while musing on all that this speech seemed to imply the varying colours on her cheek made Sidney fear he had said too much.

"Why do you hesitate? You are not displeased with your friend? You know you allowed me to call myself by that name and

> Is aught so fair
> In all the dewy landscapes of the spring
> In the bright eye of Hesper or the morn,
> In Nature's fairest forms is aught *so* fair
> As virtuous friendship?[24]

Are not these beautiful lines of my favourite Akenside's," added he wishing to divert her mind, for which purpose they had been indeed repeated.

"Yes," answered she recovering, "and Mr. Stanmore *my friend* as you call him has made me admire 'The pleasures of imagination' which on my first reading I confess I did not quite like or think intelligible. But pray what do *you* know of *my* friend Mr. Stanmore?"

"Oh poor Clara can talk of no one else with any pleasure."

"Has she been talking to you of Mr. Stanmore?" asked Selena with encreased astonishment.

"Yes perpetually, and while she thought she was only discovering to me the secret of his hopeless passion for you, she quite unintentionally betrayed her own

---

[23]   The MS editor corrects this sentence to "Whom are you looking for?"

[24]   Mark Akenside, *The Pleasures of Imagination* (1744, 1757), 2:336–41 (Tighe uses the later, expanded version).

affection, which I am sure must meet a better return should his good fortune ever again throw him in her way."

This was extraordinary Selena thought, but suspecting he only spoke thus with apparent indifference in consequence of some jealous suspicions which might have occurred to him she endeavoured to persuade him that she really believed if Clara had entertained a childish *penchant* for this singular young man that it was now entirely forgotten.

He did not contradict her opinion but with an affected gaiety which his heart was at the moment far from feeling he said looking at her archly, "I am perhaps then equally mistaken in my conjectures with respect to other people."

Selena with a glowing cheek and trembling voice asked him to explain himself.

"I am perhaps impertinent," said he more seriously, "but you see dear Selena … may I not call you dear Selena?" he paused & then repeated the question as he sought her averted eye.

"Do call me Selena," said she endeavouring to smile off her confusion … "it is indeed the name I have most right to … But what were you going to say?"

He had indeed totally forgotten what he meant to utter, so much had the expression which thus escaped her surprised him.

"What do you mean by right?" asked he eagerly.

"Oh nothing only that as my cousin and my friend, you know you have an undoubted claim to this freedom."

Satisfied with this explanation he proceeded, "Well then *dear Selena* you must not be surprised if I use the privilege of friendship and seek to examine into the secrets of my friend, nay to be offended at her want of confidence."

"What secrets?" asked Selena anxiously, not doubting that he now alluded to her marriage which she thought some circumstances might have discovered—tho' of Clara's fidelity to the solemn promise she had made of secrecy she had not a suspicion.

"Nay," said he, "I will not betray my own conjectures, perhaps ill-founded, since you refuse to understand me, but let us change the subject if you please …. tell me what do you think of our cousin Dallamore?"

More than ever now confirmed in her idea that he knew or at least guessed her situation she was too much agitated to speak and with a secret pang he gazed at her lovely features suffused by this question with the deepest blushes, the emotion which throbbed in her

> Marble neck
> Which bent aside in vain, revealing more
> What she would thus keep silent ……..[25]

and her eyes which shone like the dewy star of evening smiling in tears.

---

[25]   Mark Akenside, *The Pleasures of Imagination* (1744, 1757), 1:371–3 ("bent" should be "bends" and "she" should be "it").

He gazed at her, and he gazed in silence—a thousand mingled sensations of regret tenderness and admiration overpowering all his reasoning faculties. Deeply sighing, "It is enough," thought he at last, "it is enough. Why should I press her gentle delicacy to a farther confession. She loves him! I can no longer doubt it—and she must, shall be happy!"

While he struggled to suppress his selfish feelings, Selena resumed her composure and trying to disperse from her full eyes the tears which she trusted he had not observed she answered hesitatingly, "Lord Dallamore has many amiable qualities—do not you think so?" asked she after a moment, venturing to raise her eyes to his, surprised at his sudden pensive silence.

"What do you say—I beg your pardon," cried he starting.

"Oh you were in one of Dallamore's own absent fits," said she with a forced smile, "I see it is a family failing."

"Absent as I am however," said he exerting himself to speak with cheerfulness, "I have not forgotten that you gave me just now a tacit consent to our walking, so pray go and get on your hat."

With a sigh she left him to comply with his desire, but half reproached herself for that sigh when she found it accompanied an unuttered wish, "Oh why is not Dallamore more like his cousin!"

She was however upon reflection after this conversation anxious to discover what were the real sentiments of Clara with respect to Sidney, and thought it also expedient to give her artless mind some caution if she had indeed betrayed to him an affection for Edwin.

She took therefore the first opportunity of their being alone to say to her, "What do you think Sidney has told me about you?"

"About me! Oh I can guess he has complained how I teized him by hiding his book that he was so busy reading."

"And why did you do any thing so monky like?"

"Why he just laid it down for a moment when he saw you pass the windows, but you were gone up to your room before he went out so he came back and I had put it under the cushion of the sopha to punish him for not taking me this morning when you went to walk. Was it not that?"

"No," said Selena, "that was not it. Have you any more confessions to make of his right to complain of you?"

"Oh yes! at least a thousand but pray tell me what he has had the impertinence to say of me."

"Why then he has had the impertinence to say that you are in love with Edwin Stanmore."

The "blushing apparitions"[26] which suddenly started to Clara's face were not those alone "celestial rosy red Love's proper hue"[27] but such as burned her cheek with the deeper glow of mingled shame and indignation.

---

[26] Friar Francis in Shakespeare's *Much Ado About Nothing* (1598), 4.1.159.

[27] Milton's *Paradise Lost* (1674), 8.619.

"Oh Selena!" said she after a moment's pause, "How unlike is this to yourself. It is not kind in you

> To join with men in scorning your poor friend
> It is not sisterly, it is not maidenly
> Our sex as well as I may chide you for it.[28]

You should rather pity, than despise and betray me, and tell to every body that I am 'miserable thus to love unloved.'"[29]

"Dearest Clara what do you mean!" exclaimed Selena astonished at the bitter tears which too surely proved how seriously she had been affected, "you are mistaken, indeed you are if you can think me capable of sporting with your feelings on any subject, or that I could expose your secrets with such indelicate unkindness. So far was I from betraying you that I had myself no suspicion of your seriously remembering Edwin, and I have rather believed that you looked upon Sidney himself with a partial eye."

"Oh Selena! could you think it possible that having once known Edwin I could ever ...."

Here she stopped unknowing how to proceed and Selena gently drawing her to her, hid her blushing, weeping face in her affectionate bosom.

"Who then could have told Sidney? ... I am sure Edwin himself never suspected my folly, do you think it possible he could?" cried she warmly as she raised her enquiring eyes to Selena's face.

"No indeed my love, I do not—and what Sidney said was merely in jest because you had been speaking to him I suppose of Edwin, and that you are fond of singing his music."

"And are you not fond of his music? And must not every one that has ever heard Edwin's music love it? Surely there is nothing so extraordinary in that!"

"Certainly not nor did Sidney think it extraordinary. Nor perhaps would he have observed it, had he not felt peculiarly interested in all you like or dislike, for 'Love thou knowest is full of jealousy'[30] as I dare say you have lately read since Edwin has made you so fond of Shakespear."

"Nay," answered she smiling, "I must say now you are either not sincere Selena, or you have very little discernment."

"What do you mean Clara?"

"Why have you not perceived that Sidney loves you, how he looks at you! how he watches your every word and motion and sighs just as Edwin did?"

"No indeed, on the contrary I am sure if there is any love in the case it is for you and as for me he has certainly somehow or another heard how I am

---

[28] Helena in Shakespeare's *A Midsummer Night's Dream* (1595), 3.2.216–18. Tighe changes "friendly" to "sisterly" in line 217.

[29] Helena in Shakespeare's *A Midsummer Night's Dream* (1595), 3.2.234. Tighe changes "most" to "thus" above.

[30] Valentine in Shakespeare's *Two Gentlemen of Verona* (1594), 2.4.174.

circumstanced—and I am convinced he thinks of me in no other light but as his friend and the wife of his friend."

"Perhaps so," said Clara, "but I assure you I have never let fall the least hint of your secret, tho' I own I have fifty times been tempted to tell him not to think of you any more, since it was to no purpose now for him to love you as I am afraid he does."

"Believe me then you are mistaken," answered Selena gravely, "I have no doubt of the disinterested friendship he has so often professed, and am assured he is only interested for me as dear Mrs. Vallard is."

"I suppose you are right," answered Clara, "but it is very odd that Mrs. Vallard's friendship should seem so different, and that it should not make her attend so constantly to the most trifling word you say—and that she should not grow red always when you come into the room, and sigh when you go out of it as Sidney does ... and ... and as poor Edwin used to do."

"Oh fie Clara," cried Selena blushing deeply, "do not talk so much about love indeed it is a subject with which we have neither of us any thing to do at present you are too young yet to think of love. And for my part I must never hear of it from any one except Lord Dallamore. His affection I hope I shall be able to preserve and if so I shall be quite content."

"Well," said Clara with a deep sigh, "I am sure I do not wish to speak of love ... nor was it I, Selena, that began the subject. Come let us play some of Haydn's compositions, or yours, since I must not play any more of Edwin's while *Mr. Sidney* is here. I am sure the sooner he goes the better for all our sakes."

There was something in the latter part of this speech which struck to Selena's heart with a new and fearful emotion and perhaps the lovely sister musicians had never before exerted their abilities with less success than in the duet which immediately followed this interesting conversation.

Chapter VIII

Insolent and self-caressed
By vanity's unwearied finger dressed
Forgot the blush that virgin fears impart
To modest cheeks, and borrowed one from art—
Even just such trifles without worth or use
As silly pride and idleness produce
They stretch the neck and roll the wanton eye
And sigh for every fool that flutters by
Cowper[31]

---

[31] William Cowper, "Expostulation," *The Poems of William Cowper* (1782), lines 45–54. Tighe changes "Were" to "Even" in line 49, omits lines 51–2 ("Curled, scented, furbelowed, and flounced around, / With feet too delicate to touch the ground") and shifts the tense from past to present in lines 53–4 ("They stretched the neck, and rolled the wanton eye, / And sighed for every fool that fluttered by").

The moment Selena was alone she called herself to severe account, not only for her conduct towards Sidney but for the sentiments with which she had received his offers of a friendship so dangerous, and tho' she hoped she might hitherto acquit herself, yet she trembled at the self delusion which she had seen in Lady Trevallyn, who unconscious of any reproach, she had plainly perceived still cherished the bane of her peace, too well calculated to undermine the fair and spotless edifice of virtue and of happiness.

Tho' Selena could not absolutely credit the suggestions of Clara to whom experience had early given skill in that passion which she already felt, yet she resolved to treat the amiable Sidney with that confidence which he so well deserved and purposed that very day to consult Mrs. Vallard upon the expediency of entrusting him with her secret.

She was however prevented from entering upon this subject, to which she indeed felt an involuntary reluctance, by a letter which announcing the arrival of the new married couple on the next day put the whole house into some degree of trepidation, and busied the kind hostess in all the bustle of preparation.

Selena felt herself rather agitated at the thoughts of seeing for the first time her beloved brother in his new character—and was somewhat uneasy lest Lady Harriet whom she had been taught to consider as so fine a Lady might look upon her new sisters with contempt.

Aware of the hours to which Lady Harriet was accustomed Mrs. Vallard had not ordered dinner until six o'clock. But it was near seven before the curricle drove into the yard, in which as her Ladyship's maid had informed them (who had come some hours before to prepare her toilet) her Lady & Mr. Miltern chose to travel.

Mrs. Vallard who heard that they had but thirty miles to come on that day was really apprehensive lest some accident might have detained them, and could have no idea that this late arrival was a predetermined point on the part of Lady Harriet, who had been all day delaying Robert that they might avoid the horrors of seeing the whole family ranged in the hall to welcome her arrival by broad day light. Not that her Ladyship's modesty shrunk from the exhibition of a figure in the admiration of which indeed ever consisted her highest pleasures, but she dreaded the ceremony of receiving with the dust yet on her habit, the curls unsettled on her face and the rouge half blown off her cheeks, the salutations of the fogram Mrs. Vallard and Robert's awkward sisters of whose unfashioned rural beauty and manners in spite of his representations she had formed no high ideas.

Eager to escape this the moment she alighted she hastily enquired for her maid and desired Robert to make her apology till she had taken off her habit, or in other words "till awful Beauty put on all her arms."[32] As the present fashion however allows not those arms to consist in putting on much apparel, and as the ladies of our day, being literally "when unadorned adorned the most,"[33] have little more to

---

[32]   Alexander Pope, "The Rape of the Lock" (1712), 1.139: "Now awful Beauty puts on all its Arms."

[33]   James Thomson, "Autumn," *The Seasons* (1730), line 206.

do at the hour of dressing, than to throw aside these envious coverings in which they think it necessary during the morning in some degree to veil their charms in very little more than an hour, the butler who had been upon the watch led the way, and Lady Harriet herself entered the drawing room where had been so long assembled the impatient family, with a select company of the neighbouring gentry invited by Mrs. Vallard in order to diminish the awkward form of a small party strangers to each other. Lord Trevallyn was of course not omitted but his Lady as had been indeed expected sent an excuse.

Lady Harriet appeared with that exploring glance and conscious smile with which satisfied beauty looks round for that admiration which it has been accustomed to receive and while Robert approached to take her hand to lead her to Mrs. Vallard, advanced with an easy air saying she hoped she had not kept her waiting dinner. Robert now presented the agitated and blushing Selena, whose half offered embrace was only checked by the unbending neck with which her Ladyship while she returned her curtsey seemed to expect no farther familiarity. In the mean time Clara gazed at her with an astonishment which was not like Selena's in some degree diminished by having seen other fashionable beauties—for never before had Clara beheld any being so rouged and so dressed.

Lady Harriet's brilliant complexion indeed owed the advantages of its striking colours not to rouge alone, and the large and completely exposed neck and shoulders which dazzled the eye by their uncommon whiteness, as well as the snowy lustre of her arms, more covered by their bracelets than the small and delicate web which could scarcely boast the name of sleeve shewed as little of their natural hue as the less artificial and more acknowledged painting of her cheek. And yet it was to the shewy contrast formed by this complexion with a profusion of dark hair for which also she was not entirely indebted to Nature, that she owed her having been a much celebrated tho' questioned beauty. For except for her eyes which were large and of the very darkest hazle she possessed not one feature which could be called fine and certainly did not by the expression or animation of her countenance compensate for the want of perfect regularity.

Seated in an attitude the best adapted to display the elegance of her well turned limbs; set off rather than shaded by the soft and graceful drapery, which was taught to cling around without concealing any part of her shape Lady Harriet now appeared to take no notice of the conversation except when obliged by forced monosyllables to answer questions directed immediately to her, but her eyes wandered with an undisguised curiosity, and intently gazed by turns upon every individual, tho' the unchanged unmeaning smile which she still wore prevented the objects of her examination to guess whether it proceeded from admiration or contempt.

At length the approach of Sidney diverted her eyes from the survey which had been made with indifference to none but herself. With Sidney she even deigned to hold some conversation as he stood by her side with his back to the fire till the summons to dinner relieved Robert from the embarrassment he had experienced lest the object of his fond and proud choice should not appear in that amiable and advantageous light he so anxiously desired and hoped the friends he most loved and esteemed should now behold his beautiful bride. She was however disappointed that Sidney did not occupy the vacant chair which she left between herself and Mrs. Vallard and even with an emotion of surprise beheld him seat himself by Selena at the foot of the table. She thought the place but badly supplied by Lord Trevallyn whose ill temper had been very considerably excited by the disrespectful delay of dinner after the hour on which a person of such consequence had been appointed. Not that Sidney was a particular favourite of Lady Harriet's but as he was the only young man in company whom she had ever seen in the circle which she had been accustomed to consider as including every person one ought to know, she thought him the only being qualified to take the post of honour by her side and could not conceive what stupidity induced him to decline it.

When the ladies returned after dinner to the drawing room the silent examination once more commenced on the part of Lady Harriet, who as she stood before the fire with some music in her hand as a screen took a critical survey of the faces, dresses and even the furniture which surrounded her.

Mrs. Vallard made a few unsuccessful efforts to engage her in conversation, but finding her skill baffled now turned to pay some attention to her other guests, and Selena seeing Lady Harriet's eyes fixed upon Mrs. Vallard and the lady to whom she spoke, stood by for a while in silence. Observing that she took no other share in their conversation with a timid voice she ventured to address her, and by way of introducing some discourse asked her had she not found it rather cold in the curricle.

Lady Harriet started as she spoke; and turning round for a moment as if to see who was beside her then fixed her eyes upon the music she held while she answered, "Cold! . . oh yes … I am always miserably cold in a curricle. Indeed this is not a climate for open carriages."

Selena wondered why she had then preferred one, but would not take the liberty to ask a question which might be esteemed impertinent.

However she had no occasion to make the enquiry for after a pause Lady Harriet continued in a voice of affected languor, "But any misery is better than to be stuffed up in an odious carriage for such a length of time. Besides the smell of the leather always makes me sick, especially of a new carriage."

"You did not leave Litchfield very early I suppose," said Selena.

"Early … no not very," this answer was given after a considerably long pause for her eyes had again been busily or at least fixedly employed on Selena's hair and neck lace.

Rather uneasy at the stare which she could not avoid Selena ventured to hazard another question.

"Did you not think the George at Litchfield a very good inn?"

"Good inn, I really do not know. One inn is like another I think; They are all detestable filthy poisoned cells!"

Selena looked at her to see if she should smile but even the usual smile had left Lady Harriet's lips while she reflected on the distressing sufferings she had been obliged to undergo in these filthy poisoned cells.

"Did you not think the country you passed thro' today very beautiful?"

"Beautiful! ... no I cannot say I saw much beauty in it. It is reckoned remarkably beautiful?"

"Oh yes, I believe so. For my own part I own I am partial to Herefordshire. I hope you may like Miltern Abbey."

"Very probably I shall not ... but do not let that affront you for I am no judge."

Selena felt abashed by this reply and the contemptuous voice in which it was made but unwilling to sink again into awkward and total silence and yet ashamed to persist in asking insipid questions wished sincerely that she was acquainted with some common place topicks which it might be pleasing to Lady Harriet to converse upon, or that she knew what subjects would induce her to open herself to a freer communication. She remembered that Mr. Peters had declared her superior in life, animation and spirit to Lady Trevallyn and was afraid that contempt for her ignorance now restrained her from exercising her powers of being agreeable.

These reflections reminded her of Mr. Peters' boasted intimacy with Lady Harriet, and naturally supposing that he must be rather a favourite since he had found her so pleasant, after another long pause she said timidly, "I had the pleasure of hearing your Ladyship sometimes spoken of last summer when I was at Harrogate for a few days."

Lady Harriet now looked up with something more of satisfaction than she had before testified as she said, "from Lord Henry Ortney, was it? I saw him just before we left town, and Mr. Miltern told me you met him there."

"No," replied Selena innocently unconscious how mortifying was her answer, "it was Mr. Peters."

"Mr. Peters!" replied Lady Harriet with cold disdain. "Who is Mr. Peters?"

"I believe he is a friend of Mr. Richmond, do you not know him."

"Oh I recollect, yes, I believe I do know him, just to bow to, really I am hardly certain if I know him or not. Is this Mr. Peters a particular friend of yours?"

"No," said Selena smiling, "but I think he boasted of being well known to Lady Harriet."

At this accusation which was felt like an insult or rather the dreadful charge of some foul crime, Lady Harriet with the utmost contempt turned aside saying scornfully, "I assure you Miss Miltern you are much mistaken, he is no acquaintance of mine."

Selena was thunderstruck. Mr. Peters had never indeed appeared to her either amiable, agreeable, or elegant, but she saw him in what was called good company and she herself liked him full as well as she had done Mr. Richmond of whom she had heard Lady Harriet speak with familiarity as she listened to the little dialogue she had held with Sidney before dinner. She could not therefore conceive why the supposition of his acquaintance could be considered as an impeachment upon any one, and hardly knowing what she said, so much was she confused by the offence she was sensible she had unintentionally given she stammered out, "I suppose that is Mr. Peters' way, for he talked of Lady Trevallyn too, and she told me since that she knew nothing at all about him."

"Lady Trevallyn knows as much of him I promise you as I do. He is a horrible bore, and detestably vulgar."

Selena now completely discouraged forbore any further efforts—and Lady Harriet was the first to break the silence which now ensued by asking Selena when she had seen Lady Trevallyn and the next moment enquired whether Lord Henry had been lately in that country?

Selena coloured when she answered that he had been at Esselberrie she believed for a few days.

"Did you see him while he was there?"

Selena answered in the negative and sighed as she recollected the melancholy which oppressed her spirits at that time.

Neither the blush nor the sigh escaped Lady Harriet who tho' far from being remarkably brilliant in her understanding was yet generally pretty quick in discovering whatever had any relation to a love intrigue or could bear the slightest suspicion of such a nature. She had heard from Robert, whose violent love could not allow of any disguise towards her, of Selena's situation, with respect to Dallamore, and she was now well inclined to believe that Lord Henry whose character and powers of captivation she well knew had profitted by Dallamore's neglect to supplant him in the affections of his young and pretty bride—for pretty she secretly tho' reluctantly allowed Selena to be.

To attract to herself the envied attentions of Lord Henry had been the highest ambition of Lady Harriet during several successive winters. And in this design she had been so often thwarted by the presence of the lovely Emily and that at some times in so mortifying a manner, that, as there was no person upon earth equally hateful to her with Lady Trevallyn, so there was no circumstance she could bear with more pleasure than one she thought likely to afford vexation and humiliation to her who had in so many instances been her most formidable rival.

All the town had watched with illnatured curiosity the termination of Lord Henry's assiduities to his beautiful cousin, bets had been laid, and the certainty of their approaching nuptials circulated and denied by indefatigable gossip, never wearied of repeating the oft detected falsehood. All the town had maliciously triumphed in Lord Henry's base cruelty, and the disappointment of the innocent hopes of an unoffending lovely creature. All the town had affected to pity the "poor silly girl who was dying for love"[34] when she went abroad, but none had listened with more interest, and discussed with more constant and anxious pleasure upon this topick than Lady Harriet.

---

[34] Specific source unlocated, but variants of this phrase appear in many songs and novels, including Tobias Smollett's *The Adventures of Peregrine Pickle* (1751): "the poor young woman, who was dying for love" (chapter 7).

Emily's marriage had indeed put an end to the fears entertained that she might one day be able to bind this charming inconstant in the shackles of matrimony, but it had at the same time raised her to a rank where her unrivalled loveliness shone most conspicuous and had fixed beyond dispute her superiority in beauty and fashion above every competitor.

The first winter of a young married beauty is a second new appearance. Every tongue was now occupied by her celebrated charms. Many an eye that had past over with careless indifference the slighted Emily Montrose, mocked and defeated in her ambitious projects was now fixed with enchanted admiration upon the young Countess of Trevallyn who was indeed "The rose where all were roses."[35]

Lord Henry too had made no secret of his continued and even augmented attachment and where ever she appeared had eyes for no other object. Lady Harriet had no idea of the virtuous delicacy with which the unhappy Emily shrunk from his regard, and as Lord Henry during the last Spring had seldom remained above a few minutes at any assembly where Lady Trevallyn was not to be seen she had herself charitably entertained little doubt of their good intelligence and taken no inconsiderable pains to propagate her own opinion.

She found however little encouragement. Lady Trevallyn now stood in no envious daughter or proud mother's way—the world illnatured, false as it was seemed now to relent of its severity, and for once divest itself of its injustice in favour of the retiring modest graces of the young Countess. Royal lips had pronounced her most beautiful, and every tongue appeared ambitious to repeat the uncontested decision.

The strictest censors of the dissipated circle, who like ill-tempered gluttons at a feast, grumbling and greedy partake of all which they condemn as far as it is in their reach, these had named Lady Trevallyn as a pattern of female excellence— and envy had not been roused to protest against the approbation. Mothers with a long train of unnoticed girls, who viewed with the frown of mortified contempt, the gay chaperons engrossing all the titled partners, met with a gracious smile "the quiet Lady Trevallyn" whose silent gentleness had discouraged the advances of every fashionable coxcomb, and who in refusing to listen to Lord Henry could yet endure the attention of no other man.

Lady Harriet had indeed been told by some of her own admirers that Lady Trevallyn was "miserably stupid" and she was willing to think when she saw her unsurrounded by a train of laughing fools that "the men did not care to talk with so insipid a piece of still life," such "an inanimate picture," "so dull a set of regular features that were dressed for the day at the glass each morning," but the world in general while they admired indisputably her beauty were even indulgent enough to attribute her reserve to an amiable and domestic disposition, and to a proper sense of the peculiar propriety requisite in a situation which struck many with the same wonder it had done Selena "that one so young and so beautiful should marry such an old man."

---

[35] Thomas Moore, "Ode LXVI," *Odes of Anacreon* (1800), line 30: "The sweetest rose, where all are roses."

Lady Harriet was not however among those who gave her this deserved applause. Convinced that she loved Lord Henry, and that while Lord Henry devoted himself to her it was impossible she should resist him, she felt a secret gratification in the idea which now suggested itself to her mind that the young Selena might rival Lady Trevallyn in the fickle affections of Lord Henry.

She was too much interested in the truth of this not to take some pains to ascertain it, and therefore as the best question she could devise for this purpose she asked Selena did she not think Lord Henry a very beautiful man?

"He is very handsome," answered Selena coldly.

"Is he handsomer than Sidney?" asked Clara in a half whisper venturing for the first time to put in her word.

Lady Harriet honoured her with another stare and Selena remaining silent answered contemptuously, "very different indeed! Lord Henry is reckoned much the handsomest man in town and I never heard that Mr. Sidney was a beauty."

Selena thought within herself they were indeed very different, but as she could not truly agree with the preference which Lady Harriet had given and as she did not chuse to be thought singular in calling Mr. Sidney a beauty she was silent, and her silence confirmed Lady Harriet's suspicions.

"Have you ever danced with Lord Henry?" demanded she after some time determined not to drop the subject.

"Yes several times at Harrogate."

"Several times? He is much altered then if he is grown such a dancer. He was always one of my favourite partners but I have very seldom seen him dance otherwise tho' it is a great pity, for nobody dances so divinely. Do not you think so?"

"Yes I believe so," answered Selena who hardly remembered his dancing tho' she really had been struck at the time by its uncommon grace and agility. But her vanity did not induce her to add that she had seen him dance with no other partner but herself during her stay at Harrogate.

"What does Lady Trevallyn do with herself at Esselberrie when Lord Henry is not there?" asked Lady Harriet.

Selena was as much shocked as she was surprised at such a question, and for a moment answered only by a deep blush; indignation then supplied her with courage and eloquence, and having begun her speech by saying that her occupations were at all times the same, whatever company might be in the house, she proceeded to paint the innocent and useful employments in which her amiable friend passed her hours.

Lady Harriet listened in silence with a vacant eye and a smile which Selena could not help thinking was a smile not of satisfaction but contempt.

In the midst of her eulogium she was however interrupted by Lady Harriet's asking with a yawn, "Pray may I ring the bell?"

"Certainly, but can I do any thing for you Lady Harriet," answered Selena.

"No I thank you," answered her Ladyship who had touched the bell which was at her elbow while she spoke.

Upon the servant's entrance she said in even a lower voice than usual, "Be so good as to tell my maid to bring me my handkerchief."

"My Lady!" said the servant approaching to hear if possible the yet inaudible commands; Selena repeated her orders, Lady Harriet appearing in silent despair of making herself understood by ears so vulgar.

The maid entered with the perfumed handkerchief which she presented on a salvar, and again receiving it in a few moments retired as she had approached with an unnoticed and silent curtsey.

Selena thought this ceremony must be rather troublesome in case her Ladyship was ever unfortunate enough to be troubled with so vulgar a thing as a cold and turned her eye fearfully from the arch smile of Clara.

"Does Lady Trevallyn go to town soon?" asked Lady Harriet after another interval.

"I heard her say she was afraid they must go before December this year on account of some law business."

"Afraid!" repeated Lady Harriet, "not much afraid I should imagine, tho' to be sure it is horribly dull till after Christmas."

"Lady Trevallyn hates town at all times."

"Oh so she says, but I never saw any one seem to like it better."

"She does not go much out I believe while there," said Selena softly.

"I do not know. I think I saw her for all that every where that she was asked and I am sure she was for ever at the opera; do you know has she got a box this year?"

"I cannot tell really."

"I wish I knew, for I should like to have Lord Henry take one of my tickets, but if Lady Trevallyn has a box, I suppose *I* need not ask him."

Selena could not forgive the spiteful insinuation, and the blush it excited was once more placed to a false account.

"Do you expect to be in town next Spring?"

The unfeeling indelicacy of this speech was felt by Selena and her confusion prevented her immediate reply.

"Oh that's true," continued Lady Harriet in a half whisper, "I know you cannot tell yet, until you hear what Lord Dallamore will determine upon when he comes of age. To be sure you could not be presented without him. And pray how soon do you expect him?"

Selena was not a little relieved by the entrance of the gentlemen which prevented the necessity of answering this speech which proved so much impertinence, or so much folly.

Chapter IX

That fearful love which trembled in his eyes
And with a silent earthquake shook his soul!
But when he spoke what tender things he said!
So softly that like flakes of feathered snow
They melted as they fell—

Dryden[36]

Selena could not disguise from Mrs. Vallard the sorrow and surprise she felt that Robert had made a choice so unlike what she should have expected, and to all appearance so little likely to make him happy.

Mrs. Vallard had indeed encouraged her to this confession by expressing in pretty plain terms the dislike she had conceived for her new sister in spite of all her wish to like and love every thing that was related to her dear Selena.

"Is it not wonderful how much a shewy figure can blind a sensible man?" asked she in a tone of unusual displeasure, "and can you conceive how one so amiable as Robert, so well calculated to enjoy domestic life, could expect happiness with a companion who really seems not to possess one recommendation but beauty; perhaps however I am prejudiced against her by seeing that she wished to insinuate some very illnatured suggestions with respect to dear Lady Trevallyn. I heard poor Robert trying to amuse her, just before supper, by an account of the little school at Esselberrie, which you know we took him to look at; and I thought she listened as if it did not much delight her; at last she scornfully put up her lip and asked coolly if Lord Henry Ortney helped Lady Trevallyn to keep school? I assure you Selena I thought she looked quite ugly at that moment. Robert made some enquiring reply, but I could not hear the rest of the conversation, tho' I have no doubt of the nature of it from the different expression of their countenances."

Selena recollected what had passed between her and Lady Harriet on the same subject, but she forbore to encrease Mrs. Vallard's dislike by the repetition, and especially as she saw that her affectionate heart had been hurt, as her own had already been, by finding that any tongue presumed to censure their innocent and interesting friend.

Never was the task of entertainment more difficult to be performed than that now imposed upon Mrs. Vallard, and Selena; for never was guest so impossible to be entertained as Lady Harriet. She had at all times a coldness of manner which is the most discouraging to the efforts made by civility or kindness with an intention to please. And as Sidney paid her not that exclusive attention which she had expected, and as except from Robert she found not the constant and astonished admiration she ever looked for, she met not sufficient food for her vanity to fill up the vacuum of a country life, where the party of the evening could no longer supply matter for the conversation and meditation of the morning.

---

[36]   The Queen in John Dryden's *The Spanish Fryar or, The Double Discovery* (1681), 2.2.72–6. Tighe replaces "words" with "things" in line 74.

She was therefore wearied and discontented and took no pains to disguise her weariness and discontent. In vain did Mrs. Vallard and her new sisters exert all their powers to amuse her tedious moments. She had no resources within herself to assist them in the laborious task—and she had neither the complaisance to flatter them by apparent success, nor the mercy to deliver them for a short time from the fruitless toil by retiring to her own apartment. Tho' she boasted of being able to play a little on the harp, yet conscious that she had neither genius nor skill she would not expose herself to the criticism of those she styled judges by playing herself, and notwithstanding that when Selena or Clara had concluded she generally thought it necessary to say "you play vastly well," or "That is very pretty, pray what do you call it?" or some such cold observation, yet her yawning and inattention plainly shewing the little pleasure she received from their performance, Selena resolved to intrude upon her their accomplishments no more, and as she never solicited the exertion of their talents, music was tacitly but totally excluded in the absence of the gentlemen from the morning's employments or rather unemployments—and Clara the less regretted this restraint since she prohibited herself the gratification of playing Edwin's compositions before strangers. Lady Harriet had declared the first day of her arrival that she detested walking out in the cold, and as the cold and her complaints of the cold daily encreased no further proposal of venturing abroad was hazarded. Selena and her sister profitted however by her late rising in order to take their usual walk in which they were always joined by Sidney, tho' he too complained of the cold during the remainder of the day and with a very unusual inactivity loved to linger with the ladies after breakfast over the fire in the drawing room. Lady Harriet hated all work except netting, and her netting box had alas! been forgotten. Selena offered to supply her with silk, and the offer was after some time accepted, tho' at first disdainfully rejected upon examining the colours which were declared "horrible"—"mauvais gout,"[37] nay "perfectly beastly."

The chief resource of the yawning hours consisted in taking care to supply the fire with wood, from the basket which to save trouble to the servants lay in a corner of the room; and at the hour of *luncheon* the welcome interruption of the gentlemen, who generally returned from shooting, for tho' at other times keen sportsmen they now felt unusual attractions prevent them from pursuing their game very far from home. Robert who was yet quite a lover found indeed a thousand excuses for delaying or shortning their expeditions, and however frivolous these excuses in reality might have been Sidney never had one argument to oppose, nor ever possessed sufficient ingenuity to obviate one difficulty. On the return of the gentlemen it is true Selena might have made her escape and left to them the task of entertaining one incapable of being entertained—but the day was then broken, and she felt no spirit to recommence her interrupted studies. Besides Robert now called for a song, or Sidney engaged her attention by some ingenious criticism or the perusal of some interesting passage. In the mean time no opportunity had hitherto offered sufficiently favourable in Selena's opinion to the disclosure of the

---

[37] Mauvais gout: bad taste (French).

secret which Mrs. Vallard fully concurred with her in the expediency of imparting to Sidney. His visit had indeed been unusually lengthened, for tho' he every day declared the necessity of his going yet every day furnished some excuse to justify his delay.

One wet morning had assembled the whole party in the drawing room, Selena at Sidney's earnest request was seated at the piano forte, where his conversation as he stood leaning on the back of her chair often interrupted the brilliancy of her execution or the accuracy with which she kept time—and perhaps it was this music, not less delightful than the tones which she called from the instrument, that prevented her from hearing the request of Lady Harriet, who from the far end of the room had called upon her to extricate her from a difficulty caused by her odious silk, and entreated Selena might unravel one of the teizing knots with which it was eternally trying her patience. Robert in offering his assistance had made the work a complete chaos—and Lady Harriet throwing it aside in despair walked indolently over to interrupt a discourse which was perhaps beginning to grow too interesting.

"Is Lord Dallamore as fond of music as you all seem to be?" asked she as she crossed her arms and stood immediately opposite to Sidney and his cousin.

"Even more so I think," answered Selena as she continued to fly over the keys with increased rapidity.

"That is lucky," replied her ladyship coldly.

"Why lucky Lady Harriet?" enquired Sidney scarcely knowing what he said, so much had the meaning of this observation already agitated him.

"Oh ask Selena, you are not in the baby house I see."[38]

Selena excessively confused, and even vexed, arose, and drawing her gloves gently from under Lady Harriet's arms as she leaned on the pianoforte the more conveniently to stare upon Selena's face, walked from them.

Scarcely had she closed the door when Lady Harriet exclaimed, "I suppose I shall be quite out of favour for betraying the family secrets."

"And has Selena entrusted you with the secret of her liking Dallamore?" demanded Sidney rather doubting her having made such a confidence.

"Oh as to liking I hear there is not much of that on her part, and indeed as I suspect on any side—but you know that Lord Dallamore is rather a good match for a girl with nothing."

"And can you really imagine that Selena has such interested designs?"

"Oh poor Selena has no designs at all, but I see you know nothing about it."

"Well pray trust me with what *you* know," said he trying to assume an air of indifference.

"Oh no, I dare not, but cannot you conceive that Selena's objections, even tho' she might possibly have thought some one else more charming, might be thought very childish and ridiculous when her papa had an opportunity of making her a countess—tho' how that speculation may turn out God knows!"

---

[38]   Baby house: doll's house (OED).

"You speak in riddles, pray explain dear Lady Harriet," said he as she walked away with a significant "hush!"

Robert's approach indeed prevented him from pressing the subject any further at present but the mysterious hints which had been dropped at that time, and the recollection of some which had before this escaped from others and in particular Mrs. Vallard, inspired him with some suspicions that an engagement did subsist between Dallamore and his cousin, but as he had no idea of their being of an irrevocable nature Lady Harriet's expression had filled him with the sweetest hope that the confusion testified by Selena might not have been the effect of love but only proceeded from the secret consciousness of this engagement—and his heart trembled with delight while he cherished the idea that perhaps she now desired it to be broken. Dallamore indeed he was sensible had many advantages over him; his rank, and fortune were far superior, and he plainly saw that, if inclined to urge it, Dallamore had a prior claim to her favour seconded by the wishes of Mrs. Vallard and all Selena's own family. But then in love how much did he surpass Dallamore, and Selena's he knew was a heart that would be sensible of the claims of a faithful and ardent affection above the glittering of a coronet, or the empty gratifications purchased by great wealth.

She was left dependant, her sadness might perhaps have been occasioned by the struggles between that prudence which prompted her on this account to accept Dallamore and the want of love to justify to her delicate mind this acceptance. Oh how sweet to offer her an independence, a fortune indeed inferior to her merits but above mediocrity, to see her relieved from the weight which appeared at times to oppress her gentle spirits, and to think that every future hour of his life should be blessed with her presence and devoted to her happiness. He was not displeasing to her, he could not think he was. Their sentiments, their tastes were so similar; such tenderness, such complacency had beamed from her modest eye as often as he had expressed his friendship—would they then be armed with severity should he dare to speak of Love.

Exhilarated with the most brilliant delusions of hope his fears were all silenced; Indeed with yet more unfavourable prospects Love would have had power to silence them, for what is more constantly the attendant of Love than Hope:

Yes! Love will hope, tho' hope were lost
Tho' Heaven and earth thy passion crost
Tho' she were bright as sainted queen above
Yet if thou dost not hope thou dost not love.[39]

---

[39] "Barbauld" (Tighe's note). Anna Laetitia Barbauld, "Song I" ("Come here fond youth, whoe'er thou be"), *Poems* (1773), lines 19–24. Tighe changes line 19 ("It is to hope, though hope were lost"), omits lines 22–3 ("And thou the least and meanest swain / That fold his flock upon the plain") and changes line 24 ("Yet if thou darest not hope thou dost not love").

Selena in the mean time retired to her own apartment where the uneasy reflections on her situation, and the dislike which she could not help feeling for the wife of her dear Robert were in a few minutes strangely forgotten and all other thoughts and ideas banished or swallowed up in the remembrance of Sidney's past conversations, the looks which accompanied them, and the expectation of the important interview she was to have with him before his departure.

At length suddenly starting at the involuntary tears that rushed to her eyes as she imagined his astonishment at the intelligence she was to communicate, and the tender compassion with which he would bid farewell to the disdained wife of his friend, she reproached herself for the involuntary weakness, and with terror recollected how the thoughts of Sidney had for some time engrossed almost all her meditations.

"What have I been doing?" she exclaimed; "I accused poor Lady Trevallyn for the indulgence of a sentiment which from long habit, became almost a part of her existence, and which she yet yielded to in no conscious actual weakness—and I, a thousand times more inexcusable have suffered the first advances of a feeling equally criminal to steal into my bosom. But it is not yet too late. I owe it to the innocent affection this sociable young man has shewn for me to entrust him with a secret, which perhaps is of some importance even to him—but after that I will hold with him no particular conversation and banish him entirely from my thoughts."

Such was the resolution of Selena—and such ever are the resolutions of a virtuous mind struggling too feebly under the influence of a passion already too powerful. "I will fly from his image" says reason triumphantly. Love pretends to submit and blushing whispers "I yield—this adored this lovely image shall be no more beheld after one parting view. One more conversation is necessary and then all is over."

It was thus that Love by his usual subtle policy would have deluded Selena, and for a while she was deluded, but having called to mind the dying counsels of her mother she refused to listen to the dictates of feeling, and determined to resist the inclination she felt of shewing Sidney the grateful confidence which she placed in his friendship, and by requesting Mrs. Vallard to inform him of her marriage avoid the necessity she had at first persuaded herself there existed of one last interesting conversation in private with one so dangerous to her peace.

Having come to this resolution she quitted her fire-side where she had been indulging reflections so agitating with the intention of immediately seeking Mrs. Vallard whom she hoped to find in her own room. As she walked by the looking glass, she was struck by the flushing of her cheeks and the redness of her eyes—and as the wintry and enfeebled beams of the sun shone languidly on her windows, she took up her hat, and drawing it over her face thought she would venture to take a few turns on the gravel to dissipate her emotion and the traces which it had left on her countenance, before she met the eyes of Mrs. Vallard or encountered any of the rest of the family.

As she stole softly past the windows of the drawing room she was observed by Sidney, who with his back to the party assembled there, stood yet fixed in the posture in which Lady Harriet's speech had left him, occupied as deeply by his meditations as Selena had been by hers since her departure, tho' they had been of a more agreeable nature. No one else having seen Selena he now silently but precipitously hastened out of the room to pursue her steps.

The ground was uncommonly wet and the air damp but Selena felt herself revived by it, and her melancholy soothed by the extreme stillness which reigned around, interrupted only by the wintry song of the Redbreast who had already exchanged the lively carol in which he had greeted the spring, and had unheeded mingled in the summer concert, for the more plaintive and sweeter notes with which he alone gives melody for many months to the leafless woods.

Wishing to escape observation from the house, Selena bent her steps towards the walk which led immediately beside the river beneath the wooded bank, and as she slowly proceeded wrapt in a deep reverie Sidney overtook and spoke to her before she was aware of his pursuit.

"Are you not afraid of catching cold Selena?" said he, his voice tremulous with the tenderest agitation, his eyes sparkling with even more than their wonted lustre, and his cheek flushed not by the glow of exercise alone.

Startled at his unexpected presence, while in spite of her exertions he still occupied all her meditations, and recollecting the determination she had just formed of avoiding his society, she stopped confused and embarrassed.

He interrupted not her silence, but while enchanted hope interpreted the soft confusion his eyes sought hers with a glance of such fondness as he had never before dared to express. He took her hand, and without releasing it drew her arm beneath his.

Selena felt his heart throb violently, and for a moment had neither power to disengage herself from him nor recollection to be displeased at the freedom which their relationship had never before emboldened him to take.

The power of the infectious softness she however felt but transitory, and assuming an air of extreme reserve she withdrew from his passive and timid hold her arm saying, "It is indeed very damp and cold, and I think I had better return home."

"Nay Selena," answered he reproachfully, "it is not the coldness of the air I fear which now drives you in but the coldness of your heart to your friend. Am I not right?" added he as they walked slowly back. "Tell me how have I forfeited the little regard and confidence which I so lately flattered myself I possessed?"

"On the contrary," answered Selena extremely affected by the persuasive tenderness of his voice and manner, "far from being diminished my confidence in your friendship is so much augmented that I have been considering whether Mrs. Vallard should not entrust you with my secrets, tho' perhaps," said she with a forced smile, "you may thank Lady Harriet for this proof of my confidence since I confess I would rather have the merit of imparting it, than that it should be betrayed without my consent."

"And why must I hear it from Mrs. Vallard?" cried he impatiently, "as what relates to you is all upon earth in which I can now find myself interested, why may I not receive this inestimably prized proof of confidence from the lips which have at this moment the power to raise my soul to the sweetest hope or plunge it to despair."

As he spoke his voice at first impassioned, grew more feeble, and tho' he uttered this sentence with a rapidity that precluded all interruption yet his conclusion was scarcely articulate.

Still his eyes were fixed on her averted and glowing cheeks and she thought she felt his arm lightly thrown around her waist.

"Oh Sidney!" she exclaimed hurrying on and controlling with all her energy every emotion of sorrow, pleasure, shame, and compassion, which rushed confused and tumultuously into her bosom, "Oh Sidney you do not know what you are saying! nor how wrong it is for you to speak thus to me! But *I* know, and must not listen to such language! ..."

"Why dearest Selena! What is to prevent me from declaring, that I love you as never man before loved woman—and that you only upon earth are my first, my last, my only love—to you my heart is devoted and never, never ..." he was proceeding incoherently indeed but with ardour that forgot all restraint for he pressed her to his heart while his beautiful eyes alternately were cast towards Heaven and its most perfect earthly representative whom he held in his arms.

But Selena trembling and inexpressibly agitated with some difficulty disengaged herself from him and exclaimed, "Hush Sidney—you know not whom you speak to ...."

"What it is you mean?" cried he starting with extreme surprise mingled with fear and catching her gown as she was hastening from him. "Will you not explain yourself—for heaven's sake speak."

"Let me go Sidney," said she, "I am distressed at having exposed myself to this interview. Mrs. Vallard will tell you how wrong ...."

"Why refer me to Mrs. Vallard?" interrupted he, "tell me I beseech you yourself have I any hope?"

"You can have none from me," said Selena with firmness, while her heart sunk with the despair she imparted.

"You detest me then," cried he letting go her gown, "I see you detest me. I have no occasion to ask Mrs. Vallard more. Farewell then. I will deliver you from the sight of one hateful to your eyes. Will you not bid me at least farewell?"

"Dear Sidney do not talk thus extravagantly—your friendship will ever be valued by me but farther I must never hear."

"Must not!" repeated Sidney with a countenance that demanded explanation.

"You shall then judge yourself," replied she determined to put an end to this conversation, "you shall judge whether I must, when I tell you that all my secret is that I am married."

Language can never declare the astonishment and anguish which these words suddenly struck into the mind of Sidney—astonishment and anguish so strongly painted on his expressive face.

A faint sickness such as he had never before experienced overpowered his manly form, and Selena saw with affright the paleness which instantly veiled all the blooming graces of his countenance.

"What is the matter?" cried she almost involuntarily approaching him.

"Nothing," said he coldly and turning from her in silence ashamed of the weakness he betrayed, and wishing to hide the mortal anguish which overcame all the man within his breast. "Why are you not then with Dallamore?" said he at length, "if you are indeed his wife—or is there another? For all is mystery—all is amazement."

"I cannot now tell you particulars Sidney but once more let me entreat you will speak to Mrs. Vallard. Let her explain my singular situation." As she said this she hastened her steps, impatient to terminate a scene so painful, so critical.

Sidney in silence pursued her till coming within view of the house he suddenly turned and hurrying back into the thickest part of the wood hid his hopeless sorrows from every eye.

Chapter X

Alas from what a happy dream of Heaven
Hast thou awaked me—what is human life
A moment's meeting, a long age of absence,
One rich one precious drop of cordial joy
Drenched in a current of insipid time
Or deep affliction.

Brooke[40]

At dinner Sidney did not appear till all were seated, and his usual place beside Selena being left for him he took the vacant chair but in vain endeavoured to assume his accustomed cheerfulness; being rattled by Lady Harriet for his silence and absence he pleaded a headach.

"Have you a headach too Selena?" said she, "you and Mr. Sidney look as if you had quarrel'd. Should you not think so?" added she turning to Mrs. Vallard who looking at Selena said, "I took notice when you came in that you looked pale but I confess I have not seen or heard any symptoms of quarrelling. Are you well my Love?"

"Yes perfectly well," answered Selena much distressed at the observations, and still more that they should have been made in the presence of Sidney, who on hearing of her paleness for the first time now ventured to raise a sad and enquiring glance for an instant towards her face.

---

[40] Rutland in Henry Brooke's *The Earl of Essex: A Tragedy* (1750), 2.11.5–10. Tighe uses "life" for "bliss" in line 6, and line 8 should read "One rich and precious drop of cordial joy."

When the ladies quitted the parlour Sidney hastily arose to open the door, and as Mrs. Vallard passed took her hand and whispered a few words to which Selena heard her answer "Certainly—you will find me in my own room."

Not having a doubt that he wished to hear the particulars for which he had been referred to her, Selena now putting her arm under Mrs. Vallard's softly whispered, "I have told Sidney something of Dallamore. And you need keep nothing secret from him for as Robert has told the whole affair to Lady Harriet I suppose it would be in vain to think of concealing it. But caution him from speaking on the subject to Lord Dallamore who perhaps may not like to discuss the matter with him."

Mrs. Vallard said she was very glad she had confessed to him her situation and added smiling, "I hope it is not too late for him poor fellow."

Selena asked not for an explanation, nor acknowledged having heard the latter part of this speech. But her downcast eyes, and burning cheeks might have betrayed her, had she not taken advantage of finding herself just then at the foot of the stairs. So letting go of Mrs. Vallard's arms she hastily flew to her own room.

Mrs. Vallard in her communications to Sidney was led on by his inquisitive eagerness and the warm interest he displayed to be far more unreserved than Selena had intended or than indeed she had any idea it was in Mrs. Vallard's power to be—for having ever avoided all hints relative to her father's duplicity, and the steps which he had taken to hurry her into a consent she had so much reason to regret, Selena had no idea that in consequence of Mrs. Miltern's last letter to her friend, Mrs. Vallard had been apprised of the circumstance which Selena thought was known only to her father and herself.

The indignation felt by Sidney at the treachery which in sacrificing the lovely victim he so much adored, had blasted the hopes he might otherwise have entertained of aspiring to her love, could with the utmost difficulty be restrained in the presence of Mrs. Vallard, but in determining to serve Selena to the utmost of his ability, even if lost to him for ever, he thought it necessary to disguise from Mrs. Vallard the passion he felt for her, lest she should be influenced by the common dictates of prudence to refuse to bestow on him the confidential trust it was his resolution to fulfil with the most perfect and disinterested forgetfulness of any selfish considerations. Nevertheless when he had heard of Dallamore's strange neglect and voluntary absence, a thought darted itself across the gloom of his despair like light'ning thro' the obscurity of dreary night, that perhaps Selena might willingly suffer him to forego his claim upon her hand and think herself at liberty to receive back her unaccepted vows.

The idea was transport even as a possibility—he clasped his hands in silent extasy—and abruptly quitting Mrs. Vallard he retired to indulge the painfully agitating contemplation of a felicity so little within "the prospect of belief"[41] except to a lover such as Sidney.

He was at last resolved to make an effort to convince Selena that she was bound by no law divine or human to Dallamore, should he have the madness to

---

[41]   Macbeth in Shakespeare's *Macbeth* (1605), 1.3.74.

relinquish the invaluable gem which Fate had placed within his reach, but as he dreaded arousing her delicacy into sudden resolutions, and wished to give her time to consider a subject so difficult indeed for him to speak of without wounding her feelings or alarming her virtue, he thought it most prudent not to trust himself to a personal explanation but commit to paper his arguments without betraying his hopes.

Unable to endure society during the disorder of his mind he appeared not that evening after his conversation with Mrs. Vallard, and passed his agitated hours in framing the letter which after repeated and vain efforts of satisfying the ardor of his own mind which should not be expressed, and of restraining the impetuosity that he was convinced must weaken his cause by a suspicion of the selfishness which dictated his arguments, he at last upon hearing her foot upon the stairs just as he was beginning another attempt resolved not to delay that upon which so much depended, but folding up the letter that he had last concluded opened his door, and as she passed it alone silently put it into her hands. He was indeed unable to speak, when she almost equally agitated and hesitating whether she should receive what was thus presented asked with a trembling voice "What is this?" They were both however startled from this embarrassing silence by the sound of Lady Harriet's step upon the stairs who remained behind after they had bad her good night in order to desire Robert to find out what was the matter with Sidney.

"Take it dear Selena," said he, as she extended it towards him hastily again, "remember I am your friend." This was no time for debate. She hurried on, and Sidney softly closed his own door.

For some minutes the paper remained enfolded in her hand, as she sat confused and breathless on the side of her bed. At length impatience conquering her emotion she opened and read with a palpitating breast the following letter.

"It is the privilege of friendship to offer at all times that counsel which judgment dictates. If that counsel should now be repugnant to your feelings attribute it dear Selena to the error of my judgment and blame not the rectitude of my heart. You have honoured me with the name of friend and I here solemnly vow to devote my life to deserve that name, and to sacrifice every interested feeling which might oppose the purity and sincerity of the exertions by which as your friend it shall be my study to contribute if possible to your happiness. Listen to me then without suspicious fear, and think me not so base as to impose upon your confidence thro' any selfish designs an advice my true and unbiased opinion did not believe sanctioned by the strictest virtue and the most unsullied honour. I have heard from Mrs. Vallard *all*. If therefore in my arguments I now suppose that your conduct has not resulted from blind attachment, think not that any presumptuous hope has inclined me to form this supposition. But that your consent was extorted by unjustifiable means is surely so strong a reason for the liberty of your future choice that you must forgive my thus alluding to it for this once.

"That there exists a possibility of your being allowed this second choice nothing but my knowledge of Dallamore's extraordinary character could suffer me for a moment to imagine—and I have no fears of offending your conscious worth by the confession that I believe such a possibility does really exist. Too well you know that I at least am not insensible of that worth, which, having once beheld, Dallamore alone in all the earth would not proudly stand forth and acknowledge as his, had Heaven allowed him to make a boast so high. But Dallamore, the creature of accident, is capable of forming no exertions to obtain or preserve for himself the richest blessing which Providence has placed within his reach, and will I have no doubt submit to the really trifling obstacles, which art or malice will throw in his way to prevent his effectually calling you his as they have hitherto successfully opposed his return. Will you then contend with pride and injustice for the preservation of so uncertain a good as the possession of Dallamore's heart, whose attachment for you must be already weakened by absence and may probably be entirely alienated by the purposed intervention of some object far less wothy.

"As I cannot yet consider you the wife of Dallamore, while he at least tacitly disowns you, I think it just and right to speak with the utmost freedom of a character so well known to me that you may be the better prepared to chuse the part which you may determine to act. I have examined with the most scrupulous and impartial justice the case and solemnly declare that to me your conditional vow appears yet nugatory. But if you are resolved to abide by it, and wish not for the freedom you have a right to assert, one only way remains to induce Dallamore to acknowledge his claims; and believe me that your presence is to that end absolutely necessary.

"But can you expose your delicacy, your gentleness to the proud insults of Lord Mount Villars and dare the scorn of an unfeeling world which ever ready to take part against innocence and beauty will readily acquit the father who wishes to free a weak young man from the shackles of the imprudent connexion which artifice, tho' not in the shape of Selena, had really ensnared him to form. Thus, nay even more unjustly will it be represented and your pursuit will render the representation the more probable.

"To continue long in your present situation is impossible. Await not then the disgrace of a rejection so strange, so incredible yet so probable; Declare to your brother and to Lord Mount Villars that you relinquish all claims upon Dallamore, and silently suffer the plans to succeed which no doubt will be laid to prevent him from molesting you by any recollections of an idle ceremony which neither the laws of God or man can oblige you circumstanced as you are to respect.

"Could I believe that interest or attachment inclined you to desire the confirmation of your union with Dallamore I should even still advise you to adopt this measure. It will with safety to your brother and to him bring the awkward and to you most distressing business to a crisis, and Dallamore at the moment of losing you for ever, may exert the energy requisite to his happiness and for once deliver himself from the trammels cast around him, and again court your acceptance of the hand he now withholds. Assert your native dignity of character, and submit no more to the caprices of a man who if you suffer it may now boast a right the renunciation of which the laws will afterwards justify.

"Forgive the friendship which *now* strongly urges *your* important decision and consider I beseech you how reason and delicacy call upon you immediately to escape from the future misery and regret which a connexion with this weak character may produce. You are now free. Accidental circumstances which I can but too well foresee, may fatally diminish your liberty, and bind you, not as now with imaginary chains, to one whose natural amiable qualities cannot ensure that his future conduct shall be guided by honour and principle. Far better that you should now for ever yourself assert your freedom with a courage you are I know well capable of exerting in what you consider right, than pass some months of anxious uncertainty, and find yourself then the victim of Dallamore's weak and dishonourable conduct too much influenced by the cruel injustice of others, or at best the wife of a man you never could have chosen and indeed undeserving of your perfect esteem.

"Highly as I love and respect Mrs. Vallard I cannot submit to her as an arbitress on this occasion, because I know that her partiality for her nephew, and her own excellent heart, will never allow her to believe, in spite of his present apparent indecision that Dallamore can really ever be induced to disown a marriage which honour, and love already have in vain called upon him to acknowledge. *His* vows were voluntary. Yours were the effect of compulsion and deceit. The same delicacy, the same honour which call so loudly upon *him* to assert, command *you* to forego, the claims those vows allow.

"Motives of pride, and justifiable indignation, may prevent Robert from perceiving how much your happiness depends upon quickly submitting to the injustice which inclines Lord Mount Villars to exercise his influence in persuading Dallamore to give you up—you yourself must feel—that he who is bound to support your right, should be the last to advise you to relinquish it. Oh Selena! so young, so inexperienced as you are—how shall *I* presume to urge you to resist the counsels of two friends so dear, so valuable—and to prefer my judgment convinced as I yet am, it is for your honour and happiness, and conscious how much depends upon its being immediately adopted.

"I feel that entreaty is idle, where you are to act only as reason and your own heart shall determine; What can I say, but once more ask you to listen without prejudice, and suspect me not of wishing to blind your judgment to forward my own selfish designs. Forget if possible that I have dared to own a more presumptuous sentiment, and whatever may be your determination allow me indeed the cherished the invaluable title of your friend

Sidney Dallamore"

Selena found it impossible, after the perusal of this paper, to close her eyes during the night—but her candle burnt to the socket and her expiring fire, interrupted the profound meditations with which she held it almost unconsciously for some hours before her eyes. She was not convinced, but she was shaken in her resolutions, and looked round with terror for some guiding hand to relieve her in this critical moment of perplexity. Her Mother's dying request that she might avoid all connexion with Dallamore was now present to assist the inclination of her heart to yield to the arguments of Sidney—nevertheless she at the moment felt that these arguments were opposed by her reason and her secret conviction of the rectitude of that conduct which she had at first determined to adopt.

"I am his wife! Alas too certainly I know it, and nothing but his uniformly persisting to disown me, and marrying another woman can free me from my duty to receive and acknowledge his claims upon me as his wife. Even then my vows still preclude another choice, and having solemnly sworn to forsake all others and love only him, his rejection can never justify in me the breach of a promise made to Heaven. My lot is fixed, and my duty is now to consider it in the fairest view, and to endeavour as far as it is in my power to gain and preserve the affections of Dallamore."

She was extremely surprised at Sidney's allusion to her father's conduct, the knowledge of which, except to herself, she thought buried with him, and being able to account for it in no other way she supposed that Robert had heard from her mother some expressions which convinced him of the truth; and she dreaded lest by his manner of receiving them he might have disturbed her last moments by awaking these suspicions she herself had so carefully avoided exciting.

Various and disquieting as were her reflections poor Sidney passed not a night of greater composure—and the first rays of the morning were welcomed by both as a relief from a part of the weight of anxiety which is never so cruelly oppressive as during the inactive and tedious hours of a sleepless night.

Her first care was now to put a decisive and final end to every expectation which Sidney might secretly form, in a deliverance from the bonds which he would thus have persuaded her were not so sacred as she herself esteemed them; nor was this a task the most easy—convinced as she was that duty and honour called upon her for the exertion her heart still shrunk from renewing her vows to Dallamore and for ever renouncing all hopes of such happiness as it involuntarily pictured to itself in accepting the love of one so deserving so amiable as Sidney.

Endeavouring however to turn from the comparison she was ever ready to draw between the ardent and enchanting proof each moment given by Sidney of the purest attachment, and the cold caprice displayed by Dallamore she saw how necessary it was to shun all intercourse with him till absence should have banished from their friendship every warmer sentiment, and to this end she was now called upon to be explicit in declaring to him her unalterable resolution to fulfill her duty as the wife of Dallamore.

She arose therefore instantly upon perceiving there was sufficient light to dress herself, never being accustomed to wait for the assistance of her maid, and prepared to give in as few words as possible such an answer to Sidney as might convince him it was expedient to banish her from his thoughts and at least for the present to shun all opportunities of conversing with one he was only to consider as the wife of his friend.

She had already finished her letter, and was considering sadly how she should deliver to him the final destruction of all his hopes, when the servant entered to light her fire—and surprised at finding her so early settled at her writing desk, began to apologize for having delayed coming to her room.

"Lord Ma'am," said she as she laid the coal-box on the hearth, "I should have been in an hour ago, if I had thought you was a stirring but I thinks, as how some spirit have been abroad to disturb the house before peep-a-day. It was but just on the stroke of seven when I hears Mr. Dallamore open his door and go down stairs, and so I says to Nanny come we's best get that room done out of the way afore the rest be up, since it be empty so soon, so I thought Ma'am to be in to here afterwards, but I am sure I's sorry it have so hap'd for surely you be starved to death sitting waiting in the cold."

Having thus gained the intelligence of Sidney being already up Selena resolved not to delay giving him her answer, which she had now an opportunity of doing unobserved by Lady Harriet who so tenaciously watched her motions during the day, more from perfect idleness however than curiosity. Having therefore requested the maid not to call upon Nanny's assistance, in her absence, to begin getting *her* room out of the way, telling her that she purposed returning to it immediately she left her to kindle the fire and descended in search of Sidney.

The morning was heavy and wet, so that she guessed he had not walked out, and when she reached the drawing room door her heart beat with such violence that she was obliged to stop for some moments to recover herself before she entered where she expected to find him alone. She would indeed have stood there much longer, before she had acquired sufficient courage to enter, had she not imagined she heard his step approaching the door. Unwilling to be found in that situation she therefore hastily opened it and perceived him immediately before her as he paced the room with mingled agitation and sorrow in his countenance, which however for a moment gave place to the transient glow of delight caused by her sudden appearance.

"Is it you Selena!" said he his voice attuned by the sweetest harmony of love as he approached, while she stopped oppressed by confusion and struggling with the various emotions which deprived her of power to speak or execute the purpose for which she had sought him.

Perceiving a book in his hand, as he advanced to shut the door she at last gained strength to say while she walked from him towards the fire, "I disturb you. What have you been reading?"

Sidney who had unconsciously taken the book while the importance of his own meditations had totally deprived him of all curiosity to open it, was now obliged to look at the book in order to answer her question—it was an almanack!

"Let me look at it for a moment," said Selena unable longer to endure a tete-a-tete so embarrassing. As she took it from his hands she drew from her pocket a letter and in hasty confusion put it within the leaves, and then without venturing to raise her eyes laid the book upon the table before him and quitted the room which he had neither courage nor power of speech to oppose.

Selena having made her escape to her own room had for some time relieved her overstrained nerves by the indulgence of her tears, before Sidney acquired force to open the fatal paper upon which all his hopes depended.

At length he snatched it up and read the following lines written as he then thought by the hand of the coldest indifference, and a judgment produced by the falsest principles.

> "I hope I shall always receive with candour and gratitude the advice dictated by sincere friendship but I must not submit to another the judgment to direct my conduct in a point where my duty appears plain. I have passed the most solemn vows and must ever consider myself as the wife of him to whom I once have promised love and obedience. It is not possible for any circumstance but death to free me from this obligation, and I am convinced that the only part I have now to act is to endeavour so to gain the esteem and affection of Lord Dallamore that he may not regret the imprudent connexion which he has so early formed. I readily promise you to think no more of the few expressions which circumstanced as I am were indeed improper, but which had my situation been as appeared to you I must even in rejecting, have considered as most flattering and most disinterested."

Chapter XI

Objet du plus parfait amour,
Unique charme de ma vie,
O Maitresse toujours cherie!
Faut-il te perdre sans retour?

De Parney[42]

Selena, afraid of again encountering Sidney alone, did not go down till Clara surprised at her unusual tardy appearance came to summon her to breakfast; She need not however have delayed under such an apprehension; The farewell which hung so heavy on her foreboding heart was already made, poor Sidney was already separated by some miles from her presence, and was yet rapidly proceeding still farther, while the swiftness with which the wheels were rolled along seemed to tear him from a part of his existence.

The moment that he found himself convinced by the perusal of her letter that she was not only indifferent to him but decided in her resolution to place all her happiness on Dallamore, he was himself determined in the conduct he should adopt—and devoting himself to her service with generous ardour prepared to seek Dallamore, and influence him to deliver her by his immediate acknowledgement from a situation so mortifying, so distressing and so unworthy of her singular and extraordinary merit.

"Cruel Selena!" he bitterly exclaimed while busying himself in preparations for his journey, "I *will* prove that my friendship is sincere, and that I am not entirely

---

[42] Évariste de Parny, "Élégie X" ("Par cet air"), *Élégies* (1784), lines 25–8: Object of the most perfect love, singular charm of my life, oh always cherished mistress, is it necessary to lose you without return?

undeserving your regard tho' with such superfluous unkindness, with such cold contempt, you took care to inform me that even had you been at perfect liberty you would still have rejected my too presumptuous offers. Yes I have sworn to sacrifice my own feelings while I seek only your happiness. Oh that I may at least be able to promote that by reuniting you to Dallamore! I will see you then no more; I will not dare again to manifest the passion which you consider as criminal, which it will cost you so little difficulty to forget, and which it is impossible for me to conceal."

Full of the warmest and most generous eagerness to accomplish the design which must forever deprive him of all hopes of Selena—he would not even delay one hour his journey, being almost certain from his knowledge of Dallamore that he should find little difficulty in prevailing upon him to return with him to England, and of the powerful influence of Selena's charms if once in her presence he could not doubt.

In pursuance of this project, he desired his servant to follow him with a small parcel of what was absolutely necessary to take and walked himself to the neighbouring village to obtain a chaise with the greater expedition.

Mrs. Vallard entered the breakfast parlour with the note in her hand which he had left in order to account in some measure for his sudden departure, and with many expressions of surprise read as follows.

> "My dear Madam,
>
> "Forgive my abrupt farewell. Unexpected business which demands expedition has summoned me from Hillbarton, but as I have taken the liberty of leaving there my luggage, you will perceive that I quit you with an intention of very soon having again the pleasure of seeing you, and I hope to be able in a short time in person to make my apology to the friends I am now obliged to quit with such precipitation.
>
> Your obliged and affectionate
Servant Sidney Dallamore"

Selena in the mean time struck with sudden anguish at the prompt fulfillment of what a moment before she believed was her sincerest wish, sat in silent and cruel exertion of all her endeavours to repress the unuttered sorrow which nearly overpowered her calm strength of mind, while the rest of the party, all but Lady Harriet who had not yet made her appearance, were forming various and imaginary conjectures on the business which had thus hurried Sidney so unexpectedly away.

"See what you are doing Selena!" exclaimed Clara rising hastily to stop the overflowing tea urn, which had indeed been suffered to pour its dangerous flood not only over the tea pot but the whole table, from whence it was already fast escaping to her lap—while Selena affected to peruse the newspaper, a single line of which she had not noticed.

In the midst of the confusion this occasioned, and glad of the excuse it afforded her to retire in order to change her gown Selena flew to her own room and with shame and self reproach there struggled vainly with the bitter sensations which accompanied these reflections. That she should see him no more! That she had driven him from her, that he had left her in displeasure at her assumed coldness, and that in a short time she should probably be forgotten. Indeed what sentiments could be more painful than hers at that moment, the sense of conscious rectitude no longer supported her. She had flattered herself that she desired his absence, because reason and virtue had commanded her to desire it—and now she was cruelly convinced that the boasted wish was beyond her strength.

How painful is the discovery that our virtue is not strong enough to console us for the sacrifice it has yet obliged us to make, but which the heart in secret flatters itself will be refused! How oppressive is the sorrow which lessens us even in our own eyes, and how bitter the regret for those deprivations of which we dare not complain, and which wounded self love blushes to acknowledge as severe! Yet let not the afflicted, humbled heart even then be discouraged. The conquest is not indeed glorious, nor the success complete. But continue the resistance however enfeebled by the involuntary tenderness, persist in the contest against those feelings which virtue condemns and self content shall crown the struggle and peace assuredly reward the exertion.

Selena did not sink under the distress which had at first overpowered her, she determined to banish Sidney from her mind, and as the best means she could devise for this purpose, resolved to quit the scenes which hourly must remind her of his words and looks and to conquer the repugnance she had at first found so strong to accept Robert's invitation of returning with him and Lady Harriet to Miltern Abbey there to await the return of Dallamore, or at least the answer to a pretty warm expostulation which her brother now wrote requiring to know his real intentions with respect to Selena. To return to Miltern Abbey which had so lately witnessed her severe anguish on her irrevocable loss, and to return there with Lady Harriet, whose conduct to her was far from kind and whom she could not herself regard with esteem or affection. To behold her placed in the situation occupied within so short a time by her adored Mother was cruelly repulsive to her feelings, but to her feelings she refused to listen when they alone opposed the voice of reason which pointed out the path of duty.

Sidney had declared his intention of returning to Hillbarton and Selena had no doubt that he only waited her departure to fulfill this intention. This therefore decided her however reluctantly to comply with her brother's desire, which on many accounts now appeared the step which with most propriety she should adopt. Dependant as she was at present her brother was her most natural protector, and the only person from whom she could bear to receive the pecuniary obligations which circumstanced as she stood she was for the first time constrained to accept. To remain with Mrs. Vallard was entirely to throw herself upon her care, and Selena's noble disposition revolted against encroaching upon the kindness even of her second mother. Clara's residence had not yet been determined and Robert having acquainted her guardian Mr. Turner that for the present he wished her to return with him to the Abbey she had with tears entreated Selena not to suffer her to go alone. Every thing conspired to recommend her quitting Hillbarton, and however difficult was the task to her grateful and warm sensibility she firmly resisted all Mrs. Vallard's pressing solicitations and declared to Robert her acceptance of his kind wish that she should bear them company to her native abode.

Lady Harriet had complied with Robert's desire in giving her the final invitation without which she indeed could not have gone, but having said once that she hoped Selena would give her the pleasure of her company she never took any part in the debates which had frequently occurred upon the subject between Mrs. Vallard and Robert—nor did she seem to consider it as a matter worthy of a second thought. Selena was not insensible to this coldness, but it did not surprise her, nor could she expect that Lady Harriet would give herself any trouble to obtain the society of a person who neither afforded her pleasure nor advantage.

The day was now fixed for their quitting Hillbarton and Selena who found herself involuntarily visiting every spot where she had recollected some interesting conversation, some peculiar action of Sidney's saw how necessary it was for her to fly from the scenes of such dangerous remembrances.

On the second day after Sidney's departure a letter was brought to Selena which had been left for her at the neighbouring village, and by some neglect till then delayed.

She instantly knew the hand to be Sidney's and her emotions at perceiving it did not escape the penetrating eye of Clara, who starting from her chair, where she had been writing at Selena's side exclaimed, "Oh that is from Edwin I am sure!"

"No indeed my love, what made you have such an idea?"

"I do not know," answered she excessively ashamed at the precipitate eagerness she had so involuntarily displayed, "but you looked somehow so shocked and as if you did not know whether to open it or not; but I hope then it is from Dallamore, for it certainly contains something very interesting to you .... but why don't you open it? Shall I go away? Oh I guess now," said she with a half smile as Selena trembling and conscious broke the seal.

"What do you guess Clara?"

"Oh nothing—don't mind me, I will go and play a little since thank Heaven Robert has for once persuaded Lady Harriet to go out, and I will come back when I think you have read your letter."

Selena made no answer, and was already completely engrossed by the intelligence contained in what she read which was as follows.

"Having allowed me dear Selena the name of friend I should ill deserve so honourable a title which I have so much desired, did I not exert the little powers which I flatter myself I possess in a point where I think your happiness concerned. Your brother's interference is likely to produce so little good, and to be attended with so much uneasiness to you that I take it upon myself to render it at present unnecessary by delivering Dallamore from the artful impediments thrown in the way of his happiness. You will not I hope refuse to allow me the permission of acquainting you with my success, and if you will not gratify me with a reply yourself at least commission dear Mrs. Vallard to let me know

where Dallamore can soonest meet and personally ask forgiveness from the
woman so generously willing to pardon the neglect he has hitherto shown.
                       Your sincere friend Sidney Dallamore

I hope to find a letter from Hillbarton directed to me at the hotel Kildare Street
Dublin."

This letter written with a bleeding heart struggling with the necessary assumed
indifference brought tears of mingled gratitude, admiration, regret and tenderness
into the eyes of Selena. When she had in some degree composed herself she flew
with it to Mrs. Vallard's apartment for whose perusal she saw it was intended, and
was sensible of the delicacy which she plainly perceived suggested the hint of
Sidney's appointing her to answer it.

Delighted with his active friendship, tho' little aware how severely this proof
of it had cost him Mrs. Vallard lost no time in expressing their mutual gratitude
and acquainted him with Selena's determination to accompany Robert to Miltern
Abbey. She was now confident of Dallamore's return without any more delay,
and tho' she would with delight have witnessed the reunion of persons so dear,
yet upon Selena's promise to see her in a very few days after his arrival, should
Dallamore indeed fulfill her hopes, Mrs. Vallard did not any longer oppose her
journey to Herefordshire which might probably expedite their meeting, in case as
she supposed Dallamore would now return by Milford.

Selena checked the sighs which swelled from her heavy heart, as she made this
promise, and persuaded herself that she at length succeeded in her efforts to bring
her mind to join with Mrs. Vallard in hoping that Sidney's generous design might
be rewarded with success.

"Alas what a reward," her tenderness would have said, had not virtue
reproachfully commanded silence.

Selena could not leave Derbyshire without again seeing Lady Trevallyn tho'
all intercourse between Hillbarton and Esselberrie had for a little while been
suspended and she had distressed Selena, and mortally offended Lady Harriet by
persisting in her resolution of not paying visits of ceremony during her stay in
the country.

So much so indeed that as Selena perceived how deeply the omission had been
resented on the part of Lady Harriet, she carefully concealed her own intention of
bidding Lady Trevallyn farewell, and Mrs. Vallard furnished her with an excuse
to take Clara to Esselberrie by requesting them to chuse some trees for her at a
neighbouring nursery—a commission in which she knew Lady Harriet would not
chuse to participate.

The place in the chaise was therefore offered without much fear, and was as
had been expected scornfully declined.

The business was quickly executed and Selena with the utmost pleasure
and affection again embraced her lovely friend, whom they found in her school
surrounded by her little girls and supplying to them Mrs. Harley's place, who

was seated in a great chair at the fire side wrapt in flannels, pale and evidently extremely ill.

In answer to Selena's enquiries Mrs. Harley informed her that a severe attack of the rheumatism had at once prevented her journey to London, and rendered her stay useless, "but," added she forcing a smile, "as my sister justly said my worldly anxiety should meet its reward, and I ought to be satisfied that my going could be of no real use, or I should not have been thus detained."

"Yes," said Lady Trevallyn smiling, "and tho' I am sorry you have been thus punished, yet I hope you will now be convinced that it is your duty not to think of leaving me again and that you will in future be afraid ever to give way to such an idea."

Upon Selena's asking for Angela, Mrs. Harley said with a sigh that she had heard nothing particular from her since, and that she persisted in saying that she was better.

While Lady Trevallyn apologised to them for not having been to wait upon their new sister, Selena could not disguise her concern that she had refused to pay this trifling civility to one who she knew would repay the slight by every opportunity of throwing out malicious insinuations against her whom Selena could not help seeing she both envied and hated.

"I see you are affronted," said Lady Trevallyn smiling, "and believe me the fear of that half conquered my reluctance, but besides offending by this preference all my neighbours who hitherto have treated me with the kindest indulgence I will own to you dear Selena I really could not bear the idea of submitting to the inquisitive stare of Lady Harriet in a morning visit where there was nothing else to divert her great black eyes from counting the moles on my face, or the hairs in my eyelashes; for as she does not draw, I cannot conceive for what other purpose she always takes such an accurate survey of features which I am sure it gives her no pleasure to look at."

"That is at me I am afraid," cried Clara, "for really I am sometimes ashamed when I think how I have been looking at dear Lady Trevallyn and yet believe me I cannot help it."

"Oh," said Lady Trevallyn with a blush and a dimple, "that is quite different and I love to meet your coaxing flattering looks, but I assure you Lady Harriet's are not a bit flattering."

"No," answered Clara, "I can very well believe that for she never is pleased when she sees any thing prettier than herself, and in spite of all her conceit she must allow that is the case when she looks at you or Selena."

"I cannot thank you for your compliment," cried Selena gravely, "when it is paid at the expence of poor Robert's wife."

Clara blushed and Lady Trevallyn smiling said, "Oh Selena you would not surely treat me as such a stranger as to disguise before me your real opinion of Lady Harriet, whom I know it is impossible you can think very amiable. But tell me does she seem sensible of the value of the heart she has gained and the family she has entered?"

Selena answered that she had behaved to them with much civility and that she hoped she was sincerely attached to her brother, "but you know," added she smiling, "that my partiality for Robert will not allow me to be very easily satisfied on that point."

Clara did not again venture to make any observations but she stole a glance at Lady Trevallyn which pretty plainly told *her* opinion of her new sister.

Selena felt anxious to divert the conversation not wishing to encourage the dislike which Clara had early begun to take for the cold manners and malicious disposition she had discovered in Lady Harriet—a dislike which her open artless nature was incapable of entirely concealing.

With this intention of turning the discourse Selena asked Lady Trevallyn how soon she expected to go to town.

"Why that is at present undecided," answered she, "Lord Trevallyn must go before Christmas but I am endeavouring to prevail upon him to allow me to stay here till towards Spring, for really the thoughts of remaining in town from November till the middle of June quite terrify me. And I am certain we shall not leave it till after the birthday."

"Terrify you!" said Clara with some surprise.

"Yes," answered she with a sigh, "I might literally say *terrify* for I know the dangers of the world which I hope you never may, and tho' I am sure 'the mind is its own paradise'[43] yet I confess I am not so free from local impressions as to be able to enjoy solitude in a ball room as I do solitude at Esselberrie. As to being in town without going out, that is impossible, nor would Lord Trevallyn suffer me to attempt any thing which would appear so extraordinary to the rest of the world, who cannot conceive a young woman finding any innocent pleasures at home."

She then conversed with Selena upon the probability of their meeting saying she was sure that Lord Dallamore would not like to spend the spring any where but in London and expressed her hopes that Selena might take a house near Grosvenor's square that they might pass the more time together till observing the dejected countenance and full eyes of Selena she dropped the conversation which she saw distressed her—and having made her promise to write as soon as she had any thing important to communicate she suffered her amiable young friends to hasten home lest Lady Harriet might made some puzzling enquiries concerning their long stay.

---

[43] A reference to Milton's *Paradise Lost* (1674), 1.253–5: "A mind not to be chang'd by Place or Time. / The mind is its own place, and in it self / Can make a Heav'n of Hell, a Hell of Heav'n."

Chapter XII

Nam curiosus nemo est, quin sit malevolus.
                                          Plautus[44]

The sisters upon their return to Hillbarton found Robert sitting in the drawing room endeavouring to amuse Lady Harriet, who seated in an arm chair before the fire, with her nicely sandaled feet upon the fender, was occupied by holding a screen to preserve her face from the blaze of the wood, reading from time to time the oft perused characts which it contained.

Their intention had been to go instantly to Selena's room but as they passed the hall Robert, at Lady Harriet's desire (who had seen the carriage drive up) threw open the door and exclaimed, "Well Ladies, where have you been? I rode after you to Hodder's nursery and they told me you were gone and had not stayed ten minutes."

"You had better not be so indiscreet," said Lady Harriet with a sneer, "you see it is a secret."

They indeed stood silent in some confusion at the unexpected attack, and Selena answered in evident embarrassment, "We were paying a farewell visit."

"Were you at Esselberrie?" said Robert.

"No I suppose Selena could hardly do so mean a thing as to force her acquaintance even on the great Lady Trevallyn, or intrude her unreturned visits."

Lady Harriet said this with a voice of constrained passion and a forced smile which vainly endeavoured to assume an air of carelessness.

Selena made no answer for she was watching with uneasiness the look of displeasure which she dreaded to perceive upon the countenance of her ever tenderly beloved brother, a look so unusual from him whose eyes had always been turned upon her with kindness and approbation.

She saw that he was jealous for the wife he loved so passionately, and tho' she had no doubt that it was owing chiefly to the artful insinuations of Lady Harriet, yet she resolved to suppress every little emotion of dislike and if it was not in her power to gain her love, at least to leave her no grounds of complaint as to her conduct.

Unable to bear even his momentary slight displeasure, she conquered her dejection and with assumed cheerfulness called on his attention to listen to a strange wild song which Clara had discovered in looking over some old guitar music that Mrs. Vallard had thrown out to her from a lumber chest.

While Selena thus soothed her brother with playful endearments till the transient cloud passed away from his brow, Lady Harriet, who eyed them with scornful discontent, indignant that Robert should pay the smallest attention to any creature but herself, at length sullenly rose and retired to her own apartment where she consoled her mortification and amused her ill-temper, by ornamenting

---

[44]   Gelasimus in Titus Maccius Plautus's *Stichus* (200 BC), 1.3.55: For nobody is curious, who isn't malevolent.

with much self complacency her beautiful person, admiring the refreshed lillies and roses which glowed beneath her plastic hand, and devising some new and extraordinary form in which to twist the dark luxuriance of her tresses, by which she daily hoped to attract the attention and astonishment of the party assembled at dinner.

Scarcely were they seated on that day when addressing herself to Clara who was seated opposite she observed coldly, "Well I hope you found Lord Henry there."

"Where?" replied Clara with unaffected surprise.

"Lord child how excessively ridiculous to make such a mystery of your paying your court to Lady Trevallyn, one would really think it was Lord Henry alone that you went to see."

As her eyes were now fixed upon Selena, it is not surprising that they succeeded in their desired effect and suffused her face with the ever ready carnation.

Afraid of Clara's reply she herself softly answered Lady Harriet saying, "There is no mystery in the case, and we are quite ready to tell you all our adventures today, but I am afraid they will not prove very diverting."

"Believe me I have not the smallest curiosity. I dare say if Lord Henry is there and knows I am in the neighbourhood I shall see enough of him, tho' I don't suppose Lady Trevallyn will be very impatient to give him that information."

"He is not there I assure you," said Selena hastily.

"Dear! I am sorry you were so disappointed," cried Lady Harriet with a laugh which had in it more of malice than not.

"Why should you suppose the girls went to see Lord Henry?" said Mrs. Vallard rather hurt, "I can tell you Lord Henry is no great favourite."

"Favourite with whom Ma'am!" exclaimed Lady Harriet looking confidently up in Mrs. Vallard's face as she sat next her.

"With Selena, or indeed with me either; as for Clara, she has never seen him."

"Well really," answered Lady Harriet, continuing her interrupted dinner, "I should not have suspected that from the uncommon pains Selena took to force herself at Esselberrie, for I could not think there was such a great friendship between her and Lady Trevallyn, or her Ladyship would not so long have shewn how cool she was about seeing her."

Clara looked as if she was going to answer but was stopped by the fearfully reproving glance of Selena; and Robert was then suffered to change the conversation which had evidently been painful to his feelings.

The next morning as they were as usual seated in the drawing room and Selena having provided herself with some work was listning with apparent attention to Lady Harriet's repetition of the anecdotes, bonmots, and compliments which had been most remarkably interesting to herself in her last Spring's campaign, the conversation was suddenly interrupted by the sound of a carriage and Lady Harriet immediately exclaimed, "I protest there is Lady Trevallyn at last. I hope Selena you did not treat me so ill as to ask her to pay me the honour of a visit."

"No believe me, perhaps it is only Lord Trevallyn, how could you suspect me of taking such a liberty."

"I assure you," retorted Lady Harriet with unabated indignation, "there was not the least occasion as I did not in the smallest degree covet the honour, high as *you* may think it."

All this passed in a moment, and Selena was herself surprised on the opening of the door to see enter indeed the soft and graceful form and the beautifully blushing face of the lovely countess—who approaching Lady Harriet in the most bewitching voice and that gracious easy gentleness which was peculiarly her own, made her apologies for not having been to wait upon her immediately upon her arrival, and at the same time congratulated her upon her marriage with smiles that might have won the heart of a savage or of Lady Harriet herself had Lady Harriet possessed a heart that could be won.

But she unmoved, unmolified received this winning address with a cold indifference of manner which she herself imagined to be becoming dignity—and Lady Trevallyn then turning round to Selena softly whispered as she pressed her hand, "You see your power."

Selena blushed and fearful of Lady Harriet's scrutinizing eye occupied herself in drawing a chair for Lady Trevallyn while Clara ran to look for Mrs. Vallard. A silence of some instants ensued, while Lady Trevallyn's expressive "Hem!" told Selena how much she was suffering under the expected stare.

This silence was at last broken by Lady Harriet's enquiries respecting their removal to town, and on Lady Trevallyn's declaring her hopes of not leaving Esselberrie till spring she exclaimed, "Lord how much your Ladyship is changed! I remember when you were quite miserable ever to miss an assembly or an opera. What can be the meaning of this I wonder!"

Lady Trevallyn coloured deeply, but recovering herself instantly, answered smiling, "If I ever was so unreasonably fond of dissipation I suppose I am now wiser, I hope it is no wonder that I should gain a little wisdom as I grow old."

"You think yourself then too old to go out, is that what your Ladyship means?" said Lady Harriet while Selena laughing at the idea could not help contrasting the natural and blooming charms of her remarkably youthful looking friend with the made up beauty of Lady Harriet.

"Have you seen any thing of the Sudleys lately?" Lady Harriet while she asked this question was well aware that Lady Trevallyn having resided for some months in Derbyshire at the distance of above an hundred miles from the family she alluded to could not possibly have seen them; and Lady Trevallyn who was conscious of this might have been surprised at the question from any one except Lady Harriet.

But she was so well acquainted with her manner of introducing any subject she desired to converse upon; by some question no matter how absurd or impertinent that she only answered in the negative and patiently waited to hear what was to follow.

"I saw poor Fanny before I left town but I never met any one so out of spirits. She has certainly been used very ill. Don't you think so?"

"How so?" replied Lady Trevallyn tho' without testifying much curiosity.

"Oh Lord were not you quite sure Sir Richard meant to propose for her, he paid her such constant attention last Spring?"

"Sir Richard who?"

"Good God what a question? Do you really mean that you never heard any thing about Fanny Sudley and Sir Richard Wilmot?"

"I was out so little last year," said Lady Trevallyn coldly, "that I heard very little of what was going on in the way of scandal."

"I do not know what you call scandal but every creature talked of it, and I was in great hopes poor Fanny would have gone off at last."

"She is very young I believe," said Lady Trevallyn.

"Lord I remember her just the same thing, ever since I can remember any one."

"I have heard my Mother say that she stood for her since she was a widow, but I do not know how much younger she is than I. I was near three years old when my father died."

Lady Harriet very much provoked, well knowing that Lady Trevallyn must be sure that she herself was at least her equal in years as they at first had been introduced together peevishly answered, "Well she might have been christened at ten years old for what I know or care, however I believe she thinks herself quite old enough to be married, and you have no idea how mad all the Sudleys are with Sir Richard, I hear Mrs. Sudley was fool enough to attack him about it, and was in such a rage when he assured her that he never had the most distant idea that Miss Sudley could have imagined he presumed to think of her. I believe it has hurt poor Fanny's health very much, poor thing I pity her, nothing makes a girl look so silly as that sort of disappointment."

This was almost too much for Lady Trevallyn to bear with that composure which many a hard lesson had taught her to preserve in the eye of unfeeling malice and even now Selena's blushes, suffering, and confusion, far exceeded hers.

Selena indeed could not believe that intentional malevolence, and not folly had dictated this conversation—but she was shocked lest Lady Trevallyn should feel the indelicate introduction of a situation which might be thought to possess a similarity with her own unhappy early disappointment—but the palpable allusion was plainly seen by Lady Trevallyn and her contempt of the mean illnature which had prompted it defeated the malice of half its sting.

Quickly and coldly she expressed a doubt that Mrs. Sudley had really acted so weakly and said from what she herself knew of Fanny Sudley she could not think Sir Richard Wilmot was a likely person to gain her affections. Lady Harriet treated this opinion with a scornful laugh. The subject was however immediately changed by Mrs. Vallard, and Lady Harriet then proceeded in her scandalous recapitulation of sundry ill-founded reports all tending to the one great object of lessening the merit and ridiculing the aspiring pretentions of girls, or injuring the fame of every pretty young married woman of their acquaintance. She was not however contented that Lady Trevallyn should bear a tacit part in this discourse, appealing to her at the close of every observation for her opinion, and finding they seldom agreed she began to try what satisfaction or information she could obtain in turn from her, by all possible interrogations concerning her own private history and that of her family. Lady Trevallyn seizing on the first pause made in this very delightful and edifying conversation rose to put an end to the visit of ceremony which her great partiality for Selena had induced her so contrary to her inclination now to make.

Having curtsied to Lady Harriet she expressed, not indeed with much warmth or perhaps sincerity her hope that she would visit Esselberrie, an invitation which was haughtily declined on the part of Lady Harriet who answered Lady Trevallyn that their visit to Derbyshire was now almost over and that it was Mr. Miltern's intention to leave it in a day or two.

Having secretly thanked her stars that she had now done with Lady Harriet, Lady Trevallyn gave her hand to Selena and without letting it go gently led her towards the hall.

Perceiving that they were not followed she stopped at the hall door and throwing her arms around Selena said with a half smile, "I have done penance for your sake my love, and you must shew your gratitude by writing to me soon."

As the drawing room door was still open Selena ventured not any reply except to return her embrace and the servants standing by with the step of the carriage already down Lady Trevallyn affectionately kissed her saying, "God bless you dear Selena," and hastily left her.

As soon as Selena returned to the drawing room Lady Harriet exclaimed, "My God how wretchedly ill Lady Trevallyn looks!"

"Ill do you think," said Mrs. Vallard, "I think in my life I never saw her look prettier."

"Lord Ma'am how can you think so! I never knew any one so much altered in the time."

"Dear," cried Clara innocently, "how very beautiful she must have been! For I can hardly conceive any human creature more perfect than she is at present."

Lady Harriet's contempt and indignation prevented her reply except by a scornful smile.

Still affecting a voice of perfect indifference she observed "How much more rouge Lady Trevallyn puts on now than she did in town when first she was married!"

"Rouge!" cried all with one voice, "sure Lady Harriet you cannot think her beautiful and ever varying colour the least like rouge."

Selena appealed to Mrs. Vallard how often they had seen her quite pale for whole hours, and then recover the most lively and delicate glow, while Clara continued with all the warmth of a young and interested advocate to give a thousand proofs in support of the genuine beauty of that "red and white, which Nature's own sweet and cunning hand laid on."[45]

To all of which Lady Harriet replied with the positive assertions of the convinced yet still determined arguer and the spiteful mockery of affected disbelief until Mrs. Vallard, willing to let drop the subject of Lady Trevallyn's looks about which they

---

[45]   Viola in Shakespeare's *Twelfth Night* (1599), 1.5.234–5.

were so little likely to agree, told Lady Harriet that she hoped she would defer leaving her for some days, adding with hospitable graciousness, "you know you cannot quit the country without returning Lady Trevallyn's visit."

"You are very obliging Madam," answered Lady Harriet with a blunt quickness, "but I believe Mr. Miltern is obliged to return to Herefordshire and I shall really not think myself bound to put him or myself to any inconvenience to return a visit Lady Trevallyn took so much time to consider of. Tho' I confess I should like well enough to see the inside of Esselberrie."

"If you have any curiosity," answered Mrs. Vallard, "you may go there you know tomorrow since you are determined not to defer your journey, the place is well worth seeing."

"Oh my curiosity is not very great, and I shall certainly not appear so *pressée*[46] in visiting Lady Trevallyn. I have no ambition to be thought one of her worshippers." She said this with a sneer which left no doubt of the application that was intended, and no one being disposed to answer, a short pause ensued, after which she asked, "Pray does Lady Trevallyn draw a great deal now?"

Mrs. Vallard a little surprised at this question, tho' pretty well accustomed by this time to Lady Harriet's apparently little apropos interrogations, replied that she believed she did as she had often seen drawings upon her table when she went in.

Lady Harriet smiled significantly but as she vainly expected to be questioned she at last said, "I heard she had a master every day last Spring and I suppose Lord Henry has been endeavouring to perfect her by his instructions at Esselberrie."

At the close of this speech Lady Harriet looked for the blush upon Selena's cheek and there indeed she found it but had she glanced her eye upon Mrs. Vallard she might have seen the far less ready glow now called forth by all that resentment of which her placid spirit was susceptible.

"Lord Henry had better set up for a drawing master," answered she rather sharply, "if he possesses such uncommon talents in that way as to be able to perfect a scholar in two or three days, for he could have no more opportunities for his instructions if even as you seem to suppose Lady Trevallyn was willing to receive them."

"Two or three days!" repeated Lady Harriet emphatically, "Oh well you don't know how clever Lord Henry is! Nor how much may be done in *two or three days*, even allowing that he was at Esselberrie no longer, it was rather a long journey however for a visit of *two or three days*. I suppose Lord Trevallyn must have sent him away."

"Lord Trevallyn on the contrary did all in his power I assure you to detain him," answered Mrs. Vallard.

Selena, who had been miserable during the whole of this dialogue now left the room and Mrs. Vallard beginning also to think it could answer no good purpose to

---

[46]   Pressé: urgent (French).

contend with envy and prejudice followed her example, feeling too little kindness towards Lady Harriet to be willing to hold any conversation with her at that moment even upon subjects less disagreeable.

Chapter XIII

Sento l'aura mia antica, e i dolci colli
Veggio apparir ….
Ben reconosco in voi l'usate forme
Non lasso in me! che da si lieta vita
Son fatto albergo d'infinita doglia ……..
…. E vota e freddo 'l nido in ch'ella giacque

Petrarcha[47]

Never had Selena undertaken a journey in itself so disagreeable as that which she now made to Miltern Abbey was rendered thro' the caprices of Lady Harriet. She had been positive in her declarations of going no other way but in the curricle notwithstanding that Robert had vainly represented, that the shortness of the days must make their travelling with their own horses appear extremely tedious, especially to her who had so strong a dislike to inns; and that the cold and uncertain weather rendered an open carriage very little desirable for a woman at that time of year. However as she persisted in preferring it, she set out in this manner from Hillbarton with Robert while the sisters promised themselves an agreeable tete-a-tete in the chaise, and for the first stage Selena's dejection and anxiety were amused by the unrestrained conversation of Clara and by reading with her or singing their favourite duets in which some of Edwin's were not rejected.

But they had no sooner met on their first stopping than the miserable complaints made by Lady Harriet of the damp and cold again induced Robert to urge her to take a place in the chaise with his sisters, "Is it to go a third?" she exclaimed, "no really Mr. Miltern that is quite insufferable; I wonder how you could have such an idea!"

Selena who could not help feeling the rudeness which thus pointed out her being an incumbrance offered to change and take her place in the curricle the next stage, and Lady Harriet to Clara's no little regret accepted the offered and certainly far more eligible place considering the unfavourable weather; nor did she trouble herself to make any apology, except to ask Selena cooly as they were setting out *Whether she was sure she preferred the curricle.*

---

[47] The chapter epigraph draws from two different Petrarch sonnets: lines 1–2 are the first two lines of sonnet 320 ("I feel the aura of old times, sweet hills / I see appear where the fair light was born"), lines 3–5 are lines 9–11 in sonnet 301 ("how well I see you in your usual traces, / but not, alas, in me who from such gladness, / have now become the home of endless grief"), and line 6 is line 7 from sonnet 320 ("empty and cold the nest in which she lay"), as translated by Mark Musa.

Totally indifferent to the convenience of every other person but herself she was now extremely impatient to proceed on their journey another stage, tho' the dark November evening was fast approaching; looking with a discontented scornful eye upon the accommodations afforded, she protested it was intolerable to stay so many hours in such a wretched place, regardless of the presence of the waiter who could with difficulty restrain his indignation at the insult.

Robert ever eager to comply with all her caprices could not however indulge her in risking Selena's health by continuing their road in the dark and the thick mist which was even more soaking than a common shower, and therefore entreated her for the present to bear the inconvenience, and that in future he strongly recommended leaving the curricle to follow with the servants, and that Clara and he might then go in the hired chaise with Lady Harriet's maid while Selena accompanied her in their own carriage. They then might perform the journey as expeditiously as possible being no longer delayed by weather or their own horses.

But this arrangement could not as yet take place, the servants not having come up with them.

To this however Lady Harriet would not consent declaring that when the day was fine she could not bear a covered carriage and if Selena did not chuse it she did not want her ever to take her place.

No one liked to debate with her, but as the weather instead of improving continued to grow daily more disagreeable thro' the whole of the journey Selena tacitly occupied the curricle not suffering Clara to make the exchange she would have offered, which Lady Harriet chose to consider as a proof that Selena really preferred being half frozen and wet thro' almost every day of their tedious journey—taking care to represent on their arrival her civility in having yielded to her the very enviable place.

Not one meal passed without Lady Harriet's delicacy being shocked, and her good temper destroyed by some *horrid filth* which she discovered, or some *beastly conduct* of the waiter in her presence—and every night Selena trembled lest the contemptuous observations and haughty survey taken of her apartments, should rouse the impertinent retorts of the enraged hostess who had attended them up stairs with such officious complaisance.

Nevertheless as in spite of its apparent tediousness as St Evremond has sagaciously and consolingly observed "Le tems se passe dans le douleur aussi bien que dans le plaisir,"[48] at length the green hills scattered even to their summits by the most beautiful and picturesque trees and the thick woods of Miltern Abbey appeared in view.

Robert's prudent delicacy, by his particular orders to the steward, had prevented Selena's being shocked by any indecent expressions of rejoicing upon his nuptials and return to the Abbey in so short a time after the loss of their parents—but he

---

[48]   Charles de Saint-Évremond (1610–1703), an essayist and critic known for his maxims: "time passes during pain as well as pleasure" (specific source unlocated). "Tems" should be "temps."

could not disguise his eager anxiety that Lady Harriet should admire the beloved scenes where he had passed his childhood, where he hoped to enjoy life in the bosom of domestic felicity, and which he himself was partially inclined to believe the most beautiful residence which the world afforded. He felt a little mortified that Lady Harriet did not now offer to accompany him in the curricle, where he might have an opportunity of pointing out to her the beauties he so much wished her to discover, but the afternoon was not sufficiently fine to encourage him to make the proposal which he feared would not be agreeable.

When the road allowed him, he drove up to the side of the carriage but was disappointed to see the glasses up and Lady Harriet leaning back apparently inattentive to the scenes thro' which they past.

"Clara has surely not told her that this is Miltern Abbey," thought he, while he struck gently with his whip against the glass.

"Good Lord! How you terrified me Mr. Miltern," cried Lady Harriet as Clara put it down, "I was sure it was some banditti rushing out of this horrid gloomy forest to murder us."

"I beg your pardon my love," said he concealing his mortification, "but I wanted to know what you thought of Miltern Abbey."

"Why we are not come there yet. How can I tell you till I see it?"

"Yes both sides of the road now form a part of the domain."

"Oh very likely but I am no judge of any thing but the house and gardens."

Poor Robert made no reply but for the first time in his life began to fear that Miltern Abbey would appear gloomy and unattractive.

Selena overcome with the renewed anguish which she strove in vain to conceal, escaped from the affectionate salutations of the domestics who were all assembled impatient to welcome their young master and his beloved sisters and to behold their new Lady. Entreating Clara to leave her and return to Lady Harriet who might feel offended at their absence she shut herself up for a few minutes in her own room and gave a loose to her tears—while she almost thought the meek spirit of her Mother beheld and pitied the sorrows of her child. Once more she saw the affectionate glance and heard the mild accents of her[49] whom Earth appeared to conceal in its cold bosom but whom Heaven indeed possessed—of her who even then from the bode of eternal happiness seemed to listen to her sighs and with tenderest compassion thus reprove her sadness.

---

[49] "Lei che 'l ciel ne mostrò, terra n'asconde, / Veggio, ed odo, et intendo ch'ancor viva, / Di sí lontano, a' sospir mieir risponde. / Deh, perché innanzi 'l tempo ti consume? / (Mi dice con pietate) a che pur versi / De gli occhi tristi un doloroso fiume? / Di me non pianger tu; ché I miei dí fêrsi / Morendo eterni, e ne l'interno lume, / Quando mostrai de chiuder, gli occhi apersi! — Petrarca" (Tighe's note). Petrarch's sonnet 279, lines 6–14: "I see and hear and feel, for still alive, / so far away she answers to my sighs. / 'Why do you waste away before your time?' / she asks me pityingly. 'Why do you still / pour forth from your sad eyes a stream of sorrow? / 'Don't weep for me, for my day has become / through death eternal; into internal light / my eyes were opened when they seemed to close" (Mark Musa translation).

"Ah wherefore thus consume thy early youth in wasting affliction. Wherefore should incessant sorrows flow! Weep not for that moment which in appearing to close my eyes in death opened them indeed to eternal life and light."

Every well remembered object around her strongly brought to mind the recollection of instructions so often delivered in that spot from the lips of anxious love and the thousand nameless maternal cares never to be supplied. The little recess between the window and the fire was still occupied by the arm chair and the green desk where her Mother had been accustomed to write while her daughters drew or practised. The wax dropped by her hand was still seen upon the cloth, and the unfinished writings remained untouched within. The shelves were filled with the books marked by her pencil, and on the wall ornamented by Selena were many beautiful sentences written by the hand of her Mother.

Let those who have forever lost an object to which their hearts fondly clung for all their happiness imagine the thrilling pang mingled with a kind of sacred pleasure which attended the sight of those objects, that with silent eloquence seemed so forcibly to say "'Tis past, it never can return!"

To describe feeling is a task impossible, in attempting the description all that can be done is to awaken the forgotten memory of what we have ourselves in some degree experienced; and if there is any sensation of which we are completely ignorant the pen of a Rousseau can never by the description of that sentiment excite our sympathy. But who is a stranger to the lot of humanity which bids us enjoy our pleasures but to mourn their loss? Who has not felt the bitter anguish, the sting that accompanies the remembrance of that loss which the heart in deploring feels can never be repaired—or if there is that happy creature of indifference let him rejoice that he cannot understand. Oh anguish dear tho' hopeless! Anguish that we seem to cherish as the last memorial of our perished happiness!

> To those who know thee not no words can paint
> And those who know thee know all words are faint![50]

From the indulgence of this melancholy Selena was however in a short time aroused by the voice of Lady Harriet speaking to her maid.

Mrs. Miltern's apartment which joined that of Selena had been prepared by the housekeeper's orders for the reception of her new lady and upon her arrival she had almost immediately desired to be conducted to her own room, after having coldly expressed her satisfaction to Robert at finding the drawing room so modern and cheerful in its furniture, and appearance, "for really," she added, "one would have expected to find it all a ruin, it looks so old on the outside."

"It is a very old mansion," answered Robert, "but I hope you will think perfectly habitable, you know I told you not to expect a gay looking building or an elegant villa."

---

[50] "Miss H. More" (Tighe's note). Hannah More, *Sensibility: A Poetical Epistle to the Honourable Mrs. Boscowen* (1782), lines 251–2.

"Oh yes I thought it would look old, and I was in hopes it was just like Strawberry hill—but indeed all that great tree over so much of the walls makes it look worse than it would otherwise."

"What tree?" demanded Robert with some surprise.

"I don't understand the names of trees," answered she impatiently, "but you know I dare say what I mean, with those black leaves that quite hide one side of the house."

"Is it possible you mean, that you would take away the fine ivy that has been there these hundred years?" cried Clara shocked and astonished at the idea.

"Oh you barbarous girl!" said Robert endeavouring to laugh off his vexation, "we must reconcile you to our favourite ivy for indeed prudence as well as taste must forbid our stripping the wall of what has been for so many years its sacred veil."

"Well I shall not quarrel with you about your favourite ivy—indeed I think the outside of a house is of very little consequence, provided you make the inside nice and comfortable."

Tho' Robert could not entirely repress his disappointment that Lady Harriet had shewn so little approbation of the venerable beauties of Miltern Abbey yet he comforted himself by recollecting that she had been educated from childhood in a London boarding school and taken from thence as she had told him early to be introduced to dissipation, and that as she had never quitted the environs of town, till that time in which he met her at her uncle's, except with a gay party who brought their London with them to some fashionable watering place, it was not surprising that her sensibility to rural beauties should be yet unawakened, and he promised himself the utmost delight in opening her mind to that new and lovely source of innocence and constant enjoyment.

But alas! poor Robert might as reasonably have hoped to open the closed eyes of the blind by extolling the enchantment which reigns in the landscapes of Claude[51] as thus to inspire Lady Harriet with a taste capable of being delighted by those placid scenes his magic pencil loved so exquisitely to paint. Indeed, of the possibility that fields and groves could of themselves afford any gratification she had never been able to conceive the smallest idea—and always attributed the expression of such pleasures to affectation and nonsense. Trees and grass indeed she never willingly approached, except on a fine Sunday in Spring when she had a high triumph in exciting the universal gaze not only of the belles and beaux of her acquaintance but also of the numerous individuals of all those exterior larger circles who for once mingle promiscuously beneath the shades of Kensington.

No where perhaps did Lady Harriet's striking figure gain such flattering homage—conspicuous from her uncommon figure, shewy colours and peculiar dress, she caught every eye, and the lovely faultless form of Lady Trevallyn, shrinking from the bold eye of confident vulgarity might have past sometimes unnoticed and eclipsed, while Lady Harriet in conscious exultation overheard the frequent exclamations of the beholder who turned his head to gaze as she walked

---

[51]   Claude Lorrain (1604–82), famous for his landscape paintings.

by, saying to his equally admiring companion "Who is that lovely creature?" or "How beautiful Lady Harriet Modely looks today!" But unless there were indeed "eyes in trees and tongues in the running brooks," to feed the ever requiring vanity which insatiably called for flattery it was not to be expected that Lady Harriet could find any charm in a life "exempt from public haunt."[52]

As soon as her Ladyship had retired to her own room she desired her maid to prepare her things for dressing, and seeing that her eyes were more busily engaged in examining the furniture of the new apartment than in getting ready her toilet she asked her condescendingly "What she thought of Miltern Abbey?"

"Oh my Lady it is to be sure a very grand place."

"Grand! well your ideas of *grand* Millikin I must say are very different than mine."

Mrs. Millikin wanted no other hint freely to indulge the inclination which she already felt to abuse a residence which its distance from London made sufficiently disagreeable in her eyes. Besides the settled establishment which would probably render her superiority at least to be contested with the ancient housekeeper who already had introduced herself to their notice certainly did not contribute to her satisfaction. Dropping therefore the curtain the texture of which she had been minutely criticising, she exclaimed, "Law! my Lady it is to be sure nothing to the grandeur your Ladyship might expect and besides 'tis a sad and gloomy cloister, as a body may say and for certain the servants be the strangest sights I ever seed, quite dressed like nobody—and pray my Lady what do you think of Mrs. O'Sullivan as they calls her?"

"Heavens! where did you pick up such a name? and who is it you mean?"

"Yes I assure you my Lady that is the name of the genteel housekeeper as come into the drawing room to welcome your Ladyship;"

"What that strange being dressed out in her deep ruffles, and blue silk, with a fly cap[53] on her head stuck up a yard high."

"Yes my Lady and pray don't forget the short apron of great sprawling lace, and her high heels, I'm sure she looks just for all the world like some of the woman players at Covent garden."

"Really," answered Lady Harriet, "I took her for a mad woman and was very glad to make my escape from her, after Mr. Miltern who was gone to call you. And so that is the precious housekeeper!"

"Yes my Lady but it is no wonder she should look outlandish for I hears she be a foreigner."

"A foreigner! I am sure she spoke English loud enough while she was curtseying and wishing my Ladyship joy and telling me my Ladyship was welcome to the Abbey tho' I suppose my abrupt exit somewhat discomposed her harangue."

---

[52]   The Duke in Shakespeare's *As You Like It* (1599), 2.1.15–17: "And this our life, exempt from public haunt, / Finds tongues in trees, books in the running brooks, / Sermons in stones, and good in everything."

[53]   Fly-cap: a cap or headdress with wings forming the figure of a fly (OED).

"Oh my Lady I assure you she is a foreigner, and Mr. Miltern's own man hiself told me as how she was the late Mr. Miltern's nurse, and comes from beyond seas; all the way from Ireland, and to be sure she do speak very queer still, and not right English, like as we!"

"Well I should be content you spoke less right English so you would but brush my hair more gently. You really seem to think I have no feeling, have you been used to dress wigs on a block I should be glad to know. And do you think you have got one now to pull at?"

"Oh my Lady, there never was a wig with such lovely fine hair as your Ladyship!"

The compliment failed not of its effect, and the softened brow of her Ladyship encouraged her farther strictures upon Mrs. O'Sullivan, and her hopes that my Lady would soon go to town and provide herself with some more human figures to wait upon her Ladyship, "for to be sure my Lady such an old doting *creter* as that will never know how to order a dinner or understand your Ladyship's directions."

Lady Harriet coinciding perfectly in her hopes began now to talk with pleasure of the expected and impatiently desired removal to town determining however not to be troubled while there with the incumbrance of her sisters-in-law.

Of this toilet conversation poor Selena involuntarily heard the greatest part, while they without constraint elevated their voices, from the stillness and vicinity of her situation. Resolved to spare herself a similar pain in future she however reluctantly determined to abandon the apartment to which she had been accustomed from infancy. Lady Harriet however saved her this mortification by declaring the next day at breakfast, that she could not bear the rooms on that side of the house, the sun came in so strong in the mornings, and besides she thought the front lawn was rather less gloomy. Apartments were therefore immediately prepared for her on the other side and Selena with pleasure beheld her Mother's dressing room occupied by her own Clara instead of a daughter-in-law by whom she was so little resembled.

Being now the guest of Lady Harriet, Selena did not consider herself as obliged continually to seek entertainment for her—but endeavoured by her usual occupations in her own room to banish the cruel reflections, which her hopes of peace, and sense of duty alike forbad her to indulge. She thought that Lady Harriet, being now in her own house, might find in the novelty of domestic arrangements some employments for the mornings which had appeared so much to oppress her by their tediousness at Hillbarton.

Nevertheless, tho' pride and resentment prevented her from expressing her displeasure at the time, this conduct was highly provoking to Lady Harriet and the affront, for such she considered it, never forgotten.

Chapter XIV

As in the sweetest bud
The eating canker dwells, so eating Love
Inhabits in the finest wits of all:
And writers say, as the most forward bud
Is eaten by the canker ere it blew
Ev'n so by Love, the young and tender wit
Is turned to folly, blasting in the bud
Losing its verdure ev'n in the prime,
And all the fair effects of future hopes;
But wherefore waste I time to counsel thee
Who are a votary to fond desire!

Shakespear[54]

One morning that Selena had waited the appearance of Lady Harriet and breakfast to even an unusually late hour in a careless manner she took up the newspaper which lay unopened on the table, when her eye was suddenly attracted by the name of Inverathie and with an inexpressible shock she read the following paragraph.

"Died at Inverathie in Scotland within a few days of each other the Honourable Mr. and Mrs. Stanmore of the same infectious putrid fever which Mr. Stanmore had caught during his humane attendance upon a poor family. Tho' this amiable couple had for many years resided in Solitude their loss will be severely felt by their poorer neighbours, and their benevolent virtues long remembered. We are sorry to add that their only son a most accomplished young gentleman has been so much affected by the sudden loss of both his parents that the skill of the physicians has not hitherto been able to restore his disordered senses."

Pale and trembling the paper dropped from Selena's hands and for some time she sat motionless with horror and a half confused idea that she was in a frightful dream—till the dread of Clara's being thus suddenly alarmed with intelligence even yet more terribly interesting to *her* aroused her to recollection, she cast a fearful glance towards her, and perceiving her still seated heedless at the pianoforte, hastily crushing the paper into her pocket she retired that she might alone consider upon the best means of breaking this dreadful news to her sister.

A gleam of hope now suggested itself to her mind that the whole might be a fiction, or one of those strange misrepresentations for which she had so often heard the oracles of the day, are celebrated—and she resolved if possible to obtain some more certain account before she alarmed Clara's mind by repeating what had so much terrified herself. She fortunately recollected the name of Mr. Stanmore's old butler. To him she wrote a few lines entreating without delay to be informed of the state of the family at Inverathie and concluded with a request that if all were well

---

[54]   Proteus and Valentine in Shakespeare's *Two Gentlemen of Verona* (1594), 1.1.43–53 (Proteus speaks the first three lines, followed by Valentine's response in lines 45–52, with two exceptions: "his verdure" for "its verdure" and "That art" for "Who are").

her letter might be kept secret. In the mean time she endeavoured to assume an appearance of that tranquility which she possessed not—and her unconquerable dejection and anxiety for the arrival of the post were attributed naturally to the situation which indeed for some time had made her a stranger to happiness.

Unable to pursue her usual studies she one day accompanied by Clara, notwithstanding the heavy gloominess of the weather prolonged her walk to an unusual length and as she returned weary and languid in a silence which Clara did not interrupt, they accidentally stopped and turned round upon gaining rather a steep ascent in the path that they had taken thro' wood and were suddenly startled by the appearance of a man who the moment they beheld him darted into the wood which instantly concealed him from their sight. He was wrapt up in a dark cloak, and his hat covered his face, which the heavy mist would not indeed have suffered them at that distance to distinguish. It was however evidently not one of the workmen but some stranger of a superior rank.

Almost fainting with evident emotion Clara breathless & gasping exclaimed, "Oh Selena! did you see him?"

"Yes my love but what can so alarm you? We are within sight of the house, and surely we can have nothing to fear."

"Oh no, no, but did you not think … yes I am sure it certainly was …"

"Who do you think it was? What is it you mean?"

"I suppose it must have been only fancy," said Clara smiling, tho' still excessively agitated, "but indeed for a moment I thought I could not be deceived … in that walk … that very remarkable air …"

Selena now changed colour and perceiving plainly she thought of Edwin experienced a strong reluctance in her present uncertainty to mention his name, and felt even a kind of horror in the idea that her suspicions might possibly be well founded. Hastening home she had not power to break the deep reverie into which Clara was plunged, nor to endeavour to banish from her imagination the idea which had so engrossed it.

So strongly indeed was it impressed by the transient glimpse she caught of this object that tho' staggered at first by Selena's not appearing to have been struck by the resemblance she could not divert herself of the persuasion however improbable that it was indeed Edwin whom she had seen.

Selena observed her all day restless and disturbed. Every time that the door opened, her countenance changed, and she evidently seemed in expectation of hearing some intelligence.

At length upon Lady Harriet's repeatedly asking during the evening what made her "so uncommonly dull," she said she was fatigued by her walk and bidding them good night retired to her own room.

It was just midnight and Selena, who had been for some time sitting over her fire in melancholy conjectures respecting the fate of Edwin, and the journey undertaken by Sidney with such a true spirit of ancient chivalry, was now just preparing to commit her sad reflections to her pillow when hearing her door softly open she turned round somewhat alarmed and to her surprise perceived Clara who advancing on tiptoe whispered, "Oh you are not gone to bed then Selena! I was almost afraid I should disturb you."

"Dear child what is the matter! Have you not undressed yet?"

"No Selena but do put out your candle and let me open your window till I shew you poor Edwin."

"Edwin," exclaimed Selena starting with involuntary terror, "What do you mean?"

"Yes Selena, Edwin indeed, do not laugh at me; nor think I am ridiculously romancing but see yourself if it is possible I can be mistaken;" while she spoke she blew out the candle, and put a screen before the fire, and then going behind the curtain without drawing it up quietly opened the shutter.

Selena followed her, and would have drawn her from the window till she should hear what she had seen and her reasons for believing Edwin to be there. But Clara had already lifted up the sash without noise, and made signs to her to be silent, while putting her arm round her waist she bent her down to the window as she herself looked out.

Selena could however see nothing for the night tho' calm and still was uncommonly dark—and shocked at the possibility of Edwin's being able to distinguish them if he was really there as Clara had with so much confidence affirmed, she disengaged herself from her hold, and again retreated from within the curtain.

At length in compliance with Selena's urgently whispered entreaty Clara drew in her head saying, "He is gone now I suppose he only watched till your light was out, as I dare say he could see it thro' that shutter which is only half closed."

"Dear Clara shut the window and tell me what is all this nonsense."

Clara after having given one more vain look obeyed her, and then drawing shivering to the fire, began to account for her surmises by saying, "Why when Lady Harriet drove me away by teizing me with questions which you know I could not answer, I came up and was sitting over my own fire when all of a sudden I heard Edwin's voice singing very softly under the window."

"Oh what a fancy!" exclaimed Selena.

"Nay," continued she, "I confess I thought myself it was but fancy. However I was quite electrified, but tho' I heard only a few notes, and that very soft, I am certain it was no voice but his. Indeed who can sing at all like him? And then it was his own song, that he composed for you at Inverathie."

"Who told you he composed it for *me*?"

"Oh no matter, but you know it could be no one else that sung *that* now but himself."

"You might have been mistaken, you say you only heard a few notes, or very probably some of the workmen have an ear and certainly may have heard you sing that as often as ever you heard Edwin."

"Well," said Clara, a little hurt at this accusation, "I cannot convince you against your will, but I have myself no doubt that I have both heard and seen poor Edwin to night in the dark walk and under the great chestnut beside the house which I suppose Lady Harriet will have cut down some of these days she says it makes these rooms so gloomy."

"I hope not," said Selena smiling; "but did you go open the window as soon as you heard Edwin's voice?"

"I did certainly but he never saw me for I put out the light, and besides I daresay he knew which were your windows and so never looked at mine."

"You suppose him then to have learned Second sight or to be gifted in some supernatural manner," said Selena.

"He *has* been gifted with very supernatural talents," said Clara with a sigh, "but without enchantment or any thing very surprising he might very well have found out from any of the people about, which is your room, since it has been yours ever since you were born, and besides he might have seen your harp in the window, and perhaps you at it, if he came in the day to the grove opposite the house."

"Well, Clara let us now go to bed, I hope at all events you have not caught cold, but indeed you did very foolishly to expose yourself this way to the night air."

"Poor Edwin," answered she mournfully, "has been more exposed, and I am afraid is more likely to suffer from it."

"I trust you are mistaken, but will you promise me not to sit up any longer?"

Clara made the promise, and Selena lighting her candle accompanied her back to her own room, to stir her fire, and shut her windows, before she again bad her good night.

The sisters past an unquiet night, and perhaps Selena's rest was even more disturbed by this incident then Clara's. As soon as she thought it was light she arose and on opening her window, she beheld indeed behind the chestnut tree mentioned by Clara the same figure they had observed in their walk.

The moment she appeared he hastily vanished, and with the utmost uneasiness she could not help sharing the suspicions of Clara who in a few minutes entering her room said in a smiling whisper, "Aye I guessed you had just opened your windows, by Edwin's precipitate retreat, did you see him? And are you now convinced?"

"I certainly did see the same person that attracted your observation yesterday, but I never should have suspected him to be Edwin had you not suggested the idea."

"And can you now have a doubt?"

"Indeed I have some doubt I confess, tho' the improbability of his taking such an idle journey, and appearing in that disguised manner almost makes me ashamed of giving way to your strange surmise."

"Well *I* cannot doubt," said Clara, "tho' I own I wonder that Edwin fondly and warmly as I know he is attached to his parents should thus leave them in opposition to their judgment to be sure, or without their knowledge, much as his own inclination might lead him to be near the object of his love, which is certainly a natural wish."

Poor Selena severely felt this mention of her amiable friends who she feared were no longer able to restrain or divert the wild inclinations of Edwin, and in silence continued her dressing while Clara was still forming conjectures concerning the present residence and employments of Edwin indulging all her own romantic imagination in picturing the mingled sensations of pain and pleasure which Edwin must derive from witnessing as he thought unknown the abode and even the actions of an object so interesting to his heart.

As soon as Selena had finished her hasty toilet, which never engrossed much of her time and was this day unusually short, she invited Clara to go down with her to the pianoforte, where they might now uninterruptedly play for some hours.

But upon the arrival of the post bag she eagerly examined the contents, and seeing a letter directed to her in an unknown hand, she retired to her room to peruse what she had so much reason to dread having little doubt of its coming from Inverathie; Trembling she tore it open, and read with some difficulty as follows, written in characters scarcely intelligible, traced by an aged hand little accustomed to the use of the pen.

"Honored Miss

"This comes, to let you know, at your desire that our troubles are many and great the Lord be praised for all things; My dear good Master was always willing to serve the sick and afflicted tho' no doubt we have had a woeful loss by the means of his going to that dreadful fever where he caught his death—but the gain is his. On the eleventh day he expired and my poor Mistress was as good as gone I may say before that, for tho' she caught it by her attendance on him yet as the Doctor said her constitution was less strong to struggle with the disorder. Sick or well she would never be from him, nor would ever let us move her out of my master's room. The same grave contained them both, God rest their happy souls. But I has not told you Miss all our sad story yet; poor Mr. Edwin in spite of all their entreaties could not be kept for one minute out of the terrible chamber where they both lay—but was one moment watching my dear Master and the next kneeling beside his mother and kissing her poor hand; and to be sure his tears went to all our hearts and we would have had him away and not risk his health for the Doctors theirselves made such a do about coming into the room that it was enough to frighten the boldest.

"However Miss, the Lord be praised as I say for all things, our young Master was preserved from the fever but from the time that my poor Mistress was put into the coffin his head the Lord help us was in a terrible way; He escaped from us all, and ran out into the woods, where with all our search we could not see or hear nothing of him thro' the whole night till just towards morning, I found the poor dear gentleman quite spent and senseless on the wet ground, and then to be sure I thought my old heart would break, for I had lived too long, to see all my Master's house buried in one grave for I expected no less; However he began to recover in a day or two, tho' the fits would come on still now and again, and he would rave and talk very strangely all about you Miss and his poor parents, saying as how he had destroyed them, poor dear soul. So when I gets your letter, I thinks to my self that it would be a comfort to his poor heart to know you was well, and so good and thoughtful to us; and next time I wanted him to take some of the stuff the doctor had ordered I takes up your letter, and tells him about it promising to give it him, if he would do as the Doctor would have him.

"But to be sure he was then almost as bad as ever, and I was in a sad taking and sorry enough for having said any thing of it—being all alone with him— howsoever when he got the letter it was quite another case, and tho' he had not shed a tear since his great loss he now wept like a child and never had any return of the lunacy fits since then. Tho' to be sure he is not like as he used to be, by any means, and the doctors have ordered him from Inverathie and so Miss as I was telling you he kept your pretty letter, and put it into his bosom and tells me not for to write, as he would let you know all hisself.

"But afterwards he changed his mind and calls me to him with a piteous voice, 'David,' says he, 'you had best for to write as you were desired for perhaps my letter would be less acceptable than yours,' but. this was quite strange talk and so I would have persuaded him for to be sure Miss you must know he writes a deal better than ever I could do, at the best of times, and the Lord help me sorrow and age have now almost got the better of me but as he was pleased to order it I do my best hoping for your indulgence if I have failed in proper respect tho' I thought I would wait a bit till I could tell you Miss that my young master was quite hisself again.

"As soon as ever he was able to leave his room he said he would do as the Doctors would have him and travel abroad—bidding me take care of every thing till he came back. I made so bold as to ask him how far he might be going and he told me that his uncle Lord Stanmore had often written to desire his father might send him up to London—so that perhaps he would be glad to see him now that there was no more left of his poor brothers, as well he might be sure.

"But he said God bless his kind heart that he would write from time to time to let us know how he went on, so I trusts God will keep him for indeed I believe the like of him is not to be found on earth and if I was a fine young Lady I would rather have him than all the Lords in Christendom. Hoping honoured Miss that you will forgive my boldness I remain your dutiful servant to command.

David Preston"

Selena was but too certainly assured now what was the journey which Edwin had taken and confirmed in the idea that he was then in their neighbourhood. Extremely uneasy at the doubtful state of his health, and uncertain what steps she should take or how reveal her suspicions to her brother without exposing poor Edwin to the unfeeling scorn of Lady Harriet she was only diverted from her agitating reflections on his account by the idea of the pain she must now inflict upon Clara in communicating to her the melancholy tidings which it was necessary immediately to impart lest a meeting with Edwin might be doubly embarrassing and afflicting thro' her ignorance of the events which had taken place.

As the least distressing mode of doing this to both she prepared her by a few lines for some unpleasant intelligence and enclosing David's letter left it for her in her own room, where unobserved and unconstrained she might find relief in the indulgence of the feelings Selena well knew would be excited by the distress of Edwin. Having done this and dried her own eyes she went down with an intention of seeking and sending her to peruse the sad letter before the rest of the family had made their appearance. She was not however in the drawing room, and Selena having sought her for some time in vain, retired again to compose her own spirits before breakfast should oblige her to meet the inquisitive eye of Lady Harriet.

Upon hearing her Ladyship's voice on the stairs she went down, and on her entrance cast a fearful glance round for Clara but finding she was not of the party had no doubt of her having returned to her room and there perused the letter. The thoughts of what she then felt were almost too powerful to suffer Selena to remain at the table with any composure, and she thought it best to account for her evident emotion by telling Robert what intelligence she had received from Inverathie.

He was almost equally shocked as she had been but in the midst of their mutual lamentations and the tears which Selena could not restrain, the contemptuous smile which sat upon the silent lips of Lady Harriet could not entirely escape her wondering observation.

That she should sympathise with their regret Selena did not, could not expect, but what thus excited her scorn and even seemed in this to afford her amusement was inconceivable.

Lady Harriet was however better informed than Selena imagined or than she chose at present to confess. She had heard from Robert of Edwin's attachment to his sister, and tho' she had no idea of a young man without fashion possessing any attractions, or the possibility of such a one being able to captivate the fancy (for *heart* with her was out of the question) of one who had danced and flirted with Lord Henry, yet she had much entertainment in the thoughts of tormenting Lord Dallamore by pretending to consider Edwin as a formidable rival should he ever return to Selena.

Lord Dallamore was indeed the object of her aversion and contempt and she never spoke of him but as a fool or a madman, because on no occasion had he thought it necessary or had taken the trouble to conceal in his conversations with her that he as well as all the town thought Emily Montrose the most beautiful girl in England. That Selena had so quickly been informed of the events at Inverathie she considered as a proof of the allowed correspondence between her and Edwin, a circumstance which she failed not to treasure up against future occasions; for of David's letter which Selena had not produced she did not believe a single syllable.

As Clara did not come to breakfast Selena, however unwilling to break in upon her in the first moments of her distress, could no longer refrain from going up especially as Lady Harriet repeatedly wondered what Clara could be about. Her room was locked but upon hearing Selena's voice she opened the door at the same time averting her face to conceal the evident traces of sorrow and agitation.

"I cannot go down Selena," said she, "say I am not well indeed you may say so with truth," added she throwing herself upon the bed and sobbing violently.

Selena attempted to comfort her by expressing her hopes that as Edwin's illness had been merely the consequence of his severe shock he was probably by this time perfectly restored, and that if they had even been right in their suspicions of having seen him it was to be expected that he would proceed to his uncle's or if he remained there Robert would find him out and with greatest tenderness prevail on him to quit a life of solitude and join some cheerful society.

Clara who had listened without making any reply until she said this now started up and with an eagerness which surprised Selena entreated her not yet to mention their suspicions to Robert—"you know," cried she, "if we are mistaken how ridiculous we must appear to him and Lady Harriet."

This was indeed so much Selena's own apprehension that she readily promised to comply with her request, and then returned to excuse her absence after entreating Clara to allow her to bring her up some tea.

Poor Clara had indeed received a shock that morning of which Selena had no idea for she had herself suddenly surprised Edwin who unable to conceal himself or escape unobserved, conjured her in the most pathetic terms and with a persuasion she found it impossible to resist to keep his secret from all the house and especially Selena. He said he had no object but to be near her, and to catch sometimes a transient view of her from a distance, and on Dallamore's arrival he would for ever fly and deny himself even that gratification.

From Edwin himself Clara heard his misfortunes and too plainly perceived with inexpressible horror the yet evident disorder of his understanding. She had however past to him her most solemn promise and tho' she now lamented her own imprudence in having made the vow yet she hesitated not in her determination religiously to preserve it.

Upon Selena's alluding to her intention of speaking to Robert upon the subject, she trembled lest Edwin might accuse her of having betrayed him and the reluctance this fear had caused was perhaps even unconsciously to herself encreased by the secret unwillingness to banish him from a residence where she might occasionally see and perhaps even sometimes converse with him whom she indeed loved with the utmost purity but with the warmest ardour. She was conscious of the impropriety of secretly holding with him any intercourse, and her delicacy made her resolve to shun him as she was assured he would her. Yet chance might one day once more preclude the possibility of their totally escaping each other, and she longed to know a thousand particulars she had not dared to enquire in their last interview, so agitating to both.

In vain she dwelt with wonder on the conjectures her imagination formed as to the place of his abode. She anxiously wished to know whether he was alone and dreaded lest his solitary life and nightly wanderings might retard his recovery. While wrapt in such meditations she involuntarily past hours watching at the window for a glimpse of his form or strolled alone thro' the woods which encircled the Abbey and overhung with romantic wildness the steep banks of the Wye whose wizard stream wound thro' the extensive and beautiful domain.

But Edwin for a time no more appeared and Clara heedful of her sacred promise having ceased to mention him to her sister, Selena began to hope the idea they had entertained on the sight of the stranger was but the effort of imagination and gradually the thoughts of Edwin and his lamented parents would have faded from her mind occupied as it was by her own sorrows had not the deep melancholy which preyed upon Clara continually and painfully reminded her of the amiable family she now so much lamented her having ever known.

She saw that Clara preferred solitude and conscious how little she was at present qualified to amuse her mind she desired not to intrude upon her unemployed moments, and tho' they still languidly pursued together the regular task of their appointed studies yet their rambles were solitary and that they were sad their swolen eyes too plainly declared when they again met.

Chapter XV

Ye mysterious powers!
Whose ways are ever gracious, ever just
As you think wisest, best, dispose of me,
But whether thro' your gloomy depths I wander
Or on your mountains walk, give me the calm
The steady smiling soul, where wisdom sheds
Eternal sunshine and eternal peace.
Thompson[55]

Selena began now to be surprised that no news had yet arrived from Sidney. She was aware that some delay might naturally be expected from his ignorance of her removal from Hillbarton which she knew Mrs. Vallard had not given him reason to think would so soon have taken place, but allowing for the time necessary for the letter to make this circuit, her impatient heart, which had early made the calculation, now wondered at the protracted silence. She herself knew not what were her hopes or her wishes, but Sidney's promised letter was forever in her thoughts.

Every morning renewed her trembling agitation at the sight of the post bag, and gave her a fresh pang at the repeated disappointment. A confused sensation of terror on Sidney's account would even at some times torment her imagination, and she was then obliged to exert all herself command to drive away the horrible suggestions of gloomy dejection which would represent her as having sowed discord between these two friends, which might terminate fatally. Her disposition sweetly blended by nature with the most sanguine spirits and the most placid temper enabled her with less difficulty to turn from anxieties the contemplation of which could only produce disquietude and to look to the future with hope and cheerful resignation.

In the mean time Lady Harriet wearied of her dull guests, a bad neighbourhood, gloomy weather and above all of herself daily and almost hourly urged Robert to the performance of their promised journey to town for which her impatience to introduce him to his new relations furnished her with so fortunate an excuse.

Mortified as he was at the discontent she had plainly shewed in their retirement at the Abbey he yet considered that it was not unnatural that she should long to revisit her friends who had not seen her since her marriage, and even that she

---

[55] Masinisa in James Thomson's *The Tragedy of Sophonisba* (1730), 1.4.86–92.

might wish for those amusements to which she had been so much accustomed. Who, that really loves, does not exert a thousand times more ingenuity to cover the instances of indifference which inflict so cruel wound, than the offender? should the offender be even sensible of the fault and desirous of repairing it—but how seldom is this the case!

To indulge her was yet the fondest desire of his heart and his highest gratification, he therefore appeared to share her expectation of pleasure in spending a few months in the circle to which he had hitherto been almost a stranger. In those conversations which their purposed plans naturally produced, he would always press Selena to be of their party, but Lady Harriet never seconded the proposal and had already persuaded him to believe that it would be much more for Clara's advantage not to be seen in town for at least two winters longer, and that by leaving her at Miltern Abbey with the Governess on whom she knew they could so well depend and who had superintended their education from infancy, her improvement would be far less uninterrupted [sic] and her health which always appeared delicate might be established while it could not fail of being injured by the late hours and bad air of London.

Clara who had received Selena's promise not to separate from her was almost indifferent as to any other arrangement, contented with thus being sure of the society of her to whom her attachment was even "dearer than the natural bond of sisters"[56] and not only convinced of this, but also satisfied that she should thus be still able to indulge the imaginary charm she found in knowing herself near Edwin and treading the paths she was sure he unseen also frequented.

As to Selena, Lady Harriet ventured not openly to oppose her accompanying them, but in the absence of Robert she took care plainly to shew her she expected not her acceptance of his invitation, and Selena, who had herself no wish to quit her present situation till she changed it for one more certain found no difficulty in gratifying her in this respect by declining the kind offers of her brother and gratefully thanked him for his permission to remain with Clara at the Abbey till her future lot should be finally decided.

Mr. Turner, the uncle of Lady Harriet and guardian of Clara, was at present their guest and as he had promised to escort her to town, Robert, at her Ladyship's own desire, consented to go to London a few days before her in order to prepare a house and every comfortable accommodation against her arrival. He affectionately took leave of his sisters, desiring them in his absence to consider the house as their own and charged Selena to acquaint him as soon as possible with all she should hear from Ireland, but Selena when she embraced him at parting could not avoid some bitterness of feeling, which told her, that her brother in part estranged by his other attachments and pursuits was no longer the friend the protector to whom her dying mother had entrusted his sisters. She felt however without suffering herself to utter a complaint for she considered that in the new situation in which he stood this temporary estrangement was but too natural and she consoled herself by believing that she was not to be deprived of his affection by any circumstances.

---

[56] Le Beau in Shakespeare's *As You Like It* (1599), 1.2.267.

Every thing being now settled to Lady Harriet's content, and her Ladyship and Mrs. Millikin in the highest good humour in the thoughts of beholding their beloved London in a few days, the regret which Robert felt at this first short separation was but little shared by her Ladyship amid the bustle of preparing for her intended departure.

"Well Selena," said she gaily the first evening after Robert had left them, "I hope you will take care of yourself make the most of your time, I hope you will be as happy as possible, only I advise you to be discreet and not let Lord Dallamore find any one with you on his arrival."

The significant smile with which this was said astonished Selena and perfectly at a loss to guess the hidden meaning which she certainly wished to imply she gazed at her for a moment in silence.

"Oh don't be frightened Selena, I will not pry into your secrets, I only give you a friendly caution not to allow too much encouragement to a lover till you are quite sure of the husband."

Selena still more & more astonished gravely entreated her to explain herself, but her entreaties were in vain, while Lady Harriet escaped from her with a laugh, giving her no reply but endeavoured to hum a tune of which indeed she had very little idea few people possessing less disposition for harmony of any kind than her Ladyship.

Selena had upon two or three other occasions heard Lady Harriet drop hints which were as perfectly unintelligible as the present, but as she had never before expressed herself with an indelicacy so shocking Selena forbore to notice them in any other manner than silent wonder. She had enquired so frequently and in a way so peculiar concerning Selena's solitary rambles that the idea had once crossed her mind that perhaps Lady Harriet suspected her of making some mysterious appointments. There was however no person in the neighbourhood at all likely to occasion so strange a surmise or in the smallest degree lover-like in appearance. She therefore rejected the supposition as too wild and improbable to be countenanced even by that malice itself which is ever so ready to think all evil. Of Sidney Lady Harriet had never spoken and there alone could she have wounded and alarmed the sensible heart of Selena by a jest which implied a suspicion of attachment, for it was there alone she could suspect herself. Finding all her attempts to discover the meaning of an insinuation so gross so groundless in appearance, entirely fruitless she gave up the task and concluded that her suspicions if indeed she had any, created without cause and would probably die away without effect.

The next morning as Lady Harriet took the letters from the hands of the servant, while Selena tried to disguise the eager anxiety with which she watched her, she exclaimed in a voice of surprise as she examined the first direction which met her eyes, "Viscountess Dallamore! Rather premature! May I ask your Ladyship," continued she scornfully tossing the letter to Selena, "who is in such violent haste to seize upon the title for your Ladyship?"

With an unsteady hand and varying cheek Selena received and glancing her eye upon the letter softly exclaimed in a tremulous voice, "Lord Dallamore!"

"Oh, ho!" said Lady Harriet approaching with a look of more curiosity than satisfaction, "that indeed is something."

Clara also drew near and both eagerly gazed upon the throbbing bosom and expressive countenance of Selena as she opened the letter of which the very direction had already told her that her fate was decided.

When she had finished the perusal upon raising her eyes she met the anxious enquiring look of Clara and silently putting the letter into her hand flew to her own room to hide the torrent of tears which a thousand mingled and undefinable sensations, almost too great to be supported, had rendered so necessary for her relief.

Lady Harriet uninvited now stood behind Clara's shoulder as she read Dallamore's letter which was as follows.

> "Dearest Selena,
> "I hope we shall see each other at last and as we shall travel night and day I think you may expect us almost as soon as this letter reaches you—but Sidney says you will be glad to hear I am coming. I hope you were never so unjust as to doubt that the wish of my heart was always to be with you. Tho' one d--d thing or another has still detained me. But that is all at an end now.
> Yours Dallamore"

Chapter XVI

> Had she been mine,
> If Heaven would make me such another world
> Of one entire and perfect chrysolite
> I'd not have sold her for it!
> Shakespear[57]

Sidney in the mean time exerting all his powers in the service of Selena demands some share of our attention; Having been delayed two days at Holyhead he was much disappointed at not finding upon his arrival in Dublin the expected letter from Hillbarton which was to direct him where he might soonest join Selena, if he should succeed in the purpose for which he had undertaken this journey.

Unwilling to make any delay he left his servant at the Hotel with orders to follow immediately on the arrival of the letter and he himself directly set out for Mount Villars.

In pursuance of the plan he had adopted as soon as he had reached the village which was on the edge of the domain he would have dispatched a messenger with a note for Le Roi and a strict charge not to mention his arrival.

---

[57] Othello in Shakespeare's *Othello* (1604), 5.2.148–51 with one significant variation: "mine" for "true" in line 148.

"God bless your honour!" cried the landlord, "why the family, the Lord keep them! has been gone since Thursday."

"Gone!" exclaimed Sidney, "and is Lord Dallamore gone?"

"Aye indeed my young Lord and all, and there is not a living soul now at the house at all, at all but the Mistress, that is I mean your honour's mother."

"And where are they gone?" asked Sidney, extremely disappointed.

"To Dublin your honour, but the servants could not tell how long they should be there afore they set sail for London."

Sidney's first impulse upon hearing that he had thus come unnecessarily a journey of nearly an hundred and fifty English miles, was now instantly to return and pursue the steps of Dallamore. But the next moment, suggesting the probability of his Mother's hearing of this strange and sudden visit in the neighbourhood, determined him to spare her the anxious conjectures to which it might give rise, having left orders to have horses ready before day break the next morning, he therefore now proceeded to Mount Villars.

The astonishment expressed by the servants who met him as he entered by the back way fearful of alarming Mrs. Dallamore, made him still more sensible how much his unexpected appearance might terrify her whose health had been for some years extremely delicate, and made him resolve to send in for her confidential servant or rather friend Mrs. Ryan who he was told was then reading to her Mistress.

Mrs. Dallamore, convinced from the smiles with which the intelligence was given that no unfortunate event had occasioned his unexpected return, flew with delight to embrace her son, and when the first tumult of surprise was subsided, and that they were left alone Sidney related to her Selena's whole history and the object of his present journey, desiring to conceal nothing but his own unhappy attachment. This was however beyond his power; and Mrs. Dallamore while she admired the disinterested and generous activity with which he served his cousin secretly lamented to behold his own hopes of felicity blasted or at least obscured.

But she also saw that struggling with his own feelings he endeavoured himself to forget his selfish regret, and she trusted that his sanguine disposition would triumph over disappointment and even be rewarded by self applause in the very moment of painful trial. Often had she herself experienced that

> The softning soul
> At length shall learn what energy, the hand
> Of virtue mingles in the bitter tide
> Of passion swelling with distress and pain
> To mitigate the sharp with gracious drops
> Of cordial pleasure.[58]

From her Sidney learnt that every art having failed of detaining Dallamore at Mount Villars, after his departure, the whole party had at length to her great

---

[58] "Akenside" (Tighe's note). Mark Akenside, *The Pleasures of Imagination* (1744, 1757), 2:678–83 with one variation: "The" for "Thy" in line 678.

satisfaction fixed a day for leaving her once more to the peaceful and undisturbed possession of Mount Villars—"and indeed," added she, "this sweet place itself should not tempt me to accept Lord Mount Villars's kind solicitations that I should still remain its tenant, did I think I must yearly be obliged to suffer the visit of such a party. Not a day passed but Mr. Richmond led my nephew into some wild pursuit of pleasure, too often such as from the hints I gathered, I was astonished that Lord Mount Villars would appear to sanction. And I have heard sad tales from the neighbouring tenants since their departure."

What ever reluctance Mrs. Dallamore might have felt to part again so hastily from her son, yet she attempted not to oppose his impatience, which urged him not to delay one unnecessary moment his endeavours to free Selena from suspence and Dallamore from unjust influence.

On the road he met his servant with Mrs. Vallard's letter and finding from it that Selena was gone to Herefordshire he doubly regretted that he had not met Dallamore at Mount Villars which might so considerably have saved time and shortened their journey.

On his arrival in Dublin he sent instantly to Lord Mount Villars's house, and had the satisfaction of hearing that they were still there. His next consideration was how he should be able to see Dallamore without letting any of the party know of his return to Ireland—which might excite their wonder and suspicion. At length he resolved to write a note tho' he almost doubted whether Dallamore's indiscretion would be able to keep the secret till they met. Having made his servant write the direction he dispatched him with orders to enquire for Le Roi and desire him to deliver it when his Master was alone, which Le Roi promised to do upon his Lord's return home to dress for dinner. Sidney's note was only to request to see him as soon as possible, telling him he relied upon his friendship not to betray his being then in Dublin.

Impatiently he expected Dallamore, or at least an answer during the whole evening. Midnight came and still he would not give up the idea that Dallamore waited only for the breaking up of the dinner party to escape to him unobserved.

The night was frosty and a clear moon rendered it uncommonly light. Unable to conquer his impatience or occupy himself in any way while in momentary expectation of Dallamore, Sidney threw up the window of the parlour and spent his uneasy hours in pacing the room alternately from the window to the fire.

Some voices in the street attracted his attention more particularly as he thought he distinguished the name of Dallamore—and the next instant he plainly saw him immediately before the windows of the hotel and heard him exclaim to one of his companions who just laid hold of his arm, "What a pest you are! Why do you mind me? Have I not told you I have an appointment!"

"Oh d--m your appointment! You shan't leave us yet."

"I will drink no more tonight—I'll be d--d if I do."

"Well but come back and listen to Burrel, he was just going to sing his very best song, and you will be time enough after that. Let the dear creature wait, she will be the gladder to see you come."

"No, no, she will be glad enough without that." While he spoke he suffered himself to be led back to the door of the club which was in the same street with the Hotel where Sidney lodged.

Altho' he could not hear the remainder of their conversation yet as he saw that after some parley on the steps they all entered together, provoked and disappointed he gave him up for that night. Indeed he perceived that he was not then in a situation to attend much to his arguments and was therefore the less dissatisfied that his escape from the party had been prevented by the officious watchfulness of Richmond—for that it was Richmond he had no doubt, notwithstanding his surprise to find that this complete London fine gentleman had thought it worth his while to become a member of a Dublin club.

But during the short stay which the party had last made in Dublin Richmond had found the inconvenience of being in a manner excluded from the society of Dallamore, who liked to pass so much of his time lounging in the billiard room at Kildare Street where he was already well known having often before past some weeks in Dublin. Richmond had therefore solicited and thro' Dallamore's introduction obtained an admission not very difficult to be procured into a society hospitably prejudiced in favour of strangers.

Fearful of being met by Lord Mount Villars or his friends and continually expecting Dallamore's visit Sidney ventured not out the next morning but no Dallamore appeared nor did he hear any thing of him until about six o'clock when he received the following note.

> "Dear Sidney,
>
> "I have done all in my power to go to you both yesterday evening and today, but had not a single instant to myself and I am forced to leave town just now for a day or two. I suppose it is some cursed business about money that has brought you back and you will oblige me by using the enclosed letter in whatever way may suit. I wish your being here was not a secret that you might join our party as we shall have capital fun. You may depend upon seeing me the very moment I can come back.
>
> Yours Dallamore"

The note contained an unlimited order upon his banker to pay Sidney's draughts to whatever amount they might be.

In the first moments of Sidney's impatience, provoked as he was upon reading this, he resolved to conceal himself no longer but leave Lord Mount Villars to form what conjectures he pleased upon his appearance losing no more time in thus vainly endeavouring to see Dallamore alone. Full of this determination he flew to Merrion square but had the mortification to find that the whole party had left town at three o'clock, the messenger to whom Dallamore had committed his note having amused himself in some other pursuit and neglected its delivery for some hours. No one could tell whither they were gone, or rather there was no one to give any answer to Sidney's enquiries. Le Roi had accompanied his master, and the servants who had been left in town were already gone to seek amusement for themselves in various ways. The old woman, who had for many years had the care of the house in the absence of the family, alone remaining to answer the door. From her Sidney heard that my Lord's return was quite uncertain but that Mr. Ledron had told her my Lord's valet was to write the day before they came to town.

"And who is Mr. Ledron?" demanded Sidney.

"Why Sir Mr. Ledron is the grand french cook that was sent for from Lonnon to dress my Lord's dinner, and he came up with the family from Mount Villars."

"Then he is not gone with them now," said Sidney in hopes that the expedition whatever it was would be shortened by the want of so necessary a personage to complete their pleasures.

"Oh! not at all," answered the woman, "they are only gone on a visit to some Lord's house near town."

Not being able to obtain from her any farther information he requested that she would try and find out from the other servants the name of this Lord to whom she supposed the party to be gone; it was with some difficulty that he at length obtained the knowledge he wished and finding that they were really gone to the house of a nobleman with whom he had no personal acquaintance he thought he could now do nothing but wait the return of Dallamore; for which he determined to watch.

Few situations could be less agreeable than that in which Sidney was now condemned to pass the week. The hurry which had hitherto supported his spirits was over, and he began to doubt whether in the romantic ardour which had impelled him to this cruel task, he had not deceived himself in thinking that he was in reality by seeking thus to re-unite her to Dallamore, serving the object for whose happiness he would willingly have sacrificed his life.

"Perhaps," thought he, "it would have been more for her advantage, had things been suffered to take their fate, and surely if Dallamore on coming of age refuses to acknowledge her as his wife, she will be persuaded by reason and every judgment no longer to consider herself bound to him by any tie."

These suggestions however were quickly interrupted by the remembrance of her declaration to abide for ever by her solemn vow, and the promise which he had himself made to exert all his influence to free her at least from suspence, and to spare her those fears which the interference of her brother must occasion—an interference which, if he did not interpose, circumstances would loudly call for.

Willing to divert if possible his mind from the deliberations which he well knew his own selfish and vain hopes alone encouraged he would not indulge in the solitude which the melancholy of his present disposition was inclined to seek and forced himself to accept some of the invitations to dinner which he was sure to meet from his former acquaintances in that city as soon as he appeared in the streets or at the club.

Impossible as he found it, at such a time to attend to the conversation of the society he now joined, he was on a sudden completely aroused on the entrance of a fashionable looking young man, when in apologising for not coming in, till after they had sat down to dinner at past seven o'clock, he said he was but just returned from Clonagh Castle, a name at that time most interesting to Sidney, who well remembered it to be that belonging to the nobleman with whom Dallamore then was.

"You have had a gay party there," said the young lady at whose side the stranger now placed himself.

"Gay indeed," answered he smiling, "and if I am not much mistaken all this gaiety will come to something more serious."

"What do you mean Sir Richard?"

"Why that Lord Dallamore who is the hero of the day now at Clonagh and who to be sure is the oddest genius I ever met with, is making great play at our heiress Lady Lucy, or rather he is paying his court by proxy, and deputes his papa to make love for him which he does with great success."

The smile and the silence with which this was received, convinced the speaker who was not deficient in quickness that his tongue had outstepped discretion, and he looked round with a degree of consternation expecting to see some relation of Lord Dallamore.

Their host unwilling to encrease his confusion, but fearful of any more allusions now addressed Sidney by his family name and asked him had he seen Lord Mount Villars since he came to Ireland.

Sidney answered in the negative and added politely turning to the young man who had last entered, "perhaps Sir you can inform me how long Lord Dallamore is likely to say at Clonagh as I am obliged to wait for his return."

"I really cannot Sir," answered he hardly recovered from his embarrassment, but endeavouring to disguise it by an air of pleasantry adding smiling, "if I am to judge by Lady Lucy's attractions, their stay will be unlimited and infinite like her charms."

"Does Lord Dallamore seem much captivated?" asked Sidney assuming a careless voice while his heart throbbed with indignant agitation.

"I cannot pretend to form a judgment," answered Sir Richard, half suppressing his smiles, "for you know sir Lord Dallamore's manners are rather singular, but his intimate friend says he is amazingly in love."

"Who do you mean may I ask by his intimate friend?"

"An English gentleman Mr. Richmond, who came over with them I understand, and of whom I should advise you to caution your relation, as I strongly suspect he is well inclined to play him false with Lady Lucy, I saw a good deal of it for some days before they left town as I used to be with them at the play and at supper afterwards every night, and I always thought Mr. Richmond was himself the lover, but he says it is all pure friendship and that he is but pleading Lord Dallamore's cause, for my part I own I should not much like to have such a pleader who might be apt to remember that 'He to himself was dearer than a friend.'"[59]

"Does Lord Mount Villars seem to suspect the part Mr. Richmond is acting?"

---

[59]   Proteus in Shakespeare's *Two Gentlemen of Verona* (1594), 2.6.23: "I to myself am dearer than a friend."

"Oh not in the least, he to all appearance does the same himself, and Lady Lucy seems delighted with his attentions, but I hope sir that is for Lord Dallamore's sake; Indeed I think his friends may be well satisfied by the train things seem now to be in for Lord Clonagh highly flattered by the alliance evidently has made this party for to afford farther opportunities, and Lady Lucy independent of her personal advantages will have an immense fortune."

Poor Sidney returned home with sensations which he himself would have found it impossible to have explained—he saw the little casket in which was lodged all his precious hoard of treasure

> Given to anothers keeping
> Who did not know the value of the gem
> But threw it like a common thing away.[60]

Yet dare he not hope to profit by the insensibility, and he saw himself obliged by honour to try and restore this unguarded treasure to undeserving hands.

The conversation which had passed having completely unfitted him for society he had early quitted the party and was sitting alone in no very enviable frame of mind when a note was brought him, which to his no small surprise he instantly perceived came from Dallamore; it was to this purpose.

"Dear Sidney,
        "I am just come to town, quite alone, ill and out of spirits, no one can divert me half so well as you, so I hope you will let me see you directly.
                        Yours Dallamore"

Every reflection of selfish despondency was instantaneously banished from the mind of Sidney on the perusal of this note, and he flew to obey the summons and seize upon the favourable opportunity so unexpectedly offered him for working on the mind of Dallamore. He found him stretched upon a sopha in his own chamber before a large fire, and on the table which was covered with newspapers stood a number of candles which he had called for as if to dissipate the gloom of his own mind, caused indeed in part by having been forced by illness to quit a very lively party and finding on his unexpected return a cold and empty house.

Sidney had but little difficulty in now persuading him that his honour and happiness were alike concerned in immediately and publickly acknowledging his engagements with the lovely and amiable creature to whom he had pledged his vows and expressed his astonishment at having heard since his arrival in Dublin that he could think himself at liberty to pay his addresses to any other woman or that indeed he could hesitate about seizing the prize which he had already drawn.

---

[60] Raby in Hannah More's *Percy* (1777), 5:160–65: "I do not ask for comfort at thy hands. / I'd but one little casket where I lodged / My precious hoard of wealth, and like an idiot, / I gave my treasure to another's keeping, / Who threw away the gem, nor knew its value, / But left the plunder'd owner quite a beggar."

Dallamore protested that he had never entertained the smallest idea of any other wife but owned that Lord Mount Villars had strongly urged him to pay his court to Lady Lucy and even talked of proposing for her in his name, and tho' he denied having given his father such a permission, yet from his manner of denial, the laugh with which he answered his reproaches, and the consent he had certainly given to join the party at Clonagh as the declared lover of Lady Lucy, Sidney strongly suspected that matters had gone much farther than he allowed, or perhaps had indeed himself intended.

Sensible that no time was to be lost he pressed Dallamore immediately to set out, if he was sincere in declarations of wishing to join Selena. But Dallamore shook his head saying that was now impossible and Sidney with real sorrow and disappointment was obliged to give up now urging his departure sadly convinced that in spite of his assurances of unchanged affection for Selena it was indeed for the present impossible.

Once more with secret sighs of the bitterest anguish Sidney's doubting heart reproached him for lending his assistance to yield up to this unworthy husband the lovely innocent Selena whose worth had never been so unspeakably prized by him as at that moment when he bad himself resign every hope, and keep Dallamore steady to his declarations that nothing should be able to detain him from commanding his journey to Herefordshire the very moment that he was able to undertake it.

To Dallamore, Sidney now totally devoted himself resolving no more to quit him till Selena should herself receive him as it were from his hands; Having gained his point in being able to see Dallamore alone, and convinced that he was willing really to do all that he had intended to persuade him to, he no longer thought it necessary to conceal himself from Lord Mount Villars, well aware that the advantage of continually being in the presence of Dallamore was too great to be given up on any account, and therefore he preferred the risk of incurring their suspicions and setting them on their guard against his designs very confident that his influence was far greater than theirs and that in the present instance he was assisted by the enchanting image of Selena still powerful over the imagination and inclinations of Dallamore.

The name of Selena was now scarcely ever out of Dallamore's mouth, and Sidney, who had doubted the possibility of his ever being really in love, and had no reason from his conduct to suppose that Selena had worked such a miracle, Sidney himself could not but allow that his heart seemed truly and warmly touched by the charms of Selena, which now revived with encreasing power in his memory and imagination. However painful to poor Sidney was such a conversation he struggled against his feelings and forced himself perpetually to support it, sensible that to fulfil the duty he had imposed upon himself such a cruel exertion was now necessary.

At Dallamore's own desire he took up his abode at Merrion Square as he had always been accustomed to do in his transitory visits in Dublin, during Lord Mount Villars's absence. He constrained himself and assumed a cheerfulness very foreign to his heart to amuse Dallamore who leaned upon him for entertainment, as a child upon its nurse and was miserable if for a moment he quitted his room. He listened to his wild and contradictory projects for future pastime, talked to him of the talents the graces of Selena, played on the flute the airs so well remembered by both to which her uncommon taste and sweet voice had given a charm they possessed not in themselves, pointed out to him passages which he knew were best calculated to interest his singular attention. Without betraying one symptom of peevishness he complied with all his wearying whims, suffered him unreproved to whistle for hours while he played with him picquet or backgammon, and from his unchangeable sweetness of temper, his even cheerfulness and unsinking spirits who would not have imagined that his design, his hope was now to gain every thing from Dallamore instead of resigning to him all he loved and valued upon earth.

Chapter XVII

> Quinci l'onore e il debito, le pesa;
> Quindi l'incalza l'amoroso foco:
>
> Ariosto[61]

Lord Mount Villars felt considerably alarmed at his son's disappearance from Clonagh, for which he had left only a verbal apology promising to return the next day. Within a few hours after his departure he dispatched a messenger to enquire about him, not thinking it consistent with civility to quit Clonagh himself so abruptly as his fears of Dallamore's escape would have suggested, and having still some hopes that his son would indeed keep his promise of return. Hearing that he was actually in Merrion Square and confined to the house by a cold Lord Mount Villars was the less impatient to put an end to the visit which had been made with a view of so far engaging his son with the fair heiress that to retreat would be impossible. Nothing could be more desirable to Lord Mount Villars than this connexion, and his advances had been received so as to leave him no doubt of the wishes of Lord Clonagh to forward the alliance.

Lady Lucy herself, pleased almost equally with every new lover had constantly invited them to pass the evenings in her society wherever it might be, introduced them at every house where there was an assembly, gave them places in her box at the play and seemed charmed by their attendance upon her to Clonagh. It is true that as Mr. Richmond was infinitely the most assiduous beau, she secretly thought him far the most agreeable, but Lord Dallamore's well known high pretentions gave him a claim upon her consideration which her vanity could not possibly neglect. She well knew that as Viscountess Dallamore, the admiration of Mr. Richmond could not be diminished, and she expected still to retain his attentions in even a more brilliant circle than that in which she had hitherto moved. But to

---

[61] Ludovico Ariosto, *Orlando Furioso* (1516), 2.65.3–4: pulled one way by honor and duty, pulled the other by love's passion.

bestow her hand in return for these attentions had never once crossed her mind as a possibility, accustomed as she had been to consider herself entitled to a rank and fortune the most splendid.

Mr. Richmond however from the first moment of his introduction had formed the most decided views upon the heiress of Clonagh. Satisfied that opportunity was all that he wanted to ensure his success he had been the first to suggest to Lord Mount Villars the idea of banishing Selena from Dallamore's mind by this new object and prompted the first wish to promote such an alliance for his son. While apparently negotiating this business he had no doubt of being able to ingratiate himself so well with Lady Lucy that she would hear with satisfaction the important intelligence he secretly kept in reserve of Dallamore's prior engagement and even of the marriage which he had been well informed had taken place and tho' this marriage might not be good in law should Dallamore on coming of age chuse to anull it yet he was well convinced that it would throw a strong impediment in the way of this projected connexion.

Everything had hitherto succeeded to his most sanguine hopes; Dallamore ever unable to oppose himself singly against any scheme made no resistance and suffered all things to go on as if he had actually given his consent to the marriage— secretly reconciling his own conduct to himself (as often as the busy scenes in which he was engaged allowed him to think of Selena) by the firm resolution he made to marry no one else, and to make his escape to her as soon as possible, still imagining that possibility was not yet arrived. Lady Lucy in the mean time seated generally between him and Richmond had a smile and a ready ear for both, tho' it was far more frequently claimed by the latter. Dallamore's sudden flight from Clonagh disconcerted indeed in some degree all projects, but the arguments of Richmond had still sufficient weight with Lord Mount Villars to prevail upon him to remain there a few days, in order as he said to remove from the minds of their entertainers all idea that any slight had been intended by this precipitate retreat.

At length however Lord Mount Villars could not restrain his impatience and uneasiness in the absence of his son, and Mr. Richmond was forced to accompany him to Dublin. Lord Mount Villars had indeed desired his servants strictly to observe and acquaint him with Dallamore's movements, notwithstanding which he was not without some fears lest he should give them the slip and leave Dublin without their being able to discover his intentions. They were not a little surprised to find Sidney his companion, and took pains to ascertain whether he had as yet heard of his engagements with Selena, which they had been solicitous to conceal from him; well aware that from his strict sentiments and principles of honour he would undoubtedly oppose their design of persuading Dallamore to abandon her.

But Sidney, himself the most open and candid of mortals, now baffled all their cunning and as he was continually with Dallamore they could not from him gain this information. While thus unfortunately detained by circumstances which could not be explained to Selena, Sidney thought it best to remain silent, and it was thus that she saw with surprise post after post arrive without conveying to her the promised intelligence. He himself beheld the days pass with even infinitely more impatience, and his irksome situation grew every hour still more intolerable. The time however approached which he promised himself should free him from the restraint he imposed upon his feelings, and when having restored to Selena, the unworthy husband she was yet resolved to consider hers, he might bury himself and his disappointments in solitude and lament the irretrievable crush that had thus withered the blossoms of Hope in his hitherto sanguine bosom—for having never before experienced towards any other person the same sentiments he had felt for Selena he could not conceive it possible for another to console him in any degree for her loss.

It is perhaps a chimerical idea, that there are hearts, capable of feeling what the French call une grande passion,[62] and that in loving once love well, and love for ever, but even admitting that lovers are like gamesters and that as St Evremont has gaily said "Qui à aimé, aimera,"[63] yet this is surely certain that he is not truly and deeply enamoured who can in the first anguish of resigning the sweet object of his affections find any consolation in the assurance that time, who bears on his wings all our sorrows, shall ever bring to him the relief of indifference or exclude the dark pictures of joyless regret by the bright visions, and opening prospects presented by other hopes. In the heart of Sidney the flames of love now appeared to be for ever extinguished on the alter where the lovely image of Selena had rejected the offering. "A te principium, tibi desinet"[64] was the motto with which it had been consecrated, and the delights the comforts with which mutual affection sweetens life for ever lost to him in ceasing to hope for hers.

Nothing could now exceed the impatience displayed by Dallamore to set out upon his journey, and though to Sidney, and perhaps even to himself he attributed all this impatience to his desire of again beholding Selena, yet it cannot be denied that the weariness he experienced from confinement, not a little augmented his anxiety to depart. Sidney was himself obliged to restrain the eagerness with which Dallamore pressed him to prepare for their leaving Dublin without declaring their intentions to Richmond or Lord Mount Villars—for apprehensive of their being detained on the road, which might prove fatal to his purpose Sidney prudently postponed their journey till for some days perfectly assured of Dallamore's complete recovery. At length every thing was arranged and the better to guard against the pursuit of any of the party, which disagreeable as it would indeed have proved to both was dreaded even more by Dallamore than Sidney himself, Le Roi with the groom and horses were sent by Holyhead, with a strict charge not to mention to any of the servants their intended departure, and Dallamore

---

[62]   Une grande passion: a great passion (French).

[63]   In an undated letter to Ninon de Lenclos printed in *The Memoirs of Ninon De L'enclos: with Her Letters to Monsr. de St. Evremond, and to the Marquis de Sevigné* (Dodsley, 1761), Saint-Evremond compares lovers and gamblers: "There is a resemblance between lovers and gamblers: whoever has loved, will love" (1.21).

[64]   Virgil, "Eclogue VIII," *Eclogues* (37 BC), line 11: in you was my beginning; in you I will end.

accompanied by Sidney having seen them on board early in the evening, without returning to Merrion Square set out in a chaise and four for Waterford.

No sooner had they actually left Dublin than Sidney began to consider how he should acquaint Selena with the success of his expedition and prepare her for the arrival of Dallamore. When they stopped to change horses he retired for the purpose of writing to her—but found his soul shrunk from the task. Throwing the pen across the blotted paper he arose from the table exclaiming with a bitter kind of indignant anguish, "Why should I write? What am I to her? She will see Dallamore, and satisfied with the situation, the rank the wealth which is now hers beyond a doubt what signifies the instrument by which they have been thus secured. Let me be forgotten. Alas, wherefore should I be remembered. Could I wish that she should feel the torment with which I think upon those hours of hope of felicity passed too rapidly away and that never, never must return. Could I wish her heart to be rent with the anguish the stinging regret which these remembrances excite I should then deserve the misery to which I am doomed. No beloved Selena I would not purchase even thy love at the expence of thy peace. Oh may it never be wounded by one painful reflection caused by your unhappy friend, and may Dallamore's unthinking conduct and unsteady heart never give you cause to repent the too strict delicacy which rejected that advice which the truest friendship had dictated!" Such were the meditations by which he was occupied when the sound of the horses and Dallamore's impatient summons called on him once more to pursue his journey.

Yet notwithstanding that he thus persuaded himself that he wished not to be remembered with tenderness by Selena his heart had indeed no other consolation. The look of melancholy compassion with which she had seen his first overpowering anguish of sudden disappointment dwelt upon his imagination with a secret charm, a sweetly undefinable tenderness, which in spite of Reason, in spite of every insurmountable obstacle to his happiness, bade him be comforted with the softly whispered assurance that he was lamented, that he was beloved. It was this which insensibly to himself had sweetened those difficult sacrifices he had made for what he considered her happiness and with that inconsistency which is the very essence of Love he could bear every cruel reflection except that he might be indeed forgotten by Selena.

But this he did not believe and therefore Sidney was not quite unhappy. No it is not in the power of fortune by any combinations of circumstances to exclude all pleasure totally from that heart which at once feels love and the sweet assurance of being loved, and the idea of the sympathy with which its sorrows shall be shared, gives to those very sorrows a sweetly consoling pleasure. What human heart so disinterested, so generous as not to desire to be continually regretted by what it loves when forced to relinquish all hopes of ever being the source of its happiness? This sentiment is so intimately interwoven with love, that they who boast that they feel it not, either deceive themselves as Sidney did, or are in fact indifferent where they flatter themselves they are only delicate.

When they were again seated in the chaise Dallamore enquired what Sidney had been about but without waiting for an answer added immediately, "I'll tell you Sidney what I have just been thinking, and I am sure you will give me credit for the thought. You know Selena does not expect us in the least, and we can get some clever disguise and she will never find us out I'll bet you anything you please."

"Well, and suppose she should not," answered Sidney who felt at that moment but little inclined to enjoy any jest and not particularly seeing the humour of this.

"Oh cannot you conceive what fun we should have seeing what she was about and surprising her so confoundedly when all of a sudden there we are smack upon her when she thinks we are in Ireland. Good Lord! How pleased she will be! Don't you think she will Sidney?"

"How can you bear then Dallamore to defer her pleasure for one moment?" said he not at all approving of his masquerading plan, "you must care very little about her uneasiness of mind, or suppose her very indifferent to you, or you would long ago have written to tell her how impatient you were to see and claim her as your wife."

"Do you think she expected a letter?" asked Dallamore rather disappointed his idea had met so little applause.

"I do not know what she might have expected," said Sidney, "but certainly you cannot suppose she has any love for you without being convinced your silence is most embarrassing and mortifying to her feelings."

"Well I am sure it was your fault I did not write sooner, and so I shall tell her."

"My fault!" exclaimed Sidney with surprise, "How is that pray?"

"Why all that time we were in Dublin you never once put me in mind of it, and I thought we should set out every hour, only you were putting it off with one nonsense or another, poor thing I dare say she has almost given me up."

"Well then," replied Sidney, "the best thing you can now do is to write directly."

"Oh what good in writing now, we shall be there as soon as the letter, and besides I want to surprise her, to see how pretty she will look, as she did one day I came behind her and kissed her cheek before she knew I was in the room at what's the name of the place in Scotland?"

"I really cannot tell," said Sidney, with a peevishness which he could not entirely suppress, "but if you are so childish and illnatured as to chuse to prolong her uneasiness for the sake of seeing her look surprised, you must think differently from what I should do in your circumstances, that's all, however as I promised on quitting her at Hillbarton to let her know where she might expect you, if you do not chuse to write I shall think myself obliged to keep my word."

"Why," said Dallamore, "I will write with all my heart if you think it will give her any pleasure, but we shall travel I hope as fast as the letter."

"We may be delayed for horses," answered Sidney, "or we ourselves may require rest and at all events it is but civility to the Milterns to write."

"Oh never mind the Milterns we shall not stay very long with them I'll promise you."

"Where do you purpose going then?" said Sidney with difficulty restraining a sigh.

"No matter, any where from that cursed Lady Harriet. What the plague possessed Robert to make such a fool of himself?"

"I thought Lady Harriet was a great friend of yours."

"She the Jezebel! I would go ten miles any time to avoid looking at her."

Sidney allowed him now to pursue this subject upon which he seemed to be peculiarly eloquent, for Lady Harriet having once treated him with evident contempt he had taken care to return it and upon several occasions they had pretty plainly manifested to each other their mutual aversion. Sidney indeed felt relieved by his conversing on any subject but Selena, for as the moment of seeing her approached, that moment so critical, when his heart was as it were silently to bid her farewell for ever he found himself so cruelly agitated that he was almost unequal to the task of listening with apparent composure to Dallamore's unintentionally torturing expressions, and manner of speaking concerning Selena and their expected meeting. His health suffered under the harrassing exertion of his mind; a slow continual fever had for some days preyed upon him, and as he thought it most prudent to prepare Selena for their arrival when he had succeeded in persuading Dallamore to write, he endeavoured by seeking repose to alleviate the violence of the pains which throbbed in his temples.

Eager as Dallamore appeared, he was quickly conquered by weariness and much relieved when he heard the proposal of going to bed for a few hours, after Sidney should himself deliver to the post the letter which Dallamore declared he was so sleepy he could hardly see to write. When Sidney had for this purpose put the pen into his hands he paced the room sadly and deeply pondering on the sensations with which this important letter would be received. His meditations were interrupted by Dallamore's calling to him as he folded it up, to ask how he advised him to direct it.

"You can have no doubt surely how to address your wife," answered he as he earnestly fixed on him his fine intelligent eye with an expression from which Dallamore shrunk half abashed.

"How odd it looks!" said he as he slowly continued with his pen to paint the letters that composed the name which for the first time he now gave Selena.

"Come," said Sidney as he impatiently stood on the other side of the table, "have you done?"

"Yes," answered he slowly without however handing him the letter, "I am only thinking what a devil of a rage my father will be in, when he hears that Selena is really Lady Dallamore."

"It would have been better," said Sidney seriously, "had you thought of that before you undertook your journey to Scotland."

"Well never mind," cried he tossing him the letter and getting up to stir the fire, which he did until he had completely knocked it all to pieces whistling the whole time, till Sidney returning to the room advised him to lye down since he had complained so much of fatigue. To this he consented after having rung the bell to order a glass of hock and selzar water.

"You had better call for nectar and ambrosia," said Sidney, while the waiter advanced a few steps, the better to hear the repetition of the orders he had so little comprehended.

"Have you no hock then?" said Dallamore coolly. "Good Lord what do the people drink in this place I wonder. Be so good as to bring me a glass of water, if you have any here."

The waiter on his return said his master had desired him to say that he had some excellent claret if my Lord would please to have a bottle.

"By all means," said Dallamore who however upon Sidney's expostulations retired to bed as soon as he had tasted and gratified the waiter by his approbation of the excurable mixture presented to him as claret.

It was about four o'clock, and an extremely wet dark morning when they embarked at Cheekpoint, and the dead calm prevented their making any way for some hours. Sidney's disorder of mind and body, considerably encreased by sea-sickness deprived of his usual powers of diverting Dallamore who tho' not sick found himself dreadfully annoyed by the bad smells and continual noises around him. Upon first going on board they both lay down on the uncomfortable shelves which in a packet boat are honoured with the name of beds. But Dallamore unable to endure long the trampling over his head, the creaking of beams and the closeness of the cabin preferred going upon deck the moment it was day light, in spite of the rain which still continued.

After sunrise it however cleared up and Dallamore had the mortification of still beholding too plainly the Irish coast, from which they had scarcely yet sailed above the distance of two or three leagues.

Observing the captain and the steward occupied with the glass he enquired what they were in search of, and they then pointed out to his observation a small sloop of war which they told him had been for some days lying off Waterford and was now sailing from thence, "tho' she cannot make much way at this rate," added the captain; "for she has even less breeze than we have here, look how her sails are crowded, and not one of them has caught as much wind as would fill my hat."

Dallamore enquired the name of the vessel and upon hearing it was the Greyhound gave an exclamation of surprise and demanded if Captain Modely had still the command.

The captain said he had seen him at Waterford the very day before and that there was not a doubt of his being on board as he was informed he was then going on a cruse in the channel.

"Good God! how unlucky I am," cried Dallamore, "not to have seen him, why he is the best fellow in the world and the greatest friend I have. I would give a hundred guineas I had met him in Waterford yesterday."

While he spoke he had the glass to his eye, and then asking how far she might be from them earnestly requested the captain to allow him to take his boat and the sea being remarkably calm a sailor who heard the proposal eagerly offered to row him, with the help of one of his messmates, alongside of the Greyhound in the course of an hour. The captain made some difficulties as to sparing the men and the chance of a breeze springing up in which case he could not wait for either Dallamore or his boat, but his solicitations at length prevailed, Dallamore assuring him that he would if possible return without delay and that he might confide in his promise that if the wind should prevent this Captain Modely would set them on shore at Mitford.

The boat was nearly out of sight when Sidney ill as he was quitted his bed, surprised at the unusual disturbance which appeared upon deck occasioned by the expectation of the high reward promised by Dallamore, all hands on board being eager to offer their services and accompany him on his expedition.

The moment that Sidney perceived that Dallamore had thus strangely separated himself from him, at the time when he thought it almost impossible to have escaped from each other, had such an escape been ever so desirable, he felt as if the whole design which had cost him so much pain and to which he had sacrificed so much time and trouble was now totally defeated. And yet so unaccountable is the human heart that his first sudden involuntary emotion was that of delight. Indeed no torture could exceed his, as often as he pictured to himself the young and lovely Selena, the slighted neglected wife of Dallamore, and he had a thousand times reproached himself for his too officious interference and his endeavours to reunite those ill-paired beings, whom circumstances but for him might have finally separated. Completely roused by the agitation of his mind from the languor attendant on sea-sickness Sidney now stood upon deck watching with the glass the sloop to which Dallamore was gone when the boat which bore him was no longer visible.

In the mean time as the captain had foreboded a favourable breeze filled their sails, and Sidney began to look with anxious uneasiness at the encreasing roughness of the sea, well knowing Dallamore's rash obstinacy which would make him bribe the sailors in spite of danger should he take it into his head particularly to desire to return.

The captain however in some degree reassured him by saying that he had the utmost confidence in the men whom he had sent with Dallamore, who were the ablest steadiest seamen he had ever known. Their return indeed he very soon pronounced impossible. In a short time the vessel was no longer to be discovered even with a glass and about midnight Sidney landed at Hubbutstown with the most serious alarm and uneasy impatience for the safe arrival of the boat.

Regardless of his own health he past the night on the beach anxious to gain the first intelligence of the appearance of the sloop, which the sailors told him they could immediately distinguish by her lights and the signal she would probably make before she sent the boat on shore.

The raw and damp morning found him watching unrelieved from his anxious apprehensions, when the captain who now joined him on the beach exclaimed, "Here comes our boat, the fog I suppose will not allow us a sight of the Greyhound."

Sidney took the glass eagerly from his hand and discerned at a great distance the little black spot which the captain so positively pronounced to be his boat. As it came nearer he still maintained his opinion more strongly allowing however Sidney's observation to be just that it contained only the three sailors to whose care the captain had entrusted the boat. When they were near enough to use their trumpet they satisfied Sidney's impatient curiosity concerning Dallamore by declaring that they had left him on board the Greyhound some leagues out at sea and brought a letter from him to Mr. Dallamore.

The moment they were within reach Sidney eagerly extended his hand for the letter and read as follows while the happy sailors were exultingly recounting their adventures and displaying the generous present with which Dallamore had rewarded their exertions even beyond their desires.

"Dear Sidney,

"Nothing was ever so fortunate as my meeting Modely in this way; I have been my whole life longing to take a sail with him and missed every opportunity but this. As to Selena it makes no difference for Modely swears she is in London now with Lady Harriet for he had a letter from his sister at Waterford; so you see I shall be with her as soon as you for Modely is going to Spithead directly. However for fear of accidents I send you an order on Nesbit and beg you will assist Selena in chusing a house and every thing proper in case I should be detained. If she is not in town yet pray bring her to meet me there as soon as possible. At all events you cannot imagine what a relief it is to me to think I am saved going where I should be forced to see that cursed Lady Harriet morning noon and night, and so I have told her brother.

Yours Dallamore"

End of Volume II

Volume III

Chapter I

Make me a willow cabbin at your gate
And call upon my soul within the house
Write loyal canto's of contemned love
And sing them even in the dead of night
Hollo your name to the reverberate hills
And teach the babbling gossip of the air
To cry Olivia.

Shakespear[1]

While Sidney was considering what course he should now pursue, perplexed and mortified at the unexpected defeat of all his plans to serve Selena, and deliver her from a suspence so peculiarly distressing; while he was involuntarily at one moment reflecting with satisfaction that she was as yet unclaimed by Dallamore, and the next indignantly lamenting the levity and caprice which had so strangely frustrated all the hopes he had entertained that to his exertions Selena's gratefully compassionate heart should ever remember she owed the union which, circumstanced as she was, she esteemed desirable; while agitated by his own sorrows and embarrassed in what manner to declare to her the disappointment she could so little foresee Selena herself in hourly expectation of Dallamore's arrival dwelt with almost unconscious anxiety upon this one contemplation—"Will Sidney accompany him? Is it from his hands that I am to receive the being whom I am to regard with superior, with exclusive preference? How shall I bear to behold him sadly earnestly observing me on this dreaded meeting. Oh my father! why, why was I thus sacrificed!"

Starting at the exclamation which involuntarily escaped from her, with clasped hands and the adoring eye of meek submission she invoked the assistance of a power superior to hers not to alter her lot, but to enable her to fulfill its duties, and to expel from her heart the ideas which in spite of all her exertions were continually recurring.

Thus deeply engaged in this internal struggle as she paced her favourite dark walk beneath the venerable avenue of chesnuts which even now with their leafless branches formed a shade over her head, while the thick shrubs and underwood of laurels and holly on either side defied the attacks of winter to diminish the shelter and cheering verdure which they afforded when every other scene was stripped of beauty; her painful reverie was suddenly suspended by the appearance of the

---

[1]   Viola in Shakespeare's *Twelfth Night* (1599), 1.5.263–9 (line 266 omits "loud" after "them," line 267 uses "Hollo" instead of "Hallow," line 268 uses "teach" instead of "make," and line 269 changes "Cry out" to "To cry").

very object which had in so principal a degree engrossed for some time all her meditations, nay even her dreams.

It was indeed Sidney; tho' he had failed in his first intentions, and tho' there was little probability of Selena's accepting him as her escort to town according to Dallamore's plan, yet he had persuaded himself that entrusted by Dallamore with such a commission he ought now in person to explain to Selena the circumstances which so strangely had diverted Dallamore from appearing as he had promised at Miltern Abbey.

As Sidney entered Herefordshire and approached the place which now contained all he loved upon earth, he felt shocked at the painful idea that his presence thus unaccompanied would probably occasion much surprise to the whole family, and to Selena a disappointment the most mortifying. Unable to stand the interrogations with which he expected to be assailed and to behold the embarrassment, nay perhaps the sorrow which would speak yet more eloquently in the silence of Selena than all those interrogations, he resolved to seek her if possible alone that the confusion attendant upon a more publick investigation might be spared to each.

With this in view he purposed passing the night at a little village at the edge of the wood which encircled Miltern Abbey tho' he had arrived there at an hour sufficiently early to justify his appearance, guessing that he should then find the whole family assembled after tea. The inn presented but an uncomfortable reception, and while the maid was kindling the fire in the cheerless parlour Sidney requested permission to remain in the kitchen, benumbed as he found himself with cold after his solitary drive in a chaise whose windows excluded little of the keen air. While he stood there the landlady who was not much accustomed to entertain guests of an appearance such as Sidney's bustled to prepare his supper, and called to her daughter, whose ironing had been disturbed by the unexpected stopping of the chaise at the door, to watch the turning of the fowl, while she herself went to the press for the white sheets, which for a considerable length of time had not seen the light. As she was about to air them she perceived that the farmers who occupied the greatest part of the fire still continued their conversation over their ale not at all concerned by the arrival of Sidney, or the stir it had occasioned.

"Pray Masters," cried she, "be so pleasing as to make a little room for the gentleman."

Sidney begged that he might not disturb them, and his courteous gracious manner failed not of its always irresistible effect, tho' the sturdy boors seemed at first but little disposed to attend to the remonstrance of the hostess, and the personage already in possession of the chimney corner, taking his pipe from his mouth, was beginning a rough retort with, "I say Mistress, first come first served …" but his neighbour removing to the farther end of the settle[2] drew him towards him saying, "come, come neighbour Jenkins we's had our share … let this

---

2   Settle: chair, sitting place (OED).

young gentleman have an air of the fire. It's a mortal cold night master and you'd be the better of a pot of beer after your ride."

"Aye, aye, sit thee down," said Jenkins making room for Sidney not insensible to the beautiful smile which displayed the finest teeth in the world and illuminated his countenance as he accepted the tardy civility and approached to warm himself.

The most refined conversation could at this time have had but little allurement for Sidney, nevertheless his natural courtesy felt that having thus intruded into any society, he could not entirely resist their offers of social intercourse without an appearance of contempt which was even more repugnant to him than the interruption the uninteresting dialogue occasioned to his meditations. He therefore answered their enquiries concerning the road he had come, freely gave his opinion upon the new projected taxes and in his turn highly gratified them by some questions relative to Miltern Abbey and its inhabitants.

"It is a rare fine place indeed," cried Jenkins, "and has been in the late Madam's family as long as the memory of man."

"And it were a thousand pities," said his opposite neighbour, "that it should ever go out of it. For never was a better, tho' I say it as should not say it having been bred and born in the abbey, and for the matter of that so was my father and grandfather, and to say the truth nothing would have brought me to leave it had we had an heir of our own. But when the late Madam married, not knowing what sort he might turn out I thought it was best for me to look after my own farm and not be dependent like upon a stranger. And especially as I heard he was not even one of our own countrymen but come from the Lord knows where beyond seas where they be all almost papishes. So I thought it time I should shift for myself."

"Well," replied Jenkins; "I believe you never had cause to say wrong you did in that. The next steward had another guess[3] sort of a man to deal with than Madam's father, God rest his good soul."

"Different indeed," answered his neighbour shaking his head, "poor Madam herself had many a hard hour with him, but they are both gone now, and the young squire takes most after his mother, and all the better say I."

"Aye," cried Jenkins, "and what do you think of the young ladies?"

"They be main pretty lasses to be sure, and all as good as they are pretty."

Sidney felt his cheeks glow while the other hastily interrupted the eulogium thro' his impatience to do justice to the sweetness of disposition and the active charity of Selena, to which there was scarcely a poor cottage in the environs of Miltern Abbey that could not contribute its delightful testimony.

How *silver sweet*[4] sounds the voice which speaks the praise of what we love! Tho' shame and timid fear may prohibit the tongue from joining in the melodious strain, yet not one note is lost to the heart, but finds there its true and ready vibration, and endears to us for ever the lips from which it is uttered. How exquisite is the

---

[3]   Guess: barren (reference to cows and agriculture) (OED).

[4]   In Shakespeare's *Romeo and Juliet* (1594) Romeo says "How silver-sweet sound lovers' tongues by night / Like softest music to attending ears!" (2.2.166–7).

silence in which unnoticed, unthought of, we listen, the eyes overflowing with tenderness, and the heart enkindled with gratitude to the voice which points out the beloved perfections which we ourselves feel but dare not applaud!

Sidney was not likely to interrupt speakers gifted as they now appeared to him with eloquence so ravishing; and indeed Selena's praise was a topick upon which all seemed most willing to expatiate, and in celebration of which each had some annecdote characteristically amiable to communicate.

The landlady was the first to interpose any stop to a conversation which had been more soothing to Sidney's mind than any in which he had been engaged since he quitted Hillbarton.

She had indeed herself considered his uncommon patience with some surprise, and in acquainting him that supper was now ready, of her own accord made some apologies for the length of time which it had been preparing, confessing that she had delayed it on account of the absence of her son Tom, against whom she had been for the last hour bitterly inveighing for having taken with him the key of the wine cellar, and now added addressing herself to the farmers whom Sidney had invited to partake his supper, "I partly guess what makes him stop so long—'tis a fine night, and for certain he be gone to the wood to hear the crazy gentleman sing."

"Aye never doubt thee Tom," cried Jenkins, "let who's will work thee's sure to be idle, but what does thee let him follow the madman for, dame, mind I tell thee he will harm him afore long."

"He harm my Tom, no that he won't poor soul, not he no more than theeself; why he's as gentle as the babe just born and has no more malice in him for all he be out of his mind as they say and would have no body see him if he could help it."

"Gentle as he seems," cried the other, "there's no knowing what he may be when the fit comes on him; for my part I would no more trust myself within his reach than I would take a mad bull by the horns."

"Why sure thee be'nt so chicken-hearted," said farmer Mudge, "why thee couldst trounce three the likes of him, quite a small slip."

"I tell thee what," answered Jenkins, "I be'nt afraid to face the strongest he in the parish so he be a human christian like myself, but when once the devil gets possession of those poor crazed *creters*, there's no saying what force they do get, and I make no doubt *donny* lad as that there looks he could tear thee limb from limb as thee wouldst a spider. Why dost think," he continued, observing what an impression he had made upon the terrified hostess, "dost think now that he could sing as he does if he were in his right wits. I'll hold thee a wager no more than I could, and for my part I could take no pleasure in hearing him fine as it is when I think all that comes from the devil within him."

Sidney here interposed and requested to know of whom they were speaking, and as all were eager to give what intelligence they could, he soon learned enough to excite his interest and much more than he could believe to be true.

In the midst of this conversation Tom returned and being instantly attacked as to his stay, owned that he had been as was guessed following at a distance the nightly rambles of the madman, in order to hear him sing, "as he was sure to do when he thought no one could be at hand to listen to him," observed one of the company.

"Aye Mother, and I spoke to him too a while ago," added Tom as they went together to draw some beer; The farmers who overheard this confession were eager to know what had passed—and the boy on being again questioned told them that while following as close as he could venture, he all of a sudden struck his foot against something, and stooping for it he found it to be a book which said he, "I was main sure he must have dropt as he was just afore me in the very same path so before he had time to look about him and make off as he does the moment he spies any one I comes close up and gives him the book."

"Well and what did he say?" exclaimed Tom's auditors almost in a breath.

"Oh at first he was all in a maze like, and to be sure thought I come up out of the ground, but when he saw the book he thanked me, and asked who I was, and what I did there, so I said I had been on an errand to the Abbey, for I was afraid to let him think any thing else, so then he thanked me again and darted off like lightning."

"Aye, and well for thee he did," said his Mother; "I will have no more of this, remember I tell thee Tom, go near him no more."

"Indeed but I must Mother," cried the boy, "for lookee here be a paper that I did not see 'till he was gone, that I dare to say is part of that there book, for I found it just hard by where that lay and the poor gentleman may fret after it."

Sidney held out his hand for the paper, and was not a little astonished to behold on the first glance of his eye the beloved name of Selena. His surprise was still farther encreased, upon reading the passionate and tender sentiments conveyed in some latin verses which with all the delicacy of modern refinement might in correctness and elegance of expression have done honour to the most advanced poets of the Agustan age.

His curiosity and interest being now roused to the utmost he renewed his enquiries, anxiously demanding if he could not obtain a sight of this extraordinary person who they said had been now for some time about the neighbourhood.

"Why it is quite a chance," answered the boy, "that you can light on him in the day, for he hides himself in the woods round the Abbey if it be fine and never stirs out when the weather is bad till dark and then wet or dry out he goes, and sometimes without a hap'worth[5] on his head. Tho' when it is light he would not stir an inch except wrapt up hugger mugger[6] in a great cloak for all the world like one of them fellows that came down to the squire's funeral. And I never could see a feature in his face 'till just now that the moon shone upon it as I gave him the book. But if your honour wishes to get a sight of him, I knows where we can find him sure enough at break of day, for many a morning I have watched him just facing the Abbey, when I have been crossing the short path thro' the park to take the letters from the post boy at Newton."

---

[5]   Hap: covering (OED).

[6]   Hugger mugger: secretly (OED).

Sidney instantly agreed to accompany him, and his guide promised to call him at six o'clock assuring him at the same time that it would be to no purpose to attempt to converse with the stranger, as he would certainly make his escape the moment he perceived them, in which assurance all present agreed, each relating some adventure they had had when accident or design had thrown them in his way.

The thoughts of his approaching interview with Selena held the eyes of Sidney unclosed during the night and he impatiently awaited the expected summons from the boy who had promised to show him the way to the Abbey, and point out to his view the author of those verses which he had repeatedly read over with pity and admiration.

It yet wanted some time of the hour of sunrise when amid the gloom which thickly enveloped them his attendant vainly endeavoured to enable Sidney to discover the Abbey which he said was now immediately before them—adding, "and I shall soon have light to shew you young Misses window, that he will sit and stare at as long as there is a bit of moon in the sky to see it, for they say he be gone mad for the love of she."

Sidney was going to enquire from whom he could have had this intelligence when suddenly at some distance the softest and sweetest melody arrested the captivated attention of Sidney who while the boy whispered "There he is Sir" immediately recognized in the air now sung by a male voice with the utmost perfection of skill and taste, one which he well remembered to have heard Selena herself play as the composition of Edwin.

Melted by the tenderest recollection of those happy moments when he had listened with delight, nay even the most rapturous hope to those very notes, he felt his eyes suffused with tears and forgot for a moment the strange discovery which he had thus undoubtedly made, that the mad stranger who had excited the terror and curiosity of the village, and the romantic Edwin who had inspired with a hopeless passion the young and beautiful Clara, were but one.

The enchanting strain ceased, and the silence which reigned around was as yet undisturbed by any rural sounds which might proclaim the approach of day.

Sidney's conductor who listened with an enthusiastic admiration to the uncommon excellence of Edwin's voice, which untaught Nature had given him a taste to feel, the song being ended grew impatient at remaining longer in this cold and inactive situation, and alleging that if he delayed he should be too late for the letters, Sidney gave him leave to proceed, saying he would himself wait till he got a sight of the stranger, whom he could hardly mistake from the description he had received.

The dim morning now began to dawn from the "hazy south," and the late rising sun to "lift his pale eye unjoyous"[7] on the deflowered beauties of the landscape, which was still most interesting and lovely to Sidney as the beloved birthplace and early abode of Selena, which she had frequently described to him in the warm

---

[7]   James Thomson, "Winter," *The Seasons* (1726), lines 866, 746 ("Lifts her pale eye").

colouring of fond partiality. The venerable chesnuts which she had so often spoken of he could even now distinguish by their uncommon size and shape, as well as by their yellow leaves heaped around their huge and stripped trunks, and he felt inclined to hail them as the early companions of his adored Selena.

He contemplated the majestic towers, the heavy window, and small gothic doors with reverential tenderness, and as he gazed on the mansion which held the object of all his fond hopes and bitter regrets, forgetful of Edwin of Dallamore nay of all the world but Selena with involuntary emotion he ejaculated her name and was instantly startled by a deep sigh which seemed to escape from some person behind him.

He turned hastily round but beheld nothing, tho' the rustling among the dead leaves in the part of the wood nearest to him which was thickly crowded with hollies proclaimed to him which way Edwin had disappeared, for of its being Edwin, he could not entertain a doubt. Yet that he should thus lurk in this strange disguise around the dwelling of Selena filled him with astonishment and the most painful concern which determined him strongly to recommend her complying with the desire of Dallamore that she should remove to town.

Observing several of the windows now unclosed and some of the servants busy about the court yard, while the thick smoke from the chimneys proclaimed the new lighted fires in various parts of the house he thought he would take a short walk, and then return to the Abbey, sure of finding Selena the first in the breakfast parlour.

As he reached the entrance of the dark chesnut walk, on his return, he perceived at the extremity of the vista her light and beautiful figure, which it was impossible for him to mistake tho' turned from him and that graceful walk which was like "the music of songs."[8]

For a moment the extacy of thus suddenly beholding all he loved rushed upon his soul with a force which rivitted him to the spot, but from this he was quickly roused by the anguish of recollection which brought to his mind the painful image of Selena lamenting the neglect of Dallamore and the disappointment it was his lot to communicate.

While he stood yet motionless gazing towards her as she still slowly walked from him he beheld a figure enveloped in a large cloak stealing behind her along the edge of the walk.

Sidney instantly sprang forward scarcely knowing what was his intention, and at the sound of footsteps the person he had seen concealed himself among the underwood without even once looking round to see if he had been observed.

Selena having now turned round perceived Sidney, who confused and trembling at first hastily advanced a few paces to meet her and then suddenly stopped overpowered by mingled and indescribable emotions.

---

[8]   This phrase appears twice in James Macpherson's *The Works of Ossian* (1765): in "Cath-Loda" (Duan III) and Fingal (Book III).

Selena herself convinced by the first glance that it was indeed Sidney whom she beheld absolutely gasped for breath as she looked around for Dallamore, by whom she supposed him to be accompanied and experienced an indefinable sensation of relief on being convinced he was alone.

She was however unable to proceed and her evident agitation restored Sidney to his presence of mind and as he flew towards her he extended his hand, while he exclaimed with a forced smile and glowing cheek, "I am here Selena, but can hope for no welcome, for I come alas, alone."

"Has any thing happened?" asked she while the downcast eyes she presented to his her trembling hand.

"Nothing," replied Sidney and then pausing for a moment hesitated how he should most delicately represent to her the conduct of Dallamore, every speech which he had previously framed having vanished from his mind upon the first glimpse which he caught of the graceful form of Selena.

"Lord Dallamore then disowns me," said she calmly, as she averted her cheek crimsoned over with blushes, feeling at the same time an unusual sentiment of pride from conscious worth and offended dignity,

> As gentle spirits still are apt to do
> When cruel slight, or killing scorn assails them.[9]

"Disowns you!" cried Sidney, his full heart almost bursting thro' his lips and eyes while discretion smothered its passionate language. "No Selena he is not so blind to his most valuable possession, but he has been hurried away as usual by the impulse of the moment, and as he believed you in London hopes to meet you there; he is indeed we must confess a strange being," added he smiling, "but shall speak for himself."

As he said this he presented to her Dallamore's letter, and while she read it indulged his ardent eyes gazing on those well known, well remembered charms "While on his heart the torrent softness pours" till forced to turn away "full their dear extatic power" and even "sick with sighing languishment."[10]

"What Modely? What sailing does he mean?" cried Selena, having come to the conclusion of the letter for the second time without being able to comprehend a word of its contents or to fix her agitated thoughts upon any thing but that she had beheld Sidney, that he was at that moment actually at her side and that Dallamore was as far from her as ever.

Sidney was himself as little able clearly to explain any subject, but after a few moments they were each restored to sufficient tranquility to communicate and receive the particulars of Dallamore's unexpected voyage.

---

[9]   Emmelina in Hannah More's *The Fatal Falsehood* (1779), 4.79–80.

[10]   James Thomson, "Spring," *The Seasons* (1730), lines 982, 969–70.

Still she held the letter in her hand and as she once more perused it exclaimed, "Meet him in London! Impossible! How can I go alone, unacknowledged by his family—unsupported by my own ...." Here she stopped overpowered by confusion at the offer of protection which she seemed thus to demand from Sidney.

But his delicacy ever alive shrunk from inflicting upon hers the slightest wound, and checking the sigh with which he reflected that his protection was inadmissible he answered, "Does not your brother go to town this winter? Surely on such an occasion he will readily anticipate his removal."

"My brother is already gone," said Selena looking down, with that kind of comfortless sensation which we experience on being obliged to communicate to another, some circumstance which proves the want of that affection, the gradual diminution of which we would willingly refuse to acknowledge to ourselves.

"Gone," exclaimed Sidney, "and are you here alone?" his thoughts disagreeably recurring to the concealed attendance of Edwin.

"No," answered Selena, "Lady Harriet does not leave this until tomorrow, and my sister I hope will never quit me—at least till she marries," added she sighing as she forced a smile.

"Have I so far forfeited by my late ill-success the boasted name of friend," said Sidney, "as not to dare without too much presumption to offer again my counsel?"

Selena trembling as to what that counsel might propose coldly asked him what he would advise.

"That you should accompany Lady Harriet to town, where I hope," added he with some hesitation, "that you will find Dallamore."

Selena conscious that Lady Harriet had evidently avoided seconding every invitation given to her by Robert felt extremely reluctant to force herself into her society and especially as she could not to her show Dallamore's letter, and even wished not to express her expectation of meeting him in London, lest her disappointment, should he again fail in his engagement, might excite her contemptuous and ill-natured ridicule, the malice of which she had already more than once experienced.

The point was yet undecided when Clara who came out in order to call Selena to breakfast interrupted their conversation, and starting when she beheld Sidney, looked around with an anxious and inquisitive eye as Selena herself had already done for his expected companion.

Selena entreated Sidney to explain the matter to Lady Harriet and not chusing to be herself present at his first appearance before her Ladyship hastily retired to her own room to compose her spirits before she joined the party assembled at the breakfast table.

Chapter II

Virtue itself scopes not calumnious strokes,
The canker galls the infants of the Spring,
And in the morn and liquid dew of youth
Contagious blastments are most immenent

Shakespear[11]

As they walked slowly towards the house Sidney satisfied the curiosity of Clara who could not refrain from expressing some indignation at the conduct of Dallamore, questioning Sidney whether he thought it was really his intention ever to acknowledge the unfortunate marriage.

Sidney assured her that it was his firm persuasion that Dallamore had left Ireland with no desire upon earth so strong as to join Selena and that the step he had taken which had thus prevented their meeting was as free from all premeditated plan of separation, as it was itself sudden and unforseen, but he added that it was impossible to answer for his disposition at any future period, "for which reason," said he, "I hope My dear Clara you will assist me in prevailing upon Selena to comply with his desire and meet him in London."

Clara started. "Do you mean that she should go there as Dallamore proposes and take a house?"

"No not exactly as he proposes there is no occasion for that, for since Lady Harriet goes tomorrow why should she not accompany her?"

Clara turned pale, and the large drops fell in silence down her cheeks. They were now at the hall door and Clara stopped saying to Sidney in a melancholy tone, "Did Selena approve of your plan?"

"She has not assented to it as yet, at least she has not said so, but I hope she will; indeed there is another strong reason for her leaving this at present."

Instantly the deepest blush covered the transparent face and bosom of Clara, and Sidney gazing at her evident agitation was secretly convinced that the residence of Edwin was not concealed entirely from her.

All explanation was however prevented by the approach of a servant when Lady Harriet impatient at their unusual stay had again sent to summon the sisters to breakfast.

As Clara entered the room she was beginning in a fretful voice to enquire whether they chose to drink tea *al fresco*[12] in the dark walk that morning, when the appearance of Sidney stopped the expression of her discontent and gave a new turn to her ideas.

"Bless me," she exclaimed, "is it you Mr. Sidney? Well I am overjoyed that you are come while I am here that I may see the tender meeting of the happy

---

[11] Laertes in Shakespeare's *Hamlet* (1600) 1.3.38–42. The epigraph omits line 40: "Too oft before their buttons be disclos'd."

[12] Al fresco: in the fresh air; outdoors (Italian).

couple—but where is he? I hope there has been no unfortunate rencontre[13] already with the swain of the woods. Oh Lord I beg pardon, but never fear Clara, you need not look so excessively alarmed child, I have done."

"What is it you mean," stammered out Clara confusion and surprise almost overpowering her whole frame.

"Oh no matter … you know well enough … at *least* I believe *you* are in the secret. But where is Dallamore? Have Selena and he retired to enjoy the delicious meeting for which they have *both* been so impatient."

Clara was too much engrossed by the hint thrown out by Lady Harriet to be able to give her any answer, but Sidney in as few words as he could said that Dallamore having been informed by Captain Modely that Selena was in town was persuaded by him to sail in his vessel to Portsmouth and from thence intended to make all possible expedition to London.

At the conclusion of this speech Lady Harriet burst into a most immoderate fit of laughter and when Sidney forcing a smile demanded what had so much entertained her Ladyship she exclaimed, "Oh any thing so ridiculous I never heard! So you have actually hunted poor Dallamore from terra-firma and Arthur has rescued him at last from his wife. Well that is capital I vow! But what does Selena say to this? Does she still fancy herself Lady Dallamore? It is seriously quite too absurd in her to submit this way to such intolerable caprice. It would be an act of charity to put the thing out of the girl's head—but they are all so determined upon having a Countess."

These words in some measure restored the courage of Clara which had been terribly demolished by the allusion to *the swain of the woods* an expression which she could only think related to Edwin, and she was beginning a reply but was prevented by Sidney who colouring with indignation warmly said that, "Whether Selena should be a Countess or not was a matter already out of all dispute, and that no one could be so determined upon that point as Dallamore himself," adding, "that he could never have believed him capable of so firm an attachment but that Selena alone could work such a miracle."

"Mr. Sidney is quizzing your sister. Why do you let him Clara," cried Lady Harriet with a scornful air, always provoked when any compliment was paid in her presence of which she was not the object.

But Selena herself now appeared, and as Sidney involuntarily rose at her entrance, endeavouring to disguise his emotion by placing a chair for her at the table, Lady Harriet and her little malice vanished from his mind before the enchanting softness of these mild and modest graces upon which he dwelt with silent tenderness.

"Well Selena," said Lady Harriet with [a] suppressed smile, "when do you mean to set out—Mr. Sidney seems to think that Lord Dallamore will expect you to go to him when his voyage is completed."

---

[13] Rencontre: hostile meeting or contest (French).

"I think," answered Selena gently, while she stole an expressive look at Sidney to bid him observe that she was still uninvited to be of Lady Harriet's party, "I think it will perhaps be more prudent in me to remain here 'till I know of Lord Dallamore's arrival, especially as I have no house to receive me and could not very decently go alone to an hotel."

"I guessed so," said Lady Harriet significantly, but without taking any notice of the obvious open which Selena had left for repeating the invitation which Robert had frequently given and which Selena would now have thought it right to accept had it been made as common civility required independent of sisterly affection.

But besides the determination that Lady Harriet had long made that she would not be troubled with her sisters while in town, she had another motive for obliging Selena to remain at Miltern Abbey as she now hoped to effect. She could not bear the idea of her being presented as Viscountess Dallamore while she herself must appear but as the wife of a commoner, and secretly resolved by every means in her power to retard, if she could not entirely obviate an event so mortifying to her pride. She now hoped that Selena's preferring under such circumstances to remain at Miltern Abbey would give considerable probability to the insinuations she was bursting to throw out concerning her concealed lover in the woods, the favourite topick of all her toilette conferences with Mrs. Millikin, who had every day some new adventure or incident to invent or colour for her Lady's entertainment concerning Miss Miltern or her mad lover. Indeed except the french governess whose retired disposition and little skill in the English language kept her totally separate from the family, Selena and Robert were perhaps the only persons in the house who for some time were strangers to Edwin's residence in the neighbourhood and his nocturnal rambles. From the latter Lady Harriet had purposely concealed incidents of which she was very sure he would take some measure to prevent a repetition, however amusing they proved to her Ladyship.

The hints which she had on this and some other occasions suffered to escape her had burst forth from the overflowings of her naturally malicious mind, and nothing was farther from her intention than the very obvious effect they were likely to produce by deterring Selena from remaining at Miltern Abbey.

"And pray may I ask," said she now turning to Sidney, "whether you mean to stay here and take care of the Ladies?"

The open and manly brow of Sidney was suffused with a deep glow at the ill-breeding and indelicacy of this speech, but concealing his sensations he gaily answered, "Certainly if the Ladies will allow me so honourable a charge, unless you will confer on me a still higher honour and suffer me to escort you all to town."

"But how would you divide yourself?" replied she still resolved to disregard every hint of their travelling together conscious that it would then be impossible to shake off the sisters immediately upon their arrival in town. "For my part Selena," continued she, "I shall not dispute Mr. Sidney with you, as I am for the present content with my old beau Mr. Turner—Apropos!" cried she glad to change the subject and looking round as if she had just then missed [him] for the first time,

"I should like to know what is become of Mr. Turner all this morning. Do Mr. Sidney be so good as to ring the bell that I may enquire if he is dead."

Selena had seen enough of her airs to be pretty well convinced of the affectation of this, but Clara looking at her with surprise asked was it possible she had forgotten that he had taken leave of them the day before, which he had done having promised to visit a friend about ten miles from Miltern Abbey, and appointed Lady Harriet to meet him the next morning at the first stage on her way to town.

Selena was impatient to quit the apartment constrained by the presence of Sidney, and distressed lest in his zeal to serve her, he might still farther expose her to the rudeness of Lady Harriet by making a more direct proposal of her accompanying her in the purposed journey.

As she passed thro' the hall she perceived Mrs. O'Sullivan, the old housekeeper standing at the door which led to the back stairs and courtseying with her accustomed graciousness wished her good morning.

"I humbly thank you Miss," said she in haste to return her salutation, "but if I might make so bold I would beg leave to speak a word with you."

Selena was well used to receive the applications of all who were sick and distressed in the parish, and it had not unfrequently happened that Mrs. O'Sullivan had thus presented them.

She was not therefore now surprised but requested her to come to her room unwilling to incur the reproaches of Lady Harriet who had more than once entreated Selena "not to bring such a set of imposters and idle wretches about the house who would come to be sure and pretend to be sick, as long as they were to be pampered up with wine and broth," adding very frequently that "Mrs. O'Sullivan was wonderfully charitable of other people's goods, no doubt she found her account in it, but for her part she wondered Mr. Miltern would suffer such waste and she was sure no fortune could stand giving servants liberty to make away with what wine and provisions they pleased."

Selena now lightly tripped up before the good old housekeeper, and had stirred the fire and turned round for her the arm chair before the faithful creature entered out of breath with her unusual exertion and carefully shutting the door exclaimed, "God help me my dear child, I cannot come up those stone stairs as I used to do when I was in the habit of it to get the poor dear Mistresses orders. Ah many's the time I have seen her sitting in this very spot—well she has left none like her—the Lord help me! I did not think I should ever have served anyone else for the rest of my poor life. But who can tell what will be the will of God for us, and tho' for this many a year I expected to leave my old bones here at the Abbey; God only knows how that may be now as things have turned out."

Selena wiping the silent tears which the grateful remembrance of her Mother had called forth after a short pause (while her old servant herself wept freely) asked her had any thing happened to her unpleasant in the family.

"Oh for the matter of that my dear child enough happens every day but it is not about my own distresses that I have made so bold as to trouble you but as I may say a little business of your own like."

Selena begged to know of what nature and after some apologising preface (which Selena could not very clearly comprehend tho' she was unwilling to interrupt her) she proceeded, "I cannot bear to hear my own children, as I may call you having nursed you all, as well as your father on my knees, tho' for the matter of that I loved my poor Mistress as well as if I had nursed her myself too—but as I was a saying I cannot bear to hear you spoke of by strangers as I may call them, for what else you know Miss is Mrs. Millikin, and tho' she is my Lady's woman, I cannot but say a more idle good for nothing pratapace[14] never entered a house."

"Well but what has she said Mrs. O'Sullivan?" asked Selena.

"Oh God help you more than they should have done and when I found that you was not to go to town with my Lady I thought it right to let you know how they make so free to say as how it is all on the account of the mad young gentleman."

"What mad gentleman do you mean?" cried Selena extremely startled.

"Why he Miss that does be in the woods I hear night and day and that they say begging your pardon for speaking so free is a sweetheart of yours, tho' I knows very well," added she significantly, "that cannot be for we all heard about my young Lord tho' I never says a word as my late Master ordered. Yet to be sure often and often I wondered to myself, what can keep him away all this time and when I sees Miss Clara go past this morning with a fine clever young gentleman as ever I looked upon to be sure I jumped up to stare after him for thinks I Oh for certain that must be our young Lord, and so I axed Michael when he came into my room for the rolls who was come, but he tells me that he heard my Lady call him Mr. Sidney so I was struck all of a heap and …."

"Well," interrupted Selena colouring excessively, "you do not tell me about the mad gentleman; do you know what is his name?"

"Not I Miss, nor did I ever set my eyes upon him, but Mrs. Millikin does be for ever bothering me with one nonsense or another about his being skulking round the Abbey and under your windows of a night, and how you and Miss Clara listen to him when he does be singing and the like—and how you are for ever walking into the woods to meet him."

"Heavens, what falsehoods!" exclaimed Selena.

"I thought as much," cried Mrs. O'Sullivan exultingly, "you never then met him at all Miss!"

"Never to my knowledge, nor did I ever till this moment hear of such a person," answered Selena, when suddenly the recollection struck her of what had passed between her and Clara about Edwin and the idea she had herself entertained of having twice had a glimpse of him—and this reflection made her stop with an air of embarrassment which might have occasioned some suspicion to a more penetrating eye than that of the good old housekeeper.

---

[14]   Prate-apace: a person who talks excessively (OED).

Next to the shame of discovered guilt there is none more distressing to a generous mind than that which is felt in the consciousness that the charge (which tho' innocent of all real blame we yet cannot totally deny) will by its tacit acknowledgement bring upon us the suspicion which the heart indignantly repels.

Here was at once to Selena an explanation of all the ambiguous raillery and sneering curiosity of Lady Harriet with respect to her solitary walks and those hours which dejection had inclined her to pass alone, and whether this person was really Edwin as she trembled to think, or only some unfortunate stranger given to her as a lover by their inventive malice or silly imagination she was effectually determined by this circumstance to follow the advice of Sidney in removing from Miltern Abbey, and even preferred intruding upon Lady Harriet evidently undesired (disagreeable as this was to her own feelings) to remaining alone in a situation thus exposed to suspicion and misrepresentation.

Full of what she had just heard and her new resolution after she had returned thanks to Mrs. O'Sullivan for her friendly intelligence, she hastened to communicate it to Clara but she was not in her own room and Selena returned to seek her in the drawing room.

In the hall she was met by Sidney, who was on the watch wishing to have some conversation with her on the very same subject tho' her first appearance, and the importance of what they had discussed had completely driven Edwin from his mind during the few moments of the short interview they had already had alone before breakfast.

"Are you going to walk," said he as he advanced to meet her, "and will you allow me to attend you?"

She stopped, saying, "I was looking for my sister," adding in a lower voice, "Who is in the drawing room?" the door of which lay open.

"No one, Lady Harriet is just gone up as she said to have the pleasure of looking at the trunks packed up to convince herself that she is really going tomorrow. She has not been able to inspire you with any of her passion for London."

"Perhaps you will think I have caught the infection," answered Selena smiling, "when I tell you that I came down to consult Clara how we should manage to be of the party, for indeed I cannot leave her here alone."

"By no means—and indeed dear Selena I cannot help saying I rejoice in your present plan, as I have reason to believe there is one circumstance which now renders Miltern Abbey an undesirable residence either for your or Clara."

"What circumstance to you mean?" asked Selena colouring deeply at the idea of his having heard the reports which had only just reached her and that he possibly supposed she had been privy to the thoughtless imprudence of a conduct which exposed her to suspicions so injurious.

"Am I impertinent?" demanded Sidney as he observed the change in her speaking countenance.

"On the contrary," cried she with an ingenuous confidence which enchanted him, "I am impatient to know whether you allude to a history relating to myself, most extraordinary indeed and which I have but this moment heard for the first time; nay I must own to you it has had more effect upon me than even your advice towards altering my present plan."

"I am satisfied," cried Sidney eagerly, "you knew not then before of Stanmore's being here."

"Gracious Heaven! Is he then here indeed," cried Selena turning extremely pale, and forced to sit down quite overcome with the certainty that poor Edwin disordered probably irretrievably in his intellect had thus wildly been exposing his own health and her reputation.

Sidney hastily threw open the hall door, and was silent for a few moments fearing to betray too much the tenderness which swelled his heart.

When a little recovered she arose, and Sidney willingly followed her where they might converse more free from interruption.

Having related all he had himself seen and heard of Edwin since his arrival she on her part freely confessed to him her former suspicions suggested by Clara, and the intelligence just imparted by Mrs. O'Sullivan, who was quite sensible of the impropriety of Selena's stay after such reports, tho' as she had told Selena "the strange folk brought to the Abbey do but laugh at whatever I says to them and thinks I am doting, and indeed my Lady herself as good as told me so twice."

Nevertheless her understanding and native sensibility were unimpaired by age, and she could not bear the innocent orphan of her beloved Mistress should be exposed to the slightest attack of "back-wounding calumny" which her long experience of life had brought her without the help of books to know "too oft the whitest Virtue strikes."[15]

Selena now left Sidney in order to perform the painful but necessary task of requesting Lady Harriet to allow them to travel under the protection of her Ladyship and Mr. Turner, and at the same time to entreat that Clara might be included in this arrangement.

She found her seated at her fire with a novel in her hand, the bed strewed with feathers, gauze dresses, caps and hats without end which Mrs. Millikin seemed to contemplate with greedy eye while she seized upon the opportunity of her Lady's remarkable good humour to make such observations as these while she took them up one by one to place them in the chaise seat or imperial[16]—"Pray my Lady is this worth putting up?" "Do you think your Ladyship will ever wear this crumpled crape again?" "I am sure my Lady this old *gib*[17] of a gown is not fit for your Ladyship to appear in," "Where will your Ladyship please to have this hat put; I am sure it will but crush others," etc.

---

[15]   Duke Vincentio in Shakespeare's *Measure for Measure* (1604), 3.2.179–81: "No might nor greatness in mortality / Can censure scape; back-wounding calumny / The whitest virtue strikes."

[16]   Imperial: luggage case for the top of a coach (OED).

[17]   Gib: bale of cloth (OED).

This critical investigation (which had not proved unprofitable to Mrs. Millikin, in spite of the extreme reluctance her Ladyship always experienced at parting with any thing) was interrupted by the gentle tap of Selena at Lady Harriet's door.

But Mrs. Millikin not being desired to withdraw remained apparently very busy with her packing, but in reality much more intent upon listning to what was passing.

Selena with some embarrassment and much reluctance timidly began to make a request which she was conscious would be most ungraciously granted, obliged by circumstances to propose herself as a companion where she could not but feel she was unwished nay unacceptable.

Lady Harriet heard her with evident surprise and dissatisfaction but being unprepared with any excuse answered with some hesitation and extreme coldness, "Yes certainly if you please."

There was a silence of a moment for Selena was still at a loss how to introduce the mention of Clara whom she was quite decided not to leave at Miltern Abbey alone.

Lady Harriet shortened her debating reflections by turning round to her woman as she said in a peevish voice, "Millikin you had better go and desire Michael to send to Newton to order a chaise for you; tomorrow perhaps there is only one there and I should not chuse to be kept. For I shall positively not go three in the chaise with all these dressing boxes and parcels you have contrived to get together. I really think Selena that Lord Dallamore might at least have sent you down a carriage."

"I beg I may not put you to the least inconvenience," said Selena colouring and much agitated, "you know Clara and I can go in a hired chaise post the whole way."

Lady Harriet now lost all patience and exclaimed, "Clara! No really that is too much, to expect me to take the whole family with me to town, and I am sure neither Mr. Miltern nor her guardian will approve of bringing the girl to London. You know that was all settled, and if Mr. Sidney has made you change your mind with respect to your own conduct, believe me I shall not take upon myself thus to take advantage of your brother's absence to do what I am sure he would not consent to."

Selena's gentle spirit scarce ever knew the sensation of resentment and was incapable of suggesting a retort but she was not to be intimidated from doing what she felt right, and she therefore mildly but firmly replied, "If you have either scruple or reluctance to allowing my sister and me to travel in your suite I should be sorry to intrude, but in that case *I* shall take it upon myself to bring Clara to her guardian where you expect to meet him to-morrow; and have no doubt that when I tell him a circumstance which I did not know till this day, that he will see the impossibility of either of us remaining in this neighbourhood when you have left the Abbey."

"Oh as to my being at the Abbey or not I am sure that cannot make the smallest difference for I must say you have always behaved as if you considered this as a boarding house, and except at meals you never seemed to remember there was a being in it worth taking the least notice of but yourselves."

Selena shocked and distressed at the offence she had so unintentionally given was beginning a stammering apology but Lady Harriet abruptly turned from her saying, "Oh you were quite right to do as you liked and not throw away your time in attention to so ignorant a creature as I, but pray may I ask what is this new discovery that is to frighten you from the Abbey in such a hurry? Have you or Clara seen a ghost?" added she intending to look archly while in fact her smile had in it so much of malice that Selena felt terrified and half repented having been induced by any reasons to provoke a conversation so painful and a temper so unamiable.

"No," answered she, "we have seen no ghost but we have heard of a madman, and think our stay might be attended with danger tho' not perhaps directly from him."

Lady Harriet looked at Millikin with another smile who thus encouraged somewhat impertinently returned it.

Selena's cheeks glowed, but as Lady Harriet made no reply she let the subject drop determined to acquaint Robert with the whole of what she had heard on the very first opportunity and saying coldly, "Well Lady Harriet I hope you will have no objection to our being on the road with you tomorrow," left the room and with a heavy sigh of self pity thought upon her situation at once dependent and forlorn.

"There is yet one," she mentally exclaimed, "to whom my interest is dear as her own, and on whose affectionate sympathy I may with confidence rely."

As she said this she turned into Clara's room but her full heart had already flown to Sidney. Oh how involuntarily does the soul fly to the bosom of affection, to seek consolation upon every sorrow and at every insult which it receives from an hard world! "Yet I am loved! Oh was this known how would that heart share my grief and resent my wrongs!" Happy thrice happy! in every situation who can without any rising doubt to damp this soothing consideration, turn from the afflictions which obscure the path of life to this dear this all powerful consolation.

Chapter III

> To talk, to listen mingling sweet regards
> And looks and smiles and questions from that tongue
> Tuned as the harp of David to expel
> All anguish from the soul—delightful intercourse
> Foretaste of Heaven!
>
> Brooke[18]

The deep affliction with which Clara heard of their purposed removal from the Abbey distressed and astonished Selena, but she listened in silence to the communicated intelligence, a silence interrupted only by her sighs and her tears,

---

[18] Westmorland and Rowena in Henry Brooke's *The Earl of Westmorland* (1789), 2.5.73–7 (Westmorland speaks the first four and a half lines, to which Rowena replies "Delightful intercourse / Foretaste of Heaven!").

nor did she use one entreaty or argument to endeavour to dissuade Selena from her intention. Neither did she affect any surprise upon being told a circumstance which she had so long known.

She had herself parted from Edwin but a few moments before in a retired scene amid the wood where by tacit consent, without any fixed appointment they had more than once met unknown as they thought to any.

Their conversations had always been short, but mutually most interesting.

Edwin impatient to hear every change that might occur in Selena's situation or prospects, returned there often to enquire had any news yet reached them concerning Dallamore, and had sought this last interview that he might learn who was the young man whom he had so early that morning beheld, whose fine figure and beautiful countenance had so forcibly struck him while he watched him gazing as he had so often done himself upon the dwelling of Selena and whom he had heard with an emotion of agony he could not contain pronounce her beloved name.

Clara watched with terror and anxiety the feverish wildness that still trembled in his eyes, and the incoherent disorder of his expressions, while she vainly urged every reason and every persuasion to prevail upon him to quit a residence which filled her with the most terrible apprehensions for his safety and made her so miserable on his account in spite of the romantic pleasure it afforded her as well as herself of being thus near the object of their enthusiastic love.

But no sooner had Selena mentioned the cruel and as she called them most unfounded accusations, that charged her with being guilty of giving him private meetings in the wood than Clara turning pale and throwing herself upon her sister's neck exclaimed sobbing, "Oh Selena it is I who have injured you—I have been the cause of all this—my folly, my imprudence has brought this upon you—Selena, dear Selena can you ever forgive me?"

Selena trembling and amazed gently disengaged herself from her embrace and stooping her head eagerly sought to read in her sister's face as she held it bathed in tears from her bosom of what nature was this imprudence of which she thus bitterly accused herself.

But Clara being now released (by the discovery which Selena had made) from the vow of secrecy which she considered herself so religiously bound to observe, had scarce a thought of her pure but impassioned bosom to conceal from her sister and while she severely reproached herself for the imputation she had thus unintentionally brought upon Selena she confessed to her all that had passed at each interview and how from the first she had been too certain that it was indeed Edwin whom they had seen together in the wood and that his derangement was still terribly visible.

"Dear Selena," she sadly exclaimed, "tell me will he do you think ever recover?"

"I trust he will," answered Selena, "when he can be prevailed upon to adopt a proper manner of life and mix again with society, but nothing could be worse for him, or more unfortunate for me than your unguarded promise, indeed derangement alone can excuse his conduct, which he ought to have been aware was not only cherishing a passion at once hopeless and criminal, but exposing the object of it as well as you my dear Clara to suspicions the most injurious."

Clara tho' she could scarcely think it possible for Edwin's conduct to be wrong, even while she confessed it was not under the influence of right reason, yet did not attempt any justification of him, but said with a deep sigh, "Alas! Selena, I have been the most to blame, but little did I imagine that you should have borne the reproach of my imprudence. But had I not better," continued she hastily rising, "had I not better explain directly to Lady Harriet, the whole of the business and justify *you* at least of the folly in which you have had no share?"

Selena stopped her and kissing her tenderly advised her to let it drop silently, adding, "I am sure wilful prejudice can alone make her imagine that I could give any encouragement to Edwin situated as I am, and as we can neither of us declare positively that we have not seen him nor entertained any suspicion of his being in the neighbourhood, all we could say would have no effect on those who chuse to think I have acted in this wicked and foolish manner. Sidney knows I am innocent, and to my brother I will acquit myself as soon as we meet, but as Lady Harriet has not openly mentioned the circumstances let us not begin the subject to her. Perhaps she does not even know who the person is and I should be sorry to expose poor Edwin to her contempt."

This last argument could not fail of having its weight with Clara who agreed to say nothing of it, but Selena's principal reason for this silence originated secretly in her consciousness that her sister had really acted with great imprudence which she was particularly anxious to conceal from Lady Harriet.

The sisters then parted—Selena to prepare for her departure and Clara to consider with anguish what would be the sensations of Edwin at finding that Selena had quitted the Abbey probably to meet Dallamore, how his heart would reproach her for her apparent want of confidence in not having imparted it to him in their last conference, and how bitter would be his sorrow could he imagine he had been the means of involving Selena in encreased perplexity.

Nor could she think without extreme sadness that she had herself seen him probably for the last time, since if he did follow them to London all entrance would certainly be denied to him by Selena.

"Alas!" she exclaimed, "I shall then hear his sweet enchanting voice no more stealing on the soft stillness of the night! I shall never again catch a glimpse of his shadowy form in the uncertain twilight or the white beams of the silent moon! Yet

> My fixed mind shall gaze upon it still
> But it will pass before my fancy's eye
> Like some delightful vision of my soul
> To sooth not trouble it!
>   Baillie[19]

---

[19]   Count Basil in Joanna Baillie's *Count Basil* (1798), 1.2.203–6 ("my soul" should be "the soul").

Selena unwilling to add to the distress of Clara had forborn to speak of her own perplexing considerations, as to what was to be done on her arrival in town, as well as the difficulties which Lady Harriet had so rudely so unfeelingly thrown in her way with respect to their journey. She depended however upon Mr. Turner for protection on the road, and could not believe that Lady Harriet would actually oblige her to separate and thus force her to accept with evident impropriety the attendance of Sidney without even a servant whom she could call her own, tho' she laid her account for the journey being rendered most disagreeable by ill temper.

But what was to become of her on her arrival in town she knew not. She had hardly an idea that Dallamore would be ready to receive her there, of which she plainly saw Sidney himself entertained strong doubts, and her heart sickened whenever she figured to it the possibility of this being actually the case. Was she then to force herself upon Lady Harriet without having received the slightest invitation or the mere mockery of politeness. She felt this was impossible and after much deliberation she at length determined that Clara should request from Mr. Turner an allowance suitable to her fortune, and that she would herself borrow from her brother such a sum as might enable them to live in lodgings as near as possible to his house 'till something was decided and these she hoped Sidney would provide for her by getting to town a day before them.

There were a thousand objections to this plan, but she thought it preferable to intruding upon Lady Harriet or accepting the order on his banker which Dallamore had sent to Sidney—and except these there appeared no other alternative. The probable necessity there must now be for a constant and confidential intercourse with Sidney filled her with dread, and tho' she resolved to keep a strict watch over her own heart yet she distrusted its secret deceptions and a thousand times regretted that she had quitted Hillbarton and wished herself again with her kind and truly maternal friend. She had little expectation of receiving assistance or even friendly advice from Mr. Turner, tho' she hoped his presence on the road would obviate the impropriety and strange appearance of two such young females going to London with no other companion than Sidney.

Mr. Turner she knew was selfish and heedless of all but himself and his own convenience, disliking all trouble, and perfectly indifferent as to the interest of the Wards who had been left to his protection without his concurrence by a man for whom he had never entertained the smallest regard except as the host of a well kept table and the Lord of an extensive manor of which he had been welcome to partake the privileges during some weeks in almost every year. Narrow minded and watchful for his own interest, he had been well pleased to secure for his niece a settlement he took care to make so advantageous, and looked forward with some expectation towards obtaining for his son Clara whose £10,000 with the savings during the remaining years of her minority rendered her by no means a despicable match independent of her high connexions.

Of Selena he had never taken any notice farther than what bare civility required, but he had secretly resolved to prevent if possible Clara's residency with her as Lady Dallamore, thinking her stay at the Abbey infinitely better calculated to promote his schemes in favour of his son. On this occasion he regretted the death of his wife perhaps for the first time since that event had happened. Had she been alive, he might have insured the residence of Clara in his house and chancery would have made her guardian an ample allowance to compensate for the expence which this addition to his family might prove. As things were he contented himself with thinking that in the retirement at the Abbey, his son whom he resolved to bring on his next visit would still have excellent opportunity of making his court to his fair ward, whose beautiful person and captivating manners left him no doubt of the concurrence of the young man in his scheme.

Neither he nor Robert had said one word to either of the sisters at their departure on the subject of money. It had not occurred to Robert who tho' generous and good-hearted was thoughtless and too apt to be entirely engrossed by whatever at the time occupied his imagination. Full of his London journey and anxious to execute all Lady Harriet's preparatory commissions completely to her satisfaction, he had forgotten that Selena absolutely pennyless would be restrained by delicacy from asking him to supply her however she might dislike being thus left totally destitute of money until the arrival of Dallamore. Mr. Turner not having been applied to by Clara (since he had sent her at her desire a small sum on her first coming to the Abbey) thought perhaps reasonably that she could have no want of money thus situated and that it would be time enough some months hence to settle with her brother what allowance she should in future regularly receive.

For the first time in her life Selena now felt some share of that uneasiness which torments so large a portion of the world, where the want of money involves with it every complicated distress, so that this may as properly boast the name of the *Golden Age* as that in which Tasso declared

> Veramente il secal d'oro e questo
> Poiche sol vince l'oro & regne l'oro.[20]

She was sensible indeed that there was no reason why she should not accept of it from Dallamore, since she so undoubtedly considered herself as his wife—and had he sent it to her as such, she could have had no scruple in receiving it—but the order was to Sidney, and he himself had never recommended that she should follow Dallamore's directions and settle herself previous to his arrival in this unprotected manner.

Sidney had indeed entertained no doubt of her being able to remain at her brother's house until she could be publickly acknowledged as the wife of Dallamore and be sheltered at least by his nominal protection, for with many a sigh and many

---

[20] "Vide Ovid Art: Amat: lib II—Aurea sunt vere nunc saecula: plurimus auro / Venit honos: auro conciliatur amor" (Tighe's note). Tighe quotes Satiro in Torquato Tasso's *Aminta* (1573), 2.1.57–8 in the text above ("Truly this may be called a golden age, because only gold prevails, only gold reigns") and footnotes Ovid's *Ars Amatoria* (ca. 1 BC) 2:277–8: "Truly now is the golden age; the highest honour comes by means of gold; by gold love is procured."

a cruel pang he thought how little probability there existed that in Dallamore she should find thro' life the protector the friend she deserved.

Selena had already completed her little arrangements for this sudden departure from the Abbey when they met at dinner—that she might be able to remain in the drawing room during the evening, resolving as little as possible to absent herself from Lady Harriet whenever she should be her guest since she found that this sacrifice was expected as a tax from civility.

Lady Harriet was evidently out of humour and on the first word which was spoken by Sidney in allusion to their journey she turned to Selena and said, "Pray how do you mean to go on from Oxfordshire to town if my company is so necessary to your safety, for I mean to spend two or three days with Lady Harston. I suppose you will not chuse to stop there if you are not acquainted with the Harstons."

"No certainly," answered Selena looking with uneasiness at the deep crimson which glowing on the cheeks of Clara plainly shewed that she was in a moment sensible of Lady Harriet's reluctance to be troubled with their company.

Sidney could hardly contain his indignation and while he continued to heap the plate which the servant held to him asked with some hesitation, "pray does Mr. Turner stop at Sir John Harston's?"

"I really am not Mr. Turner's guardian nor he mine thank God, but bless me Mr. Sidney do you think I can eat all that veal? Do take it away Michael the sight of such a quantity has really made me quite ill."

Little was said during the remainder of dinner, and Lady Harriet as if anxious to avoid any conversation with Selena or her sister retired to her own room immediately upon quitting the parlour, nor appeared in the drawing room until long after the usual hour of tea.

During her absence Clara had entreated Selena that they might proceed to town (if it was indeed absolutely necessary for them to quit the Abbey) without attaching themselves to Lady Harriet, or that they should accept of Mrs. Vallard's invitation of making Hillbarton their home now that they had in fact no other.

Sidney who had joined them after a few minutes in the drawing room was included in this consultation, and Selena with delighted satisfaction saw that he approved of her intention of trusting to Mr. Turner's apparent protection until she could meet her brother, without paying any attention to the incivility of Lady Harriet.

"You must suffer me," said he, "to be Dallamore's banker till we arrive in London and you see your command of money there is unlimited."

Selena told them what was her present plan but Sidney could not imagine it possible that her brother would suffer her to quit his more immediate protection until he could place her under that of Dallamore.

The extreme cold of the day which seemed to threaten a fall of snow, as the party on the next morning quitted the Abbey contributed not a little to the ill temper of Lady Harriet which was encreased when on arriving at the end of the first stage where she had appointed to meet Mr. Turner she found that he was not yet come.

She however refused Sidney's invitation of coming into the parlour of the inn to warm herself, saying she would sit in the carriage till Mr. Turner arrived, and when the Landlady came out to repeat the invitation with her best curtsey Lady Harriet made no other reply than peevishly to desire Millikin to "pull up the glass that they might not be teized to death."

But as the other chaises were to be changed Sidney handed out Selena and her sister; and with them awaited the arrival of Mr. Turner with somewhat less impatience than was experienced by her Ladyship.

Clara whose melancholy seemed rather to encrease than diminish at every step they had taken from the Abbey, unable to join in their conversation now took from her work basket a small Petrarch which had been her beloved and constant companion ever since she had received it as a gift from Edwin during his residence at Hillbarton.

As they had not set out on their journey till late she had entertained a latent hope of again meeting and explaining to him in some degree Selena's motives for quitting the Abbey and her discovery of his having been so long concealed in the neighbourhood, but resolved to spare him the pain of knowing the malicious reports which it had excited.

But it was in vain she wandered round the spot in which she had been accustomed to meet him—Edwin appeared not, and she was returning sad and hopeless, fearful of being condemned by Selena for her long absence, when she caught a glimpse of Mrs. Millikin herself hastily retreating from among the shrubs at some distance.

Instantly she perceived who had been the reporter, and spy of those interviews so wilfully misrepresented and laid to the charge of Selena, and her own self accusations conquered for a time even the cruel regret which she experienced at being thus obliged to leave Edwin without at least one farewell.

Still as they passed rapidly thro' these woods which had so often echoed to the melodious sound of his nightly sorrows her eye looked for him incessantly, and she eagerly wiped the mist from the glass as it gathered on the windows of the carriage.

Selena perceived the anxiety with which she watched on all sides and even continued to look from the back window of the chaise for some time after they had past thro' the last gates of the domain, easily guessing the object which her eyes thus inquisitively sought. But she forbore to speak to her of Edwin or even to press her into any conversation when she observed the deep melancholy in which silently she sunk into the corner of the carriage after a turn in the road shut out from their view the wood embosomed towers of Miltern Abbey.

Yet unwilling that any, even Sidney, should perceive her dejection, Selena was pleased on his joining them to behold her assume a degree of cheerfulness, and have recourse to her Petrarch to excuse her little inclination to take part in their conversation.

After some time passed Sidney started to the window on observing the ostler leading out the horses for Lady Harriet's carriage, and at Selena's desire went out to see if Mr. Turner was arrived. The servants who stood at the door said their Lady was going on to Glocester and intended leaving a message for Mr. Turner. While they were speaking Lady Harriet upon seeing Sidney put down the glass saying, "I suppose Mr. Dallamore you will chuse to stay with the girls, and if so pray be so good as to tell my Uncle that he will find me at the Bell at Glocester but cannot answer for his seeing me alive after keeping me starving here so unmercifully."

"Do not you think," said Sidney hesitating, "that Selena .... that my cousins had better come on now with you [—] the days are so short, and they will find it unpleasant to be on the road these dark cold nights, without a servant particularly."

"That is their business," answered Lady Harriet, "I really never pretend to give any advice to Selena who always thinks herself so much wiser than any one else."

Sidney turned from her hastily and hurried on to inform them of her intentions advising them without delay to follow. Meanwhile they saw Lady Harriet drive from the door attended by her two servants on horseback, neither of whom she had offered to leave with Selena who after some hesitation resolved to wait a little longer for Mr. Turner, without whose consent she hardly felt authorised to proceed with Clara and was likewise impatient to consult with him on the subject of money, but she had not very long to consider of this delay before Mr. Turner's servant arrived to inform Lady Harriet that having been alarmed by some appearance of gout he was afraid to venture on a journey in such severe weather, and that when able to travel he should be obliged to visit his physician at Bath.

Selena in the utmost perplexity now cast an involuntary look at Sidney that penetrated to his very soul while she thus seemed to say "Am I not cast by Heaven and all the world upon your protection?" With difficulty could he restrain himself from opening his arms and exclaiming "Oh my beloved! here forever find your shelter and defense! Be not disturbed at any abandonment—

> Lodge that and all thy cares within my breast
> Where every gesture word and look inspire
> The spirit of purest Love!"[21]

Selena however saw that no time was now to be lost, and entreated him to hasten and order the chaises.

When he left the room she consulted with Clara who agreed with her in the expediency of her writing herself to her guardian and that for the present Selena should borrow from Sidney what was necessary to defray their expences, which must be done immediately Lady Harriet not having given any orders they

---

[21]   Herod in Elijah Fenton's *Mariamne* (1723), 5.6.50–52.

observed to her servant to pay for the horses which had brought them from the Abbey.

In a few minutes Sidney returned and with evident uneasiness acquainted them that one pair of horses only was to be procured, Lady Harriet having insisted upon having the pair which he had himself ordered directly on arriving, as she refused to go with less than four horses, and when the ostler told her they were engaged she assured him that Mr. Dallamore had bespoke them for her intending himself to proceed with the ladies.

This was thought by her Ladyship and Mrs. Millikin an extremely good joke "to puzzle the prudes" but it threw poor Selena into the greatest embarrassment. To invite Sidney to take a place in their chaise was not only exposing them to the malicious raillery of Lady Harriet, but was encreasing that intimacy, which tho' circumstances had rendered it impossible for her to shun she continually trembled at as dangerous to the virtue and peace of both. Yet to proceed without him at that late hour was hardly safe, independent of the rudeness and excessive nicety to which he might attribute such a reserve.

But there were no such deliberations in the breast of Clara who freely confessed her satisfaction at the circumstance, "that is," said she turning to Sidney with a smile, "if *you* have not such an objection as Lady Harriet to go a third in a chaise."

Selena colouring entreated her to make haste and conclude her letter which Sidney's news had interrupted saying that already it began to look dark and that it was seventeen miles to Glocester.

"Perhaps," said Sidney, "tho' I could not get a saddle horse at this house there may be one to be had in the village and in that case I need not crowd you, but indeed you must not leave this till I can attend you."

Clara again interfered objecting to such a delay, and Selena herself felt the cruelty of obliging him to ride in such severe weather even if a horse could be procured.

She therefore timidly said it was needless to make the search if he would accept the seat they could offer him and Sidney for a little while gave himself up without constraint to the delightful sensation of finding himself thus as it were separated from all the rest of the world with the being he most loved.

"Those few precious moments," he cried internally, "I will give to happiness. When we are parted there will be then time enough to exert my strength and my fortitude to conquer a passion which tho' I will endeavour to resist I feel never can be banished. But for the present I will forget every other consideration but that I can behold her, watch every motion of her lips, every glance of her eyes, listen even to her breath and exult in the certainty that her thoughts must in some degree be occupied constantly on me!"

Chapter IV

Amitié, confiance, intimité douceur d'âme!
que vos assaisonnements sont délicieux!
Rousseau[22]

Clara had gained but little in the way of entertainment by their additional travelling companion. Little was said. Sidney satisfied with his happiness, felt not much inclined to communicate in speech with any one—yet his heart was unusually opened to benevolence towards the whole world and he could with pleasure have imparted to the peasants as they passed them on the road all the wealth he possessed had he then held it in his hands. But as the great master of the human heart has well said "Silence is the perfectest herald of joy"[23] so it is ever the case that, that species of pleasure which sensibility at times bestows upon her favourites to compensate for the more numerous pains she so frequently inflicts will give to the whole countenance and appearance

Such a cast
As folly might mistake for want of joy.[24]

Selena was on her part as little disposed to conversation. Uneasy at her situation, oppressed with melancholy and tormented with self upbraidings for the regret and tender emotions which however repulsed continually returned she caught the silence of Sidney without sharing the pleasurable sensations to which she refused like him to yield.

The evening closed fast upon them and a few thin flakes "light wavering thro' the saddened air"[25] foretold a fall of snow which Sidney thought was not unlikely to detain them some days on the road, and in his present turn of mind indulged this idea as a hope, while with a sigh he endeavoured to drive from him all thought of a separation he more than ever considered as most dreadful. Every thing was soon enveloped by the whitening shower and earth's universal face lay buried under one wide waste. Sidney had nothing to regret in the deepening shades of night (which seemed at once to overwhelm them) except the sight of those beautiful features which however near him he could no longer behold. Deprived of this gratification he became more ambitious to hear the soft accents of her voice.

---

[22] Jean-Jacques Rousseau, *Confessions* (1782), part 2, book 8: "Friendship, trust, intimacy, sweetness of soul, your seasonings are delicious!"

[23] "Shakespeare" (Tighe's note). Claudio in Shakespeare's *Much Ado about Nothing* (1598), 2.1.292.

[24] Edward Young, *Night Thoughts* (1745), 8.953–4.

[25] James Thomson, "Winter," *The Seasons* (1726), lines 229–30: "Thro' the hushed air the whitening shower descends, / At first thin wavering."

At length he succeeded, the conversation grew animated and interesting, occasionally interrupted by the compassion which they expressed for the postilion condemned to endure all weathers and never ceasing toil at the caprice of his more affluent and restless fellow creatures—while Selena secretly congratulated herself that Sidney was not now exposed on horseback to the inclement night, and Clara sighed as she thought on Edwin who was perhaps at that moment idly gazing upon the projecting windows of Selena's deserted apartment at the Abbey.

Their consideration for others was however suddenly diverted for the moment by their own danger. The postboy confused by the snow and the unusual obscurity of the night had taken a wrong track over a common which they were to cross, and after proceeding for some time over an extremely rugged and broken sod, the unusual and violent jostling they experienced causing Sidney to suspect they were not on the high road he put down the window to ask where they were, and it was fortunate that he did so, for almost at that same moment they descended with such violence down a deep rut that the wheel was instantly smashed to pieces and the chaise overset on that side where Sidney (who sat himself in the middle) had just let down the glass.

Before they had time for recollection, or mutual enquiries the door on the opposite side was violently forced open, and Selena who was next it felt herself snatched out and in the arms of a man who exclaimed in a breath with Sidney, "Oh Selena are you hurt!"

Astonishment and terror with the shock she had just received held her dumb, but the voice of Clara on a sudden explained the mystery, who while the others continued their eager enquiries to Selena sadly exclaimed, "Edwin! Is it you! Oh what a night!"

"Sidney! Clara are you safe? Are you not hurt?" cried Selena, as she clung trembling to the arm of Sidney who tenderly supporting her thought not at that moment of another being upon earth while in incoherent sentences, he now blessed Heaven for her safety and now required from her fresh assurances that she had sustained no injury.

In the mean time Edwin perceiving that Selena was indeed unhurt assisted Clara from the chaise who with tears fell upon the neck of her sister and while she congratulated her upon their safety softly whispered, "Oh will not you speak to poor Edwin?"

"Heavens Mr. Stanmore! What can have brought you here … on such a night … and on foot …" said Selena turning round to her unfortunate lover whose snow-covered hat and coat presented a most deplorable picture of suffering—but whose soul at that moment felt that it was not in the power of any of those external inconveniences from the elements at which "delicate felicity" so shrinks to add to his wretchedness.[26]

---

[26] The Countess in Horace Walpole's *The Mysterious Mother* (1781) says "'Tis delicate felicity that shrinks / When rocking winds are loud" (2.3.5–6), lines that Charlotte

"I was not on foot," answered he mournfully after a moment's silence looking round, "but my horse has I conclude wisely gone to look for some shelter while I was occupied in endeavouring to assist you."

"The best thing we can all do now is to try and follow his example," said Sidney while he wrapt his own great coat over Selena, and endeavoured to protect her from the snow which was still falling without intermission.

"What is to be done my fine fellow," said he turning to the postboy who was still muttering curses over his horses, as he disentangled them from the shattered carriage.

"I am sure I can't say Sir," said he sullenly, "but I suppose we shall be pretty nigh buried alive if so be we's obliged to bide here all night."

The ladies heard with silent terror this very comfortable supposition, but Sidney impatiently exclaimed, "Here all night! Impossible. What nonsense! Come man think of something better than that. Is there no house on this common whither we can carry the ladies until we can get a chaise from Glocester? For I suppose we can do nothing with this."

It was however no easy matter to obtain any information from this their companion in misfortune, who not having like the rest of the party that secret internal consolation of being in the presence of those most dear to their hearts had already found his whole stock of good temper totally forsake him, and seemed better inclined to grumble over his broken carriage and beat his horses than to discover any method of assisting the distressed travellers.

Sidney himself now thought he discovered a light at some distance and entreated Selena to allow him to carry her towards it in his arms, convinced that she could not possibly reach it thro' the snow on foot.

To this however she would by no means consent and after much time spent in deliberation and debating various plans it was at length agreed that each of the ladies mounted like the dames of old upon one of the horses taken from the chaise attended by their squires on foot should proceed towards the light, while the postboy was desired to go on before and explore the ground on Edwin's horse which had not strayed far, to which plan the boy did not indeed consent until Sidney had been obliged to add some threats to his eloquence of persuasion and even his ready promises of reward.

When Sidney had placed on the steed his lovely charge (already wet thro' altho' protected by his great coat buttoned over her own habit) he asked her in a whisper, "if it was quite safe to trust Clara to the care of the madman."

"We must all keep close together," said Selena aloud. "Pray Clara let us not be silent a moment for fear we should lose each other on this frightful common."

Smith annotates in "Sonnet LXX: On Being Cautioned Against Walking On An Headland Overlooking the Sea, Because It Was Frequented by a Lunatic," *Elegiac Sonnets*, 5th ed. (1797), Vol. 2, lines 11–12 ("*He* has no *nice felicities* that shrink / From giant horrors").

She was nevertheless the only one of the party whose mind was not so much agitated by the strange situation in which fortune had thus placed them as to be totally regardless of the danger and inconvenience they themselves suffered.

While Sidney in one hand held the bridle of the poor animal very little accustomed to his new honourable office of carrying a lady, the other yet retained the chilled hand of Selena which she had in vain gently sought to withdraw from his after he had assisted her to her uneasy and very insecure seat, where he persuaded himself that the slight support he thus afforded was absolutely necessary for her safety. Full of solicitude on her account and dreading lest she should suffer from an expedition so hazardous, this consideration alone prevented him from esteeming this moment as the most delightful of his life.

Edwin on the contrary beheld placed in a situation he would have purchased with the remnant of his existence not Dallamore, but a rival who from even the transient glance he had taken of him when startled by his pronouncing the name of Selena he had seen him beneath her window, he was convinced was a thousand times more captivating as well as captivated. He had heard her also in the softest accents of concern for his safety address him by the familiar name of Sidney, and he had listened to his tender expressions of alarm for her, with an anguish which can alone be conceived by those who have tasted the bitter cup of jealousy.

Nor was the young bosom of Clara calm tho' less cruelly agitated than that of Edwin—the first sentiment of her soul had been love for Selena, it had almost absorbed every other affection during her childhood and the romantic passion which had early occupied her heart for Edwin was perhaps first excited by the sympathy which existed between them in love and admiration of Selena. As she had never beheld him in any other light than as the hopeless lover of her sister, this passion seemed to her as a part of himself, and she even felt pained as well as surprised when she discovered almost before Selena herself suspected it, that it was possible, that she who had listened with indifference to the vows of Edwin could be susceptible of affection for another which her sense of duty and her reason condemned. To be the friend of Edwin, to see him happy, and to see him constantly was almost all the bliss to which even her imagination had ever aspired. But tho' in fancying that she could have rejoiced in his joys and in completion of his desires she probably deluded her warm and inexperienced heart yet it is certain that she shared in all his pains, and suffered with him at that moment, in the evident preference which Selena felt justified in bestowing upon Sidney, from the situation in which he stood as their common friend and relation, as well as the person to whom Dallamore had apparently entrusted the charge of her conduct in his absence.

That he had ever been more, Selena at his own desire had promised that she would endeavour to forget, and tho' to effect this had indeed been a task impossible, yet they had mutually appeared to suppose the other had been more successful.

The little party who tho' thus constrained to smother their sensations were yet in fact the whole world to each other at length reached the cottage from whence the light had so far attracted them, and as they stood dripping at the door to request admittance, they beheld thro' the casement window what struck their hearts as the most lively picture of comfort and contentment, which presented a striking contrast to the desolation of Nature without. A bright blazing fire with the family circled around it and a table already spread for their supper seemed to invite to repose and shelter—and tho' at first somewhat alarmed at this unusual knocking at so late an hour yet when Sidney in a few words explained their situation they were instantly admitted, and received a cordial welcome from the good housewife who at Sidney's request without delay busied herself in preparing the bed in her own apartment to which he entreated Selena to retire.

But Selena infinitely more uneasy about her sister whose constitution had always been more delicate could not be prevailed upon to give the least attention to herself till Clara had consented to lye down and take something warm while their kind hostess bustled about to provide some change of cloaths for her and the rest of the party.

Selena having wrapt herself up in a large dry cloak again returned to the kitchen. Sidney had accepted the offer of one of the farmer's coats but Edwin refused to change any of his cloaths, and having only thrown aside the great coat which was no longer useful to him as a disguise for his figure he sat silently with his arms folded in a corner of the fire place while Sidney was busy apologising to the good people for the interruption they had given, and sending into Selena and her sister some burnt brandy which he himself prepared, being strongly recommended by the farmer and his wife, as the best preservative from cold. On Selena's entrance they both eagerly arose to approach her, but Edwin soon gloomily shrunk back in silence when Sidney took her hand and anxiously bent over her with an expression of fondness which could not be mistaken as he enquired after her health.

Never had he seen her look more beautiful, her naturally delicate complexion heightened to the deepest carmine by the exercise and cold thro' which she had past, added brilliancy unusual to the bewitching softness of her clear blue eyes. The coarse dark cloak which was wrapt round her figure concealed indeed its exquisite perfection but added by a whimsical contrast new grace to the delicacy of the ancle which appeared beneath it and the throat under which it was tied—a throat which in loveliness of shape could only be equalled by that of Lady Trevallyn and which even if possible exceeded hers in its dazzling whiteness of colour. Part of her thick and beautifully silky hair unconfined by a ribbon had escaped from the comb under which she had carelessly collected all its bright curls and fell in graceful wildness over her transparent temples and behind on her polished neck. The dimpled smiles and modest confusion with which on her first entrance in this new dishabille[27] she half retired from the gaze of admiration encreased the loveliness of its attraction and quickly sensible of the too evident effect upon Sidney she hastily withdrew her hand asking him what he had done towards procuring a conveyance from thence.

"I have done nothing," answered he endeavouring to suppress his emotions, "the post boy is ready here to go to Glocester which is five miles from this, but no

---

[27]   Dishabille: partially or casually dressed (French).

chaise can be had nearer. I have only waited thinking you had better send by him some message to Lady Harriet who doubtless will be much alarmed at your not coming to night."

Selena smiled incredulously but agreed that it was certainly proper to acquaint her with the cause of their delay and also to send Mr. Turner's letter which might possibly require an immediate answer. She accordingly enclosed it and having with some difficulty procured a pen and ink wrote a few words in the cover to inform her of the accident and their present situation. Having no doubt that Edwin would accompany them as far as Glocester she wished to spare herself the embarrassment which she must feel at his unexpected appearance with them in the presence of Lady Harriet and therefore in mentioning the accident she added their surprise at having been joined by Mr. Stanmore.

It was not indeed Selena's wish now to part from Edwin until she had an opportunity of speaking to him in private, and representing to him as she meant to do the injury he did both to her and himself by a conduct so wild, and this opportunity she could not expect to find until their arrival at Glocester.

Detesting the idea of all disguise, and conscious that the innocence of her heart and rectitude of her actions required it not, she felt no reluctance at being seen in the company of Edwin (even by Lady Harriet) except what arose from the expected illnature of her raillery and the contempt with which she was sure he would be treated.

By the time that their hospitable entertainers had spread the clean tablecloth, and set before them a supper of such homely fare as their cottage afforded Clara joined them equipped in a manner so grotesque from the motley wardrobe of the farmer and his family that involuntary gaiety diffused itself upon her appearance.

Selena herself touched with the sincerest compassion for Edwin, and hoping in a few hours to convince him of the necessity of giving up all thoughts of her for ever, now assisted Sidney in endeavouring to chace the gloom from his brow by all those little soothing attentions so grateful to a sensible heart. His was not one upon which such efforts could be lost—accustomed from his infancy to the voice of tenderness he had cruelly felt the want of it when his state of health rendered peculiarly necessary all those cares which affection is so ready to afford. Softened by the kindness which was now shewn him, and which his heart was at all times incapable of resisting he was ready to fall at the feet of Selena and was filled with gratitude tho' more than ever devoid of hope.

Placed between him and Sidney at supper she did the honours of the little feast and never had Sidney tasted of one so exquisite—"Un repas apprêtè par l'amour peut-il jamais être insipide?"[28] Clara (too happy to find herself seated at the side of Edwin, and to listen to him sharing in some degree in the conversation which Selena seemed desirous to encourage) had the satisfaction of thinking she had been deceived in considering him as not entirely restored to the perfect use of that

---

[28] "Rousseau" (Tighe's note). Jean-Jacques Rousseau, *Julie, ou La Nouvelle Héloïse* (1761), Letter 26: "A meal prepared with love can never be dull."

eminently fine understanding with which nature had gifted him and which even now shone forth so as to strike Sidney with astonishment and admiration. Clara's eyes sparkled as she observed this and she would have given the world for courage to ask him to sing.

Whether it was that Sidney's discernment made him desirous of thus gratifying her, or whether he really wished to shew their host and his wife their inclination to bestow in return all the entertainment in their power for their cheerful hospitality, but he now turned to the farmer and with a smile said gaily, "If you are fond of singing my good friend you should have made a bargain before you admitted us that it should be 'No song no supper.' These ladies have sweet voices, and I am sure are too generous to refuse you now."

"Oh my Master does love a song in his heart," said their hostess quite overjoyed, "do pray Miss if I may make so bold do indulge us."

"Aye," said the farmer putting another block on the fire as he spoke, "and that will help us watch 'till your chaise come, which I doubt will not be for one while."

Selena smiled an assent and saying, "Come Clara, Mr. Stanmore will join us in this," began a trio which they had been accustomed at Hillbarton to perform together.

Edwin was at first unable to join them, and when he did the tremulous sweetness of his notes proclaimed his agitation, but the charm of melody ever powerful over his mind soon restored him to himself, and the night wore away as they listened thoughtless of sleep to the ready exercise of his talents so singularly captivating, and of which Sidney had been able to form only a faint idea in spite of all he had heard of them from Clara and even Selena herself, a less partial encomiast.

Before it was quite daybreak (the chaise not having yet arrived from Glocester) the farmer suggested the expediency of sending one of his boys to watch the luggage which they had been forced to leave with the broken carriage, but as they could not exactly describe the spot they were obliged to wait till there was sufficient light for him to discern where lay the debris. Soon after this messenger had been dispatched the expected chaise arrived and the delay was excused by the pretence of there not being horses at home at the time the post boy arrived to order them, tho' the truth was the driver preferred repose to the encountering at that late hour the severity of the weather. It was some time before all things could be arranged for their resuming their journey after having taken a grateful leave of their entertainers who themselves positively refused all pecuniary compensation for the trouble their benighted guests had given them—so that all Sidney then could do was liberally to reward their servants.

As poor Edwin stood with a look of envy observing Sidney hand the sisters into the chaise and place himself between them Selena in a hesitating voice asked him which way he was now going.

"I am not sure," answered he in some confusion, "but I believe to London."

"Shall we see you in Glocester?" she continued, resolved to have with him before they parted the conversation she had been meditating.

"Certainly," answered he his animated countenance resuming for an instant that bright look of enthusiastic pleasure which his fond parents had so often contemplated with delighted sympathy during twenty years of happiness at Inverathie.

"Well that is a wonderful young man!" said Sidney as the chaise drove from the door.

"Is not he!" cried Clara eagerly her bosom glowing with delight at this tribute of admiration to the object of its warm affections "While her breast trembled to that sweetest music" for true it is indeed that

> The heart of woman tastes no sweeter joy
> Is never flattered with such dear enchantment
> ('Tis more than selfish vanity)—as when
> She hears the praises of the man she loves.
>   Thompson[29]

But those pleasurable sensations were instantly checked by the dread of having betrayed herself when she perceived the arch smile that played round the lips of Sidney, for which tho' it covered her for the moment with the deepest blushes of confusion she nevertheless quickly forgave him, while she listened to the voluntary encomiums he passed upon the talents and interesting manners of Edwin.

Chapter V

> Potrai dunque amor mio
> Potrai da me partire
> E vedermi morire
> O core! O Vita! O fin d'ogni desio!
> Come puoi dirmi Oime si lungo adio?
> Perche perche te'n vai
> Se togliendoti a me morte mi dai
> Dove, dove e l'amore? Ahi che mercede
> Della mia bella fede?
>   Rinuccini[30]

It was nearly eleven o'clock before they reached Glocester but Selena remembering the late hours at which Lady Harriet had been accustomed to set out on their former journey together had no apprehension of having now occasioned her

---

[29]   Sigismunda in James Thomson's *Tancred and Sigismunda* (1745), 1.1.106–9 (in line 106 "sweeter" should be "truer").

[30]   Ottavio Rinuccini, *Poesie* (1622), p. 82: "Could you then my love, / Could you leave me, / And see me die? / Oh heart, oh life, oh object of every desire! / How can you tell me, dear me, such a lengthy farewell? / Why, why do you go? / If by taking yourself away from me, you make me die? / Where, where is love? Ah, what recompense / For my fine faithfulness?" (Lucia Greene translation).

any delay. Great then indeed was her surprise on enquiring for her at the Bell to hear that she had been gone nearly three hours, and that without having left for Selena the smallest apology or even any message whatever.

Sidney was at first inclined to think that not having received the letter which they had sent from the cottage she might have suspected that something had befallen them or Mr. Turner and perhaps had returned in search of them—but upon farther enquiry they found that the waiter had delivered the letter on the night before while Lady Harriet was at supper.

He said that she immediately asked whether the post-boy intended to return that night, and upon hearing that he could not take the chaise till early next morning, had said it was very well and ordered her carriage and servants to be ready before eight o'clock. But he was positive in saying that her Ladyship had left no message.

Once more poor Selena looked round perplexed and uncertain what course she should pursue. Lady Harriet had evidently seized upon this opportunity of shaking her off, and Selena had no doubt that she would so represent it to Robert that this separation should appear the choice of Selena herself. To attempt to overtake her was useless, even had they been so inclined, since she had declared her intention of visiting in Oxfordshire, and to proceed to London thus with no other attendants except Sidney and Clara (even if she could as she hoped get rid of Edwin) appeared to Selena after the accident of the preceding night more than ever improper.

Edwin in the mean time had joined them, and while breakfast was preparing, Sidney endeavoured by promoting a gay and general conversation to dispel the cloud of distress and care which at this new mortification he perceived hung upon the beautiful brow of Selena tho' usually serene as the summer Heaven.

The pale and languid countenance of Clara, bespoke her need of repose, and Selena alarmed lest she should suffer from the fatigue of the last night, insisted upon her lying down for a few hours, and hoped this would afford her a favourable opportunity for the conference which she wished to have with Edwin. She saw that to treat him with reserve, or to repulse him with harshness was not the method by which to effect his cure, and her aim was now to gain his confidence and preserve him for a friend while she convinced him that to her he could never be more. It was thus he might restore his talents to society which they were so well calculated to adorn and it was thus she hoped one day to behold him deserving of that heart which Clara young as she was had probably already irrevocably given him.

The chambermaid apologised for bringing the ladies across the court yard to the room which she had prepared for them but as the inn was very full Sidney would not suffer them to cross it alone, and waited at the foot of the stairs until Selena returned after leaving Clara to her rest.

As they went towards the parlour she explained to him in a few words her design with regard to Edwin.

"You are right Selena," said he with a sigh, "ever most wise, ever most good, but the malady of poor Edwin is not one which you can expect to cure in an hour by a little prudent advice."

"No assuredly," answered she forcing a smile as she disguised the confusion which his evident agitation had communicated while his hand trembled in hers as he held it under his arm. "No I am certain that 'Therein the patient must minister unto himself.'[31] All that I hope to do by my prudent advice [is] to make him sensible how much his wild imaginations if thus indulged may injure me."

"*Imaginations!*" repeated Sidney in a mournful and half displeased voice of reproach, but without turning his face towards hers which she held averted from him as she spoke.

All farther communication was prevented by the violent noise occasioned by a chaise and four, which that instant rapidly drove under the arch and stopped at the door which Selena had just reached.

She was impatient to get out of the way and Sidney was vainly endeavouring to keep her from being pressed upon by the crowd of waiters, ostlers and chamber-maids who from all parts pushed forward to surround the chaise door, when Selena involuntarily looked back as the step was furiously let down by the waiter who had won the race, and suddenly exclaiming, "Lady Trevallyn!" found herself in an instant embraced in her arms.

"Dearest Selena! how fortunate I am!" she cried as they entered together the little parlour, the door of which Sidney had thrown open for them, no one attending to the waiter who was bustling in exclaiming, "This way my Lady if you please"—but Lady Trevallyn's inquisitive eyes were at that moment too busy to heed any thing save the search they made for Dallamore. Selena instantly caught their meaning and half dreaded the expected enquiry.

"But where are you going and who is with you?" she continued still looking round tho' without resting either upon Sidney or Edwin.

"I am on my way to London," answered Selena, "and Lady Harriet left Glocester but a few hours ago."

"And are you here now alone?"

"No," said Selena in some confusion, "Clara is with me."

"Yes and Sidney Dallamore also," interrupted he smiling, "tho' I perceive Lady Trevallyn refuses to acknowledge him."

"I beg your pardon Mr. Dallamore. I saw you immediately, but I was looking I own to who else I was to expect. Tho' believe me I am quite satisfied and have met no such pleasant surprise for a long while."

"You will see no one else of your acquaintance now," said Selena in a low voice perceiving that she still looked in expectation of Dallamore, and then added aloud, "but here is a gentleman whom you must allow me to introduce to you. You have heard Mrs. Vallard speak of him and I know you wished to see the nephew of your friend Lady Stanmore."

The awkward embarrassment of poor Edwin had not escaped Selena, and she who never was indifferent to the uneasiness of another nor heedlessly prolonged for a moment the pain she could relieve, was in haste to deliver him from a situation

---

[31]   Doctor in Shakespeare's *Macbeth* (1605), 5.3.47–8.

where he might conceive himself past over with mortifying neglect, or considered as an impertinent intruder. She well knew that she had but to direct the attention of Lady Trevallyn to ensure for the object of it that delighted enchantment which the soft and attractive fascination of her countenance and the grace of her manner could not fail to inspire in a breast gifted with such sensibility as Edwin's. In fact he *was* charmed, and the gentle sweetness of her voice and the gracious softness of her smiles as she addressed him had an effect which her beauty eminent as it was for all loveliness never could alone have performed—for a moment his admiration was diverted from Selena.

After a few minutes general conversation in which Lady Trevallyn informed them that she was on her way to Bath where she expected to meet her Lord, Sidney invited Edwin to walk, judging rightly that their presence was a restraint upon the friends and that Lady Trevallyn in particular must be impatient to hear wherefore Selena was thus unattended by Dallamore.

The moment they had closed the door her eyes indeed demanded the explanation and Selena after some little embarrassment communicated to her all that had past in the last two important days and asked her advice where and how she thought it most prudent for her to proceed.

Lady Trevallyn listened to the end in silence with an impatient and interested curiosity which precluded all interruption, but no sooner had Selena concluded than she warmly and affectionately urged her to accompany her to Bath.

Selena at first started, while the sudden emotion of her heart said secretly but forcibly, "What part from Sidney … so soon … oh no! This unexpected stroke may at least be avoided," but the next moment pointed this out to her better judgment as the most convincing argument that their separation was expedient.

Lady Trevallyn mean while pressed every reason for her adopting her plan, reminding her that at Bath she would probably in a few days see Mr. Turner and Clara might then if necessary consult him upon her residence, and that in the mean time the house which Lord Trevallyn had ordered for their reception was sufficiently large for their mutual accommodation—"and we can all travel together so pleasantly," continued she, "I have room enough as you may observe for you and Clara in the chaise—for the maids have the coach to themselves as Lord Trevallyn never suffers me to take even my own little Fanny in the carriage, tho' he is not himself with me. So now I have come from Derbyshire quite alone and you may judge by this time I am almost tired of my solitary meditations."

"And is Lord Trevallyn now at Bath?" enquired Selena.

"I believed he arrived there yesterday. He went to London a fortnight ago, and I was preparing to follow him when he wrote me word that his physicians had recommended it to him to try the Bath waters, and that he had resolved to follow their advice, in consequence of which dearest Selena we have so happily met, and I shall think it one of the most fortunate circumstances in my life if I can tempt you for some time to make choice of a residence which it shall be my chief delight and study to make you find agreeable."

"But Lord Trevallyn!" said Selena timidly.

"Oh," interrupted she smiling, "you know your poor Emily very little if you think she has courage enough ever to propose to herself even so great a pleasure if not quite sure that it would meet no opposition there. No my love be assured if there was the least danger of my plan meeting with his disapprobation I would never have ventured thus to expose you or myself. I could better endure that my Selena should suffer from the rudeness of Lady Harriet than what I should in some degree feel as my own. But there is nothing Lord Trevallyn so much likes as company; and so there are bodies enough around him he is contented, tho' they so seldom I should think administer any thing to his entertainment. But come dear Selena consent. I see a yielding softness in your eye. Give me this little triumph over Lady Harriet. It is all I seek. For I know she will envy you to me, tho' she could not value your society as I do."

Selena overcome by her kindness, and oppressed at the same time by the commands of cautious Virtue and the secret sense of unacknowledged sorrow could only answer her by her tears and the tenderest caresses, which Lady Trevallyn joyfully accepted as the tacit signal of her compliance, and asked her how soon she would be ready to leave Glocester, saying she hoped that Clara would make no objection to the London journey being thus postponed.

Selena requested that she might not be disturbed for some hours which Lady Trevallyn willingly consented to wait, and even pressed Selena to take some repose herself before they should proceed.

But never was poor Selena less inclined to sleep. Yet she resisted but feebly her offers of going no farther that day and upon Sidney's return which interrupted the debate felt her heart shrink from communicating to him the plan she was about to adopt, which should thus suddenly and unexpectedly separate them at the very moment when she appeared abandoned by the whole world to his protection.

Lady Trevallyn however spared her the painful task, for the instant he entered the room she exclaimed, "Oh Mr. Dallamore congratulate me! I have prevailed and Selena is mine at least till she is claimed by higher authority."

She was proceeding but the expression of surprise, disappointment and anguish which suddenly darted from the tell-tale eyes of Sidney as he instantaneously comprehended what had passed betrayed all that he himself most wished to disguise and which Selena never could have confessed even to the tender Emily the chosen friend of her heart.

From the hasty impulse of her sensibility, which in Lady Trevallyn was always triumphant over prudence she now eagerly added, "But surely Mr. Dallamore you will not I hope forsake your charge, at least you must conduct us in safety to Bath."

The bosom of Sidney once more throbbed with revived pleasure, but it was but like the transient flush from the expiring taper, for his eye met the speaking glance of Selena and there he read the impossibility of his accepting a proposal which had been seized upon with such avidity by despairing Love.

Endeavouring to assume an air of tranquility he constrained himself to make some apology, saying that his presence was necessary in London, and then advancing to the back of Selena's chair said in a lower voice, "Do you go immediately?"

"No I believe not, I think Clara is asleep," answered she not daring to look round and scarce venturing to trust her voice.

"Oh we will go no further this day positively," said Lady Trevallyn, "do not you think she wants rest Mr. Dallamore? You will therefore be so good as to order dinner for us, and in the mean time I will make her lye down a little."

This was at least some reprieve, but when the door closed upon them as she quitted the room, and that his eye could no longer gaze fondly upon hers "E'l nettar amoroso indi bevea"[32] he sunk with despondency upon the seat which she had just quitted, and resting his head upon the marble of the chimney piece, gave way to all the bitterness of his emotions, heedless of Edwin who viewed him with a mixture of compassion and surprise.

"He loves her," he mentally exclaimed, "He loves her, and yet he can forsake her! He loves her and he can yet listen to the dictates of prudence and fly from his ruin; oh he loves her not then like me! Or he would like me pursue her and tho' hopeless of her favour find life only in her presence."

To Edwin indeed this change of plan was of little consequence, except from a degree of satisfaction which it afforded him in thus separating Sidney from Selena a satisfaction which was unacknowledged even to his secret heart. The universe to him seemed divided in but two parts, where she was, and where she was not, and to him all places were in every other respect indifferent.

They had both spent some time in silence when the unexpected return of Selena at once put to flight all other ideas from the bosom of each.

"Sidney," said she, as she entered, "do you think you can get us a messenger who will go to the cottage of our friends who received us so kindly last night, Clara has left her workbasket behind, and is very anxious to recover it."

Sidney had his hand on the bell in order to entrust this commission to the waiter, when a look cast by Selena from him towards Edwin, reminded him of her wish to speak to him before they parted. With a sigh he therefore slowly walked to the door, but held the lock for a moment in his hand, and then said hesitating, "Shall I find you here on my return?"

"I will stay here till Lady Trevallyn comes down," answered she, "I left her writing a letter in the room with Clara who has not slept and is uneasy about her workbasket, pray write a letter by the messenger."

Sidney reluctantly retired to obey her, but in this reluctance was mingled no portion of jealousy notwithstanding that he was thus excluded intentionally by Selena that she might have an interview in private with his very captivating rival.

---

[32] Giovanni Battista Guarini, "Tirsi morir volea" (1581), line 12: "and drank the nectar of love."

Chapter VI

Give me thy hand
That I may dew it with my mournful tears,
Nor let the rain of Heaven wet this place
To wash away my woeful monuments.
Oh could this kiss be printed in thy hand
That thou mightst think upon these, by the seal,
Thro' whom a thousand sighs are breathed for thee
…………………………...................…………..
So get thee gone that I may know my grief
'Tis but surmised while thou art standing by.
Shakespear[33]

No sooner had Sidney left the room than Selena found her courage almost fail her at the embarrassing conversation which she was now to begin, and dreading lest the awkward silence of such a tete-a-tete should entirely deprive her of power to avail herself of the only opportunity which might occur, she hastily did violence to her natural extreme timidity and without giving him time to utter a word, she turned towards Edwin with a serious countenance as he appeared just ready to address her and said, "I think Mr. Stanmore you told us you were going to London, will you think me impertinent if I request that you will not alter your intention, nay that you will even if you have no objection to the society of my cousin Mr. Dallamore, oblige me so far as to perform this journey in his company."

Observing that he looked at her with surprise, and was preparing to reply she continued, "You perhaps think me very extraordinary, but I am not afraid to treat you with confidence, nay even to ask you a favour as a friend. I have already obligations to your family which alas! I can now never repay, and the memory of my lamented friends at Inverathie must for ever gratefully bind me to promote as far as it is in my power the happiness of one so dear to them."

Edwin softened by this affectionate remembrance, and tribute of tenderness to his beloved parents burst into tears, and seizing her hand exclaimed, "*My* happiness! What is there left upon earth for me! And do you really interest yourself for such a wretch! Oh no!" he cried (vehemently while he covered his face with both his hands), "the tomb hides all that could ever listen with any interest to the sorrows of Edwin."

"You wrong your friends Edwin," answered she in a softer voice, "the best proof I can give you that you wrong us is my thus speaking to you, when your late extraordinary conduct has almost rendered it necessary for the preservation of my good name to avoid and shun you."

Edwin started.

---

[33]   Queen Margaret in Shakespeare's *Henry VI, Part II* (1590), 3.2.339–47. Although the manuscript indicates an elision, there is none.

"You have unintentionally I allow, but very imprudently," continued she, "exposed me to the worst of suspicions. It has been confidently affirmed that I was no stranger to your residence in our neighbourhood. You bound my sister by an indiscreet promise to conceal her accidental knowledge of it until it was too late to serve me. Her interviews with you have been watched and attributed to me. Never can I justify myself, since innocent as she really is, this can only be done at her expense by apparently casting upon her such an accusation. You know my situation, you know how critically I stand at this moment uncertain whether I am an entirely rejected or neglected wife. In either case I am a wife—and tho', I trust, I as such shall ever so conduct myself as to be approved by Heaven and my own conscience, yet it is now peculiarly necessary for me, delicately as I am circumstanced to give scandal no grounds for misrepresentation, nor Lord Dallamore in particular any cause to doubt my virtue and prudence.

"But this is not all .... let me speak while I have this opportunity," pursued she as she perceived him ready eagerly to interrupt her, "Clara and I sensible of your value would wish to preserve you as our friend. It is your own conduct that in fact separates us. What society can we have with one who lurking like a spy or an outlaw is himself anxious to be concealed from those whose friendship might if he did not thus reject it, be a mutual and lasting source of pleasure and advantage. Lose not your best days in a wild delusion and believe me you will no sooner endeavour to rouse yourself from it than you will find it suddenly disperse. I have heard that your own favourite Rousseau has himself said 'On n'aime point si l'on n'est aimé du moins on n'aime pas longtem[p]s.'[34] This is an authority which I am sure on such a subject you cannot dispute."

"Hold Selena," interrupted he no longer able to restrain himself, "I have been delirious, I have been criminal. With my life I would most gladly expiate the injury my folly has done the woman I adore, but it has been no common passion, no imaginary or transient inclination thus easily to be dispersed by the exertion of a little cold philosophy, which has driven me to seek in solitude the only consolation which earth can now afford me. But every thing is now at an end. Never will I again purchase relief from the despair which consumes me, at the risk of injuring your peace. Do not however insult me by supposing that I have deluded myself by the vain idea of a passion I did not feel, that I could not have felt if there existed a possibility of my ever ceasing to adore you. No true Love, Love such as I have known is incapable of change and this heart tho' broken will still reflect in every part the one only image which it can ever retain."

"Forgive me Mr. Stanmore," said Selena coldly rising, "I have offered you my friendship but you reject it by speaking to me a language which I never will listen to. All I can now do is to wish you well but I must not expose myself to hear you boast of sentiments as weak as they are criminal, and which from me above all others you would most carefully conceal had I really your esteem."

---

[34] Rousseau, *Julie, ou La Nouvelle Héloïse* (1761), Letter XVIII: "One doesn't like it if one is not loved, at least one doesn't like it for long."

She would have left him but throwing himself at her feet before the door he exclaimed, "Oh leave me not in anger. How bitter to part upon such terms and part for ever! I will say, I will do any thing you command let me but think you do not hate nor if possible despise me."

"Rise then I beg of you," said she turning from him, "& promise me that this is the last time I shall be obliged to recollect your follies ... for I really can give some of your actions and words no milder name—and be assured it is for the last time that I will ever converse with you on this subject. I have treated you as my friend, I have solicited your friendship—but you are unworthy of my confidence if after this you require a repetition of these reproaches which it has been so painful to me to make."

Edwin answered only by a deep sigh, but after a moment's silence extending his hand he said in a calm but mournful voice, "You will not then banish your friend, you will allow me to see you on your own conditions."

"Most assuredly!" replied Selena readily as she gave him her hand, "when I can do so with safety to my character, which you have yourself for the present rendered impossible."

"Oh Selena! Here then (at least for that offence) may your reproaches end. Surely it has brought its own punishment."

"I have done with reproaches you know," answered Selena with a smile, "and when we meet in London I hope to feel proud of my friend, whose talents if rightly exercised must ensure him reputation."

"Reputation in London," cried Edwin smiling bitterly, "Yes Selena, if you are ambitious of hearing that your friend is applauded on the stage where perhaps my voice may please while it is a novelty."

"Ridiculous!" said Selena, "you could not imagine that I meant that, nay I should be sorry to hear that you yielded to the solicitations of those who will call themselves your friends and the natural impulse of vanity by devoting your time to the exhibition of your musical talents even in a less public manner. Grieved indeed should I be to know that you were ensnared in that dangerous and *bruyante*[35] society, to which you will undoubtedly be courted, and which it will I am sensible cost you some courage to resist. It is not in scenes of dissipation and at the tables of riot that I wish my friend to seek for applause—it is in the fruits of your study that I hope you will taste the sweeter and more valuable praise of genius and of virtue."

"Alas Selena," answered he after some pause, "this flattery from you soothes indeed my ear but it reaches not my understanding, nor can it inspire my heart with any thirst for a fame which I can neither hope nor desire. On what subject could I write, occupied but with one hopeless pursuit, every thought centered on one object I have indeed relieved myself, by uttering my complaints in verse and partiality has extolled the harmony of those complaints

---

[35]   Bruyante: noisy, boisterous, debauched (French).

Ma certo ogni mio studio in quel tempo era
Pur di sfogare il doloroso core
In qualche modo, non d'acquistar fama
Pianger cercai, non già del pianto honore.[36]

"Even in those happier times when I looked with grateful fondness for a parent's smile, I have never felt much alive to the pleasures of an unlimited confidence, and this has the rather inclined me to write my sensations—for oh how soothing is it to fix upon paper and to behold with my eyes the feelings deeply engraven on my heart but known only to myself. This embosoming of my soul affords indeed a charm sweet and consolatory, far superior to that which could arise from a detail of sentiments to ears which never can fully understand and still less sympathise with our emotions for vain is the effort to communicate by any expressions the ideas which memory and sensibility can sometimes reproduce to the mind by a single line."

"Well," replied Selena, "tho' you may despise the vanity of authorship, or not feel inclined to undertake any work which might benefit others, yet I hope you will never lose in dissipation or indolence your taste for literature, nor forget the instructions of your father, nor the prayers of your mother—and that for the sake of those friends whom you still possess, you will pay some attention to your health, which has been so near suffering irreparably by your neglect."

The voice of Clara enquiring for the room here put a stop to the conversation and Selena perceiving Edwin about to escape said hastily, "You will then allow me to tell my cousin that you will take a place in his chaise to town."

Before he could reply Clara opened the door accompanied by Sidney who had been impatiently waiting in the passage for the termination of this tete-a-tete, every moment of which (while it robbed him of Selena's company during the little time they were yet to remain under the same roof) seemed taken from the only few precious hours which he now valued in life.

Edwin rushed past them, and Clara first anxiously gazing after him, and then inquisitively at Selena fearfully and in a low voice demanded, "What is the matter? where is he gone?"

Selena pressed her hand with a look of tender caution which she instantly understood and then in haste to relieve her mind turned to Sidney & said smiling, "I hope you will not be angry with me for having without your leave disposed of a place in your chaise to town."

"Have you prevailed then with poor Edwin?" cried Sidney, "I really rejoice, and that not merely even on your account; I feel now sincerely interested for himself and as far as it concerns me thank you for the arrangement."

---

[36] "Petrarca" (Tighe's note). Petrarch's sonnet 293, lines 9–12 (with "Ma" for "Et" in line 9): "At that time, certainly, my only care / was to release, somehow, the grief that filled / my heart, and not to win myself some fame" (Mark Musa translation).

"You would probably have gone in the mail but for this," observed Selena, "I did not think of that, however this is only a slight addition to the many many obligations I have to you."

Sidney endeavoured to smile, but his emotion constrained him to relinquish the soft hand which he had just taken and turning to the window he thus spared poor Selena the confusion she would have suffered had he perceived the tears which at that instant trembled in her eyes.

She saw that Clara was cruelly impatient to hear what had passed between her and Edwin and taking her arm invited her to go in search of Lady Trevallyn promising Sidney that they would return in a few minutes.

The day passed but too quickly. Except Lady Trevallyn there was not one of the party but anticipated with a kind of secret terror and anguish the moment of separating for the night and all the cheerfulness which each had endeavoured to assume vanished when the waiters who had removed the supper after having placed the glasses upon the table at length closed the door.

Lady Trevallyn herself ever tenderly inclined to sympathize with all who suffered seemed to catch the melancholy infection tho' her heart had opened unusually to the hope of pleasure in the society of Selena with whom alone she had felt inclined to converse with unrestrained confidence since the irreparable loss her heart had sustained in her fond Mother.

She was yet the first to break the sad and tender silence that now reigned and turning to Selena with a soft voice reminded her of their want of rest after the preceding night.

Selena arose in silence with a beating heart, and as Sidney put the candle into her trembling hands scarce ventured to trust her voice with the good night which they had so much dreaded.

Edwin without rising from his seat mournfully echoed it while his head rested on the table.

"We shall meet at breakfast," said Lady Trevallyn addressing Sidney whom she saw unable to speak and as she kissed Selena's cheek on leaving her in her own apartment and felt it wet with the tears which she had laboured almost to suffocation to suppress, she softly sighed and in a voice scarcely audible whispered, "Alas Selena! our cousins are too amiable!"

Had Lady Trevallyn uttered volumes of sermons with the persuasive eloquence of a Massillon[37] she could not more effectually have touched the heart of Selena with self humiliation and conviction, than by those few words which had escaped from the overflowings of a sensibility too tender.

She had then alas! surely betrayed herself and was it to be hoped that Sidney's eyes had been less penetrating than those of Lady Trevallyn, or that she had been able to conceal from him during the days which they had past together in continual

---

[37]   Jean-Baptiste Massillon (1663–1742), the French Catholic bishop and preacher famous for his sermons on the workings of the human heart.

intimacy those sentiments which a few hours had discovered to Lady Trevallyn a far less interested observer.

Nor was this all; hurt and shocked by the comparison she saw that Love had been able to cloath with every perfection him whom she considered as a mean and palpable deceiver, a vile and worthless seducer. She saw that Lady Trevallyn endowed with an understanding she allowed superior to her own, thought this being (in Selena's eyes so despicable) worthy to be ranked with Sidney, with Sidney whom she thought gifted with every virtue adorned with every grace!

"And have I also," she secretly exclaimed, "been thus grossly deceived? Are those perfections but the work of a deluded and sick imagination? Is he in my heart alone all that is excellent, all that is amiable? And am I whom he has appeared to love with such pure such disinterested affection, am I but the object of his temporary caprice, or can he cruelly design to effect the ruin of her whom he has appeared to serve. Oh no dear, too dear but deserving Sidney forgive the injurious comparison. It is impossible that any can exist between a heart the most depraved & one of the noblest that ever warmed a human breast."

Amid such contending reflections, and in self reproach for the weakness which had betrayed her, added to the secret pang with which the thoughts of their separation still thro' all other cares most oppressed her heart this night could ill compensate by the serenity of its repose for the loss of sleep during that which had preceeded it.

Towards morning however exhausted by fatigue she fell into a profound sleep from which Clara aroused her who surprised at her not having yet appeared came to inform her that Lady Trevallyn had just sent to request they would make breakfast, and that she herself had been sitting for some time with Sidney and Edwin in the parlour.

Selena hastily dressing herself endeavoured to fortify her spirits to support without an appearance of confusion or oppression the last moments of her perhaps ever beholding Sidney until she saw him in the presence of Dallamore—to prepare for which she determined during this absence to study by every means to forget him.

She knew not that in forming this determination and in the continual endeavour to practice it, the idea she sought to banish was but the more strongly impressed upon her mind, and that while she for ever said to herself, "I will think of him no more," she in fact ceas'd not thus for one moment to have him present to her heart.

She was not now sorry that she had escaped the distressing interview which she must probably have had with Edwin and Sidney had she risen at the early hour which she had intended—while each would naturally have desired the absence of the other, and perhaps ever after feel the less pleasure in each other's society from the disquiet occasioned by this hour's impatience.

There was nothing Selena thought more desirable for Edwin than the friendship which Sidney appeared inclined to cultivate and tho' at first Edwin had shrunk from his advances, yet she had no doubt that the talents, the virtues and the amiable graces conspicuous in the conversation, manners nay in the very countenance of

Sidney could not in the end fail of captivating the ingenuous soul of Edwin. His friendship she knew would all be exerted to turn the warmth of Edwin's affections towards Clara, for whom Edwin himself already felt a grateful attachment, while he beheld her with a brotherly love and admiration. The judgment and experience of Sidney, might she hoped preserve Edwin from the dangers of the world, of which his extreme ignorance, the artless impetuosity of his temper and his singular powers of pleasing all rendered him peculiarly exposed to perils where genius and virtue have so often fatally perished.

On the preceding evening, in a short but interesting conversation in private which Sidney after anxiously seeking had at last obtained, she had recommended Edwin to his care and even delicately hinted her wish that he might one day be worthy of Clara. He had promised to cultivate his regard and on this promise she relied with confidence. Sidney then enquired concerning her own plans, and heard with pleasure that if Lady Harriet, or even her brother wrote to advise her coming to town, & invited her to their house she would without delay accept their invitation even tho' Dallamore were not yet arrived there. Nor did she refuse Sidney's request to be allowed to write in case he should hear any thing concerning him on his arrival in town.

The carriages were ready before Selena went down, but the breakfast tho' it had been some time prepared remained as yet untasted. She was however herself anxious to shorten a scene so painful to all and having swallowed some tea told Lady Trevallyn in a trembling voice that she was ready and then pretended to busy herself in looking for the books and parcels which had been brought into the parlour, her eyes all the time fearfully avoiding those of Sidney whose anxious and melancholy glances watched her with earnestness as if they feared to lose one motion of that graceful form which was so soon to be torn from their sight, or as if now that the hour of sorrow was indeed come, he wished to heap up treasures in his memory which henceforth were to be his only consolation "Breve conforto a si lungo martiro."[38]

Lady Trevallyn at length enquired if every thing was in the carriage and arose to depart.

Selena in silence gave her hand first to Edwin and then breathless and trembling to Sidney withdrawing it however instantly while she desired Clara to take leave of her friends, as if she wished to prevent either of them from accompanying her to the carriage, the door of which was held already open surrounded by waiters and ostlers. In an instant she was seated in it while Sidney silently assisted Lady Trevallyn and Clara with difficulty restrained her tears, when she felt her hand covered with those of Edwin as he pressed it gratefully to his lips.

"We shall meet in London, shall we not!" said she as he put her into the carriage, less desirous of comforting herself than him by the suggestions of this hope.

---

[38]   Petrarch's sonnet 14, line 14: "take some brief solace for long martyrdom" (Mark Musa translation).

Edwin answered only by a deep sigh, and as they drove from the door his soul felt annihilated to all hope as to all pleasure while he listened motionless to the sounds of the retiring wheels now fainter as they bore all he loved upon earth so rapidly away.

"In the dark void, the wild waste of future existence," he cried, "there shines not now for me one sunny spot—

> What is mine after life?
> My day is past the gloom of night is come
> An hopeless darkness settles o'er my fate!
> I've seen the last look of her heavenly eyes
> I've heard the last sounds of her blessed voice
> I've marked her fair form from my sight depart
> My doom is closed."[39]

And did Sidney mean time look with indifference upon her departure? Oh no! but yet a sweeter sensation mingled tenderness and even tender melancholy pleasure with his sorrow.

In their last interview, in those few precious moments dearer than "a long thousand years of vulgar hours"[40] the softest emotion of sudden delight had stolen into his heart when in the midst of her expressions of gratitude for his friendship she stopped overcome with her own feelings while she observed the cruel agitation which he in vain attempted to disguise. He saw her calm beautiful eyes suffused with tears as she for an instant fixed them upon him with a melancholy smile and oh in that instant with what enchantment did they not speak to his soul while they seemed to say

> Il core e noi siam tuoi
> Tu bramar più non dei[41]

It is true that the sudden expression which lightened in his countenance recalled her to herself, and that "discretion strove to check the rising joy,"[42] yet in spite of all his bitter regret and the sighs which said "Ah, Why was such happiness not given me pure?" in spite of the virtuous resolutions he had so often made never to injure her peace by seeking to gain those affections she considered due to another the softest secret consciousness of being beloved diffused the delicious balm of consolation thro' his soul, the source of which was scarcely acknowledged even to himself.

---

[39] "Miss Bailllie" (Tighe's note). Basil in Joanna Baillie's *Count Basil* (1798), 4.3.219–25 (with "past" for "closed" in line 220).

[40] Jaffeir in Thomas Otway's *Venice Preserved* (1682), 4.1.85.

[41] "Tasso" (Tighe's note). Dafne in Torquato Tasso's *Aminta* (1745), 1.1.214–15: "My heart and I are yours, desire no more."

[42] Bertrand in Hannah More's *The Fatal Falsehood* (1779), 1.1.199 (with "dash" for "check").

It was this that enabled him to support an appearance of composure and even endeavour to inspire Edwin with a degree of cheerfulness during their journey, which he was however far from being able to effect tho' his attentions were received with a grateful and even affectionate sensibility.

Chapter VII

Why was I ever blest! why is remembrance
Rich with a thousand pleasing images
Of past enjoyments, since 'tis but to plague me?
When thou art mine no more what will it ease me
To think of all the golden minutes past
To think that thou wert kind, and I was happy.
Rowe[43]

Never had Lady Trevallyn appeared so lovely, so animated, as in this little journey. All her powers of pleasing were exerted to chace away the melancholy which she saw hung over the brow of her young companions. Her natural languor with her habitually pensive reserve vanished before her affectionate endeavours to inspire her beloved Selena with the cheerfulness which no longer sparkled in the enchanting softness of her bright blue eyes or dimpled round the glowing coral of her lips in playful smiles.

Lady Trevallyn did not indeed affect a gaiety to which her disposition had never been much inclined, nor was her conversation brilliant with the sallies of wit or the challenge of mirth. Even in her happiest moments, and when her heart had been most alive to the fairy visions of hope, her spirits had been ever gentle and her demonstrations of pleasure calm. The unvarying sweetness which sat upon her regularly beautiful features and the exquisite symetry of her form truly bespoke the softness of that nature which was as incapable of being ever intoxicated by joy as of being inflamed by passion. The cruelty of unkindness, the bitterness of disappointment and the anguish of hopeless regret preyed upon her heart but found no utterance on her lips. Mocked and affrighted by clamorous affectation, Tenderness and Sensibility took refuge in her gentle bosom and sheltered themselves in her silence. Yet there was in that silence something of a sympathy which was ever ready to speak kindness to sorrow, and of all the children [of] affliction who had approached Lady Trevallyn Angela alone had shrunk from her with reserve. Always attentive to sadness, which however unobtrusive it might be seldom escaped her feeling observation, never had she been so anxious to afford consolation as on the present occasion, and no conversation could be better calculated to sooth the melancholy by which both sisters appeared oppressed than that with which she quickly captivated their attention and interested their sensibility.

---

[43] Axalla in Nicholas Rowe's *Tamerlane* (1701), 3.1.27–32.

Tho' her mind owed but little to education, yet her imagination was lively, and her natural elegance of taste had stored her excellent memory with the most beautiful passages from almost all the works to which she had been led by her heart the only guide she had ever had for her studies, as it had been her chief instructor in the path of Virtue. The soft melody of her voice and the grace with which she introduced what ever she repeated, as the expressions or the sentiments of her favourite authors occurred to her in their conversation added to all a new charm, and in her own ideas there was a refinement, a delicacy, as well as a melancholy tenderness which spoke most sensibly to the soul.

The subjects on which they now conversed were indeed apparently general, but all bore some secret allusion, some interesting connexion with the sorrows or the objects that reigned predominant in the bosom of each. The images most beloved appeared in every sentiment tho' their names dwelt not on their lips and while Selena listened with sympathy and compassion to the natural description of sensations of tenderness she forgot for awhile the worthlessness of the being who had inspired her with this touching eloquence by dearly purchased experience.

Selena failed not to enquire for Mrs. Harley and Angela.

"Alas!" answered Lady Trevallyn, "my poor Mrs. Harley has been extremely ill this whole autumn, and as the hard weather came on continued to grow worse so that she has now almost entirely lost the use of her limbs. I shall never be able to supply her place, but she still superintends my little girls, tho' I do not like to think how much they may suffer from not having either her eye or mine constantly over them for so many months as I shall be obliged now to leave all my little occupations at Esselberrie at sixes and sevens."

"I dare say," said Selena, "Mrs. Harley frets at not being able to go to poor Angela."

"No doubt," answered Lady Trevallyn, "but upon the whole I am not sorry that Angela left Esselberrie for tho' she is certainly very uneasy about her, yet I am sure she is less miserable than when she had her constantly before her eyes such a picture of gloomy discontent. But apropos Angela; Do you know that I have found out the cause of her unhappiness?"

"Indeed!" cried Selena eagerly.

"Yes and in spite of all her wise Aunt's self congratulations that she should bring no young man dancing after her to her house, it is just as dear Mrs. Vallard first guessed and the poor thing is in love."

"Has she opened her heart then at last?" demanded Selena whose suspicions of Lord Henry had frequently since recurred to her mind when thinking with pity on her former conversations with Mrs. Harley.

"No," said Lady Trevallyn, "but I have found out her secret and when I tell you how," added she with a deep blush, "I know you will smile and think of Clara's lullaby—but that I assure you was quite different and no such inference was to be drawn from those silly verses."

"Does Angela write verses too?" said Selena smiling.

"I have at least good reasons for suspecting it I think as you shall hear. I was sitting lately one day with poor Mrs. Harley when I began to talk to her of Angela tho' I rather avoid the subject in general as I do not think that she herself loves to introduce it, but I happened that day to ask her could she imagine what was the reason that Angela was not to be prevailed upon to take a pencil in her hand while at Esselberrie, and I was lamenting that I had never seen any of her drawings of which I had heard so much. Mrs. Harley could not account for this whim, but she told me that since her departure she had found a little portfolio in a table drawer containing some sketches in pencil and water colours but that she was sure they had not been done during her residence at Esselberrie. I expressed a wish to see them for you know Selena how very fond I am of drawing tho' I have so little genius for it, and between you and me, as poor Angela was a little perverse I rather suspect that was the reason I was never to be indulged in that way."

"Oh no, I am sure you wrong her … indeed I am dear Lady Trevallyn."

"Well that is no matter," continued she smiling, "perhaps so, for I do not think I ever felt as partial to your favourite Angela as I am sure I ought, tho' I trust I did all in my power to comfort her, but you know she was one of those who refuse to be comforted; but let that be as it will I must go on with my story. Her dear Mother at least never was unwilling to give me every gratification in her power, so upon my saying I should like to look at this portfolio she shewed me the drawer where I might find it, not being able herself to get up to reach it for me. No sooner had I opened it than I was indeed struck with astonishment at the beauty of the style as well as the uncommon cleverness of the touch and the skill displayed in the design which I could have no doubt was her own. But it was the style that so peculiarly arrested my attention … it was just what I so much admire … what I have so long imitated and vainly wished to attain. Oh Selena if you knew all the melancholy remembrances that rushed upon my mind as I gazed upon the first sketch which presented itself to me! It brought back the happy, happy, days of my youth, the endearing images of those hours the sweetest of my life passed in copying drawings done in that style! You smile Selena! You think I have made but little progress."

"Not in drawing, but in Angela's story," answered Selena still smiling tho' her swimming eyes spoke the tenderest compassion.

"You are right, my love," said Lady Trevallyn with a deep sigh, "my thoughts were all gone far, far away from Angela, or any thing but what was most delightful, most dear but it is well to call me back tho' how can

> I but remember that such things were
> And were most precious to me.[44]

---

[44] Macduff in Shakespeare's *Macbeth* (1605), 4.3.224–5: "I cannot but remember such things were, / That were most precious to me."

Oh that I had died, that I had been laid beside my darling Mother before it became a bitter punishment as well as a crime to dwell upon those hours! Or that I could now forget what it has since become my constant torment to remember! How true is that my past enjoyments are my present anguish—

> Felicité passée
> Qui ne peut revenir
> Tourment de ma pensee
> Que n'ai je en te perdant perdu le souvenir
> Helas il ne me reste
> De mes contentemen[t]s
> Qu' un souvenir funeste
> Qui me les convertit a toute heure en tourmen[t]s[45]

But this is sad egotism," said she wiping her streaming eyes after a moment's pause, "and I am sure you are both longing to hear Angela's verses."

"Have you got them then?" cried each with one voice.

"Patience we are not come to that yet," continued she smiling, "Mrs. Harley saw me so much taken with the contents of the portfolio that she requested I might carry it hence if I thought any thing in it worth acceptance. I gladly availed myself of her offer, that I might look over it at leisure but determined to restore it again lest Angela should enquire for it hereafter. There were none of the drawings finished, but genius and the hand of a master were stamped upon even the most imperfect outlines—and as such every scrap was interesting. In the inside of the cover was a little silk pocket which I did not observe until I had looked over all the papers which had been thrown loosely into the portfolio. I found in it a few pieces of ivory ready for painting miniatures and one folded paper which I at first thought contained a picture. There certainly had been one wrapt up in it as the oval impression remained still evidently in the folds, but I suppose in taking the portrait out she forgot the lines which she had written in the envelope. As soon as I had read them I became doubly anxious to return the portfolio lest she might recollect the circumstance and therefore brought it to Mrs. Harley the very next day shewing her the accidental discovery which I had made, for I thought it well she should know it, that she might be on her guard never to let Angela suspect I had seen the portfolio which you may be sure she was very ready to promise. But with her permission I retained one sketch which I found torn across, because I felt as if I had a sort of right to it. For however extraordinary it may seem I assure you there is not a doubt that it is my own portrait; I have it in my writing desk and will shew it to you when we come to Bath. I did not think it fair to copy the poor girl's verses but I am sure I have them exactly by heart and it is no breach of confidence

---

[45]   Jean Bertaut, "Les cieux inexorables," *Recueil de Quelques Vers Amoureux* (1602), lines 37–44. "Happiness past, which will never return, tormenting my thoughts, because I lost you but not your memory; alas it doesn't let me rest, because even in contentment a sad memory converts all hours into torment."

to let *you* hear them, as she seemed so much more inclined to open her heart to you than any one else."

After a few moments recollection Lady Trevallyn then repeated the following lines.

> Yes, these are the features already imprest
>> So deep by the pencil of Love on my heart;
> Within their reflection they find in this breast,
>> Yet something is wanting—Ah where is the art
> That to painting so true can that something impart?
>
> Oh where is the sweetness that dwelt on that lip?
>> And where is the smile that enchanted my soul?
> From those roses no sweet dew of Love can I sip,
>> Nor meet the soft glance that with magic controul
> O'er the chords of my heart so bewitchingly stole.
>
> Cold, cold is that eye unimpassioned its beams,
>> They speak not of tenderness Love or delight!
> Oh where is the heart-thrilling rapture that streams
>> From the heavenly blue of that circle so bright
> That sunshine of pleasure which gladdened my sight.
>
> Yet come to my bosom oh image adored!
>> And sure thou shalt feel the soft flame of my heart,
> The glow sympathetic once more be restored
>> Once more it shall warm thee, Ah cold as thou art,
> And to charms so beloved its own feelings impart.
>
> Oh come and while others his form may behold
>> And he on another with fondness may smile;
> To thee shall my wrongs, shall my sorrows be told,
>> And the kiss I may give thee those sorrows the while
> Like the memory of joys which are past shall beguile![46]

"Alas, my dear Lady Trevallyn!" cried Selena extremely affected by what she had heard, "if poor Angela did indeed write those verses, I fear she is lost not only to happiness and her poor Mother, but even to innocence. What virtuous girl could bear thus openly to boast a passion for which it is evident she even then doubted of meeting a faithful return? But I can hardly think they are her own; perhaps she has only copied them, tho' even that would incline me to join with you in thinking you had discovered the source of all her misery. Had you found the portrait perhaps we might have made a still more important discovery."

---

[46]   Tighe titles this lyric "The Picture. Written for Angela. 1802" in *Verses Transcribed for H.T.* (Brompton, 1805); it is first published in *Psyche, with Other Poems* (1811).

Fig. III.1   Illustration for "The Picture" in *Verses Transcribed for H.T.* (Brompton, 1805), MS Acc 5495/C/8/1, National Library of Ireland, Dublin.

"Oh I have no doubt," cried Lady Trevallyn without observing the extremely thoughtful air with which Selena uttered the last words, "I have no doubt as to the verses being her own, Lady Anne Ortney used always to tell me how fond her little Angela was of reading and poetry. Besides there were one or two lines scratched out and others to the same purpose written over them evidently done for the sake of the rhyme which followed; but I do not quite agree with you as to the necessary conclusion you have drawn from them, for I know when the fit of writing seizes a person who is in the habit of this dangerous indulgence, one is inclined to express in even stronger language than the heart at other times feels the sentiments we scarce allow ourselves in plain prose to speak. Not but that I own in this case I strongly suspect as you do that there may be some remorse mingled with poor Angela's regret for the loss of her lover. Why else that extreme dark reserve and that strange obstinacy to return to her cross aunt; whom I could be half glad she has outwitted she looked so bitter and so wonderfully convinced of her own superior sense and piety to all the rest of the world, only that in this affair (if it is as we suppose) the poor child has in fact deceived herself far more than her aunt."

"Did Mrs. Harley make any observations on the verses?" asked Selena.

"Oh she was at first extremely eager to search for the portrait as you would have been I perceive Selena, tho' I can hardly think we should have been any of us much the wiser, and most probably our eyes might have met those 'heavenly circles of blue' without discerning where lay their powerful enchantment which stole away poor Angela's heart."

"Perhaps not," replied Selena but in a manner so *distract*[47] and with a look so unusually absent that Lady Trevallyn could not help suspecting that fond memory had fixed her thoughts just then on the beautiful blue eyes of Sidney—and yet perhaps their ever present beams had never shone upon her heart with less irresistible power, from the time she had beheld them fixed upon her with tender sadness at the door of the inn at Glocester unto that very moment.

Diverted entirely from herself all her imagination was busy in forming suspicions and conjectures upon Lord Henry and she even wondered that Lady Trevallyn did not appear in the least to advert to what she thought so probable tho' she could not be a stranger to his opportunities of intimacy with Angela at Lady Anne's.

The truth is that the possibility of Lord Henry's loving another woman during the time that his eyes had told her such unutterable tales of love and fidelity entered not into the artless unsuspicious bosom of his deluded Emily who saw in his mind so many imaginary graces as in fact adorned his person, and dreamed not that truth, affection, generosity, and honour in forsaking his depraved heart still hovered on his *Love* formed lips and illuminated his countenance to assist the deception with which fondness delighted to paint him as all that was fair and excellent in man.

The doubts which had been revived in Selena's bosom by the relation of this little circumstance for a while entirely engrossed her, but Love possesses truly the chemic secret of quick transmutation; so that every subject which occupies the mind is immediately found to bear some analogy to the one chief object and to this constantly reverts by some almost imperceptible link. Selena therefore from her suspicions of Lord Henry's cruelty to Angela and the consideration of his base and treacherous conduct towards his cousin was soon led to form comparisons most favourable to Sidney. How differently had he acted! How generous were his offers when he knew her portionless and thought free. Alas! had Lady Trevallyn's affections been won by such an object, had her love been as justly placed as it was in itself pure and exalted how might it have caused her pride and happiness instead of her misery and shame!

From these meditations she was at length in some degree diverted by the account which Lady Trevallyn was giving to Clara of Mrs. Aston whom she expected to meet at Bath. Selena having seen her at Harrogate was now surprised

---

[47] Distract: distracted (obsolete use).

to hear that she was niece to Lord Trevallyn but that having married as it was considered by that high born family in a manner far beneath her, her uncle had for many years refused to have the smallest intercourse with either her or her husband who had been chaplain to the late Lady Trevallyn.

"Upon our coming over to England immediately after our marriage," said Lady Trevallyn, "Mrs. Aston whom I had known a little some time before applied to me to exert my influence in restoring her to her uncle's favour, from whom I believe she had once had great expectations, or rather perhaps I should say her husband for her spirit is really noble and I believe she prides herself upon despising wealth which assuredly is not his case. I did my best in this affair but was a long time without being able to succeed. However just before we left town we had a grand dinner of reconciliation, and to their great joy they received an invitation to Esselberrie. Soon after you Selena left Derbyshire this visit was paid upon Mrs. Aston's return from Harrogate, I do not know where she picked up her husband for I know she could not prevail upon him to accompany her to a place where he was exposed to such demand for money—for a greater miser you never heard of, and that in the oddest way. He will often go to great expence in matters of serious consequence but is wretched if he sees the smallest trifle wasted and never parts with a penny without displaying the most ridiculous reluctance. Mrs. Aston told me that she saw you at Harrogate and I assure you she enquired very particularly for your brother Robert. I forgot since to ask you what was your opinion of her."

"Oh," answered Selena laughing, "I must take care what I say of Lord Trevallyn's niece and your protegée, perhaps it was very fortunate I got this preparatory information."

"You need not be to the least cautious about it," answered Lady Trevallyn, "for I am sure say what you will, you must think as I do that she is the most absurd ridiculous animal that ever lived; but in spite of that she has many good qualities and I shall be extremely happy if I can completely restore her to the favour of her uncle which she terribly forfeited by her love match, for such as you may suppose she said it was, tho' the love must have gone off wonderfully if that was really the case."

"What else could have induced her," said Selena, "to have disobliged her family by marrying beneath her?"

"Why certainly," answered Lady Trevallyn with a smile, "Mr. Aston's birth was not altogether just the thing to please the house of Trevallyn but in other respects I do not think she could have looked much higher. I put the man himself out of the question for his oddity had not at that time broke out, tho' he must always have been a miser at heart—he has a large living in the church and besides that a little property of his own. She was not very young and tho' she had been reckoned pretty you know the memory of that does not go for much. Her fortune was but small and she had the odious character of being a very learned Lady which I have heard was more against her than even her want of wealth. I have no doubt she has taken care already to inform you of her great acquirements."

"I know her very little," answered Selena, "but Robert used to amuse us with her oddities sometimes, tho' Lord Dallamore never could bear to have her mentioned: indeed," added she with a sigh as she recollected the consequences which had hence arisen to herself, "I think it was rather unfortunate for Miss Richmond that Mrs. Aston happened to be in her party, as I have no doubt the violent dislike which he took to her often made him dread going where he thought she would be found."

"And can you tell me the reason of this," asked Lady Trevallyn, "Had she offended him, or was it one of his unaccountable antipathies?"

"Oh I really do not know but I believe she used to teize him asking him questions about greek books and reading him long lectures on chemistry and botany. Robert quite delighted in her, but she put every one else to flight tho' I really believe, a great many women envied her the learning which they pretended to despise. I have seen her attack Lord Dallamore sometimes when he was in one of his absent fits and as she did not very often meet a patient hearer it was amusing enough to watch her astonishing volubility. In the midst of it however if she insisted upon his giving an answer he would give a great yawn, and only say 'I protest Ma'am I do not know, I really cannot say' and then walk off to some other sopha where she generally pursued him to his extreme misery till he left the room or till Robert's entrance drew her off from him."

"Oh," cried Lady Trevallyn, "I can imagine them both so well. I think I see her looking so *great* when she began her harangue to your brother but did he really think her very clever?"

"No, I should think not. But he said she had read a vast deal and had in fact more knowledge than she knew what to do with, tho' the pompous manner in which she talked of common things that every one knows as if she thought they were never heard of before till her discovery often made people suspect she was in fact ignorant with all that pedantic display of learning."

"Why I think I can account for that in some degree and to her credit too," answered Lady Trevallyn. "She is entirely self taught, educated in great retirement with a very confined circle of illiterate, self conceited ignorant card players her mind really superior to all around took its ideas wholly from books. No one took any pains either to amuse or improve her time, and as she had naturally an inquisitive turn and that there happened to be a large old library at Trevallyn hall where the first five and twenty years of her life were exclusively past reading became almost her sole occupation. As all her knowledge cost her equal trouble, and as she is conscious of the infinite pains and labour which by undiverted study she has paid for that general knowledge which almost every one acquires as soon as they can read and that is fixed in our memory by continual allusions in conversation, it is not unnatural that she should appear to herself a miracle of learning and be ambitious to display to others what she gained with such patience and difficulty. When at length she escaped from her confinement and mixed with the world, she saw that even among the most distinguished literary characters there were perhaps none who sacrificed to study so large a portion of their time as she had been accustomed to devote to her vague pursuit of knowledge—and as all listened with astonishment and many with admiration to such unusual learning from the lips of a female possessing still some share of the more common attractions of youth and beauty, it is not surprising that her vanity at perceiving herself the object of universal attention in all companies should nearly turn her poor brain."

"She must have been much mortified then," cried Selena, "I should imagine at Harrogate for no one minded a word she said and it was generally thought that she was a little deranged, I believed so myself until Robert who knew her better undeceived me."

"Oh," replied Lady Trevallyn, "it is many years since she could command this flattering attention—but my poor Mother has often described to me the surprising effect she produced, when first brought out into the world by the late Lady Trevallyn upon the death of her parents. But alas! the novelty soon wore off and what was still worse a scorbutic complaint prematurely destroyed her beauty, had it even remained unimpaired tho' she might more readily have retained her hearers yet I have heard nothing could be more disadvantageous to her establishment than all this parade of learning which whether real or imaginary served to terrify from her the fine young men, a class of beings in general themselves very illiterate. And tho' extremely irritated by her marriage I have frequently heard Lord Trevallyn say that Mr. Aston's was the only proposal she had ever had."

"I hope he at least is well qualified to admire her attainments," said Selena.

"I believe he is a good scholar," answered Lady Trevallyn, "but alas! I fear her supposed expectations from her uncle were her chief charms in his eyes. Nevertheless her strong mind and really generous disposition has obtained a happy ascendency over him so that she prevents I am told his exposing himself in a thousand instances where his extreme parsimony would lead him into the most ridiculous meanness. I have heard a great many stories about them which I have no doubt are much exaggerated, yet I have seen enough to be convinced that she does govern with a pretty high hand."

Chapter VIII

> All that can softly steal, or gaily charm
> The heart of Woman—hence dear sad ideas!
> Destroyers hence! and dare you tempt me still
> When your false charms have wreck'd my peace, for ever!
> Thompson[48]

As it had been rather late when Lady Trevallyn and her young friends left Glocester it was already nearly dark when they arrived at Sodbury.

"Dear Selena how happy I have been this day," exclaimed Lady Trevallyn, "perhaps it may be long before I shall be able again to enjoy uninterruptedly your society. Let us go no farther to night. I wrote from Glocester to Mrs. Aston, so even

---

[48]   Clytemnestra in James Thomson's *Agamemnon* (1738), 1.1.57–61. The epigraph omits line 60: "Perfidious Syrens! in that very moment."

if Lord Trevallyn is arrived they will take care not to let him be alone. Besides we may be overturned in the night, and we shall hardly meet such protectors as you had in your last adventure of this kind."

Nothing could be more agreeable to Selena than this proposal, as her spirits began already to sink at the idea of encountering strangers and still more while she anticipated the reception which she might meet from Lord Trevallyn, about whom the repeated assurances of her friend could hardly satisfy her apprehensions or inspire her with courage.

It was near two o'clock when they drove into Bath, and a fine frosty day gave this beautiful town every advantage. The gaiety and novelty of its appearance struck Selena and her sister with surprise and admiration and even surpassed their expectations in spite of all they had already heard of this grand resort of those whom idleness duly disperses around the kingdom in search of health or amusement.

As the carriage which conveyed them to the house that had been prepared for their reception turned the corner of Milsom street an involuntary and half suppressed ejaculation turned the eyes of her companions upon Lady Trevallyn whose face was covered with the loveliest blushes and brightened with an unusual lustre of beauty.

In an instant the chaise was stopped and the doors opened by Lord Henry himself, who holding out his hand to his cousin with some expressions of surprise and pleasure at this unexpected meeting presented a countenance glowing with every charm of manly beauty, animation and delight.

Lady Trevallyn uttered not one word, but the heart of Selena ached with pity and trembled with apprehension while she anxiously read the soft expression which too visibly spoke in the downcast eyes of her friend beneath their long silky lashes as she presented him her hand. Tho' his first glance had caught (with perhaps mutual dissatisfaction) that of Selena, on his hastily opening the door of the carriage it was some moments before he appeared to notice her, nor was it till Lady Trevallyn had gently withdrawn her hand that he turned round to pay Selena his smiling compliments. After which again impatiently addressing the still silent Emily he enquired whether she was come to make any stay in Bath and where she resided.

"We have a house in this street I believe," said she in a voice tremulous with agitation, but whose soft tones vibrated upon his delighted, his exulting heart.

"Will you go to the rooms tonight?"

"No certainly," answered she smiling; "I am but just come and am not even certain that Lord Trevallyn is arrived."

"Will you give me leave to call this evening to hear how he is?"

Lady Trevallyn was silent but as he said this he again held out his hand and having pressed hers for a moment closed the door without requiring another answer.

No sooner was he gone than Clara who had lost not one word or look which had passed eagerly enquired if that was not Lord Henry Ortney? Lady Trevallyn left it to Selena to satisfy her curiosity who coldly answered that it was.

"I thought so," replied Clara smiling. "Indeed I could not mistake him after all Lady Harriet has said of him. Besides no one else could be so much handsomer than Sidney."

The eyes of both her auditors were turned towards her at this speech, but with far different emotions. Selena's countenance spoke nothing but surprise while tenderness and pleasure shone in the mild beams which yet seemed to retain some of that unusual animation which they had reflected from the enkindling glances of Lord Henry. But whatever might have been the secret thoughts of each neither spoke and the next moment they found themselves at the door where the Butler already stood to announce that my Lord was arrived and waited in the drawing room to receive her Ladyship and his expected guests.

As she ascended the steps Lady Trevallyn looked round, but the gentle confusion painted in her suddenly withdrawn eyes betrayed to Selena who followed her that they had encountered those of Lord Henry and on her turning in the same direction which they had taken she in fact perceived him retiring from the spot where he had waited to see them alight. Neither of the ladies had any doubt but that he had done so with a view of ascertaining the house, yet probable as this supposition may appear they were mistaken. Lord Henry had indeed spent the greatest part of that and the preceeding morning in watching that house for a sight of her whose arrival he had with impatience expected.

From the far end of a large table at which they had dined together a few days before in London, he had overheard Lord Trevallyn declare his intention of going to Bath for a few weeks, while at the same time he informed his far less interested hearer for whom this intelligence was meant the day upon which he had appointed Lady Trevallyn to meet him at the house which he had already sent his Butler to take for them in Milsom street.

Transported at the tidings which he appeared not to notice Lord Henry immediately determined to join a party of his friends lately gone to Bath, whose pressing solicitations he had hitherto refused from his unwillingness to absent himself from town at a time when he might expect Lady Trevallyn's arrival. No event could have taken place more fortunate, more correspondent to his wishes. The continual opportunities which he hoped the confined society of Bath (added to their natural connexion from relationship) would afford him filled him with the most confident expectation of being almost constantly in her presence and presented the fairest prospects of success in the fondest wish of his cruel and unworthy heart, that too well knew his influence over hers.

The rapture of present joy and anticipated triumph which throbbed in his bosom when first he perceived the carriages and servants of Lady Trevallyn as they rapidly approached him now in some degree diminished when he discerned that she was accompanied by Selena. Instantly did he foresee the interruption of those morning tete-a-tetes which he had planned with such delight; he already dreaded that interfering eye which in every glance spoke sense and purity and the rather as he entertained no doubt that Mrs. Vallard had inspired her young friend with those suspicions which he plainly perceived she herself had conceived.

Besides the uncommon beauty of Selena, and the singular situation in which rumour whispered she now stood with respect to Dallamore, rendered her an object too interesting to escape the designs of Lord Henry should opportunity ever throw her in his way at a time when he could not urge the pursuit of his first chief object, the only lovely attractive being who had really ever touched his naturally cold and hardened heart. To behold them therefore thus together obliged him to consent to the entire relinquishment of one—and tho' he could not hesitate in the choice, yet it was with reluctant disappointment that he resigned his hopes of ever captivating the affections of this slighted wife whose youthful beauties even now nearly equalled and must soon eclipse the charms of his long loved Emily which hitherto had stood unrivalled in every circle.

But if he had received but little gratification from this unexpected sight of Selena, she on her side was equally inclined to consider their present meeting with regret and displeasure and as she slowly followed Lady Trevallyn upstairs felt a sad and secret suspicion that on Lord Henry's part it was not altogether so accidental as had been represented.

Timidity however quickly dispersed all her reflections when the servant flung open the drawing room door and the confused sound of voices issuing from thence proclaimed it to be full of company. Lady Trevallyn started back, and turning round a piteous look at Selena regretted that they had not retired to her own room at least till they had heard who was in possession of the house.

Nevertheless to escape now was impossible. Exerting herself therefore as well as she was able she received the salutations of a swarm of connexions and acquaintances whom the fame of her expected arrival had already drawn to the door which they looked upon not only as the happy means of destroying the present hour but as the pass-port to future entertainment, all of whom male and female at the express order of Lord Trevallyn had been admitted, nor did Mrs. Aston who was now reinstated in some degree as an inmate of her uncle's house venture to oppose this cruel interruption to all her usual occupations.

Lord Trevallyn received his lovely wife and their two abashed guests whom she gracefully presented to him, with the same ceremonious bow and having desired the servant to place chairs for them near the fire once more seated himself at the upper end of the sopha which was occupied entirely by his Lordship and a dowager lady of quality. After a short time past in general conversation during which Lady Trevallyn spoke but little and his Lordship not at all the company gradually dispersed leaving only Mr. Guise whom Selena remembered to have seen at Esselberrie and who now at Lord Trevallyn's desire took up a newspaper to read aloud. Mrs. Aston mean while had already begun to question Clara as to the extent of her studies but this was at length interrupted by Lady Trevallyn who having enquired whether there was any company expected to dinner made an apology to her Lord and Mrs. Aston for leaving them to change her dress.

She then withdrew requesting Selena and her sister to accompany her that they might visit their new apartments, an invitation which they gladly accepted. Having seen that every thing was provided she had previously ordered which could be thought of for their comfort and accommodation and offered the assistance of one of her women which Selena declined Lady Trevallyn left the sisters to unpack and settle themselves in their present habitation while she retired to calm the agitation of her own spirits if this could possibly be effected while all her thoughts dwelt upon the unexpected vision which had met her eyes and the promised evening visitor.

But this not a task the most easily performed, and when she joined the sisters to summon them to descend to the drawing room Selena, struck with the deep and vivid glow which suffused her cheek, recollected Lady Harriet's positive assurances that her friend had always worn rouge, and for a moment questioned the superior beauty of that complexion which she had so often beheld with admiration, for her taste unspoiled by fashion refused all tribute of praise to any charms which the features could owe to art. But this suspicion was indeed that of a moment. It was not long before the dying roses surrendered one cheek to the sole dominion of the Lily while the other still retained that flush of feverish perterbation which seemed to beat in her very eyes and independent of this incontestable evidence of Nature in support of her own cause Selena had an assured confidence that her friend unsolicitous of beauty and incapable of deceit could never secretly have recourse to an art for which she openly expressed her dislike.

After Selena had thanked her for the attention with which she had ordered her room to be furnished with a harp, musick and a number of books from the various circulating libraries she observed her dress more particularly, as she had doubted whether Clara or herself were sufficiently ornamented to appear before the company whom they were prepared to expect at dinner. She saw with some surprise that it was if possible even more simple than usual consisting only of a thick muslin gown drawn up close to her neck and encircling her beautiful arms even to her wrists.

This in the hurry of unpacking had first presented itself to the hands of the maid who bringing it to her Lady twice demanded "if *it would do*" before she succeeded in rousing her from the profound reverie in which she sat before her dressing table.

At length Lady Trevallyn (ever ready to atone for unintentional neglect) hastily arose saying, "I beg your pardon Fanny, I was thinking of something else, what did you say?" and immediately approved of all she proposed upon her again repeating the question.

Having received her gloves from Fanny's hands she thus appeared before Selena with the modest concealment which the present fashion allowed only to what is called *undress* having completely covered all but her lovely face with no other ornament than its own bright golden hair twisted negligently around her head.

The branches were already lighted and Lord Trevallyn seated in the drawing room (with Mr. Guise) when the ladies entered. Lady Trevallyn approached his Lordship and began in a low voice to make some enquiries concerning his health. He paid them however no attention but surveying her during some moments in silence at length said, "I should think Lady Trevallyn that politeness required you to be dressed before the arrival of your guests. I hope it is not your intention to insult the company whom I have invited by receiving them in a habit at all times unfitted for Lady Trevallyn and which I must this instant request that you will part with to one of your women."

The gentle Emily withdrew in silence casting a glance upon her figure as she passed reflected in the long glass that was opposite the door as she thought for the first time on the appearance it should make in the eyes of the self invited guest who yet of all who were expected could alone for an instant occupy her thoughts.

"Fanny," said she as her maid answered the summons of the bell, presenting to her at the same time the gown she had hastily thrown off, "our taste has not been approved to day but Lord Trevallyn desired me to give you this to compensate for your trouble in this second dressing."

While Fanny paid her smiling thanks and prepared the more splendid toilet she secretly as usual attributed all the kindness to her Lady while all that was like caprice was given to her Lord.

The countenance of Lord Trevallyn brightened on her reappearance as he seemed to contemplate with pride and something approaching to pleasure the beauty raised by him to rank and surrounded with a blaze of diamonds whose value he well knew might purchase a principality.

He presented her with ostentatious politeness to some of his guests who were as yet personally unknown to his beautiful countess and looked around with an haughty air of self congratulation (which the fair object was herself far from sharing) on the universal gaze of astonishment and admiration which her loveliness surpassing even itself at that moment excited.

The sombre silence which reigned at dinner was but little interrupted except by the usual civilities of form required at such a repast, nevertheless Lady Trevallyn who appeared lost in meditation was in no haste to quit the parlour.

Selena indeed had been not only the attentive but the pleased auditor of Mrs. Aston who having been accidentally seated beside her congratulated herself upon having found in her a better hearer than she usually met with. Selena tho' well aware how much Mrs. Aston thus mistook in her aim of obtaining general admiration yet felt herself internally rather inclined to respect the uncommon acquirements thus obtrusively displayed, than to treat them with that contempt which they in general alone could obtain. Naturally diffident she had never been accustomed to introduce her studies into conversation but being now questioned she in a low voice acknowledged her acquaintance with many of Mrs. Aston's favourite authors and listened with that look of flattery which is always irresistibly captivating, to her dissertations and criticisms which she thought ingenious and amusing.

"As you are fond of poetry," said Mrs. Aston, "I will read to you tomorrow, my friend's Proclus's commentary upon the very learned hymn to the Gossamer by Dr Dunce have you seen it?"

Selena confessed her ignorance of both those authors.

"Heavens," exclaimed Mrs. Aston suddenly, heedless of the silence which had reigned around during their whispering dialogue now bursting forth in an audible voice, "Heavens what a pity that a soul formed like yours in the prodigality of Nature should remain yet a stranger to the writings of those great men which as the animated rival of Plato expressed himself *shine forth like the sun with a brightness not subject to diminution ever new and ever the same—the source of mental life vigour and fecundity! Hebe the Goddess of youth presides at their entertainments! They comprehend with the eye of intellect the whole sensible world and by a sublime intention of mind which is never warp'd or turned aside they fill all things by the power of their creative and youthful divinity!*"[49]

The eyes of all were instantly turned upon poor Selena who sinking with confusion regretted at the moment that her curiosity or her politeness had induced her to pay her enthusiastic orator that attention which had thus exposed them both to the ridicule of an assembly so formidable.

Lady Trevallyn roused from her reverie looked at Selena with her own enchanting smile and rising that she might deliver her from her present embarrassment said turning to Mrs. Aston, "So I perceive you and Plato have quite given me up. I shall never be able to read myself I fear into your good opinion."

No sooner had the ladies retired to the drawing room than impatient to escape from the irksome task of forcing a conversation with her uninteresting guests to which she now found it impossible to attend, Lady Trevallyn lost no time in placing them at the card table.

As she herself never played she was now at liberty to indulge her own reflections seated by the side of Selena who perceiving her friend little inclined for conversation had retired to the pianoforte in the adjoining apartment.

Her eyes which incessantly watched the door that lay open between the rooms at length sufficiently announced the entrance of Lord Henry to Selena, who directed by their sudden brilliant expression and the glow with which her features were instantaneously suffused, turned her head and beheld him advancing with the most animated smile of pleasure while in his very step there appeared that delay of satisfied delight with which when actually in the presence of the most beloved object, even tho' surrounded by others the heart full of its own contentment will sometimes seem to pause upon its happiness and to dwell with luxury on the blissful certainty of approaching what it has so long desired so fondly loved.

---

[49] A translation of Proclus's *Commentary on Plato's Timaeus*, which might be taken from Thomas James Matthias's *The Shade of Alexander Pope, on the Banks of the Thames. A Satirical Poem, with Notes. Occasioned Chiefly, but not Wholly, by the Residence of Henry Grattan, Ex-Representative in Parliament for the City of Dublin, at Twickenham, in November, 1798* (1799): "Hebe, the goddess of youth presides at their entertainments. They comprehend with the eye of the intellect the whole sensible world; and by thought and intention of mind, which is never warped or turned aside, they fill all things by a species of creative wisdom and foreknowledge. They have always a youthful divinity; and the power of their understanding shines forth with a brightness not subject to diminution" (59).

The grace of this movement was well remembered and deeply felt by Lady Trevallyn. How often when seated at the most distant part of the crowded assembly room had her eye caught his first glance upon his entrance and directed his gradual progress as the pole star rules the obedient vessel, while her heart which as yet was unsubdued by disappointment and unawed by reluctant vows had watched impatient and doubtful of the coming of him it might then innocently acknowledge the lord of all its wishes, now throbbed with confidence of joy at his appearance, assured that tho' arrested by the impertinence of friends or the coquetry of the beauties whom he passed his destination was unalterably fixed, and for the rest of that evening at least he was her own.

Alas! with what different sensations did she now behold him, no longer the fond object of every hope, but the cruel source of all her anguish, self reproach, shame and bitter regret. She beheld him however and in spite of virtue she was for the moment blest.

Let not the severe moralist condemn the weakness of my Emily till they can recall to mind if ever they have felt the enchantment of reading love in the eye of the object they adore; if they have let them pronounce with sincerity whether it is in the power of any circumstances at the instant to free the soul from its bewitching charm—but if their tranquil breasts are strangers to this enchantment they cannot know the situation in which Lady Trevallyn was then placed, and till then let them forbear to judge.

From the more impassioned gaze of those expressive eyes she nevertheless now turned with a kind of fearful self distrust after the moments of first salutation and while he leaned on the back of Selena's chair and requested her to proceed in the song which he had interrupted, Lady Trevallyn taking no share in the conversation which he attempted to promote sunk into the pensive silence which she had before held.

From this however she was after some time aroused by Clara who approaching with a volume of the Botanical magazine[50] open in her hand asked Lady Trevallyn if the flower she pointed out was not like that of her favourite geranium, adding, "I wanted to compare the leaves and was sure of finding one in your bosom, I really believe this is the first time that ever I saw you without one."

The burning flush of shame which instantly shot over the face of Lady Trevallyn can but poorly be compared to the blushes with which the rose returns the caresses of the amorous sun or the glow with which aurora hails his approach.

Lord Henry too blushed, but it was such a blush of triumph as sits on the cheek and lights with new lustre the eyes of the young and popular candidate when he at length beholds himself raised upon the shoulders of the shouting multitude. Once more he sought to meet her averted eye, while Selena with more uneasiness than curiosity gazed upon a scene which tho' unable entirely to comprehend she had yet too much reason to interpret as most dangerous to her friend.

---

[50]   *The Botanical Magazine; or Flower Garden Displayed* is an illustrated serial that has been continuously published (under various names) since 1787.

But the appearance of the gentlemen now interrupted the embarrassing silence which had succeeded a confusion so evident—a silence which Lord Henry had not attempted to break. Instantly he assumed an air of the utmost carelessness while with the ease of fashion (blended with all that respectful ceremony which he knew was required) he advanced to pay his compliments to Lord Trevallyn with whom he commenced a conversation upon the state of his health and from thence entered into a political discussion which did not terminate until the supper tables were brought: he would then have taken his leave but being invited by Lord Trevallyn to remain he contrived to place himself as it appeared accidentally at the side of his fair cousin.

"You are cold," said he softly as he pressed his hand upon hers for a moment under pretence of saving her trouble by taking from her the spoon with which she was about to help him from the dish before her, "You are cold Emily! but you are in the right not to complain since it is I that must suffer."

At the name of Emily thus pronounced the tears of sudden and tenderest remembrances rushed to her eyes and Lord Henry fearful lest others should observe what he himself appeared not to notice secretly satisfied with his power, instantly called upon himself the attention of all around by some lively and unexpected remark. He well knew that no instance of delicacy was ever lost upon the heart of Lady Trevallyn and fearfully he marked the mildly penetrating eye of pity with which she was observed by Selena.

Chapter IX

> Oh dio! sparger cosi d'oblio
> L'ardor che un alma ha per gran tempo accesa
> È difficile, è dura è lunga impresa!
> L'augellin dall visco uscito
> Sente il visco fra le piume
> Sento i lacci del costume
> Una Languida Virtu
>
> Metastasio[51]

It was not Lord Trevallyn's custom to appear at breakfast. He nevertheless entered the drawing room the following morning on his return from the pump room while the ladies were at breakfast and after having paid his compliments in the most

---

[51] Valeria in Pietro Metastasio's *Romolo ed Ersilia* (1765), 3.5.5–8, 13–16: "Oh God! To scatter into oblivion / The ardor that my soul for so long has set on fire / Is a difficult, hard, and lengthy endeavor! / The little bird escaped from the slimy snare / Feels the slime between its feathers / I feel the ties of my dress / Like a feeble virtue." The epigraph elides lines 9–12: "Un istante al cor talora / Basta sol per farsi amante; / Ma non basta un solo istante / Per uscir di servitù": "Sometimes an instant is all the heart / Needs to fall in love; / But an instant only is not enough / To escape the slavery" (Lucia Greene translation).

solemn voice to Selena and her sister he turned to his lady and enquired whether she had ordered her carriage.

Lady Trevallyn replied in the negative, saying she had not as yet thought of going out.

"There is one point Lady Trevallyn," resumed he with an accent of the most grave authority, "to which I must desire your attention and I hope you will remember during our stay in this town that I highly disapprove of the very indecent custom which I am told prevails here tolerating the women of such high situation in life as yours at present is to assume so far the manners of the meanest of the people as to be seen to jostle with them in the public streets. For my part I declare that I could never after look without disgust upon a female of a particular rank who could thus indelicately expose herself to come in contact with those vile and filthy things who there obtrude themselves upon our sight and that by so doing she must degrade herself irretrieveably in my opinion."

Lady Trevallyn was going to assure him of her readiness to comply in this respect, with his desire but profoundly satisfied with the impressive period which he had utter'd he once more bowed to Selena and looking round with an air of sullen dignity slowly quitted the room.

Lady Trevallyn immediately turned the conversation without appearing to notice the smile which in spite of all the gravity around her and her own efforts half dimpled the lips of Clara and rising to open her writing desk said to Selena, "I must shew you that sketch of Angela's which I mentioned to you and see whether you will not acknowledge the resemblance, allowing something for the flattery always to be expected from the pencil."

"Oh yes, there is no mistaking that figure," cried Clara as she looked over Selena's shoulder to whom Lady Trevallyn had presented the torn paper.

"And the face," continued Selena, "is also extremely like, and yet I almost wonder you knew it instantly. I am sure I should not recognize my own portrait if I were to see it unexpectedly."

"Oh no!," answered Lady Trevallyn, "it was not the resemblance which at first struck me—but I could not doubt that white hat and blue feathers with the blue scarf trimmed with lace were intended for mine, besides I so well recollect the moment this represents and the spot which is here so exactly drawn."

"May I ask you what the view is taken from?"

"Why the scene is Kensington gardens;"

"And what do you look down upon, with such a sweet kind expression—I wish it had not been torn off so unluckily just there," cried Clara still attentively gazing upon the beautiful drawing.

"Is it a kind expression?" said Lady Trevallyn deeply blushing, "I suppose it was at the geranium which you see in the hand but I was in the very act of giving it away at the moment Angela must have seen me, as you would have discovered had you seen the other figure which I dare say she tore off from not being able to do it so well from memory as mine with which she was so much better acquainted. I suppose the poor thing was standing by me and perhaps felt hurt I would not acknowledge her,

I am sure it was most unintentionally. But you must do me a favour," added she in a hurried voice of encreasing confusion, "and never mention that geranium again at least before any body but ourselves for *thereby hangs a tale*."[52]

"And must not we hear it?" demanded Clara timidly.

"No, no," interrupted Selena hastily, "we will not speak or think of it any more," tho' in saying this she perhaps rather expressed her wishes than her expectations. Indeed assured as she was that this tale related in some way to Lord Henry she felt not disposed to dwell upon a topick painful to herself and certainly affording a dangerous indulgence to her friend, who she could not help seeing scarcely ever talked with interest upon any subject which did not bear some relation to the secret poison the nature of which is to diffuse itself into every thought.

"Nay," said Lady Trevallyn, "there is nothing to be ashamed of in the matter, but it is a long story and worth repeating only to shew you particularly when I wish not to have my geranium alluded to. I must get my work however before I begin my history," and as she spoke she handed to each her work basket.

Nor did she thus furnish their eyes with employment entirely perhaps without design, since hers had already more than once fallen with confusion beneath the glance of her partial indeed, but yet quick sighted friend.

"I must begin then," said Lady Trevallyn, "by telling you that my sister-in-law Mrs. Montrose is wonderfully fond of going out with me ever since I was married."

"There is nothing very wonderful in her being fond of that I should imagine," said Selena with a smile.

"You would perhaps think otherwise dear Selena if you knew what pains it has often cost her to avoid taking me out with her while I was a girl—but that is not much to the purpose. I was going to say that one night last spring she had asked me for a place in our box at the opera and ...."

"Pray," interrupted Clara somewhat abruptly, "had Lord Henry a place in your box last year?"

"No indeed," answered Lady Trevallyn colouring with some surprise at this sudden demand for which she was so little prepared, "Lord Trevallyn never shared his box even before he was married."

"I beg your pardon dear Lady Trevallyn," said Clara now conscious of her apparent rudeness, "but when you mentioned the opera I could not help thinking how excessively anxious Lady Harriet is to have Lord Henry subscribe to her box only she said ...."

"Well but never mind Lady Harriet now," said Selena observing the air of uneasiness with which Lady Trevallyn listened and unwilling to encrease her dislike of her sister-in-law, "Dear Clara what is that remark to the purpose?"

"Why Clara's question was rather apropos too, just then," continued Lady Trevallyn with a little embarrassment, "for tho' he had no *right* to a place in our box he certainly was there the night to which I alluded and was sitting between

---

[52]   Jacques in Shakespeare's *As You Like It* (1599), 2.7.28.

me and Mrs. Montrose when she bent across him to ask me had I been at any of the nursery gardens on the Kings road that year, as she knew I was always so remarkably fond of flowers; Upon my answering that I had not she begged me to take her there the next morning. I pleaded engagement not being particularly anxious to have the pleasure of her company if I did go; besides I felt it looked so like making an appointment with Lord Henry. But my excuse did not save me for she named another and another day till I was obliged to give up, and indeed I might have known from the first that she some how always carries her point in the end—at least I know she has the art to make me for ever do what I most dislike— accordingly I called for her and on our way to Chelsea Lord Henry overtook us and rode by the side of the carriage till we came to Shepherd's garden where we alighted.

"A sickly looking woman decently dressed followed us as we entered the shop and enquired concerning her son in a voice of modest distress which attracted my attention tho' it gained her none from the men who were entirely engrossed by their expectations of receiving our orders. She looked so little able to stand that I could not help repeating her question to the man who stood waiting my directions; he then turned to her impatiently saying 'Good woman, pray do not crowd the shop your son has not been at work here these two days.' I own I felt greatly interested for her when I saw her turn away with a look of subdued anguish that I think has always the most powerful claim upon pity. I was going to ask something about her when Lord Henry darted forward to assist her without which she would have fallen to the ground—for just as she passed the step of the door she staggered and sunk quite senseless in his arms, as he eagerly flew to assist her."

"How pretty that was of Lord Henry!" said Clara.

"Oh it was so like himself!," cried Lady Trevallyn with a glowing cheek and glistning eye while she felt this second interruption of Clara's fully atone for the last however painful it had been to her feelings.

"Mrs. Montrose however did not think as you do," continued she, "for she screamed out 'My God what is he about! Oh Lord Henry for heaven's sake do not bring her in here, I shall die if I see a person in convulsions.' Lord Henry indeed did not seem to mind this terrible threat for in spite of it he lifted in the poor fainting woman and desired the man to bring her some water instantly. I gave him my salts and he held them to her himself, bathing her temples with a look of the most solicitous compassion. In a few moments she recovered her senses and after a violent burst of tears began to overwhelm us with excuses and acknowledgments. Lord Henry interrupted her by desiring to know where she lived and then turning to me proposed that I should let the carriage take her home. I confess I was ashamed to refuse, nor could I tell him that I knew Lord Trevallyn would be displeased at such a use being made of his carriage but after a moment's hesitation I desired him to send one of the footmen for a hackney coach and took that opportunity to put a trifle into the poor woman's hand with my direction begging of her to let me know how I could be of use to her or her son.

"She wept bitterly and was unable to speak, but Shepherd himself who was now standing by told us that her son a fine young man and the best workman he had ever had was her sole support—that she was but just recovered from a fever and that he was afraid some ill must have happened to the young man as it seems he had left home without saying a word either to his mother or him who had been so long his employer. The coach was soon got and I desired the servant to go home with her that I might know where to find her. Upon looking round then for Mrs. Montrose I perceived that she had hurried away from a scene which she thought so little amusing and hearing that she was gone to the green house we followed her thither thro' the gardens which never look so beautiful I think as just at that time of year when one has been so long shut up in town and every thing in the country is so sweet and so fresh.

"The first thing that struck Lord Henry's eyes as we entered the green house was a beautiful plant of the very geranium with which you are now so well acquainted tho' I then saw it for the first time when he pointed it out to me and indeed never before had I seen or smelt a flower so charming. I applied directly to the man who attended us and heard that Mrs. Montrose had just bought it, that it was a very expensive plant and the only one they had been able yet to rear. I felt really disappointed and was not deterred by delicacy from expressing my regret for I know Mrs. Montrose was not the least likely to offer to yield up her prior claim for my gratification; in fact she only replied with a sneer 'Aye Emily, you lost that by staying behind you see to flirt, or by your charity if you please, I am very glad that poor wretch had the fit just then, or you might have come in here first and seized upon my beautiful flower that is worth all the rest of the green house.' While she was speaking Lord Henry with a smile broke off a small but blossoming branch, which I was rather ashamed to receive from him as Mrs. Montrose much displeased desired the man to take it out of the way directly and to be sure to send it to her that very evening.

"I thought of the geranium more than once that day and the next, for its very peculiar fragrance as I kept the little branch in my bosom perpetually reminded me of the disappointment which I childishly regretted. But I was sitting alone in my dressing room after dinner the following evening when Fanny entered with the very plant as I believed in her hand. 'Did that come from Mrs. Montrose?' exclaimed I with astonishment. 'No my Lady,' answered Fanny, 'but the porter called me down just now to a poor woman in the hall who wished to speak to my Lady's own woman and gave me this flowerpot and a note' which note she produced from her pocket as soon as she had laid down her lovely burden on my table. It was only a few lines signed Margaret Williams thanking me for my goodness to her on the day before and saying that having heard from Shepherd that I expressed a wish for the plant she begged I would not refuse to accept one which her son had himself rear'd and which she was so fortunate as to be able to send me. You may be certain I read this with some doubt, however I again examined the geranium and was but the more convinced that it was the very individual plant which I had envied to Mrs. Montrose. But to put the matter beyond all dispute

I took from my bosom the branch and found it exactly fitted to that part of the stem from whence Lord Henry's hand had broken it. The woman was gone but I resolved to send Fanny to her the next day and in the mean time enjoyed the delicious fragrance of the plant which remained on my writing table and perfumed my whole apartment.

"I accordingly sent Fanny the next morning herself to Chelsea in a hackney coach with directions to bring Mrs. Williams to see me, but she returned with a long story the substance of which was that Lord Henry was the best and most charitable of men, that the people where Mrs. Williams lodged could talk of nothing but his praises and indeed I think that Fanny had caught the infection for she told me in such an enthusiastic manner of his goodness to poor Mrs. Williams that he had given her money to set off in the stage to follow her son who it seems wrote to her from Chatham that he had been made drunk and in that state enlisted by a recruiting party whom he unfortunately met with on his return from work. Lord Henry had paid her lodging and promised to procure immediately her son's discharge. All this and a great deal more I heard from Fanny but not a syllable of my geranium which indeed she had totally forgotten.

"On Saturday evening Mrs. Montrose was to be again in our box. As I was dressing I perceived on the table the little branch still fresh in the glass where I had left it to be revived by water. Certain that it would introduce the subject which I knew I never should have courage to do myself however curious I might be, I put it into my bosom and accordingly the first thing that Mrs. Montrose said as I entered the box [was] 'Oh I see you have got my poor branch still. How do you think Shepherd has served me after all, like a blockhead as he is, gave my nice geranium to some common fellow that never came near me and has stolen it—absolutely stolen it! Shepherd declares he knows not where upon earth to find him out—but it was excessively impertinent of Shepherd. I shall take care never to deal with him again and I beg it as a favour Emily if you will not either. It was quite lucky I had not paid him for the plant or I dare say he would have cheated me of that too.' I was going to confess having received the stolen goods when something prevented me."

"What was that?" asked Clara while Selena's speaking eye made the same enquiry.

"Why to confess the truth," resumed Lady Trevallyn after a little pause, "I saw it could not be done without betraying to my sister and of consequence to the whole town the part I was sure Lord Henry had in the business. He at the moment was at my side standing behind her chair. I met his eyes for an instant and he smiled with an archness that overpowered all my courage while he put his hands together with an air of supplication. I turned from him and looked towards the stage but worlds could not have induced me at that moment to say a word. I never acknowledged to him that I had any suspicion from whom my geranium came but as he handed me that night to the carriage he begged I would return him the little branch adding 'it *is* very sweet indeed, I am not surprised that Mrs. Montrose is so much provoked at its being lost. I will do all in my power to get her another and have no doubt I shall succeed.'"

"I suppose," said Clara, "that this was to quiet your conscience."

"I am sure it was," answered Lady Trevallyn, "and in fact a few nights after this Mrs. Montrose came up to me with high exultation to tell me that Lord Henry had been so exceedingly polite and obliging as to send her a charming little plant of the very geranium we had both so much coveted, dwelling with considerable triumph upon the trouble which he must have taken to find for her what was so very hard to be procured."

"I hope hers did not flourish as well as yours has done at least," cried Clara.

"The wish I must say Clara is good natured," observed Selena.

"It is one however which I can gratify," answered Lady Trevallyn smiling, "for her plant died in a few weeks and mine has been multiplied with wonderful success. All the cuttings we have taken from it were alive and spreading delightfully when I left Esselberrie. The original plant was our travelling companion as it is the most hardy and I like the smell so much I could not leave them all behind."

Selena sighed but was silent, after a short pause Clara enquired whether she had ever heard any more of Mrs. Williams to which Lady Trevallyn replied that she had been told by Lord Henry that he had got the young man discharged and that Shepherd had not only consented to take him again but assured him of a higher salary so that when they returned to town the poor mother was enabled to live a little more comfortably.

"Fanny," continued she, "went to visit her and found her happy with her son and full of gratitude to her kind benefactor."

"And did you thank her for the geranium?" asked Clara somewhat slyly.

"No," answered Lady Trevallyn, "but I thought myself bound to make her some return for my valuable present and when Fanny in my name thanked her for it she was quite silent making her no sort of answer which gave me a higher opinion of her sincerity than it did Fanny (who had no suspicion of the truth) of her politeness."

Their conversation was here interrupted by the very person whom it had so much concerned and Mrs. Aston entering the room almost at the same moment Selena, who felt something of her friend Mrs. Vallard's disliking to look upon Lord Henry immediately retired to her own apartment.

Clara soon followed her thither protesting that she had been obliged to make her escape while Mrs. Aston went in search of a dictionary in order to convince her that she had made use of a word improperly.

"Probably she was right," observed Selena.

"Not a doubt of it my dear," answered Clara, "but it was in vain for me to protest myself perfectly satisfied. 'Never take any thing for granted my good friend that is my maxim' she insisted and off she went to hunt for a dictionary among her books in the next room."

"Is Lord Henry gone?" asked Selena.

"Oh no! but he was talking to Lady Trevallyn so I had all the benefit of Mrs. Aston's instructions to myself—but I really could bear it no longer!"

"Do you recollect what Solomon says?" interrupted Selena smiling.

"Oh I know you would say in your wise voice *A fool hateth instruction*[53] but dear Selena what upon earth did it signify whether I said the servant *took* or *brought* the book to Ball's library?"

"Nothing except that one is right and the other wrong and it is always better to confound as little as possible words not quite synonymous, but I see you meditate making your escape from me as you did from Mrs. Aston if I go on with my lecture, so come let us play some of poor Edwin's music to put you into proper harmony."

The sisters remained together till some time after four o'clock, and as the sky was unusually heavy they were then obliged to desist from their occupations for want of light.

Selena left Clara at the harp saying that she would go to the drawing room in order to ring the bell for candles. Upon her entrance she was a little startled to see Lord Henry in the same spot in which she had some hours before left him.

He had a book in his hand which he threw down on the table as Selena approached and observing that it was growing too dark to read took his leave, an observation which indeed he might have made some time before tho' most probably it had been still longer deferred had not the appearance of Selena reminded him that it was time to retire.

Chapter X

> Who knows the joys of friendship?
> The trust, security and mutual tenderness
> The double joys where each is glad for both
> Friendship our only wealth! our best retreat and strength!
> Secure against ill fortune and the world.
>   Rowe[54]

Lord Trevallyn had more than once hinted to his lady since her arrival at Bath that it was expected she should make her public appearance at the rooms, dwelling with the ostentation of condescending affability upon the necessity of her not seeming to scorn the mixt society which as he said must unavoidably be then tolerated.

"I have no doubt," he continually repeated, "that Lady Trevallyn's own dignity and sense of delicacy will prevent her from forming any lasting acquaintances at which she must hereafter blush."

Mrs. Aston whose fondness for study was perpetually at variance and on all opportunities conquered by her extreme desire of admiration warmly seconded the opinion that this appearance in public was necessary.

---

[53]   Proverbs 1:7 (KJV): "fools despise wisdom and instruction."

[54]   Lavinia in Nicholas Rowe's *The Fair Penitent* (1703), 4.1.331–5 (line 334 should read "Friendship, the Wealth, the last Retreat and Strength").

Lady Trevallyn who had privately consulted with Selena excused herself from complying with an advice she both disliked and dreaded, by alleging that ceremony would not permit her to leave her guests, explaining at the same time with Selena's permission to Lord Trevallyn in confidence the delicate circumstances in which her young friend stood which rendered it highly improper for her to appear in public, while the extreme youth of Clara was a sufficient objection to her being yet as it is called taken out.

Lord Trevallyn whose pride was never so highly gratified as when he heard the world bear testimony to the superior beauty of his countess, her jewels and her equipage now for the first time expressed his discontent at her having without his permission burdened herself with guests, who imposed upon her a restraint so unreasonable and disagreeable.

After a day or two of unusual sullenness he then declared that not finding the Bath waters agree with him he was resolved to return to town in a week and desired Lady Trevallyn to write that the house might be prepared for their reception.

In the mean time he passed his mornings with his constant attendant Mr. Guise either airing upon the downs, at the pump room or in the library—and every day a large and sumptuous dinner assembled at his table in turns all that Bath could boast of rank and fortune.

Lord Henry was a constant guest, but this was not all; Selena with grief and uneasiness beheld that no morning passed without his visit, that he was always admitted and that when able to sit out all others as was too generally the case, the approach of darkness alone reminded him that it was time to go home and dress that he might again be at the side of his fair cousin at dinner.

Selena occupied as she was by her own singular situation and uncommon present anxiety, felt all that tender solicitude for her friend which Mrs. Vallard had formerly expressed. Witness as she now found herself of a conduct which she could not help considering as dangerously imprudent and highly reprehensible, she thought it incumbent upon her to repay the confidence which Lady Trevallyn had formerly conferred upon her by candidly confessing her fears lest she should suffer not only in the opinion of the world but her own peace by thus constantly allowing the visits of Lord Henry.

Yet as often as she entered her presence for that purpose or endeavoured when tete-a-tete to lead their conversation to this point her heart shrunk from the delicate the painful task and she dreaded almost equally wounding the gentle feeling disposition of her friend and the risk which she was sensible she herself incurred of thus diminishing the partial fondness with which she was now regarded.

But no sooner did the well known knock kindle the cheeks and agitate even to view the lovely bosom of Lady Trevallyn then Selena with self reproach and that strong sense of courage inspired by conscious rectitude firmly resolved to address her friend the moment of his departure. Nevertheless all this courage seemed to die within her when once more alone with the unhappy Emily she plainly perceived the oppression of her spirits and the uneasiness with which she now carefully shunned all conversation relative to Lord Henry—the caution with which she even avoided alluding to any circumstance however indifferent in which his name was to be mentioned, and the eagerness she shewed to speak on Selena's own interesting affairs as a kind refuge from the subject which she appeared to dread.

Ashamed of a weakness to which she was determined no longer to yield Selena at length left her room purposely to seek Lady Trevallyn, having requested Clara not to interrupt their conversations. She entered the drawing room prepared to meet Lord Henry as it was an hour which he was accustomed to chuse knowing that the sisters were then usually occupied in their own apartment. He appeared to have been reading but stopped on Selena's entrance, and as Lady Trevallyn did not desire him to proceed there was a silence of some minutes after his first salutation. Selena took her seat and drew from her basket her work.

Lord Henry hemmed, looked at his watch rose struck a few notes on the pianoforte then walked to the window in order to introduce some observation upon the weather, again sat down, attempted a forced conversation and at length after asking the ladies if they were going out took his leave. The moment the door was shut Selena out of breath with agitation and sick with reluctant dread of the task which she had imposed upon herself but decidedly resolved not again to sink beneath her selfish apprehensions, threw aside her work and rising to embrace Lady Trevallyn would have spoken but suddenly quite overpowered burst into tears.

"What is the matter my love," said her friend as she kissed her head while she felt her tears upon her bosom, trembling at the same time with a secret consciousness of the explanation she feared would follow. "I heard the post-man knock; you have got letters I am sure; what accounts have you heard from Sidney?"

"No dear Lady Trevallyn," answered she struggling with her emotions, "I thought not of myself at that moment tho' I have indeed got letters—and may have much to think of …."

"But what Selena?" interrupted she with more impatience from fear than curiosity, "pray say something till you satisfy me with respect to what you have heard. Is Dallamore in London?"

"I will give you the letters," said Selena drawing them from her pocket, "but you think me unworthy of your friendship if you will not allow me to tell you all my thoughts even when I dare to think my dearest, dearest Lady Trevallyn can act wrong."

Lady Trevallyn pressed her hand in silence as she extented hers to receive the offered papers. She attempted not however to open them but resting her head upon the table covered her face as she leaned it upon her arms.

"I am sure," continued Selena timidly, "I am sure you know what I mean, and I am also quite sure that your own judgment is on my side, if you will only listen to it, and what pleasure is there upon earth (supposing this to be a pleasure) which can be worth purchasing by turning a deaf ear to conscience and to reason."

"What can I do?" whispered Lady Trevallyn deeply sighing but without raising her head.

"Do as you did formerly," answered Selena hastily, "you did not admit his visits in London and why here?"

"Oh that was different!" cried she lifting up her glowing face tho' she still averted it from the eye of her friend, "the orders were there general with no exceptions. Here every one is let in and you would not have me expose myself, to the servants by this singular exclusion."

"Well then," said Selena, "let us drive out every morning. We know the hour of his visits."

"I will do whatever you wish me," answered she after a while, "But that will be a cruel penance and I really do not see the necessity of it. What is it you fear dear Selena?"

"Every thing," exclaimed she warmly. "The ill natured world, a being whom you see in much too partial a light, the loss of Lord Trevallyn's esteem but above all yourself, the peace of your own heart which I see suffers already from this indiscreet renewal of an intimacy which you ought to avoid above every danger which can threaten you."

"You are mistaken my love," interrupted Lady Trevallyn, as she wiped the tears from her eyes, "Believe me you are mistaken, it is his image not himself that is terrible to my peace. When absent he is a thousand times more powerful over my heart than when he is before my eyes. I feel it is only by continually being in his society as a common acquaintance that I can by degrees forget what he has been so long, what but for this I am assured he would ever be to my heart. I see you do not believe me—but you cannot understand me, I cannot express myself so as to convince you as I know I might—but read that passage which I have marked there, it was only this morning that it struck me so exactly what I myself feel."

As she spoke she pointed to a page in La nouvelle Heloise which as Selena had observed Lord Henry had laid upon the table at her entrance and while Selena now softly read these lines Lady Trevallyn leaning over her shoulder followed her with her eyes—"Si l'on n'est pas maitre de ses sentimens au moins on l'est de sa conduite. Sans doute je demanderais au ciel un coeur plus tranquille, mais puissai je á mon dernier jour offrir au souveraine juge une vie aussi peu criminelle que celle que j'ai passe cet hiver! En verite je ne me reprochais rien aupres du seul homme qui peuvoit me rendre capable—il n'en est plus de meme depuis qu'il est parti—en m'accoutuemant á penser á lui dans son absence J'y a pense a tous les instans du jour & je trouve son image plus dangereuse que sa personne."[55]

---

[55]   Jean-Jacques Rousseau, *Julie, ou La Nouvelle Héloïse* (1761), Part 6, Lettre II: "If one cannot control one's feelings, at least one can control one's conduct. Without doubt I would ask the heavens for a more peaceful heart, but may I on my last day offer the supreme judge a life as little criminal as I passed last winter. In truth I reproach myself with nothing concerning the only man who could make me feel guilt. It is not the same since he left: accustomed to thinking of him in his absence, I think of him every moment of the day and I find his image more dangerous than his person."

"So much dear Selena," resumed she as she closed the book, "for what concerns my own peace—my peace did I say! Alas! I have but little terms to keep with peace which has so long ago for ever quarreled with and abandoned me."

"Oh do not say so dearest Lady Trevallyn. Seek for it in virtue and in yourself and there you will assuredly find it!"

"Well let me try this one experiment to regain it," cried she with a faint smile, "since I have sought so many others in vain."

"But in the mean time consider what a risk!"

"Not of my virtue again," interrupted Lady Trevallyn hastily, "you cannot think that at least in danger."

"No," said Selena, "but tho' I hate to quote an author I never read I know that your own favourite Rousseau has somewhere said 'Les apparences memes sont au nombre des vertus d'une femme verteuse.'"[56]

"It is very true Selena and you know how I avoid the world for that very reason, and should do so entirely but for that unfortunate passion which Lord Trevallyn has to have me seen or known as he calls it."

"Lord Trevallyn always seems to place in you the most unlimited confidence," replied Selena, "and I am sure you are too generous to repay it by giving him uneasiness."

"I hope I am," answered she coldly, "but allow me now to satisfy myself and read your letters. I wonder at my own forbearance."

"You are not however offended with me," said Selena extending her hand.

"With you Selena!" cried she warmly as she tenderly embraced her, "Oh no! That is impossible! Certainly I could not be so ungrateful as to repay in such a manner your affectionate friendship. Be my monitor, my guardian ever, speak to me with confidence unbounded and if ever you think me reserved attribute it not to my want of love or gratitude towards my dearest, my best friend."

Once more she wiped her eyes as she unfolded the letters but Selena's tears continued to flow while she hung over her again perusing with her the papers which she had put into her hands. The letter which first presented itself was from Sidney and contained the following intelligence.

> "My first care Selena on my arrival in town after setting down Edwin at his
> uncle's was to hasten to Upper Brook street that I might be myself the bearer
> of your letter to your brother. He was not at home but upon enquiring for Lady

---

[56]   Selena seems to be adapting the following famous quotation from *Julie, ou La Nouvelle Héloise* (1761) Part 12, Lettre XVIII—"Une femme vertueuse ne doit pas seulement mériter l'estime de son mari, mais l'obtenir; s'il la blâme, elle est blâmable; et, fût-elle innocente, elle a tort sitôt qu'elle est soupçonnée: car les apparences mêmes sont au nombre de ses devoirs" ("A virtuous woman must not only earn the respect of her husband, but maintain it; if she is at fault, it is reprehensible, but if innocent, she is at fault as soon as she is suspected, for appearances themselves are among her duties")—when she warns Lady Trevallyn that "appearances themselves are among the virtues of a virtuous woman."

Harriet I was immediately admitted to the drawing room where I found her completely engaged in the most delightful confusion formed by two or three young men of fashion assisting her to puzzle a number of tradesmen who had so scattered the room with muslins and various other articles of whose use I could form no guess but it was with some difficulty I could make my way up to her Ladyship and the fire. I will not however trouble you with the particulars of my reception because I confess it did not please me, but finding that Dallamore had not yet called there and that I was not likely to get any information concerning him I was glad to escape from the scene of noisy stupidity which appeared to reign there in an unusual degree I suppose because I was not then in the happiest disposition to be amused.

"You will no doubt hear from your brother in consequence of the letter which I left for him with the servant, but if I have any discernment I imagine that Lady Harriet is too much piqued by your desertion to Lady Trevallyn to write herself.

"I have ever perhaps usurped too much the privilege of the friendship you allow me to boast; bear with me then when I once more presume to offer you my advice, tho' conscious it will oppose your inclination. Suffer me to represent that your brother's house situated as you are, is your best asylum, and do not let Lady Harriet's coldness, or your own excessive delicacy deprive you of the protection which in the eyes of the world is the most eligible.

"It is unnecessary after this to say that of Dallamore I have heard nothing.

"Upon my enquiring for him at his lodgings Le Roi looked confounded, having expected hourly to see him arrive in company with me. As soon as I communicated to the faithful fellow all I knew of his master he shook his head and expressed in a few simple words such sincere interest in your cause that from that moment my heart numbered him among its friends. He accompanied me immediately to the Admiralty office where all the intelligence we could gain was that the Greyhound was under orders for a cruise in the channel. Le Roi then consulted me as to the expediency of his going to meet his Master who had declared his intention of quitting Captain Modely at Spithead. But I thought it most prudent that he should not be out of the way and set out myself without delay for Portsmouth desiring him to watch at my lodgings and have an express to send after me should any letter arrive there from Dallamore. At Portsmouth I received as little satisfaction as in town, except the certainty that the Greyhound had not yet arrived there and as the winds of late could not have prevented this I confess I much fear that Captain Modely out of a frolick (which I know is in his own style) has engaged Dallamore to accompany him on his cruise.

"I am now on my return to town and in a day or two hope to have some more certain intelligence to communicate to you at least concerning the Greyhound. I happen to know one of Modely's lieutenants who is engaged to a very interesting orphan now living with his family about ten miles from town. He takes every opportunity I am assured of letting them know his destination and even if he has not been able to write since they left Waterford I can at least be able to learn from them what were Modely's intentions or rather orders.

"The little information which I have to impart can I fear scarcely now authorise me to avail myself thus of the permission you gave me at parting. But after this impatience to profit by it for the first time you need not be apprehensive that I shall hereafter trespass. I will confine myself to the one subject so important to us both and oh dear Selena never deprive me of a name I so much value till you have new cause to judge me unworthy of so high a title as

Your faithful friend,

Sidney Dallamore

"P.S. I obey Dallamore's desire in sending to you the enclosed order on the bank. I am sure you will do him the justice to believe that he would at least wish to save you all inconvenience of such a nature and as long as you consider yourself as his wife you can have no scruple to command what is your own."

"Excellent Sidney! Incomparable generous friend!" exclaimed Lady Trevallyn, "Oh Selena he only deserves you. Why are you not his?"

Agitated by a thousand contending emotions Selena laid her soft fingers gently upon the lips of her friend and for a moment hid her face upon her bosom.

Lady Trevallyn felt the delicate reproof and pressed her to her heart in silence.

Selena at length raising her head said with a forced smile, "Come will you not read Robert's letter—that other is from Mr. Turner, Clara's guardian."

"I hope at least they are not unfavourable to my interests," said Lady Trevallyn, "and that you will not desert me in spite of Sidney's advice, which is the only part of his letter I cannot admire."

"Read them," answered Selena gratefully, "and give me your real opinion what I should do, you cannot have a doubt which way my inclination leads when your kindness is opposed to Lady Harriet's unsisterly reluctance to receive us."

"Well let me hear what they say," cried Lady Trevallyn as she opened Robert's letter which was as follows.

"My dear Selena,

"I must say you write kinder than you act towards me or you would never have suffered Harriet to come to town alone, and prefer the company of a stranger; at least one comparatively so, to that of your sister. She feels a good deal hurt at this preference and is so fearful of your not finding yourself comfortable with her that you must not be surprised if she does not herself write to renew her invitation to you. I hope however that this little misunderstanding will be completely done away when you meet and that you will take up your abode with us till something is settled. Dallamore's conduct is infamous and proves him either a fool or a villain. Whichever that may be I have every reason to regret you have any thing to say to him, but the more vexatious your situation is the greater is the necessity of your acting with the utmost circumspection. I am glad Clara is with you but wish we were all together. I have written as you desire to Mr. Turner with regard to her allowance. Sidney tells me that he has Dallamore's orders to supply you with money. I am glad he had at least so much consideration.

Your affectionate brother

Robert Miltern"

Lady Trevallyn observed too plainly the keeness with which Selena already felt the evident coldness of this letter to suffer her to make any reflection upon it, she returned it therefore in silence, but her soft eyes sufficiently explained the sympathy with which she had marked the indifference of a brother so tenderly loved.

"Oh," cried Selena bursting afresh into tears, "you must not judge of Robert from that letter—it is not his—how unlike, how very unlike his own generous affectionate heart."

"He is under influence my love," answered Lady Trevallyn, "and you cannot be surprised at that. I fear he will but too soon discover how unworthy of his heart and judgment has been their choice, and your brother will then be restored to you."

"Oh never, never, at that price," exclaimed Selena warmly, "rather may I be completely estranged from his affections if there must be so cruel an alternative!"

"But surely," resumed Lady Trevallyn, "you do not consider yourself bound to comply with such an invitation as that, at my expence."

"I hardly know what I ought to do," answered Selena, "Lady Harriet certainly wishes not to have me as her guest, that is very plain, but see what Mr. Turner says. Read this very extraordinary answer to the letter which I told you Clara wrote, it is addressed to her, but you will see it all at me."

Lady Trevallyn read aloud as follows.

> "Dear Miss Miltern,
>
> "I cannot but say I am much surprised at the extraordinary step taken by your sister, and sorry that in this instance she should have had so much influence over my ward—two such young ladies travelling about the world under the protection of two young gentlemen (as I am informed has been the case) wears the appearance I confess not the most desirable for their reputation. My niece writes me word that your sister has chosen to take up her residence with the young Countess of Trevallyn, but I hope you will not think I usurp too much of the authority of a guardian if I declare my entire disapprobation of your remaining any where except in your brother's house or under the care of a respectable lady of character accustomed to superintend the education and conduct of young persons in your situation. Such a one as my niece tells me she can point out. I shall be glad to receive your acquiescence in this opinion and shall then settle an allowance suitable to your fortune. I am detained here at present by an unfortunate fit of the gout otherwise I should have joined you at Bath—the charge committed to me by my late friend rendering me extremely anxious for your welfare.
>
> I remain etc.
>
> Edward Turner"

Lady Trevallyn's comments on the letter of this affectionate guardian were interrupted by the sudden entrance of a gentleman whose tall and strikingly fine figure bore at once the stamp of fashionable confidence and haughty impertinence.

He advanced carelessly to Lady Trevallyn exclaiming, "So Emily, how do you do? how long have you been at Bath?" and coldly touched her cheek while at the same moment he fixed the assured eye of insolent curiosity upon Selena.

Lady Trevallyn who had risen to receive him evidently with more surprise than pleasure having returned his first cold salutation and enquired for Mrs. Montrose now presented him to Selena as her brother; she then requested to know what business could have brought him to Bath a place which she had so often heard him declare he detested.

"Oh I shall not stay long here I promise you but Louverney persuaded me to come with him and give him my opinion of a damned fine hunter that he heard was to be sold here. Curse the fellow we were just one hour too late! A rascal of a groom belonging to Lord Dallamore paid two hundred for it this very morning and tho' we offered him ten guineas for his bargain the blackguard scoundrel would not let us have it, yet he owns he does not know where the devil his master is or where he shall see him, notwithstanding he is obliged to keep his horses in hunting order the whole season, not knowing the day he may write for them. Did you ever hear such a cursed fool as that Dallamore is? And what do you think was the last good thing I heard of him?"

Lady Trevallyn dreading lest Selena should now hear her own story told in no very pleasant manner endeavoured to change the conversation by interrupting him to ask where he had left Mrs. Montrose.

"Why at Rose park to be sure, where would you have her? And you must come and see us too I forgot to tell you that."

"Is that a settled point?" said Lady Trevallyn smiling somewhat incredulously.

"Fixed as fate for your Jove has nodded his assent my little Juno."

"What do you mean?" exclaimed Lady Trevallyn surprised.

"Why I met his Lordship not ten minutes ago and he has done me the honour to promise to call at Rose park on his way to town. My servant has a letter for you too from Isabella to beg you may come and bring whoever you like as we are to have a gay party at Christmas. Not Lord Henry however I must beg. I hear he lives here constantly now."

Accustomed from her infancy to the imperious tyranny and rude insults of an unfeeling brother, the extreme softness of Lady Trevallyn's nature had perhaps never before been roused to an emotion which so much resembled indignation as that of the present moment.

This earth could not then produce two bosoms more gentle or who less knew the throbbings of resentment than those which Mr. Montrose had thus found the secret at once to agitate, and the deep blush which shot across Selena's face might have very naturally excited in him a suspicion similar to what Lady Harriet had formerly entertained and led him to imagine that Selena at least believed that the visits of Lord Henry were not solely for his fair cousin, had not the eyes of Mr. Montrose been just then too irresistibly engaged in an opposite mirror to suffer him to notice the starting tear or the burning glow which his cruel speech had called forth from his auditors.

"I should be glad," said Lady Trevallyn in a tremulous voice after an instant's silence, "I should be glad if you have really heard any such falsehood that you would tell me who ..."

"Psha Emily," interrupted he rising to stir the fire, "do you expect that I can give you an exact gazette account of all the gossip I have heard in this confounded place with my authorities like the examination of witnesses. All I can tell you is that I have heard of it every where I went. I never interfere with women, not I, that is not my way damn it—only I think any thing of eclat[57] should be avoided, so I beg to be excused having him at Rose park at present that's all, Emily. But who do you think I have asked," added he with a laugh and without waiting for a reply, "those damned fools the Astons, and they have promised to come too, you will never catch the miserly dog refusing free quarters so we are sure of some sport. Louverney has thought of fifty ways of quizzing them already. There he is," cried he starting up as a loud knock announced some impatient visitor, "I desired him to call upon me here."

As he spoke he threw up the sash and began to address his companion as he stood at the door, regardless of Lady Trevallyn who entreated him to shut the window as the air was uncommonly cold and damp.

Lord Louverney the young man thus introduced to Selena under no very favourable auspices now entered hastily presenting a countenance and appearance of a far more conciliating and gracious promise than those of his forerunner. After paying his compliments in a hurried manner to Lady Trevallyn and asking a few "generous questions" which waited for no answer he turned to Mr. Montrose and begged of him not to delay him a moment as he was in the greatest hurry imaginable.

"Oh d--n your hurry!" answered he as he drew on his gloves and settled his neck cloth, his eyes still fixed upon the glass which had indeed engrossed far the greatest share of his attention since he entered the apartment.

At length perceiving that Lord Louverney was already gone he prepared to follow him saying to Lady Trevallyn, "That is {true} Emily what time do you dine as I have promised to feed with you. I hope you have ordered a turbot. I saw a devilish fine one just now," and then without noticing Selena in the least he walked down stairs leaving the door wide open and striking his cane against the banisters as he went, as if ambitious to proclaim his progress towards the hall.

Selena rose in silence to shut the door while Lady Trevallyn gave free course to the tears which she had with difficulty for some time restrained but whether they sprang from the unkind insult which she had just received from one who ought to have been her tenderest protector, or from the secret idea that her present situation was soon to be changed for one she so much disliked and dreaded, is a point which perhaps she herself would have found it not very easy to decide.

---

[57] Eclat: ostentatious display, brilliant show (OED).

Indeed the society of her brother had been for many years so continually productive of disagreeable sensations that she never saw him approach without an emotion of terror, or could for a moment find herself at ease while in his presence.

Before her marriage the vain attentions paid her by Lord Henry had afforded an unfailing subject for his cruel mockery and tho' he affected to condemn the consent she had given to yield her hand to Lord Trevallyn ridiculing the great disproportion of their ages, yet he in fact shared all the little envy which Mrs. Montrose had felt on beholding the magnificence of his sister's establishment which was every way suitable to the vast wealth and high rank to which she had been elevated. No person knew better than Mr. Montrose the advantages of wealth or felt more sensibly the various mortifications and the many uncomfortable privations of domestic luxuries which are necessary to support the constant miserable struggle of endeavouring with a moderate fortune to appear on an equal footing with the wealthiest of families of the wealthiest nation upon earth, with whom alone he could endure to associate in habits of intimacy.

The humblest and saddest day of Emily's life in her own consideration was therefore in the eyes of her brother that of her highest triumph and from the moment in which he presented her hand at the altar to the Earl of Trevallyn he no longer looked upon her as the slighted insignificant Emily whom his selfishness dreaded as a future weight upon his purse but as the young and beautiful Countess with whom his connexion was henceforth to be his proudest boast, whose notice was to bestow the stamp of fashion and whose smile was to be the signal of universal approbation. Artful and interested in his disposition with a very small portion of understanding, he yet possessed all the cunning which was necessary with much apparent carelessness and candour to flatter and ingratiate himself with Lord Trevallyn from whose favour he expected a thousand advantages but was infinitely less solicitous to gain the affection of his sister, trusting to the well known softness over which he had ever ruled with a high hand; and well convinced that she could not resist his advances however disagreeable or forward she might esteem them.

"And is this really Lady Trevallyn's brother!" ejaculated Selena mentally as in one instant she felt the whole of his selfish character and saw insolence and folly render hateful features in themselves singularly beautiful.

Shocked at the reports which he had so grossly repeated she felt more than ever the imprudence of her friend tho' she shared in the vexation and regret with which Lady Trevallyn was at that moment anticipating the meeting of Lord Henry and her brother at dinner, a meeting which it was not now possible to avoid.

The painful meditations which held each silent were in a short time interrupted by the entrance of a servant with the letter of ceremonious invitation from Mrs. Montrose which had been already announced and Lady Trevallyn having read it aloud was warmly expressing her earnest hope of being suffered to decline it, when Selena fearfully and delicately suggested the danger of such a refusal being attributed to a motive by which of all others she should most avoid appearing to be influenced.

Her friend was silent and the return of Lord Trevallyn accompanied by Mr. Guise precluded all farther discussion of a point which he immediately proclaimed was already absolutely decided.

Selena perceiving that the dejected Emily received in silence the views of their promised departure in a few days for Rose park retired to consult with Clara upon what they had now to do, defenceless and deserted as their situation appeared.

Chapter XI

Hast thou brought to light a weakness
I would have kept in darkness from all eyes
Ev'n from myself—or wept in silence o'er it—
My last unconquerable fondness!

Mallet[58]

If the image of Edwin suddenly arose to the palpitating heart of Clara, or if the idea of beholding Sidney again prompted the soft sigh which heaved the bosom of Selena upon the first suggestion that a removal to town was now necessary, the sisters must not therefore be accused of voluntary disguise tho' neither confessed the instantaneous reflection since it was to each almost self unacknowledged.

There were however many difficulties and unpleasant circumstances to oppose their performing this journey thus unattended and to balance this secret and unallowed yet promised pleasure.

Selena especially shrunk with dread from the new scene which was to expose her heart to trials which she felt but too severe, and she knew well that once in London to avoid Sidney or to behold him with indifference were equally impossible. Besides she was by no means satisfied to encounter Lady Harriet and offer herself as an unwelcome guest unwished nay uninvited and Clara while she embraced her even with tears entreated that she would suffer no power to separate them.

Selena assured her that there was but one circumstance and that the most improbable upon earth which should oblige her to forsake her and that nothing but Dallamore's positive commands could alone so influence her.

In the midst of their deliberations Lady Trevallyn flying upstairs with an unusual vivacity of step, softly opened the door and displaying a face all radiant with celestial smiles asked leave to come in.

"Congratulate me dear Selena," cried she, "I have got leave to write my apology and say you are glad that we are not yet to part. Do Clara tell me that you are pleased—half as pleased as I am."

---

[58] Mustapha in David Mallet's *Mustapha* (1739), 3.7.97–100.

Selena's heart could not resist this affectionate call upon it for sympathy of satisfaction, tho' she had more than one cause secretly to diminish her hopes of pleasure at this time in her friend's society and she could not help expressing a fear least her continuing her guest had been aledged as the ostensible reason for refusing an invitation which prudence perhaps declared should have been accepted.

Lady Trevallyn did not deny that she had made use of the obvious apology which thus presented itself for at least delaying a visit in every respect disagreeable—knowing that in conformity to the laws of ceremony she was sure of obtaining Lord Trevallyn's concurrence. He had therefore she said desired her to write immediately to Mrs. Montrose, insisting upon her being prepared still to go to Rose park should a second invitation include her guests.

"You have then gained nothing I fear, My dear Lady Trevallyn," said Selena, "since in three days at farthest I suppose you may have that invitation. There can be scarce a doubt that Mrs. Montrose will not ask your friends when you thus name them after having desired you to bring whoever you liked."

"Oh that was all talk! They know very well I would bring no one and I am sure I can prevent her asking you by describing you both exactly as you are, since there is nothing that Mrs. Montrose less covets to have around her than youth beauty and talent eminently conspicuous in her own sex. So now eloquence assist me while I go draw a faithful portrait of each of my dear girls!"

Notwithstanding that nothing could be more true than this observation of Lady Trevallyn with respect to the general envious disposition of Mrs. Montrose she was yet in the present instance mistaken in the inference which she had drawn from thence. For tho' the company of the two lovely sisters would gladly have been dispensed with by the Mistress of Rose park yet in spite of her little inclination to do so she now invited them to occupy a principal apartment in her crowded house aware that they would also draw off a share of that attention which she desired herself entirely to engross. Nay a greater sacrifice had it even been required would now have been made, to obtain a point on which both she and Mr. Montrose were for once equally determined.

One of the members for Lord Trevallyn's borough had been for some time in a state of health the most precarious. Mr. Montrose had hitherto vainly endeavoured to sound his Lordship's intentions as to the future representation and the most agitating hopes perpetually presented themselves to his fancy as to the probable successor to a post he so much coveted. Splendid visions accompanied the idea of emolument and encreased consideration in that circle out of which he could not exist tho' with his present income he felt it impossible much longer to maintain in it even the uneasy situation which he had hitherto held. He was himself convinced and had assured Mrs. Montrose that upon this visit every thing depended

"Let me alone," cried he "with the old fool and I will get about him and seem to think himself and his damned wealth of such consequence that he will never be able to do without me. I know that's the way Guise manages him. Sure he can never be so absurd as to think of bringing in that cursed rascal even tho' he be his bastard."

Such was the real motive of Mr. Montrose's journey at that time to Bath, who now returned with all expedition to Rose park upon finding that this unexpected impediment, in spite of his first promised success, was invincible—and seeing that Lady Trevallyn was not in the least moved by the contemptuous expressions with which his spleen had overflowed, against her suffering herself as he said "to be fettered by two insignificant girls whom nobody knew who chose to fasten themselves upon her."

Immediately upon his return home the required invitation, ceremonious as Etiquette herself could dictate was dispatched and the following morning was received with sorrow and surprise by Lady Trevallyn, vexation and disappointment by Lord Henry and the utmost perplexity by Selena who was herself little more inclined to accept it than her sister who eagerly besought her to proceed at once to London tho' she found herself somewhat puzzled to advise what was to be done when once arrived there.

Lady Trevallyn's extreme dejection of spirits, the tears with which she listened to Selena's doubts of accompanying her to Rose park with her assurance that it was Lord Trevallyn's determination not to remain there longer than a week at length prevailed upon Selena to comply with the earnest intreaty of her friend that she would not quit her until they arrived together in town.

The day was now fixed and the party arranged for quitting Bath. Lord Trevallyn had taken upon himself the chief care of these preparations, anxious that the expedition should be performed in a manner suited to his own ideas of appropriate splendour indeed his sole wish in paying this first visit to the brother of his wife was to display all the pride of his princely equipage as he had already done his sumptuous domestic magnificence.

In the mean time Lord Henry continued as usual his morning visits and his constant attendance at the dinner table of Lord Trevallyn.

"It was surely not worth while for those few days to prohibit his coming or order him to be excluded."

The excuse thus made with downcast eyes and voice scarce audible for the disregarded admonitions of friendship Selena heard in silence and sensible that she could not be of use avoided as much as possible the presence of Lord Henry, whom she never beheld without the most painful uneasiness whether he addressed her lovely and innocent but imprudent friend with that peculiar softness which his manner to her so conspicuously displayed, or gazed upon her with the fixed eye of passionate tenderness which followed incessantly her every motion even when he was apparently engaged with others.

On the morning previous to that allotted for their departure to Rose park Selena having a few purchases to make and unwilling to annoy her friend by obliging her to drive out contrary to her inclinations, took a chair the streets being too dirty to admit her to walk even had she been inclined to subject herself to Lord Trevallyn's charge of indelicacy.

While seated in the chair at a shop door she was suddenly startled by seeing an immense head with erect ears and two enormous eyes staring upon her close to the glass, She had not however much time to be terrified for almost instantly she recognized the well remembered (and in spite of all her efforts) very feminine voice and laugh of Lady Greysville who having spied Selena had now seated herself upon the pole of her chair holding in her hand the reins of a welch poney whose head had at first so much surprised Selena thro' the window.

She now tapped at the glass which Selena hastened to let down in order to return her warm and affectionate salutations—yet she could not repress a smile and some expression of surprise at her companion.

"Oh my dear," replied Lady Greysville while she scratched with her delicate fingers the forehead of her favourite, "I am but just arrived and on my way met with that booby Richmond who had brought this sweet little poney with him from Wales. Did you ever see a nicer limb'd animal. Look what a shoulder and observe what a forehand. There is not a better goer in my stable; but this is not fat you see, all carcase ... depend upon it."

"And how did you prevail upon Mr. Richmond to part with it," said Selena laughing at the panegyrics which she so little comprehended. "I did not think you were such good friends."

"Oh that was just the very reason. I bullied him out of it child. I luckily sohoed[59] him coming from Ireland on a fresh scent and swore I would spoil his fortune for ever and publish all over Bath his adventure at Harrogate with Fanny Ludlow if he would not swop this little Devil here with me for an old cat of a blooded mare all broke down before and touched in her wind with the hard riding my groom gave her this season while following me when I was so much better mounted. But there is the Sadler waiting for me, I was just going to fit Patch with a proper saddle, but I got a glimpse of you. Where is Mrs. Vallard? Well I hope," so saying she hardly waited for a reply as she shook hands with Selena; Then tucking up her habit and displaying a nicely booted and admirably shaped leg to an astonished mob whom she had collected round poor Selena's chair she skipped across the street amid the thickest part of the mud to the shop on the other side where the grinning sadler composed his features to receive obsequiously her orders given in terms and a manner so little appropriate to the minute delicacy of her figure.

Selena on her return home after relating this comical rencounter to Clara sat down to read and answer a few lines written by Sidney simply stating that he as yet had received no new intelligence and thus engaged she allowed the remainder of the morning imperceptibly to pass away.

Ashamed of herself for the hours which she had suffered to elapse in dwelling with a weakness she judged unpardonable upon ideas too powerfully seductive she started on hearing the clock strike four and wishing to divert the train of her thoughts had taken by some active employment she began to collect her books and clothes preparative to her journey the next morning. Missing a volume which Mrs. Aston had sent for her perusal she went down stairs in order to seek for it in the

---

[59]   Sohoed: to shout or cry "soho" (OED).

drawing room, and for that purpose as it was already nearly dark lighted the little candle which lay upon her writing table.

On her entrance she stopped for an instant shocked, surprised and embarrassed when she distinguished by the help of a large blazing fire which afforded almost the only light the lofty but heavy windowed apartment then contained, Lady Trevallyn seated beside her little work table and Lord Henry on his knees at her feet. Involuntarily Lady Trevallyn without rising moved back her chair, but Lord Henry without altering his position said coolly, "Will you not finish your silk?" and at the same time raised his hands surrounded with the skein which he appeared to have been thus assisting her to wind.

Lady Trevallyn made no reply and as Selena advanced Lord Henry after stooping for the ball which lay upon the floor, arose and depositing the silk upon the back of a chair addressed a few unnoticed words to Selena after which observing that it was uncommonly dark he made his bow to the ladies and withdrew.

A silence of a few minutes succeeded, during which Selena apparently occupied in search of the book struggled in fact with emotions which trembled in her whole frame and beat in her bosom with a violence that almost impeded respiration.

Unable to speak, confused and uncertain as to what she ought to say she was about to retire without having uttered a syllable when the soft and broken voice of Lady Trevallyn faintly pronouncing her name arrested her ere she reached the door.

Selena perceived that she wept, and touched with a tenderness of compassion which deprived her better judgment of all its power to condemn she approached and mingled her tears with hers.

"I know you must blame and despise me," whispered Lady Trevallyn, "but pity me dearest Selena. Think of what I have lost—lost by my own folly! How happy I might have been and what a wretched creature I am now for life!"

"My dearest Lady Trevallyn," interrupted Selena, "this is all very wrong and ..." she was proceeding but with an emotion of impatience unlike herself her friend prevented her by exclaiming as she clasped her hands together, "I know, I know it is wrong! But it is something stronger than myself believe me it is—however now it is all over! After this evening ... this one last evening I shall see him no more and all the happiness of my life is sacrificed to a duty I detest! Oh forgive me dear Selena I talk very wickedly, but do not hate, do not forsake me. I am not worthy of such a friend but your affection is all I have left upon earth."

While she spoke the agitation of her mind was so visible in her whole convulsed person that Selena intent only upon soothing her to peace endeavoured to speak comfort giving her the tenderest assurances of a love that nothing could diminish while she internally reflected with hope upon what had thus fallen from her friend, trusting that the intimacy which she so much disapproved was to be now at least suspended, tho' she ventured not to make any enquiries or express such a satisfaction.

Unwilling to quit her in a state of such disordered spirits they did not separate till a loud knocking at the door announced the arrival of company and obliged them hastily to retire in order to make some alteration in their dress.

Dinner was on the table and Lord Trevallyn extremely out of temper had twice sent an impatient summons to the fair hostess before she made her appearance, for which her heavy eyes and pale countenance alone pleaded her silent apology. Lord Henry had taken his accustomed place but Selena could not but observe the unusual gloom which sat upon his generally most animated features. During the evening the dejection of Lady Trevallyn appeared rather to encrease than diminish. More than once she quitted the room and upon her return her swolen eyes too plainly evinced what had been her employment.

Selena who had been requested to sing remained at the piano-forte principally to avoid the necessity of supporting a conversation with Mrs. Aston which her want of spirits then rendered unusually irksome. Lady Trevallyn had seated herself behind and her head reclined languidly upon the back of Selena's chair. Lord Henry approached and stood at her side but so quietly that Selena knew not he was there until she heard half indistinctly his voice thus softly addressing his cousin.

"Oh Emily! Is it thus that we are to part—say then must it be for ever! Will not you speak—Emily speak. Ah if we must part let it be as those who have so loved should part—who have loved so long—so well."

Selena's agitation was but too evident; the tremulous notes died upon her lips and her fingers hesitated powerless upon the keys. Instantly Lord Henry perceived he had been overheard and in a louder voice abruptly began to speak on some indifferent subject. Lady Trevallyn was still silent—and as Selena ceased playing she left her seat and approached the fire.

Lord Henry did not follow her but apparently gay and unembarrassed would then have engaged Selena in conversation. But having given a forced smile to the light remark with which he began to address her she turned from him the softness and sweetness of her manners struggling almost vainly with sincerity to disguise the sensation that she just then felt towards him which extremely resembled hatred.

Certain of pursuing Lady Trevallyn to the corner whither she had now retreated and uneasy at witnessing the evil which she could not remedy Selena hastened into the other apartment and before supper returned to her own, dwelling with some degree of hope nevertheless upon the words which she had involuntarily overheard seeming to promise a lasting separation. She suspected not the art which had suggested this pretended self-banishment to Lord Henry as the surest method of arousing all the latent tenderness in the bosom of Lady Trevallyn, altho' he in fact never had less idea than at the present of forsaking the gaieties of London and his beloved Emily.

Lady Trevallyn still more unsuspicious than Selena listened to the romantic pictures of melancholy exile and solitude with which he interested but too keenly all her sensibility, and considered every word he uttered as the purest and truest proof of a love insurmountable struggling with esteem for her and the principles of exalted virtue which appeared to kindle every sentiment and glow in every expression.

By this feigned flight he hoped to ensure a Parthian[60] victory. It was indeed no common conquest that he meditated—and the more intimately he read into Lady Trevallyn's heart the more convinced he became of the difficulty it would cost in spite of all its tenderness to subdue its purity and to silence its virtue. As the most certain means of deluding her vigilence he affected to share every scruple, and while he appeared to be involuntarily hurried away by the resistless impulses of a sentiment he vainly endeavoured to suppress he was in fact systematically pursuing what he judged the most infallible measures for corrupting that pure and generous heart which had so unworthily bestowed itself upon him.

In taking leave of Lady Trevallyn at present he purposely inspired her with an anxious uncertainty whether it was indeed his resolution they should meet no more. He wilfully was silent to this question so eloquently made by her speaking eyes as she involuntarily returned the pressure of his hand at parting with difficulty restraining her tears altho' a thousand mingled sensations prevented her from uttering even the farewell which her heart fainted while it believed it might be eternal.

Chapter XII

While I am compassed round
With mirth, my soul lies hid in shades of grief,
Whence like the bird of night with half shut eyes
She peeps and sickens at the sight of day.
Dryden[61]

The morning was far advanced before the party assembled at Lord Trevallyn's and the splendid retinue he had prepared set off from Milsom street upon the intended expedition to Rose park and in the arrangement which preceeded their departure upon which Lord Trevallyn had debated with that importance of consideration which a general bestows on an attack, Lady Trevallyn contrived with some difficulty to retain Selena as her companion.

As they past the York Hotel a travelling chaise with four post horses stood at the door.

"Do you know the carriage?" asked Selena whose attention had been excited by the eagerness with which Lady Trevallyn had gazed upon it.

"It is Lord Henry's," answered she in a voice scarce audible, withdrawing at the same time her eyes in some confusion.

---

[60] Parthian victory: designating a pointed glance, cutting remark, etc., delivered by a person at the moment of departure (OED).

[61] Julia in John Dryden's *The Rival Ladies* (1664), 3.1.62–5.

"He leaves Bath then today," observed Selena.

Lady Trevallyn hurt at the tacit reproach conveyed in these words hesitating replied, "I heard him say that the party he came with meant to stay here no longer."

Selena could not help doubting the exact coincidence of time but was silent. While Lady Trevallyn plunged in a mournful reverie profitted for some time but little by the pains which she had taken to procure for herself in this journey the society of her friend.

Gradually however Selena succeeded in her efforts to rouse her from a train of thought she rightly judged not the most favourable to her peace, and having of late more than once noticed the visible restraint and coldness of her manners whenever she was obliged to converse with Mr. Guise, which she indeed seemed at all times most studiously to avoid Selena ventured to enquire had she any reason for the dislike—Mr. Guise having always appeared to her a young man of inoffensive and obliging manners.

"I cannot like him Selena," replied Lady Trevallyn, when observing her smile at this little satisfactory mode of accounting for evident dislike she continued after a little hesitation, "I have seen some ugly traits in his character, and I know him to be artful and illnatured. Lord Trevallyn's marriage was a measure most opposite to his interests and one which he had more than once successfully opposed. It would I am sure never have taken place had he not been unfortunately prevented by a fever from accompanying his patron abroad. But the business was all fixed before he was able to join Lord Trevallyn. He did every thing in his power as I have been informed to break off the marriage on his arrival at Nice where we then were. This I can easily forgive him, but I confess I cannot pardon his affectation (to me most offensive and indeed shocking) of love while I know he does all in his power toward injuring me in the opinion of the world."

"You amaze me dear Lady Trevallyn; in what way do you mean?"

"By talking every where of what he knows the illnatured will be so eager to consider in the worst light; you heard the contemptuous allusions of my brother and I can be at no loss to discover the author of these reports which he so readily caught at."

Selena could not refrain from expressing some doubts and said that perhaps Mr. Guise had been misrepresented, as for her part she had never heard him speak of her friend but in the highest terms, "and indeed," added she, "I thought he seemed quite anxious that Lord Henry should be invited to Rose park from several little things I heard him say to Lord Trevallyn."

"Oh I have no doubt of it," replied Lady Trevallyn in some agitation. "Our visit would then have furnished him with some precious anecdotes."

"But how is it possible you can know this?" enquired Selena rather surprised.

"I cannot be mistaken on that head I have heard it from such certain authority," answered Lady Trevallyn while her faultering voice and evident reluctance to name this authority convinced Selena that it was no other than Lord Henry himself.

Painfully struck with the obvious familiarity and mutual confidence which must have produced conversations of so delicate a nature Selena once more secretly rejoiced at her separation from a companion so dangerous and fervently prayed that it might be lasting and complete while Lady Trevallyn sunk again in melancholy silence dwelling upon that eternal separation at one moment with all the despair of hopeless tenderness and again with the resignation of courageous virtue, at times suspended by the sudden palpitation which throbbed to her heart when her imagination presented the possibility of her still beholding him once more upon her arrival in town.

It was already dark before the party reached Rose park and each being shewn to their several apartments to prepare for dinner Lady Trevallyn at Selena's request promised to call for her when dressed in order that her presence might give her courage upon her introduction to Mrs. Montrose of which both the sisters were in some dread.

The first dinner bell had rung before they entered the drawing room where they found a large and shivering circle of ladies while the fire remained totally eclipsed by a more than proportionate number of gentlemen.

Mrs. Montrose advanced to meet them and after coldly saluting Lady Trevallyn received Selena and her sister (who were then presented to her) with a silent courtesy. Her eyes however were not silent for while they alternately and quickly glanced from one to the other they seemed already to say "Are those *your* beauties Emily?" a question which in fact she seized the first opportunity to make in a whisper which Lady Trevallyn feared was but too audible.

She was however impatient to return to her seat at the corner of the fire place which to her surprise she beheld now occupied by Lord Louverney with whom she had been conversing before the entrance of her new guests.

As Mrs. Montrose herself was the only person who did not seem to consider this impertinence as wit, in the silent circle where dullness languished for any interruption, the temporary amusement it afforded encouraged Lord Louverney to persist in affecting to disregard her orders to him to rise, while he continued to converse with the lady who was seated on his right hand, till in real displeasure Mrs. Montrose turned away saying with a voice of scornful anger, "I see Lord Louverney has reasons for his rudeness I shall not disturb so interesting a conversation."

Lady Trevallyn mean time who had seated herself on a sopha near the door between the astonished sisters now received the compliments of a few whom the attraction of the beautiful Countess had drawn from the important discussion of the morning's sport which engrossed the gentlemen over the fire, close to which in an arm chair was seated Lord Trevallyn—placed there immediately on his entrance by the master of the house who taking his station by his side paid to him exclusive attention—and indeed Lord Trevallyn alone of all his guests on any occasion ever appeared to share in the slightest degree his consideration except so far as they administered to his own entertainment while Mrs. Montrose on her part equally occupied by her selfish attention treated all except Lord Louverney with perfect indifference bordering upon rudeness.

Perhaps it may be thought that they with some justice considered that the difficulties in which they involved themselves to keep up the expensive shew with which they esteemed it necessary to live during the reception of company was a sufficient tax upon the entertainers and that what they purchased at so high a price should at least produce them their own gratification without additional trouble or self-denial.

Nevertheless their guests unfortunately were for the most part of a different opinion and little sensible of the obligation they resented the inattention and derided the poverty which in spite of every exertion peeped out at a thousand openings from the scanty covering of brocade which the hand of Pride laboured vainly to extend.

The general commotion occasioned by the summons to dinner at length relieved the silent circle and found Lord Louverney once more so far reinstated in the good graces of Mrs. Montrose that having seated herself at the head of the table he was called upon to take his usual place at her side.

Selena had now for the first time an opportunity of seeing her hostess the obscurity of the drawing room having prevented her being able to distinguish more than that she was little and appeared to be ill proportioned and ungraceful in her figure. This might however have been amply compensated for in the judgment of most eyes by a very beautiful face had not ill temper manifestly injured every feature and strongly marked her countenance with that disgusting union of silliness and illnature, weakness of mind and violence of passion.

Her eyes tho' small were exquisitely shaped, and of the most dazzling brilliance. Nay there were not wanting many in the high circle where for a time they had moved together who preferred their dark lustre ever animated with a kind of searching fire to the meekly chastened radiance of Lady Trevallyn's eye which tho' seldom raised from the shade of its own long and darkly silken veil, an eastern would have loved to compare to his favourite gazelle or the flowers of the blue lotus bathed in the dew of the morning.

If Selena beheld Mrs. Montrose with mingled dislike and admiration, she on her part was not deficient in observing the two young and lovely sisters but during a kind of sparring flirtation with Lord Louverney who amused himself by provoking her bitter retorts she busily scrutinized with prying curiosity the faces and ornaments of her new guests after having recourse for this purpose to her glass and by this means displaying to advantage the whiteness of a very beautiful hand and arm.

This was at length interrupted by Lord Louverney who in a grave voice asked her "could she really see thro' that glass."

"What nonsense you do talk Lord Louverney!" cried she excessively discomposed, "I should like to know what you think I use it for?"

"Oh nothing gives one such an air, as the lifting of a glass to the eye and besides it has this advantage which should be not inconsiderable to some of my friends that all the staring before and after may be supposed to go for nothing, since it must be taken for granted you can only see we will suppose now Miss Miltern at the moment your glass is to your eye. Is that the case Mrs. Montrose?"

"I wish Lord Louverney you would not mind whom I look at," answered she indignantly, "It shall not be at you I promise you."

"Oh yes for you cannot help that," interrupted he smiling carelessly, "but there are a thousand other advantages which I dare say you find from your glass such as twisting that pretty Venetian chain when you are angry, as you are doing at this minute. See there now … but take care … Oh Lord you have really broken it … I am so sorry—but it was your own fault."

While he was saying this he had attempted to take the chain from her hand, but her voice at all times harsh and loud assumed a more than usually unpleasing tone as she desired him to "be quiet," snatching it from him at the same time with a violence which really broke it.

Her anger was now at its height and his playful entreaties for pardon could procure him nothing but reproaches for awkwardness and impertinence or sullen negatives. Finding his endeavours were ineffectual and his supplications for reconciliation answered only by scornful looks he turned after some time to Selena and asked her with an arch smile "where was her glass?"

"I long," added he, "to see if I could make you so angry … do let me break it …"

Selena surprised at this scene and somewhat embarrassed told him that she was not short-sighted.

"Oh that is nothing to the purpose as to wearing a glass. I have just been telling you some of the advantages and there are many more. I wore a glass myself as long as I could."

"And pray what prevented you?" cried Mrs. Montrose who irritated as she was could not bear to see him engaged in conversation with another and in particular Selena whom she had already heard him declare was a lovely little angel. Her curiosity at all times irresistible was also excited by his assertion and finding that without attending to her he continued leaning towards the other side of the table to address Selena she again impatiently repeated her question.

"Oh," replied he still without looking at her, "it grew so vulgar there was no possibility of continuing to wear what no person of fashion would be seen with any longer!"

"I like to hear you say any thing so absurd. It is really too ridiculous. Do you pretend then to tell me that no person of fashion must now be shortsighted. And pray what do you call Lady Languish, or the Duke of Loden or Mr. L—? Is he vulgar I should be glad to know?"

"All quizzes depend upon it!" answered he his attention to all appearance completely occupied in peeling walnuts and placing them on Selena's plate.

Mrs. Montrose could endure this no longer but hastily turning to Lady Trevallyn proposed retiring and casting a terrible glance at Lord Louverney as she passed followed the ladies into the drawing room.

They were scarcely seated there before Mrs. Montrose began a long meditated attack upon Lady Trevallyn, having for some time determined in her own mind that nothing could be more agreeable than to spend the spring in Grosvenor square and that no means should be left untried to obtain this invitation either from Lord or Lady Trevallyn.

Mr. Montrose who on more occasions than one had felt ashamed of her palpable meanness and dreaded the disgust which Lord Trevallyn might thence conceive had cautioned her in pretty strong terms against meddling with him which added to the awe his haughty and forbidding manners inspired kept her at such a distance that all her hopes at present lay upon the gentle Emily from whom she had so often extorted what she wished at the expence of her own inclinations ever ready to bend to those of others.

"How soon do you go to town Emily?" enquired she with more eagerness than civility.

"Immediately from this. Next Thursday I think Lord Trevallyn said he should be obliged to bid you farewell."

"Oh I hope you will not leave us so soon," answered she coolly, but without waiting for a reply instantly added; "Do both the Miss Milterns go with you to Grosvenor square?"

"Certainly," said Lady Trevallyn with a smile tho' secretly hurt at a question which she saw disconcerted Selena.

"Oh I did not know but they might have gone to Lady Harriet. Pray has not she taken a house in town?"

"I believe she has."

"And pray can you tell me what they pay for it for the winter?"

"No really."

"Perhaps you can inform me Miss Miltern."

Selena expressed her concern that she could not.

"Well really I hope I shall be able to persuade Mr. Montrose to buy a house when we go to town, for nothing is so uncomfortable as to have every year the same teizing work looking out for one to hire and uncertain this way where we are to be. And besides one is often a length of time in town before one's friends can find one out. Lord Emily how I wish I was settled some where near you in Grosvenor square. Do you think we are likely to get a house there?"

"I hope so," answered Lady Trevallyn faintly, her heart at the same time giving the lie to her words and dreading the illnatured vigilance of her indefatigable curiosity.

"Perhaps when you go to town you would be so good as to look round, and write us word Emily if you see any thing that would suit, We could come upon chance to some of our friends—or sleep for a few nights at an hotel, tho' to be sure that is very uncomfortable. I detest an hotel—don't you?"

"No indeed," said Lady Trevallyn, "I never was pleasanter than I have been sometimes at an hotel."

"Well," resumed Mrs. Montrose with an affected laugh, "we may manage nicely then to change, I will take your delightful apartments in Grosvenor square and you shall have mine at Lothian's in Albemarle street since you have such a fancy for an hotel."

In hopes that this hint would succeed Mrs. Montrose looked full in Lady Trevallyn's face expecting her reply but some dear associations, some melancholy remembrances had now fixed her mind on scenes of other times and bid

> A thousand images awake,
> A thousand little tendernesses throb.[62]

Observing her inattention to what she had said, Mrs. Montrose who was not deficient in cunning the sense of little minds, began to consider what had been said likely to produce this reverie and enquired eagerly on what occasion she had slept at an hotel in London.

"I have often been there for a night or two in the summer," said Lady Trevallyn with a tremulous voice, "on our way between this and poor Lady Anne Ortney's."

"Oh yes I remember!" cried Mrs. Montrose her curiosity sufficiently satisfied, "your Mother was very fond of going there and Lord Henry was always of your party."

Selena trembled for her friend whose sudden paleness shewed her suffering and agitation.

One sigh however which was all her Mother's dispersed it and in a moment she was enabled to disguise her feelings from the hard and prying eye which examined her.

"So the Miss Milterns stay all the Spring with you, do they?" enquired Mrs. Montrose after a little pause.

"Yes I hope so," answered Lady Trevallyn annoyed at the impatient question.

"Oh no Madam!" interrupted Selena colouring but stopped short uncertain what she should say.

Mrs. Montrose waited an instant expecting a farther explanation but seeing that she was not likely thus to obtain it she demanded addressing herself to Selena, "Whether she was to go to Lady Harriet's upon leaving Lady Trevallyn."

Selena in a hesitating voice replied she believed she should—an answer which only the more excited Mrs. Montrose's desire of finding out a truth which thus appeared involved in some mystery and she in secret determined to discover the history of Lady Trevallyn's connexion with these apparently neglected girls.

"You will be a great loss to my sister when you leave her; Won't she Emily?"

"Oh I do not intend to let her leave me," said Lady Trevallyn

"Why certainly," said Mrs. Montrose, "it is vastly pleasant to have a young person at one's call as I may say in town. I assure you I have often stayed at home rather than be at the trouble of looking for a party to go to the play, or the opera or Ranelagh or to walk in the gardens or any place where we cannot go alone.

---

[62] Cassandra in James Thomson's *Agamemnon* (1738), 4.3.7–8 (the lines should read "At this ten thousand images awake; / Ten thousand little tendernesses throb").

Well I do envy the men that may do as they please and are not obliged to ferret out a stupid companion or else stay at home. But that could never happen if you had some one you liked in the same house. Lord how I should like that."

Lady Trevallyn who had no idea to what this tended, but thought the conversation not much calculated to set Selena at ease now took the advantage of a pause to ask Mrs. Montrose to give them a little music telling her that she was sure that Selena or her sister would have pleasure in playing if she would set them the example.

Mrs. Montrose with a bluntness which disconcerted Selena positively refused to comply with their united request and but very coldly seconded Lady Trevallyn's desire that Selena should then herself sit down to the piano-forte who unaccustomed to refuse felt some unwillingness at this exhibition.

Lady Trevallyn glad to escape from her unamiable questioner took refuge at her side. Indeed she was the only person who seemed to pay Selena's musick much attention and yet it is certain that not one in the room gave it fewer thoughts however it might insensibly have had an effect in soothing the sensations of bitter regret and hopeless dejection with which Lady Trevallyn saw herself once more for the first time since her Mother's death in the scene of her bright her early years and in the apartment where she had so often listened to the accents of tenderness and beheld the eye of maternal fondness sparkle at her approach with delight and admiration. Not a chair, not a picture but seemed to speak to her of all the hopes and pleasures which she had consigned for ever to the cold grave of her Mother.

While the confused voice of unfeeling mirth or insipid tattle struck upon her ear from the other side of the apartment she sat indulging a mournful train of thought and many a sad comparison between her past and present prospects. Those prospects which an idolising Mother had but too much cherished and which seemed to Emily to die with her—"and I have forever lost him!" and "I might have been his" were the perpetual exclamations of her heart which her opening lips could scarce refrain from uttering, while the painful sensation in her throat and a stagnant tear in either eye she gazed on the heartless group to whom she knew her anguish could they have read it at that moment would have afforded joy or at least amusement.

But the most bitter, the most cruel of all the reflections which oppressed her heart were those which in spite of all his subsequent protestations would sometimes suggest the doubt that Lord Henry had never wished that she might call him by any dearer more sacred name than that of Lover! In vain she tried to banish the too painful recollections of those mortifying those terrible moments when the anxiety of her Mother, the scorn of the malicious world, and above all her own wounded heart pointed out the palpable neglect in some cruel instances of him who might then boldly have professed himself her lover.

It has been fancifully said by a french author that in the distribution of Nature to the sexes she has given to man a cell more in the brain but to woman a fibre more in the heart.[63] The character of Lady Trevallyn might appear strikingly to support this observation.

The blandishments of Lord Henry since her marriage and his artful misrepresentations might easily have deceived her judgment, but her heart felt that all was not fair and right. For tho' even to Selena, nay scarcely to herself would she confess that she had been wrong'd by the only man she loved upon earth the secret conviction of this was her sorest torment. So truly has it been said

> Se plaindre de ceux qu'on adore
> C'est le plu grand de tous les maux.[64]

Upon the entrance of the gentlemen Lady Trevallyn pleaded fatigue and retired for the night.

Lord Louverney immediately advanced to Selena and would have pressed her to continue at the piano-forte from whence at their appearance she had risen.

But Mrs. Montrose who had no ambition to set off the talents of her fair guest to the disadvantage of her own abruptly interrupted their conversation saying she had been commissioned by the rest of the party to request Selena would have the goodness to play a country dance. With the utmost cheerfulness Selena instantly obliged her and in spite of Lord Louverney's remonstrances to Mrs. Montrose herself with a few couple[s] stood up and danced without interruption till supper.

Selena indeed who was excessively fond of dancing and whose young and innocent heart for a moment could forget all its sorrows and vexations while her eyes and feet involuntarily danced in cadence with the cheerful sounds of her flying fingers, at length yielded to the importunities of Clara and Lord Louverney, allowing her sister to take her place for one set, during which the glances of her gay partner spoke his admiration too plainly to escape the angry eyes of Mrs. Montrose who indeed observed them with infinitely more attention than Selena herself.

Chapter XIII

> To a soul enamoured
> There is a sort of local sympathy,
> Which when we view the scenes of early passion
> Paints the bright image of the object loved
> In stronger colours than remoter scenes

---

[63] "Champfort" (Tighe's note). Nicolas Chamfort (1741–94), *Maximes et pensées* (1795), chapter six ("Des femme, de l'amour, du marriage, et de la galantrie"): "Il y a dans le cerveau des femmes une case de moins, et dans leur coeur une fibre de plus que chez les hommes."

[64] Arnaud Berquin, "Plaintes d'une Femme Abandonnée Par Son Amant, Auprès du Berceau de Son Fils," *Idylles et Romances* (1776), lines 41–2: "Complaining about those we love is the greatest of all evils."

Could ever paint it—realizes shadow
Embodies vacancy—lends shape and being
To airy fantasy.

Miss H. More[65]

Immediately after breakfast the following morning Lady Trevallyn who
complained of a head-ach and whose pale countenance sufficiently justified the
excuse, retired to her own apartment. The day was too cold and gloomy to tempt
the ladies from the fire. The gentlemen indeed dispersed but Lord Louverney had
followed Selena into the billiard room whither she had accompanied some of the
ladies having heard from Lady Trevallyn that this was also the library and hoping
to find there some amusing book with which she might escape to her own room
feeling herself treated with marked slight by both Mr. and Mrs. Montrose and
totally neglected by all the party except Lord Louverney whose attentions were
thus the more strikingly particular.

Selena could not but be sensible how disagreeable those attentions were to
Mrs. Montrose and seeing with what a scowling eye they were observed she was
desirous of avoiding Louverney tho' she had at first felt amused by the lively
raillery with which his conversation abounded. She therefore stole from the
billiard room the first moment that she could do so unnoticed by him certain that
no other person would make any efforts to detain her in their society.

Tired of the confinement which she had had for some time in Bath she long'd
once more to find herself at liberty in the open air to which she had been from
infancy accustomed at all seasons. Wrapping herself therefore in her great coat in
spite of the unpleasing aspect of the day she found her way to the shrubbery at the
back of the house.

The walks were in the wildest disorder, the fences broken and all the shrubs
torn and destroyed except those whose woody and naked stems had overgrown
the injurious attacks of the cattle. The heaps of bark piled on a rising ground to
the north and the stripped and fallen timber declared that it had once been shaded
by a venerable wood, nay even of the few magnificent elms upon the lawn which
had hitherto been spared some now bore upon their trunks the numbers which
marked them devoted by their fall to contribute to the luxuries of their master
whose boyish sports they had so often shaded.

Selena delayed by no agreeable objects around walked fast in order to defend
herself from the extreme cold of the air and quickly reached the end of the shrubbery.
Finding there an open door she proceeded into a flower garden which was grown
completely wild and overrun with weeds among which a pig was unmolestedly
rooting who had stolen thither thro' a large gap in an adjoining fence.

At the extremity of this little garden was a terrace open to the south and
commanding an extensive and beautiful view of the country beneath bounded by
the Dorsetshire hills. In the centre of this was built a kind of Portico where stood a

---

[65]   Percy in Hannah More's *Percy* (1778), 3.1.31–8.

number of orange and myrtle trees in tubs half of which were already dead and all had evidently suffered from neglect.

Here Selena entered but started upon seeing Lady Trevallyn seated at one end upon a broken chair—her head reclining upon her hand while torrents of silent tears fell upon a book which lay open on her lap. Selena stopped for a moment but upon her advancing a step Lady Trevallyn hastily rose and wiping her eyes continued in much agitation tho' her momentary terror at hearing a footstep was relieved upon perceiving that it was only that of her friend.

"Have you been reading?" asked Selena unwilling to notice her tears.

"No," answered she, "but I had left behind me locked up in that little press some drawings and I was impatient to see whether I should find my papers as they were."

As she said this she went over to some shelves which were made in the wall upon which lay a few unfinished drawings, specimens of plants and botanical books.

"I knew not," she continued while her tears streamed afresh as she examined them one by one, "I knew not that I was never to return to this once favourite spot with those whose memory must still endear it to me . Alas my poor mother! How would she lament to see her dear walks, her beautiful flowers and her beloved trees thus totally destroyed—all changed, all lost like her poor Emily! Here have we sat for hours on a summer's evening or a calm autumn morning. Here I used to draw while she worked and some one read to us." These last words were added in a fainter voice and Selena needed not to be told that the image of Lord Henry had been thus recalled.

As she spoke she held her back to Selena and her eyes were fixed upon the drawings while she wiped away the drops that so quickly renewed again obscured the dear traces of past pleasure. Selena mean time no unmoved spectator of this scene which she so justly considered as most prejudicial to the mind of her friend had taken up the book which she had observed on their first entrance in Lady Trevallyn's lap.

It was a volume of Withering's botany[66] and in the title page she read the name of Henry Ortney. Several common wild flowers were marked in the same hand with a date implying that they had been then found at Rose park. Observing a paper between the leaves and supposing it to contain a dried plant she unfolded it but perceiving it to be verses and written by Lady Trevallyn she presented it to her asking her permission to read them.

"You know already all my weakness dear Selena!" cried she returning them to her, "it was that wretched paper that I was reading just before you entered. Take it, but do not read it now and never let me again behold so sad a monument of my folly. It was written as you will see the autumn before I was married and in this very spot. See those Acacia's and that poor Platanus—how lovely were they

---

[66]   William Withering, *The Botanical Arrangement of All the Vegetables Naturally Growing in Great Britain* (1776).

then. I myself planted them and it is right perhaps that they should thus miserably sympathise with me! Look Selena at these hills—oh how often have I been desired to remember as I gazed upon them that on the other side they were nearly the same outline seen from the windows of Ortney castle! But come let us carry away these sad relicks I often wished for an opportunity to recover them and I have reason to be thankful that my little deposit was never surprised by the present possessors, I should say destroyers of poor Rose Park."

The moment Selena was alone she with a sigh drew from her bosom the paper which Lady Trevallyn had given her, the nature of which she already guessed from what had passed. The verses were such as shall be now given but the reader must have witnessed the beautiful Emily in the sorrow amidst which Selena surprised her to read them with that interest which she then felt.

> Fled are the summer hours of joy and love!
>   The brilliant season of delight is o'er
> Alone mid leafless woods I silent rove
>   The voice so dear enchants these bowers no more!
> Yet sweet the stillness of this calm retreat,
>   As toward the sunny bank I pensive stray,
> The muse affords her consolations sweet,
>   And sooths with memory's charms my lonely way—
> Here led by Flora o'er the pathless wild
>   I woo sweet Nature in her private haunts
> The rarer flower which long neglected smiled
>   My curious eye unspeakably enchants—
> Ev'n now the season our mild Autumn yields
>   Forbids not yet my timid foot to roam,
> A languid Sun illumes yet verdant fields
>   And many a lingering blossom yet can bloom—
> While smiling science shews her Withering's page
>   And half unveils her most attractive face,
> Reveres the memory of the Swedish sage
>   And bids me nature's charms delighted trace
> But if the gloomy clouds or northern blast
>   Endear the comforts of our social hearth,
> How swift the calm domestic hours are past!
>   How far superior to the hours of mirth!—
> Oft when my heart the call of joy would spurn
>   By sad involuntary gloom opprest,
> To thee my plaintive harp I languid turn
>   Thy silver sounds can sooth my soul to rest—
> Or wrapt in loved imagination's dream
>   I hear the voice I see the form so dear,
> In visionary charms they present seem
>   The well known accents vibrate on mine ear—
> I see those eyes of bright celestial blue,
>   Those laughing eyes beam love and sympathy,
> And o'er the mantling cheek the rosy hue

The blush of kindling hope and tender joy—
I have not lost thee then my soul's best part!
    I still can hear thee talk of love and bliss!
Can pour out all the fulness of my heart,
    Oh what felicity can vie with this!
How oft will fancy thro' the watchful nights
    Picture thy form my sorrows to beguile,
The glance of soft affection now delights
    Now archly gay I see thy sportive smile
I see thee oft with pensive tender eye
    Mark our blue hills thy gay horizon bound
While fond imagination with a sigh
    Measures the space of the far distant ground—
Beyond those hills constrained a while to dwell
    Full many a lonely hour the thought can cheer
The shades of sorrow oft it can dispel
    And turn to tenderness the saddest tear—
But thou whose image never quits this heart
    Art thou unmindful of thine absent love
Ah no! I bid the cruel thought depart
    And each suggestion of distrust reprove—
And yet too oft awaking from my trance,
    My brilliant day-dream of unreal joy,
I think with anguish that thy tender glance
    Has charmed in vain my captivated eye—
Sad victim of each heart forboding care
    I think with pity on my future lot
Even now some happier eye thy smiles may share
    Thy vows of tenderness to me forgot—
On such sad doubts each trembling thought employed
    Oh what a dreary silence there appears!
Life offers nothing but a joyless void
    While my youth wastes in unavailing tears—
Thou canst not see me in those cruel hours
    Thou knowest not Love but as he smiles and charms
Thy stronger mind feels not dejection's powers
    Nor knows the pang which tenderness alarms—
Yet let thine heart the pains of absence share,
    Oh! be but constant and I yet am blest,
Alive to each suspicion kindly spare
    The trembling feelings of this anxious breast![67]

Occupied by the melancholy reflections which were excited by what she had just witnessed, and which insensibly led her to her own situation Selena thought not of again quitting her apartment till she was aroused by the entrance of Clara.

---

[67]   Tighe titles this lyric "Elegy. Written for Emily. 1802" in V*erses Transcribed for H.T.* (Brompton, 1805).

Fig. III.2   Illustration for "Elegy. Written for Emily. 1802" in *Verses Transcribed for H.T.* (Brompton, 1805), MS Acc 5495/C/8/1, National Library of Ireland, Dublin.

"Oh Selena," cried she as she opened the door, "how glad I am to get to you again! I have been so catechised by Mrs. Montrose with respect to the whole of our past history and future intentions! But I have given her very little satisfaction so I suppose she will attack you next. And there is Lord Louverney has been making her furious by enquiring for you a thousand times. But what it the matter?" cried she with a look of earnest concern, "you can have had no letter. Surely the rudeness of these people who are so indifferent to us cannot make you seriously unhappy. For my part it only amuses me when Mr. Montrose looks down upon us over his shoulder with half shut eyes as if we were not worth speaking to and when his *sweet mild* Isabella looks bursting with spite because she cannot prevail upon Lord Louverney to think you are a fright and an idiot."

Selena smiled and assured her sister they had occupied but a small share of her thoughts since she had left the drawing room, "tho' I confess," said she, "the rudeness which they have certainly shewn us has not in the least amused me but on the contrary rendered my stay at Rose Park extremely disagreeable. But Thursday I hope will put a termination to this trouble and in the mean time we must not seem to notice or give any cause for offence by staying away since we are missed."

No sooner had Selena entered the drawing room than Lord Louverney advanced to meet her, quitting his station near the piano-forte at which Mrs. Montrose was now seated who however ceased playing the moment she perceived Selena.

"Where have you been this whole morning little truant?" cried Lord Louverney gaily, "We have been all disconsolate in your absence—and even Mrs. Aston has been in search of you with some learned commentary in her hand. I take it for granted she has made you a perfect Greek scholar."

Selena smiled while she denied the charge but observing the sullen air of Mrs. Montrose approached her, not without some little dread and with the most graceful softness requested her to proceed.

"Oh Lord no indeed I shall not! Do you think I could have the presumption to play before so great a performer. You want to turn me into ridicule I suppose."

Selena extremely disconcerted at the words and still more the voice in which they were uttered, coloured and was at a loss how to reply—but Lord Louverney interposed a seasonable interruption exclaiming, "Well Ladies if you will not play tell me what you think of my wager?"

"Your wager, what wager?" said Mrs. Montrose eagerly.

"Lord has not Montrose told you of our bet."

"No, that he has not, but if it is with him I can tell you that you will most assuredly win for he is always losing his money that way with one nonsense or another."

"Well I am at least sure of your good wishes and if I succeed I think I shall deserve the thanks of the company for the treat I shall exhibit to them. You know that famous old wedding suit that Montrose found the other night in the great wardrobe."

"What with those frightful orange velvet ...."

"Velvet what?" said Lord Louverney smiling at the pause made by Mrs. Montrose ... "proceed or I will tell you how a lady of my acquaintance used to express herself and spare your delicacy—you may in future call that nameless part of our dress *le vetement necessaire*."[68]

"Well but what of them?"

"Why what do you think of seeing Aston tricked out in those frightful *orange velvet*—with the white Lyons silk coat, the embroidered sattin waistcoat coleur de rose and all its appurtenances?"

"Think? why I think it would be a charity to give them to the wretch the cloathes he has on are so thread bare."

"That was just what I said to Montrose and I have laid him a dozen of Champaigne he wears them while he stays if he will promise to give them to him on those conditions."

"Lord what a fool Edward is! Does not he know the odious brute would do any thing that was mean and ridiculous so that he was to get a shilling by it and I dare say he can sell the gold frogs that are on the coat for more than it would cost him to maintain his family for a month. You never heard of such a beast as he is. If it was not for Mrs. Aston he would not allow a morcel of fire to be burned in his

---

[68] Le vetement necessaire: the necessary clothing, a polite phrase (here for breeches).

house. He keeps the key of the coal cellar in his pocket and reckons the pieces as he gives them out."

"Oh I know his ways pretty well," interrupted Lord Louverney laughing, "I assure you I have not much fear of losing my bet except for the interference of his lady. I was on a visit last winter in their neighbourhood and have often seen him trudging about dressed in an old uniform that I was told belonged to a brother of his that was in the army who died some time before, with great wooden shoes and worsted stockings all over darns. We used to watch him poking about for old bones to boil into soup and pieces of green wood to keep alive his miserable fire. But the most comical thing was to see him bringing home his prize and sneaking in for fear of being discovered by his wife. I have known her stand at the window on purpose to shame him and when he has looked up he would drop his load and sculk away like a thief."

The sudden entrance of Mrs. Aston instantly suspended the mirth with which the greatest part of the company anticipated the adoption of such antiquated finery by a person whose character was too well known to leave much doubt of Lord Louverney's success.

Selena indeed was the only person who goodnaturedly felt for the gross rudeness with which she had already seen him treated whenever Mrs. Aston was not observing what passed, for of her upon her uncle's account they were in some degree of awe.

She now advanced with a large book in her hand covered with very old vellum, from which she had yet scarcely rubbed off all the dust tho' her hands and gown had already acquired a pretty considerable share. She looked around for Mr. Montrose but perceiving that he had not yet joined the company then assembling before dinner she approached his lady saying, "Do you think Madam that I might venture to borrow this very valuable work. If I thought Mr. Montrose had any immediate occasion to consult it I should not make the request, but you may perhaps inform me whether he can without inconvenience allow me to take it to town for about a week, it will I am sure be the utmost service to assist me in the researches which I have undertaken to make for my friend Dr Proclus towards forwarding his glorious efforts for the revival of the ancient Polytheism and the divine philosophy of Plato."

As she said this she presented the volume to Mrs. Montrose who surveyed it contemptuously for an instant and then throwing it from her declared that she was poisoned with the dust, but that she was sure she was perfectly welcome to take it, as Mr. Montrose she "believed knew as little about them Hebrew books as herself."

"The work Madam is not Hebrew, but as I perceive for the most part at least very pure classical Greek," said Mrs. Aston respectfully taking up the venerated pages which contained some of the writings of the divine Plotinus.[69] "You my Lord will I am sure taste the beauty of this sublime passage," added she turning to

---

[69]   Plotinus (204/5–270) is generally considered the founder of Neoplatonism.

Lord Louverney who listened with a face of the most profound attention to a pretty long sentence of which it must be confessed he understood not a syllable.

"That is very fine upon my honor Ma'am," said he, "and perhaps when you and Dr Proclus have entirely read through that volume which I take it for granted you will do in a few days, you will have the goodness to make interest with Mrs. Montrose that I may be allowed to peruse so incomparable a performance."

Mrs. Aston extremely delighted with the hopes of making a new convert to the incomprehensible doctrines of her friend immediately offered to resign in his favour at present the work which she was really impatient to examine.

A contest of civility ensued carried on with a great appearance of earnest gravity on both sides which furnished considerable amusement to the rest of the company until Lord Trevallyn who had unperceived entered with Mr. Montrose during a debate which occupied so much of the attention of all present now stalked up to his niece and with a frown demanded how she could continue to make such a fool of herself.

"I have frequently told you Jane that people of a certain rank and women in particular should have nothing to do with Pedants and scholars who are for the most part people of low birth and in no respect such as we should like to associate with."

"Faith my Lord it's very true," cried Mr. Montrose, "I wonder for my part how people can have any pleasure in poring over books and besides one must get so d--d sick of all these old stories about the Gods and one stuff or another of that kind over and over again for the same stupid nonsense these thousand years I dare say."

It was very long since Jane had hazarded the danger of contradicting her uncle, so that altho' now touched in the tenderest part she did not even dare to defend her darling Dr Proclus or his still more darling philosophy. In silence therefore she looked down with sovereign contempt on the profound and stupid ignorance with which she was surrounded congratulating herself upon the superior energy of her mind irradiated by the serene illumination of intellectual truth which as she frequently declared "had gradually enabled her to despise all terrene advantages all merely corporeal forms, so that her soul being filled with constant and ineffable light rendered all its images pure and pellucid perfectly abolishing the obscurity of sensible impressions."

It is true the dissipation of assemblies or a few flattering words upon her looks from the most illiterate and insignificant coxcomb could often cloud this intellectual splendor and disturb this contemplative enjoyment, but a few hours conversation with the learned Dr Proclus, or an essay upon the hymns of Orpheus[70] restored her speedily to philosophic dignity—while she lamented with him the blindness of the present age to whom their united efforts had not yet been able to demonstrate the stupid prejudice which induced them to embrace so dull so insipid a religion in preference to the truth and purity of the Grecian philosophers.

---

[70] The hymns of Orpheus are a set of pre-classical compositions said to be composed by Orpheus which were famously translated by the Neoplatonist Thomas Taylor in 1792.

Lord Louverney found but little eloquence necessary in order to prevail upon Mr. Aston to suffer him to win his wager. The richness of the velvet and the quantity of tarnished gold with which it was ornamented were as had been expected irresistible and tho' somewhat afraid of the contemptuous glances of his wife he resolved to fulfill the conditions and had hopes of being able to carry it off as a jest. Lord Louverney himself attended his toilet and when he judged the greatest part of the company were assembled before dinner descended in triumph to the dining room with his victim. Throwing open the door the effect which was instantaneously produced on the appearance of a figure so grotesque may be better imagined than described. Lord Louverney had indeed anticipated it and found no small difficulty in restraining his risibility as he followed him down stairs but the burst of laughter on his entrance was universal.

Lady Trevallyn alone excepted who having heard nothing of the design gazed with silent amazement at the strange figure without being able to comprehend to what purpose he was thus uncouthly attired. She was the first to interrupt the merriment which had been excited and looking round enquired was there to be a masquerade in the neighbourhood.

He himself stood yet disconcerted at the door having totally lost the degree of spirit with which he hoped to have repelled derision and the first tumult had scarce subsided before the attention of all, was in some measure diverted from Mr. Aston by the appearance of his lady who gazing with dismay at the transformation of her husband enquired in no very amicable voice, "What was the meaning of all this nonsense."

"Nay my dear Madam," cried Lord Louverney, "you who are such an admirer of antiquity cannot be displeased with me for having provided Mr. Aston with a dress that has surely nothing to do with our times and if you will but give your sanction to my taste I do not despair of being able to procure for you the complete suit of a Roman Matron, or perhaps you would prefer the Spartan petticoat. Indeed that is better calculated to display the symetry of your shape."

The latter part of this speech as Mrs. Aston had really a fine figure in some degree mollified the rage which had begun to flash from her eyes at its commencement in the idea of its being intended to insult each and that owing to his instigation Mr. Aston had thus exposed himself to the ridicule which she saw plainly was excited.

She was nevertheless beginning a pretty sharp reply when the door suddenly flew open and Lady Greysville rushed into the room dressed as usual in her dark habit her beaver hat in one hand and a large driving whip in the other.

"Here I am my good friend," cried she as she ran to shake hands with Mr. Montrose without paying the smallest regard to the cold salutation with which she was received by his Lady when suddenly her eyes being attracted by the farcical figure of Mr. Aston she stopped short exclaiming, "What in the devil's name have you got here? How Mr. Aston! I'll be shot if ever I saw any thing half so comical. My god! Where's Tom? Cross as he is if he can help laughing at that I will be divorced from him as something unnatural for 'tis not in human nature I'll swear to resist that."

But the gloomy sullenness which sat upon the brow of Sir Thomas who now entered resisted every attack of the open gaiety which surrounded him and it was sufficiently obvious that the unexpected visit for such it to all appeared to be was as little agreeable to his wishes as it could be to those of Mrs. Montrose. However so long as Lady Greysville could carry her point which with a kind of childish obstinacy she generally effected, her enjoyment was never to be disturbed by the ill-temper of others (a disorder to which indeed she was herself totally a stranger) and regardless of the frowns of her husband and the cold incivility of Mrs. Montrose she now collected around her by her strange and lively sallies a laughing and admiring group, while she humourously enumerated to them all the difficulties she had surmounted and all the stratagems it had cost her to induce Sir Thomas to accept of an invitation which they had received some months before from Mr. Montrose to visit them at Rose Park about Christmas.

Her narrative was from time to time interrupted by renewed exclamation of surprise and delight as often as she cast her eyes upon the fantastic habit of Mr. Aston, which proved by no means agreeable to him and if possible still less so to his cara sposa,[71] who in a low voice teized him with entreaties to retire and put off that ridiculous fool's coat, all of which he either pretended not to hear, or endeavoured to silence by changing his place, or by nods and significant looks. But her wishes were opposed by all the party and in particular by Lord Louverney who reminded Mrs. Aston that it was beneath a philosophic mind to pay attention to such trifles as the ornaments of the person.

"True Lord Louverney," interrupted Lady Greysville, "and you see what a philosopher I am; I drove Tom off from Bath in the curricle at a moment's warning and have left all our rags to follow us as they can. For my part I never desire to wear any thing but an old habit as long as I live—and as for Tom if Mr. Aston will but lend him that irresistible dress I am sure it cannot fail to restore his good spirits. What do you say Tom? Don't you think it would exactly suit you? So do dear Mr. Aston promise to let him have it tomorrow and then I hope we shall have no more sulks."

The angry retort which seemed to menace Lady Greysville and the confusion of the scene was suspended by the summons to dinner, tho' the mirth of the company was again revived by observing that it was fully shared by the assembly of the lower house.

Mrs. Montrose who felt peculiarly desirous to put Mr. Aston out of countenance and if possible prevent Lord Louverney from obtaining his bet had given the hint to her maid, so that besides the servants usually ranged in the hall thro' which they past to the dinner parlour, not a domestic was wanting male or female from the housekeeper to the scullion in the group whom curiosity and malice had assembled

---

[71] Cara sposa: dear wife (Italian).

at the doors of the passages and happy were they who over the heads of their grinning fellow servants could get a peep at the strange figure who sneaked along busying himself in calculations upon the value of his frogs in order to support him under his present disgrace.

Chapter XIV

Do not you stick to Truth! she is seldom heard
A poor weak tongue she has, and that is hoarse too
With pleading oft in vain—none understands her.
                                    Beaumont & Fletcher[72]

The ladies had no sooner returned to the drawing room than Lady Greysville taking out of her pocket a small comb began without ceremony to arrange with taste those graceful curls with which she was conscious Nature had authorised her to affect despising all the assistance of art.

Mrs. Montrose who had before heard her declare the extent of her present wardrobe now enquired whether she would not like to go take off her odious habit which after so long a drive she must find particularly disagreeable adding, "Indeed Lady Greysville my house is at present so full and your Ladyship's visit such an agreeable surprise that I am quite ashamed of the apartment I am afraid my housekeeper must be obliged to give you."

"Oh I am pretty indifferent as to how I lodge," answered Lady Greysville, "and as to dressing you may thank your stars if you see any thing but this *odious habit* for these three days and then I am much afraid that Tom will deprive you at once of the pleasure of seeing it and me."

As she spoke these words an arch smile plainly demonstrated that however indifferent to it she was not unconscious that at least to her hostess her visit was unwelcome. Turning from her with a careless air she now addressed Selena expressing her pleasure at again meeting her and then enquired for Lord Dallamore saying, "Lord my dear I have heard such extraordinary stories about you both, one time you were positively married and at another as positively unmarried, I have taken an oath never to believe gossip since one fine day that I heard I had eloped from poor little Tom with one of Astley's riders. The lie was probable enough I allow but notwithstanding it *was* a lie so I have religiously kept my vow and never believed any one story that I heard since, accordingly these exact contraries alternately have had precisely the same effect on me as they could have had on the most faithful and implicit believer of the tattling tribe. When Fanny Ludlow wrote me word that you were assuredly married at Gretna green I could have sworn you were a sober spinster at Miltern Abbey and when my Aunt Rolleham wasted her lungs to prove to me you were unmarried at Hillbarton I was in my own mind

---

[72]   Clarinda in John Fletcher's *The Lovers' Progress* (1647), 3.6.103–5. The epigraph omits "Madam" at the end of line 103 and substitutes "oft in vain" for "at the bars" in line 105.

convinced that my pretty Selena was gone to town Lady Dallamore. But now do tell me truly about it, and what have you done with Dallamore."

"Lord Dallamore is gone a cruise with Captain Modely is not he?" eagerly interrupted Mrs. Montrose all her curiosity on the stretch as she fixed her searching eyes upon Selena who thus suddenly interrogated lost for a moment all her presence of mind and felt ready to sink with confusion.

Trying to recover herself she stammered out, "I believe so," "I hardly know," "I have not seen Lord Dallamore for some months."

Mrs. Montrose was not thus easily to be answered but was proceeding with her investigation when Lady Greysville perceiving that she had unintentionally annoyed Selena and unwilling that Mrs. Montrose should thus be gratified at her expence now called off the attention of all by abruptly exclaiming, "Oh but pray have you heard the strange affair between the old Dutchess of Portville and her son's tutor."

"No not a syllable do tell me," cried Mrs. Montrose her whole countenance brightening with sudden animation and pleasure.

"Lord where have you lived? Why you must know the Duke caught them at last, fairly caught them!"

"Oh the horrid old beast!" cried her delighted auditor. "Well I declare I always thought something shocking would come out she was such a detestable prude and such a canting hypocrite."

"Well this proves your discernment of characters my dear Madam," said Miss Lemon a lady who seldom spoke but to utter an assent to some good natured observation of this sort dropped from the fair lady of the mansion, "but I am amazed you should not have heard something of that shocking business before."

"You knew it then Miss Lemon," said Lady Greysville turning to her quickly, "why then did you not gratify the ladies here before this?"

"Oh I should be the last person upon earth to tell any thing of the poor Dutchess we were the most intimate friends she was always so good to me and used to ask me to all her assemblies."

"And pray how did you know this story?"

"Dear I really cannot tell reports were so contradictory, besides I promised not to speak of it," answered Miss Lemon in some confusion.

"Well but dear Lady Greysville," impatiently interrupted Mrs. Montrose, "do you I beg tell us all about it."

"Oh," replied she assuming a very demure look, "I assure you ladies it is quite too bad to tell, but you will believe that she was quite shameless when you hear that there is not a footman in the house who is not to give evidence."

"Impossible!" exclaimed Lady Trevallyn, "my dear Lady Greysville where did you pick up this most improbable of all histories. You have forgotten your oath I am sure strangely if you can give credit to it. I know the Dutchess intimately and a purer mind lives not on earth."

"Lord Emily what nonsense you talk," interrupted Mrs. Montrose, "I am sure I think nothing in the world is more likely, only she is so old and so ugly I wonder who could think of her. But I suppose she used to give the fellow money."

"Oh you may depend upon it," replied Lady Greysville, "indeed I know a person that saw a fine suit of linnen that she had made up for him and marked it all with her own hair—there is not a doubt of that."

"A great many doubts indeed," said Lady Trevallyn smiling, "and I am sure you do not yourself believe one word of that ridiculous falsehood."

"Not believe it my dear Lady Trevallyn! Do I believe that the sun shines, or that you are the prettiest woman in England? You see Miss Lemon can vouch for the truth of it. Why is it possible you did not hear it?"

"Never upon my word," replied Lady Trevallyn, blushing and smiling a thousand new beauties at the abrupt compliment.

"Nor you Mrs. Montrose?"

"No not before this but I have long suspected that something was not right."

"Well really," cried Miss Lemon, "that is extraordinary enough tho' I confess I was not myself quite free from some suspicions."

"I give you both infinite credit ladies for your sagacity," said Lady Greysville, "and especially as there is not one syllable of truth in all I have told you."

"How! what do you mean Lady Greysville?" exclaimed Mrs. Montrose.

"Why that I have not heard one word of the Duke or Dutchess of Portville since I dined with them last spring and had the happiness to see them on the best possible terms and that it is my opinion their Son never had a tutor at home."

"Do you mean then that *you* have invented all that?"

"Every tittle and all for your amusement."

"Oh you will never persuade me of that," said Mrs. Montrose recovering her first surprise, "and besides you hear Miss Lemon knew of it before."

"Yes," replied Lady Greysville, "but you know Miss Lemon is the *poor* Dutchess's particular friend so we cannot expect to have the story from her I am afraid."

Miss Lemon thus appealed to from both sides stammered out in some confusion "that she was sure she had heard something but perhaps it was of some other person, she really had not been told the name and she only supposed it must allude to the Dutchess as it was so like the story which Lady Greysville had invented."

"Aye perhaps so," said Lady Greysville (smiling archly at Lady Trevallyn), "and depend upon it," continued she looking round, "half the scandalous stories you hear are told like mine for the sole purpose of your entertainment, only those who relate them have seldom the sincerity to own as I do their true origin. Lord what a difference it would make if after every story, one was to tell candidly exactly how much of it we ourselves disbelieved, as well as the motives which induced us to repeat it. We should see then how far a fashionable partner or a pretty feather can sometimes go towards the destruction of a woman's character when Envy was obliged to shew her ugly face without any veil."

"Half the effect would certainly be destroyed by these means," said Lady Trevallyn smiling.

"Half! Oh say all my dear Lady Trevallyn! Who ever tells any story simply as it is and when the luxuriant branches of exxageration, malice or interest, or the mere desire of exciting astonishment are lopped off who will pay any attention to the dull unornamented trunk that is left, if even any thing whatever should remain."

Mrs. Montrose who by no means liked the turn which the conversation had taken still contended that nothing good was to be expected from the Dutchess of Portville and upon the entrance of the gentlemen proposed cards, but Lady Greysville protesting that she should go to sleep if she looked at them invited Mr. Montrose to a game of back-gammon.

"Oh for Heaven's sake," said Mrs. Montrose peevishly, "let us have any thing rather than that detestable noise of dice. I really cannot stand it."

"Well then Montrose," cried Lady Greysville, "let us come into the next room."

Unable to refuse the challenge Mr. Montrose rung the bell to order candles in the other room, while with an affected laugh and a voice of evidently stifled vexation Mrs. Montrose turning to Sir Thomas Greysville asked him did he approve of the tete-a-tete?

"Lady Greysville seldom troubles herself to ask my opinion," answered he peevishly.

"Why what can we do Tom? Mrs. Montrose has very fairly acted as a bore and turned us out, so you see we have no defense and must sound a retreat."

"Psha! Lady Greysville," cried he pretending to read a newspaper which he had held before his face during the whole debate, tho' his eyes had never ceased watching his Lady until the moment she now addressed him.

"Psha!" repeated she, "Aye that always means *you are quite in the right my love*. So come Mr. Montrose let us lose no time that I may gammon you before supper."

So saying she led the way and after shutting the door violently proclaimed her triumph aloud by a laugh which was indeed intended for the room which she had just quitted.

Having listened with evident uneasiness to much spiteful raillery from Mrs. Montrose upon his very convenient easiness and indifference, Sir Thomas unable longer to endure the torments of his suspicious disposition, at length followed his wife into the adjoining apartment.

Lord Louverney upon this began immediately to attack Mrs. Montrose and swore she was jealous, or she could not so ill-naturedly have disturbed the tete-a-tete—an assertion which she vehemently denied affecting to treat the whole as a jest of the most perfect indifference to her while every word and look evinced her secret vexation.

"Mr. Montrose I can assure you," cried she, "does as he pleases without my giving myself the smallest uneasiness and I am sure I should never trouble myself about his laughing at such a little flirt as Lady Greysville who makes a set at every man she sees."

"She is a charming little woman however," cried he, "don't you think so? Miss Miltern," he added turning to Selena with whose scissors and silk he had for some time been doing all the mischief which her vigilance would allow him to effect.

"I think she is very pretty indeed and seems excessively good-tempered."

"And do you think her pretty too my Lord?" cried Mrs. Montrose with a contemptuous voice.

"Yes upon my soul I do amazing pretty, and especially when she is driving those mad horses she has got now in her curricle I expect they will kill her some day and that makes her appear to me quite interesting. She looks then so stout while in fact she is trembling from head to foot for she is a devilish coward in her heart as all women ought to be."

"I wonder from what fool she got these horses," exclaimed Mrs. Montrose with a malicious sneer.

"Whoever parted with them rather shewed their wisdom in my mind," cried Lord Louverney, "for they are confoundedly dangerous animals."

"Do you know how she contrives to have always such expensive horses," said Mrs. Montrose, "for every one knows how extremely distressed they are and I fancy it would be long enough before Sir Thomas would indulge her in such extravagance, even if he had the power."

"More shame for him then, don't you think so?" replied his Lordship, "but for God's sake my dear Mrs. Montrose if you have any secret for getting good horses without money do let us have it for the public benefit. I for one should find it particularly convenient just at present."

"Oh I don't know whether we can profit by it or perhaps would like to adopt Lady Greysville's method—but you may depend upon this being absolute matter of fact as I tell it to you. Lord Dallamore had an amazing fine hunter that she insisted upon trying and after riding it several times she declared she could not live without insisting upon his selling it to her. Lord Dallamore tho' particularly fond of his horse was just the kind of ideot to be bullied out of any thing, accordingly as she no doubt expected he offered it to her as a present."

"Oh I daresay, that I can easily believe for Dallamore is generous as the winds," interrupted Lord Louverney, "but as you say I am afraid that would not succeed quite so well with me. I could hardly expect to coax even Dallamore out of a favourite horse whatever a pretty woman might do."

"But you have not heard the best part of the story yet," cried Mrs. Montrose, "for Lady Greysville did not accept his offer. 'No, no,' says she, 'Tom (as she calls that poor stupid wretch) Tom is so jealous that he will never let me take it, and so stingy that he will never buy it at a just price but ask him fifty guineas for it and all the world will tell him it is well worth a hundred and advise him not to lose such a bargain.' The affair was soon settled as her Ladyship desired but Lord Dallamore saw neither the hundred nor the fifty guineas. Some months after this Lady Greysville having entirely knocked up her fine hunter declared the absolute necessity of purchasing another. Sir Thomas as you may suppose expostulated and upbraided her with having so lately got one of her own choice. She assured him that the horse she had had from Lord Dallamore was unsound upon which Sir Thomas insisted upon its being returned observing that Lord Dallamore must certainly have known it from his willingness to part with it apparently so much beneath its value. What was now to be done?"

"I do not understand your story perfectly," cried Lord Louverney somewhat surprised.

"Nay," continued she, "wait till I tell you how her Ladyship managed. You know she is always reckoned vastly clever. Without the least shame she flew to Lord Dallamore and confessed to him that she had received from Sir Thomas the fifty guineas and having long since spent them, she was lost if he did not save her from his fury by receiving the horse and consenting to refund the money which he had never seen; and this he actually did, tho' he was so provoked to see his favourite horse so completely ruined that he shot him thro' the head the moment he was brought home."

"Oh bravo! bravo!" cried Lord Louverney bursting into a loud laugh, "well I give you credit for that. Upon my soul you would make a most excellent swindler if that story is your own invention."

"Nay I declare," replied she, "I had it from Lord Dallamore himself, I hope you will allow him to be a good authority."

"From Lord Dallamore!" exclaimed he, "why that is the most incredible part of your whole tale my dear Mrs. Montrose, for I could have sworn that Dallamore never by any chance remembered any thing in half an hour after it had happened. I heard that he married some girl in Scotland last summer and forgot it so completely that his wife has not yet been able to prevail upon him to establish her rights and I really don't in the least doubt it."

"I am sure," said Mrs. Montrose, "she has no loss of him, for a greater fool I never saw."

"Pray," said Lady Trevallyn seizing the first pause that had for some time occurred, "when was it that Lord Dallamore told you that story of poor Lady Greysville?"

"Oh I really cannot exactly remember but I know that it was at Harrogate that the last part of *poor Lady Greysville*'s story happened for Mr. Richmond told me of it as well as Lord Dallamore?"

"And have you seen Lord Dallamore since he was at Harrogate last July?"

"Yes certainly," answered she peevishly.

"May I ask you where you met him?"

"Lord Emily how you catechise me about Lord Dallamore have you taken him into favour?"

"No not yet," answered Lady Trevallyn with a smile, "but I did not know he had been in this part of England lately."

"No but I saw him when I was in town. I will swear it if you please."

Lady Trevallyn stole a glance at Selena who could so easily have detected the palpable falsehood. But Selena trembling and agitated dared not to lift her eyes from her netting dreading to meet the inquisitive & keen eye of Mrs. Montrose.

It had indeed been directed to her by the glance of Lady Trevallyn which had not escaped Mrs. Montrose. But it was not her eyes only that were at that moment fixed upon Selena. Lord Louverney a yet more interested observer gazed with earnestness upon the lively and beautiful carnation which had been thus called up and still mantled over her expressive face. Uneasy at the attention which was drawn upon her and under which she suffered Lady Trevallyn endeavouring to account for her evident agitation playfully observed, "Take care I advise you what you say of Lord Dallamore for I can tell you he is first cousin to my girls."

To Lord Louverney who remembered how freely the character of her relation had been handled this was a sufficient and satisfactory explanation, but Mrs. Montrose who had a better reason to recall with some confusion speeches so destitute of good manners troubled not herself with self recollections while totally engrossed by the discovery which she thought she had made she now believed or at least resolved to declare that Miss Miltern had set her cap at her cousin and had been sent by her friends to Lady Trevallyn in order to conceal her mortification in consequence of the disappointment of all her schemes. Determined if possible to satisfy her curiosity and sift this matter to the bottom she soon after this took an opportunity of catechising Mr. Guise, and from him she contrived to extort under a strict promise of secrecy all he knew of Selena's story—which indeed amounted to no more than this, that some engagement had passed between the cousins which Lord Dallamore did not now appear very willing to fulfill. For as to his having been actually drawn in to a marriage they agreed in pronouncing the idea perfectly ridiculous, "As if," cried Mrs. Montrose, "Lord Dallamore fool as he is would think of tying himself at his age to a little insignificant girl that no body knows!"

Chapter XV

> Ah base the sport that lightly dares defame
> The sacred honors of a Lady's name.
> > Mickle[73]

Notwithstanding the promise of secrecy which Mrs. Montrose had made to Mr. Guise (a promise indeed which no curious person ever yet sincerely and absolutely intended to keep) upon the very first opportunity that occurred she eagerly communicated her important intelligence with respect to the situation of Selena to Lord Louverney, and saw with a vexation which she could not disguise the evident anxiety with which he listened in spite of his efforts to assume an air of indifference and the unwillingness he appeared to entertain to give any credit to the assurances which had been made that some engagements subsisted between Lord Dallamore and his cousin, still less could he be persuaded to believe that any designs had been formed on the side of Selena.

---

[73]   Luis de Camõens, *The Lusiad*, translated by William Julius Mickle (1776), 6.324–5.

Indeed he scarcely avowed to himself the interest which he already found so strongly attach him to whatever related to Selena and without considering his motives or asking himself what were his views he was restless and eager to discover the truth. The gentle reserve and retired silence of Lady Trevallyn gave so little encouragement to that familiarity of manner with which Lord Louverney usually addressed women that altho' few thought more highly of her superior beauty and graces yet he felt rather less at his ease in conversing with her than with many whom he admired less. When he would have questioned her with respect to Selena he therefore found himself unusually embarrassed, and as she shewed no inclination to continue this conversation he gave up all hopes of receiving from her the satisfaction which he wished.

At one time he was upon the point of acknowledging to Selena herself part of the intelligence he had heard, and resolved to ask her if indeed her lot was really decided; but the recollection of the question which might naturally be expected to follow, should she to the first reply in the negative, prudently prevented his uttering what in any other light might certainly wear the appearance of impertinence. To Lady Greysville therefore he at length determined to apply. She had been with them at Harrogate as he had already heard and surely must have observed had an attachment on either side existed. He easily found an opportunity of conversing with her alone, and having challenged her to a game of billiards led her without any apparent effort to speak of Selena.

"She is a lovely girl," cried she; "and upon my soul Louverney I recommend it to you strongly to marry her. Take my word for it she will be more admired and have a greater run than any one if she has luck enough to marry a dashing young man of rank like you that has spirit enough to go on his own judgment before she has been criticised by the town. You are just the knowing fellow to do it and you can afford to take a girl without a sous."

"Or what do you think of Lord Dallamore?" asked he with a smile.

"Oh d--m the cold hearted '*lilly livered* loon' he fights shy they say."[74]

"What you think she likes him then?" said he with more secret vexation than he liked to confess.

"Why faith I don't know how that is. I rather think not myself, but the good natured world at Harrogate said they did all they could to get him and even ran away with him to Scotland, but that as ill luck would have it on their way they were overtaken by Lord Mount Villars. I can hardly tell what to think for certainly they did go together to the North for Tom had some business at Borrowbridge and he met them on the road as he returned."

"Alone!" interrupted Lord Louverney eagerly.

"Oh God no! Her father and her brother were both with them besides two chaises filled with Dallamore's dogs and servants, for my part I really think it most probable they were only on a shooting party."

"With Miss Miltern?"

---

[74] Fight shy of: avoid (OED).

"Aye why not, I should have gone myself to the mountains last August only for Tom I am no bad shot I can assure you."

"And do you think that little Selena is so well accomplished?"

"Why no I should rather doubt that however I should be more surprised to find that she could have fallen in love with Dallamore than with his little double barreled gun. I never saw any thing the least like flirting between them at Harrogate and indeed it is scarcely possible that any girl could like Dallamore he is so strange a mortal. I ought not to say that however for he is a great friend of mine ever since he offered me a beautiful thorough bred chesnut mare that I took a fancy to, and I would have given one of my eyes to Tom with pleasure if he would but have allowed me to keep her, but nothing could prevail upon him, so after two days riding I sent her back with a heavy heart. But any thing for a quiet life you know. I took care however to make my complaint to Dallamore and what do you think he did?"

"Gave her to his groom I dare say."

"Oh I wish to Heaven he had. No but the savage took a pistol and shot her thro' the head before Tom's face, I really cried with vexation when I heard it."

Lord Louverney smiled at the strange misrepresentation with which this annecdote had so lately been repeated and he might perhaps have been tempted to betray Mrs. Montrose at least in part to the revengeful lash of Lady Greysville's tongue had not the interest he powerfully felt to hear farther of Selena conquered the impulse of this spiteful justice. After a short pause he therefore exclaimed, "So you really do not think then that Miss Miltern is engaged."

Lady Greysville now smiled in her turn and indeed it required but little penetration to see that his inclination for Selena wanted only encouragement to assume the name and pretentions of Love.

As she was good natured in general to all and really liked Selena she immediately felt anxious to promote an establishment so desirable—and being of a disposition warmly and eagerly to engage in whatever struck her fancy she after a few more conversations actually brought Lord Louverney before they left Rose Park to authorise her to sound the sentiments of Selena whom she had very little doubt of being able to persuade graciously to receive an offer which so few young women of the first rank would have rejected.

In the mean time Lord Louverney endeavoured to gain her affections by all these little constant flattering attentions which to almost every woman are universally agreeable from the other sex, but which from one alone could reach the heart of Selena with that fascination which attends the most apparently indifferent actions when they point out the unceasing devotion of the beloved object. These are even involuntary and never can be imitated where the heart is in fact disengaged. They are the genuine fruits of Love and to a sensible mind are of infinitely more value than the most ardent professions or the most shewy sacrifices—for it is not by those tokens of affection by which the lover studies to please that we can best judge of his attachment, it is from the most trifling occurrences, it is from the most insignificant movements to which none but the eye of love could pay the lightest attention that we draw the most infallible and the most irresistibly enchanting proofs.

But while Lord Louverney was thus seeking to win the heart of Selena, he himself with thirsty eyes drank so largely of love's intoxicating potion that his growing attachment was observed not only with secret envy and indignation by Mrs. Montrose but from both Clara and Lady Trevallyn Selena received warnings of what a proposal she might expect.

The generous and feeling heart of Selena would at all times have shrunk from giving the most distant encouragement to offers which she could not accept, and lamented inspiring sentiments which she could not share; but in her present situation the idea seemed to convey to her delicate mind a species of criminality from which she felt it revolt with a dread which made her, altho' extremely unwilling to believe those foreboding suspicions, yet resolve to shun as much as possible during the remainder of their short visit all conversation with Lord Louverney.

The rudeness with which Mrs. Montrose treated both sisters encreased to a degree that was extremely painful to them and was even still more felt by Lady Trevallyn. That rudeness was now extended to Lord Louverney and from the moment that she thought that he no longer admired her exclusively she could not command her temper so as to address him even in the common terms of civility.

It is true that as Lord Louverney possessed in unusual degree the talent of keen and delicate repartee she in general suffered whenever she ventured to attack him but there was one subject by which she found the secret of distressing almost equally him and Selena, and when in her presence Mrs. Montrose assailed him with gross and spiteful mockery upon his obvious attachment his embarrassment encreased by that of the interesting object of his love deprived him for the moment of all his presence of mind and all desire of revenge yielded to his wish of relieving Selena by an immediate change of subject.

There is no species of persecution by which girls are more frequently tormented than this and too often has envy succeeded by these very means in her efforts of easily separating those whom a growing inclination might (had not intimacy been thus discouraged) have in time rendered mutually happy.

Selena felt it perhaps less than she would have done had Lord Louverney been the secret object of her heart, nevertheless her confusion was extreme every time that Mrs. Montrose opened her lips to address her after casting the contemptuous and sarcastic glance upon her and Lord Louverney which was the sure forerunner of some malignant and offensive jest.

She beheld herself by this intentional cruelty and affected merriment exposed continually to the observation of the whole party and the rather as the society at Rose park had suffered a considerable loss by an inexhaustible fund of amusement in the desertion of the Astons.

On the morning after the obsolete magnificance had made its appearance with so much revived eclat an apology was delivered to Mrs. Montrose for their sudden departure alleging that unexpected business called them immediately to town.

The truth was that Mrs. Aston not being able to endure the contempt which she conceived in some degree attached to her from the ridiculous meanness of her husband endeavoured to prevail upon him to relinquish his newly acquired prise, and to quit what she considered as the scene of his disgrace. And to this notwithstanding his reluctance he was after some contention apparently obliged to consent. After every thing was packed up however and Mrs. Aston already in the carriage deeply engaged in her philosophical studies he contrived unperceived by her to thrust his bundle under the seat and the secret satisfaction of having thus been able to bear away his contested treasure rendered him unusually amiable during some stages in spite of the monstrous impositions which never ceased to excite his wonder as well as indignation at every inn upon the London road.

The day fixed for the breaking up of the party assembled at Rose park now approached, and approached unregretted by any if we except Lord Louverney and Lady Greysville. Yet altho' Lord Louverney could not without sorrow lose those opportunities which he had there enjoyed of constantly addressing the ever graceful, ever lovely object whom he so much admired, yet he consoled himself by the hopes which he indulged in spite of all Selena's reserve, hopes which Lady Greysville so confidently encouraged that when his disinterested declaration should be made his assiduous attendance whereever she might be would assuredly be allowed and that their present temporary separation would deliver them both from the persecuting malice or ill bred folly under which they had there suffered.

Lady Greysville perfectly at her ease notwithstanding the ill humour of her hostess and the displeasure of her husband was gratified by the admiration of Mr. Montrose amused by all around her and warmly interested in the match which she hoped to bring about and the passion of which she was the confidant; a passion which she had indeed in so large a share contributed to raise by timely cherishing the hasty and tender plant that it is not surprising she should consider it as entirely of her own creation and ardently desire its success. Hitherto she had however contented herself with only hinting to Selena her noble conquest and in the triumph of her heart could not refrain from speaking of it in her absence to Mrs. Montrose whom she thereby never failed provoking to some contemptuous observation upon the innocent object of her envy, before whom she often took an opportunity to assert that "Lord Louverney was not at all a marrying man," which observation was constantly made to Lady Greysville's sanguine hopes while she heard her with an incredulous toss of her head or a forced smile generally concluding with "No, no I promise you it will be no such easy matter to draw in Lord Louverney! He knows a little too much of the world for that."

Altho' from motives of delicacy and prudence Selena sedulously shrunk from the conversation of Lord Louverney and as much as possible retired from his admiration, yet she considered him with that degree of interest and gratitude which every heart of sensibility will naturally experience towards an amiable object the voluntary gift of whose affections it cannot return.

Nature in all her varied loveliness, all her attractive graces possesses nothing so beautiful or so engaging to a mind susceptible of tenderness as the artless testimonies of innocent affection, and it is the coldness of coquetry or the dullness of insensibility alone that can with pleasure or with complete indifference resist that impression which Nature bids them make upon the heart of her favourite Woman.

But all the favourable colouring which might thus have been cast upon manners and a disposition which were in themselves far from deficient in grace and warmth was in one moment obscured when Selena heard him (with that thoughtless levity too common in the conversation even of those most free from all ill natured designs) let fall some unlucky pleasantries upon the well known attachment of Lady Trevallyn for her profligate cousin. The countenance of Selena instantly spoke her wounded her indignant feelings. Struck with the conviction that he had thus unintentionally offended the only woman upon earth whom he now desired to please Lord Louverney vainly sought to retract, but in continuing the unfortunate subject his confusion but plunged him deeper in disgrace, till without trusting herself to utter a reply in a cause the weakness of which she too painfully felt Selena silently arose and quitted the apartment leaving Lord Louverney ready to curse his own tongue for those unseasonable expressions which were yet only such as he had been accustomed to see excite a smile from the lips of those who styled nay perhaps considered themselves the dearest friends.

It was in this inauspicious moment that Selena was met by Lady Greysville who tho' not absolutely commissioned by Lord Louverney was in search of her to lay at her feet as she abruptly expressed herself rank, fortune and a charming young fellow.

Impatient as she had been to perform this office Lord Louverney had hitherto resisted her arguments by representing that Selena might justly feel hurt at the appearance of confidence which so hasty a proposal would perhaps wear.

But when she found that they were actually to separate on the following day she determined that she would at least have the satisfaction of announcing to Selena his declared attachment and to this he willingly consented not however without much trepidation for its reception.

Amazed at the decisive manner in which (when at length convinced of the sincerity of his professions) Selena gave the most serious negative to listen to this proposal Lady Greysville could not at first comprehend what could induce a girl thus inconsiderably to reject advantages so brilliant when suddenly recollecting the reports which related to Dallamore she shook her head and exclaimed, "Ah my dear child do not throw away your happiness for a little romantic nonsense! And believe me if you had every thing at your call it is far better to take the man who loves you than him you love."

Selena perceived the mistaken idea and felt hurt at being thus suspected of cherishing an unreturned partiality. But unable to explain the real truth she hung her head in silent mortified confusion and Lady Greysville continued, "Love is a mighty silly thing, take my word, and a first Love the silliest of all; I do think that the most unfortunate thing that can happen to a poor girl is to have a flirting cousin. I say with Hotspur 'The Devil take such cozeners!'[75] ever since poor Lady Trevallyn suffered so much from that wretch Lord Henry who is but too charming since one cannot hate him as he deserves."

A tear started to Selena's eye, and a gentle sigh almost escaped her bosom when the image of an amiable cousin banished for the moment every idea but that of excellence remembered with the softest tenderness.

This was not unmarked by Lady Greysville and all the resentment and indignation she really then felt towards Dallamore she openly let fall upon Lord Henry, whose conduct (while she now considered it as the counterpart of Dallamore's) she made no scruple of declaring had not only destroyed Lady Trevallyn's health and happiness but irreparably injured her reputation.

At this Selena replied with some warmth, "Oh dear Lady Greysville! You who spoke so well the other day against cruel slander can you condescend to repeat yourself the illnatured misrepresentations of Lord Louverney or any other thoughtless accuser of innocence which I am sure you are yourself convinced is purity itself?"

"Lord Louverney?" repeated Lady Greysville in astonishment. "Why what has Lord Louverney been saying of Lady Trevallyn?"

Selena sorry for what she had said coloured in silence.

"You have surely misunderstood him my dear! for I know he admires her more than any woman upon earth except yourself."

"Then I am sure," replied Selena blushing still deeper and with some hesitation, "his principles as to woman's conduct cannot be very strict for I have just heard him myself imply that she gives encouragement to the love which he says Lord Henry still professes for her. Nor can I feel much flattered at the preference of a man who could admire one he thought capable of such a crime."

"And is it thus that poor Lord Louverney has forfeited your favour?" demanded Lady Greysville with a smile.

Selena assured her that her rejections had reasons much more invincible but could not deny that she considered him in a less favourable light from this which she esteemed a wanton injury towards her amiable friend.

"Oh my dear Miss Miltern you little know the world," exclaimed Lady Greysville, "and in particular the young men of fashion. They accuse us females of being fond of gossip and scandal—and say that we love to destroy the characters of each other when in fact there is hardly a malicious story which has not its first origin in the desire some idle young man has of amusing the circle around him; or gratifying the vanity or illnature of the woman he addresses by some detracting anecdote for which he does not himself expect credit and which he then perhaps dismisses from his memory for ever. Lord Louverney with the best heart in the world must be some such stupid unnaturally perfect monster as

---

[75]   Hotspur in Shakespeare's *Henry IV, Part 1* (1597), 1.3.253.

Sir Charles Grandison[76] if he could have entirely escaped this fashionable vice, but I will pledge my existence you will never find one more free from it and every other thing like illnature."

Selena smiled perhaps incredulously for Lady Greysville looking archly added nodding her head, "No, not Dallamore himself. Come my dear, nobody could be more ready to defend Lady Trevallyn from the nasty cats that would tear her to pieces than I would be, but between ourselves poor thing she has given the world some right to talk and we cannot expect that people will be so delicate as to look in silence upon what they think wrong. We must be content either to act for the good opinion of the world or else disregard its censure. I would not say this only to be free with you I think she affords you a strong warning in her example. How much happier would she have been, how much more estimable if she had acted wisely and given up her foolish love and her wicked cousin when she saw he had no intention of acting fairly by her. If she had not so imprudently surrendered herself and all her hopes to him and looked so cold upon every other man and so miserable when he spoke to any woman but her, there was scarcely a young man in town whom she might not have attracted, for who is half so beautiful or so attractive? And she might now have been blooming and gay with a little family of her own to educate and love instead of those little beggar brats that she would spend all her life with now, if Lord Trevallyn would but let her have her own way. Let me give you a little advice my dear Miss Miltern—there is no man worth being unhappy about believe me. A lover is a very charming thing but when he begins once to give you a pain, good bye all that is charming, let him go without a struggle. Treat him as you would a pen knife—nothing looks more brilliant at a distance but where it dazzles most if clasped too closely nothing can give a sorer wound. Handle it rightly nothing is more useful, but attempt not to detain it if withdrawn for if you do depend upon it, it will cut you most severely."

Selena smiled but assured her that the lecture was misapplied.

Lady Greysville nevertheless finding that all her arguments were without effect retir'd discomfitted and much disappointed to reproach Lord Louverney for his imprudent tattle, upon which she chose to lay the whole of her defeat. He however saw too plainly that he had been able to make no impression upon the heart of Selena and regretting his hasty declaration separated from her with but little hope, tho' he resolved (if suffered to claim any intimacy upon their meeting in London) to persevere in his efforts to banish from her mind the remembrance of Dallamore which he believed was the present obstacle to his happiness.

---

[76] Sir Charles Grandison is title character of Samuel Richardson's 1753 epistolary novel.

Chapter XVI

Happy my eyes when they behold thy face!
My heavy heart will leave its doleful beating
At sight of thee, and bound with sprightful joys:
Oh smile as when our loves were in the spring
And cheer my fainting soul!

Otway[77]

Clara did not disguise the transport which she experienced as she entered London. The certainty of soon seeing Edwin of whom she had never heard one syllable since Sidney and he had arrived there together lent such an additional brilliant charm to the pleasures of novelty that all was enchantment. Every object upon which her eye beamed was a new delight and this hour was one of those bright spots that to the end of life are never to be forgotten but continue to shine "Amid the dreary waste of time o'er past."[78]

Nor was the more placid mind of Selena entirely free from this impression of pleasure tho' mingled with disquieting and sorrowful reflections. She too was sure that her eyes in a few hours should once more behold the form whose image her heart had never ceas'd to present from the moment of their separation. And tho' she trembled at the anticipated joy and knew not what intelligence Sidney might now have to communicate yet the certainty of seeing his beautiful countenance animated with delight at their meeting shed an exquisite drop of tender joy over all her meditations which was more than sufficient to conquer every bitterness.

Far different were the sensations of Lady Trevallyn as they approached London—the scene to her of so many lively enjoyments so many cruel disappointments, where she had sparkled in all the triumph that youth beauty and the homage of an admiring world, with the still dearer flattery of the man she loved could bestow, where she had sunk oppressed by the bitterest of mortifications, insulted by secretly rejoicing envy, and neglected by him she adored. All reflections on the past were however now swallowed up in the agitating uncertainty whether she was here again to meet that fatally beloved object. A sickness almost to fainting seized upon her more than once as they drove thro' Hyde park and it was with the utmost difficulty that she dispersed the tears which perpetually rushed to her eyes, or restrained the deep sighs that appeared to oppress her bosom even to suffocation.

Scarcely however had the carriage turned into Piccadilly when the sight of Lord Henry's horses (which were too remarkable not to be recognised by one whose heart was indelibly impressed by all that related to him) at once decided all her doubts, and tho' it encreased the perturbation of her spirits insensibly and unconsciously calmed the anguish of her soul.

---

[77]   Belvidera in Thomas Otway's *Venice Preserved* (1682), 1.1.316–20.

[78]   De Montfort in Joanna Baillie's *De Montfort* (1798), 1.1.182 (Tighe uses "Amid" for "Which" and "waste" for "gloom").

As the carriage past, the groom who slowly led his master's horses put his hand to his hat and Selena's eye read in the quick changing colour of Lady Trevallyn's cheek by whose servant she was thus acknowledged.

But Lady Trevallyn at that moment heeded not her observations; her whole soul looked forth at her eyes in search of him whom she thus concluded separated from her but a few paces; they sought nevertheless in vain. Happily for the present ease of her too sensible heart they could not penetrate the walls of the splendid the dissolute mansion of fashionable vice which they at that moment passed. She was spared a sight of the most keen torture that the feeling mind is ever destined to endure, she was for this time at least spared the conviction that he whom she loved was at once unworthy and unmindful of their love.

Roused from the deep reverie into which this accidental circumstance had plunged her by the stopping of the carriage Lady Trevallyn exerted herself to welcome Selena and her sister to their new abode, but her exertions were soon rendered unnecessary by the sudden entrance of a visitor who at once engrossed all the attention of her guests.

Early that morning Sidney had called, and having been informed of their expected arrival in town found it impossible during the remainder of the day to quit the neighbourhood of Grosvenor square. The lamps just beginning to be lighted he was however slowly returning homewards when his heart beat violently as he perceived the carriages for which he had so long watched drive rapidly into the square.

Urged immediately onwards he found himself nearly at the door at the same instant with the chaise which contained all he loved. He caught a glimpse of that adored countenance which was then turned from him and overcome with the violence of contending emotions he stopped short; then suddenly recollecting the strange appearance it might have if he were perceived thus as it were awaiting their arrival he hastily retired some paces from the door where unobserved he gazed upon her as she alighted with unutterable fondness and regretted that by his idle prudence he had lost the opportunity of pressing that hand the right to which he would have considered cheaply purchas'd by worlds had they been at that moment in his possession.

Again his feet with involuntarily speed led him to the door; the servants were busily engaged in the tumult of untying luggage and dismissing post boys, when amidst the idle crowd that collects instantaneously upon such occasions of bustle Sidney was unexpectedly recognised by Lady Trevallyn's servant who had attended them during the day which they had spent together at Glocester. Bowing respectfully he seemed to expect some enquiries, or at least Sidney glad to seize upon the excuse to himself for making them was persuaded they were expected.

"My Lady is very well Sir I thank you and is just gone in, will you please to walk up stairs?" It was an invitation not to be resisted and almost breathless he followed him to the apartment where the strong light of a large blazing fire and the branches already lighted over the chimney could shew his enraptured eyes but one lovely object, the beautiful the interesting Selena pale, trembling, and motionless overcome with delight and bewildered with surprise at this his sudden appearance.

When the agitation of the first moments had abated, and after the usual general solicitations had past Selena read in his countenance that he had some intelligence to impart; tho' the presence of Lord Trevallyn and Mr. Guise prevented her from making any enquiry. Restless and embarrassed he evidently sought an opportunity of speaking to her unobserved, but as no prospect of this appeared to offer after a few minutes forced conversation he rose to withdraw. Lord Trevallyn invited him to dinner but as he at the same time apologis'd for doing so and added that he feared he must before this be already engaged Sidney with some little hesitation excused himself and asking leave from Lady Trevallyn to call the next morning gave Selena one look that spoke more than years of eloquence could utter, and retired.

As the ladies quitted the dinner parlour a letter was delivered to Selena which she instantly perceived to be from Sidney and retiring to her own room to conceal her agitation she sunk upon her knees and piously sought the assistance of Heaven to calm and tranquilise her mind which she at first found unequal to support her courage in opening what she doubted not contained some decisive sentence of her lot. She had no sooner broke the seal than her collected fortitude once more forsook her upon perceiving that it enclosed a letter written in the hand of Dallamore. A flood of tears having in some degree relieved her she cast her eyes over the lines in the envelope which as she saw were Sidney's. They were merely to inform her that the letter which was received but on the day preceding, to account for his not having sent it to her before her arrival in town. With a trembling hand she then unfolded Dallamore's letter. It was not dated but on the cover Sidney had desired her to observe the post mark from which they might conclude it had been written from Mount Villars ten days before. The letter was as follows.

> "Dear Sidney,
>
> "I suppose you thought we had been taken by the french but it was all Modely's fault, and I'll be damned if ever I step into a ship again except a Holyhead packet as long as I live; I never was so cursed sick of any thing since I was born. When I got sight of the irish coast if the scoundrel had not lent me his boat I would have swam ashore and was just preparing to do it. I hope you have got a nice house and carriage for Selena and that she finds London very gay. I expect to see her in a few days but I must first decide a wager of five hundred guineas upon our Woodcocks for I met Burton and the Dunbars at Bantry and if Burton and I don't kill a hundred brace in a week I lose, but there is not a doubt of our doing it if this weather lasts.
>> Yours &c
>>> Dallamore"

While Selena was yet again and again perusing this letter so little calculated to inspire her with pleasing ideas or flattering hopes Clara softly entered. She had observed Selena's agitation upon receiving it and certain that it came from Sidney was impatient to learn what intelligence it had produced.

When her indignation had in some degree subsided, which in spite of Selena's silent tears, she found it impossible entirely to suppress as she read this wild proof of inconsistent and inconsiderate folly the sisters consulted together upon what conduct they were now to pursue.

Clara was strongly inclined to remain with Lady Trevallyn till Dallamore's arrival, but uncertain as Selena still considered this she represented to her sister that kindness to Robert and propriety of appearance required them to accept of his invitation should either he or Lady Harriet give them the power of removing to upper Brook street—and the rather as Clara's guardian had made some objections to her remaining under the protection of Lady Trevallyn.

Poor Clara who could not conquer her dread of being separated from her sister reluctantly yielded to her opinion and a note was immediately sent to inform Mr. Miltern of their arrival in which Selena enclosed Dallamore's letter.

In less than an hour Selena's affectionate heart overflowed at her eyes in tears of tenderness and pleasure as with open arms she flew to meet the embrace of her brother.

"You are welcome dearest girls," cried he, "but we must not again separate Selena till Dallamore in person claims you."

He then in the warmest and most affectionate manner insisted upon their immediate removal to his house, so that Lady Trevallyn who at first strongly opposed his wishes was at length obliged to consent to their quitting her on the following morning but she did not acquiesce in this arrangement till she had received from Selena a promise that no day should pass without their meeting while they remained in town.

When the hurry of this debate was over, Selena observed with concern that her brother was much changed in his appearance, that he had lost the gaiety which used to animate his countenance and was become absent and thoughtful.

Upon her enquiring for Lady Harriet he said that she was not at home when Selena's note had arrived & she was not again mentioned during his stay which he prolonged till Lady Trevallyn's evident fatigue after supper reminded him that he should allow the ladies to retire. Slowly therefore rising he wished them a good night and excused himself for having kept them up so long by saying that he had been used to such late hours since he came to London that he had scarcely yet seen the light of day there.

The high spirits with which Clara entered for the first time the great city were by this time considerably abated. She dreaded the haughty tyranny of Lady Harriet and felt it strange that she should have been so many hours in the same town with Edwin and as yet her ear have vainly and impatiently expected to hear his name which no lip had even mentioned. No sooner was she alone with Selena, after having parted with Lady Trevallyn for the night, than blushing and hesitating she expressed her surprise that Sidney should not have spoken of their friend who had been in a manner recommended to his care, and eagerly asked Selena did she think Lady Harriet would suffer her to keep her promise in admitting his occasional visits.

Selena smiling sought to relieve her anxiety on this head, assuring her that as far as she was concerned he should never be repulsed.

Clara's uneasiness from these apprehensions joined to the agitation her spirits had felt during the whole day deprived her of rest, an uneasiness which the ensuing morning convinced her she might well have spared herself, since Lady Harriet had long since determined that neither Selena nor her sister should be placed with her in town as spies upon her conduct and rivals with her for the admiration which in her own house at least she was resolved to engross. The art of turning the thoughts from "the fashion of uncertain evils"[79] is indeed one of the greatest secrets to preserve peace of mind—and it seems strange that in a world of so much real pain and sorrow we should not at least have wisdom enough to prevent our suffering by the anticipation of distress which may never arrive or "run to meet what we should most avoid."[80] But it is all men's office to preach that philosophy which would

> charm agony with words [....]
> But no man's virtue nor sufficiency
> To be so moral[81]

when it shall become him to put his own lessons into practice.

While they were at breakfast the next day Selena received from her brother the following note.

> "My dear Selena,
>
> "It is a very sensible mortification to myself to give up the hopes I had indulged of enjoying your society at home for some time as Harriet seems to fear that you do not feel yourself so comfortable with her as you do in your present very agreeable situation and as you expect Dallamore so soon perhaps you will hardly think it worth while to make any change until you can settle yourself according to your own choice. I hope you will at least contrive to let me see as much of you as possible and consider me always as
>
> Your most faithful friend and affectionate brother,
>   Robert Miltern
> P.S. Harriet dines out today but perhaps you and Clara will come to me as I shall be alone."

Selena felt her colour rise and her heart sink as she read these words and perceived herself thus totally cast by her brother upon the protection of a stranger. It is true that the affection and tenderness which Lady Trevallyn had shewn was indeed more than sisterly, and that Selena could not so keenly feel the conduct of her brother on this occasion as she must have done had she not been convinced

---

[79]   John Milton, *Comus* (1634), line 360.

[80]   John Milton, *Comus* (1634), line 363 ("And run to meet what he would most avoid").

[81]   Leonato in Shakespeare's *Much Ado about Nothing* (1598), 5.1.26, 29–30 (line 26 should read "Charm ache with air and agony with words").

that he acted not according to the dictates of his own inclination but under the influence of one whom Selena could not love and who never had shewn to her even the semblance of affection or indeed the common decencies of civility.

With some little embarrassment Selena handed to Lady Trevallyn her brother's note, who with cordial sincerity expressed with her own peculiar powers of fascination her pleasure at this their relinquishment of what she had so reluctantly sacrificed to a superior claim.

Clara also with a lightened heart unaffectedly congratulated Selena and herself upon their escape and fixing her sparkling eyes upon the piano-forte already in fancy beheld there Edwin and listened to his mellifluous voice that in every note poured forth the very soul of melody.

The ladies had not yet left the breakfast table when Sidney was announced but tho' his soul languished to pour forth all its fondness to the ears of Selena yet he now scarce ventured to address her. Satisfied to be thus near, to gaze upon her downcast eyes nay even sometimes for an instant to catch their timid glance

> As when the blue sky trembles thro' a cloud
> Of purest white[82]

To watch the movements of her hurried pulse as they fluttered thro' the pure lawn that shaded her purer bosom, or beat beneath the beautiful whiteness of her transparent throat and temples.

And even when the fear of observation forced him to withdraw his ardent eyes yet the consciousness of being at her side diffused a calm delight thro' his soul as the casket still retains the fragrance of the exhausted perfume, and his heart yet felt the sigh of peace that seemed to whisper some nameless pleasure, some undetermined prospects of flattering Hope.

Mutually engaged upon no one object upon earth except each other, they yet exchanged but few words.

Sidney indeed fearful of betraying his feelings exerted himself to support a general conversation but Selena remained almost silent until wishing to indulge Clara she at length assumed courage in a tremulous voice to ask him after Edwin.

The countenance of Sidney ever the interpreter of his soul was ever loaded with generous concern as he replied that he had not seen him for some time;

"Is he ill?" exclaimed Clara eagerly turning pale with an apprehension which she thought not at the moment to disguise.

"No," replied Sidney with a half smile, "but Edwin is too much sought after by all the world to be easily seen except in circles of the very haut ton where I have not sought admission since I came to town. When you go out Lady Trevallyn you will hear of no one but Edwin Stanmore, the object of every woman's attention and the envy of the men, the hero of every assembly and the soul of every pleasure."

---

[82] Narva in James Thomson's *The Tragedy of Sophonisba* (1730), 1.1.77–8.

The brow of Clara which had once more brightened with hope was again shaded by anxiety and Selena herself was not without uneasiness at this account of Edwin which seemed so plainly to imply his having been drawn into the vortex of dissipation. The conversation was however here critically interrupted by the entrance of a servant who presented to Lady Trevallyn Mr. Leeson's compliments of enquiry with a message signifying that he was then in my Lord's study and wished if permitted to have the honor of paying his respects in person.

"There is no avoiding this now," said Lady Trevallyn with a smile as she dismissed the servant and Sidney congratulated them upon the visit that they were about to receive, "which," said he, "will last you may depend upon it, till every syllable of news and battle true or false which the town affords is completely exhausted."

While he spoke the little bustling figure thus announced hurried into the room apparently out of breath with his glass held up to his eye in one hand and in the other extending at arm's length his hat and cane. After a quick motion round the room of his erect and well powdered head he singled out Lady Trevallyn and with the cordiality of a most intimate friend welcomed her to town.

With the volubility of a torrent that rolls over an impeding rock he then expressed his satisfaction at seeing her look so charmingly, enquired after their friends at Rose park, repeated all that had just passed between him and Lord Trevallyn informed her where he had been the night before and where he was to dine that day and all in a self satisfied and even jocular strain which far from calling for any reply left for it indeed not the smallest space.

In the midst of this wearisome and insipid continuation of sound without sense their attention was suddenly recalled by a piece of intelligence which Sidney in a lower voice confirmed to Selena adding that he was about to communicate it when his thoughts were diverted by her enquiry after Edwin.

"Well but my dear Madam," continued Mr. Leeson, for no pause whatever had occurred in his address to Lady Trevallyn, "You have not said anything of your opinion of our friend Richmond's wonderful luck which I take it for granted you must have heard. Well for my part I always said that fellow would make his fortune by marriage. But they tell me that not one shilling of the estate is settled unless Lord Clonagh has a son so that Lady Lucy may be no heiress after all—and especially if the old gentleman really marries again, which will be a sad take in for our poor friend and indeed ..."

"Is Lady Lucy O'Brien married to Mr. Richmond?" interrupted Lady Trevallyn much surprised.

"*God* bless my soul," cried the delighted Mr. Leeson half rising from his seat thro' eagerness to pour forth his information, "is it possible you have not heard that extraordinary business, and your Ladyship just come from Bath. Oh true as you are going to say you must have been gone to Rose park I suppose before it happened. Well my dear Madam you shall have the exact truth at least as far as I have been able to collect it from the various accounts which I have heard, for really nothing else has been spoken of for these three days past. It was Lady

Vellum that I first heard it from. Oh, no, I ask your Ladyship's pardon it was Miss Blabbit told it me at Lady Vellum's last Monday evening where all the world was assembled to hear that young Stanmore sing—a very wonderful genius he is upon my honor—pray has your Ladyship heard him. Oh no I recollect you have not been out since you came to town, but to go on with my story, you must know then that some time last summer—no, no, I remember now it was about the beginning of autumn, or it might be later Richmond went over to Ireland with Lord Mount Villars, you Mr. Dallamore can probably tell exactly the time as I believe my Lord has the honor to be your uncle, not that the particular month signifies much in my story, but if I am wrong while speaking of your family affairs have the goodness to set me right, but you know I say nothing that all the world does not talk of—indeed for my part I seldom listen to gossip and almost make it a rule never to repeat it for you know my dear ...."

Here Sidney with some difficulty stopped him for an instant by entreating him to allow him to satisfy Lady Trevallyn's curiosity dreading lest he should say something of Selena's story.

"Oh by all means my good sir but I beg your pardon allow me first to say a few words till I let Lady Trevallyn know some circumstances of which you may perhaps not be so well informed as I can assure you I have had my information from the very best possible authority."

"At least I hope then you will be so good as to recollect Lady Trevallyn is impatient to hear about Mr. Richmond and not mind for the present my family affairs."

This Sidney was obliged to say at the same time for he plainly perceived that Mr. Leeson was decided not to suffer him again to find a pause.

"Certainly, certainly," cried he with impetuosity, "nothing upon earth can give me greater pleasure than in any possible manner to obey her Ladyship but indeed Mr. Dallamore you must excuse me as to passing over entirely what relates to some of your family since it is so connected with my history as you shall judge yourself my dear Madam, but to come to the point with all possible expedition for I see your Ladyship's curiosity is raised as well as that of both these young ladies who I conclude are acquainted with Mr. Richmond, indeed he is very generally known and a very gentleman like young man in his manners as can be, and so Lady Lucy thought I do suppose. Perhaps your Ladyship may have seen Lady Lucy—a very charming girl as I am told; sings plays, dances to admiration with all those little accomplishments absolutely necessary you know to set off youth beauty and ten thousand a year—ha, ha, ha.

"But as I was saying on their arrival in Dublin Lord Mount Villars found his son going to make a sad foolish connexion with some fair Hibernian much below him, indeed quite out of the way; your Ladyship understands me and probably must have heard of it. You smile Mr. Dallamore, but I appeal to you, I dare say you were all very uneasy at the thoughts of your cousin being drawn in so imprudently. However I hope our young friend has quite given up that foolish idea, tho' at the time I have been told he was very much smitten, nearly caught faith—and that was Lord Mount Villars's chief motive for endeavouring so strongly to bring about a match between him and Lady Lucy. Every thing went on swimmingly Lady Lucy's charms triumphed in spite of all the arts of the fair adventurer the settlements were signed and the wedding cloaths all bought, when as ill fortune would have it who should come into the bay of Dublin but young Modely in the ship that he had just got the command of.

"Well I vow to God it is a shame in such times as these to trust our wooden walls with such wild fellows, boys I may say that have no more prudence or discretion than your Ladyship's little dog. By the bye that young pickle's sister Lady Harriet goes on at a fine rate. You know I for my part detest slander but she is really quite shameful. Poor Miltern, your Ladyship don't know him a poor soft lad ...."

"Well but Mr. Leeson," hastily interrupted Lady Trevallyn, "where is Mr. Richmond all this time?"

"You had better let me finish the story if you please," said Sidney turning towards her when Mr. Leeson eagerly raising his voice continued, "Oh by no means I am just come to the very critical part for the day was fixed when our comical friend Madam, for begging your pardon my dear Sir your cousin is a very odd young man and gave a very remarkable proof of his oddity on that occasion, for what does he do, but sails off with Captain Modely without paying either of his brides elect the compliment of a farewell visit or a card of apology.

"There was a strange uproar I hear when it was discovered and both ladies considered themselves as extremely ill used. But now observe comes Richmond's part, for seizing the golden opportunity while Lady Lucy's indignation was at its height he contrived so well to recommend himself to her good graces that she told her Papa she never could be happy unless he consented to their marriage. The old Peer was furious for indeed it must be confessed that our friend Richmond is no very advisable match for a young lady of her high expectations but by way of amusing her mind and driving away a billious attack which vexation had brought upon him he carried his daughter to Bath whither Richmond followed them and a few days ago whipped off the fair heiress of Clonagh in a chaise and four to Scotland. I am assured that her father would not hear of their being pursued but swears he will never see her face, and some go so far as to say that he has already married the daughter of his Landlady at Bath, a blooming young widow who has three fine children to shew as the fruit of her former Hymen which lasted but for two years. This however I do not give you as positive fact as for the rest you may depend upon it.

"But bless me what o'clock is it? I vow it is nearly three; and I promised Lady Vellum to be in Manchester square exactly at two. But really your conversation has been so uncommonly entertaining my dear Madam that I was quite insensible to the swiftness with which Time flew past. I am enchanted to see your Ladyship in such excellent spirits; It is positively a great journey from this to Manchester square and I must run all the way or Lady Vellum never will forgive me. I am going in her Ladyship's carriage to introduce her to a charming painter in crayons. She is going to have her portrait and that of young Stanmore in full length in one miniature while he accompanies with his voice her harp—or he is to be supposed accompanying her I should say for her Ladyship does not play the harp—that is only for effect. The harp is an extremely graceful instrument you know Ladies. But this between ourselves. I would not for the world it should get about. People are so censorious and say such illnatured things of poor Lady Vellum and her young beau whom she has netted so completely. For my part I never say anything. But you will detain me all day. Farewell I hope we shall meet this evening at Lady Rout's. Stanmore has promised faithfully to be there and I know Lady Vellum is to call for him where he dines to ensure him. Good morrow ..."

He was by this time on the stairs and had not yet ceased his liberal loquacity, but Clara heedless of all except the insinuation which respected Edwin with anguish and eager impatience turned to Sidney and demanded who was Lady Vellum.

"Oh my dear," cried Lady Trevallyn smiling, "she is a very terrible old creature—but she gives the best assemblies in town and has two or three balls every Spring a masquerade and concerts without end. She has a faro table too so that there is no house better filled."

"But is she married?" asked Clara with naivete.

"Yes my dear these thirty years at least."

"Then what does Mr. Leeson mean?" said Clara blushing but recovering herself in some degree, "and what can she mean by having herself drawn in that ridiculous manner."

"Pooh that was some nonsense I dare say of Mr. Leeson's. You must have seen enough of him already to be convinced one ought never to mind a word he says."

Sidney was however silent and Clara still anxious, endeavoured to gain from him an explanation of the hints which related to Lady Vellum when the door once more opened but not before the throbbing bosom of Lady Trevallyn had already assured her that Lord Henry was about to enter.

Distressed confused or surprised at this appearance not a countenance in the room but plainly spoke the agitation of each mind as he advanced, while he himself with more command of features expressed nothing but pleasure though he in fact shared something of each of these emotions. He had hoped that on their arrival in town the sisters whose presence at Lady Trevallyn's he justly considered so inimical to all his hopes should have been placed under the natural protection of their brother. Great then was his disappointment at finding them thus settled in the place where of all others he least desired to see them. Nor was he much less annoyed to behold Sidney not only thus admitted apparently as an inmate but so assiduous in early availing himself of this admission from which Lord Henry would gladly have excluded all others beside himself.

Sidney on his part looked on his designs with an eye of suspicion and indignation. Interested for Lady Trevallyn not only as he must naturally have felt from her own beauty and innocence but more particularly as she stood the chosen friend and seemingly only protector of Selena whose delicate situation called for such peculiar prudence; he trembled for the lovely object thus exposed to the persevering and cruel views of her profligate cousin and felt a conscious sting of humiliation and self reproach at the obvious tho' he was sensible unjust parallel which severity or malice might draw between his present conduct and that of a seducer whom he abhorred. Selena with more grief than astonishment beheld the renewal of those visits which her heart lamented and her judgment condemned as dangerous and unjustifiable—while even Clara provoked at the interruption of a conversation so interesting to all her hopes looked upon the sudden entrance of Lord Henry with an eye of displeasure which was too evident to escape observation had not each at this moment been so completely engrossed by their own emotions.

In the mean time Lady Trevallyn who in momentary expectation of this visit had impatiently watched the length of Sidney's stay and of Mr. Leeson's harangue her eyes incessantly turned towards the clock that stood upon the chimney piece from the tines its silver bell had struck one, now oppressed with mingled joy sorrow and confusion scarce raised her dejected eyes as she returned the salutation of that beloved voice whose softest accent shot thrilling to her heart.

After a few minutes Selena, who in spite of Sidney's presence now found her situation uncommonly disagreeable retired to her room and Sidney as may well be supposed remained not long after her departure while Clara having unsuccessfully tried to engage him to speak of Edwin's present pursuits followed Selena to pour into her sympathising and affectionate bosom all her fears and disappointments leaving Lord Henry at length to congratulate himself upon having once more an opportunity of appealing to the fatal sensibility of Lady Trevallyn to pardon the weakness which he confessed rendered it impossible for him as yet to tear himself for ever from her presence.

Chapter XVII

Consumed in riot all that Life adorned
For joys unrelished shared with those he scorned.
                              Knight[83]

New sorrows and disquietudes awaited poor Selena on that day. As she was impatient to see her brother and converse with him freely upon her little cheering prospects she requested Lady Trevallyn to order the carriage before five o'clock and accompanied by Clara drove to Upper Brook street. Both the servants who appeared in the hall were strangers to her and indeed had she been able instantly to survey the whole household she could not have recognised one face but that of Mrs. Millikin.

To her surprise she was informed that neither their Lady nor Mr. Miltern were at home but as she said she would go in to await her brother's return, the servant after some hesitation as he proceeded her up stairs said he believed his Lady was at home—but he did not know whether she was not dressing. As he opened the

---

[83]   Richard Payne Knight, *The Progress of Civil Society: A Didactic Poem in Six Books* (1796), 3:497–8 (the epigraph substitutes "he" for "I" in line 98).

drawing room door a large screen prevented their entrance from being noticed and Selena before she saw to whom they were addressed heard these words from Lady Harriet uttered in a tone of much vexation and anger, "Upon my word I shall not again wait at home for you to this hour and I wonder at …"

Here to their mutual surprise and confusion Selena once more met the eye of Lord Henry and the deep rouge that then disguised the conscious flush of shame upon the cheek of Lady Harriet rivall'd not the glow which for an instant overspread the face of her companion who could scarcely have felt more consternation at the sudden appearance of any monster most hideous to sight, than was thus caused by the entrance of a form lovely as that in which the young imagination of a painter would wish to cloath his favourite nymph.

The cold embrace which was timidly offered and ungraciously accepted having been exchanged between Lady Harriet & her sisters she expressed her surprise at seeing them saying that she understood they were to dine with Robert and therefore did not expect to have the pleasure of a visit till dinner time.

"Is not my brother come in?"

"Lord no child did you think we dined in the middle of the day. I suppose you expect us to copy your stupid Mrs. Vallard's primitive hours."

Lord Henry who had not again seated himself after Selena's entrance now took his leave saying as he looked at his watch that he supposed it was nearly time for her Ladyship to dress, to which she only replied by an angry glance with which she followed him to the door—and then stirring the fire enquired from Selena whether Lady Trevallyn was going to dine abroad that she had turned them out so early.

Clara coloured but Selena prevented her reply by saying, "I had some business with my brother and I thought he would probably return home when it grew dark, but I beg we may not prevent your going to dress."

"Oh Lord it is time enough this half hour. Well pray what are we to call you? Are you Lady Dallamore yet? Or have you given up that pretty piece of nonsense."

"Lord Dallamore intends to be in town in a few days I believe," said Selena quietly, "and till then you may call me what you please."

"And in the mean time I suppose you may have all your beaux about you at Lady Trevallyn's. I dare say she had a crowded leveé□ this morning."

Selena was silent and the question was then put more directly.

"Who have you seen pray since you came to town?"

"Mr. Leeson called."

"Mr. Leeson! Oh my God Lady Trevallyn must be sadly at a loss for visitors to let in that fool, and had you no one else?"

"Yes Sidney."

"Hrumph! And was that all?"

Selena who guessed that the object of this curiosity was to find out whether Lord Henry had been at Grosvenor square was resolved not to gratify her by this intelligence and therefore only replied, "I left Sidney in the drawing room and did not come down till just before I came out. There was no one there then but Mr. Guise."

"Oh, I suppose Lady Trevallyn likes tete-a-tetes and you are accommodating enough to withdraw upon such occasions."

"I have never yet had any reason to suspect that my presence was unwelcome to Lady Trevallyn or to fear that my choosing to be sometimes alone should give her offence," answered Selena colouring deeply at the odious insinuation.

There was something in this reply which highly provoked Lady Harriet and it was surely not want of will to inflict pain that no more poignant repartee presented itself than that "it was a pity two such prodigies of wisdom should ever separate."

Selena returned no answer to this observation and there was a short pause which Lady Harriet interrupted by saying, "So you have not had a visit from young Stanmore yet! But I dare say he intends to cut you now that he is grown such a wonderful fine man I suppose you must have heard what a ridiculous fool he makes of himself with that old set of harridans and odious Vellum in particular."

"How do you mean," cried Clara her voice scarcely articulate while happily for her the obscurity of the room at present concealed the paleness of her countenance.

"Oh Lord! Is that all you know? Why they have got him completely into their set and as to Lady Vellum she never stirs an inch without him at her elbow. He is a fine deary duck for their faro tables for he is at all their parties and brings the whole town after him, just because he is something new and will make a fool of himself for the public entertainment, for I am sure as to his music it is no such great things, but I suppose you will not allow me to give any opinion, however I can assure you I have heard some very good judges say the same. But I must bid you good bye now. I intend to look in for a minute at Lady Rout's tonight and I dare say I shall see him stuck up in the middle of the room with a parcel of affected fools all crowded round and pretending to be in tears of sensibility. It is really the most ridiculous scene as Lord Henry says that ever was exhibited; I have heard him every night now this week. Lord Henry and I have agreed that we are quite sick of him."

While she was speaking she rung the bell and the servant here coming in she ordered Millikin to be sent to her room and enquired whether Mr. Miltern was come in. Upon being answered in the affirmative she desired he might be told that his sisters were in the drawing room and then retired but not without having left a sting in the bosom of each of her gentle auditors.

There are some people who in their conversation have the happy talent of perpetually giving pain, who possess the secret of selecting the most unpleasing subjects, nay on these which are in themselves of a nature the most agreeable can yet speak in a disagreeable manner. Never was mortal endued with this amiable qualification in a superior degree to Lady Harriet and it was hardly possible for her to utter a sentence which did not tend to wound the feelings of those who heard her even when she intended not any particular insult or malice. In the present instance however this was not the case. All the rancour of her soul had been called forth during the course of this day. On her return in the morning from a late supper party at about five o'clock she had been informed by Robert of the guests whom she was to expect, and after much violence of debate the result was such as has been already seen. But tho' Lady Harriet was determined to avoid the company of her husband's sisters she yet felt a secret and unaccountable regret and mortification, that they should have found another asylum and one in every way so respectable and so agreeable.

But this was not all her vexation. Her conduct had been already loudly censured by a world which she had not sufficient rank to set at defiance and where the haughtiness of her manners had conciliated few friends. But on the arrival of Lord Henry in town she immediately discarded every former favourite & thought no sacrifice would be too much to make could she seduce from the long envied and detested Lady Trevallyn her lover whose constant attachment was so greatly the theme of every tongue. He had always appeared to admire Lady Harriet and now met her advances with an ardour which flattered all her hopes. He had accepted with the utmost appearance of grateful pleasure the offered place in her box. He had followed her in her evening rounds; excited universal attention by his assiduities at every assembly, danced with her and her only to the envy of many an unpartnered girl—attended her each night at supper and spent the greatest part of his mornings in Upper Brook street where at his wish all other visitors were now excluded, and until this decisive day no doubt had occurred but that her charms had been victorious.

The appointed hour on this morning arrived and brought not with it Lord Henry to confirm the triumph which she had anticipated over her slighted rival. He came not. Too well could she suspect where he was detained and without love she knew all the heart devouring tortures of jealousy. At length he appeared but tho' he denied having been with Lady Trevallyn, and treated her suspicions as ridiculous there was a kind of respect with which he shrunk from hearing her mentioned and declined from the conversation which struck her with the mortifying conviction that Lady Trevallyn was still loved and loved with a passion different from that which she had been able to inspire—that she had herself been but the passing amusement of his disengaged hours and would now be sacrificed to the very rival whose misery her malevolent mind had exulted in the hopes of causing. The interruption which had been given by Selena and her sister, with the idea that they had perhaps overheard some words of her conversation contributed not much to the affectionate sweetness with which she might already have been inclined to receive them.

The confusion which Lord Henry had displayed on their entrance, proceeded not as might naturally enough be conjectured from the probable discovery of his falsehood by some allusion to his last visit. His thoughts were entirely engrossed by the far more interesting apprehension lest Lady Trevallyn might suspect his heart or even his attention could for a moment be diverted by another woman. His vanity and the necessity he found of having his mind for ever occupied by some intrigue had alone engaged him to meet the advances of Lady Harriet, and as the conquest had cost him no trouble he felt that to maintain it was not worthy of the smallest sacrifice, nay had he even esteemed it a nobler prize he would not scruple its instant relinquishment when it could interfere with his grand design.

Indeed he had at first engaging in this affair some idea that it might contribute to his wishes by exciting the transient jealousy of Lady Trevallyn, notwithstanding that his heart now failed him and shrunk trembling from so dangerous an experiment. Convinced that Lady Trevallyn would avoid as much as possible meeting him in public he calculated upon being able without difficulty for some time to persuade each of his entire devotion. His mornings whenever he could gain admission he consecrated to his Emily, while he might still amuse himself and flatter the vanity of Lady Harriet by his faithful attendance at the evening assemblies. But should any circumstance occur to render this impossible no doubt remained but that by the immediate sacrifice of all intercourse with Lady Harriet he should be able amply to remove or compensate for any suspicion which might cloud the gentle bosom of his Emily.

Inexperienced as Selena was in the profligacy of the fashionable world and little inclined as her benevolent and pure mind ever was to imagine evil, yet there was something in the countenance of Lady Harriet and yet more in that of Lord Henry which recalled to her remembrance the words of Mrs. Vallard, "Tho' Emily has ever been his chief she is not believe me his only object," and her heart sank as she considered the unfortunate lot which her beloved brother had so imprudently drawn for himself.

Indeed it was obvious that his eyes were already opened and that convinced of the worthlessness of the object of his choice he vainly struggled to hide from the world and particularly from his sisters the misery which followed this conviction. But Selena alas read it on his pensive brow, his eye so often fixed in gloomy meditation and the hopeless indifference with which he seemed now to speak upon every subject and especially on all that related to futurity so different from his natural gaiety and the ardour of his sanguine disposition.

Lady Harriet's name, as if by tacit consent was never mentioned, but while with affectionate interest he enquired whether his sisters really felt themselves in every respect comfortable in their present situation he appeared anxious by peculiar tenderness to remove all painful doubts which might have arisen from the seeming unkindness of refusing to receive them.

Occupied as he evidently was by his own unhappiness Selena felt but little inclined to add to his cares by speaking much of Dallamore. Indeed what he did say on that subject she found extremely agitating, as he seemed now decidedly of opinion that she might rather at once to get rid of so unfortunate a connexion than be tied for life to the caprices of one who might prove a weak tyrant, that heaviest scourge by which Heaven can afflict those over whom it gives him power.

After such an opinion expressed, tho' not in direct terms yet too plainly to be misunderstood Selena felt some confusion as she informed him that she had already accepted Sidney's offer of becoming Dallamore's banker and at the same time requested her brother to settle with Mr. Turner so that Clara without being separated from her should receive a suitable allowance, as Clara herself was anxious to profit by the opportunity of being in town to receive the assistance of masters.

Robert recollected with shame and regret his negligence and warmly declared, "There is one thing dear Selena which I never shall forgive myself. In my impatience for the precipitation of our hasty marriage I left the whole care of the settlements to our mutual guardian—and scarce knew till it was too late that I had thus deprived myself of the possibility of doing you the justice I ever intended. There was no reason that you should not have been as well provided for as Clara and tho' unfortunately I must now only regret my folly and indeed I may call it my crime in this omission yet the interest of the £10,000 which I consider as yours, you shall always receive during my life let me be involved in what difficulties I may."

While Selena protested against this generosity she expressed her hope that he might never be involved in any such pecuniary difficulties as those he seemed to allude to & his answer convinced her that he had already been led into great imprudences.

"But that is a matter of little consequence," added he again sinking into gloomy despondence. "I am so hampered by settlements that I can do my heirs at least no harm, be they who they will—and as I never intend to see London after this Spring I don't care how privately I shall be obliged to live at the Abbey provided I am let to stay there while I pay my debts."

As they went down stairs to dinner upon Selena saying that she feared he had staid at home that day on their account he replied hastily, "Oh no I have nothing to do with their parties. As to formal dinners, and large assemblies I am sick to death of them, but from the private set I am excluded and indeed have no ambition to be admitted among them. I assure you I was not even invited to day."

"What set?" demanded Clara with surprise.

"The less you know of it the better," answered he with so much unusual asperity that both sisters were completely discouraged from all further questions.

While Selena was making tea a double knock announced a visitor and Robert immediately said, "I dare say that is Sidney he often calls on me at this time when he dines in the neighbourhood and he knows we were to be together this evening for I recollect I mentioned it to him when I saw him to day."

As he spoke the door softly opened and half ashamed but quite delighted Sidney stopped for an instant to survey the little party and ask permission and pardon for the intrusion.

"Oh come in," cried Robert with evident satisfaction, "there is no one on earth whose face I would be so glad to see. We will let you into our baby house and you shall enliven us."

As he said this he pointed towards the corner of the sopha that remained vacant between the tea-table and the fire—where Sidney gladly placed himself forgetting for the moment every thing but that he was once more seated beside Selena. The contentment of his soul diffused itself around him and tho' the cares which darkened each bosom could not effectually be dispersed, yet the serenity of his countenance and the persuasive eloquence that smiled upon his lips did indeed enliven and cheer the little circle.

Tho' Selena feared that the conversation would not be productive of much satisfaction to poor Clara yet she rightly guessed that she was watching with impatience for the introduction of Edwin about whom she had entreated her to interrogate Robert.

Unconscious how deeply the subject interested the heart of one of his auditors he expatiated with freedom upon the profligacy into which he had been hurried.

Sidney softened all that was said and endeavoured to account for it by informing them how, "Lord Stanmore had overwhelmed him with kindness on his arrival in town, insisted upon his taking up his abode in his house and seemed anxious by favours to the son to atone for the slight with which he too late reproached himself for having treated the father. The ill conduct of his own son who had squandered in the vilest debauchery enormous sums and even sold the reversion of his property contributed not a little to the eagerness with which Edwin was received by his uncle and by him instantly introduced to what is called the best company in town ...."

"That is," interrupted Robert warmly, "you should say the most unprincipled and profligate."

Sidney smiled and continued, "Nothing can exceed the admiration which his talents have excited; indeed you can form no idea of the crowd which the very report of his presence collects every where and it is not surprising if the novelty of the scene and the boundless flattery he meets with should have turned his brain. At first his melancholy and a small degree of wildness the consequence of his illness which was visible to every one but rendered him the more interesting, some attributed this to the sudden loss of his parents...."

"No, no," cried Robert, "I assure you it was generally said to be an unhappy passion and you Selena can I am told decide best to which of those causes it was most justly attributed—but whatever it might have been as it was the ambition of half the women in town to disperse this melancholy and restore this mind craz'd by hopeless love your vanity cannot reasonably be much hurt that they should have succeeded as I suppose is the case, for tho' at first anxious to be much in our society he now evidently avoids me and is never to be found even in the mornings. But except Lady Vellum or some of those old Ladies (who for the sake of filling their assemblies have made so famous an attack upon him) succeed in gaining his heart I do not believe he has any thoughts of forming attachments; and I fancy you will not think they have much chance of success when you have seen those painted she devils. It would be well for him that he could fix his warm imagination upon some deserving object for I hear he is ruining himself with his Bacchanalian music meetings and the worst kind of dissipation."

"And does not Lord Stanmore," asked Selena, "exert himself to prevent his inexperienced nephew from falling into the same dangerous path which has already proved so fatal to his son?"

"Oh Lord Stanmore," answered Sidney, "is full as much intoxicated as Edwin himself can possibly be by the attention which it has been the fashion to pay his talents: for singularly striking as those talents really are, it is in fact fashion which gains him one half of his admirers, tho' his style of singing is indeed generally captivating yet how few of his auditors have taste in that high degree to feel what they affect to declare so *exquisite, delicious, enchanting, ravishing*! Of this Edwin himself is perfectly aware, for it is impossible for Genius to be mistaken as to its own powers over the minds of others—and the very praises which ignorance and dullness bestow must in themselves be betrayers of the want of sensibility and judgment which bestowed them but Lord Stanmore swallows every flattery and believes in good faith that the universe has never yet produced a prodigy such as Edwin."

"But can his vanity so far conquer his own regard for his nephew as to allow him to encourage what you say will prove his ruin."

"Why as to that," said Robert, "I believe Lord Stanmore is one of those who think that what is fashionable must be right and so long as Edwin associates only with the profligates of high rank among whom he lives his uncle is perfectly satisfied, dreading nothing but the low vice which has been destructive to young Stanmore."

"And is it possible," exclaimed Clara, "that Edwin's polished mind can find a charm in such associates!"

"You would not feel surprised at this," rejoined Sidney, "if you knew how much genius and talent are thus squandered. I will venture to say that it was not the lustre of high rank, nor the tables of revelry that first seduced Edwin into this society I know that he was courted to add grace to licenteousness by men whose abilities could hardly have been exerted in any cause without success. Is it then surprising that so susceptible a mind should have been led away upon first emerging from seclusion into all the glare of courtly dissipation and polished seduction. Few could have withstood the flattery by which Edwin has been beguiled, and much firmness was hardly to be expected from one so inexperienced and so ardent—but his dream of folly will not last long you may depend upon it, and all I fear are those moments of gloom in which when in company with him amidst the gayest scenes I have seen him perpetually sink and only rise at length by an evident struggle. I know he already sickens at the life in which he is engaged and despises his companions and you will see how soon these impediments to virtue and honour

> Shall like the dew drops on the lion's mane
> Be shook to air."[84]

The heart of Clara gratefully listened to those flattering hopes with which Sidney then prognosticated the future eminent situation in which the talents of Edwin better directed would hereafter deservedly place him, and tho' the picture set before her eyes by Lady Harriet perpetually recurred to her imagination while during the whole evening she beheld Edwin surrounded by all that was seductive all that possessed dangerous fascination yet Sidney's prophetic promises returned

---

[84] "Shakespear" (Tighe's note). Patroclus in Shakespeare's *Troilus and Cressida* (1601), 3.3.225–6 (the first line should read "And like a dew-drop from the lion's mane").

to cheer her despondence and encourage her yet to trust that Edwin's amiable disposition and virtuous principles would never disgrace in her own eyes that tenderness with which her romantic mind had formed all its luxury of idea in cherishing his remembrance for life unknown to all the world and unsuspected by himself.

While she believed him yet occupied with a pure and hopeless passion for Selena she had adored him with a secret delight which perhaps surpasses all that the completion of a lover's hopes can ever bestow. But Edwin a profligate Edwin abandoned to vice and engrossed solely by despicable vanity! Edwin unworthy of her love! This was a new and unexpected overthrow of all her ideal pleasures, and as they returned to Grosvenor square she anxiously sought from Selena's lips her repetition and confirmation of Sidney's well remembered and consoling promises.

Chapter XVIII

> Dare not th'infectious sigh, the pleading look
> Downcast and low in meek submission drest,
> But full of guile. Let not the fervent tongue
> Prompt to deceive with adulation smooth
> Gain on your purposed will.
>
> Thompson[85]

For more than a fortnight after their arrival in town, during which Selena observed with augmented concern the daily visits of Lord Henry; Lady Trevallyn excused herself on account of a slight cold from going out but perceiving that her seclusion was the source of perpetual ill temper from Lord Trevallyn with much persuasion from Selena she at length prepared for her appearance at the drawing room. She was accompanied by Lord Trevallyn who in the morning papers of the ensuing day read with all the exultation of triumph the elaborate description of their dresses which were too singularly magnificent to escape such celebrity. He saw not however the paragraph which the withering hand of malice had traced for his eye and which slander had published with that cruel wantonness which loves to throw her poisoned darts at random ever against unoffending objects.

But altho' it had escaped the glance of Lord Trevallyn engrossed as he was with the little pride of dazzling the vulgar by the grandeur which they can never imitate it was not unobserved by Selena, whose sudden paleness and evident agitation as she hastily put the paper into her work basket struck the eyes of Lady Trevallyn. A kind of presentiment as to the nature of what had thus affected her friend fell instantly upon her heart and with a sick and fearful tremor she gazed upon her in silent anxiety while Selena with scarcely less terror continued to examine the remainder of the papers which overspread the breakfast table and then taking her basket in her hand, quitted the room with hurried and trembling steps.

---

[85]   James Thomson, "Spring," *The Seasons* (1728), lines 972–6.

As soon as she could do so without observation Lady Trevallyn followed her to her own room the door of which she found locked, and when Selena opened it upon hearing her voice she perceived she had been in tears. "Which of us my Love have they attacked and where is the paper?" said she as she held out her hand with the sensation of a criminal when he stands arraigned at the bar.

"I thought to have spared you the shock my dear Lady Trevallyn," answered Selena, "but perhaps it is better you should see it. We may extract a precious jewel even from the venemous animal that would sting us—at least Shakespear[86] would comfort us by saying so," added she smiling thro' her tears as she half reluctantly put the paper into her friend's trembling hands and pointed out to her those hateful lines:

> "We hail with pleasure the reappearance of a most distinguished and beautiful luminary which we feared intended not to shed its lustre this season upon our courtly sphere. The attachment of a certain lovely countess for her own family has been long our admiration and we cannot but regret that the exclusive constancy with which she still devotes her hours to retirement and her noble cousin even in Grosvenor square should not have been rewarded by a more permanent connexion."

While shame yet burnt upon the cheek of Lady Trevallyn and her timid and truly feminine heart sunk gasping under the terrible prospect of being thus violently held forth to public scorn and censure it was not in the nature of Selena to utter a syllable which could encrease the bitter self reproach by which she saw her unhappy friend was at that moment stung and tho' she felt the necessity of enforcing future prudence she reserved her counsel to some calmer hour and employed the present in endeavouring to sooth the agitated bosom of her friend.

But when of herself Lady Trevallyn confessed the indespensibility of less frequently allowing those visits which had been thus strangely noticed Selena with tears of joy and tenderness embraced her friend and applauded the resolution which by every argument she strove to confirm; seizing on the important moment she entreated her to begin by immediately giving orders to have no one admitted.

"What not even Sidney!" asked Lady Trevallyn with a half smile in the midst of the anguish which pressed heavy on her heart.

"We will make no exceptions whatever to avoid suspicion," answered Selena colouring deeply, "and indeed dear Lady Trevallyn since you have mentioned Sidney excuse me for saying that I would rather you did not invite him so continually to dinner."

"Poor Sidney!" said Lady Trevallyn with a deep sigh. "Well I believe you are right—but *you* at least have nothing to fear you are so wise and so prudent."

Selena once more recalled her to the immediate painful task and unable to go back from her own declaration Lady Trevallyn with an aching heart gave the orders which her friend required.

---

[86] "Like the toad—ugly and venomous / Bears yet a precious jewel in his head" (Tighe's note). Duke Senior in Shakespeare's *As You Like It* (1599), 2.1.13–14.

The remainder of the morning Selena passed with her in her dressing room and observed with pain the dejection into which she was plunged while she watched perpetually the window and listened to every noise with impatient eagerness repeatedly enquiring in a half whisper "Was not that a knock at the hall door Selena?" Having at length sent to enquire from the porter who had called and hearing with a stifled sigh the name which could alone interest her she requested Selena to play who gladly complied with her desire tho' from time to time she stole a melancholy glance upon her friend as she sat with her head reclined upon the arm of the sopha neither attempting to conceal or restrain her tears.

It was not without the utmost reluctance that Lady Trevallyn exerted herself that day to fulfill an engagement which she had been constrained to make and while she dressed to accompany Lord Trevallyn to a large and splendid dinner given to them by a nobleman high in office she had need of all Selena's gentle offices of friendship to support her spirits which more than once failing her she was about to send an excuse that Selena well knew would be peculiarly displeasing to Lord Trevallyn.

Ever attentive to promote the gratification of her beloved guests Lady Trevallyn had invited Robert to spend this day with his sisters, and without having consulted Selena had desired him to bring Sidney. While Clara was engaged in conversation with her brother Sidney seized an opportunity to ask Selena had she seen the paragraph which had so palpably insulted Lady Trevallyn. Selena informed him that she had and of the good consequences which she hoped would result from it. While he candidly confessed the urgent necessity for the resolution which she told him her friend had taken and entreated her to exert all her prudent care in strengthening it he ventured not to request an exception for himself from the general exclusion. Yet he severely felt the deprivation and more than once sighed at the reflection that no other asylum appeared open for Selena. Indeed his words and still more his looks so seriously impressed upon her mind the danger of her friend that she determined to suffer no tenderness of inflicting pain to prevent her from fulfilling her duty and exerting all the means in her power for her rescue—& she was convinced that if those failed it was her part at least not to share her criminal weakness by tacitly beholding what she condemned.

Anxious to hear from her how she had passed the dreaded day she awaited her return home tho' it was nearly midnight in her dressing room. As she entered Selena beheld with pleasure the soft and delicate rose which had resumed its station upon each lovely cheek and the ray of cheerfulness that once more beamed from the mild azure of her beautiful eyes. She instantly dismissed her maid and impatient to communicate the intelligence which she seemed yet at a loss to express, she in silence drew from her pocket a small paper dirtied and extremely tumbled.

"What is the meaning of this?" said Selena surprised as she cast her eyes over it and perceived what it contained. "This is nothing but the copy of what we have seen already."

"The *copy* Selena! No that is the original and do you know the hand?"

"I have surely seen it but cannot recollect where."

"What do you forget the writing of Mr. Guise? Could you not swear to that *T* and that *R*. But to convince you here is the song he wrote out for me the other day compare them. Can you have a doubt now?"

Selena acknowledged the resemblance but enquired with astonishment how she had become the possessor of this paper and how it proved Mr. Guise to be the author not the copier. Hesitating and blushing Lady Trevallyn was evidently unprepared for the interrogations which however obvious and naturally to be expected the artless Emily in her impatience to display her discovery to her friend had never once anticipated.

Selena at length gathered from her tho' she confessed it with evident reluctance that Lord Henry whom she had met at dinner had found an opportunity unobserved to inform her that immediately upon seeing the abominable libel as he termed it he had gone to the publisher & threatening him with vengeance had received from him as some expiation the paper which he gave her, and which he said he had no doubt from the description had been left there by Mr. Guise himself.

Selena made no comments on this story to which she listened with the deepest concern and Lady Trevallyn glad to turn the discourse from the means by which it had been obtained to the discovery itself exclaimed, "How fortunate that he should have betrayed himself by leaving thus his own hand writing with the printer. We might otherwise never have suspected his wickedness, indeed I could not have believed any one capable of such deliberate malice."

"Wicked indeed must be his heart," replied Selena, "but what great advantage is it dear Lady Trevallyn that we know this, now that the mischief is done?"

"Oh Selena is it nothing to be thus delivered from the shocking idea that the world in general censored my conduct and watched me with such vigilence of malice. I never thought of concealing Lord Henry's visits from those whose intimacy in our house could certainly have detected them, but that they should have been remarked by strangers was horrible! I hold not myself accountable to one so every way despicable as this my treacherous foe; and I think that it would be a kind of meanness and a confession of guilt should I thus sink under the dagger which he has struck at me in the dark. Should he now be successful what may he not next attempt. Shall I teach him the mode by which he may at once blast my name and terrify me from every comfort?"

Selena perceived that she had not now to reason with the pure and docile mind of her friend; simple in its own views, open to conviction & alarmed at the shadow of guilt, but with the specious arguments of vice retailed from Lord Henry himself. She saw the feind had been at work,

> for all was false and hollow tho' the tongue
> Dropt manna and could make the worse appear
> The better reason, to perplex and dash
> Maturest councils.[87]

---

[87] "Milton" (Tighe's note). John Milton, *Paradise Lost* (1667), 2.112–15 (description of Belial).

Selena witheld not from her friend her real opinion to the dangerous situation in which she stood, who once more driven from every subterfuge where the weakness of her heart involuntarily lingered listened in silence drowned in tears and covered with confusion. At length Selena declaring with gentle firmness that "delightful and necessary to herself as was her friendship and society in her own deserted and doubtful condition, she was yet determined to forego it, if Lord Henry's visits were still to be suffered and that she would prefer seeking an asylum in any situation the most unpleasant to remaining the witness and partaker of her friend's voluntary disgrace."

"Oh unkind Selena!" cried Lady Trevallyn covering her face with both her hands, "do not threaten me so harshly, I will do whatever you please, but pity me and do not abandon me. You do not know the misery I feel. You never *can* know—you can always act right with so much ease—you who are not a poor weak wretched creature lost for ever to happiness and hope like me."

Poor Selena's throbbing heart and overflowing eyes acquitted her of insensibility, that inflexible unfeeling virtue of which this speech appeared to accuse her. She heard it however with sensations only of the tenderest compassion and left not her friend until she had exerted every art to pour balm into the subdued and afflicted spirit which she half reproached herself for having however involuntarily contributed to wound.

Upon their being joined the next morning at breakfast by Lord Trevallyn and Mr. Guise Selena in silence observed with some astonishment and much contempt the conduct of this monster—for such she could not help considering him towards the lovely object of his secret malice. His artful features wore only flattering smiles and whenever he addressed Lady Trevallyn his voice put on an unusual softness. Attention and a kind of half expressed admiration followed the grace of all her movements and hung upon the music of her accents. The coldness and reserve of her manners and her averted eye spoke no suspicion to his coward heart. It was thus she had ever received his hypocritical homage and it was thus she had added venom to the desire of revenge which gnawed his heart.

After a short time having received some commissions from Lord Trevallyn to execute in the city he withdrew and Selena in the vain hope of diverting the mind of her friend which she saw plainly rested with melancholy dejection upon one object, proposed to her that they should that morning put into effect their meditated visit to poor Angela of whom they had heard nothing since their arrival in town.

The timid glance and heightened colour of Lady Trevallyn instantly apprised her of the imprudence of her proposal at that time while Lord Trevallyn instantly throwing aside his pen and pushing from before him his unfinished letter demanded whether it was possible his lady could have had any such intention and whether she had not servants who might more properly be sent upon such an errand.

"You say right," answered Lady Trevallyn with a forced smile, "I have been guilty of a strange omission in not having sent before this to enquire after poor

Harley and Angela. I will defer it however no longer and will this moment send Thomas to Kensington."

The gentle Emily who dreaded no punishment equal to an argument of this nature, hoped by this hasty submission to put an end to the subject so unfortunately started, but Lord Trevallyn was not thus easily to be silenced, and a lecture ensued not less painful to Selena than to her to whom it was addressed.

Happily for them however it was interrupted by a note which a servant delivered to his Lord who having read it exclaimed, "Very obliging indeed this of Mr. Sidney Dallamore, I mentioned to him the other day that I had some desire to see Mrs. Jordan in Viola[88] but that I disliked the promiscuous associations to which one is necessarily subject in the public boxes of the Theatre, to which I should certainly never willingly suffer any woman with whom I am connected to be exposed and he has now sent me Mr. —'s order for his private box at Drury lane. I am concerned that the impertinence of the business which I have to discuss this day with the Duke of P— will probably detain me till a late hour but if possible I will join you at the Theatre where I hope Lady Trevallyn that you will have no objection to await me."

"Surely Lord Trevallyn you would not wish me to go there alone."

"By no means, the Miss Milterns I have no doubt will accompany you and I will desire Mr. Dallamore and Mr. Guise to give you the pleasure of their company at dinner in order to attend you in, as it is impossible for females of any rank or delicacy to enter a theatre without the protection of some men who from some family connection may claim a respectable degree of intimacy."

Having thus settled matters to his own satisfaction, and dispatched the invitation to Sidney he left the room and Lady Trevallyn then consulted Selena as to her inclination with regard to this arrangement.

Selena felt a secret unwillingness to disappoint Sidney conscious that he had most probably exerted himself on this occasion from having heard her carelessly express a wish to see this celebrated actress without an idea of her being able with propriety to do so at present. She considered also that it might be an advantage to Lady Trevallyn to appear unattended by Lord Henry as there was no possibility of his knowing of their intentions in time to profit by them, and that the party might also serve in some degree to amuse the gloom which evidently oppressed her mind.

Lady Trevallyn on her part shewed a desire to avail herself of the offered box which she was in fact far from feeling, for she considered it natural that both Selena and her sister might find charms in the novelty of the scene, tho' independant of their gratification and that which she well knew it must afford to Sidney, few things in her present state of mind could be more wearisome and insipid than the mere shew of a public amusement, which had long ceased to yield her any pleasure

---

[88] Dorothy Jordan (1761–1816) was celebrated for her portrayal of Viola in Shakespeare's *Twelfth Night*, from her first performance at Drury Lane in 1785 through the 1800s.

except that which resulted from meeting there him whose society could have rendered the wildest desert to her imagination blooming as the garden of Eden.

The wishes of Lord Trevallyn were therefore without difficulty complied with and Clara's heart once more panted with hope in the expectation that Edwin might now possibly behold Selena and that this sight by reviving the slumbering flame would restore to him all his former eagerness to be admitted to her society, from which her sanguine mind could easily deduce every delightful prospect of advantage to Edwin and felicity to herself.

It happened that on this night an audience of uncommon rank had honoured with their presence the theatre which in the gay season is usually so totally deserted by all who move in that higher circle which dignifies itself exclusively with the title of the world. Nor was this solely to be attributed to the attractions of the charming actress who might upon that night as heretofore have exerted her inimitable talents for the gratification of more vulgar beings who are not ashamed to prove that a whole evening could thus be spared from the multiplicity of their engagements, nay a part of what is termed morning be thus sacrificed to the necessity of an early dinner, had not the caprice of an high born fair decreed that thro' her influence a considerable portion of the tide of fashion should flow hither at her command. Struck with the splendour and the magnitude of the exhibition both sisters for an instant stood motionless on their entrance which was not till the house appeared completely full the first act being just at an end.

Wishing to escape observation Selena and her sister remained at the back of the box from whence unseen they beheld not only the stage but the brilliant assembly with a delighted admiration which in some measure communicated itself to their companions. Sidney who could now have seen but one object had the universe been extended before his eyes, gazed upon Selena with that interest which on every occasion, in every new circumstance seems to cloathe with new beauties, and point out new charms in the adored mind and person. Clara with eyes yet dazzled and confused was vainly wandering from tier to tier and from box to box with almost hopeless anxiety to distinguish amidst the mass of living faces these features she so eagerly desired to behold and as she surveyed with bewildered curiosity the immense multitude she could almost fancy that all London was collected before her except the one only individual whom she had desired to meet.

Mean while Selena whose whole attention was fixed upon the stage, charmed to it by the silver tones of Mrs. Jordan's voice willingly yielded to her sister the opera glass which Sidney on their entrance had put into her hands and Lady Trevallyn pointing to her observation the second box from the stage enquired whether she could not there distinguish Lady Harriet. Her figure, her dress, her air were all too singularly striking ever to be mistaken and the glass quickly confirmed Lady Trevallyn's discovery. But she had no occasion for its assistance when sometime afterwards, towards the conclusion of the third act her eye was by one glance assured that it was no other but Lord Henry whom she beheld entering that very box. Lady Harriet who with some little difficulty had kept the place, and whose eye with impatient vexation had been hastily turned round each time that the door had opened now made room for him and Lady Trevallyn beheld the smiling salutation, the pleased whisper, the fixed and flattering glance with which he instantly took his seat at her side.

From that instant the stage, the audience, her companions, all that surrounded her was equally and totally annihilated for Lady Trevallyn save that only object which fixed her whole soul while her temples beat, and her heart sickened as under the influence of some terrible distemper when first it seizes on the brain.

Nor was she roused from this till Mr. Guise having vainly attempted to gain her attention by his casual observations at length following the undiverted course of her eyes at once discovered what had thus engrossed all her faculties and with a smile of affected carelessness remarked, "Pray do I not see Lady Harriet Modely opposite—that Lady you may observe with the bandeau of diamonds and very dark hair. Oh yes now that I look at her neck I am quite sure it must be she. But who is that gentleman on her right who looks so entirely engaged with her conversation. He seems to admire her very much. There his face is turned this way now. Pray is it not a friend of yours. Surely it is Lord Henry and if I am not much mistaken he is looking at us too. I think he is trying to make us out. Does not your Ladyship think so?"

Poor Lady Trevallyn scarce able to articulate with mingled anxiety, confusion and very agitating emotion having at length removed her eyes faintly demanded "where?"

"*Where!*" repeated he with a smile sufficiently expressive of incredulity, "Oh have not you seen them yet? Well I will try and point them out, look at the front row a little to your left and the ...." then suddenly turning his eyes upon her he continued, "There now you are looking at the very spot. Have you found them out at last. He has his opera glass to his eye you see. But what it the reason that he does not seem to mind his companion as he did just now. Look how she talks to him and he pays her not the smallest attention. I really believe she has just spied out Miltern in the box over us for he appears as if he was afraid they were watched by some jealous eye."

Lady Trevallyn with difficulty kept her seat and Selena whose attention he had at length attracted now enquired whom they were looking at—but Sidney who had overheard and with indignation perceived the malice of his remarks now entreated Mr. Guise if possible to be silent for a few minutes as Mrs. Jordan was just about to sing her favourite song.

"I beg your pardon Mr. Dallamore I assure you she does not introduce it in this act but I cannot persuade Lady Trevallyn that that is Lord Henry who is sitting there opposite to us next to your sister Miss Miltern. Pray don't you think it is he? And if you had seen him just now when he was speaking to Lady Harriet and seemed to be animated you could not have had a doubt, there is something so very peculiar in the manner he moves his head and a sort of trick he has with his shoulder. I have heard it noticed as remarkably graceful by some ladies. Do *you* know what I mean Lady Trevallyn?"

Selena with pity and apprehension turned hastily her mildly sympathising eye from the sight to which she had been thus directed upon her friend and trembled as she marked her quick varying colour, difficulty of breathing, and every symptom of sudden faintness.

"It is extremely hot Sidney," cried she wishing to draw off their attention from her friend, "pray open the door of the box, I feel quite ill."

With Clara and Sidney this indeed succeeded who in their concern for her overlooked her design, but Mr. Guise saw thro' it and fixing his eyes upon Lady Trevallyn observed, "I am afraid your Ladyship is not very well, your paleness really alarms me, shall I get you a glass of water? Or perhaps you would like to leave the box with Miss Miltern who finds it so hot, tho' I am surprised at that as for my part I have felt it so uncommonly cold. Are you any thing better?" continued he, "pray Miss Miltern let Lady Trevallyn have those salts for a moment"—then with all the parade of anxiety he would have held them to her himself alternately glancing his eyes from her to the opposite box as if anxious that the little bustle should be observed which he evidently tried to make.

Lady Trevallyn penetrating with terror into his malicious design exerted all her strength to throw off the languid sickness which had indeed seized her and repeatedly assuring him that she was perfectly well gratefully availed herself of the excuse which Selena had afforded by endeavouring to turn the attention upon her.

In the mean time the arts of Mr. Guise had succeeded the doubt which had before struggled in Lord Henry's mind whether he should by quitting his post mortally and irreparably offend Lady Harriet or by remaining excite the uneasy suspicions of his beloved Emily was instantly decided by the appearance which he thought he saw of her sudden illness, for the cause of which his vanity left him in no uncertainty. He seized the opportunity of the curtain being now let down between the acts and promising to return shortly, left the box and filled the breast of Lady Harriet at once with all the envenomed serpents of rage, mortification, jealousy, revenge, envy, hatred, malice and in a word with all uncharitableness.

This was not unmarked by Mr. Guise who immediately exclaimed, "Oh here is Lord Henry coming I am sure to see how you are Miss Miltern. He has been watching us I dare say tho' when he comes here I am afraid he will suspect it is you Lady Trevallyn who are not well, for really Miss Miltern you look as blooming as ever and if I was censorious I should be apt to say you owe your fine colour to the perfumer, it has been so proof to illness."

Here his impertinence was at length silenced by the entrance of Lord Henry. Gracefully saluting all his eye with eager interest was fixed upon the pallid countenance of his lovely Emily and tho' with that presence of mind which never forsook him he contrived so as to place himself as that the curtain might screen him from the view of the opposite boxes, yet who that looked upon the unutterable tenderness, the fondly ardent devotion which beamed from his expressive eyes could have imagined that his heart could cherish a single idea but that of the beautiful being upon whom he then gazed with a delighted fondness which was indeed but too infectious.

Nor was Lord Henry the only visitor whom the sight of Lady Trevallyn attracted to their box. Lord Louverney who had made more than one ineffectual attempt to see Selena since her arrival in town no sooner perceived Lady Trevallyn than he eagerly sought to discover by whom she was accompanied and not being able to satisfy himself entirely, at length after some hesitation availed himself of the degree of intimacy which a residence together for some time in a country house he hoped might allow to justify his intrusion into her box.

Tho' received with civility by all he had too much feeling as well as discernment not to discover that he was a welcome visitant to none. Each seat was occupied and no person being inclined or thinking it necessary to resign his place he stood for a while at the back of Selena's chair and vainly endeavoured to disguise his chagrin and the awkwardness of which he was conscious, by some questions which were but coldly answered and general remarks which remained unseconded. There is no situation in which a person of sensibility appears to less advantage than when convinced that those they wish most ardently to please desire their absence.

Selena felt for what she saw he suffered—and was only restrained from endeavouring to relieve his uneasiness, by her wish to discourage him from all farther thoughts of so idle a pursuit, and her conviction of the necessity of her total silence at present was perhaps strengthened by observing the inquisitive anxiety with which Sidney fixedly watched his looks without uttering a syllable.

It was therefore with pleasure that she saw Lord Louverney retire after a few minutes of the most painfully uncomfortable sensations he had ever experienced.

"Pray Miss Miltern," demanded Mr. Guise with a sneer, "may I ask which was Lord Louverney's visit intended for you or Lady Trevallyn? In either case I suppose his Lordship must have found himself *de trop*[89] from his speedy decampment." Here Lord Henry darted a look of such expressive fury at Mr. Guise that in spite of his affected coolness he remained filled with confusion and smothered malice effectually silenced for the rest of the evening "Ready to wound but yet afraid to strike."[90]

Sidney mean while continued plunged in the deepest reverie. Selena tho' she herself could not immediately shake off her secret concern for the pain she had involuntarily caused yet trusted that the departure of Lord Louverney would restore Sidney to cheerfulness. But in vain he now tried to smile, again to affect a gaiety to which his heart had in reality been long a stranger. A train of the most afflictive meditations, not entirely unmingled with self reproach had been aroused by the emotions of jealousy which the first glance of Lord Louverney upon Selena had instantly excited.

"What is my aim!" exclaimed he as he returned home after having complied so far at least with the dictates of his conscience as to resist the invitation of Lady Trevallyn when she would have brought him back to supper. "How am I plunging myself deeper into folly and misery by cherishing a passion which

---

[89] De trop: too much, superfluous (French).
[90] "Pope" (Tighe's note). Alexander Pope, "An Epistle to Dr. Arbuthnot" (1735), line 203 (the line should read "Willing to wound and yet afraid to strike").

I must not call innocent, and which I knew will never be returned! And yet Selena we might be happy! Virtue itself could not disapprove in such a case the assertion of your liberty; Oh if you loved but as I do. Something of delicacy might surely be sacrificed and happiness unclouded, years of unabated felicity confidence and union of soul that time never could diminish but every hour must encrease might then be ours! What if the unjust the idle world should dare to attack the sacred purity of thy name! What is the world to us! In the approbation of our own hearts, in the tenderness, the full affection of each other oh how amply blest!

> Tu sorella e Sposa
> Tu mia ricchezza mia grandezza e regno!
> Tu mi saresti il ciel la terra e tutto!
> Io ne' tuoi sguardi e tu ne' miei felice
> Come di schietto rivo onda soave
> Scorrer gli anni vedremmo, e fonte in noi
> Di perenne gioir fôra la vita![91]

"Oh delicious picture! Oh delirium of happiness! Why must I resign thee? Why must I awake to the cruel conviction that the bliss I have thus imagined not only never must be mine but is desired, thought of by me alone! All in Heaven and earth conspire against my wishes. And they are not even shared by her! What then is left for me? One only part—Reason and Virtue both forbid this waste of life in self torment. Let me strengthen my mind and in spite of fate recover contentment and peace by abandoning and forgetting this hopeless love.

"But while I thus behold her every hour and every hour behold her yet more lovely can I indeed ever find this peace? Oh no, I must fly! Fly from thee dear Selena! From thee whose image will eternally pursue me! From thee whom I must but too soon resign for ever!

> How shall I live without thee?
> How forego thy converse sweet[92]

and thy presence which seems to form for me the whole of life? Oh sentence too rigorous, Oh stroke worse than of death! No Selena never can I thus violently tear myself from thee. Rather suffer me by a gradual effort gently to wean myself from all that casts sunshine on existence that the gloom of my future life may be rendered at least supportable."

---

[91]   "Monti" (Tighe's note). Vincenzo Monti, "V" ("Oh se lontano dalle ree cittadi"), *Pensieri d'amore* (1782), lines 4–10: "You sister and bride / You my wealth, my grandeur, my kingdom! / You are to me heaven and earth and everything! / I am happy in your gaze and you in mine / Like the sweet ripple of a pristine brook / We will see the years go by, / And life will be for us / A source of eternal joy" (Lucia Greene translation).

[92]   John Milton, *Paradise Lost* (1667), 9.908–9 (the lines should read "How can I live without thee, how forego / Thy sweet converse").

Chapter XIX

Oh she is gone! The beauty of the earth
All that in woman could be virtue called
Is lost—corrupted are her noble faculties
The temper of her soul is quite infected.
Lee[93]

It was in such meditations as those which closed the foregoing chapter tho' uttered in no words that Sidney past hours of watchful melancholy devoted to reflections equally sad on the part of Selena, who not only considered her own future lot with a kind of patient sorrow, but felt anxious to escape from her present situation which she was conscious must prove injurious to her own mind as well as that of Sidney for whose happiness she was scarcely less interested than for her own.

Nor was this all her partiality for Lady Trevallyn could not blind her so far as to prevent her from beholding her weakness and tho' she had for the time yielded to her urgent and strong representations against admitting the continued visits of Lord Henry yet she could have little hope that friendship should obtain that which was refused to virtue, or that Lady Trevallyn would for her sake relinquish a pleasure for which she had seen her sacrifice fame and conscience and Selena unequal to the hopeless task of perpetual censure wished to be spared the sight of that self-incurred misery which she so deeply lamented without power to alleviate.

It was with pleasure she however heard Lady Trevallyn on the following morning order the carriage which proved as Selena trusted an intention of dissipating her thoughts from the unfavourable subject upon which they had so long dwelt and on this account she also received with approbation her announced purpose of obeying Lord Trevallyn's wishes, by accepting some of the numerous invitations with which the chimney was overspread.

But from the caution which prudent friendship was about to dictate Lady Trevallyn evidently sought to escape and in this she was for the present assisted by the entrance of a servant who delivered to Selena the following letter from Dallamore addressed to her by the title of Viscountess Dallamore but enclosed by Sidney in a blank cover.

"My dearest Selena,

"I have just heard from Sidney that you suspect me of indifference and as I cannot account for this extraordinary and unjust suspicion except by supposing that he has never told you how impatient I am to see you I think it best not to trust to him any more but to tell you so myself. Believe me there is nothing in

---

[93] Ziphares in Nathaniel Lee's *Mithridates, King of Pontus: A Tragedy* (1678), 3.2.528–31 (line 528 should read "The King! she's gone; the Beauty of the Earth").

the world I long for so much as our meeting & if you wish it as I do you will consent to the plan I have in my head for which I refer you to Sidney, as I am now in great haste.

Ever Yours &c

Dallamore"

Having shewn this letter to Lady Trevallyn and her sister, Selena hastened to send it to Sidney inclosed in a few lines requesting he might inform her what was this plan to which Lord Dallamore thus alluded.

Lady Trevallyn gave orders that when Sidney called he should be admitted & all with impatience awaited his arrival each forming various conjectures, none of which however wild were secretly thought too strange to be the project of Dallamore.

But Sidney himself came not. His spirits exhausted by the watchful sufferings of the preceding night were ill prepared to assume that degree of cheerful composure with which he thought it expedient to speak of Selena's affairs before witnesses and he wished besides gently to hint to Lady Trevallyn how much his judgment approved of the general rule which she had given by his unwillingness to infringe it. He therefore returned by the messenger the following note.

"I received no letter from Dallamore but that which I enclosed nor can I conceive what plan he has formed or what can detain him in Ireland. The moment he informs me you may be certain I shall communicate my intelligence to you.

Yours &c

Sidney Dallamore"

Thus once more cast upon the waste of uncertainty and expectation poor Selena again sought refuge in the consolatory arms of her mild associate patience, and innocently flattering herself that she rejoiced in the determination which she suspected Sidney had formed of absenting himself from Grosvenor square she strove to occupy her mind with the books which Lady Trevallyn delighted to supply and to charm her sorrows and disquietudes with musick.

She assisted at the toilet of her lovely friend and wondered not at the smile of complacence which for a moment illuminated her exquisitely fine features when Fanny proud of her labours entreated her Lady to take a parting glance of self admiration at the perfect loveliness which the hall mirror presented ornamented with all the blaze of luxury which the graceful hand of taste did not withhold or the modest eye of Delicacy forbid.

"Remember dear Lady Trevallyn," whispered Selena as she arrang'd the pearls which encircled the rival fairness of her clear and spotless neck, "remember what my favourite Fenelon has said, 'The world is a severe censor and happy for us that it is so.'"[94]

---

[94] François Fénelon (1651–1715), *The Spiritual Letters of Archbishop Fénelon to Women* (London: Rivington, 1877), Letter 126: "To One Living in the World. On the

Lady Trevallyn forced a smile as she pressed her hand in silence and then hurried away to conceal the conscious tear which rushed to her eyes dispers'd by Love at the next moment with the heart thrilling certainty that the wheels which bore her so rapidly along were already awaited with impatience and that alone upon her entrance amid hundreds joy and pleasure should sparkle in those eyes which till that instant were fixed upon the door.

"How beautiful Lady Trevallyn looks tonight!" exclaimed Clara while they watched her from the window as she stepped into the illuminated carriage.

"Oh yes," said Fanny with a sigh, "my Lady looks tonight as she used to do when my poor Mistress that is dead used to say '*Fanny look at my Emily, not the tongue of Envy itself can find a fault in the face or figure of my Emily*,' and then my Lady used to smile so sweetly and say '*Pray Fanny let us believe Mama for I am afraid no one else will*' tho' God knows my Lady thinks less of herself in every way than any body else. For indeed if possible her mind is more perfect than her face, and that I am sure ladies you know very well."

Here another sigh from poor Fanny's affectionate heart as she left the room seemed to sympathise with the secret wish of Selena that a happier and less dangerous lot had awaited so much native excellence.

At Clara's entreaty Selena consented to sit up for the return of Lady Trevallyn 'till overcome with fatigue she said at last with some surprise "Dear Clara are you not sleepy? Had we not better go to bed?"

"No Selena I never felt less inclined to sleep—and I long to hear who Lady Trevallyn has seen."

"Why how can that possibly interest you when all are alike unknown?"

"Oh no, not all," replied Clara with a deep blush which instantly convinced Selena that Edwin was in her thoughts tho' as if conscious of having betrayed herself she immediately added, "I know Lord Henry and I dare say she will meet him, and I know Sidney tho' I do not suppose he goes out much now."

"Probably not," answered Selena, "for you may remember he said last night that he had not seen Edwin since we came to town and Lady Harriet says that Edwin is at every assembly."

"Oh I don't mind Lady Harriet," cried Clara, "but we shall hear whether Lady Trevallyn has met him."

Selena now plainly perceiving what was her object contentedly bore her company 'till near four o'clock when Lady Trevallyn with some astonishment found them sitting in her dressing room.

As she herself did not appear much more disposed to rest than Clara she willingly began to tell her adventures while they assisted her in taking off her ornaments, for she had accustomed herself never to allow her maids to watch to a late hour for her return home. But in the little history of her night she took care to

---

Lawfulness of Amusements": "True Christians have cause to be thankful that the world is so severe a censor; inasmuch as that makes it more urgently incumbent on them never to give the least cause for scandal" (241).

omit the name of Lord Henry tho' to avoid this she was more than once obliged by her unpractised artlessness to leave the sentence which she had begun unfinished.

Selena however who but too well guessed the cause pursued her with no examination and Clara only intent upon discovering whether she had seen Edwin overlooked all but what she hoped would lead to this grand object of her curiosity.

Nor was she disappointed, for with a smile Lady Trevallyn at last turned to her & demanded why she had not enquired whether she had had the good fortune to meet her much admired friend?

"Edwin do you mean?" stammered Clara deeply blushing from mingled shame and eagerness for what should follow.

"Yes poor Edwin, I saw him in all his glory. I told you I had promised to sup at Lady Racket's so I went there last, and was surprised at the stillness of the room as I entered, till I heard the sound of a soft piano-forte and seeing the crowd gathered around it guessed that they were waiting to hear Edwin sing.

"Lady Racket as soon as she saw me came upon tip-toe and simply took me by the hand and by way of being very obliging made way for me thro' the crowd, and whispered and fussed till she settled me in a chair close to Edwin who saw nothing of what was going on. For while he was wildly running over the notes he appeared totally abstracted from the scene in which he was so conspicuous a figure and entirely engrossed by his own thoughts in spite of all the arts of Lady Vellum and a very pretty woman somewhat younger who seated on either side of him exerted their utmost graces to attract his attention. At last he seemed suddenly to recollect himself and turning hastily to Lady Vellum asked what he should sing in a voice I fancied expressive of the utmost weariness and disgust. She was asking for some song amidst a torrent of the most affected compliments when his eye happened to glance towards me, and instantly starting up as if struck by a sudden dart he eagerly looked round expecting I am convinced to see you Selena. He was pale as death but recovering himself in some degree he was going to address me when enquiries of surprise and concern pouring upon him from all sides he was recalled to recollection upon the strange appearance of his conduct and requesting to be excused singing at that time pleaded a sudden illness. I overheard a great many men who I am sure envy him his success and the admiration of our sex declare he was perpetually seized with such fits but that his disorder was nothing else but affectation. After all I assure you men are more envious than women and I never heard a man reckoned handsome that he was not immediately pulled to pieces and treated with contempt by every other in company. The ladies however all pressed eagerly round our young bard and in the confusion this occasioned the anxious solicitude all affected and the numerous remedies proposed you may suppose he despaired of being able to speak quietly to me, indeed I am sure he thought himself only to make his escape."

"So you did not speak to him!" exclaimed Clara much disappointed.

"Speak to him my dear—how was it possible I could get in a word when I am sure at least twenty voices were all exerted to claim his attention, but I am asked to Lady Vellum's tomorrow night and there I suppose I shall see him again, and

I shall take care," added she smiling, "not to come upon him by surprise when he is[95] going to sing, that I may not disappoint the company as I did to-night and 'break the good meeting with most admired disorder.'"[96]

Clara with scarcely less impatience awaited Lady Trevallyn's return on the following night, but at Lady Vellum's Edwin had vainly been expected, and for many a succeeding evening the disappointed circle loudly complained of the failure of the favourite guest.

In the mean time post after post arrived and Sidney received not yet the promised letter from Dallamore, while Selena's uneasiness with respect to Lady Trevallyn's danger was far from diminished upon observing that tho' her advice was complied with in excluding Lord Henry in the mornings yet this compliance had but precipitated her imprudent friend into worse evils, since unable to forego his society she purchased it by exposing herself in public to the loud reproaches of a world but too ready to catch the tale of infamy which Lady Harriet with implacable revenge and envy studiously sought to circulate.

A few days had now hurried Lady Trevallyn into all the dissipation of the higher circles where those who spoke loudest against her errors were those by whom she was most courted to perpetual engagements. No evening was now passed at home and Lady Harriet took care to inform Selena who had at every assembly been Lady Trevallyn's unfailing attendant.

Yet if the hours for which she thus sacrificed her reputation, alas her virtue too! if those hours were indeed the hours of pleasure whence the paleness of that faded cheek? Why sparkles not that dejected eye with its former mild celestial lustre? Why does it bend its mournful sweetness on the ground? Whence that sadly conscious look (averted from the compassionating bosom of friendship) as of one

> Betrothed to loneliness in whom
> The pride of beauty was no more remembered,[97]

Are these the traces of pleasure? Is this happiness! Ah sweeter far sweeter are even the very sacrifices of Virtue (painful tho' they may be) than are those indulgencies which she condemns!

Selena (however unwillingly she owned it to herself) was at length convinced that her friend now avoided all private conversation with her—and this confirmed the resolution which her mind had for some time adopted tho' her affection for Lady Trevallyn and the expectation of Dallamore's letter had hitherto delayed its execution. She now wrote to Mrs. Vallard wishing to avail herself of her friendly offers of protection and having done this awaited her reply before she

---

[95] MS: "his" (my correction).

[96] Lady Macbeth in Shakespeare's *Macbeth* (1605), 3.4.110–11.

[97] Nottingham in Henry Brooke's *The Earl of Essex* (1761), 3.1.12–13 (the citation should read "Betroth'd to loneliness; in whom the pride / Of power, and beauty, was no more remember'd").

communicated either to Clara or her friend a determination which she feared would meet with some opposition from both. Her brother whom she alone consulted approved highly of her intention, and offered himself to escort her to Derbyshire, but to this proposition she would by no means consent having already independently settled the little plan of her journey and resolved to perform it under the protection only of Le Roi whom she looked upon in the light of a faithful and sincerely attached friend.

While she was yet expecting Mrs. Vallard's answer Dallamore's long promised and impatiently awaited letter at length arrived containing the following lines which Sidney hastened to communicate to Selena.

> "Dear Sidney,
>
> "By the merest accident I find that I forgot to send you the letter which I meant to enclose with Selena's. Never was any thing so provoking. I might just as well not have written it for I must now tell you every thing over again and besides we were preparing all matters for you and I dare say you have not thought of setting out yet. But I hope you will lose no time now and that Selena may have no objection to come with you to meet us in Dublin. We are all longing till you come, there is not a better fellow in the world than Bently; but as for Barton and his wife they are the pleasantest people you ever knew and I am sure Selena will like them of all things. They are coming with us to Merrion square and I have ordered the house to be quite new furnished in the best possible style on purpose that it may be fit for Selena so pray make haste.
>
> Yours &c Dallamore"

Nothing could exceed Selena's astonishment at a proposal so extraordinary; Sidney on his part felt more vexation and displeasure than surprise, the conduct of Dallamore having long taught him to expect every folly that wild caprice could invent.

But a painfully predominant sense of shame oppressed Selena as she again and again perused this letter. She doubted not but that her situation had been exposed to the contemptuous ridicule of these his new friends who from interested motives or perhaps in the wantonness of sport had probably with a view of detaining him in Ireland suggested the idea of Sidney's attachment for her which she felt assured that this proposal was intended to insult for that Dallamore could seriously imagine she should comply with a scheme so repugnant to all delicacy all decency of situation she could not believe.

But this suspicion she avowed to no one and it entirely vanished during the first conversation which Sidney held with her upon the subject, by his setting forth the thoughtless inconsistent character of Dallamore in the true light. She now imparted to him her design of seeking an asylum with Mrs. Vallard and requested him to write immediately to Dallamore to inform him of it having little doubt of receiving the kind welcome of her benevolent maternal friend.

Sidney while his heart ached at the dreaded yet desired separation expressed himself in favour of a scheme which his better judgment could not but approve and then enquired how she would persuade Lady Trevallyn to suffer her to depart.

Selena sighed but answered only by saying that she hoped they should soon meet at Esselberrie.

"Has she then any thoughts of leaving London?" demanded Sidney pleased at the idea.

"Not at present I think, but a few months will soon be past and they are determined to go there early in Summer."

"In Summer!" repeated Sidney, "why do you give up Dallamore's return, or do you think he will not be impatient to bring you back to town when once in England."

"It is difficult for me," said Selena while a forced smile sickened on her cheek, "to form any conjectures as to what may be Lord Dallamore's plans."

"True," cried Sidney with a deep sigh and a momentary swell of indignation, "or if you know those plans it would still be as uncertain what was to be his conduct. But in the mean time," added he in a lower voice, "wisdom and goodness will ever be *your* guides; it is a pity you should deprive poor Lady Trevallyn of their counsels."

"She has a better monitor than I in her own mind," said Selena, "and I trust she will never silence its voice."

Sidney was silent and Selena saw that he struggled with his reluctance to communicate what was unpleasant. She guessed that he thought it expedient to warn her of the harsh censure which awaited her friend and already but too well informed of this by the officious malice of Lady Harriet she spared Sidney a task which he wished not to fulfil and changed the conversation with an eagerness that convinced him that the caution which prudence had dictated was unnecessary and that Selena had already done all that virtuous friendship & courageous affection could perform.

The following day brought Mrs. Vallard's answer which declared her satisfaction in the prospect of seeing her dear children as she called Selena and Clara, excusing her long silence by saying she had been ill during the whole of the last month and was still confined, concluding with a desire to be tenderly remembered to her dear Emily. In a postscript she added, "I hear that poor Mrs. Harley is extremely ill and unable to go close the eyes of her dying Angela. I am sure it would bring comfort to the unhappy Mother could you see her child before you return to us."

A request with which Selena's compassionate heart determined to comply.

Chapter XX

How wretched they
Who feel, but cannot save their dying Virtue!
Thompson[98]

With a view of preparing Lady Trevallyn for their separation Selena had more than once hinted her intention which had always been received with the bitterest tears and followed by fits of such extreme dejection as almost terrified Selena.

"You are my good Angel," she used to say, "whom Heaven itself sent in human form to guide and cheer my dark life and when you are taken from me I shall know I am indeed lost and abandoned!"

With a heavy heart Selena now entered her dressing room to announce the day fixed for her departure and armed herself with firmness to persist in what she considered the path of her duty however painful she might feel the task of withstanding the importunities of tenderness. She was pleased on her opening the door to observe an unusual air of cheerfulness had banished for a while the languid melancholy of Lady Trevallyn's countenance and congratulated herself upon having found the fit season for announcing her intelligence which she had so long dreaded to declare.

"Oh Selena you have surprised me," cried she with a smile, "you were not to have seen our work till Fanny and I had completed it; we were just going to have this little stand left in your room. It is entirely my own design, and I think you will not love the gift the less on that account especially if you could know how happy I have been while selecting and arranging these books."

Selena's eyes filled as she gazed with admiration on the little bookcase of the most exquisite workmanship where the hand of taste itself had directed an elegant and fanciful combination of well chosen authors in their most highly ornamented dress intermingled with small but beautifully adorned baskets of the most rare and fragrant plants.

"Come Fanny," continued she, "let us have it moved in I will shew you where I think it will be most comfortable to fix it. I think between your harp and the fire. Do not you Selena?" Fanny had run to obey her lady's orders, as proudly delighted with the gift as tho' it had been made under her own immediate directions and Lady Trevallyn who saw that amid Selena's tender tho' scarcely articulated expressions of gratitude there was some latent cause of sadness which she was about to utter fearfully demanded with an altered countenance, "What is the matter my Love."

"Nothing new dearest Lady Trevallyn. But what must I be could I behold without the sincerest regret the hour approach that even for a time must part us?"

"Part us!" exclaimed her friend, her pale lips quivering while the last volume which she was preparing to place upon the stand dropped from her trembling hand, "Oh Selena will you leave me? Then am I indeed abandoned!"

---

[98]   Clytemnestra in James Thomson's *Agamemnon* (1738), 1.4.136–7.

"Say not so dear Lady Trevallyn," cried Selena throwing herself upon her neck, "we shall soon meet again at Esselberrie. Happier hours, hours of tranquility and self approbation are I trust in store for us both."

"No not for me," said Lady Trevallyn in a low and mournful voice, receiving without returning the embraces of Selena, "I have seen happiness depart for ever, and

> helpless, hopeless heard her say
> Farewell! we meet no more![99]

Oh my poor Mother why did you forsake your child. Why leave your lost your wretched Emily in a world of strangers where none feels, none can understand my anguish. How gladly would I hide my head in thy cold bosom could I thus resign this being hateful to myself and wearisome to others."

"You are angry with me my dearest Lady Trevallyn or you would not talk so cruelly. But you will not be so when you reflect that tho' you are and ever will be inexpressibly dear to me I have yet other kind friends to whom I owe some consideration and that we can comparitively now enjoy but little of each other's society while you are shared by so many and constant engagements."

"And will Lady Harriet be less engaged? Or will she value your society as I do?" hastily interrupted Lady Trevallyn.

"Lady Harriet!" repeated Selena with surprise, "I have not thought of Lady Harriet. It is to poor Mrs. Vallard that I mean to go—my dear Mother's only friend! our kind Mrs. Vallard! who has been ill and confined without a companion to comfort or cheer her lonely hours of sickness. See here is her letter!"

Lady Trevallyn now taking it from Selena dried her eyes apparently consoled in some degree by finding that Selena had not been seduced from her by one whose malice had lately been manifested more than once so as to terrify the gentle spirit of Lady Trevallyn and fill her breast with a presentiment of some unknown purposed injury.

Nevertheless as Selena found it impossible to reconcile her friend to their separation she thought it better to spare them both the painful farewell scene and silently appearing to yield to her entreaties of remaining at least one week longer she in secret resolved to arrange all things for her departure on the second day after their explanation.

It now remained for her to acquaint Clara with her purpose, but this task was far less difficult. Clara indeed wept at the thoughts of quitting London without once beholding the face of him whose image as she entered it had filled her with such lively delight, such enchanting hopes, but despairing now of his return to Selena since he had met Lady Trevallyn without one effort to see or even to speak of her who he well knew was under her protection, she now promised herself only the melancholy pleasure of retracing the scenes where her young heart had first

---

[99]   William Cowper, "Ode to Peace" (1782), lines 23–4.

been captivated by Edwin, where she might dwell upon that Edwin with all the admiration and tenderness we give to the memory of a departed friend and forget that lost to her for ever he yet existed careless and unworthy of her love.

While Selena observed with some secret mortification that in spite of Lady Trevallyn's dejection, she at the usual hour mournfully resumed the labours of her toilette preparatory to fulfilling the engagements of the evening she was hence but the more confirmed in the expediency of withdrawing herself from witnessing what her influence was insufficient to check even at the moment when it must be the strongest over the affectionate feelings of the tender Emily.

Should any question the sincerity of Lady Trevallyn's distress at parting from her friend and the reality of that friendship which at such a time could deny a sacrifice apparently so trifling let them recal to mind whether they have ever felt the torment of being constrained to disappoint a beloved object without the possibility of accounting for the unexpected failure.

Reluctant as Lady Trevallyn was to leave Selena and appear with swelled eyes and an aching heart to a crowded assembly room, she yet could not endure the image of Lord Henry anxious, alarmed nay even offended at her absence, or perhaps consoling himself for it by the conversation of another, of Lady Harriet! The debate which she held in secret with herself was at length decided as too many had hitherto been by temporising with the foe; "this one engagement must be fulfilled and the remainder of my time shall be all Selena's while I can yet preserve her."

Who is surprised at the result of this debate? If ever they have found themselves in such circumstances and can yet feel surprise their friendship has owed its triumph only to their insensibility.

On the following day Selena requested Lady Trevallyn to allow her to visit Angela at Kensington. The carriage was instantly ordered but Lady Trevallyn sighed when she considered that this visit was preparatory to the journey she anticipated with such sorrow. She however requested Selena might enquire whether any thing could be done to render Angela's situation more agreeable and to offer whatever medical assistance which she or her friends might hope to afford any relief.

As Selena drove into Park lane she perceived Sidney on horseback a few paces before her, and felt for an instant rejoiced at this opportunity of once more seeing him before she left town tho' she had in her coolest moments resolved against bidding him farewell.

Upon hearing the sound of the carriage immediately behind him he looked round and joy darted from his eyes while the smile of inexpressible delight played over his cheek which was instantly suffused with the deepest glow while his heart swelled with that unutterably sweet sensation ever attendant upon the sudden and unexpected sight of what we love.

At his desire the coachman stopped and Sidney then putting his hand upon the door apologised for thus delaying her by telling Selena that he wished to shew her a letter which he immediately produced and told her to peruse it at her leisure, adding, "I have just received it from my old friend Bently the father of the young Lieutenant who I told you was on board the Greyhound with Dallamore, who had been engaged to marry Ophelia Lawder his father's ward. I was just going to ride to Bently farm to answer it in person."

Perceiving that he was now ready to pursue his way Selena involuntarily sought to prolong the conversation for some moments thinking it probable it might be the last.

"Shall I return this to-day," asked she.

"Oh no, do not trouble yourself," answered Sidney, "I am to dine at Grosvenor square tomorrow and we can talk it over then."

"I hope to be half way to Derby by dinner time to-morrow," answered Selena endeavouring to force a smile.

"To-morrow!" repeated Sidney! with an emotion which he could not disguise.

"Yes," continued Selena observing he remained silent, "but I have made no one my confident yet except Le Roi; so if you should meet Lady Trevallyn take care you do not betray me. Will you not bid me good bye?" said she extending her hand while he stood yet silent and motionless with his eyes fixed upon the seat of the carriage.

"Will you allow me to call upon you this evening?" said he at length, as if awaking from his reverie, "I want to have your opinion of that letter."

"You must take care then to preserve my secret," answered Selena after some hesitation.

"You may depend upon my discretion," cried he and then having heard whither she was going he desired the coachman to drive on.

While Selena dwelt unconsciously upon this rencounter and the promised evening some minutes elapsed before she recollected the letter which Sidney had left in her hands for her perusal. With a sigh she then called back her imagination from ideas where she allowed them not to wander and unfolding the paper read as follows.

"My dear Sir,

"I am impatient to communicate to you the important service which your noble relation Lord Dallamore has conferred upon my son being assured from your friendly disposition to my family that the news will afford you satisfaction. I have just had a letter from Charles which I shall be happy to shew to you when you can allow me the pleasure of seeing you here. In this he informs me with all the enthusiasm of gratitude we might expect from his very ardent mind that having (while on board his ship) told Lord Dallamore his story and that of our poor deserted Ophelia, his Lordship instantly promised to remove all impediments to their immediate union by exerting his influence to obtain leave of absence for Charles and then in the most generous and friendly manner presented him with the promise of a lease for ever at a meer nominal rent of a very beautiful farm in Oxfordshire with an excellent house completely furnished.

"My Son is I hope determined to avail himself no farther of his liberal friendship than he can do with honour which assuredly will not suffer him to accept the farm on any other terms than what may be considered a reasonable rent. I have written to him my ideas on this subject but from your knowledge of us you will easily judge how rejoiced I am at this proposal of seeing Charles settled with one so peculiarly fitted to make him happy. I trust he will ever retain a sense of the obligation and that the domestic felicity of the young couple may prove the best reward to their noble benefactor. Captain Modely has given my son permission to go on shore with Lord Dallamore and Charles writes me word that tho' he cannot quit his friend while he continues in Ireland yet he hopes very shortly to accompany him to London.

"I shall be much gratified to converse farther with you on this business and to let you see the innocent joy of our young people who have long looked upon the little Ophelia as their sister and now anticipate with the highest exultation the prospect of Charles's return and her establishment. Your friendly congratulations seem only wanting to complete the satisfaction of my dear Sir

Yrs &c

H: Bently"

What were the sensations which filled with tears the eyes of Selena as she read this new proof of the benevolence of Dallamore's disposition? Alas! Dallamore himself was at the moment forgotten so entirely was she absorbed in the consideration of that superior generosity which had prompted Sidney's eagerness thus instantly to impart it to her.

But it was not long before she once more commanded her thoughts, which are perhaps more obedient to the will than we weakly chuse to acknowledge, and dwelling upon the many amiable traits she had already known in Dallamore's character she contemplated with pride and satisfaction this new addition to the list which she loved to enumerate to herself and those friends who she perceived considered her lot with pity and regret. In the midst of such meditations she was interrupted by her arrival at the small house where the servant who attended the carriage informed her he had already been to enquire for Miss Harley.

The maid who opened the door upon being asked for Angela offered instantly to call her to the carriage, but Selena not chusing that she should be thus summoned got out and entered the little hall.

A middle aged woman of gentle and pleasing manners in a few minutes came down stairs and with many excuses for her being thus left standing requested Selena to walk into the parlour saying that she hoped her Ladyship would forgive her niece Angela for not waiting upon her, as at that time she had lain down and she was unwilling to disturb her being so extremely unwell.

Selena expressed her concern and perceiving that she was mistaken for Lady Trevallyn she repeated the kind commissions with which she had been charged and requested Mrs. Harley to inform Angela that she would send a messenger that evening in case she wished to have any thing conveyed to her Mother whom she hoped in a few days to see.

"You are very good Madam," answered Mrs. Harley, "but we have been expecting my sister every day."

Selena shook her head and told her how poor an account she had had of her health which she feared would not suffer her to move from Esselberrie.

Selena's offers of a Physician Mrs. Harley gratefully accepted saying however that Angela already had had advice but tho' she did not obstinately refuse to take any medicines yet she believed she had herself little faith in their prescriptions and never swallowed any thing but in compliance with her entreaties.

Selena was sorry to be obliged to quit the house without seeing Angela but as Mrs. Harley still appeared unwilling to disturb her she at length returned to Grosvenor square and having privately consulted with Clara after dinner she dispatched a messenger with a few lines to Angela offering to take her home to her Mother if she thought herself able to undertake so long a journey by short stages.

Selena resolved in case she refused this proposal to leave her in some degree in the charge of Sidney and he cheerfully promised to visit and offer every assistance in his power to the afflicted family at Kensington, gladly seizing the pretence it afforded of writing sometimes to Selena in order to inform Mrs. Harley thro' her of Angela's health.

Before supper a small sealed packet arrived from Angela directed for her Mother, with the following lines for Selena.

> "You are too good, dear Madam, to an unhappy creature but I shall never more behold my poor Mother. You who are all benevolence and pity will I know try to comfort her for the loss of an undutiful ungrateful child who living or dying could only repay her love with care and sorrow. I have however obeyed her last request as you will see when you have the goodness to deliver to her the papers with which I take the liberty to trouble you. Tho' my prayers are of no avail Heaven will reward *you* for your tenderness to my afflicted Mother.
> Angela Harley"

Melancholy as this note appeared to Selena she could not help considering the sense which Angela had of her danger as a symtom rather favourable having heard the reverse always accounted a sure and fatal attendant upon a hopeless consumption.

As Angela had omitted the name of Lady Trevallyn in her acknowledgements Selena silently put the note into her writing box, with the little parcel without communicating its contents and exerted herself to display a cheerfulness she was in fact far from feeling.

Nor was Sidney on his part wanting in the firmness with which he had prepared his mind to support with smiles the anguish of those hours of constraint, the last he might ever spend in the presence of Selena, for he had secretly vowed in future to shun the dangerous indulgence of her society which under circumstances so hopeless served only to encrease his misery.

The moment so dreaded at length arrived. Selena yet felt the pressure of his hand but the door had already closed upon him which she knew was never more to gladden her soul by opening to his entrance.

If thy sinking heart thrills with the sad remembrance of a like sensation, if thou hast listened to the departing step that must approach no more, if thy fancy still loves to dwell upon the looks that shall never again smile upon thee, if thou hast not dared to lament, if thou hast deplored thy very sorrow as the worst of thine evils, if thou hast worn the smile of serenity upon thy lips, while the desolate gloom of Melancholy settled around thy heart thou wilt then look with more tender compassion upon Selena than her own sense of duty allowed her to bestow herself upon her feelings.

Yet when she pressed Lady Trevallyn in her arms and while she bade her good night indulged her affectionate heart with a parting embrace and a farewell breathed in secret, she could no longer restrain her tears, but hastening from her concealed the sorrow which she feared might betray her intended departure.

Lady Trevallyn whose eye or rather heart was ever ready by a kind of native delicate instinct to understand and share the unuttered distress of others, was not now insensible to the unusual sadness which hung over Selena's mind. But attributing it to her approaching separation from Sidney she suspected not, or at least willingly rejected the transient suspicion, that the parting was already over, and that she herself had already lost the society which she so fondly so justly valued. She retired therefore to her pillow where exhausted by the dissipation of so many preceeding nights, her sorrows, her self-upbraidings, her past regrets, and anxious forebodings were awhile suspended in the placid arms of sleep.

Selena feeling herself but little inclined for repose past the greatest part of the night in preparations for her journey having previously requested Le Roi to be ready at the door with the hired chaise as soon as it was light.

Before she quitted Grosvenor square she wrote a grateful and affectionate farewell to Lady Trevallyn and at the same time entreated her in the tenderest and most delicate terms to beware of the dangers to which she now exposed herself in the scenes of dissipation, injurious to all, but chiefly fatal to the most amiable minds and those whose artless sensibility must render them so open to receive the most lively impressions.

Having laid the letter upon her friend's dressing table she cast a glance of soft melancholy around, where every thing seemed to wear the sweet interesting charm of the gentle Emily. The very air of the apartment breathing the peculiar fragrance of her favourite plants still appeared to partake something of her presence. The lovely Rose was missing indeed but its perfume seemed to remain! The book which she had been reading as she undressed lay open. It was a volume of Florian. Selena took up the gloves which on drawing them off Lady Trevallyn had placed within it as a mark and casting her eye upon the page read these words marked by the pencil of her friend:

"Oh quelle tourment de s'etre condamnée de combattre sans cesse un sentiment que sans cesse occupe son ame! d'arracher lentement de son coeur l'image cherie qui le remplit toujours."[100]

Selena replaced the gloves but not till a tear had dropped upon them as she pressed them to her lips and breathed a prayer for her erring her unhappy friend, pure and acceptable even as the prayers of her superior guardian angel.

Nor was it without emotion that Selena as she softly stole down stairs perceived the drawing room door open; all the house was still, the chambermaid had not yet been there and the chair which Sidney had occupied remained unmoved as he had left it. At its foot, she perceived a small and half withered branch of myrtle which she recollected to have seen him take from the chimney piece and it still retained the circular form into which he had twisted it while engaged with her in conversation. Involuntarily she advanced and stooping for it was about to place it in her bosom when the conscious sense of her weakness stung her with a sensation of shame and self reproach which prompted her to relinquish the aromatic plant more suddenly than if she had held the most rank and poisoness weed. She felt the air of this place was but too favourable to those painful remembrances which she studied to banish & hastily quitting the room waited for Clara in the chaise and in a few moments they commenced their journey attended by Le Roi on horseback.

End of Volume III

---

[100] Jean-Pierre Claris de Florian, *Gonzalve de Cordoue, ou Grenade Reconquise*, 3 vols. (Paris, 1791), 3:9, page 175 (the citation substitutes "sentiment" for "amour"): "Oh what torment to be condemned to fight without cessation the feeling that constantly occupied one's soul; to slowly tear from one's heart the cherished image that always filled it."

Volume IV

Chapter I

Sweet Peace and heavenly Hope, and humble Joy,
Divinely beam on the exalted soul
With incommunicable lustre bright
Life take thy chance but oh for such an end!
Young[1]

Selena endeavoured to enliven the dreariness of the wintry scenes thro' which
they past and their own hopeless comfortless prospects by every effort which
her naturally cheerful disposition and lively fancy could suggest. Banishing all
considerations of a more selfish nature she now felt herself called upon to supply
to Clara the place not only of natural tenderness but of those social amusements
and those elegancies of luxury which Lady Trevallyn had with a caressing grace
studied to provide for her guests during their residence with her.

It was early in the day when they reached Hillbarton where they had the
satisfaction of finding Mrs. Vallard considerably better tho' yet unable to leave
her room. Selena anxious to execute Angela's commission had no sooner received
her first kind welcome and tender salutations, and satisfied her eager enquiries
concerning her own situation with respect to Dallamore, than she dispatched a
messenger to Mrs. Harley enclosing the parcel which Angela had sent as well as
the note she had received from her on the evening before she left London.

Selena herself wrote a few lines promising to see her on the next day, and
acquainting her with the proposal which she had made to Angela.

"I fear," said Mrs. Vallard, "that you will find poor Mrs. Harley greatly
changed, I have not been able to visit her for a month but hear she has never left
her bed during that time and Mr. Graves the apothecary who visits the school by
Lady Trevallyn's orders in her absence tells me he has not the least hopes of her
recovery, tho' she may linger yet for some time."

Selena always an early riser was but just up when Mrs. Vallard's maid tap'd at
her door. On being admitted she told her that Mr. Mason (whom Selena had heard
of as the curate of an adjoining parish) was below and wished to speak to her from
Mrs. Harley who was at the point of death. Selena hastened to the parlour where
she was told he waited her coming. As she opened the door he turned from the
window at which he stood and advanced to salute her.

---

[1]   Edward Young, "Night II," *Night Thoughts* (1742–45), lines 693–7, The epigraph
substitutes "the" for "his" in line 694, omits line 695 ("Destruction gild, and crown him for
the skies"), and includes line 697, generally omitted after 1749.

Never had Selena beheld a countenance so heavenly! Candour, humility and peace sat upon his brow whose unwrinkled serenity seemed to deny the years which had yet marked their course by a few silvery hairs but thinly scattered over his temples. Universal benevolence beamed in his placid eye where the traces of tears bore witness to his sympathy with suffering humanity. A smile innocent as that of infantine simplicity and a voice mild as that of Charity herself at once engaged all the confidence, & the esteem of Selena. The chemical affinities of bodies are not more real nor more strong than those which attract some minds instantly to each other, and Selena felt in meeting him for the first time; as tho' she again beheld a long known and valued friend.

"I fear my good young Lady," said he, "that my errand will appear but a melancholy one; the bed of death is terrible to the apprehension of the gay and the young. But yet believe me that of Mrs. Harley is exempt from all terrors; your presence for a few moments will free her from her last earthly anxiety and she has sent me to entreat that you will suffer her to impart to you in person her dying request."

Selena declared her readiness instantly to accompany him, and as they went eagerly demanded, "Were there no hopes of her recovery?"

"Say rather fears, dear Madam," replied he with a gracious smile, "Our hopes for her are all fixed upon a better world and she has not many hours of patient suffering to endure."

He then continued to acquaint Selena with the situation of Mrs. Harley's health for some time past and informed her that he had been sent for on the preceding night, the remainder of which he had passed by her bedside as it was not expected she could live till morning, but that Death yet lingered with exhausted Nature and that she appeared only unwilling to leave the world till she had imparted to Selena her dying injunctions with respect to her child and her beloved benefactress.

Selena replied that she feared nothing now remained for poor Angela but to conceal from her the death of her Mother when it was most probable she could not many days survive. From Mr. Mason's answer she perceived that he had been already made better acquainted with the particulars of Angela's situation than she was herself, and from some peculiarity in the term of his expressions she recalled to mind that Mrs. Vallard ever reluctant to censure had yet mentioned him as a dangerous enthusiast while Lady Trevallyn had been recounting some uncommonly amiable instances of benevolence which she had heard of him from Mrs. Harley.

When they reached the school-house Mr. Mason fearful of the least surprise in her weak state went in to prepare Mrs. Harley for the visit which she had so ardently desired. Selena took this opportunity of enquiring into the state of the little school in which she felt peculiarly interested as a favourite object to her friend and one worthy of a disposition so kind and generous. She found that Mrs. Harley had for the present provided a decent looking woman who in some measure supplied her place but Selena resolved during her stay at Hillbarton to superintend with her own eye the conduct and improvement of the children.

Mr. Mason now introduced her to the apartment of his dying friend. The curtains of the bed were undrawn and the windows were not darkened, while the pallid and emaciated countenance of Mrs. Harley alone announced this to be the seat of death or sickness. She sat erect, supported by pillows and a faint smile spoke her pleasure at the entrance of Selena.

"Approach my dear," said Mr. Mason in a low voice, "you may do so fearlessly and our friend is unable to utter very distinctly."

Selena sat down on the side of the bed and taking Mrs. Harley's hand pressed it to her lips, while the image of her own dying Mother too forcibly oppressed her bosom with tenderness and grief to allow her to speak any language but that of tears. Selena at first found it extremely difficult to understand the words of Mrs. Harley but Mr. Mason having retired to the window, she at length heard her distinctly pronounce the name of Lady Trevallyn.

"Is there any thing my dear Madam," said Selena, "that you would have me say for you to Lady Trevallyn?"

"Oh watch her! Save her!" cried she exerting herself and clasping her hands with energy.

Selena somewhat surprised thought she might now possibly allude to Angela and repeated her request to know whether she had any message—or if there was any thing she wished to have done for her child.

Mrs. Harley raised her eyes to Heaven and with an expression of humble, joyful confidence said in a stronger voice, "My child is gone before me! But oh my poor Lady! Save her from the misery of guilt, save her from the wicked one!"

She then made an effort to move and Selena offering her assistance she pointed to some papers which lay half covered by the pillow. Taking them from Selena she pressed them for a moment to her bosom and her countenance for the first time assumed the expression of agony. But the pang was transient and her placid eye was once more raised with sweet submission and a divine satisfaction more blessed than Hope itself. After a short silence she put the papers again into Selena's hands and said something scarce audibly of which Selena could only distinguish, "I leave you all …. never betray my poor …. Save! Oh save! …"

Here her strength failed and Mr. Mason advancing took her hand and said in a soft but solemn voice, "Enough my sister … Depart in peace! Trust to the mercies of our loving father. Remember all his children are alike his care."

A smile of infinite contentment proved that her heart received this truth with confidence. He continued to address her with exhortations to rejoice in the glorious exchange she was about to make and her last words were an expression of this joyful assurance. After this she made a sign to him to pray by her and while they kneeled down she closed her eyes without a groan so that it was some moments before they perceived that the spirit had departed into the bosom of its creator.

Selena inexpressibly affected at the awfully pleasing scene remained upon her knees while her venerable companion in the pathetic eloquence of the heart, gave thanks for the happy release which they had just witnessed and implored for themselves that "*they also might die the death of the righteous and that their last end might be like hers.*"[2]

As soon as Selena had given what orders she thought necessary in the name of her friend with respect to the steps immediately to be taken, she was impatient to return to Hillbarton, fearing that her long absence might excite uneasiness in Mrs. Vallard or her sister. Before she left the school she however strongly recommended the woman to follow the advice of Mr. Mason, who entreated that the utmost quietness should be preserved and that nothing might be said to create an impression of terror on the minds of the children.

While she was employed in carefully putting up the papers which had been entrusted to her in so sacred a manner, she perceived that they were all written in the hand of Angela—and rightly guessed that they had been contained in the parcel of which she had been the bearer.

"I fear," said the person who had attended as she observed Selena, "those writings (be they what they may) contain no good, they shortened poor Mrs. Harley's days that much I can answer for. It would have made your heart ache Sir," said she turning to Mr. Mason, "had you seen the poor soul while she was reading them. She fainted twice and was only a little composed after we had sent for you at her desire."

"We should remember," said Mr. Mason mildly perceiving Selena inexpressibly shocked at the idea, "we should remember that her days could not be shortened without the will of God, and when I saw our departed friend last Sunday she was to all appearance rapidly approaching to her last moments."

This in some degree relieved Selena from the reproach which she had felt ready to make to herself for imprudently executing her commission, tho' in the state in which she had left Angela she could hardly have justified to herself the wilful delay even of a few hours.

As she parted from Mr. Mason he affectionately blessed her and in a lower voice desired her never to forget the dying and important charge which she had received. Selena who had as yet but a confused and faint idea of its meaning, wished to converse farther with him upon the subject but deferred it to another opportunity, finding her spirits at present unequal to the task of any farther exertion. She thanked him therefore for his admonition adding that she hoped to meet him shortly where they might consult what was to be done about Angela. He bowed in silence and Selena with languid steps returned to Hillbarton nearly exhausted with fatigue of mind and body.

Terrified at her paleness Mrs. Vallard insisted upon her lying down for a few hours after having taken some refreshment, nor would she for the present allow her to repeat to them any particulars of the awful scene.

But no sooner had Selena recovered her calm composure in the stillness of solitude of her own room; where Mrs. Vallard had strictly desired that she might remain undisturbed, than she found it impossible to resist her impatience to know

---

[2]   Numbers 23:10 (KJV).

the contents of those papers, which she doubted not might explain the nature of the charge so solemnly committed to her.

Seating herself therefore on the bed she opened as much of the window as was necessary to give her light to peruse the manuscript, but was more than once obliged to lay it aside overcome with the emotions of pity, indignation, and terror which it excited, while the pale and interesting figure of the once beautiful and innocent Angela appeared itself to utter each melancholy sentence.

Chapter II

Angela's narrative
Written for her Mother

Ah me from real happiness we stray
By vice bewildered: Vice which always leads
However fair at first to wilds of woe!
                                    Thompson[3]

Alas my too kind Mother why should I record the sorrows of your wretched child whom no guilt, no folly can make an object of indifference to your too pitying heart. Abandoned as I am of God let me rather hide this devoted head from the eye of compassion as well as of scorn and since I am born to be miserable and hated let me fly from the voice of tenderness which should never meet this ear. But my full heart longs to unburthen itself, and in the cruel blank which existence every moment presents to me, incapable of any other employment I can at least consume some of my miserable hours in retracing scenes too deeply painted on my agoniz'd bosom. When I attempt to paint the fatal image my heart which is so ready to afford the pictures seems for a moment relieved of the cruel weight with which they so continually oppress it.

Oh my Mother why did you abandon your unfortunate child? Why expose me to dangers, to miseries which beneath your watchful eye, your loved protection I had never known. But it is not for me to dare to utter a reproach. You did all for Angela's good, Heaven willed all for Angela's destruction! Miserable worm is it for thee to reproach the will of Heaven? But where slept the wrath which had marked me from my birth for misery when every morning my eyes opened to meet the glance of Love and every night they closed but to dream of those glances which Hope whispered should again illumine the morrow? Alas I now feel that those hours of delight were but bestowed to give the sting of Memory without which sorrow possesses not half its force. Oh past felicity! delusions of Hope, scenes so exquisite to every feeling why when lost to me for ever why will you leave behind those ever torturing remembrances? Terrible indeed are the phantoms of departed pleasures amid the gloom which hangs over my despairing soul!

---

[3]   Clytemnestra in James Thomson's *Agamemnon* (1738), 2.7.18–21.

Oh that in endeavouring to describe the scenes of my happiness I could yield up for ever the fatal ideas and cease to remember the sensations I record.

The years of my childhood were devoted to peaceful study and the solitude in which they were passed almost without interruption nursed the softness of a sensibility so deadly to my peace. Nay the pure enthusiasm of the very religion with which my benefactress sought to inspire my soul by teaching me to despise the vanities of life and those frivolous amusements so generally captivating to youth rendered my heart more susceptible to receive deeply the impressions of a passion which quickly assumed the sole dominion of my mind.

Unnoticed I had seen and admired the beautiful niece of Lady Anne and been the unheeded witness of a thousand scenes of tenderness between her and Lord Henry. How often have I joined with my indulgent mistress when she has expressed to me her hopes of seeing one day united two beings so beautiful, so amiable, so formed for each other. Did one wish rise in this presumptuous bosom to disturb such felicity? Oh no! Why then was I doomed to be the victim of its not being accomplished? Why did this too much loved seducer abandon the far more lovely object of his first choice to turn his eyes upon the humble being whom his fondness has destroyed? And did he then indeed ever love the poor Angela? Oh can I now believe that this despised form possessed ever in his eyes one charm? Could I yet believe that I was not always deceived and that he indeed felt for me the passionate tenderness he expressed the flattering idea would sooth even now the anguish of my soul and cheer the desolate gloom of my deserted hours.

Bear with me my Mother. I know that I should drive from my heart the sentiments which have betrayed me into guilt and abandoned me to misery. But it is impossible. I have vowed, I have prayed to Heaven; but my vows have been fruitless and my prayers are disregarded. I have indeed sinned but my punishment is greater than I can bear! To you my Mother I now pour out my full heart as I have hitherto done to that Heaven which has been as brass to the voice of my sorrows.[4] Little did you think when you read with pride and satisfaction the letters of your poor Angela that the time would come when you should wish that instead of placing her youth in scenes of polished society, where her mind should be cultivated and her faculties improved, you had left her in the poorest cottage on the wildest mountain, and to the casual protection of the rudest unknown peasant.

Oh Angela how ungrateful has thy own guilt rendered thee to the love of the tenderest of Mothers, to the care of the most indulgent of benefactors! Seated at the side of my beloved Lady Anne encouraged to declare every feeling of my heart how often have I blessed Heaven and you for the happy situation I enjoyed, and those letters which you declared so pleasing overflowed with the contentment

---

⁴   Angela may be invoking Deuteronomy 28:22–3 (KJV): "The Lord shall smite thee with a consumption, and with a fever, and with an inflammation, and with an extreme burning, and with the sword, and with blasting, and with mildew; and they shall pursue thee until thou perish. And thy heaven that is over thy head shall be brass, and the earth that is under thee shall be iron."

which reigned unclouded in my soul. In the beautiful secluded villa from whence we never stirred Lady Anne saw no company except that of a few chosen and pious friends and her own family, whom she considered herself bound to receive with courteous and endearing welcome, as often as her gentle amiable manners invited them for a while to exchange the gay scenes of pleasure or of business for our sweet retirement.

Mrs. Montrose and her much admired daughter were among our most frequent visitors, for there they always met Lord Henry the fascinating and beautiful nephew of Lady Anne. While the lovely cousins who seemed indeed formed for each other wandered thro' the plantations or were seated in the garden, my presence in the chamber of my kind Mistress never prevented Mrs. Montrose from conversing with the utmost freedom with Lady Anne whom she well knew to favour her hopes of a serious attachment on Lord Henry's part and that a marriage so probable and so desirable might at last take place.

Lady Anne who had some reasons for being less sanguine in these expectations in vain cautioned her upon the danger to which she exposed her daughter till his designs were more explicitly declared. She continued not only to countenance but encourage every intimacy and feared nothing but the interruption of their present happiness persuaded it tended rapidly to their lasting union.

One day in particular I remember that returning from our evening's walk with Lady Anne and Mrs. Montrose we passed a little seat shaded by the spreading branches of a large tree, and perceived it occupied by Miss Montrose, while Lord Henry seated on the short grass at her feet, fed her in a playful manner from a leaf of cherries which he had placed beside him. While she bent down her beautiful lips to catch the offered fruit, the fond Mother entreated us to stop that we might unseen contemplate a picture surely more perfect in loveliness than any ever painted by the hand of a master .Lord Henry's expressive eyes were raised to her face, and one hand held the half offered cherry while the other gracefully supported his body almost reclined upon the grass. For a moment he held it beyond her reach and gently approaching at the same time he presented to her lips not the fruit which they expected but others of a vermillion softness infinitely more perfect, and a sweetness how much more enchanting! A deep blush suffused her glowing face and rising hastily she prevented our joining her by the quickness of the steps with which she quitted the spot where Lord Henry was still reclined calling upon Emily with a smile and in a soft voice entreating her to return. Then springing up he lightly pursued her and when we (who were the unknown witnesses of this scene) entered the drawing room Miss Montrose was seated with her back to the window while Lord Henry standing at the outside read aloud over her shoulder the book which she held in her hand.

Oh my Mother! In recalling images which I beheld at the time without interest, nay even with pleasure, a pang of the severest jealousy even now rends my soul and I think that I would gladly purchase the united torments I have myself endured and those comparitively so light which Lady Trevallyn has suffered to be for one hour the object of those soul-penetrating glances which he then bestowed upon the young and lovely Emily and by which he afterwards fascinated my heart.

Lady Anne looked with painful apprehension on circumstances which filled Mrs. Montrose with the utmost confidence of expectation and the innocent victim of her Mother's imprudence received with more trembling doubt and with less exultation the demonstrations of an affection which Mrs. Montrose still flattered herself was daily strengthening.

Year after year renewed the hopes which appearances would so often render doubtful: At length I understood that Miss Montrose's health had suffered and that the physicians had ordered her if possible to try a warmer climate.

Lady Anne visibly affected with sorrow on her account entrusted me with the mortifying secret; Miss Montrose's health was really in danger, but she would never have consented to quit the Kingdom which contained all her hopes, had not the advice of Lady Anne and the persuasions of her Mother which that advice had stimulated, powerfully urged her.

"This will put my Nephew," Lady Anne would say, "to the test, and why waste your sweet Emily's youth and even life in vain expectations?"

They yielded to her reasoning and with difficulty obtained from government a permission for Mrs. Montrose to pass thro' France into Italy. The names of those who accompanied her were to be particularly inserted in the pass-ports and Lady Anne took upon herself to ask Lord Henry if he chose to be of the party.

The answer was decisive to all their hopes. He declined it positively and even avoided taking a farewell so distressing on all sides by suddenly quitting town some time previous to that fixed for their departure. Nor did he return until assured of its having taken place.

Mrs. Montrose miserable at the situation to which she thought her own impatient imprudence had reduced her daughter deferred their journey from day to day, still nursing a fond and lingering hope that Lord Henry might return and by his declaration restore them both to health and joy.

It was Miss Montrose herself who at last urged her Mother to delay no longer and refused to listen to her proposal of entirely relinquishing a plan which had so completely failed in its principal object—"No my Mother let him not think that we wait for him, let him never know the misery I suffer, or for a moment imagine that he has the power which he wishes not to exercise of restoring your poor Emily to peace. Oh force him not again to refuse me!"

It was Lady Anne who told me that she would thus reply to her Mother's doubts respecting the preparations for their departure—and never shall I forget the day when she accompanied Mrs. Montrose to take leave of Lady Anne. I thought I had never seen her look more beautiful—her illness had rather encreased than diminished in any degree the naturally soft colour of her cheeks and lips, but nevertheless had given to her an extreme appearance of delicacy which her more dazzling beauty in the days of health and earlier youth had not possessed.

When Lady Anne folded her to her arms, and whispered her fondly an ardent blessing entreating her to trust for happiness and place her affections in those divine objects which can alone give peace and comfort to the troubled spirit her tears which she had with difficulty restrained during their whole visit now freely burst forth and laying her sobbing face upon Lady Anne's neck she exclaimed in a voice scarcely audible, "Oh pray for me! Pray for the poor, despised, mean Emily! that I may forget the good that never must be mine!"

She had never said so much in my presence before this, and fearing that she might repent having thus betrayed herself I retreated unobserved and I think Lady Trevallyn never knew that I had been made acquainted with her secrets thro' the imprudence of her Mother and Lady Anne's confidence in my silence as to the affairs of her family; these she indeed never concealed from me on any occasion, and has often with flattering condescension consulted me upon many points where her own humility made her diffident of her own judgment.

When Lord Henry returned she received him with undisguised coldness and displeasure but as he still enquired with the fondest interest about Emily and spoke of her to Lady Anne his eyes beaming with the softest tenderness, she yet entertained a latent hope that when tired of the gay scenes of folly and dissipation in which he was engaged, Emily as a wife would be alone his choice. But this latent hope she took care to conceal from her too credulous Mother.

We heard with pleasure that the health of Miss Montrose was nearly reestablished, and Lady Anne smiled while she observed how Mrs. Montrose loved to fill her letters with the compliments bestowed upon her daughter's beauty, the admiration and homage it had received from foreign princes and nobility and the many lovers it had procured her in their present society. Among the rest she enumerated the Earl of Trevallyn who had actually proposed for her tho' his ill health and unsuitable age had induced her positively to reject those proposals.

In the mean time Lord Henry continued his visits to Lady Anne which were the more frequent as since Miss Montrose quitted London the assemblies of fashion and the places of public amusement ceased to afford him the same charm which he had been accustomed to find in frequenting balls concerts and crowded rooms where his sole object had indeed seemed to be the conversation of his lovely cousin. Lady Anne was on her part pleased to behold him devote so many of his hours to the retirement which she thought so well calculated to cherish his tender remembrances of her favourite Emily of whom she was always careful to entertain him.

When I read he listened with attention and his remarks full of taste and the nicest judgment delighted us both. To me however he paid in the presence of Lady Anne but little attention, tho' whenever a moment's opportunity presented itself of speaking to me alone, his voice then assumed the softest tones while he assured me that his stay with his Aunt was solely that he might share my society. I did not then believe him and would have seemed offended at this jest which I could not but consider as an insult. He heard my timid and ill-expressed reproof in silence and repeated the declarations which had caused it no more, but his eyes left me no doubt that he had been in earnest, and for the first time I had to reproach myself for having a thought purposely concealed from my dear benefactress:

She loved to encourage those talents which she partially fancied I possessed, and tho' our distance from town did not conveniently allow the constant visits of masters yet she had procured me occasional instructions in drawing and singing and was delighted to applaud the improvements I made in practising untaught. Lord Henry drew with a masterly hand and offered to give me some instructions an offer which my dear Lady Anne perhaps imprudently accepted. While she worked or read Lord Henry seated at my side past hours in cultivating the unfortunate taste which I owed in some degree perhaps to Nature but for which it was his too delightful lessons that had inspired me with such an enthusiastic desire of excellence. Yet slowly did the poison steal into my as yet untainted bosom; At my birth I had received a disposition timid and reserved, and it was not with intentional art that I deceived mine indulgent benefactress.

She saw the little inclination which I shewed to hold conversation with Lord Henry, the care I took to avoid all approaches to familiarity and the prudent foresight with which I was ever on my guard to shun every opportunity of being alone with her nephew. She confided then in my coldness and indifference, an indifference which was even more displayed when I began to be sensible of its diminution. I trembled indeed at finding how much she was deceived, but how could I acknowledge to her sentiments which I studied to hide even from myself, and the rapture with which I secretly received the proofs as I then thought them of Lord Henry's ardent love, which he ceased indeed to profess by words while every look every action spoke it to my heart. I know not whether I even then betrayed myself to his penetrating eyes, but I am well convinced that long before my lips dared to utter the passion which consumed my soul he was already assured of its full force.

When he entered the room I did not indeed meet him with my eyes, I had no occasion to convince myself by them of his presence, my heart had already declared his approach and throbbed responsive to every step. A delightful sensation of contentment seemed to overflow my heart at his entrance; I wished not that he should address me, satisfied to breathe the same air to know that his thoughts were occupied by me, unobserved to see his most trifling motions, to hear his soft voice and above all to behold his bewitching smile, these were the enjoyments the most exquisite that my imagination could picture, and which indeed exceeded all that more rapturous moments where love could be expressed without constraint could bestow.

When he quitted the apartment where in silence I had shared the unutterable pleasure of beholding him seated near me, or when any person approached so as to interrupt for the moment my view of this beloved object, it appeared to me as if the sun had quit the horizen and that my existence was suddenly envelloped in a dark and chilling cloud and when he again appeared, life and light instantaneously seemed to diffuse itself over my soul. At night I lay down with the cheering reflections that the same roof sheltered us, my dreams again presented to my view the love inspiring smile, and my first thoughts as I awoke were those of tumultuous delight that in a few moments that smile should indeed bless my waking eyes.

When he left us for a few days together, which to prevent suspicion he still continued frequently to do, my imagination was calmer, and allowed my reason to combat in some faint degree these feelings which over powered it in his presence. Yet while I sighed at the justice of its forebodings and formed resolutions for conquering my hopeless love, every desponding reflection was secretly consoled by the idea which forever presented itself to the dear expected moment fixed for his return. How as that moment approached did my heart throb with impatience. In vain I endeavoured to occupy myself—my eyes pursued the lines of the book which I held, or my hand sought to trace the images I had placed for its imitation, but while my heart panted with breathless agitation it was not in the power of any genius or fancy to arrest my attention and my trembling hand sketched with thoughtless inaccuracy.

Oh delightful days! Days too happy and too much prised even then! But of whose full enchantment over my soul I knew not yet the force. Days passed so rapidly away never never can ye return! Never must those eyes again behold the soft beams of inexpressible tenderness with which he was then wont on his return to meet their timid glance. Never more must I meet those looks which thrilled in every nerve. Even now in the hopeless darkness that has settled over my fate I can look for some instants on those bright spots in the gloamy waste of my existence and fancy realises them to me once more till reflection with a sudden pang bursts suddenly upon my short dream with these fearful sounds, "they are lost to thee for ever."

I sometimes look around in a wild consternation at the change of my destiny, I wonder to see the morning dawn and the soft air breathe freshly as it used to do—the hours roll tranquilly along in the same regular succession, the evenings close with the same shades and the sun rises with the well remembered brightness which it wore in the time of my felicity.

Nature is the same and I wonder that days so similar in themselves should be to me so different. It seems to me as if the universe which to my view now presents but one bleak and desert solitude should share in the gloom with which I am oppressed. In every sound I seem to hear but the echo to the cry of despair which my heart is ready to utter—but that cry reaches not to thee, Oh object of my vain regret! I am forgotten, I am no longer loved! And I live to feel the torments of that cruel certainty! Yet believe me my Mother in spite of these bitter expressions of regret the severest punishment of my guilt is the consciousness of its magnitude and if I had preserved my innocence all other sorrows nay even the loss of that affection so madly prised would have been more supportable.

But I now look round in vain for one source of consolation and heaven and earth are alike to me objects of terror and despair!

It was while I yet struggled with my unhappy passion endeavouring but vainly to hide it from the view of its adored object that I lost my guardian my benefactress. Lord Henry was at that time absent. It was but the day before that sudden stroke which deprived me of her loved protection that he left us with every mark of the strongest reluctance to join his regiment which was ordered to Ireland but he had in private assured me that his return would certainly be speedy as he was resolved rather to sell out immediately than be thus banished from all he loved—and that this was a step upon which he was determined if he could not obtain in a very little time a leave of absence.

His words and the look by which they were accompanied are yet marked indelibly upon my heart and the tear that swam in his beautiful eyes as he fixed them upon me at parting even from on horseback after he had secretly pressed my hand, was forever present to my view. Not even the awful bed of death upon which I so soon beheld laid my second Mother, the friend of my youth, my sole support and all my hopes of independence could for one moment banish that lively image of unfeigned affection as my deluded heart fondly considered it—and tho' I hated myself for being comforted yet in the midst of all my sorrows my soul listened to the soft, the enchanting sounds of consolation whispered, "He loves me! I shall see him again! I am not abandoned! My interest is still dear to one and that one is the whole world to me!"

As my beloved benefactress had died without a will the Marquis her brother who so quickly after followed her to the grave, immediately came as her natural heir to seal up her papers and take possession of her effects. I have no reason to complain of his behavior towards me. He respected the affliction into which I was thus suddenly plunged and I saw him but once during his stay—this was a few hours previous to his departure when he sent a message requesting to speak with me on the subject of my future intentions. I had indeed but one resource which was to go to my aunt at Islington provided she would receive me, for of my Uncle Harley I knew at that time nothing as he was as yet in Cumberland. I was therefore constrained to address my aunt for an asylum and ask her to receive me till I could hear from you my dear Mother and know what your advice would direct. I trembled at the idea of being ordered by you to quit England but I entertained a hope that my skill in drawing might perhaps enable me rather to assist than be a burden upon my friends, and therefore my aunt might wish me to reside with her, a companion at her time of life being I should imagine desirable.

The Marquis approved of my plan and gave me as you know a liberal present to buy mourning and the promise of the same sum annually or an equivalent upon my marriage. This generosity enabled me to write to my Aunt with more confidence as I was now at liberty to promise her a certain compensation for the expence I should prove to her, but my heart I will confess felt humbled at being thus obliged to receive the bread of dependance from the hand of Lord Henry's father.

My Aunt's answer I well remember; it contained but the following words.

> "Dear Child,
>
> "As it appears that it is the will of Providence I should take charge of you, I dare not decline it as long as you submit yourself in all things humbly to your duty in that state of life in which it has pleased God to call you—but no longer.
> "Your Affectionate Aunt
> Gertrude Blightal"

When the chaise arrived that was to convey me for ever from the scenes of all my happiness my soul sunk within me; my tears which had flowed incessantly since the dreadful moment which convinced me that my indulgent friend would never again smile upon me now ceased. I looked round with a bewildered sense of consternation upon the dear objects I was to behold no more and my heart seemed bound with a tight cord which almost prevented respiration. It was not till a turn in the road gave me the last view of those beloved, those love endeared shades, that I could again weep. I felt as if I was then torn from every earthly good—my hands involuntarily stretched towards the objects I had quitted and I uttered a piercing cry. It was this movement of extreme distress that awakened me to recollection, Lord Henry's fondly cherished image which I had seemed for ever to leave in that dear spot where he had last bad me farewell now returned to sooth & calm the horrors of my situation and Hope once more whispered those sweetly consolatory words, "He loves me and I shall yet see him;"

Oh my Mother if you could at that moment have known the relief afforded your unhappy Angela by the tears which that soft reflection of tenderness excited could you have been able to wither the last faint blossom of comfort by the cold suggestions of prudence?

At the Marquis's desire I brought with me all that my bountiful Mistress had allowed me to consider as my own except a piano-forte, bookcase, and some other articles which could not conveniently be removed; and these he had ordered the housekeeper to preserve carefully as mine till I might wish to have them sent to me. My drawing box and a few books I had brought with me so that when the chaise stopped at the entrance of Mount Row where it had been accustomed to alight when sent by Lady Anne to pay a yearly visit to my aunt, I was obliged to desire the postillion to wait till I should send him some assistance to lift in the parcels.

My Aunt was at chapel, and the little girl whom she had left to take care of the house in her absence was unwilling to quit it contrary to her orders.

I recollected that tho' it was impossible for a carriage to drive up to the front door yet the back of the house being in the little private road which was a continuation of Wentworth buildings it was probable there might be some entrance upon that side.

Upon enquiring the girl told me that there was a door and shewed me where the key now hung but that her mistress never suffered it on any account to be opened except once a year to lay in her coals.

I hesitated, but not seeing any other method of bringing in my little luggage I concluded there could be no crime in opening the door for that purpose if I took care to fasten it again; I therefore ordered the postillion to drive round and with the assistance of the little maid we lifted into the hall my trunk and a number of small parcels which I had thrown into the chaise without much attention.

While we were thus employed my Aunt knocked at the front door and upon entering uttered an ejaculation of surprise and displeasure at the disturbance which she found in her house.

"What is all this to-do Sally? and what upon earth have we got here?" she exclaimed staring around without seeming to notice my offer to embrace her. "How dare you I say you saucy slut open that door! Don't you know very well it is what I never allow?"

I did my best chilled as I was by so rude a reception to exculpate the poor trembling Sally, and to excuse the liberty which I had so unfortunately taken in her absence but it was in vain to attempt to stop the torrent of reproaches I had thus brought upon the innocent girl and my spirits unequal to a contest so new I could no longer restrain my tears but seating myself upon the trunk which the postillion had set down in the little hall sobbed violently.

My Aunt then turned towards me and softened in some measure perhaps, took my hand and said in a milder tone, "Come, come child it cannot be helped for the present and indeed it is not you I so much blame seeing you do not as yet know my ways, but you must never in future open that door without my leave. I do not chuse to have fellows rush in and blow out my brains as they might so easily serve a poor defenceless woman in so remote a place."

She then desired me to make haste and dismiss the post-boy expressing at the same time her surprise that I had not come in one of the stages which past every day thro' Esher.

I dried my eyes and obeyed her in silence; she then fastened the door and deposited the key in her bureau, ordering Sally to help me in removing all that trumpery out of the hall.

I was pleased to find that she had allowed to me an apartment for myself. It was indeed without a fireplace and the furniture consisted only of a turn-up wooden bedstead, two oak chairs and a very old table which as it was not small I found very convenient for my books and portfolio.

Observing that I was in deep mourning my aunt asked me with an illnature which I could scarcely forgive whether I had paid that compliment to Lady Anne in gratitude for the vast legacy which she had so generously taken care to bestow upon me.

I answered with truth that the gratitude I should ever bear her memory could not have been encreased had she made me heiress of all that she possessed and that the least of my misfortunes in consequence of the cruel stroke was the impossibility of her providing for me so suddenly had Death deprived me of the best and dearest of friends.

"Don't tell me," interrupted she harshly, "don't tell me of such impossibility. Every christian should prepare for death—not knowing when it may call the healthiest or youngest of us away. I always think of that for my own part. Your Mother little thought child that after all Lady Anne's pretended love for her Angela (as she profanely would have you called) that she would have left you a beggar at last. I often warned her but she was always for taking her own way I must say that."

Observing that I wept again at the unfeeling taunt she added, "but come child don't be a fool, you must now make the best of your situation seeing that it is the will of God to humble you I have no doubt on account of the hardness of your heart. So take it patiently. We will think what can be done best for you and in the mean time you are welcome to such fare as I can give you as long as you behave as you should do."

I assured her it was my intention to give her as little trouble as possible, and that as far as the Marquis's benevolence enabled me I would gratefully contribute towards our expenses.

"I don't speak with regard to that point child, to be sure that will be only fair, but I would not receive into my house a princess except under conditions of her conforming to what I think necessary for her salvation. I shall therefore expect you will constantly attend family prayer with me and that you give up that idle propensity of gadding abroad which I know most silly folk of your age love to indulge. Very likely Lady Anne might have been less strict in that point as I fear her worldly connexions were a great injury to her poor soul."

I interrupted her strictures upon the conduct of my lost friend by assuring her that I never should desire to leave the house except my health required a degree of air & exercise which I had certainly been used to, but that without her permission I was ready to promise never to stir abroad.

She appeared satisfied with my assurances and asked me was I hungery after my ride, I had indeed not tasted a morsel since at the entreaty of the housekeeper I had swallowed a cup of tea in the deserted chamber of my sainted benefactress, where I had watched thro' the melancholy night that preceded the morning when I was for ever to leave a spot endeared by so many grateful remembrances.

I was exhausted and without feeling any desire for food yet I suffered all the pain and weakness of hunger & wishing not to sink under the depression of spirits it encreased I accepted her offer of hastening supper on my account.

I will not my dearest Mother dwell upon the unkindness of my Aunt who doubtless thought that she acted for the best in trying to humble a proud heart, but I will own that her asperity rendered my abode with her so irksome that I was often tempted to seek for some other situation where I might cheaply purchase a peaceful residence, but from this I was dissuaded by the fear of increasing your displeasure, and a latent idea that Lord Henry would soon seek for me and that it was from my Aunt he would naturally expect to receive information. This idea supported me thro' all the mortifications I endured and the humiliations with which she delighted to load me.

While it was day-light I indeed prevailed upon her to suffer me to remain chiefly in my own little apartment where I enjoyed comparative happiness, but as we were not allowed the luxury of a second candle I was condemned to pass my evenings, except during the hour which she usually spent at chapel, either in reading to her some religious treatise in which alas! my heart was but little engaged, or to listen as we worked to conversation far less pleasing, for I dare not produce in her presence any of the books from which I might derive pleasure assured that thereby I should draw upon the sacred memory of my beloved friend some harsh and unmerited censure for my Aunt condemned all reading as profane, or at best idly unprofitable, except such as treated on the one important subject and while she indulged me in so many hours of solitude I did not chuse to contend with her.

It was not however without some struggle on my part that she at length gave up desiring me to accompany her constantly to the Tabernacle; I respected the sacred worship which she thus constantly attended too much to bring there the mockery of a prostrate body and an inattentive spirit poluted with earthly hopes and desires—and I felt an unconquerable reluctance to pass so many hours in apparent devotion when my wandering heart was occupied by far other objects, or my spirits sickened under the languor of the tedious ceremony in which I felt unable to join.

My mornings were past away in secret expectation of some intelligence from Lord Henry and I endeavoured to divert the insurmountable impatience with which in spite of all myself reasonings [insertion missing] this idea was attended by the exercise of my skill in drawing. Gradually peace and a cheerful self contentment began to obliterate those melancholy regrets which embittered my memory. The image of him I loved would still return with a thrilling tenderness but when I reflected upon the immense distance by which Nature had separated us I could even then look to Heaven with gratitude for having snatched me from those paths of enchantment which might have led me to my ruin.

When I had finished two or three drawings of my own design I requested my aunt to enquire among her acquaintances for some artist who would purchase or dispose of my works; she consented and even asked me to accompany her that I might be convinced she did her best to answer my expectations on which she freely declared she had very little dependance, tho' she owned that she was not well qualified to judge never having given much of her attention to such vanities thanking God that *she* had learned to employ herself more profitably. I told her that I would rely on her endeavours and that I was not myself sanguine of success so should not attribute my failure to her want of exertion.

She returned home one day that she had taken with her my drawings considerably pleased with the reception which she had met with, telling me that she had been directed to a miniature painter in great business who had expressed himself so well satisfied with the execution (tho' he pretended to doubt of their originality) that he said he would certainly purchase them at what she deemed an extraordinary price and offered to furnish me with constant employment if I chose to engage to sell my labours only to him and to work as he should point out.

I was glad to have some occupation by which I might innocently divert my mind, contribute to my independence, save myself from the more menial duties required from me by my aunt and justify my passing my hours in solitude. I therefore without hesitation accepted the proposal. The use he had for my pencil was to finish the hair, drapery, and in fact all except the faces of the portraits for which he received a high price and for this he paid to my aunt a weekly sum with which she was well content. Day after day past over in this manner. My health began to suffer from the continual close application, and my aunt proposed that in future I should be myself the bearer of the pictures to my employer, which would afford me exercise and save her and Sally the trouble of the continual messages which were necessary.

I felt an invincible repugnance to walk thro' the public streets and besides I had never seen the artist who employed me; for without confessing my reasons to my aunt I entreated her to spare me the personal intercourse of a trafick which I could not but feel humiliating. I therefore now alleged with truth that the time this must necessarily take from my labours would considerably diminish the profit, and this was an argument to which she was selfishly well inclined to listen. Influenced by it she yielded to my representations that it would be of far more advantage to me and save my time to walk for half an hour early in the little garden which was before our door. She would have made no objection to my extending my walk at those times to the fields within view of the house and which joined the garden I have mentioned, but I feared to walk alone and tho' she laughed at my apprehensions I believe they gave her confidence in my discretion.

I had been now nearly two months at my aunt's when I one day received from the painter a portrait which I immediately believed to be that of Miss Montrose, but her features are so regularly beautiful that the likeness was not very strong and I thought it might perhaps be a fancy picture done from some of the grecian models for I was sure no other living face but hers could be so perfect. I cannot express the sensations by which I was agitated as I began to work at this picture. The most melancholy ideas crowded into my mind. Every repressed and smothered emotion seemed to revive with redoubled power. I could bear our separation but to be forgotten was indeed intolerable. This beautiful object whom I had dared to rival was then returned to England and this very picture might be intended as a pledge of renewed attachment between her and Lord Henry.

In vain I endeavoured to proceed. My hand refused the task—and my heart sickened as I surveyed the enchanting features. At length I resolved rather to disoblige my employer than perform a labour so irksome. I knew not what excuse to make, but returned it to my aunt and requested her to make some enquiries for Mrs. and Miss Montrose but without mentioning me. She brought me back intelligence which filled me with surprise and for the moment overwhelmed me with a joy which I dared not to analyze.

I heard indeed with some regret the death of Mrs. Montrose, but that her daughter was now countess of Trevallyn filled me with unspeakable satisfaction. It is true that I represented to myself how idle were those feelings—that tho' Lord Henry had indeed lost her for ever, he was not thereby sunk to the level of the humble Angela—or that her aspiring hopes might for that cause dare to look towards him.

Still I reflected with pleasure that they were now irrecoverably separated and Heaven hath severely punished that envious sentiment. Lord Henry however appeared not and the secret hope that every night would whisper promises of intelligences for the morrow began to fade in cheerless despondency. Still self-deceived I flattered myself that I wished not to behold him but only to be assured that I was not forgotten and tho' I was confident of my own power to fly I could not endure that he should thus easily relinquish all pursuit.

One morning unusually dejected I laid the little parcel which Sally had just brought for my daily task upon my table; and meditating on some of those hours of happiness which had left behind such indelible traces I forgot my business which tho' at first I had found uninteresting was now my chief pastime. I had seated myself as usual at the window but the languid melancholy which devoured me banished all inclination to prepare for my accustomed occupation or even to examine what was the present task allotted to my pencil.

Once more I was seated beside Lord Henry, his hand again for a moment rested upon mine and my cheek glowed and my heart thrilled subdued by the power of the sweet deception. Not only his beloved image was before mine eyes and the spot still so dear, but all the surrounding objects became present, I seemed to breathe the well remembered air, the peculiar odour again saluting my enchanted senses and all the local impressions returned with the force of reality. I know not how long I cherished this day dream of my disordered imagination but it was my Aunt's harsh voice in the adjoining room which roused me from my fool's paradise. I started—and once more I was in my solitary chamber and once more I was separated from all that could give value to life. The tears which I sought not to restrain relieved my bursting heart and after a few moments indulgence to their free course I collected my spirits to repel the bitter reflections which had overpowered them by having recourse to occupation that most invaluable blessing which can be bestowed upon the hopeless sufferer.

As I opened the packet, the sketch, for it was no more, fell from my hands and for an instant I felt an indescribable sensation of terror lest I had yielded to imagination till it had injured my understanding. But I indeed beheld the well known and striking likeness of features too beautiful to be mistaken and pressed them to that bosom where they were far more accurately painted. In that countenance so expressive were painted grief, anxiety, and tenderness, his graceful figure but slightly traced was represented as trampling upon his uniform while he appeared ready to place his broken sword upon an altar which bore this inscription—*For thee alone.*

I gazed with emotions too powerful for utterance incapable of moving. I scarce breathed while I seemed to fear lest the enchantment should be dissolved, or some unseen hand should snatch from my trembling grasp the treasure which it contained. "He loves me! I shall again behold him!" were the captivating sounds that burst from my heart with new force and my bosom throbbed with tumultuous and uncertain expectations without considering upon what they were founded. In a few moments I grew more calm and the first use I made of my recovered faculties was to fly to the door that I might fasten it against every intruder; I dreaded lest any eye but my own should share the transport I felt at beholding those adored features.

As I returned towards the table with the portrait still pressed to my lips, I perceived on the floor a folded paper, which in my first agitation I had dropped from the packet. I supposed it to contain the directions of the artist, but upon taking it up all the emotions and tumult of my soul were redoubled by the sight of Lord Henry's seal, which alas I too well remembered. The paper was without address but I had no doubt from whom it came, and in the midst of the ecstacy which overflowed my heart and eyes, no whispering conscience was heard to forbid my opening with transport the adored herald of such enchanting tenderness. The letter is still in my bosom but I have no need to look there for those expressions which are so deeply engraven within that death only can obliterate the characters.

"Angela beloved Angela! Thou art at length discovered! Thine own inimitable talents have restored thee to thine anxious and almost despairing friend! We shall meet again after a separation so cruel to me and which I began almost to fear must prove eternal. On the first news of your distress I sacrificed every thing to the hopes of affording you shelter and consolation. To those hopes I have given up for ever all my prospects of promotion and would have thought them cheaply purchased had I been able to realize them. But I arrived too late. I could find no traces of my Angela—and I feared to injure her by my too eager inquiries. Lady Anne's housekeeper either would not, or could not inform me of your Aunt's residence and I came to town hopeless of receiving any better intelligence from my father.

"Chance & the unrivalled excellence of my Angela's pencil have at length relieved me from the anxious sorrow under which I laboured. On entering casually a print shop yesterday what were my emotions at seeing two drawings never to be mistaken by my heart. I had scarce presence of mind to find words in which to express my eagerness of enquiries. I was referred to the Artist who had passed for his own perfection I knew he never could obtain. No I could not be deceived they were indeed my Angela's alone.

"I flew to his lodgings and hastily enquired for the lady who had executed the drawings which I produced. Observing that he coloured and hesitated I feared by my impetuosity again to lose you and changing the subject proposed sitting instantly for my picture. You see how love has succeeded in its most ardent and anxious desire; the painter has no idea of the motive of my request but has promised to convey this letter. He does not even know the person who has demanded from him this favour and thinks that acquainted only with your talents this paper contains simply directions for the finishing of the sketch which he took upon the spot and for which I am again to sit this morning before it accompanies to you the burning sighs breathed upon this paper by your adoring and now happy Henry.

"Impatient as I am for an answer which I trust will enable me to find means of again beholding my lovely Angela I even now feel the most exquisite delight in the idea that your eye shall dwell upon my image and your soft hand be employed in tracing a form which breathes only to adore you. And you will tell me dearest Angela—that I may see you. You will not blast by chilling indifference the rapture I felt on again finding you. You have nothing to apprehend in writing and can surely find no difficulty in conveying a letter to the post. One line, one word my Angela by giving me the hope of a meeting so ardently desired will raise to the summit of felicity your inexpressibly adoring—
Henry."

Tears of delight and love bathed my cheeks as I read again and again characters so dear.

Blinded as I was by the excess of my passion I thought not at first upon the convincing proof this might have given me of his cruel designs. He addressed me not as a friend he dared to own himself a lover, a secret lover! Wherefore indeed should he have recourse to strategem to see the object of his aunt's affectionate cares and of his father's bounty? Might he not boldly have presented himself had he not feared to encounter the prudence of the sole protector I now possessed. It was plain he meant not to visit me and I dare not propose it, tho' my heart sickened with impatience once more to behold him. Yet my natural timidity would not suffer me to write altho' I might easily have done so by the method he proposed.

But I was in a delirium of joy, he knew my abode, he was resolved to see me, his love was unabated! What would it not achieve! And once more my heart replied to every suggestion of fear. He loves me and I shall again behold him! With what vexation did I quit when obliged by the gloom of the early closing evening my beloved occupation, with what ecstacy did I again resume it on the first dawn of morning.

I blessed with an idle gratitude that fatal talent which had again thrown me in the way of my beloved seducer; I recollected with a delighted remembrance every line of those dear drawings which had caught his view: it was indeed impossible for him for a moment to have doubted the hand which had executed them.

Too faithful memory was ever ready to present to my pencil the perfect form of my lover, and I had indulged my imagination by drawing him in a thousand well remembered graceful attitudes until my pencil refused to return another image. One of the drawings which he had now seen represented the beautiful cousins as they are described by Rousseau receiving the lessons of St. Preux in whom I had too faithfully pourtrayed my own more irresistible instructor[5] while the other contained an equally true resemblance in the character of Romeo at the moment of separating from the enamoured Juliet.[6] I blushed when I considered that this was what convinced him of my hand even more than the style which he himself had formed. I continued now to embellish with all the art of which I was capable the professed portrait of those graces which I had been so accustomed to copy— and while daylight lasted spared not a moment from my task without extreme reluctance.

It was now late in autumn and the fogs which at this time of year hang over London shortened cruelly my light. The neighbouring clock had just struck five when the gloom of the evening already began to deprive me of the beams of a sun which I had never before so much valued. For the first time I withdrew my eyes from the object which had fixed all their attention for so many hours. I turned to the window and opened it to observe with regret the heavy sky faintly tinged with

---

[5]   In Rousseau's epistolary novel *Julie; ou la Nouvelle Héloïse* (1761) Saint-Preux tutors and falls in love with Julie, who corresponds initially with her cousin Claire.

[6]   Shakespeare's *Romeo and Juliet* (1594), 3.5.1–9.

the dark red hue of the setting sun struggling amid the fogs which even before his departure hastened the shades of evening.

I looked out and the first object which met mine eyes was Lord Henry! Never to the end of my existence can the impression of that moment be effaced or even in the smallest degree forgotten! Even now it is present as tho' mine eyes indeed could again behold the glance which had enchanted them.

In my first transports of surprise and joy I knew not what I did, but when I again recovered my bewildered senses I found myself sunk upon my chair and I heard the voice of Love softly pronounce the name of Angela. I started up and again beheld him beneath my window.

"One word," said he, as I approached, "I must not be observed but say you will meet me on this road at some hour to-morrow."

"Impossible!" I exclaimed softly.

"What do you never leave the house?"

"I walk alone no where but in the garden."

"That opposite to the front door."

"Yes."

"At what time."

"As soon as it is light."

"I will see you there tomorrow."

He waited not my reply but darted from me suddenly and mounting his horse which his groom held at some distance was out of sight in a moment. I listened to the sound of his retiring steps till they faded from my ear, and after all was lost in silence I yet remained in a kind of stupefaction which admitted not of reflection upon the past; or consideration for the future. I had seen him! I had heard his voice! This one idea occupied my whole faculties and reason, virtue and prudence vanished before it.

Who that listens to the seductive and at first apparently gentle persuasions of a sentiment which circumstances have rendered imprudent or criminal can say with confidence, *Hitherto will I go and no farther*,[7] or boast that in the moment of severest trial Virtue shall possess that power of resistance which it should then chiefly have exerted, when it first perceived the advances of a passion which indulgence alone can render a Tyrant.

To what purpose have I been endowed with understanding when my feelings have ever had power to silence its suggestions while they could be of use to direct my conduct and it is only upon objects uninteresting to my heart that my judgment has ever been heard? Hurried by my too warm sensibility to the edge of the frightful chasm with a rapidity which I had no power to resist, Reason ever too late in her warning admonitions has served but to shew me the inevitable danger when I could no longer avoid it and precipitated my destruction by rendering me giddy with the view of the immense gulph into which I am constrained to plunge.

---

[7]   Job 38:11 (KJV).

The purposed meeting was attended with every hazard to my good name but I had not been able to refuse, and could not now disappoint him.

Mine eyes closed not during the night and frequently I found myself obliged to rise to be relieved from the suffocating sensation which oppressed my agitated heart—"For this once," I rashly cried, "I will meet him, I will bid him at least an eternal farewell! I will hear his promise of a tender remembrance, and that moment shall afford me a source of perpetual consolation!"

It was thus I silenced every representation of hesitating prudence and blinded myself wilfully to the obvious danger that he who could thus prevail upon my weakness in the first important step would never forbear to exert his influence till my innocence should be the sacrifice.

Yet when the moment arrived my natural timidity had nearly arrested my steps. On the first appearance of the long-watched for dawn I arose and while preparing for my accustomed early walk the agitation of my spirits seemed to support my courage; but when I was ready to descend my trembling limbs refused their assistance and my heart beat with such violence that unable to breathe I was obliged to seat myself before I reached the door. I shuddered with a sudden glimpse of the fearful consequences of this imprudent act and I was for a few moments determined to relinquish my design.

As the windows of my room were to the back (my aunt occupying the front bed chamber while Sally slept on the floor in our parlour) I had no means of watching Lord Henry's arrival or of making signs to him to depart. The idea of his impatience stung me to the soul and my hand which had for some time rested motionless upon the lock now suddenly pushed back the bolt and in one instant the misty brightness of the morning sun and the peculiar odour of the fine autumnal morning saluted and revived my senses. I crossed the court looking round with a fearful eye when seeing no one and finding the garden door as usual locked I concluded Lord Henry was not yet arrived.

Slowly I advanced along the ground moistened with the heavy dews and when I had reached the far end I started at hearing the well known soft voice again repeat the name of Angela. I gazed around not being able for a moment to imagine where he had concealed himself when at length I beheld the most adorable the most passionate of lovers stretched upon the wet grass in the adjoining field that he might the better be screened from the eye of curiosity or casual observation. At the extremity of the garden was a little arbour and it was behind this that he had placed himself, having bent the branches of the willows which formed it, so as to make a temporary gap nearly large enough entirely to admit him.

How partially does the eye of Love see tenderness and grace in every occurrence capable of receiving such a colouring! I saw in this action nothing but the delicacy of true affection which feared to injure the object on which it was determinately fixed, and never then considered that it might only proceed from the dread lest any future meetings might be prevented by the premature discovery of the first. How at that moment was he endeared to my fondly grateful heart by this instance of disregard to personal convenience which to a person possessing less sensibility might perhaps have appeared as trifling! Trembling I approached and sinking on the seat beside him shed the sweetest tears while he held my hand and covered it with his kisses.

But the moments were precious—and he lost none nor spared any intreaties and solicitations to allow him some more secure and satisfactory method of conversing. He pointed out what was indeed too obvious, the extreme risk which we thus ran of being observed and proposed admitting him during my Aunt's absence. I shewed him the impossibility of doing this without her knowledge and this he said he was determined to avoid lest he should be thus put upon her guard to prevent his ever being able again to meet me.

Tho' it was dark indeed when my aunt went to chapel yet our little court was so much exposed to the observation of our neighbours that even if she was accompanied by Sally which was not always the case, it was yet most probable that a visit from Lord Henry would excite their curiosity and reach her ears. He then mentioned the little door which he had noticed in the back, but besides my reluctance to admit him thus clandestinely I told him of the care with which the key was detained. At length we were obliged to separate and his powerful solicitations prevailed upon me to promise him a similar meeting on the following morning.

I left him and he desired me to hold my aunt in conversation for some time after I entered that he might the more certainly retire unobserved. But this was impossible! Oppressed with shame and remorse, my soul which was alone supported by his presence, sunk into the deepest dejection the moment that he was withdrawn. I shrunk from the eye of the maid who just risen met me in the hall and stealing to my own room there flung myself upon my bed, wrapping my face in the coverlet as tho' I feared the light of Heaven should discover in my guilty countenance the shame by which I was degraded. Yet even in these very moments of severest self reproach the idea that I had not seen him for the last time would intrude itself with a charm of consolation which I had no power to resist—and with impious doubts I sometimes questioned the possibility that those sensations could be imputed to me as guilt which were stronger than myself. I strove to banish reflection by continuing to occupy myself and having completed the task assigned me began to copy for my own consolation the figure in which I found an unutterable charm from the idea that it had been drawn immediately from him, and that while he thus stood I was the object of his thoughts.

When I again saw him he urged yet more strongly his entreaty that I would even for once admit him where we might converse in security, for here I was every moment startled by imaginary voices and our eyes incessantly wandered around in fearful anxiety. He then produced a key and confessed that he had during the night employed an ingenious workman who owed every thing to him to procure it so that I had now nothing to do but to raise the latch. I looked with mingled terror and love upon this proof of his perseverance and with astonishment at the quickness with which he had conquered this difficulty. Indeed so silently and cautiously had it been effected that altho' I past a watchful night almost immediately over the door which had been thus examined and fitted I had not noticed the least unusual noise.

Why should I dwell on the progressive steps by which your wretched child was precipitated into guilt and despair? Yet I refused, yet I struggled against the inevitable misery of my fate, I resisted with shame his reproaches of my distrust in his solemn promises, I resisted his tears which fell upon my heart like burning drops of liquid fire, I left him in anger which my sorrows appeared rather to irritate than sooth and retired in anguish fearful that I should never behold him more. All day I watched at my window, every step filled me with tumultuous expectation and as it approached sickened me with disappointment. A latent and scarce acknowledged hope remained that I might in the morning find him at the spot which had already been the witness of our fatal interviews. But in vain I timidly entered the arbour, in vain I looked around with a fondly eager eye. I was then convinced I had for ever lost him and the bitter tears of regret fell in torrents which I was unable to restrain. As it was impossible to disguise the anguish with which I was overwhelmed, I shut myself up in my own room and pleaded an illness which was indeed unfeigned. I was unable to do any thing, or to remain for a moment in the same place, and a sickness almost to fainting seized me upon the slightest noise beneath the windows for which my ears were yet incessantly upon the watch.

The miserable day at length was over, and it was near six the hour at which my aunt was accustomed to go to chapel, when I heard the door close upon her. Ashamed of the sorrow to which I had thus yielded, I rose from the bed on which I had sunk in despondency and taking the candle she had left resolved to seek for some oblivion of myself by reading. I had scarcely taken up the book when I started at the voice which I yet scarcely believed I heard so softly pronounce my name. Breathless I listened. All was silent. I approached the window and again it was repeated. Gently I raised the sash and placing my candle behind the bed looked out. The night was so dark that I could distinguish no object, but I heard the beloved sounds to which my heart seemed to vibrate.

"Dearest Angela open the door but for one word, I will not ask to come in I swear by all my hopes on earth and heaven."

I was silent.

"Will you not believe me? If not for mine at least for your own sake do not hesitate. Do not expose yourself thus. For Heaven's sake leave the window. But here will I stay till you allow me to say but one word."

Well aware of the risk I did indeed thus run of being observed I closed the window and sunk breathless upon the floor.

In a few moments I again heard the whispered name and at length confiding in his sacred promise I decended in order to hear him at the door. My hands refused to obey the but half voluntary design. My senses seemed bewildered and it was many minutes before I could draw the bolt or even find the latch. In the mean time I heard the key on the outside gently turn and my efforts hastened by still more gentle whispers of encouragement. The moment that decided my fate was alas arrived. Nothing now was interposed and in a transport of love and gratitude he caught me in his arms, and saved my terrified form from sinking to the earth.

Struck with no sensation but that of horror I disengaged myself from him but pressing my cold hand to his palpitating heart he whispered—"Fear nothing my Angela! I ask nothing but to tell you that I live only for you and if we are discovered nothing shall ever separate us and you are my own for ever."

He kept his promise and we stirred not from the spot which first admitted him beneath our roof. A step in my Aunt's room convinced me that Sally had not that evening accompanied her abroad as I had imagined. I communicated my fears and pressing me for a moment to his heart he silently withdrew.

Oh wretched Angela! dost thou dare pollute the ears which never listened to the protestations of guilty love with the circumstances of thy infamy. The words he had uttered were for ever repeated by my deluded hopes, and the discovery which I looked upon as inevitable was at once the object of my terror and my fondest expectation. I should be his for ever! There could be but one explanation to those delightful words, and in the madness of my voluntary self delusion, I was fondly persuaded that Lord Henry who had shrunk from a lasting union with the unrivall'd beauty who had possessed his first affections, now meditated a sacrifice of himself to the humble being whom worthless and unattractive as she was he had yet taken so much pains to captivate.

Scarcely credible even to myself does this excess of folly now appear; when my eyes are opened to the infatuation which then led me on to ruin. But in the moments of tenderness how often did he vow that he had never loved before as he loved now and tho' he never mentioned his former attachment, and that delicacy restrained me from uttering the fears which still secretly oppressed me, yet by a thousand delightful expressions did he seek to convince me that his heart was now solely occupied by me as it had never been by any other object. He had called me his Angela, his wife! And taken Heaven to witness that he would never own another! My heart answered with delicious sensations of contentment to the dear appellation and felt that as it never could be another's he was indeed its wedded Lord.

I endeavoured by such specious consolations to banish the horrors which reason from time to time presented to my conscience, yet my soul abhorred the situation in which I found myself. Every sentiment of delicacy, every principle of virtue, was repugnant to the means by which I could alone see the sole being whom I valued in creation. To admit in the hours of privacy a *lover* unsanctioned by sacred vows, and to deceive the person whose hospitality afforded me shelter degraded me in my own esteem below the vilest female who purchased with infamy the bitter bread of guilt and misery.

How gladly would I have forsaken my present abode and hid myself in some obscure cell of poverty, could I there have indulged without these stings of remorse the exquisite delight of beholding myself beloved by the object whom I so passionately adored. A thousand times have I been upon the point of declaring this to my lover, for still I imagined that delicacy for my reputation alone prevented the proposal, but timid reserve arrested my lips and I knew not how of myself to offer what I so joyfully would have accepted. Besides the moment of discovery for which he seemed alone to wait might not be far distant, yet while I anticipated it with a fearful pleasure the idea of your anguish and shame my Mother when you should hear of your lost child's crime and humiliation overwhelmed me with sorrow and confusion.

Hours of the bitterest reflection have suspended my wretched narrative. Unable to proceed in the description of scenes for ever impressed upon my heart I threw from me the pen and have only now resumed it to deplore the glimmerings of reason which unable to save me prevented me from fully tasting happiness even at that time for ever and for ever to be regretted.

Is it then possible! I believed myself loved! I gazed without suspicion upon the glances of impassioned tenderness which beamed from his eyes on *me* yes on me alone, and yet I dared to repine! Alas in the despair which has forever crushed me I feel that remorse itself could not now have power to take from me one moment of the rapture with which I should enjoy that felicity which never never can be restored—*never* …. Ah they alone can tell the meaning of that cruel word who have seen love perish in the bosom they adore as I do!

Wretched Angela is this repentance? Is there then no medicine for a guilty mind! Will Heaven never be appeased and remove the scourge of an involuntary criminal sentiment from my bosom, and at length say to my heart

> be at peace
> Forget the transports of encreasing passion
> And all the pangs I felt at its decay.[8]

Often did he regret the cruelty of our situation *prevented* the possibility of our meeting except in this secret manner and suggested a thousand mild and impracticable schemes which in spite of all my inclination to compliance I was obliged to reject. One night however before we parted he told me with an air of playful mystery that he was determined on the next day to write himself to my aunt and "I do not despair," cried he, "of engaging her to trust you to my care for a few days."

Alas, even now I remember the unutterable sensation of mingled hope, wonder and confusion with which I listened to those ambiguous words, he seemed instantly apprehensive of my interpreting them too fondly, from the haste with which he explained his design of addressing my aunt in the name of Lady Anne's housekeeper and entreating her permission to suffer me to spend a week with her at Richmond.

"I thought it right," continued he, "to warn you of my plan lest you should yourself refuse to consent."

---

[8]   "Rowe" (Tighe's note). Calista says "be at peace" in Nicholas Rowe's *The Fair Penitent* (1703), 4.1.217; Jane Shore utters the next two lines in Rowe's *The Tragedy of Jane Shore* (1714), 1.2.141–2 (the citation above substitutes "I felt at" for "we feel for").

My heart was at that moment but little able to share the transports with which he appeared to anticipate this week of Love and Liberty. I even opposed with all my resolution a plan which I abhorred as a new species of deceit more than from the dangers it seemed to threaten of discovery which on my own account I looked upon with but little dread. Humbled as I was in the sight of Heaven and in my own eyes I reflected with a kind of indifference upon the disgrace which the world might cast upon me, but love and delicacy witheld me from revealing what I too plainly saw he wished me to conceal.

He reproached me for the coldness with which I listened to the delightful pictures he then drew with such bewitching eloquence of our unrestrained happiness and he knew not that my heart was then in secret trying to smother the anguish with which it received the too cruel conviction that he desired not that happiness to be perpetual. We parted mutually dissatisfied with each other and in the tears which burst from me after he had left me, the most bitter were those which flowed from the idea of having inflicted upon him one moment's pain.

I was uncertain whether my reception of his project had obliged him to relinquish it, but towards evening my aunt entered the room with a letter which I instantly knew to be written by a hand the most beloved.

"Here child," she cried without observing my evident perturbation, "you must help me to make out this fine scrawl as it is from one I know you call your friend, I think it is signed Margaret Hernon was not that Lady Anne's housekeeper. See here what is all that she says about a turkey and a hare?"

As she spoke she put the paper into my trembling hand pointing out towards the conclusion the line which had most powerfully interested her attention. The letter contained only a civil invitation to me for to spend a week with her near Richmond without particularizing the lady with whom she lived and who she said in her absence from home had allowed her to take this liberty. The time was fixed at which a returned chaise she said should call for me and the letter concluded with a request that my aunt should accept the hare and turkey which the bearer who waited her answer had orders to deliver to her. This present completely gained her propitious assent to the request, and the messenger was immediately summoned into our presence. In him I directly recognised Lord Henry's groom tho' in some degree disguised by the dress which he had assumed.

My aunt scarce consulted me on the occasion and dismissed the pretended country boy with many commendations for the care he had taken of the present committed to his charge, desiring him to return her best thanks to Mrs. Hernon and that her niece should wait upon her whenever she was so obliging as to send. As she spoke she was too much occupied in the examination of the newly acquired store of provision (sufficient as she reasonably expected for her household during the next fortnight) to pay any attention to my confusion or the sly glances which overwhelmed me with shame when I ventured to raise my eye to the countenance of the artful messenger.

With an heart palpitating with terror, delight, remorse and love I ascended the chaise which as its pannel proclaimed came from the Star at Richmond, but had not proceeded above a mile before I was overtaken by Lord Henry. He gave his horse to his groom and taking his seat beside me invited me by the tenderest caresses to resign every care and sorrow and give the ensuing hours to happiness, unmingled with any embittering reflections.

Alas how easily is Love persuaded to forget that futurity which must too certainly destroy its present delights! Of all the passions which reign over the human heart Love is the least anxious to penetrate into ought beyond the present hour. Infinitely curious and delicately sensible on the most minute circumstances which attend that, it willingly shuts its eyes against the uncertain gloom which hangs over the consequences of its imprudent confidence, and future fate.

I saw myself the sole object of his undivided attention for whom alone in Heaven and Earth I existed, and whom alone in Heaven and Earth I loved nay, worshiped with impious and fatal idolatry. The luxuries, the delights, that I shared with him in this enchanting Paradise were all beheld by me but as so many proofs of his love, and as such Oh how exquisite did they appear to my heart as well as to my senses.

The retreat itself possessed almost every beauty which in so confined a spot could be concentrated. The pavilion was small but light and beautiful and furnished with all that art or taste could devise for ease and ornament. It stood in the midst of a soft green watered by a lively stream and entirely surrounded by thick evergreens and fragrant shrubs over which appeared on every side a wood. The distance could not have been above five miles from town, as to avoid the curiosity which his absence might excite, he rode in there during the morning, leaving me not till two o'clock and returning before it was quite dark. The same motive induced him he said to wish just to make his appearance for a few minutes at the different assemblies. I willingly agreed that we should drive into town four of the evenings and I waited at his lodgings while he flew thro' the streets, looking as he told me on his return into about twenty apartments all equally splendid, brilliantly illuminated and subject to the vapid power of dullness. For the first three evenings his absence lasted less than an hour and was compensated by his lively description and endearing caresses on his return—but on the Saturday evening which closed this transient scene of my happiness we left our retreat at an earlier hour and I set him down at the Haymarket about ten o'clock proceeding as he desired to his lodgings where I waited for him with an impatience not unmixed with the tortures of jealousy until long after the watchman had cried midnight.

The incessant roll of carriages for nearly an hour had proclaimed the conclusion of the opera and kept alive my continual hopes while each as it rapidly hurried past the door conveyed to my heart a fresh sting of disappointment. A circumstance which had that morning occurred contributed not a little to poison the bitter hours of expectation, and I dwelt upon my suspicions till my natural timidity alone restrained my strong desire of flying myself to the Haymarket to watch whether the image which haunted my soul was indeed real, and that if so I might in beholding him assisting Lady Trevallyn to her carriage acquire fortitude at once, to forsake him and my guilt for ever. The morning had been unusually fine and he had requested me to enjoy the first sweets of the early promised spring accompanying him on horseback round some of the retired roads which intersected that part of the country on all sides. I was unaccustomed to the exercise and of a coward disposition, but his tender cares dispelled all my fears and as we were slowly proceeding, his right hand laid upon the neck of my horse while I listened enchanted to the sweetest eloquence flowing from the most beautiful lips that were ever formed by Love, he suddenly broke off, and drawing in his horse, as he kept his eyes fixed on a party at some distance, I beheld the paleness of Death instantly succeed the vivid glow of health and beauty which the moment before so brightly suffused his fine features.

Terrified and unable to speak I perceived him quicken his pace as he led down another lane which then crossed that which we had at first pursued, calling to me in an eager voice to come on. I followed with my anxious eyes still turned to the direction which his had taken, as it appeared so unhappily for his peace, and had soon no longer a doubt what was the object which had so much disturbed him. In the midst of a gay and numerously attended group I distinguished a form which was never equalled by any other in female grace and perfection; and I also perceived that we had instantly attracted the attention of Lady Trevallyn who as it seemed involuntarily had urged her horse a few paces before the rest of the gay party, while her head bent forward to survey us with eager curiosity. Already by a turn in the road Lord Henry was out of sight, my confusion and terror deprived me of any power to move but the animal that carried me unwilling to be left behind pressed on with a speed which quickly bore me to his side while it deprived me of all sense or recollection.

His activity alone saved me from being thrown with violence and his soothing tenderness soon restored me to life, but my heart sunk with a sensation never to be forgotten when I perceived he avoided with displeasure all allusion to the object which had thus betrayed his confusion and the unfortunate meeting which we had thus barely escaped. In silence I endeavoured to conquer the confused oppression of a misery which I could not define, for tho' I doubted, yet the idea that I was not loved, or that another shared his heart was too dreadful to be even admitted for an instant.

After some attempts to resume a cheerful conversation, observing the tears which I in vain sought to conceal he asked me in a voice of less tenderness I thought than vexation, "What was the matter!"

Unable to constrain myself I hid my face upon the back of the sopha on which we were seated and with an involuntary expression of anguish exclaimed, "Alas you love her still! Oh why deceive me!"

"I love nothing as I love you Angela," cried he with displeasure, "and to see what I have sacrificed for you should rather raise your vanity."

As he said this he would have left me, but the careless tho' unintended unkindness, the want of delicacy which I felt in this speech overpowered me with such affliction that compassion at least, if it was not indeed as I then believed a softer sentiment brought him once more to sooth me by the tenderest assurances of unalterable love. His caresses and his irresistible powers of captivation soon restored me to the joys which his presence was accustomed to inspire. But all that I had before experienced of fear and sorrow returned with redoubled force in those cruel hours which seemed to exceed all I had hitherto known of tedious suspence.

At length my tears ceased and my heart throbbed as I beheld the lamps of his carriage drive furiously beside the pavement as it drew up to the door. Exhausted by all which I had suffered, I had not power as usual to fly to meet him and yet my heart noticed and bitterly reproached the tardy steps with which he ascended the stairs unlike the impatience of a lover to embrace the beloved being from whom he had been separated only by reluctant necessity. His first words as he entered the room I shall never forget! Instead of the ardour of affectionate pleasure which I so much needed to compensate for all I had endured he now exclaimed with a voice expressive only of surprise and disappointment, "Good God! have you let the fire go out!" I had indeed stood at the window chilled as I was, heedless of the cold of the night during the whole time of his absence, and my tears which had only ceased on the well known sound of his long expected chariot wheels now again flowed with renewed anguish.

Struck with my silence—the silence of despair—he now flew to embrace and console me excusing his involuntary stay by assuring me that the unexpected presence of his own family had obliged him to remain till the opera was over by a combination of the most provoking little accidents, and that he had not been able to find his carriage a moment sooner. He ordered fire and refreshments and while the warmth revived my half expiring frame his tenderness poured balm upon my afflicted heart. When in some degree restored to peace and confidence he proposed our return the night being already so far advanced and during our little journey endeavoured to charm the melancholy which yet hung upon my spirits by the liveliest sallies of wit which were yet less effectual than the endearing expressions of love by which they were accompanied.

As his arm encircled my waist and my head reposed upon his shoulder I perceived by the light of the lamps an uncommon and strikingly beautiful branch of geranium in his bosom. Its fragrance was equal to its beauty and as I would have taken it from him to examine it more closely by an involuntary movement he prevented me. Instantly a cruel suspicion darted across my mind which he no doubt perceived as I disengaged myself from him.

"What a child you are Angela! I stole the geranium from my sister," said he in the tenderest voice, as he held it to me, "Why thus embitter the few moments we have yet for happiness by groundless jealousies and capricious quarrels. Let us not quarrel, why should lovers quarrel; life is too short for that, too precious time!"

My heart was but too ready to yield to the apparent justice of this complaint calculated to touch it most forcibly by the warmth of affection with which it seemed accompanied. Why should I doubt his love I asked myself. To what purpose would he seek to deceive me? And from that moment I studiously drove from me every thought upon these circumstances which yet returned perpetually to my memory suggesting doubts it was so much my interest to believe unjust. But in spite of all my efforts the season of confidence was but of short duration. Once more I returned to the dreary solitude or the wearisome society which I was obliged to endure at my Aunt's;

The illness of the Marquis at some distance from town obliged Lord Henry as he told me to make frequent visits to —. When he left me, the night fixed for his return was always named and during some time in spite of my entreaties no severity of weather ever made him fail in his appointment, so that he has often rode fifteen miles in the wetest or coldest nights that he might be in time to give me the expected, beloved signal, without exciting any suspicions in the family with whom he had dined.

Gradually his absences grew more frequent and his return less faithful. Without suffering myself to doubt the fidelity of his unabated affection, my heart silently but with stifled anguish lamented the change which I could only attribute to the want of that delicacy of tenderness which made love in me so sensible of every action, word, or look which it observed in him. In a thousand instances of which it was impossible to complain my heart was cruelly wounded by some thoughtless expression, some mark of inattention which he observed not that I noticed while it cost me hours of bitter anguish, wept in secret, or when my tears could not be disguised he treated them and my complaints as captious and unjust.

When night after night had passed away in impatient and vain expectations, when the neighbouring clock had struck the dreaded hour after which he ventured not ever to come, and that I at length sought my pillow wearied with watching, sick with disappointment torn with a thousand suspicions and without one consolatory reflection, how often have I then resolved never again to admit him! But alas, I lived but for that moment alone! And the joy that bounded in my heart when I indeed heard his never mistaken silent footfall approaching under the window seemed at that moment to compensate for all the misery of the remainder of my existence.

"'Tis him," I cried, "he comes, and every doubt's at once dispel'd, ''Twas fancy all he never meant to wrong me.'"[9]

In vain I endeavoured to reason myself out of this imaginary pleasure, the deprivation of which gave me such real misery, In vain I represented to myself How short were the moments of his transient visits! and even these how mingled with unnumbered bitterness of present pain and future disquiet. I marked the gradual but too certain change which a few months had made with a hopeless and secret pang, which no words can ever describe. I perceived or trembled in the apprehension of perceiving indifference usurp the place of rapture while he now rather received my love than sought to inspire it or to express his own.

There was besides a want of confidence between us the most fatal to Love. The subject of my continual alarms I dared not utter tho' during every interview it was perpetually present to my heart. I saw he carefully avoided imparting to me in what manner he spent his hours and the image of Lady Trevallyn tho' her name

---

[9]	Emmelina in Hannah More's *The Fatal Falsehood* (1779), 3.1.14.

pass'd not our lips appeared as a mournful veil suspended between me and that heart upon which alone I leaned for hope or consolation. Often have I felt as if I desired him to repose in me confidences even at the expence of all my remaining flattering delusions—and that I could have preferred to this sad and cruel silence hearing him confess that he no longer loved me, that he indeed felt the passion which I still suspected he cherished for another.

But the time approached when suspence and uncertainty were no longer to be numbered among my tortures and when I was to experience that I could yet suffer a misery worse than ever they had been able to inflict. The advancing Spring and the encreasing length of the days necessarily shortened our interviews and rendered them more hazardous. He had prepared me for an absence of some weeks and a few days before it was to take place I thought I could no longer delay to apprise him that some circumstances convinced me that the suspicions which I had for a time entertained with regard to my own situation were well founded.

To you who have experienced the unutterable sensation of delight and tenderness which accompanies the first throb of maternal solicitude need I attempt to paint the sentiments which swelled my heart at this conviction. Already my heart opened to another passion equally violent and my love without being diminished appeared to be shared with the creature which was to owe its existence to that love. The pleasure which I experienced had even power to subdue every terror, every shame which hung threatening over my head, and all the future consequences which awaited the guilty wretch who thus beheld herself a mother with no sanctioned claim upon the tender exultation of another being who might equally feel interested in the hopes and anxieties of that moment.

The tumult of my soul was however unutterable. I saw the period arrived which was to determine the fate of my future life and I suffered myself to form no conjectures upon the change which must necessarily ensue. Now was the time to put his affection indeed to the test and while shame and agitation deprived me of all power to reveal the important secret I waited with trembling anxiety to observe the impression it would make upon his soul.

His penetrating eye instantly perceived the unusual perturbation of my spirits, and having vainly questioned me at length the truth flashed upon his imagination from my blushes, my confusion and the expression which I suppose he read in my eyes as I sought with anxious tenderness to see in his the first emotions of his heart. Alas! one instant was sufficient to convince us both. I saw that regret, vexation, and embarrassment were all the sentiments of his soul and despair from that decisive that fatal moment took possession of mine.

I shed not a tear, we were silent. At length I sunk upon my knees and clasping my hands with agony exclaimed, "Oh Heavens! you can then lament it!" He was still silent and appeared lost in a gloomy reverie. "My God," I continued, "if I may yet invoke thy pity, deliver me. It is all I ask, deliver him and me from this wretched burdensome existence." The faint and deadly sickness which at that instant overpowered my whole frame made me for a while assured that my prayer was indeed heard. But I had not yet fulfilled the measure of my sufferings in this world which have been so great that I can fear no change except the assurance that they must be perpetual which hitherto my soul refuses to believe.

Affrighted I think more than softened at the state in which I lay he raised me in his arms and said while he embraced me, "How can you thus torment yourself Angela, or feel hurt at what should be to you the utmost proof of my disinterested love? Is it not on your account that I lament? Could I be selfish enough not to feel for the consequences which I have thus brought upon you is it then you should indeed hate me?" Every word he uttered was but a fresh dagger to my soul, in the violence of my affliction I lost sight of all prudence and restrained not the sobs which seemed the only method of respiration to relieve my suffocated breast.

"I must leave you Angela," said he after in vain entreating me to be composed and consider the risk to which I exposed myself should I alarm my Aunt, "I must not let you be the victim of the rage which a discovery now would produce, and which you are so little able to bear at present."

"Yes," I exclaimed, "leave me, and let me never again behold you, it is all I ask from Heaven and it is all you can now do for my peace."

"Calm yourself my Love," replied he, "and think that there is nothing upon earth which I would not do for your peace except resigning you for ever—and that I cannot do."

He left me with those sweet those consolatory words upon which my soul hung with the fond eagerness of an expiring wretch. In spite of conviction itself they blinded my reason. They shot a gleam of hope even thro' the gloomy gulph of despair into which I had been plunged and made me feel that life was yet supportable since I had not for ever lost him. To this I willingly turned my broken heart and would gladly have forgotten every other idea of my soul. I strove to persuade myself that he still loved me. I recollected all that I had ever heard of the power of jealousy which gave Love groundless miseries and I sought to believe it possible that I was the martyr but of my own unjust suspicions. I soothed myself also with the consideration that the irksome life of deceit and constraint which I had been obliged to lead for some months must now of necessity terminate in some manner. My situation could not be long concealed, and whatever were Lord Henry's intentions I should at least be delivered from this worst of all punishments, where I was condemned to wear in some degree the appearance of contentment and innocence while my soul was devoured by anguish and remorse.

Earlier than the accustomed hour on the ensuing night, my heart once more leaped with transport at the approach of its Lord; perceiving me calm he exerted unusual tenderness to complete my restoration to peace and by his entreaties extorted from me a promise that I would make no discovery nor take any step with respect to my situation till I should consult with him. After having obtained this he then in a voice of chilling indifference told me "he was glad to see me more reasonable and that he hoped I would always believe he loved me most sincerely and not give way to melancholy ideas and passions which could only torment myself, injure my health and poison all the pleasure which otherwise it would ever give him to see me as often as he could."

As I was unable to make any reply he continued but in what cruel words I knew not. My soul was stupified by the excess of my grief and I was only aroused by his saying something of having already arranged in his mind how I could retire when it became necessary to the villa at which I had before been upon pretence of again visiting Mrs. Hernon and that he would take care I should be satisfied as to the attention paid one who should always be equally dear and valuable to us both. At this my indignation which I then for the first time experienced towards his cruelty gave utterance to my despair.

"Oh no! no!" I cried as I wrap'd the curtain around me to conceal myself from his sight, and which I would so gladly have exchanged for the more effectual veil of my shroud, "No, I will trouble you no more! But never, never will I abandon my child; nor be the mistress of a man who no longer loves me. Oh my God," I continued while I clasped my hands round my neck with a violence which covered it with blood, tho' unconscious of it at the time, "Let me bear every punishment it is thy will to inflict I only ask that I may never again behold the author of my misery."

"Well Angela," he replied, "since it makes you so unhappy to see me I must the less regret that I must leave town tomorrow and I hope you will remember your promise and be more cheerful next time I come."

"Oh never, never!" I exclaimed while I shrunk from his offered embrace and refused to raise my head from the concealment which seemed in some degree to screen me from my shame. He opposed not my wishes but as he departed pressed a kiss upon the curtain which even then thrilled to my subdued and broken heart.

But when convinced he was indeed gone, I flew to the window with a kind of frenzy, listened gasping to his departing steps and shuddered as they had left me entombed within a living sepulchre. All my resolution forsook me; in vain I struggled with my ill-placed tenderness. The woman, the weak, the mild, the fond, the coward woman, could not bear to yield him up—tho' certain that his love was lost to me for ever. I could not believe that he would take me at my word and abandon me in a state of mind so terrible. I watched with inconceivable misery for his return the following night; when the agony of suspence was over all hope had fled, "leaving my bosom colder than the grave."[10] The terrors of an unknown judge, whose sentence against guilt I had already so severely felt, and whose hand was even now heavy upon me, alone witheld me from putting a period to my existence, that I might once more at least awaken in his bosom a sentiment of compassion for the wretch he had destroyed.

Three weeks he had appointed for his stay and that time must now pass before I could be assured whether his indifference would suffer him again to witness my sorrows. My purposes and resolutions varied every moment. Sometimes I acquired strength to determine yet to struggle with my destiny, and fly to some obscure retreat, where I might exert myself to procure a wretched subsistence for myself

---

[10]   Athenais in Nathaniel Lee's *Theodosius* (1680), 2.1.572 ("Has left my Bosom colder than the Grave").

and my infant even then inexpressibly dear to my imagination, and hide myself where I should never again hear the sound of a name so fatally adored. The next moment his image in all the enchanting loveliness of his first endearments melted me to the softest weakness and I thought all punishments could be endured except eternal separation from him whom I loved alone upon earth, and I then resolved to smother the anguish of my soul, consent to all that he desired and conceal from him the sight of my misery that he might not hate or totally forsake me.

It was in this deplorable state of mind that your letter my dear unhappy Mother found your child, and the intelligence which it announced of your speedy return to England, terrible as I should have felt it a few weeks before had now no power to add to my affliction. My mind was so entirely engross'd by the idea of my next interview with Lord Henry, and torn with the uncertainty whether I should indeed again behold him, that no other consideration in life had for me the smallest interest, and I heard of the expected arrival of a mother whom I had never seen from the years of childhood with the same indifference that I listened to the sound of the knocker when it declared the return of my aunt from her daily exercises of devotion. In the mean time my health suffered visibly, and as I found it impossible to continue my usual occupation with any profit my Aunt began to grow impatient at its decline which she was constrained to notice.

My Uncle Harley was now come to Kensington and had often invited us to spend some days there with his family. My Aunt who hitherto had refused upon the pretence of its being an unprofitable waste of time and from the fear lest she might be expected to give some invitation in return, now thought it advisable to try, whether the change of scene might not restore me to the abilities I had hitherto exercised with such success almost entirely for her emolument. As this visit was to be made during the time in which I had no expectation of seeing Lord Henry I felt a pleasure in the idea of watching the way which he had so often passed, as I knew that my uncle's house was situated on the direct road from St James to — where the Marquis had a villa and there I at that time supposed Lord Henry.

My Aunt Harley received us with kindness and the whole family appeared to look with compassion upon my pale and altered looks, and the melancholy which was marked upon my countenance. We had been there two days and I had already begun to find my spirits somewhat soothed by the look and voice of kindness to which I had of late been so much a stranger when as we were returning from afternoon service on Sunday my Aunt Harley (with a view of diverting by the gaiety of so novel a scene the sadness which she thought seemed to prey upon my health) whispered her daughter to shew me the gardens while she would take my aunt to hear another sermon before they returned home. All places and all scenes were indifferent to me but I opposed not what I saw was the design of kindness and leaning upon my cousin's arm I was led by her to a scene where I was to endure moments of the most acute anguish which in a life of suffering had yet I think been inflicted.

We entered at the great gate near the Palace and the day being uncommonly fine my heart seemed unexpectedly to open to the sensations of a soft and melancholy pleasure from the peculiar sweetness and beauty of Nature at that season—the thorn, the Syringas, and the other flowering shrubs were already exhaling almost premature odours, and the fresh verdure of the magnificent chesnuts and elms filled me with an unlook'd for pleasurable admiration. As we advanced to the great grass walk the scene became more lively. Crowds of beautiful women dressed with every advantage that taste & luxury could devise attended by an innumerable swarm of all that was young and gay appeared to offer the most brilliant picture of what the world esteems felicity. Every heart seemed alive to joy but mine, and tho' I had not been insensible to the charms of Nature yet I sickened at the scene of splendour and gaiety which was now presented to my view.

My cousin was here joined by some of her young acquaintances, I saw innocent joy sparkle in her eyes & modest pleasure suffuse itself over her cheek as she was addressed by a youth whose candid and ingenuous brow promised her a far happier lot than mine. A dark sentiment of envy seized upon my soul with a consciousness of my vileness and while I compared myself to the fallen spirit intruding into Paradise I more than once withdrew my arm with an intention of separating myself from innocence, when the kind and encouraging voice of my cousin again induced me to proceed while my sadness and silence which were looked upon as the effect of bad health were soon overlooked.

When we had reached the end of the walk and were arrived at the small door resorted to by all who came thither from town I was struck by the number of gentlemen on horseback who were ranged at the outside of the wall and stood to take a view of the company as they passed in procession before them. Instantly my eyes were fixed upon one object and it was impossible again to withdraw them. I indeed beheld the perfection of manly grace and beauty & at the same time received the cruel conviction that I had been deceived by the idol whom I adored. He might however have returned unexpectedly to town—returned perhaps with the wish of affording me consolation. The idea was too exquisite to be easily relinquished and I was debating whether I should offer myself to his view when he made a sudden and hasty turn and alighting instantly gave his horse to the groom while he approached the door with an eager step and an animated countenance.

My eyes followed his too surely! and I beheld as my heart had already forboded the too lovely being that unconsciously was the cause of all my anguish; She was in the midst of a large party and the reception which she gave him on his first address might have deceived by its affected coldness all eyes but those of Love and jealousy. I saw in the blush which glowed on her brow as she averted it from his empassioned gaze the agitation of a combatted indeed but a triumphant passion which in spite of virtue exulted in the certainty of being beloved and the conscious transport of being in the presence of the adored object. His eye was not less penetrating than mine. I saw it beam with those glances of living fire which had once kindled in my soul these flames which yet consumed it.

The bench opposite to the door was that moment vacant. I saw Lady Trevallyn and the ladies who accompanied her approach it and an instant after she was seated, beheld Lord Henry place himself at her feet on the grass. He raised his eyes to hers and extended timidly his hand to take from her bosom a branch of that very geranium which had once before excited my suspicions. It was of so singular a species that I could not be mistaken. This moment seemed to be the crisis of my fate; I thought I had suffered my last. A deep groan escaped me I met his eyes for an instant and the night of Death seemed then for ever to overtake me.

When I recovered I found myself surrounded by crowds whom curiosity or pity had assembled about me while I lay apparently lifeless on the ground, but my eyes in vain sought the only object which my memory or my imagination retained. I exerted myself to rise. I cast an anxious glance around but the whole party was gone and all had vanished like some dreadful vision sent to appal the expiring sinner with the prospect of the horrors which should await his guilty soul. My terrified companions now expressed their joy at my recovery and all eagerly pressed around me with enquiries & offers of assistance.

"Good God!" exclaimed my cousin, "What will Mrs. Blightal say when we return at our long stay and the condition you are in! Are you able Angela to walk home?"

"Mrs. Blightal! Angela!" repeated a middle-aged gentleman who appeared officious among the foremost to support me. "Is this young lady then the niece of Mrs. Blightal of Islington?" My cousin was surprised but answered to his enquiries while I sat bewildered and almost insensible of all I saw & heard.

As it was evident that I was not yet able to move far less to reach my cousin's which was at some distance from the palace, and as I was without power of resistance to any thing which was proposed the gentleman prevailed upon my cousin to allow him to convey me to a carriage which was waiting in the park offering to set us down where ever she directed. At the same time he informed her that his name was Deverel and that he was well known to Mrs. Blightal.

Of this I have been since informed for my brain then appeared on fire and I had no perception or sensation but a confused idea of having suffered some intolerable misfortune.

When we reached my cousin's we perceived my Aunt at the door awaiting our return in the utmost rage, and the violence of her invectives was I think the first thing which aroused me from the torpor in which I had been plunged and the kind of insensibility which still remained after I had been recalled in some degree to life.

Mr. Deverel who as I found afterwards was the painter who had so long known me only by my drawings, now attempted to pacify my Aunt, by representing the illness with which I had been so suddenly seized—but she persisted in declaring that it was a judgment upon me for having dared to enter the gardens without her knowledge which she said was at once an horrible breach of the Sabbath and an act of unpardonable disobedience and deceit. Her reproaches appeared a kind of relief to me by calling off for a moment my mind from the fatal picture which yet seemed to swim before mine eyes. I listened with a dumb sadness which I believe pleaded more in my favour in the eyes of the spectators than the most clamorous sorrow. My Uncle Harley interfered and words ran so high that my aunt protested "that if from that moment I should once again enter their door hers should for ever be closed against me."

Mr. Deverel now advanced to offer his carriage to convey us home, an offer which my aunt instantly accepted—my cousins embraced me and with tears in their eyes entreated me to forgive the pain which they had unintentionally brought upon me by having seduced me to take this unfortunate walk. Alas! how little could they know the mortal anguish, the irreparable blow with which it had pierced my heart! How little would they imagine how deeply those moments were impressed for ever upon my soul!

On my return home I found myself with the utmost difficulty able to reach my bed from whence it was some days before I could again rise and too surely I perceived that all which I had hoped might yet remain to me as a sad memorial of my perished happiness, had been destroyed by the fatal agitation of my mind. This circumstance which might perhaps have been considered justly as the fortunate preservation of my character and the deliverance of an unoffending creature from a wretched existence of expiation I deplored as the completion of my despair. The ignorance of the girl who attended me and the total neglect which my aunt shewed me during this illness from the apprehensions which she entertained that it was infectious entirely exempted me from all the suspicions which otherwise must certainly have been excited not only from my situation but from the unguarded expressions of bitter lamentation which I since recollect to have frequently uttered.

The certainty that I was abandoned for ever—that he could then be enjoying pleasure while I was suffering the tortures of the damned, that he would cruelly rejoice as in a deliverance from expected embarrassment at that calamity which I now thought filled up the measure of my afflictions were ideas too bitter to be endured. Night after night however I continued to watch for his signal remembering his parting words which in desiring me to be more cheerful on his return implied a promise of again seeing me. He had besides beheld me fall apparently lifeless in his presence and staid not to be assured of my recovery! Was it in human nature to treat with such harsh cruelty the being whom he had so long professed to love. He came not however! And distracted with the idea that I should never again behold him I thought that I would suffer every other sorrow with patience could I but hear him say farewell! and give him one parting embrace!

This idea haunted me so perpetually that it seemed to subdue every sentiment of modest dignity which I had hitherto in some degree preserved amid all the humiliations of my guilt.

I left my bed as soon as I was able to crawl to my writing desk and having with difficulty traced a few lines I sealed the paper illegible and blotted as it was with my tears and giving it to the maid bid her run with it to the bell man as soon as I heard him at some distance. What I wrote was I think to this purpose.

"Do not read this with dislike or fear. It contains no reproaches, nor will I even request again to see you; but however I condemn myself for the weakness which thus urges me to break the eternal silence which should in future separate us I cannot part for ever with one so loved without a last farewell. If it is your wish I am content to see you no more! Alas: in my despair I have even desired it! But oh! by all the love which you so long professed for your unhappy Angela let us part in peace, and as you have no right to despise or hate me think of me without aversion or contempt. Farewell then forever! Oh let me at least imagine that I have softened you to some little tenderness and thus unburden my full heart in wishes for *your* happiness."

My oppressed heart did indeed appear in some measure lightened of its intolerable load when I had dispatched this letter. The state of desolation in which I had appeared abandoned was now changed by expectation into one of mere agitation but free from such gloomy despair. You whose peaceful life has only experienced the calm joys and patient sorrows of innocence can never imagine the emotion with which I distinguished on the ensuing night his beloved step. As I sunk upon his bosom and once more felt his arms clasped around me, my very heart melted within me, seemed to flow dissolved in the tears which I shed in silent torrents—while the only wish I felt was that I might at that moment fall dead without a wound before him.

"Oh Angela," he cried softly whispering as he was wont to do, "how could you ever imagine that I would see you no more? I staid away only to allow you time to compose your spirits which you agitate so dreadfully by this indulgence of your sensibility, since I found that my presence only encreased your pain."

My tears only replied to this unfeeling attempt at consolation. Alas his presence did indeed encrease my pain, which hourly augmented, but his absence he too well knew was agony insupportable. Nevertheless as I was conscious that complaints could never inspire him with sensibility or restore that love which too surely I felt was for ever withered in his breast *I* uttered no reproach, stifled every pang of anguish and asked for no sympathy while I communicated to him that event which had blasted every faint prospect of future consolation, silently consented to receive his *promise*, not his *request* still thus to see me and suffered tenderness and hope to flutter idly on my lips while melancholy brooded alone over my heart and there forever told her wrongs and her despair.

When I met my aunt for the first time after my illness she gave me a letter, and informed me that she had had a visit from Lady Trevallyn who desired that immediately upon my Mother's arrival this might be communicated to her adding that it contained, in consequence of the recommendation of our late benefactress, an offer of a settlement with her which she hoped would not prove unacceptable.

I had hardly time to reflect upon this strange circumstance (and to listen to my fears lest I should be included in this plan of dependance upon the last person upon earth from whom I could bear to receive assistance) before I was interrupted most disagreeably by a visit from Mr. Deverel. My aunt introduced him to my room at his desire upon pretense of having some directions to communicate respecting a picture which he brought for me to finish. There was something to me highly offensive in his looks and manners—and upon my representing this to my aunt she commended my prudence and refused on his repeating his visit the following day to admit him again to my presence.

In the course of a few hours I received as usual a packet containing as I supposed his orders for my next employment, but judge of my confusion and indignation when I found it to be a letter filled with the most shocking professions of a disgraceful passion and the humiliating proposals of commanding his fortune offering to take me home to his house where I should in all respects be treated as its mistress.

But this was not all, and what most cruelly affected me was a hint at the unmerited constancy with which I reserved myself for a lover to whom I was become indifferent and who was the open and received admirer of a Lady of rank even at the time he had taken most pains to discover my retreat—"and lest," added he, "my beautiful Angela should doubt the truth of this assertion I will impart to her a circumstance which must at once convince her of the treachery of the heart she should despise. It was accidentally hearing that I was employed to paint Lady Trevallyn's picture that brought him first to me and at his entreaty I let him have that copy which you with instinctive reluctance refused to finish. He then commissioned me to paint that portrait which he afterwards so basely made use of to deceive you; it was intended for Lady Trevallyn and I myself consulted her as to its resemblance by his orders—tho' I found from his letter to you that he meanly and falsely persuaded you that you were then his sole object. I happened to shew two of your drawings whose striking likeness to him had appeared to me but accidental and the beautiful designs instantly discovered you. I confess my curiosity was excited to read his letter from the anxiety which he expressed to find you tho' I know his heart was devoted to another and he himself had furnished me with the means of opening it without suspicion by leaving in my hands his seal, of which he desired me to copy the impression to place upon the altar but not until after the picture had been returned by you."

I repeat the very words which made so horrible an impression upon my mind. The mystery of the seal I had little difficulty in solving most cruelly to myself. I recollected having heard Mrs. Montrose formerly tell Lady Anne that Lord Henry had stolen from her daughter a favourite ring: often had that returned to my remembrance even in the happiest hours of confidence, and never did I cast my eye upon the finger where he tenaciously preserved it without a secret pang. I once carelessly asked him who had given it to him and with a carelessness equally affected he answered that he had bought it.

Many months after this I attempted gently to draw it from his hand and as he bent the finger on which it was placed in order to prevent my design I repeated the question which I had formerly made—and was answered that it was the gift of his sister. In silent sorrow and shame with something too like an emotion of contempt to dare to express I received this confirmation of my suspicions that this was indeed the very stolen ring, but never would humble the being whom I adored, by suffering him to see I had discovered his duplicity.

The information which I now received from the odious Deverel while it degraded the object of my idolatry gave me for the moment a kind of false courage to support my misfortune which I yet considered as augmented by the discovery.

"At least," I cried, "if I could have preserved for him some esteem even in losing his affection I should not be thus utterly desolate and wretched." But I determined to yield no longer to the meaness which had forced me still to see the man to whom I felt I was indifferent and who had seduced and betrayed my innocence without having ever loved me.

Yet with what agony of mind, with what contending passions did I on the ensuing night listen to the long loved signal repeated with impatience and more surprise no doubt than disappointment.

When I found my resolution fainting under the dreadful struggle between offended and relenting Love I stopped my ears and hid my head beneath the cloathes that I might no longer be tempted by the sounds which even thus seemed to continue to strike upon my heart. I listened again, but all was still: all was silent: in a sudden frenzy I rushed to the window and even uttered the beloved name— the stillness of despair and night surrounded me. Oh never, never was I again to hear the sounds of love and joy! I felt that all was over! I felt that I should never embrace him more! That we were for ever parted! And my heart did not break! And I am yet alive to breathe forth the accents of my despair!

I need not recall to your remembrance the situation in which you found me, nor the distress with which you perceived my want of health to which you attributed the melancholy of which it was indeed but the effect. You will not now wonder at the weakness which made me faint in your arms upon your first embrace when you know that you arrived on the day which succeeded a night of such cruel agitation terminated by a despair which never can diminish. Your determination to accept of Lady Trevallyn's proposal was accelerated by the idea that the change of scene and the benefit of good air would contribute to the restoration of my health and spirits. In vain I entreated to remain with my aunt thinking that my situation was preferable to dependance on Lady Trevallyn. The surprise and grief with which you heard my strange and unnatural request deprived me of all power to persevere in my opposition to your will and I submitted, firmly convinced that Death would soon deliver me from this irksome existence which with hourly impiety I reproached my Creator for having bestowed upon me only for my misery, unsolicited unchosen by me happy as I comparatively was in my insensibility.

One more night of torture I was condemned to pass in vain expectation. I determined for the last time to behold Lord Henry should he again seek admission. Alas he came not! He was perhaps during those hours so memorably wretched to me, exulting in the soft smiles of the beautiful object of his love, or sharing the more tumultuous pleasures of his gay companions.

Impatient to remove me from an abode which you considered as injurious to my health on the following morning we commenced our melancholy journey.

Heavens! with what despair did I look for the last time upon the distant view of that town where I had left all that was capable of interesting me upon earth. When the possibility of again beholding him was thus totally lost I bitterly reproached myself for having listened to the dictates of pride and resentment in refusing him admittance. I would have given worlds once more to be permitted to tell him all that I had heard, implore his compassion, ask to be if possible again deceived and receive the promise which I knew the gentleness of his nature would readily bestow of an eternal remembrance. The promise could indeed have yielded no conviction to my understanding but it would have soothed my heart.

Time brought no consolation to my grief for regret and remorse were for ever now. The only sensation of pleasure which I ever experienced since his last embrace was in hearing of Lady Trevallyn's quitting London. They were then separated I was assured and the baneful passion of envy was at least satisfied. Yet this passion, odious as it is, was surely not natural to my heart which loathed its inmate. And the satisfaction which this assurance gave me if such it might be named, was accompanied by self detestation—and abhorrence, and the cruel idea of being hence obliged perpetually to behold her whom I could never *now* approach without an involuntary shuddring as of mingled with shame and terror.

When with a view of cheering my dark despondence you repeated to me her kind and generous request that I should become an inmate of her house, an exclamation of horror which it was impossible for me to restrain struck you with astonishment and I well remember the expression of your countenance which convinced me that you suspected the derangement of my intellects. I took no pains to undeceive you, and even wished to confirm the idea to save me from the pain of hearing your entreaties to discover my secret.

Doubtless my beloved Mother your ill-squandered tenderness & too great indulgence must long ere this have extorted from me my confession but your confidence in Lady Trevallyn placed an insuperable bar between you and mine.

When urged by your entreaties I at length forced myself to obey your orders and wait upon her the day after her arrival at Esselberrie all my exertions were necessary to withold a cry of anguish as I cast my eyes upon her dressing table covered with a profusion of that well remembered geranium, the peculiar odour of which now for the second time met me on my entrance. The plants she had brought down in her own carriage and I have watched the singular care with which she has preserved and multiplied them convinced as I was that the interest and unusual particularity with which this seemed to inspire her above all other plants were derived from some circumstance relative to the object so intimately connected with every spring which governed each of our hearts.

Far from experiencing myself soothed in any degree to peace by the calm tranquility of the scenes which now surrounded me the restless misery of my mind seemed to encrease in proportion to the quiet which every other object appeared to enjoy. A terrible void had laid desolate my soul and in vain I looked round for some external assistance to tear me if possible for a moment from myself. Perpetually dwelling upon the images which Lady Trevallyn's voice & appearance, nay her very name was sufficient ever to renew with fresh torture I persuaded myself that could I quit the presence of an object so fatal to my peace, could I be relieved from the insufferable load of humiliation under which her bounty crushed me, could I against revisit the scenes where I had fancied myself most blessed by his fondness and once more breathe the same air and inhabit the same town with him whom I must hope no more to behold I idly imagined I should enjoy comparative contentment.

I was besides exposed continually to the most dreadful agitations from the apprehension I entertained of his visiting Esselberrie and I almost expected this with a horrible kind of desire convinced as I felt that I should not survive the moment of witnessing him again smiling upon Lady Trevallyn and watching with the rapturous gaze of love that expression of delight which darted from her downcast eyes. Yet when assured of his actual arrival at Esselberrie a terror amounting to frenzy seized me at the idea of meeting again so cruel an image, and could I have avoided it by no other means I was determined rather than witness it again to run every risk of eternal misery by self destruction.

You no doubt remember that morning when my sudden illness so much terrified Miss Miltern. We were returning from a walk in which I was almost allured by the irresistible softness of her attractive benevolence (as I had more than once before experienced) to unveil to her my guilt and my despair—when on a sudden I beheld before mine eyes Lord Henry's well known horses led by the groom I had so much reason to remember. From that instant I can recollect nothing till that in which I beheld you my Mother prostrate at my feet imploring me to relinquish my obstinate design of leaving the house. My reason had certainly for a while yielded to the sudden shock and this alone can palliate the ingratitude of my undutiful cruelty. When I became sensible of the pain I had inflicted upon the tenderest of parents, I abhorred myself but could not endure your presence.

When at length you consented to my ardent desire of escaping from every eye I flew to the spot where he reposed in those slumbers of careless contentment which never more should visit my sad eyes. At this early hour every being was wrapped in sleep save those to whom sorrow had forbidden all relief from the sense of their woes. Unobserved I thought to enter the stable that I might caress the animal the sight of which had so often filled my bosom with transports no language can express. The hand so beloved had been laid upon his neck as he alighted and I longed to imprint a kiss upon the spot thus rendered sacred to my imagination. Finding that all the doors were locked and that my wild hope was thus defeated I remained within view of the walls which contained all so dear to my soul until the dread of being exposed to observation drove me to a more solitary retreat. I called to mind the rock from whence I might watch all who quitted the house and anticipated the anguish of beholding Lady Trevallyn attended by Lord Henry issue from the door at her accustomed hour of exercise. But this at least I was spared, and at length the chaise, the well known chaise where I had rested my head on the fondly trusted bosom of Love, now announced to me the unexpected preparations for his immediate departure.

I saw him my Mother! Once more I gazed upon his adored form and as he ascended the steps of the carriage, no secret instinct turned his eyes towards the forgotten and wretched victim whom he had abandoned to despair. Stung with a mad impatience, I pursued with all the force I could exert the path which brought me quickly to the high road, as tho' I wish'd or that it was possible for me to overtake his wheels. But they had already passed and as I marked the traces which they had left in the dust I felt as if I had at that moment for the first time been certain of the loss of all I valued in existence.

When again capable of reflection I could not but attribute this his sudden departure to the intelligence which his groom might have given him of my residence at Esselberrie. He shunned me—he sought not to afford me consolation, or to hear the particulars of my wretched fate—and this fresh proof of his indifference appeared the most cruel of all I had yet suffered. The idea that my removal from thence would encourage his return, far from diminishing my desire of quitting an abode I so much detested confirmed me in my resolution. Tho' I could have endured the rack to have been assured of the eternal separation of those two persons I had once thought formed but for each other, Yet I could not support the idea of being considered by him as an impediment to his happiness.

"Shall I then stand in the way of his desires?" I exclaimed. "I who would think life so poor a sacrifice were it possible for me thereby to promote his most trifling pleasure."

Having extorted from your yielding indulgence the consent which your judgment and your heart alike refused, I escaped from your arms, by which I never was encircled without feeling a stab of remorse which made me shrink involuntarily from the embrace. With a tenderness I so little merited you entrusted me with many a charge to the protection of my fellow travellers.

On the second day as we drove thro' a beautiful country my companions desirous of rousing me if possible from the gloom in which I appeared plunged desired me to observe the delightful situation of a magnificent house which we passed at a small distance and at the same time a stranger whom we had just taken in informed us that the fine seat she admired belonged to the young Marquis of Ortney who had just come to the title. My heart leaped at the name which it had never heard without unutterable emotion and I bent my head towards these scenes where Lord Henry had doubtless passed so many hours. We were then within view of an iron gate which opened into the avenue and just at that moment the confused voices of mirth and joy saluted my ears and the striking figure of Lord Henry mounted on his beautiful chesnut horse was conspicuous among the gay and gallant troop with which he was surrounded.

As the loaded stage in which we travelled drove past, the party gave way and stopped to let us proceed. I saw him with that grace in the action peculiar to himself step forward and place himself between us and the Lady at whose side he had been riding but at the same time as he held his hand upon the bridle of her horse he turned his face towards her so that I in vain sought the adored countenance which now unconsciously was thus once more so near that being upon whom for some time it had never beamed without delight and love. I trembled as I had been accustomed to do in happier hours when his unexpected presence suddenly had met mine eye—but we passed! The joyous band rode on. He saw not the dying paleness which came over my face, he heard not the cry of terror which this paleness extorted from my companions. I was to him as tho' I had never existed!

A strange sensation of tumultuous pain bewildered my senses and as I recovered not my reason until I found myself laid on my bed at my aunt's I cannot to this hour certainly declare whether the whole of this last sudden apparition was not the sole work of my disordered brain. The sight of the well known objects around me marked by such dear such bitter remembrances recalled me to myself. I seemed by a violent effort to struggle from a state the most shocking to nature. I strove to resume my former occupation from which I had been obliged to refrain while at Esselberrie from the impossibility which I found of tracing any other images but those for ever present to my mind.

As you had taken care that my aunt should not require from me any labour for profit I found the only supportable moments I passed were those devoted to the melancholy employment of fixing upon paper the scenes engraven on my heart. I visited each morning the arbour where in evil hour I had first consented to meet him—the autumnal air, the damp and yellow leaves, the distant early cries all renewed to memory the first endearments of Love. I only am changed and all that were then hopes and pleasures are turned tormentors to me—strong diseases! The hours that used to be marked by love again struck, my heart seemed to await the signal for joy while night after night passed in watchful anguish as tho' I yet expected his approach.

How often have I started from a disturbed slumber and flown to the window scarce convinced by the pang of recollection that his beloved voice had not indeed saluted my ears! This was too miserable to be long endured and at the price of my already irrecoverably injured constitution I purchased forgetfulness for a few hours each night by opiates the strength of which I was obliged continually to augment, as from habitual use they failed in their effect.

By this means I feel that without the wilful guilt of self destruction the period of my earthly suffering is nearly arrived. My stomach consumed by the slow poison which I have been obliged to swallow in such large quantities now obstinately refuses all solid food. In vain are my efforts now to preserve life. I suffer all the faintness all the craving of famine and frequently desire with eagerness the food at the sight of which I have fainted with disgust and loathing.

The wish of beholding but once again him who is still so dear in spite of the near image of Death for ever haunts me. Could I but for one moment fix mine eyes upon his and read there the soft glance of pity which they would assuredly bestow I should then have nothing earthly to desire and my thoughts should at length be able to rest upon the mercy of my God! This one idea which has consumed my youth, blasted my peace and at length destroyed life itself pursues me to the very gates of an unknown existence and stands between me and the forgiveness of Heaven itself.

Revolving perpetually a thousand wild schemes all alike impracticable for appearing suddenly in his presence without subjecting him to embarrassment or exposing myself to the unfeeling scorn of strangers, I yet timidly reject each at the moment I had resolved to put them into execution. In vain I seek to turn my thoughts upon the horrors which perhaps await my resignation of a life which has been so long only an intolerable burden. An eternal separation from him is all I can regret or fear.

Oh sole possessor of a heart too keenly sensible! Thou first, and last, and only object of those tumultuous affections that even yet throb and will not be at peace—

receive the last sighs of the bosom which contains alone thine image! In pity draw a veil over the terrible truth, let the delusion for which alone I lived sooth if possible the agonies of Death. Abandon me not! Oh yet a little! a little longer let mine eyes behold thee and I shall then close them in peace! Alas I am already abandoned! I am forgotten! He flies me! He loves me no longer! Oh horrible idea! Why could not the first weight of this overwhelming conviction crush me at once into dust.

A ray of hope has darted into my soul! Something whispers I shall yet once more behold him and my languishing soul that longs to be dismissed and seems yet enchained to earth by this one only desire shall be allowed at length to depart in peace. My Uncle Harley hearing of my illness has invited me to Kensington remembering no doubt with compassion the harshness of my Aunt. I know not from whence I derive my hope, but any change is now desirable convinced as I am that he will never more approach those scenes that have witnessed a thousand perjured vows and blasted hopes. I kiss each sad memorial of our divided loves— for never again shall the dying Angela press them to her heart or bathe them with her tears. The clock to which I have so often listened with the throb of impatience, or the faint sickness of disappointment I have just heard strike for the last time and my heart yet echoes to the funereal sound. In quitting for ever those scenes where I hourly met the ghost of my departed joys I feel something approaching to hope and pleasure in the consideration that every step shall bring me nearer to his abode. Ere long perhaps my heart shall hail the remembered trampling of his horse's feet. Ah when it shall no longer acknowledge that beloved sound it hath then for ever ceas'd to beat! I shall at least gaze upon the way he hath so often trodden and my eyes may visit the objects which he hath been so long accustomed to behold!

The hour so long desired at length approaches. I leave not yet with my sad existence all the tormenting passions and affections which still seem to bind my soul in some degree to earth! Something will yet survive! I have obeyed you my Mother! I have acknowledged my sin and my misery as to the ear of Heaven itself. Not for your sad Angela do I implore your pity and indulgence—too well I know the tenderness of your love which will condemn and deplore but can never hate your unhappy child. But there is yet another being whom you must forgive. If the wretched guilty Angela still is dear to thee hear her dying request and hate not, curse not the beloved of her soul—him whom she has espoused in the sight of Heaven. Forgive him! Bless him! When this cold heart this silent tongue no longer can breathe prayers for his happiness do you my Mother perform their last their *dearest* office; never let your unavailing complaints expose the shame of your lost Angela. Oh let our mutual faults be buried in my grave—nor ever let Lady Trevallyn know that the unfortunate wretch upon whom she desired to lavish favours had dared to rival her in the possession she prised above all wealth and rank.

Oh never let her hear the part she had in my miseries!

My beloved Mother farewell! Few and evil have been the days of my pilgrimage and my soul is yet weary of thinking upon her affliction and her misery the wormwood and the gall!

But Heaven is yet merciful! I bow before its decrees and feel that it will quickly give me peace and from my bleeding heart wash out my sorrows.

Oh for one parting look—One dying last farewell!

But in vain I have hitherto watched! He comes not my Mother! And my reluctant soul struggles still with Death and refuses to depart unblessed. One effort & all is over! I will breathe out these sad remains of life in his arms or at his feet!

Chapter III

> Ev'n in death's last pangs
> My closing eyes shall view thee! and my ears
> Drink in the music of thy charming accents!
> The dear loved name shall cool upon my lips
> The last—or die unfinished on my tongue!
> Trapp[11]

> Oh may those ravished beauties fall to earth
> Gently! as withered roses leave their stalks!
> May death be mild to thee as Love was cruel
> Calm as the spirits in a trance decay
> And soft as those who sleep their souls away
> Lee[12]

Selena had locked herself in before she commenced the melancholy task of perusing this Manuscript; and as she answered not to the soft enquiries of Clara who after some hours whisperingly demanded if she slept, she was left to herself till she had sufficient time to assume a degree of composure before she joined her friends. She was yet uncertain how far she was at liberty to impart the story of Angela to any and determined before she mentioned it to consult with Mr. Mason whether the dying and scarcely heard injunctions of Mrs. Harley were to preserve the secret of Angela's misfortunes which she herself appeared so anxious to hide

---

[11] Pyrrhus in Joseph Trapp's *Abra-Mule: Or, Love and Empire* (1708), 4.2.150–54 ("accents" should be "accent" in line 152, and "The" should be "Thy" in line 153).

[12] Ziphares in Nathaniel Lee's *Mithridates* (1678), 4.1.596–600.

from the knowledge of Lady Trevallyn to whom Selena thought it of the utmost importance that they should be communicated.

The agitation of her spirits and the evident traces of sorrow which it was impossible for her to disguise were naturally attributed to the scene which she had so lately witnessed and Mrs. Vallard felt secretly some alarm, lest Mr. Mason had seized upon this opportunity to disturb the mind of Selena by the infusion of some of his own peculiar religious opinions which prejudice had taught her to consider as so highly dangerous. Deeply therefore did she lament, that her maid had as she thought so imprudently allowed Selena to see Mr. Mason and severely did she condemn herself for not having dispatched a messenger immediately upon being informed where she was with her earnest entreaties to her to return, which might thus as she believed have spared her a scene too distressing for her nerves to bear without receiving a shock under which it was evident they yet violently suffered.

Selena had hardly yet recovered her tranquility so far as to arrange in her mind what steps she should take to induce Angela if yet alive to unite her endeavours with hers towards rescuing her friend from the same misery to which Angela had herself fallen a victim when she met her sister the following morning who presented to her a letter from Sidney which she had just taken from the post bag— upon the perusal of which every emotion which she had before felt from the story of Angela was revived and if possible even augmented. The letter was as follows.

"Allow me dear Selena to seek from the compassionate tenderness of your nature that soothing sympathy which I so much need to compose my mind agitated as it has been for some hours with the melancholy scene to which I have been witness and which I am going to recount to you.

"Yesterday while pursuing your journey to Hillbarton I rode to Bently farm not having been able to complete my intention the day before when you may recollect you overtook me as I was preparing to ride thither in compliance with Mr. Bently's wish to see me. Night was just falling as I approached town and as I was engaged to dine in Grosvenor square where I had thought it best not to send an excuse, I pressed my horse and preferred going thro' the park that I might be the less impeded by carriages. As I came opposite to a small gate which opens into Kensington gardens I perceived indistinctly several people running towards it and thinking I heard one enquire 'Did she drown herself?' a sentiment of pity and horror made me follow their steps and tho' this was soon contradicted I continued to advance no one being able to give any certain information as to the object of their curiosity except that it related to some accident to an unfortunate woman.

"Having the advantage of being mounted I soon made my way thro' the crowd which even in so retired a place was almost incomprehensibly collected and I perceived in the arms of a common rough looking fellow a female figure apparently lifeless. She was wrapp'd in a large coat and as they had thrown off her straw bonnet as they told me to rub her temples her thick dark hair fell on each side her face and covered her beautifully formed neck and shoulders. I demanded of this man some account of the poor creature whom he thus supported, I found that he was the person appointed to lock that door and that about an hour before as he was going as usual to execute his office he perceived this unfortunate being extended on the grass at the foot of the bench opposite the door. As he approached she called to him in a faint voice for the love of Heaven to assist her, but that he in vain had sought to gain from her any reasonable answer when he offered to conduct her home—that all she could utter or that at least he could distinguish was the name of Lord Henry and St James's street, but that when she attempted to walk upon his raising her up she had fainted in his arms. She had been already recovered out of this fit but relapsed after a short time and to me she appeared at first to be quite dead. However before we could get a carriage she once more opened her eyes and repeated the name of Lord Henry.

"'Shall we take you to Lord Henry Ortney's?' demanded I supposing she must mean him as I recollected he has lived for some time in St James street. I had no sooner said those words than she exclaimed, 'Oh yes! yes!' clasping her hands and casting upon me a look of wildness and entreaty that struck me to the heart.

"Tho' I affected to suppose what was indeed possible that she was connected with the people who kept Lord Henry's house in his absence and that she probably resided with them, yet I confess from his well known character and the appearance of this young creature who in spite of the horrors of death bore the traces of much beauty, I had but little doubt that she was some unfortunate girl whom he had deluded and abandoned. I was nevertheless determined to comply with her request, but as she again relapsed into insensibility on the first motion of the carriage, affrighted at her situation I gave my horse to the honest man whose humanity had been exerted in his efforts to save this unhappy girl and sent by him a line written with my pencil to Dr. P— intreating him to meet me instantly at Lord Henry's. I then drove myself with my poor unconscious charge directly to St James street. Tho' she was unable to speak and appeared insensible to what we said, yet her deep sighs and the movement of her lips and pulse shewed that she was restored to life before we reached the door.

"On enquiring for Lord Henry the servant answered that he expected him in to dress every instant. I requested to have the housekeeper summon'd and without waiting for her appearance I lifted into the hall my poor companion in whose miserable fate I already found myself too much interested not to feel some degree of indignation against the very fine Lady who at length answered my call for the housekeeper, who after looking with a scornful eye upon the dying countenance which might have touched with pity the heart of a savage declared her perfect ignorance of 'any such creter' and insisted in pretty strong terms against my bringing into 'my Lord's house some trumpery trollop out of the street who she had no doubt was only shamming ill to extort money—a very common practise I can assure you Sir' said she addressing me with no very gracious air and then observing that the coachman and one or two others crowded in, thro' curiosity and perhaps pity she called in a loud voice to the footman to 'turn these fellows out and not suffer a mob to gather this way about my Lord's door.'

"In the midst of this while I was holding a glass of water to the pallid lips that seemed incapable of receiving it, Lord Henry himself appeared. He entered with a face of astonishment and was beginning to ask the meaning of all this bustle when his eye glancing upon the form which I supported, he started back, but the next instant advancing eagerly said in a disturbed voice of confusion and pity, 'What's the matter?' At this sound which seemed instantly to pierce the heart which had almost ceased to beat, with a convulsive groan she opened her eyes and feebly stretched forth her arms as if to embrace him.

"'Angela! my poor Angela!' he exclaimed bending over her with an expression of such genuine compassion and tenderness that for the moment I acquitted him of the cruelty which must have brought to this terrible situation so young and lovely a creature. 'Oh thus yet once again most beloved! and kind!' she faintly cried attempting to throw herself at his feet while he caught her in his arms and carrying her into the parlour would have laid her on a sopha but her hands thrown round his neck clung with convulsive grasp to his coat while she attempted for a few moments vainly to speak.

"At length we distinguished some broken accents. Those which I heard are forever fixed upon my memory as they filled me at the time with the most painful sentiments of compassion which I ever experienced. With expressions the most tender and the most grateful she implored blessings upon him who thus soothed she said her last moments and rendered her death far happier than her life.

"After an instant's silence I heard 'Oh my poor Mother!' and then 'My God forgive!' As she said this her hand loosened from its hold when Lord Henry gently disengaging himself from her she again extended her arms and with a smile that I thought something more than human faintly cried, 'Mercy! dearest! …' Her eyes then closed, and the next moment we plainly perceived that all was over.

"As we stood around this awful scene in silent consternation Lord Henry was the first to break silence, 'Good God what is to be done!' cried he, 'with this poor creature and how shall we have her taken home?'

"'Do you know her home my Lord?' said I.

"He coloured the deepest scarlet as he answered this very natural enquiry with much hesitation saying, 'Why this is a poor girl who used to live with Lady Anne Ortney and since her death I understand she has been at her Aunt's in Islington. But curse me if I know what brought her here. Do you know any thing of it Mr. Dallamore?'

"I told him in a few words what I had just witnessed, during which in spite of all his efforts I more than once saw his countenance change but he interrupted me hastily by saying, 'Well we had best have her carried instantly to Islington or we shall have the coroner and the Devil to do here.'

"'She must not be moved however,' said I shocked at the unfeeling air which he assumed, 'until Dr. P— comes. I have sent for him and am sure he will be here immediately.'

"'You are very humane and charitable I make no doubt Mr. Dallamore,' cried he with a sneer and as I could see extremely piqued at my interference, 'but I confess I should like to know why you have honoured my house on this occasion.'

"'I wish my Lord,' answered I, 'that this poor unhappy girl had directed me to another, but as it was her dying request I shall never regret having complied with it.'

"'I hope your humanity then Sir may extend to her aunt and that you will prepare her for this sad business.'

"He then spoke to a servant to see if the hackney coach was still at the door and ordered Michael his groom to be called into the hall that he might accompany the body to Islington. Upon this I again interposed and protested against any steps being taken till Dr. P—'s arrival.

"'You have a vast deal of faith in Dr. P— to suppose he can be of service to the dead,' said he warmly, 'but as I am not quite so credulous and have no ambition to afford him subject for his d--d tattle all over the town tomorrow. I shall certainly not suffer Dr. P— nor any other Doctor to set foot in my house to night.'

"I commanded my temper as well as I could but resisted all attempts to have the body yet removed with so much obstinacy that Lord Henry who is himself I think naturally cool seeing me resolute and that as things were his opposition would only encrease the noise which this melancholy affair was likely to excite continued silent tho' evidently agitated with impatience and vexation. I begged of him to give himself no trouble about the business telling him that he need not appear in it at all, as I would myself take charge of having the body brought to Islington if Dr. P— declared there were no hopes of restoring her to life.

"After taking a few turns from the window to the fire biting his lips he at last said that he was sorry he was obliged to leave me since I was determined upon staying, as he was very particularly engaged that day but that he advised me to let his groom attend the body to Islington, 'as he had heard his father say that on Lady Anne's death he had sent Michael with the chaise to escort Angela to her aunt's so that he would have no difficulty in finding out the place.' He staid a few minutes in the hall giving some orders which I did not hear and then I believe left the house, at least I heard the door shut as I supposed after him.

"Upon his quitting the room all the servants with the exception of the housekeeper alone crowded round the wretched remains of what once was the lovely temple of innocence and beauty. All expressed their compassion for her fate, and one maid servant who had continued weeping from the time she had first seen her, with a natural emotion of courage and delicacy which I own I looked not to find in this assembly declared that she would herself accompany the body to Islington. This voluntary offer with the feeling which she had already evinced, interested me highly in her favour and I instantly accepted the proposal which a sense of decency had prompted promising to share myself the melancholy office intending literally to follow Lord Henry's advice and prepare her aunt for an event so awful even to the most hardened and insensible heart.

"I wondered that from the lively description which you had more than once given me of poor Angela she did not immediately occur to my mind upon her mentioning the name of Lord Henry, but interested as I was even at the first view of this poor girl my concern for her was encreased tenfold from the moment he pronounced the name of Angela. All that the compassionate and feeling bosom of Selena would on this sad occasion have experienced had she been present seemed instantly devolved upon me, and standing as I proudly imagined at that moment in your place the pity which before was but a painful instinct became now a sacred duty mingled with sensations not entirely devoid of pleasure. It was not long before the arrival of the Doctor confirmed the certainty we had already received that life had for ever forsaken that quiet immoveable breast which should never more throb with affliction.

"The housekeeper upon this appeared again and said the body must instantly be removed and Michael in consequence as I suppose of the orders which he had received advanced to let me know that a coach waited and that he had given the coachman such directions that his attendance was unnecessary but upon hearing the voluntary declaration which Hannah had made he appeared ashamed of having thus hung back, answering her reproaches with a warm assertion that 'he would go to the Land's end if he could serve Miss Harley, but that he saw no use in venturing himself alone with a dead corpse that could never be the better of it and know any thing about it bad or good,' and especially as it was to go to the house of her aunt who 'for certain,' he said, 'was the bitterest fowl upon God's earth.' However as he found that he was not expected to go alone he now readily offered his attendance and having wrapt the dead body of poor Angela in her own great coat we proceeded together to Islington.

"On our road thither I questioned Michael as to his Master's knowledge of Miss Harley, but he was too well tutored to give me any information protesting that he had only known her himself during her residence at Lady Anne's. I observed however that Hannah whose tears had not ceas'd shook her head and on my enquiry whether she had ever seen Angela before that sad evening she replied, 'Oh yes sir, I was once for a week in the house with the poor dear soul, and a kinder sweeter creature never breathed and that you know right well Michael … the more's the sin I say to them who wronged her.' 'Hannah,' retorted Michael warmly, 'you had best keep your tongue quiet and not speak of things that you don't know nothing at all about.' 'I knows more than I wish,' replied Hannah provoked, 'that I promise you and should be sorry my conscience had so much to answer for as you, aye or some great folk either.' As I thought this was no time for questioning her I put an end to their altercation resolving to take some other opportunity of enquiring into poor Angela's wrongs—and in this I hope you will acquit me of malicious curiosity and if I have liberty I will hereafter explain my motives to your better judgment.

"Mrs. Blightal's house was at the far end of the court into which the carriage could not possibly enter. I therefore left my companions and advanced alone to be the first messenger of these sad tidings. After knocking vainly at the door several times the window was at length cautiously opened and a shrill voice proceeding from beneath a white night-cap which was all that I could distinguish demanded what I wanted. 'I have business with Mrs. Blightal of some consequence. Pray allow me to see her for a few minutes.' 'I know of no business you can have with me at such a time; or if you have any you may tell it there.' 'I am sorry Madam to be the bearer of ill news but as you must have been already alarmed for your niece you are the better prepared for the melancholy event I have to communicate.' 'If you mean my niece Angela Harley I have nothing in the world to do with her, nor do I ever expect to hear any good of her since she chose to leave me and go to her profane carnal relations.' 'But Madam I beg leave ….' and I was about to begin my speech when she interrupted me in a still louder and shriller key. 'Let her keep with her aunt Harley I say! and if you have any thing to do with her you may go to Kensington. But I desire you will not torment me— for I wash my hands of her.' While she said this she closed the window with violence and as I found it quite in vain to persist in asking admittance I thought I had nothing for it but to pursue our way to Kensington and endeavour to find out Mrs. Harley thinking myself fortunate in having obtained even this information.

"After some difficulty we at length discovered the house where we were in search of, and met with a far different reception. Mrs. Harley and her daughters were watching with tears and anxiety for Angela's return and her uncle had gone out as I heard in search of her. They heard of her fate with more sorrow than surprise tho' they could not comprehend many particulars which I told them and as I saw they suspected nothing of Lord Henry's villany I thought it best to let them imagine as they seemed inclined to do that I had brought her thither from my previous knowledge of her dependence on the Ortney family. 'Poor child!' said Mrs. Harley as she herself assisted on placing the body decently on her bed, 'I expected little better when she insisted upon going out to walk alone this morning. But what firmness could stand out against her eloquence of solicitation. Heart breaking news for her poor Mother.'

"I gave into her care a little sealed parcel which had fallen from Angela's bosom round which it appears to have been fastened by a string which was probably loosened while Lord Henry's servants were busied in assisting her as I found it on the floor while awaiting there the decision of Dr. P—. It seemed to me to contain a picture but perceiving it directed to Mrs. Harley, Esselberrie, I put it in my pocket and her sister has promised that it shall be speedily conveyed thither.

"You dear Selena are the person best fitted to break the melancholy news to the unhappy Mother and surely if grief like hers can admit of any earthly consolation I have provided it for her in such a friend,

Sidney Dallamore"

Chapter IV

Hélas! que cet amour croit tôt ce qu'il souhaite,
En vain la raison parle, en vain elle s'inquiète,
En vain la défiance ose ce qu'elle peut
Il veut croire & ne croit que parce qu'il veut.

Corneille[13]

What ever obligation of secrecy Selena might feel with respect to the communications made thro' Mrs. Harley it was certainly no way incumbent upon her to conceal Sidney's letter, nor would it indeed have been possible for her to have done so from her present companions, without exciting in them strange suspicion. Its unusual length immediately upon her opening it had caused a degree of alarm which her agitation as she cast her eyes over it considerably encreased, so that she was obliged before she had half finished the perusal to satisfy the eager enquiries of Clara who already began to tremble for Edwin and of Mrs. Vallard who suspected some dreadful accident must have befallen Dallamore or Lady Trevallyn.

"Surely," thought Selena while Clara perused the letter for Mrs. Vallard, "surely this will in itself be sufficient to open the eyes of my deluded friend and if even Mr. Mason confirms my fears that Mrs. Harley objected to having the errors of her child exposed this I am free to communicate and this will for ever separate her from the vile seducer who has so blinded her eyes and infatuated her soul."

---

[13]   Camille in Pierre Corneille's *Othon* (1664), 3.1.73–6: "Alas! how easily does this love believe what it wishes, / In vain reason speaks, in vain it worries, / In vain doubt does all it can / This love believes only because it wants to believe."

Mrs. Vallard's tenderness of disposition was evident in the tears which she shed at the fate of the lost Angela and when she had finished the melancholy account she eagerly exclaimed, "Well Selena my dear, I hope that you will let our poor Emily hear all this. It may not be without its use for I am sure she will never hereafter have any connexion with a person capable of seducing and abandoning an innocent young creature such as I am sure poor Angela must have been."

Selena told her that she was determined to write that very day but she concealed from Mrs. Vallard the doubts which yet suggested themselves that Love reluctant to condemn would still find some palliation or totally disbelieve the hateful charge which it was yet unable to refute. Painful as Selena found the task of communicating intelligence to Lady Trevallyn which she knew would fill her bosom with the utmost anguish, she yet determined not to omit a word of Sidney's relation which might be likely to lead her mind to the discovery of the truth. Nor was she to be deterred from this by the danger of which she was well aware that her friend might accuse both her and Sidney of unjust prejudice and that by Lord Henry they should be represented as malicious propagators of scandal.

In her little narration of the death of Mrs. Harley she also threw out some hints concerning her knowledge of Angela's story but felt in doing so a sacred fear of betraying the trust reposed in her by the dying saint.

It was on the very next visit which Selena paid the schoolhouse that the mistress now there delivered to her a little packet which had been just left directed for Mrs. Harley. As it did not appear to be a letter after some hesitation Selena took off the outside cover and perceived in it a few lines written from Mrs. William Harley of Kensington before she had received the account of her sister's death. They were intended to inform her that the enclosed parcel contained all of Angela's papers which had been found in her room, as well as the little packet directed by herself for her Mother which Mr. Dallamore had entrusted to her care.

Selena doubted what she should do, but at length without proceeding any farther in her examination sealed up the whole and sent it with a few lines to Mr. Mason.

He returned it by her messenger with the following reply.

"My dear Madam, it was our late friend's particular desire that all which concerned her child should be entrusted to you and you alone. I know it is unnecessary for me to remind you of the sacred office which she thus committed to you, your mind is already too deeply impress'd with its importance to suffer you to betray her confidence and my prayers shall not be wanting for its success.
                    G: Mason"

Selena returned home with the parcel reserving its examination till assured of being uninterrupted and shed abundance of tears over its contents.

The first thing which met her eye was the beautiful and lively resemblance of Lord Henry, which poor Angela had worn in her bosom with a lock of his hair and two letters written in his hand. These she had herself sealed up and directed to her mother unwilling to part with them to the last and dreading lest another eye should behold them. The papers which Mrs. Harley had collected were chiefly fragments both in prose and verse expressive of the deep melancholy and despairing fondness which consumed her soul. The following are selected not for their merit but as being the most complete and these may serve as a specimen of the whole the sentiments being nearly similar in every fragment.

Sonnet
'Tis past the cruel anguish of suspence
 Shall vex my soul no more—I know him lost
 For ever lost to me—and all that most
On earth I valued, bought with dear expense
Of peaceful nights, and days of innocence
 Lies withered in my grasp—oh idle cost
 Of squandered hours! oh vows of anguish tost
To the wild winds, that mocked the eloquence
 Of grief indignant, yet constrained to speak!
Now all is past, the desolating storm
No longer may the bowers of bliss deform
 Its furious malice has no more to seek
 Each high aspiring hope lies all laid low
Sweep on ye powerless winds, o'er your fall'n trophies blow![14]

The following verses tho' without any date yet evidently appear to have been written during her first residence at Islington while tortured by suspicions and agitated by remorse the first delirium of love had already given place to the torments of jealousy.

Oh seal my sad and weary eyes
 Sleep soft suspence of human woe!
The day's long hours may sure suffice
 For sighs to swell and tears to flow!

Oh be the night to sorrow dear
 Sacred to cheering calm repose
Nor let the secret wasting tear
 Forbid the watchful lid to close.

Let me resign this load of grief
 In thy divinely soothing arms,
For thou canst yield some short relief
 Ev'n to the soul Remorse alarms.

How blest are they who lay them down!
 And sleep to wake in life no more!
At least if dreams of power unknown
 Haunt not Death's dark, and silent shore.

---

[14] Tighe titles this sonnet "Written for Angela. 1802" in *Verses Transcribed for H.T.* (Brompton, 1805); it is first published in *Psyche, with Other Poems* (1811).

What hope in life for me remains?
    What prospect cheers the dreary gloom?
Ungrateful heart! forget thy pains
    Love shall some future night illume!

Banish the agonising thought
    How swift the parting hour must come,
Be future woes no longer sought
    Nor thus anticipate thy doom.

I yet may hope some blissful night
    Shall bring me all in life I prise,
And to my captivated sight
    Restore the joy of these fond eyes!

His tender voice I yet shall hear
    His eye shall beam delight and love!
The happy hour that brings him near
    Awhile shall every pang remove.

Breathless with trembling joy once more
    This agitated heart shall leap,
The hours of long impatience oer
    Shall hail once more his well known step!

Assured his heart is only mine
    On this dear hope enchanted dwell,
And let its influence benign,
    Suspicious dreary clouds dispel

Come dear delusions! loved deceit
    This weight of fear awhile remove
With flattering dreams my reason cheat
    Hide every form that threatens Love!

O say in bonds of happiest fate
    Our days united yet shall live!
Oh say that peace and love await
    The fairer hours our hopes shall give!

Let me forget the cruel truth
    That peace with innocence is gone
That ceaseless tears shall waste my youth
    All hope, all bliss, forever gone.[15]

---

[15]   Tighe titles this lyric "Stanzas. Written for Angela. 1800" in *Verses Transcribed for H.T.* (Brompton, 1805), where the final word is "flown" (not "gone").

Fig. IV.1   Illustration for "Stanzas. Written for Angela, 1800" in *Verses Transcribed for H.T.* (Brompton, 1805), MS Acc 5495/C/8/1, National Library of Ireland, Dublin.

Selena resolved for the present to conceal these papers from every eye, but carefully preserved the irrefrable proof which they had afforded her of the villany of Lord Henry in his own hand writing.

"Yet why," thought she, "were these papers committed to me with a charge to watch over my friend if I am not at liberty to use them for her protection from the threatened danger." The more she pondered over this in her own mind the more anxious she felt to converse upon this head with Mr. Mason who might perhaps know what were the intentions of her whose confidence in her last moments he seemed to possess in an unbounded degree.

But how to obtain a conference with him she knew not. In the account which she had given to Mrs. Vallard of the solemn scene which she had witnessed his name had often occurred and the more warmly her lips had poured forth his commendations and the more anxious she appeared to interest Mrs. Vallard in his favour the stronger grew the good old lady's apprehensions, lest the artless mind of Selena should be seduced by an imposter or at best an enthusiast to become a convert to the dreaded principles of Methodism.

Selena saw the prejudice which she almost despaired to conquer and unwilling to vex her amiable and worthy heart by opposition to her little failings she determined to trust to accident for the interview which she so impatiently desired to have with the venerable pastor.

Before it was possible for her to receive an answer to her unwittingly afflictive letter, the post brought her from Lady Trevallyn one whose contents gave her more pain than surprise.

After tenderly reproaching her for her treacherous flight and many expressions of the most affectionate regret for her loss she proceeded thus.

> "I suppose you have heard from Sidney of the strange and melancholy office he performed for poor Angela. You must have been surprised at the house in which she chose to breathe her last and as I know *somebody* is no great favourite of yours I dare say your busy brain has already been at work and formed many an unjust suspicion. And from what I have heard Sidney was not wanting I am sure in assisting you to this. Notwithstanding dearest Selena you will I know be the first to rejoice when you find you were in this instance carried away by unfavorable appearances and it is but common justice to let you know the truth—tho' he himself entreated me never to say any thing in his justification thinking I suppose that it would be a cruelty to the memory of the poor girl.
>
> "You would have pitied him had you seen as I did the agitation she has excited in a breast which is indeed dear Selena Pity's resting place, and as Angela was considered in some measure under my protection, he whom she thus constrained to witness her melancholy death was anxious to communicate to me all he knew of the unfortunate Angela.
>
> "You were always partial to the poor soul so I am not afraid of wearying your patience by repeating what he now thought himself obliged to reveal.
>
> "As she had a talent for drawing her dear kind benefactress who doated upon her wished she should profit by the opportunity which she thought so fortunately offered of receiving instructions in the country from one you know so uncommonly skilful in that accomplishment. But alas dear Selena she never reflected on the obvious dangerous consequences. And can we wonder that what is really so amiable, what you, even *you* must confess to be so unlike all other human beings; can we wonder that so much gentleness, so much grace, should have captivated fatally her inexperienced heart. He himself at last perceived it but unwilling to excite Lady Anne's suspicions by at once entirely forsaking his pupil, he rejoiced in the excuse which presented itself of accompanying his regiment to Ireland.
>
> "From this time he heard and I suppose thought no more of the unhappy girl whose romantic mind cherished such a hopeless passion until on his return to London he received a note from her entreating him to pay her a visit at her aunt's as she had a request of the utmost importance to make him. He says that the style of her letter plainly shewed him that her mind still dwelt upon her unfortunate prepossession and that on this account he thought it most prudent to decline seeing her but returned an answer offering any pecuniary assistance it was in his power to bestow.
>
> "You know dear Selena this cannot be a falsehood for had he then seen her it is most certain that her aunt when questioned as she so often was as to her visitors during Angela's stay would not have omitted mentioning one so remarkable.
>
> "She however continued to write to him still supplicating him to call till her Mother carried her into Derbyshire. You remember my love, how miserable she was to return to London especially after she had heard of his short visit at

Esselberrie. She nevertheless made no more attempts to see him till this last sadly successful effort. He says he is convinced that her intellects were disordered even during the time of his first acquaintance with her and indeed I cannot doubt this from all I myself remember.

"Poor thing my heart aches when I think what her sufferings of mind must have been added to her ill health before she saw him—and methinks I would not for worlds that she had been deprived of this satisfaction which she seemed so ardently to desire. Poor Angela! the arms of compassion were extended to receive thy last sigh and thine eyes which closed in peace had nothing to desire! Her lot miserable as it will be esteemed was yet far happier than that of many who are looked upon as the objects of envy.

"Dearest Selena! those are indeed happy who have done with the labours the sorrows of life and sleep at last in peace! How often do I think of a speech I have somewhere read that begins 'Oh Heaven! I think it greatest happiness, never to have been born, and next to that to die'[16]—for surely existence is to most a sad, sad burden. I am confident that you will do all in your power to alleviate poor Mrs. Harley's distress.

"I had a thousand little commissions to give you before you left town but your stolen flight shall not entirely save you; I have written to the steward to give you my key which I left with him; and as I hope you will often visit the children at Esselberrie I think you will find it pleasant. You know it will admit you into the garden and from thence thro' the greenhouse into my dressing room and study. I have also desired Rawlins to send the harp to Hillbarton. You will keep it in order for me and whatever books you like to have, leave out and he will send them for you. He will shew you where are the keys of the bookcases—and whatever the house or gardens can afford for your gratification will possess for me a value they never had before."

The rest of the letter was chiefly addressed to Mrs. Vallard and Clara with some directions which she wished Selena to have executed for her at Esselberrie. And from the whole her friend saw with concern that her heart was totally free from all suspicion of the falsehood of him by whom she had been thus grossly deluded.

Clara after having read this letter declared her satisfaction that Lord Henry was not so bad as they had suspected and wondered how for a moment they could have supposed him unfaithful to the lovely being to whom he seemed only too ardently attached.

Indeed, as the object of Lady Trevallyn's unconquerable love Clara had ever secretly felt interested in his favour. This idea seemed to cast upon him a partial and favourable lustre which the fascination of his soft manners and beautiful countenance in no small degree assisted.

Even Mrs. Vallard ever ready to give credit to the shallowest pretence of innocence now seemed inclined to believe that Lord Henry was not so criminal in this respect or he would not have been in such haste to speak of it himself to Lady Trevallyn.

---

[16] Ziphares in Nathaniel Lee's *Mithridates* (1678), 1.1.499–501.

Selena who thought it would answer no good purpose to undeceive them would have been silent had not her affection for the memory of the ill-fated Angela constrained her to observe that there was a peculiar delicacy of reserve and native dignity about Angela which made it extremely improbable that she could ever have declared a passion for any one (still less one so much her superior in rank) unless some pains had been taken to induce her to believe that it had been at first returned.

To this they both agreed and indulged their amiable dispositions by forming conjectures how this unfortunate affair could have been with the least possible fault on either side while Selena was on her part secretly projecting schemes for again seeing Mr. Mason without grieving Mrs. Vallard by opposing her prejudices.

The harp which was sent from Esselberrie within a few hours after the receipt of this letter was a most welcome acquisition to both sisters but more especially to Clara who had bitterly lamented the deplorable state in which they found Mrs. Vallard's piano forte and the time that must elapse before they could have it put into order. She had no pleasure so great as in playing the musick which she had learned from Edwin in the spot where he had first captivated her heart. She fancied she yet beheld him there and forgot during these moments of sweetest melancholy that she had been ever painfully obliged to acknowledge him less deserving of her love and admiration.

Chapter V

Pleasure has charms but so has Virtue too!
One skids the surface like the swallow's wing
And scuds away unnotic'd—'Tother nymph
Like spotless swans in solemn majesty
Breasts the full surge and leaves long light behind
                          Walpole[17]

Selena now passed the greatest part of her mornings in the school of Esselberrie when the weather allowed her to walk thither, nor was she easily discouraged by cold or the damp of the ground from performing what she not only considered as a duty but felt a source of great consolation and what afforded her the happiest moments in her present situation.

The children loved her as a mother. She superintended their little works; she instructed them in reading and writing and joined her voice in their harmonious chorus which poured forth the acceptable incence of love and gratitude to their common parent.

---

[17]   Florian in Horace Walpole's *The Mysterious Mother* (1781), 2.4.26–30 (line 26 should read "Pleasure has charms; but so has virtue too" and "Skids" should be "skims" in line 27).

She was not without expectation that in some of her visits to the school she might at length meet Mr. Mason, but on enquiring found that except when particularly summoned by Mrs. Harley he had never been at Esselberrie and Selena doubted not that his absence was the effect of prudence conscious that his character of Methodist was to many an object of the utmost aversion, nay even terror.

Chance however as Selena had hoped for in a few days brought them together and in a manner which encreased their mutual esteem and the interest which each had already found in the other's welfare.

Having from her childhood been accustomed to visit the cottages of her poor neighbours Selena had already made herself known to several of those within the limits of her walks during her former visits at Hillbarton: By a thousand little offices of kindness she was remembered there with affection: the infants had not yet overgrown the dresses which her beautiful fingers tho' well skilled in finer works had not disdained to make for them even before their little eyes had opened upon the light—and their older brothers still shewed with pride the books they had received from her in reward for their diligence.

But there was one cottage which had more than all the rest with grateful love preserved her remembrance. An industrious couple with a young family struggled, and at times struggled with difficulty to keep an aged grandmother from the disgrace of being assisted by the parish of which she (who had seen better days) had conceived the utmost dread. She had long lost the use of her limbs and of late was unable to be of use to them even in any degree as she had been accustomed to render herself before her eyesight failed.

The kindness with which she was treated by her grandchildren and her own contented piety had not only called on Selena for such assistance as she could afford but obtained her admiration and reverence. No sooner had she pointed out their merits than Mrs. Vallard had been most ready to take them under her protections and Selena herself had many an hour sat by the side of old Margaret when she had been placed on a bench in the sun and read to her from the old Bible the family treasure. Since her return to Hillbarton she had been so much engrossed as deputy in Lady Trevallyn's favourite charities that she reproached herself for her neglect of poor Margaret upon hearing Mrs. Vallard's maid one evening request her mistress's leave to take her a bottle of Port wine as she had been for some days in a very weak state.

Early the next morning Selena arose and hastened to the cottage of old Margaret, who welcomed her with tears of pleasure tho' unable to rise from her bed and apparently fast declining. She recalled to mind with so many expressions of gratitude the hours which Selena had devoted to reading to her and seemed to dwell upon them with such delight that Selena cheerfully offered to renew her pleasing office. The Bible was taken from the press, where it had been for some time deposited, and Selena placing herself on a little stool at the window, with her face to the bed, had just commenced when Mr. Mason entered the cottage.

As her back was to the door he stood unperceived by her for a few minutes surprised at the graceful figure and sweetly modulated tones which unexpectedly struck him.

Perceiving that dame Barnwell was about to speak he made a sign to her to be silent and continue her occupation of rocking the cradle where her infant reposed while she watched something which she had placed on the fire for Margaret's nourishment. He then quietly seated himself beside her letting her see that he wished not to disturb what was going on. Selena however had not long proceeded before a little boy running in eagerly to demand his Daddy's breakfast interrupted the lecture and starting at an involuntary "Hush!" uttered by Mr. Mason she turned and beheld the reverend pastor, his eyes glistening with tears and upon his lips the cordial smile of satisfied benevolence.

Blushing deeply she arose and expressed her pleasure at meeting him, not without some graceful confusion which added to every charm that already made her appear in the sight of the good old man as the very earthly representative of one of those celestial spirits with whom he in fancy held daily converse.

A few simple words expressive of his real joy at seeing her, and seeing her thus, spoke more flattery to Selena's heart than all the exaggerated effusions of courtly homage could ever accomplish.

Unwilling to lose this opportunity of the conference she had desired, she now lingered in the cottage till he had performed the pious offices for which he had visited Margaret, and when they had taken leave of her after having risen from their knees Selena timidly requested to speak a few words to him as they walked towards the village at some distance where he resided.

"You have heard I suppose Sir," said she, "that poor Angela did not live to receive the account of her Mother's death and I dare say you are not unacquainted with her melancholy story."

"You are right my dear young Lady and I have yet to communicate to you what I daresay you can pretty well guess from the incoherent words of my departed friend was her chief earthly desire—tho' as she had before feared when you arrived she had already lost the power of expressing herself very plainly."

Selena's countenance shewed her extreme attention and eager desire of information and he proceeded.

"Her faith for her lost child could only lie in the mercy of God, but there is another who may yet be saved, and for whose preservation her dying prayers and last worldly anxieties were all exerted; and for this purpose it was that she at length determined to entrust to you the confession it appeared so necessary should be known."

"I am then at liberty," eagerly interrupted Selena, "to produce this testimony of baseness and wickedness that perhaps could never otherwise be credited."

"To you," resumed he in an impressive voice, "to you it was confided with a solemn entreaty that the memory of her child should never be exposed in a manner so repugnant to her own wishes unless you shall judge it absolutely necessary to snatch another from the same vice and misery. We heard her dying lips implore you to save one whom she considered as her child, and never to betray her suffering penitent. If possible comply with both those earnest injunctions, but do not for any earthly consideration sacrifice the first important charge. This was her heart's chief desire let us trust in Heaven for its accomplishment and never lose sight of your friend."

Selena now understood the full force of Mrs. Harley's last words and having nothing more to learn from Mr. Mason felt the delicacy of the theme restrain her tongue.

He saw and respected the reasons for her silence and changing the subject dwelt with eloquent enthusiasm on the confidence and peace which had sweetened the latter hours of Mrs. Harley's life.

Selena listened to him with a delight which made her forgetful of time till he himself suddenly stopped saying, "Well but my dear I have carried you a long way out of your road and I doubt you have not breakfasted."

Selena looked round with some consternation as she had indeed never before wandered so far and the sun was already high.

"What say you," continued he with a smile, "shall I bring you home to my good dame? She knows you already by report and I can promise will give you a kind tho' not courtly welcome."

Selena thanked him for his hospitable proposal which she longed to accept when he pointed out to her at a little distance his neat and humble cottage the abode of piety and happiness. But she was obliged to deny herself saying she already had exceeded her bounds and feared she should be waited for impatiently.

He suffered her not however to return alone but accompanied her till they came to a stile which led to the path thro' the fields to Hillbarton and then taking her hand affectionately blessed her saying with somewhat of archness in his countenance, "Take care how you confess what bad company you have been in— you may chance to get the name of Methodist."

Selena who thought of Mrs. Vallard's prejudices scarce knew what reply to make, He however waited not for any, but bowing turned towards his contented dwelling while Selena with the lightness and grace of a Woodnymph flew hastily across the fields and in a few seconds joined Clara who had begun to feel some alarm at her long absence, but Mrs. Vallard as Selena was pleased to hear had not yet risen.

Selena now wrote to Lady Trevallyn and endeavoured by the strongest reasoning to open her eyes upon the improbability of Lord Henry's story, leaving nothing unsaid except the positive avowal of Angela's confession which she reserved as her last resource.

This letter Lady Trevallyn was slow to answer and then declining all argument plainly shewed Selena that she considered her as a prejudiced judge and was herself fatally resolved to disbelieve that any thing ill could reside in so fair a semblance, but while Selena yet debated on the gentlest means of imparting to her conviction so terrible, circumstances in an unexpected manner were preparing to produce the dreaded eclaircissement.[18]

Mean while her own affairs wore not an aspect more promising. She had been now a fortnight at Hillbarton and in that time had heard nothing from Dallamore. Even Sidney had not written since his account of Angela's death to which she had not indulged herself by making any reply. She was indeed self persuaded that she hoped absence would restore each to the calm of indifference, but many a sad and lonely hour which she past, were unconsciously embittered by the idea of being really forgotten by Sidney.

Her favourite retirement for some days after her return to Hillbarton was the walk by the river where he had for the first the only time confessed his love. But convinced of the dangerous tendency of this indulgence in a weakness for which she severely condemned herself, after one sweetly silent shower of tender sorrow she made the sacrifice which Virtue demanded and on the spot so well remembered solemnly resolved never again to visit it until her heart could do so without the shadow of reproach or one emotion at which she ought to blush.

But it was in Lady Trevallyn's study at Esselberrie that her thoughts seemed to feel a delightful liberty of reflection. It was indeed a scene calculated to nurse and sooth tranquility. As she could admit herself here at all times, and that these apartments were kept constantly warm by the fire which supplied the hot houses the fragrance and beauty of the plants with the various luxuries around gave Selena an idea of these enchanted palaces described by Eastern poets, and to this the uninterrupted stillness of the scene much contributed; remote as it seemed from every sound except the voice of the red-breast who still thrilled his wintry song from the shrubs that bloomed around with perpetual verdure.

It was here that Selena especially loved to write to her friend, accompanying every letter with tears of affectionate solicitude and ardent supplications to Heaven in her behalf. It was here that contemplation had indeed her fill

'Twas here she oft retired to read
And oft retired to pray.[19]

From her brother she had received more than one letter. In the first which he wrote to her after her departure from town he thus mentioned his introduction to the family at Bently farm.

"I am sorry dear Selena, that you had not an opportunity of seeing the objects of Dallamore's generous kindness. Very fortunately as I think it, I overtook Sidney the other morning as I was going to ride and was invited to accompany him in his visit to his friends. Mr. Bently is a man about sixty of pleasing manners and when Sidney presented me as a near relation of Dallamore's you may judge he received me with peculiar attention. Mr. Bently was educated for

---

[18]   Eclaircissement: clearing up or explanation (OED).
[19]   Hannah More, "Sir Eldred of the Bower" (1774), lines 151–2.

a physician and practised for some years as Sidney tells me with considerable success, but unfortunately a tedious fever not only interrupted his course but left behind a weakness of constitution which prohibited his remaining in town. He retired therefore to his farm near Richmond where he has since resided. His skill is there highly esteemed while his amiable character insures him the love and respect of all who know him.

"With strict oeconomy he has contrived to provide for four sons the third of whom Charles is Dallamore's friend. He has still at home two boys whom he educates himself and three very fine girls. But the favourite and adopted daughter of the family and as I am told the affianced bride of Charles is indeed lovely. I am not sure that you would allow her to be beautiful and she is certainly not so perfect a model as Lady Trevallyn, but a sweeter dimpled smile nor a finer natural complexion it is impossible to shew. Add to these a profusion of flaxen ringlets with the softest clear blue eyes—and you may form some idea of Ophelia Lawder's person. But the innocent interesting expression, the playful childish grace which accompanies all her words, looks, and actions, and to which her foreign accent perhaps contributes—you certainly cannot imagine for I never saw any thing like it except with herself. I have more than once seen infantine naiveté affected and turned from it with disgust, but this peculiarity in the simplicity of Ophelia's manners are as perfectly unattainable as the features of her face. Of her history I have only heard that her family originally English had been long settled in France that her father had suffered by the guillotin early in the revolution while her mother escaped to England without being able to preserve any thing but her little Ophelia. The consequences of grief and terror proved fatal to a delicate frame and it is near five years since the orphan was received into the protection of Mr. Bently. How she gained so fortunate an asylum I have not been able to discover and delicacy has prevented me from enquiries from themselves. They never speak of her but as she now stands the darling adopted and affianced sister of the young people.

"Harriet very obligingly complied with my wishes and visited the ladies of Bently farm giving them an invitation to dine with us offering to take the girls to the opera. This was however politely declined and indeed they appear to have no wish to enter into the gaieties of London."

Robert continued to expatiate on the captivating beauties of the fair Ophelia and dwelt so much on his curiosity to know whether she was really attached to the son of her benefactor that Selena felt rather uneasy lest he should have been making some comparisons not the most favourable to Lady Harriet.

But she took care not to mention those fears to Mrs. Vallard or Clara to whom she read Robert's letter and no sooner had she finished it than Clara hastily exclaimed, "I wonder what scheme Lady Harriet has laid against these poor girls."

"What do you mean my dear?" asked Mrs. Vallard.

"Why sure Selena you cannot think that it was out of good nature to them or to oblige Robert that she put herself out of the way to drive ten miles and for once in her life do what was civil. No, no depend upon it she has something in view, but I hope by their refusing that they have defeated her spiteful design for spiteful it must be I am sure in some shape or another."

"Oh fie Clara," said Selena gravely. "How can you speak so ill-naturedly?"

"Nay my dear Selena there is no denying that she has a bad heart and can that ever produce any thing that is good?"

"Well Clara I hope for poor Robert's sake that you are wrong but at least," added she smiling, "we ought to be just and confess that we cannot be fair judges since we are not favourites and I suppose of course are prejudiced against her, and if we speak thus, who as sisters might be expected to look on her with partiality, what must others think, candour therefore should oblige you to declare when talking of Lady Harriet (if you must talk of her) as you remember Montesquieu did when he quarrel'd with his friend 'N'écoutez ni le père de Tournemine ni moi, parlant l'un de l'autre, car nous avons cessé d'etre amis.'"[20]

Selena however had soon cause to suspect that Clara's accusation of Lady Harriet's designs in this instance was not unjust.

Robert's letters continued to speak of nothing but Ophelia, and his visits to Bently farm; and from the pains which Lady Harriet evidently took to forward this intimacy it could not be doubted that she wished by engaging her husband in some other pursuit to draw off his attention from too closely canvassing her pleasures.

But from her anxiety for her brother and her friend placed in the midst of such peril Selena was now called more directly to herself by the sight of Sidney's hand.

He told her that he had just received an answer from Dallamore, expressive of his disappointment at not seeing them in Dublin and especially as it was impossible for him then to quit it Lord Mount Villars being there and so ill as to be confined to his bed. Sidney concluded with expressions of his concern for Edwin who appeared consumptive and was not to be prevailed upon to take that care of himself which his situation required.

Selena wondered that Sidney had not sent her as he had been accustomed to do Dallamore's letter.

But the truth was, this would have been impossible—its contents strange and licentious were delivered in so incoherent a manner, that Sidney rightly concluded they were written when he was half intoxicated and Selena's name throughout the whole was not once mentioned, nor was she even alluded to, unless indeed she might have been included in the first sentence which thus began "I am sorry *you* will not come."

Nevertheless his account of the illness of Lord Mount Villars was confirmed by another hand in the next post and Sidney immediately (but without acquainting Selena) set out for Dublin, once more resolved at this critical period to bring Dallamore to declare positively his intentions towards his injured unacknowledged wife.

---

[20] Rousseau cites this saying in *The Confessions* (1782), Book X: "Listen neither to Father Tournemine nor I when we speak of one another because we have ceased being friends."

He had not left London many days when the intelligence arrived of the death of Lord Mount Villars, which Robert instantly announced to Selena adding his hopes that one great bar was now removed to the return of Dallamore.

He informed her also that Sidney was gone over to Ireland and Selena could not doubt the object of this journey.

Mean while poor Clara's spirits, colour, and appetite forsook her and she seemed sympathetically to droop as the being still so ardently beloved declined in health.

Selena lost every thought of her own cares in her apprehensions for her sister and knowing how vain it was to argue with some feelings and that "Raissoner sur l'amour c'est perdre la raison,"[21] she employed herself continually in studying to amuse her mind and prevent it from dwelling constantly upon what gave it pain.

But her endeavours appeared vain and in order to satisfy her anxiety Selena entreated Robert to send them a particular account of Edwin's health.

His reply was as follows.

> "Poor Edwin is acting a miserably foolish part. I fear he has for ever disobliged his uncle who himself complained to me of his strange wild conduct. Lord Stanmore having centred all his hopes upon him for the support of his family, expressed as was natural his wish that he should marry and I believe mentioned some one to him, when Edwin indignantly burst forth into the most ridiculous displeasure and as if on purpose to grieve his uncle made the strongest declarations that nothing upon earth should ever induce him to marry. He left Albemarle street upon the spot as if his liberty was menaced and they have not spoken since. As to his health it is evidently fast declining, and as he has not any kind of prudence while he lives in the most expensive society in London—I fear that poor Inverathie (should he even recover) must quickly change its master. What a pity! Abominable London! Every day I live here I see fresh cause to curse the profligacy into which it hurries all ranks of men and women it is only in the innocent tranquility of Bently farm that I find a consolation for my disgusts and disquietudes."

"Poor Edwin!" cried Clara with streaming eyes. "Oh Selena! *what a noble mind is here o'erthrown.*"[22]

Selena tried to comfort her by assurances that she had no doubt that Robert would be able to bring about a reconciliation between him and Lord Stanmore and that she would instantly entreat him to exert himself for that purpose and to endeavour to prevail upon him to visit Inverathie for the recovery of his health.

But a few days after this Selena had a letter from her brother written evidently in the utmost depression of spirits and disturbance of mind. Tho' he did not confess the cause both sisters thought they plainly discovered that affairs were coming to a crisis between him and Lady Harriet.

---

[21]   Stanislas Jean, Chevalier de Boufflers, "Le Coeur," *Oeuvres* (1781), line 12: "To reason about love is to lose one's reason."

[22]   Ophelia in Shakespeare's *Hamlet* (1600), 3.1.153.

He said he was on the point of leaving London and that he went alone to Miltern Abbey but promised to write more fully on his arrival there—which he accordingly did in a few days to the following purpose.

"My dearest Selena,

"You have no doubt received with surprise the intelligence of my quitting London while Lady Harriet remains there, but many circumstances have conspired to render my longer stay there highly imprudent as well as insupportable.

"Harriet has promised to follow me hither, as soon as the house can be properly prepared for her reception; I have now written to inform her that all which I can have done at present is done and have declared my firm purpose of returning no more to London. If she does not comply with my request of seeing me here before the end of this month *we meet no more.*

"I have said so much dearest Selena to prepare you for an event which I think but too probable and can rely with perfect confidence on your discretion. You may perhaps attach some blame to my conduct and think that I at first encouraged and now deserted her in error and I will confess that I did act weakly in not resisting with steadiness that torrent of dissipation which has proved so fatal to my domestic comfort but I soon found that all endeavours were vain and that what I most valued was lost beyond redemption. From absolute guilt however I yet hoped she might be free & was willing to receive as a concession made to my solicitations her renunciation of an intimacy with Lord Henry which I have since reason to believe proceeded more from pique than from love to me, or a sense of returning Virtue.

"Her subsequent conduct has indeed but too well proved how little influence either of these motives can have upon her mind. My expostulations have been in vain and she has even had the malignity to endeavour by way of palliation to her own errors to asperse the character of an innocent and unoffending creature, by accusing me of an improper connexion with Ophelia Lawder. In justice to myself and the amiable victim of her calumny I must assure you that the reports which I know she has circulated with the utmost diligence are absolutely without foundation. I do not deny that I think Ophelia Lawder all that is lovely and excellent in woman, and that I consider the lot of the man to whom she shall be attached as the happiest which can await a mortal; but if ever the purity of Angels appeared in the shape of female beauty it dwells in the bosom of Ophelia. From what I say you will I am sure perceive and approve of the powerful motives which compelled me to fly from London where I had already remained long enough to resign every hope of happiness upon earth."

The remainder of this letter contained many serious arguments to Selena upon her own situation, urging her to write a formal renunciation of her claims on Dallamore and offering her an asylum at Miltern Abbey tho' he lamented that her residence there must be attended by some unavoidably disagreeable circumstances. Selena tho' in some measure aware of the situation of her brother with Lady Harriet from what she had herself seen in town; and tho' she had feared the evils which she now perceived had followed his admiration of Ophelia yet experienced much painful emotion from the perusal of this letter the contents of which she prudently concealed even from Clara.

The most agitating moments of her present life were those in which she received from the hands of the servant the post bag (or rather as was oftener the case, watched the more eager Clara as she opened it) with anxiety and a presentiment of uneasiness which almost deprived her of power to break the seal of the letters which were addressed to herself.

But with what unusual trembling is she seized as the black seal of a well remembered form announced to her from across the table the hand of Sidney ere it met her eyes. Clara saw that she struggled to conceal her emotion and in silence retired that she might with liberty at first peruse a letter which was probably the herald of Dallamore's intentions, nay of Dallamore himself.

No sooner was Selena alone than the tears which she before felt ready to burst forth had she uttered a single word now flowed plenteously affording a sweet and salutary relief. Fearful of interruption she put the letter into her bosom and hastened to a sheltered spot in the shrubbery where she seemed to breathe more freely and there eagerly examined the contents of Sidney's letter who thus addressed her as he believed for the last time.

Dublin March

"My dear Selena,

"The fate which has still seemed to frustrate every intention that I may have had in any way to serve you has now pursued me hither and on my arrival at Merrion Square I found that Dallamore had a few hours before sailed for Holyhead. The object of my journey is however doubtless fulfilled and Dallamore, who heard from me of your retiring to Derbyshire, has probably reached Hillbarton before this. Nevertheless is it possible that in his usual inactive mode of reading letters this intimation may have escaped him in which case he may have proceeded to London. I think it therefore better to acquaint you that he has left Dublin that Robert may inform him where you are. As my Mother will now think it expedient to remove from Mount Villars I am under a necessity of immediately joining her. I can hear nothing that is pleasant of young Bently nor can I discover whether he accompanied Dallamore but for his own sake and that of poor Ophelia I sincerely hope he has not remained in Ireland. Your lot is now for ever decided, may you my dear Selena never regret that you rejected the counsel of him who was not merely selfish, since he would have perished with joy could he thus have purchased happiness for you and tho' now condemned never to witness it, that happiness shall still be the object of his most ardent wishes.

"Farewell!

Sidney Dallamore"

The bitterness with which Sidney had written the cruel word which closed his letter seemed to have left behind some portion of its poison.

Selena looked around her with a kind of fearful anguish.

She seemed already to hear the step of Dallamore's approach and to hear faintly uttered the last sigh of this eternal farewell from Sidney whom she was never again to behold. Every object around her looked gay; the soft gales of an almost premature spring breathed on her keenly shooting temples. The deep blue stream danced gaily in the sunbeams that called forth the early fragrance of the first violets, primroses and the young shoots of the sweet briar hedge while the hepeticas and the crocus in large spots formed a splendid mixture of the most glowing gold and purple. The robin had resumed his cheerful song and seemed to vie with the blackbird who should first hail the Spring from the branches of the hazel which profusely hung out the tender green of its calkins in graceful festoons.

Who has not experienced at times as tho' the cheerfulness of nature mocked his sadness? To Selena these lively scenes of universal animation appeared oppressive as the song of joy or the tale of mirth to the suffering ear of the agonising patient. She seemed as if no longer alone—her feelings were restrained and bewildered and when a sudden pang again reminded her that she was not her own, that enchained for life she had lost even the privilege of lamenting him whom she was no more to see, she started from her seat resolving to fly from Dallamore and a fate which appeared to her at that moment worse than Death.

Gradually the calm of resignation once more stole into her bosom; Her soul which a few minutes before had sunk despondent and desolate now called forth all its energy in self consolation which in so many situations is the great part of Virtue.

"I shall see thee no more dear Sidney," she continued, "deservedly dear! amiable, generous as thou art! I have lost thee then for ever! But all is not lost in life, much yet remains: the remembrances that now torment me, the idea that I might have been more happy shall soon fade away, my heart again shall open to enjoyment! & I shall smile to think how an imagination a dream has been able to render it thus cast down and disquieted."

Yet it was vainly that she repeated this incessantly to herself, a secret internal power seemed mournfully to deny the possibility of future pleasure, nay to revolt with disgust from the hope of ever being comforted by the medicine of Indifference.

Chapter VI

> Domestic bliss! thou only good
> Of Paradise that has survived the fall!
> Thou art not known where Pleasure is adored
> That reeling Goddess with the zoneless waist
> And wandering eyes—Still leaning on the arm
> Of Novelty, her fickle frail support.
> Cowper[23]

---

[23] William Cowper, *The Task* (1785), 3.41–2, 51–4 (line 41 should read "Domestic happiness, thou only bliss").

While Selena thus struggled by every effort of Reason, Virtue, and Religion to tranquilise her mind, and prepare herself to receive with affection and cheerfulness him whom she considered herself bound chiefly to love, the young Earl of Mount Villars now hastening to London forgetful of Selena and impatient only by change of scene and continual hurry to get rid of the melancholy and troublesome impression by which the scene he had last witnessed still tormented his mind.

There was nothing which Dallamore had ever so much disliked as being compelled to remain any where, let the situation be in itself ever so well suited to his inclination. But to feel himself constrained not to quit the chamber of suffering and of sorrow was a pennance too heavy to be long endured and had not death in a few days released them both from their misery Lord Mount Villars had been denied in his last moments the consolation of beholding the tears of unaffected grief which bathed the cheeks of a beloved son as he received the dying pressure of his hand.

Anxious as Lord Mount Villars had formerly been to divert Dallamore's mind from Selena he yet never once alluded to her during his last illness, tho' perfectly aware of his own danger and Dallamore wholly engrossed by the new and disagreeable sensations which assailed him in the strange shapes of confinement and affliction, thought of nothing but how he might soonest escape from his own uncomfortable reflections, for which purpose he had with indecent precipitation left the abode which now appeared to him the most gloomy and detestable he had ever inhabited—hurrying to London, with all the speed which a fair wind and four post horses could effect.

The rapidity of motion, the many hours sleep which Leader's softest cushions and easiest springs naturally afforded, and the amusement found in the profligate pages of a new french romance all combined to aid his own endeavours so that by the time he approached his usual lodgings in Pall Mall the late Lord Mount Villars was as little regretted, as tho' his title and estate had descended to the most rapacious heir.

We must nevertheless do Dallamore the justice to affirm that this oblivion of indifference would as surely and as speedily have arrived had he by the death of his father lost a property equal to that of which this event now gave him the possession.

Indeed Dallamore was gifted by nature in a most eminent degree with that happy independence with which it is the highest effort of piety and has so often been the vain boast of philosophy to arm the more feeling soul, upon which

> Or grief or joy,
> Should leave no deeper prints than air retains
> Where fly alike the vulture and the Dove
> And leave no trace.[24]

---

[24]   Mariamne in Elijah Fenton's *Mariamne* (1723), 1.4.110–13 (line 111 uses "make" for "leave" and line 112 uses "fleet" for "fly").

It was early in the evening when Dallamore arrived at Pall Mall. Le Roi who had returned to town to await his master's orders (after having conducted Selena safe to Hillbarton) now with surprise beheld him unaccompanied by his lady. He followed him up stairs and perceived that he had thrown himself in an arm chair by the fire and was continuing the book which he had brought from the chaise in his hand. After some hesitation Le Roi ventured to enquire whether My Lord had dined. A single no was all the reply and that pronounced in a manner so *distrait*[25] that Le Roi doubted if the question had even been heard. After stirring the fire he therefore again took courage to interrupt his studies and enquired in rather a timid voice, "Whether my Lord would please to dine at home and if my Lady was expected that day?"

"Good God that's true," cried Dallamore starting up and throwing aside the book, "where does Selena live?"

"My Lady," answered Le Roi suppressing his astonishment, "has been at Hillbarton near a month and Mr. Dallamore informed me that he had written to acquaint your Lordship and that your Lordship would call for my Lady on your way from Ireland."

"I'll be hanged if he did tho'," impatiently interrupted Dallamore tho' but half assured of the truth of this asseveration adding eagerly, "get me a hackney coach directly, I must go look for Sidney."

"Mr. Dallamore left London last week and I am surprised your Lordship did not meet him on the road."

"Why is he gone to Ireland then?"

"So I understand my Lord."

"Was there ever any thing so provoking! And is Selena gone with him?"

"Oh no my Lord she is with Mrs. Vallard in Derbyshire. I rode down there after my Lady and Miss Clara—and my Lady expected that your Lordship would have called there."

Le Roi added not without design this latter supposition which it is most certain Selena had never expressed to him. He indeed thought it extremely probable that the orders for horses would immediately follow—nor was he deceived.

"Well Le Roi," said Dallamore resuming his book and his seat, "we must set off tomorrow: see that you have every thing ready at twelve o'clock."

"When will your Lordship please to have dinner?" Dallamore began to whistle. "It is very near seven o'clock my Lord," continued Le Roi.

"What day is this?" demanded Dallamore after a long pause.

"Tuesday My Lord."

"Where's the newspaper? Does Banti[26] sing to night?"

---

[25]   Distrait: distracted (OED).

[26]   The celebrated Italian singer Brigada Georgi Banti frequently performed in England during the 1790s.

"She does my Lord," said Le Roi hesitating as he handed him the paper whether he should take the liberty to remind him of the extreme indecorum of his yet appearing in public.

But while he was debating his master exclaimed, "Get the room ready and order a coach I will go dress, and I can dine at Brookes's since it is so late."

Le Roi depended upon some other interference and was willing to save himself a remonstrance so delicate.

In the coffy-room where Dallamore now ordered his dinner he was accosted by a Mr. Rainsford who was just arrived in London from abroad and who not meeting there as he had expected his family was well pleased to see Dallamore whose character he well remembered would allow of his fastning himself upon him while he remained in town. Dallamore had liked him from a boy and met his salutation with almost equal pleasure. After dinner by mutual consent they adjourned to the opera, to which indeed Dallamore had every year been able to admit several, from the total impossibility he found to resist the request of any Lady who required his name to complete her subscription.

"For Heaven's sake Dallamore who is that lovely creature in mourning?" asked Mr. Rainsford as he pointed to one of the pit boxes nearest the door where Lady Harriet displayed her charms with the least possible disguise save that which her great grandmothers the Picts were accustomed to employ at once as ornament and covering.[27]

Dallamore for an instant turned his eyes as directed and as hastily withdrew them, making use of an exclamation so little to the credit of his politeness or respect for one of the fair sex that we shall not venture to repeat it lest the reader (tho' we trust less an admirer of Lady Harriet than Mr. Rainsford) should yet possibly prove more fastidious and not like him receive it with a smile.

"She has been cruel to you I conclude Mount Villars," replied his friend, "for I can account for your dislike of so fine a woman in no other way."

"Cruel! no d--m it! I'll bet you a hundred guineas that she is in love with me before I leave the house if I chuse it."

Mr. Rainsford declined the bet, thinking it not improbable that to all appearance (which alone could decide the bet) the attacks of the young Earl might not prove unsuccessful upon an object whose dress and manners certainly did not justify the supposition that she possessed any of that outrageous virtue which would repel an insult of this nature with indignation, nor even that delicacy which might shrink disgusted from the assurance of impertinence.

But he was not the less anxious for an introduction and expressed for this purpose so many provoking doubts of the possibility of Dallamore's being well received that he at length succeeded in engaging him to make the trial

---

[27]   The Picts were a group of Celtic tribes who inhabited Scotland from before the Roman invasion till the tenth century (when they were assimilated), sometimes described as wearing little clothing to conceal their painted and tattooed bodies.

Arm in arm they approached Lady Harriet's box, who being fortunately unattended by any except Mr. Leeson, received the new Earl of Mount Villars with more gracious looks than she had been used to bestow upon Dallamore.

"Pray my Lord," said she with a contemptuous half suppressed smile after the first salutations & expressions of surprise at seeing him in town, "may I ask you what you have done with your wife?"

Here Rainsford (who had already exchanged some expressive glances with her Ladyship which sufficiently declared his ambition of being better known) seized on this opportunity of becoming a party in the conversation by exclaiming in an audible whisper to Dallamore while his eyes remained fixed on Lady Harriet, "What the Devil are you married then?"

"Has not Lord Mount Villars introduced you to his lady?" said Lady Harriet rolling her large majestic eyes upon Mr. Rainsford as Homer has so frequently represented his Juno while addressing her Thunderer.[28]

Mr. Rainsford now approached nearer to that part of the box occupied by her Ladyship and ventured upon this encouragement in a half timid half smiling manner to ask her some information with respect to Lady Mount Villars.

Lady Harriet all condescension leaned over the box and continued the conversation with her new beau in a strain of raillery which piqued Dallamore who had approached her with the professed view of proving his powers of insinuation.

He therefore exerted himself unusually to interrupt the attention which she devoted to Mr. Rainsford, and engross it on himself.

Lady Harriet failed not to perceive this; indeed what is there (that is at all capable of being construed into flattery) which can ever escape the notice of a vain woman? And on this occasion her vanity was singularly flattered and the more perhaps from her having so little expected a compliment from Dallamore.

She hesitated not therefore to accept his overtures with a marked preference and turning from Mr. Rainsford said with a gracious smile, "Are you not tired of standing there my Lord?"

"Most confoundedly."

"Besides you are just in the way and now the dance is going to begin you will be pushed to death."

Dallamore had already begun to feel his situation irksome and was on the very point of retiring to a bench which he perceived vacant in the pit at some distance when Lady Harriet made the well timed offer of a place in her box which after some hesitation he accepted not meeting any thing to divert his intention of so doing in the passage between the pit and the door of her Ladyship's box.

Mr. Rainsford kept his station till at the instigation of Dallamore he was properly presented to Lady Harriet and invited to her box where a very animated conversation commenced and was carried on with more spirit than wit, decency or good nature.

---

[28]   A quick reference to Homer's treatment of Juno in *The Iliad* (800 BC).

Mr. Leeson who consoled himself for the total neglect with which he was treated by collecting anecdotes where with to embellish his future volubility having gathered to his extreme surprise that Lord Mount Villars was actually married to the sister-in-law of Lady Harriet, now requested to know whether he had yet taken a house and if her Ladyship was come to town.

"A house!" exclaimed Lady Harriet, "no I assure you, Lord Mount Villars chuses that *his* wife should live toad eater[29] to Lady Trevallyn."

Dallamore whistled, his usual reply when annoy'd.

"Is Lady Mount Villars then in Grosvenor square?" asked Mr. Leeson.

"No, no, I suppose he has ordered her off now that he is come to town himself."

"I shall not be many hours in town however," said Dallamore dryly.

"Why where are you going?" eagerly exclaimed both Lady Harriet and Mr. Rainsford in one breath.

"Down to Derbyshire for Selena to be sure."

"And pray where do you mean to bring her to?" asked Lady Harriet with a displeasure she vainly sought to disguise. This was a point Dallamore had not considered. "I think it would be as well if your Lordship were to take a house before you go," continued she maliciously resolving to oppose what she thought tended to Selena's happiness.

"Oh I can easily get a house tomorrow morning."

"Nothing upon earth more easy," eagerly cried Mr. Leeson, "if your Lordship will but allow me to call upon you after breakfast I think I can shew you two or three of as pleasantly situated houses as any in London and your Lordship may chuse ...."

"No bad plan faith," interrupted Dallamore ever caught by any scheme likely to produce expence.

"Take my advice then," said Lady Harriet disdainfully, "and let some one else give their opinion or ten to one Selena may not like either your choice or Mr. Leeson's."

"Well will you chuse it?" said Dallamore carelessly.

"With all my heart," answered Lady Harriet triumphing in the success of her malice. "I will call on you in the carriage at about two o'clock to morrow."

"I shall take care to meet your Ladyship at my Lord's lodgings punctually," said Mr. Leeson. "Two o'clock my Lord," repeated he unwilling to let drop a bustling appointment like this so much to his heart's content.

"Oh I shall be gone before two o'clock."

"Pooh! ridiculous!" cried Lady Harriet, "you have a thousand things to do before you can leave town. I dare say you have not bespoke a carriage yet and no time is to be lost if you have a mind Selena should have it while she is in town."

"You will allow me my Lord," again interrupted Mr. Leeson, "to accompany you to Long Acre—there is a carriage at Godsals that the Dutchess of ..."

---

[29] Toad eater: humble friend or dependant; specifically a female companion or attendant; used contemptuously (OED).

"Well, well," said Lady Harriet impatiently, "never mind your dutchesses we will go there tomorrow after you have brought us to those wonderful houses."

"I beg I may be allowed to be of the party," said Mr. Rainsford smiling.

"By all means," answered Lady Harriet, "you shall give us a breakfast Lord Mount Villars at your lodgings and you shall dine with me tomorrow that we may settle all about what servants we should hire for Selena and a thousand things that will be necessary before she can come to town. In the evening I am to have a rehearsal and you shall be one of us if you like."

"A Rehearsal!" cried Dallamore, "why are you going to act?"

"Oh Lord we have been acting all the winter and we are just now going to get up the prettiest farce in the world in two acts written for us on purpose by Mr. L—. You have no idea how beautiful our dresses are. I assure you they are infinitely more magnificent than any you see there on the stage."

"What for the farce?"

"Oh Lord you don't imagine we act any vulgar low-life characters."

"And does Miltern act?" asked Dallamore considerably taken by the novelty thus offered.

"Oh Good God no; what could he act. Besides he has left town; otherwise I promise you there would have been no rehearsal in Upper Brook street tomorrow. We are to meet to settle about it at Lady Vellum's to night, you shall come and sup there with us and I can tell you who you will hear sing there …"

"Yes," interrupted Mr. Leeson, "I can answer for young Stanmore's being there positively to night, for I dined with him in a large party to day, and Lord Antry and Colonel Sutton swore they would not stir without him and they have resolved he should go."

"Young Stanmore is a friend of yours, is not he?" said Lady Harriet to Dallamore who in the midst of a freely indulged yawn answered, "Upon my soul I don't remember."

"You don't remember! Well you are the saddest animal! Why you have spent God knows how long in his house."

"Very possibly."

"Fortunately for him however," said Lady Harriet significantly, "Selena's memory is not quite so short, I fancy she has not forgotten her residence at Inverathie and Mr. Edwin Stanmore's compliments."

"Good Lord I remember Edwin Stanmore to be sure. What brought him to London?"

"Nay," said Lady Harriet, "I believe you must ask Selena that."

"Well," cried Dallamore without attending to her, "I would go any where to hear him sing again tho' I had as lieve be d--d as see Lady Vellum. It makes me so cursed sick to look at her."

Determined to obstruct his joining Selena Lady Harriet exerted all her powers to amuse Dallamore, and proposed numerous plans to all of which he acceded thoughtless of the impediments which they must throw in the way of his journey.

She brought him in her carriage to Lady Vellum's where they entered just as all was hushed and still in expectation of Edwin's song.

Surrounded as he was by his enthusiastic admirers, he perceived not Dallamore who irresistibly enchanted remained motionless till Edwin arose from the piano-forte and was then advancing to shake hands with him when Edwin suddenly started and overwhelmed with a tumultuous tide of recollections which Dallamore's appearance had at once excited, trembling at the possibility of beholding Selena and totally mastered by his feelings, without attempting one excuse rushed out of the assembly.

Lady Harriet who had not quitted the side of Dallamore burst into a loud laugh. "You have terrified him my Lord, can you guess how?"

"Upon my soul I cannot conceive," answered he still looking after him, tho' more entertained than surprised, since surprise was an emotion he scarcely ever experienced, observing for the most part literally Horace's universal receipt for happiness.[30]

Lady Harriet failed not now to profit by the opportunity which this precipitate retreat had afforded to throw out hints which might certainly have aroused the curiosity of a more suspicious or a more attentive auditor, but on her examining the countenance of Dallamore to discover the effect produced by her artful insinuations, she had the mortification to be convinced that he had not even heard one syllable she had uttered, so completely was he engrossed by tracing carefully with his little switch the minute pattern of a very beautiful Axminster carpet.

Lady Harriet was not long before she discovered that to support a lively tete-a-tete conversation with Dallamore in public required powers which she at least possessed not, and that the secret of amusing him lay in performing a kind of farce of which he should be the sole theme; This was indeed the only method of keeping alive his attention, while without feeling constrained to supply any part of the conversation, he should be insensibly inclined from the gaiety around to furnish by his occasional singular remarks subjects for a sort of universal raillery which seldom fails to flatter the self love of the object to whom it is addressed, if their self confidence assures them that they are not a but for contempt. Gratified by the hopes of retaining in her suite an admirer of so much consequence as the young Earl of Mount Villars, Lady Harriet employed all her talents to provide him with amusement. Nor was it without some kind of success, since he remained to a late hour in her circle and if he thought of her at all as he returned home, it was as an "uncommonly clever pleasant woman."

As Le Roi had received no contradictory orders, he had prepared every thing with secret satisfaction for his master's departure, and at eleven o'clock the following morning entered his apartment and opened his shutters.

Perceiving that Dallamore heard his intonation of the hour without betraying the least inclination to rise he after waiting impatiently for some time ventured to

---

[30] "Nil admirari": In *The Epistles* (20 BC), 1.6 Horace advises Numicius "To marvel at nothing."

remind him of his having a journey to perform—adding, "I daresay my Lady will expect to see your Lordship every hour."

The lovely gentle image of Selena which had gradually faded from the mind of Dallamore was yet occasionally revived and always with a kind of sweet and pleasing emotion more delightful to him than any other idea which his senses or imagination ever suggested.

Totally forgetful of the engagements which he had formed the preceeding evening & stimulated by the words of Le Roi he now conquered the reluctance he felt to rise occasioned by the late hour at which he had sought repose and had nearly breakfasted when Mr. Rainsford entered the room exclaiming, "Why what the Devil whim is this? Do you drive about town in the morning with four post-horses?"

"No," answered Dallamore with the utmost indifference as he fastened his knee buttons, "Do not you know I am going to Derbyshire?"

"To Derbyshire! What before you have looked at the house and bought the jewels you were talking of! Sure you can't do any thing so shabby?"

"Oh curse the house! I should like indeed to get these Emeralds Lady Harriet told me of—where did she say they were?"

"Oh quite close at Wirgman's here in St James's street, let us come."

Dallamore hesitated and Le Roi who listened not without some fears of the delay now hastened to announce to his master that every thing was ready.

"And pray have you sent an apology to Lady Harriet?"

"Not I. Do you think she expects me?"

"Do I think it? Well I never heard any thing so savage in my life! Oh here is Mr. Leeson," continued Rainsford as they already heard their loquacious companion on the stairs with impetuous volubility enquiring from Le Roi for what purpose the chaise had been ordered.Lady Harriet who was not totally unsuspicious of Dallamore's departure in spite of his promised attendance, had given Mr. Leeson a hint to call on him early and he now poured forth such a torrent of intelligence with respect to houses, jewellers, equipage &c that poor Dallamore totally unable to reply or resist was forcibly overcome and tacitly consented to the orders which were heard by Le Roi with a regret and indignation which it required the utmost efforts of his discretion to disguise.

Thus day after day was Dallamore seduced to pass in the most vicious part of that society esteemed good company in London. He was indeed deluded into the idea that he was acting towards Selena in the most generous and flattering manner because he had sanctioned every order for the most expensive ornaments, equipage, and establishment that Luxury could devise. He had dispatched expresses to Hillbarton absolutely loaded with trinkets of immense value; but unaccompanied by a single line. He had indeed tormented and wearied the patience of Lady Harriet by the incessant repetition of messages which he had not the smallest doubt she faithfully delivered to Selena and he had received in return many imaginary commissions of the most absurd and expensive nature which were executed with scarcely less satisfaction than the invention of them had afforded amusement to Lady Harriet and her confederate—Mr. Rainsford, who entered greedily into all her schemes even before he was aware of the extent of her design. They were also considerably assisted in the project of detaining Dallamore by the co-operation of Mr. Richmond who was returned to London with his pretty, silly, but alas! *un heiress'd* Lady Lucy.

Lord Clonagh who had long remained a widower thro' partial fondness for his daughter had indeed married a captivating young woman in the first transports of his indignation at her undutiful and deceitful conduct and had been impatient to announce to the world the prospect in which he already exulted of his lineage being strengthened and his title preserved. The disappointed Richmond defeated in all his deep laid strategems gladly seized upon an opportunity of once more sharing Dallamore's superfluities and supported with all his ingenuity every effort made towards disuniting him from the innocent Selena against whom he secretly bore the most inveterate malice.

The magnificent preparations which with the busy assistance of the officious Mr. Leeson had already been made for the reception of the young countess who tho' so many months a wife was now to commence her state of bridal splendour filled the breast of Lady Harriet with an envy which she not only found insurmountable, but was resolved to gratify. The many valuable presents which during her selection of beautiful trinkets she had already received from Dallamore, had but inflamed her desire of commanding for ever the rich fountains of this overflowing generosity. Her efforts to ensnare Dallamore had hitherto been rewarded with the most flattering success. Every scheme which she had laid for the direction of his conduct had been adopted and every bait for his seduction to expensive riot swallowed if not with eagerness at least without resistance.

Mean while she was not without some apprehensions lest Mrs. Vallard should bring Selena to town, or that Sidney's return might at once demolish all her well laid structure and annihilate her hopes. She had also received from Robert a pretty peremptory refusal of supplying her with remittance while he reminded her of her engagement to follow him to Miltern Abbey. The Easter holidays too were fast approaching which occasioned a division of their more private society from the number of parties formed for passing a few days with those who possessed villas near town. All these reasons urged Lady Harriet to form a plan which with some difficulty she at last effected—a select set was invited to Miltern Abbey, of those whose scrupulous delicacy did not oppose their accompanying the lady without having received a direct invitation from the master of the mansion. Among these were of course included Mr. Richmond and Lady Lucy with the great projecter Mr. Rainsford.

Splendid dresses, and expensive scenery for the continuation of the private theatricals were the theme of every conversation at which Dallamore was present and Lady Harriet having assured him of Selena's cheerful consent to meet them at Miltern Abbey which she always preferred to London, Dallamore was easily prevailed upon to consent to drive her Ladyship thither in his curricle. The splendid dresses and the expensive scenery became then something more substantial

than the mere theme of conversation for no sooner was Dallamore engaged in
a scheme than all difficulties which money could obviate vanished into air. The
costly decorations, for the projected theatre, with the party, which was composed
of such as knew no pleasures but these of vice and extravagance were already on
the road with the deluded Dallamore before Lady Harriet apprized her husband of
the guests he was to expect, apprehensive lest he should take some measures to
defeat her intention.

The indignation of Robert at the imprudent depravity of his wife and her
associates could only be equalled by the astonishment with which he perceived
them accompanied by Dallamore.

"I should have expected my Lord," said he in a voice of suppressed displeasure
as the Earl advanced to shake hands with him, "I should have expected that my
sister might have been your companion in the first visit with which you should
have honoured me."

"Good God," cried Dallamore who now for the first time since they left London
was reminded of Selena, "Why I thought she would have been here before us!
What is not she come yet?"

"Here!" replied Robert with surprise, "had you any reason to expect she should?"

"To be sure I have, Lady Harriet settled every thing for our meeting here, it was
Selena's own choice or I am sure I should not have thought of it."

Incredulous as Robert was as to Selena's approbation of so strange an
arrangement especially considering her total silence to him, he yet forbore any
farther comments at present until he should be able to receive from Lady Harriet
some explanation of the reasons which had induced her to include Dallamore in
the group of vice and folly by which she was surrounded.

Lady Harriet had however a thousand reasons to dread a private interview
with her husband which she avoided with all imaginable care and in the riotous
confusion which it was her interest to promote the gloomy displeasure with which
Robert shunned his unwelcome guests and refused to partake of their amusements,
was but little noticed by some among whom was Dallamore and to those who
possessed more penetration it afforded only matter for derision.

Mean while Lady Harriet was not idle—the moments were precious, and the
golden opportunity was improved with more eagerness from the dread of some
eclaircissement between Dallamore and Robert which would so probably defeat
all her plans. The weather for the early season was uncommonly fine—and even
admitted of a party being formed upon the water the day after their arrival. Robert
declined accompanying them as Lady Harriet indeed wished—and at her orders
they were rowed to a romantic spot buried in wood upon the edge of the Wye. Here
they came on shore, and found a table spread with refreshments in a kind of hut
which appeared a temporary addition to another not much larger inhabited by one
of the wood rangers.

After some time Lady Harriet had the address to separate the party and having
then desired Dallamore to observe the various inscriptions which the table, the

trees and the bench on which they were seated yet bore, she asked him with a malicious smile "could he guess to whom this passionate language was addressed."

While she spoke her finger which pointed out the name of Selena precluded the necessity of his exercising his sagacity to divine who had been the Goddess of this idoletry.

"It was here," continued Lady Harriet, "that the all seducing Edwin Stanmore consol'd Selena for your absence. It was here that he concealed himself during her residence at the Abbey and it was in this very hut that he passed the severest weather of last winter."

"Pooh," cried Dallamore incredulously still occupied in endeavouring to read some lines which he had just discovered on the table, "you don't mean I hope that he slept in this hole."

"I can easily convince you of that," said Lady Harriet advancing to the door of the adjoining cottage desiring Dallamore to follow her.

Here she interrogated the wood ranger and his wife who both confirmed her assertion, adding many particulars with respect to Edwin's strange conduct and his nightly rambles among the woods which encircled the Abbey. Lady Harriet failed not to represent to Dallamore that a young man of Edwin's profligate character could hardly be supposed to sacrifice himself thus without some reward for the hardship he endured and indeed the romantic passion which Edwin then felt could be but little comprehended by either.

But this was not all. The note was then produced written by Selena from the cottage near Glocester where she mentioned her overturn and her having been obliged to pass the night there with Clara, Sidney, and Edwin. This Lady Harriet had carefully preserved and it now served to corroborate her testimony that Edwin had been the companion of her journey, while in the most artful manner she misrepresented their separation from her.

She had yet another proof. Mrs. Millikin was called upon as a witness to declare that she had repeatedly seen Miss Miltern meet the young gentleman in the wood, who lived in that hut.

Dallamore felt secretly assured in his own mind of the innocence of Selena, but he could not reply to evidence so strong and had they been much weaker he had not the smallest inclination to be at the trouble of sifting the affair to the bottom in order to be convinced of the truth. Lady Harriet's personal attractions had bewilder'd his senses, and given her a transient ascendancy over his mind which she was herself conscious could be but of short duration. It was her object to bring every thing therefore speedily to a crisis, and taking it for granted that he was now satisfied that by renouncing Selena he could do her no injustice, it only remained to prevail upon him to accept the compensation which Lady Harriet was willing to offer him for the wife whom she had so fully proved to be undeserving of the title.

Chapter VII

Her lovely downcast eyes
That used to gladden each beholder's heart
Now wash the flinty bosom of the earth,
Her troubled breast heaves with incessant sighs
Which drink the purple streams of life, and blast
Her bloom—as storms the blossom of the spring.

Lillo[31]

Selena mean time totally ignorant of all which had passed was almost wearied with the various conjectures formed by Mrs. Vallard and her sister, who vainly strove to solve the mystery of Dallamore's conduct, while presents of such value continually arrived all addressed to the Countess of Mount Villars and all unaccompanied by any explanation or apology for the absence of him who to all appearance should have been their fittest bearer. Selena herself attempted not to account for what was indeed inexplicable and silently endeavoured to seek composure by diverting her mind from what she could not but esteem so glaring an absurdity and such an evident token of indifference in him whom she wished if possible to love and honour.

Her anxiety for Lady Trevallyn was a still more insurmountable bar to her tranquility. Her last letters which contained several hints as to her knowledge of Lord Henry's baseness to Angela for which she was prepared to be called to an account by her friend remained on the contrary unanswered, and Selena was considering how far (circumstanced as she was, separated from Lady Trevallyn and uncertain of the extent of her danger) she was authorized to communicate all she knew when the papers announced that the Earl and Countess of Trevallyn had quitted town with an intention of spending the Easter at Trevallyn hall. That the Earl should undertake such a journey at a time of year so unusual, and that her friend should leave London without informing her of their intentions, appeared so improbable that Selena was inclined to suppose there must surely have been some mistake in the assertion, tho' the strange silence of Lady Trevallyn rendered her quite uncertain what she should believe.

The preceding day had been so extremely wet that it precluded the possibility of Selena's visiting the school according to her daily custom, she therefore intended to devote to the girls the whole of this morning and as soon as breakfast was over hastened to Esselberrie having put a few books in her workbasket which she wished to exchange for some others in Lady Trevallyn's study.

Her little pupils crowded around her upon her entrance each ambitious to express their joy at again seeing her and to inform her how much they had been disappointed the day before when they heard that Lord Trevallyn had arrived during the preceeding night but found that my Lady had not come with him.

---

[31]   Maria in George Lillo's *Arden of Feversham* (1762), 4.2.3–8.

"Are you sure," said Selena to the Mistress, "that Lady Trevallyn is not also arrived?"

"Oh for certain Madam, she would have been down here long afore this time had she been with my Lord."

"Yesterday was so wet," answered Selena, "that it might possibly have prevented her going out."

"True Madam, but I saw my Lord's own gentleman and he informed me, as how my Lady was still in town, and besides just after you were gone from here on Tuesday Mr. Rawlins came in and told us that he had orders to prepare every thing for my Lord's reception that night, but no mention whatever was made of my Lady, and Mr. Rawlins thought as how if he could have seen you Madam that perhaps you might have heard somewhat."

While they were yet speaking, the sound of a carriage attracted their attention and Selena in the sudden idea of the possibility of beholding her friend just arrived sprung forward to an opening in the plantation from whence she could distinguish whatever passed the gate of the avenue. The instant she reached it the chaise drove out and she plainly distinguished that it contained only Lord Trevallyn and Mr. Guise. Unwilling to be seen by them she shrunk back and upon enquiry found that Mr. Guise had alone attended Lord Trevallyn from town the night before and that they were now only gone some miles from Esselberrie.

She resolved to seize the opportunity of their absence to go to the study, recollecting that she had left there a little manuscript book in which she had copied some passages which had particularly pleased her from the books she had read during her visits at Esselberrie. Having reached the end of the green house she stopped thinking that she heard a noise in the dressing room within. She listened a while but all was still and as she remembered to have observed from the lawn that the windows of those apartments were unopened she advanced with the less fear of meeting any of Lord Trevallyn's attendants; but determined to retreat should she hear any one she unlocked the door cautiously with as little noise as possible, and softly putting by a part of the thick silk curtain which hung before it looked in and beheld to her astonishment by the light of a single candle which stood on the bible the figure of Lady Trevallyn, seated on the floor, wrapped in a long white dressing gown. Her beautiful hair negligently fell over her shoulders till it swept the ground and her head supported by the sopha reclined upon those arms whose transparent delicacy exceeded the purity of the dew-bleached wax, and in a whiteness rivalled the unsunned snow.

The shutters being close shut the gloom of the chamber as Selena entered from the full glare of day made her for a moment suspect the evidence of her eyes. Breathless with a sudden dread she remained motionless awhile but on her exclaiming, "Heavens! what is the matter?" Lady Trevallyn instantly started and turning round to gaze on Selena clasped her hands with an emotion of joyful surprise.

Selena flew to embrace her weeping friend who while she flung her arms around her and fondly pressed her to her heart in a soft voice entreated her to be cautious lest they might be overheard and then hastened to fasten the door which led from thence to the study.

She then in broken sentences answered the eager enquiries of Selena respecting the sad mystery which hung over her concealment at Esselberrie, confessing to her that Mr. Guise had at length succeeded in his malicious designs of awaking the jealousy of Lord Trevallyn who after much reproachful language insisted upon her taking a solemn oath that she would never again speak to Lord Henry.

"And you refused!" exclaimed Selena grasping her hand and gazing upon her with a look expressive of earnest and fearful tenderness.

"Oh Selena," cried Lady Trevallyn as she hid her face upon her shoulder, "I could not! indeed I could not, never, never will I make such a promise. Besides what would that have been but a confession of the guilt with which I was innocently charged. I never injured Lord Trevallyn! While I am called by his name, while he claims me as his wife, I never could be another's, but my heart was wedded, early wedded to its only, its eternally espoused love! Of one single act do I reproach myself when in an evil hour I perjured myself by uttering in the sight of Heaven vows which my heart abhorred and solemnly renounced him for whom alone I live. Never no never will I repeat the hateful promise."

Selena shuddered at the consequences of this fatal derangement of mind, for which she considered her indulgence of so miserable a sentiment, and after a short silence enquired what were Lord Trevallyn's intentions.

"I know not exactly," answered she, "he has not condescended to explain himself, but in the fury which succeeded my refusal he talked of perpetually confining me; at Trevallyn hall I think it was."

She then continued to inform Selena that this demand had been made on her return from an assembly; and that having watched her strictly as she supposed lest she should write to any one she was at that late hour compelled to accompany him and Mr. Guise to Northampton where they remained till the next evening Lord Trevallyn not chusing that they should be seen upon the road. That on their arrival at Esselberrie she found a strange female servant was appointed to attend her, but she had the satisfaction to perceive that her own apartments were those now allotted for her reception, probably on account of their being separated from the rest of the house by the corridore. Lord Trevallyn she observed had certainly sent down an express with orders previously, as the windows which opened on the ground were all made fast with bars and locks to prevent as she supposed her escape.

"Oh," cried Selena secretly trembling at the idea, "he could not surely think you meditated any thing so rash, but perhaps he feared you might be seen, since your being here is I believe known to very few servants. But how can you account for the door to the green house being thus unsecured?"

"I know not," answered she, "when first Lord Trevallyn came in he examined that door and finding it locked enquired for the key. I referred him to Rawlins, who I suppose gave him his own key and either forgot mine or was afraid to mention his having sent it to you."

Selena endeavoured to sooth the agitation, and comfort the affliction in which she found her friend by the prospect which accident thus happily afforded them of being able to pass the greatest part of their hours together even should Lord Trevallyn persist in his design of totally secluding her from society, and she secretly felt assured that the required promise would speedily be given when she had communicated Angela's Manuscript, which she as yet forebore thinking that already, "Fate had rebuked her sharply for her easiness"[32] and that the first shock of her present situation was in some measure abated, she might be better able to bear the salutary but cruel conviction of how greatly she had been deceived.

But vain were all of Selena's efforts at consolation! Even her promise of devoting all her hours to cheer her solitude, were received with silent tears and looks of hopeless speechless anguish, tho' at every motion to retire which Selena hinted, fearful of being surprised, she fell into an agony which terrified her friend.

Selena observed that tho' she detained her hand with tenacious fondness, yet abstracted in her own meditations she listened to her with evident inattention and appeared engrossed by her unuttered sadness.

At length after a long silence she requested Selena would if possible herself see Mr. Rawlins immediately and intrust him with the important key desiring him to come to her while Lord Trevallyn was at dinner, but to be cautious and not enter without being assured that she was alone.

Selena, surprised at the confidence which she was about to repose in the steward as it appeared so unnecessarily, remonstrated and expressed her fears lest he might betray her and thus deprive them both of the satisfaction of meeting.

Lady Trevallyn for some time replied only by her tears but when pressed by Selena's tender arguments she at length said that she had always considered Rawlins as particularly attached to her, and had reason to expect much from his gratitude for some services which she had rendered him formerly.

"I have something of consequence," continued she, "now to communicate to him, besides I wish to tell him what he should say, should Lord Trevallyn think of enquiring further respecting this key."

Selena knew not how to refuse but it was with the strongest reluctance that she promised to execute her commission. "So you wish," cried she mournfully, "to exclude me you are weary of my friendship!" Lady Trevallyn's tears fell fast upon the hand of Selena which she held to her lips, but she made no reply.

Alarmed and surprised at what she thought a tacit acknowledgement of so strange an intention Selena exclaimed, "Dearest Lady Trevallyn will you really refuse me the power which chance has so fortunately allowed me of seeing you, can you be so unkind as to wish me to give up the key?"

"Rawlins shall return it to you to-morrow," said Lady Trevallyn at last.

"Do you promise me that faithfully?"

"I do," answered she after a moment's hesitation.

---

[32] Leontine in Nathaniel Lee's *Theodosius* (1680), 2.1.514–16: "Fate is in all our actions, / and methinks, / At least a father judges so, it has / Rebuk'd thee smartly for thy easiness."

"Well then dearest Lady Trevallyn let me now go for fear I should be seen."

"Oh will you! can you leave me!" cried she embracing and clinging to Selena with an earnestness which astonished her, who the moment before had feared that she was willing entirely to renounce her society.

But after a minute relinquishing her grasp, she shrunk back and covered her face with her hands as she cried in a low voice, "Go Selena, I am not worthy to detain you."

"My dear Lady Trevallyn," answered Selena once more seating herself beside her, "you know how gladly I would stay with you for ever, but should we now be surprised ...."

"Yes, yes, you are in the right," interrupted she. "Go Heaven bless you, let what will become of me."

She then sunk upon the sopha reclining her head languidly upon the cushions, and Selena imprinting a kiss upon her forehead retired, softly closing the doors and hastening across the garden fearful of observation.

Returning to the school she enquired where she should be most likely to find Mr. Rawlins and was directed to his office in the yard where he usually past his mornings.

Her long stay had excited no surprise as she was already so much in the habit of spending so many hours in Lady Trevallyn's study; fortunately she found Mr. Rawlins alone; the moment he saw her he appeared aware of what might be the purport of her visit and advancing with an air of mournful mystery closed the door. He then awaited her orders in silence as if fearful of committing himself before he knew how far he might safely venture. Selena took from her pocket the key and with some hesitation presented it to him with his Lady's directions, and requested he might return it to her early in the morning.

With a thoughtful look he remained holding his eyes fixed upon the key and Selena trembled lest he was meditating to deliver it up instantly to his Lord.

At length in a timid voice she asked him softly whether he would certainly not neglect to bring her the key.

"That must be as my Lady pleases Madam."

"But Mr. Rawlins if she wishes it as I am sure she will, you cannot surely deprive her of this small consolation. You will not be so cruel as to betray her."

"Betray her!" repeated he as it were roused from his reverie. "God forbid, I should be such a base monster. No I would serve my Lady to the ruin of myself as well I might, since I owe everything to her goodness, but Madam what will become of my poor family if my Lord should find out, as he must for certain, that I brought about my Lady's escape."

"Escape!" exclaimed Selena absolutely gasping at the idea, the possibility of which she had not dared to suffer into her imagination. "Oh no, no be assured she has no such thought. Where would she escape to?"

Mr. Rawlins shook his head.

"Nay," cried Selena after a pause, "depend upon it you may go in safety. Lady Trevallyn will not treat you ungenerously, and should she hint a desire of your assisting her in this way to fly from Esselberrie, I charge you at your peril as you shall answer for it to Lord Trevallyn and to Heaven itself do not obey her without informing me of it and think me not too presumptuous if I answer for prevailing upon her contentedly to remain. Or should it be otherwise I solemnly promise to take all upon myself and Lady Trevallyn never shall accuse you of infidelity to her, nor my Lord suspect your having any concern whatever in the business."

Tho' Mr. Rawlins did not appear entirely satisfied by her assurances yet he declared his resolution to obey Lady Trevallyn let what would be the consequence and promised instantly to communicate it to Selena should any thing pass between them such as he fearfully anticipated.

Selena then hastened home and as Lady Trevallyn had permitted her immediately informed Mrs. Vallard of what had passed, which confidence she was desirous of making from the impossibility of her otherwise spending as she fully purposed nearly all her time with her unhappy friend till matters wore a more hopeful aspect.

Mrs. Vallard struck with terror at the strange and melancholy situation of her poor Emily saw not at first the fatal errors of her conduct which Selena, keenly as she herself felt them, had been far from pointing out. Prompt to succour the distressed Mrs. Vallard thought only by what means she could snatch Lady Trevallyn from the hands of her tyrant and eagerly entreated Selena to return and offer her an asylum at Hillbarton.

Selena represented prudently how much better it would be if possible to reconcile her to Lord Trevallyn—"let this," cried she, "be her last rescource [sic] as if she must quit Esselberrie happy is it for her that in your friendship she may find such a protection, so soothing for herself so respectable in the eyes of the world such," added she with a tender smile, "as you have already afforded to your poor Selena."

Chapter VIII

> Oh! give me leave awhile! allow
> A little time for Love to make his way
> Hardly he won the place, and many sighs
> And many tears and thousand oaths it cost him
> And Oh I find he will not be dislodged
> Without a groan at parting hence for ever—
> No, no he vows he will not yet be razed
> Without whole floods of grief at his farewell
> Which thus I sacrifice—and Oh I swear
> Had he proved true I would as easily
> Have emptied all my blood and died to serve him
> As now I shed these drops and vent these sighs
> To shew how well, how perfectly I loved him!
>
> Lee[33]

---

[33] Athenais in Nathaniel Lee's *Theodosius; or, The Force of Love* (1680), 2.1.545–57 (the epigraph transforms the first line of Athenais's speech, which reads as "Ah, sir, allow").

Selena concealed from Mrs. Vallard the suspicion which Rawlins had suggested but felt secretly far from satisfied that some such designs had not been agitated in the bosom of her friend, when she reflected on the disposition in which she had left her.

She therefore resolved no longer to defer the full declaration of Angela's story, determining not to wait for Rawlins but the moment it was light the following morning to take with her the important papers and demand from the steward the key that she might lay them before her yet deluded, infatuated friend.

While she was sitting at tea with Mrs. Vallard Selena was told that a person wished to speak to her. She instantly started up, and prepared as she was for some intelligence from Esselberrie she was not surprised to meet Mr. Rawlins on her entering the parlour where he awaited her coming.

"I have made bold Madam," said he looking round carefully to see if they could be overheard, "to trouble you as you desired My Lady being determined to quit Esselberrie." Selena struck to the heart clasped her hands as she sunk upon a chair but had only power faintly to ask him what she had said and he continued, "Why Madam I went to my Lady as you desired as soon as the family were gone to dinner; for My Lord and Mr. Guise went this morning to Sir Hugh Trevor's and are not to return for two days. All was quiet at that part of the house, for my Lady's woman had brought away her dinner untouched some time before, and so as I came to the green house door and found every thing was still I knocked softly as you desired and my Lady who was watching immediately came over and told me as how I might come in; but to be sure I was shocked to see my Lady so much altered. Why she does not look the same as she did no more than any thing and the tears were starting in her eyes all the while as she was talking to me and she trembled from head to foot.

"'Rawlins, said she, speaking low and in a hurried kind of way, 'will you do me a favour of the utmost consequence, which can injure no one but myself and I will reward you to the utmost of my ability. That is not great at present but,' she was pleased to say, 'I know your heart Rawlins and that you will be content in the knowledge of having saved me from death.' 'From Death my Lady,' said I quite terrified, thinking to be sure that my Lord had some very terrible design, for anger will carry some great folk frightful lengths. 'Yes Rawlins,' said she very sad, 'I cannot live this way and you can easily assist me to get way from this prison without any one's knowing you had the least to say to it.'

"I said nothing, for you know Madam, it was not my place to speak, tho' I grieved to think that my Lady who was always so good should intend such a thing that all the world will be for crying shame upon. But it went to my very heart when she cried, 'Oh Rawlins! Sure you will not refuse me! Can you wish me to be buried alive?' Then I ventured to say that I hoped it would please God that my Lord would think better of it; 'No,' cried she, 'you know his disposition too well to think that he will ever give up what he is once fixed upon;' and indeed Madam I could say nothing again that, so I was silent. And my Lady then gave me two letters and bid me put one of them into the post directly; and be careful to take it myself which I did …."

"You did," interrupted Selena with extreme concern and guessing but too well to whom it was addressed. "Oh why would you do that till you had spoken with me?"

"Why Madam to say the truth, I considered that I had no right to betray my Lady's secrets any farther than was absolutely necessary for her own safety and besides she made me promise to take it directly on leaving her otherwise it would have been too late for this night's post, for the mail was just making up when I went."

"And what became of the other?" asked Selena.

"The other Madam is for yourself and I was to give it to you to-morrow with the key, but if you please to take it now here it is"—saying while he presented it to Selena who after some hesitation refused the offer saying, "Mr. Rawlins, it is not mine untill then and Lady Trevallyn may perhaps enquire for it when you return," and then requested Rawlins to tell her what his Lady had farther required from him.

"Why Madam she was pleased to give me a note for the innkeeper at Barton bridge ordering him to have a chaise in waiting, at this side of the turnpike by twelve o'clock tonight."

"To-night!" exclaimed Selena eagerly. "You do not mean this very night."

"Yes Madam for when I made bold just to ask her would not she please to wait even till she had seen you—she shook her head and said, 'Oh no! Rawlins, I have no right to involve Miss Miltern in my misfortunes!' So she would have had me leave the key then with her that I might not come any more, for fear that some one should chance to see me, and so my Lord might come to hear how I was engaged in the business, but I could not think of my Lady's waiting at that late hour alone on the high road for better than a mile, so I told her that I could not do as she would have me, unless she would allow me to see her safe at least to the chaise, and so on considering the matter she was pleased to consent, and I promised to do all as she ordered—tho' I fear my Lady will repent the step she is taking the longest day she lives."

"You have then ordered the chaise!"

"I did Madam, for as I was at the post-office I thought it best to give the note to a young man who did not know me by sight, who chanced to come that way for fear my Lord should hear that I had given it, as he will no doubt send there to make enquiries."

"Well," cried Selena after some consideration, "if you will entrust me with the key, I will go speak to your Lady and return it to you in about an hour."

Rawlins however declared that he could not bear that his Lady should suspect him of having betrayed her, as she assuredly must, should Selena return there at that time.

While he spoke Selena had herself reflected, that she might spare her friend the confusion of ever knowing that she had been privy to her rash intention, and with this view she requested Rawlins might wait a few minutes and that she would write a note to himself desiring him to deliver the parcel which should accompany it immediately to his Lady and that this note he might shew to her as an excuse for his intruding upon her again before the appointed hour. He complied with her request while Selena readily repeated her promise that Lady Trevallyn should never know of his communication.

In less than a quarter of an hour Selena returned to Rawlins after having sealed up Angela's manuscript, with the letters written in the hand of Lord Henry, and the following lines hastily traced by herself in the cover.

> "My dearest friend, you have I know listened with incredulity to my hints respecting the real character of a person whose conduct not only towards the unfortunate Angela but yourself these papers will but too clearly explain. The internal evidence of truth which they so strongly bear must totally preclude any doubt which might diminish the due weight they should have with you. I received them from Mrs. Harley on her death bed, who expressed so much reluctance to have the memory of her child exposed that I did not think myself at liberty to impart her confession sooner, tho' it appears to me now necessary to undeceive you and prevail upon you no longer to refuse that promise which duty and virtue so loudly call upon you voluntarily to make, even tho' undemanded by one who has certainly a right to your obedience. Dearest Lady Trevallyn do not hate your Selena for the cruel task which friendship has imposed. Allow me to see you early tomorrow; I have much still to say to you and trust that fairer days await us and sweeter from the very remembrance of what we have suffered."

Selena had no sooner dismissed Rawlins than she began to consider that it was not impossible that in the hurry of her spirits, and preparations for her flight Lady Trevallyn might defer opening the parcel till she had left Esselberrie, when it might be too late to save her from the impending ruin. She was also uncertain what she should say to Mrs. Vallard being determined against letting her know what was her friend's present purpose—confident from her knowledge of the purity of Lady Trevallyn's heart, that she would now tear from thence the unworthy object tho' the struggle were to prove fatal to her life.

She was however so anxious from the idea which had now seized upon her that her friend might defer the perusal of the papers, that she resolved upon telling Mrs. Vallard that Mr. Rawlins had come from Lady Trevallyn and that it was of consequence that she should go see her right after the family were gone to bed and as it was a fine night she beg'd to be allowed to take Philip her old confidential butler to walk thither with her.

Mrs. Vallard would have insisted upon her taking the carriage, but as this would totally have defeated her scheme, she so earnestly declined accepting it, that Mrs. Vallard gave up, only begging of her to wrap herself up carefully.

A little before twelve she sallied out upon her chivalrous expedition attended by Philip, and taking the high road turned towards Barton bridge which lay about half a mile from the avenue gate on the London side.

"Lord bless you Ma'am you are turning quite wrong," cried her attendant somewhat surprised.

"No Philip," answered she, "I cannot go to Esselberrie yet, till I see Mr. Rawlins, whom I expect here about this time."

She very soon beheld the chaise waiting as it had been ordered, and satisfied that so far at least all was safe and that her friend had not as yet taken the irremediable step, she felt her mind relieved from some anxiety tho' as she walked up and down she watched not without uneasiness for Rawlins, who she was sure must soon come in order to dismiss the carriage. But the patience of the postilion was exhausted before that of Selena, or perhaps thinking he had only been made a fool of, he at length after two or three hearty curses bestowed on he know not whom, drove back into the village and the night being remarkably still, they distinctly heard him turn into the inn yard.

Selena then in spite of Philip's remonstrances who assured her that it grew very late, and that he was certain she should take cold determined to proceed to Esselberrie and try if possible to see Rawlins. Every thing about the house and offices was shut up and quiet and not a person to be seen, she was therefore on the point of returning when as she came to the little green gate of the garden, thro' which she had so often pass'd she thought she would just try if it was unlocked, tho' with but little idea of really finding it so; she lifted the latch and gently pushing it, in an instant all the fragrance of the garden burst upon her senses.

"Come in Philip shut the door and wait for me here," said she flying with hasty steps towards the greenhouse.

That too was open and she had no sooner entered it, than a confused sound of voices from within the dressing room arrested her feet.

The image of Lord Trevallyn unexpected returned and falling with all his fury upon the gentle Emily and her faithful domestic struck her with terror. Her first emotion was to fly from a scene of such dreadful confusion but the idea of her friend's distress urged her more powerfully to approach. She put her hand to the door and distinctly heard the voice of Rawlins saying, "Oh my God she will never never!"

Selena waited for no more but rushing in beheld Lady Trevallyn stretched on the sopha, pale, motionless and apparently without life.

Rawlins was on his knees rubbing her hands, while several women were busied around, some burning feathers while others chaff'd her temples or endeavoured to revive her with hartshorn and salts.

"Oh she is quite gone?" cried Selena as she sunk on the floor with her hands clasped in an agony of terror.

"No Madame, I trust in God she will come to herself," said Rawlins, "but she has been from one fit into another as the women say for these two hours;"

"Fly," exclaimed Selena, "this instant fly for Mr. Graves, do not I beseech you lose a minute." Observing that each looked at the other with the fearful dread occasioned by Lord Trevallyn's strict orders, Selena continued in a more peremptory strain to insist upon Mr. Graves being immediately sent for—adding while the tears streamed from her eyes, "Oh Mr. Rawlins would you let Lady Trevallyn perish for want of assistance!"

"No," cried he hastily rising, "not for the wealth of the first Lord in the land. I will go myself, and not return without Dr. Graves and with the help of God I trust she will recover."

Selena took his place and while she supported the head of this fair drooping lilly her own tears as she hung over her, fell in showers upon her pallid cheeks.

After a few minutes she seemed to revive and tho' unable to speak yet her deep sighs gave at once symptoms of life and suffering, companions alas too faithfully connected!

Selena now observed the table covered with the scattered writings of poor Angela and had but little doubt what had caused this violent effect upon her spirits already too much exhausted by the agitation of so many preceeding hours. Having collected the papers, she then assisted in undressing and placing her in her own bed during which she once more fainted in her arm. But upon her again reviving she knew Selena and expressed her satisfaction in seeing her; talking however so much and so wildly that Selena was seriously alarmed for her head, especially as the burning heat of her hands and her parched lips announced a high degree of fever.

She now wished to speak to Philip since she feared Mrs. Vallard might not sleep till she had heard of her safety, but when for this purpose she would for an instant have relinquished the hand she held the violent reluctance her friend expressed and the impossibility of convincing her that she meant not entirely to forsake her obliged Selena to give up the design.

But being informed that Philip who had been met by Rawlins now waited in the dressing room she sent by him a message to Mrs. Vallard signifying the necessity for her remaining that night at Esselberrie.

In little more than an hour Rawlins returned with Mr. Graves who pronounced his patient in an ardent fever, ordered her to be kept perfectly quiet, and seemed anxious that farther assistance should be sought without delay.

Selena much alarmed by his words and still more by his countenance would have instantly dispatched a messenger to Derby for Dr. O— but Graves himself suggested the expediency of sending first to inform Lord Trevallyn of the situation of his Lady and to desire his orders.

In spite of Selena's reluctance from various reasons to see Lord Trevallyn, and her dread lest his return should banish her from her friend, yet sensible of the propriety of this proposal she did not oppose its being put into immediate execution, and even complied with the request of Rawlins, that she should herself write a few lines to account for her admittance to Lady Trevallyn in such a manner as might exempt Rawlins himself from blame, which she easily managed and she at the same time requested permission to retain her office of nurse tender till her friend should be entirely recovered.

Nothing could be more opposite to the intentions of Lord Trevallyn than the interference of Selena; but as his sole object had been to preserve himself from the shadow of dishonour and to prevent the world from daring to suspect the wife of Lord Trevallyn he would not even to Selena betray the deep and implacable resentment by which he was actuated, lest it might defeat the plan which offended pride and revenge so firmly meditated.

Mr. Guise indeed whose natural timidity (from the fear of unpleasant consequences which might result to himself) had shrunk from affording his patron the assistance which his purpose required, heard with the utmost satisfaction of the chance there now seemed that death might at once deliver him from an object he ever considered as the great bar to his ambitious expectations and remove it in a way attended with far less difficulty than that which the indignation of Lord Trevallyn had projected.

No sooner had Lady Trevallyn's refusal to comply with the promise suggested by Mr. Guise convinced the enraged husband of his wife's infidelity, then he resolved upon saving himself from disgrace by instantly removing her from all possibility of intercourse not only with her lover but any other person. And this he thought could easily be effected by conveying her to an estate which he possessed in a retired part of south wales at some distance from Trevallyn hall giving out that she had died there suddenly.

She had been brought to Esselberrie only as a temporary retreat while proper measures might be taken to prepare for her reception the ruinous old mansion where she was condemned to pass the remainder of her existence, since Lord Trevallyn resolved to ensure her confinement beyond his own life, by leaving the whole of his immense property to Lady Trevallyn and in case of her death before the opening of the will to Mr. Guise; well convinced of his knowledge of his disposition that the self interest which he thus engaged in the execution of his orders was the surest bond for the fulfilment of the vows by which he intended to bind him.

Tho' he had not yet positively explained his purpose to Lady Trevallyn, yet enough had escaped him in the moments of violence to convince her what was to be the nature of her punishment. Her horror of vice and her native delicacy had hitherto preserved her innocence in the midst of her most perilous situation, in spite of all the arts of her adored seducer, all the weakness of her own heart.

There were moments indeed when afflicted by his reproaches of distrust and coldness, when softened by his entreaties and his tears she felt that had he urged her to fly with him into perpetual seclusion and banishment she could not have resisted the fatal persuasions. Nor was Lord Henry a stranger to this silent unacknowledged triumph of Love over Virtue, fame, wealth and Honour. Nay there were times when he himself hesitated not generously whether he should accept this sacrifice, but whether he himself should resign to his lovely fond Emily all his ambitious hopes, all his prospects of fortune and all the pleasures of London; the struggle was however but transient—the world the victorious world, subdued the softer impulse and he resolved to persist, confident of success in the end even on his own terms; Hitherto his arts had all been baffled; Lady Trevallyn's whole soul shrunk from the vile treachery, the horrible crime of bearing to the world and to an injured husband a brow of innocence while her conscience could reproach her with the most atrocious of crimes, and had her virtue for one moment yielded, the next would have beheld her self banished for ever from the roof of her Lord. But while she listened with a tenderness that could not be disguised to the insidious tongue of him whose presence she no longer had the force to shun, while his power was so evident in all those sacrifices which she had hitherto made what had he not a right to expect?

Mean while the severe internal combat, the scenes of daily agitation and the nights of sleepless misery thro' which she had passed had already laid the seeds of that violent fever which appeared with every mortal symptom, hurried on by the overwhelming shock which terminated that dreadful fatigue of body and mind which during the last cruel days and nights she had endured.

But among all those tumultuous hours which she had yet passed were even more agitating than those which succeeded her interview with Selena.

The moment that her entrance proclaimed the possibility of escape, her soul opened with a kind of agonising rapture to the idea of seeking protection and shelter in the bosom of Love. The anguish with which she had just considered the probability of their eternal separation, the tenfold force which affliction ever adds to Love, all conspired to hurry her into a sudden and violent resolution to seize on their unexpected opportunity and fly to those dear generous faithful arms which she had no doubt would open with sympathizing rapture to receive her.

Her plan was instantaneous as the impulse which prompted it, and as may naturally be expected was as little under the guidance of prudence. Had she been unfortunately suffered to put it into execution there can be but little doubt that her steps might easily have been traced and before Lord Henry could have arrived at the retreat which she had appointed for their meeting, she could most probably have been surprised by Lord Trevallyn or his emissaries.

To Selena she had written an eternal farewell and the tears of remorse and shame, if not of salutary contrition blotted the paper whereon she acknowledged herself undeserving of ever holding any correspondence with the friend to whom her heart was so fondly attached.

Nothing now remained and she waited for the appointed hour in an agony of mingled fear and impatience which almost amounted to frenzy before Rawlins entered with the packet which at Selena's desire he delivered to her and there awaited her farther orders in the green house. Here he was after some time alarmed by the hysterical sobs which proceeded from the dressing room and upon entering found her in a situation which obliged him fearfully and instantly to summon her women to her assistance in spite of his reluctance to let them see how he had now entered.

As Lady Trevallyn had opened the packet the first paper which met her eyes was in the hand writing but too well acknowledged by her heart. The horrible conviction of the treachery of that breast upon which she had reposed all her hopes struck her at once as with a mortal irrecoverable blow. She continued to examine the papers—all was confusion, her bewildered brain incapable of receiving another impression saw but one object. Nature sunk beneath the shock which her reason sustained from this sudden this violent subversion of every long cherished idea which from the very years of childhood had coloured every thought so that not one moment of her existence but bore some reference to the one all reigning image cloathed by fond fancy with every excellence as it was in reality adorned with every superficial grace. Confused already with a disordered and fevered brain she turned over the dreadful papers from an unaccountable idea that some explanation of this overpowering mystery should at length arrive. Phantoms of terror mingling visionary with real evils swam before her eyes, the horrible papers were yet grasped in her convulsed hand but the characters could no longer be traced and while she uttered abrupt and faint cries she sunk powerless from her seat while she seemed[34] with every thing around her by an irresistable and violent motion.

Chapter IX

> Alas the pain
> We feel whene'er we dispossess the soul
> Of Love; tormenting tyrant, yet exceeds
> The rigour of his rule.
> > Fenton[35]

For ten days the delirium of Lady Trevallyn continued without one hour's decided intermission. Yet for the greatest part of this time she spoke little and even appeared to know Selena being always more calm and apparently easier when she was by her side.

The name of Lord Henry never once passed her lips, but Selena was at no loss to discover to whom all her conversation was addressed. At one time pouring forth the softest sentiments of unbounded tenderness while her disordered imagination made her believe that he shared with her the enchanting prospects and delicious fruits of Paradise, and at another moment while suffering the violent pains of the fever she would entreat him in the most pathetic terms to save her from the cruel hand of Angela, who she fancied tore open her side or pressed upon her temples with violence an iron crown. To all attendants except Selena these appeared but the incoherent and unmeaning ravings so commonly produced by the disorder under which she laboured. She alone listened to them with an aching fearful heart, knowing them to be the fruits of that cruel internal malady to which she solely attributed her present dangerous situation.

As Lord Trevallyn and Mr. Guise apprehensive of infection returned not to Esselberrie, Selena was not opposed in any of her friendly wishes. Lord Trevallyn had left every thing to the direction of Mr. Rawlins, ordering him to pay every proper attention to his Lady, and twice a day he dispatched a messenger to enquire concerning her state and the progress of the fever.

---

[34]   The manuscript contains an insertion sign with nothing inserted.

[35]   Herod in Elijah Fenton's *Marianne* (1723), 5.1.19–22 (the epigraph inserts "Love" in line 21, which should simply read "Of that tormenting tyrant, far exceeds").

Rawlins thus left to his own discretion rejoiced in having Selena to share in some measure his responsibility at a period so critical. By her desire Dr. O— was sent for and she found the utmost consolation in the benevolent interest which he seemed to take in the situation of two females so young, and so beautiful, one to all appearance at the very point of death and the other voluntarily exposed to all that toil and danger from which the hireling nurses shrunk with terror.

It was not without the strongest daily remonstrances from Mrs. Vallard and her sister that Selena was thus allowed to fulfil the dictates of her warmly sensible heart. But she had more than one motive for resisting their importunities. Independent of the importance of the service in which she was now engaged she felt the utmost dread lest she should convey infection to Hillbarton peculiarly trembling for the consequences for Clara when she considered the weak state of her present health. She therefore resolved no more to quit Esselberrie till she could do so with the most perfect confidence, yet for herself she felt no fear, and indeed this may almost universally be observed to be the case where there is strong affection.

Unable to prevail upon her to return Mrs. Vallard complied with her entreaties, and exercised all her authority over Clara to restrain her from obeying the impulse which led her to share with her sister the fatigue which the delicacy of Clara's constitution so little qualified her to bear.

Selena on the contrary, tho' in her mind and figure the very perfection of female delicacy, was yet gifted by Nature with a vigour of health and spirits which might carry her uninjured thro' an extreme of sorrow and of suffering, beneath which many must have sunk who possessed not half her sensibility, and the hope of administering consolation to her friend should she ever again have an interval of Reason supported her thro' the melancholy task of watching the wild and wretched wanderings of uncontrouled fancy.

On the eleventh day Dr. O— had prepared her to expect a decisive crisis, and tho' obliged from the duties of his profession to return to Derby where his presence was daily necessary he promised again to visit Esselberrie before the following morning.

For some hours during that terrible night every hope appeared lost, but life yet lingered reluctant as it appeared to leave its so lately perfect mansion; tho' urged to retire by the advice of the attendants who were convinced that all was now over Selena remained endeavouring to restore warmth to those limbs on which the coldness of Death had already seized, and to call back, by reanimating cordials, the spirit which each moment seemed to waver as the expiring taper trembles in every breeze. A gradual diffusion of vital heat a stronger pulse and freer respiration rewarded Selena's pious cares, and revived her hopes while she watched the countenances of those around fearful of enquiry lest they should contradict her scarcely trusted wishes.

All however confirmed the evidence of more favourable symptoms and tears of grateful, fearful joy bathed the cheeks of Selena as she felt the gentle pressure of Lady Trevallyn's hand, and listened to her name feebly pronounced while her mild eyes in calm languor were fixed upon the face of that incomparable friend whose care she now acknowledged.

Trembling with anxiety Selena awaited the opinion of the physician, he saw the hopes she cherished and apprehensive of their disappointment, declared it impossible absolutely to pronounce that the disorder had taken a favourable turn.

But in his benevolent countenance Selena flattered herself that she could read his own reviving courage, and strictly observed his injunctions to resist all conversation which Lady Trevallyn now appeared to desire.

Satisfied in observing the hourly amendment which Dr. O— now feared not to confirm tho' he yet refused to affirm that his patient was absolutely out of danger, Selena silently administered to her when waking, and watched the prolonged slumbers which after so many sleepless hours now closed her eyes uninterruptedly for days and nights.

Lady Trevallyn herself complied without reluctance to Dr. O—'s orders of perfect silence, tho' upon her first return to reason surprise and gratitude towards Selena had prompted her impatient enquiries. She now only insisted upon Selena's quitting her during the hours of refreshment necessary for her health and at night was always careful to enquire the time in order that she might be satisfied that her friend retired to the bed which Selena had for herself prepared in the dressing room.

Except this her silence continued unbroken till Dr. O— apprehensive that the disorder might fall upon her nerves, thought it advisable to recommend Selena if possible by cheerful conversation, to arouse her from this state of languor, but in this all her efforts failed. At length she was able to sit up and Selena having brought her some of her favourite early flowers Lady Trevallyn in a low voice demanded whether they were alone. Selena trembling for what was to ensue replied in the affirmative.

"Dear Selena," continued she after a pause, "I have had such strange dreams since I have been ill, that I knew not what to believe, but I am at Esselberrie and therefore I think that I am indeed a prisoner here, but where is Lord Trevallyn and how is it that I am blessed with your presence?"

Selena reminded her of the key, and of their first interview, but some dreadful images the meer creatures of fancy were so interwoven with her recollection of all that she had seen and heard in the dressing room that Selena could with difficulty convince her of the reality of what had passed.

Lady Trevallyn however did not impart what floated upon her mind in this uncertain form, and Selena who too well knew to what they alluded forebore all enquiry.

But Lady Trevallyn's anxiety was now become too intolerable to be suppressed.

During the first days of her recovery she had willingly persuaded herself that the afflictive images which yet remained were but like those wild and unconnected horrors from which she found it impossible to separate them. What indeed could be more remote from the very "prospect of belief"[36] than the black falsehood, the

---

[36] Macbeth in Shakespeare's *Macbeth* (1605), 1.3.74.

perfidious infidelity, the unfeeling cruelty of him whose bosom she fondly thought the abode of truth and excellence.

Yet a fatal presentiment restrained her tongue and she trembled at every approach which her curiosity would make to pierce the mysterious uncertainty which still involved her retrospections tho' they incessantly occupied all her thoughts.

But having once commenced the agitating enquiry her doubts were too important to suffer her to stop before she should relieve her mind from the images of horror which oppressed it, or indeed find her worst fears confirmed by a reality which should leave her nothing but despair.

After some minutes of silent expectation (nearly as terrible to Selena as to herself) she therefore ventured in a faultring voice to ask "Whether Angela was really dead?"

"Dead! My dear Lady Trevallyn how can you possibly doubt it? Do you not remember the melancholy account which Sidney gave us of her last hours?"

"Well but tell me now truly & do not let any idea of saving me from being disturbed prevent your answering me as if called upon by Heaven did not some one else come to me when I was very ill?"

"No one I solemnly declare but those whom you have seen this day about you. I never left these two rooms for more than ten minutes together and no one could possibly come in without my knowledge."

"Well that is strange," cried Lady Trevallyn, and again sunk into a silent reverie.

"Rawlins indeed," continued Selena, "was with you when first taken ill, but he has not been farther than the door since that night." Lady Trevallyn started and was preparing to speak, but Selena observing her tremble and breathe with difficulty dreaded the effects of this disquieting conversation on her yet weak frame, and entreated her to divert if possible her mind from the thoughts of what she had suffered.

"One more question," interrupted she eagerly grasping Selena's hand, "did Angela send me from the grave a dreadful tale of perfidy?"

Selena burst into tears at the anguish which she read in the pale quivering lips that pronounced these words but endeavouring to resume a tranquility so necessary at this time to support her friend she answered, "No but poor Mrs. Harley when dying entrusted to me the history of her child's misfortunes, and I thought that the knowledge of these might enable you better to support your own and convince you how little you have to regret."

As she spoke Lady Trevallyn seizing instantaneously the whole terrible truth was at once overwhelmed with confusion at having loved and despair at having lost him and letting go her hand sunk back upon her chair exclaiming in a low hollow voice, "Then all is over! I shall never, never see him more."

Selena knelt by her side and strove to soften her by every endearing expression of sympathy to tears, by which she hoped to gain her some relief.

But it is the very nature of despair to close the heart against all tenderness, and at that moment even Lady Trevallyn received her caresses with coldness and in silence.

At length she spoke but it was only in a few words to ask for the papers.

"My dear Lady Trevallyn you could not possibly read them now, your eyes are still weak and I am sure your spirits are not equal to the task. They are all in your own cabinet and when you are able to peruse the melancholy story, you will I am sure find your heart overflow with gratitude to Providence for your deliverance from one who never merited your affection even when it was innocently devoted to him. How little my dear friend can we judge for ourselves! How often do we bitterly lament the very circumstances which are the greatest blessings which infinite mercy can bestow upon us! How truly is it said that

> We ignorant of ourselves
> Beg often our own harms, which the wise powers
> Deny us for our good, so find we profit
> By losing of our prayers.[37]

Never would I have afflicted you by so painful a conviction had I not thought it necessary for your future contentment, to see that the lot which you regretted as, so fair and so desirable, had it been granted to your wishes must have afforded you only misery and disappointment."

"Oh no, no!" cried Lady Trevallyn clasping her hands over her head in an agony, "Oh that I had never been undeceived! Oh my God why did I not perish in that sad bed, before I lost the only hope, the only consolation of my miserable life!" Selena saw that this was not the moment to speak the language of sound reason, or to tell her of the comforts which earth might yet afford: but there are superior hopes, higher, and more powerful consolations, which in the most desolate hour of extreme despondence may yet be held out by Piety, and happy is that mourner whose broken spirit humbly submits to receive support where alone it should seek for it under the chastisement of fatherly compassion.

Thus, and thus only was the bosom of Lady Trevallyn softened into gentler sorrows.

The tears of gratitude and contrition mingled with those of anguish while Selena eloquently described the heavenly peace and confidence which crowned the latter hours of Mrs. Harley in spite of all her worldly cares and afflictions—but when she thus concluded, "Had you dear Lady Trevallyn beheld her then as I did, I should not be surprised at your desire of thus exchanging a life of difficult combat for so happy a rest."

Lady Trevallyn struck with shame and remorse exclaimed, "Oh Selena the case is far different! I am a wretch unworthy to live, and unfit to die, no wonder I am so miserable it is what I deserve, for no one is so guilty; and but for you I should be lost indeed."

Selena saw she was about to enter into the particulars of her intended escape, and as she wished not to receive this farther humiliating confession of weakness she entreated her to forbear all farther conversation at present and to prove her

---

[37] Menas in Shakespeare's *Antony and Cleopatra* (1606), 2.1.5–8.

gratitude to Heaven in endeavouring by patience and resignation to regain health of mind and body.

Lady Trevallyn yielded to all that Selena required, but for many succeeding days her excessive weakness prevented her from quitting her bed.

Her tears during all that time flowed incessantly, but tho' she spoke only in answer to the enquiries of those around, her heart evinced all and even more than all its usual softness and tenderness, gratefully acceding to every proposal made by Selena for her comfort and advantage.

As soon as it was possible she exerted herself to rise, and at Dr. O—'s desire was assisted into the dressing room.

As she entered it she shuddered, and the recollection of these moments the most dreadful of her life, which she had there passed, seemed to awake with new force.

Selena saw with the utmost pity her emotion, as well as the struggle which after a short time she evidently made to subdue her feelings, nor could she doubt what was the object of her meditations while she observed her eyes constantly fixed upon the little cabinet, where Selena told her lay the lasting witness of guilt, the monument of misery.

She did not however insist upon opening it, and appeared to be conscious of her own weakness; but after some time she expressed a wish to see Mr. Mason, and asked Selena would she venture to send for him: Selena hesitated, doubtful whether Lord Trevallyn might not be displeased at this step, and make it an excuse for banishing her from the society of her friend.

Lady Trevallyn instantly saw the justice of these apprehensions and shared them herself too seriously to run any risk, but as she spoke of him so frequently and seemed so delighted to listen to the particulars of Mrs. Harley's last moments, Selena voluntarily offered to be the bearer of any commission which could afford her satisfaction. Lady Trevallyn gratefully declined her proposal of writing a note to Mr. Mason but said she wished to speak for a few minutes to Rawlins. Selena rightly guessed that she was anxious to know had he sent the fatal letter with which she had entrusted him on the first day of her illness and which she indeed only clearly remembered when she again entered the dressing room, where it had been written.

Selena therefore judged it better not to accompany Rawlins, but having sent him to his Lady, enjoyed the delicious season, which had already not only filled the garden with fragrance but encouraged the whole country to burst forth into beauty. Upon her return to Lady Trevallyn she found her, as she had indeed dreaded, plunged in the deepest dejection, upon finding that the letter had been sent which must have exposed her weakness to him, of whose unworthiness she was now but too well assured. Selena at first attempted to amuse her mind, but perceiving that her distress seemed rather to encrease than to diminish by those efforts to turn her thoughts into another channel, she gently besought her to consider how ungrateful she was to Heaven in thus refusing to be comforted.

"Oh Selena you mistake me," cried she earnestly while her tears streamed afresh, "you think that I can yet regret the object of my love, when it is that love itself that I deplore. It is not that I have for ever lost all that my fond soul doated upon that I now mourn; No believe me—

> All kinder thoughts are fled for ever from me
> All tenderness, as if I ne'er had loved
> Has left my bosom colder than the grave.[38]

But I grieve and ever will grieve that I could thus have been the victim of this wilful blindness, this fatal self deception. What mercy can I expect from Heaven when I so obstinately resisted all that its gracious Providence interposed to save me, all that you dear Selena had so often urged, and refusing to listen to any thing but my own miserable folly have exposed my gross credulity, my wicked infatuation to the very being from whom of all others upon earth I should wish it most to be concealed. No never can I hope for forgiveness and the remainder of my life is, and should be devoted to the bitterness of remorse and shame."

Selena endeavoured to speak hope and comfort to her wounded spirit, and while they were thus engaged Rawlins asked to be readmitted.

Lady Trevallyn desired him to come in, and on his entrance he advanced and spoke a few words in a low voice to his Lady.

"It is very well Rawlins," said she, "you may go now, but give orders that I may be told the moment he comes."

When he had closed the door Lady Trevallyn turned to Selena and with a faint smile bid her not to be surprised that without consulting her she had sent for Mr. Mason.

"I have the strongest desire to see him," added she, "and wished to take upon myself all the blame which may possibly arise from this step."

Selena recollected Mrs. Vallard's prejudices, and tho' she had herself the highest esteem for the character of this amiable and pious curate, she could not but feel some sorrow that her friend should risk incurring farther the displeasure of Lord Trevallyn, to whom she had no doubt the name of Methodist was at least as obnoxious as it could be to the mild and indulgent Mrs. Vallard.

Nevertheless while she was so painfully sensible of her own inability to restore peace to the afflicted bosom of her friend, she could not oppose any scheme from which she herself appeared to expect consolation.

Early on the following morning Mr. Mason paid his expected visit. After a few minutes general conversation with respect to Lady Trevallyn's recovery, Selena rose to retire and as her design was not opposed she took this opportunity of seeing her anxious friends at Hillbarton, who could not without much reluctance consent to her prolonged absence, tho' they acknowledged the justice of those claims with which friendship yet called for her attendance upon Lady Trevallyn; and indeed now that the danger appeared over Mrs. Vallard found much satisfaction in thinking that her poor Emily had the comfort of Selena's cheerful society.

---

[38]   Athenais in Nathaniel Lee's *Theodosius; or, The Force of Love* (1680), 2.1.570–72.

When she had communicated as far as she could the particulars of her friend's situation she turned the conversation upon her own affairs asking them with a smile "Did they think she might give up all hopes of ever hearing from Dallamore?" There was something in the manner of both Mrs. Vallard and Clara which convinced her that they knew or at least suspected more than they chose to explain tho' they declared without hesitation, that no letter had arrived since she left Hillbarton containing any intelligence of interest.

The dread lest some evil had befallen Sidney struck a chill upon the heart of Selena and in faltering accents she enquired concerning him, but on this head she was quickly reassured, and judging with more of philosophy than is usual at so early an age, she reflected that if they really had heard any tidings which they wished to conceal it was probably for the interest of her own peace not to enquire too eagerly, since by remaining in ignorance of an uncertain evil she might perhaps save herself much vain disquietude.

Mrs. Vallard had indeed heard from London of Dallamore's constant attendance upon Lady Harriet and that he had now accompanied her to Miltern Abbey, in consequence of which Clara had written to Robert; but the whole story had come (thro' a neighbour celebrated for her curiosity) in so questionable a shape and was in itself so incomprehensible that they thought it best to spare Selena the mortification of hearing it until the truth could be more clearly ascertained. They therefore suffered her to return to her affectionate and tender duties at Esselberrie without disturbing that serene tranquility that "Sweet peace which Goodness bosoms ever."[39]

Chapter X

> For true repentance never comes too late,
> As soon as born she makes herself a shroud
> The weeping mantle of a fleecy cloud,
> And swift as thought her airy journey take—
> Her hand Heaven's azure gate with trembling shakes
> She tells her story in so sad a tone
> That Angels start from bliss and give a groan
>
>   Lee[40]

On Selena's entering the dressing room she perceived that Mr. Mason had not yet taken his leave; the tears which remained on the cheeks of each bore testimony how interesting to both had been this interview.

---

[39]   John Milton, *Comus* (1634), line 368.

[40]   Genius in Nathaniel Lee's *The Massacre of Paris* (1690), 5.1.20–27 (the epigraph transforms past tense to present, uses "A" for "For" in line 20, uses "As" for "So" in line 21, omits line 25, "The Stars did with amazement on her look," and uses "her" for "thy" in line 26).

Perceiving that Selena hesitated whether she should yet interrupt their conversation Lady Trevallyn desired her to come in adding with her own sweet smile, "Mr. Mason has promised to be no longer a stranger at Esselberrie while we are allowed the privilege of his society."

Selena's eyes beamed upon her friend with cordial satisfaction as she listened to the silver tones of her melodious voice now for the first time assume a degree of cheerfulness.

Mr. Mason's heart seemed full and after a few moments he withdrew to pour it forth as he returned home in prayers for that sweetly contrite and humbled spirit into which he had already sought to pour the balm of consolation.

"I will tell you Selena," said Lady Trevallyn when they were alone, "what I have done, and you must not think me ungrateful or suspect that I do not most highly prize your judgment when I confess that I was not at rest until I asked counsel from another in a point which has lain very heavy upon my mind."

"My dear Lady Trevallyn," interrupted Selena smiling, "I should almost think you meant this as a reproof to me for self conceit did I not know your partiality, but believe me I am fully sensible how little qualified I am to guide you. If you have had any doubts with respect to your conduct I am rejoiced you consulted good Mr. Mason and I beg that you will not think it necessary to repeat to me any matter of confidence in which I can be of no use, and which it may only be painful to us both to dwell upon."

"No," replied Lady Trevallyn with a deep sigh, "I will have no reserve from my best, my most faithful earthly friend. You know not dear Selena the full extent of my obligations to you, nor that but for you I should be at this moment self-plunged in the very depth of guilt and misery, exposed to the contempt of the whole world as well as of my own heart."

She then fully informed Selena of her intention, from the execution of which she had been so providentially rescued, and bitterly regretted that she had by her letter betrayed her willingness to become the victim of Duplicity.

"But the point dear Selena," continued she, "which I feared your tenderness to me might prevent you from rightly judging was whether I am now required to confess to Lord Trevallyn the whole of my criminal design and the extent of my infatuation. That my heart was fatally wedded to another, I never disguised, so that on that head I have no farther confession to make, but as I already knew your opinion would be to spare me the humiliation which I feared my conscience dictated, I could not rest satisfied till I had consulted a less prejudiced judge."

"And I trust," cried Selena earnestly, "that he considers so hazardous a confidence by no means expedient;"

"He thinks as you do my love, that to enter into particulars with one who cannot understand my feelings, would only excite unjust suspicions of my past and future conduct grievous to us both; but I must no longer delay an acknowledgment of my faults, and that proof of obedience which he has hitherto vainly exacted for I can now without hesitation promise never willingly to behold, the sight of whom is the earthly punishment which I most deprecate."

She then called for a pen and ink, and having traced with her feeble hand the following lines she presented them to Selena, upon whose approbation they were immediately sent to Lord Trevallyn.

"I wish my Lord that the first act of my restored life may be some reparation and acknowledgment of my errors. I have no longer any reluctance to renew my vows of obedience by which I am already bound to comply with your orders, and my most ardent wish is in future by the fulfillment of my duties to atone for their past neglect.

> Emily Trevallyn"

Selena felt more anxiety than her friend to know what would be the reception of this letter. Tho' she had never mentioned her fears yet since Lady Trevallyn had begun to recover many an uneasy moment had Selena passed in the dread of their future separation, and the melancholy solitude which she trembled to think was prepared for her friend at Trevallyn hall. She knew that in the present temper of her mind, a total seclusion from the world was the only earthly consolation for which her soul languished; But she dreaded lest when left to herself, unsupported by the soothing cares of friendship, and uncheered by the voice of affection, the depression of spirits which must naturally ensue from the remembrances of past suffering, would prove fatal to her already deeply injured constitution.

As to Lady Trevallyn herself, she awaited with the most perfect indifference the declaration of her future lot. She had drank the cup of worldly affliction to the very dregs. The sudden shock which had all at once obliged her to convert the tenderest love into the strongest abhorrence, and the most unbounded confidence into the contempt of detected treachery had rent from her all hope of earthly happiness, and it was in the calm tears of penitence that she alone aspired to seek resignation and tranquility.

Her gentle heart to which all violent passions were naturally foreign quickly subsided into these silent sorrows which however deep betray no external agitation. She resisted not the hand of chastisement and tho' she sunk beneath its heavy weight her soul even then refused not to listen to the voice of duty while it promised future peace. Her letter to Lord Trevallyn had been penned by its dictates, and totally occupied by the past, she thought not upon what destiny awaited her; it was not till the following day that she received his answer.

Selena who was present when the important letter was delivered into her hands, eagerly watched her countenance as in a hurried manner she ran her eyes over it and the paper which it enclosed. She could read there however nothing but a kind of bewildered astonishment, a vague expression, such as a tale of yet unintelligible calamity might excite, while it strikes the heart, ere it can reach the brain. At length the letter falling from her trembling hands she sunk upon her knees and pressing her arms across her bosom exclaimed, "Merciful God! I thank thee; I am indeed delivered from my fear! My prayers are heard, for never, never shall I see him more!"

As she uttered these last words the divine energy which had for a moment illuminated her countenance with a celestial beauty vanished and struck perhaps instantaneously with some softer recollections of long cherished ideas, tears silently streamed from her dejected eyes, as she bowed her lovely drooping head.

Selena who had conceived with a sensation of horror the idea of Lord Henry's death and perhaps by the hand of Lord Trevallyn, snatched from the ground the papers, but was quickly relieved from her terror by the words of his short letter which were as follows.

> "It is well Madam, but it might have been better, and your boasted sense of duty and repentance might have worn a greater semblance of sincerity, had it preceeded your knowledge of the desertion of the contemptible villain whom you refused to sacrifice at my desire. That you may see that I am not the dupe you hoped and that I am already acquainted with the circumstances which have had so powerful an effect upon your conduct I enclose you the information which I received at the same time with your tardy submission.
> Trevallyn, Castle Morne &c&c&c"

"What is the meaning of all this?" cried Selena relieved from the fearful idea which had at first so much shocked her tho' still at a loss to comprehend to what an answer so harsh could allude.

Lady Trevallyn faintly desired her to read the letter which it had contained but appeared herself scarcely able to articulate as she remained motionless with her face buried in the cushions of the sopha. The first lines were torn off as well as the conclusion, but Selena perceived that it must have been addressed to Mr. Guise and what remained was to the following purpose ....

> "The whole affair has been now made public by her tenacious obstinacy in insisting upon her title as wife being acknowledged. I have it from Mr. Moore the lawyer whom she had employed so that you may depend upon my accuracy in spite of the many contradictory reports which are in circulation.
> "It seems that it is some months since Lord Henry was privately married to this Miss Daniel, who has certainly very few personal or mental advantages to recommend her. But his Lordship's inducement was pretty obvious as this Lady some time previous to that in which she received the address of Lord Henry became by the death of her maternal Grandfather possessed of nearly one million sterling and the utter ruin of her noble suitor's affairs is now pretty well known. The immense property was as it appears entrusted to the care of old Soloman Daniel, who was himself believed to be scarcely less wealthy tho' as it has turned out he was in fact but a needy and fraudulent schemer.
> "At his Lordship's own desire his enamoured bride consented that their nuptials should remain a profound secret, until he could obtain the approbation of the Marquis his brother, from whom as he pretended his expectations were prodigious. He had nevertheless drawn from the reluctant hands of old solomen [sic] some thousands, in order to satisfy the demands of his most clamorous creditors. Notwithstanding this, upon the sudden and terrible crash which involved the whole of the unfortunately deluded daughter's property,

with that of her unjust and foolish father Lord Henry absolutely refused to acknowledge his marriage and offer'd in order to obtain his freedom by their silence, not only to refund the sums which he had already received but to settle upon her a very considerable annuity, a promise which on the examination of his affairs he was proved to be totally unable to fulfil. Nothing can now console the ruined heiress but the complete enjoyment of her rights as Lady Henry Ortney, but the disgrace of being obliged to acknowledge such a wife his Lordship considered quite intolerable and immediately exerted all his influence to procure a trifling appointment in India. Actually leaving London at night he embarked at Portsmouth in a vessel just ready to sail with a fair wind, so that before his creditors had arrived there in pursuit of him he was already many leagues beyond their reach."

Selena's heart overflowed secretly with gratitude to Heaven for an event which she esteemed so singularly happy for the gradual but certain restoration of her friend to peace. But she too well understood the sensations of mingled shame and regret which naturally overpowered the breast of Lady Trevallyn at this new proof of the worthlessness of the object whom she had so long adored, to be inclined to express any of her own feelings upon this occasion.

A few exclamations of surprise alone escaped her and Lady Trevallyn still preserving silence she for the present forebore all farther comments.

After a considerable pause having once more perused Lord Trevallyn's letter Selena expressed her wish that her friend should justify herself from the charge of duplicity, which she thought might easily be done, as Selena could herself witness that she had received no letter whatever since her illness until this from Lord Trevallyn himself.

"No Selena," answered she languidly, "I will bear this reproach in lieu of those with which he might more justly load me."

"Nay dear Lady Trevallyn," replied Selena, "independent of justice to yourself is it not your duty to deliver him from the pain which must necessarily ever result from suspecting those with whom we are so nearly connected?" Lady Trevallyn shook her head in silence, but Selena without appearing to notice it continued, "What reliance can he ever have upon your sincerity while he thinks you capable of so much art. Convince him of his error, and ashamed of his injustice he will restore to you his confidence and he will see that between mortals mutual forbearance and forgiveness must always be necessary."

"Oh Selena," cried Lady Trevallyn, with a little impatience, "you do not know him. Believe me you could not require from me any thing more impossible than that I should convince Lord Trevallyn that he had been mistaken."

"At least," said Selena, "you can have the consolation of knowing that you have done your part."

It was not in Lady Trevallyn's nature to resist importunity, and had she been of a less yielding temper, her respect for the opinion of Selena would in this instance have been insufficient to conquer the extreme reluctance with which she once more addressed Lord Trevallyn upon a subject most torturing to her soul, while she solemnly assured him of her total ignorance of these transactions which had past during her illness until she received his own communication.

To this however no answer was returned and Selena who from this derived no promising hopes of Lord Trevallyn's purposes watched her friend's slowly returning health, and the extreme weakness which yet continued with a trembling but silent solicitude which scarcely allowed her for a moment to quit her presence. And when Lady Trevallyn fearful of her suffering from the confinement would compel her by her entreaties to taste the freshness of the garden, or under pretence of some message to Mrs. Vallard or the school-house, engage her to quit for a short time the chamber where she wished to pass all her hours, Selena considered the moments she was thus separated from her, as taken from the few which were probably the last she was ever to share with the interesting friend whose misfortunes nay whose very errors had but wound her still more closely round her heart.

But tho' this idea oppressed her with a melancholy which often made it extremely difficult to her to restrain her tears even in the presence of Lady Trevallyn, she never uttered her fears, but in silence wondered at the tranquility of indifference with which her friend seemed to forget the gloomy solitude which might be intended for her future lot.

On the next visit which Selena paid to Hillbarton she found Mrs. Vallard and Clara in the utmost astonishment at a paragraph which they had just read in one of the morning papers remarkable for its eagerness to record the vices and follies of the fashionable circle.

Immediately upon Selena's entrance they pointed it out to her attention and being ignorant of the complete and violent revolution which before this had taken place in the mind of Lady Trevallyn both expressed their fears lest the knowledge of this extraordinary business might prove injurious to her health while yet not perfectly restablished.

The paragraph stated the circumstances of Lord Henry's conduct pretty nearly as Selena had already heard them, but in terms sufficiently intelligible it attributed his desire of concealing his marriage to his attachment for his lovely cousin and represented his sudden departure from England as the consequence of the despair which he had felt at her refusing all farther intercourse with him upon its discovery—and concluded by affirming that Lady Trevallyn's recovery was still extremely doubtful stating her illness to have taken place at Trevallyn hall.

When Mrs. Vallard heard from Selena that their dear Emily had been already informed of the affair and had borne the news with composure she heartily thanked God for the removal of one she had so much feared and disliked, and seemed in no wise to participate with the compassion which Clara could not help expressing for the fate of "poor Lord Henry."

To all her good natured lamentations for his being thus banished for ever by his unfortunate connexion with this horrid woman Mrs. Vallard made no other reply than, "My dear it will do him a great deal of good. He deserved nothing better for his conduct to poor Emily. If he had married her four years ago he might have been happy and respectable now."

Selena who had read still farther into the depravity of his heart thought silently that it was happy for her friend that his ambition had stifled his love, as had they been united she believed it most probable that his profligacy and infidelity would before this have broken the affectionate heart of the gentle and tender Emily.

Nothing surprised Clara so much as that Lord Henry could have left England during the illness of Lady Trevallyn while even her life was in such extreme danger; Selena indeed suggested the probability of his not having heard this circumstance and in this she was right and we must at least acquit him of this additional instance of that hardness of heart and cruel insensibility even towards those who for him would have sacrificed existence which were concealed beneath the softest manners and a shew of exquisite feeling the most seductive.

He had received the incoherent and scarcely intelligible lines which Lady Trevallyn had penned nearly under the influence of delirium, while he was perplexed and overwhelmed by the disgrace and ruin brought upon him by his unfortunate marriage no longer possible to be kept secret. No sting of conscience smothered the sudden resolution which his selfish passion formed that his beautiful fond Emily should be the partner of his ruined fortunes.

As soon as it was dark he quitted London and flew to the house appointed for the meeting. It was at a village some miles beyond St Albans where resided an old servant of the Ortney family, long and faithfully attached to Mrs. Montrose and her lovely Emily. Disappointed at not finding her and aware of all the fatal consequences which must attend his delay, he yet remained there in a state of mind not the most enviable during the whole of the ensuing forty eight hours. Conscious of the imprudence of his conduct, certain that his imprisonment for life must inevitably have followed their being overtaken by Lord Trevallyn he endeavoured to console himself for the eternal relinquishment which he was now constrained to make (not without the bitterest pang he had ever experienced) of his long dearest favourite object, the first and only love which his cold and vicious heart had ever really known.

Still selfish in his sorrows as in his pleasures he regretted his own disappointment with all the impotent fury of vexation but without shedding one tender tear for the deplorable situation in which it was manifest to him he had now for ever abandoned that soft and faithfully constant bosom who would to him have sacrificed all that is valuable in life, and who as he could have no doubt was now exposed to all the shame and misery attendant on her discovered and prevented flight.

But if his heart bled not for the sufferings which he had caused the lovely and innocent victim of his cruel artifices, he yet quitted England overwhelmed with an intolerable anguish which might well prove how equally Nature distributes her portion of calimity, so that those to whom she has denied that sensibility which is so prone to sympathise, are not spared from sharing affliction the universal lot of mortality where all are

Alike condemned to groan,
The tender for another's pain,
Th'unfeeling for his own.[41]

Chapter XI

Perhaps there is in wisdom, gentle wisdom
That knows our frailties therefore can forgive,
Some healing comfort for a guilty mind
Some power to charm it into peace again
And bid it smile anew with right affection.

Thompson[42]

As Selena could not but observe that Lady Trevallyn appeared less absorbed in her own oppressive tho' uncomplaining sorrows, after each visit from Mr. Mason, she rather encouraged the inclination which her friend shewed to have them repeated, tho' she took care to conceal this circumstance from Mrs. Vallard who she well knew would consider those visits in scarcely a less dangerous light than those of Lord Henry. Selena on the contrary hoped from them the most salutary consequences, for tho' upon the whole she trusted that composure was restored to her friend, there were still moments of sad reminiscence for the effects of which she yet trembled thinking that

The colour of our fate too oft is tinged
Mournful or bright but from our first affections.[43]

One morning she perceived her friend deeply occupied in reading over and arranging the papers contained in her writing desk. Many of them having been torn across she threw into a little heap at her side which from time to time at Selena's desire (who feared the strong smell of the burnt papers might over power her) she gave to her to carry to the fire in the dressing room. While thus engaged the torrents of tears which she silently shed, and the sighs which seemed to proceed from the very depth of a broken heart convinced Selena upon what painful subjects her attention was employed and the cruel recollections which she thus revived. Gently therefore expostulating with her upon this weakness, she entreated her to defer an examination so afflicting till she should be better able to bear the sight of those images which were thus with renewed force presented to her memory;

"My dear Selena," replied Lady Trevallyn endeavouring to conquer her melancholy, "do not accuse me of wilfully recurring to scenes dreadful indeed to memory and which cover me with self humiliation that I have dared to repine, and

---

[41]   Thomas Gray, "An Ode on a Distant Prospect of Eton College" (1747), lines 92–4 (line 92 should read "Condemned alike to groan").

[42]   Clytemnestra in James Thomson's *Agamemnon* (1738), 1.1.111–15.

[43]   Jacqueline in Robert Jephson's *The Count of Narbonne* (1781), 2.2.22–3.

to consider my lot as undeservedly hard, and my situation as unfortunate when I have all my life been the artificer of my own sorrows. But my soul has been for some time busy about a strange work.

> She now comes home,
> Like a long, absent man and wanders o'er
> Each room a stranger to her own.[44]

Dreary indeed are the ruins which she has there discovered, but let her at least expel all traces of the destroyer. Nevertheless dear Selena I am as you see unfit for the task. You my better self shall perform it for me. Take from this wretched heap all the memorials of my shame, that no hard eye may view them with scorn at my death, or if life is to be prolonged that I may be at least for ever hereafter spared these bitter remembrances. But separate and preserve for me all that you will find written in the hand of my poor Mother, who felt too tenderly felt with her unhappy Emily."

While she spoke she gathered up the scattered fragments and threw them into Selena's lap who promised ere she slept that night to execute her wishes and immediately retired to her own room where having locked them up, she hastened back to her friend, whom she wished not at that time to leave to her own melancholy meditations. Upon her return she found her at a table surrounded by the wild flowers and grasses which Selena had that morning before her rising gathered for her inspection in the

> Wood-walks wild
> By Springs luxuriant hand then strewn anew.[45]

While she complacently smiled on the returning tranquility which she saw beam in every mild and beautifully placid feature Selena could not forbear a secret sigh while she recollected a conversation which she had had with her on the subject of botany during the time of their early acquaintance when she observed her often employed in this manner in her first visits to Esselberrie.

"How just," thought she, "were the reasons which she then gave me for her preference of this peaceful occupation which I was then tempted to consider as a waste of the hours which thus stole insensibly away!"

She had indeed since felt the full force of what Lady Trevallyn then repeated to her as the sentiments of an author in whose fascinating writing she was but too conversant and often had she congratulated her friend on her having imbibed a

---

[44] Dolabella in John Dryden's *All for Love* (1677), 3.1.124–6 (line 124 should read "She's new come home").

[45] Charlotte Smith, "Sonnet ["Farewell, ye lawns!—by fond remembrance blest"]," *Celestina* (1791), lines 5–6 ("Ye wood-walks wild!—where leaves and fairy flowers / By Spring's luxuriant hand are strewn anew"), reprinted as "Sonnet L" in *Elegiac Sonnets* (1800).

taste for this innocent recreation which while it leads the soul to adoration and gratitude towards the Creator so wonderful in all his works can at the same time repose the heart by a suspension of its pains and in misfortune divert the mind from the remembrance which pursues it.

"Botany," Lady Trevallyn used to say after her favourite enthusiast, "is a study adapted for the solitary and the unhappy. The earth is strewed with a profusion of plants, as the Heavens are set with innumerable stars to invite our curiosity. But the study of astronomy is often beyond our reach while the flowers of themselves seem to solicit our hands and are born under our very feet. Even the nature of the objects render this amusement more seductive: the sweetest fragrance, the most vivid colours, forms of inimitable elegance seem to vie with each other to attract our attention. The love of pleasure is in itself sufficient to incline me to a study which cherishes sensations so sweet. Attracted by those beautiful objects which surround me, I contemplate and compare with incessant delight the prodigious variety which accompanied with an astonishing regularity and constant analogy reigns in the organization of the vegetable world: I seek for those simple amusements which can charm alone in the silence of the passions, which I can taste unmingled and which can divert me from my discontents."

These were rather sentiments which Lady Trevallyn had caught from the spirit of the visionary recluse of the island of St. Pierre[46] than an exact quotation of his words—but when Selena since reminded her of the disputes which they used to have upon this subject, owning herself now a convert to her opinion and determined to study botany Lady Trevallyn with a smile expressed her satisfaction and repeated to her a passage which she said she had accidentally met with a few days before.

"In the study of natural history no cause ever presents itself to complain of inconstancy or treachery. An attachment is easily contracted for objects which afford enjoyment alone—and those connexions are as pure as their objects, as durable as their nature—and stronger in proportion to the exertions which have been made to establish them."[47]

When Selena had embraced her friend for the night and retired to the adjoining apartment which she still continued to occupy she commenced the melancholy task which she had undertaken for her friend and past the greatest part of the night in tears while she read over the various testimonies which these papers contained of the fond and then innocent attachment which had been squandered on this unfeeling object of her young affections—an attachment which had been so fatally cherished by a tender but imprudent Mother.

All that was written in the hand of Mrs. Montrose Selena considered as sacred and returned unopened to her poor Emily and from the many unfinished scraps

---

[46] The French chemist and statesman Jean-Antoine Chaptal (1756–1832) was born in Saint-Pierre-de-Nogaret, Lozère.

[47] "Chaptal" (Tighe's note). Jean-Antoine-Claude Chaptal, "Preliminary Discourse," *Elements of Chemistry*, trans. William Nicholson, 3rd ed., 3 vols (London, 1800), 1:lxv.

which at her desire she committed to the flames she ardently wished to preserve the following verses, which she thought painted so exactly that state of anxious and harrassing uncertainty in which she had spent her brightest years while she was indeed fairest of the fair. They were written on the back of a very passionate song which bore the title *Translated for Emily*, and even tho' Selena had not known the hand she could have had no doubt from the style and from this address that Lord Henry had been the translator. By the date on the song it appeared to have been written about two years before her marriage. Lady Trevallyn's verses which were on the other side had no date but they were no doubt produced by the cruel conduct which at that time loved to sport with the purest affections and most amiable feelings.

Selena ventured not to renew them in the memory of her friend by asking for that permission without which she could not reserve them for herself, but before she reluctantly consigned them to perpetual destruction she had so often repeated them over with partial tenderness that involuntarily her retentive memory had seized upon every line.

> Peace, peace, nor utter what I must not hear
>   Too much already hast thou been believed
> Think not thy words can reach alone mine ear
>   In this weak heart too easily received.
>
> Why dost thou mock me with a vain complaint?
>   Why speak of feelings which thou dost not know?
> Too well thy lips can fond affection paint
>   But from thine heart those accents never flow!
>
> What dost thou wish what would this language mean
>   What can the idle boast to thee avail?
> To wound my peace, to blast my hours serene
>   O'er every hope of future bliss prevail.
>
> Is this thy sport? ah thoughtless and unjust?
>   For I have marked thee with a jealous eye,
> Since reason first forbad my heart to trust,
>   And Virtue called me from the snare to fly.
>
> Why should I tell the struggles which have torn
>   This simply credulous, this trusting heart?
> As down the stream of fond affection borne
>   I saw the tranquil shores of peace depart.
>
> As the light flag when borne against the breeze
>   Looks back and trembles with reluctance vain,
> My vanquished soul reflects on former ease
>   Yet powerless sinks submissive to the chain.

Oft when my friendly fate had bad us part
    Thy well feign'd sorrow could prevent my cure,
And absence cherished in my grateful heart
    Friendship it called so innocent and pure.

Yet when returned I saw this friend advance
    Expecting joy to sparkle in his eye,
Chilled I beheld the cold averted glance
    And proudly checked the involuntary sigh

Then how with scorn my weakness I despised
    The folly which was lur'd by falsehood's tale
When other smiles than those I thought were prised
    Could o'er thy false or changeful heart prevail.

Back then with trembling haste to wisdoms side
    Offended delicacy, bade me flee,
Accept my peace restored by wounded pride
    And think no more of tenderness or thee

Why then with cruel art and idle pain
    Revive the sentiments I still deplore?
Why seek what thus you slighted to regain
    And swell this breast with anxious sighs once more

In vain the foldings of thine heart I seek
    At length by reason, or by truth to trace,
Conjecture cannot from thy conduct speak
    But baffled yields to sad surprise her place.

I sought no arts to captivate thy soul
    To blast the prospects of thy opening youth
Such selfish vanity could ne'er control
    The heart which loves with innocence and truth.

Torture no more this agitated breast
    With false seductive hopes of joy and love,
Suffer in calm indifference to rest
    The feelings Prudence bids me disapprove.

Yet a short while and this sad timid eye
    No more shall meet thee with reproachful glance
No claims have I to make or thou deny
    For ease alone this wearied bosom pants[48]

---

[48] Tighe titles this sonnet "Written for Emily" in *Verses Transcribed for H.T.* (Brompton, 1805).

Selena taking the opportunity of Mr. Mason's attendance on her friend endeavoured to raise her own uncommonly dejected spirits by the freshness of the air, and the beauty of the surrounding scenery. With slow and languid steps she turned towards the school house whither she thought her duty led her, tho' never had she felt less disposed for mental exertion. She had plainly perceived and could not banish from her remembrance that her friends at Hillbarton knew something which they were reluctant to communicate and could have but little doubt of the painful or humiliating nature of that intelligence which friends so affectionately attached to her interest were anxious to conceal from her in whom their confidence was at all times so unbounded. Her heart was weighed down by a sense of her situation, despised and abandoned as she appeared to be by him to whom she was enchained, and perhaps now forgotten by the amiable the tender Sidney whose warm friendship and sympathy had secretly tho' unconsciously supported her thro' all her cares.

There is nothing which human nature finds it so hard to sustain with dignity as contempt. Selena felt herself despised, and this sensation as is ever the case, deprived her of the soothing consolation which the afflicted may find in silently lamenting and enumerating their own sorrows. When misfortune assails the tender heart it naturally seeks refuge in the bosom of affection and if even not inclined to utter complaints yet it secretly enjoys a pleasure in dwelling upon the woes which it is conscious have ensured for it compassion. But from mortification and from slight however unjust we seek for no shelter, a kind of despondence and self dislike ever accompanies it; we sink hopeless under its oppression; we wish to hide it even from ourselves and if possible forget our humiliation. But in vain, for the remembrance in spite of all our efforts is for ever new, for ever stinging. Selena's constant and close attendance upon her unhappy friend had in some degree subdued her natural cheerful spirits, so that she had lost some of her accustomed firmness to bear up against the acute sense of suffering to which her lively sensibility always exposed her.

"Why," thought she with somewhat of bitter regret, "Why should I have relied upon my own judgment in opposition to that of others surely far wiser than mine, when in doing so I have cast from me every prospect of earthly happiness. Oh dear Sidney thy generous wish has not been fulfilled! Already I reproach myself for not having listened to consel [sic] so sweet, so delightful, and in refusing to be guided by such advice I may perhaps have been suspected of interested motives, an avaricious attachment to splendid fortune, or the childish ambition of possessing a title. Perhaps he thinks that I sought to ensnare him who now rejects me, and that I cherish for him an unreturned passion. He knows not how my bleeding heart has struggled with inclination in following the powerful voice of conscience. He knows not what I yet feel; Alas he thinks not of me! How easily can men get rid of those little weaknesses which torment us in our allotted solitude. Continual interruptions of various sorts, business, amusements, a thousand cares, and a thousand pleasures of which we know nothing must divert their minds—even undesignedly from the happiest love, how much more when all the efforts of reason and virtue are exerted to banish recollections and sentiments which can yield nothing but pain.

"Besides he has no right to think of me as even deserving his generous attachment. He knew not, he never must know what it cost me to forgo the dear pictures of Love and felicity which my heart was but too ready to represent might be shared with him in the humblest situation and could be my portion with him alone. But can I repent having acted as I still know and feel was right? Could I have been happy in any circumstances while pursued with the consciousness of guilt. Oh no! I should then have indeed deserved my misfortunes and my punishment might have been to have found Sidney unworthy, or to have beheld him indifferent to my love—and either of these I feel would have been indeed insupportable."

In the midst of such meditations she found herself at the door of the school and wiping the tears of which she was before almost unconscious, with a suppressed sigh she endeavoured to give her attention to the various claims which were now eagerly and joyfully made upon her by the little noisy group to whom the appearance of Selena ever proclaimed a holiday of pleasure, a signal of enjoyment.

Chapter XII

> That thou art here beyond all hope
> All thought, that all at once thou art before me!
> And with such suddenness hath hit my sight!
> To such surprise, such mystery, such extacy
> It hurries all my soul and stuns my sense.
> Congreve[49]

Notwithstanding that Selena had ever found her best consolations in the performance of what she looked upon as her duty, and that in a peculiar manner her superintendence of the little school at Esselberrie proved to her a source of the sweetest pleasures, yet in consequence of the melancholy train of thought which she had just indulged, she now entered it with an oppression of spirits that rendered her really for the moment unequal to the exertion of giving to each of her animated little claimants that attention and cheerful regard which she had accustomed them to demand; she therefore proposed to them to sing with her, as it was now some time since she had been able to lead their simple chorus.

Gladly they assented to her desire, and Selena having placed herself in the seat of the projecting window that she might the more unobserved avert from the careless yet prying circle her still tearful eyes, found her own mind gradually composed and tranquilized while to notes of plaintive and simple melody she adapted some words of feeling piety which Lady Trevallyn had received a few days before from Mr. Mason and expressed a desire to hear the children repeat.

---

[49] Almeria in William Congreve's *The Mourning Bride* (1697), 2.7.87–91 (the epigraph substitutes "hath" for "hast" in line 135 and "To" for "Is" in line 136).

Selena wished to surprise her on her first visit with her favorite hymn and having explained this wish to the children they listened in all the stillness of attention to catch from her beautiful lips those lingering notes which then appeared of more than earthly melody.

Nor were they heard by dull ears alone. The very infants listened with a sacred and home felt delight, but there was an auditor upon whose heart they fell with a rapture that took possession of every sense "And in sweet madness robbed it of itself."[50]

Suddenly a general start, an half whispered exclamation, a suppressed titter, and a look of innocent surprise interrupted the mute silence of Selena's little auditors. She stopped and with a smile demanded what they had seen, every eye being still fixed with the avowed eagerness of curiosity upon the door which lay open to the sunny green.

Native politeness abashed them all when sensible of the involuntary disturbance by which they had silenced their lovely songstress and hesitating and blushing they pleaded their having been frightened by the sight of a young gentleman.

Selena's heart died within her. Lord Henry, Dallamore, at once rushed upon her uncertain apprehension. Nay the beloved and graceful form of Sidney failed not at that moment to usurp its ever predominant place. But this was wild and but the transient mockery of improbable fancy. The idea of Lord Henry was also instantly rejected and she remembered with satisfaction that he had already sailed, and it was scarcely possible that if he were even in England he would now dare thus openly to appear at Esselberrie. Upon Dallamore then her thoughts her terrors rested. Yes he was assuredly come! This surprisal, this vanishing, all was consistent with his character; he meant indeed to claim her; She was his for life! She must resign the shadow of liberty which she had apparently enjoyed; she must think of Sidney no more! And altho' a few minutes before she had considered her desertion as a disgrace and a calamity it was now indeed that she felt utterly undone.

Scarcely knowing what she did, unable to speak and with difficulty to support herself she advanced trembling to the door, but she looked around in vain, the shrubs on all sides had totally concealed the person whoever he might have been from their view at present, and Selena once more resumed her composure and began to reassure herself by trying to suppose, that it might in fact have been an entire stranger who had wandered into the demesne from some of the neighbouring roads. In hopes of being confirmed in this persuasion she began to interrogate the children concerning this apparition.

"Oh he was a very beautiful tall gentleman," they all agreed, but Selena who knew how easily such eyes are taken by an appearance of superior rank and an air of gentility relied not much upon this description which indeed might have well applied to either Sidney or Lord Henry—nay even to Dallamore, who was certainly in features and complexion remarkably handsome tho' an extreme vacancy of countenance rendered him far from captivating. That he was dressed in

---

[50]   John Milton, *Comus* (1634), line 261.

black from top to toe, was not a more decisive distinction the mourning for Lord Mount Villars was common to both.

"And he had nice brown hair darker than yours, but all glossy and in little curls about his face," observed one of the eldest girls who had been seated opposite to the door.

Selena's heart throbbed once more—Dallamore it was not; his hair as well as that of Lord Henry was of a lighter shade and both wore powder.

The image of Sidney was yet more forcibly recalled while little Agnes continued, "Yes and he had the sweetest dark blue eyes I ever saw, tho' he looked almost as tho' he was crying while he kept staring at you as you were singing and never seemed to mind us looking at him till you stopped and then he jerked away all of a sudden growing as red as any thing."

"I dare say we could see him yet if we might run to the little mount in the new plantation," said another of the girls somewhat timidly as this spot, being rather exposed, was not within the limits of their prescribed reign.

Selena faintly smiled consent and followed their more eager steps at a distance her prudence hardly sanctioning the permission which her indulgence had granted.

She had not however proceeded many steps before she stopped, struck by the idea that if it should indeed be Sidney her thus pursuing him with curiosity might if he beheld her wear a strange appearance, and nearly overcome with emotion she seated herself on a bank behind her, surrounded with thick evergreens. While the confused voice of merriment that proceeded from the delighted little troop died faintly away and while her eyes were still fixed on that part whither her wild companions had hastened, she on a sudden perceived emerging from the shade and within a few paces of her the very object of all their curiosity. His face indeed was turned from her, as he also earnestly pursued their steps eager to behold by whom they were accompanied but could she longer doubt? Oh no! it was indeed Sidney himself!

Motionless, breathless she remained intently gazing upon the form, till having cast a hasty glance around without chancing to alight upon that little spot where he might indeed have found all he loved upon earth he retired with quick steps taking the path which led thro' the park to Hillbarton.

When he was no longer in sight Selena involuntarily started up and exerting all her strength advanced rapidly a few steps with streaming eyes, till faint and sick with agitation, she supported herself against a tree, and burst into a violent shower of tears. It was then that having in some degree recovered her bewildered senses, she began to doubt if the whole was not indeed a dream—a vision of fancy and could not persuade herself that she had indeed beheld Sidney that he also had beheld her and was now gone without seeking an interview or explaining wherefore he was there.

The romantic and imprudent conduct which Edwin had pursued while he concealed himself in the woods of Herefordshire, was too unlike Sidney, to suffer her for a moment to suspect that he could act in so wild a manner, so idle and criminal in itself, so injurious to her reputation. That he should come to Hillbarton at this time without an intention of seeing her was impossible, since if he had even desired to visit Mrs. Vallard, he might without difficulty have previously informed himself whether she had yet quitted her, and that he should desire again to see Selena after the decided farewell which she had so lately received she knew not how to believe nor was such a supposition indeed justified by his sudden disappearance from the schoolhouse and the concealment which he now evidently design'd.

Lost in conjectures with a palpitating heart and trembling steps she returned to Lady Trevallyn starting at every breeze which rustled in the young leaves, and at every opening in the walks anxiously looking round with uncertain expectation. Once she had almost determined to hasten to Hillbarton that she might communicate to her sister what she had seen or thought she had seen and hear from her whether this vision had also appeared to them and for what strange purpose it was come. But the apprehension, nay almost certainty of meeting Sidney there, Sidney who now avoided her instantly diverted her steps and involuntarily quickened them as she returned to Esselberrie, so that she was already in the presence of Lady Trevallyn before she had considered whether she should speak to her of the apparition which had so much agitated her whole frame.

Chapter XIII

> While thou art present my sad heart seems lighter;
> Thy gentle eyes send forth a quickning spirit,
> And feed the dying lamp of life within me:
> But oh when thou art gone, and my fond eyes
> Shall seek thee all around, but seek in vain
> What power what angel shall supply thy place
> Shall help me to support my sorrows then
> And save my soul from death.
>
> Rowe[51]

Selena on her entrance perceived that her friend was occupied with a book which Mr. Mason had left for her perusal, and felt for the moment relieved that she was thus allowed time for recollection.

Silently she advanced to the window, and remained there motionless her head resting upon the frame and her eyes fixed upon the lawn till the sweetly plaintive voice of her friend roused her from her reverie.

"Well Selena," said she closing her book and placing it in her work basket, "you have brought me no violets I think this morning. But have you been to visit my little girls?" Selena turning round with a deep sigh was about to make some reply when Lady Trevallyn looking earnestly at her exclaimed, "Oh Selena how pale you look my love! What is the matter?"

---

[51]   Aribert in Nicholas Rowe's *The Royal Convert* (1708), 2.1.440–48 (the epigraph omits line 441: "I gaze, and gather Comfort from thy Beauty").

"Nothing dear Lady Trevallyn," answered she forcing a smile and a cheerful accent, but finding her courage absolutely fail her to account for her evident agitation and confess that it was occasioned by the sudden appearance of Sidney.

"You have walked too much," said Lady Trevallyn affectionately pressing her hand, "the sun seems to be very hot to day, and I dare say you feel this room oppressively close just coming in from the sweet freshness of the air, I long myself to taste once more the gales of Spring, and see if they can still seem to me 'Redolent of joy and youth.'"[52]

Selena encouraged her to venture into the air, wishing if it were possible to open her heart again to these sensations of calm pleasure which the parent of Nature allows all his children to enjoy in the "Breath of Heaven fresh flowing pure and sweet."[53]

'Tis man alone who in the absence of positive pain and surrounded by agreeable objects rejects the present pleasure and obstinately tenacious of misery dwells upon the memory of departed sorrows, anticipates the distant nay the uncertain pain, or brings the bright comparison of lost enjoyments heightened by regret to make us esteem as dull and obscure those blessings which yet remain.

Unfortunately as Selena supported the feeble steps of her friend thro' the greenhouse her eyes were instantly attracted by her beautiful plants of geranium, whose fragrance like those subtle poisons whose very odour is so fatal suddenly communicated to her heart a death like anguish.

She stopped however gently repulsing Selena who would have led her on, and in silence extending her hand after a moment's reflection gathered one of the most perfect blossoms, and examining it with a sadly earnest eye inhaled the odour.

She then suffered Selena to conduct her to a seat in a small marble portico open to the south. For a few moments each was silent, but as Selena perceived that her whole soul was still intently fixed upon the little branch over which she bent with a look of unutterable melancholy she ventured softly to draw it from her hand repeating in a half whisper the pathetic exhortation of Petrarca "Deh non rinovellar quel che n'ancide!"[54]

"Oh! Selena," replied she raising her swimming eyes, "*You* do not know, *you* cannot conceive the change. To you that is still the same, still beautiful, still fragrant; but think what it was to poor Angela! The airs of Paradise could not be sweeter to my soul than that once appeared, while to her baneful and torturing it imparted only those sensations which are now my just but heavy punishment. Poor Angela! I knew not the bitter feelings I thus excited, but surely my bleeding heart has paid them back, and if we meet, and that the remembrance of our short and troubled voyage still survives we may meet in peace and with mutual pity. And you my best friend, my preserver, my good angel in human shape, pray that I may

---

[52] Thomas Gray, "Ode on a Distant Prospect of Eton College" (1747), line 19.

[53] Milton, *Samson Agonistes* (1671), line 10.

[54] Petrarch, Sonnet 273, line 9: "Ah, don't renew what tortures us to death" (Mark Musa trans.).

be forgiven that the remainder of my punishment may be remitted and that I also may find at last that rest which I trust ere this poor Angela has gained. And when our prayers are heard dear Selena will you not look after my little girls and watch that no canker may devour those poor innocent blossoms."

Selena struck with the conviction that her friend felt the approach of that release from life which she so much desired was unable to reply to her with the cheerfulness that she thought expedient and could only press her hand in silence while she vainly endeavoured to conceal the tears which overflowed from her bursting heart.

At the sound of a slowly approaching footsteps behind the greenhouse they both started, once more the idea of Sidney took possession of the soul of Selena and banished from thence every other thought, nevertheless the next moment presented an object far different indeed, but one at that time scarcely less agitating even to her eyes.

"There is Lord Trevallyn," exclaimed her friend endeavouring to rise as he advanced but trembling and unable to support herself she once more sunk upon the seat.

Selena distressed, terrified and embarrassed could with difficulty return the salutation which he made with an air of cold and haughty gravity which Selena felt more expressive of insult than respect—then turning to Lady Trevallyn with a look of scornful displeasure, "I congratulate you Madam," said he, "upon your complete recovery, and altho' you have not thought proper to announce it to me you see you have not been able to prevent my return to witness so joyful an event."

"It was my intention my Lord," replied she with a feeble and tremulous voice, "to have desired Rawlins this evening to let you know that I had been out so that all danger of infection is probably over, but this is the first time that I have left my dressing room."

Selena quickly recovered her composure and shocked at the situation in which she perceived her friend now advised her to return in saying, "I shall never forgive myself if you suffer by taking my advice."

"Your advice Miss Miltern," said Lord Trevallyn with a sneer, "is at all times so prudent that I should rather suppose they must suffer who do not always regard it."

Selena could not doubt that this speech was intended to convey some reproach but was at a loss to know how she had merited his dislike except by her attachment to her friend. She made no reply but whisperingly urged Lady Trevallyn to suffer her to support her in.

But this was impossible; conscious of her weakness she wished to defer the attempt till she had in some degree recovered the faintness which had overpowered her on this surprise and when in compliance with Selena's entreaty she made an effort to rise her powerless limbs refused to obey her wish.

A half smile that sat upon the hard features of the Earl as he gazed upon Selena and her friend plainly evinced his opinion of the affectation which he really believed was displayed in this scene. Disdaining to offer any assistance he at length said coolly, "Perhaps Lady Trevallyn may recover the strength which in my absence she appeared to enjoy when I retire, and when she is able to allow me a few minutes conversation without the necessity of a third person to afford her support I shall take it as a favour of Miss Miltern to inform me."

The stress which he laid upon those words plainly told Selena how peculiarly undesirable was her presence, and made her dread that the hour was at length arrived when her unhappy friend was to be deprived of the consolations of her society.

Nor was Lady Trevallyn herself insensible to the loss she was about to sustain. She knew not how great had been the comforts and the soothing pleasures which she had hitherto received from the attendance of Selena in what she had felt a state so desolate, until she saw that desolation could be yet so much encreased by the absence of her silently sympathising eye, or the soft accents of her tenderly cheering voice. She nevertheless resolved neither to murmur nor resist but patiently submit to whatever Lord Trevallyn might propose, even tho' she must thus as she feared relinquish totally all communication with Selena. For from some words which he had before dropped, as well as from the expression of his countenance as he now addressed her gentle and affectionate friend she had indeed too much reason to apprehend that he had resolved upon their entire separation.

Nor was she mistaken. Mr. Guise, who dreaded lest her penetration should discover his interference had long since urged the expediency of her removal, representing her as the great promoter of Lady Trevallyn's intimacy with Lord Henry and dwelling upon the art with which no doubt at her instigation the obstinately refused promise had at last been given with such affected submission immediately upon hearing of the flight which had in fact rendered it so unnecessary and superfluous.

Selena herself now waited with fearful anxiety the result of Lord Trevallyn's interview with her friend. She watched impatiently till he had quitted the dressing room and then hastened to learn their fate. As she opened the door Lady Trevallyn in silence extended her arms and Selena who too well understood the melancholy signal falling on her knees hid her tears in the bosom of her weeping friend.

"We must part Selena," cried she, "I have given you up for the present that I might not be constrained to lose you entirely. I have told Lord Trevallyn that you would return to Hillbarton this day, and as he appeared satisfied with my ready concession he will not I hope oppose your visits."

Altho' Selena's heart ached thus to be constrained to leave the sad Emily in melancholy weakness and dejection, at a moment when she so much required to be soothed and supported she could yet oppose nothing to the prudent submission which acquiesced in the will of Lord Trevallyn, a submission which her own judgment could not but approve.

But while she still lingered with reluctant tenderness and melancholy foreboding while they mutually formed plans for their daily and constant meetings which the heart of each sadly and secretly foretold must never be realised Lord Trevallyn's servant abruptly entered with a message to Miss Miltern to inform her that his Lordship's carriage awaited her orders.

Selena coloured at the more than hinted dismission, Emily pressed her hand in silent anguish but after a moment's hesitation Selena arose and addressing the servant desired him to return her thanks to Lord Trevallyn and requested him to inform his Lordship that "she was just setting out but that it was her intention to walk to Hillbarton," then turning to her silently sorrowing friend she added immediately in order that the servant might hear it, "I will send a messenger in the evening for my cloaths and a few books which I have brought here."

When he had closed the door and they saw themselves perhaps for the last time alone they now felt they must indeed part and once more mingled their tears in a last embrace. They exchanged scarcely a few broken words, but those who have held to their heart the friend whom they feared they should meet no more, those who have listened to the interrupted blessing, the half uttered farewell can alone imagine the anguish with which they then separated.

End of Volume IV

Volume V

Chapter I

But when that sex leave Vertue to esteem
Those greatly err who think them what they seem,
Their plighted faith they at their pleasure leave
Their love is cold but hot as hell their hate,
On whom they smile they surely those deceive,
In their desires they be insatiate;
Them of their will there's nothing can bereave,
They lay by fear when they at ruin aim;
They shun not sin as little weigh they shame

Drayton[1]

Amidst the sadness which oppressed Selena in being thus constrained to abandon her friend in a situation so terrible, at a moment so critical, it is not to be denied that her heart beat tumultuously, when she thought upon what might perhaps await her on her return to Hillbarton; But it was not until she had slowly closed the little gate which separated the park of Esselberrie from one of the fields belonging to Hillbarton that she had leisure to turn her consideration from the sorrows of Lady Trevallyn to her own perplexities. As she approached the wood the dread of meeting Sidney and thus appearing to pursue him conquered every emotion of curiosity and impatience to learn for what purpose he had returned. Fancy cloathed every distant object with his form, every sound appeared to her ears to be his footsteps and her heart beat with a violence which made every breath a sigh. The road lay on her right hand but a high hedge screened it from her view, the trampling of horses suddenly arrested her attention.

"It is Sidney!" thought she instantly. "He has been at Hillbarton in my absence and now quits it fearful of the return of her he must avoid for ever."

It is impossible to conceive the pang with which this idea was accompanied and which urged her to fly towards the hedge thro' which with some difficulty and totally insensible to the briars which tore her arms she at length obtained a view of what had so forcibly attracted her thither.

But it was not Sidney! And her heart which had so strongly pictured his beautiful form felt for a moment a sensation which resembled disappointment upon perceiving her mistake; But as she gazed upon the objects which had now passed the spot where she stood feelings of a far different nature were excited upon the conviction that the post horses which she beheld were assuredly returning from Hillbarton after having left there a carriage. The two post boys, the harness that

---

[1]   Michael Drayton, *The Barons' Wars* (1603), 3:79–88 (the epigraph omits line 86—"Their anger hath no bound; revenge no date"—and uses "hell" for "fire" in line 82).

hung loose upon the horses all declared it. But Sidney was not accustomed to travel alone in his own chaise with four horses. Dallamore was now beyond a doubt his companion. Alas! to what a scene was she returning? How little was she prepared for what she had to encounter! Sidney was however there! In a few minutes she should probably behold him and might again listen to the sweet voice which she had so lately considered as lost to her for ever. There was in this assurance a pleasure which subdued the pain, the anxiety, of this tumultuous moment. Quite overpowered by her agitation she sat herself down to consider how she should steal to her own room unobserved until she had conversed with Clara.

She had not been there many minutes before the dinner bell gave her notice of the family being assembled and thinking that this afforded her an opportunity of entering unseen she exerted all her courage and hastened forward. She had now entered the grass walk beneath a fine avenue of limes which led immediately along the lawn towards the house at one end. The dinner parlour was to the front and there were but few windows on that side which looked to the avenue, nevertheless as she approached she fixed her eyes upon these while she stole fearfully along.

"Selena!" cried a voice which vibrated to her heart, "Selena! dear Selena!" and her feet were rooted to the ground while she beheld indeed Sidney, breathless with eagerness, surprise, and delight advancing with extended hand his whole soul sparkling thro' his enraptured eyes. Seizing her trembling hand discretion scarcely could restrain him from casting himself at her feet and clasping her in his impatient arms while he exclaimed in incoherent sentences, "Is it indeed you dearest Selena? Shall I not awake from this delightful dream? Will it not fly like all the rest? Forgive me dear, inexpressibly dear Selena but I am happy, yes in spite of all things I am happy, I must confess it, I can lament nothing, that restores me to your presence, no were it the dissolution of empires that was threatened instead of those rashly formed ill suited ties I could not be insensible to the joy of this moment. Alas, you are grieved, you are shocked! And I, selfish wretch! am happy, still I am happy! Do you hate me? Selena can you forgive me?"

"What is the matter with you dear Sidney?" cried Selena trembling and overcome with the transport which his burning hands and empassioned glances seemed in some degree to have communicated to hers while lost in the sudden delight of gazing indeed upon the very "*hourly image*"[2] of her thoughts. But tho' carried away for a moment while she involuntarily returned the pressure of his hand with such tumultuous emotions of a joy in which reason had no participation she was quickly restored by painful recollection to the consciousness of her situation and she gazed upon the incomprehensible Sidney with astonishment not unmingled with terror as she eagerly repeated, "what is the matter?"

The expression of her countenance seemed instantly to calm the excess of his transports; "you think I am mad I believe Selena, and my want of delicacy I see distresses you, believe me I knew not myself till this instant how selfish I was nor[3]

---

[2]   Belvidera in Thomas Otway's *Venice Preserv'd* (1682), 2.3.162.

[3]   MS: "now" (my correction).

could I have believed how the delight of seeing you would have at once banished from my mind every painful reflection, every sensation but that of joy. And yet Selena do me the justice to believe that a few hours ago I fled from your presence without courage to be the bearer of intelligence which I trembled to think might render you unhappy. But now that you are apprised of it; now that I am convinced you wish not to shun me ...."

"Apprised of what?" exclaimed Selena who had gazed upon him earnestly during this speech, unable to comprehend its meaning, and too much bewildered to know what enquiries to make. She could however no longer restrain her impatience and interrupting him with this eager interrogation Sidney at once perceived that the task which he had so much dreaded, the painful office he had avoided, was now necessarily imposed upon him and that he had to communicate to her intelligence not less important to himself than to her—that from his lips she was to hear of her brother's dishonour and of her own rejection in the elopement of Lady Harriet with Dallamore and his decisive declaration that he considered not Selena as his wife.

Nor was this all that now overwhelmed Sidney with the conviction that she was yet a stranger to these events. Unable to appear with calmness he had excused himself to Mrs. Vallard for his absence at dinner and impatiently watched for the return of the messenger who had been sent to Selena with her brother's letter who having missed her by taking a shorter path had arrived at Esselberrie almost immediately after she left it. His heart bounded with ectasy when he beheld her approach from the sudden assurance that had this intelligence been as severe to her heart as his fears sometimes suggested it might prove, she could not thus hastily have returned where she was informed he had arrived. All the rapturous hope which from this idea Love pour'd in a torrent upon his soul fled at the instant that he perceived that she was yet uninformed of the strange occurrances which had taken place.

Embarrassed and hesitating he relinquished her hand and remained for a moment silent till upon her repeating her question he said faintly, "Then you have not received Robert's letter."

"No, I am but just come from Esselberrie, shall I find it here?" added she advancing some steps towards the house.

He gently detained her while he said in a tremulous voice, "No but you will find there Robert himself. We arrived together this morning."

"Robert here!" exclaimed Selena while the first emotions of joy were instantly checked by the dread of some misfortune which she felt assured had caused this unexpected journey.

"Oh Sidney," cried she turning pale at the ideas which crowded in fearful tumult into her mind, "tell me I beseech you what has happened. Who else is at Hillbarton?"

"No one dearest Selena," answered Sidney judging but too surely that her thoughts were fixed on Dallamore. Nevertheless other apprehensions now seized upon her mind and had urged the question already anticipating her brother's separation from his unworthy wife.

"And where," cried she eagerly, " is Lady Harriet?"

"Selena how shall I tell you where she is. I know not, but she has quitted Miltern Abbey for ever and Dallamore is her companion!"

"Oh poor Robert!" exclaimed Selena her expressive eyes fixed upon the face of Sidney with a mixture of consternation, wonder, and pity, while quite overcome with the sudden shock she would have sunk to the ground had he not caught her in his arms and leaning against a tree supported her as her head reclined upon his shoulder in a state of confused insensibility.

Sidney meanwhile pressed her to his beating heart internally repeating the dear consoling words which had at first escaped her lips involuntarily proving that the loss of Dallamore was only felt in the disgrace and crime which had occasioned it. "Oh she will be mine!" thought he, "Angel of bliss if thou hast not reserved for me such happiness let me at least expire whilst I cherish so exquisite an hope!"

Recovering her recollection she now disengaged herself from his arms and once more attempted to hasten to the house in order that she might collect her spirits before she met Robert or heard the particulars of this surprising event.

Sidney followed her in silence for a few steps, and suddenly exclaimed, "Stay Selena one moment, rest yourself upon that seat, I see the messenger is returning with your brother's letter."

As he spoke he flew to meet him and having put it into her hands assisted her to reach the house which she entered unobserved and immediately retired to her room where she perused the following letter.

> "My dearest Sister,
>
> "All is over. Your fate as well as mine has come to a crisis. Heaven has in a wonderful manner at once broken those inauspicious ties which it judged unworthy of us. The discussion is yet so painful to me that I wished Sidney my friend my brother to have spared me the task of communicating to you this event but that delicacy which made him so long conceal even from me the love he bears you shrunk from being the bearer of intelligence at which you might accuse him of selfishly rejoicing. I wish however to avoid for the present all conversation on the subject and that you my dear Selena may for a few days give me no answer upon the important point which I now desire to submit to your consideration before we meet, that I may be at liberty to enjoy the consolation of your society unmingled with any distressing retrospections any painful reference to unpleasant topicks.
>
> "In hourly expectation of your arrival at Miltern Abbey, as I was deluded to think was your intention, I separated myself as much as possible from the abominable society which was assembled there without my consent. I will not sully your pure mind with an account of what passed there in the course of a few days of riot and confusion which it was the interest of vice at that time peculiarly to promote. I saw enough to oblige me to demand from Dallamore an explanation and upon my rising early before the appointed hour on the following morning I found that he had already quitted the house with the vile woman from whom in

the course of a few hours I received the insolent and abominable lines which I enclose for your perusal. In the first fury which seized upon my mind I was fool enough to pursue the worthless objects of my resentment, that the villain who had thus injured and insulted me might not at least escape punishment from my hand. My wise good Angel met me in the person of Sidney.

"By the most fortunate accident he had arrived at Ross on his way from Ireland not an hour after this abandoned pair had left it. Doubtless with the view of preventing pursuit should any be intended they had taken with them every horse which could be procured in the town, and Sidney being informed of this upon ordering a chaise was astonished to hear the name of Dallamore. The confused and uncertain account which he then received of this strange journey so much excited his curiosity that he determined to walk to the next village and from thence procure a horse that he might reach Miltern Abby and there learn the real truth.

"On the road he met and restored me to myself. In the tumult of his first astonishment his secret escaped him and I perceived that by adopting the plan which this infamous woman herself desires and by giving Dallamore the power to unite himself to his proper mate for life I shall at once free us both from unworthy bonds and indulge the hopes of the most amiable of men. Dearest Selena never was there a more tender a more noble heart than that of Sidney.

"I am sensible how inestimable is its value or never would I consent for the doubtful prospect of future happiness to submit to the disgrace of a public trial; but if you are resolved not to profit by the freedom which Dallamore's marriage would indisputably restore you, if you can still wish to retain your claims upon him, I shall think it my part to prevent the possibility of his forming this far more suitable union and will never procure that divorce which they desire. I will not attempt to advise you; your own delicacy and prudence which have hitherto so well conducted you in a path so intricate are better guides than your rash, ill-judging, and unfortunate brother who has no wish now more strong than to promote your happiness. I will confess Selena that at times my courage shrinks from exposing to the world the shameful tale of my dishonour, and the guilt of her whom I once loved; but on the other hand there are moments when a fierce indignation gets possession of my soul and it is bitter to me to think that young as we are our lives must be devoted to a disgraceful and deserted widowhood, deprived of all the consolations of mutual tenderness, all the sweets of domestic affections, which our hearts warm and susceptible are well calculated to feel.

"Is it not hard Selena? And shall we not assert our freedom and seek the bosom which Heaven has destined to be the pillow where we may yet recline in peace and find our future happiness and the sweet forgetfulness of our past griefs? At all events dearest Selena, your determination shall decide mine; our lot is interwoven together and if you still consider it as your duty to abide by your unfortunate and rejected vows I will take no steps to be absolved from mine."

Lady Harriet's letter which was enclosed in this had fallen to the ground when Selena hastily unfolded the papers, and it was some time before she thought of perusing it so entirely was her whole soul engrossed by the agitating consideration of Robert's proposal. Nor is it to be wondered at if poor Selena, tho' the least selfish of mortals, found every emotion of curiosity suspended and forgot for the moment every idea but that there was offer'd to her a possibility of devoting her life to receive the love and form the happiness of the beloved the amiable being with whom alone she could conceive felicity.

"Meek spirit of my mother!" she exclaimed, "look down from Heaven, and behold your last wishes at length accomplished! Behold the unlooked for deliverance of your child who never now can be Lord Dallamore's."

The tender remembrance of the prayer for her happiness in a union with one whom she should love which had accompanied this anxious wish of her expiring mother now returned with fresh force to her mind, which for the first time since those prayers had been uttered now suffered itself to dwell upon the sweet hope of their being ever realized.

But how quickly was she called back from this day dream of delight to the painful reflections upon her brother's situation and the doubtful part which now remained for her to act.

While thus overwhelmed and bewildered by emotions which she could not define and by thoughts which had no fixed object Clara who had heard of her return from the messenger who had delivered her brother's letter entered impatient to embrace and welcome her.

Perceiving Selena whose spirits were quite overcome, unable to speak for her tears she looked at her with a concern mingled with surprise and eagerly exclaimed, "Oh Selena! surely you do not lament Dallamore, he never deserved you!"

"But have you no consideration for poor Robert?" cried Selena, "and can you not feel our common disgrace?"

"*Poor Robert*! do you say?" returned Clara with an accent of surprise, "why Selena I think it the most fortunate event that could have happened to him; and never did I feel him less the object of compassion since that moment that I saw heartless pride and illnature lowering on her scornful brow when she first entered the drawing room below! And as to our disgrace surely her ill conduct must reflect less both upon us and Robert now that she has I will say thank God separated herself from us for ever than when we might appear to give it at least tacit encouragement. No, no, Selena I cannot regret any thing whatever in this business that has put an end to the torturing suspence in which that wretched Dallamore held us, and has now at once both delivered you and Robert from the bondage that threatened to form the misery of your whole lives."

While she spoke thus with some warmth almost unconscious what she was doing she stooped for the paper which she perceived at her feet and unfolding it was instantly struck with surprise by the hand writing of Lady Harriet.

"Good Heavens! Selena what is this?" she cried as she cast her eyes over the contents which Selena with almost equal eagerness perused at the same moment over her shoulder. The letter was as follows:

> "I shall not give you or myself the trouble of attempting to excuse my conduct, which however it may oppose some illiberal prejudices, your own heart will tell you may be sufficiently justified by your indifference to me and attachment

to another. But for fear *you* should suffer any thing from my absence I wish to afford you all the consolation in my power and I think I cannot do this more effectually than by furnishing you with the best evidence for the removal of all difficulties which might lie in the way of your obtaining a divorce, for which I take it for granted you will be as desirous as Lord Mount Villars, myself or even Miss Ophelia Lawder. I have to this end remained at this house the greater part of this night and have brought hither Millikin who will be ready to give her testimony that those hours have been passed with him whom for the future I esteem my husband. It is my Lord's request that you will have also the goodness to question her (but this may be done in a less public manner Selena having always pretended to greater delicacy than myself) upon the conduct of the person whose matrimonial claims upon him he never did nor ever will acknowledge; during her residence last winter at Miltern Abbey and it is our mutual wish that the seducing Edwin Stanmore may amply compensate for the loss of Lord Mount Villars—a loss which she may have the injustice to lay to my charge.
                     Harriet."

Words can never paint the emotion visible in the whole agitated frame of Clara as she continued to keep her eyes fixed upon the paper which was not only shocking to her as a proof of such depravity as she conceived not possible in woman, but conveyed to her heart the severest reproach for her own imprudent conduct, which by preserving the secret of Edwin and meeting him in private had thus injured the pure character of Selena and perhaps occasioned the desertion of Dallamore, which now that she accused herself as the cause she was timidly inclined to consider as the most terrible disgrace and misfortune to Selena, tho' the moment before she had represented it rather as a subject of congratulation.

Selena was now constrained to exercise all her powers of consolation to restore Clara to peace with herself, and to this end confessed to her what she had hitherto scarcely ventured to acknowledge to her own heart, that she could never have been happy united to Dallamore and that tho' she could not yet think herself free to form a new engagement yet that his marriage with another would relieve her from an inexpressible load of apprehension by delivering her for ever from his caprices and the duty of loving him exclusively, which she had found it so hard to fulfil.

Perceiving that Clara was about to argue in favour of her complete liberty she prevented her with a smile saying, "Do you wish me then to follow Lady Harriet's advice? and endeavour to console myself for my loss in the manner she recommends?"

"Oh dear Selena! Edwin was once worthy of you, but alas! what, is he now?"

As she spoke her voice trembled and the deep sadness of her countenance made Selena anxious to turn her mind from the subject which she blamed herself for having once more introduced. She felt therefore relieved by the entrance of Mrs. Vallard who the moment that she heard of Selena's arrival hastened to her eager to unburden her heart full as it was of indignation and regret.

Perhaps of the whole party whom it concerned Mrs. Vallard felt the most unmingled affliction in consequence of Dallamore's conduct, and as was natural, while she severely condemned him in her own mind she endeavoured in some degree tacitly to justify or at least excuse him by pouring out all her indignation and reproaches upon his shameless seducer as she perhaps not improperly styled Lady Harriet. Nevertheless her kind heart, which quickly inclined her to sympathise with all Robert's sufferings upon this occasion, readily agreed to the desire he had expressed to Selena which her own delicacy had indeed already discovered and it was determined that nothing should be said in his presence relative to an affair so painful.

While they awaited his joining them in the drawing room Selena's heart almost reproached her for involuntary hypocrisy as blushing she listened to Mrs. Vallard's warm eulogium upon the gentleness with which she bore this injury and the calm and composed fortitude with which she had received the intelligence which by degrading her from a countess with the united wealth of splendid revenues to the simple rank of a portionless girl, Mrs. Vallard considered as the complete disappointment of all her prospects of worldly felicity.

"Alas," thought Selena, "how little does my indulgent unsuspicious friend see into the windings of this deceitful heart! Ah had it been Sidney who had thus deserted me! Had I once been suffered to indulge the hope of passing my life with him and calling myself his own for ever, could I thus resigned and tranquil have borne a desertion like this?"

But this was a self examination from which she even in thought now shrunk, for even to herself she wished not to own that tho' a hope had never been indulged, tho' an idea of mutual bliss and mutual confidence had never been cherished, yet the very supposition of Sidney's ceasing to love her, ceasing to display an interest for her, let fall a chill and heavy weight upon her heart more insupportable than any sensation which it was in the power of Dallamore by any conduct to inflict.

But he was at this instant separated from her only by one appartment. He was engaged with Robert in conversation of which she was perhaps the object, he was perhaps expressing his hopes and forming plans of happiness which tho' they might never be realized were yet even in contemplation delightful. His thoughts at least were assuredly fixed upon her, in a few moments the door upon which she now fixed her eyes should open, she should behold him enter, and his first glance she well knew would be for her! If he did not immediately approach her, if he seemed at first to address another, yet some movement involuntary, and to all others imperceptible would convince her beyond the power of words that she and she alone possessed his whole attention while there. All this she felt, and in vain did she persuade herself that she lamented the wicked action of Dallamore and that her thoughts were occupied by him and her unfortunate brother.

Chapter II

There is in love a power,
There is a soft divinity that draws
Even transport from distress—that gives the heart
A certain pang excelling far the joys
Of gross unfeeling life

Thompson[4]

There was a degree of embarrassment in the appearance of Robert as he first entered; Placing himself beside Selena on the sopha with his arm thrown around her waist while she affectionately retained his hand in hers, the tears rushed to his eyes and in spite of all his efforts to dispel them fell in large drops upon her hair, as he leaned his face upon her head, which reclined on his shoulder, to conceal the unmanly emotion. In vain he struggled to bear some part in the conversation, his oppression every moment encreased at length while they were still seated round the tea table he quitted the appartment.

Sidney who had endeavoured to support the apparent cheerfulness of the party by many an unseconded observation now approached Selena, and addressing her in that soft voice of inexpressible tenderness with which Love so easily penetrates the soul he gradually soothed or banished from her sweetly harmonized bosom every painfully anxious thought, 'till nothing remained but the gently agitating consciousness of beholding and being beloved by him in whose presence alone the universe could smile.

It was not till some casual interruption had suspended for a few moments this enchanting eloquence of the soul, that the recollection of her brother returned with distressing force, and she instantly quitted her seat with the intention of seeking him and endeavouring to cheer his dejected spirits. He was not however in his own room and upon enquiring from Philip she heard that he had taken his hat and walked towards the wood.

It was yet scarcely dark, one star alone twinkled with feeble lustre and above it appeared the moon not with the silver splendor which she wears in the deep blue vault of night but rather like a crescent of wanish gold in the midst of the serene sky, which overspread with one clear uninterrupted canopy, gradually melting from the purest blue to the light tints of the most pale and delicate green except where the still blushing horizon glowed thro' the dark shades of the western grove. It was an evening so still, so sweet that it would have irresistibly allured Selena to a solitary walk, when the remembrance of Sidney, had Sidney been far away, must have accompanied the gentle sigh which said in secret "oh how delightful to taste with those we love an evening such as this!" No wonder therefore that he was now present to her heart as she advanced along the path where she hoped to meet her brother.

---

[4]   Eltruda in James Thomson's *Alfred: A Masque* (1740) , 1.6.34–8.

But there she found him not and unwilling to venture alone into the wood at so late an hour, she slowly returned and had not advanced many paces before she was joined by Sidney whose walk she instantly recognized upon seeing the figure at a distance which the obscurity prevented her from accurately distinguishing.

"Are you determined upon solitude Selena?" said he with some hesitation, "Or may I share your walk this sweet evening?"

"I came to look for Robert," answered she timidly accepting his offered arm, "that I might if possible dissipate some of his melancholy. He is sadly altered since I saw him last."

"He has certainly past thro' some hours of the most severe suffering and vexation that a man can endure, but believe me dear Selena this last blow was scarcely felt in comparison to what preceeded it of internal struggles in his mind and after the first tumult (in which I so fortunately met him) had subsided, I have not seen him so dejected as since he arrived here and we can easily account for that by reflecting how different was his situation when he last visited Hillbarton."

"Ah true," replied Selena, "and I myself felt inexpressibly shocked at the unavoidable comparison when I saw him just now enter the very drawing room where he introduced to us the first choice of his warm affectionately feeling heart. How terrible must it be to be forced to change love and admiration into hatred and contempt! I have alas but too lately seen this attended with effects nearly fatal."

"I know to whom you allude," answered Sidney, "but you will allow dear Selena that the case is by no means parallel. Your lovely interesting friend had from her very childhood been seduced by the most artful species of villains, possessed of every charm that woman could love except true excellence of heart, nay even his heart may have been naturally amiable had he not been early corrupted by the worst principles."

Selena who knew that heart perhaps better than Sidney (tho' less acquainted with the profligacy of Lord Henry's life) shook her head and Sidney with a smile proceeded.

"Well I can forgive you for not thinking it possible that he was ever really amiable, but she whom for years he deceived was justified in believing that she knew him well, and if any thing has been able to open her eyes to his true character, it is still impossible that she should ever love another. The sentiment and the object were identified in her heart, and in order to banish the one it was absolutely necessary to root out every trace of the other. How different is the case of your brother! The transient inclination which rashly prompted him to offer his hand to Lady Harriet would certainly in his amiable and virtuous mind have ripened into the truest affection had she deserved his esteem, but ill-temper and want of sympathy hastened even prematurely the destruction of passion and there was there no gentler dearer sentiment to take its place. She herself designedly and for the worst of purposes encouraged his intimacy with one of the most captivating young woman I ever saw."

"You mean Ophelia Lawder?"

"Robert has then already told you of his attachment; he gave me liberty to speak to you of it, saying he would have nothing secret from *us*." His voice faultered and he almost insensibly pressed the hand of Selena as he pronounced those last words while the twilight screened the deep blushes which they called forth, for her heart trembled like his at the dear association.

She was a moment silent before she had power to answer, "no he has told me nothing, but from his letters some time ago Clara and I entertained suspicions which we wished not to encourage. But she is engaged, is she not. I thought every thing was settled for her union with young Mr. Bently."

"What you have never heard of Charles Bently's strange marriage?"

"Marriage, is it possible he has then deserted Ophelia whom he loved so long?"

"Oh it was all together a most unaccountable business. He ran away with a young Lady from Ireland. Poor Dallamore assisted him very foolishly and the business vexed Mr. Bently extremely at first, more than it did our friend Ophelia, but it is a long story and Robert will tell it to you at full length. Perhaps one day you may hear it from Ophelia herself if you will but assist me in my plans for your brother's happiness."

Sidney had once more taken her hand and now pressed it to his throbbing breast. Understanding the full force of his words, overwhelmed with confusion and agitated beyond the power of utterance she would have disengaged herself from him, but with a gentle force he retained her hand saying in a voice of fondness mingled with some degree of archness, "We were talking only of your brother you know dear Selena. Do you not desire his happiness? Oh say you do! That you desire it as I do; tell me but that ...." A sound of an approaching step behind them silenced Sidney and relieved Selena from her embarrassment. They both hastily turned round.

"There is Robert!" cried Selena suddenly releasing herself from Sidney's hold, and hurrying towards him endeavoured to conceal her confusion by some trifling observations to which Robert replied in a voice of more cheerfulness than she had yet heard him assume.

He expressed his pleasure at meeting them and seemed to wish to prolong their walk until Selena feeling her own flagging spirits require some moments of solitude, complained of the heavy dew, and seeing with satisfaction that Robert was engaged with the little party in the drawing room in some conversation she retired to consult with her own heart how she should now conduct herself towards Sidney.

So much had her ideas been perplexed and hurried by the strange and agitating intelligence of this day that she could scarcely believe herself awake and as yet had formed no distinct judgment upon her situation. She saw that Sidney had returned with revived hopes, that he looked upon her with far other eyes than those which had been so often sadly averted from her in their former constrained interviews. She was convinced that he now considered her as free and Robert had already declared his opinion that she might be so. Mrs. Vallard herself who had hitherto never borne the supposition seemed now to speak of her separation from Dallamore as final and to think their re-union impossible.

Nevertheless all the feelings of Selena seemed to shrink from the acceptance of the proffered liberty, and having so long considered Dallamore as her husband it still appeared to her a crime to think with complacency upon the love of another. In vain did she strive to reconcile those instinctive principles with the visions of felicity which had already opened to her palpitating heart. Her solemn vows, her long respected and sacred duty, still asserted their invincible force, their irrevocable claim. Yet she was still conscious that this decisive act of Dallamore's had delivered her from a dreadful weight of anxiety, and tho' delicacy nay perhaps virtue forbad her to give herself to him whom she loved, she was now at least relieved from the terrible idea of belonging to another.

She resolved to take the first opportunity to communicate her resolutions to Robert and thro' him to Sidney, and in the mean time to behave with such reserve that the hopes of Sidney might gain no additional strengths by the knowledge of those struggles which internally agitated[5] her breast. She was indeed impatient for this explanation with Robert, in order that she might discover more certainly than she could do from his letter whether he thought his happiness depended upon obtaining his liberty and seeking another union better suited to his heart; and in this case she determined to urge him to take the unpleasant steps necessary for this freedom, for as every feeling both of principle and inclination at once concurred in her total renunciation of all claims upon Dallamore after the connexion which he had now formed, she saw no reason why her refusal to make new engagements should be an obstacle to her brother's breaking these shackles which he found so heavy, and suffering the guilty and deluded Dallamore to pursue his inclinations and unite himself to the woman who had sacrificed so much in order to obtain the false splendour which rank and fortune can bestow upon a blasted character.

It was not long before the meditations of Selena were interrupted by Clara who in summoning her to return to the drawing room to assist in amusing their brother, was in fact more prompted by her own wish to gratify Sidney and relieve him from that state of restless impatience which he could so ill disguise during this voluntary absence of Selena.

Unbounded contentment and delight once more overflowed his soul at her return and it was impossible that the complete satisfaction of one should not in some degree communicate a share of his light-hearted felicity to all who now surrounded him and whom he was so solicitous should sympathise in his sensations of pleasure.

Selena now longed to relate all which had passed to Lady Trevallyn, convinced as she was that circumstances so important to herself could not fail of powerfully interesting her affectionate friend, and would assuredly call her mind in some degree from the contemplation of her own afflictions. She therefore told Mrs. Vallard before they parted for the night that she proposed walking to Esselberrie before breakfast, that her absence might cause no surprise should she be detained. Lady Trevallyn had given her the key of the green house before they parted and it had been agreed that early in the morning was the best time for Selena's visits,

---

5   MS: "agitate" (my correction).

which might thus entirely escape observation, as long as she was allowed to continue in her present apartments.

Selena who had not closed her eyes during the night, hailed with joy the intruding beams of the bright sunny morning, and found no reluctance early as it was to quit her pillow, from whence sleep appeared to be totally banished while Sidney's "*good night*" still seemed to sound sweetly in her ears and thrilling to her heart. Apprehensive that there was as yet no one stirring to unlock the doors of the house she made no haste to dress herself but threw open the window to enjoy the sweetness of the morning air so peculiarly refreshing after a sleepless night.

But she had scarcely finished her simple toilet before she perceived on the lawn at some distance Sidney; who had not passed a night of greater tranquility or enjoyed more undisturbed repose during those hours which had been counted by Selena in impatient watchfulness. Tho' her heart bounded at the sight she withdrew in haste from the window upon which she could not doubt his were fixed—tho' she was by seeing him assured that the doors were open she yet loitered with timid reluctance, since he could not fail of seeing her as she quitted the house and would most assuredly join her.

The visit to Esselberrie however could not be long deferred, if she would avoid all risk of again encountering Lord Trevallyn and she at length descended to the back door intending thus to escape the observation of Sidney or perhaps we should rather say that she would thus avoid the appearance of seeking his attendance—for it is certain that no sensation could be more remote from regret or pain than that which suffused her cheeks with the most beautiful carnation upon perceiving that as if from anticipation of her design Sidney had taken a circuit and just reached one extremity of the lime walk as she entered the other.

Slowly as she advanced he was in a moment at her side—"You are an early riser Selena! I have seen your windows open a long while and since the morning has tempted you out I congratulate myself upon my own mistake."

"Did you expect your breakfast at this hour?" demanded Selena with a smile.

"Why the fact is I did not know the hour, till I came down stairs, for I confess I do not in general get up at six o'clock, but I forgot last night to wind up my watch and having no guide but my own impatient temper I thought it could not be less than ten o'clock, even when I opened my windows every thing looked so bright and gay that I still imagined it must be much later than it was. But is this your usual hour of rising?"

Selena explained to him her purpose and was insensibly led from the unaffected interest which he displayed to speak with confidence of the situation of her friend and tho' Sidney foresaw that her attention to Lady Trevallyn would necessarily deprive him of many of those precious hours of Selena's society to which he now almost felt a right, yet he anxiously and generously wished that her unhappy friend might not be deprived of this most soothing consolation.

Never had the walk to Esselberrie appeared so short to Selena[;] they were now at the garden gate, and Sidney not without a sigh relinquished the arm of Selena as she gently withdrew it from his. An unaccountable emotion of sadness oppressed her heart as she locked the door which now separated them. The transition seemed to be the most instantaneous from love, security, and confidence to gloomy reflection, obscure presentiments, and solitude the most dreary. Convinced that he had not yet stirred from the door in spite of herself she on the other side lingered near it.

"Alas!" thought she sighing deeply, "Do I feel this temporary exclusion? What should I then suffer if it were to be eternal? If we had now parted never more to meet!" She stood wrapt in such meditations till the large drops fell from her eyes, and half surprised and ashamed of the weakness she started from her reverie and hastened across the garden to the green house.

All was silent within—and Selena seeing no one in the dressing room, passed thro' it and knocked softly at the door of the bed chamber. No reply being made to the repeated signal Selena ventured to enter and was not a little surprised to find there neither Lady Trevallyn nor any of her women; nor was there even the appearance of any one having slept in the room the curtains being all undrawn and the bed settled.

A fearful suspicion seized Selena that all was not right and that she should see her friend no more. She knew not what to imagine but again returned to the dressing room in the faint hope that Lady Trevallyn weak as she was had perhaps ventured out to walk, or that she had been summoned to the apartment of her lord tho' this was scarcely possible considering the unusual early hour. In a state of mind the most uneasy she wandered round the garden and once more entered the house, nay even ventured along the corridor to the hall without yet meeting a living creature.

Restless and impatient as she paced the dressing room forming a thousand wild conjectures and debating with herself what she should do, with a movement natural in a state of watchful disquietude she opened a musick book which lay before her on a table. It happened to be one of her own which she had sent for to Hillbarton at the desire of her friend who loved to hear her play out of it some beautifully affecting passages of Haydon. Selena sighed at the recollection of those hours of sadness, not unmingled with a sweetly pensive pleasure, which she had thus devoted to soothing the melancholy of her friend and as she let fall the leaves which she had carelessly turned over the hand writing of Lady Trevallyn in the first page suddenly struck her eye while the cover closed upon it. Eagerly she again opened it and perceived the following lines written with a pencil.

> "Adieu my best, my most amiable friend! I have but a moment to bid you this last farewell—and even this may never reach you but my prayers my blessings unworthy as I am will yet reach the ever ready ear of our tenderly pitying father and he will assuredly in the hour of sorrow remember your protecting love to the poor lost Emily. All is bustle—the carriages are already at the door and I knew not till about an hour ago that we were this night to leave Esselberrie. I could not write to you dearest Selena but my heart told me you would not charge me with ingratitude. Nor can I now bid you write but you may rest assured that if it is possible for me to receive your letters I will lose no time in claiming those dear consoling marks of your remembrance. Think of my poor girls if they are deserted and tell good Mr. Mason …."

Here it broke off and it evidently appeared that she had been abruptly interrupted. Again and again Selena read over the dear characters of her beloved and interesting friend while tears of sorrow and compassion fell in showers from her eyes, till suddenly starting at the sound of a footstep advancing from the passage she snatched the book from the table and would have hastily retired. But before she could make her escape to the green house she perceived in the person who entered the room only Mr. Rawlins.

Relieved by his appearance and anxious to obtain from him farther information she was yet at the first moment unable to utter a sentence or restrain her tears.

He himself appeared much affected by her presence and closing the door behind him cautiously, advanced exclaiming with a look of deep concern, "Oh Miss Miltern! My Lady is gone, they set off last night at ten o'clock and my lady I am sure will never be able to bear the journey!"

"Do you know where they are gone?" demanded Selena eagerly.

"My Lord was pleased to tell me they were going for Trevallyn hall when he ordered every thing to be got ready with the utmost haste for the journey."

"Did you know his intentions Mr. Rawlins when I left yesterday?"

"Oh no Madam! and if I had I could hardly have obeyed my Lord's orders who charged me to say nothing of it in the house till all was ready; for I am certain it would have been a great comfort to my poor Lady to have had you with her for a bit before she left us."

"How did she seem to be?" said Selena in a tremulous voice.

"Poorly enough God knows," answered Rawlins mournfully shaking his head, "and while she was leaning on Mrs. Harris coming along the passage I could not help saying so to my Lord. But he did not please to notice it only looked very fierce."

"She left no message for me with you Mr. Rawlins—did she?" asked Selena.

"Bless you dear Miss she could not get to say a word, not so much as to bid me good bye as she was always pleased to do when my Lord was not in the way. I tried all in my power to get to see my Lady alone for I did think she might have somewhat to say, to me either about you Madam, or the school that she used to take such delight in. But I was kept so busy there was no such thing as coming at her."

"Perhaps," said Selena, "she might have desired some of the maids to let me know."

"I doubt not Miss for I heard them all wondering this morning how they knew nothing of the journey, nor they are sure did my Lady either till about half an hour before the carriages came to the door and then my Lord came into the dressing room and sent one of the women away who happened to be with her Lady and they none of them were suffered to come in after that."

"Did Lady Trevallyn take a maid?"

"None but Mrs. Harris Madam, I am afraid she often wishes for Mrs. Frances who was left in town. She was always my Lady's favourite and indeed I believe she would walk from this to Edinburgh to serve my lady, aye on her hands and knees."

"Poor Fanny!" cried Selena the tears again streaming from her eyes, "what would I give that you were now with your mistress."

"Indeed my poor Lady wants some comfort I doubt [not] my heart ached to think of her not having any cheery body with her and I could not but long to know if I could be of any service so as soon as I could leave what my Lord had given me to do I made bold to step to the dressing room and I listened awhile at the door, so hearing no one I was in hopes she was alone and being afraid to knock I ventured to open it softly. But when I saw my Lord was there I would have gone back only he called out and bid me come in. Tho' my Lady held her face from me I saw afterwards plain enough that she had been a weeping poor soul, she was locking up her cabinet and when she had done that my Lord without saying a word handed her a small writing box that stood on her table, and she immediately locked that also and then gave him her little bunch of keys. My Lord put them into his pocket making no answer but desired me to take the writing box to his study, with a little china ink stand and some paper that lay on the other table and then asked me what I wanted, but indeed Madam looking at my poor Lady and grief for her had put me quite beside myself so I stood like a fool till my Lord repeated his question in a way that to be sure was enough to frighten me, so I stammered out as well as I could some directions that my Lord's gentleman had given me and begged to know had I done right and then made all the haste off I could—tho' I made another trial and the more because I saw plain enough how it was that my Lord would not have her write. But it was to no purpose. My Lord never stirred from the dressing room or the corridore till he and Mr. Guise followed my Lady into the travelling coach."

"And do you really believe they are gone to Trevallyn hall?"

Rawlins confessed he had some reason to suspect the contrary but added that on account of his Lady's extreme weakness he could not but hope that they might not take so long a journey.

While they were thus engaged in conversation Sidney had accidentally overheard one of the gate keepers talking to one of his companions of the unexpected departure of the family over night—and finding upon enquiry that Lady Trevallyn had actually been thus precipitably removed from Esselberrie he returned and waited for Selena with considerable impatience fearful of her being severely afflicted by this event. He could only account for her[6] delay by supposing that ignorant of what had happened she now waited anxiously in the dressing room for the appearance of Lady Trevallyn and desirous of abridging those painful moments of suspence he resolved to go seek Selena at the house.

She perceived him from the windows as he advanced and guessing what had occasioned his return she joined him at the hall door as soon as she had entreated Mr. Rawlins to impart to her whatever intelligence he should hear of his Lady which he promised instantly to do.

Selena put the musick book into Sidney's hand and sorrowfully pointed out to him the lines traced by her friend as they slowly proceeded towards Hillbarton,

---

6   MS: "he" (my correction).

and while he sympathised in all her distress and while she imparted to him all her fears and anxieties for her friend's health & the melancholy which preyed upon her delicate constitution she herself found the sweetest consolation in the warmth and tenderness with which he shared all her feelings. What sadness indeed can resist the soothing powers of sympathy when in the presence of those eyes upon whose beams of fondness our dearest happiness is fixed! How sheltered how supported do we feel in every sorrow, in every difficulty when we are confident that the heart whose affection we are most solicitous to preserve is near us to take as it were our part "Against ill fortune and the world."[7]

Yet exquisitely powerful as may be this consolation, the philosopher will perhaps never abandon himself to that weak sensibility which opens the heart to receive it since it is certain that when deprived of that external support by any of the thousand chances to which mortal attachments are liable it is then infinitely less able to struggle with the afflictions or the mortifications of life. It is like the plant which fostered in factitious warmth and covered by the protecting glass is encouraged to expand its delicate leaves and unfold its feeble and premature blossoms to the heat of the reflected sun. But suddenly expelled from the green house, exposed at once to the nipping frost or the overwhelming tempest its pride its beauties instantly languish, its withering branches by degrees drop off and the perishing stem alone remains, stripped sapless and faded the encumbrance of the garden; while its more hardy companions, natives of the same soil but accustomed unshielded to "bear the pityless storm"[8] are still able to defy its keeness and resist its force.

Bosoms endowed with sensibility! who now repose upon affection and enjoy the balmy sweets of mutual confidence, can the foreboding mind envy your felicity? Too well assured that the time must come when one at least will bitterly feel how insupportable is such a deprivation—will it not rather be inclined to utter the selfish but prudent precept of the inconsistent Rousseau "O Homme resserre ton existence en dedans de toi & tu ne seras pas plus misérable."[9]

Chapter III

> Such is the product
> Of those illmated marriages ….
> Where good with bad are matched, which of themselves
> Abhor to join
>
> Milton[10]

---

[7]   Lavinia in Nicholas Rowe's *The Fair Penitent* (1703), 4.1.335.

[8]   A reference to Lear in Shakespeare's *King Lear* (1605), 3.4.29: "bide the pelting of this pitiless storm."

[9]   Jean-Jacques Rousseau, *Émile, ou, De l'éducation* (1762), Book 2 (the quote should be "au dedans" rather than "en dedans"): "O man, constrain your existence within yourself, and you will no longer be miserable."

[10]   John Milton, *Paradise Lost* (1667), 11:683–6.

For some days after his arrival at Hillbarton Selena had not courage to address Robert upon a subject which she could not but see he was evidently studious to avoid.

The public papers informed them that Lord Mount Villars had left the kingdom with his fair fugitive and had hired a vessel to sail for Hambourg after having been disappointed in his project of obtaining permission from his friends in power to visit France which had indeed been by far the most potent inducement held out by Lady Harriet and her confederate Mr. Rainsford to prevail upon Dallamore to undertake this *frolic* for such he himself alone considered it, and so far was he from dictating the letter which Lady Harriet had written to Robert, or from desiring that divorce which she conceived to be the inevitable consequence of this expedition, that he never doubted the probability of Rainsford's representations which so artfully corresponded with his own wishes, that the innocent and soft Selena would easily be reconciled, and that his return in a few weeks would set all matters right while his affectionate conduct upon their meeting, and the well chosen ornaments which he might have an opportunity of bringing to her from Paris would be a very sufficient proof that he had never ceased to love her; Dallamore's own ideas were upon all subjects so confused, his principles so flexible and his usual associates so profligate in opinion as well as practice that he prided himself upon the sacrifice which so fine a woman as Lady Harriet was ready to make for the pleasure of accompanying him for a few weeks to Paris and even thought a circumstance so flattering could not fail of rendering him of infinitely more consequence in the eyes of Selena herself, while he felt secretly satisfied that after his character as un homme des bonnes fortunes[11] was thus established with such eclat he must in future be irresistible to every female.

Nevertheless many a sudden secret pang the result of a naturally amiable heart which had been really touched with love for the very lovely Selena reproached him for the pain which he was now inflicting upon her, for tho' he could answer nothing to all the false anecdotes and malicious bon mots[12] of Lady Harriet upon the subject of Edwin Stanmore he never could for a moment believe that he had in fact a favoured rival.

Those transient stings of conscience were however quickly smothered by the hurry and perpetual dissipation which his companions industriously provided for him.

Yet he was more than once upon the very point of escaping their vigilence particularly when he found that instead of the expeditious trip which he had schemed by Calais and Dover he should be obliged to trust himself to the chance of another tedious sea voyage the confinement of which he yet remembered with horror.

And altho' Rainsford assured him that they should not find the smallest difficulty in procuring passports into France thro' Germany as he had himself tried this with success the preceeding summer yet Dallamore detested the thoughts of the sandy roads and lazy postillions which they must thus previously encounter.

---

[11]   Un homme des bonnes fortunes: a man of good fortunes (French).

[12]   Bon mots: clever sayings (French).

He however saw no possibility of being off, and assisted all their efforts to banish reflection by every wild device that folly or extravagance could invent.

Lady Harriet's great aim and only anxiety was to retain him in her power and under her influence until Robert should solicit the divorce which there could be no doubt of his obtaining. For after this she was assured that Lord Mount Villars from his natural generosity of disposition, and the established point of honour might easily be persuaded that it was absolutely necessary to make her the customary compensation for a life of infamy by a marriage without esteem, that only basis upon which lasting affection and connubial felicity can ever subsist.

In her labours to amuse or rather perpetually to occupy Dallamore she was considerably assisted by Rainsford who worthless and grossly profligate as he was disguised the most odious tempers under some agreeable talents and possessed powers of satire which gave him an almost unbounded influence over Dallamore who while he was diverted by his cutting sarcasms on others was yet kept in constant tho' unconscious subjection in his presence from the fear of incurring his ridicule.

Lady Harriet secretly gloried in the conviction that she had inspired this hero of a thousand intrigues with the most violent passion and his artful flattery had conspired with her own vanity in persuading her that her strong mind and great talents must forever enchain with the most indissoluble bonds those whom the dazzling beauties of her alluring person had captivated.

Their intercourse was however carefully concealed from Dallamore who was made to believe that to his eloquence of persuasion and the personal attachment which Rainsford pretended to entertain towards him he was now indebted for the society of this pleasant fellow in their expedition.

Rainsford's great passion was the love of intrigue. He never had an enjoyment which was not obtained by strategem, nor a thought which did not bear some reference to a project. With an understanding beneath mediocrity, strong passions and a cold heart, destitute of every feeling but those of appetite, he thus imposed not only upon others but himself and was firmly assured that his talents might have raised him to the most eminent situation, had not the warmth of his sensibility devoted him entirely to Love. It is true upon his first setting out in life taking Alcibiades[13] for his model, he aimed at being a universal Hero. But his ambitious views meeting early with some peculiarly mortifying disappointments he had since avoided the walks of Glory preferring this voluntary relinquishment to the chance of a disgraceful defeat.

The facility with which his addresses had been received by Lady Harriet might have soon rendered this pursuit insipid had it not been for the constant exercise which her project upon Dallamore had supplied his mind so fertile as he esteemed it of invention. He was not long in discovering what was her design and from the first exerted all his cunning to encourage and promote it. So far was his

---

[13]   Alcibiades (c. 450–404 BC) was an Athenian general who served with Socrates in the Peloponnesian War, and was well known for strategically shifting his political allegiances.

passion from professing any of that troublesome train of scrupulous delicacies and exclusive jealousies which attends a more sentimental connexion, that he appeared on the contrary generously to concur with eagerness in every effort to ensure to her for life the possession of Dallamore's wealth the sweets of which they both at present so largely tasted.

But as no sentiment of generosity had ever yet been harboured in his selfish bosom it may be well supposed that he had his own views upon the victim of their united arts, nevertheless his were in fact of a more temporary nature than Lady Harriet entertained, for egregious dupe as he esteemed him he secretly never believed it possible that she would be able to ensnare Lord Mount Villars into marriage. This was however a point of much indifference to him who in the mean time amused himself at the expence of both and certainly with justice considered himself bound to her Ladyship by no ties but those of transient inclination.

Their voyage was tedious and Dallamore found his reflections in an unusual degree obstinately troublesome. His companions languid with sea sickness struggled ineffectually to supply him with entertainment while the image of Selena in all its innocent and attractive beauty perpetually returned to reproach him for his conduct. In order to get rid of this internally tormenting monitor he employed himself in composing a letter which thus singularly described his hopes and sentiments.

> "Dearest Selena,
>   "Do not be uneasy whatever gossip you may hear, nor ever for a moment believe that I could love any woman upon earth but my own Selena. I curse myself every hour of the day for having been so foolish as to quit England without you and cannot tell what the devil bewitched me. But for the future you may depend upon it I will never do any thing but what you shall advise and like best, so do not make yourself unhappy about this short absence, nor think unkindly of me for it, for I assure you you have no right.
>   Yours ever Mount Villars"

Having once written this which he considered a full and satisfactory account of his conduct and a complete compensation to Selena he found himself more at ease and as Lady Harriet called for his attendance upon their landing and that all were in high spirits in the exhilarating confusion and bustle which accompanied it this letter remained in his pocket unthought of till the following morning at breakfast when it happened accidentally to come into his hand, and tossing it upon the table he desired the servant who waited upon them to convey it to the post office.

Lady Harriet and Mr. Rainsford exchanged a glance while the latter in consequence of what they had observed and well comprehending her Ladyship's commands followed the messenger out of the room and saying that he was himself going to the post office he took from his hands the indisputable testimony that their strange companion still considered Selena as Countess of Mount Villars. However mortifying this was to the vanity of Lady Harriet as well as blasting to her hopes, she appeared to join in the unbounded mirth which so absurdly curious a composition could not fail to excite in Mr. Rainsford who however concealed from her how entire a confirmation he now received of the folly of her Ladyship's speculations.

Thus by the interference of those worthy associates this letter occasioned none of that agitation and astonishment which it was assuredly well calculated to create had it been suffered to reach its intended destination. Nothing indeed could appear less likely to the whole party at Hillbarton than that Dallamore the voluntary companion of the abandoned fugitive, still maintained an intention of claiming that wife whom he had in so decisive a manner rejected and whose brother he yet so grossly insulted, and amidst all the scruples which combatted in the bosom of Selena with her love and her lover against that consent for which they so powerfully pleaded this apprehension had never intruded an argument so wildly improbable.

Chapter IV

How many deaths are in the word *Depart*!
………………………………....................
Take off the edge from every sharper sound
And let our parting be as gently made
As other loves begin.

Dryden[14]

After many ineffectual struggles Selena had at length declared to her brother that her resolution was fixed against forming any connexion inconsistent with those sacred vows which she had already so unfortunately pledged in the sight of Heaven and in the gentlest manner she entreated him to prevail upon Sidney for both their sakes to absent himself till he could see her without any of these painful emotions which must now interrupt his enjoyment of her sisterly friendship.

Robert listened to her in a fixed mournful silence until she who had perhaps expected to hear her purposes, combatted, and had to this end prepared all these arguments upon the weakness of which her heart so much wished to be if possible convinced finding that he opposed nothing to her determination hastily changed the subject urging him to take the unpleasant but necessary steps to deliver himself and them from a connexion so disgraceful.

But no sooner had she commenced this subject than in a manner the most decided and a tone of the deepest melancholy he told her that this was a point which nothing could change—his resolution. That while she looked upon herself as the wife of Dallamore no personal considerations should ever enduce him to assist their separation and tho' he might think she acted unwisely for her happiness or that she was influenced by a false delicacy yet he felt that in this point he was too much interested to give her any advice in opposition to her own judgment.

---

[14] Antony in John Dryden's *All For Love* (1677), 4.1.5, 20–22.

He therefore entreated that the subject might entirely be dropped and declared his resolution of returning to Miltern Abbey which he hoped she would consider as her own and that in the society of each other and their endeavours to promote the happiness of those around them they might find that peace

> Which nothing earthly gives or can destroy
> The souls calm sunshine of eternal joy.[15]

Selena tho' at a loss how to express her feelings, yet was painfully conscious that she was the unwilling bar to the only plan from which Robert had too plainly expected all his felicity.

She saw no reason why it should be so, esteeming herself as totally separated from Dallamore by his present connexion as if the ceremony of marriage had passed between him and Lady Harriet, but when she attempted to convince him of this he abruptly stopped her saying, "No my dear Selena, do not argue with me about this, recollect that I now act from a sense of duty, and you are yourself so invariably directed by this guide, that you will not I am sure expect me to obtain happiness by opposing what I think it commands."

Then affectionately pressing her hand he left her with some precipitation, and Selena's heart sunk with the sensation of him who hears the despairing Physician pronounce the sentence of death upon the earthly idol of his soul, when in a few minutes after this conversation she perceived Robert advancing to Sidney who was sauntering beneath the limes upon the lawn, and putting his arm under his led him away apparently in deep conversation.

As soon as they were out of sight she burst into tears while in the conviction that she had now banished from her the chosen of her heart, she bitterly exclaimed, "I have lost him! and he knows not he never must know the anguish which it costs me!" At this moment no idea appeared to her more insupportable than this, and it seemed as if she should be happy even in their separation could she but once relieve her heart by unfolding it to him with unbounded confidence, could she but tell him how earth afforded to her but one image of pleasure and of felicity which was that which duty now compeled her to reject, could she but confess how severely she herself shared the pain which she knew this rejection must inflict, might she convince him how she prized his love and esteemed his virtues and could they even in the dark silence of absence be cheered by assurances of mutual sympathy.

These were however but the involuntary feelings of Love, who is never so strong as when struggling impatiently beneath the shackles of constraint. But her reason and her strict principles of Virtue alike convinced her that nothing was more necessary for the recovery of the tranquility of each, than that Sidney should remain ignorant of the real situation of her mind and the difficulty which she found

---

[15]   Alexander Pope, *An Essay on Man* (1733–34), 4:167–8 (line 168 should read "The soul's calm sunshine, and the heart-felt joy").

in acting as she now did. She armed herself therefore with resolution to meet him with an appearance of indifference and to behold him depart without discovering any emotion which might betray her weakness. Having spent the remainder of the morning in her own room she decended with a trembling heart upon hearing the dinner bell.

Robert did not join them till they were seated at table. An unusual cloud of melancholy sat upon his countenance and in a suppressed voice of agitation he said a few words to Mrs. Vallard to tell her that Sidney had taken a long walk and entreated to be excused for not returning to dinner.

Poor Selena who was instantly struck with the idea that he was gone from Hillbarton and that she should see him no more with the utmost difficulty could conceal the faint sickness which suddenly overpowered her. But it was impossible for her to eat and when (upon perceiving the eyes of Clara fixed upon her) she carried a morsel to her lips she felt as if in the attempt to swallow it she must have been suffocated. Several times she was upon the point of quitting the room, and relieving herself by giving loose to her tears, but as often the dread of exposing her weakness enabled her to struggle against it.

The conversation was forced and languid and as soon as the servants had withdrawn Robert expressed his gratitude to Mrs. Vallard for her kindness to them all at a season when they stood so much in need of the consolations of friendship, adding that he must not any longer trespass on her hospitality, and that he hoped she would forgive him, for prevailing upon Selena to return with him to Miltern Abbey where the presence of his sisters was become so necessary to him.

Mrs. Vallard scarcely suffered him to proceed and warmly opposed his determination. Nothing could be in her opinion worse calculated for the dissipation of that sadness which her affectionate heart lamented to perceive was thus preying upon the spirits of those two amiable young persons, than this plan of dismal seclusion at the very scene which had so lately witnessed the disgraceful misfortune to which alone she attributed their present melancholy.

She had even been considering during the time of dinner how she should bring about some amusement to divert their minds from dwelling on those unpleasant subjects and now expressed herself in such urgent terms, pleading her own dreary situation if they should thus leave her in perfect solitude that Robert was obliged to consent as a compromise that they should all remain at Hillbarton until the arrival of a young Lady a distant relation to Mrs. Vallard who had already been invited to pass a part of the summer with her—"and remember," cried their kind-hearted hostess, "that you have promised for Sidney in this bargain, for I can by no means part with him."

"I don't know how that will be," replied Robert evidently agitated, "but I am afraid Sidney will be obliged to return to Ireland in a few days."

"Oh he dare not go without my leave," returned Mrs. Vallard, "and tho' he is the best son in the world, we shall be able I think this time to keep him from good Mrs. Dallamore a little longer."

All Selena's courage had suddenly revived at the words of Robert which convinced her that she had not yet seen Sidney for the last time, and so entirely did this idea occupy her that Mrs. Vallard's speech which however unintended would at any other moment have covered the cheeks of Selena with the deepest blushes now past unnoticed as well as the arch smile with which it was heard by Clara.

They now rose to quit the parlour and Robert at the same time inviting Selena to walk she prepared herself to hear with composure the conversation which had just past between him and Sidney. In this expectation she however deceived herself; not once did he allude to the subject which doubtless occupied all their thoughts. He spoke to her of his impatience to return to Miltern Abbey, of his plans of improvement there and the manner in which he intended to employ his hours. He explained to her the embarrassed state of his affairs as far as he himself knew the extent of their involvement. Tho' his settlements precluded the possibility of selling any part of his estates, or of his borrowing a sum sufficient at once to pay off all his other debts, yet he hoped by a prudent arrangement to satisfy for the present his creditors and that the strict economy of a few years retirement would free him from all pecuniary difficulties without his being obliged in any respect to injure Miltern Abbey, nay even without their being sensible of any inconvenience from the retrenchments necessary to be made.

In all his little projects for the advantage of his neighbouring peasantry from which he appeared to expect his chief consolation Selena was included and he consulted with her upon the plan of their future studies which he entreated might be in common and for the present chiefly directed for the improvement of Clara, whom he considered as placed under their mutual charge and to whom he thought they were bound to endeavour by every exertion to compensate for the many advantages of which their seclusion must deprive her.

Not once did he hint at the possibility of their situation being otherwise and if he alluded to the misfortunes which condemned them to this life of solitude it was as tho' they were inevitable and rather to be if possible forgotten than remedied or lamented.

Selena saw that he exerted himself to maintain a kind of cheerfulness and she vainly struggled to catch the tone which he wished to assume. She felt as tho' her brother to a false delicacy upon her account sacrificed to her all his hopes of happiness in life and she could not avoid fancying that all those schemes of domestic peace and retirement had already been illuminated in his imagination by the presence of the lovely and innocent object of his second choice, and that in omitting this dear and enchanting image nothing but the most dreary blank remained in his future prospects; yet cruel as this sacrifice appeared, she could say nothing to oppose it without seeming to repent or waver in her own resolution.

She wished him also to speak of Sidney and the image of his first despair & disappointment which Robert was desirous of sparing her became almost intolerable to her fancy from this very silence.

She blamed herself for a thousand involuntary looks and actions which during the few last days she was but too sensible had betrayed her tenderness and in spite of all her reserve cherished his hopes. She blamed herself also for having timidly shunned these private interviews which he had assiduously sought for, and she earnestly wished that she had herself explained to him the reasons by which she was directed. Had she at least she thought

> with gentle friendship
> Since they must part at last their parting softened[16]

he might have been convinced of the rectitude of her conduct and soothed by her kindness his remembrance of her (for she could not wish him to forget her) might be free from all bitterness.

A conversation under such constraint and while her mind was so preoccupied by the idea of that affliction in which she bore so large a share was not much calculated to raise poor Selena's spirits; and upon their return to the house she would have retired but felt she could not do so without some appearance of unkindness to her brother as upon their entering the drawing room they found no person there. She was however pleased that he expressed a desire to hear her play as he had been accustomed to do in more cheerful hours and particularly as she had taken notice that since he had been at Hillbarton he had never seemed to take that pleasure in her music which he had formerly evinced, nor ever seconded Sidney's solicitations to obtain it.

She therefore willingly assented to his proposal and seated herself at the harp which stood near the window that she might at the same time not lose the beauty of the setting sun. Unembarrassed by the necessity of attending and replying to conversation Selena now gave a free loose to her sad reflections while she played their most favourite airs occasionally accompanying them with her voice while Robert listened in silence, his head and his arms reclined on the back of a chair at some distance.

Music which has a power so irresistible in disposing the happiest mind to a delightful and tender melancholy, tho' it may sooth distress can never for a moment divert the heart from the memory of its sorrows. The unhappy may court its aid but they will never find it like the amusing companion who dissipates grief by presenting gayer objects, nor even as the philosophic comforter who enables by the force of reason the sorrowing heart to struggle with calamity, but rather like the sympathising fellow sufferer who imprudently recals every source of affliction, awakens every emotion of too painful sensibility, paints in yet more lovely colours the lost and lamented good and softens the bosom already but too much enervated by melancholy. Every remembrance which music excites is regret, every feeling is that of wounded tenderness. Scenes of pleasures the most mingled, hours perhaps embittered by many a painful sensation when recalled by music are presented to memory as the only delicious season of enjoyment which was granted to life

---

16 Sigismunda in James Thomson's *Tancred and Sigismunda* (1745), 3.1.8–9 ("they" and "their" is "we" and "our").

and which gone for ever can no more be renewed; while the aching heart looks forward with cheerless despondence upon future existence as tho' exhausted of sweets it could henceforth yield no more. Selena had long ago discovered this secret and in former times had often encouraged Lady Trevallyn to employ herself in drawing or writing, or else in those botanical researches which however trifling they may appear to the uninitiated observer can yet so completely captivate the attention, rather than indulge her pensive meditations by listning to the exercise of her musical talents, which Lady Trevallyn would most frequently demand from her friend when peculiarly oppressed by her own melancholy.

Nor had Selena alone exercised her prudence in this instance for her friend. Many a time had she abruptly risen from the instrument, and flown for protection to some more active employment or some study which called for application however painful she might find the exertion when her heart melted by the sweet sounds awakened by her own fingers[17] dwelt with overflowing sadness upon her pitiable lot, her fatal vows, and the happiness which seemed just placed in her sight but beyond her reach and which never must be hers.

And such were now her meditations accompanied with the yet more powerful ideas of Sidney's present distress and their approaching separation while in compliance with her brother's request she indulged her own inclination which uncontroled would ever in sorrow have led her to the "song that was lovely but sad"[18] which Ossian has so justly compared to "the memory of joys that are past, at once pleasant and mournful to the soul."[19]

But while Selena and her brother were thus employed Mrs. Vallard had been unexpectedly engaged with Sidney in conversation the most deeply interesting, She had enquired concerning him from Philip who was on all her household affairs her prime minister, and who was as solicitous as herself that Mr. Dallamore should by no means lose his dinner, and when he now informed her that he was just returned and gone to his own room he added with a look of much concern "that he was sure he had not tasted bit or sup since breakfast tho' he would not allow him now to get any thing ready."

"Silly boy," cried Mrs. Vallard, "I suppose he thinks much of giving them a little additional trouble as dinner was over when he came in."

"Bless you Ma'am what signifies that but I was a thinking so myself and so I begged leave only to bring him a slice of cold beef and a drop of Madeira for he looks quite low and dull, but he would not so much as touch it, not he."

Mrs. Vallard then gratified Philip by saying that she would herself go up and press him to have some refreshment after his long walk; she was also desirous of speaking to him alone upon some means of raising the still depressed spirits of her children as she always styled them.

---

[17]   MS: "finger" (my correction).

[18]   James Macpherson, "Carric-Thura," *The Poems of Ossian* (1765, 1773), 219.

[19]   James Macpherson, "The Death of Cuthullin," *The Poems of Ossian* (1765, 1773), 385.

She therefore knocked at his door, and was shocked to find the state of extreme sorrow in which he appeared to be plunged; As he could not disguise his emotions and that he saw she was terrified with the apprehension of some new and dreadful misfortune he attempted to relieve her from her uneasiness by telling her that he alone was the sufferer incoherently exclaiming that his presumptuous hopes, his infatuated imaginations deserved the bitterness of that disappointment which now awaited them.

Mrs. Vallard was some time before she could comprehend his meaning, for the generous ardour with which he had pursued Dallamore, and the labour which he had vainly spent in endeavouring to restore him to Selena had totally taken from her all the suspicions which on their first acquaintance she had conceived of his feeling for Selena a more than friendly attachment or brotherly affection.

It was not in Mrs. Vallard's nature at any time to behold distress without sympathising with the unhappy and wishing to afford relief; and as there existed few persons upon earth for whom she felt that lively interest with which Sidney's amiable manners and excellent heart had ever inspired her it is not surprising that she on a sudden warmly and strenuously espoused his cause and seconded his desires with her own most ardent wishes. The conduct of Dallamore which had for ever deprived her of all hope of seeing him united to Selena dissolved in her opinion all those ties which she had hitherto encouraged her young friend to consider as irrevocable, and the language of passion which is ever eloquent instantly transferred to Sidney all those anxious wishes which had formerly and impatiently looked forward to the union of her nephew with Selena, while it convinced her that if Sidney once pleaded his own cause it would be impossible for Selena to resist the warmth and energy of his arguments. She now recollected a thousand little circumstances which confirmed her in the assurance that Selena was not herself insensible to his love.

All these she placed in the strongest light and repeated to his enraptured ears inspiring him with a momentary hope which vanished with the delightful sound which had created it. She had however succeeded in making him relinquish his design of immediately quitting Hillbarton, and having gathered from him that his purpose was to obtain a commission in a regiment about to embark for the West Indies, she constrained him by her urgent entreaties and the remembrance of his Mother to promise that he would not take so rash a step under the first violent impulse of passion tho' she could not prevail upon him to say that he had completely relinquished all such design.

She had at length with much difficulty prevailed upon him to accompany her to the drawing room but as they approached thro' the hall he started at the sound of Selena's harp and fearful of exposing to her the violence of those feelings at which he inwardly blushed he was tempted impetuously to rush from the house and never again to obtrude himself upon her presence.

Mrs. Vallard saw the momentary but cruel conflict and having no doubt of the success of his perseverance feared nothing but the consequence of his present desponding temper, dreading that he should defeat all her good-natured hopes by this sudden flight.

But his sense of shame and perhaps tho' unacknowledged the influence of some yet more tender emotions enabled him to resist this desperate impulse and when Mrs. Vallard entered leaving the door open she was followed in a few moments by Sidney who walked slowly towards the window at the other side of the room from that where Selena was placed and seated himself in silence. Selena paused and would have risen to join Mrs. Vallard at the tea-table but the kind old lady who felt ashamed to discover the traces of tears which the conversation she had just held had still left upon her countenance prevented her by saying, "Go on my dear. Clara will make tea presently, and do you play that sweet pretty Italien song which I love so much."

Selena hesitated, it was an air which she had learnt from Sidney, during the time of their first unconstrained and delightful intimacy, before they had mutually been forced to disguise the pleasure which the society of each other inspired. Tho' seperately they had both remembered with delight the beloved music, yet the conscious fear of recalling images too tender had never since that period suffered Selena to play it in his presence and Sidney had not dared to ask for it. How then could she now discover to him that in his absence it had been her oft practised, her favourite theme, faithfully cherished in her memory by frequent repetition.

Upon Mrs. Vallard's repeating her innocently embarrassing request Selena would have diverted from it her attention, and hoped to satisfy her by commencing a Venetian ballad whose affecting simplicity she thought best calculated to attract her taste.

But Mrs. Vallard interrupted her expressing her astonishment at her imagined mistake, and having endeavoured to describe the song she wished for by reminding her how frequently she played it, she added, "Dear Selena is it possible you do not know what I mean? How stupid I am not to know the words!" The heart of Selena which was the seat of truth itself suggested not the possibility of a denial to the lips which had never yet been stained by the utterance of a deliberate falsehood and with a trembling hand she lightly struck the chords with which she accompanied a beautifully plaintive air adapted to those words of Metastasio

> Fra tutte le pene
> V'è pena maggiore,
> Son presso al mio bene
> Sospiro d'amore,
> E dirgli non oso
> Sospiro per te.[20]

---

[20]   Egle's aria in Pietro Metastasio's *Zenobia* (1740), 3.9.8–13: "Among all punishments there is none greater than to be so near to my love, to be sighing for love, and dare not say I am sighing for you."

The tremulous sounds which her agitation half repressed, the melting tenderness of the voice which uttered those expressive words thrilled instantly to the soul of Sidney; he had not yet ventured to look at her, tho' the candles which were just brought in shone full upon her beautiful brow, covered with the lovely blushes of the softest confusion; but as he stood leaning against the window he now turned his head and for an instant met the involuntary the unutterable glance of love. It was indeed suddenly withdrawn and her modest eyes fell beneath the beams of rapturous fondness which they had enkindled but Selena was herself conscious that ages of restraint could never recal that moment, nor the power of language obliterate its effects.

Shocked at wearing an appearance of that coquetry which might seek to defeat by the encouragement of the eye the decisive denial of the lips, she now in vain during the remainder of the evening studiously avoided the timid efforts which he made to address her; Robert, who scarcely hoped that Sidney would again join their society from the successless endeavours which he had made to sooth his impetuous despair, was now surprised to behold the command which he exercised over his feelings in assuming an appearance of cheerfulness which he secretly owed to the revival of some degree of Hope, in the persuasion that Selena acted not from indifference, but from a mistaken principle of delicacy which Mrs. Vallard had promised by every argument to oppose.

Once more his sanguine temper ever inclined to meet hope upon her very first approach and view all objects in the fairest light, was again cheered by the delicious visions presented for future days of love and bliss by his lively imagination. So absorbed was he in those sweet contemplations that as he gazed upon the averted countenance of Selena, he with unconscious vehemence frequently clasped[21] his hands and longed to pour forth to her ear the fullness of his soul; nay once he was upon the very point of uttering to her the lines which he had so often internally repeated and which now most forcibly recurred to his remembrance:

What a new paradise were there! to know
No pangs of parting; see thee every day,
And sometimes all the day! sweet holy day!
Peace round my pillow and my morning sun
Cheered by thy presence, and thine eyes to speak
Love's language and thy smile to interfuse
The swell of cordial joy! that life indeed were bliss![22]

Selena mean while oppressed at once with the consciousness of her own weakness in his presence and the dread of that separation which she still resolved

---

[21] MS: "clapsed" (my correction).

[22] "Brooke" (Tighe's note). The Countess of Rutland in Henry Brooke's *The Earl of Essex* (1761), 2.276–82 (lines 282–3 should read "The swell of cordial joy—O, my lov'd Essex, / That life indeed were blest").

to enforce, stifled her sighs and struggled with her sorrows to assume an air of indifference against which her heart powerfully revolted.

She retired early to her own room and excused herself from coming to supper by pleading the fatigue which she really felt from her long walk.

Mrs. Vallard who had impatiently longed for an opportunity of speaking to her alone upon that subject in which she now felt herself so deeply interested, was disappointed at being thus prevented from claiming her attendance as she was sometimes accustomed to do while she undressed, when in those hours of unbounded freedom she communicated to her all her own little anxieties and all which she benevolently felt for others, while she listened with admiration and tenderness to the pure sentiments, the clear and just opinions, and the amiable feelings of Selena's excellent judgment and untainted heart.

As soon as supper was over Mrs. Vallard accompanied Clara to her sister's room, but Selena not feeling as yet disposed to converse with either upon what had had occupied her mind during the day extinguished her candle when she heard their voices on the stairs and seating herself upon the bed drew the curtains around her, so that upon opening the door they supposed her to be asleep and softly retired.

Mrs. Vallard now found it impossible to remain any longer silent, and relating to Clara all that had passed between her and Sidney they mutually declared their ardent wishes for the union of two so dear to each and who seemed to be

> So paired; so suited in their minds and persons
> That they were formed the tallies for each other.[23]

As Selena had never confessed her affection for Sidney, Clara considered it as no breach of confidence while she disclosed to their warm hearted friend the discovery which she had long since made, and delighted her by the repetition of a thousand innocent proofs, by which Selena had continually confirmed her suspicions ever since their first acquaintance with Sidney in spite of all her endeavours not only to conceal but to conquer her love.

Chapter V

> I had so fixed my heart upon her
> That whensoe'er I framed a scheme of bliss
> For time to come, she was my only joy
> With which I wished to sweeten future cares,
> I fancied pleasures none but one that loves
> And doats as I did can imagine them
>   Otway[24]

[23]   Dorax in John Dryden's *Don Sebastian* (1691), 5.1.209–10 ("formed" should be "framed").

[24]   Pierre in Thomas Otway's *Venice Preserved* (1682), 1.1.168–73.

While they were at breakfast the following morning Mrs. Vallard requested Selena to accompany her in an airing of a few miles.

"My old friend Mrs. Rolleham," said she, "called here yesterday morning while I was at the farm seeing how poor Anne was going on. Philip tells me that she was extremely anxious to see me and that she was much disappointed at his not being able to find any of us for her."

"Yes I can answer for that," cried Clara, "for I am sure she staid a full hour at the door with her head first at one side of the carriage and then at the other peering about to try if she could make any discoveries."

"And how did you escape Clara since you were not inclined to indulge the poor old Lady?"

"Why my window was open and as I guessed what Philip was going to do, I made such a face when I saw him look up towards my room that I am sure he blessed himself and did not dare to come near me and then I heard her charging him a thousand times to tell you how sorry she was not to see you, and how glad she was to hear you were able to walk out; I was convinced poor Philip could never remember all, so I intended to divide the message and tell him to keep the sorrow and I would take charge of the joy."

"Come, come," said Mrs. Vallard half smiling herself, "I will not have you laugh at my poor friend. She is the oldest neighbour I have now alive and a very good sort of body I assure you, Tho' I will allow she must appear ridiculous sometimes to those who do not over look her peculiar ways, she is so very eager about trifles. But I am not afraid of you Selena, you never laugh at any one, so if you will come with me there in the chaise this fine warm day I think I will venture with the new horse—Philip says it is so very quiet."

"Oh Mrs. Rolleham and I are old friends!" answered Selena unwilling to make any objection to Mrs. Vallard's proposal tho' she somewhat dreaded the interrogations of the inquisitive old Lady.

"Yes indeed Selena," replied Mrs. Vallard, "and you would be very ungrateful if you did not return some of the good will she bears you, she often says that she sees no young person like you, and I am sure she will take it very kind of us to go visit her especially as she knows I have been out."

Nevertheless Mrs. Vallard's fears had almost defeated this projected expedition, for being remarkably timorous she had not ventured into her carriage since the loss of one of her old steady horses, and it now required the utmost persuasion of her postillion and Philip to give her courage to trust herself with a stranger whom after repeated trials they assured her to be perfectly gentle and well trained.

Her attention was for a while completely taken up in watching his steps but she soon forgot him and her terrors when once she had begun to open to Selena upon the subject so near her heart, to declare to her the concern she had felt in the distress of Sidney and to expostulate with her in his behalf.

She could not comprehend her scruples and Selena with astonishment beheld her a thousand times more eager for his success, than she had formerly been for her union with Dallamore.

Knowing her partiality for her nephew and remembering how strenuously and decidedly she had formerly opposed the advice given to Selena no longer to consider herself bound by her unfortunate vows, Selena could not believe that she would ever thus encourage her to form another connexion.

"Alas!" cried she to herself as she sighed in secret, "why must I alone consider this in the light so opposite to my wishes? Could I dare thus to act contrary to the advice of all whom I love and respect if my judgment in this instance coincided with my inclination? And why must I then relinquish happiness by obstinately adhering to my own opinion? I am not infallible. Why may I not in this as well as so many other points be mistaken?" Nevertheless in vain did she thus argue against conviction; Her vows had been unconditional and her conscience refused to repeat them to another.

Their arrival at Mrs. Rolleham's interrupted her meditations and Mrs. Vallard's arguments which had in them more of urgent persuasion than deep reasoning. For indeed the good Lady at all times argued more from her heart than her head and in her own case those who failed to influence the former could have but little chance to succeed in their effect upon the latter, tho' from the gentleness of her temper she often appeared to yield while her little prejudices quietly remained in their full force. Those prejudices were however of a nature the most amiable, tending to promote the happiness of others tho' in a manner which the proud or selfish might denominate absurd for "Ev'n her failings leaned to Virtue's side."[25] And never had Selena been tempted to contend with them except when she observed her uneasy at the ascendency which Mr. Mason had gained over the mind of Lady Trevallyn, nay even then the dread of giving her pain by an opposition of sentiment forced her to listen to those apprehensions in a silence for which she almost reproached herself as a want of courage to support the excellent character of their pious friend.

As they drove up to the house Selena entreated Mrs. Vallard to suffer her to remain in the carriage during her visit for she trembled lest Mrs. Rolleham's curiosity should constrain her in spite of all good breeding to some enquiries concerning Dallamore or Lady Harriet, which she knew in her presence would shock Mrs. Vallard and make her repent having required Selena's attendance.

This hope was however defeated by Mrs. Rolleham herself who hurried to greet them the moment that the carriage drove up to the hall door. With her little polished crutch in one hand and her glass in the other (which as she was excessively shortsighted she kept almost continually to her eye) she hobbled along and welcomed Mrs. Vallard with the most hearty expressions of satisfaction mingled with enquiries.

While the servant assisted Mrs. Vallard from the chaise Selena shrunk back, trusting to her blindness for escape from her scrutiny; but she quickly found her mistake, for no sooner was Mrs. Vallard out than Mrs. Rolleham putting her head into the carriage exclaimed, "And whom have you got here my dear? Oh is it you Miss Miltern? I beg your pardon my good child but you know what a poor buzzard

---

[25]   Oliver Goldsmith, *The Deserted Village* (1770), line 164 ("her" should be "his").

I am. What good creatures you are both to come to me! … you cannot think how I have longed to see you all since ….." Here she checked herself directing her eyes with a significant glance towards the servants and then towards Mrs. Vallard as if claiming applause for her singular discretion.

She now followed them into the drawing room apologizing all the way for the filth into which she was bringing them, altho' both the hall and the apartment itself were of a neatness the most exact. Having narrowly examined with her glass the chairs which she presented to them declaring she supposed they were all covered with dust she expatiated for some moments upon the invincible carelessness of housemaids, and the extreme difficulty there was to be tolerably decent; Mrs. Vallard looking round her naturally replied by the encomiums which these disparaging speeches seemed to demand.

"Oh my dear soul," she cried, "you are very good to say so, I know you were always the most indulgent creature upon earth."

While she spoke she was still fussing round the apartment, continuing her minute investigation whether every thing was in its proper place and before she sat down once more opened the door, in an angry voice repeatedly vociferating for Nanny Bonsy.

The housemaid tho' accustomed to such calls appeared reluctantly and Mrs. Rolleham then pointing out an almost imperceptible soil upon the floor, poured forth a torrent of reproaches mingled with apologies to her guests.

At length sitting down and adjusting by turns each sleeve she once more extended her hand to Mrs. Vallard saying, "I am so glad to see you my dear, but come tell me now, how you all are and who is with you at Hillbarton?"

Mrs. Vallard answered her enquiries in a few words and then attempted to divert the discourse by asking in her turn some questions respecting her own family—during which Mrs. Rolleham was busily occupied in examining carefully sundry articles of Selena's dress which she alternately took up and held close to her eye occasionally observing, "This is a pretty lace in your cloak my dear, pray now what did it cost a yard? Where did you get that nice straw hat. Oh in London I dare say. I got one the other day for my little grand daughter Harriet but it does not sit like yours at all to be sure Harriet's head is not so small as yours. I beg pardon my dear, what's that you say about Charlotte?" Mrs. Vallard not without a smile repeated her enquiry after Lady Greysville her niece.

"Oh my dear I had a letter from Charlotte the other day. My son came down here with a friend of his from Greysville lodge. They have been here two or three days, and I have a great piece of news for you which I am sure you will be glad to hear." Mrs. Vallard was well accustomed to the important manner in which her busy neighbour generally announced intelligence the most insignificant, so that she felt but little curiosity as to this "great piece of news" and could hardly imagine that it was one really so pleasing and of so much consequence as the prospect of an heir to the house of Greysville which had been for some time despaired of.

Mrs. Vallard was expressing the surprise and delight which she really felt on this occasion, but Mrs. Rolleham whose mind appeared quite occupied by some thing else which she was impatient and yet knew not how to bring forward, unable any longer to restrain herself turned to Selena and asked her would she like "to take a turn in her wilderness, for indeed my dear I cannot call it a garden it is in such dirt and disorder."

Selena assented with a smile and opening the little glass door which led into a very nicely dressed flower garden felt grateful for the degree of consideration which she believed made Mrs. Rolleham wish to get rid of her while she gratified the curiosity which could not be repressed. The sun was however hot and in its full power while the gravel walks afforded little shade and Selena observing the key in the garden door was tempted to advance to the shrubbery and there await the termination of the conference. The shrubbery was open to the lawn of which it formed a ring fence. She had not proceeded many steps before she was determined to return again to the garden upon finding herself in view of the servants who were collected round the carriage at the door; and the rather as she observed among them a groom leading a horse which she supposed might be Mr. Rolleham's. She had not however quite reached the door when at the sound of hastily approaching footsteps she turned her head, and beheld to her no small surprise that she was pursued by Lord Louverney.

As he was still at some distance her first impulse was to escape without appearing to notice him and she involuntarily quickened her pace, but as she closed the garden door the manifest rudeness of excluding him when he must be certain she had seen him made her hesitate in spite of her reluctance to such a meeting at this time when she had no doubt that the events connected with her brother and herself were become a pretty general topick of conversation.

While she stood for an instant irresolute her hand yet on the key he advanced and gently pushing open the door his delight at beholding her was better painted in his sparkling eyes and the kindling glow of joy which overspread his face than by those incoherent expressions with which he vainly attempted to utter what he felt.

Selena in some confusion returned his salutation but she had recovered her composure before she reached the house while that of her companion seemed every moment to encrease, and tho' he had infinitely less reason to be surprised at this unexpected meeting, it completely bewildered all his faculties so that he would have found it utterly impossible to explain how Selena had happened to be there, tho' in answer to his embarrassed questions she had repeated to him more than once that she had come with Mrs. Vallard and at Mrs. Rolleham's desire walked out to look at the hyacinths which she observed were still in great beauty.

They now entered together. Mrs. Rolleham who was in close conversation being thus interrupted was obliged most reluctantly to break off and having had recourse to her glass now introduced Lord Louverney in proper form to Mrs. Vallard as the particular friend of her son.

Selena could not help feeling some embarrassment at the very significant smiles and nods with which Mrs. Rolleham alternately examined Lord Louverney and herself. She affected however not to observe her, and sat silently and secretly longing for Mrs. Vallard to put a conclusion to this visit. But of this she saw no prospect for some time.

Mrs. Vallard had begun to speak of Lady Greysville to Lord Louverney, and was delighted by the account which he gave of the quiet life which she was leading and the favourable change which already appeared in the temper of Sir Thomas.

Lord Louverney had a remarkable talent for easy conversation, so that without possessing in an eminent manner any other abilities it was impossible to be in his company without paying to him constant attention and admiring the peculiar turn of his expressions or rather the pleasing manner in which they were delivered. His bon-mots were never repeated, and had any one attempted to recollect what had charmed in his conversation they would have been puzzled to describe in what it consisted or even to discover it themselves. Yet every party smiled at his approach and dull indeed must be the society which was not enlivened to animation by his presence.

No one was more sensible to the pleasures of conversation than Mrs. Vallard and the confinement in which she had passed many of her years with an infirm husband had calculated her the better to enjoy society while it contributed to the cultivation of her mind, tho' it for a time obliged her to renounce those social pleasures which she always loved even when she cheerfully relinquished them without one exception. With the strong wish to render himself agreeable which Lord Louverney now possessed it is therefore not surprising that he and Mrs. Vallard were mutually much pleased with each other, and as her health did not permit her to accept of Mrs. Rolleham's invitations to dinner she found great difficulty to restrain herself from complying with the pretty plain hints which that Lady now threw out that her party might be invited to Hillbarton. But she had already promised Robert to bring thither no strangers during his stay and the remembrance of this promise now witheld her lips from uttering the request, for which Mrs. Rolleham awaited with evident impatience.

Mrs. Vallard was not ignorant of the constant attachment which upon hearing of Dallamore's elopement had given Lord Louverney new hopes, and urged him to undertake this journey to which Lady Greysville's strong persuasions had contributed to encourage him, and tho' Mrs. Vallard could not wish him success and honestly confessed to Mrs. Rolleham her certainty that Selena's affections were already engaged, yet while she conversed with him, and observed his pleasing manners and prepossessing countenance she could not help lamenting his disappointment and wishing that she could transfer his attachment to the unengaged Clara, since Selena could not alas! complete the happiness of Sidney and at the same time reward the love of another however worthy and amiable he might be.

Mrs. Rolleham as well as Lord Louverney attended them to the carriage and as she perceived his horses still on the gravel she enquired for her son. Lord Louverney answered her inquisitive demands by saying that he had rode on and that he had promised to follow him. He accordingly mounted his horse and prevented for the present Mrs. Vallard from entering into any particular conversation with Selena by his occasional remarks as he rode by the window, in which Mrs. Vallard found considerable entertainment.

They proceeded in this manner until they came to a long and pretty steep hill about a mile from Hillbarton. The postillion accustomed never to press his horses ascended in his usual creeping gait and Lord Louverney observing the servant with prudent caution alight to let down the drag staff demanded without any intention of terrifying Mrs. Vallard whether her horses ever baulked adding that the road in this part would be very dangerous under such circumstances.

Mrs. Vallard instantly took the alarm and calling to the servant eagerly asked "Did he think there was any danger?"

Lord Louverney instantly alighted officiously advancing to the horses's heads and ready to offer his assistance, while the postillion half angry at the insinuation had to reassure his mistress and at the same time smartly exercised his whip and spur turning them from the edge of the steep bank.

The high fed creatures impatient of the unexpected discipline made a violent plunge toward the other side of the road and unfortunately the new horse upon which the postillion was mounted lighting upon a large loose stone stumbled and nearly fell. Tho' he instantly recovered himself and that Selena as well as the servants with one voice assured Mrs. Vallard that she had nothing to fear she was not to be convinced, particularly as they were seconded by Lord Louverney who had already opened the chaise door and stood ready to assist the ladies out.

Mrs. Vallard eagerly accepted his aid and suffered him to lift her out while Selena followed her with less precipitation, for tho' "a true maid" she possessed none of that cowardice which Shakespear[26] seems to consider as the indispensable attribute of that character, but on the contrary was gifted with more real courage and presence of mind than many a hero who had distinguished himself in the front of a battle.

She now left the carriage with much reluctance, perceiving no real cause for terror and foreseeing the difficulties which would thus attend their return home; Mrs. Vallard protesting that she would never again hazard their lives with the poor animal who had thus unfortunately incurred her displeasure. Selena fearful of her suffering from a walk of such a length in the heat of the sun, knew not what to propose when she saw her determined not to resume her place in the chaise and therefore offering her arm advised her to take the shady side of the road. Lord Louverney giving his horse to his servant presented her with a more able support on the other side and after they had proceeded some time Mrs. Vallard recommended Selena to accept the offer of his other arm which she had at first declined. Ashamed strongly to persist in this rejection, and the rather as she feared Mrs. Vallard would remember that she was not accustomed thus to refuse the

---

[26] "Vide Midsummer's night's dream" (Tighe's note). In *A Midsummer Night's Dream* Helena declares "I am a right maid for my cowardice" (3.2.302). In *As You Like It* Rosalind uses the phrase "true maid" when she tells Celia to "Speak sad brow and true maid" (3.2.211–12).

assistance of Sidney, she consented and the reproaches of Lord Louverney for her unwillingness served but to heighten her blushes and add to her uneasiness.

At length tho' with much fatigue on the part of Mrs. Vallard, they had nearly reached the termination of their journey when Selena perceived Sidney at some distance on the lawn who was impatiently watching for their return and now advanced hastily to meet them.

Her first involuntary movement was to withdraw her arm from Lord Louverney but restored in an instant to recollection by his stopping and looking round upon her inquisitively, she coloured deeply and once more resumed her place at his side.

Sidney, who had upon first observing the carriage slowly following thought some accident had befallen them, could now behold but one object his modest his adored Selena, hanging on the arm of his acknowledged rival whose eye seemed at that moment to meet his with the insolent confidence of rapturous triumph.

There was not a feeling of his heart which did not instantly pass to that of Selena, and in beholding the anguish which he suffered she forgot how little right she had yet given him to express his jealousy and how trifling was the cause which had now excited it.

How did she long to address him! to banish the gloom which overspread the manly beauty of his speaking countenance, to tell him that all her tenderness was his, and that when compared with him Lord Louverney and every other being upon earth appeared to her fondly occupied fancy but as objects of the most entire indifference, as the very dust of the ballance.[27]

She was however not only silent but conscious of her weakness she feared to trust her eyes, lest they should confess too much and held them fixed upon the ground, while the confusion which he read in her glowing face seemed to him but the declaration of the delight which she felt in the presence of the lover who now at liberty to assert his claims and offer his vows had hastened to pour them at her feet and whose arrival she had greeted with such apparent eagerness.

He was nevertheless restored to self command by Mrs. Vallard who little guessing the cause of his manifest perturbation suddenly exclaimed, "Oh Sidney! You need not be frightened, you see all is safe; but I assure you we have been in the greatest danger, tho' I dare say Selena will not allow it. But if Lord Louverney had not been on the spot to help us out I do not know what might have happened."

She then proceeded to give an account of their accident which her fears magnified unintentionally far beyond the bounds of simple truth.

Selena who of all people upon earth was the least inclined to the spirit of contradiction and who at present was peculiarly disposed to silence interrupted not her narrative which she hoped would at least convince Sidney that they had not alighted merely for the pleasure of walking with Lord Louverney.

Indeed this was almost the only part which made any impression upon Sidney, for the danger of their situation he could not comprehend, and his knowledge of Mrs. Vallard made him on that head somewhat incredulous.

---

[27]   Dust of the ballance: reference to dust on the scales, from Isaiah 40:15 (KJV).

Relieved from this first idea which however absurd had yet for the moment the full power of torturing his mind in an indescribable manner, Sidney disguised the uneasiness he still experienced, assuming an air of frigid indifference which in him appeared the most constrained and unnatural he returned Lord Louverney's salutation and resolved if he discovered in Selena that preference (which he began to dread she might too justly entertain for his rival) that he would hide from her and every eye upon earth his affliction, and relinquish for ever those imaginary hopes which in spite of fate had hitherto supported him.

Mrs. Vallard was now willing to conceive herself absolved by circumstances in this instance from her promise and could not suffer Lord Louverney to accompany her to her own door without inviting him to dinner, an invitation which he instantly accepted to the infinite mortification of Selena, who not only felt for the vexation she knew his presence gave Sidney and her own embarrassment but was also apprehensive of the distress which Robert must now experience on the intrusion of a stranger.

But she endeavoured to disguise her feelings and as Sidney during the whole day affectedly shunned her conversation, and even avoided meeting her eyes she was not betrayed into any weakness which could at least to him recal the pain that in secret oppressed her with an almost insupportable weight.

Once indeed she was upon the point of exposing herself to the eyes of all and it was with extreme difficulty that she refrained from bursting into tears. When they entered the dinner parlour she took her usual place; Robert who had not before made his appearance, came in at the same instant with Lord Louverney and while they exchanged salutations in some degree awkward on both sides Selena's heart beat in the assurance that Sidney would profit by the momentary pause to advance behind the chair at her side which he had ever occupied. He remained however motionless, and as she ventured to raise her eyes he instantly turned his head towards the window—while Lord Louverney impatiently approached and seized upon the vacant seat which he at that moment considered as the most enviable spot upon earth satisfying for the present the full extent of his wishes.

The heart of Selena sunk with a more cruel sensation of disappointment than the certainty of far greater and what might be esteemed more real misfortunes could have for the time inflicted. But having subdued her emotions she argued herself into imagining that she approved of Sidney's conduct which she doubted not proceeded from his determination no longer to persevere in a pursuit from which he could hope no happiness and she firmly resolved that she would not give him cause to suspect that she weakly regretted his thus at length submitting to what her principles had obliged her to require. In conformity to this resolution, she struggled to bestow apparent attention to the conversation which Lord Louverney continued assiduously to address to her and even supported her share in it with some cheerfulness.

Mrs. Vallard at length began to perceive how vain were her projects on behalf of Clara, since it was totally impossible for Lord Louverney in the presence of Selena to bestow one interested thought upon another female, and the gloomy and silent sadness of Sidney convinced her that he thought she had not acted with fidelity to his cause in this reception of his rival.

Selena herself therefore expected the departure of their new guest with scarcely less impatience than Mrs. Vallard, an impatience which his Lordship however shared not in the least, and tho' he was sensible that something was wanting to his happiness and that there was a coldness more than that of bashful reserve in the manner of Selena, which chilled all the ardor of his hopes yet he could not resolve to tear himself from the domestic scene, to which a secret presentiment made him tremble for his re-admission until the lateness of the hour and Mrs. Vallard's faint invitation to him of an apartment for the night shamed him into retiring.

Never had Selena felt a melancholy more oppressive or for which she would have found it more difficult to account, than that which she this night experienced. She could bear to part from Sidney. She had even desired it, but to part in coldness, to behold a premature indifference chill in the very moment of her warmest sensibility the tenderness of that friendship which even in absence she had hoped to preserve as her chief consolation thro' life this was indeed insupportable! The bitterest tears bathed her pillow and her unquiet slumbers were incessantly broken by that sense of suffering which those acquainted with sorrow well know can still continue to oppress the heart when the memory of its cause is suspended by sleep or if blunted for a moment it is but to sting with augmented force at the moment of awakening.

When, impatient to quit her uneasy bed she beheld the sun rise, she said sadly to herself that its orient beams should never more open her eyes with the exhilarating hope of being able to fix them upon that soft smile of delighted fondness that had ever spoken love and pleasure to her soul. She was assured that Sidney would now leave Hillbarton for she had watched in vain for that relenting weakness which might constrain him to linger in spite of the resolution which she was certain he had taken. She endeavoured therefore during those tranquil hours to fortify her mind to bear the severe trials which she expected should that day await her, but she had not been long risen before she was convinced that he also was up, for as his room was adjoining to hers, she could plainly distinguish his steps as he paced the floor in an hurried and unequal manner which plainly spoke the agitation of his mind.

They met not however till all were assembled at breakfast, and yet Selena was in the parlour for above an hour alone. She knew not herself that she had expected to find him there until the pain she experienced at the disappointment and her impatience as the tedious moments rolled away convinced her of the self mortifying truth. They past! These precious moments which she thought he might like herself have considered as the few that were yet left to the possibility of feeling their existence shared together! Oh! if he indeed loved could he bear at such a period willingly to absent himself? No! he had already succeeded in his efforts, and she was already banished from his heart!

He spoke not to her during breakfast. Intending to assist his purpose of avoiding her, or rather perhaps hurt at his not entering until all were seated, Selena placed herself between Mrs. Vallard and Clara and before he came in offered to attend the former when she spoke of visiting one of her patients who resided at the farm yard at some distance from the house.

After Mrs. Vallard had left the room to prepare herself for the little expedition Selena arose and opened the window. Without looking round she knew that Sidney now left his chair and was hesitating whether he should join her. Her heart palpitated violently and she was so conscious of her agitation that she did not dare to turn tho' Clara (who had not heard her engagement with Mrs. Vallard) asked her would she walk. As she continued silent Clara repeated her question and Sidney then advancing leaned on the open window as he sought her glowing and averted face while he with difficulty articulated, "Will you?"

"I am going out with Mrs. Vallard," answered Selena and having said this she for the first time that day met the eyes of Sidney. Oh! at that moment her soul felt that indifference had no part in his. How weak, how slow, is language to utter the eloquence of lovers' eyes!

Lightened of an inexpressible load she appeared in one instant delivered from every sorrow of her own and nothing remained but the compassion she felt for his, and the almost irresistible longing to express the tenderness which overflowed in her bosom.

But she tore herself from the dangerous scene, and flying to her own room awaited the call of Mrs. Vallard. Having remained there above an hour she went in search of her and found then from Clara that she had left a message advising her to walk with her younger friends as upon consideration she did not chuse to take her to a sick room. Selena sorry that she had suffered her thus to walk alone immediately hastened by the shortest path to the farm yard.

But Mrs. Vallard had just left it and was returned hence by a shady walk thro' the wood.

Selena prepared to follow her and being obliged to cross the road had just opened the gate when she perceived Lord Louverney within a few paces advancing on horseback. This rencounter was in every respect unpleasant to her, but particularly annoying from the idea which instantly struck her that Sidney might suspect it had been preconcerted. There was however no possibility now of avoiding it; Lord Louverney had already given his horse to his servant and was in a moment at her side expressing a delight at this meeting in which she could so little sympathise.

Her silence and coldness struck to his heart and unable to disguise his feelings he profited by the opportunity which this tete-a-tete afforded and with that tender embarrassment ever the attendant on Love, entreated her to allow him to visit her in Herefordshire as she had before mentioned her purpose of speedily returning thither with her brother.

Perceiving by her blushes and hesitation that she comprehended the full force of his request, he proceeded passionately to declare how from the time of their first acquaintance he had never ceased to think of her with an ardour of attachment which nothing had been able to discourage but the report of her engagement, and that the moment he was convinced of the falsehood of this, he flew to discover whether the most entire devotion and the most faithful love might obtain for him some hope of indulging the fondest desire of his soul which for the rest of his life should be only to please her.

In the midst of the painful confusion which oppressed Selena she was yet not displeased that he had thus early given her the power in an explicit manner to put an end to the business which could only terminate in his disappointment and that she might at once crush those hopes which the longer they were indulged must the more effectually injure his happiness.

Her candid and generous disposition therefore in a few moments enabled her to conquer her natural timidity and in terms at once the most graceful and the most decided she told him that she never could otherwise express her gratitude for the disinterested regard he had shewn than to regret that it should have been thus vainly squandered upon one whose lot for life was already cast before he had even seen her and tho' circumstances precluded the possibility of entirely explaining to him her situation, yet thus much she thought he was entitled to know and hesitated not to tell him that she was no longer at liberty to dispose of herself.

He heard her almost without interruption, but gazed upon her as she spoke, with sentiments of mingled regret, admiration and tenderness which made it impossible for him to withdraw his eyes while every instant he felt more strongly and painfully the value of what he despaired ever to obtain, sighing to himself, "Lost, lost for ever lost, and now 'tis gone. How beautiful!" At length subduing the emotions which rose to choak his utterance he replied, "One question allow me to ask and pardon some impertinence in a man who has nearly lost every hope that can sweeten life! Is your heart at liberty to regret those mysterious bonds?"

Selena's whole frame betrayed her agitation. How was she to reply to a question which it was almost impossible to answer with sincerity? How shameful, nay even criminal did she at that moment seem in her own eyes while she reviewed at one glance the situation which she could not explain!

"Shall I tell him," thought she, "that considering myself solemnly wedded to another I have yet suffered my heart to sigh for liberty only to assume new bonds which with culpable self will it has already chosen for itself? Or shall I by a half confession while I own that I regret my lost freedom falsely imply that my heart has reserved itself for another Lord?"

The love of truth which ever prevailed over every other sentiment in the bosom of Selena overpowered her reluctance and seeing that he awaited her reply with earnest impatience, watching with anxious solicitude the struggling emotions evident in her countenance she with glowing brow and dejected eyes pronounced, "I will not deceive you, you have a right to my confidence as far as relates to myself tho' to you alone have I said thus far; I am not free, and there is one being upon earth who before I knew you had fixed for ever in himself all my ideas of earthly felicity. Insurmountable bars separate us but never will I voluntarily be another's!"

She ceased and for some moments each was silent. Overcome as she was with confusion she ventured not yet to raise her eyes, but at length she suddenly stopped upon perceiving that they were within view of the house and her feet were rooted to the ground as she beheld Sidney leaning against a tree at some distance intently gazing upon them.

Lord Louverney started! Not that he had also discovered his rival, but suddenly aroused by this pause from the gloomy reverie into which her words had plunged him he saw the decisive moment was arrived in which he must for ever bid adieu to the chosen lovely object of his warm affections.

"I understand you," he cried, "I will persecute you no more! Yet think of me sometimes with pity and God bless you, sweetest Selena God bless you for ever!" As he said this ashamed of the unmanly expression of grief that rushed to his eyes and in haste to hide himself from sight he snatched her hand and pressing it eagerly to his lips repeated in hurried accents his ardent blessing mingled with entreaties for forgiveness and then disappeared leaving Selena with but one idea, one image, that of Sidney whom she at the same instant beheld rush violently from the spot on which he had stood overwhelmed with every painful every indignant feeling of despair and jealousy inspired by the scene which he had just witnessed.

Chapter VI

> Spite of my vulgar duty I will speak
> With all the dearness of a parting lover;
> Farewell most lovely, and most loved of men!
> Why comes this dying paleness o'er thy face?
> Why wander thus thine eyes? Why does thou bend
> As if the fatal weight of death was o'er thee?
>   Lee[28]

For some moments Selena remained motionless, overpowered as she was by the idea which now for the first time seriously presented itself to her mind that Sidney suspected her of favourably listening to another and that from hence proceeded his conduct during the last four and twenty hours which she had felt so cutting to her heart. She recollected how many circumstances had tended to confirm to a jealous eye such a suspicion, and eager to explain them, and acquit herself as she thought justice to her own character required, she no sooner recovered her powers, stunned as they seemed to be, by this overwhelming discovery than she hastened towards the drawing room where she hoped to find Sidney. No one was there, and unable to conquer her impatience, or the ardent wish which she now had for another interview with Sidney, she returned to the lawn and continued within view of the house, in the faint hope that he would (as he had till now ever been accustomed to do) upon perceiving her from the windows hasten to join her. She was persuaded that she only desired to free herself from the charge which his heart had been too

---

[28]   Athenais in Nathaniel Lee's *Theodosius* (1680), 4.2.524–9 ("vulgar" should be "rigid" in line 515, "parting" should be "dying" in line 517, "thine" should be "thy" in line 520, and "was o'er thee" should be "were on thee" in line 521).

ready to credit tho' appearances might half justify the suspicion; But her reason having once allowed that she was excusable in desiring this last interview she suffered inconceivably from its delay and tears of an impatient vexation to which she was almost a stranger accused him of indifference and neglect in thus wilfully avoiding the explanation which she now so ardently longed to give, tho' had he at the moment appeared before her she would have found it totally impossible to utter a syllable.

The moments appeared immeasurably tedious, and she could scarcely believe that they had not forgotten to ring the labourers bell at the usual hour, at length wearied out, ashamed, and mortified at the vain expectations in which she had worn away the morning she slowly returned towards her own apartment, forming a thousand plans how she should conduct herself upon their unavoidable meeting at dinner. As she was ascending the stairs her feet were arrested by the sound of steps hastily passing thro' the hall, but her heart which had in this case never deceived her told her this was not Sidney, she nevertheless waited with a kind of unaccountable fearful foreboding and was almost instantly joined by Robert in whose countenance she read disquietude and grief.

He held a letter in his hand and telling Selena as he passed that he wished to speak to her he advanced to his own room. Leaving the door open he threw himself mournfully on a seat and hid his face as he leaned his head upon the table on which he left the letter for her inspection.

With a trembling hand she took it up and perceiving that it was the writing of Sidney the sudden testimony that he was indeed gone, that he was gone without a wish to see her overpowered her with a silent anguish. She grew very sick, and sinking upon the seat nearest to which she stood it was some minutes before she could distinguish the characters of the following lines.

> "Do not blame me my dear friend for a conduct I feel necessary. Would to God I had at first followed the dictates of prudence! I am at length convinced there is no hope for me. Alas! long ago I might have seen it, had not my own folly blinded me. To what purpose therefore should I linger here? prolonging my own torments and a burden upon the compassionate kindness of others. When my destination is decided I will write to you but for the present I cannot speak of my intentions since they have no other fixed object than to fly from what my soul has so long, so fatally loved. I cannot bid Mrs. Vallard farewell but you have all borne with me too long and it is time to deliver you from the sight of wretchedness which you cannot relieve. Heaven bless you my dear Robert! My soul can for itself form no desires so strong as those which it incessantly breathes for the happiness of Selena but I wish her not to know the anguish with which in tearing myself from hence I look with envy at the very stones upon which she may tread when I shall be banished far, far for ever from her sight!"

Never had Selena until that moment known the extent of her love for Sidney, and while her tears flowed with unconstrained abundance, she felt as if deprived of every hope, and incapable of consolation.

The idea of his absence, nay even of his being lost to her for ever affected her not with half such bitterness as that with which she internally exclaimed, "Alas did he indeed love, he never could have thus abandoned me! He could not have borne to quit me without one last farewell, one parting blessing! Could I have done so? Oh never, never! It is then plain he has deceived me or himself. He loves not alas as I do!"

Poor Selena overwhelmed with this terrible conviction considered this as an argument unanswerable, but woe to the woman of sensibility who places her happiness on the love of one of the other sex, if she suffers herself to draw conclusions from such a comparison! Could she possess the whole heart of the most passionate, most delicate lover that ever languished at the feet of beauty, how often must her soul be wounded by disappointment and her bosom torn with unjust suspicions! Is it that men are better fortified against the weakness of feeling? Or is it that women love with a delicacy more refined? But the affection of a man is not to be estimated by the same proof that might be incontestible in a female, and let her whose fond breast would desire peace never yield to the timorous suggestions of distrust which would thus point out the deficiency in what it receives by the consciousness of what it bestows!

While Selena's spirits were yet fainting under the first oppression of her grief Clara hastily rushed into the room and bathed in tears exclaimed, "Oh Robert! How could you let poor Sidney go! And you Selena did you know it?" Selena in silence handed to her the letter.

Having cast her eyes over it—"Alas," cried she eagerly, "too well I know what that destiny will be if he is not rescued from destruction! Dearest Selena! Let me conjure you as you would save yourself from everlasting self reproach and misery the most dreadful let not Mrs. Dallamore accuse you of the murder of her son. Do something instantly to prevent him from going to the West Indies to perish in that horrible yellow fever!"

Selena shuddered. Her tears no longer flowed, but pale and unable to articulate she looked to Robert for the confirmation of tidings which her fears were but too prone to credit.

"Speak to her Robert," said Clara, "she does not believe that Sidney has this shocking intention. Yet Mrs. Vallard assures me there is not a doubt of it. I have left her in the utmost agony of mind writing to entreat him to return, but Heaven knows whether her letter will ever reach him."

"Does she know where to direct to him?" demanded Robert starting.

"Alas no! Her only hope rested upon you."

"I have not the most distant idea," replied he sighing, "I am just returned from Barton bridge. He had not been there himself but his servant had left it in a chaise before I arrived and was gone to Derby. The probability is they are now on their way to town."

"And will you not endeavour to find him out?" interrupted Clara, "and dissuade him from thus exposing himself to certain Death. You know what dreadful accounts there have been lately from the West Indies and Mrs. Vallard says she is sure the very thoughts of his going will kill Mrs. Dallamore."

"And what reason have you to suppose he has any intention of it?" asked Selena at length in a tremulous voice, her heart sinking with terror.

"She has but too much reason," replied Robert, "He had already almost determined upon it when I first told him of your unalterable resolution to abide by your unfortunate vows, I succeeded in making him for the time abandon the project, less I believe by my persuasions than by declaring my purpose of accompanying him if he was determined to put it into execution and it is I am sure to prevent this that he has thus suddenly quitted us."

"And how could you dear Robert," said Clara reproachfully, "thus think of abandoning us in such a manner?"

"I will tell you my reasons my dear girls for wishing to be poor Sidney's companion, if I could not prevail upon him to relinquish a plan which appears to me so wretched. He can have no view in preferring such a service but from a desire to expose himself to danger. The disorder which so justly terrified you, is fatal to the imprudent. I may prevent his rashness and I owe him too much poor fellow, not to make my sacrifice in order to preserve his health and if possible restore his mind to tranquillity. I am therefore decided to follow him to London where I can hardly fail of discovering him should he be employed about such a purchase. I will exert myself to persuade him to come with me to Ireland and if I fail he shall at least not cross the Atlantic without a friend!"

Selena who had until now listened with an indescribable sensation of horror, was unable longer to endure a conversation so dreadful to her feelings, and looking upon herself as the miserable source of all this distress which she already beheld and of those more terrible misfortunes which her heart foreboded, she wished to bury herself from every eye and dreading to meet Mrs. Vallard as tho' she merited the reproaches of all she thought only of seeking some retirement where secure from interruption she might pour out the smothered anguish of her bursting heart.

Afraid of being pursued by Clara she went not to her own apartment but with hurried steps heedless of the briars and high weeds which intercepted the path, she tore her way amidst the thickest part of the wood thro' which she knew there were no walks and which was of course most wild and unfrequented.

The quick motion of her feet and the suffering of her body seemed in some degree to drive from her mind the sense of its pains for she felt not all the weight of her affliction until exhausted and almost fainting from fatigue she sunk upon the rough ground amongst the high grass and scraggy branches that nearly closed her round.

Her grief uttered itself in no complaints, her tears did not flow, but a confused and indistinct sensation of dread and anguish seemed to suspend all her recollection and with her hands closed she looked around with despondency as tho' left alone upon earth, and for ever separated from all that she loved in life.

Mean while Sidney whom her heart during the last hours they had passed together had more than once accused of indifference, was a prey to all the cruel conflicts which can distract the soul torn between the hopes promised by Love and the despair threatened by jealousy.

No sooner had he quitted Hillbarton than he was entirely forsaken by all the firmness and courage which had supported him in this determination from the moment he beheld Lord Louverney seal, as he imagined, his hopes on the soft hand of Selena, and at every step he reproached himself with encreasing regret that he had not alleviated the anguish of this separation by giving vent in one last adieu to all that ardour of passion which like a devouring fire had so long in silence consumed his soul. In pursuance of the plan which he had formed to avoid Robert and all pursuit he arrived on foot at the village two miles distant to the north of Hillbarton. Here he could however procure no horses, and was informed that four had been just sent to Rolleham hall to convey Lord Louverney to Derby. A ray of joy shot across the mind of Sidney as he heard this casual intelligence. From what trivial circumstances will not the tide of animal spirits suddenly turn in the bosom of the sanguine lover? This detested rival was then gone! and now at least should not triumph in his absence.

It was now that he recollected all the arguments which he had intended to use to Selena in order to prevail upon her for the sake of her brother's happiness totally to renounce all claims on Dallamore which could no way be effectually done but by declaring to Robert that she conceived herself free to form a new connexion.

While Sidney now blamed the precipitousness of his flight he almost persuaded himself to think that the friendship which he owed to Robert required that he should return to seek an interview with Selena to paint to her the strengths of his attachment to Ophelia and urge her to deliver him from those false scruples which now prevented him in consideration of her from obtaining his own freedom.

"Yes," cried he passionately, "it was my duty to represent to her motives so powerful over her feeling heart, even tho' I were convinced that her acceptance of another was to be the immediate consequence."

Stung with these thoughts and unknowing whither he wandered, he hurried along at one moment ardently urged to return and throw himself at the feet of Selena, and the next blushing at his weakness he felt impatient only to abandon every scene which could renew the remembrance of his last hopes and dreams of happiness.

Upon his leaving the village he struck into the grounds of Esselberrie thro' which he had purposed to take his way to Barton Bridge, wishing to avoid the high road which led by Hillbarton gate. But heedless of what surrounded him, he had bewildered himself in the paths and on a sudden started from his profound meditations upon beholding himself at the little gate which opened into the woods of Hillbarton from the park of Esselberrie.

It was here that he had so often walked with Selena; some large stones projecting in the wall at one side formed a kind of style, and here they had frequently seated themselves to enjoy the beauties which that elevated situation commanded. Here on both sides was presented the most delightful variety of ground in two parks which lay immediately beneath, bounded by a rich and extensive country. The river half concealed by plantations beautifully wound thro' the highly dressed valley before them, while the high rocky grounds of Esselberrie park almost covered with oaks rose immediately behind. On a calm evening Selena particularly loved this spot, and from her partiality Lady Trevallyn had formerly called it her own, a name which had been adopted both at Esselberrie and Hillbarton, so that Selena's seat became the well known and favourite scene of many a mutually delightful conversation. In an agony of grief Sidney now gazed around; Every sweet, and silent object seemed to smile with the same tranquility as they had worn in the hours of his most exquisite felicity, and all maintained its immoveable beauty and serenity while his soul was torn with tumultuous and torturing agitation.

"Alas," cried he, "what is this superiority which we boast over inanimate objects but the capacity of suffering? I am but as others! I daily see afflictions greater than mine oppress humanity and yet even I am tempted to exclaim, oh that I were but as those stones! that this heart might cease to beat and these temples no longer throb with this intolerable anguish! Creator of the world why hast thou made man in pain?"

Scarcely had he dared to utter the bold reproach of involuntary impiety than a secret voice within him thus reproved his blind injustice. "Ungrateful accuser of wisdom and of goodness which thou canst not comprehend is then thine existence limited to that of the perishable dust which thou canst now behold? Recollect that thy real life commences not until thou hast reached the goal where all the delusive phantoms of cares and of sorrows which now vex thine imagination shall vanish and Virtue alone remain permanent. Offspring of a benevolent Being, created for happiness, feel in thy very sufferings the conviction of thine immortal nature. Fulfill the part allotted to thee, enter into thyself for thy peace thy consolations, and despise the transient evils of which thine own distempered fancy has been the sole artificer!"

A train of more composing reflection followed and an emotion of softer melancholy diffused itself over his soul as he leaned upon the gate and surveyed the well known objects around while all the pleasures which he had there enjoyed seemed to rise before him and "beat thick on his remembrance."[29]

"They are then past," he cried, "for ever! those moments the sweetest of my life, when seated here beside thee I might listen to thy voice, gaze upon thy smiles, and occupy thy thoughts! I shall see thee then no more! Oh pardon sweet image! Yes I shall see thee for ever! In the nightly gloom of the most deserted forest, or in the confused din of the full peopled camp I shall behold thee and thee only! Oh could I at least know that thou my beloved wert happy, the assurance would render me contented tho' separated far from thee for ever, tho' banished for ever from thy remembrance!"

His meditations lasted long and would have probably still longer continued had not his attention been suddenly aroused by observing a female figure advancing thro' the trees at a little distance. Tho' he could only distinguish the white drapery yet the step, the air could belong to none but Selena. Breathless and intently stretched to gaze upon the form he remained for some minutes without power or thought of motion even after the deep shades into which she entered entirely obscured her from his eye.

"Now," thought he at length starting passionately from his trance, "Now has friendship offered to me this opportunity and I will employ it for Robert.

---

[29]   Antony in John Dryden's *All for Love* (1677), 2.1.457–8 ("his" should by 'my").

Yes surely when I speak not for myself, she will not refuse to hear me plead for the happiness of her brother!" Then with a violent bound he vaulted over the gate and rushing towards the spot which had thus concealed her, in an instant beheld her seated on the ground within a few paces of him as he stood arrested in his pursuit and fixed to the earth by the unexpected lovely apparition of what he had sought.

She heard not his approach, but continued her face raised towards the other side and her hands clasped as they rested on her knees.

He heard her sigh deeply and shuddered while he thought upon Lord Louverney when she faintly articulated these scarcely audible sounds—"Never never shall I see thee more! my brother, my friend, my beloved! Ah why must vows abjured by my soul thus separate us for ever?" Odious to think himself in the part of spy which he thus unwillingly acted while intruding on her secret retirement he armed himself with a kind of indignant fortitude and hastily stepping forward she started from the ground and stood pale and trembling at once overwhelmed with confusion, terror, and astonishment at this strangely sudden vision. For in the surprise joy had as yet found no part and tho' the moment before she felt as if she could have resigned her life with contentment to purchase but one parting interview all pleasurable emotions were now excluded by the shame of having betrayed herself and the deep sadness and disquietude which she yet read in every feature of Sidney's countenance.

Without daring to fix on her his eyes he began in an hurried voice of smothered emotion to declare his satisfaction at thus meeting her accidentally, as he had a few words of consequence which he wished to utter before they should part for ever; "There is no one," continued he, "who knows as I do the secrets of your brother's heart, and now that you can no longer suspect me of interested motives you will perhaps believe me when I assure you that he cherishes a passion which I know to be powerful enough to destroy all the future happiness of his life, yet no consideration will be able to induce him to deliver himself totally from the vile woman who is still by the laws of man his wife, except the persuasion that you will accept the liberty which her marriage with Dallamore will assuredly give you. Selena sacrifice not your own happiness and that of your brother to an imaginary scruple, a false delicacy unworthy of your sound judgment. Think not that I plead for myself! That is all at an end; The hopes which I had madly indulged have for ever vanished but may he upon whom you can look with tenderness be worthy of that precious heart which I would have died to obtain. Selena farewell! Remember the last counsels of your friend and think upon what a proof he has given of their sincerity in his voluntary exile from all his soul adores—in tearing himself away from your sight for ever!"

He had pronounced these words with a rapidity only interrupted at times by a difficulty of breathing which made him gasp for utterance. He now advanced one step, desiring once more to press her hand to his lips but a cold sickness that ran shivering thro' his heart and affected every limb with a faint tremour made him relinquish the attempt and turning from her he leaned against a tree waiting a moment for strength to retire.

But Selena, who amidst the overwhelming sorrow that confused all her powers had comprehended in this whole speech nothing but that they were now to part and part for ever; when she beheld the deadly paleness which suddenly overspread his beautiful countenance and perceived him ready to depart felt at once every other consideration perish in her mind but the desire of relieving him from the mortal anguish beneath which he seemed oppressed. Timid bashfulness, suspicious delicacy, cautious prudence, nay the strict voice of duty itself would at that moment have spoken unheard within the soft bosom of Selena which yielding wholly to the irresistible dominion of love and compassion urged her to throw aside every reserve and at once confess to him all that tenderness which so long had struggled within her most secret soul.

She would have approached him, but with that painful sensation which is sometimes experienced in a troubled dream, her feet refused to move and bending towards him with earnest sadness as tho' she feared his escape she mournfully exclaimed, "Stay Sidney leave me not till you have heard the only vows my heart has ever seconded. Leave me not until I say that altho' I cannot be yours, and tho' you abandon one thus for ever yet if I am indeed free I never will be another's."

As she spoke she sank upon her knees to make the solemn appeal to Heaven, but a cloud overspread her eyes, and exhausted with the violent exertion of her mind she remained insensible till recalled to life and love by the warm tears and passionate embraces of Sidney, who held her in his arms and while he poured forth the incoherent transports of rapture and of gratitude, mingled his ardent supplications that she would repeat the words which had thus beyond all comprehension restored him at once from despair to extasy unutterable.

Almost frantic with impatience at her silence and the tears which now flowed abundantly from her eyes, he vehemently exclaimed, "Oh speak Selena, for the sake of Heaven I conjure you, tell me did I rave, am I in a dream, or did you indeed say that your heart was mine and never can be another's!"

"Never, never dearest Sidney, and let that assurance, let our mutual confidence in each other's affection sweeten the painful hour of parting ...."

"Parting!" eagerly interrupted Sidney as he pressed her hand to his heart which beat high with unutterable transport, "no we will never part! Why should we part? Life is too short to part even for a moment. Where should I go? My joys, my only joys are centered here."

"Alas my dear friend," cried Selena while a tender smile beamed thro' her tears, "how have I deceived you if from this foolish weakness you imagine that you have convinced my reason because you have conquered my resolutions and detected my want of strength to resist those feelings which I yet condemn."

He suffered her not to proceed but passionately exclaimed, "Say not so, dearest, purest of beings! Diminish not by one word of ungenerous regret the full tide of joys that overflows my heart in this hour of extasy. I ask you nothing more, suffer me but to taste my happiness! Dispose of me, command me, make me what you will. I am henceforth all your own! Nor will I even breathe a wish that shall offend you. Only speak not of separation, be my sister, my friend, my best adviser, and let our hearts for ever united rejoice in the sweet prospects which I will open to your view of confidence unlimited and sympathy unalterable!"

Selena softened herself into unspeakable tenderness was but too willing to banish every reflection that might dissolve the delicious enchantment of that hour.

"Supremely happy in th' awakened power of giving joy"[30] they mutually indulged the sweet certainty of being beloved, and beloved with an affection which they believed was in its very nature unalterable—for Love that abounds with delusions, has no delusion half so powerful as that which represents its charms eternal and unfading and he does not truly love who can credit the possibility of those warmly glowing feelings ever being chilled into the frost of indifference. Seen thro' this medium what could life present but faint visions, while all nature "Wore to the lover's eye a look of love."[31]

How light appeared the afflictions, the cares which they might thus suffer together! Selena indeed still wept, but those were vernal showers

> Lovely, gentle, kind
> And full of every hope and every joy.[32]

How softened was every theme in which they conversed! With what complacency did each agree to the plans devised by the other for the restoration of the mind of Robert to perfect happiness, while Selena consented that suspending for the present in silence every scruple which yet remained to obstruct their own union, Sidney should employ every argument which her confessed attachment might suggest to urge her brother to that measure upon which she could not but believe from all the circumstances which she now heard his happiness so entirely depended.

Chapter VII

> Were my whole life to come one heap of troubles
> The pleasure of this moment would suffice
> To sweeten all my griefs with its remembrance—
> Oh happy hour! if I not set thee down
> The whitest that the hour eye of time e'er saw,
> Let me ne'er smile when I remember thee
> Nor ev'n in wishes offer at a joy!
> > Lee[33]

Ev'n such were the sentiments that breathed from the happy Sidney's lightened heart, as they wandered together, heedless whither their footsteps bore them while every painful reflection for the time suspended, the passions gently soothed away,

---

[30] James Thomson, "Summer," *The Seasons* (1727), lines 1184–5.

[31] James Thomson, "Spring," *The Seasons* (1728), line 935.

[32] James Thomson, "Spring," *The Seasons* (1728), lines 152–3.

[33] Ziphares and Semandra in Nathaniel Lee's *Mithridates, King of Pontus* (1678), 2.1.331–7 (Ziphares speaks lines 331–3; Semandra speaks lines 334–7).

Sunk to divine repose and love and joy,
Alone are waking, love and joy serene
As airs that fan the summer![34]

But from this delightful trance of newly indulged happiness Selena was on a sudden awakened when upon looking around she perceived that hitherto unnoticed by each they had taken the path thro' the wood which led along the river and had just then reached the very spot where Sidney had first breathed the vows inspired by Love and prompted by Hope.

It was a spot which had long for Selena possessed many a secret powerful charm—many a sweetly pensive joy of memory, many a dear impression of treasured tenderness, all of which she had sacrificed by a solemn promise to the shrine of duty when she considered it a crime to indulge any sentiments injurious to those required from the wife of Dallamore. Having vowed never again to visit the scene of such dangerous recollections until she could do so without self reproach, she now after such an absence beheld herself unconsciously led thither at the very moment when after so severe a struggle she at length yielded to the arguments of strong affection and suffered herself to be convinced that duty no longer forbad her to receive the love of him, so long the chosen of her heart.

Struck by the circumstance, a momentary self examination called her to account for the rectitude of her present conduct, and the cloud which past over her sweet countenance was instantly observed by the ever watchful eye of love so ready to take alarm.

"What is the matter," exclaimed Sidney. "Oh Selena surely you do not already regret that you have recalled me from anguish worse than death to happiness? a happiness that if not entirely complete I will yet never wish to perfect at the expence of your peace. Have you already lost your confidence in my moderation my total submission to your will?"

"No dearest Sidney," answered she gently pressing his hand as she withdrew it from his grasp, "my confidence in you is unbounded, it is my dearest support in this moment of doubt and perplexity, when my soul suspicious of herself scarcely trusts the dictates even of that internal voice to which she has hitherto listened without daring to hesitate."

"Whence then my beloved Selena, whence was that shade which so suddenly overcast our dawning happiness?"

For a while she was silent, till urged by his earnest importunity she with glowing cheek and broken accents confessed to him her former resolution and the enraptured Sidney beheld in the sentiments which had called for that resolution all that secret tenderness which beyond his most presumptuous hope had long combatted for him with virtue in the soft bosom of Selena.

---

[34]   Mark Akenside, *The Pleasures of Imagination* (1744, 1757), 1.130–32 ("Sunk" should be "Sink").

Their tete-a-tete was at length interrupted by the appearance of Robert, who was indeed in search of his sister uneasy at her long absence.

Before he perceived them Selena hastily made her escape and retired to her own room totally unequal to any farther exertions at present and covered with sudden confusion at thus returning as it were in triumph with the captive fugitive.

Amidst the mutual congratulations and joyful surprise which the unhoped for recovery of the lost Sidney occasioned at Hillbarton no one entertained a doubt that his speedy marriage with Selena was to be the certain consequence notwithstanding he forbore all allusion to any farther hope than was consistent with their brotherly union which she confessed she had promised should in future subsist between them and with which he on his part had agreed to remain satisfied.

But tho' Sidney in the first hours of tumultuous joy which succeeded his certainty of being beloved could behold nothing but contentment, nay delight in whatever circumstances Selena's will should place him, she was herself scarcely retired for a moment to her own meditations before she was sensible how impossible it was for her to continue long within these terms upon which she now stood with Sidney; and fully convinced that having once confessed her fondness, Virtue and delicacy alike required her to give herself totally to him whom she had thus chosen from all the world, or if the objections to their union were yet insurmountable to separate herself from his society.

(This for a time at least) she was resolved to do, and this she at length effected after some hesitation on her own part and a thousand obstacles on his, all of which were strongly seconded by Mrs. Vallard who could see no reasons why those so dearly united should ever again be parted. Selena was however furnished with an excuse for gaining the temporary absence of Sidney which even he could scarcely withstand.

Robert having once more given his imagination leave to indulge in the new opening prospects of Hope was seized again with all that ardour of sanguine impatience which had ever distinguished his early youth, and found it impossible to resist the longing desire which he experienced to share these lovely visions of unexpected felicity with the tender Ophelia of whose affection tho' hitherto unacknowledged he could yet scarcely entertain a doubt. He resolved instantly to take the steps which however attended with pain and disgrace were yet preparatory to his liberty and his happiness, and also as he hoped to that of Selena, which was indeed hardly less dear to him than his own.

As he could not conceal his inclination to visit Richmond Selena prevailed therefore upon Sidney to accompany him and after a few white-winged delicious days, the fondest and while they lasted the happiest too of lovers, tore himself from the presence of Selena boasting of his submission, and secretly inspired with hope that by this obedience he was hastening the time when they should meet never more to part in life. They were also mutually consoled in the sad hour of separation by the promise of a regular and frequent correspondence, and by the comparison which they could not forbear drawing between their present tender and not undelightful sorrow with that hopeless anguish which each had for a while suffered when parted as they thought for ever.

Nevertheless an indescribable and almost unaccountable sadness overwhelmed Selena, as she listened to the gradually fading sounds of their retiring wheels and slowly trod alone those walks, where every stone appeared to stand as a memorial of love, and every tree seemed to be hung "With some fond record of some happier hour."[35]

The dreary blank which pleasure had left when it departed with Sidney was felt by her at every moment, and to this she was herself willing to ascribe the uncommon dejection which oppressed her spirits while a mournful presentiment incessantly pursued her with the idea that hours of such enjoyment must never more return for her.

Often would she with a kind of violent effort escape from her dejection and comfort herself with that Hope which still whispered, "We are not for ever parted!"

> Shall we not meet again? Why then hangs my heart thus heavy
> And cold like death within my bosom? Oh 'tis well!
> The joy of meeting pays the pangs of absence
> Else who could bear it?[36]

But the feelings of the lovers and what occurred to each during their separation having been mutually and without constraint imparted to one another, may be perhaps painted in the most lively colours by the following short extracts from their letters. It will indeed be necessary to retrench much of what fell from their pens, for as a french writer has justly observed "Un amant n'a jamais tout dit"[37] and those exact details and eternal repetitions which constituted so large a share of the merit of those compositions and rendered them most interesting to the heart for which they were alone destined must infallibly appear tiresome to the eye of indifference.

> Sidney to Selena.
> How my beloved Selena are you at this moment employed? Where are you my soul perpetually exclaims and why am I not with you since it is no longer possible for me henceforth to conceive one single good idea or perform one action with self contentment deprived of the angel of Heaven who has for a while been given to me as the guide the companion of my steps. Expect nothing from me Selena! I can neither afford assistance nor consolation to Robert in this absence which is the more insupportable to me from my constant recollection that it is voluntary on your part. Consider my beloved Selena that prudence itself forbids you to punish me with unmerited banishment lest I should repent the ill rewarded self denial with which while in your presence, I respected those very scruples that with sorrow and surprise I behold you still retain.

---

[35] Possibly a reference to Michael Wodhull's "Epistles, Book II, Epistle III. St. Preux to Julia, On Her Marriage. From Rousseau's New Eloise" (1768), *Poems* (1772): "Beneath yon jasmine bowers, / Each fond memorial of our happier hours" (lines 84–5).

[36] Moneses in Nicholas Rowe's *Tamerlane* (1701), 2.1.54–7 (line 54 adds "again").

[37] Un amant n'a jamais tout dit: a lover never says everything (French).

Had I followed the impulse of my heart, had I urged the arguments that almost burst from my lips at every happy interview, had I suffer'd all that earnestness to escape from the fullness of my soul which I so often found it nearly impossible to restrain, had I implored you to give me a right to call you by that tenderest dearest name, a name more prized than even that of friend or lover, had I uttered all that struggled within my bosom when I felt that yet you were not mine how could I have been more severely punished? Unjust Selena what have I earned by mine unexampled submission? It is in vain that you have prohibited me with such cruel indifference from speaking of my feelings and desired me only to describe what passes around me. I am in a land of strangers! No one understands me and I for my part cannot comprehend how objects so perfectly insipid as those by which I am surrounded can interest the attention of those with whom I converse.

I am impatient even with Robert and can sometimes scarcely disguise my unreasonable ill humour when he converses with me on any subject but that which has forever engrossed my whole soul.

> Tout ce qui n'est pas vous me devient odieux
> J'ai perdu tous les goûts qui me rendaient heureux
> Vous seul me restez oh ma douce amie![38]

Suffer me then to return to you! Never was my society less necessary to Robert. Never was I less able to contribute to his happiness. He has already taken a lodging in Richmond within a little distance of Bently farm and tho' he goes to town every morning to expedite his business, yet his evenings are all passed in the presence of Ophelia. It is true that he has already received some hints from Mr. Bently that prudence and delicacy require that his visits should be less frequent, but as he has firmly resolved never openly to declare his attachment until every impediment to their union shall be removed, I am certain that he will not be prohibited from enjoying the only society in which assuredly he can now feel happiness.

To what purpose therefore am I condemned to look with envy on his far happier lot, and to compare your unnecessary and cold reserve with that tenderness which triumphant over her native extreme delicacy evidently constrains his Ophelia to embrace every opportunity of seeing and conversing with Robert and makes her regret every moment which he is obliged to devote to other objects. Ah Selena! love can boast but little authority over that heart where scrupulous discretion uniformly guides and governs.

But to you the sacrifice has been nothing. Calm and contented you pass those hours, which constrained by impatience and devoured by regret, I wish blotted from my existence; conscious at the same time how precious they might be were I not suffered but behold you. You feel not as I do the terrible idea that we are in fact during the present moment nothing to each other—that in absence those we

---

[38] "Du Parnez" (Tighe's note). Evariste Parny, "L'absence," *Poésies Erotiques* (1778), lines 15–18 (the quote omits line 16—"Ah! vous m'avez ôté toutes mes jouissances"—and replaces "ô mon Eléanore!" in line 18 with "oh ma douce amie"): "Anything that is not you is odious to me; I have lost all the tastes that made me happy; you alone remain to me oh my sweet friend."

love exist for us only in our memory or by anticipation—that while I am most wretched you are unconcerned; that you may be suffering at the very instant my lips are profaned by a smile and that it is even possible you may have ceased to live while I now write. Oh spare me an imagination so horrible! Never, never let us again separate, and I will be contented to relinquish every other expectation that my more aspiring hopes have sometimes indulged. Do not again silence me by an idle threat of the censure of others.

No Selena, dear as your virtue is to my heart, your honour is scarcely less dear, and I would willingly perish rather than propose to you for my own gratification any thing at the expense of either. Confide therefore in my prudence; do me justice my beloved. Remember with what restraint I watched my lips, nay my very looks while I considered you as the wife of another. Did I once express a sentiment that the severest virtue could forbid from the moment in which you declared your resolution to adhere to your unfortunate vows until that which so beyond all hope all prospect for ever dissolved those ties and gave me liberty to adore my Selena without a crime? How often have I done violence to every feeling and tore myself from your presence to avoid the observation of the illnatured, or the reproaches of my own heart? And when the sweet and innocent softness of Lady Trevallyn's character led her to seek for my indulgence inviting me to join your evening circle how many a time have I refused the offer'd bliss detesting the false excuse that died upon my faultering tongue! You know not, you shared not in the bitterness which I then felt! You thought not on the self excluded wretch who hovered round the dear walls he dared not enter, who unable to free himself by one desperate struggle and fly to a distance from the scene of such continual tortures, was perpetually exposed to the severest trials which his nature was capable of enduring.

How little have you imagined when seated in your usual place beside the little table near the window how eagerly the graceful moment of your smallest action was watched, while heedless of the weather or only desirous of its severity to encrease the desertion of the streets, I have passed hours in the square, esteeming those as fortunate nights on which the windows of the drawing room were left unclosed after the candles had brightened the scene within. How often have I congratulated myself upon the peculiar fancy of Lady Trevallyn, who reluctant to exclude the nightly sky on which she loved to gaze from the balcony, had so often unconsciously presented to my eyes the mild and beautiful star whose influence must for ever guide my destiny!

But why should I dwell upon the remembrance of those hours of hopeless melancholy, when my memory is now so rich with those of happiness? Blest hours! of whose value I was sensible even while they flew past with such swiftness and which while I regret my heart now overflows with unutterable delight in the anticipated removal ....

Selena to Sidney

My heart reproaches you my dearest friend for the ingratitude and want of sympathy in thus accusing me of enjoying contentment in our separation. I feel as if you ought to know all that I experience, and that words should never be necessary to enable us to penetrate into the sentiments of each other. Alas! it is this want of sympathy that can indeed effectually separate us! Have you forgotten what you yourself said on the evening before you left us? How you repeated to me those beautiful passages where the exalted nature of friendship is so well expressed by some of the greek philosophers who used to admonish each other never to divide the divinity that was within them? Surely without being too fanciful or enthusiastic we may really believe that true affection can communicate one spirit into the hearts of those who are truly united, by which we may instantly perceive how each will feel if only informed of the circumstances in which we are placed. For my part I could even imagine more than this. And I feel a secret persuasion that were any change to take place in your sensations towards your friend I should not need your pen or your lips to inform me of my fate, and that my heart would have already sunk beneath its affliction before any proof could testify your coldness. And why should this be considered as an absurd idea because it cannot be accounted for by reason? Can reason then account for the infallible vibration of its own truly responsive tone which one note of my harp will call from every other instrument around it? And why must we deny as visionary all influence upon our feelings for which we are unable to assign a cause when we are obliged to acknowledge such on sensible objects in a thousand instances? But perhaps you do not understand me, and I am to blame in desiring you to know how much I share in all that regret which you feel as the hours pass heavily along which are no less counted among the number allotted to our existence than those which appeared to fly from us with such irresistible precipitation.

Yet it is certain dear Sidney that you never seemed less absent to me than since the last time I beheld you kiss your hand to me from the chaise before the turn in the avenue hid you from my sight. You have accompanied me in every walk, I see you take your place at my side with every meal, I listen to your judgment at every sentence which I read and fancy that you share the pleasure that I derive from whatever I admire, I hear your voice in every song and as I go over our favourite music your flute still sounds in my ears as soft as sweet as ever. But all this is attended with a melancholy that sometimes terrifies myself and I frequently feel the utmost exertion necessary to escape from the oppressive pang of those gloomy forebodings which tell me that we shall meet no more.

I confess to you all this weakness that you may be convinced how vainly you urge me to consent to your return since I have been able to conquer myself. Do not I beseech you add to the unavoidable pain of our separation by unmerited reproaches and importunities with which I well know you would not yourself desire me to comply could you understand the strong principle by which I am governed in this refusal. I am persuaded dear Sidney that you will spare me for the future those vain and afflicting solicitations when I thus declare to you my whole heart which suffers so cruelly in the resistance, but my determination is unalterable and I will not scruple to confess to you the full extent of my purposes. Never dearest Sidney will I voluntarily see you until Dallamore has passed his vows unto another woman. The laws of God and man must alike render irrevocable those which he shall henceforth make at the altar. But I deny not my beloved friend that in pronouncing the solemn resolution of my soul my hand trembles and my eyes overflow with tears at the uncertainty of that character upon which our happiness still hangs.

If however, in spite of all these my dark presentiments, if Dallamore shall indeed fulfil your expectations why should I oppose the scruples of a perhaps false delicacy and idle superstition to the wiser judgment of my friends?

Sidney if we meet again it is for ever! Oh if your heart swells like mine at those words how well shall that moment compensate for all the sorrow and anxiety we have endured. Console me then by presenting to my fancy for ever a hope so dear. Speak of it with all your own bewitching eloquence; teach me to rest upon it with confidence notwithstanding all the sadness of my fears, but harass me no more with entreaties to what I feel to be impossible.

Why have you not gratified me by the exact history of your hours and even the description of your abode. Let me be as little a stranger to all that concerns you as our situation will permit. I hate to perceive how ignorant I am of all that you look upon so that my imagination cannot fix you in any known scene. I often wish that since we must be parted it had been at least your lot to remain where we had been happy once together. Where ever I wandered I should then have known whither to suffer my heart to flee for consolation and I might fancy you less excluded from me where every thing necessarily reminded you of our former interviews.

You have also disappointed us both by not mentioning Edwin. I am convinced you have not forgotten our commission and that your silence is too surely caused by having nothing pleasant to communicate. But I do not say this to Clara, who would herself I think rather hear any thing than remain longer so entirely ignorant of his health and situation. Tell us therefore what you can least painful of our illjudging unfortunate friend. I have heard nothing of Lady Trevallyn. Rawlins has received no tidings and unable longer to restrain our impatience by Mrs. Vallard's advice I have written to Trevallyn hall, but my heart anticipates with but little satisfaction the result of this letter.

Selena to Sidney

I thank you my generous friend for your tenderness. It has fulfilled all my expectations. Your warm hopes have animated mine. Your assurance of happiness has given me confidence and your encouraging representations have reconciled me to myself. With your consolatory letter I received one from Robert in which he urges me to come to Richmond with Clara kindly solicitous to introduce us to the Bentlys. I have for the present been obliged to reject this proposal but I will confess to you dear Sidney that some inducements incline me take this journey relying as I shall do with confidence upon your promise of forbearing to visit it during our stay. But the circumstances which must direct me in this point are in the disposal of Providence and as yet I must not have even the imaginary pleasure of diminishing the distance which now divides us.

But is it possible that in speaking of myself I can thus forget the subject upon which I was so impatient to write to you. I sat down with my heart full of our dear Lady Trevallyn when the sight of your letter once more banished every other idea but that of affection due to that tender and amiable heart which had generously dictated it for my support and consolation. Not that I have any thing satisfactory to impart to you about our interesting friend, but I cannot bear the idea that you should be unacquainted with any thing which occupies my thoughts. I now feel how justly you have said that absence suspends the power of that sympathy which ought for ever to unite our hearts.

I walked yesterday to the school and on my entrance was not a little surprised to see the girls assembled in a group at the door, their attention apparently fixed upon a stranger of a noble and striking figure who was engaged in conversation with their Mistress. As they made way for me to enter he turned round, and never shall I forget the strange emotion that I experienced as I gazed upon him for a moment in a state of bewildered amazement and perplexity. It was not Lord Henry but such a resemblance, and at the same time so strange a contrast never can be imagined to any but those who may have seen these two brothers, for you already I am sure guess that it must be the Marquis whom I then beheld. He is certainly not so regularly handsome as Lord Henry, nor has he that fashionable (perhaps I should call it graceful) manner for which he is so remarkable. Besides he looks many years older, and has none of that gaiety and lively animation which I have heard was so universally captivating in Lord Henry. I speak in this after Mrs. Vallard and Clara for you know dear Sidney I have so little partiality for him whose worthless cruel heart in my eyes looks out at every feature that I find it difficult to confess he possesses even any personal advantages over his amiable excellent brother.

I am not unwilling to acknowledge that resemblance which so completely overwhelmed me upon his first appearance that when he advanced to address me on hearing my name, I remained without power to comprehend what he uttered or to disguise the astonishment with which I surveyed his face and listened to the sound of his voice. I am now surprised how I could have been so much struck by a likeness which every moment diminishes. The false smile of dissembled softness that perpetually sits upon the countenance of Lord Henry can never surely be compared with the candour and benevolence, which seems mingled in that of his brother with a considerable degree of reserve, a reserve that appears to proceed not from pride or even bashfulness but a retired a pensive disposition.

Observing my embarrassment he took some pains I believe to apologise for his intrusion, while Rawlins, who I now perceived attended him, made me understand who the Marquis was and I at length began to recollect myself sufficiently to be able to answer his enquiries respecting Mrs. Vallard and afterwards to tell him what I then could of his cousin. I found that having come to Esselberrie, Rawlins anxious to furnish him with as much information as possible with respect to Lady Trevallyn had given him all the particulars of her illness, of which the Marquis had heard something on his arrival in England, and which had indeed as he says hastened his journey to Derbyshire. In the course of his narrative Rawlins having repeatedly mentioned me it was natural for the Marquis to enquire who I was, and when he heard that I was the guest of his old friend Mrs. Vallard he expressed his intention of proceeding immediately to Hillbarton. By the advice of Rawlins he however walked to the schoolhouse in the probability of meeting me there on my daily visit, and as you will easily imagine found himself irresistibly attracted by the sight of those engaging little creatures, the memorials of the kindness, the benevolence of his once adored and still I am sure fondly beloved Emily. I could not but observe the interest with which he looked upon every object and all that seemed so peculiarly to relate to her, and as he returned with me to Hillbarton the eagerness with which he questioned me concerning her situation and illness.

I felt a degree of awkwardness in this conversation, for tho' the nearness of their relationship might of itself sanction the curiosity he displayed, yet the knowledge I had of his former attachment and the principal part which his brother had borne in the misfortunes of dear Lady Trevallyn secretly embarrassed me strangely in my answers. I felt therefore not a little relieved when I could refer him to Mrs. Vallard and retired immediately after their first salutations had passed. You who have heard her speak of the Marquis can well imagine the pleasure with which she welcomed him. Indeed she received him as a long lost son and I was not surprised when I came down to dinner to behold him settled as an inmate. I am convinced she had been very free in her communications and has not only told him all that she knew of our dear friend's situation but every thing that we have even surmised.

His melancholy seemed to encrease during the evening and he spoke but little while we were together but when we retired after supper Mrs. Vallard repeated to me all that he had said to her with respect to his cousin's misfortunes. He told her that he had been resolved never to return to England had she married Lord Henry, but upon hearing of her establishment in another family which might preclude the necessity of continual intercourse and feeling his mind sufficiently restored to peace to hazard an interview he turned his course homeward after an absence from England of more than six years. On his arrival in London he had the mortification to hear confirmed the strange and improbable history of his brother's disgraceful marriage and his still more disgraceful conduct. Nor were these the only unpleasant tidings which saluted him on his return.

Everywhere he heard of the dangerous illness of the young Lady Trevallyn whose beauty and sweetness were as he said the theme of every tongue while her early fate excited universal compassion. The Marquis eagerly flew to obtain some certain information from Mr. Montrose, but the unconcerned manner in which he avowed his perfect ignorance of his sister's situation with the utmost apparent indifference on the subject filled him with abhorrence and disgust. "I know nothing of Emily since she left town," answered he carelessly to the Marquis's inquiries. "I heard indeed that she has been ill but neither she nor Lord Trevallyn have taken the trouble either to let us know where they are, or what has been the matter. I dare say however that she is only nervous. She will soon get over it I have no doubt and I confess I am not sorry that things have come to a crisis and think she is well off to have been not more blown upon."

"The malicious smile with which he spoke," said the Marquis to Mrs. Vallard, "left me without a doubt that he alluded to Henry and unable to disguise my indignation I hurried from him abruptly." He then enquired at Grosvenor square and what is singular enough was there told that Lady Trevallyn was dangerously ill at Esselberrie and it appears to me obvious that the servants there must have been purposely deceived. From the warmth with which he described the anxiety that he felt at receiving accounts so unsatisfactory Mrs. Vallard says that she has no doubt that this revived all that tenderness which years of absence, and all his efforts to forget the first impressions of his youth could not entirely eradicate.

You may be certain that what he heard here has not tended to quiet his solicitude and the same motives which irresistibly urged him to take this journey into Derbyshire now powerfully prompt his hastening to Trevallyn hall. Tho' I have not been present at any of their conversations, yet I can easily perceive that Mrs. Vallard has encouraged him to pursue his inclinations in this point, and I myself cannot but feel somewhat more contented than I have been for some time in the unprotected state of my unhappy friend. I did not last night expect again to see the Marquis as I heard it was his purpose to leave this at an early hour it is however now nearly breakfast time and his carriage has not yet been ordered to the door. I will therefore write a few lines which he will perhaps be able to deliver to our dear Lady Trevallyn.

Tell me dearest Sidney what you think of this conduct of the Marquis. Interference in such a case is so dangerous, and that of one who had himself formerly pretented[39] to her love so peculiarly delicate, that I almost tremble for the consequences, yet when I think on the protracted silence of my friend, the circumstances which attended her removal and the unnatural indifference testified by her brother I cannot but bless the Providence which has thus opportunely as it appears sent to her a protector from cruelty or tyranny in one of her nearest relations so highly respectable in every light, endowed with so much discretion and feelings so amiable.

Selena to Sidney

Oh Sidney how deeply do I regret the strange infatuation which could blind the eyes of our poor friend to the merits of this excellent young man and made her prefer that false and unworthy heart to him whose soul seems the very abode of truth and honour and whose affection for her has been so long unshaken! How can I avoid bitterly lamenting her lot and thinking how blest she might have been in such constant tenderness had not her breast been early poisoned by this fatal prepossession.

I have but just parted from the Marquis and am impatient to tell you as nearly as I can what has passed between us. A few moments after I had sealed my letter I met him alone in the breakfast parlour. He was pacing the room with so much agitation in his countenance as I entered, that I was on the point of again retiring in order to call Mrs. Vallard whom I believed him impatiently waiting to see before he commenced his journey. He perceived my design and with some embarrassment prevented me saying he requested to have a few moments conversation with me before his departure.

I felt myself a good deal confused, certain as I was that his wish was to obtain some information with respect to Lady Trevallyn's sentiments having heard from Mrs. Vallard of our intimacy. Indeed in that extreme respectful attention which he had paid to me I could easily perceive that he looked upon me as the favoured friend of his lost Emily. "Can you my dear Miss Miltern," said he, "forget for a while that it is a stranger who takes the liberty to demand your confidence. Consider only how we are united by a common interest and that never brother more truly and ardently desired to serve his sister than I do my cousin. From Mrs. Vallard as well as the servants at Esselberrie I have heard that to your generous care she owes her life, and with you she has no reserve. Tell me then has the world spoken with truth and is it thro' the villainy of my brother, or the causeless jealousy of Lord Trevallyn that she is unhappy?" His whole frame was agitated as I stood for a moment unable to reply, but thus called upon I found myself irresistibly prompted to free him from a suspicion which might rend his noble heart and not only this but to entrust him with all my fears for her present situation.

"There breathes not," I replied, "upon earth a more pure and virtuous heart than that of Lady Trevallyn. A fatally cherished partiality has been the bane

---

[39]   Pretented: obsolete variant of pretended in the sense of intended (OED).

of her life, but that sentiment no longer existed when once convinced of the unworthiness of its object. She loved with weakness but she loved with innocence, she loved the semblance of Virtue and when at length the mask was removed no trace of that love remained in her pure bosom but self humiliation at having ever been deceived."

It is impossible dear Sidney for you to conceive the effect which these words produced upon him, and tho' during our long conversation he never alluded to his more than brotherly attachment for his cousin, yet there was not a word or look which did not breathe a portion of that generous, that beautiful disinterestedness of affection that it is the happy lot of your Selena to feel she has herself inspired. From such friendship ought I, dear Sidney, to have concealed any thing at the time when I have so much reason to fear its dear object suffers under injustice and oppression? No it was impossible! I entrusted to him therefore her refusal to give the promise which Lord Trevallyn required, her illness, her sincere repentance, the change which providentially and suddenly took place in her heart and her judgment, her humble submission and the offered vow which was rejected with such an accusation of artful duplicity so unjust and severe. I saw him tremble and turn pale as he perused the melancholy lines traced by her hurried and feeble hand in the music book and when he found that I had since received no letter and that Rawlins had never heard of their arrival at Trevallyn hall his impatience to set out and satisfy his fears was no longer to be restrained.

Upon my expressing some anxiety lest Lord Trevallyn might look with a jealous eye upon the manifest interference even of a relation he told me I might rely upon the coolness which should guide him—that his passions had never been violent and that the study of his life had been completely to subdue them. He also acquainted me with what he himself esteemed as a fortunate circumstance that his visiting Cardiganshire could never appear strange a considerable part of his property lying in that country. Mrs. Vallard heard with much pleasure the result of our conversation and his promise of acquainting her with the result of his enquiries.

Sidney to Selena

This moment I have received a letter from Ireland, my poor Mother is ill and requires my attendance; I cannot hesitate in my obedience but I hate myself for the undutiful reluctance with which I execute her wishes. I had a thousand projects in my head for putting an end to the state of wretched uncertainty which I am condemned to suffer with respect to the situation and conduct of him upon whom my Selena has made me thus dependant. I must now abandon all and quit England without once again beholding you or having even the satisfaction of learning where are those persons whose union I must so ardently desire. Alas dearest Selena the hopes with which till now I have supported this our tedious absence begin to be obscured! Compelled to fly still farther from you there are moments in which I think we are indeed to meet no more—when a secret voice seems to tell me that I have for ever lost all which I love upon earth and that I have hoped and prayed in vain. This idea is so terrible to me that I confess to you Selena I have been ready to murmur against my lot & to wish that I had never beheld the excellence which has destroyed my tranquility; nay I feel at these times as if I should have been less miserable had I never indulged the rapturous hope of being beloved than having once tasted such felicity be forced to resign you and relinquish all those enchanting prospects for our united lives.

> Ma in que' vergini labri, in que' begli occhi
> Aver quest'occhi inebriati, & dolce
> Sentirmi ancor nell' anima rapita
> Scorrere il suono delle tue parole;
> Amar te sola, & riamato amante
> Non essere felice, & veder quindi
> Contra me, contra te, contra le voci
> Di Natura & del ciel sorger crudeli
> Gli uomini, I pregiudizi & la fortuna:
> Perder la speme di donarti un giorno
> Nome piú sacro che d'amante, & caro
> Peso vederti dal mio collo pendere,
> E d'un bacio pregarmi, & d'un sorriso
> Con angelico vezzo: abbandonarti ...
> Obliarti, e per sempre.—Ah lungi, lungi!
> Feroce idea![40]

No! no! it must not be! We are not forever separated! Let my Selena continue but to smile and hope shall never quite forsake her Sidney's heart.

---

[40]   It is but justice to say that the following translation can give but an imperfect idea of the tenderness expressed in those lines which Sidney has quoted from Monti:
> But to have hung enamoured on those lips
> To drink the poison of those beaming eyes!
> Yet, yet to feel th'intoxicating power
> Which stole into my heart at every word
> Of that soft voice that vibrates in my ear -
> Thus to have loved and loved to extasy
> And be beloved again—Oh rapturous bliss!
> Destroyed and lost! Yes all on earth conspired
> Against the voice of Heaven; against my hopes;
> And must I never more indulge the dreams
> That love to call thee by a name even yet
> More fond more sacred more endeared than lover?
> Must I resign the image of delight
> When in the gentle pressure of thine arms
> Methinks I hang upon that neck adored
> Gaze on thine angel smile or taste thy kiss?
> Forced to abandon thee to give thee up!
> Forget the hopeless and forever lost! ....
> Hence! hence ye terrible ideas hence! .... (Tighe's note).

Vincenzo Monti, "Don Sigismondo Chigi" (1783), lines 150–65. Tighe titles her 117-line translation "To — Imitated from Monti 1804" in *Verses Transcribed for H.T.* (Brompton, 1805).

Fig. V.1   Illustration for "To — Imitated from Monti 1804" in *Verses Transcribed for H.T.* (Brompton, 1805), MS Acc 5495/C/8/1, National Library of Ireland, Dublin.

The Marquis of Ortney to Mrs. Vallard

My dear Madam,   Trevallyn April 12

I scarcely know how to communicate to you and Miss Miltern the unsatisfactory end of my journey, but as I am convinced you expect with impatience the fulfillment of my promise I will not delay informing you what has been my success, little as I fear the account will afford you pleasure. You will guess already that I have not seen my cousin nor indeed have I hitherto been able to discover where she is.

Immediately on my arrival at the inn in this little village I enquired for Lord Trevallyn and was told that he had been at the hall for some time, but that he had come there alone and had seen no one except a gentleman who came several times in a hired chaise, and having spent there the day, quitted him again in the evening. Upon my farther enquiry they expressed their opinion that as they knew my Lord had been ill since he came down, this must be a physician, but they knew not his name nor from whence he had come. All however were agreed that Lady Trevallyn had never been in this country.

As it was then about noon I thought it most prudent to proceed directly to the Hall and hoped to be able to surprise his Lordship before he could be prepared in what manner to receive me. The doors of the magnificently gloomy old mansion were all closed and it was with difficulty that I at length by means of the great bell obtained an entrance to the court. With evident reluctance the servant at length admitted me having listened for some time to my enquiries with an air as if conscious he was thereby incurring the displeasure of his Lord and yet knew not how to avoid it. He said his Lady was at Esselberrie, that my Lord was ill and he was sure could see no one and at first refused to bring him any message whatever until he had heard my name which, if it could not procure for me the information I wanted, obtained at least some of his respect. In a few minutes he returned declaring that his Lord was not yet up and must not be disturbed. I thought it best to return hither and write the following note which I instantly dispatched to the hall.

"My Lord,
"After an absence of six years I am ambitious to renew as soon as possible my acquaintance with my cousin, and thro' her to be introduced to the nobleman who has honoured us by his alliance. I was disappointed at not having the pleasure of finding Lady Trevallyn at Esselberrie but as the business which has brought me to Cardiganshire will not I hope detain me long I request your Lordship will have the goodness to inform me where I may be allowed the honour of presenting myself to my cousin.
I am My Lord Yours &c&c
Ortney"

My servant was detained some hours as I had ordered him not to return without an answer for which I waited in a state of suspence not the most agreeable. I at length received the following reply.

"The Earl of Trevallyn presents his compliments to the Marquis of Ortney and is extremely concerned that the state of his health will not allow him the honor of entertaining his Lordship in a manner suitable to the Marquis's rank and the high respect which Lord Trevallyn entertains for his Lordship's person. Lord Trevallyn will however esteem himself honoured if the Marquis will take up his abode at Trevallyn hall during his stay in Cardiganshire which may perhaps afford Lady Trevallyn the opportunity of receiving the high honor which the Marquis proposes to confer upon her by his Lordship's visit."

At this absurd and evasive reply I scarcely knew how to conduct myself but disagreeable as it was to me to think of remaining under the roof of a man whom I suspected of such mean and treacherous cruelty I yet resolved to return an answer by which I left myself at liberty to visit Trevallyn hall in the course of a few days—and I did so in the view of prosecuting my discovery should I fail in the endeavours I now mean to exert.

Chapter VIII

What cannot lenient gentle time perform?
I eat my lonely meal without a tear,
Nor sighed to see the dreadful night descend,
In my own breast a world within myself,
Where e'er I studious looked I found companions—
But chief *Religion* lent her softening aid
At her enchanting voice my sorrows fled
Or learned to please — while thro' my troubled breast
She breathed the soul of Harmony anew.

Thompson[41]

There existed not perhaps upon earth a man better fitted for the delicate task he had now undertaken than the Marquis. The cool firmness that he possessed and the determined resolution with which he at all times resisted the attacks of passion whether from within or without gave him a command over himself and a superiority over others that were sure to render him successful in every enterprise. The affection which he still retained for his lovely cousin tho' unshaken and tender as in his earlier youth was yet ever subordinate to his love of virtue and his principles of honor.

The implacable desire of revenge which had been excited and cherished in the bosom of Lord Trevallyn by his deceitful flatterer Mr. Guise, was less the offspring of jealousy than the dread of that contempt which the known ill-conduct of his wife must procure him from the world. At that critical moment when the Marquis arrived their plan was nearly matured and in a few days the death of the young Countess at Trevallyn hall was to have been announced in London while Mr. Guise was himself to conduct the magnificent mock funeral which the domestics and neighbours were to believe conveyed from Esselberrie the remains of all that was most beautiful upon earth to be interred with the ancestors of her proud Lord in the superb Mausoleum annexed to the chapel of this their ancient abode. The gentle and unresisting victim was herself unacquainted with the extent of their project but was contented to remain in the perpetual confinement and total seclusion to which she believed herself to be condemned.

After the first few stages from Esselberrie upon their arrival at a considerable town her Lord separating himself from her proceeded with the attendants to Trevallyn hall and in a few hours afterwards according to the orders which she had received Lady Trevallyn patiently submitted to continue her journey under the direction of Mr. Guise. His conduct towards her indeed called for no opposition but was respectful and attentive. And as she forbore all questions and indeed all

---

[41] Melisander in James Thomson's *Agamemnon* (1738), 3.1.85–97. The epigraph omits lines 89–92 ("In Streams, in Groves, in sunny Hill and Shade; / In all that blooms with vegetable Life, / Or joys with kindred animal Sensation; / In the full-peopled Round of azure Heaven") and substitutes "Religion" for "the Muses" in line 94, "breast" for "heart" in line 96, and "her" for "their" in lines 94–7.

conversation he on his part was equally silent and reserved. Her extreme weakness precluded the possibility of their travelling with expedition and he never urged her beyond her strength, so that it was more than a week before they reached the place of their destination.

Lady Trevallyn for the first time during their journey voluntarily broke silence when Mr. Guise appeared at the door to assist her in alighting as the chaise stopped late in a gloomy evening at a dwelling large but ruinous which seemed to have been in former days the residence of grandeur and opulence, but was now for the most part suffered to go to decay except a small portion which was tenanted by a farmer.

"This is surely not Trevallyn hall," exclaimed she as she gazed on all that wore the air of desolate poverty around.

"Trevallyn hall!" repeated the post boy (who had advanced to the door in spite of Mr. Guise having rendered his assistance needless by opening it himself), "Trevallyn hall! Lord love you Miss! We be five mile from the turn to Grydery vaun and that I take it is pretty nigh five more to the left of Trevallyn hall."

The meek Emily checked the enquiries which had been nearly extorted by the first emotions of terror at her dreary situation when Mr. Guise taking from his pocket a letter (which by the seal she instantly knew to be from Lord Trevallyn) entreated her in a whisper to be silent until she had perused that, and for the present not to object to enter an abode where she should find herself more comfortable than from the exterior she might suppose.

Lady Trevallyn pressed her hand to her trembling heart and for a moment raised her swimming eyes to Heaven in silence while she offered up her present fears and sufferings as an atonement for her past errors and instantly found that sweet confidence with which submission ever cheers the heart of humbled penitence. Having travelled on that day farther than she had done hitherto she felt herself so much exhausted that she suffered Mr. Guise to support her up the broad and broken staircase by which they ascended to a large unfurnished gallery leading them to a number of apartments which from the damp and musty smell seemed to have been untenanted for years.

From the number of windows blocked up and the heaviness of the evening the house was completely dark and the single light that was held by the old woman who preceeded them gave but little power to distinguish the objects thro' which they past, but the carpeted floor and fresher air of the room which they at length entered convinced her that it had been prepared for her reception. The attendant having set down the light upon a heavy black table that stood in the midst advanced to shut the casements.

Mr. Guise looking round desired her to bring more candles and then turning to Lady Trevallyn who had seated herself upon one of the high backed chairs at the entrance of the room, enquired if she would like a fire or any refreshment.

Upon her faintly replying by expressing a wish to be alone he advanced and with his accustomed smoothness of speech begged her to excuse his presuming to offer her his advice that she should repose herself after her fatigue before she perused the letter which he had been under a necessity to deliver. He then repeated his orders for light and fire adding in a lower voice, "Do not suffer your spirits to be depressed by this gloomy appearance; I hope we shall soon be able to make it look more cheerful."

In fact when the wood was kindled the two adjoining apartments which opened into each other, displayed a mixture of modern convenience with the relicks of ancient magnificence by no means uncomfortable. The furniture of the bed in the inner room, as well as the carpet and a well filled bookcase evidently shewed that care had been taken of late to fit up the habitation and Lady Trevallyn already understood her intended destiny before she had examined the contents of this letter which Mr. Guise had put into her hands.

> "It is not my desire Madam to inflict punishment but to restrain you from dishonour. To the world you are now dead, and all attempts to escape are utterly vain. If your repentance be sincere you will embrace with satisfaction the means I have discovered for hiding your shame and enabling you to pass the remainder of your life in security and retirement. Your attendant believes you the wife of him to whose friendship I have entrusted the management of this affair and you will do well to evince the sincerity of your late professions of duty by holding with her no unnecessary conversation. For the future I renounce with you all communication whatever and shall receive from you no message, but my orders are that he who will deliver this into your hands shall comply with every wish which you may express consistent with your absolute seclusion."
>
> "Trevallyn Castle Morne &c&c."

The situation in which she now beheld herself inspired not Lady Trevallyn with that horror which it might be expected to create in the bosom of a naturally soft and affectionately dependent female, yet in all the bloom of unrivalled beauty, and accustomed from her infancy to receive the homage of flattery and listen with but too much susceptibility to the voice of tenderness. Her soul no longer sought its happiness in the vanities of life and the delusions of affection; she received her lot as the immediate gift of protecting Heaven and

> Blessed the hand divine which gently laid her heart at rest
> Beneath Death's peaceful silent cypress shades,
> Unpierced by Vanity's fantastic ray.[42]

Having committed herself to the charge of that kind Providence whose presence she in this solitude peculiarly felt and whose still voice seemed to breathe in this silence of elemental nature, she laid herself down to sleep and tasted that tranquility which had so often been a stranger to her breast, when scenes of gaiety courted her approach, when the splendid circle brightened at her appearance and

---

[42] "Young" (Tighe's note). The first line comes from Night IV of Edward Young's *Night Thoughts* (1742–45), lines 80–81 ("Blest be that hand divine, which gently laid / My heart at rest"); the next two lines come from Night V, lines 313–14 ("peaceful" should be "gloomy").

the murmur of admiration, or the sigh of envy burst from every lip as the crowded assembly opened to receive her on her entrance.

She had not yet awakened from this restoring slumber when old Mary knocked at her door with a message from Mr. Guise requesting to know was she ready for breakfast.

Hearing that he was but just arrived and in the adjoining apartment she desired to have tea in her own room intending not to quit it until she found that he had again left the house. Towards noon however Mary brought her the following billet which after some hesitation determined her to grant him the interview he sought.

> "Do not dearest Madam refuse to allow me a few minutes conversation. I have had the honour of seeing Lord Trevallyn last night and there are some farther intentions of his that he has commanded me to explain but which I shall only execute with satisfaction when I can know your wishes.
> Your obedient and most devoted servant
> Ed: Guise"

There was however something in his manner when they met which (flattering and officiously eager as were his professions of service) Lady Trevallyn found peculiarly offensive and made her resolve on no pretence whatever again to admit him to her presence. She trembled indeed to reflect how entirely she was in his power, but the confidence which she could not obtain from his disposition or his principles she securely reposed in the guardianship of Heaven, and felt an assurance that his wicked designs whatever they might be could never harm her.

As soon as she appeared he began vehemently tho' with some confusion to justify the share he had taken in this treacherous affair, solemnly protesting his only motive for obeying the commands of Lord Trevallyn was that of serving her, and that there was nothing which she should order him that he would not instantly execute.

She now interrupted him by refusing to listen to any thing on this subject, coldly declaring that his motives were indifferent to her, that she was satisfied in their effects and that she only met him in order to be informed what farther was the plan of Lord Trevallyn by which she might regulate her future conduct.

Abashed at a reply for which he was but little prepared he stood awhile silent until Lady Trevallyn again repeated her enquiries what was now expected from her requesting to know whether she might be allowed pen and ink, and the liberty of walking out at stated hours upon her promise never by either of those indulgences to seek her escape or intercourse with any person.

Mr. Guise with a smile of malicious triumph informed her that in both those particulars he was especially prohibited to comply, but that she had only to pronounce her pleasure and at the risk of all his own advantages he would obey claiming no other remuneration than her gratitude.

Lady Trevallyn without hesitation rejected the offer, and was then told that she was permitted to walk during the day thro' all the apartments of that floor at the extremity of which were those fitted up for her residence; and that whatever books she desired should be immediately provided.

Mr. Guise then proceeded to inform her that the woman appointed to attend her had for many years inhabited this long forsaken mansion once a favourite abode of some of the Trevallyn family—that she and her son had received instructions from their Lord to consider themselves for the present as his servants and that they were given to understand that this place had been lent to him for the purpose of affording a safe retirement to his wife who was at times unfortunately deranged in her understanding.

Lady Trevallyn started at this cruel falsehood and somewhat hastily demanded its utility.

"I may lament but cannot be surprised," replied her artful persecutor, "that you should receive with such evident displeasure a claim so presumptuous by which alas I must not hope to profit. But recollect that by no other means could your cruel Lord furnish me as was his purpose with authority to contradict your assertions and prevent your escape should you resist his tyranny. This is however unnecessary; in me you have a friend of whom no power arbitrary as it may be shall ever deprive you, and when you wish for liberty I will fly with you to the farthest part of the earth."

More indignant than amazed Lady Trevallyn looked upon him with an eye of cold aversion and would have retired in silence to her own room, had he not opposed her passage, and conjured her to treat him with less reserve and consider him not as her gaoler but as one who lived only to devote himself to her service.

Unwilling to provoke him to throw aside the mask by open reproaches she contented herself with thanking him for his offers of service telling him they would best be exerted by protecting her retirement from all interruption. She then hastily withdrew and having secured her door firmly resolved to exercise all her courage in refusing ever again to listen to him let his pretences be what they might. In pursuance of this resolution she refused to attend his invitation to dinner and resisted all solicitations to quit her own room until assured that Mr. Guise had indeed departed by her quiet attendant, whose stupid but honestly good natured countenance had inspired her with much confidence.

Far from feeling resentment towards Lord Trevallyn she more than ever reproached herself for the injury she had done him in suffering herself to be prevailed upon to give him a wife whose whole soul had been devoted to another, and she plainly saw how criminally she had acted by cherishing in secret that fatal partiality even after she had passed her vows to him whom she now thought of with gratitude for the retirement he had provided for her. Nor was this gratitude unmingled with a sentiment of affection; she lamented that she had for ever lost his esteem and regretted nothing in her situation but that he had prohibited her to address him and had been so deluded as thus to commit into the hands of an artful & malicious hypocrite a power which he might exercise so injuriously for each.

Desirous in every respect to fulfil the wishes of Lord Trevallyn she made no enquiries from Mary, and was more amused than irritated by the kind of curiosity and terror which she evidently perceived had been excited in her old servant by the representations of her occasional madness.

In spite of her confinement her health was rapidly reestablished. The calm that reigned around penetrated to her heart and diffused itself sweetly over her whole soul. She almost wondered at the happiness which to her so strange a guest seemed imperceptibly to have now stolen into her bosom. Those who have suffered extreme anguish can alone justly appreciate the value of an exemption from pain, or know how delicious is that serene repose which succeeds when the storm of passion and the black clouds of despair are chased by the mild sun of peace and resignation.

She found means so to occupy her silent hours that she feared not the approach of ennui and during those contented nay cheerful occupations if sentiments of forbidden tenderness were at times awakened by the sudden recollection of "scenes in strong remembrance set"[43] in her thrilling heart, she felt that the true object of those warm affections existed not on earth and she was enabled to transfer and repose them all in Heaven:

> If haply from her guarded breast
> Should steal the unsuspected sigh
> And memory an unbidden guest
> With former sorrows filled her eye
> Still pious hope and duty praised
> The wisdom of unerring sway
> And as these eyes to Heaven she raised
> Their silent waters sunk away
>   Cartwright[44]

Her restored strength of body no doubt contributed much to this internal tranquility, and even her glass told her that Health, the true Goddess of Beauty, had spread over all her features that fresh and vivid lustre which dissipation and consuming anxiety had for some time banished from them.

Mr. Guise finding that she continued with firmness to resist his repeated efforts to obtain another interview sought to work upon the softness of her disposition by proving in a thousand attentions his wish to contribute towards promoting those comforts and amusements which her solitude could allow her to enjoy. The materials for drawing with which he now supplied her she had not demanded considering that they might strictly speaking have been included in the prohibition which he had declared Lord Trevallyn had given to her liberty of writing, but when offered she did not reject them determined never to avail herself of those means for that purpose.

---

[43]   Robert Burns, "The Lament. Occasioned by the Unfortunate Issue of a Friend's Amour" (1786), line 73.

[44]   Edmund Cartwright, *Armine and Elvira* (1771), lines 5–12 ("her" should be "His" in line 5, "sorrows" should be "passions" and "her" should be "his" in line 8, "still" should be "then" in line 9, "as these eyes to Heaven she raised" should be "while his eye to Heaven he raised" in line 11, and "Their" should be "Its" in line 12).

She profitted every morning by the permission given her of ranging thro' the suite of apartments for exercise, and on a fine day enjoyed the sweet freshness of the vernal breezes from the open windows. Observing the wild green behind the house which had once been a garden covered with primroses, violets, and cowslips she requested Mary to gather her from thence a nosegay and was not a little surprised on the following day to find one of the rooms that opened to the south suddenly converted to a kind of green house by the profusion of plants with which it was filled, glowing with all the gay flowers of the season and breathing all the sweets of spring.

It was not possible to have presented her with a gift more acceptable and while she was admiring and arranging her little garden she felt a wish that she might now owe this testimony of good-natured consideration to Lord Trevallyn who well knew her remarkable fondness for flowers; trusting that the same generous sentiment would prompt him to provide still for the little orphans whom she had left dependant on his bounty.

But while thus engaged she was struck with a degree of surprise and terror to find her meditations abruptly interrupted by Mr. Guise. She had always locked the outside doors during her morning's walk and was now shocked to find that she had not the power to exclude him whose entrance convinced her that he possessed a master key to all. She however concealed the emotion of fear which this conviction had excited, and affecting that composure which she could not feel, desired that he would express her acknowledgments to Lord Trevallyn for the kindness which had thus sought her gratification.

"Ungrateful Emily! you owe him nothing!" replied the odious hypocrite, "why will you refuse your thanks and your confidence to him who is indeed ambitious to please you?"

Lady Trevallyn roused to indignation at the insolence with which he addressed her, heard no more, but repulsing him as he approached to take her hand, rushed past him with a sudden spring and flew to her own room which she hastily double locked and then sinking on the ground placed her back against the door panting and listening for pursuit like the terrified hare.

She was however quickly relieved from her immediate apprehension, convinced that he at present meant no farther to intrude and in a few minutes Mary asked for admittance and gave her the following billet from her dreaded persecutor.

> "Why do you fly me Madam with such aversion and contempt? Only suffer me
> to explain to you in a few words my conduct and you shall be convinced that
> you have nothing to dread."

Lady Trevallyn who had already begun to repent that thrown off her guard by the terror of the moment, she had betrayed to him whom she had too much reason to fear her consciousness that she was so much in his power. She therefore after some struggles with her timidity and aversion resolved to collect her fortitude to see him once more and declare her determined purpose to comply in the strictest manner with the intentions of Lord Trevallyn which he had explicitly announced to be her total seclusion from all society and that she should therefore consider all intrusion upon her solitude not only as a treacherous breach of trust to him, but as an insult to herself. The firm dignity and coolness with which she expressed her resolution surprised him into an awe that was unaccountable to himself, nevertheless he once more repeated his offers of entire devotion and urging her to comply with his proposal of escape, to enforce his entreaties shewed to her a copy of Lord Trevallyn's will which he had procured for that purpose.

Whatever might have been the natural emotions of her mind upon seeing with how much care her imprisonment had been secured even after the death of her tyrant, she had yet sufficient self possession to subdue or at least disguise the momentary impulse so that to the scrutinising eye that fixedly observed her she betrayed no symptom of terror or regret while to his insolent professions and proposals she made no other reply than calmly to assure him that she would never resist the will of Lord Trevallyn while it allotted to her the solitude which was indeed her soul's best choice she was yet resolved to exert every effort to deliver herself from a situation where she should be condemned to suffer his intrusions. The smile of contempt with which he heard this threatened escape convinced her how powerless he esteemed her of being able to effect it notwithstanding which she left him feeling internally a calm confidence that his villainy should be defeated and that if pushed to extremities she should be able either to convince her credulous attendant of the truth of her representations or else elude her vigilance.

Chapter IX

He was a man then boldly dare to say
In whose rich soul the virtues well did suit
In whom so mixed the elements all lay
As all did govern, yet did all obey
He of a temper was so absolute
As that it seemed when Nature him began
She meant to shew all that could be in man—
So thoroughly seasoned and so rightly set
....
That those rough storms whose rage the world doth prove
Ne'er injured him who sat them far above.
                                        Drayton[45]

Nothing could be more remote from the real intentions of Mr. Guise than the proposal of flying from the power of Lord Trevallyn which he had made to the unprotected Emily and which he had hoped her desperate situation would have inclined her to embrace with credulity, but the unexpected arrival of the Marquis having rendered for the present impracticable every scheme which they had at first

---

[45]   Michael Drayton, *The Barons Wars* (1603), 3:321–9, 3:335–6. The epigraph omits line 324 ("That none to one could sov'reignty impute") and replaces "raught" with "injured" in line 336.

adopted Mr. Guise had exerted all his influence to prevail upon Lord Trevallyn to consent to one which was infinitely safer as well as more feasible. He now proposed that with the same secrecy which had been already observed he should attend Lady Trevallyn abroad and that if the Marquis should persist in his officious enquiries he might be informed in confidence that his cousin was really living but that having eloped with Lord Henry this fiction of her supposed death had been employed to save them both from disgrace and infamy.

Lord Trevallyn nevertheless felt an extreme reluctance to accede to this atrocious plan, and it was in vain that Mr. Guise represented to him that they had every reason to believe this had been her real intention and as they alone had prevented this elopement by their timely interposition they should be in fact guilty of no unjust calumny in asserting to the Marquis that it had actually taken place. Lord Trevallyn still found himself in the utmost doubt and perplexity; it was manifestly impossible to carry on a mock funeral and the absurd falsehoods he had proffered while the Marquis just arrived from Esselberrie and assured that his cousin had neither been there nor in town was now on the spot. To delay it rendered the whole affair obvious to detection and yet not only his conscience but his pride revolted against the only method which was thus suggested by his grand adviser. He however saw himself absolutely necessitated totally to relinquish his purposed vengeance and restore his fair Countess to the rank in society which he thought she had justly forfeited, or conquer his reluctant scruples and by a false confidence engage the Marquis tacitly to concur in a design calculated to rescue his cousin from disgrace and hide their common shame—since circumstanced as they were at this critical period it was impossible to delude him by the ridiculously fabricated tale of her death.

The arguments of Mr. Guise at length prevailed. The plan was arranged and the place of her retirement agreed upon, so that all which was now wanting to complete the success of Mr. Guise was to obtain Lady Trevallyn's gratitude by persuading her that in carrying her abroad he was activated only by the desire of delivering her from confinement tho' in doing so he hazarded the loss of all his patron's favour.

Her indignant rejection of his odious proposals did not deprive him of all hope that when she should find herself still a prisoner in a foreign country she might be induced to accept the means of recovering her liberty by consenting to a union with him when the death of Lord Trevallyn had rendered him apparently the sole heir of his immense property. Indeed there was no other plan by which he could enjoy the inheritance with security since to ensure her perpetual confinement the will was so worded that her escape or even the possibility of her writing by proving she yet existed gave to her the whole wealth and must at once deprive him of all he had laboured with so much artifice to obtain.

Lady Trevallyn terrified at the encreasing audacity of his declared views resolved to try every means to procure an interview with her deluded Lord, or at least to convey to him a representation of her situation, and to this end she watched for the moment of Mr. Guise's departure who she knew returned before night to Trevallyn hall. No sooner was he gone than she summoned her attendant and entreated her to listen to her story. She then in the simplest manner she could devise told her that having offended Lord Trevallyn she had willingly retired to this solitude but that Mr. Guise having abused the confidence which had been placed in him it was absolutely necessary she should explain the matter and requested her to supply her with pen and ink and convey a letter instantly to her Lord.

As this was the very language that Mary was taught to expect from her insane mistress she listened to her with distraction and terror, taking care to place herself near the bell by which she could summons her son to her assistance should this be necessary. Lady Trevallyn saw what were her thoughts and in vain would have argued her into a conviction of the truth. Perceiving that she might as well have uttered the most incomprehensible ravings a despondent melancholy seized upon her heart and for a moment she felt herself persuaded that she was indeed deranged, an effect which is perhaps not uncommonly produced upon the unhappy victims of that most attrotious oppression which has been exercised in private madhouses.

But tho' she had failed in convincing the head of stupid Mary her tears and extreme tho' gentle sorrow easily touched her heart which was made of more penetrable stuff, and persuading herself in spite of her orders to the contrary that she could do no harm by indulging her she soothed her by promises of compliance with affected submission and real tenderness. She left her therefore to seek for the pen and ink, Lady Trevallyn waited a while till impatient at her long delay she at length stepped along the passage leading to the stairs. As she had never testified the least desire of passing the prescribed limits of her confinement Mary was but little on her guard and having now purposed an immediate return she had not taken the precaution to lock the door. Lady Trevallyn expected not to find it open but almost without thought turned the bolt and instantly perceived herself at liberty to descend.

Her first emotion was to profit by this accident but reflecting that she should probably meet Mary on the stairs, and that at all events the outside doors were certainly fastened she stopped and hearing noises stood silent to listen. She could however distinguish nothing but presently a loud knocking at the hall door gave her a violent start. She then heard Mary say in a more distinct voice, "Why do not you answer the man at once and tell him to go about his business. He must be sure there is some one within and he will keep pounding there all night till you speak."

"Mother have done with your nonsense," retorted Owen in a harsher key, "don't I tell you once for all I will do as I was bid. Did not you hear the master hiself desire us to let no strange body in or even make believe to hear them."

The knocking was again repeated while Mary still argued the case saying, "Bless my soul what an uproar is here about nothing the poor dear lady will be disturbed and God help her poor head it is bad enough already tonight. Besides it is a shame and a sin to keep any christian standing out in this rain."

The remainder of her speech was drowned in the noise of the knocking which being now redoubled with violence, in spite of all her son's remonstrances she opened the casement and demanded who was there. Lady Trevallyn could not hear the answer, but understood from Mary's reply that it was some traveller who overtaken by the storm requested shelter for the night, as she heard her directing him to a public house at some distance. He expostulated as it appeared by her seeming inclined to admit him but her son now advancing to the casement roughly interposed to put an end to the parley.

Lady Trevallyn seeing them thus engaged was powerfully prompted to seize on the opportunity of delivering herself from the danger of Mr. Guise's perfidious designs and fearing that the stranger would have retired discomfitted should she delay a moment lightly descended the stairs and finding herself in the hall tried to unfasten the lock. But this her own confusion and the obscurity around her rendered impossible.

She now heard the casement of the adjoining room at which Mary had stood violently close and knowing that the next instant she must be discovered she felt as her last resource for the window and with that precipitate force with which impatience and fear almost supernaturally supported her she at once flung aside the bar of the shutter and pushed the casement open.

The first story was only raised about three feet from the ground but Lady Trevallyn had not an idea how the hall was placed having never seen the front except on that dark evening in which she at first arrived.

She however ventured to spring forward having called for assistance to the stranger who as she hoped was still at the door and in an instant was caught in his arms before she reached the ground while he exclaimed, "Heavens! Emily dear Emily is it you?"

Lady Trevallyn shuddered. A thousand tumultuous emotions of terror and astonishment seized upon her brain as the voice struck upon her heart and disengaging herself from him with vehemence she uttered in a faint accent, "Merciful God who are you?"

"Have you then forgotten me Emily? Have six years quite banished from your mind your cousin?"

"Lord Ortney! Oh gracious Heaven what has brought you here?" cried she bursting into tears of joy and affection as she pressed his offered hand while her terrified attendants having opened the door entreated her to return in, Mary still endeavouring to keep back her son who appeared somewhat roughly inclined to enforce her entreaties.

The rain mean while poured in torrents and the Marquis demanded from his still weeping cousin what she wished to do and whither he should conduct her.

"Come in," she replied, "I have a letter which I wish you to deliver for me to Lord Trevallyn and you must dry yourself before I speak any farther to you."

The Marquis still detained her hand but suffered her gently to lead him in and with a voice of authority desired Owen to put up his horse whom he had left at the outside gate, which he had vainly tried to open after having himself clambered over.

"What is the meaning of all this?" said he strangely as he entered and looked round on the ruinous abode the broken stone floor and lofty black walls scarcely visible by the light which proceeded from the chamber on the left hand now used as a kitchen.

Lady Trevallyn perceived that Mary and Owen remained motionless with surprise and uncertain in what manner they should act.

"Tell this good woman my name," said she with her soft bewildering smile, "I have my reasons for it which I cannot now explain, but she is a good creature and will I am sure receive you hospitably when she knows that you are my cousin my own dear cousin whom I have not seen for six years."

Lord Ortney was still silent, but wonder at all he saw was not the most powerful emotion which held him dumb. He gazed on the lovely object of his early hopes, his first and only love, from whom he had been so long separated and tears of the purest affection coursed each other down his manly cheek as he secretly vowed to her a friendship as sacred as it was ardent. It was indeed Emily! the beautiful Emily! and if possible more perfectly lovely than when glowing in the first bloom of promised beauty. Once more her enchanting voice struck on his ear soft as the western wind that trembles thro' the forest. If her eyes sparkled not with the fire of youthful animation they yet beamed upon him with that gentle lustre which had first stolen his heart, while the smile of tender melancholy added a thousand charms to the cheek

> Sweet as the damask rose
> Wet with cold evening dew.[46]

"What do you say Emily?" said he at length upon her repeating her request that he might speak to Mary who stood gazing at them in stupid wonder.

"Do you not know Lady Trevallyn then my good woman?" demanded he. "Tell me dear Emily what is this you mean?"

"Oh never mind now," returned she her eyes beaming with sweet contentment. "But come Mary will not you provide some supper for Lord Ortney—see how wet he is—and I am sure you will give us a good fire."

But Mary was as yet unable to move or understand any thing except that she was in the presence of a Lord and a Lady and when restored to the power of speech could only utter ejaculations of surprise and entreaties for pardon.

Owen however still doubted, and having received the positive orders of Lord Trevallyn was apprehensive of the consequences of this involuntary admission, resolving at all events not to suffer the Lady to leave the house till Mr. Guise should return, he even hesitated whether he should not endeavour forcibly to oblige the Marquis to quit his station, but rightly judged that this would be an hazardous attempt, tho' provided with a blunderbuss.

While debating this matter within himself the Marquis perceiving that he still delayed at the door took from his waistcoat his pistols and laying them on the table

---

[46]   Herod in Elijah Fenton's *Mariamne* (1723), 3.6.2–3 (the lines should read "Tears make her cheek feel like a damask rose, / Wet with the cold evening dew").

before which he stood repeated his orders with respect to his horse. Impatient to learn the particulars of the singular situation in which he found his cousin whose hand he yet held with tenacious earnestness he now entreated her to speak. She saw he was agitated and bewildered by uncertain apprehensions for her safety and desiring Mary to hasten supper conducted him to the apartment which had been fitted up for her as a study.

As soon as they were alone she told him that she had nothing to complain of Lord Trevallyn, that her retirement was voluntary, but that a person in whom he had unfortunately placed his entire confidence had abused it basely, and prevented her from being able to transmit any letter which might undeceive him. "All therefore that I wish you to do," added she, "is to take one from me and deliver it yourself to my Lord."

"Oh unkind Emily," interrupted he eagerly, "why do you refuse to treat me with your native candour; do you fear to tell me how cruelly how treacherously you have been treated? No never must you again hold correspondence with the contemptible tyrant who not satisfied with thus burying you alive would have defamed your innocence."

Lady Trevallyn would have stopped him, but he vehemently proceeded.

"Emily, dearest Emily do not refuse to hear me; deny not to me that confidence of which I was not esteemed unworthy by Mrs. Vallard and your friend Miss Miltern whose uncommon understanding might …."

"Selena," exclaimed Lady Trevallyn softened into tears at the sweet and tender remembrance, "Oh have you then seen my sweet Selena, and did she think of her poor lost Emily?"

"She has not ceased to think of you be assured and with the most extreme degree of anxiety. It was at her desire that I came hither. Behold my credentials," cried he smiling as he presented to her Selena's letter which she pressed unopened to her lips as he continued, "tho' she could not imagine the extent of your wrongs, she yet dreaded the necessity of an interference which indeed Emily you must suffer me to make."

He then related his first reception at Trevallyn hall and the ineffectual effort he had made to learn where she was.

He proceeded afterwards to tell her that having desired his servant to watch Mr. Guise during his nightly journeys he had traced him to this old mansion which he informed her was Llandura house as she had already guessed knowing that Lord Trevallyn possessed a place of that name in Cardiganshire. From the poor neighbours among whom he now enquired he was able to hear nothing of its present inhabitants except that they believed it was lent to a Gentleman who had a sick wife or Mother. Immediately a strange suspicion seized the mind of the Marquis that here he should find his cousin and urged by this idea he hastened to the house. The gates were all locked and it was with much difficulty that he at length brought Owen to the door to answer his repeated summons.

Asking for Mr. Guise he was told that he was at Trevallyn hall. He then desired to see the lady of the house and was bluntly answered "there was no lady there and if he had any business with Mr. Guise he should go to the hall as none of the family was here nor did they expect to see any more of them while my Lord or Mr. Guise staid in the country." This was evidently a lesson which the man had been taught by heart nor could all the enquiries of the Marquis produce any thing except the same reply in literally the same words.

Confirmed more than ever in his suspicions he determined to employ some strategem in order to get admission and therefore retired for the present without betraying too much curiosity which might only set Owen more on his guard. Nevertheless reason would sometimes reject the idea which had thus forcibly seized on his imagination and once more he returned to Trevallyn hall determined to insist upon a positive answer with respect to his cousin's present residence.

As Lord Trevallyn still refused to see him on the pretence of illness the Marquis sent up a card requesting to know where he could have the honour of waiting upon his cousin immediately.

After remaining a considerable time Mr. Guise appeared and presented to him a few lines from Lord Trevallyn announcing that from his inability to receive the visit of the Marquis he had desired his friend to explain to him the unfortunate reasons of Lady Trevallyn's absence.

Lord Ortney received Mr. Guise coldly and listened to him with a fixed countenance while he began lamenting the distresses of his noble friend which he said had reduced him to a state of such extreme weakness that he not only found it impossible to speak to his Lordship on the wretched business but gave him reason to tremble lest Lord Trevallyn should never recover [from] a blow so dreadful. Observing that the marquis expressed not the expected concern and condolence he proceeded in a confused and hesitating manner to inform him that her Ladyship had suddenly and privately quitted Esselberrie and that all their efforts had not been able to discover her retreat, but that from her openly avowed attachment to Lord Henry and from his secret flight at that very period they could have little doubt that she was his companion which a thousand circumstances had since corroborated.

Mr. Guise then dwelt upon the tender indulgence with which Lord Trevallyn had conducted himself upon the first discovery of her guilt, that he had only required her solemn promise of giving up her profligate lover a promise which she refused with an obstinacy that compelled him to confine her to her apartments at Esselberrie from which she had made her escape with ease her lord's gentleness not suffering her confinement to be rigorous after her illness. Somewhat disappointed that the Marquis should yet continue silent expressing neither horror nor astonishment Mr. Guise proceeded to declare the method by which Lord Trevallyn intended to conceal their common disgrace, hoping that a project formed for their mutual screen from infamy would meet with his approbation, adding that Lord Trevallyn meant to place in the hands of her noble relative a promise of a very considerable settlement should his unhappy cousin ever stand in need of assistance upon condition of her voluntary exile and change of name.

The Marquis had not once interrupted this harangue; nay so far from it that he condescended not to make one observation even tho' Mr. Guise had more than once paused to observe its effect upon his auditor. As soon as he had apparently concluded he however made this short reply. "As I know it to be absolutely impossible that Lady Trevallyn could have accompanied my brother it is evident to me that there is some strange misrepresentation in what I have heard, and I should be glad to demand from his lordship personally whether he had really ever conceived the idea of associating me in a project of villainy, cruelty, and deception."

Shame, rage and terror quivered on the pale countenance and livid lips of the confounded ambassador. Unable to articulate he rose from his seat at the same moment with the Marquis who approached the bell. At length stammering he demanded, "Am I to understand my lord that it is your intention to insult …."

"You are at liberty Sir," replied the Marquis holding the bell rope in his hand as he turned around to address him, "to demand an explanation of my words in any manner you please at another time, but at present my business is with Lord Trevallyn or an officer of justice." So saying he pulled the bell and on the entrance of the servant said in a firm voice, "Tell your Lord that the Marquis of Ortney desires to be admitted to his chamber on business of consequence for a few minutes."

"I will have the honor to be the bearer of your Lordship's message," said Mr. Guise precipitately retreating before the servant had closed the door.

The Marquis employed the time during which he was now detained in collecting all his powers of self command to display that dignified composure that his delicate office so much needed.

At length Lord Trevallyn's valet entered the room and presented his Lord's compliments with many expressions of regret that his extreme illness at that moment could not suffer him to converse with any one but that on the following morning he should be prepared if possible to receive his Lordship. He then repeated his Lord's request that in the mean time the Marquis should remain at the Hall offering to conduct him to the library, or the dressing room prepared for his lordship's reception.

The Marquis sent a polite refusal of an invitation made with so much courtesy and appointed twelve o'clock the following day for the promised interview. Leaving his servant to keep a strict watch he then rode to a cottage in the neighbourhood of Llandura house where he remained till his servant informed him that Mr. Guise had just quitted it and was returned on horseback toward Trevallyn hall.

He then sallied forth determined to force an entrance at Llandura house and desired his servant to follow him thither in case he did not return within an hour.

All this he now repeated to Lady Trevallyn who concealing for the present every emotion of tender gratitude towards the generous friend who had evinced such active zeal in her behalf, contented herself with assuring him that her present retirement was entirely her own choice—that Lord Trevallyn had (she believed firmly) been deceived by Mr. Guise and that she entreated him to interpose his good offices no farther than to convey the letter which she would write to her Lord. In vain were the Marquis's arguments, persuasions, and remonstrances. She resisted his offers of conducting her either to Mrs. Vallard's or his own sister Lady Frances Reddale either of whom he well knew would receive her with open arms. Nay she even declined going to Trevallyn Hall which he at last proposed as being at least more secure from the insults of Mr. Guise than her present defenceless situation. She persisted in remaining in that retreat which Lord Trevallyn had chosen and her own inclination approved, declaring herself perfectly released from all fear, now that her attendants no longer gave credit to the assertions of Mr. Guise and were convinced she was indeed Lady Trevallyn. The entrance of supper terminated their debate after which the Marquis returned to his cottage declining Mary's offers of the lodging which she had prepared with such alacrity, since the arrival of his servant had fully informed her of the rank and consequence of her noble guest.

Lady Trevallyn did not second Mary's hospitality observing that she feared the beds were damp, but the Marquis left his servant upon whose discretion and fidelity he could depend and extorting a promise from his cousin that she would see him at breakfast when he would return for her letter he bade her good night relieved in some degree of his anxiety for the uncertain fate of the beautiful and interesting Emily and resolved to expose to the whole world the base conduct of Lord Trevallyn if he could by no other means deliver her from his tyranny.

Chapter X

I see there is no man but may make his paradise
And it is nothing but his love and dotage
Upon the world's foul joys that keep him out on't
For he that lives retired in mind and spirit
Is still in paradise.

                                    Beaumont & Fletcher[47]

When the Marquis again met his cousin the following morning he failed not to renew his expostulations that she should not submit to that cruel injustice which might require from her a total renunciation of the world, reminding her of the claims which her affectionate friends and Selena in particular had upon her society. Softened as she evidently was at the remembrance of her beloved friend she yet earnestly persisted in assuring the Marquis that her present retirement was her own choice conjuring him never to acknowledge to Lord Trevallyn that he had any suspicions of the contrary and to forbear all interference except that of delivering into his hands her letter which was the only service she had to desire, or that he could possibly render her.

She then committed it to his care and finding that she was decided to await there the event, he lost no time in returning to Trevallyn hall in order to execute her commission.

The letter contained a simple statement of the conduct of Mr. Guise, without any complaint, or even allusion to the cruel aspersions which had been thrown upon her in the false account given to Lord Ortney, or the unjustifiable method

---

[47]   Shamont in Francis Beaumont and John Fletcher's *The Nice Valour; or, the Passionate Mad-man* (ca.1615–16), 5.2.3–7.

employed to secure her intended imprisonment for life. She only entreated Lord Trevallyn to confide in her solemn assurance that complete solitude was her own desire and represented that as the place of her retreat was at his own disposal and that she would never hold correspondence with any, there could be no reason for his committing the charge of her conduct to another, or refusing himself to signify his wishes which she should ever consider it as her duty strictly to fulfil.

Mean while Owen apprehensive of the consequences which might proceed from the occurrences of the night hastened early to Trevallyn hall in order to acquaint Mr. Guise with all that he had seen and heard. The consternation which instantly seized upon him was so overwhelming as tho' he had never foreseen the possibility of that confusion which is ever the pursuer of guilt or as tho' he had not known "this of old ever since man was placed upon earth, that the triumphing of the wicked is short and the hope of the hypocrite as but for a moment."[48]

He was now convinced that he must not only suffer the disgrace of their defeated project but that he was himself exposed assuredly to the vengeance of Lord Trevallyn to whom he could never by any artifices be able entirely to justify his conduct to his prisoner. From the hour of the Marquis's first arrival he had foreboded the impractibility of effectually concealing their victim and had more than once cursed his own folly for acceding to a plan which his timid and cunning disposition ever opposed in spite of all the allurements of interest.

He had even felt strongly impelled to take advantage of the power of attorney which Lord Trevallyn had given him and abandon all his future prospects, but had been hitherto restrained by some considerations happily still powerful over minds however destitute of virtue and principle.

Nevertheless in the terror and perplexity which at this moment bewildered his soul, desperate at seeing himself for ever blasted and undone he listened to the rash impulse which hurried him in spite of all the threatened punishments of justice to secure the possession of wealth far short indeed of that with which he had fed his late golden expectations but yet sufficient to ensure him the luxuries of life in a foreign country.

Preparatory to his projected journey to the continent with Lady Trevallyn he had been already provided with an unlimited letter of credit to his Lordship's banker in London and a request that he should furnish him with a similar order upon his correspondent in Hambourg.

Without delaying a moment for consideration he therefore now hastened with four horses to London conveying with him about four hundred pounds which he had but the day before received from the agent. From the banker he demanded ten thousand pounds which he had reason to think was the sum actually in his hands on Lord Trevallyn's account. Tho' somewhat surprised at the magnitude of the draft the banker who had been accustomed to transact with him on all occasions his Lordship's business made no difficulty of paying it satisfied in his knowledge

---

[48]   Job 20:5 (KJV).

of him as the confidential friend of Lord Trevallyn whose letter fully justified the demand which was now made.

He presented him at the same time with letters of credit and recommendation which Mr. Guise received with abundance of thanks notwithstanding his secret consciousness of their inutility. He spent not many hours in London but having procured as many guineas as he could conveniently carry proceeded to Bristol and thence embarked in a trader bound to New York. Tho' persuaded that he has been able to excite but little interest in the breast of any reader it may yet perhaps gratify some who cannot forgive him for his malevolence towards the gentle Emily to hear that the vessel in which he sailed being taken by a french privateer and carried into Brest he was reduced to the most extreme indigence and suffered some years of a far worse imprisonment than that to which he had doomed the unoffending object of his malice to whose amiable and forgiving charity he afterwards owed his chief support in the obscurity of his voluntary exile.

No sooner was Lord Trevallyn informed that the Marquis was arrived than he sent once more in search of Mr. Guise whose assistance and counsel he now so much needed and whom he had already repeatedly summoned with all the fury of impatience. No one had seen him and after a second message from the Marquis, Lord Trevallyn finding that he could by no means prevail upon him to quit the house again without being heard at length consented to admit him to his dressing room.

The state of wretched agitation which had so evidently disordered his whole debilitated frame inspired the Marquis with a compassion mingled with contempt that rendered almost unnecessary the gentle cautions of Lady Trevallyn, and his noble generous nature which firmly resolved to support his cousin's rights shrunk from offering any insults to an opponent so miserable.

Courteously therefore he accepted his Lordship's laboured apology for his inability to rise from his great chair and then presenting to him the letter in a few words expressed his hopes that the recovery of his Lordship might be accelerated by the arrival of Lady Trevallyn and that he himself should be allowed the honor of waiting upon them in a few days.

Having said this he retired without stopping for an answer, or even to behold the astonishment and confusion with which Lord Trevallyn gazed at the well known characters that had been put into his trembling hands.

But no sooner had he cast his eye upon the contents than every other emotion gave way to that indignation and rage with which he was seized at the insolence and treachery of the man in whom he had so entirely confided.

Totally unable to account for the interview which the Marquis had obviously obtained with his cousin, bewildered by doubts as to what he should do or say and furious at the incomprehensible absence of the villain whom he desired to overwhelm with his reproaches it was yet some hours before the slightest suspicion of the truth flashed upon his mind, and the terrible situation into which he was thrown upon its first recurrence convinced all around that those strange and to them unaccountable paroxysms of fury were but the symptoms of delirium.

Messengers were now dispatched for Physicians, but it was not until his orders had been repeatedly delivered (and that the steward himself began to reflect on the sudden disappearance of Mr. Guise) that Lord Trevallyn was obeyed and that expresses were sent off if possible to discover and overtake his flight.

His flight was nevertheless but a secondary consideration. The most terrible apprehension had seized upon him however really really wild and improbable that the vile traitor had carried with him Lady Trevallyn, an idea so terrible to his pride, that in spite of every remonstrance from the apothecary who was already with him he would have insisted upon being himself placed in the chaise and carried to Llandura house.

Feeling however upon making the attempt that this was absolutely impossible in the situation in which he now was, and too proud to impart to any one his fears, he at length consented to suffer the servants to take the carriage for Lady Trevallyn, announcing to them that he had just heard of her arrival there. As few things appeared more unlikely than this, his attendants even in the obedience that was extorted by fear were convinced that the orders were but the meer effects of frenzy and had not the smallest idea of really being able to bring home their Lady.

The Marquis who had kept a careful watch not only at Llandura house but also at Trevallyn hall being now informed of what had passed entertained the greatest apprehensions as to the intended removal and failed not to accompany the carriage that he might be assured whether it indeed conveyed Lady Trevallyn. He was also eager to converse with her upon all that had occurred since the morning and entreated her to allow him to see her early on the following day that he might be relieved from a portion of his solicitude on her account.

Lady Trevallyn was not herself entirely free from some dread as to what reception awaited her, and the confused relation that she heard from Lord Ortney and the servants of the state of things at the Hall prepared her for a scene of tumultuous agitation. But there is a sweet associate Patience, who with "Her meek hands folded o'er her modest breast" can lift "the adoring eye even to the storm that wrecks her!"[49] There is a serenity of soul, a tranquility of Resignation which can preserve self composure amidst the tempest of surrounding objects and a portion of this Lady Trevallyn had lately gained which enabled her to look upon all future trials with gentle firmness and to consider with cheerfulness her opening prospects tho' they should wear the darkest frown conscious that the virtuous mind is its own Heaven.

Upon her arrival she would immediately have sent to demand permission to see Lord Trevallyn but was prevented by the attendants who feared to shock her by the terrible state in which he appeared more in consequence of his disordered mind than body. Nevertheless the Physician who had heard him repeatedly and furiously enquire for Lady Trevallyn recommend[ed] her appearance and arming herself with courage she entered his chamber. No sooner had he beheld her than

---

[49]   The Chorus in William Mason's *Caractacus* (1759), lines 320–22: "Patience here, / Her meek hands folded on her modest breast, / In mute submission lifts the adoring eye, / Even to the storm that wrecks her."

he became instantly calm and ordering all out of the room she entreated him if he was able to listen to her and then expressed her sincere regret at the agitation and distress of which she had been the unfortunate cause declaring her earnest desire to repair the mischief she had occasioned.

His satisfaction at seeing that she was yet secure and that his character might still be uninjured in the eyes of the public made him hear her with some complacency, but at length he eagerly interrupted her demanding how she had met the Marquis and what she had told him.

Lady Trevallyn repeated without disguise all that had passed, suppressing only those parts of the Marquis's conversation which must prove the most offensive and in particular his allusion to the false tale made to him by Mr. Guise of her elopement.

A variety of emotions combatted within his breast as he listened to her narrative and compared the artful villainy of the wretch by whose counsels he had submitted to be guided with the candid and generous conduct of the erring but repentant Emily. He however disguised his feelings and contented himself with signifying his desire that she should not write to any person whatsoever and that she should send to inform the Marquis of her arrival at Trevallyn hall and invite him to come thither on the following day. He however continued for some days so extremely ill that Lady Trevallyn whose constant attendance he appeared to suffer with pleasure confined herself exclusively to his apartments, during which time as she strictly observed his injunctions of not writing the Marquis received only verbal messages in answer to his perpetual enquiries, but he had the satisfaction of hearing from the Physicians a thousand anecdotes of the amiable devotion of the beautiful Countess to their noble patient, and as her cares were accepted with complacency, he had good reason to hope that the heart of Lord Trevallyn convinced of the falsehood of her secretly malicious foe, and softened by remorse nay perhaps tenderness was ready to embrace her dutiful offers of reconciliation.

He delayed not to inform Mrs. Vallard of all that had passed and tho' Selena wondered at the continued silence of her friend she yet shared the consolotary hopes of the Marquis and her heart readily acquitted her of all wilful neglect.

Before Lord Trevallyn was able to leave his chamber he with much evident perturbation and extreme embarrassment in his utterance expressed his gratitude to his gentle nurse for the unremitting and kind offices with which she had contributed to his recovery and added that "he was willing to forget all that had passed if she would consent to reside for the future exclusively at Trevallyn hall, pass her solemn promise never to quit the domain in his absence and to renounce all correspondence with Lord Henry and Miss Miltern."

Lady Trevallyn started at the strange association which seemed to imply so unjust an impeachment of that incomparable friend. But perceiving that her hesitation seemed to revive all his former suspicions and that the critical moment might for ever destroy or confirm that confidence which for their mutual happiness she so ardently desired to restore she professed her joy at his intention of making Trevallyn hall her residence and renewed the solemn promise of obedience which she had already given. With this however he was not satisfied but insisted upon her expressly abjuring all intercourse for ever with Lord Henry and Selena. With a faultering voice and pallid cheek Lady Trevallyn pronounced that fatal name which he first demanded, but added in a firmer tone what she thought due in justice to her friend.

"As to Miss Miltern My Lord, allow me to say that you do not know her if you can think it necessary to bind me by any promise to forego her correspondence since to inform her that such is your desire would always be sufficient to make her of herself decline it. Suffer me to relate to you the whole history of my errors and misfortunes that you may know on what grounds to rest your future confidence and that you may see how much I owe to this friend against whom forgive me for saying you are so strangely and unjustly prejudiced." Observing that the subject agitated him with tumultuous passions, and that this was not a moment to contend with him she thus proceeded, "For the present however I am silent when I have sworn to you in the most sacred manner that till I have obtained your free permission I will relinquish every advantage and pleasure I might hope from Selena's friendship nor will I since such is your command even explain to her the reasons of a silence she must esteem strange."

Lord Trevallyn declared himself satisfied and then required her to repeat to the Marquis her inclination to continue at their present residence and to invite him to pass some days with them that he might be convinced of her freedom and contentment.

To the affectionate and grateful heart of Emily, this was a requisition the most pleasing, nor did she display a cheerfulness and satisfaction to which her soul was a stranger. Internal peace diffused a smiling charm on the venerable magnificence of her abode and the hopes of benevolence once more animated her plans of active employment.

On the morrow which succeeded this important conversation the Marquis had the gratification of beholding his cousin restored securely to her proper station while pride and complacency triumphed on the brow of the convalescent Earl as he gazed upon the fresh bloom of beauty and sweet smiles of placid serenity which illuminated with more than their wonted lustre every lovely feature of the graceful female who presided over his magnificent table.

Chapter XI

> Behold the clouds that have eclipsed my sun
> And view the crosses which my course do let
> Tell me that ever since the world begun
> So fair a rising had so foul a set.
> Drayton[50]

---

[50]   Michael Drayton, "Sonnet LX ["Define my weal"]" from *Ideas* (1594), lines 9–12 (line 9 uses "that" for "which" and line 11 uses "that" for "if").

Selena had not only the comfort of hearing from the Marquis of her friend's apparent contentment in her present situation, but found from Mr. Rawlins that Fanny had been permitted again to attend her Lady, and that he himself had received constant orders which came immediately from her own hand, relative to the school and several other subjects in which she and Selena had mutually taken an interest. Tho' her name was never mentioned yet she could plainly perceive that her friend had studiously alluded to every thing in which she had been formerly associated and Selena was not dull in comprehending that her silence was the effect of a prohibition which tho' she could not exactly account for she could easily imagine. There was a magnolia against the wall of the greenhouse that Selena had herself planted and Lady Trevallyn had loved to call it her own. Rawlins received not now a single letter in which she did not send some message with respect to this magnolia and she had ordered that a cutting might be taken from it and sent with the utmost possible care to Trevallyn hall. She was also particular in her enquiries whether her little girls continued to sing and sent them some verses expressive of tenderness and gratitude for the affection of friends which she desired them to learn. All of these implied remembrances conveyed as was intended a pleasure the most sweet to the feeling bosom of Selena. Indeed except the hours devoted to her correspondence with Sidney she found none more delightful to her heart than those past in receiving and imparting by a thousand little mutual actions those dumb testimonies of an affection by which in spite of all division from distance or time they were forever indissolubly united.

Her correspondence with Sidney was it is true the chief solace of her life, yet it was not unembittered by many a painful reflection, many a dark presentiment and on his side especially the most anxious impatience and solicitude poisoned almost every charm. He was still in Ireland and the unavoidable irregularity that at times delayed the letters of Selena harassed him with perpetual alarms, while the illness of his beloved his only parent, who had on earth no other object to divide with him her tenderness, and of whose recovery he now almost despaired oppressed his spirits and precluded the possibility of his return to England. Yet mingled as now was the pleasure which Selena found in the perusal of his passionate complaints and tender reproaches, she yet too surely felt that her existence seemed counted by those precious moments marked by the arrival of the letters which appeared the sole objects of all her impatience and the centre of almost every thought. The post on which she might expect to behold the beloved seal, the herald of love, was anticipated with delight and the disappointment occasioned by their delay produced only the sweet hope that internally whispered "C'est pour demain."[51]

Nevertheless this consolotary promise had been for some days repeated and a painful foreboding accompanied her anxiety at a silence which she began to think unaccountable, when one morning as she was seated at breakfast alone with Clara, Mrs. Vallard being confined to her room by a slight illness, she found herself so unusually low, that her sister who guessed the cause of her depression ventured

---

[51]   C'est pour demain: it is for tomorrow (French).

to argue with her upon the unreasonableness of suffering the casual peevishness of the winds to destroy that contentment which the assurance of being beloved by him whom she so justly valued ought to diffuse over her soul.

"Dear Selena!" she warmly exclaimed while her own emotion tinged her cheek with a deeper glow, "possessing such a sweet consciousness I think there are no circumstances that could possibly interrupt the happiness of an affectionate heart such as yours! Is it not indeed

> Life's best sunshine
> The warm blaze in the poor man's hut
> That when the storm howls o'er his humble thatch
> Brightens his clay built walls and cheers his soul?"[52]

As Selena listened in silence she felt her eyes overflow while her sister proceeded eloquently to paint those visions of bliss which innocent love always promises to a young and credulous mind.

At length the event which had been so impatiently expected interrupted the harangue and starting from her seat as she heard the pully of the door which led from the back hall Clara exclaimed, "Here are the letters I am sure and Sidney himself shall say the rest."

While she spoke she flew out of the room and as she had not closed the door Selena looked for her instant return while a mixture of strange sadness and anxious terror held her still silent and motionless.

But Clara did not come back and supposing that she had gone out to enquire after the postbag, for whose arrival she was so disinterestedly eager Selena continued for some time not displeased to be thus left alone to indulge the train of melancholy reflections which succeeded each other thro' her mind in an obscure and languid suspicion.

At length surprised at her long stay she slowly ascended the stairs with an intention of seeking her in her own room.

As she passed Mrs. Vallard's door she listened for a moment and being assured by the voices within that she was not asleep she softly entered to enquire concerning her health.

The moment she opened the door Clara who had been seated on the bed hastily started up and would have hurried past her without speaking, but Selena, terrified at her averted countenance and the agitation that spoke in her very steps, stopped her gazing on her face bathed as it was with tears in an agony of terror which for the moment deprived her of all speech.

Clara attempted to speak but flinging herself in her arms could utter nothing but sobs until perceiving Selena's pallid lips, fixed eyes and cold trembling limbs she supported her to the sopha exclaiming, "Oh I have killed you my poor Selena! Heavens what shall we do, see she is dying."

---

[52] Austin in Robert Jephson's *The Count of Narbonne* (1781), 4.1.106–9 (line 107 should read "'Tis the warm blaze in the poor herdsman's hut").

Mrs. Vallard half distracted herself with apprehension violently rang the bell repeating in incoherent sentences, "My dear girls do not terrify yourselves in this manner. How can you Clara give way to your feelings to such a degree? Selena my love be composed. All will be well yet. I am sure all will be well. We must not mind this foolish boy."

"Sidney!" exclaimed Selena in a low voice, under the bewildered and terrible conviction that some frightful accident had for ever deprived her of what was dearer to her than life. "Tell me I beseech you tell me what has happened."

"Nothing dearest girl; we have heard nothing from Sidney and I trust in God you will yet pass many happy years together."

A torrent of tears burst from the oppressed heart of Selena and relieved her from the faintness occasioned by the sudden transition which instantly took place from the extreme of terror and of anguish to gratitude and confidence in Heaven.

"What *is* the matter then," she then eagerly demanded with a secret consciousness of courage to suffer every disaster except that from which she was thus delivered beyond her very hope.

"Give her the letter my dear she will be better when she knows the worst," said Mrs. Vallard returning to Clara the unopened letter whose very direction had presented to them the too certain proof that Dallamore still intended to claim as his own the only true Countess of Mount Villars.

Philip had himself beheld it with so much painful surprise that he had feared to deliver it to Selena and with a look of inquisitive concern gave it into the hand of Clara.

Inexpressibly shocked and afflicted as she was herself she shuddered at the idea of Selena's feelings and flew to consult with Mrs. Vallard carrying with her the fatal paper.

That it was the writing of Dallamore they could not doubt and the English postmark assured them of his immediate return but their deliberation as to examining the contents were suddenly suspended by the appearance of Selena.

With trembling anxiety they now watched her countenance as they put into her hands the too quick interpreter of all their mysterious distress.

Hastily she glanced her eye over the address and pausing for a moment as she gazed on the unbroken seal, with a faint smile of tender melancholy uttered in a half whisper, "Poor Sidney! my heart was but too true a prophet! happy for us both had we listened to its first forebodings."

"What does he say dearest Selena?" impatiently cried Mrs. Vallard glad to perceive with how much unexpected calmness she had received the agitating herald of approaching trials and the delay if not total overthrow of all her promised bliss.

Selena kissed the sobbing Clara whose head still rested on her shoulder while she prepared to satisfy their curiosity. She had intended to read it aloud but in spite of her gentle resignation and calm firmness she felt her voice faultering and her eyes blinded. Resigning it therefore to Clara and requesting her not to follow her for some time she retired to implore from Heaven for Sidney and for herself those consolations and counsels which they should so much need.

Mean while her friends filled with the most eager disquietude and dread of future consequences read the following lines.

> "Dearest Selena,
>
> "If it was not for the cursed wound the villain gave me I should have been with you before this but do not be frightened for I do not mind it now thank God I have got rid of them both for ever—and when I can see you I shall be quite well. Bush insists upon my writing to you to meet me here for he says it will kill me to travel night and day as I have done since I left Frankfort but if I do not see you here before tomorrow night all the surgeons and fools in London shall not keep me any longer from Hillbarton and my own sweet little Selena.
>
> Yours Mount Villars"

Totally incomprehensible as was this letter to both Mrs. Vallard and Clara they in vain tormented themselves with devising solutions for the impenetrable mystery in which it seemed involved. In vain did they repeatedly exclaim after every improbable guess, "What can he mean! Can he expect that Selena would receive him without apology, without explanation, and where is it that he thus requires her attendance?" for his letter had as usual no date.

Nevertheless Mrs. Vallard was seriously alarmed by the allusion to the wound and the surgeon's prohibition of travelling while all the affection she had ever bore her strange nephew seemed by those fears to revive in her tender heart irritated as it had justly been by his late conduct.

So entirely were they engrossed by this letter which Philip had impatiently presented to Clara that they thought not of examining the post bag, and it was not until after a considerable time that he at length brought up to Mrs. Vallard's room along with the newspaper another letter which it had also contained.

Clara perceiving that it was that very letter for which she had watched with such impatience found every painful feeling redoubled at the sight but thinking it might for the moment divert Selena from the contemplation of the cruel surprise she had just received she delayed not to deliver it.

Whatever were the emotions of Selena she now at least appeared to have recovered her composure only requesting Clara once more to leave her alone to peruse both her letters.

And she had indeed need of all her fortitude to support her thro' the agitating task. It was in the utmost affliction that poor Sidney had sought the soothing sympathy and tender consolations of his friend while he informed her that he had just lost his excellent and fondly loved Mother and he concluded by entreating with the most melancholy and eloquent importunity that she might not deny him the only pleasure upon earth to which his heart could look forward with any hope but allow him to spend one day at Hillbarton on his road from Dublin. He promised however to wait at Derby for her permission, but conjured her not to add to the wretchedness of his sad and melancholy situation by a cruelty so unnecessary, nor deny him the consolation of a few hours which was all he even asked.

Quite unable for the present to see either Sidney or Dallamore and convinced of the urgent necessity of preventing their meeting which thus appeared to be immediately threatened and which she apprehended with a degree of terror that she found almost insupportable Selena resolved instantly to quit Hillbarton, and to take some measures if possible to obviate a danger she so much dreaded.

She had no doubt of being able to prevent Sidney from coming thither, but the chance of his accidentally encountering Dallamore in the neighbourhood was what filled her with uneasiness. With a trembling hand and bleeding heart she at length traced the following lines and having communicated her design to Mrs. Vallard dispatched them by a messenger on horseback to wait for the arrival of Sidney at Derby.

> "Would to Heaven my dearest Sidney that I could afford you consolation but I resign you to the care of him who can alone speak peace to the troubled soul. Do not come here. It could answer no good purpose and I am obliged to leave our dear Mrs. Vallard for a few days; you will essentially serve me by hastening to Nottingham where you shall find the full explanation of this request or at least you shall not wait long for its arrival.
>
> Ever beloved Sidney adieu!"

Selena who upon every occasion beheld him prompt to sacrifice his own desires to her service had no doubt of his instant compliance with her request and as she was persuaded that Dallamore was now in London and would hasten from thence by the shortest road, should he indeed fulfil his threat of seeking her at Hillbarton, she trusted that by sending Sidney to Nottingham she precluded the possibility of their meeting unless they were so peculiarly unfortunate as to arrive at the same moment at Derby. She was decided in her choice of Nottingham not only by its vicinity but by knowing that one of his most intimate friends resided close to this town and she was anxious that at a season so melancholy he should not be absolutely destitute of all society.

She now began to consider whither she should herself flee for a temporary retreat not only from the man she loved but from him who now asserted a claim which she had for some time suffered herself to be persuaded he had decisively renounced

She felt that by this unfortunate caprice the happiness of her life was for ever lost, but in her anxious solicitude to soften the severe blow to Sidney and to avert the impending evils which from Dallamore's rashness she might expect, all her own personal sufferings appeared to be swallowed up, or at least for the present suspended.

Eager as she was now to escape from Dallamore she yet unhesitatingly and unalterably resolved never to dispute in public a right which she felt he ought not to relinquish.

The mutual solemn engagement for life that they had already taken she had been ever internally persuaded nothing should dissolve and tho' the peculiar circumstances of her desertion convinced her that Dallamore could not again renew the claims which he had abjured with such aggravated insult her heart had never ceased to forebode that her union with Sidney would be troubled by his caprices.

Nevertheless had he indeed bound himself by another connexion she might hope that every motive would have engaged Lady Harriet to detain him abroad till years might bestow upon him a degree of that prudence the total absence of which rendered his natural understanding almost useless to him.

But now that he had returned to England, and as it appeared from his letter had returned without his companion, Selena saw no alternative but to consent to expose herself publicly to a contest the most painful to delicacy and which might risk lives far dearer to her than her own, or submit with patience to that lot from which her gentle spirit would never have violently freed itself while she believed it allotted to her by Heaven.

She was however not without hope that Mrs. Vallard might be able gently to divert Dallamore from the pursuit, and from her knowledge of his inconstant and pliable disposition she thought it not improbable that she might be yet allowed unthought of to pass a life of seclusion, or at least that their meeting might be retarded until time and those exertions of virtue which she was resolved to employ, should have subdued every strong emotion that now so powerfully resisted all ideas of accepting another as her husband even while her heart submissively resigned the possibility of ever being Sidney's and bore with resignation that sudden stroke by which her youth's dearest only hopes were for ever lost.

But in consenting to the good offices of Mrs. Vallard she earnestly cautioned her against confessing any thing relative to the attachment of Sidney, prudently representing to her how much any idea of rivalship or opposition might encrease his ardour in asserting his right, while she acknowledged to Mrs. Vallard that her chief solicitude was to prevent as long as possible their meeting, and that one great motive of her impatience to reach Richmond was the certainty she entertained of Robert's compliance with her wishes in persuading Sidney to absent himself for a time by which means she might as she hoped be able to keep them both at a distance from Dallamore in this critical period.

Nor did she despair of being able quickly (when once satisfied of their security) to free herself from that intolerable weight of anguish which for the present clouded her mind. "Will not virtue and philosophy," thought she, "be able to anticipate for me the work of time who can in the weakest minds gradually efface the remembrance of affliction."

Most difficult was yet the task which she had now to fulfil. She had not only to combat with her own feelings but with those of Sidney more empassioned and in this instance not subdued as were hers by the consciousness of duty. She was also prepared to struggle against the counsels and entreaties which she well knew would assail her on all sides, but having once debated the matter between her own heart and her reason she had but little hope that any arguments could be suggested by others or any means discovered that might in this point reconcile her inclination with her conscience. She therefore avoided for the present all discussion with Mrs. Vallard or Clara and they both assented to the necessity of her quitting Hillbarton and the expediency of her consulting with Robert in person and preventing him from seeing Dallamore in the first moments of his surprise and disappointment from this extraordinary sudden return.

All things were therefore arranged for the instant departure of Selena for Richmond accompanied by Clara and a servant on horseback. Mrs. Vallard would fain have induced them to suffer Philip to be their escort but Selena did not dare to accept this protection or the convenience of her carriage lest it might betray them on the road should they be met by Dallamore. Sad on all sides was the hasty farewell, but the tranquility displayed by Selena, and the presence of mind with which she was alive to every caution for others almost convinced her friends that she was now decided never finally to abandon the chosen of her heart, while to Heaven and that heart alone was known the anguish with which preparatory to her leaving Hillbarton she had dictated and sent to Sidney the following letter.

"All is over my most beloved, my most amiable friend. The dream of happiness in which we have too long indulged our flattered hopes has vanished and we must awake to the sad reality of our fate. We must forget the delusion with which we have voluntarily deceived ourselves in the vain idea that we were at liberty to form prospects of felicity inconsistent with the duty of my irrevocable vows. Yes we must indeed part! But in the certainty that this separation can only last during the short and troubled period of a few years I can even now in this hour of extreme sorrow look forward with a sweet hope to the moment of our eternal reunion. How comfortless, how bitter indeed would be this farewell had I in losing you been constrained to think that I owed my affliction to the guilt or the inconstancy of my Sidney. But it is no fault of thine my once dear love tho' hopeless that I no more must call thee so all the store of our sweet affections

> Lye now exhaust and spent
> Like sums of money into bankrupts lent

and that

> We who did nothing study but the way
> To love each other in which thoughts the day
> Rose with delight and with it set

must now only learn 'The hateful science of forget.'[53]

---

[53]   Selena quotes and paraphrases the first eight lines of Henry King's "The Surrender" (1657): "My once dear love, hapless that I no more / Must call thee so, the rich affection's store / That fed our hope lies now exhaust and spent, / Like sums of treasure unto bankrupts lent. / We, that did nothing study but the way / To love each other, with which thoughts the day / Rose with delight to us and with them set, / Must learn the hateful art, how to forget."

"Yet spare me dearest Sidney all expressions of disappointment and generously remember that as your hopes originated but in my weakness on me must fall every pang which their defect can occasion. Spare me then the only insupportable affliction upon earth, spare me self reproach.

"Remain where you are until you shall hear from me again thro' Robert, and rest assured that every effort that you could make to see me or to exert your influence over my feelings in opposition to my duty will but force me to take at once the decisive step which I am for the present solicitous by delay to avoid and which I may possibly for ever escape. But my heart reassures me, and tells me that tho' lost to you for ever my peace my virtue are still dear to you beyond all selfish considerations and that I shall never repent the confidence that I have reposed upon the pure and disinterested affection of my generous friend.

"Dearest Sidney farewell! My prayers for your happiness will I trust be heard tho' Heaven has forbidden me to hope that I may contribute to it by any other means."

Chapter XII

Nature affords no object of concern
So great, as to behold a generous mind
Driven on by passion's gust and dashed on guilt
     Young[54]

Selena having commenced with Clara her melancholy journey ventured not to take the direct road to London in the dread of encountering Dallamore and her consideration for the delicate state of her companion's health retarded her speed in spite of her impatience to join Robert whose accidental meeting with Dallamore she anticipated with such horror, so that the second day was pretty far advanced before she reached Richmond.

She had frequently heard that the Star was a place of great resort and wishing to avoid such a bustle as she might there expect she requested the post boy to take them to a quieter inn. The boy who had no idea what she meant by this proposed their going to another saying it was a very civil house, to this Selena tacitly assented who knew not that it was nearly equal to that she had objected to in the honour of receiving crowds of gay parties from the bosom of the silver Thames. She however felt considerably embarrassed as they drove up to the door and saw the carriage instantly besieged by a swarm of waiters who looked contemptuously on the hired equipage as one advanced to let down the steps. But it was now too late to retreat and Clara taking hold of her arm they followed their conductor timidly and hastily thro' the crowded passage into a small room which looked into the garden at the foot of which flowed the river.

---

[54] Mandane in Edward Young's *Busiris, King of Egypt* (1719), 3.1.374–6 (line 376 should read "driven by a sudden gust").

Selena lost no time in sending to enquire for her brother with a line to announce her arrival and waited impatiently for above an hour the return of her messenger, when she had at length the mortification to hear that he had been obliged to give up his house the day before on the return of the family in whose absence it had been let. All she could learn farther was that he was gone to town but no one could inform her of his direction as he had ordered his letters to be taken to Mr. Bently.

Selena now felt awkward in sending thither in her own name without an introduction aware that they might think it necessary to return an invitation. She therefore desired her messenger if possible to procure Mr. Miltern's address without mentioning from whence he came; but by the time she had received it, it was too late to think of going that evening to an hotel in town on the chance of finding their brother there, so unprotected as they felt themselves.

Nevertheless their situation grew every moment more unpleasant. The noise and confusion of the house and the little attendance which they obtained was indeed accounted for by their being told that a large party of above thirty young persons had come that day from town to dinner, and having remained longer on the water than they had intended, the weather proving so uncommonly fine they had declared their intention of passing the night at that house. The servant who rode with Selena from Hillbarton informed her that the ladies of this party were "player folk and such like but that they had been brought there by some of the finest young lords and dukes in town as their grooms had let him know" and indeed the novel society of these deputy lords and dukes of the stable seemed to possess so many captivating charms for Mrs. Vallard's simple Frank that Selena tho' she had gently requested him not to be out of the way, in vain enquired for him during the rest of the evening.

In passing from their chamber to the little room where they dined Selena had seen the long assembly room laid out for the reception of those gallant guests and as this was immediately adjoining to their apartment they had now the pleasure of hearing the confused and riotous sounds of tumultuous merriment which encreased from the moment of the loudly proclaimed entrance of the jovial troop, and more especially from the time that the dinner was removed till it amounted to a degree of clamorous vociferation that could to a disengaged listener give no other idea than that of Bedlam liberated from its keepers.

On a sudden all was chill as death and after a moment's pause a voice was heard more soft than the aerial music which by the spell of Prospero crept upon the waters "Allaying all the fury of the tempest"[55] when as it sweetly breathed its melodious and at first tremulous notes Selena started and Clara clasping her hands with a look of inexpressible anguish exclaimed, "Oh Edwin!"

---

[55]   In Shakespeare's *The Tempest* (1611) Ferdinand describes Ariel's song as follows: "This music crept by me upon the waters, / Allaying both their fury and my passion / With its sweet air" (1.2.395–7).

"It is indeed poor Edwin!" sighed Selena. But tho' she had uttered those words only in a whisper Clara with a movement of impatience grasped her hand expressively to demand silence scarcely breathing while with extreme earnestness she silently listened to the close of the heart thrilling melody.

A burst of loud applause aroused her from this delicious trance which had seized her prisoned soul, painfully recalling to her remembrance the contemptible scene of vice and folly where Edwin now bore so conspicuous a part.

"Alas dearest Clara!" cried Selena, "how little did we imagine we were ourselves interested in that rude revelry which so much disgusted and shocked our ears. But let us come my love to our chamber, we shall there be less annoyed by these disquieting sounds and at least we shall not be able so plainly to distinguish a voice we must both of us try henceforth to forget since its unhappy possessor is no longer worthy of our remembrance."

Clara answered only by her tears but resisted the entreaties of her sister to retire; and remained in a silence of the most accute agony, listening to every voice that mingled in the roar of barbarous dissonance, anxious in vain to catch the beloved tones for which her heart languished. Dreadful were those hours to Selena. For a while she sought to divert if possible the attention of Clara, but perceiving that she heard her with a fretful impatience, preserving herself a mournful silence while totally engrossed by the tumult of the neighbouring chamber Selena hopelessly relinquished the vain endeavour and sunk herself in the most dreary melancholy, her spirits wearied with the confusion and agitation by which she found herself oppressed.

Once more the din of "ill managed revelry" was hushed. Again the sweet and gently breathing strain

> Rose like a stream of rich distilled perfumes
> And stole upon the air.[56]

"Oh it is too much!" cried Clara as she hid her pale cheek and streaming eyes in the bosom of her sister and stopping her ears exclaimed, "let me not hear it."

"Come then dear Clara," replied Selena as she gladly arose to accompany her from this most painful scene but again dissolved in softest tears and insensible to all but the deliciously compulsive enchantment of the song Clara clung to the chair which she had left as tho' she feared to be torn violently from the spot where her heart was irresistibly rooted.

Quite unequal to contend with her however she might blame her imprudent weakness Selena exhausted by her own sufferings had reseated herself at the door resting her head languidly upon a table which had been placed there as a sideboard. In this position she continued for some time and insensibly stealing from the rude festivity which again besieged her ears with a violence that seemed redoubled by the suspension and even from the anticipation of the agitating

---

[56]   John Milton's *Comus* (1634), lines 172 ("revelry" should be "merriment"), 556–7.

scenes which she had to dread from the contending passions of boisterous spirits her heart flew back with tender fondness to the sweetly tranquil hours of love and happiness which she had passed with Sidney in the woods of Esselberrie or by the placid stream that crept thro' the meadows of Hillbarton. Alas! those hours were for ever past, nor must she ever again hope to renew such delights. She had perhaps for the last time seen the beloved source of all their charms, and her situation was so cruel that she was even condemned to desire this, yet still remembrance poured o'er her conscious heart the dear ideas and every lost treasure that had made life precious.

Mean while midnight had been long past unheeded. Other voices had asserted the claim of interrupting the tumultuous clamour but attention so still was no longer produced and even female accents were heard with indifference or disgust while those of Edwin yet vibrated upon the ear.

Clara now of herself proposed their retiring and Selena taking her arm followed the chamber maid who proceeded them at a little distance with a light thro' the passage which was long and dark; when on a sudden the folding doors of the assembly room at once burst open and amidst the blaze of light a scene of what to Selena appeared frightful riot presented itself to her view. Vainly she stove to conceal herself from observation while a large party issuing from the room in various directions completely encircled the terrified sisters. Clara clung nearly fainting to Selena who supported her in her arms, at that instant nearly equally shocked for close beside them they beheld the pale and emaciated figure of Edwin and hanging on his arm a female whose bold and intoxicated aspect might have done honour to the court of Comus. In the wanton audacity of swelled insolence she had no sooner caught a glimpse of the trembling sisters than she snatched the light from his hand and held it with a loud laugh up to the face of Selena.

An exclamation like that of mingled agony and horror escaped from Edwin while Selena darted on him a glance of indignant contempt as she shrunk affrighted from the bold rudeness of his impudent companion; quick as lightning and with a look of sudden frenzy Edwin violently cast from his arm his astonished Bacchante[57] and rushing thro' the throng instantly disappeared.

Amidst the shout of general surprise Selena sought to make her escape but one young man more intoxicated or more insolent than the rest advancing caught her in his arms, swearing that she was beautiful as Hebe[58] and her lips should be his nectar.

Indignation and disgust restored to Selena all her courage, and with more than her usual strength she repulsed the brutal freedom, and sprung lightly from his grasp, but Clara pale and motionless continued leaning against the rails of the gallery totally insensible to the boistrous insults to which she was now exposed and Selena shocked and distracted at the situation from which it appeared impossible at the moment to extricate her, was on a sudden overwhelmed by the

---

[57]   Bacchante: a priestess or female votary of Bacchus (OED).

[58]   Hebe: the goddess of youth and spring.

violent contending emotions of joy, terror, and astonishment at the sight of Sidney who just alighted from his horse rushed impetuously from the stairs.

Looking wildly around bewildered and amazed he eagerly exclaimed, "Heavens! What is all this. Selena whom are you with?"

Restored instantly to a portion of her accustomed calmness Selena with admirable presence of mind took the arm of Sidney cautious of embroiling him with the intoxicated party and without appearing to notice by what a group they were surrounded said softly as they approached her sister, "Come dear Sidney, support poor Clara, she is not well" and then added in a yet lower tone, "We have just seen Edwin."

Apprehensive that some impertinence had been threatened Sidney had cast a fierce eye around on the flushed associates of intemperance but at the touch of Selena's hand instantly trembled alive to nothing at that moment but the softest tenderness.

With the air of gracious politeness natural to him, but which he would assuredly not have worn had he known the insult his Selena had just suffered he addressed them as he made way quietly with his hand amid those who prest upon them, "I ask your pardon Gentlemen, be so good as to let us pass." Awed by the gentleness and dignity so gracefully conspicuous in all his movements they in silence retreated and suffered them unmolested to return to the room which Selena had just quitted.

No sooner had Sidney placed on a seat the half fainting Clara than falling at the feet of Selena he passionately seized her hands, and pressing them to his lips and eyes as they burst forth with unmanly sorrows he exclaimed, "Oh Selena will you, can you indeed forsake your truly wedded love! No it is impossible—you are mine, mine only, and no power on earth shall ever tear you from me."

"Cruel Sidney!" interrupted she endeavouring to hide the tears that choaked her utterance, "I thought we might both have been spared a moment so painful as this. I trusted that you would have been satisfied by the assurances which my letter contained and that you would have respected the entreaties of my heart."

"I have received no letter," cried he vehemently, "I waited for none. I arrived at Derby yesterday evening and met there Philip who told me all. I have been on horseback ever since."

Selena involuntarily pressed his burning hands and looked with anxious compassion on his fevered eyes, pallid countenance and disheveled hair which plainly spoke that he had indeed taken no repose while he passionately proceeded.

"I have heard nothing from you—I will hear nothing but that you are my own—that you remember the solemn vow registered in Heaven, as well as in my heart that you will never be another's."

"Alas Sidney!" she replied, "do not unkindly upbraid me with the weakness which prompted me too eagerly to grasp at the shadow of freedom in which I for a while rejoiced, and by making this conditional promise raise hopes which even at the time my heart foreboded must end in disappointment. Too well you know that

I am not yours nor alas my own! But oppose not the claims which are now made, and you will see how easily they may again be relinquished."

"Not oppose them," warmly interrupted Sidney, "yes with all the vigour of which my whole soul is capable, I will oppose them, and to the last drops of blood that warm my heart."

Selena sick at an idea which tho' for ever present to her mind she had yet never dared to utter, struggled with the faintness that overpowered her soul and earnestly taking hold of his arm replied with a voice of impressive energy, "Sidney listen to me. Hear the firm purpose which no violence can ever shake from which no horrible threats shall ever intimidate me. Never will I look upon the hand by which the safety of Dallamore is endangered, and the first effort which you shall make forcibly to break those bonds which now unite us only in idea, shall compel me to seek our mutual peace and security by claiming him as my protector and soliciting that meeting which I now promise you to shun, at least till more reasonable motives shall appear to decide my lot than that transient caprice by which he is now activated. But this is no time for such discussion. Poor Clara has already been but too much agitated—and can you bear to see her thus? We must all now seek repose. Promise me to conform to my wishes as to what respects myself in these important moments of my life and I will see you early tomorrow. If you refuse me this promise never will I again voluntarily meet you."

"Ah Selena how vain, how superfluous is the promise you require! You know your empire over me is more powerful than that of reason or even of passion—and I must obey you tho' my life were to be the sacrifice."

While he spoke he assisted Selena to support Clara to her room, who as if insensible to all that had passed spoke not to her sister as she suffered her to undress and lay her in bed, except to complain of extreme cold and in her fears for her situation Selena almost forgot the despair of Sidney and his altered appearance which so plainly announced how dreadfully his mind and body had been harassed during the last four and twenty hours.

So anxiously did she watch the feverish starts and uneasy slumbers of Clara that she thought not of undressing and only occasionally laid herself down on her own bed during the remainder of the night. Day had not long dawned when she heard a gentle tap at the door.

Her heart throbbed in the sudden assurance that it was Sidney but considering the untimely hour and that the bustle of the house instead of diminishing had continued nay even seemed to encrease she listened with some disquietude. Nevertheless as the door was locked she resolved to answer and enquire who was there before she opened it. Unwilling to disturb Clara she approached close to the lock when her soul instantly recognised the soft sweet voice of Sidney as he whisperingly pronounced her name.

Assured that some strange and important cause had thus induced him to intrude at an hour so unseasonable the thought of Dallamore's arrival instantly occurred to her and with a trembling hand she drew back the bolt, tho' she did so with the utmost caution lest Clara might be aroused to new disquiets, for ever sensible to the feelings of others, no terror, no affliction of her own had the power on any occasion to make her heedless of inflicting a wound that could be spared to another.

She spoke not until she had gently closed the door but was by no means reassured as she eagerly gazed at the distress and consternation painted on the brow of Sidney.

"I am glad dearest Selena," said he preventing her enquiries, "that you are already up, I wish to caution you not to let Clara come from her room this morning till you can quit the house entirely. Edwin has hurt himself, not I hope materially, but there are some circumstances attending it which she cannot fail of hearing if she stirs out and that we should not if possible let her know at present she seems so very nervous."

"Merciful God! What has happened?" cried Selena convinced that there was more in this than he wished to tell and terrified with the apprehension that Edwin had perhaps destroyed himself.

"Do not be alarmed dearest Selena! I trust he will be well enough in a few days, but there has been a sad uproar here, and the poor unfortunate fellow has indeed had a miraculous escape. Just after he had met you last night, seized no doubt with a fit of sudden frenzy he leaped into the river from the terrace and would unquestionably have been lost for ever had it not been for a boat which providentially lay directly under him almost filled with water so that he could not see it. He struck his head however severely and was found quite insensible about an hour after I had parted from you. I heard the tumult underneath my windows as they were carrying him across the garden and thinking immediately of poor Edwin ran out to see what had happened. His companions whom he had come with from town were all too much intoxicated as well as their servants to afford the least assistance. I have therefore been obliged to give what orders were necessary. The apothecary is with him already and says the hurt is not of consequence, but as he is quite delirious I am going to request Mr. Bently to visit him. Promise me that you will not leave this till I return and that you will then hear me speak."

Selena pressed his hand as she gave him the assurance he desired and bidding him hasten back to the unhappy Edwin returned to keep her sad vigil of sorrow and anxiety beside the restless pillow of the already too much agitated Clara.

Chapter XIII

> Didst thou but know what 'tis to love like me
> And to be so beloved ....
> Yet to be past all hope of happiness
> Of ever tasting those desired beauties
> Of any dawn least glimpse or spark of comfort
>   Lee[59]

Drearily did the intervening hours pass with poor Selena while she watched for the return of Sidney.

Bently farm was above two miles from Richmond yet he still found on his arrival there that none of the family were yet risen and however impatient at the delay he found himself compeled to wait for some time before he could see Mr. Bently and request his attendance.

No sooner had he mentioned the name of Stanmore than preventing all his apologies he eagerly demanded if he meant Edwin and evinced for his safety considerable interest and concern saying that the family of Stanmore was nearly connected to that of his wife and altho' he had himself never met this extraordinary young man of whom he had heard much he had been indebted to his father formerly for so many good offices that anxious to save him he with the utmost alacrity hastened to accompany Sidney.

Unwilling to mention the arrival of Selena at Richmond Sidney found it absolutely impossible to continue any conversation with Mr. Bently so entirely did she of whom he could not speak engross at that time his whole soul.

Impatient to return to her he quitted him as soon as he decently could leaving him with the apothecary and their patient, after having been assured that his life was in no immediate danger, and promising to return in a few moments flew to her apartment and once more summoned her by his quiet signal.

She had just given Clara her breakfast and desired the chamber maid not to come in again till called for; "It is Sidney dear Clara," said she while her heart beat fast. "You know I promised to see him, allow me to leave you for a quarter of an hour and do not get up till my return."

Clara consented to her wishes feeling herself indeed scarcely able to rise but detaining her hand with a meaning eye Selena saw that she was anxious to say something which she yet knew not how to express.

"Do you wish for any thing my love?" demanded she.

"No Selena, unless perhaps you would gratify me, I know it is very foolish and indeed I do not mean to think of him any more, but I should like to know and Sidney could tell you if *he* is still here."

Selena could with difficulty restrain her tears, but pressing her hand as she withdrew it promised to bring her the intelligence she desired and then with those

---

[59]   Ziphares in Nathaniel Lee's *Mithridates* (1678), 5.2.75–9 (the epigraph omits "O Archelaus!" at the end of line 76).

strangely mingled emotions of dread, confidence, affection and delight which her love contending with her unhappy circumstances excited she met Sidney and eagerly enquired what had been Mr. Bently's opinion.

Sidney acquainted her with what he had said on first seeing his patient, but added, that he was still with him.

"Have you told him of our being here?" enquired she and Sidney in confessing that he had not could not disguise his earnest reluctance to her suffering the friend of Dallamore to be acquainted with her present abode. He did not however explain the motives of this reluctance but she herself secretly felt and shared them. Hesitating for a moment she without directly replying enquired Where was her brother? Sidney had not thought of asking.

Selena's eyes filled while she smiled from her heart for it told her how his had been occupied.

"You had better then go back to Mr. Bently and bring me word where I may hope to find him, but you need not say any thing of me as I should be sorry to be delayed here if he is not to return immediately."

Sidney now found his benevolent friend extremely busy in preparing a method of removing Edwin to his house, he declared that nothing was so necessary for him as quiet, and that by having him immediately under his own eye, he hoped to administer relief both to the mind and body of the darling child of that accomplished pair whose virtuous attachment and amiable manners had captivated the enthusiastic friendship of his early years and had never ceased to interest his riper judgment.

Sidney was convinced that this kind arrangement would afford satisfaction to Selena but he could give her little with respect to Robert who had been obliged to go in search of Mr. Turner without exactly knowing where to find him in order to get some papers relative to his marriage which his lawyers required, and tho' Mr. Bently expected his return in a few days he could not supply Sidney with his address.

Extremely disconcerted by this unfortunate absence which happened so peculiarly malapropos[60] for poor Selena she remained awhile quite uncertain what conduct she should now pursue. Hastily revolving in her mind every circumstance she at length determined upon confiding herself to the protection of Mr. Bently, who would provide her no doubt with some secure retirement where she might hide herself for the present as well from Sidney as from Dallamore. To this end she now desired Sidney to carry to him a message signifying her wish to be introduced.

But in him she found the most extreme repugnance to comply with this desire. Vehemently did he conjure her to consider how strange must appear her refusal to take up her residence with his family until her brother's return, and that her compliance with this request which would assuredly be enforced with all the violence of persuasion must expose her to the probability nay almost certainty of a surprise from the intrusion of Dallamore. Hearing as he must do of Robert's

---

[60] Malapropos: inopportune (OED).

intimacy where but at Bently's farm would Dallamore first seek Selena when disappointed of finding her at Hillbarton?

She persisted however in her intention but assured Sidney that the single circumstance of Edwin's reception would be sufficient to deter her from accepting that invitation which in every respect was so unadvisable that Mr. Bently himself could not press it.

Perceiving that she was not to be induced to give up to his arguments and that she was ready to send her message by the waiter detaining the hand with which she held the bell he passionately exclaimed, "Selena if you are indeed determined for ever to divide yourself from me let me at least on my knees conjure you do not give yourself up to eternal repentance by rashly devoting your life to the man who was born with more than human frailties and folly that he might prove the punishment of my sins."

She would have spoken but eagerly preventing her he continued, "I claim your promise. Listen to me tho' it be for the last time! Hear me at least for once in this critical moment plead for the only rescue that remains for the happiness dearest Selena I will say the happiness of both our lives! You are now to chuse between those extorted, those rejected vows and those offered by your heart and accepted by Heaven and your only truly wedded spouse. To morrow may be too late. Selena there is frenzy in that thought! and Edwin has taught me a dreadful way to seek relief. Look not upon me with horror my gentle, my beloved Selena! No, my soul despises the cowardly refuge. I can bear my anguish like a man, and never shall he whom you have once chosen disgrace you by any crime. But Selena shall I suffer alone? Alas, while the knowledge of my despair shall add to your regrets, the conviction of your sorrow will be the most insupportable part of mine. Have pity upon us both, beloved, only object of all my tenderness! Blush not to assert your freedom. Be not ashamed to confess the accepted husband of your choice. Yet if your timid gentleness shrinks from the short contest that might possibly ensue, then let us instantly fly. United by secret but sweetly indissoluble bonds I will find with you a retreat where malice itself shall never trace our happy steps, and where we may repose sheltered in the downy nest of love until other objects shall have obliterated from that capricious breast the memory of his insulted his oft slighted vows. Selena we have yet known Love only by its pains or its anxieties! And yet can you bear to resign it for ever? Oh let us prove its innocent joys and life will be to us a paradise. Contented in each other, in the confidence of affection, in the peace of virtue, in the delicious certainty that we shall pass our hours for ever together, and that our duties are inseparably interwoven with our pleasures, is there an affliction that can oppress the more than doubled strength of our bosoms while they thus lean upon each other?"

Selena's heart trembled as he spoke and hastily withdrawing her hands from his empassioned grasp she covered her eyes with her gown and stopping her ears interrupted the persuasive fallacy of his arguments.

"Oh Sidney I must not hear you! Speak not of a happiness that Heaven has forbidden us to taste, and that never could be realized while my soul was a prey to self reproach and perpetual terrors for your safety."

He was again eager to speak but gently laying her soft hand upon his lips she suffered him to detain it while she continued in a firmer tone.

"No dear Sidney. Confide in me. I solemnly assure you my present purpose is to avoid Dallamore, and doubt not that I shall be able to accomplish it, unless your interference drives me on that rock where all our hopes must forever perish. Our immediate union is impossible but fairer prospects may again open to our view. Once more exert yourself in my service. Promise me that you will not converse with Dallamore and that you will seek Robert and engage him to accompany you to Miltern Abbey till you shall hear from me—and suffer me in peace to pursue the only path to which my conscience nay even my feelings can now direct."

It is not to be supposed that Sidney could be induced easily to consent to a plan which thus separated them at a moment so critical, nor could she at length prevail until she had past her word that while he submitted to this absence she would entrust to him the place of her retreat and that he should see that she was sincere in her acknowledged reluctance to be discovered by Dallamore.

He had besides afterwards the satisfaction to hear her decidedly reject Mr. Bently's expected offer of an asylum in his own house.

She was charmed with the ingenious and kind manners of her new friend but having entreated him to preserve her secret and promised to see and consult with him as to her plans in the afternoon she left Sidney to explain to him her reasons for this secrecy and returned to communicate to Clara what were her intentions.

She could now tell her with truth that Edwin had left the house and endeavoured to turn her attention from the remembrance of the past night by conversing with her on her own important affairs, and so deeply did they interest her more than sisterly love that Selena in effect quickly succeeded, tho' her languid spirits and weak frame yet visibly suffered by the late agitation.

Selena had now time for recollection and feeling herself unequal to the task of again parting from Sidney she resolved to abridge those trying moments and declared to him in a few lines that she could not again leave Clara entreating him to lose no time in fulfilling the office which he had accepted and repeated her promise that while he complied with the conditions she had imposed and intruded not on her retirement he should not cease to hear from Robert all that so materially concerned them both.

As he found that all his eloquence of persuasion to obtain another interview was in vain, and that impatient of his delay she at length refused to answer his repeated notes he impetuously quitted the house, a momentary emotion of resentment mingling with his despair, as he threw a last look upon those walls which concealed from him by her own consent all he valued in life, the object of his soul's idolatry, her whom he so unjustly accused of cruelty nay even then of caprice.

Scarcely knowing whither he directed his course he walked along with hurried steps, heedless of all that surrounded him wrapt in his own bitter meditations until he on a sudden found himself amid all the concourse and confusion of the full peopled regions of Piccadilly before he was conscious of his having proceeded a mile.

Suddenly starting he looked around with a strange kind of distaste and aversion upon all who past him, whether they wore on their countenances the idle curiosity of vacuity, or the unobserving thoughtfulness of preoccupied attention.

For the first time he now asked himself by what means he might probably soonest fulfil his promise of finding out Robert and for this purpose however reluctant he felt to converse with any one, he got into a hackney coach, and proceeded to the city to enquire from Mr. Turner's banker where he might hear of him. There he learned that he was expected from Essex that evening or the next day, and that he usually took up his abode while in town at Ibbetson's hotel in Vere street.

Thither accordingly Sidney went thinking it probable that Robert would accompany Mr. Turner to town, and feeling himself totally exhausted by the fatigues, watchings and sufferings of the two preceeding days and nights he lay down tho' not till a late hour to take repose, leaving a strict charge that he should be immediately called if Mr. Turner arrived before he rose.

Sleep as some one has justly said is respected by every anguish, every affliction which torments the soul. Passively they resign their prey to its sweetly restorative suspension. Remorse alone triumphs over her gentle rights and despises her consolotary efforts.

Sidney awoke on the following morning astonished himself that he had been able thus for some hours to forget his vexations, his sorrows and his perplexities.

He now hastened to make enquiries among the lawyers employed by Robert, but received from them no farther information than that which Mr. Bently had already given him and having prosecuted his fruitless search until about noon he returned to the hotel to see if they might be arrived.

As he was proceeding along Oxford Street with those hurried and heedless steps which bespeak agitation of mind, he on a sudden rather roughly encountered some person who moving with equal precipitation was too busily occupied in watching the carriages to take much precaution against whom he might jostle. Raising his eye from the ground Sidney was about to make the apology which habitual courtesy prompted when his ears were instaniously [sic] saluted with a torrent of excuses and expressions of pleasure at the unexpected and somewhat brusque encounter.

No sooner did Sidney perceive that he was accosted by Mr. Leeson than he was seized with a kind of horror at the persecution to which he was now infallibly exposed, in being constrained to listen to the insipid nay probably most impertinent discourse of the never ceasing talker who would now inevitably fasten himself upon his victim. Slightly bowing and muttering some unintelligible excuse for his haste, tho' almost hopeless of escape he hurried on, anticipating what indeed instantly took place while the indefatigable orator seizing hold of his arm announced his declaration of accompanying him.

Poor Sidney who to an uninterested spectator might now have presented a ludicrous image of a truant detected by the unexpected appearance of his master in vain employed every stratagem that his invention could devise for his escape, in vain did he urge his adhesive companion not to come out of his way declaring that he for his part could not possibly make any delay, he suffered him not to say more but overpowering all his efforts replied, "I can walk pretty fast my dear Sir, and as I have nothing very particular to do this morning I cannot relinquish the pleasure of your company now that I have been so uncommonly fortunate as to meet you. Besides you are the very person I wished most to see, and I want to have some very particular conversation with you and to complain to you of the remarkable indeed I may say unaccountable bad treatment I have received from your most extraordinary kinsman Lord Mount Villars;"

Sidney encreased the rapidity of his steps from an emotion of instinctive impatience that was excited by this name and the throng amid which they moved rendered it impossible for Mr. Leeson in spite of all his struggles to retain his hold and out of breath as he was to pursue his narrative.

"My dear friend," cried he at length when with the utmost exertion he had again seized on the arm which the interposing crowd assisted by Sidney's good will had for a moment forced him to forgo, "My dear friend this throng is very intolerable. Which way are you going. Might not we as well turn down some of these quiet streets where we could have a little comfortable chat and not be knocked about in this deplorable manner. Which side does your business lye?"

Sidney (who had passed Vere street under the apprehension of his establishing himself with him should they once enter a house together) was now obliged to declare that he was going to call on a friend in Manchester street where he hoped to shake off his self offered attendant who however eagerly interrupted him with, "Well that is the very luckiest thing that could have happened. Why I had positively forgot the very thing I principally came out for this morning and Lady Vellum never would have forgiven me if I had not called to enquire after her. So I can drop you in Manchester Street to do your business with your friend and call for you there again after I have just left my name at her Ladyship's door. I shall not go in so that I cannot possibly miss you even if you are impatient to wait for me, I will keep my eye on the house, Lady Vellum's is in the square you know poor soul she takes on I hear sadly for the dreadful accident that happened to her cher ami,[61] young Stanmore. I suppose you know how he had a quarrel about a lady of a certain description the night before last and got a severe blow on his temple that has put out his right eye. A great pity that poor young man should have ruined himself as he has done. Quite done up—not a shilling left in the world and his constitution quite gone. His uncle too has given him up and I am told will never see him again and then this sad business at Richmond, but very true I dare say

---

[61] Cher ami: dear friend (French).

you can tell me all the particulars of that. We all know you were not very far from thence. The neighbourhood of Richmond possesses I have been told at present certain powerful attractions for some folk … well well don't look so strange. If you had put me in your secret I would never have betrayed your confidence. No one so close as I am, but you see I know more than you suspect, and tho' I might happen to have been the first unluckily perhaps that mentioned it to Lord Mount Villars yet I assure you the whole town …."

"Mentioned what Sir?" exclaimed Sidney with a warmth of eagerness which disconcerted but could not silence his tormenter.

"Why my dear friend just give me leave to tell you exactly how this whole affair happened, for it was upon the very business I wished to speak to you having no doubt that your cousin will try and misrepresent me to you in this particular, a thing I should be extremely sorry for, as upon my word of honour I have always considered you as one of my very best friends. But I beg your pardon I see you are impatient and I will lose no time to clear myself in your opinion as there is no character I so much detest and despise as a busy body and a tatler."

"Excuse me Mr. Leeson," interrupted Sidney impatiently, provoked beyond the power of endurance, "I have really no leisure at present but beg you may be so good as to let me know what it was you have said to Lord Mount Villars."

"Lord Sir I protest I said nothing that he must not have heard from every soul that visited him, even if I had not been unfortunately let up to him yesterday morning … indeed my great anxiety to hear exactly how he was and what had really happened in that cursed business at Frankfort made me partly force my way to his room and much concerned I was to …."

"I must wish you good morning Mr. Leeson," cried Sidney in despair, "I see a friend of mine that I must speak with."

While he spoke he forcibly disengaged himself and sprung to the other side of the street to address an acquaintance trusting that this accidental meeting might deliver him from his persecuter, but closely following him with his glass to his eye he watched his movements and in a moment was again at his elbow.

"I am sorry to intrude my good friend," said he, "but you must positively allow me to explain to you this little business so I will wait with pleasure till you have concluded what you have to say to this gentleman."

Commanding his temper and really anxious to know what had past between him and his cousin, Sidney passively suffered him to resume his post at his side and continue thus—"I see you want to get rid of me, but I will not delay you a minute, and I must entreat you will not believe that I had the most distant intention of making any mischief between you and Lord Mount Villars when I happened unfortunately to let slip how matters stood at Richmond."

"I do not understand you Sir," said Sidney with suppressed indignation.

"Oh my good friend you cannot suppose that we did not all hear of your very allowable and indeed I may say laudable endeavour to compensate to Miss Miltern for the slight with which she must have felt herself treated by her former admirer. Some people to be sure went so far as to say that they were even married, but for my part I never believed it and used always to see that Lady Harriet meant only to quiz us when she would have persuaded us that Lord Mount Villars was married to the pretty Selena."

Sidney's whole frame shook while he heard the name of his soul's beloved thus lightly profaned, but despising the contemptible object of his resentment too much to display it he in silence suffered him to continue.

"But my dear Mr. Dallamore I wish to Heaven you had but seen the extraordinary fury that your cousin flew into without the smallest provocation upon earth. Upon my life Sir his treatment of me was such as no gentleman ought to put with, and if it was not for the very peculiar situation in which I found him, and the circumstances which attended our interview I should really feel myself obliged to require some explanation for his language and behavior. Do you know my dear Sir that he absolutely desired his servant to turn me out, and called me by some very disagreeable names which I shall not repeat; upon my word it was most extremely unpleasant, I never met with such treatment in my life and I had no idea of it. But I am sure my Lord has one of the best hearts in the world and I have no doubt that he will make me an apology when he finds that all I said was true and as soon as he comes back from Richmond if he is able"

"Comes back from Richmond!" exclaimed Sidney starting back impetuously. "What do you mean?"

"Why Sir he insisted upon having a chaise and four ordered to the door directly, and I doubt all the efforts of his servant (who by the bye is a very saucy jackanapes I must say) but with all his efforts and his lies I am sure he was not able to hinder him. I will venture to promise he has got there long ago and found that I am"

"An impertinent fellow," cried Sidney casting him from him with irresistible violence while he ran forwards with an impetuous speed as if seized with a sudden frenzy, leaving him to declare with a mixture of astonishment and resentment as he recovered his feet and gazed after him thro' his glass, "Well if ever I saw such young men in my life! there must certainly be madness in the family"—while the pleasant idea of circulating this sudden opinion reconciled him in some measure to the mortification and disappointment which he had just suffered.

For more than a mile Sidney continued without diminishing the swiftness of his course rushing on with inconceivable velocity in spite of all interruptions and impediments which he met with, impelled by a confused desire of escaping from his tormentor and the idea of snatching Selena from the arms of Dallamore—his almost irrevocably lost Selena! Gradually his impetuosity subsided and tho' he still resolved to proceed to Richmond yet he felt a confidence in the prudent caution of his beloved to escape from the impending ruin which now threatened all his hopes and began to deliberate how he might excuse to her, the apparent breach of their agreement in this hasty return. This he hoped he might do without difficulty, since he had engaged to seek her brother and he now really persuaded himself that having executed his business with Mr. Turner Robert without stopping in London had already hastened back to rejoin his Ophelia.

Sidney now for the first time recollected how ridiculously he had acted and that the utmost speed he could exert would not bring him to Richmond as quickly as the first horse he might probably have hired. Unwilling however to turn back he continued his way expecting to be overtaken by some of the stages that so perpetually ran on that road.

He had just taken a place on one of the boxes when he perceived riding towards him a groom whom he instantly remembered to belong to Dallamore and eagerly desiring the coachman to stop demanded, "Where is your master?"

"My Lord is near Richmond Sir at Mr. Bently's."

"How long?" exclaimed Sidney tho' hardly able to articulate.

"Since yesterday Sir."

The anxious doubts which now burned within the bosom of Sidney found no utterance on his lips as he trembling gasped for breath. The groom observing his silence put his hand to his hat and the coachman once more whipped on his horses with a rapidity that might have satisfied all impatience but that of Sidney.

With difficulty could the representations of reason prevail on him to keep his seat and on the first interruption which delayed their progress as they entered the town he leaped from the box and flew to the inn.

Yet as he entered the hall the dread of hearing that what he had feared had indeed befallen him made him shrink back from the enquiry which might in one sudden crush annihilate his every hope. Speechless and half suffocated he gazed around as if a misfortune so terrible to him must have left behind on all some monuments of desolation which might at once declare it to his soul. Just at that instant he saw Mrs. Vallard's servant (who had attended Selena from Hillbarton) alight from his horse and in a voice which struck upon his heart as tho' it had been the groan of sepulchral horrors he heard his demand why the luggage had not yet been sent to Bently farm.

Oh she was lost! lost to him for ever! gone irrevocably! Cold drops of dew stood upon his throbbing brows and every limb appeared stretched upon the rack while he listened for the terrible confirmation of all his fears. As he stood thus fixed immoveable, and almost stupified to thought Frank withdrew from the door without having perceived him. His absence seemed to afford a temporary relief.

"It cannot be," cried he starting from the spot, "my fears have unmanned me! How can I doubt my Selena! She could not have thus deceived me, and Heaven has not abandoned us both and betrayed her into the power of another against her own will!"

Conquering his weakness he now rushed from the door expecting to find Frank in the stable yard, but he perceived him already at some distance having taken the road to Bently farm, and followed by a cart which undoubtedly contained the luggage for which he had been sent. His situation was now intolerable. No certainty however dreadful could exceed a suspence like this.

"Where are the Ladies," cried he with quivering lips as he met the waiter.

"Oh sir Mr. Bently came for them yesterday evening in a vast hurry. They did not stop to take their things and the servant has just been for them, you might have seen him not a minute ago."

"And did she go!" exclaimed Sidney in a hollow voice unconscious what he uttered.

"Oh Lord yes she went to be sure," replied the waiter with a half simper. "Lord Mount Villars sir came to the farm so Mr. Bently came off directly to fetch my Lady. My Lord's servants were here last night."

Sidney heard no more. Resolving to be assured of what in spite of conviction he still wished to doubt, he took the pass across the fields to Bently farm which he had so often been accustomed to tread with Robert.

But his steps were no longer precipitated with the fervour of impatience; Hope had almost died within his bosom, and her faint promises were overpowered by the desponding voice which threatened the confirmation of his terrors while he internally exclaimed, "Away, away wretch that thou art! There is no hope for thee!" He was now in the meadow which was separated from the shrubbery by a high thorn hedge alone. The voice the soft sweet voice of his adored his lost Selena struck upon his heart and the sickness that instantly overpowered him obliged him to lean against the bushes for support.

At that moment she passed, Mr. Bently whose arm she held had just pronounced some words of which Sidney only heard, "Let the consciousness of acting right sustain your spirits." But in the answer he then distinctly distinguished the accents that pierced to his inmost soul.

"Ah my dear Sir tho' I have acted as my heart tells me is right how can it be at peace until I shall know how my brother will consider my conduct and how Sidney will bear the intelligence of my thus coming to meet Dallamore in spite of all my solemn promises."

Her voice scarce reached him as she uttered the last words and he felt that it was broken by her tears, but he had now too terribly received the assurance which he sought and had no wish remaining upon earth but to bury himself from every hope, to fly from the whole world and above all Selena.

Having wandered for some hours in a state of wild distraction, the first use he made of his recovered senses was to write the following billet to Selena, and having done this he proceeded immediately to put his sudden but determined purpose into execution.

> "We are forever separated. The grave itself cannot now unite me to the Selena whom I adored! You have betrayed me, you have betrayed yourself! You have resigned me without one struggle and never shall the knowledge of my fate disturb your tranquility. I renounce a world that I abhor and tho' the voice of Heaven forbids me to free myself from the burden of life I can at least terminate its miserable course where I can molest you only as the dead of my remembrance. Selena forget me—forget the happiness that might have been ours, and be if possible free from every feeling which now rends my soul in saying Farewell for ever!"

Chapter XIV

Yet have they many baits, and many wicked spells,
To inveigle and invite th' unwary sense
And under fair pretence of friendly ends
Wind them into the easy hearted man
And hug him into snares.

Milton[62]

But while the wretched Sidney was anxious only to bury himself where all that related to the union of Selena with Dallamore might never reach his ear, his rashness inflicted on her an additional weight of anguish which for a time nearly equalled the overwhelming load that had so entirely overthrown his manly spirit.

She was indeed under the roof with Dallamore who tho' emancipated from his late worthless companions was yet in fact severely suffering from the consequences of his fatal connexion with the abandoned Lady Harriet and the profligate Mr. Rainsford. Unable to enter France they had kept the deluded Dallamore in perpetual motion by still holding out this or some other ridiculous project to his imagination until they reached Frankfort; as it was their interest as much as possible to exclude from his mind all lively remembrances of what he had left in England they had studiously tho' secretly kept him at a distance from the society of such of his compatriots as were at that time abroad. But on the day after their arrival at Frankfort as they were sitting at dinner a servant entered and presented Sir William Johnson and Captain Rowley's compliments to Mr. Rainsford with a request that he might give them leave to wait upon him.

Suppressing his discontent Rainsford returned a polite reply signifying his intention of calling himself at their hotel by which he hoped to avoid their intrusion. But Dallamore ever fond of novelty, and already heartily weary of his companions with eagerness desired that they might immediately be invited to join their party. Lady Harriet in vain objected. Open opposition had ever upon Dallamore the precise contrary effect to that which it desired.

Rainsford had often foreboded that the illtemper which Lady Harriet in spite of herself so frequently testified would in the end defeat her projects and thinking it now high time for him to interpose assured Lord Mount Villars that he would find not the smallest pleasure in the addition of two such stupid old fellows, as he might be convinced if he chose to accompany him to visit them, declaring that he wished with all his heart that he could depute him to go in his place. Rainsford hoped by this to satisfy him for the present and that by entertaining him in other ways he might be able to make him forget the unfortunate intrusion of those two young men who from their shewy attractive manners and wild dispositions he well knew were exactly calculated to ensnare Lord Mount Villars, which he had indeed no doubt was their aim in this impertinent self introduction.

---

[62]   Milton's *Comus* (1634), lines 537–8 ("many wicked" should be "guileful"), 160, and 164–5 ("them" should be "me").

But Dallamore with impatient and pertinacious eagerness at every proposal that was devised by Rainsford for delay perpetually repeated, "Well but come first to these men," or, "I'll be hanged if I do any thing till you come and see your friends."

Despairing of satisfying him by any other means Rainsford with apparent cheerfulness at length consented to accompany him and conducted him (fearless of detection from the heedless Dallamore) to an hotel at the opposite side of the town from that to which the servant had directed him in his presence.

Here upon enquiring for the persons who had kindled such an obstinate and totally unaccountable curiosity they were informed by a man previously sent thither for that purpose by Rainsford, that the gentlemen had quitted the town some hours before.

Nothing could exceed Dallamore's disappointment. He iterated with the most tiresome sameness his reproaches to Rainsford for his delays, and was not to be aroused from this unfortunate subject by all the subtleties of his companions, nor in any degree to be contented till they readily agreed to the idea which on a sudden violently laid hold upon his fancy that they should pursue these fugitives whom as he said there could be no difficulty in tracing.

Pleased at the proposal which completely restored him to good humour Rainsford listened with apparent patience for the remainder of the evening to the various conjectures and absurd plans relative to their pursuit, on which he now delighted to expatiate. All things were arranged for their leaving Frankfurt at day break but Rainsford resolved not to awaken him until he had met Sir William and his friend at nine o'clock the next morning as he had secretly appointed fearful of any farther intrusion and wishing to ascertain what was their route that he might take care and not unfortunately clash with them in future.

He was well assured that he had nothing to apprehend from the voluntary early rising of his intended dupe who was with the utmost difficulty ever prevailed upon to quit his bed before noon.

But Dallamore on this occasion seemed to be urged with an almost supernatural impulse.

All his dreams were of his two countrymen whom he had thus been prevented from seeing and in spite of Lady Harriet's efforts he ordered the carriages and would have set off at ten o'clock had it not been for the provoking absence of Rainsford for which he could not account.

However upon Lady Harriet's suggesting the probability of his having gone to enquire the route which Sir William had taken, he instantly espoused the idea and was not to be any longer detained from following his example—tho' it was a precaution which he had himself never once before this had thought of the necessity of taking.

As he strolled indolently along the streets, hardly conscious of his own design and watching the bounding swiftness of Rollo his constant companion, he suffered himself to be led by the sportive direction of his favourite in his perambulations which tho' apparently more sober were in fact determined as little by any fixed purpose.

On a sudden his frolicsome guide eagerly springing forward darted into a court yard and by his barking and demonstrations of the most lively joy induced Dallamore to hasten his pursuit, who immediately perceived Rainsford engaged in conversation and apparently taking leave of two handsome gay looking young men whose air and dress indisputably announced them to be English men of fashion.

"Ho ho! Rainsford!" cried Dallamore quickly advancing, convinced at once that he had discovered the object of his search, "So you have found out your friends I think."

Rainsford excessively annoyed and somewhat embarrassed was preparing his reply and yet considering if it were possible to avoid the introduction which he saw was on both sides anticipated with pleasure and impatience. In the mean time while for an instant he hesitated Rollo (whom his constant caresses had been accustomed to encourage to familiarity and grateful affection) continued somewhat roughly to jump upon him, and gifted with as little discernment and discretion as his master neither perceived that this was an unpropitious moment for testifying his satisfaction, nor that by those sincere testimonies he very liberally communicated to the white waistcoat and new leather breeches of his friend Rainsford a large portion of the mud which he had collected in his wild gambols thro' the streets.

Provoked at the detection which the innocent Rollo had unwittingly caused, and teazed by his rude endearments into a moment of forgetfulness and ungovernable ill-temper, Rainsford seemed suddenly to send all his spite into the foot which directed so severe a kick to the fawning favourite that he ran piteously howling to his master and crawling on the ground looked up in his face as if to complain of the insult, and to shew the full extent of what he had suffered opened his jaws covered as they were with blood by the unlucky blow.

Those who had seen Dallamore in that habitual languor and placid indolence with which his love of ease and dread of all exertion usually inclined him to yield with suavity to every companion, never could imagine the violence of those sudden starts of irresistible fury with which he was at times seized. A paleness more horrible than that of death instantly overspread his face, his livid lips quivered while gasping for utterance, fires seemed to flash from his distorted eyes and his whole frame trembled with the most frightful agitation.

Rushing with [the] rapidity of lightning upon Rainsford he seized him by the throat and when able to articulate uttered a torrent of abusive epithets mingled with curses too horrible for repetition and all these absurdities which the delirium of passion is so ready to supply, swearing that on his knees he should demand Rollo's pardon with a thousand other threats equally ridiculous and calculated to inspire laughter, were it not for the shocking frenzy by which they were accompanied.

The spectators assisted by Sir William and his companion at length succeeded in separating them, but while he struggled in their arms, and felt himself restrained from inflicting a part of the revenge for which he so much desired, no symptom of returning reason could prevent him from descending to the weaker demonstrations of Billingsgate fury.[63]

At length Sir William prevailed upon Rainsford to retire with him who literally kicked, spit upon, and insulted by the grossest abuse was at the moment cool enough to deplore nothing with so much inconsolable regret as the absolute impossibility which he at once perceived of escaping a duel with Lord Mount Villars, such a scene having taken place before so many witnesses and above all his two young countrymen as he was obliged to resent or submit to eternal ignominy and the future insults of every brutal coward.

With too much justice did he secretly curse the hard laws of false honour, which render it necessary for a man to expose his own life because he has already suffered an injury, and the greater that injury the more impossible do they pronounce it to escape the dangerous hazard.

Many a time, while his friend Sir William was in silence considering how he could avoid making these offers of service he would on such an occasion naturally expect, did the dark mind of Rainsford meditate the assassination of Dallamore and his own flight and as often did the recollection of the present destitute condition of his purse, by precluding the possibility of hasty escape terrify him with the horrors of ignominious death.

Mean while Captain Rowly giving both the slip and publickly declaiming that he was not at all surprised that Lord Mount Villars should have been highly provoked at an action at once so rude and so savage, considering the dog was known to be such a favourite, resolved to secure this opportunity of cultivating what he hoped would prove a most useful acquisition to himself and following his Lordship into the apartment to which they had hurried him by appearing to take part in his resentment he at length in some degree soothed the fury which had indeed began to subside from the moment that its detested object had been removed from his sight.

After some time Captain Rowly invited him to adjourn with him to another Hotel, that they might avoid the crowd which curiosity had already gathered around them, expressing his extreme regret at the disagreeable circumstances that had attended their first introduction and assuring Lord Mount Villars of his anxious desire to accommodate matters if possible amicably, or at all events to give him every assistance of which it was too probable he might stand in need since it was hardly to be expected that Mr. Rainsford would silently suffer the affair thus to rest.

Still violently agitated by the tempest which had with such unexpected vehemence shook his soul Dallamore tacitly followed the guidance of his new counsellor for some time, but at length suddenly recollecting himself he declared that he must go back "to tell Lady Harriet what had past, for fear the rascal should return before him and be received again under the same roof."

---

[63] Billingsgate fury: scurrilous vituperation, violent abuse; the fishmarket near Billingsgate was noted for vituperative language (OED).

Captain Rowly continued to hint that honour and delicacy both required that the affair should be kept secret from the lady, at least till they could assure her that every thing was peaceably over and that to alarm her might be judged by some in a manner the most unpleasant. He however trusted that the business would be settled without affording just cause for her Ladyship's fears and in the mean time requested permission to wait on him to his hotel and to be introduced to Lady Harriet.

Dallamore readily assented and her Ladyship after expressing some surprise at his long absence and making a few enquiries for Rainsford was satisfied for the present by the easy and insinuating answers of the young man who immediately engrossed her whole attention and whom she received with the utmost graciousness.

But Dallamore full of his own quarrel, bore with a manifest impatience this trifling conversation, and Rowly perceiving that his secret was every instant ready to burst from his lips at length proposed to shew him an English horse which he wished to dispose of [&] on this pretence retired with him to another apartment, after receiving with a smile and a glance of infinite meaning her Ladyship's facile permission to hope that he should again be permitted to present himself to her gracious presence.

Dallamore tho' somewhat ashamed of his own conduct was in no disposition to accede to any solicitations for reconciliation even could they have been made and far less to think of offering the slightest apology. Indeed he was himself eager to prevent Rainsford by sending a challenge. But while Captain Rowly was representing to him how little this could be justified, their debate was interrupted by the entrance of a servant introducing Sir William Johnson, who almost started upon discovering Rowly thus established as the confidential friend of the young Earl. A movement of resentment mingled instantly with his envy at his having thus supplanted him in the post which those fashionable swindlers had previously agreed to share together, and this could with difficulty be disguised, or give him leave with his accustomed assurance to announce that he came on the part of Mr. Rainsford from whom he presented the expected billet desiring him to name his time and place for their meeting.

Dallamore impatiently started up and pointing to his pistols declared that he was ready in person to give him the only answer he should ever again receive from him. Captain Rowly interposed, but in vain—and Sir William desiring an hour in order that his friend might have the time to settle some business of consequence, appointed as the place of their rendezvous a retired garden on the banks of the river Nid which tho' only a few miles distance from Frankfort was yet belonging to the little city; [blank] and this was selected as being in a territory subject to the state of Montz, a circumstance which the seconds thought advisable as it might facilitate an escape which the troublesome interference of government it was too probable might render necessary for one of the parties.

Nothing could be more unfavourable for the friendly offices which might serve to compromise the business than the ill terms upon which the seconds now stood towards each other and a few faint suggestions on the part of Sir William for its termination in an amicable manner having been hastily rejected by Lord Mount Villars the ground was measured and shots were mutually exchanged.

Dallamore's passed at a harmless distance, but Rainsford better practised in the horrible science of murder levelled his arm with such justice that the ball entered his adversary's breast and passing thro' his body without injury to his shoulder or reaching any vital part, saved him the painful operation of extraction.

As he instantly fell apparently lifeless Rainsford without waiting for the exhortations of Sir William, or the opinion of the surgeon prudently mounted the horse he had prepared and was out of sight in a moment, a precaution which his second thought it advisable also to adopt for the preservation of his liberty leaving the fainting Lord Mount Villars to the care of Captain Rowly who with some self reproaches and much uneasiness saw himself (as he certainly might have foreseen) in a situation the most disagreeable and indeed the most dangerous in the case of the death of the unfortunate young man whom he held in his arms before he could testify his innocence.

But having procured the assistance of the surgeon who had been ordered to wait at some distance, he was in a few minutes relieved from his fears by his assurance that Lord Mount Villars was not (at least for the present) in danger and that if unattended with fever, the wound would even probably prove of little consequence. Apprehensive however of being put under arrest till Dallamore's recovery he committed him into the charge of the surgeon and his servants and retired to some distance from Frankfort, intending to return thither in a few days if he should hear that the Earl was pronounced out of danger.

Chapter XV

But evil on itself shall back recoil

Comus[64]

Terrified at her situation, irritated by the imprudent conduct of Rainsford and eager to engage Dallamore by will to provide for her future interest, Lady Harriet was obliged to disguise all her own ill-temper while she undertook the new and strange employment of nurse-tender.

Affecting the utmost concern for the safety of her patient, she listened to the abuse of Rainsford with which he continued almost perpetually to entertain her and in which he required and obtained her assent and assistance.

She had however in a short time the consolation of hearing from Rainsford and being able to communicate to him the intelligence so satisfactory to them both that he might return to Frankfort without fear. His loss had indeed most grievously afflicted her; not only from the injury it might be to her schemes, but from the personal regret she felt from his absence in circumstances so vexatious. He had actually acquired over her mind as much influence as can ever be produced by a

---

[64] Milton's *Comus* (1634), line 593.

connexion so profligate, so totally destitute of all mutual esteem, all delicacy of tenderness, and tho' she despaired of being able again to profit by that ascendency which he had persuaded her his talents had given him unboundedly over Lord Mount Villars, she was yet secretly determined not to relinquish his society.

The surgeons had prohibited Dallamore from leaving his bed and recommended the utmost quietness and abstinence.

The former part of these prescriptions Lady Harriet enforced with all her power and tho' careless of the protraction of a confinement she had no inclination to abridge she opposed not the indulgencies which his appetite required she yet strictly and with every persuasion of affected solicitude restrained him from that liberty for which his restless disposition so much languished. She was sensible that his recovery must destroy that security with which she could now that he was a prisoner enjoy the presence of the man to whom she pretended so much resentment and detestation during those hours that she with such reluctance sacrificed to her irksome attendance on Dallamore while with impatience she anticipated those more pleasurable moments which she could devote to the object of all this real and counterfeited aversion whom she had retained concealed in her own apartments.

She had one evening retired earlier than usual from the chamber of Dallamore. At his desire she had taken up a volume of one of those modern works which under the announced character of romance, are intended to convey the principles of the most pernicious tendency and disquisitions of the most profound and stupid ignorance.

Wearied by the dullness of the metaphysics which he could not comprehend and to which he listened with as little interest as tho' it had been the most stupid homily that ever churchman pened or Kirkman spoke, Dallamore was quickly lulled into the most composing slumbers.

No sooner did Lady Harriet perceive this than taking advantage of her unexpectedly anticipated liberty she hastened to make herself merry with Rainsford upon the happy effects produced by the soporiferous pages which she desired him to kiss with gratitude.

At an early hour the following morning Dallamore awoke, and surprised at finding himself alone and the chamber totally dark endeavoured for some time to compose himself again to sleep. In this he however could not succeed and pulling his bell with a sudden jerk he deprived himself for that time of its assistance.

Having waited with considerable patience for the entrance of his attendants, and feeling himself quite stout and heartily wearied of his confinement, he at length arose and opened his windows. The sun was already high, and putting on his dressing gown he went into the adjoining apartment where his servant had slept during his illness, but he was now risen and was gone to amuse himself till summoned by his Lord's bell as Dallamore had rightly imagined from his having called in vain to know the hour.

Prompted by the desire of affording Lady Harriet an agreeable surprise (ever a favourite motive with him for many an absurd and unlucky enterprise) he now proceeded to her dressing room where he had no doubt of finding her at her solitary breakfast; But if to produce an agreeable surprise was now indeed his object it may [be] confidently affirmed never was design more completely and miserably defeated. Yet the consternation and astonishment which his sudden appearance excited could not surpass that which Dallamore himself felt as he cast a glance of rage and horror upon the very being who had so powerfully filled his distempered fancy with a more than rational abhorrence, without the possibility of doubting that this was the intimate and chosen companion of the deceitful woman who had professed for him a passion so exclusive and had affected so ardently to participate in his resentment.

Unfortunately in a moment so critical his eye rested on the pistols which Rainsford had placed on the pier table and seizing one of them without uttering a word instantly fired it in the face of the wretched Rainsford as he stepped forward to discharge the other, having followed his example in instantly seizing the instrument of death, but felt at the same moment that his ball grazed the shoulder of Dallamore.

The shrieks of Lady Harriet and the horrible exclamations of the agonizing Rainsford quickly brought together the whole house, but as all were inclined to favour the generous young Nobleman who had been so treacherously treated his escape was effected before the arrival of the officers of justice, by the advice and assistance of his Valet de place an active intelligent lad who filled the station from which Le Roi had been excused during his Lord's expedition, which being intended for France Le Roi as an emigrant was afraid to undertake.

Wilhelm, who was well assured that the risk which Lord Mount Villars now ran by the incessant and extreme speed with which he travelled, was infinitely greater than what he might incur by delay, even if they were indeed pursued, often urged him to consider his health and take some repose, but Dallamore who had no dread but that of again beholding the hateful faces of his former companions, and no desire so strong as to tell his injuries to the artless and tender Selena and to receive her sympathy, would listen to no prudent representations but embarking at Hambourg in a high fever had been more than once delirious before he reached the magnificent palace which had been taken and embellished for the reception of the young Countess of Mount Villars in Arlington Street.

Le Roi inexpressibly shocked at the apparent situation of his master eagerly exclaimed as he assisted him from the chaise, "Oh my Lord what is the matter?"

The voice of sincere affection scarcely ever fails of penetrating the heart. Dallamore contrary to that silent reserve with which he usually conducted himself towards his domestics, now gave vent to all the indignation which still boiled in his bosom against Lady Harriet and her worthy associate. This reserve had indeed proceeded neither from pride nor a principle of supposed propriety, but merely from a want of that exertion which is at the first always necessary to encourage the freedom of such well taught attendants as he had been ever accustomed to have about his person.

The true interest which Le Roi felt in the situation of his master now broke thro' that respectful distance which he had always maintained, and the eagerness of his enquiries, and the hearty reproaches he bestowed upon the worthless beings who had so injured and deceived his Lord gave him so much influence over his irritated mind that he submitted to his entreaties that he should go to bed, and on the arrival of the surgeon for whom Le Roi had sent without delay, the possibility of Lord Mount Villars pursuing his journey to Hillbarton was declared for the present absolutely out of the question.

Le Roi who had already heard the reports of Selena's proposed marriage with Sidney, secretly trembled for the effects this intelligence must produce while he endeavoured to sooth his master who incessantly and impatiently harassed him with enquiries respecting both, which Le Roi scrupled not to answer with more regard to prudence than to truth.

Having taken every precaution to exclude from his master's chamber all whom he had not previously cautioned, his vexation may easily be conceived, when he beheld the very individual whose admission he would have been justly most anxious to prevent, having out-argued the porter, and forced his way by dint of perseverence, now actually posted at his side and besieging him with every interrogation which his curiosity could suggest in spite of the discouraging monosyllables that he received in reply.

Le Roi no sooner cast his eye on Mr. Leeson than he foreboded the agitating eclaircisement which would ensue, but venturing to approach his ear softly acquainted him that the surgeon had positively forbid his Lord to be disturbed by conversation.

With a redundancy of words Mr. Leeson commended his discreet solicitude but seemed by no means inclined to quit his post, and in the hope of disposing Lord Mount Villars to a more free communication he most liberally imparted to him the various reports which had been circulated concerning him during his absence.

In vain were all the significant shrugs and grimaces of the provoked and terrified Le Roi; he resolutely proceeded in his self delighting harangue to which the taciturnity of his patient auditor for a while afforded him no interruption.

But no sooner had he alluded to the successful passion of Sidney, and hinted that he was at present with Selena at Richmond than starting up with fury Lord Mount Villars exclaimed that it was an infernal lie, fiercely demanding from the astonished little orator "how he dared to utter such abominable falsehoods?" Perceiving Le Roi who wished if possible to interpose he impetuously ordered him instantly to send for horses that he might himself fly to Richmond and detect the scoundrel swearing that he would cut off his ears on his return.

Once more Le Roi endeavoured to repair the mischief entreating his master to be calm and not listen to such nonsense, while by signs and whispers he would have urged Mr. Leeson to retire assuring him that, "My Lord's life depended upon his being now kept quiet."

Not a little displeased at the freedom of speech into which the roused zeal of Le Roi had hurried him, and being possessed of nearly as little discretion as Dallamore himself, Mr. Leeson with some warmth desired the officious Le Roi to hold his tongue and then assured his Lord that "what he had told him was very far from being a falsehood, that he had it from the very best authority that Mr. Miltern had taken a house at Richmond, and that his sister and Mr. Sidney were either actually married or only waited till the settlements should be drawn."

He would have continued to corroborate his pleasing intelligence by a thousand testimonies, but Lord Mount Villars in a paroxysm of rage finding himself without strength to move, roughly gave orders to Le Roi to kick out that lying rascal, orders with which the perplexed and irritated Le Roi might perhaps have felt well disposed to comply had not Mr. Leeson saved him the trouble by a precipitate retreat.

No sooner had he vanished than Dallamore in spite of the vague and hesitating assurances of Le Roi, felt the information which he had just received with such resentment so powerfully lay hold of his mind that no persuasion could avail and in the absolute delirium of an ardent fever and so weak that he was unable to support himself to the chaise, he insisted upon being carried that afternoon to Richmond.

Nothing could exceed the surprise and distress of Mr. Bently when he saw arrive at his house in so terrible a situation this strange and imprudent young man to whose generous friendship he considered his family to owe so much grateful regard.

Le Roi declared to him in a few words the purport of his Lord's visit, which his own incoherent language could never have explained.

It was with the utmost difficulty that Mr. Bently could prevail upon him to go to bed, and perceiving that his wound required the immediate assistance of the surgeon he thought it necessary to send an express to town to induce Mr. R—- if possible to attend his patient there whom he pronounced it absolutely death at present to remove.

Nevertheless Dallamore continued in the most violent manner to rave for Sidney and Selena, declaring he must seek them at Hillbarton and would pursue them to the extremity of the earth nor ever rest a single night until he had found them. Nor could Mr. Bently's assurances satisfy him that they were not married, nor even together until he at length thought it well to confess that he knew of Selena's retreat and that if he would consent to remain there quietly and submit to what was absolutely necessary for the preservation of his life, he had no doubt she would visit him and declare herself that she had formed no new engagements.

This had instantly the desired effect, and yielding himself up to the direction of Mr. Bently exhausted nature no longer buoyed up by the tide of his impulsive passions sunk at once into a kind of torpid insensibility and resisted not the effects of the composing draught administered by Mr. Bently.

Satisfied with his present state he now left him under the watchful care of Le Roi and hastened to inform Selena of what had passed, assuring her that the life of Lord Mount Villars already in extreme danger could not without a miracle be saved should he now undertake another journey and that he could not answer it to himself not to employ every means in his power to preserve this rash and unfortunate young man from the destruction which threatened his imprudence.

Selena inexpressibly shocked, hesitated not a moment in acquitting Mr. Bently for this apparent breach of confidence towards her, and to approve of all that he had hitherto done. She then in a faultering voice asked him what conduct he should now advise her to adopt.

"My dear Madam," replied he, "thus called upon I must freely declare that independent of your doubtful duties, humanity demands from you that you should by your presence afford that temporary relief to his disturbed mind which seems absolutely necessary to his life. Satisfy him for the present, the safety of those so justly dear to you cannot be menaced by your meeting him and when he is capable of listening to reason we may be able either to persuade him peaceably to relinquish his claims, or you may avoid his persecution by concealment according to your first intentions. I promise you my assistance and every effort in my power to reconcile those unfortunate differences."

The internal monitor within the bosom of Selena had from the first instant decidedly pronounced sentence and left her not in doubt as to the part she was to act, but her heart shrunk from the painful exertion and remembered the promise which she had passed to Sidney. She was indeed aware that the unexpected circumstance which now required her attendance upon him who claimed her plighted duty, must have acquitted her of her promise to avoid his presence, had this promise been even more unconditional than her cautious prudence had on this occasion dictated. She was also assured that Sidney himself, generous and tender-hearted would not oppose the dictates of humanity nor refuse his consent to what Mr. Bently proposed for the relief of the unhappy Dallamore. But still the anticipation of future contests and the dread of Sidney's uneasiness if he should hear, as he too probably might, of the step she was about to take before she could explain to him her reasons for it, filled her with a terror and anguish which she could scarce suppress or disguise. Nevertheless Mr. Bently had no necessity to urge her decision, and in spite of every feeling she delayed not the performance of a duty which she thought the most painful that had ever yet been imposed upon her gentle and oft afflicted heart.

In a few words she declared her readiness immediately to attend him and then hastened to acquaint her sister with what had passed and the necessity of their instant removal. Clara who was convinced that Mr. Bently either deceived or deceiving had magnified the danger of Dallamore, would warmly have opposed a resolution which she foresaw would render the deliverance of Selena from his unjust caprices only still more difficult, but gently stopping her mouth Selena entreated her to spare them both an argument so distressing since it was impossible for her to act otherwise than what she had now resolved upon and then entreating her to prepare for their accompanying Mr. Bently without delay she returned to him that she might enquire for Edwin and caution him not to mention his accident before Clara, delicately accounting for this caution by representing her weak state of health and her dread of agitating her nerves.

Mr. Bently promised to be on his guard and told Selena that he had himself concealed from his family all the shocking circumstances of this event which they believed merely accidental, and he said that Edwin appeared so much composed that he hoped his delirium was not occasioned by the wound on his head as he had at first feared and then added with an encouraging voice, "With your assistance I hope I shall be able to perform wonders on both my patients."

With a faint smile Selena expressed her wishes that her presence might indeed contribute to aid his benevolent exertions, but could not at the same time avoid confessing her fears lest the sight of her at such a moment and the questions which Lord Mount Villars might require her to answer would not prove favourable to his tranquility.

Mr. Bently reassured her by declaring that he must not allow of any conversation which could prove in the least degree agitating.

When they reached the farm Mr. Bently brought his guests immediately to the apartment he had ordered to be prepared for them, saying that he was sure they would as yet dispense with an introduction to his family; it was a small but pleasant chamber fitted up with simplicity and that cheerful union of neatness and comfort which especially on a first impression has most assuredly an influence upon the spirits.

Clara at once felt at home and tho' Selena was much too agitated to observe the objects by which she was surrounded, yet insensibly there can be no doubt she thence felt less unhappy than if she had been placed in a dark and dirty apartment.

Leaving Selena to prepare herself for the intended interview Mr. Bently returned to Lord Mount Villars whom he found wildly contending with Le Roi while he demanded his cloaths insisting that he was[65] well enough to rise and follow Mr. Bently who Le Roi assured him was really gone for Selena.

"Is she come?" exclaimed he on his entrance. "Where is Selena? Did you tell her what a cursed way I am in, and that it is not my fault that I ever left her?"

"Patience my good sir," interrupted Mr. Bently, "she is here but I shall not permit her to visit you unless you prove to me that you better remember the silence and composure that you have promised."

"Oh I will do whatever you would have me, if you will but bring me Selena, and let me hear her say all that rascal Leeson said about Sidney was only a pack of lies."

"Her coming here is a sufficient proof of its falsehood and give me leave to say my young friend, that considering all things you should rather begin with some apologies for your own conduct than what she may naturally think an indelicate allusion to the malicious reports to which by your desertion of her she has been so long so cruelly exposed."

Dallamore was eagerly beginning to justify his actions by the declaration of his intentions but Mr. Bently again stopped him saying,

---

[65]   MS: "wall" (my correction).

"Well, well this is no time for explanations on either side, we must think of nothing now but to get you stout again, and prevent you from feeling hereafter the consequences of that ugly wound and your own rashness. Will you see the young lady, and promise not to agitate her or yourself for the present by any conversation but such as I will allow to attend those affectionate salutations which she has generously consented to receive and bestow?"

No sooner was Dallamore satisfied that Selena was actually waiting for admission to his chamber than all his jealous apprehensions of Sidney having subsided, he began to feel a degree of embarrassment at the thoughts of thus meeting after an absence on his part so strangely prolonged, her who in spite of all his self justifications he was secretly fearful might reproach him for neglect to herself and insult to her brother.

Perhaps more from an unconscious wish of delaying that interview which to the imminent hazard of his life he had just sought with such eagerness, than from any delicate ideas of propriety, he now so earnestly insisted upon being suffered to rise in order to receive Selena that Mr. Bently at length tho' with reluctance consented, thinking the contest more prejudicial than the exertion.

He was however unable himself to rise, or to bear being lifted and after two or three ineffectual struggles abruptly and somewhat peevishly desired Le Roi to let him alone and sinking into gloomy silence Mr. Bently who guessed the awkward apprehensions which had now taken possession of his mind thought it better to put an end to a distress which must only encrease by delay and which was in fact instantly and totally dispelled by the appearance of Selena, who on the first summons entered with that placid and gentle grace which he had ever seen her wear and by which her beautiful image had never entirely ceased to captivate his remembrance even in the midst of the mad roar of profligacy and of folly into which he had been enticed.

On her serene brow and in that mild smile of angelic tranquility were yet visible the more than human assistance and consolation which she had indeed received, while with resignation and pious confidence she had prepared herself for an interview so long the object of all her terror and now attended with every doubtful every agitating concomitant.

Approaching his bed she offered him her hand which he pressed to his lips not without some strange emotions of tenderness and sensibility, while shocked at the inconceivable alteration that illness had made in his countenance she could with difficulty utter some expressions of the sincerest concern for his situation.

"Oh never mind Selena. Do not be at all uneasy about it, I shall be quite well now if you will stay with me and let me hear you sing. What do you think, I got the prettiest music for you that ever you heard, of some german opera I forgot the name, and after all I left Frankfort in such a cursed fuss that we were obliged to forget every thing behind us. But it was all Rainsford's fault and that infernal b-- Lady Harriet's. Come sit down here beside me till I tell you how it was and all about what Leeson said too."

"No, no I will have no histories at present," said Mr. Bently observing the distress of Selena, who looked with mingled horror and compassion on the thoughtless unconcern which yet so strongly marked his character even at a time she felt his situation so awfully dangerous.

But the arrival of the surgeon relieved her from the necessity of reply and she was suffered without opposition to retire upon her assurance that she had accepted Mr. Bently's hospitality and was ready to return to him whenever he desired her attendance.

She had now leisure to reflect on those gentle precautions, those delicate cares which others so dearly connected to her heart should next require from her in those painful communications which it was her severe task to make.

She was to account to Sidney for her conduct and prepare him for the total and peaceable relinquishment of those hopes that he still persisted to cherish, since she too certainly foresaw that the circumstances which had in spite of herself thus reunited her to the long absent Dallamore would prevent the possibility of his ever resigning except with life those claims which she was now constrained apparently to sanction. She knew not where to find Sidney and had therefore sufficient time to meditate that letter which Sidney was alas! never fated to receive.

Nor was it alone to him that she was to justify the part she had now acted. The man who above all others upon earth had most outraged and wronged her brother was at present received into the house of one of his dearest friends, under the same roof with the woman he adored, and was attended and forgiven by the sister to whom he was so tenderly attached and from whom he had been so anxious forever to separate him. Selena was also sensible that the bar which Dallamore's reception at Bently's farm must unavoidably place to his enjoying for some time that society in which he so much delighted would tho' perhaps unconsciously render it more difficult for her to reconcile him to her conduct. She dreaded his displeasure— she dreaded yet more the despair of Sidney—but she could not repent of having followed the dictates of her best judgment.

There was yet another duty which it was more immediately necessary for her to fulfill. Clara was now in the house with Edwin and it was not possible to suppose that this could be long a secret from her. Selena therefore in the tenderest manner acquainted her with every circumstance attending his residence there except that the event which had occasioned it was the consequence of an horrible and voluntary crime. At the same time she gently and delicately cautioned her lest the too warm feelings of her sensible heart should betray her into expressions which by the eye of strangers might be misinterpreted.

Consoled by Selena's assurances (in whose undeviating truth she placed a confidence that nothing could weaken) that Mr. Bently considered him not in danger Clara experienced an unacknowledged but delicious satisfaction in being thus once more sheltered by the same roof with Edwin and her heart already anticipated for him a thousand blessings in the friendly guidance of their benevolent host.

The night was by this time far advanced, poor Sidney unconscious as yet of the events which had taken place since he left Richmond, was just laid down to seek a few hours repose at Ibbson's hotel, when Selena having heard from Mr. Bently that Dallamore was satisfied in being told she had retired for the night, composed herself by the side of her sister and having recommended to the protection and comfort of Heaven those who were most dear to her she resigned herself and her sorrows to the sweet influence of these silent balmy dews which Innocence sheds upon the wearied eyelids of affliction.

Chapter XVI

> Where such grace
> The soul of beauty? where such winning charms?
> Where such a soft divinity of goodness?
> Such faith, such pity, tenderness unequalled?
> Such all that Heaven can give.
>   Thompson[66]

For some succeeding days the situation of Dallamore wore no visible alteration. His fever continued but he had no delirium and tho' he could hardly be restrained from incessantly repeating to Selena his complaints of the injuries he had received from Lady Harriet, yet his conversation was not more wild than she had been accustomed to hear from him in the uncontrolled hours of health. Amidst all his misfortunes there was nothing he seemed so perpetually to lament and with so much inconsolable vexation as the loss of the music of Mozart's beautiful opera which had charmed him so highly at Frankfort, and which even then to the no small provocation of Lady Harriet he had avowedly anticipated the delight of hearing Selena play.

Nothing could induce him to silence but the magic of Selena's harp, which to gratify his earnest desire she had been advised to have placed in the adjoining room and this she scarcely quitted except during the hours necessary for refreshment.

Never was mortal gifted by nature in so eminent a degree with the talents and dispositions necessary for a nurse as the young and lovely Selena—patient, calm, quiet, unmindful of herself, regardless of trouble, unterrified by danger and keenly feeling for others—contented in tedious solitude, cheerful in calamity, quick to foresee and dextrous to obviate any difficulty her native handiness and courage had served a painful but well rewarded apprenticeship in her attendance upon Lady Trevallyn, and she was now again ready to sacrifice herself and forget her selfish anxieties in those cares and pious offices which duty and compassion alike required for Dallamore.

---

[66] Edward in James Thomson's *Edward and Eleonora* (1739), 3.5.83–7 ("pity" should be "love" in line 86).

She had as yet seen but little of any of the family except Mr. Bently; Judging that the presence of so many strangers to whom she might feel it necessary to make apologies and express gratitude must be oppressive at such a time, he had himself encouraged her to decline joining the domestick circle which was however rendered exquisitely captivating to Clara, whose warm and affectionate disposition ever susceptible of tender impressions was ready to hail them all and the gentle Ophelia in particular as the sisters of her heart while as may well be imagined she shared with them in all their carefully benevolent attentions for the accommodation as well of Edwin as of their noble patient.

Mr. Bently had prudently disguised not only from them but from Edwin himself that any suspicions had been entertained that this accident which had so nearly proved fatal had been caused by any thing more dreadful than intoxication and Edwin softened and humbled by the kindness which he felt to have so little merited received it with grateful tenderness. To account for the little time which he could now devote to him, and to amuse his mind which he saw more indisposed than his body Mr. Bently related to him the singular circumstances which had obliged him to offer shelter at that time to other guests who like him had hitherto been personally strangers, little conceiving how deeply his hearer was interested in his narrative.

Edwin however listened to him in silence secretly assured that what he now heard was but like these temporary delusions of his fancy to which he was conscious he was occasionally subject ever since his malady occasioned by the sudden death of his parents. For even while Mr. Bently yet spoke the distant sound of Selena's harp appeared like the song of angels sent by pitying Heaven to promise future forgiveness and returning peace. Tears bathed his cheeks, the softest emotions took possession of his soul, he feared to awake from a delirium so sweet and every evil spirit seemed to fly from his couch, while like the harp of David, those magic numbers soothed and calmed his mind, seeming to recall to his remembrance as tho' repeated from the lips of Selena herself the instructions of his father, the prayers of his Mother.[67]

On the day after Selena had come to Bently farm, as soon as the family had finished their early dinner, her kind host hastened to invite her to refresh herself in the sweet breezes of that delicious afternoon which tho' the sun was yet powerful fanned the light branches of the cool colonade formed by the walks thro' the well planted shrubbery. He there communicated to her a letter which he had only just then received from her brother tho' it had been written from town two days before and manifested evidently the most extreme agitation. He told Mr. Bently "that he had learned to his inexpressible surprise the return of Lord Mount Villars, that on calling at his door he found that the just reward of his infamous association for the present secured him from all his interrogations, but that for fear of his being

---

[67] 1 Samuel 16 tells how David soothed Saul with his harp: "And it came to pass, when the evil spirit from God was upon Saul, that David took an harp, and played with his hand: so Saul was refreshed, and was well, and the evil spirit departed from him" (KJV).

troublesome to his sister he thought himself obliged to lose no time in going to Hillbarton that he might himself inform her of an event so unforseen and take her under his more immediate protection." He then requested Mr. Bently to engage a house for him in his neighbourhood to which he might carry his sisters and tho' he mentioned not Ophelia, Selena could read her name in every line of suppressed bitterness and vexation.

She saw that the kind hearted Mr. Bently shared all the uneasiness with which she looked upon the situation in which her brother now stood, all these sad terrors with which for him she anticipated the future. Her hopes for his comfort and preservation next to Heaven lay all in Sidney and in the secret appeal which her heart made to his generous friendship, his kindly active prudence; every nerve thrilled in the tender remembrance tho' no unaccountable instinct, no supernatural emotion told the tender heart that at that very instant her voice struck upon his soul with a pang of such mortal anguish as years of felicity could scarcely repay or obliterate the dreadful impression.

It was not till the following day that she received the cruel lines which that anguish had dictated. Unable to discover from whence they came, or to comprehend what intelligence had been given him or when he had heard it, she for a while suffered the most lively sorrow, as she hung upon every heart rending expression of resentment and despair, each bitter declaration of an eternal absence. And yet after some time she was enabled even from a cup so bitter to extract some salutary good. However violent was the stroke which had thus driven from her the beloved of her soul she could even now bless the hand by which they were separated, and thus had rendered her duty less difficult to be fulfilled, while at the same time it snatched him from a danger her heart had considered with such horror. She could not imagine that he would be able to conceal himself from Robert and she despaired not by these very means to remove her brother from a scene where his presence could only encrease the perplexity and distress of those to whom he was most dear.

She had now every reason momentarily to expect his return to Richmond since Mrs. Vallard would assuredly send him thither in quest of her; & tho' Selena had written to inform her of what had happened immediately on her removal to Bently farm yet she could not expect that Robert would delay at Hillbarton long enough to hear that letter, and indeed she rather rejoiced in this improbability as she wished herself to communicate to him her conduct in order that she might explain to him her motives and justify Mr. Bently for a kindness and humanity which she was but too sure Robert would on this occasion feel misplaced.

She therefore entreated her friends to watch for his approach and sending instantly for her leave them together.

Nevertheless before he reached the farm Robert had already heard from busy report a confused account of the events which had occurred there; and before he hazarded encountering Dallamore in the presence of Selena he wrote to her from Richmond a few lines to know "if it was indeed true that she had forever abandoned the amiable the deserving Sidney and chosen for the partner of her days, the seducer of her brother's wife the destroyer of his happiness—and whether he was to consider himself indeed banished for ever from her society and from that of the man whom he had wished to esteem as his more than friend, his adopted father, since he had for ever excluded him if he had indeed received into the domestic intimacy of Bently farm the villain by whom he had been so basely injured."

Selena was prepared for all this, she yet cruelly felt the bitterness of every word and in terms of the most caressing tenderness entreated him to come to her, promising that he should see none but those he loved, and that were attached to him by the warmest affection. He obeyed her summons and found her anxiously and almost fearfully watching for his arrival in the hall having left Mr. Bently to calm Lord Mount Villars in her absence which was at times a matter of no small difficulty.

Robert received her endearments with a coldness nay almost severity which struck to the gentle heart of Selena tho' she affected not to notice it, and suppressing even her tears, while she observed his eyes fill with regret as he wandered over every love-endeared spot, she entreated him to listen to her while she explained the reasons by which she had been directed.

She then in the first place painted the situation of Dallamore when he had been received by Mr. Bently and Robert who well knew the strictness of her sincerity which never suffered her to exaggerate on any occasion, with generous warmth confessed that his friend had acted well and that he had accused him unjustly since thus circumstanced he could not have refused his hospitality even to his most fatal enemy. Nay Selena beheld him touched with compassion for the misfortune of the rash being whom from his heart he forgave, tho' in the most solemn manner he declared that never again would he see him unless it were to demand satisfaction for the insult which he had received a demand which he assured the terrified Selena he meant not ever to seek opportunity to make; and that the business of his life should be to avoid him.

Selena with an aching heart looked forward to the time when she should be too deeply interested in their perfect reconciliation to omit any means for their re-union, but for the present she contented herself with this resolution and telling him that altho' the surgeons had little hopes of a very speedy restoration to strength and even feared his perpetually suffering some painful consequences of his neglected wound, yet they had declared that in a few weeks his removal would be attended with no danger, and that Dallamore ever restless impatiently expected the arrival of this period however grateful for the kindness he had here received.

She then shewed to him the letter which Sidney had written and conjured him to employ that time of necessary exile from the society of his friends, in the consolation of one so deservedly dear to them both.

Here Robert eagerly interrupted her and with all the energy of passion natural to his warm temper entreated her not to sacrifice Sidney and herself to a false and foolish scruple.

She heard him with sad but patient composure while her heart secretly exclaimed, "Oh vain waste of torturing persuasion! Oh anguish vainly roused! Have I not resisted Sidney? What arguments can now prevail?"

When he suffered her to speak she repeated to him all that she had before said to a yet more deeply interested pleader and having convinced him that it was impossible for her to give herself to Sidney without incurring the reproaches of her own heart and exposing to the whole world that shamefully disputed claim, as well as risking a life dearer to her than her own, she added the motives which had compelled her to relinquish her first design of concealing herself from Dallamore whose very existence seemed to depend upon her not adhering to this resolution. She now declared that tho' she devoted herself to his preservation, which she was decided to do even to the loss if necessary of her own health, the opinion of the world, nay the esteem of Sidney, yet she was with equal firmness resolved never to suffer Dallamore to call her his wife until by some consistency of conduct he had proved that his choice was not the transient caprice arising from the ascendency her cares had now produced over his gratitude and affection; and she added in a broken voice "until her heart had ceased thus obstinately to refuse another lord than him whom it had rebelliously chosen."

"Incomparable Selena!" cried Robert clasping her to his bosom and bathing her with his tears, "Oh why must the sins of the father be thus visited on his most perfect child?"

"Hush dear Robert," whispered she gently, "the memory of those who gave us birth is sacred, and I complain not of my lot, had I chosen it for myself I could not have ensured happiness but we can always have the satisfaction of feeling that we have not deserved our misfortunes by our ill conduct, and believe me dear Robert I have even now internally the sweetest consolation in my conviction that happiness depends not so much on outward circumstances as we are ready to imagine in the moments of disappointment. Poor Sidney I have no doubt thinks that life has lost all offered[68] enjoyment because he suffered his heart too fondly to cherish a visionary scheme of love and bliss, which, alas this world never could have given him pure. Convince him dearest Robert that he has yet left in life pleasures as well as duties—and remind him that as surely as love falls short of what it promises, so surely does Virtue promise infinitely less than she bestows."

Selena then embraced her brother and having received his solemn word that he would devote all his time and all his exertions to seek out Sidney and restore him to himself she left him to take his farewell of Ophelia and returned with an heart lightened of half its anxieties to give herself with undivided attention to those cares which Dallamore so constantly demanded.

Weariness, peevishness, nay pain and sickness seemed to fly at her approach; The medical attendants who observed with some surprise and continual admiration her patient and indefatigable assiduities with the gentle power which she possessed of charming his unquiet spirit now told her confidently that her cares

---

[68]   MS: "afford" (my correction).

were rewarded with almost assured success and that tho' the recovery of Lord Mount Villars might probably be tedious, his life could absolutely be pronounced out of danger.

He himself in spite of all his inconsistent carelessness of character was not insensible to the obligations which he owed his angelic nurse, promising never again to leave but be guided by her in every action of his life and frequently asked her with a tone of sentiment which penetrated to Selena's aching heart "could she love him, and forgive the folly of his past conduct?"

Every moment convinced her yet more strongly that nothing could now induce him to relinquish her, and tho' she could not but feel sadly anxious for the peace and safety of Sidney, while Robert's letters brought only disappointment and lamentations at his ill success in discovering his retreat, yet in general trusting that he was under the peculiar protection of Heaven Selena could rejoice that unshaken by his solicitations or his sorrows she was at liberty to pursue the difficult path allotted to her and was left to contend with no passions but her own gentle as they were by nature and subdued by reason and religion.

Mr. Bently who knew enough of Sidney to be well convinced that if Selena had ever been attached to him no earthly good could ever compensate for his loss, felt the most sensible uneasiness at the impossibility which he now foresaw of her being able peaceably to escape from Lord Mount Villars, or ever to reconcile him to the idea of yielding her up. And tho' he could not doubt that to her attendance and influence her cousin owed his life, he could not forbear at times reproaching himself for the part he had acted when he thought her happiness must be the sacrifice.

Nevertheless the even cheerfulness, the kindness, nay the pleasure with which she evidently performed all those wearisome offices which could amuse and meliorate his confinement persuaded Mr. Bently that her feelings suffered not acutely from the surrender which he saw she had made of her inclination and he was willing to believe that with the affection which she bore to Lord Mount Villars and the sweet internal consciousness of performing her duty she could even in this lot enjoy much happiness.

However as he now judged Dallamore's life in safety he thought it incumbent upon him to speak with her on this subject and taking the opportunity of her expressing her gratitude for the hospitality on which she said she thought they should not much longer trespass since Lord Mount Villars she trusted would soon be in a situation to remove without hazard, he reminded her of the promise which he had made to assist in her concealment should she think it prudent to withdraw herself, and hinted that if resolved on this measure it was expedient it should be adopted before Lord Mount Villars should remove where she could no longer with propriety afford him that attendance which he required without assuming his name and sanctioning his rights as her husband.

A mournful silence made Mr. Bently for some minutes imagine that Selena hesitated, and he was beginning to explain in what manner he thought she could best retire, and where he had projected her temporary retreat, when interrupting him with a deep sigh [she] told him that for the present at least she could not justify to herself her witholding from Lord Mount Villars any of those attentions from which he derived comfort or benefit, and that she had already written to Mrs. Vallard, who she had no doubt would if possible meet them at her nephew's house in the town when he could be carried thither. But that if her friend's health would not suffer her to undertake this journey, her own resolution was still fixed, that she had spoken to her sister who was willing to be her companion while she should pursue the conduct which she had thought it right at first to adopt.

Mr. Bently whose cool and dispassionate judgment approved of all her purpose except her declining as yet to assume the name to which he thought her now pledged, admired in secret the sacrifice to which he yet forbore to allude, convinced that the firmness of her character sought not for relief in the compassion which others might bestow upon those weaknesses over which she could so well triumph.

He only insisted upon her giving up all idea of removal until Mrs. Vallard should be able to join them in Arlington street, and indeed the very tedious recovery, and great weakness of Lord Mount Villars rendered this delay expedient and while alleging this he added with a smile, "I cannot possibly yet spare our little Clara, for she is almost as good as yourself and her attendance tho' not quite so exclusive is almost as necessary for my other patient."

Selena was surprised and perplexed. She had occasionally heard from Clara that Edwin was now sufficiently recovered to pass a part of the day in the drawing room with the family, but had no idea how much Edwin owed that recovery to the officious and friendly cares with which he had been watched and soothed by every female in the house except herself, and what influence this cheerful and innocent society had had in dispersing from his soul the gloom which dissipation ever leaves upon a sensible mind when at length aroused from its dream of folly. To Clara who had ever been his confident he had without scruple opened his whole heart, and while she shuddered with an horror that shook almost to dissolution her whole frame at his confession of a crime which had been so providentially defeated the pang was nearly compensated by the contrition which he evidenced and the detestation with which he declared he for ever renounced a society which while it had allured him with the vain promise of dissipating his sadness, had but encreased the melancholy and disorder of his fevered brain and enfeebled spirits.

From Clara he heard the particulars of Selena's present situation and learned that virtue can give a force to the gentlest heart by which it can triumph over its sensibility and enjoy peace even in the very struggle.

Mr. Bently who perceived the charm with which Edwin yielded himself unreservedly to those confidential conversations had no doubt that their attachment was lively and mutual; he had therefore urged her to exert her influence in prevailing upon Edwin to make some concessions to his uncle who languished for a reconciliation which Edwin haughtily refused to seek, his independent spirit revolting from the idea of courting the favour which might be esteemed so necessary to his interest.

The blushing Clara melted to the softest tenderness at the dear flattery so exquisitely sweet to her heart obliged, and with that delicate prevailing art which women so peculiarly possess from nature, intended as they are for the peace makers, the healers of humanity, she at length quietly induced him to blush for his past ungrateful conduct, and write a conciliating letter which was received by Lord Stanmore with all the joy of relenting affection.

He delayed not many hours to fly himself to embrace his nephew and testify his cordial forgiveness in person as well as to make acknowledgments to Mr. Bently and every individual of his family—in which the lovely and modest Clara would assuredly have been included had she not retired from his presence with conscious bashfulness.

He had however nearly spoiled all by sending to his nephew immediately after a bank note of considerable value which it was with the utmost difficulty Clara could prevent the wounded pride and delicacy of Edwin from disdainfully returning to the unintentionally offending Lord Stanmore. Occupied as Selena had been with Dallamore, and supposing Edwin to be still chiefly confined to his own room she had not interrogated her sister, and no opportunity had hitherto occurred to encourage the timid Clara to the confession from which she half reluctantly shrunk, of that intimacy with which she had received and returned the confidences of Edwin.

Selena therefore now for the first time heard of an intimacy so dangerous from Mr. Bently, who she plainly perceived considered it as the truest of acknowledged affection; and it was not without alarm that she reflected on the situation to which however involuntarily she had been the means of exposing the too susceptible Clara; With terror she thought on the rash wild character of Edwin the dissipated life into which he had on the first temptation plunged with such weakness, His constitution injured by the most cruel malady, and his own errors and follies to use no harsher word, as well as the little probability there was for happiness to the warm and feeling bosom of Clara if united to a man, over whose affections she possessed not an undoubted undisputed right.

Mr. Bently who in her speaking countenance instantly read the uneasiness with which she considered this dangerous friendship ventured to plead in Edwin's favour, assured her of his firmly purposed reformation, enumerated many instances which might prove how his mind retained all its noble sentiments and virtuous principles even while ensnared by the profligacy which he had always detested and had now for ever abjured. He even hinted at the great expectations which Edwin might justly boast as the presumtive heir to the title and estates of Lord Stanmore.

Selena who could not explain even to Mr. Bently the situation in which they stood, contented herself with saying that she hoped her sister would not rashly think of forming any engagements with one to whom so many objections might certainly be made, and that her extreme youth was a sufficient reason for her to feel distressed at the circumstances which had thus interested her for one however captivating from his manners and talents was yet assuredly not such as could be reasonably recommended by her brother or her guardian.

Mr. Bently understood the hint, and promised that he would not encourage Edwin to remain at the farm, but suffer him to depart as soon as he was satisfied he should not materially suffer by the deprivation of their society and attendance.

In the mean time Selena delayed not to question her sister as to the terms upon which she stood with her friend, and saw beyond the possibility of doubt that Clara herself "pure in the last recesses of her mind"[69] entertained no hope or idea of captivating ought but his friendship, which she indeed exulted and gloried in having obtained, while Selena could hardly persuade her to believe (or indeed make her comprehend) how such an exalted sentiment, a union so sacred could ever expose her to censure or ridicule.

At her sister's request she however promised to be more cautious in displaying an affection which she acknowledged nothing could diminish and which even now formed her greatest happiness.

Chapter XVII

> Vengeance is still alive—from her dark covert
> With all her snakes erect upon her crest
> She stalks in view.
>
> Young[70]

When the kindness of his benevolent heart and the compassion which the state of the unfortunate Edwin excited, had induced Mr. Bently to remove him to his own house he had given him the only apartment which was usually reserved for the reception of strangers, tho' his family cheerfully concentrated themselves afterwards upon the unexpected demands made on their hospitality by those whom they so much desired to serve.

Ophelia had claimed the privilege of giving up her room as the most agreeable to the lovely sisters, and the favourite saloon on a level with the lawn, where the girls had been accustomed to work and read in social enjoyment was instantly appropriated to the accommodation of Lord Mount Villars, being judged the most convenient for that purpose as it opened into another smaller apartment.

Selena had been now upwards of a month with unremitting assiduity watching the slow but gradual progress of Dallamore's recovery to whom her presence was yet every moment as necessary as on that of her first arrival. Tho' secure of his safety, the surgeons appeared themselves weary of his prolonged weakness and continual relapses while his impatient temper could scarcely be prevented from openly reproaching them with want of skill or willingly retarding his complete recovery.

---

[69] John Dryden, trans., "The Second Satyr," *The Satires of Aulus Persius Flaccus* (1693), line 133 ("her" should be "the").

[70] Isabella in Edward Young's *The Revenge* (1721), 2.1.43–5.

One afternoon that Lord Mount Villars after enduring many hours of disquietude & uneasy watchfulness had at length yielded to the influence of a composing draught, Selena who perceived him at rest advised Le Roi (exhausted as he appeared by his constant careful attendance) to retire and obtain refreshment by some hours of repose promising to call him should his master enquire for him.

Rollo the companion as he had been the unfortunate cause of his Lord's sad illness was asleep at his feet & Selena had seated herself between the curtain and the half closed window, but tho' she had taken with her a book her attention was diverted from it by the plaintive minstrelsy of the thrush who chanted his wild vespers from the laurel hedge beside the window while her eyes were fixed upon the beautifully vanishing glories of the evening sky with melancholy contemplation, while fancy soothed by the repose around formed many a tender comparison between those and the hope painted visions of Love which had faded before that impenetrable gloom that had quickly overclouded even the morning of her days. Abruptly interrupted she suddenly started upon hearing the door burst open uncautiously, and Rollo aroused by the unusual noise flew to greet the intruder somewhat roughly.

Selena had already sprung from behind the curtain but had scarce uttered the whispered Hush! when she was struck with instant terror and amazement at perceiving by the uncertain and feeble light admitted from the open door a stranger his face nearly covered with a black handkerchief and a pistol in his hand step towards the couch from whence Dallamore now started exclaiming, "Who is there Selena!"

She shrieked for at that moment the pistol was discharged close to his head—she beheld him fall—she heard his dying sigh and involuntarily rushed forward as if to save him from inevitable fate, but a second had not elapsed before the villain drawing another pistol from his bosom levelled it as Selena then imagined at her. Grasping the lifeless arm of Dallamore she sunk breathless at his feet and when she recovered found herself amidst the shrieking and affrighted family in another apartment in the arms of Mr. Bently while Edwin at her side supported in his her apparently expiring sister.

"Are you hurt? Are you wounded?" burst at once from every lip while yet speechless she gazed alternately with bewildered amazement at all that surrounded her and her own disordered dress.

Glancing her eye on the death like form of Clara the remembrance of the dreadful instant seemed to return like a terrific dream and shrieking with new horror as she stretched forth to her, her arms she exclaimed, "Oh has the villain then killed her also!" Nor was she without difficulty to be convinced, that extreme terror had alone reduced her to that situation. "But where is Dallamore?" cried she struggling as they witheld her, "Why did you take me from him? Oh let me see him again I beseech you. I am sure he is not quite gone. Let me try and revive him. Oh do not detain me."

The look of dismay, the dreadful silent pause, and the continued resistance made by Mr. Bently to her efforts convinced her that all was indeed over and a flood of tears relieved her from a second fit.

Clara at length restored to sense was the first to enquire how and what had happened eagerly renewing the oft repeated question, "Are you sure that you have not been wounded?"

But Selena was unable to reply, and remained in deep and silent horror gradually recalling each of those dread moments, marked by events so shocking to nature, so tremendously impressive to memory. In this awful pause Le Roi abruptly entered, looking round inquisitively and seeing Selena restored to life he exclaimed, "Who is the villain?"

The eyes of all equally earnest tho' with more gentle caution now seconded the important enquiry and Mr. Bently incoherently pronounced his own suspicions, "Was there indeed any villain, or did the unfortunate …."

"Yes, yes," cried Selena passionately, "but I know not the murderer, he burst in, he fired on us and Dallamore oh poor Dallamore." She could not proceed, but her hands were clasped with trembling energy while her convulsed features proclaimed to Mr. Bently the danger of pressing her as yet to speak.

Making signs therefore to Le Roi to follow him he desired his girls to persuade her to lye down and that she should be kept as quiet as possible and then withdrew to make all possible enquiries into this strange affair and take what steps he could to secure the assassin.

Mr. Bently accompanied by Clara and his family had been walking in the shrubbery adjoining the house and Edwin encouraged by the softness of the air was for the first time suffered to share their evening stroll when alarmed by the report of the pistol and Selena's horror-breathing shriek they hurried home.

Clara out ran all but found the hall door which usually lay open now closed. While she continued eagerly to ring, and call for admittance the rest of the party came up. All the men belonging to the house were out except Le Roi, who starting from his sound slumbers at length flew to the door with the female servants.

Dallamore's apartment lay open to the hall and rushing in at once they beheld a spectacle which it is no wonder proved nearly fatal to Clara, since no being however firmly nerved could look upon it without feeling chilled with sudden and terrible consternation.

Selena prostrate on the floor without sign of life yet retained her grasp of the mangled form of Dallamore as he lay extended on the sopha, while the wounded and faintly yelling Rollo licked with expiring tongue the cold and insensible hands of his fatally loving Lord. For a moment all was confusion and the screams of general horror were alone echoed thro' the chamber of death. At length Mr. Bently besought Le Roi to assist him in bearing Selena to the stronger light and freer air, declaring his hopes that she had received no injury as he could discover on her no trace of a wound.

Clara was however no longer able to hear consolation but inanimate as her sister required the same cares; But Le Roi was too soon convinced that to secure his murderer and avenge his death was the sad and only duty which he could now perform for his lamented master. Furiously looking round he called upon Wilhelm to assist him in the pursuit. Wilhelm was no where to be found and desiring the other servants to fly in every direction he himself hastened to the little lodge at the gate occupied only by an old woman. In answer to his questions she said that she had seen no one pass except Wilhelm who a few minutes before had called to her impatiently to open the gate, and had then galloped towards London on a horse which she had particularly noticed was without a saddle.

Full of the strange suspicion which this account excited Le Roi flew back in order to get a horse and if possible gain some information from Selena. Having heard her declare that she knew not the villain he informed Mr. Bently of what the old porter had said and they went together to the stable from whence they perceived that the fleetest horse had been taken and a watering bridle which Mr. Bently recollected to have seen hanging up at the stable door not many minutes before the alarm.

They now examined the pistol, which they discovered on the floor, and which (as it was so remarkably small that Dallamore might easily have had always in his dressing box) had at first suggested the idea which Mr. Bently entertained until Selena's declaration that either from accident or sudden frenzy the unhappy young man had been his own destroyer.

In spite of that declaration Mr. Bently could not avoid for a moment again resuming that suspicion when Le Roi letting it drop with astonishment exclaimed, "Merciful God it is my Lord's own pistol!" Snatching it from the ground Mr. Bently perceived that it was of remarkably nice workmanship inlaid with gold in a curious and beautiful manner but what identified it beyond a doubt, on the stock was engraved in the gold a small cornet and beneath it the initial of Lord Mount Villars's title.

But no sooner had Mr. Bently betrayed by some incoherent expressions his natural conjecture than Le Roi starting from his amazement solemnly and positively protested that his master had indeed taken those pistols abroad but that he was certain he had not brought them back with him on his return and that however extraordinary and unaccountable was such an unprovoked murder he was persuaded that it could only have been perpetrated by his german servant Wilhelm whose sudden disappearance justified the suspicion. Mr. Bently who well knew that to his fidelity and active exertions in the most critical moment Lord Mount Villars owed his escape from imprisonment at Frankfort, could not in spite of the strong presumptive evidence give any credit to the possibility of his now committing so atrocious a crime against a master who had behaved to him with the most generous gratitude and to whom he appeared to be so warmly attached. As to his disappearance he reminded Le Roi that on the first alarm occasioned by the shot he had come as it seemed from the stable yard to the hall door at the same instant with the whole affrighted party. And while he was trying to persuade the incredulous Le Roi that Wilhelm had now gone in pursuit of the real murderer, a number of breathless curious persons seen running towards the house from various directions convinced them that the alarm had already been given to the neighbourhood.

Le Roi advanced to meet them and with mutual eagerness they exchanged interrogations. Amid the general confusion Mr. Bently at length gathered that Wilhelm flying along the London road on his unsaddled horse and enquiring from all he met for a stranger whose remarkable appearance he in a few words described had raised a universal and tumultuous curiosity. But neither Mr. Bently nor Le Roi could any longer hesitate in pronouncing whom they now believed to be the assassin when all agreed in repeating Wilhelm's description of Rainsford as horribly disfigured by having lately received a shot in the lower part of his face, while they declared that such a person had been seen that morning lurking about, covered entirely except his eyes with a black silk handkerchief, and mounted on a very beautiful bay mare.

The old female porter who had joined the group now deposed that a man answering to this description had questioned her about two hours before very inquisitively respecting the family at the farm—enquiring what servants Lord Mount Villars had with him there and who attended him. She saw that he fastened his horse to a tree near the lodge on the outside and asked her leave to walk thro' the farm which was never refused. That while she was busy about something a long while after she all of a sudden heard the horse gallop off and as the gentleman had not past the gate she went out in haste thinking the horse had got loose and ran away. She however saw that he was mounted and had taken the London road, tho' she had forgotten the circumstance so much had she been some time after surprised by the precipitate flight of Wilhelm.

Le Roi desired them to describe the horse and was soon assured that it was an uncommon swift hunter which Lord Mount Villars had taken over with him and which he had often since his return heard him regret that he had given to the scoundrel Rainsford.

By the advice of Mr. Bently Le Roi now repaired immediately to the Bowstreet officers who in a few hours brought to him in Arlington street the very horse that he had so accurately described, which had been left at an hotel in Piccadilly by a lad who was easily found out and who gave oath that he had received him from a gentleman muffled in the manner already described, and who giving him a shilling desired him to leave the horse at that hotel with orders to have it taken care of till called for.

Wilhelm who had made himself conspicuous by his enquiries and his broken English was without difficulty traced to Yarmouth. He had indeed from the first moment of general suspicion not entertained a doubt that Rainsford was the murderer, which the wounded Rollo and the sight of the pistol that he instantly discovered and recognized had indisputably confirmed. The pistols he indeed too well knew—they like the horse had been the gift of his Lord to Rainsford and it was with this very pistol which now terminated his ill-fated days that Dallamore had so frightfully mangled the face of his revengeful implacable foe. In his ardour for justice the hotheaded Wilhelm was convinced that all present saw those circumstances so palpably evident to him in the same clear light with himself, and he lost not a moment in taking counsel or asking assistance for the pursuit of the wretch who he concluded must have fled to Yarmouth altho' he was able to trace him no farther than London.

Nor was he mistaken in this conjecture, for Rainsford relying on the advantage which a few hours must have given him hurried on with all possible expedition tho' not by the direct road to Yarmouth where he expected to find a vessel ready to sail. In this however he discovered that he had unfortunately miscalculated, and the tide serving one hour sooner than he had reckoned the packet had just sailed as he arrived.

Little as he now valued the life which he considered as worse than lost by the horrible wound which had been inflicted by the detested Dallamore, he yet felt the natural instinct of self preservation powerfully stimulate him to escape from an ignominious death and the avenging ministers of justice who he had no doubt were already at his heels.

Offering a large reward which he paid into the hands of a poor fisherman's wife, he with some difficulty prevailed upon him to follow the vessel still in sight, notwithstanding the high wind which blowing very hard and quite fair for the opposite coast must render a return extremely laborious nay hazardous.

They had not long embarked on their daring voyage when Wilhelm arrived, but tho' he offered madly, double the sum given by Rainsford yet the wind every moment encreasing he could not prevail upon any of the fishermen to risk their lives with him on such a pursuit.

The distress of the poor women whose sons and husbands were out in this tempest and in particular the agony of the wife of the unfortunate man whom Rainsford had bribed can only be imagined by those who have stood among them as Wilhelm then did watching from the beach at a distance the billow beaten boat, now seen and now lost while yet labouring with the black weltering waves or vainly seeking amidst the wide o'erwhelming waste for that little speck which "Eye had marked upon the gleaming main" but also

> Night heard the parted waters close
> Morn oped her pitying eye and sought that speck in vain.[71]

Wilhelm felt his humane heart so deeply interested in the scene of woe so near to him and so terrifying to those accustomed to the dangers of the sea, that he forgot even the object of his pursuit while he entirely participated in the hopes and fears of those around him until the arrival of Le Roi accompanied by the bow street officers newly aroused his grief for his master and the vexation and disappointment which he had felt on finding that his treacherous destroyer had so narrowly escaped his impetuous diligence.

---

[71]   Thomas Gisborne, "Solitude: An Ode," *Poems, Sacred and Moral* (1798), 2.2.14–16.

As there could be no doubt that the person whom they sought was actually clear of British ground the messengers of justice returned to town, but Le Roi passed the day on the beach anxiously awaiting the sight of the fisherman whose testimony he discreetly resolved to receive upon oath before a magistrate.

Towards evening the storm subsided and the wind shifting to the east many a sad heart was lightened of its load as it welcomed the return of all those joys which the greedy waves had nearly devoured.

But no such rapturous moment rewarded the anxious terrors of the disconsolate mourner who cursed the bitterly earned reward which had thus tempted her unfortunate sailor to encounter the fury of the threatened hurricane.

Vainly did her pitying neighbours urge her to return home when night at length precluded all hope of her being able to discover his boat at a distance—and when Le Roi and Wilhelm overcome with weariness retired to rest, they carried with them the melancholy image of her despair as they left her pacing the strand, or hiding herself among the rocks while her little boy clinging to her gown pierced her heart with his complaint and his cries produced more by her grief and his present uneasiness, than from his sense of that loss the magnitude of which he could not conceive.

Early in the morning Le Roi was awakened by a sailor who came with information that the body of the gentleman who had been described, had been cast upon the rocks at some miles distance and that he and some of his companions had brought it to Yarmouth claiming the reward which had been offered by the Bow-street officers for the apprehension of the murderer.

Mangled as the body was, it was yet incontestably proved to be that of the miserable Rainsford by the wound in his face which had not been perfectly healed when his impatient thirst for revenge drove him to seek the destruction of the unfortunate Dallamore for which he alone desired to live, hateful as existence was now rendered to himself by one intemperate moment of rage dooming him to pass a life of perpetual misery, an object of horror to every eye.

The natural benevolence of Le Roi would not suffer him to quit Yarmouth without enquiring for the poor widow that he might afford her at least the consolation of pity and administer as far as he could to her present wants in which he was seconded by Wilhelm.

Their charity was not unrewarded. They arrived at the moment when the shouting sailors by every rudely delighted demonstration of joy shared the extacy with which she welcomed as from the dead her lost husband, rescued from that dreary grave by his own uncommon force and the exertions of the seamen on board a vessel which he had observed at a considerable distance after a tremendous wave had at once overset his little boat. He said he had never beheld his companion more and that he himself nearly exhausted by contending for several hours before he could reach the vessel with the billows that rolled mountain high, had scarcely strength to catch the rope which the sailors extended to him.

Chapter XVIII

Ev'n now in dark affliction's troubled days,
Teach me to wait in Quiet's friendly bower
The future sunshine of a fairer hour.

Hayley[72]

Robert delayed not a moment to hasten to his sisters as soon as he was informed of the dreadful event which had taken place in the presence of Selena from the effects of which she still severely suffered, so that she whose nerves were from nature and habit regularly firm and composed could not now hear the slightest unusual noise without experiencing a terror such as might be expected to result from the most violent shock.

The tenderness with which she was treated, and the growing attachment which her grateful and affectionate heart felt for every member of the amiable family who united in devoting themselves in every way to her restoration and comfort contributed to her recovery and made her reluctant to express the impatience with which she desired to quit scenes that she could never look upon without horror and a society which however delightful and captivating was she feared so injurious to Clara.

She had now personally an opportunity of observing her intimacy with Edwin, which as may well be imagined all her delicate admonitions and prudent cautions had not been able to restrain. And yet tho' convinced of the expediency of their separation until some time had elapsed to confirm the real and perfect restoration of Edwin's mind, and his steady return to these paths of Virtue from which he had so far strayed, Selena would often secretly indulge the hopes that his heart amiable and noble might at length reward the fidelity of attachment which had been so purely so disinterestedly lavished upon him. And she beheld with a delighted sensibility which it was impossible for her entirely to conceal the warm tribute of gratitude and admiration with which Edwin even in the presence of Selena herself devoted nearly his whole attention to the interesting graces of his enchanting friend, her darling Clara. For even while she disapproved and even dreaded the idea of her being united to a character so wild, she yet exulted with a kind of vanity which she was incapable of feeling for herself that a love so pure, so true should at length be requited with the sensibility it merited.

It is true that Edwin still wore the habits of melancholy, spoke of himself as the most unfortunate of beings and entertained "*his friend*" with his resolutions of perpetual seclusion at Inverathie.

But it was easy for all but Clara to observe these complaints were sweet to him from the unaffected and tender interest which they ever created in the soft

---

[72] William Hayley, "Epistle 2" of *An Essay on Sculpture* (1800), lines 394–8. The epigraph transforms line 394 ("Teach me, like you, in dark affliction's days"), and omits lines 395–6 ("Now while the lyre, by sorrow's stern command, / Sinks in forc'd silence from my troubled hand").

bosom of that friend, and the bewitching looks of mild sympathy which would at these moments beam upon him with irresistible fascination, and in spite of these projects of seclusion he could not disguise the concern with which he anticipated the departure of the lovely sisters which Selena now announced as indispensable, her presence being necessary to the consolation of Mrs. Vallard from whom it had been impossible to withold the shocking circumstances of her nephew's death with which the whole kingdom now resounded.

Nevertheless as the moment of the departure approached Selena and even Robert found it impossible to resist the request of Edwin that he might be allowed to accompany them to Derby on his way to Inverathie saying that tho' he wished not to intrude upon Mrs. Vallard at a season of such affliction yet he was anxious to testify his solicitude for her health and to prove by every attention that he had never forgotten the eternal claims which her kindness and friendship had upon his gratitude—adding in a softer voice while he addressed himself to Clara and secretly pressing her hand to his lips, "It has been my lot to find all my consolations in friendship and if I must not hope to inspire love is not the misfortune compensated in a matchless friend?"

Clara replied not but her full eyes and glowing cheeks gave testimony how sweet to her heart was the flattering homage.

Before they left Richmond Mr. Bently strongly urged Robert to press Selena to assume the title and claim the rich position to which she had so just a right, but this her brother forbore to do, when he perceived the invincible reluctance which at the first hint she evinced to hear him speak a word on this subject, positively declaring that however doubtful it might appear in the opinion of others, there existed not the possibility of her committing any act of injustice which her whole soul should more utterly abhor, and that while she had a brother and a sister such as she was blessed with she could never feel that dependance to which she was doomed irksome or degrading.

Selena did not oppose the delicate scruples of Edwin who parted from them at the gate leading into Hillbarton avenue when they were told that Mrs. Vallard continued much indisposed. But the regrets of Clara on this separation were considerably sweetened by a conversation which she had with him on that morning when he informed her that he intended to pass some time in the neighbourhood of Matlock at some retired cottage, where he might enjoy the romantic scenery with the tranquility of solitude. He had asked her advice whether at the end of some weeks his visit would be considered as an indiscreet intrusion and received her promise that if inexpedient she would prohibit his coming, having already obtained her permission to write to her that information concerning himself which in secret she had so much languished to require from him.

Mrs. Vallard tho' dreadfully affected at the first sight of Selena yet found herself gradually revived by her presence, and in the approbation which she expressed of her conduct, and the tears of gratitude with which she thanked her for those pious cares she had given to sooth the last hours of the lost and unhappy Dallamore Selena felt a sweet additional reward to that which her own heart had already bestowed.

Nevertheless her uneasiness with respect to Sidney became every moment more cruel and his total silence more extraordinary. It was impossible that he could be in any part of the British islands and yet ignorant of the wonderful event which had at once restored Selena to complete liberty and given to him a rank and wealth nearly princely. Was this a moment when he would voluntarily hide himself from her whom he had loved with such passionate devotion, or at least could he withhold from her thro' her brother the assurance that he yet lived for her?

But in vain had he been sought for with all the diligence of enquiry. In vain had advertisements respecting his affairs been inserted in the public papers both at home and abroad with a view of urging his return. The only information which they had been at all able to procure was from his agent in Ireland to whom Robert had applied immediately on his first interview with Selena at Richmond when convinced that Selena would not abandon the suffering Dallamore. To this he quickly received the following answer.

"Sir,
"I am honored with yours of the 26th—and am sorry it is not in my power to satisfy you with respect to the present residence of Mr. Dallamore. Some days ago I received a letter from him dated the 20th inst[73]—in which he mentioned his purpose of quitting England without delay, but did not further communicate his intentions. The letter was at his desire delivered to me by a gentleman to whom as he informed me he had given a power of attorney in future to receive his rents on his estate in Kerry where he had promised to reside during Mr. Dallamore's absence from Ireland. Your cousin has expressed the utmost confidence in his friend and desired that his conduct may in no wise be interfered with.
"I have the honour to be &c&c,
James Plunkett"

To this Robert instantly replied enclosing a letter for Sidney entreating him in the strongest terms to allow him to share his exile or retirement. He mentioned not indeed Selena's name since what could he say but that in spite of all his efforts she was then devoting herself to what she esteemed her melancholy duty in her attendance on Dallamore. This letter he requested Mr. Plunkett to forward thro' the gentleman to whom he had alluded and from Mr. Plunkett he received the following answer.

"Sir,
"I have the honour to enclose for your perusal a faithful copy of the letter of instructions which I have received from Mr. Dallamore, by which you will see that I am not authorised to do as you direct. I have nevertheless complied with your request but have reason to fear that your application to Mr. Alesen may not be attended with the success you desire, as I understand that it was Mr. Dallamore's wish that no letters should be received for him in his absence."
"I am &c—James Plunkett"

---

[73]   Inst is an abbreviation for "instant," meaning this same month.

The letter from Sidney which was enclosed was to this purpose.

"Dear Sir,

"Some particular circumstances have occurred which render my return to
Ireland extremely uncertain, and as I cannot exactly say what is my present
plan or where I shall first proceed on my leaving this country I do not wish to
receive any letters or applications whatsoever. Mr. Alesen the gentleman who
will transmit this to you is acquainted with my wishes on the subject of my
affairs, and as I had not an opportunity of communicating with you personally,
you will not I am sure unjustly feel hurt that I have profitted by this occasion
of materially serving myself and at the same time obliging my friend, who has
reasons for wishing at this time to retire to Ireland, and now purposes to take up
his residence exclusively at Loughlaven where he will save you the trouble of
collecting my rents, managing all my affairs with the tenants and he will remit
regularly to my banker such sums as will give me credit with his correspondents.
I shall take it as a favour if you will as far as you are able, prevent his being
molested by letters and applications, as it will not be in his power to forward
any thing to me, and I wish him to act towards the tenants in the manner I have
explained to him without any interruption. Should he wish hereafter for any
assistance or introductions I have no doubt that you will oblige me thro' him to
the extent of your power but for the present your kindness will be best shewn
in leaving him to himself. He will continue to remit to you each half year your
accustomed salary, as I should be sorry to think I had lost the services from
which I have always derived such advantage and which I now only wish you to
consider as suspended."

"Yours &c Sidney Dallamore"

As Mr. Plunkett had prognosticated, Robert received no reply whatever to the
letter which he sent to Mr. Alesen and his application to Sidney's banker in London
proved equally idle. He had received no remittances on Mr. Dallamore's account
(who had no letters of credit from him) since he had settled his affairs and closed
his accounts with him some weeks before, and it was evident that Sidney had to
avoid discovery now determined to transact his business at some other house.

All this unsatisfactory as it was Robert communicated to Selena when they
met, and his distress at this unaccountable concealment was encreased by the
perplexity in which he now found the affairs of Lord Mount Villars, which
he immediately undertook to settle in trust for Sidney as his nearest relation,
expecting every moment that he would return and by his smile once more lift
up the light of gladness in the dejected eyes of Selena, and restore peace and joy
to that sadly desponding heart, which in spite of all its natural firmness, and the
comforts which her friends endeavoured to impart seemed silently to sink into
the very earth with sorrow.

Convinced from this strange abandonment that Sidney had ceased to live,
or ceased to love her she suggested no plans for his discovery, nor even spoke
of him voluntarily. She uttered no complaints, and buried in secret solitude that
consuming anguish which she could not suppress. She however urged Robert to

return to London and he whose business called him thither, and who hoped to be able more effectually there to prosecute his enquiries, left her with the less reluctance to the consolations of Clara.

Edwin too, by his occasional visits, tho' he declined taking up his residence at Hillbarton yet by every soothing art endeavoured to administer cheerfulness to their little society and Mrs. Vallard prognosticated to Selena the unenvied rivalship of her sister. Restored as Edwin now appeared to be to health and tranquility of mind and testifying towards her no sentiment but those of the tenderest friendship, mingled with admiration as if something of more than mortal excellence Selena could not wish to banish him tho' she often considered with dread and pity the lot which awaited those two amiable bosoms who unshielded by insensibility, unarmed by firmness should encounter together the thorny and difficult path of life.

Day after day; and week after week rolled heavily away while poor Selena shunning every eye and yielding for the first time in her life to the sadness which she at least thought herself at liberty to cherish, rejected every consolation and indulged the regrets which every surrounding object was so well calculated to inspire. But it was in that love-consecrated seat beside the river that she especially loved to linger and wear away the melancholy hours: for here had Sidney first spoken the sweet impassioned accents of purest tenderness which even yet seemed to thrill to her heart, and it was here that she had at length confessed to him that love which however combatted she had found it impossible to subdue.

Early on the morning which had succeeded that fairest day Sidney had planted on the beloved spot two young limes, Selena's favourite tree; at the foot of the little rock which rose behind he placed honey suckles and the sweet scented clematis and he himself had formed a seat of rustic woodwork and covered the bank between the river and the rock with violets, mezerions and every fragrant shrub and flower that Selena peculiarly loved. Not a day had passed during Sidney's last happy visit at Hillbarton in which they had not together visited this their favourite garden, still embellished by him with some new offering as a grateful memorial of every endearing grace, every kind expression that testified the fondness of his Selena's heart, which ingenuous as it was, yet reluctantly betrayed those sentiments which Virtue had so long smothered, and even then in the hours of softest happiness Love delicately veiled within her breast by blushing timidly and retired modesty scarce dared to trust itself to the gradual view of him whose felicity it promised to ensure thro' a long train of smiling years. Not a leaf, not a stone was here which did not speak of joys departed never to return—and inflict those bitter stings with which Memory tortures the heart still obstinately clinging to the sepulchre of bliss.

Here she sadly revolved in her mind not only each past proof of affection, and the vows of tenderness which still seemed in her ear to promise unalterable love, but also every improbable conjecture which she incessantly formed to excuse his absence. But formed in vain! while desponding Reason rejected each in its turn and mocked the fallacious efforts by which flattering hope sought to find an asylum in her bosom to tranquilize her fears. How often wearied with the disappointed expectations which in spite of her own hopeless dejection, the anxious suggestions

of Clara would perpetually excite, how often would she fly to this her solitary
bower to hide the tears with which she bitterly exclaimed,

"No he returns to me no more! The fairest years of my life are doomed thus
to pass in wasting regret, tortured by consuming uncertainty. If he indeed lives,
he lives not for me but devoting himself to new pursuits he flies all traces of our
divided loves that have no more a name.

> Oh toi qui me fuis! toi que j'adore!
> Où veux tu chercher la bonheur!^{74}

I shall see thee beloved Sidney no more! And the cold dark days of oblivion and
insensibility can alone restore to me my peace!"

Chapter XIX

> We'll unlock
> Our fastest secrets, shed upon each other
> Our tenderest cares; and quite unbar those doors
> Which shall be shut to all mankind besides
> Lee^{75}

From this state of extreme despondency Selena was however at length aroused
in some degree by an event which restored to her all those soothing endearments,
those flattering caresses which had been lost to her with the strangely interrupted
friendship of Lady Trevallyn.

She had continued constantly to visit the school, for tho' no longer alive to the
pleasures of life, even these the most pure which benevolence bestows, she yet
forgot not its duties.

Mr. Rawlins who always took an opportunity of paying her his respects and
acquainting her with whatever he heard from his lady met her there one morning
with the account which he had just heard of the dangerous illness of Lord Trevallyn
and that a Physician had been sent for from the hall to Bath.

In a few days after this while Mrs. Vallard was hesitating whether she should
not make one more effort to obtain some intelligence from her dear Emily, the
news arrived at Esselberrie of his Lordship's death, which was confirmed the
following morning by the public papers.

A day or two after this Mr. Rawlins sent to inform Selena that he had just
received a letter from Fanny with orders to him immediately to prepare the house
for her Lady's reception whom he might expect without delay.

---

^{74} Isabella de Montolieu, *Caroline de Lichtfield* (1786), 2:123: "You, who flee me, you
whom I love, where are you seeking happiness."

^{75} Varanes in Nathaniel Lee's *Theodosius; or the Force of Love* (1680), 1.1.317–20.

Her friends at Hillbarton had scarcely time to congratulate themselves on the prospect of again beholding her from whom they were once as they feared for ever separated before a second messenger brought to Selena the following note.

"You are then indeed so near me dear Selena; oh do you not in some degree share the impatience of your friend who has never for a moment forgotten that she owes to you more than life? Hasten to me that in one embrace I may be assured that no unjust suspicions has yet banished from your heart the apparently ungrateful Emily. Tell dear Mrs. Vallard that I knew not until I reached Esselberrie that the true angel of comfort was already with her, and that the vain hope of administering to her consolation by my presence urged the precipitancy of my journey hither. Our house of mourning should be but one, and she will not deny her Emily while she claims a participation in her sorrows."

Words can never paint the mingled emotions of grief and joy with which those two lovely friends wept in each other's arms the mutual hours of terror and of anguish which each had past during their cruel and involuntary but total separation.

With what tender interest did they demand the particulars of those awful moments those unlooked for events which had thus restored them widowed to each other? But it was now Lady Trevallyn's turn to be the comforter and to preach that calm resignation, that piously contented dependence which even in moments of doubtful vexation, and disquieting suspence, yet "leans with unexhausted hope in Heaven."[76]

With confidence did she forebode the return of Sidney, and tho' unable to devise any probable conjecture as to the reasons of his absence yet the heart of Selena soothed with the sweet images of possible tho' unlikely bliss sighed its fondly credulous assent and yielded once more to the soft almost forgotten sentiment of pleasure while she listened to the feeble accents of nearly expiring hope.

The greatest part of the night they thus past together in the overflowings of a friendship and confidence which knew no bounds, where each thought might pass pure from soul to soul "As light transmitted thro' a crystal glass."[77]

Lady Trevallyn then taking the hand of her friend led her to her dressing room which Selena perceived had been fitted up for her reception.

"Ah Selena!" cried she as she lighted the candles on the toilet decorated with striking elegance, "Best and dearest of friends! This room is for ever your own. I have consecrated it to friendship and never was there so perfect a representative as my Selena of that dear sentiment to which I devote from henceforth all those too warm feelings which but for you had been my destruction. Dearest Selena! I can now look round with far other sensations than those of horror, on this memorable chamber where your protecting care first opened my eyes to the fearful precipice which gaped beneath my feet, arrested me ere I plunged headlong with giddy desperation, and then with all the pious heroism of faithful friendship risked your health, nay life, thro' days and nights of laborious watchfulness for the preservation

---

76　William Hayley, "Epistle 6" of *An Essay on Sculpture* (1800), line 42.

77　Berenice in John Dryden's *Tyrannic Love; or The Royal Martyr* (1670), 5.1.460.

of mine. Here then shall the remainder of that life, which you have thus preserved be past, and all that can in future charm my imagination shall be destined to adorn this little temple. Too happy when I can allure hither the beloved image of that virtue I adore!"

Selena listened with smiles to the grateful expressions of her beloved friend and once more blessed that Providence whose protecting care had indeed rescued her from misery and restored her to that peace from which her gentle spirit had been almost a stranger from earliest youth. Nevertheless her own health and spirits had suffered so cruelly from the confinement and toils which during her attendance upon Dallamore she had patiently sustained, terminated at last by a moment so terrible and succeeded by such perpetual anxieties, disappointments, and sorrows that she was no longer able to bear with her native firmness and serenity any unusual scenes of agitation and she felt herself so much affected after this interview with her friend that she found it impossible to close her eyes during the remainder of the night.

Early in the morning Lady Trevallyn was at her side and softly demanding if she was awake. Selena immediately arose. "I thought it was but a dream dear Selena," cried she, "and I could not persuade myself I had you indeed within my reach till I came thus and disturbed you. But look how sweet the morning is, every thing seems to sympathise with my lightened heart and I long to go into my garden."

While she spoke, she had herself undrawn the curtains and opened the windows, and Selena gazed with pleasure and admiration on the animated bloom of health which seemed to spread the vivid brilliancy of new youth and beauty over the graceful form and perfect features of the more than usually lovely Emily.

The dazzling resplendency of her complexion and lustre of her eyes had struck Selena on the preceeding evening but she had attributed this to some degree of fever caused by her journey and the agitation of their first interview as well as to the strong contrast formed by the gloomy sables in which she was enveloped.

But she was now in her white dressing gown and Selena could no longer question the obviously heightened beauty with which tranquility new to her heart and established health had cloathed her friend. That beauty had even changed its character and with its former languor and melancholy had perhaps lost some interesting charms which in the eyes of some could scarcely be compensated by freshness and vivacity.

Every proportion of her delicate and naturally slender frame had assumed an additional roundness, and the luxuriant beauty of those Magdalen tresses which her severe illness had ravished from her head was not yet replaced, but the silky curls of a darker shade that now clasped with innumerable tendrils the polished and transparent whiteness of her neck and temples gave to her small and delicate features an almost infantine grace.

"Dear Lady Trevallyn!" cried Selena, "How fat you are grown. Mrs. Vallard will certainly send me to Wales as soon as she sees how blooming you are she has been so uneasy at the loss of my good looks as she says."

"You have indeed lost all your sweet roses my love, care and sorrow have stolen them from their most lovely seat but believe your Emily's prophetic heart that those envious usurpers shall soon be put to flight and all their thefts shall be restored."

As they walked together Lady Trevallyn imparted to Selena her intentions with respect to the immense property which had now devolved upon her.

Lord Trevallyn had made no alteration in the will which he had formerly written except to obliterate all remembrance of Mr. Guise. Nor was it only by the wealth which he had thus entrusted to her that he proved the restoration of his confidence in his fair Emily, for he had been so much touched by the cheerful sacrifice that she made of all society in her attendance on him and her endeavours to contribute to his health and amusement that he had laid on her no restrictions as to the choice of her future friends and residence and altho' pride forbad him to name Selena or acknowledge his error he had been long secretly convinced of his unjust suspicions and even desired the renewal of that friendship which his arbitrary commands had suspended.

The last words which he uttered when he perceived his end inevitably approaching was to advise Lady Trevallyn's immediate removal to Esselberrie where she might have the protection and comfort of Mrs. Vallard's society, a circumstance which entirely relieved her delicate mind from every scruple she might otherwise have entertained of instantly acting in defiance to the power he had formerly exerted in her separation from those dear friends.

The aversion which Lord Trevallyn had ever entertained towards his own relations had been a great inducement to his making his late second marriage, when the degrading connexion formed as he imagined by his niece Jane's union with Mr. Aston had estranged her also from his favour.

Nevertheless Lady Trevallyn now considered it as an act of injustice to deprive his natural heirs of those landed estates to which she was conscious they had ever looked with anxious expectation.

The large settlement which at the demand of her relations had been made upon her at her marriage was fully sufficient for every wish of her benevolent heart and elegant mind in that retirement which was her present choice, and from which she desired not to be ever allured by business or by pleasure; To Esselberrie she was attached with a fondness which would have made her regret the relinquishment of it, and the last wish of Lord Trevallyn had sanctioned her resolution to make it her abode. But she lost no time, nor waited for the counsel of any to execute what her heart dictated and with the exception of Esselberrie park alone she therefore made a formal surrender of all the family estates and houses in an equal division between the next male heir and Mrs. Aston whose high expectations had been formerly allowed by the declared partiality of her uncle.

Yet tho' banished for ever from her heart, or remembered only as those vanished phantoms that disturb our fevered dreams Lord Henry even in his disgraceful exile was tortured with fresh stings of vexation and selfish regret at the intelligence that fame quickly brought to his ears of the freedom and wealth which he vainly imagined would finally have been devoted to him, had he not as fatally sacrificed himself by his irrevocable connexion. How bitterly did he curse his own folly which had thus excluded him from all those enjoyments of love and fortune which he might otherwise now have shared with his beautiful fond Emily! In vain did he endeavour to drown her image in perpetual scenes of the most abandoned debauchery and riotous intoxication. The unconquerable fiends of remorse, disappointment and disgrace pursued him with unremitting vigilence, and the graceful insinuating being whose well shadowed semblance of all the virtues had captivated the young and innocent Emily could no longer be traced in the diseased and bloated tyrant who with a body disfigured by vice and a temper soured by vexation vented his cruelty upon all whose ill fortune placed them in his power and at length fell in the prime of life a victim of intemperance, pitied by few and lamented by none.

In the superintendence of her favourite school, in administering to the health, instruction and comfort of every individual that inhabited the cottages in her happy neighbourhood every stranger that sought from her relief, in the pious conversations of Mr. Mason and the society of her beloved friends at Hillbarton— in the improvement of her own intelligent mind and the cultivation of her curious and beautiful gardens, fancifully adorning with all her own natural elegance of taste the little temple which she had consecrated to friendship Lady Trevallyn now passed a life of the purest happiness uninterrupted except by the impatience which she could not but feel at the strangely protracted absence of Sidney, and her observation of that deep and silent melancholy which pressed upon her Selena in spite of all her tender efforts to sooth and cheer her desponding soul.

Seriously alarmed at the visible alteration in her health and spirits which mutually affected each other, she now seconded Mrs. Vallard's advice that Selena should comply with the entreaty of her brother who pressed her to accompany him in the journey to Ireland which he now thought it expedient to make in order the more effectually to settle the affairs he had undertaken to manage.

They all agreed in judging that the scenes in which Selena now perpetually passed her hours kept alive the keeness of her regrets by presenting to her every instant fresh remembrances of her vanished happiness.

The sanction of Parliment [sic] was alone wanting to complete the liberty of Robert, but as that could not now be obtained till the following session which could not be expected for some months Mr. Bently hinted that delicacy required his temporary absence from Richmond altho' he did not prohibit his occasional visits, and the anxiety which Robert himself felt to discover if possible the retreat of Sidney made him earnestly desire to see and converse with Mr. Alesen from whom he had never been able to obtain any answer to his repeated letters however urgent.

He therefore resolved to take this opportunity of going over to Mount Villars for a month in order to settle the affairs belonging to the Irish estates which had been left in strange confusion and at the same time determined to visit Loughlaven

Sidney's paternal property situated in the neighbourhood of Mount Villars, where he hoped to meet Mr. Alesen.

But this which was indeed the chief object of his journey he confessed not to Selena, for anxious to induce her to accompany him he justly feared her delicacy would shrink from this pursuit of him who now appeared to fly her.

She yielded at length to his persuasions and the disinterested counsels of her friends, and tho' she left those so dear to her with extreme reluctance yet it was but for a month and her heart fondly promised to itself a melancholy pleasure in visiting the birth place of Sidney, the beautiful scenes he had so much loved, where he had passed his childish years and which had so lately witnessed his filial piety.

Clara could not without the utmost regret consent to this separation, the second which she had ever known from her beloved sister. Nevertheless she trusted that better consequences would result from this, than from that inauspicious visit which she had formerly made without her to Hillbarton, she trusted that the spirits of Selena would be raised by this change of scene and that it might wear away the time of that tedious and unaccountable absence the termination of which she every moment expected. And unconsciously she felt a secret satisfaction that the necessity which called for her remaining to console and cheer Mrs. Vallard, detained her in the society of Edwin who passed many of his hours at Hillbarton and whose presence was always welcomed with cordial pleasure and affection by Mrs. Vallard.

Chapter XX

Esser non riedi! ohime che fai, che pensi?
Qual destin, qual vaghezza & qual dilette
Lungi da me di ritenerti ha ferza?
Chi m' invidia 'l mio ben e chi m' l toghe
Si lungamente? e come il soffre amore?
Lasso ch' io sen dall 'aspettar si stanca
Che lusinghiera speranza entro l mio sen
Piu non trova ricetto in vain pur fingo
Del tuo lungo tardar ragioni & scuse
Che nulla so trovar che puo me acqueti
Rinuccini[78]

---

[78] Rinuccini source unlocated, but likely a corrupt sample of his unrhymed endecasillabi, translated by Lucia Greene as follows: "And if you do not return! Dear me, what are you doing, what are you thinking? / What destiny, what whim, what delight / Has the power to keep you away from me? / Who is jealous of my love and deprives me of it / For so long? And how my love suffers? / For a long time I have been tired of waiting, / And my bosom accepts flattering hope no longer / In vain I pretend there are reasons and excuses for your long delay / But I can find nothing to give me peace."

How sharp the point of this remembrance is!
Irreparable is the loss; and Patience
Says it is past her cure.
Here then will I put off my hopes and keep it
No longer for my flatterer.

Shakespear[79]

Selena exerted herself during their journey to reward with an appearance of grateful success the affectionate and unremitting endeavours of her brother to afford her consolation, or at least supply her with amusement. But she paid dear for these exertions in the dark hours of solitary gloom when the image of Sidney for ever lost to her pursued her imagination with a force encreasing in proportion with that depression which ever succeeds when the vain hope is faded and the firm mind at length subdued.

A painful sensation of resentment mingled with the bitter anguish of tender regret which pressed upon her heart while she lamented an absence that she a thousand times exclaimed to herself never could have been, had Sidney really loved her, as she had once believed, since however he might have been affected upon first hearing of her removal to Bently's, yet the circumstances which obliged her to this step must surely have excused it even in his eyes and of these he could not have remained ignorant except by obstinately refusing to listen to all that related to her, a resolution which she felt it impossible for true love, however hopeless or irritated long to maintain.

The days she spent at Mount Villars were to her peculiarly sad, she had indeed desired to behold those scenes which during their last separation at her own command Sidney had in his letters so well described. Every spot was hailed as sacred & dear to her heart, which loved to imagine that the remembrance of her had then at least occupied his thoughts and had left her some traces of love upon every hallowed tree that had shared the meditations inspired by tenderness. Yet now that she was indeed there, the idea that he no longer thought of her as he had then done embittered every sadly pleasing recollection of his fondness and she could have wished to fly from all that spoke to her of past hopes of the fond confidence of love.

The agent who was appointed to meet Robert at Mount Villars occupied him in a great measure and Selena left alone wandered wrapt in the deepest melancholy over the magnificent and romantic scenery of the extensive park amid woods and rocks alive to no pleasurable emotion even from the aspect of Nature then coloured with all the variety of beauty which the first hints of autumn luxuriantly bestow.

Robert who perceived the dejection which she in vain struggled to disguise hastened to transact his business with the agent, and having arranged every thing in a train of some regularity he proposed to Selena that they should now proceed

---

[79]   The epigraph begins with Alonso in Shakespeare's *The Tempest* (1611), 5.1.138–41 (omitting line 139, "My dear son Ferdinand. [Prospero] I am woe for 't sir") and continues with Alonso in 3.3.7–8 (changing "Even here I will" in line 7 above).

to Loughlaven urged by that strong tho' secret motive, which had principally prompted him to undertake the journey to Ireland and anxious as he was to converse with Mr. Alesen.

The beautifully circumstanced estate belonging to Sidney which took its name from the small lake around which it was situated, lay at but a little distance from these justly celebrated scenes of unequalled picturesque beauty, in the neighbourhood of Killarney.

The weather was peculiarly clear and serene and as this was the season when the mellowing year gave even additional charms to the landscapes possessing in themselves such varied grace as pen or pencil could never paint, Robert resolved to conduct thither his sister, from whence he might easily ride over to Loughlaven and make the enquiries he wished; as Selena had objected to accompanying him to the estate of Sidney.

Exaggerated as had been the accounts which they had heard of the charms at once sublime and softly delicious which Nature in a moment of magnificent prodigality had lavished upon those scenes, they were yet not disappointed in the lively effect which the first view excited on each, as they gained the summit of a hill that overlooked Killarney and at once beheld that most beautifully grand amphitheatre which bursts upon the eye. The blue lake carved by the sweet and cunning hand of Nature lay spread beneath them, separated and encircled with hills clothed to the very summit with the richest woods, and the pure bosom of each sapphire flood was scattered with innumerable islands each worthy to be the favourite residence of some fairy Queen—while the high Rocks mountains of the deepest purple and gigantic size raised their grotesquely pointed crowns to Heaven and bounded the magnificent horizon as with a magic chain which imagination itself could not overpass.

An exclamation of delight and astonishment burst from the lips of Robert as he involuntarily stopped his horses at this unexpected prospect exceeding all that his fancy had ventured to picture from past descriptions.

Selena was silent but tears of thrilling admiration trembled in her eyes, mingled with that sting of regret which instantaneously accompanied each pleasing sensation and whispered, "Oh he is not here! The fair face of nature wears for me one dark impenetrable veil! Oh thou who canst alone remove it will thou never never appear! and teach my heart once more to open to enjoyment?"

Nevertheless she longed to taste that tranquility promised by the sight of the setting sun, amid scenes of such inviting softness, by the side of those clear and peaceful waters, and felt therefore disappointed on arriving at Killarney to find that the town was placed at some distance from the lakes, so that it was impossible for her to visit them on that evening as by the time they had dined the moon was already struggling vainly to repulse the approaching shades of twilight, but as her mild splendour irresistibly allured them out their steps were directed to the gardens adjoining Lord K—'s residence,[80] situated at the extremity of the little town.

---

[80]   Lord Kenmare was the largest landowner in the Killarney area.

Here they were permitted to enter, and while Selena leaning on the arm of her brother slowly walked upon the terrace, inhaling the odorous gales which the mild west wind wafted over the orange trees, her heart melted within her at the tender remembrances that the perfumed air seemed to breathe of those enchanting evenings when with Sidney she had enjoyed the same fragrance in the dear bowers of Esselberrie.

Mean while Robert entered into conversation with a young man who encouraged by the courteous affability with which he had questioned him at the gate, had ventured to be their guide.

With a smiling countenance Robert listened for some time to sundry astonishing memoirs of the great O'Donahoe, and his supernatural appearances on his white horse from his pearly paved caves beneath "the silver and translucent lake."[81] But at length taking advantage of some pause he demanded how far it was from thence to Loughlaven.

The interesting name recalled Selena's attention & with a beating heart she listened for the reply.

Her brother then enquired whether he knew the place and could direct him the best road as he understood it lay in a wild part of the country which was but little frequented.

"Is it know Loughlaven your honour? Indeed I do know it well, for I was born and bred on that land, and wish I had never quit it. But as ill-luck would have it I left home before all the good came among 'em."

"And what good to you mean?"

"Why you must know Sir, as may hap you do already that the estate all round the Lough belongs to squire Dallamore, but as the family lived for the most part abroad the old house that is on it was let to go to rack and ruin till some time back that it was all put to rights and made quite neat and clever as you'd desire to see for the old Madam that the talk was intended to come live there. But howsomever afore the jobs were quite done and the workmen well out of the house the poor Madam was gone to her long home and the more's the pity for there never was a better lady. Oh she was a great loss and if she had lived she would have done a power of service to the poor God bless her, as she had always done about the great place where she used to be."

"You had the less reason then to regret your having quitted the estate," observed Robert.

"Aye so I thought then your honour but there then comes one Alesen from England, as agent for the young Squire who is gone as I hears beyond seas, that has been so good to the tenants and so very kind to every soul on the land that there is not a sad heart left upon it, it's my belief. He has put chimneys and glass windows into every cabin, and new thatched and white washed them all so that you would not know the place, and besides he is building a school-house and in the mean

---

[81]   According to legend the great chieftain O'Donoghue walked upon lake Killarney and disappeared in its middle on the first of May, when he sometimes reappears at sunrise.

time he has all the children in the parish taught in the long hall, aye and they get their dinner of a Sunday old and young whoever will go for it, and there is not a labourer but he gives work to. But the best of all your honour," and as he spoke the significant grin told how much he was himself interested in the account, "the best of all is that he has promised ten guineas and a milch cow to every girl in the land that is married within the year."

"And you mean to assist in qualifying one of the lasses to claim this?" interrupted Robert.

"Why they shan't say, but Shamus Moon has done his endeavour," replied the lad.

"This Mr. Alesen must be a great favourite with your young ladies Shamus?" said Robert.

"Would you believe it Sir there is not one of them ever so much as heard him open his lips, and if they see him, it is but a chance."

"And did you ever see him?" cried Selena eagerly.

"Never Miss—tho' I do be there as often as I can and of a Sunday particularly. But being a stranger I did not like to intrude myself up at the house, yet I partly hope I shall soon get work there, tho' they have employed none yet but such as were on the land. Howsomever as I was born there, may hap I may be able to settle among 'em for life afore long."

When Robert afterwards made some further enquiries with respect to the road saying he intended to ride thither the following morning, his guide again offered to act in that capacity but added that Mr. Alesen never saw any strangers and was very particular that none should be let into the house in his absence.

"The servants," added he, "never know when he is at home or not. I am told he often goes away for days together shooting as I suppose on the mountains for he takes his dogs and a gun on his shoulder, and when he comes back if he finds the hall door shut he goes in at one of the windows, and as he always has dinner laid out in the parlour he never calls any one and may be they do not know he has been in till he is gone again."

"He has not much communication then as it appears with the tenants to whom he is so good a friend."

"Oh yes your honour! for there is a young man that he brought down there with him as steward that teaches them all the new fangled farming, and whenever any of them wants a favour, if they do but speak a word to him he lets the master know and then Mr. Alesen comes to them himself and hears all that they have to say, and if it is any way reasonable at all, they are sure to get whatever they want."

"Well," said Robert as they parted at the door of the inn to which their loquacious guide gratified by their attention had accompanied them, "if you will come to me tomorrow we will ride together to Loughlaven and if I cannot see Mr. Alesen I will at least leave a message for him with his steward."

The candles were lighted as they entered the room Selena drew her hat over her eyes but Robert instantly perceived the large drops that hung upon the faded roses of her cheeks.

"Dearest Selena!" he cried, "Who is this Alesen this chosen brother of our Sidney's heart? who executes his benevolent wishes like his second self, and to whom alone he entrusts the secret of his retreat?"

Selena trembled. Strange suspicions, tumultuous ideas hurried thro' her mind but shrunk from utterance. A pause of some moments ensued.

At length starting from his seat in agitation Robert unable to conceal the doubt that burst from his bosom exclaimed, "Could it be possible that this is indeed Sidney himself?"

"Oh no! no!" cried Selena bathed in the tears which she had not any longer the power or even the wish to disguise, "No 'tis wild! 'tis impossible conjecture! Sidney is far, far from hence and never shall we see him more. He has rather found some deserving friend oppressed by fortune, and struggling with debts, he has relieved him from difficulties, provided him with a safe and delightful retreat and to him he has entrusted the care of his property determined never to revisit these kingdoms."

"I will see him however," cried Robert unconvinced tho' wavering in the improbable hope which at least "bade his thoughts yet dally a while with false surmise."[82] "In this I am decided that I will not quit the country till I have by some means obtained the interview I desired."

Fearful of encreasing the agitation which Selena betrayed he spoke no farther on the subject, but he passed a night of nearly as restless perturbation and impatience as Selena herself.

They met at an early hour and while waiting for breakfast (of which they hardly partook any thing) Robert walked to the post-office in hopes of finding a letter from Richmond which he had vainly expected at Mount Villars and had ordered to be forwarded hither, should it arrive after his departure from thence.

The post master appeared doubtful whether he had not received some with the direction he enquired for, and while turning over the unclaimed letters Robert whose eyes followed him inquisitively, beheld with astonishment his own hand and snatching it up perceived it to be a letter which he had written long since to Mr. Alesen.

"What is the meaning of this?"

"Oh Sir!" answered the man with a half smile, "that is but one of many, sent to the same gentleman since he has been in our neighbourhood, but he don't chuse to have them sent."

"How do you mean."

"Why he is rather a particular kind of gentleman I believe, for as soon as I found out where he was I had a boy on purpose to run to Loughlaven with the first letters that came for him, and he took them, but at the same time sent me a note to desire I might do so no more, so here they lie ever since, for he never asks for them and no one that comes from Loughlaven dares to take them without orders."

"Have you got the note?" demanded Robert eagerly.

---

[82]   Milton, "Lycidas" (1637), line 153: "Let our frail thoughts dally with false surmise."

"Indeed I have so," replied the man, producing it from between the leaves of an account book, "for thinks I, as the gentleman is that sort of fanciful body perhaps he may one day or another forget and be coming upon me for not having done my duty."

"Allow me to look at it for a moment." He handed it over to Robert, but alas, it was not the hand of Sidney and his affectionately warm heart sunk with that disappointment which the sanguine perpetually feels, but from which it can always spring with such elastic vigour.

In fact had Sidney thus anxiously concealed himself at Loughlaven he would assuredly not have hazarded discovery by sending thence his own handwriting, and altho' the argument could not occur to suppress his hope, it failed not quickly to come to the consolation of his disappointment.

Selena passed a day of the most unquiet impatience that she had ever experienced.

The market which was held immediately underneath her windows discouraged her from venturing out alone in order to divert her uneasiness and calm her agitation in those lovely scenes which tantalized her by their vicinity. While the wrangling concert of discordant and unmelodious voices beneath, added to the confusion of her spirits and depression of her heart, she could settle to nothing, her eyes pursued the page which she held for their perusal, but her memory received not a single image. In vain did she open her writing box with the intention of commencing a letter to Clara. Involuntarily she was again each moment at the window, as tho' the sound of every horse's foot awakened her expectation, while the pen remained motionless in her heedless hand; At length the weary hours were at an end.

With that superstitious movement which all have at times felt, she had at last left the window exclaiming, "I will not look again, my watching but retards his coming."

As this resolution is seldom formed until impatience is exhausted by delay, and the moment anticipated for promised happiness long past it is not justly surprising that it so often seems to produce the desired effect as it then did in that instance. But alas tho' Selena had scarcely seated herself at the far extremity of the room till her heart leaped at the sound of her brother's voice upon the stairs, yet no sooner had he opened the door than she was at once convinced as her eager eye met his, that he had been disappointed in the visionary hope which he had suffered his imagination fondly to cherish.

Her heart sank within her but as she had never confessed that she shared that hope she was ashamed to acknowledge the disappointment.

With a melancholy countenance he approached and having kissed her seated himself in silence, languidly resting his elbow on the table which separated them.

She therefore exerted herself to speak, and with a forced smile and faultering voice said as she fancied cheerfully, "Well Robert have you seen Mr. Alesen?"

"I have Selena."

Once more a weight of intolerable anguish fell upon her heart and constrained her to a short pause, till at length recovering herself she begged of him to tell her how he had spent his morning, and kissing away the affectionate tears that rushed to his eyes at the question she turned away, to conceal her own. Then ringing the bell to divert him from the painful contemplation she said she was sure he wanted some refreshment.

"I *am* tired dear Selena—have you dined?" Selena confessed that she had eaten nothing and they agreed to defer all farther explanation till the waiter should have left the room.

Robert's spirits gradually rose as he finished the repast which he had so much needed impatience and vexation having prevented him from as yet tasting any food during that day.

Selena tho' she sickened at every morsel which she forced herself to swallow, yet affected to sympathise with his returning cheerfulness, and when the cloth was removed hardly ventured to renew the question lest she should again distress him by recalling his disappointment.

He was however himself anxious to communicate to her all that he had seen and heard, tho' conscious how little satisfactory his intelligence would prove. He therefore hastened to inform her how much his conversation with his guide as they rode to Loughlaven had served to strengthen his suspicions. To whom but Sidney himself could he indeed attribute traits of such amiable such generous kindness as those he now repeated to her.

Even Selena confessed with tears that the heart of Sidney could alone have prompted them and that he had assuredly breathed his warm and feeling spirit into the bosom of his friend.

The appearance which every thing wore upon the estate was calculated to confirm the strange idea. The graceful hand of taste which marked every improvement tho' there was nothing done but what evidently tended to the comfort of the tenantry; the attention to the wants of all, and the air of serene tranquility and order that seemed to diffuse itself on each object, all spoke as he fondly thought the amiable heart the accomplished mind of Sidney.

Having entered two or three of the cottages and heard from all the grateful praises of their cherished benefactor he advanced trembling with eagerness to the hall door.

It lay open and striking it with his whip in a few seconds a servant appeared.

"Can I speak with Mr. Alesen?"

"Please to walk in Sir and I will let my master know," replied the man as he opened the door of a small parlour and having closed it retired leaving Robert to examine with the most anxious interest every thing which he trusted might tend to establish his flattering imagination.

The room however contained nothing which could direct his conjectures. It had no furniture but a few chairs and a side board, it was covered with a floor cloth which also appeared new and not a book nor a paper was scattered about. The side board was spread with a cloth on which was laid glasses and the usual apparatus for dinner. Upon raising one end of the napkin which had been thrown lightly over all Robert perceived the refreshments which he had been told were daily prepared for the return of the wandering master who was considerately desirous that his liberty should incommode none.

A loaf of bread, with some cold meat a covered vessel of milk some wine and a decanter of water furnished the repast which Robert had sufficient time to examine while almost breathless with anxious impatience he awaited the entrance of Mr. Alesen.

A length a quick step approached.

Robert involuntarily sprang to the door, it opened, and presented to his view a young man of an ingenuous countenance and pleasing manners, but alas how unlike the object of his vain hopes.

Aghast and overpowered by the sudden overthrow of all his air built castles Robert stood motionless and silent, leaving the stranger full leisure to announce himself as the friend whom Mr. Dallamore had honoured with his confidence, requesting at the same time to know in what manner he could now serve the gentleman who had favoured him with his visit.

Having at length in some degree recovered himself Robert informed him of his relationship to the present Lord Mount Villars, and that the only purpose of his journey to Ireland was to endeavour to discover where he at present was and to arrange the affairs belonging to those estates which he had accepted in trust for his cousin but which he now wished to deliver up into his Lordship's own hands or if that was not possible into those of the gentleman whom he had alone considered worthy of his confidence.

He then expressed his surprise at finding that he had never received his letters and ventured to enquire whether Sidney had prohibited him from all intercourse with his family.

Mr. Alesen listened to him in silence and with the most fixed and inquisitive attention. He then replied in a few simple but energetic words to the following purpose.

"I assure you upon my honour, I am as entirely ignorant of your cousin's retreat as you are yourself. I have acted exactly according to his instructions and my solemn engagements. I am not at liberty to impart these to any person, but what intelligence I may hereafter be allowed to give you you shall receive if you will let me know where I can have the honour to address you. You will yourself perceive that my situation cannot admit of my accepting the farther trust which you would wish to repose in me, but I give you mine honour the moment that Lord Mount Villars gives me the power I will communicate to him this conversation and if suffered repeat to you the result of this communication. Confiding therefore in this promise I hope you will respect the privacy of that retirement which your cousin has provided for me, and not molest its tranquility by forcing upon me a correspondence which may prove the total destruction of my future peace."

The cool and gentlemanlike air of resolution with which he delivered this discourse precluded all farther remonstrance or enquiry.

Robert therefore took his leave after he had given him a direction to Hillbarton, which place he had proffered as thinking that there the intelligence so much desired might probably soonest meet Selena, and having declined the courteously offered refreshments he returned with a heavy heart to communicate his disappointment to that gentle bosom whose happiness he now almost feared was for ever lost.

Chapter XXI

Lo! I am here to answer to thy vows
And be the meeting fortunate! I come
With joyful tidings; We shall part no more!
Akenside[83]

Tho' Selena now languished to quit Ireland where she had no longer a latent hope of receiving any news of what could alone interest her heart, yet she would not appear insensible to the tender and watchful exertions with which her brother studiously sought to divert her from the contemplation of her sorrows. She therefore concealed the mental languor that rendered her secretly so reluctant to comply with his proposal, and appeared to share the pleasure with which he beheld the serene and beautiful lustre of the following morning.

At an early hour she accompanied him to the edge of the lake and they embarked together at Ross castle. As they purposed to leave Killarney on the ensuing day Robert was anxious to reach the wilder magnificence of the upper lake; they therefore without landing passed the softly enchanting island of Inisfallen, and the swelling lawns of Muckross, where the ruined abbey scarce revealed its ivied turrets from amid the deeply sombrous shades, with many a more retiring grace which encircles these lakes and which a residence of a month could scarcely be sufficient entirely to discover to the industriously delighted eye.

They had now proceeded along the sweeping range of wooded hills, which covered with oak and arbutus presented one immensely extensive mass of shade, varied with the rich scarlet of the glowing berries and broken by the fantastic shapes of the abruptly prominent marble rocks, which seemed struggling to escape from beneath that luxuriant mantle of wood that Nature had spread even from the aerial horizon to the very edge of the silvery lake.

Nevertheless lovely as were the surrounding scenes which gave varied beauties at every stroke of the oar Selena found it impossible entirely to disguise her internal suffering. The sun was now intensely hot, and her pale cheek and languid eye plainly betrayed her encreasing faintness and lassitude.

"You are ill, dear Selena," cried Robert mournfully, "Had we not better return. You who are so alive to the charms of Nature take no pleasure in all those exquisite pictures and I am only tormenting you by my appeals to your admiration. I see you are fatigued and I have myself no longer an inclination to behold more let us then return."

---

[83] Mark Akenside, *The Pleasures of Imagination* (1744, 1757), 2:644–6.

Selena however urged him to pursue his first intention and assured him that she should in future reproach herself if they now lost an opportunity so favourable.

Their pilot here interposed and remonstrating against their return proposed that they should land on the island of Dymas beneath whose woods they were now slowly winding, and rest there till they had dined and that the heat of the day was over.

To this Robert assented but it was yet so early that Selena would not consent to an arrangement which by losing so much of the day would she foresaw render it impossible for her brother to reach the object of his curiosity. It was at length decided that Selena who had brought her maid to enjoy the fine scenery, should land with her and the other servants and remain on the island till her brother's return from the upper lake.

Leaving her happy attendants to prepare in the sylvan scene the little feast which they had brought Selena now indulged the melancholy liberty of her sad solitude.

Seeking refuge from the sun which was now in full possession of the sky she found a mossy seat beneath the unpierced umbrage of the leafy labyrinth where was indeed presented to her view a very paradise, "so lovely seemed the landscape."[84]

The black turf underneath her feet was covered with the luxuriant verdure interspersed with every native plant that spreads her green leaf to the morning ray the large loose stones scattered around were richly clothed with moss and clusters of the delicate rose heath which grows here in such abundance. Thick tufts of the wild myrtle scented with its balmy aromatic gales the rugged bank which sloped to the margin of the lake upon whose reluctant bosom floated in beautiful pride the water lily whose raiment may indeed justly be said to exceed that of Eastern monarchs "in all their glory."[85] The rocky shore that lay below was profusely covered with the gay arbutus, but nothing added more considerably to the singular beauty of this forest scenery than the young shrubs which shot their vigorous branches from the huge mossy trunks of the most grotesque form that lay overthrown and decayed by age.

Before her the lake forming a small bay was enclosed by the circular unanimity of loftiest shade. Directly opposite to her eye rose Tomys extending to the right its woody theatre "stage above stage high waving"[86] until it reached Glena. The light foliage of the birch and mountain ash hung over the lake that seemed to hold its crystal mirror to the fringed bank—and a dark chasm in the centre of the woods proclaimed the deep glen where O'Sullivan's cascade headlong rolls its white dashing torrent

---

[84] Milton's *Paradise Lost* (1667), 4:152–3 ("the" should be "that").

[85] The quotation invokes Matthew 6:28–9 ("Consider the lilies of the field, how they grow; they toil not, neither do they spin. / And yet I say unto you, That even Solomon in all his glory was not arrayed like one of these" [KJV]) as well as John Wesley's commentary on Matthew 6:29: "Solomon in all his glory was not arrayed like one of these—Not in garments of so pure a white. The eastern monarchs were often clothed in white robes" (*Explanatory Notes Upon the New Testament* [London, 1755]).

[86] James Thomson, "Summer," *The Seasons* (1727), line 650.

from the gelid caverns from whence it rushed. To the left the river which connects the lakes suddenly turned its rocky channel'd course beneath where with bold outline stood in vast majesty the Eagle's nest. Huge masses of white projecting rocks burst from among the wood that darkened the shaggy steep and behind this in wild and savage beauty appeared the mountains of Turk and Mangeston.

Astonished at a picture so sublime whose strong features seemed to wear a solemn frown, Selena who loved tranquility turned her peaceful eye from thence to the milder softer graces that hung over the smooth surface of the gently swelling Glena, whose uninterrupted sloping woods were now varied with hues such as expression cannot paint. Here while she gazed her sadness seemed soothed by the lovely scenes then surrounding with innumerable songsters. In still silence she listened to the sprightly mildness of their notes contrasted with the melancholy murmur of the stock dove that every now and then breathed forth its plaintive melody.

"Alas," thought she, "Poor complainer! How unheeded are thy lamentations amid the song of universal gladness! So fares it with the sons of sorrow thro' the bustle of the unfeeling world. I only can attend to thee! For I alone am sad!" Then while remembrance thrilled with many a proof of recollected love, the deep sigh heaved from her swelling heart as she exclaimed but half audibly, "Oh Sidney! I have then for ever lost thee! I am remembered no more! And this anguish that consumes my heart is shared by none, is known by none!" A torrent of tears flowed from her as with self pity she considered the fairest hours of her life thus devoted to pining regret and insensibility even to all the purest pleasures.

When suddenly a voice so soft, so sweet struck upon her heart, "bathing her drooping spirits with delight," "Beyond the bliss of dreams."[87]

"Selena! beloved Selena! Look upon me my own Selena! Lost, but for ever restored! Behold your happy Sidney! Oh 'tis extacy too much to bear!"

She heard not what he spoke, but she had heard his voice! She had seen him at her feet bathed in tears and wild with unutterable rapture—and she now dreads to breathe or move lest the delightful vision should vanish into air!

Pale, silent, and motionless as the marble statue that enchants the world she remained for a few moments overwhelmed by the full tide of astonishment and joy, insensible to all his raptures and assured that this tumultuous and bewildering impression of bliss which seemed but the lively repetition of so many preceeding dreams would suddenly dissolve like them, and like them leave her once more to all the regret of awakening misery.

But he clasped her in his arms, she felt his heart beat violently against hers, and on her cheek the warm tears of the purest sensibility. The tender shower seemed to melt her first amazement into the softest tenderness of unspeakable felicity. Her own flowed freely.

"Oh Sidney!" she at length exclaimed as she gently pressed him in her modest arms and reclined her face upon his shoulder, "dear Sidney! you are then alive, and you have not forgot me."

---

[87] Milton's *Comus* (1634), lines 812–13 ("bathing her" should be "will bathe the").

"Forgot thee! No beloved Selena, ever since I first beheld thee my soul has not been without thee for one single moment! by day, by night, the only object of my wishes, the dear centre of every thought! Cruel have been the hours of my exile from all I loved, but this happy moment recompenses all. But tell me, are you indeed my own? All my own? Have you never been another's? And do we now meet like the severed waves that mingle together and part no more?"

"Never, never dearest Sidney!" cried Selena in broken accents while her tears impeded all the eager enquiries that her full heart longed to make.

He saw her nerves agitated by excess of bliss even to agony, and seating himself at her feet, he prest her soft hand in silence to his lips, and suffered her tears uninterruptedly to flow that they might relieve and restore her to tranquility.

Oh it was a silence sweeter than Apollo's lute, more eloquent than the Muses' tongue! At length with accents of sweet reproach Selena entreated him to say wherefore he had concealed himself, and to what end he had thus tortured them with fears and suspence, then without waiting his reply she impatiently demanded, "and who is this new favoured friend that has thus engrossed you to himself and banished us all from your heart and from your confidence, for whom you abandoned us even in the hour of terror and affliction, for whom you have neglected nay abjured the world, your family and your poor Selena! Who is this Alesen, this my powerful rival?"

A sweet smile of inexpressible delight played over the arch dimples, and danced in the sparkling eyes of the happy Sidney as he interrupted her tenderly inquisitive expostulations.

"Selena! your lover and your rival are but one, and both are now your own for ever! But where is Robert, I am impatient to express to him my gratitude, for without him what a wretch should I yet be?"

Selena told him that she waited there for his return, and in the mean time besought him no longer to delay accounting for his unkind and strange concealment

Their mutual explanations now commenced and Sidney having listened with every mingled emotion to the eagerly demanded recital of Selena's sufferings since their absence commenced his own melancholy narrative interrupted by many a fond endearment, and rewarded by many a sympathising expression of grateful consolation, many a soul penetrating glance of beaming tenderness from his sweetly captivated auditor.

Having related the misery he had experienced on his unfortunate return to Richmond, in finding that in spite of her promise to him she had removed to Bently farm where he was too well assured from her own lips she had indeed met Dallamore, he then confessed the resolution which he in consequence formed in the bitterness of his despair for ever to fly from all who might pronounce her name or impart to him the detested tidings which he already but too certainly anticipated and having acknowledged how much of his anguish was due to his own impatience which had thus prevented him from hearing the motives of his Selena's conduct he thus proceeded.

"I rode post thro' England with a precipitation that succeeded in some measure to stifle those bitter reflections which I so much dreaded and when I reached Haverford west was almost driven to frenzy upon finding that I must wait four and twenty hours before another packet should sail. My impatience was as intolerable as tho' I could have expected on the opposite shore some relief from the horrible anguish which pursued me. I trembled lest I should be seen by any, in the dread of that impertinence which might pronounce in my ears, these sounds from which my soul shrunk with an agony of terror that I can never describe.

"Nevertheless as I wandered along the shore, burying myself among the recesses of the rocks I could not but observe that my desire of retirement was shared as my disappointment on finding that the packet had sailed had already evidently been by a young man who arrived at the inn at the same moment with myself. Whether it was from the ingenuous expression of his countenance, or because

> Misery delights to trace
> Its semblance in another's face[88]

I know not, but I found my heart warm to him with a sentiment of pity and benevolence which are the only pleasurable sensations to which I was ever alive from the instant that I parted from you at Richmond until a vague hope once more revived in my soul as I yesterday beheld your brother."

"You saw him then," exclaimed Selena. "Is it possible but how was this—for Robert surely could not have deceived me."

"He did not deceive you my beloved Selena, but suffer me to continue, and you will see with what precautions I studiously sought to preserve my own misery and prolong my despair.

"While revolving in my mind the plan which I had already formed for avoiding all communication with those whose friendship might desire to seek me out and offer consolation, I perceived at a distance two or three ill-looking fellows who seemed to watch my motions. It was still daylight, but as the spot that I had chosen was peculiarly desolate, I thought it not impossible that their designs were not fair in thus lurking about. In the disposition in which I found myself at that moment I should certainly have parted with life without regret but my spirit revolted from suffering indignity from the hands of ruffians. I therefore broke off a large branch from a dead thorn which I perceived near the shore and determined to defend myself as well as I was able. Mean while I saw that they had forsaken me and were apparently advancing towards the young man whose evident dejection had so much interested me.

"I followed their steps resolved to afford him what protection I could when on a sudden he looked round and discovering his pursuers and the impossibility of escape as they instantly surrounded him, he at once submitted himself to be hurried

---

[88] "Cowper" (Tighe's note). William Cowper, "The Castaway" (1799), lines 59–60 ("face" should be "case").

with them towards the town. I then guessed that those were bailiffs and unable to resist the impulse of compassion which seized upon me I flew towards them and taking hold of his arm abruptly separated him from their grasp. They exclaimed with one voice, 'Do not attempt a rescue. He is our prisoner by law,' and produced not their writ but their more powerful coadjutors, their pistols. 'Allow me to speak a few words to the gentleman,' replied I, 'I give you my honour I do not intend a rescue, and I have no doubt that you are acting legally.'

"They acceded to my request with a courtesy I hardly expected and even made some apologies for the step they had taken retiring as I wished to a few paces distance from us. I then endeavoured to excuse my conduct which I feared might appear to him impertinent and naming the sum which I had at present with me offered its assistance towards procuring his liberty. My name I could not give without risking the discovery of my own secret which I then considered of such importance. Fortunately I succeeded in my wishes and having conquered the generous and delicate scruples with which young Esmund himself at first rejected my offers, and got rid of the fiends of justice, he imparted to me the history of those misfortunes which had exposed him to the situation in which I had then found him and which still threatened his liberty.

"He had early in life married secretly and against the will of his father an amiable young woman and tho' in consequence of this he had struggled for awhile with the difficulties of poverty, yet her affection and his own sanguine enterprising temper had sweetened every thing. In fact dearest Selena! what situation can be felt as painful while cheered with the dear association of those we love and the sweet confidence that even to share those difficulties and sorrows is to them greater happiness than could be enjoyed in a separation from us?

"The inclination of each fixed them to the country, and as he possessed not only a passion for agriculture, but had also acquired considerable skill and even experience, he for some years reaped a large profit and a still larger crop of hopes from the improvement of an extensive farm which he had been fortunately able to get at a moderate rent. He drew a picture of their innocent felicity which at the time seemed to rend my heart and whatever might henceforth be his lot, I esteemed him but too much blest since he had at least for a time known happiness so perfect and so pure. But alas Selena! my soul shuddered as he continued his sad tale. His prospects of success encreased until encouraged to embark in some more hazardous speculations he in one season lost not only all which he had been able to realize but to the whole value of his remaining stock. Nevertheless the cheerful sweetness, the patient consolations of his beloved partner supported him thro' all. He had received a classical education and her refined and cultivated taste had given a spur to his pursuit of literary enjoyments.

"As they had no young family their hours of leisure were entirely devoted to the studies which they prosecuted together and which thus afforded them the sweetest pleasures, and the tranquilizing charm amid all the perplexities and harassing cares of fortune. One evening as she leaned upon his bosom, while his arm was thrown around her waist, he read to her an affecting passage which had just soothed his own mind. His attention and his feelings were deeply engaged when he had finished he looked round as usual for the applauding smile, the sympathetic ray of beaming approbation which ever confirmed his own. Oh Selena! He looked! She was in his arms a corpse!" Sidney paused and eagerly clasped the hand of his beloved his lips quivered, and his whole frame shook as tho' the angel of Death hung indeed threatening over the lovely innocent object in whose restoration to his despairing wishes he yet fearfully and tremblingly rejoiced.

Selena was herself shocked at a relation so terrible and pressing his hand as tho' she shared his fears, and dreaded even now to lose for ever that dear treasure which she had so lately regained, they continued for some moments silent.

At length Selena whisperingly entreated him to proceed.

"You will not wonder dearest Selena that such a shock for a while should totally have deprived him of all ability to think or act with prudence. His affairs fell prone into ruin and disorder; he freely confessed to me that even at the first he had engaged in schemes which it required years of industry and close attention to render productive. The farm was however even now far more valuable then when he had taken it, but he was not permitted to sell his interest, and leaving every thing to his creditors, he abandoned a scene become horrible to him, and anxious only to escape the dreary confinement of a prison, cared not in what manner he should seek to support a life not merely indifferent but miserably irksome to him. The indefatigable cruelty of one of his creditors who had thus pursued him was the source of his consolation.

"Our mutual misfortunes and sorrow endeared and united us to each other. I could not indeed communicate to him my motives for desiring concealment but satisfied that such was my desire, he devoted himself to my service and solicited not my confidence. I did not even declare to him my real name but informed him that having reasons to disguise my own I wished to be called Alesen, and this I chose to assume because it appeared sweet to me that I should thus bear the adored name of my Selena concealed as was her image for ever in my heart. It never met my ear without exciting a thrilling sensation of a pain that I wish not to avoid —'Il volgo non intendemi, ma tu m'intendi Amore!'[89] I told him that under this appellation I had been appointed agent to the estate of Loughlaven, acquainting him with the real name of its possessor whom I described as my friend. I offered him a share of all that liberty and retirement which this promised to me and he gave me his word to preserve my secret and assist me in my projects for promoting the comforts of the tenantry and their instruction in what might prove of lasting benefit to themselves and their neighbourhood.

"I confessed to him my determination never to receive any letters, and the more certainly to avoid all discovery it was agreed, that if in spite of our endeavours our retreat should be penetrated into by intruders, he should present himself as the friend of your Sidney. As I had never before visited Loughlaven no one looked at

---

[89] "Alfieri" (Tighe's note). Not Alfieri but Vincenzo Monti, "Per Nozze Illustri" (1787), lines 19–20: "The common people do not understand me, but you do my love."

me with suspicion. I had no sooner entered heartily into our projects for improving the estate and meliorating the wretched condition of the tenants, (who destitute and ignorant rather resembled savages than peasants) than I found a degree of returning peace dawn upon my soul. Man is born to a life of trial and condemned to bear a repetition of perpetually new sorrows and vexations; He is therefore gifted with a natural propensity to escape each misfortune so that however heavy be that calamity it cannot continuously oppress him."

"You were then soon comforted dear Sidney," said Selena softly, a reluctant smile of playful fondness half defeating the glance of sweet reproachful displeasure which she beamed upon him as he spoke.

"Unjust ungrateful Selena! What does not that deserve? Beware how you provoke me to persecute you with the sad repetition of my sufferings and claim from you who were their source their full recompense. No Selena that peace of which I boasted in the exertions that I thought duty still required was interrupted by recollections of anguish almost intolerable and fled at every pause of laborious activity. In vain did I represent to myself that being thus suddenly rent at once from all the ties of habit and affection, I was become another being, and might commence anew a life which possessing as I was conscious I still did many positive advantages, must surely in itself contain some pleasures. In vain did I persuade myself that being thus violently separated from all that could locally remind me of my disappointments I had indeed drank the waters of oblivion. Certain that you were for ever lost to me, that you had willingly embraced that part which rendered it even a crime for me to regret or desire you I in vain wished to esteem the past as annihilated for me, and that free from all anxiety I might form new views and looking only to the future forget the feelings which even while I considered them innocent had been the perpetual source of anguish to my soul.

"Alas those feelings still existed, and existed for my torment. Independent of the reasons by which my judgment prohibited me from imparting my sorrows to my companion my heart felt no inclination to place him farther in my confidence. Possessing almost every amiable disposition and even strong sensibility young Esmund was yet but little qualified to sympathise with a melancholy which could resist the consolations of time and new pursuits. I saw him eagerly embrace every scheme which I encouraged, and animated with a never failing spring of unconquerable vivacity it was not long until he appeared to have shaken off every trace of his misfortunes, and I was often obliged to fly to solitude from the overpowering flow of animal spirits which I could not indeed with unfeeling brutality check by reminding him of his misfortunes but under which my soul was oppressed and even disgusted.

"Nevertheless his grateful attachment, his actively[90] benevolent disposition and the ardour with which he prosecuted every wish that I expressed, or that he could even divine endeared him to me by bonds of the most sincere regard and esteem. His talents, his love of doing good to all around us and above all his natural cheerfulness of temper precluded every fear of his growing weary of our solitude,

---

[90]   MS: "activity" (my correction).

and I was confident that should he even languish for change he was capable of sacrificing himself to the gratitude by which I knew he generously considered himself bound to me for ever.

"But of this I was under no apprehensions, for his imagination wild and ardent, produced for him by its perpetual magic an enchanted world that mocked the dullness of confinement and continually procured for him that variety which a less lively fancy would have sought with restless discontent. With the same eagerness that he engaged in our rural labours he more than shared in every literary pursuit and tho' always ready to partake of my employments he opposed not the perfect liberty of my solitude. Apparently devoid of all curiosity he anxiously protected my concealment still led by his ardent desire for my gratification. We were by turns masons, poets and labourers, whatever I had recourse to in the vain hope of excluding the sense of my misery he pursued as the favourite object of his life and it created for him a thousand pleasures while it became to me irksome and insipid. Assured of his acting in every thing as I would myself I have often been absent from home for days together, and I have wandered over all those beautiful scenes with the independent freedom of a savage.

"But this romantic paradise where indeed

> To all delight of human sense exposed
> In narrow room[91]

is nature's whole wealth of loveliness had for me no charms and believe me dearest Selena, my heart is not capable of boasting in your absence any sensation that resembles pleasure save that which results from the imagination that I in some degree administered to the happiness of others. I dreaded nothing so much as to hear that name which I could not doubt you had now assumed and for this reason obstinately persisted in refusing to receive all letters except those which officiousness at first forced upon me and which I committed unopened to the flames.

"I have now nothing to relate to you except those tumultuous emotions of incomprehensible hope and uncertainty which after having since yesterday almost worked me up to frenzy have now at length brought me into the haven of felicity where in the bosom of my only beloved my wearied soul may repose itself for ever. You will smile my Selena when I tell you in what manner I was employed when your brother entered my farm. Esmund had undertaken to instruct one of the men whose cottage we were repairing, to thatch in a more durable manner. Dissatisfied with the progress of his scholar he had entreated me to assist him in proving the advantage of his new method and conquer the prejudice of habit which is sometimes no easy task. Indeed, 'Oh sir it was always done that way!' is the constant reply and they generally think it a sufficient and convincing argument against every recommended improvement, so that it requires some ingenuity and patience to persuade them that things might yet be better than they have hitherto been. We were mounted upon the roof of the cottage and our characters being at

---

[91]   Milton, *Paradise Lost* (1667), 4:206–7.

stake were exerting our utmost abilities as thatchers when I suddenly perceived your brother slowly riding thro' the far gate. The confusion of my mind totally overpowered for the moment all my senses. I was about to throw myself from the place where I stood that I might hide myself from his sight, but Esmund (who was at my side and had observed me closely from the time that the sound of the horses feet had called his attention as well as mine) now hastily seized my arm and restored me to recollection by asking with eagerness what I was about to do.

"I was for awhile unable to determine but observing that your brother entered one of the cottages at some distance we had time to consider and arrange what conduct we should pursue. I was anxious to prevent his entering the house where I thought it most probable that he would find no servant to answer him and as the hall door I was sure lay open he might proceed to my study and there discover a thousand indisputable traces of him whom I had no doubt he sought. Thither therefore I hastened by the shortest path and desiring Esmund to come to me for farther information, after he had prepared our servant whom he went to look for in the stables, I locked myself in, and endeavoured to recollect every caution with which it might be necessary to furnish my intelligent representative. How he conducted himself I dare say Robert has already told you, who I believe entertained no farther suspicion, altho' from all I have since heard I cannot doubt but that till Esmund entered the room, his kind affectionate heart had felicitated itself upon having detected the apparently ungrateful insensible Sidney.

"I had no fears in the discretion of Esmund. I had already sent him in this character to transact some business with my former agent on our first arrival in Ireland and while he now repeated to me each word that had passed between him and Robert, while my panting heart trembled

> in vast suspence
> Between unruly joys and chilling fears[92]

he with generous delicacy forbore to add to the torments of my bewildered mind by one hint of that curiosity which he must unquestionably have experienced. The unfortunate being who had ever been more the object of my pity than abhorrence even while he was the destruction of all my peace and the tormenter of her I loved, the ill-fated companion of my childhood was then no more. Selena, will you again reproach me for the tears which I gave to his memory? Angel of tenderness! These precious drops of sympathy are my dear pledges of absolution, suffer me to receive them on those lips that in our hopeless absence have still 'virgined our last kiss'[93] and 'Oh my souls joy!'

> May after every tempest come such calm."[94]

---

[92]   Amestris in Nicholas Rowe's *The Ambitious Stepmother* (1702), 3.2.11–12.

[93]   Coriolanus in Shakespeare's *Coriolanus* (1607), 5.3.46–8: "that kiss / I carried from thee, dear, and my true lip / Hath virgin'd it ever since."

[94]   "Shakespear" (Tighe's note). Othello in Shakespeare's *Othello* (1604), 2.1.184–5.

"Go on dear Sidney, and if you can excuse your tardy coming and say wherefore you did not spare us at least this last night of affliction and disappointment."

"Consider dear Selena, I knew not that you were here. I should not even perhaps have been able to trace Robert so immediately had it not been for the indefatigable exertions of Esmund. Early this morning he discovered and brought for my examination the young man who had been your brother's guide. Alas dear Selena! What were the contending emotions of my soul when I could no longer doubt that you were indeed the companion of Robert? My heart melted within me as the boy simply repeated your melancholy looks, your gentle words, and the sweetly broken voice which demanded 'had he ever seen me?' And yet intoxicated as I was with the rapture of that moment shall I confess all beloved Selena? Shall I tell the insupportable idea which even then intruded with a violence that almost vanquished all delight? Convinced that you had been another's, my heart revolted invincibly against the joy, which was to be snatched as it were from the grave of him to whom it had once belonged. I could not yet forgive the easiness with which I thought you had abandoned me and thrown yourself into the arms of another, even tho' that rival could no longer oppose me. Struggling with my peevish discontented scruples which I in vain condemned, I at length resolved to send for the letters which I knew remained for me at the post office. Afraid to enter the town lest I should be seen by Robert or his servants I waited at some distance with inconceivable agitation for the return of my messenger. Richly were those torments of suspence overpaid by the conviction I there received that my Selena had never injured that spotless faith which with a purpose fair as her pure self she had once pledged to the espoused of her heart.

"Impetuously I flew to the house, I pronounced that dear name which you had even until now preserved unchanged for your happy Sidney, that name which had so long been buried in my heart nor past my lips except in the darkness of the night, or the deep solitude of embowering forests. You were gone! No never in my life had I known impatience, until that which seized upon me at this intelligence. It appeared to me as if I was in one of those disturbed dreams where we are mocked by the sight of what we desire, without the power of ever attaining it. I could not believe that you had not even now escaped me for ever—or that I should indeed again behold you.

"While hastening to the edge of the lake I enumerated in my mind every possibility which could prevent or retard our meeting and could scarcely persuade myself that some unforseen circumstance, some terrible misfortune would not arise to intercept even at the very goal my arrival at felicity so beyond all hope. Happily I found a fisherman's boat close to Ross island and having learned which direction you had taken I concluded you were gone to the upper lake, when just as I was exerting all my strength to row round that point I perceived a group assembled at a little distance from the shore. I believe I could not have supported a disappointment at that instant. I was unable to strike the oar.

"'Land me,' I articulated with difficulty, breathless and without power to move while my eyes were eagerly strained to distinguish the features. They first rested upon your little Sophy. She uttered an exclamation of surprise and joy. 'Where is she?' I cried as I leaped on shore. I knew not if she answered me, but a confused idea that I heard her say you were on the island urged me on and springing forward on a sudden Selena, I only know I saw you. Finish for me this dear, this transporting moment & tell me that you shared the unutterable rapture with which it filled my soul and which even yet overflows my eyes in these unmanly showers."

There is no eloquence so divine, so powerful as the conversation of happy lovers, but there is also none that in repetition retains less of that sweet perfume and suppliance of the moment—its charm is of too fine an essence to be fixed by ought but memory and eludes all the chains of recitation.

The reply of Selena, and those mutually enchanting confessions of delight and tenderness, with their renewed vows of pure and perfect faith must not therefore be recorded.

They were however quickly interrupted by new joys in the arrival of Robert. Scarcely was he landed when his servant hailed him with the unexpected and almost incredible tidings. Eagerly flying to meet each other Selena sunk in his arms and hiding her sobbing face in his bosom, once more wept the extacy which she could not speak.

Sidney retained her hand but his joy was nearly as silent as her own, while pressing her hands which were thus united Robert poured forth his affectionate heart in congratulations and every demonstration of joyful tenderness.

"Oh welcome," he exclaimed, "My brother my friend! Never may we again feel the cruelty of such a separation!"

Once more explanations ensued and when the happy party sat down to their repast it may be well said that "Altho' they had neither many serving men nor vessels of gold nor silver, yet was that a sweet meal upon the grass amid the forest."[95]

Chapter XXII

> Love on this earth the only mean thou art
> Whereby we hold intelligence with Heaven!
> And it is then that only dost impart
> The good that to mortality is given.
> Oh sacred bond by time that art not broken!
> Oh thing divine, by Angels to be spoken!
>
> Drayton[96]

> Look here and weep with tenderness and transport,
> What is all tasteless luxury to this
> To those best joys which holy love bestows.
>
> Thompson[97]

---

[95] "Amadis" (Tighe's note). Robert Southey, trans., *Amadis of Gaul*, 4 vols (1803), 2:8.

[96] Michael Drayton, *The Legend of Pierce Gaveston* (1596), lines 85–90 ("then" should be "thou" in line 87).

[97] Agamemnon in James Thomson's *Agamemnon* (1738), 2.3.41–3.

Tho' they did not part until a late hour Selena's agitated spirits were but little disposed for sleep. Restless and disturbed she dreaded to lye down lest dreams of terror such as she had for some time frequently experienced might deprive her of the consciousness of that happiness which she could yet scarcely believe really existed. But having past the greatest part of the night in writing to her affectionately sympathising friends in Derbyshire she poured forth her gratitude to Heaven and in thus doing found the most delicious tears come to her relief composing her mind to an almost divine tranquility.

What sensation upon earth can equal that, with which she awoke the following morning? When starting from a sweetly restoring slumber, the beloved sound of her Sidney's voice as he spoke to her brother in the adjoining chamber, at once brought to her soul the full sense and recollection of all her bliss and convinced her that she had indeed beheld him, that they had passed the night under the same roof, that in a few moments his eyes would speak unutterable fondness and that their mutual lives should be spent in the presence of each other.

Tho' she had resisted the proposal made by Sidney that they might now return with him to Loughlaven, she nevertheless eagerly desired to visit the scene of that retirement to which the most amiable most tender of lovers had devoted himself for her. The fruits of that benevolent activity wherein he had alone sought his virtuous consolations were to her heart the sweetest pledges of a love so pure, so faithful that her confidence reposed on it with tender assurance for years of unabashed felicity.

They wandered over every part of the well cultivated farm and no object met Selena's eye that was not interesting to her sensibility. In every thing she saw her beloved, nor was this all, for in every thing she saw how fondly, how constantly she had occupied his soul with sad regret during their cruel separation. At each step she found fresh planted, or flourishing in young beauty her favourite flowers, the trees beneath whose branches she had peculiarly loved to repose. His melancholy pleasing occupation had been to form by art a spot which exactly resembled that at Hillbarton which had been consecrated to happier love. Not a flower not a shrub but was here exactly imitated, nay she even here beheld the overhanging rock. She looked for the twin limes which Sidney had planted emblems of their lives, memorials of their loves. They were indeed here but separated by a rough portion of rock against which he had found a sad gratification in placing the cypress, the yew, the deadly nightshade and every plant of sombrous growth. Selena saw her own tree vigorous in its beauty, while wounded and lopped and severed in the midst its miserable associate withered in decay.

"Ah unjust unkind Sidney!" exclaimed she pressing his arm and smiling thro' her tears. "How little did you know that heart which you alone have ever possessed when you accused it of insensibility or want of sympathy!"

"Alas beloved Selena!" replied he inexpressibly moved by this acknowledgment of invincible love, "Even while I thus indulged my fancy in idly sporting with my own anguish those reflections which I could least endure were those which told me that your heart could never more know peace on earth, and that even duty itself could never smother that compassion and regret with which the remembrance of him who was thus lost would perpetually pursue your gentle tenderness. But away with these recollections. Love presents us with a present moment of exquisite enjoyment and a cloudless future. I have now nothing upon earth to desire except that blest hour when my generous Selena will give me indeed an undisputed right to call her my own for ever."

Her glowing cheek and downcast eye forbad him to proceed, but pressing her hand to his heart, in the soft glance which at length met his with slowly modest fondness, he read that promised vow which Heaven had already heard and resolved to crown with every nuptial blessing.

Selena was however resolved in secret that the months which as next heir were for Sidney dedicated by custom to the ceremonial of mourning habits should never be intruded upon by him with hymeneal festivities.

She therefore desired Robert to inform him of her determination and prevent [him] from even speaking to her upon the subject during the short period which yet remained till its expiration.

Sidney was for the present too happy to murmur at any wish of his Selena's and satisfied in the assurance that she desired never more to separate from him he resigned into her hands every moment of his present and future existence.

On the following morning Robert proposed that they should set forward towards Hillbarton. But Sidney requested the delay of a few days wishing to arrange before his departure some transactions for the convenience of his friend Esmund to whom he gave a lease of Loughlaven and at the same time advanced him a sufficient sum to pay all his creditors so that he might return to England with liberty and honour.

But Esmund whose head was full of projects for his new and beautiful farm preferred to remain at Loughlaven and Sidney delighted in the certainty that he would pursue every benevolent and useful plan which he had himself pointed out.

With the consent of the smiling blushing Selena he promised to visit him a part of every year and received in return his assurance that he would join them whenever they made Mount Villars their residence, and give his assistance towards the improvements which they might there undertake.

Warm and ardent in every thing he beheld Selena as an angel of Heaven and her brother as next to Sidney, the first of all that was amiable and excellent among men.

Sidney who had vowed in secret never more to seek repose but under the same roof which sheltered his beloved, returned with them that night to Killarney where Esmund joined them while at breakfast.

They proceeded together to the edge of the lake where Sidney had already prepared every thing for their arrival.

Selena was surprised at the new dresses of the rowers and the gay appearance of the boat, furnished with a silk awning and all that could contribute to the unalloyed pleasure of those happy days.

But what most added to this enchanting scene was the attendance of a band which Sidney had procured from Lord M's regiment quartered at the neighbouring town.

Placed in another boat kept to the windward of theirs at some distance and when they landed to dine on the little lawn beside the river, immediately beneath the Eagle's nest, the harmony of Heaven could alone surpass that produced by the echoes which were awakened by the unseen flutes and clarionets placed behind the wooded rocks.

Tears of thrilling extacy bathed the cheeks of Selena as she returned the soft pressure of her Sidney's hand while he gazed in her speaking eyes to read the effect of this celestially surprising melody—unutterable indeed by any language and inconceivable by any but those to whom Memory may faintly yet return the unexpressive[98] sounds.

Unable to quit a spot so delicious they lingered there until the sunny evening had tinged with all its yellow lustre every steep descending grove, and did not return to the lake till the moon rode sublime in the pure cerulean sky. Never did the deep dark shades of the wooded mountains look so magnificent, as while thus contrasted with the pure silver sheet that reflected her quivering beams while from the cloudless height of the blue dome she shed over all the lake her "long levelled rule of streaming light."[99]

"Oh Sidney we must not leave this yet!" exclaimed Selena sighing with excess of pleasure each evening as they returned from their new delights. Not an instant but had now witnessed their felicity and Selena could scarcely credit that she had been indeed conducted to those bewitching scenes before the presence of Sidney had so embellished their beauties that they were even to her eyes another face.

Esmund who was besides interested to detain his lovely friends devised a thousand new entertainments and after a fortnight's residence it was with the utmost difficulty that he was constrained reluctantly to part from those whom he then believed so twined around his heart, that when severed from thence his happiness must perish in the violence of separation.

Nevertheless while Selena expressed her compassion for him thus left in a strange country, bereft of the society of such a friend, she had herself seen enough of his character to assent to the opinion of Sidney that a few days would reconcile him to the loss, and that new objects would quickly occupy his imagination and his heart.

The justice of this their confidence in the consolations of his sanguine mind, was confirmed in less than two months by the intelligence communicated by himself with all the raptures of delighted love that he was about to unite himself to one whose charms of mind and person fully justified his second choice made under far happier auspices than his last.

The morning before the happy party left Killarney Esmund presented to Selena some complimentary verses and when rallied by Sidney on the subject with playfully counterfeited jealousy he retaliated by upbraiding him with his silence when love and beauty called so powerfully upon his Muse. Selena joined in this reproach, and reminded him of his confession that before her arrival in Kerry they had both been poets.

---

[98]   The manuscript shows a large "X" over "unexpressive."

[99]   Milton, *Comus* (1634), line 340.

"True dearest Selena! But my moments are now too precious to employ one of them in recollecting insipid rhymes."

"Nay," cried Esmund, "that is but a lame apology. For as to recollecting your verses, had you indeed composed any, it is impossible but you should have communicated them to us during our many moonlight excursions."

Sidney smiled; and Selena looking at him half reproachfully said in a soft voice, "I have heard that satisfied assurance ever leads to indifference and that indifference contracts the ideas, and by its dullness can blunt the finest genius."

"Well Selena," replied he while a momentary glow suffused his beautiful brow, "on your head shall lie all my poetical sins, and if you smile I care not for the Muses' frown, but you must allow me some moments to call back the lines that have really escaped my memory, for in spite of Esmund's assertion it *was* possible to compose bad verses and yet not impose them on your indulgence."

He then called for a pen and ink, and amidst abundance of mirth caused by his mistakes and affected impatience he at length completed three sonnets, which he in due form laid at his Selena's feet and half surprised and half obtained his reward upon her soft cheeks. Two of these are here presented to the reader because they attempt some description of scenes indeed that surpass all language, scenes which are surely ever dear to memory and cannot therefore fail to please in some degree those who have once enjoyed them.

But the third was instantly concealed by the blushing Selena from every eye but hers which swam in delighted tenderness as they beamed upon him a grateful confession of sympathy in the love and rapture which they had so sweetly expressed.[100]

> Sonnet Written at the Eagle's Nest
> Here let us rest, while with meridian blaze
>   The sun rides glorious o'er the cloudless sky,
>   While o'er the Lake no cooling zephyrs fly,
> But on the liquid glass we dazzled gaze,
> And fainting ask for shade—Lo where his nest
>   The bird of Jove has fixed—the lofty brow,
> With arbutus and fragrant wild shrubs drest,
>   Impendent frowns nor will approach allow—
> Here the soft turf invites; Here magic sounds
>   Celestially respondant shall enchant
> While melody from those steep wood rebounds
>   In thrilling cadence sweet—Sure life can grant
> No brighter hours than this—and memory oft
> Shall paint this happiest scene with pencil soft![101]

---

[100] The third sonnet is Tighe's "On Leaving Killarney. August 5, 1800," transcribed in her manuscript collection *Verses Transcribed for H.T.* (Brompton, 1805) and first published in *Psyche, with Other Poems* (1811).

[101] This sonnet is titled "Written at the Eagle's Nest. Killarney. July 26, 1800," in *Verses Transcribed for H.T.* (Brompton, 1805) and first published in *Psyche, with Other Poems* (1811).

Fig. V.2   Illustration for "Written at the Eagle's Nest. Killarney. July 26, 1800" in *Verses Transcribed for H.T.* (Brompton, 1805), MS Acc 5495/C/8/1, National Library of Ireland, Dublin.

          Sonnet Returning at Night
How soft the pause! the notes melodious cease,
      Which from each feeling could an echo call—
      Rest on your oars that not a sound may fall
To interrupt the stillness of our peace!
The fanning west wind breathes upon our cheeks
      Yet glowing with the suns departed beams;
      Thro' the blue Heavens the cloudless moon pours streams
Of pure resplendent light—in silver streaks
Reflected on the still, unruffled lake—
      The Alpine hills in solemn silence frown
      While the dark woods night's deepest shades embrown—
And now once more that soothing strain awake!
Oh ever to my heart with magic power
Shall these sweet sounds recal this rapturous hour![102]

---

[102] This sonnet is titled "Written at Killarney. July 29, 1800" in *Verses Transcribed for H.T.* (Brompton, 1805) and first published in *Psyche, with Other Poems* (1811).

Fig. V.3   Illustration for "Written at Killarney. July 29, 1800" in *Verses Transcribed for H.T.* (Brompton, 1805), MS Acc 5495/C/8/1, National Library of Ireland, Dublin.

Before Selena quitted Ireland, or could receive an answer to the joyful intelligence which she had communicated to Hillbarton, she got a letter from Clara confessing in terms of sincere astonishment mingled with a kind of regret that Edwin had professed to her sentiments too warm for friendship and ardently solicited her to give him hope that when his constancy and his perseverance in prudence should have expiated his shameful errors he might be allowed to offer her a heart which however unworthy of hers, was yet entirely and for ever her own.

Clara did not repeat these expressions. Too much agitated to say much, she contented herself with intrusting to her sister the strange proposal which she said a thousand invincible reasons obliged her without hesitation decidedly to reject.

Selena was however little surprised to behold Edwin on her arrival at Hillbarton among the happy group assembled to hail their return with all that cordial glow of pleasure which attends the meeting of dearest friends long separated and at length reunited for ever.

The houses of Esselberrie and Hillbarton had combined their inhabitants as one family and Mrs. Vallard had consented to the earnest proposal of the lovely widow (whom she considered as her own child and who loved her as a tender Mother) that they should henceforth reside together. And they had mutually concerted that while the young Earl and Countess of Mount Villars could be detained in Derbyshire, Hillbarton should be exclusively their own. For Mrs. Vallard wished during her life to endear to them a place which she loved to think her Selena would ever prefer, not only on account of its vicinity to Esselberrie but also in remembrance of her by whom it should be bequeathed.

There was also another visitor at Hillbarton whom Selena met with considerable pleasure. She had before heard from Clara that the Marquis of Ortney occasionally enlivened their society. She had ever considered him as amiable and worthy of her regard and she now looked upon him with grateful interest for the services he had rendered her beloved friend.

The acknowledged tenderness and unreserved friendship which subsisted between him and his cousin almost destroyed all suspicions that she was at first ready to entertain of his designs upon the liberty of Lady Trevallyn, and when she ventured gently to hint to her friend the probability that he might now seek some recompense for his long attachment, that look of pensive sadness, which they had once been accustomed to wear, when "sorrow seemed pleased to dwell with so much sweetness,"[103] again clouded the beautiful features of the fair Emily for the first time since she had welcomed the return of her dear and happy Selena.

"Ah never, never," she exclaimed with a mournfully determined voice, "never may my ears be wounded by another profession of a sentiment that has no existence for my heart. No Selena, be assured my cousin has too much delicacy, too much true feeling to think of me otherwise then as an unfortunate sister preserved by Heaven, and her Heaven sent friends, and restored to that happiness, which her weakness deserved not. But could Lord Ortney ever foolishly cherish a wish so injurious to himself, he knows my whole heart; and he is well assured that no motive upon earth could ever induce me to make new vows. He has demanded my friendship, and offered me all that protection which the best of brothers could bestow and which his excellent judgment and amiable heart render so valuable to my folly, and imprudence. His advice shall be my oracle. I am not fit to conduct myself, but never dear Selena will I take in future any step without your approbation. Happy Emily! blessed with the dearest, wisest, best of friends!"

The proposals of Edwin were after some time again renewed, and seconded without his knowledge by the warmly officious interference of his uncle Lord Stanmore who had heard from Mr. Bently of the obligations which he owed to the tender cares of Clara, and had been told of Edwin's attachment to her before he was himself conscious it existed.

Not contented with expressing his approbation of his choice, Lord Stanmore in his eagerness to accelerate a business upon which he found Edwin slow to communicate with him, now applied to Robert immediately on his return, and with many flattering expressions of satisfaction in the proposed alliance promised to make settlements beyond his utmost demands.

---

[103] Dolabella in John Dryden's *All for Love* (1678), 4.1.64 ("seemed" should be "seems").

Robert who had himself only faint suspicions of the change which had taken place in the sentiments of Edwin, which by the earnest desire of Clara was kept a profound secret was amazed at these offers and could not forbear expressing some doubts; he nevertheless declared his acquiescence with whatever his sister might determine and confessed himself highly obliged by proposals so generous on the part of his Lordship.

Robert lost no time imparting what had past to Selena, and desired her to consult with Clara on the subject. In the mean time Edwin who heard from his uncle what he had done, felt all that anxious timidity which never fails to accompany love, and fearful of being banished from the only society in which he could exist entreated Selena that what had passed might be considered not as his act and that he might not be denied these opportunities thro' which he trusted in time by constancy and assiduity to prove the sincerity of his attachment, and gain those affections upon which he now indeed felt all his happiness depended,

"Do not dear Selena," cried he earnestly, "Judge me of a fickle disposition, and that my love is of a transient nature because I have proved it possible to be transferred. The sentiments, the graces that I have loved and yet love with a passion which never can be changed are the same. You are all that is lovely, all that is excellent upon earth, I know, I feel it, but give credit to my sincerity when I declare that had I seen Clara at Inverathie, my unfortunate folly should never have tormented you and injured myself as it has done. I blush for what has past, but not for that love which has never changed, for in you I did but love the virtues and the charms of Clara."

Selena heard him with a partial pleasure, and a hope that guided by the gentle influence and pure principles of Clara, his character established in virtue might form the happiness of the sister she so tenderly loved. And having found that her delicacy alone opposed the suit which she feared was more the effect of pity for her betrayed fondness, than the dictates of his own passion, Selena trusted to time and the eloquence of love to convince her of the sincerity of Edwin's attachment and thought that the extreme youth of Clara was of itself a sufficient reason to encourage the delay of their union.

Robert was therefore commissioned to represent this to Lord Stanmore, and to request him not to urge the affair at least for some months, and in the mean time the society of Edwin who had taken up his abode near Esselberrie added a thousand charms and graces to the happy circle amid which he resided, while every hour strengthened that mutual innocent affection which inspired the heart of Clara with all that confidence it had at first wanted and sweetened every moment of their existence.

The happiness of Robert was now unclouded except by the occasional remembrances of his disgraceful and unfortunate connexion and the delays which unavoidably attended his complete liberation. The abandoned woman whom he had so rashly chosen to be the companion of his life had indeed obviated most of the difficulties of their final separation by assuming the title of wife to the possessor of a celebrated gaming house in Paris, whom her personal attractions and the large settlement made on her by the lavish generosity of Robert had allured to an association which might in those regions of licentiousness be dissolved at pleasure. No sooner was she assured of the final desertion of Rainsford than she had sought consolation from the offered protection of Captain Rowly. Having accompanied him to Paris and discovered that his resources were even yet more uncertain than her own, they parted by mutual consent their union being no longer cemented by interest or inclination. Brilliant was now her reign, and for a while untroubled by remorse and insolent in all the luxury of vice she would perhaps have looked down with unenvying contempt upon the insipid tranquil felicity of the dear contentedly domestic circle assembled around the social blazing hearth at Esselberrie.

Leave her in her short career of splendour [—] disturb not with the anticipation of her inevitably hastening calamity the gentle bosom that loves to rest on the sweet pictures of innocence and love presented to the imagination from the union of their two most beautiful and spotless earthly representations!

The happy morning at length dawned whose return was to be for ever beheld with encreasing affection and gratitude thro' the united lives of the faithful amiable Sidney and his most adored, most lovely bride.

It was the wish of Selena that Mr. Mason should join their hands and that from his pious lips they might receive the nuptial blessing. As they entered the little church of Esselberrie a half sorrowful glance from the happy Sidney accompanied the whispered reproach, "Selena! beloved Selena! Do you weep?"

"Ah Sidney these are sweet tears, they flow from the remembrance of a saint in Heaven. Surely the eyes of my Mother are at this moment fixed upon her happy children! Oh how would she have loved my Sidney!"

How exquisite are the tears excited by tenderness and wiped away by the hand of Love! How precious are those sacred vows sanctioned by the heart which ensure to us even until Death itself alone must part the beloved society, the protection, the common interest of the being we have chosen from the whole world! All that Sidney had ever formerly uttered of the joys inseparably attached to their united duties and pleasures dwelt at this solemn moment upon Selena's heart and no doubt disturbed her confidence in their perpetual affection. Happy lovers! Revolving periods find you more endearing, more endeared unto each other, for you there is no honey moon! Your love knows how to perpetuate itself, and built upon the solid basis of just esteem has nothing to fear from time which can but strengthen the beautiful and perfect edifice, as the weight which oppresses the arch adds to its firmness and ensures its durability.

The End

Works Cited

Akenside, Mark. *The Pleasures of Imagination*. 1744; London: Dodsley, 1757.

An act to dissolve the marriage of John Blachford ... with Maria Camilla Blachford, his now wife, and to enable him to marry again; and for other purposes therein mentioned. London: Clayton & Scott, 1812.

Anderson, John. "Mary Tighe." *The Encyclopedia of Romanticism: Culture in Britain, 1780s–1830s*. Ed. Laura Dabundo. New York: Garland, 1992.

Archives of the Longman Group, MS 1393, Reading University Library, Reading, UK.

Ariosto, Ludovico. *Orlando Furioso*. 1516; Oxford: Oxford University Press, 1974.

Armstrong, Isobel, et al., "Mary Tighe." *Nineteenth Century Women Poets*. Oxford: Clarendon Press, 1996.

Baillie, Joanna. *Count Basil: A Tragedy* and *De Montfort: A Tragedy*. *Plays on the Passions*. Ed. Peter Duthie. 1798; Ontario: Broadview, 2001.

Barbauld, Anna Laetitia. *Poems*. London: Johnson, 1773.

Beattie, James. *The Minstrel; or, the Progress of Genius*. London: Dilly, 1771.

———. *Original Poems and Translations*. London: Millar, 1760.

Beaumont, Francis and John Fletcher. *The Dramatick Works of Beaumont and Fletcher*. 10 vols. London: Sherlock, 1778.

Bell, Eva Mary. *The Hamwood Papers of the Ladies of Llangollen and Caroline Hamilton*. London: Macmillan, 1930.

Berquin, Arnaud. *Idylles et Romances*. Paris, 1776.

Bertaut, Jean. *Recueil de Quelques Vers Amoureux*. Paris, 1602.

Blachford, Theodosia. *The Life of the Baroness de Chantal*. Translated from the French. London: Fry and Couchman, 1787.

———. "Observations on the Foregoing Journal by Her Mother, Mrs. Blachford." *The Collected Poems and Journals of Mary Tighe*. Ed. Harriet Kramer Linkin. 227–43.

Blackburne, Elizabeth. "Mrs. Mary Tighe." *Illustrious Irishwomen*. 2 vols. London: Tinsley Brothers, 1877.

Blain, Virginia, Patricia Clements, and Isobel Grundy. "Mary Tighe." *The Feminist Companion to Literature in English*. New Haven and London: Yale University Press, 1990.

Bourke, Angela, et al. *Irish Women's Writing and Traditions*. Vols 4 and 5 of *The Field Day Anthology of Irish Writing*. Cork: Cork University Press, New York: New York University Press, 2002.

Brooke, Henry. *The Earl of Essex: A Tragedy*. London: Davies, 1761.

———. *The Earl of Westmorland: A Tragedy*. London: Sewell, 1789.

Buchanan, Averill. "'Selena,' the 'New Favorite of My Imagination': Mary Tighe's Unpublished Novel." *Irish University Review* 41:1 (2011): 169–82.

Burns, Robert. *Poems, Chiefly in the Scottish Dialect*. 2 vols. Edinburgh: Creech, London: Cadell, 1793.

Camões, Luis de. *The Lusiad, or, the Discovery of India*. Trans. William Julius Mickle. Oxford: Jackson and Lister, 1776.

Cartwright, Edmund. *Armine and Elvira: A Legendary Tale in Two Parts*. Oxford: Murray, 1771.

Cervantes, Miguel de. *Don Quixote*. Madrid: Robles, 1605, 1615.

Chakravarti, Debnita. "The Female Epic and the Journey Toward Self-Definition in Mary Tighe's *Psyche*." *Approaches to the Anglo and American Female Epic, 1621–1982*. Ed. Bernard Schweizer. England: Ashgate, 2006. 99–116.

Chamfort, Nicolas. *Maximes et Pensées*. Paris, 1795.

Chaptal, Jean-Antoine-Claude. *Elements of Chemistry*. Trans. William Nicholson. 3rd ed., 3 vols. London: Robinson, 1800.

Chevalier de Boufflers, Stanislas Jean. *Oeuvres*. Paris, 1781.

Chorley, Henry. *Memorials of Mrs. Hemans with Illustrations of Her Literary Character from Her Private Correspondence*. 2 vols. London: Saunders and Otley, 1836.

Congreve, William. *The Mourning Bride*. London: Tonson, 1697.

Corneille, Pierre. *Othon*. Paris, 1664.

Cowper, William. *The Poetical Works of William Cowper*. London: Bell and Daldy, 1800.

———. *The Task*. London: Johnson, 1785.

De L'enclos, Ninon. *The Memoirs of Ninon De L'enclos: with Her Letters to Monsr. de St. Evremond, and to the Marquis de Sevigné*. London: Dodsley, 1761.

DeShazer, Mary K. "Mary Tighe." *The Longman Anthology of Women's Literature*. New York: Longman, 2000.

Drayton, Michael. *The Works of Michael Drayton*. Ed. J. William Hebel. Oxford: Basil Blackwell, 1931.

Dryden, John. *All for Love*. London: Herringman, 1678.

———. *The Conquest of Granada*. London: Herringman, 1672.

———. *Don Sebastian: A Tragedy*. London: Hindmarsh, 1690.

———. *The Rival Ladies*. London: Herringman, 1664.

———. *The Spanish Fryar, or, The Double Discovery*. London: Tonson, 1681.

———. *Tyrannic Love, or, The Royal Martyr*. London: Herringman, 1670.

Dryden, John, trans. "The Second Satyr." *The Satires of Aulus Persius Flaccus*. London: Tonson, 1693.

Feldman, Paula. "Mary Tighe." *British Women Poets of the Romantic Period*. Baltimore: Johns Hopkins University Press, 1997.

Fénelon, François. *The Spiritual Letters of Archbishop Fénelon to Women*. London: Rivington, 1877.

Fenton, Elijah. *Mariamne*. London: Tonson, 1723.

Florian, Jean-Pierre Claris de. *Estelle et Némorin*. Paris, 1787.

———. *Gonzalve de Cordoue, ou Grenade Reconquise*. Paris 1791.

Gambold, John. *The Works of the Late Rev. John Gambold*. London: Robinson, 1789.

Gisborne, Thomas. *Poems, Sacred and Moral*. London: Cadell and Davies, 1798.

Goethe, Johann Wolfgang von. *The Sorrows of Young Werther*. 1774; London: Dodsley, 1779.

Goldsmith, Oliver. *The Deserted Village*. London: Griffin, 1770.

Grant, Elizabeth. *Roy's Wife of Aldivalloch*. London: Dale, 1798.

Gray, Thomas. *Ode on a Distant Prospect of Eton College*. London: Dodsley, 1747.

Greene, Lucia. Italian Translations for *Selena*. 12 April 2011.

Greenshields, John Boyd. *Selim and Zaida*. London: Longman and Rees, 1800.

Guarini, Giovanni Battista. "Tirsi morir volea." *Rime*. Venetia, 1581.

Hamilton, Caroline. *Anecdotes of Our Family Written for My Children*. MS 4810. National Library of Ireland, Dublin.

———. "Mary Tighe." *The Collected Poems and Journals of Mary Tighe*. Ed. Harriet Kramer Linkin. 247–67.

Hayley, William. *An Essay on Sculpture*. London: Cadell and Davies, 1800.

Henchy, Patrick. "The Works of Mary Tighe: Published and Unpublished." *The Bibliographic Society of Ireland* 6.6 (1957): 1–14.

Horace. *Odes*. 23 BC.

Irish Women Writers of the Romantic Era. 9 reels. Marlborough: Adam Matthew, 2005.

Jephson, Robert. *The Count of Narbonne*. London: Cadell, 1781.

Kelly, Angeline. "Mary Tighe." *Pillars of the House: An Anthology of Verse by Irishwomen from 1690 to the Present*. 1987; Dublin: Wolfhound Press, 1997.

King, Henry. *Poems, Elegies, Paradoxes, and Sonnets*. London, 1664.

King James Bible. London, 1611.

Knight, Richard Payne. *The Progress of Civil Society: A Didactic Poem in Six Books*. London: Nicol, 1796.

Kotzebue, August von. *Count Benyowsky; or, The Conspiracy of Kamtschatka: A Tragic-comedy, in Five Acts*. London: Richardson, 1798.

Lee, Elizabeth. "Mary Tighe." *Dictionary of National Biography*. Ed. Sidney Lee. Vol. 56. New York: Macmillan, 1898.

Lee, Nathaniel. *The Massacre of Paris: A Tragedy*. London: Bentley and Magnes, 1690.

———. *Mithridates, King of Pontus: A Tragedy*. London: Magnes and Bentley, 1678.

———. *Theodosius, or, The Force of Love: A Tragedy*. London: Bentley and Magnes, 1680.

Lillo, George. *Arden of Feversham*. London: Davies, 1762.

Linkin, Harriet Kramer. "Mary Tighe: A Portrait of the Artist for the Twenty-First Century." *A Companion to Irish Literature*. Ed. Julia M. Wright. Oxford: Wiley-Blackwell, 2010. 1:292–309.

———. "Mary Tighe and Literary History: the Making of a Critical Reputation." *Literature Compass* 7:7 (July 2010), 564–76.

———. "Mary Tighe and the Coterie of Women Poets in *Psyche*." *The History of British Women's Writing, 1750–1830*. Ed. Jacqueline Labbe. Vol. 5 of *The History of British Women's Writing*. Ed. Cora Kaplan and Jennie Batchelor. 10 vols. England: Palgrave Macmillan, 2010. 301–20.

Loeber, Rolf and Magda Loeber with Anne Mullin Burnham. *A Guide to Irish Fiction, 1650–1900*. Dublin: Four Courts, 2006.

Lyttelton, George. *The Poetical Works of George Lord Lyttelton*. London: Cadell, 1801.

Macpherson, James. *The Works of Ossian*. 2 vols. London: Becket, 1765.

Mallet, David. *Mustapha*. London: Millar, 1739.

Mason, William. *Caractacus*. London: Knapton, 1759.

Matthias, Thomas James. *The Shade of Alexander Pope, on the Banks of the Thames. A Satirical Poem, with Notes. Occasioned Chiefly, but not Wholly, by the Residence of Henry Grattan, Ex-Representative in Parliament for the City of Dublin, at Twickenham, in November, 1798*. London: Becket, 1799.

Mercier, Louis-Sébastien. *Tableau de Paris*, vol. 5. Neuchâtel, 1783.

Metastasio, Pietro. *Romolo ed Ersilia*. Rome, 1765.

———. *Zenobia*. 1740; London: Woodfall, 1758.

Milton, John. *The Oxford Authors: John Milton*. Ed. Stephen Orgel and Jonathan Goldberg. Oxford: Oxford University Press, 1991.

Montagu, Lady Mary Wortley. *Poetical Works of the Right Honourable Lady M—y W—y M—e*. London: Tonson, 1781.

Monti, Vincenzo. *Poesie di Vincenzio Monti*. 2 vols. Pisa: Cappuro, 1808.

Montolieu, Isabella de. *Caroline de Lichtfield*. Dublin: Luc White, 1786.

Moore, Thomas. *Memoirs, Journal, and Correspondence*. Vol. 2. Ed. Lord John Russell. London: Longman, 1853.

———. *Odes of Anacreon*. London: Carpenter, 1800.

More, Hannah. *Cheap Repository Tracts*. London, 1795–1997.

———. *The Fatal Falsehood: A Tragedy*. London: Cadell, 1779.

———. *Percy: A Tragedy*. London: Cadell, 1778.

———. *Sacred Dramas: Chiefly Intended for Young Persons: The Subjects Taken from the Bible. To Which Is Added, Sensibility, A Poem*. London: Cadell, 1782.

———. *Sir Eldred of the Bower, and The Bleeding Rock: Two Legendary Tales*. London: Cadell, 1776.

Mountain, Arthur Harcourt. "The Romantic Elements in Mrs. Tighe's 'Psyche,' with an Account of Her Life and a Review of Her Reliques." M.A. Thesis, University of Chicago, 1921.

Mulvihill, Maureen. "Mary Tighe." *Irish Women Writers: An A-to-Z Guide*. Ed. Alexander G. Gonzalez. Westport, CT: Green Press, 2006.

Otway, Thomas. *Venice Preserv'd*. London: Hindmarsh, 1682.

Ovid. *Ars Amatoria*. Ca. 1 BC.

Parny, Évariste de. *Élégies*. Paris, 1784.

———. *Poésies Erotiques*. Paris, 1778.

Perkins, Pam. "Mary Tighe." *The Oxford Dictionary of National Biography*. Oxford: Oxford University Press, 2004.

Petrarca, Francesco. *Le Rime di Francesco Petrarca*. 2 vols. Leghorn, 1778.

Petrarca, Francesco and Mark Musa. *The Canzoniere, or Rerum vulgarium fragmenta*. Bloomington: Indiana University Press, 1996.

Plautus. *The Comedies of Plautus*. 5 vols. London: Lister, 1767.

Pope. Alexander. *An Epistle to Dr. Arbuthnot*. London, 1735.

———. *An Essay on Man*. London, 1733–34.

———. *The Rape of the Lock*. London: Lintott, 1714.

Pope, Alexander, trans. *The Illiad of Homer*. 6 vols. London: Bowyer, 1715–20.

Porter, Anna Maria. "After Having Seen a Lovely But Miserable Girl." *The Poetical Register and Repository of Fugitive Poetry for 1801*. London: Rivington, 1802.

Report of the trial ... between Robert Tighe ... plaintiff, and Dive Jones ... for crim. con. with Esther Francis Tighe, otherwise Wade ... Dublin: William Folds, 1800.

Rinuccini, Ottavio. *Poesie*. Florence: Giunti, 1622.

Roberts, Adam. *Romantic and Victorian Long Poems*. England: Ashgate, 1999.

Rousseau, Jean-Jacques. *The Confessions*. Neuchâtel?: Fauche-Borel, 1782.

———. *Émile, ou, De l'éducation*. Amsterdam, J. Néaulme, 1762.

———. *Julie, ou La Nouvelle Héloïse*. Amsterdam: Rey, 1761.

Rowe, Nicholas. *The Ambitious Stepmother: A Tragedy*. London: Wellington, 1702.

———. *The Fair Penitent: A Tragedy*. London, 1703.

———. *The Royal Convert*. London: Tonson, 1708.

———. *Tamerlane: A Tragedy*. London: Tonson, 1701.

———. *The Tragedy of Jane Shore*. London: Lintott, 1714.

Saint-Pierre, Jacques Henri Bernardin de. *Paul et Virginie*. London, 1788.

Schiller, Frederich. *Kabale und Liebe*. Mannheim, 1784. *Cabal and Love*. Trans. P. Colombine. London, 1785.

Seward, Anna. *Llangollen Vale, with Other Poems*. London: Sael, 1796.

Shakespeare, William. *The Complete Works of Shakespeare*. Ed. David Bevington. 5th ed. New York: Longman, 2004.

Shattock, Joanne. "Mary Tighe." *The Oxford Guide to British Women Writers*. Oxford: Oxford University Press, 1994.

Smith, Charlotte. *Elegiac Sonnets and Other Poems*. 8th ed. 2 vols. London: Cadell and Davies, 1797–1800.

Smith, Mrs. Richard. *The Life of the Rev. Henry Moore; The Biographer and Executor of the Rev. John Wesley; including the Autobiography; and the Continuation, Written from His Own Papers*. London: Simpkin, Marshall, 1844.

Smollett, Tobias. *The Adventures of Peregrine Pickle*. London: Wilson, 1751.

Southerne, Thomas. *Oroonoko: A Tragedy*. London: Playford, 1696.

Southey, Robert, trans. *Amadis of Gaul by Vasco de Lobeira*, 4 vols. London: Longman, 1803.

Sowerby, James. *English Botany*. 36 vols. London: Davis, 1790–1814.

Tasso, Torquato. *Aminta*. Venetia, 1573.

Thomson, James. *Agamemnon: A Tragedy*. London: Millar, 1738.

———. *Alfred: A Masque*. London: Millar, 1740.

———. *Edward and Eleonora*. London: Millar, 1739.

———. *The Seasons*. London, 1730.

———. *Tancred and Sigismunda*. London: Millar, 1745.

———. *The Tragedy of Sophonisba*. London: Millar, 1730.

Tickler, Timothy. "Noctes Ambrosianae XXI." *Blackwood's Magazine* 18:104 (September 1825): 381.

Tighe, Mary. *The Collected Poems and Journals of Mary Tighe*. Ed. Harriet Kramer Linkin. Lexington: University Press of Kentucky, 2005.

———. "Letters to Joseph Cooper Walker." MS 1461. Trinity College Library, Dublin.

———. *Mary, a Series of Reflections During Twenty Years*. Dublin, 1811.

———. *Psyche; or, the Legend of Love*. London: Carpenter, 1805.

———. *Psyche, with Other Poems*. London, 1811.

———. "Reading Journal." MS 4804. National Library of Ireland, Dublin

———. *Selena*. MSS 4742–4746. National Library of Ireland, Dublin.

———. *Verses Transcribed for H.T.* Brompton, 1805. MS Acc. 5495. National Library of Ireland, Dublin.

Tighe, Wilfrid. "The Tighe Story." MS D/2685/14/1. Public Record Office of Northern Ireland, Belfast.

Tighe, William. *The Plants*. MSS 4752–4753. National Library of Ireland, Dublin.

———. *Statistical Observations Relative to the County of Kilkenny*. Dublin: Graisberry and Campbell, 1802.

Trapp, Joseph. *Abra-Mule: Or, Love and Empire*. London: Stephens, 1708.

Virgil. *The Works of Virgil*. Ed. Joseph Warton. 3rd ed. 4 vols. London: Dodsley, 1778.

Walker, Joseph Cooper. "Letters to William Hayley." MS 146. Gilbert Collection, Dublin City Library, Dublin.

Walpole, Horace. *The Mysterious Mother: A Tragedy*. London: Dodsley, 1781.

Weller, Earle Vonard. *Keats and Mary Tighe: The Poems of Mary Tighe with Parallel Passages from the Work of John Keats*. New York: Modern Language Association, 1928.

Wesley, John. *Explanatory Notes Upon the New Testament*. London: Bowyer, 1755.

Withering, William. *The Botanical Arrangement of All the Vegetables Naturally Growing in Great Britain*. 2 vols. London: Robinson, 1776.

Wodhull, Michael. "Epistles, Book II, Epistle III. St. Preux to Julia, On Her Marriage. From Rousseau's New Eloise" (1768). *Poems*. London: Bowyer and Nichols, 1772.

Wu, Duncan. "Mary Tighe." *Romantic Women Poets*. Oxford: Blackwell, 1997.

Young, Edward. *The Brothers: A Tragedy*. London: Dodsley, 1753.

———. *Busiris, King of Egypt*. London: Johnson, 1719.

———. *Night Thoughts*. London: Hawkins, 1745.

———. *The Revenge: A Tragedy*. London: Chetwood, 1721.

Index